WHITAKER'S LONDON ALMANACK 2002

Whitaker's London Almanack
2002

LONDON
THE STATIONERY OFFICE

© The Stationery Office Ltd 2001

The Stationery Office Ltd
51 Nine Elms Lane, London SW8 5DR

ISBN 0 11 702274 8

A CIP catalogue record for this book is available in the British Library

All rights reserved. No part of this publication may be reproduced, stored in a retrieval system, or transmitted in any form or by any means – electronic, mechanical, photocopying, recording or otherwise – without prior written permission of the publisher, to be obtained from: the Contracts and Right Manager, The Stationery Office Ltd, St Crispins, Duke Street, Norwich NR3 1PD.

Crown copyright material is reproduced with the permission of the Controller of Her Majesty's Stationery Office.

Whitaker's Almanack is a registered trademark of J. Whitaker and Sons Ltd. Registered Trade Mark Nos: (UK) 1322125/09; 132212/16 and 1322127/41; (EC) 19960401/09; 16, 41, licensed for use by The Stationery Office Ltd.

Publisher: Tim Probart
Consulting Editor: Gyles Brandreth
Editor: Vanessa White
Editorial team: Inna Ward, Tom Brundle, Debbie Paola, Tara West, Sharon Taylor, Chris Sadowski

Contributors: Jon Asworth (Finance); Clive Longhurst (Insurance); Paul Hammond (Education); Lauren Hill (Law); Karen Harries-Rees (Environment); David Warwick (Index)

Typeset by The Stationery Office Limited, Parliamentary Press, London.

Printed and Bound in Great Britain by The Stationery Office Limited, Parliamentary Press, London.

Jacket designed by Compendium
Jacket Photographs © PA Photos Ltd.

Published by The Stationery Office Limited
and available from:

The Stationery Office
(Mail, telephone and fax orders only)
PO Box 29, Norwich NR3 1GN
General enquiries 0870 600 5522
Order through the Parliamentary Hotline
Lo-call 0845 7 023474
Fax orders 0870 600 5533
Email book.orders@theso.co.uk
Internet www.clicktso.com

The Stationery Office Bookshops
123 Kingsway, London WC2B 6PQ
020-7242 6393 Fax 020-7242 6394
68–69 Bull Street, Birmingham B4 6AD
0121 236 9696 Fax 0121 236 9699
33 Wine Street, Bristol BS1 2BQ
0117 9264306 Fax 0117 9294515
9–21 Princess Street, Manchester M60 8AS
0161 834 7201 Fax 0161 833 0634
16 Arthur Street, Belfast BT1 4GD
028 9023 8451 Fax 028 9023 5401
The Stationery Office Oriel Bookshop
18–19 High Street, Cardiff CF1 2BZ
029 2039 5548 Fax 029 2038 4347
71 Lothian Road, Edinburgh EH3 9AZ
0870 606 5566 Fax 0870 606 5588

Accredited Agents
(See Yellow Pages)

and through good booksellers

PREFACE

By Gyles Brandreth, Consulting Editor

As a journalist and broadcaster I get around – usually at somebody else's expense. Over the past twelve months assignments for ITN Radio, Sky TV, the *Sunday Telegraph* and CBS News have taken me to some of the world's most fascinating cities—Paris, Rome, Edinburgh, Cape Town, New York, Columbo, Dubai – but wherever I go, whatever the reason, and however good the weather when I get there, I still want to come back home. The more I see of the world, the more I realise that London is – without doubt—the most exciting and rewarding city on earth.

I have lived and worked here all my life and, despite the chronic state of the public transport infrastructure (I travel on the bus and underground most days and the experience is not a congenial one), despite the unsettling crime rate (Scotland Yard reported that street crime in London soared in 2000, with offences reaching the 50,000 mark for the first time), despite the weather (in the winter of 2000/2001 London suffered its wettest six months since 1697), there is, overall, a richness and quality and variety to London life that cannot be rivalled anywhere in the world. Whatever your priorities – business, commerce, sport, the arts, fine food, good music, cultural, ethnic or social diversity – my experience is that, if you look for them, in terms of facilities, services, places and people, you will unfailingly find what you need in London. Whatever the world has to offer us at the beginning of the third millennium, it can be found here, in this unique and extraordinary capital.

With the arrival of the elected mayor, with the advent of the Greater London Authority, on top of the continuing and developing role of the thirty-two London boroughs and the City of London, the governance of London has never been more complex. The sheer scale of the capital, too, has never been greater. Over the past fifteen years London's population has grown by around 400,000 people. Within the next fifteen years, the expectation is that it will rise by a further million.

Whitaker's London Almanack is designed to help you find your way through the maze that is the modern management of London. It does much more than that, of course, covering everything from public services to the voluntary sector in London, from the law in London to cultural London, from the religious life of the capital to the astronomical and tidal data you would properly expect to find in an almanac. I like to think this is the definitive handbook for those in search of the DNA of our capital city.

Proudly, I can claim to have made a direct impact on the quality of London life in two distinct ways. When I was a member of parliament, as a Private Member's Bill I introduced a modest piece of legislation called the 1994 Marriage Act. This changed the law so as to allow civil weddings to be conducted in venues other than Register Offices. As a consequence of this legislation, Londoners seeking a civil wedding can now be married in a wide variety of interesting and historic settings, including, since January 2001, the London Eye, the slowly revolving wheel on the South Bank, and the Tate Modern, the undoubted success of London's millennial celebrations. (Recently I happened to meet one of the two architects who conceived and designed the London Eye: I was intrigued to discover that the co-creator of London's newest landmark shared a birthday with Gustave Eiffel, the progenitor of the Paris Eiffel Tower).

My other contribution to the quality of London life relates to this book. This is the second edition of *Whitaker's London Almanack* and I am proud to be associated with a volume that has established itself immediately as the indispensible reference book for anyone who lives or works in – or does business with – the United Kingdom's capital city. As Consulting Editor, I cannot claim to have to have undertaken the detailed research and painstaking legwork that have gone into producing the book (that has been achieved by more expert, experienced and reliable hands, under the leadership of Tim Probart as publisher and Vanessa Taylor as editor), but as someone whose working life is and has been wrapped up in various aspects of London life over many years I have tried to ensure that the contents of the book provide the breadth and depth of information you might require, whether you are a foreign diplomat newly posted to London or a disgruntled consumer in search of the name and address of a particular 'ombudsman', whether you are an active citizen wanting to take action on an issue concerned with education, planning or the environment, or simply an enquiring mind wanting to explore unexpected aspects of this formidable city, what it is and how it works.

The start of the third millennium on 1 January 2001 (the 'Millennium Dome' at Greenwich was a year premature) certainly saw one encouraging development in the history of the capital: scientists released figures showing that London air is cleaner now than at any time since the Industrial Revolution. This is good news if, like me, you are someone who enjoys walking the streets of London. I am fascinated by the architectural heritage of London and by the thought of those who have walked the streets before. Armed with my copy of this book, with my thumb wedged in the section that lists the commemorative plaques that adorn so many London buildings (page 345),

I find there is no part of the capital that has not been home to some extraordinary figure from history, whether it is William Blake in Barnet or William Pitt in Westminster, whether it is Charles Dickens in the centre of town, off Holborn, or Enid Blyton on the outskirts, at Kingston. There is only one significant figure I can think of who does not yet appear to have a blue plaque to commemorate his contributiuon to our national life and that is Joseph Whitaker, the London publisher who produced the original *Whitaker's Almanack* in 1868. I see it as my millennial mission to remedy this oversight. How successful I have been I shall report in the next edition of *Whitaker's London Almanack* in a year's time. Meanwhile, I trust you will find this handbook as reliable, practical, up-to-the-minute and comprehensive as we have aimed to make it. If there are additional features you would find useful in a future edition, please let us know. Our ambition is to create an authoritative and accessible work of reference that truly serves its readership.

Gyles Brandreth
London, June 2001

INTRODUCTION

By Vanessa White, Editor, Whitaker's Almanack

Welcome to the second edition of Whitaker's London Almanack.
    London is truly a diverse and complex capital city. To people visiting London, a guide book of attractions, hotels and events is a pre-requisite. But to those eager for a more in depth perspective of London, for example those who choose to live and work in the capital so much more information is necessary. Whitaker's London Almanack provides readers with all the essential facts and figures in sensibly defined sections, exploring all the component parts which enable London to function as a vibrant, economically successful and socially diverse city.
    Readers can explore how London is governed, starting with clear explanations of the roles and functions of the Greater London Authority and expanding to examine the structures of Local, Central and European government. The Business London section provides a detailed commentary of the past year in London's financial and commercial sectors, enhanced with statistical evidence of business trends. For those wishing to understand how public sector bodies operate in London such as the health service, educational institutions, the police and transport, the Public Services London section provides a clear and comprehensive overview. Whitaker's London Almanack goes on to describe the elements which make up London's media community; there is also a detailed section dedicated to examining the diversity of Religion in London. For those with a fascination with London's historical roots, the role of the monarchy in London and for those who wish to find out more about London's many historical landmarks, the Cultural London section provides information on this and much, much more.
    As a sister publication of Whitaker's Almanack we endeavour to also make Whitaker's London Almanack a snapshot of the past year and an essential reference work for the year to come. We have incorporated to this end the new *London Events of the Year* section. This is a chronological profile of the significant news stories which have made an impact on London, ranging from the controversy surrounding the closure of the Millennium Dome to the trial of Barry George for the murder of Jill Dando.
    This is just the tip of the iceberg and I hope readers will enjoy discovering all that Whitaker's London Almanack offers as an accessible and comprehensive reference tool. May I also take this opportunity to thank the editorial team for their hard work and all those who have contributed to the compilation of Whitaker's London Almanack.
    As with all the publications in the Whitaker's series we would be most grateful to receive your feedback. Please write with your comments to:

Vanessa White
Editor
Whitaker's London Almanack
The Stationery Office
51 Nine Elms Lane
London SW8 5DR
Tel: 020-7873 8442
Fax: 020-7873 8723
Email: whitakers.almanack@theso.co.uk
Web: www.whitakers-almanack.co.uk
       www.clicktso.co.uk

WHITAKER'S LONDON ALMANACK – NOTES FOR READERS

The London Almanack investigates the structure of London within the following categories:

Statistical London
Governed London
Public Service London
Business London
Legal London
Media London
Cultural, Historical and Recreational London
Environmental London
London and the World
Religious London
Societies, Institutions and Charities
Events of the Year and Forthcoming Events
Astronomy and Tides

As well as the main contents page at the front of the book, each section has a contents page which breaks down the key elements of that section. Readers should note that listings such as 'Public Relations Agencies' will not comprise all the agencies in London as there are just too many to list. Such listings are in no way an endorsement of the quality of the services provided by each company but are purely representative of those companies responding to our enquiries and questionnaires. Other listings such as 'Police Forces' in the Public Services section, are to our knowledge fully comprehensive.

As with all the Whitaker's family of reference books, we are always keen to hear your comments and suggestions. Further, if you have ideas for a subject or entry you would like considered for inclusion in future editions, please get in contact with us.

Please write to:
The Editor
Whitaker's London Almanack
51 Nine Elms Lane
London
SW8 5DR

CONTENTS

Preface	v
Introduction	vii
STATISTICAL LONDON	1
Population	3
Births and Deaths	4
Migration	5
Deprivation	5
Household Expenditure	6
GOVERNED LONDON	7
Greater London Authority	9
Cabinet	9
Election Results	15
Assembly Members	30
London Borough Councils	33
General Election Results	89
European Parliament	99
Government Departments and Public Offices	100
PUBLIC SERVICES LONDON	115
Education	117
Emergency Services	136
Ambulance	136
Fire	136
Police	137
Health Care	145
Housing	152
Libraries	155
Transport	175
Utilities	187
BUSINESS LONDON	189
Banking	195
Financial Services Regulation	197
Insurance	200
London Stock Exchange	204
Ombudsmen	205
Business and the Workforce	205
Trade Unions	211
Employers' Associations	214
Training and Enterprise	216
Charity and the Voluntary Sector	218
Conference and Exhibition Venues	226
LEGAL LONDON	235
Legal System	238
Circuit Judges	239
County Courts	241
Crown Prosecution Service	242
Crown Courts	243
Magistrates' Courts	244
Coroners' Courts	247
Tribunals	247
Prison Service	249
Probation Service	250
Legal Bodies	251
Legal Notes	254
MEDIA LONDON	279
Television	281
Radio	283
Press	285
Advertising	314
Public Relations	319
Telecommunications	325
Postal Services	331
CULTURAL LONDON	333
History Timeline	335
English Kings and Queens	339
Order of Succession	343
Order of Precedence	343
Scenes and Sights of London	345
Blue Plaques	345
Clubs	379
Museums and Galleries	386
Theatres	400
Tourism	408
Sport	409
Cultural, Historical and Leisure Organisations	427
ENVIRONMENTAL LONDON	431
Introduction	433
Nature Reserves	434
Sights of Specific Scientific Interest	435
River Thames	436
Environmental Bodies	437
Waste Minimisation and Recycling	439
LONDON AND THE WORLD	445
Tourist Boards	448
Embassies	452
International Organisations	462
European Union	463
Time Zones	463
Air Distances from London	466
International Direct Dialling Codes	468
RELIGIOUS LONDON	471
Christianity	474
Bahá'í Faith	474
Buddhism	474
Hinduism	475
Islam	476
Jainism	477
Judaism	477
Sikhism	478
Zoroastrianism	478
Churches	479
SOCIETIES AND INSTITUTIONS	487
EVENTS OF THE YEAR	531
FORTHCOMING EVENTS	548
ASTRONOMICAL AND TIDAL DATA	551
MAPS	564
INDEX	567

STATISTICAL
LONDON

**POPULATION TRENDS
BIRTHS AND DEATHS
MIGRATION
DEPRIVATION
HOUSEHOLD EXPENDITURE**

STATISTICAL LONDON

London boasts the largest metropolis within the European Union and is culturally diverse. Almost 50 per cent of Britain's ethnic minority population live and work in London. The capital is one of the world's top financial centres and is home to an abundance of businesses, educational establishments, leisure and cultural facilities, transport links, communities . . . the list is vast.

Within this section you will find a wealth of data aimed at providing a statistical insight into the people and population of London.

POPULATION TRENDS AND PROJECTIONS OF LONDON 1961-2021 (000s)

	1961	1971	1981	1983	1991	1997	2001*	2011*	2021*
Inner London	3,481	3,060	2,550	2,523	2,627	2,727	2,765	2,863	2,963
Outer London	4,496	4,470	4,255	4,242	4,263	4,395	4,450	4,607	4,773
Total London	7,977	7,529	6,806	6,765	6,890	7,122	7,215	7,470	7,736
UK	52,807	55,928	56,362	56,377	57,808	59,009	59,618	60,929	63,642

*1996-based London and 1998-based United Kingdom projections.
Source: Focus on London 2000, Office for National Statistics © Crown Copyright 2001

POPULATION OF LONDON BY AGE 1971-2021 (PERCENTAGES AND 000s)

Age	London						UK					
	1971	1981	1991	1998	2011[1]	2021[1]	1971	1981	1991	1998	2011[2]	2021[2]
0-4	7.3	5.8	7.0	7.0	6.4	6.4	8.1	6.1	6.7	6.2	5.6	5.6
5-10	—	—	7.2	7.9	7.3	7.0	10.0	8.1	7.6	7.9	6.8	6.7
11-15	—	—	5.2	5.7	6.0	5.5	7.4	8.0	6.0	6.3	5.9	5.5
16-19	—	—	4.6	4.8	5.0	4.6	5.5	6.7	5.3	5.0	5.0	4.5
20-24	8.7	8.8	9.1	7.4	7.6	7.2	7.7	7.6	7.8	5.9	6.7	5.9
25-44	24.9	27.5	33.2	33.9	30.4	29.7	24.1	26.2	29.4	29.9	26.6	25.4
45-59/64[3]-74	22.3	19.5	17.2	18.2	23.0	23.5	20.9	19.4	18.8	20.6	23.7	24.0
60/65-74[4]	11.8	12.1	9.8	8.7	9.0	10.5	11.6	12.0	11.4	10.8	12.0	13.6
75-84+	3.9	4.9	5.1	4.4	3.8	4.1	3.9	4.7	5.4	5.4	5.5	6.3
85+	1.0	1.2	1.5	1.7	1.5	1.5	0.9	1.1	1.5	1.9	2.2	2.5
Pensionable age[5]	16.7	18.2	16.3	14.9	—	13.2	16.3	17.8	18.3	18.1	19.3	19.2
All ages (000s)	7,529	6,806	6,890	7,187	7,470	7,736	55,928	56,352	57,808	59,237	61,773	63,642

1 1996-based sub-national projections.
2 1998 based on national projections.
3 Age band covers from 45 for both genders to current state retirement age: 64 for men and 59 for women.
4 Age band covers from current state retirement age: 65 for men and 60 for women, to 74 for both genders
5 The pensionable age population covers those over the state retirement age. The 2021 figure takes account of planned changes in state retirement age from 65 for men and 60 for women at present to 65 for both genders. This change will be phased in between 2010 and 2020, as a result the London figure for 2011 is unavailable.
Source: Focus on London 2000, National Statistics © Crown Copyright 2001

4 Statistical London

POPULATION[1] OF LONDON BY ETHNIC GROUP, 1998-99[2] (PERCENTAGES AND 000s)

Ethnic Group	Inner London	Outer London	Total London	Great Britain
Black Caribbean	5.8	2.9	4.0	0.8
Black African	7.2	2.5	4.3	0.7
Black other	3.4	1.6	2.3	0.5
Indian	2.3	7.4	5.4	1.6
Pakistani	1.0	2.0	1.6	1.1
Bangladeshi	4.0	0.7	2.0	0.5
Chinese	0.9	0.5	0.7	0.3
Other Asian	1.5	2.0	1.8	0.3
Other	3.8	2.4	3.0	0.7
All ethnic minority groups	29.9	22.0	25.1	6.6
White	70.1	78.0	74.9	93.4
All persons (000s)	2,696	4,309	7,005	56,857

1 The population includes residents in private households, students in halls of residence and those in NHS accommodation
2 Four quarter average: Autumn 1998 to Summer 1999
Source: Focus on London 2000, National Statistics © Crown Copyright 2001

LIVE BIRTHS, DEATHS AND NATURAL CHANGE IN LONDON 1971-1998 (THOUSANDS AND RATES PER 1,000 POPULATION)

	London			UK		
Year	Live births	Deaths	Natural Change	Live births	Deaths	Natural Change
Thousands						
1971	113.1	85.0	28.1	901.6	645.1	256.5
1981	92.4	77.6	14.8	730.8	658.0	72.8
1991	105.8	68.9	36.9	792.5	646.2	146.3
1996	105.4	65.4	40.0	733.4	636.0	97.4
1997	106.2	63.5	41.8	726.8	629.7	97.1
1998	105.3	62.1	43.8	717.1	627.6	89.6
Rate per 1,000 population						
1971	15.0	11.3	3.7	16.1	11.5	4.6
1981	13.6	11.4	2.2	13.0	11.7	1.3
1991	15.4	10.0	5.4	13.7	11.3	2.5
1996	14.9	9.2	5.7	12.5	10.8	1.7
1997	14.8	8.9	5.9	12.3	10.7	1.6
1998	14.7	8.7	6.0	12.1	10.6	1.5

Source: Focus on London 2000, National Statistics © Crown Copyright 2001

AGE-ADJUSTED MORTALITY RATES IN LONDON*, BY CAUSE** AND GENDER, 1998

	Males		Females	
	London	UK	London	UK
Circulatory diseases	351	384	331	381
Respiratory diseases	144	134	156	149
Cancer†	255	259	230	233
Injury and poisoning	38	41	19	21
Other causes‡	124	120	146	156
All causes‡	911	939	882	939

* Rates are standardised to the mid-1991 UK population for males and females separately
** Deaths at ages under 28 days occurring in England and Wales are not assigned an underlying cause
† Malignant neoplasms only
‡ Including deaths at ages under 28 days
Source: Focus on London 2000, National Statistics © Crown Copyright 2001

Statistical London

MIGRATION TO AND FROM LONDON: BY AGE, 1997-8* (000s)

Age	Within the UK To London	From London	International** To London	From London
0-15	15.6	37.4	8.1	4.0
16-24	66.6	45.4	53.8	30.7
25-44	71.7	95.1	47.0	6.6
45-64	10.9	27.8	4.0	-0.7
65+	4.9	15.6	0.2	-0.3
All ages	169.5	221.3	113.1	40.3

Mid-1997 to mid-1998
** Excludes asylum seekers/visitor switchers and movements to and from the Irish Republic
Source: Focus on London 2000, National Statistics © Crown Copyright 2001

LONDON HOUSEHOLDS, 1998

	Average household size	Household Type % Married Couple	Co-habiting Couple	Lone-parent*	One-person	Other multi-person	All house-holds (= 100%) (000s)
Inner London	2.18	27	10	10	39	14	1,239
Outer London	2.40	45	9	6	30	10	1,822
Total London	2.32	38	9	8	34	12	3,061

* Lone parents with dependent children
Source: Focus on London 2000, National Statistics © Crown Copyright 2001

MOST SEVERELY DEPRIVED DISTRICTS IN ENGLAND, 1998*

Ranking*	Districts	Ranking*	Districts
1	Liverpool	16	Nottingham
2	NEWHAM	17	CAMDEN
3	Manchester	18	HAMMERSMITH & FULHAM
4	HACKNEY	19	Newcastle-upon-Tyne
5	Birmingham	20	BRENT
6	TOWER HAMLETS	21	Sunderland
7	Sandwell	22	WALTHAM FOREST
8	SOUTHWARK	23	Salford
9	Knowsley	24	Middlesbrough
10	ISLINGTON	25	Sheffield
11	GREENWICH	26	Kingston-upon-Hull
12	LAMBETH	27	Wolverhampton
13	HARINGEY	28	Bradford
14	LEWISHAM	29	Rochdale
15	BARKING & DAGENHAM	30	WANDSWORTH

* Based on the Index of Local Deprivation
Source: Focus on London 2000, Office for National Statistics © Crown Copyright 2001

6 Statistical London

WHERE LONDON'S RESIDENTS WORK*, 1991 (PERCENTAGES AND 000s)

	1991
Percentage of London's residents working...	
...in central London**	23.1
...elsewhere in London	71.6
...outside London	5.3
Total residents (000s)	**2,826**
Percentage of in-commuters working	
...in central London**	38.6
...elsewhere in London	61.4
Total in-commuters (=100%) (000s)	**673**

* The figures are derived from 10% data and relate to residents who are employed
** Defined as the West End and the City of London
Source: Focus on London 2000, National Statistics © Crown Copyright 2001

HOUSEHOLD EXPENDITURE, BY COMMODITY AND SERVICE, 1996-99* (£ PER WEEK AND PERCENTAGES)

	£ per week		As a percentage of average weekly expenditure	
	London	UK	London	UK
Housing (net)†	69.3	52.50	18	16
Fuel and Power	11.70	12.50	3	4
Food and non-alcoholic drinks	63.10	57.40	17	17
Alcoholic drinks	14.10	133.80	4	4
Tobacco	6.00	6.10	2	2
Clothing & Footwear	22.80	20.20	6	6
Household Goods & Services	50.80	45.30	13	14
Motoring & Fares	56.40	55.20	15	17
Leisure Goods & Services	65.40	55.80	17	17
Personal Goods & Services	15.40	12.60	4	4
Miscellaneous	1.50	1.10	-	-
Average Household Expenditure	376.40	332.60	100	100
Average Expenditure per person	157.70	140.20		

* Combined data from the 1996-97 and 1997-98 and 1998-99 surveys.
† Net of Housing Benefit and Council Tax Benefit (rates rebate in Northern Ireland)
Source: Focus on London 2000, National Statistics © Crown Copyright 2001

GOVERNED
LONDON

**GREATER LONDON AUTHORITY
LONDON BOROUGH COUNCILS
MEMBERS OF PARLIAMENT
MEMBERS OF EUROPEAN PARLIAMENT
GOVERNMENT DEPARTMENTS**

8 Governed London

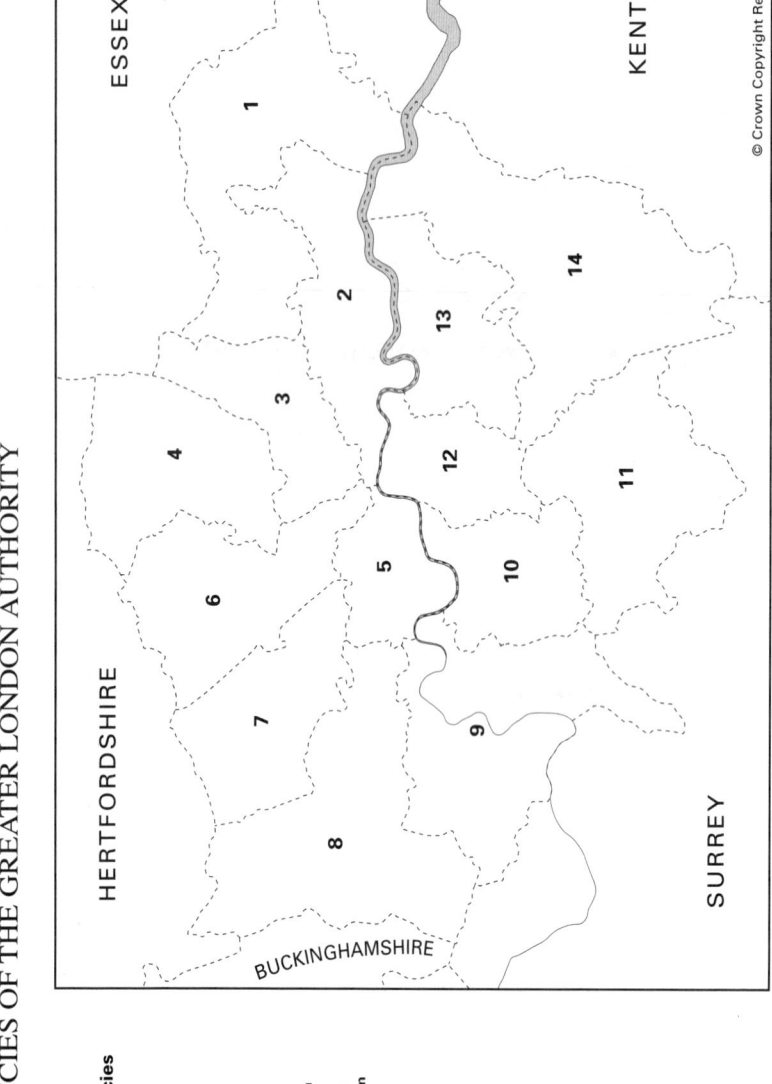

CONSTITUENCIES OF THE GREATER LONDON AUTHORITY

London Constituencies

1 Havering & Redbridge
2 City & East
3 North East
4 Enfield & Haringey
5 West Central
6 Barnet & Camden
7 Brent & Harrow
8 Ealing & Hillingdon
9 South West
10 Merton & Wandsworth
11 Croydon & Sutton
12 Lambeth & Southwark
13 Greenwich & Lewisham
14 Bexley & Bromley

GOVERNED LONDON

GREATER LONDON AUTHORITY (GLA)

Romney House, 43 Marsham Street, London SW1P 3PY (Tel: 020-7983 4000; Press Office: 020-7983 4071/4072/4090/4067/4228; Email: mayor@london.gov.uk; Web: www.london.gov.uk).

OVERVIEW

On the 7 May 1998 London voted in favour of the formation of the Greater London Authority. The first elections to the GLA were on Thursday, 4th May 2000 and the new Authority took over its responsibilities on 3rd July 2000.

The structure and objectives of the GLA stem from its eight main areas of responsibility. These are transport, planning, economic development and regeneration, the environment, police, fire and emergency planning, culture and health. The bodies that co-ordinate these functions and report to the GLA are: Transport for London (TfL), London Development Agency (LDA), Metropolitan Police Authority (MPA), London Fire and Emergency Planning Authority (LFEPA). The GLA absorbed a number of existing London bodies, such as the London Planning Advisory Committee, the London Ecology Unit and the London Research Centre.

The GLA consists of a directly elected mayor, The Mayor of London, and a separately elected assembly, The London Assembly. The Mayor has the key role of decision making with the Assembly performing the tasks of regulating and scrutinising these decisions. In addition, the GLA has around 400 permanent staff to support the activities of the Mayor and the Assembly, overseen by a Head of Paid Service. The Mayor may appoint two political advisors but may not appoint the Head of Paid Service, the Monitoring Officer or the Chief Finance Officer. These must be appointed by the Assembly.

The Mayor is also responsible for appointing a Cabinet. The Cabinet functions as part of the Mayor's objective of eliminating barriers to effective decision making and enabling the GLA to speak with one voice on behalf of London. The function of the Mayor's Cabinet is to provide the Mayor with the most sound advice on policy and strategy. Meetings of the Cabinet are designed to be a powerful forum for discussing the issues affecting Londoners. The Cabinet is not intended to fit the Whitehall Cabinet model in that GLA members will not be bound by the convention of collective responsibility, the absence of which does not mean that the Mayor will devolve or federalise his powers. All decisions are made by the Mayor acting on the honest advice of his Cabinet. Cabinet members can be broadly categorised into (a) those with specific policy brief (e.g. in the areas of planning, policing or fire and civil defence and (b) those who have been chosen to give advice and/or reflect political breadth.

Mayor's Advisory Cabinet:
Nicky Gavron (Deputy Mayor), (Spatial development and strategic planning)
Toby Harris, (Police)
Graham Tope, (Human rights and equalities)
Valerie Shawcross, (Chair of the London Fire and Emergency Planning Authority)
Darren Johnson, (Environment)
Judith Mayhew, (City and business)
Glenda Jackson, (Homelessness)
George Barlow, (Chair of the London Development Agency)
Kumar Murshid, (Regeneration)
Lee Jasper, (Race relations)
Diane Abbott, (Women and equality)
Richard Stone, (Community partnerships)
Sean Baine, (London Voluntary Services Council)
Caroline Gooding, (Disability rights)
Yasmin Anwar, (Chair of Cultural Strategy Group)
Richard Rogers, (Urban strategy)
Sue Atkinson, (Health issues)
Rod Robertson, (Trade union issues)
Lynne Featherstone, (Liberal Democrat representative)
Angela Mason, (Lesbian and gay issues)

The role of the mayor can be broken down into a number of key areas:
- To represent and promote London at home and abroad and speak up for Londoners
- Devise strategies and plans to tackle London-wide issues, such as transport, economic development and regeneration, air quality, noise, waste, bio-diversity, planning and culture
- To set budgets for Transport for London, the London Development Agency, the Metropolitan Police Authority and the London Fire and Emergency Planning Authority
- To control new transport and economic development bodies and appoint their members

10 Governed London

- To make appointments to the police and fire authorities
- To publish regular reports on the state of the environment in London.

The role of the Assembly can be broken down into a number of key areas:
- To provide a check and balance on the Mayor
- To scrutinise the Mayor
- To have the power to amend the Mayor's budget by a majority of 2/3
- To investigate issues of London wide significance and make proposals to the Mayor
- To provide the Deputy Mayor and the members serving on the police, fire and emergency planning authorities.

ELECTIONS AND THE VOTING SYSTEMS

The Assembly will be elected every four years at the same time as the Mayor and consists of 25 members. There is one member from each of the 14 GLA Constituencies topped up with 11 London members who are representatives of political parties or individuals standing as independent candidates.

The GLA constituencies are: Barnet and Camden; Bexley and Bromley; Brent and Harrow; City and London East, covering Barking and Dagenham and the City of London; Newham and Tower Hamlets; Croydon and Sutton; Ealing and Hillingdon; Enfield and Haringey; Greenwich and Lewisham; Havering and Redbridge; North East, covering Hackney, Islington and Waltham Forest; Lambeth and Southwark; West Central, covering Hammersmith and Fulham, Kensington and Chelsea and Westminster; South West, covering Hounslow, Kingston upon Thames and Richmond upon Thames; Merton and Wandsworth.

Two distinct voting systems were used to appoint the Mayor and the Assembly. The Mayor was elected using the Supplementary Vote (SV) system. With the SVS electors have two votes; one to give the first choice for Mayor and one to give the second choice. Electors cannot vote twice for the same candidate. If one candidate gets more than half of all the first choice votes, he or she becomes Mayor. If no candidate gets more than half the first choice votes, the two candidates with the most first choice votes remain in the election and all the other candidates drop out. The second choice votes on the ballot papers of the candidates who drop out are then counted. Where these second choice votes are for the two remaining candidates they are added to the first choice votes

these candidates already have. The candidate with the most first and second choice votes combined would become the Mayor of London. Ken Livingstone was voted the first Mayor of the Greater London Authority using this system on the 4th May 2000.

The Assembly was appointed using the Additional Member (AM) system. With AMS electors have two votes. The first vote is for a constituency candidate. The second vote is for a party list or individual candidate contesting the London-wide Assembly seats. The 14 constituency members were elected under the first-past-the-post system, the same system used in general and local elections. Electors vote for one candidate and the candidate with the most votes wins. The Additional (London) Members were drawn from party lists or were independent candidates who stood as London Members.

The Greater London Returning Officer (GLRO) was the independent official responsible for running the election in London. The GLRO had overall responsibility for running a free, fair and efficient election. He was supported in this by Returning Officers in each of the 14 London Constituencies.

GLRO: Robert V. Hughes CBE.

FUNCTIONS AND STRUCTURE

Every aspect of the Assembly and its activities must be open to the view of the public and therefore accountable. Assembly meetings are open to the public and the reports it produces are available to the public. Other measures such as a twice yearly 'people's question time' also takes place. The meetings where the Assembly questions the Mayor will also be open to the public.

Funding

The GLA is responsible for funding Transport for London, the London Development Agency, the Metropolitan Police Authority and the London Fire and Emergency Planning Authority. Budgets are set by the Mayor, and scrutinised by the Assembly. Funds are allocated subject to safeguards on service standards. The GLA inherited its funding from the existing bodies that it replaced. This amounted to around £3bn. The GLA also received a government grant to cover the cost of the Mayor, Assembly and additional staff. The contribution of the London taxpayer to the cost of the GLA is around £1.70 a year, (3p per day).

Greater London Authority

Transport for London (TfL)
(Email: enquire@tfl.gov.uk;
Web: www.transportforlondon.gov.uk)

The mayor is responsible for forming an integrated transport strategy for London. The Assembly is consulted on the strategy. TfL is the new body responsible for most transport in London and it is accountable to the mayor. The government has proposed that London Underground will be modernised through Public Private Partnership, however the current mayor is opposed to this.

The role of TfL is:
- to manage the buses, Croydon Tramlink and the Docklands Light Railway (DLR).
- to manage the Underground once control is passed from central government
- to manage an important network of roads to be known as the Transport for London Road Network
- to regulate taxis and minicabs
- to run the London River services and promote the river for passenger and freight movement
- to help to co-ordinate the Dial-a-Ride and Taxicard schemes for door-to-door services for transport users with mobility problems
- to take responsibility for traffic lights

London Borough Councils maintain the role of highway and traffic authorities for 95% of London's roads.
Commissioner, Transport for London: Bob Kiley

TfL Board members: David Begg; Prof Stephen Glaister; Kirsten Hearn; Mike Hodgkinson; Ollie Jackson; Jimmy Knapp; Susan Kramer; Prof Robert Lane; Joyce Mamode; Paul Moore; Steve Norris; David Quarmby; Tony West; Dave Wetzel.
Special Advisers to the Board, Bryan Heiser and Lynn Sloman

For further information see the entry for TfL in the Public Services section.

Spatial Development Strategy (SDS)
The Mayor of London is responsible for strategic planning in London in the form of a Spatial Planning Strategy. This sets priorities and provides direction for the future development of London. It replaces regional planning guidance provided by the Secretary of State. The SDS incorporates the key aspects of the many other areas of the Mayor's responsibility including sustainable development, transport, economic development, housing, the built environment, the natural and open environment, waste, town centres, cultural and community facilities, London's Capital and World City roles and the River Thames.

London Borough Councils continue to deal with all planning applications and produce Unitary Development Plans (UDP) which conform with the SDS. The Mayor is however a statutory consultee for planning applications of 'potential strategic importance'.

London Development Agency (LDA)
(Email: info@lda.gov.uk; Web: www.lda.gov.uk)

The LDA promotes economic development and regeneration. It is one of the eight regional development agencies set up around the country to perform this task.

The key aspects of the LDA's role are:
- to promote business efficiency, investment and competitiveness
- to promote employment
- to enhance the skills of local people
- to create sustainable development

London Boroughs retain powers to promote economic development in their local areas.
Chief Executive: Michael Ward

LDA Board members: Victor Anderson (London Assembly Member); George Barlow (Chair); Honor Chapman (Vice-Chair); Mick Connolly; Len Duvall (Vice-Chair), (London Assembly Member); Michael Frye; Tamara Ingram; George Kessler; Judith Mayhew; Kumar Murshid; Lord Paul; Andrew Pelling, (London Assembly Member); Cllr Sally Powell; Mary Reilly; Yvonne Thompson.

The Environment
The mayor is required to formulate strategies to tackle London's environmental issues including:
- air quality
- biodiversity – the protection and enhancement of flora and fauna
- waste management
- noise
- energy use and London's contribution to climate change targets
- ground water levels
- traffic levels and emissions

12 Governed London

Metropolitan Police Authority (MPA)
(Email: enquiries@mpa.gov.uk;
Web: www.mpa.gov.uk)

This body, which oversees the policing of London consists of 12 members of the assembly, including the deputy mayor, 4 magistrates and 7 independents. One of the independents is appointed by the Home Secretary. The role of the MPA will be:
- to maintain an efficent and effective police force
- to publish and annual policing plan
- to set police targets and monitor performance
- to be part of the appointment, discipline and removal of senior officers
- to be responsible for the performance budget

The boundaries of the metropolitan police districts have been changed to be in line with the 32 London boroughs. Areas beyond the GLA remit have been incorporated into the Surrey, Hertfordshire and Essex police areas. The City of London has its own police force.

Members of MPA (Total: 23)
Tony Arbour, (London Assembly Member); Jennette Arnold, (London Assembly Member); Reshard Auladin, (Magistrate Member); Richard Barnes (Deputy Chair), (London Assembly Member); John Biggs, (London Assembly Member); Cindy Butts, (Independent Member); Roger Evans, (London Assembly Member); Lynne Featherstone, (London Assembly Member); Nicky Gavron, (London Assembly Member) (Deputy Mayor); Toby Harris (Chair), (London Assembly Member); Peter Herbert (Deputy Chair), (Independent Member); Elizabeth Howlett, (London Assembly Member); Darren Johnson, (London Assembly Member); Jennifer Jones, (London Assembly Member); Nicholas Long, (Independent Member); Cecile Lothian, (Magistrate Member); R. David Muir, (Independent Member); Sir John Quinton, (Independent Member); Angela Slaven, (Independent Member); Richard Sumray, (Magistrate Member); Graham Tope, (London Assembly Member); Abdal Ullah, (Independent Member); Rachel Whittaker, (Magistrate Member).

London Fire and Emergency Planning Authority (LFEPA)
20 Albert Embankment, London SE1 7SD (Tel: 020-7582 3811; Email: info@london-fire.gov.uk; Web: www.london-fire.gov.uk)

From 3rd July 2000 the existing London Fire and Civil Defence Authority became the London Fire and Emergency Planning Authority. It consists of 17 members, 9 drawn from the new assembly and 8 nominated by the London Boroughs. The role of LFEPA is:
- to set the strategy for the provision of fire services
- to ensure that the fire brigade can meet all the normal requirements efficiently
- to ensure the fire brigade is properly trained and equipped
- to ensure that effective arrangements are made for the fire brigade to receive emergency calls and deal with them promptly
- to ensure that information useful to the development of the firefighting is gathered

Members of the LFEPA (Total: 17)
Liaquat Ali; Louise Bloom, (London Assembly Member); Brian Coleman, (London Assembly Member); Lynne Featherstone, (London Assembly Member); Peter Forrest; Anne Gallop; Maurice Heaster; Samantha Heath, (London Assembly Member); Jennifer Jones, (London Assembly Member); Janice Long; Robert Neill, (London Assembly Member); Eric Ollerenshaw, (London Assembly Member); Trevor Phillips, (London Assembly Member); Philip Portwood; Roy Shaw; Valerie Shawcross (Chair), (London Assembly Member); Toby Simon.

Health
Healthcare in London continues to be the remit of the NHS and the London Ambulance Service. The NHS London Regional Office of the NHS Executive is supported by the GLA in its development of strategies to improve the health of Londoners. The Mayor has also set up an independent London Health Commission to tackle health inequalities and improve the health of Londoners.

Membership of London Health Commission
Henry Abraham; Dr Sue Atkinson; George Barlow; Bolanji Bank-Anthony; Dr Ian Basnett; Jane Belman; Jonathan Bland; Mark Brangwyn; Chris Bull; Jo Cleary; Neale Coleman; Anna Coote; Liza Cragg; Dr Deirdre Cunningham; Helen Davies; June Dawes; Dr Adrian Eddleston; Janet Fyle; Dr Clare Gerada; Prof. Andy Haines; Terry Hanafin; Elizabeth Howlett; Anthony Jacobson; Dr. Bobbie Jacobson; Lee Jasper; Hermine Kelly-Hall; Dr Zarrina Kurtz; Cllr Bernadette Lappage; Elizabeth Manero; Prof. Michael Marmot; Mary Ney; Christine Outram;

John Owen; David Peters; Trevor Phillips; John Riordan; Steve Roberts; Hilary Samson-Barry; Daniel Silverstone; Richard Smith; Richard Sumray; Rashmi Varma; Melba Wilson; Ansel Wong (Chair).

The Cultural Strategy Group for London (CSGL)
The GLA aims to provide a wide ranging culture strategy, encompassing the arts, sport and tourism. The CSGL provides advice and guidance to the GLA on this matter. It works with a number of regional agencies such as English Heritage, London Arts and the London Sports Board. Its role is:
- produce a cultural strategy for London
- support a programme of events across London, in partnership with a number of agencies
- to develop a co-ordinated approach to funding and support of the cultural sector
- to pro-actively foster partnerships with other sectors

Membership: Esrah Ahmed; Chinedu Aniedobe, Yasmin Anwar (Chair); Jennette Arnold, (London Assembly Member); Wozzy Brewster; Cllr Lyn Brown; Cllr Raj Chandarana; Maya Even, Eenasul Fateh (Aladin) (Vice Chair); Piers Gough; Sally Hamwee, (London Assembly Member); Cllr Bob Harris; Paul Hopper; Elizabeth Howlett, (London Assembly Member); Nicolas Kent; Ben Knowles; Diane Henry Lepart; Yvonne Marson; Martin McCallum; Bev Randall; Nicholas Serota; Belinda Sosinowicz; Richard Sumray; Mike Weber.
Official observers: Lady Sue Woodford Hollick; Jack Amos

The GLA will be housed at the temporary address shown above until its new premises are complete. The new GLA building is being built on a brown field site on the south bank of the river Thames, adjacent to Tower Bridge. The building is a distinctive glass globe with a purpose built assembly chamber and offices for 400 people. It will stand fifty metres high, with 21,700 square metres of floor space.

THE MAYORAL CANDIDATES
In the build up to the election of the Mayor for London, there were a number of controversial issues which dogged the main parties in the nominations of their Mayoral candidate. Each party held an internal ballot to appoint their official candidate the results of which are given below. There were also a number of independent candidates running whose details are also given.

Conservative Party
Ballot Date: 17th January 2000
Chosen Candidate: Steven Norris
Rival Candidate: Andrew Boff
Voting System: One member one vote.
Result of Ballot: 12,903 in favour; 4,712 rebuff

Labour Party
Ballot Date: 20th February 2000
Chosen Candidate: Frank Dobson
Rival Candidates: Ken Livingstone*; Glenda Jackson
Voting System: Votes split into three sections. One was for the 41,000 London party members. The second was for the unions and societies affiliated to labour; the third was for MPs and MEPs and GLA candidates.
Result of Ballot: Membership vote: Dobson – 35.3%; Jackson – 9.8%; Livingstone—54.9%; Unions Vote: Dobson—26.9%; Jackson – 2.1%; Livingstone – 71.0%; MPs, MEPs and GLA candidates: Dobson—86.5%; Jackson – 1.3%; Livingstone – 12.2%
Totals after reallocation of Glenda Jacksons' votes: Dobson – 51.5%; Livingstone – 48.5%

*On the 6th March 2000 Ken Livingstone announced in the Evening Standard that he would stand as an independent candidate.

Liberal Democrats
Chosen Candidate: Susan Kramer
Rival Candidates: Donnachadh McCarthy; Mike Tuffrey, Keith Kerr.
Percentage of vote won: 62%

14 Governed London

CANDIDATES FOR GLA MEMBERSHIP

Labour Party
Trevor Phillips
Samantha Heath
David Lammy
Jeanette Arnold
Joe Docherty
Diana Johnson
Abdul Asad
Pam Wharfe
Talal Karim
Katy Thorne
Navin Shah

Conservative Party
Bob Neill
Eric Ollerenshaw
Syed Kamall
Rhodri Harris
Roger Evans
Tony Arbour
Andrew Pelling
Irene Kimm
Elizabeth Howlett
Lurline Champagnie
Richard Barnes
Victoria Borwick
Bernard Gentry
Michael Flynn
Patti Komlosty
Bob Blackman
Peter Forrest
Diane Henry
Robert Moreland
Harry Stokes
Piers Wauchope
David Williams
Cheryl Potter

Liberal Democrats
Sally Hamwee
Graham Tope
Lynne Featherstone
Louise Bloom
Mike Tuffrey
Geoff Pope
Meher Khan
Duncan Borrowman
Chris Noyce
Monroe Palmer
Meral Ece

Green Party
Darren Johnson
Victor Anderson
Jenny Jones
Noel Lynch
Shane Collins
Hilary Jago
Ashley Gunstock
John Street
Jayne Forbes
Simone Aspis
Catherine Mukhopadhyay

London Socialist Alliance
Paul Foot
Greg Tucker
Janine Booth
Christine Blower
Theresa Bennett
Anne Murphy
Kate Ford
Tobias Abse
Jean Kysow
George Taylor
Mark Steel

UK Independence Party
Damian Hockney
Christopher Pratt
Anthony van der Elst
Anthony Scholefield
Gregory Sylsz
John de Roeck
Robert Bryant
Gerald Roberts
James Feisenberger
Mark Lester
Penelope Weald

Socialist Labour Party
Arthur Scargill
Amanda Rose
Harpal Brar
Margaret Sharkey
Hardev Dhillon
Nicola Hoarau
Geoff Palmer
Novjoy Brar
Robert Siggins
Ella Rule
John Hayball

Natural Law Party
Geoffrey Clements
Richard Johnson
Judith Thomas
Alexander Hankey
Gerard Valente
Jeanie Livesley
Juliette Taylor-Elwes
Jonathan Hinde
Michael Mears

Campaign Against Tube Privatisation
Patrick Sikorski
Oliver New
Catherine Effer
Robert Law
Pam Slinger
Enoh Iterjere
Brian Monroe
Arwyn Thomas
Lewis Peacock
Graham Campbell
Davey Lyons

The Christian Peoples' Alliance Party
David Campanale
Sue May
Andrew Farmer
Ellen Greco
Deepak Mahtani
Nigel Poole
Stuart MacPherson
Philippa Berry
Tim Ward
Peter Wolstenholme

British National Party
David Hill
Peter Hart
Ken Francis
Michael Davidson
Paul Ferguson
Frank Walsh

Communist Party of Britain
Nick Wright
Sandra Lusk
James Beavis
Monty Goldman
Salvador Urdiales-Antelo
Anita Halpin
Anita Wright
Kevin Halpin
Richard Maybin

Pro-Motorist Small Shop
Geoffrey Ben-Nathan
Brian Bartle
Russ Conway
Joseph Pronckus

Other Independent Candidates
Peter Tatchell

GLA Election Results 15

THE MAYORAL AND ASSEMBLY ELECTION RESULTS

BARNET AND CAMDEN

Mayor

Name	Party	1st Pref	%	2nd Pref	%
Ken Livingstone	Ind	51,649	38.8	13,368	12.0
Steven Norris	Con	36,826	27.7	14,858	13.4
Susan Kramer	LD	17,096	12.8	33,144	29.8
Frank Dobson	Lab	16,978	12.8	17,125	15.4
Darren Johnson	Green	3,564	2.7	16,621	15.0
Ram Gidoomal	CPA	2,336	1.8	3,649	3.3
Michael Newland	BNP	1,451	1.1	2,285	2.1
Geoffrey Ben-Nathan	PMSS	1,055	0.8	2,865	2.6
Damian Hockney	UKInd	972	0.7	2,832	2.6
Ashwin Kumar Tanna	Ind	708	0.5	2,938	2.6
Geoffrey Clements	NL	397	0.3	1,388	1.2
Turnout	Total Votes: 133,032 (35.0%)				

Assembly
First Past the Post

Name	Party	Votes	%
Brian Coleman	Con	41,583	32.9
Helen Gordon	Lab	41,032	32.5
Jonathan Davies	LD	22,295	17.6
Miranda Dunn	Green	14,768	11.7
Candy Udwin	London Socialist Alliance	3,488	2.8
Magnus Nielsen	UKInd	2,115	1.7
Diane Derksen	Maharishi's Natural Prog.	1,081	0.9
Majority	Total Votes: 551 (0.4%)		
Turnout	Total Votes: 136,384 (35.0%)		

Top up seats (London wide)

Name	Votes	%
Conservative	37,795	29.4
Labour	37,352	29.1
Liberal Democrats	19,376	15.1
Green	16,789	13.1
Christian Peoples' Alliance	3,258	2.5
London Socialist Alliance	2,421	1.9
British National Party	2,217	1.7
UK Independence Party	2,037	1.6
Peter Tatchell	1,908	1.5
Campaign Against Tube Privatisation	1,517	1.2
Pro-Motorist Small Shop	1,381	1.1
Socialist Labour Party	1,115	0.9
Natural Law Party	677	0.5
Communist Party of Britain	632	0.5
Turnout	Total Votes: 127,475 (35.0%)	

16 Governed London

BEXLEY AND BROMLEY

Mayor

Name	Party	1st Pref	%	2nd Pref	%
Steven Norris	Con	57,193	39.3	18,552	15.3
Ken Livingstone	Ind	41,679	28.7	12,935	10.7
Susan Kramer	LD	20,610	14.2	38,691	31.9
Frank Dobson	Lab	11,975	8.2	14,898	12.3
Michael Newland	BNP	3,785	2.6	5,569	4.6
Ram Gidoomal	CPA	3,678	2.5	5,093	4.2
Darren Johnson	Green	2,673	1.8	13,335	11.0
Damian Hockney	UKInd	2,149	1.5	5,593	4.6
Geoffrey Ben-Nathan	PMSS	749	0.5	1,847	1.5
Ashwin Kumar Tanna	Ind	617	0.4	3,366	2.8
Geoffrey Clements	NL	286	0.2	1,385	1.1
Turnout	Total Votes: 145,391 (37.3%)				

Assembly
First Past the Post

Name	Party	Votes	%
Bob Neill	Con	64,879	47.2
Charlie Mansell	Lab	30,320	22.1
Duncan Borrowman	LD	29,710	21.6
Ian Jardin	Green	11,124	8.1
Jean Kysow	London Socialist Alliance	1,403	1.0
Majority	Total Votes: 34,559 (25.2%)		
Turnout	Total Votes: 137,436 (35.3%)		

Top up seats (London Wide)

Name	Votes	%
Conservative	59,019	41.8
Labour	29,776	21.1
Liberal Democrats	23,302	16.5
Green	11,021	16.5
British National Party	5,060	3.6
Christian Peoples' Alliance	4,621	3.3
UK Independence Party	3,746	2.6
Pro-Motorist Small Shop	1,167	0.8
Peter Tatchell	759	0.5
London Socialist Alliance	721	0.5
Socialist Labour Party	701	0.5
Campaign Against Tube Privatisation	656	0.5
Natural Law Party	443	0.3
Communist Party of Britain	321	0.2
Turnout	Total Votes: 142,072 (36.4%)	

BRENT AND HARROW

Mayor

Name	Party	1st Pref	%	2nd Pref	%
Ken Livingstone	Ind	47,044	43.7	11,847	13.6
Steven Norris	Con	25,293	23.5	11,240	12.9
Frank Dobson	Lab	15,279	14.2	15,372	17.6
Susan Kramer	LD	10,797	10.0	23,718	27.2
Ram Gidoomal	CPA	2,841	2.6	3,902	4.5
Darren Johnson	Green	1,809	1.7	9,959	11.4
Michael Newland	BNP	1,362	1.3	2,022	2.3
Ashwin Kumar Tanna	Ind	1,200	1.1	4,002	4.6
Geoffrey Ben-Nathan	PMSS	905	0.8	2,198	2.5
Damian Hockney	UKInd	788	0.7	1,945	2.2
Geoffrey Clements	NL	424	0.4	1,102	1.3
Turnout	Total Votes: 107,742 (32.5%)				

Assembly
First past the Post

Name	Party	Votes	%
Lord Toby Harris	Lab	36,675	37.6
Bob Blackman	Con	32,295	33.2
Chris Noyce	LD	17,161	17.6
Simone Aspis	Green	8,756	9.0
Austin Burnett	London Socialist Alliance	2,546	2.6
Majority	Total Votes: 4,380 (4.5%)		
Turnout	Total Votes: 97,433 (29.4%)		

Top up seats (London Wide)

Name	Votes	%
Labour	37,818	36.5
Conservative	28,622	27.6
Liberal Democrats	13,551	13.1
Green	9,763	9.4
Christian Peoples' Alliance	3,541	3.4
British National Party	1,955	1.9
UK Independence Party	1,943	1.9
London Socialist Alliance	1,299	1.2
Campaign Against Tube Privatisation	1,267	1.2
Pro-Motorist Small Shop	1,068	1.0
Peter Tatchell	975	0.9
Socialist Labour Party	816	0.8
Natural Law Party	545	0.5
Communist Party of Britain	534	0.5
Turnout	Total Votes: 103,697 (31.3%)	

18 Governed London

CITY AND EAST

Mayor

Name	Party	1st Pref	%	2nd Pref	%
Ken Livingstone	Ind	46,236	40.6	13,638	14,7
Frank Dobson	Lab	24,832	21.4	18,998	20.5
Steven Norris	Con	19,026	16.7	12,188	13.1
Susan Kramer	LD	9,919	8.7	20,468	22.1
Michael Newland	BNP	5,081	4.5	4,839	5.2
Ram Gidoomal	CPA	3,009	2.6	3,192	3.4
Darren Johnson	Green	2,383	2.1	10,740	11.6
Damian Hockney	UKInd	1,264	1.1	2,848	3.1
Geoffrey Ben-Nathan	PMSS	1,123	1.0	1,480	1.6
Geoffrey Clements	NL	816	0.7	1,568	1.7
Ashwin Kumar Tanna	Ind	783	0.7	1,568	1.7
Turnout	**Total Votes:** 114,022 (28.5%)				

Assembly
First past the post

Name	Party	Votes	%
John Briggs	Lab	45,387	45.9
Syed Kamall	Con	19,266	19.5
Janet Ludlow	LD	18,300	18.5
Peter Howell	Green	11,939	12.1
Kambiz Boomla	London Socialist Alliance	3,908	4.0
Majority	**Total Votes:** 26,121 (26.4%)		
Turnout	**Total Votes:** 98,800 (24.7%)		

Top up seats (London Wide)

Name	Votes	%
Labour	44,329	40.4
Conservative	19,116	17.4
Liberal Democrats	12,526	11.4
Green	10,079	9.2
British National Party	7,763	7.1
Christian Peoples' Alliance	4,001	3.6
UK Independence Party	2,977	2.7
London Socialist Alliance	1,844	1.7
Peter Tatchell	1,835	1.7
Campaign Against Tube Privatisation	1,710	1.6
Socialist Labour Party	1,149	1.0
Pro-Motorist Small Shop	818	0.8
Communist Party of Britain	784	0.7
Natural Law Party	672	0.6
Turnout	**Total Votes:** 109,603 (27.4%)	

GLA Election Results

CROYDON AND SUTTON

Mayor

Name	Party	1st Pref	%	2nd Pref	%
Ken Livingstone	Ind	41,818	32.9	12,935	12.2
Steven Norris	Con	41,794	32.9	15,534	14.6
Susan Kramer	LD	18,331	14.4	32,418	30.5
Frank Dobson	Lab	12,399	9.8	14,223	13.4
Ram Gidoomal	CPA	4,925	3.9	5,911	5.6
Michael Newland	BNP	2,389	1.9	3,686	3.5
Darren Johnson	Green	2,201	1.7	11,322	10.6
Damian Hockney	UKInd	1,578	1.2	4,238	4.0
Ashwin Kumar Tanna	Ind	716	0.6	3,149	3.0
Geoffrey Ben-Nathan	PMSS	647	0.5	1,725	1.6
Geoffrey Clements	NL	309	0.2	1,197	1.1
Turnout	Total Votes: 127,107 (34.8%)				

Assembly
First past the post

Name	Party	Votes	%
Andrew Pelling	Con	48,421	40.6
Anne Gallop	LD	30,614	25.7
Maggie Mansell	Lab	29,514	24.8
Peter Hickson	Green	8,884	7.4
Mark Steel	London Socialist Alliance	1,823	1.5
Majority	Total Votes: 17,807 (14.9%)		
Turnout	Total Votes: 119,256 (32.7%)		

Top up seats (London wide)

Name	Votes	%
Conservative	43,666	35.4
Labour	29,221	23.7
Liberal Democrats	23,837	19.3
Green	9,658	7.8
Christian Peoples' Alliance	6,039	4.9
British National Party	3,206	2.6
UK Independence Party	2,902	2.4
Pro-Motorist Small Shop	1,028	0.8
London Socialist Alliance	907	0.7
Peter Tatchell	803	0.6
Campaign Against Tube Privatisation	779	0.6
Socialist Labour Party	675	0.6
Natural Law Party	440	0.4
Communist Party of Britain	354	0.3
Turnout	Total Votes: 123,515 (33.9%)	

20 Governed London

EALING AND HILLINGDON

Mayor

Name	Party	1st Pref	%	2nd Pref	%
Ken Livingstone	Ind	48,192	37.6	13,243	12.2
Steven Norris	Con	34,948	27.2	13,879	13.4
Frank Dobson	Lab	19,566	15.2	17,357	16.8
Susan Kramer	LD	14,011	10.9	29,281	28.3
Ram Gidoomal	CPA	3,127	2.4	4,256	4.0
Michael Newland	BNP	2,679	2.1	3,700	3.6
Darren Johnson	Green	2,612	2.0	12,344	11.9
Damian Hockney	UKInd	1,266	1.0	3,335	3.2
Geoffrey Ben-Nathan	PMSS	841	0.7	1,784	1.7
Ashwin Kumar Tanna	Ind	666	0.5	3,052	3.0
Geoffrey Clements	NL	386	0.3	1,332	1.3
Turnout	Total votes: 128,294 (30.7%)				

Assembly
First past the post

Name	Party	Votes	%
Richard Barnes	Con	44,850	37.4
Gurcharan Singh	Lab	38,038	31.7
Mike Cox	LD	22,177	18.5
Graham Lee	Green	11,788	9.8
Nick Grant	London Socialist Alliance	2,977	2.5
Majority	Total Votes: 6,812 (5.7%)		
Turnout	Total Votes: 119,830 (30.7%)		

Top up seats (London wide)

Name	Votes	%
Labour	40,551	32.7
Conservative	38,191	30.8
Liberal Democrats	16,575	13.4
Green	11,863	9.6
Christian Peoples' Alliance	3,846	3.1
British National Party	3,823	3.1
UK Independence Party	2,387	1.9
Campaign Against Tube Privatisation	1,474	1.2
London Socialist Alliance	1,261	1.0
Peter Tatchell	1,067	0.9
Pro-Motorist Small Shop	973	0.8
Socialist Labour Party	950	0.8
Natural Law Party	531	0.4
Communist Party of Britain	529	0.4
Turnout	Total Votes: 124,021 (30.7%)	

GLA Election Results 21

ENFIELD AND HARINGEY

Mayor

Name	Party	1st Pref	%	2nd Pref	%
Ken Livingstone	Ind	50,250	43.0	12,067	12.7
Steven Norris	Con	28,522	24.4	11,691	12.3
Frank Dobson	Lab	16,469	14.1	16,119	17.0
Susan Kramer	LD	12,113	10.4	26,092	27.5
Darren Johnson	Green	2,762	2.0	15,095	15.9
Ram Gidoomal	CPA	2,398	2.0	3,317	3.5
Michael Newland	BNP	1,967	1.7	2,784	2.9
Damian Hockney	UKInd	928	0.8	2,524	2.7
Geoffrey Ben-Nathan	PMSS	667	0.6	1,411	1.5
Ashwin Kumar Tanna	Ind	475	0.4	2,552	2.7
Geoffrey Clements	NL	369	0.3	1,216	1.3
Turnout	Total Votes: 116,920 (33.6%)				

Assembly
First Past the Post

Name	Party	Votes	%
Nicky Gavron	Lab	34,509	32.2
Peter Forrest	Con	31,207	29.2
Sean Hooker	LD	14,319	13.4
Richard Course	Ind Pro-Livingstone	12,581	11.8
Peter Budge	Green	10,761	10.0
Weyman Bennett	London Socialist Alliance	3,671	3.4
Majority	Total Votes: 3,302 (3.1%)		
Turnout	Total Votes: 107,048 (30.8%)		

Top up seats (London wide)

Name	Votes	%
Labour	37,191	33.0
Conservative	29,807	26.4
Green	14,673	13.0
Liberal Democrats	13,824	12.2
Christian Peoples' Alliance	3,277	2.9
British National Party	2,634	2.3
London Socialist Alliance	2,564	2.3
UK Independence Party	2,278	2.0
Peter Tatchell	1,803	1.6
Campaign Against Tube Privatisation	1,424	1.3
Socialist Labour Party	1,213	1.1
Pro-Motorist Small Shop	895	0.8
Communist Party of Britain	718	0.6
Natural Law Party	571	0.5
Turnout	Total Votes: 112,872 (32.5%)	

22 Governed London

GREENWICH AND LEWISHAM

Mayor

Name	Party	1st Pref	%	2nd Pref	%
Ken Livingstone	Ind	47,522	45.9	11,413	12.9
Steven Norris	Con	19,822	19.1	10,204	11.6
Frank Dobson	Lab	15,124	14.6	15,365	17.4
Susan Kramer	LD	10,880	10.5	23,439	26.5
Darren Johnston	Green	2,679	2.6	14,335	16.2
Ram Gidoomal	CPA	2,668	2.6	3,105	3.5
Michael Newland	BNP	2,562	2.5	2,987	3.4
Damian Hockney	UKInd	932	0.9	2,285	2.6
Ashwin Kumar Tanna	Ind	570	0.6	2,934	3.3
Geoffrey Ben-Nathan	PMSS	531	0.5	1,106	1.2
Geoffrey Clements	NL	302	0.3	1,144	1.3
Turnout	Total Votes: 103.592 (31.6%)				

Assembly
First Past the Post

Name	Party	Votes	%
Len Duvall	Lab	40,386	42.6
Rhodri Harris	Con	22,401	23.6
David Buxton	LD	16,290	17.2
Terry Liddle	Green	11,839	12.5
Ian Page	London Socialist Alliance	3,981	4.2
Majority	Total Votes: 17,985 (19.0%)		
Turnout	Total Votes: 94,697 (29.0%)		

Top up seats (London wide)

Name	Votes	%
Labour	37,200	37.0
Conservative	20,450	20.3
Green	13,269	13.2
Liberal Democrats	12,704	12.6
Christian Peoples' Alliance	3,729	3.7
British National Party	3,487	3.5
London Socialist Alliance	2,274	2.3
UK Independence Party	2,117	2.1
Peter Tatchell	1,592	1.6
Socialist Labour Party	1,215	1.2
Campaign Against Tube Privatisation	903	0.9
Pro-Motorist Small Shop	798	0.8
Natural Law Party	464	0.5
Communist Party of Britain	390	0.4
Turnout	Total Votes: 100,592 (30.7%)	

GLA Election Results 23

HAVERING AND REDBRIDGE

Mayor

Name	Party	1st Pref	%	2nd Pref	%
Ken Livingstone	Ind	39,277	33.8	10,927	11.5
Steven Norris	Con	38,088	32.8	13,903	14.6
Frank Dobson	Lab	14,549	12.5	14,355	15.1
Susan Kramer	LD	12,719	11.0	27,913	29.3
Michael Newland	BNP	3,938	3.4	5,231	5.5
Ram Gidoomal	CPA	2,784	2.4	3,579	3.8
Darren Johnston	Green	1,815	1.6	9,934	10.4
Damian Hockney	UKInd	1,619	1.4	3,865	4.1
Geoffrey Ben-Nathan	PMSS	618	0.5	1,670	1.8
Ashwin Kumar Tanna	Ind	511	0.4	2,726	2.9
Geoffrey Clements	NL	287	0.2	1,179	1.2
Turnout	Total Votes: 116,205 (32.9%)				

Assembly
First past the post

Name	Party	Votes	%
Roger Evans	Con	40,919	37.6
Chris Robbins	Lab	32,650	30.0
Geoffrey Seeff	LD	14,028	12.9
Ian Wilkes	Residents' Association	12,831	11.8
Ashley Gunstock	Green	6,803	6.2
George Taylor	London Socialist Alliance	1,744	1.6
Majority	Total votes: 8,269 (7.6%)		
Turnout	Total votes: 108,975 (30.8%)		

Top up seats (London Wide)

Name	Votes	%
Conservative	40,350	36.0
Labour	32,717	29.2
Liberal Democrats	13,691	12.2
Green	8,280	7.4
British National Party	5,170	4.6
Christian Peoples' Alliance	3,658	3.3
UK Independence Party	2,974	2.7
Campaign Against Tube Privatisation	1,087	1.0
London Socialist Alliance	967	0.9
Pro-Motorist Small Shop	939	0.8
Socialist Labour Party	740	0.7
Peter Tatchell	678	0.6
Natural Law Party	384	0.3
Communist Party of Britain	345	0.3
Turnout	Total Votes: 111,980 (31.7%)	

LAMBETH AND SOUTHWARK

Mayor

Name	Party	1st Pref	%	2nd Pref	%
Ken Livingstone	Ind	52,028	47.6	12,769	13.7
Steven Norris	Con	18,437	16.9	9,651	10.4
Frank Dobson	Lab	15,863	14.5	16,073	17.3
Susan Kramer	LD	13,139	12.0	25,497	27.4
Darren Johnson	Green	3,061	2.8	15,974	17.2
Ram Gidoomal	CPA	2,917	2.7	3,416	3.7
Michael Newland	BNP	1,572	1.4	2,050	2.2
Ashwin Kumar Tanna	Ind	815	0.8	3,654	3.9
Damian Hockney	UKInd	616	0.6	1,723	1.8
Geoffrey Ben-Nathan	PMSS	469	0.4	1,028	1.1
Geoffrey Clements	NL	323	0.3	1,116	1.2
Turnout	Total Votes: 109,240 (31.3%)				

Assembly
First past the post

Name	Party	Votes	%
Valerie Shawcross	Lab	37,985	37.6
Peter Facey	LD	22,492	22.3
Irene Kimm	Con	19,238	19.0
Storm Poorun	Green	13,242	13.1
Theresa Bennett	London Socialist Alliance	6,231	6.2
Tony Robinson	Humanist	1,261	1.2
Jonathan Silberman	Communist League	536	0.5
Majority	Total Votes: 15,493 (15.3%)		
Turnout	Total Votes: 70,983 (29.0%)		

Top up seats (London Wide)

Name	Votes	%
Labour	35,957	33.8
Liberal Democrats	18,065	17.0
Conservative	17,245	16.2
Green	16,130	15.2
Christian Peoples' Alliance	4,237	4.0
London Socialist Alliance	3,305	3.1
Peter Tatchell	3,241	3.0
British National Party	2,412	2.3
UK Independence Party	1,700	1.6
Campaign Against Tube Privatisation	1,264	1.2
Socialist Labour Party	1,123	1.1
Pro-Motorist Small Shop	705	0.7
Natural Law Party	507	0.5
Communist Party of Britain	486	0.5
Turnout	Total Votes: 106,377 (30.5%)	

MERTON AND WANDSWORTH

Mayor

Name	Party	1st Pref	%	2nd Pref	%
Ken Livingstone	Ind	46,125	38.4	12,530	12.4
Steven Norris	Con	36,237	30.1	13,928	13.7
Frank Dobson	Lab	14,436	12.0	16,330	16.1
Susan Kramer	LD	13,752	11.4	29,863	29.4
Ram Gidoomal	CPA	3,162	2.6	4,310	4.2
Darren Johnson	Green	2,713	2.3	14,049	13.8
Michael Newland	BNP	1,468	1.2	2,259	2.2
Damian Hockney	UKInd	979	0.8	2,931	2.9
Geoffrey Ben-Nathan	PMSS	502	0.4	1,320	1.3
Ashwin Kumar Tanna	Ind	496	0.4	2,673	2.6
Geoffrey Clements	NL	325	0.3	1,265	1.2
Turnout	Total Votes: 119,197 (35.5%)				

Assembly
First past the post

Name	Party	Votes	%
Elizabeth Howlett	Con	45,308	39.5
Maggie Cosin	Lab	32,438	28.3
Siobhan Vitelli	LD	12,496	10.9
Mark Thompson	Ind Lab Pro-Livingstone	11,918	10.4
Rajeev Thacker	Green	8,491	7.4
Syeed Manzoor	Ind Pro-Motorist	1,465	1.3
Sarbani Mazumdar	London Socialist Alliance	1,450	1.3
Terence Sullivan	Ind Pro-Transport	1,049	0.9
Majority	Total Votes: 12,870 (11.2%)		
Turnout	Total Votes: 114,615 (34.1%)		

Top up seats (London wide)

Name	Votes	%
Conservative	38,122	33.0
Labour	34,167	29.6
Liberal Democrats	14,199	12.3
Green	13,631	11.8
Christian Peoples' Alliance	3,969	3.4
British National Party	2,176	1.9
UK Independence Party	2,122	1.8
Peter Tachell	1,703	1.5
Campaign Against Tube Privatisation	1,393	1.2
London Socialist Alliance	1,264	1.10
Socialist Labour Party	863	0.8
Pro-Motorist Small Shop	843	0.7
Natural Law Party	494	0.4
Communist Party of Britain	441	0.4
Turnout	Total Votes: 115,387 (34.3%)	

26 Governed London

NORTH EAST

Mayor

Name	Party	1st Pref	%	2nd Pref	%
Ken Livingstone	Ind	63,333	48.0	14,422	13.3
Steven Norris	Con	21,676	16.4	11,632	10.7
Frank Dobson	Lab	20,075	15.2	19,708	18.1
Susan Kramer	LD	14,731	11.2	28,230	26.0
Darren Johnson	Green	4,253	3.2	20,678	19.0
Ram Gidoomal	CPA	2,791	2.1	3,472	3.2
Michael Newland	BNP	2,454	1.9	3,078	2.8
Damian Hockney	UKInd	986	0.8	2,331	2.1
Geoffrey Ben-Nathan	PMSS	720	0.6	1,367	1.3
Geoffrey Clements	NL	494	0.4	1,443	1.3
Ashwin Kumar Tanna	Ind	463	0.4	2,372	2.2
Turnout		Total Votes: 131,976 (32.3%)			

Assembly
First past the post

Name	Party	Votes	%
Meg Hillier	Lab	42,459	36.1
Paul Fox	LD	24,856	21.1
Eric Ollerenshaw	Con	20,975	17.8
Yen Chit Chong	Green	18,382	15.6
Cecelia Prosper	London Socialist Alliance	8,269	7.0
Paul Shaer	Ind Universal Justice	1,501	1.3
Erol Basarik	Reform 2000	1,144	1.0
Majority	Total Votes: 17,603 (15.0%)		
Turnout	Total Votes: 117,586 (28.7%)		

Top up seats (London wide)

Name	Votes	%
Labour	43,382	33.9
Conservative	20,923	16.3
Green	20,449	16.0
Liberal Democrats	19,790	15.4
London Socialist Alliance	5,556	4.3
Christian Peoples' Party	3,869	3.0
British National Party	3,515	2.7
Peter Tachell	2,981	2.3
UK Independence Party	2,156	1.7
Campaign Against Tube Privatisation	1,572	1.2
Socialist Labour Party	1,435	1.1
Communist Party of Britain	979	0.8
Pro-Motorist Small Shop	817	0.6
Natural Law Party	644	0.5
Turnout	Total Votes: 128,068 (31.3%)	

GLA Election Results

SOUTH WEST

Mayor

Name	Party	1st Pref	%	2nd Pref	%
Ken Livingstone	Ind	52,457	36.3	15,974	13.0
Steven Norris	Con	41,618	28.8	17,525	14.2
Susan Kramer	LD	23,745	16.4	38,124	31.0
Frank Dobson	Lab	15,719	10.9	18,033	14.6
Ram Gidoomal	CPA	3,195	2.2	5,000	4.1
Darren Johnson	Green	2,916	2.0	15,154	12.3
Michael Newland	BNP	1,862	1.3	2,977	2.4
Damian Hockney	UKInd	1,397	1.0	3,962	3.2
Ashwin Kumar Tanna	Ind	658	0.5	3,209	2.6
Geoffrey Ben-Nathan	PMSS	637	0.4	1,689	1.4
Geoffrey Clements	NL	356	0.2	1,466	1.2
Turnout	Total Votes: 144,560 (37.6%)				

Assembly
First past the post

Name	Party	Votes	%
Tony Arbour	Con	48,248	35.4
Geoff Pope	LD	41,189	30.2
Jagdish Sharma	Lab	31,065	22.8
Judy Maciejowska	Green	13,426	9.8
Danny Faith	London Socialist Alliance	2,319	1.7
Majority	Total Votes: 7,059 (5.2%)		
Turnout	Total Votes: 136,247 (35.4%)		

Top up seats (London Wide)

Name	Votes	%
Conservative	43,258	30.6
Labour	35,538	25.1
Liberal Democrats	31,585	22.3
Green	14,966	10.6
Christian Peoples' Alliance	4,115	2.9
UK Independence Party	2,772	2.0
British National Party	2,625	1.9
Peter Tatchell	1,257	0.9
London Socialist Alliance	1,251	0.9
Campaign Against Tube Privatisation	1,089	0.8
Pro-Motorist Small Shop	1,029	0.7
Socialist Labour Party	906	0.6
Natural Law Party	583	0.4
Communist Party of Britain	459	0.3
Turnout	Total Votes: 141,433 (36.7%)	

28 Governed London

WEST CENTRAL

Mayor

Name	Party	1st Pref	%	2nd Pref	%
Steven Norris	Con	44,954	38.8	13,256	14.1
Ken Livingstone	Ind	40,176	34.7	10,741	11.4
Susan Kramer	LD	11,609	10.0	27,937	29.7
Frank Dobson	Lab	11,070	9.6	14,139	15.0
Darren Johnson	Green	2,680	2.3	13,224	14.1
Ram Gidoomal	CPA	2,229	1.9	4,387	4.7
Michael Newland	BNP	999	0.9	1,870	2.0
Damian Hockney	UKInd	850	0.7	3,260	3.5
Geoffrey Ben-Nathan	PMSS	495	0.4	1,531	1.6
Geoffrey Clements	NL	396	0.3	1,384	1.5
Ashwin Kumar Tanna	Ind	337	0.3	2,307	2.4
Turnout	Total Votes: 115,795 (30.9%)				

Assembly
First past the post

Name	Party	Votes	%
Angie Bray	Con	47,117	44.2
Kate Green	Lab	28,838	27.0
Jon Burden	LD	14,071	13.2
Julia Stephenson	Green	12,254	11.5
Christine Blower	London Socialist Alliance	2,720	2.6
Stephen Smith	Homeless and Addicted	1,600	1.5
Majority	Total Votes: 18,279 (17.2%)		
Turnout	Total Votes: 106,600 (30.9%)		

Top up seats (London Wide)

Name	Votes	%
Conservative	44,489	39.6
Labour	27,675	24.6
Green	13,339	11.9
Liberal Democrats	12,530	11.2
Christian Peoples' Alliance	3,032	2.7
Peter Tatchell	2,260	2.0
UK Independence Party	1,943	1.7
British National Party	1,627	1.4
London Socialist Alliance	1,439	1.3
Campaign Against Tube Privatisation	1,266	1.1
Socialist Labour Party	789	0.7
Pro-Motorist Small Shop	787	0.7
Natural Law Party	604	0.5
Communist Party of Britain	517	0.5
Turnout	Total Vote: 18,279 (17.2%)	

OVERALL RESULTS

First Pref	Party	Votes	%
Ken Livingstone	Ind	667,877	39.0
Steven Norris	Con	464,434	27.1
Frank Dobson	Lab	223,884	13.1
Susan Kramer	LD	203,452	11.9
Ram Gidoomal	CPA	42,060	2.4
Darren Johnson	Green	38,121	2.2
Michael Newland	BNP	33,569	2.0
Damian Hockney	UKInd	16,234	1.0
Geoffrey Ben-Nathan	PMSS	9,956	0.6
Ashwin Kumar Tanna	Ind	9,015	0.5
Geoffrey Clements	Natural Law Party	5,470	0.3

Second Pref	Party	Votes	%
Susan Kramer	LD	404,815	28.5
Frank Dobson	Lab	228,095	16.0
Darren Johnson	Green	192,764	13.6
Steven Norris	Con	188,041	13.2
Ken Livingstone	Ind	178,809	12.6
Ram Gidoomal	CPA	56,489	4.0
Michael Newland	BNP	45,337	3.2
Damian Hockney	UKInd	43,672	3.1
Ashwin Kumar Tanna	Ind	41,766	2.9
Geoffrey Ben-Nathan	PMSS	23,021	1.6
Geoffrey Clements	Natural Law Party	18,185	1.3

Note: Percentages throughout the GLA Election results have been rounded to the first decimal place.

30 Governed London

THE MAYOR AND ASSEMBLY

The Mayor: Ken Livingstone
Political and Career History: Member of Lambeth LBC 1971-8; Member of Camden LBC 1978-1982; Member of the Regional Executive of the Greater London Labour Party 1974-1986; became a member of the GLC in 1973; elected leader of the GLC in 1973; Labour candidate for Hampstead and Highgate at the general election; elected MP for Brent East 1987; elected Mayor of the first Greater London Authority in May 2000.

CONSTITUENCIES AND MEMBERS

Constituency: Barnet and Camden
Member: Brian Coleman (Conservative)
Political and Career History: Councillor, London Borough of Barnet (Totteridge Ward) 1998 – date.

Constituency: Bexley and Bromley
Member: Bob Neill (Conservative)
Political and Career History: Barrister (specialising in criminal law) since 1975; Councillor, London Borough of Havering 1974–1990; Chairman of Environment and Social Services Committees, London Borough of Havering; GLC Member (Romford) 1985-1986; Leader, London Fire and Civil Defence Authority 1985–1987; parliamentary candidate, Dagenham 1983–1987; Chairman, Greater London Conservatives 1996–1999.

Constituency: Brent and Harrow
Member: Lord Toby Harris (Labour)
Political and Career History: Labour Councillor since 1978; Leader Haringey LBC 1987–99; Chair, Association of London Government; Director, Association of Community Health Councils 1987–1998; Appointed 'working peer 1998.

Constituency: City and East
Member: John Biggs (Labour)
Political and Career History: Tower Hamlets LBC councillor 1988—date; Opposition Council Leader, Tower Hamlets LBC 1991-1995; Labour spokesperson on Transport, GLA.

Constituency: Croydon and Sutton
Member: Andrew Pelling (Conservative)
Political and Career History: Croydon LBC councillor 1982–date; Chairman of Croydon Education Committee (1988–1994); Deputy Leader, Croydon Council Conservative Group 1996–date; President, Oxford University Conservative Association 1980; Secretary and Librarian of Oxford Union Society Autumn 1979–Spring 1980.

Constituency: Ealing and Hillingdon
Member: Richard Barnes (Conservative)
Political and Career History: Conservative Leader of Hillingdon LBC; Vice-chairman of Hillingdon Health Authority; Member of the Metropolitan Police Authority and the GLA Standing Orders Committee.

Constituency: Enfield and Haringey
Member: Nicky Gavron (Labour)
Political and Career History: Councillor, Haringey LBC 1986; Labour leader of the London Planning Advisory Committee and Chair since 1994; Vice-chair of the Planning Committee of the Local Government Association; Chair of the National Planning Forum; Member of Commission for Integrated Transport; Advisor to the Government's Urban Task Force.

Constituency: Greenwich and Lewisham
Member: Len Duvall (Labour)
Political and Career History: Deputy Leader, Greenwich LBC 1990; Leader, Greenwich LBC 1992–2000; Deputy Chair of the Association of London Government; Member of the London Fire and Civil Defence Authority; Chair, Thames Gateway London Partnership; Vice-chair, Local Government Information Unit 1994–96; Non-executive Director of the New Millennium Experience Forum; awarded OBE in 1998 for contribution to London Local Government.

Constituency: Havering and Redbridge
Member: Roger Evans (Conservative)
Political and Career History: Waltham Forest LBC councillor 1980–date; Waltham Forest LBC Opposition Deputy Leader 1993–1994; Waltham Forest LBC Opposition Leader 1994–1998.

Constituency: Lambeth and Southwark
Member: Valerie Shawcross (Labour)
Political and Career History: Former Leader Croydon Council; Commonwealth Development Project Manager; Labour Party's National Women's Officer.

GLA Biographies 31

Constituency: Merton and Wandsworth
Member: Elizabeth Howlett (Conservative)
Political and Career History: Professional opera singer 1961-1988; Professor, Royal College of Music 1988 – date; Deputy Chairman, Putney Conservative Association 1984-1986; Elected Councillor for Wandsworth London Borough Council 1986; Chairman – Social Services, Wandsworth LBC; Chairman – Education, Wandsworth LBC 1992-1998; Mayor, Wandsworth LBC 1998-1999; Chief Whip, Wandsworth LBC 1999-2000; Freeman of the City of London 1999.

Constituency: North East
Member: Meg Hillier (Labour)
Political and Career History: Reporter for the *Yorkshire Times*, 1991; Petty Officer, P&O Ferries, 1992; PR Officer, Newton Housing Group, 1993; Reporter, *Housing Association Weekly*, 1994; Features Editor, *Housing Today* 1995 – 1998; Councillor, Islington LBC 1994 – date; Mayor, Islington LBC 1998 – 1999.

Constituency: South West
Member: Anthony Arbour (Conservative)
Political and Career History: Councillor, Richmond upon Thames LBC 1968; Magistrate, Richmon upon Thames 1975; Chairman, Hampton Wick United Charity 1975; Vice-chairman, Kingston and Richmond Family Health Services Authority 1990-1996; Leader Conservative Group, Richmond upon Thames 1994; Senior Lecturer, Kingston University Business School, 1983.

Constituency: West Central
Member: Angie Bray (Conservative)
Political and Career History: Radio presenter/reporter for British Services Broadcasting 1979 – 1980 and for LBC 1980-1988; Head of Broadcasting for Conservative Central Office 1989-1991; Press Secretary to Chairman of the Conservative Party (The Rt. Hon. Chris Patten) 1992-1992; Manager of Media Unit, IGA 1992-1995; Senior Consultant for APCO Ltd 1995-2000.

LONDON LIST MEMBERS

Member: Victor Anderson (Green)
Political and Career History: author of Alternative Economic Indicators and Energy Efficient policies; researcher for Plaid Cymru at House of Commons and Welsh Assembly.

Member: Jennette Arnold (Labour)
Political and Career History: former nurse, health visitor and regional director of the Royal College of Nursing; Deputy Mayor of Islington Borough Council.

Member: Louise Bloom (Liberal Democrat)
Political History: Researcher to Liberal Democrat Candidates, Royal Borough of Kingston 1991—93; Voluntary Sector Employment 1994—97; Information Officer, Richmond Advice and Information on Disability 1998—2000; Vice Chair, Green Liberal Democrats 1995—present.

Member: Lynne Featherstone (Liberal Democrat)
Political and Career History: A strategic design specialist; author of Marketing and Communication Techniques for Architects; Opposition Leader of Haringey Council.

Member: Baroness (Sally) Hamwee (Liberal Democrat)
Political and Career History: Councillor, London Borough of Richmond upon Thames (Palewell ward) 1978-98; Chair, London Planning Advisory Committee 1986-87; Member Joseph Rowntree Foundation Inquiry, Planning for Housing, 1991; appointed Life Peer 1991 (Liberal Democrat Lords spokesperson, Environment Transport and the Regions); Member Liberal Democrat General Election Team 1992 and 1997; Appointed Deputy Chair of Greater London Assembly, May 2000.

Member: Samantha Heath (Labour)
Political and Career History: trained as a civil engineer; lecturer at University of Greenwich; Wandsworth councillor.

Member: Darren Johnson (Green)
Political and Career History: Joined Green Party aged 20; Served on Party's National Executive from 1993—95; graduate of Goldsmiths College, London in Politics and Economics.

Member: Jennifer Jones (Green)
Political history: worked in London as a financial controller; Chair of National Executive, Green Party 1995-1997.

32 Governed London

Member: Eric Ollerenshaw (Conservative)
Political and Career History: Chairman of Hackney North and Stoke Newington Conservative Association 1991—1999; member of ILEA from 1986-1990.

Member: Trevor Phillips (Labour)
Political and Career History: former President of the National Union of Students; worked for the BBC and London Tonight; Chairman of Greater London Assembly.

Member: Graham Tope (Liberal Democrat)
Political and Career History: Leader of the European Liberal Democrat and Reform (ELDR) group on the Committee of the Regions, Vice President of the Local Government Association; Liberal Democrat MP for Sutton and Cheam 1972-74; Deputy-General Secretary for Voluntary Action Camden 1975-90.

London Borough Councils, Map 33

LONDON BOROUGH COUNCILS

London Boroughs

1 Barking & Dagenham
2 Barnet
3 Bexley
4 Brent
5 Bromley
6 Camden
7 City of London
8 Croydon
9 Ealing
10 Enfield
11 Greenwich
12 Hackney
13 Hammersmith & Fulham
14 Haringey
15 Harrow
16 Havering
17 Hillingdon
18 Hounslow
19 Islington
20 Kensington & Chelsea
21 Kingston upon Thames
22 Lambeth
23 Lewisham
24 Merton
25 Newham
26 Redbridge
27 Richmond upon Thames
28 Southwark
29 Sutton
30 Tower Hamlets
31 Waltham Forest
32 Wandsworth
33 Westminster

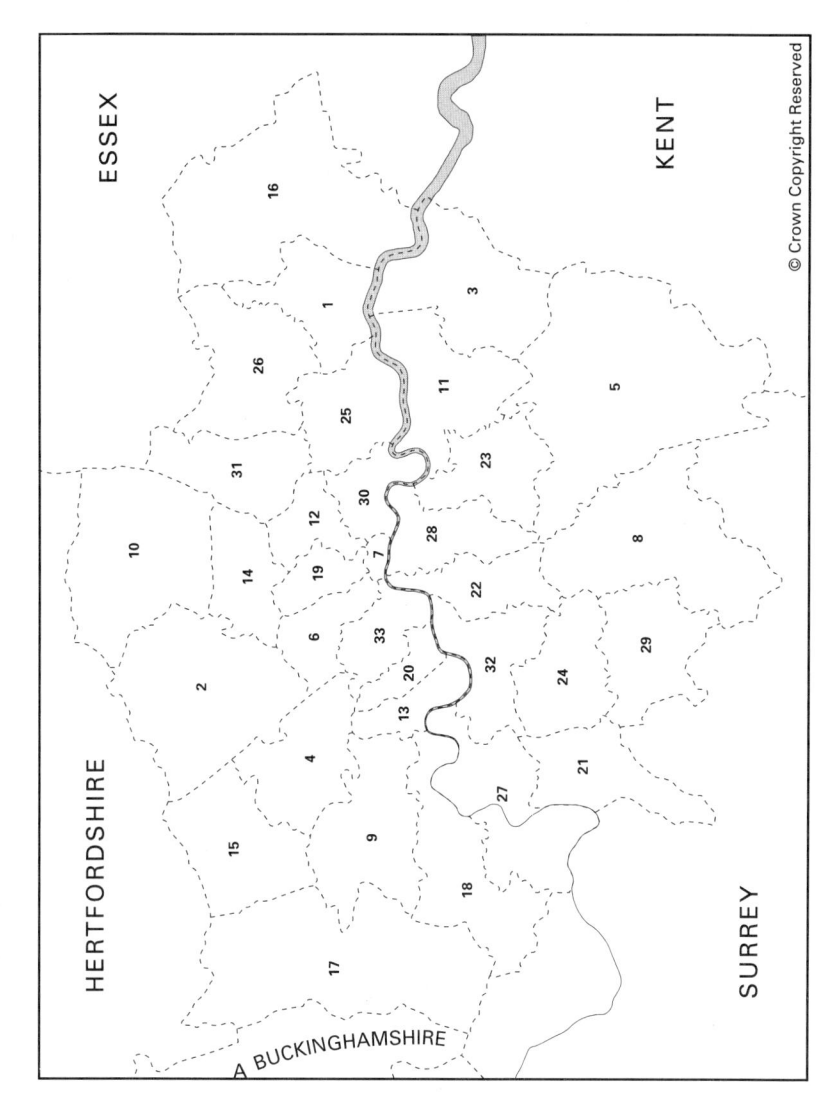

© Crown Copyright Reserved

LONDON BOROUGH COUNCILS

By virtue of the London Government Act 1963 the Greater London Council and 32 chartered boroughs came into existence in April 1965. The GLC ceased to exist in 1986 by virtue of the Local Government Act 1985. Currently in London there are 32 boroughs plus the Corporation of London. In this section we have provided maps and main contact information for each borough along with listings of the chief officers and councillors. Political composition, parliamentary constituency and council tax details are also included. Please note that non-domestic council tax rates are derived from the value of property as at 1 April 1993 and further information on this can be acquired directly from individual boroughs. London borough councillors have four year terms of office retiring together – the next elections will be held in May 2002. The listings of councillors were correct as at April 2001.

BARKING AND DAGENHAM

BARKING & DAGENHAM

Civic Centre, Dagenham RM10 7BN
(Tel: 020-8592 4500; Fax: 020-8227 2806;
Web: www.barking-dagenham.gov.uk).
Director of Housing and Health: 2 Stour Road, Dagenham RM10 7JF.
Education Officer: Town Hall, Barking IG11 7LU.
Contracts Services: Valence Depot, Becontree Avenue, Dagenham RM8 3BU.
Librarian: Central Library, Barking IG11 7NB.
Valence House Museum: Valence House, Becontree Avenue, Dagenham RM8 3HT.
Registration of Births, Deaths and Marriages: Arden House, 198 Longbridge Road, Barking IG11 8SY (Tel: 020-8270 4742).

CHIEF OFFICERS

Chief Executive: Graham Farrant
Borough Finance Officer: Barry Pummell
Borough Officer for Community Learning and Chief Inspector of Schools: Roger Luxton
Borough Officer for Democratic Support and Legal Services: Roy Cottle
Borough Officer for Policy and Review: John Tatam
Borough Personnel Officer: Alan Beadle
Controller of Leisure and Environmental Services: Jack Knowles
Director of Housing and Health: David Woods
Director of Social Services: Julia Ross

MEMBERS OF THE COUNCIL

Councillor	Ward
Mayor: P. A. Twomey, Lab.	River
Deputy Mayor: P. J. Manley, Lab.	Eastbury
Leader of the Council: C. J. Fairbrass, Lab.	Heath
J. L. Alexander, Lab.	Abbey
M. G. Baker, Lab.	Longbridge
D. F. Best, Lab.	Village
J. Blake, Lab.	Parsloes
E. E. Bradley, Lab.	Becontree
G. J. Bramley, Lab.	Abbey
S. Bramley, Lab.	Longbridge
J. E. Bruce, Lab.	Valence
L. E. Bunn, Lab.	Eastbrook
H. J. Collins, Lab.	Fanshawe
L. A. Collins, Lab.	Eastbrook
J. Conyard, Lab.	Manor
A. Cooper, LD	Eastbury
V. W. Cridland, Lab.	Valence
R. J. Curtis, R.	Chadwell Heath
W. Dale, Lab.	Village
J. Davis, Lab.	Triptons
M. A. R. Fani, Lab.	Abbey
K. J. Flint, Lab.	Gascoigne
C. Geddes, Lab.	Triptons
A. Gibbs, R.	Chadwell Heath
N. S. S. Gill, Lab.	Longbridge
S. P. Gill, Lab.	Parsloes
K. A. Golden, Lab.	Village
I. Jamu, Lab.	River
R. J. E. Jeyes, R.	Chadwell Heath
F. C. Jones, Lab.	Fanshawe
S. Kallar, Lab.	Heath
J. H. Lawrence, Lab.	Heath
M. E. McKenzie, Lab.	Gascoigne
B. M. Osborne, Lab.	Valence
R. B. Parkin, Lab.	Fanshawe
R. A. J. Pateint Lab.	Thames

C. T. W. Pond, Lab.
J. W. Porter, Lab
J. E. Rawlinson, Lab.
R. P. Rogers, Lab.
V. M. Rush, Lab.
G. H. Shaw, Lab.
L. A. Smith, LD
S. Summerfield, Lab.
A. G. Thomas, Lab.
J. M. Van Roten, Lab.
T. G. W. Wade, Lab.
J. P. Wainwright, Lab.
M. M. West, Lab.
E. J. White, Lab.
M. M. Worby, Lab.

Marks Gate
Campbell
Campbell
Manor
Gascoigne
Thames
Goresbrook
Eastbrook
Goresbrook
Campbell
Alibon
Becontree
Triptons
Alibon
Marks Gate

Political Composition: Lab. 46; R. 3; LD. 2.
Population: 154,786
Area: 3,611 hectares.

ABOUT BARKING AND DAGENHAM

Barking and Dagenham lies on the north side of the River Thames to the east of the City. It is a mainly residential area, however, a variety of industry is based in the borough, notably Ford Motor Company's factory in Dagenham. Barking Town Centre is home to the Vicarage Field Shopping centre which has a large pedestrianised area and the Borough has nearly 1000 acres of parks and open spaces and two nature reserves – The Chase Nature Reserve and Barking Reach Nature Reserve. There are numerous leisure and sporting facilities in the borough including a theatre, swimming pools, leisure centres and community halls.

COUNCIL TAX BANDS 2001-2002

Band	Market Value of the Property	Council Tax
A	Up to £40,000	£566.62
B	£40,001 to 52,000	£659.89
C	£52,001 to 68,000	£754.16
D	£68,001 to 88,000	£848.43
E	£88,001 to 120,000	£1136.97
F	£120,001 to 160,000	£1225.51
G	£160,001 to 320,000	£1414.05
H	£320,001 or more	£1696.86

London Borough Councils 35

BARNET

Town Hall, The Burroughs, Hendon NW4 4BG (Tel: 020-8359 2000; Fax: 020-8359 2480; Email: info.centre@barnet.gov.uk; Web: www.barnet.gov.uk).
Chief Executive: Town Hall, The Burroughs, Hendon NW4 4BG (Tel: 020-8359 2021; Fax 020-8359 2579).
Strategic Director of Community Development: Town Hall, The Burroughs, Hendon NW4 4BG (Tel: 020-8359 2462; Fax 020-8359 2025).
Strategic Director of Education and Children: Town Hall, The Burroughs, Hendon NW4 4BG (Tel: 020-8359 2283; Fax 020-8359 2284).
Strategic Director of Environment: Town Hall, The Burroughs, Hendon NW4 4BG (Tel: 020-8359 2116; Fax 020-8359 2561).
Strategic Director of Resources: Town Hall, The Burroughs, Hendon NW4 4BG (Tel: 020-8359 2123; Fax: 020-8359 2581).
Strategic Director of Social Affairs: Town Hall, The Burroughs, Hendon NW4 4BG (Tel 020-8359 2714; Fax 020-8359 2284).
Registration of Births, Deaths and Marriages: 29 Wood Street, Barnet EN5 4BD and 182 Burnt Oak Broadway, Edgware, Middlesex HA8 0AU (Tel: 020-8731 1100).

CHIEF OFFICERS

Chief Executive: Leo Boland
Strategic Director, Community Development: Rita Dexter
Strategic Director, Education and Children: Vacant
Strategic Director, Environment: Anne Lippitt
Strategic Director, Resources: Jeremy Jaroszek
Strategic Director, Social Affairs: Brian Reynolds

36 Governed London

MEMBERS OF THE COUNCIL

Councillor	Ward
Mayor: Anita Campbell, Lab.	Arkley
Deputy Mayor: Pauline Coakley Webb, Lab.	Arkley
Leader of the Council: Alan Williams, Lab.	Burnt Oak
Steven Blomer, Lab.	Hale
Maureen Braun, C.	Hendon
Wayne Casey, LD	Mill Hill
James Chapman, C.	Friern Barnet
Danish Chopra, Lab.	Colindale
Usha Chopra, Lab.	East Barnet
Jack Cohen, LD	Childs Hill
Melvin Cohen, C.	Golders Green
Brian Coleman, C.	Totteridge
Pam Coleman, Lab.	Arkley
Geoff Cooke, Lab.	Brunswick Park
Katia David, C.	Hadley
Jeremy Davies, LD	Mill Hill
Aba Dunner, C.	Golders Green
Kevin Edson, C.	Totteridge
Olwen Evans, C.	East Barnet
Michael Freer, C.	Finchley
Anthony Finn, C.	Hendon
Vanessa Gearson, C.	Garden Suburb
Arun Ghosh, Lab.	West Hendon
Brian Gordon, C.	Hale
Helen Gordon, Lab.	East Finchley
Eva Greenspan, C.	Finchley
Christopher Harris, C.	Golders Green
Lynne Hillan, C.	Brunswick Park
Sean Hooker, LD	Mill Hill
Anne Jarvis, Lab.	East Barnet
Malcolm Lester, C.	Edgware
Victor Lyon, C.	Totteridge
Kitty Lyons, Lab.	St. Paul's
John Marshall, C.	Garden Suburb
Linda McFadyen, Lab.	Burnt Oak
Katherine McGuirk, Lab.	St. Paul's
Alison Moore, Lab.	East Finchley
Jazmin Naghar, C.	Garden Suburb
Ruth Nyman, Lab.	Hale
Monroe Palmer, LD	Childs Hill
Susette Palmer, LD	Childs Hill
Kanti Patel, C.	Hadley
Beverley Pearce, Lab.	Woodhouse
Wendy Prentice, C.	Hadley
Barry Rawlings, Lab.	Woodhouse
Paul Rogers, Lab.	Woodhouse
Nathaniel Rudolf, Lab.	Colindale
Brian Salinger, C.	Friern Barnet
Joan Scannell, C.	Edgware
Gill Sargeant, Lab.	Colindale
Andrew Sherling, C.	Hendon
Agnes Slocombe, Lab.	West Hendon
Anthony Spencer, C.	Edgware
Ansuya Sodha, Lab.	West Hendon
Leslie Sussman, C.	Finchley
Andreas Tambourides, C.	Brunswick
Jim Tierney, Lab.	St. Paul's
John Tiplady, C.	Friern Barnet
Allan Turner, Lab.	Burnt Oak
Philip Yeoman, Lab.	East Finchley

Political Composition: C: 28; Lab. 26; LD. 6.
Population: 331,548
Area: 8,663 hectares.

ABOUT BARNET

Barnet is one of the largest local authorities in London. It was created in 1965 from the former urban districts of Chipping Barnet and East Barnet, previously in Hertfordshire and Friern Barnet and the boroughs of Finchley and Hendon, previously in Middlesex. It lies on the edge of London's green belt and contains 14 conservation areas. It is crossed by three major roads from London to the North, The Edgware Road, Watling Street or A5 and the Great North Road renamed the A1000 after a bypass was built in the 1920s. Barnet has a number of areas of architectural and historical interest including the RAF Museum at Hendon and the Jewish Museum in Finchley.

COUNCIL TAX BANDS 2001-2002

Band	Market Value of the Property in 1991	Council Tax
A	Up to £40,000	£582.86
B	£40,001 to 52,000	£680.00
C	£52,001 to 68,000	£777.15
D	£68,001 to 88,000	£874.29
E	£88,001 to 120,000	£1068.58
F	£120,001 to 160,000	£1262.87
G	£160,001 to 320,000	£1457.15
H	£320,001 or more	£1748.58

London Borough Councils

BEXLEY

Bexley Civic Offices, Broadway, Bexleyheath, DA6 7LB (Tel: 020-8303 7777; Fax: 020-8301 2661; Email: customer.services@bexley.gov.uk; Web: www.bexley.gov.uk).
Environmental Services: Wyncham House, 207 Longlands Road, Sidcup, DA15 7JH.
Education, Leisure, Social and Community Services: Hill View, Hill View Drive, Welling, DA16 3RY.
Registration of Births, Deaths and Marriages: Manor House, The Green, Sidcup DA14 6BW (Tel: 020-8300 4537).

CHIEF OFFICERS

Chief Executive and Director of Corporate Services: Christopher Duffield
Chief Educational Services Officer: Ms. Pauline Maddison
Chief Engineer: Peter Morley
Chief Works and Contract Officer: Mike Frizoni
Controller of Finance and Personnel Services: Dave Berry
Controller of Legal Services: Alan Short
Director of Environmental Services: Melvyn Checketts
Director of Social and Community Services: Paul McGee
Head of IT: Steve Ripley

MEMBERS OF THE COUNCIL

Councillor	Ward
Mayor: A. M. Beckwith, C.	Lamorbey
Deputy Mayor:	
G. A. Bacon, C.	Sidcup West
J. Antenbring, C.	Blendon and Penhill
R. F. Ashmole. C.	Upton
Linda. J. Bailey, C.	Christchurch
C. Ball, Lab.	Thamesmead East
N. P. Betts, C.	Falconwood
G. Blowers, Lab.	St. Michaels
Beryl Brand, LD	St. Michaels
Donna Briant, Lab.	Thamesmead East
Joel Briant, Lab.	Cray
M. Brooks, C.	Barnehurst
J. Browning, Lab.	Erith
D. B. Cammish, C.	Upton
P. Cammish, C.	Blackfen
C. E. Campbell, C.	St. Mary's
A. W. Catterall, C.	St. Mary's
I. S. Clement, C.	Bostall
A. Deadman, Lab.	North End
J. W. Eastaugh, Lab.	North End
W. Flint, C.	Sidcup East
Sylvia Fortune, LD	Danson
D. Francis, Lab.	Belvedere
Liz French, Lab.	Barnehurst North
Mick French, Lab.	Thamesmead East
R. H. French, C.	Brampton
C. J. Garland, C.	Blackfen
R. M. Gillespie, C.	Barnehurst
G. Hacker, Lab.	Northumberland Heath
C. F. Hargrave, Lab.	North End
P. Hollamby, Lab.	Belvedere
G. R. Holland, C.	Lamorbey
G. Johnson, C.	Christchurch
R. J. Justham, Lab.	Cray
Tonya Kelsey, Lab.	Crayford
M. Ketley, C.	Sidcup West
J. Lawrenson, Lab.	East Wickham
Ann Lucas, Lab.	Northumberland Heath
Richard Lucas, Lab.	Belvedere
Sharon Massey, C.	Christchurch
K. McAndrew, C.	Sidcup West
R. A. Morgan, C.	Bostall
L. S. Newton, C.	Upton
N. O'Hare, LD	East Wickham
B. W. Oliver, LD	East Wickham
M. A. O'Neill, Lab.	Erith
Teresa O'Neill, C.	Brampton
Ann Partington, C.	Blendon and Penhill
R. J. Passey, C.	Lamorbey
Teresa Pearce, Lab.	Erith
Wendy Perfect, Lab.	St. Michael's
T. Perrin, Lab.	Crayford
Cheryl Potter, C.	Brampton
N. Sayers, C.	Blendon and Penhill
J. D. Shephard, Lab.	Crayford
E. J. Shrimpton, LD	Danson
June E. Slaughter, C.	Sidcup East

38 Governed London

M. A. Slaughter, C.
Kathryn Smith, Lab.
B. C. Standen, LD
C. L. Tandy, C.
J. P. Wilkinson, C.
Sidcup East
Northumberland Heath
Danson
St. Mary's
Bostall

Political Composition: C. 32; Lab. 24; LD. 6.
Population: 219,311.
Area: 6,065 hectares.

ABOUT BEXLEY

Bexley is situated in the south east of London. It is within easy reach of the major road, rail, air and sea networks including the M25, A2 and A20; Heathrow, Gatwick, Stanstead and City airports are all within an hours distance away. Links to Europe via the Channel Tunnel and Dover are also around an hour away. The borough is home to more than 4,000 businesses ranging from large-scale manufacturers to small and medium scale commercial ventures. Bexley contains over 90 parks and gardens which are open to the public. Sites of architectural and historical interest include Hall Place at Bexley, Danson Mansion in Danson Park and the Red House at Bexleyheath.

COUNCIL TAX BANDS 2001-2002

Band	Market Value of the Property	Council Tax
A	Up to £40,000	£588.00
B	£40,001 to 52,000	£686.00
C	£52,001 to 68,000	£784.00
D	£68,001 to 88,000	£882.00
E	£88,001 to 120,000	£1078.00
F	£120,001 to 160,000	£1274.00
G	£160,001 to 320,000	£1470.00
H	£320,001 or more	£1764.00

BRENT

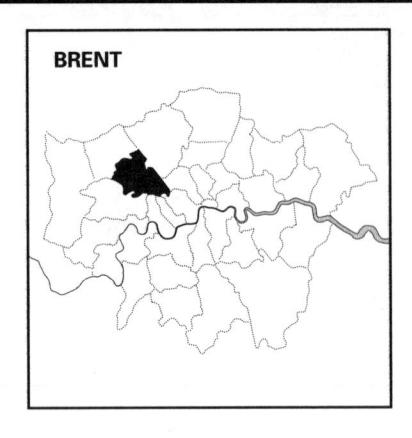

Main Address: Brent Town Hall, Forty Lane, Wembley, HA9 9HD (Tel: 020-8937 1237; Fax: 020-893 1444; Web: www.brent.gov.uk).
Chief Executive and Corporate Services: Brent Town Hall, Forty Lane, Wembley, HA9 9HX (Tel: 020-8937 1007).
Education Office: Chesterfield House, 9 Park Lane, Wembley, HA9 7RW (Tel: 020-8937 3130).
Environmental Services: Brent House, 349-357 High Road, Wembley, HA9 6BZ (Tel: 020-8937 5006).
Trading Standards: Quality House, 249 Willesden Lane, London, NW2 5JM (Tel: 020-8937 5500).
Housing: Mahatma Gandhi House, 34 Wembley Hill Road, Wembley, HA9 8AD (Tel: 020-8937 2341).
Corporate Finance: Town Hall, Forty Lane, Wembley, HA9 9MD (Tel: 020-8937 1423).
Libraries Service: Chesterfield House, 9 Park Lane, Wembley, HA9 7RW (Tel: 020-8937 3146).
Principal Curator: Grange Museum, The Grange, Neasden Lane, London, NW10 1QB (Tel: 020-8937 3600).

CHIEF OFFICERS

Chief Executive: Gareth Daniel
Director of Community Development: Gerry Davies
Director of Corporate Services: Bernard Diamant
Director of Education: Jacky Griffin
Director of Environmental Services: Richard Saunders
Director of Finance: Stephen Hughes

London Borough Councils 39

Director of Housing (Acting): Martin Cheeseman
Director of Human Resources: Francesca Okosi
Director of Policy and Regeneration: Phil Newby
Director of Social Services: Jenny Goodall

MEMBERS OF THE COUNCIL

Councillor	Ward
Mayor: Ramesh Patel, Lab.	Queensbury
Deputy Mayor: Akber Sarguroh, Lab.	Brentwater
Leader of the Council: Ann John Lab.	St. Raphael's
Andrew Ammerlaan, Lab.	Manor
Mary Arnold, Lab.	Carlton
Joyce Bacchus, Lab.	Roundwood
Ian Bellia, Lab.	Mapesbury
Lincoln Beswick, Lab.	Wembley Central
Nicola Blackman, C.	Tokyngton
Robert J. Blackman, C.	Preston
Daniel Brown, LD	Alperton
Dr. Alec Castle, Lab.	Tokyngton
Reg Colwill, C.	Kingsbury
David Coughlin, Lab.	St. Raphael's
Mary Cribbin, Lab.	Kilburn
Paul Daisley, Lab.	Harlseden
Orugbani Douglas, Lab.	Tokyngton
William Dromey, Lab.	Roe Green
Uma Fernandes, C.	Sudbury
Keith Ferry, Lab.	Brondesbury Park
Gideon Fiegel, C.	Sudbury Court
Ralph Fox, Lab.	Brentwater
Moore Giwa, Lab.	Manor
Helga Gladbaum, Lab.	Kensal Rise
John Godfrey, Lab.	Chamberlayne
Robert Hamadi, Lab.	Stonebridge
Richard Harrod, Lab.	St. Andrew's
Vanessa Howells, C.	Sudbury Court
Havard Hughes, LD	Barham
Lesley Jones, Lab.	Willesden Green
Bertha Joseph, Lab.	Kensal Rise
Gabrielle Kagan, Lab.	Brondesbury Park
Suresh Kansagra, C.	Barnhill
John Lebor, Lab.	Carlton
Peter Lemmon, Lab.	Chamberlayne
Dorman Long, Lab.	Church End
Janice Long, Lab.	Mapesbury
Paul Lorber, LD	Barham
Michael Lyon, Lab.	Gladstone
Eric McDonald, C.	Queensbury
Colum Moloney, Lab.	Stonebridge
Cormach Moore, C.	Sudbury
Neil Nerva, Lab.	Queens Park
James O'Sullivan, C.	St. Andrew's
Sean O'Sullivan, C.	Kenton
Martin Harshadbhai Patel, C.	Preston
Kantibhai J. Patel, Lab.	St. Raphael's
Tullah Persaud, Lab.	Wembley Central
Maureen Queally, Lab.	Roe Green
Neil Rands, C.	Sudbury
John Rattray, LD	Alperton
Ann Reeder, Lab.	Harlesden
Abdul Sattar-Butt, Lab.	Gladstone
Jack Sayers, C.	Cricklewood
Carupiah Selvarajah, C.	Kingsbury
Asish Sengupta, Lab.	Fryent
Ahmad Shahzad, Lab.	Willesden
Carol Anne Shaw, C.	Cricklewood
Arthur Steel, C.	Kenton
Tom Taylor, C.	Preston
Bobby Thomas, Lab.	Church End
Noel Thompson, Lab.	Kilburn
Irwin Van Colle, C.	Barnhill
Sarah Walker, Lab.	Queens Park
Mohammad Zakriya, Lab.	Roundwood

Political Composition: Lab. 42; C. 19; LD.4.
Population: 250,611
Area: 4,421 hectares.

ABOUT BRENT

Brent is situated in the North West of London. It is connected to the West End of London and the City by a network of 26 over and underground railway stations. Heathrow airport is also around 30 minutes away by car or train. Brent is home to the world famous Wembley Stadium which has hosted an array of events including the World Cup and Olympic Games. Regeneration is the key objective of Brent Council. The Borough consists of a number of deprived regions and has received investment in recent years in order to achieve the aim of long term social and economic revival. Projects that have evolved include the Wembley Park Single Regeneration Budget, The Park Royal Partnership and Brent Reading Recovery Project.

COUNCIL TAX BANDS 2001-2002

Band	Market Value of the Property	Council Tax
A	Up to £40,000	£532.99
B	£40,001 to 52,000	£621.83
C	£52,001 to 68,000	£710.66
D	£68,001 to 88,000	£799.49
E	£88,001 to 120,000	£977.15
F	£120,001 to 160,000	£1154.82
G	£160,001 to 320,000	£1332.48
H	£320,001 or more	£1598.98

40 Governed London

BROMLEY

BROMLEY

Civic Centre, Stockwell Close, Kentish Way, Bromley, BR1 3UH (Tel: 020-8464 3333; Web: www.bromley.gov.uk).
Director of Leisure Services: Central Library, High Street, Bromley, BR1 1EX (Tel: 020-8460 9955).

CHIEF OFFICERS

Chief Executive: D. Bartlett
Director of Education: Ken Davis
Director of Environmental Services: G. N. Hayward
Director of Social Services and Housing: Jeremy Ambache
Director of Leisure and Community Services: R. Stoakes
Borough Secretary: W. Million
Borough Treasurer: P. Dale

MEMBERS OF THE COUNCIL

Councillor	Ward
Mayor: John Holbrook, Lab.	St. Mary Cray
Deputy Mayor: Colin Willetts, Lab.	St. Paul's Cray
Leader of the Council:	
Chris Maines, LD	Orpington
Graham Arthur, C.	Hayes
Peter Ayres, LD	Martins Hill and Town
Peter Bloomfield, C.	Darwin
Katy Boughey, C.	Chislehurst
Joan Bryant, C.	Chislehurst
I. A. Buckley, C.	Bickley
Cathy Bustard, C.	Plaistow and Sundridge
Stephen Carr, C.	Bromley Common and Keston
Alan Carter, LD	Bromley Common and Keston
Gill Charmarette, LD	Chelsfield and Goddington
David Crowe, LD	Clock House
Martin Curry, LD	St. Paul's Cray
Ernest Dyer, Lab.	Mottingham
Chris Elgar, C.	Kelsey Park
Peter Fookes, Lab.	Penge
John Gallop, C.	Bickley
Chris Gaster, LD	Anerley
Jamie Gillespie, LD	Plaistow and Sundridge
Steve Gosling, LD	Plaistow and Sundridge
Geoff Gostt, LD	Biggin Hill
John Gray, C.	West Wickham South
Jane Green, LD	Eden Park
Mike Hall, LD	Chelsfield and Goddington
Bill Hawthorne, LD	St. Paul's Cray
Jenny Hillier, C.	Farnborough
Carole Hubbard, C.	West Wickham North
Brian Humphrys, C.	West Wickham North
Tara Huntington-Thresher, C.	Petts Wood and Knoll
Malcolm Hyland, C.	Shortlands
John Ince, C.	Petts Wood and Knoll
Gordon Jenkins, C.	Bickley
Philip Jones, C.	Lawrie Park and Kent House
John Lewis, C.	Lawrie Park and Kent House
Martin Lockwood, LD	Clock House
Bill MacCormick, LD	Anerley
Anne Manning, C.	Hayes
David McBride, LD	St. Mary Cray
Russell Mellor, C.	Copers Cope
Alexa Michael, C.	Bromley Common and Keston
Mike Norris, LD	Orpington
Graem Peters, LD	Chelsfield and Goddington
Tony Phillips, LD	Eden Park
Sue Polydorou, Lab.	St. Mary Cray
Helen Rabbatts, LD	Crofton
Neil Reddin, C.	Hayes
Karen Roberts, Lab.	Penge
Viv Ross, LD	Crofton
Bob Shekyls, LD	Biggin Hill
T. C. Stevens, C.	Farnborough
George Taylor, C.	Shortlands
Michael Tickner, C.	Kelsey Park
Len Tutt, C.	West Wickham South
R. P. Warner, LD	Martins Hill and Park
Tony Wilkinson, C.	Copers Cope
Peter Woods, C.	Petts Wood and Knoll
Joan Wykes, C.	Chislehurst
Rob Yeldham, Lab.	Mottingham

London Borough Councils

Political Composition: C. 30; LD. 23; Lab. 7
Population: 297,118
Area: 15,179 hectares.

ABOUT BROMLEY

Bromley is the largest of the London Boroughs and is home to many commuters, especially as London train stations can be reached in under half an hour. The borough has considerable historic pedigree – Scadbury Park Estate in Chislehurst was the home to Sir Thomas Walsingham and Charles Darwin wrote his renowned book 'On the Origin of Species' at Downe. Shopping and leisure facilities are diverse in the borough with The Glades shopping centre being rated amongst the best in the country. There are numerous recreation centres, sports courses, libraries and theatre-goers can visit the borough's Churchill Theatre.

COUNCIL TAX BANDS 2001-2002

Band	Market Value of the Property	Council Tax
A	Up to £40,000	£550.92
B	£40,001 to 52,000	£642.74
C	£52,001 to 68,000	£734.56
D	£68,001 to 88,000	£826.38
E	£88,001 to 120,000	£1010.02
F	£120,001 to 160,000	£1193.66
G	£160,001 to 320,000	£1377.30
H	£320,001 or more	£1652.76

CAMDEN

Camden Town Hall, Judd Street, London, WC1H 9JE. For all Departments (Tel: 020-7278 4444; Web: www.camden.gov.uk) Register Office (Tel: 020-7974 6002).

Financial Services Branch, Town Hall Extension, Argyle Street, London WC1H 8NL.
Environment Department, Town Hall Extension, Argyle Street, London WC1H 8EQ.
Housing Department: 20 Mabledon Place, London, WC1H 9BF.
Leisure and Community Services: Crowndale Centre, 218-220 Eversholt Street, London, NW1 1BD.
Social Services Department: 79 Camden Road, London, NW1 9ES.
Education Department: The Crowndale Centre, 218-220 Eversholt Street, London, NW1 1BD.

CHIEF OFFICERS

Chief Executive: Steve Bundred
Assistant Chief Executive (Communications): Deirdre Colledge
Assistant Chief Executive (Personnel): Ms. Tracey Dennison
Assistant Chief Executive (Policy and Partnership): Dennis Skinner
Borough Solicitor: Alison Lowton
Controller of Financial Services: John Mabey
Director of Education: R. J. Litchfield
Director of Environment (Acting): Tom Jeffrey
Director of Housing: Neil Litherland
Director of Leisure and Community Services: Ian McNicol
Director of Social Services: Jane Held

MEMBERS OF THE COUNCIL

Councillor	Ward
Mayor: Roger Robinson, Lab.	St. Pancras
Deputy Mayor: Judith Pattison, Lab.	Gospel Oak
Leader of the Council: Jane Roberts, Lab.	Highgate
Penelope Abraham, Lab.	St. John's
Richard Arthur, Lab.	Highgate
Peter Brayshaw, Lab.	Bloomsbury
Bill Budd, Lab.	Chalk Farm
Patricia Callaghan, Lab.	Bloomsbury
Ewan Cameron, C.	Belsize
Maggie Cosin, Lab.	Highgate
Edward Cousins, Lab.	Brunswick
Martin Davies, C.	Fitzjohn's
John Dickie, Lab.	Grafton
Julian Fulbrook, Lab.	Holborn
Dermot Greene, Lab.	Camden
Michael Greene, C.	Frognal
Janet Guthrie, Lab.	South End
Bob Hall, Lab.	Swiss Cottage
Aileen Hammond, Lab.	Belsize
Gerry Harrison, Lab.	South End

42 Governed London

Charlie Hedges, Lab.
Stephen Hocking, C.
Dave Horan, Lab.
Peter Horne, C.
Barbara Hughes, Lab.
Ernest James, Lab.
Heather Johnson, Lab.
Bernard Kissen, Lab.
Deirdre Krymer, Lab.
Gloria Lazenby, Lab.
Margaret Little, LD
Sidney Malin, LD
Andrew Marshall, C.
Andrew Mennear, C.
John Mills, Lab.
Keith Moffitt, LD
Honora Morrissey, C.
Pat Nightingale, Lab.
Richard Olszewski, Lab.
Flick Rea, LD
John Rolfe, Lab.
Nirmal Roy, Lab.
Jane Schopflin, LD
Roy Shaw, Lab.
Sybil Shine, Lab.
Nick Smith, Lab.
Dawn Somper, C.
Huntly Spence, C.
Anne Swain, Lab.
John Thane, Lab.
Heather Thompson, LD
Jim Turner, Lab.
Phil Turner, Lab.
Tim Walker, Lab.
Barbara Ward, Lab.
Piers Wauchope, C.
Brian Weekes, Lab.
John White, Lab.
Brian Woodrow, Lab.

Kilburn
Swiss Cottage
St. John's
Adelaide
King's Cross
Somers Town
Kilburn
Caversham
Castlehaven
St. Pancras
Hampstead Town
Hampstead Town
Adelaide
Fitzjohn's
Gospel Oak
West End
Swiss Cottage
Camden
Regent's Park
Fortune Green
Priory
Bloomsbury
Fortune Green
Grafton
Somers Town
King's Cross
Frognal
Belsize
Caversham
Highgate
West End
Regent's Park
Priory
Kilburn
Regent's Park
Adelaide
Brunswick
Chalk Farm
Holborn

Political Composition: Lab. 42; C. 11; LD. 6.
Population: 192,000
Area: 2,200 hectares.

ABOUT CAMDEN

The London Borough of Camden stretches from Covent Garden to Hampstead and Highgate. It is home to numerous famous museums, historic houses and contemporary art galleries including the British Museum, the British Library, Kenwood House and London Zoo. It also contains a number of parks and open spaces including Regent's Park, Waterlow Park and Hampstead Heath.

COUNCIL TAX BANDS 2001-2002

Band	Market Value of the Property	Council Tax
A	Up to £40,000	£633.25
B	£40,001 to 52,000	£738.79
C	£52,001 to 68,000	£844.33
D	£68,001 to 88,000	£949.87
E	£88,001 to 120,000	£1160.95
F	£120,001 to 160,000	£1372.04
G	£160,001 to 320,000	£1583.12
H	£320,001 or more	£1899.74

CORPORATION OF LONDON

CITY OF LONDON

PO Box 270, Guildhall, London EC2P 2EJ (Tel: 020-7606 3030; Web: www.cityoflondon.uk).

The City of London is the historic centre at the heart of London known as 'the square mile' around which the vast metropolis has grown over the centuries. The City's residential population is 5,500. The civic government is carried on by the Corporation of London through the Court of Common Council.

The City is an international financial centre, generating over £20 billion a year for the British economy. It includes the head offices of the principal banks, insurance companies and mercantile houses, in addition to buildings ranging from the historic Roman Wall and the 15th-century Guildhall, to the massive splendour of St Paul's Cathedral and the architectural beauty of Wren's spires.

The City of London was described by Tacitus in A.D. 62 as 'a busy emporium for trade and traders'. Under the Romans it became an important administration centre and hub of the road system. Little is known of London in Saxon times, when it formed part of the kingdom of the East Saxons. In 886 Alfred recovered London from the Danes and reconstituted it a burgh under his son-in-law. In 1066 the citizens submitted to William the Conqueror who in 1067 granted them a charter, which is still preserved, establishing them in the rights and privileges they had hitherto enjoyed.

THE MAYORALTY

The Mayoralty was probably established about 1189, the first Mayor being Henry Fitz Ailwyn who filled the office for 23 years and was succeeded by Fitz Alan (1212—14). A new charter was granted by King John in 1215, directing the Mayor to be chosen annually, which has ever since been done, though in early times the same individual often held the office more than once. A familiar instance is that of 'Whittington, thrice Lord Mayor of London' (in reality four times, 1397, 1398, 1406, 1419); and many modern cases have occurred. The earliest instance of the phrase 'Lord Mayor' in English is in 1414. It was used more generally in the latter part of the 15th century and became invariable from 1535 onwards. At Michaelmas the liverymen in Common Hall choose two Aldermen who have served the office of Sheriff for presentation to the Court of Aldermen, and one is chosen to be Lord Mayor for the following mayoral year.

LORD MAYOR'S DAY

The Lord Mayor of London was previously elected on the feast of St Simon and St Jude (28 October), and from the time of Edward I, at least, was presented to the King or to the Barons of the Exchequer on the following day, unless that day was a Sunday. The day of election was altered to 16 October in 1346, and after some further changes was fixed for Michaelmas Day in 1546, but the ceremonies of admittance and swearing-in of the Lord Mayor continued to take place on 28 and 29 October respectively until 1751. In 1752, at the reform of the calendar, the Lord Mayor was continued in office until 8 November, the 'New Style' equivalent of 28 October. The Lord Mayor is now presented to the Lord Chief Justice at the Royal Courts of Justice on the second Saturday in November to make the final declaration of office, having been sworn in at Guildhall on the preceding day. The procession to the Royal Courts of Justice is popularly known as the Lord Mayor's Show.

REPRESENTATIVES

Aldermen are mentioned in the 11th century and their office is of Saxon origin. They were elected annually between 1377 and 1394, when an Act of Parliament of Richard II directed them to be chosen for life.

The Common Council, elected annually on the first Friday in December, was, at an early date, substituted for a popular assembly called the Folkmote. At first only two representatives were sent from each ward, but the number has since been greatly increased. The Corporation is reducing the number of Common Councilmen from 130 to 100 through natural wastage. The Government has introduced legislation to remove anomalies from the election system and to extend the non-resident franchise.

OFFICERS

Sheriffs were Saxon officers; their predecessors were the wic-reeves and portreeves of London and Middlesex. At first they were officers of the Crown, and were named by the Barons of the Exchequer; but Henry I (in 1132) gave the citizens permission to choose their own Sheriffs, and the annual election of Sheriffs became fully operative under King John's charter of 1199. The citizens lost this privilege, as far as the election of the Sheriff of Middlesex was concerned, by the Local Government Act 1888; but the liverymen continue to choose two Sheriffs of the City of London, who are appointed on Midsummer Day and take office at Michaelmas.

The office of Chamberlain is an ancient one, the first contemporary record of which is 1237. The Town Clerk (or Common Clerk) is mentioned in 1274.

ACTIVITIES

The work of the Corporation is assigned to a number of committees which present reports to the Court of Common Council. These Committees are: City Lands and Bridge House Grants Estates, Policy and Resources, Finance, Planning and Transportation, Central Markets, Billingsgate and Leadenhall Markets, Spitalfields Market, Police, Port and City of London Health and Social Services, Libraries, Art Galleries and Records, Board of Governors of City of London Freemen's School, Music and Drama (Guildhall School of Music and Drama), Establishment, Housing and Sports Development, Gresham (City side), Hampstead Heath Management,

44 Governed London

Epping Forest and Open Spaces, West Ham Park, Privileges, Barbican Residential and Barbican Centre (Barbican Arts and Conference Centre).

The City's estate, in the possession of which the Corporation of London differs from other municipalities, is managed by the City Lands and Bridge House Grants Estates Committee, the chairmanship of which carries with it the title of Chief Commoner.

The Honourable the Irish Society, which manages the Corporation's estates in Ulster, consists of a Governor and five other Aldermen, the Recorder, and 19 Common Councilmen, of whom one is elected Deputy Governor.

The Lord Mayor 2000-2001
The Rt. Hon. The Lord Mayor, Sir David Howard, Bt.
*Note: The Lord Mayor assumes office in November each year. The elections for the Lord Mayor 2001-2002 take place at the end of September.

The Sheriffs 2001-2002
Alderman Michael Savory (Bread Street); David Mauleverer.

Officers
Town Clerk: Tom Simmons
Chamberlain: Peter Derrick
Chief Commoner: Anthony Eskenzi, CC

The Aldermen
Richard Agutter — Castle Baynard
Nicholas Anstee — Aldersgate
Sir Clive Martin, OBE, TD, DL
David Brewer, CMG — Aldgate
John Hughesdon — Bassishaw
Michael Oliver — Billingsgate
Michael Savory — Bishopsgate
Sir David Rowe-Ham, GBE — Bread Street
— Bridge and Bridge Without
Sir Christopher Collett, GBE — Broad Street
Sir Richard Nichols — Candlewick
Anthony Bull — Cheap
Robert Finch — Coleman Street
Sir Brian Jenkins, GBE — Cordwainer
The Rt. Hon. The Lord Mayor,
 Sir David Howard, bt — Cornhill
Gavyn Arthur — Cripplegate
Sir Christopher Leaver, GBE — Dowgate
Sir Christopher Walford — Farringdon Within
Simon Walsh — Farringdon Without
Sir Alan Traill, GBE, QSO — Langbourn
Vacant — Lime Street

The Lord Levene of Portsoken, KBE — Portsoken
Sir Alexander Graham, GBE — Queenhithe
Richard Agutter (Sheriff) — Castle Baynard
Sir Roger Cork — Tower
Sir John Chalstrey — Vintry
Sir Paul Newall, TD, DL — Walbrook

The Common Council
George Abrahams, CC — Farringdon Without North Side
John Absalom, CC — Farringdon Without North Side
Lionel Altman, CBE, CC — Cripplegate Within
Ernest Angell, CC — Cripplegate Without
Wilfred Archibald, Deputy — Cornhill
Kenneth Ayers, CC — Bassishaw
Derek Balls, CC — Castle Baynard
John Barker, Deputy — Cripplegate Within
Stephen Barter, CC — Langborn
William Baverstock Brooks, CC — Billingsgate
Michael Beale, Deputy — Lime Street
John Bird, OBE, CC — Bridge and Bridge Without
David Bradshaw, CC — Cripplegate Without
Michael Bramwell, CC — Langborn
John Brewster, OBE, CC — Bassishaw
Roger Brighton, CC — Porsoken
Joseph Byllam-Barnes, CC — Cheapside
Daniel Caspi, CC — Bridge and Bridge Without
Michael Cassidy, Deputy — Coleman Street
Benson Catt, JP, CC — Farringdon Without North Side
Roger Chadwick, CC — Tower
Jonathan Charkham, CC — Farringdon Without North Side
Mrs Christine Cohen, CC — Lime Street
Dennis Cotgrove, CC — Lime Street
Miss Stella Currie, Deputy — Cripplegate Without
Roger Daily-Hunt, CC — Cripplegate Without
George Darwin, CC — Farringdon Without South Side
Barry Davis, CC — Bread Street
William Dove, MBE, JP, CC — Bishopsgate
Simon Duckworth, CC — Bishopsgate
Alfred Dunitz, JP, CC — Porsoken
Anthony N. Eskenzi, Deputy — Farringdon Without South Side
Robin Eve, CC — Cheap
Kevin Everett, CC — Candlewick
Fergus Falk, TD, CC — Broad Street
Martin Farr, CC — Walbrook
Michael Farrow, Deputy — Farringdon Without
Bruce Farthing, CC — Aldgate
Rodney FitzGerald, Deputy — Bread Street

London Borough Councils   45

Graham Forbes, CC
Stuart Fraser, CC
William Fraser, Deputy
Archibald Galloway, Deputy
George Gillon, CC
Stanley Ginsburg, CC
Alison Gowman, Deputy
Colin Graves, CC
Clifford Green, CC
Robert Hall, CC

Mrs Pauline Halliday, Deputy
Dr Peter Hardwick, QHP, CC
Brian Harris, CC
Maurice Hart, Deputy

John Haynes, CC
Michael Henderson-Begg, CC
John Holland, CBE, JP, DL, Deputy
Mrs Elizabeth Holliday, CC
John Hooke, CC
Thomas Jackson, CC
Mrs Maureen Kellett, JP, CC
Derek Kemp, CC
Alastair King, CC
Keith Knowles, Deputy
Gregory Lawrence, CC

Geoffrey Lawson, CC
Peter Leck, CC
Mrs Vivienne Littlechild, CC
Edward Lord, CC
Ian Luder, CC

Julian Malins, QC, CC

Peter Martinelli, Deputy
Deputy Judith Mayhew
Jeremy Mayhew, CC
Ms Catherine McGuinness, CC
Ian McNeil, CC
Mrs Wendy Mead, CC

Christopher Mitchell, Deputy
Douglas Mobsby, Deputy
Bryan Montgomery, CC
Brian Mooney, CC
Anthony Moss, CC
Sylvia Moys, CC
Joyce Nash, OBE, Deputy,
Mrs Barbara Newman, CBE, CC
Mrs Janet Owen, Deputy
John Owen-Ward, CC

Dr Andrew Parmley, CC

Bishopsgate
Coleman Street
Vintry
Broad Street
Cordwainer
Bishopsgate
Dowgate
Bishopsgate
Aldersgate
Farringdon Without South Side
Walbrook
Aldgate
Broad Street
Bridge and Bridge Without
Cornhill
Coleman Street

Aldgate
Vintry
Walbrook
Bread Street
Tower
Coleman Street
Queenhithe
Candlewick
Farringdon Without South Side
Portsoken
Aldersgate
Cripplegate Without
Coleman Street
Farringdon Without North Side
Farringdon Without South Side
Bassishaw
Queenhithe
Aldersgate
Castle Baynard
Lime Street
Farringdon Without South Side
Castle Baynard
Bilingsgate
Dowgate
Queenhithe
Tower
Aldgate
Aldersgate

Aldersgate
Langbourn
Bridge and Bridge Without
Vintry

Mrs Ann Pembroke, Deputy
John Platts-Mills, QC, CC

Edward Price, CC

Gerald Pulman, JP, Deputy
Christopher Punter, CC
Stephen Quilter, CC
Richard Regan, CC

Peter Rigby, CBE, JP, Deputy

Miss Dorothy Robinson, CC
Patrick Roney, CBE, Deputy
Mrs Iris Samuel, MBE, Deputy
Keith Sargant, CC
John Scott, CC
Richard Scriven, CBE, JP, CC
David Shalit, CC

Robin Sherlock, CC
Michael Snyder, Deputy
Steve Stevenson, CC
John Taylor, TD, CC
Clive Thorp, CC
David Thorp, CC

John Trotter, DL, CC
Douglas Warner, CC
Philip Willoughby, JP, Deputy
Tom Wilmot, CC

Cheap
Farringdon Without South Side
Farringdon Without North Side
Tower
Cripplegate Within
Cripplegate Without
Farringdon Without South Side
Farringdon Without North Side
Bishopsgate
Bishopsgate
Portsoken

Cornhill
Broad Street
Candlewick
Farringdon Without North Side
Dowgate
Cordwainer
Cripplegate Within
Bread Street
Billingsgate
Farringdon Without South Side
Billingsgate
Cripplegate Within
Bishopsgate
Cordwainer

COUNCIL TAX BANDS 2001-2002

Band	Market Value of the Property	Council Tax
A	Up to £40,000	£386.50
B	£40,001 to 52,000	£450.92
C	£52,001 to 68,000	£515.34
D	£68,001 to 88,000	£579.76
E	£88,001 to 120,000	£708.60
F	£120,001 to 160,000	£837.44
G	£160,001 to 320,000	£966.26
H	£320,001 or more	£1159.52

THE CITY GUILDS (Livery Companies)
The constitution of the livery companies has been unchanged for centuries. There are three ranks of membership: freemen, liverymen and assistants. A person can become a freeman by patrimony (through a parent having been a freeman); by servitude (through having served an apprenticeship to a freeman); or by redemption (by purchase).

46 Governed London

Election to the livery is the prerogative of the company, who can elect any of its freemen as liverymen. Assistants are usually elected from the livery and form a Court of Assistants which is the governing body of the company. The Master (in some companies called the Prime Warden) is elected annually from the assistants.

THE CITY GUILDS

The Worshipful Company of Mercers
Mercers Hall, Ironmonger Lane, London, EC2V 8HE (Tel: 020-7726 4991; Fax: 020-7600 1158; E-mail: mail@mercers.co.uk;
Web: www.mercers.co.uk)
Clerk: C. H. Parker
Master: R. C. Cunis

The Worshipful Company of Grocers
Princes Street, London, EC2R 8AD (Tel: 020-7606 3113; Fax: 020-7600 3082; E-mail: beadle@grocershall.co.uk;
Web: www.grocershall.co.uk)
Clerk: Brig. P. P. Rawlins, MBE
Master: J. G. Tregoning

The Worshipful Company of Drapers
Throgmorton Avenue, London, EC2N 2DQ (Tel: 020-7588 5001; Fax: 020-7628 1988; E-mail: mail@thedrapers.co.uk;
Web: www.thedrapers.co.uk)
Clerk: Rear-Admiral A. B. Ross, CB, CBE
Master: R. W. P. Beharrell

The Worshipful Company of Fishmongers
Fishmongers' Hall, London Bridge, London, EC4R 9EL (Tel: 020-7626 3531; Fax: 020-7929 1389; E-mail: clerk@fishhall.co.uk;
Web: www.fishhall.co.uk)
Clerk: K. S. Waters
Prime Warden: Sir Thomas Stockdale, Bt

The Worshipful Company of Goldsmiths
Foster Lane, London, EC2V 6BN (Tel: 020-7606 7010; Fax: 020-7606 1511; E-mail: the.clerk@thegoldsmiths.co.uk;
Web: www.thegoldsmiths.co.uk)
Clerk: R. D. Buchanan-Dunlop, CBE
Prime Warden: B. L. Schroder, DL

The Worshipful Company of Merchant Taylors
30 Threadneedle Street, London, EC2R 8JB (Tel: 020-7450 4440; Fax: 020-7588 2776)
Clerk: D. A. Peck
Master: Sir Jeffrey Holland, KCB

The Worshipful Company of Skinners
8 Dowgate Hill, London, EC4R 2SP (Tel: 020-7236 6590; Fax: 020-7236 6590; E-mail: clerk@skinners.org.uk)
Clerk: Capt. D. Hart Dyke, CBE, LVO, RN
Master: G. B. Thompson

The Worshipful Company of Haberdashers
39–40 Bartholomew Close, London, EC1A 7JN (Tel: 020-7606 0967; Fax: 020-7606 5738; E-mail: enquiries@haberdashers.co.uk;
Web: www.haberdashers.co.uk)
Clerk: Capt. R. J. Fisher, RN
Master: B. E. Shawcross, FRICS

The Worshipful Company of Salters
4 Fore Street, London, EC2Y 5DE (Tel: 020-7588 5216; Fax: 020-7638 3679; E-mail: company@salters.co.uk; Web: www.salters.co.uk)
Clerk: Col. M. P. Barneby
Master: The Rt. Hon. Lord of Berwick

The Worshipful Company of Ironmongers
Shaftesbury Place, Barbican, London, EC2Y 8AA (Tel: 020-7606 2726; Fax: 020-7600 3519; E-mail: beadle@ironhall.co.uk;
Web: www.ironhall.co.uk)
Clerk: J. A. Oliver
Master: W. L. Weller

The Vintners' Company
Upper Thames Street, London, EC4V 3BG (Tel: 020-7236 1863; Fax: 020-7236 8177; E-mail: theclerk@the-vintners-livery-co.org.uk)
Clerk: Brig. M. Smythe, OBE
Master: H. J. Newyon

The Worshipful Company of Clothworkers
Dunster Court, Mincing Lane, London, EC3R 7AH (Tel: 020-7623 7041; Fax: 020-7283 1289; E-mail: enquiries@clothworkers.co.uk;
Web: www.clothworkers.co.uk)
Clerk: M. G. T. Harris
Master: Vacant

The Worshipful Company of Actuaries
81 Worrin Road, Shenfield, Brentwood, Essex, CM15 8JN (Tel: 01277-261110; Fax: 01277-261110)
Clerk: Mrs J. V. Evans
Master: P. J. Derry

London Borough Councils 47

The Guild of Air Pilots and Air Navigators
Cobham House, 9 Warwick Court, Gray's Inn, London, WC1R 5DJ (Tel: 020-7404 4032; Fax: 020-7404 4035; E-mail: gapan@gapan.org; Web: www.gapan.org)
Grand Master: HRH The Prince Philip, Duke of Edinburgh, KG, KT, OM, GBE, PC
Clerk: Capt. J. G. F. Stoy, CB
Master: M. Grayburn

The Society of Apothecaries
14 Black Friars Lane, London, EC4V 6EJ (Tel: 020-7236 1189; Fax: 020-7329 3177; E-mail: clerk@apothecaries.org; Web: www.apothecaries.org)
Clerk: Lt.-Col. R. J. Stringer
Master: J. Briscoe

The Company of Armourers and Brasiers
81 Coleman Street, London, EC2R 5BJ (Tel: 020-7606 1199; Fax: 020-7606 7481)
Clerk: Cdr. T. J. K. Sloane, OBE, RN
Master: The Venerable C. Wagstaff

The Worshipful Company of Bakers
Harp Lane, London, EC3R 6DP (Tel: 020-7623 2223; Fax: 020-7621 1924; E-mail: clerk@bakers.co.uk; Web: www.bakers.co.uk)
Clerk: R. E. B. Sawyer
Master: J. W. Tompkins

The Worshipful Company of Barbers
Barber and Surgeons' Hall, Monkwell Square, Wood Street, London, EC2Y 5BL (Tel: 020-7606 0741; Fax: 020-7606 3857; E-mail: clerk@barberscompany.org.uk; Web: www.barberscompany.org.uk)
Clerk: Brig. A. F. Eastburn
Master: Mr W. S. Shand

The Worshipful Company of Basketmakers
48 Seymour Walk, London, SW10 9NF (Tel: 020-7351 2918; Fax: 020-7351 6559)
Clerk: Maj. G. J. Flint-Shipman, TD
Prime Warden: N. E. Woolley

The Worshipful Company of Blacksmiths
48 Upwood Road, London, SE12 8AN (Tel: 020-8318 9684; Fax: 020-8318 9687; E-mail: hammerandhand@supanet.com)
Clerk: C. Jeal
Prime Warden: Col. Sir Neil Thorne, OBE, TD, DL

The Worshipful Company of Bowyers
11 Aldermans Hill, London, N13 4YD (Tel: 020-8882 3055; Fax: 020-8882 5851; E-mail: john@owen-ward.u-net.com; Web: www.bowyer.com)
Clerk: J. R. Owen-Ward
Master: E. J. Burnett

The Worshipful Company of Brewers
Aldermanbury Square, London, EC2V 7HR (Tel: 020-7606 1301; Fax: 020-7796 3557)
Clerk: Brig. D. J. Ross, CBE
Master: W. R. Lees-Jones, TD, DL

The Worshipful Company of Builders Merchants
4 College Hill, London, EC4R 2RB (Tel: 020-7329 2189; Fax: 020-7329 2190; E-mail: wcobm@aol.com)
Clerk: Miss S. M. Robinson, TD
Master: D. C. E. Ridgeon

The Worshipful Company of Butchers
Butchers Hall, 87 Bartholomew Close, London, EC1A 7EB (Tel: 020-7606 4106; Fax: 020-7606 4108; E-mail: clerk@butchershall.com; Web: www.butchershall.com)
Clerk: G. J. Sharp
Master: J. F. Jackman

The Worshipful Company of Carmen
8 Little Trinity Lane, London, EC4V 2AN (Tel: 020-7489 8289; Fax: 020-7236 3313)
Clerk: Cdr. R. M. H. Bawtree, OBE, RN
Master: B. H. Owen

The Worshipful Company of Carpenters
Carpenters Hall, 1 Throgmorton Avenue, London, EC2N 2JJ (Tel: 020-7588 7001; Fax: 020-7638 6286; Web: www.thecarpenterscompany.co.uk)
Clerk: Maj.-Gen. P. T. Stevenson, OBE
Master: R. S. Miller

The Worshipful Company of Chartered Secretaries and Administrators
3rd Floor, Sadler's Hall, 40 Gutter Lane, London, EC2V 6BR (Tel: 020-7726 2955; Fax: 020-7600 5699)
Hon. Clerk: C. H. Grinsted
Master: M. J. Dudding, OBE, DL

48 Governed London

The Worshipful Company of Chartered Surveyors
16 St Mary-at-Hill, London, EC3R 8EF (Tel: 020-7623 2761;
Web: www.wccsurveyors@talk21.com)
Clerk: Mrs A. L. Jackson
Master: H. D. C. Stebbing

The Worshipful Company of Clockmakers
Room 66–67, Albert Buildings, 49 Queen Victoria Street, London, EC4N 4SE (Tel: 020-7236 0700; Fax: 020-7236 0800;
E-mail: clerk@clockmakers.org;
Web: www.clockmakers.org)
Clerk: Gp. Capt. P. H. Gibson, MBE
Master: Sir George White, Bt

The Worshipful Company of Constructors
181 Fentiman Road, London, SW8 1JY (Tel: 020-7735 1459; Fax: 020-7735 1459)
Clerk: L. L. Brace
Master: J. M. Burrell

The Worshipful Company of Cooks
Registry Chambers, The Old Deanery, Deans Court, London, EC4V 5AA (Tel: 020-7593 5043; Fax: 020-7248 3221)
Clerk: M. C. Thatcher
Master: P. A. P. White

The Worshipful Company of Coopers
13 Devonshire Square, London, EC2M 4TH (Tel: 020-7247 9577; Fax: 020-7377 8061;
E-mail: clerk@coopers-hall.co.uk)
Clerk: J. A. Newton
Master: J. W. S. Clark, RD

The Worshipful Company of Cordwainers
8 Warwick Court, Gray's Inn, London, WC1R 5DJ (Tel: 020-7242 4411; Fax: 020-7242 3366);
E-mail: office@cordwainers.fsbusiness.co.uk)
Clerk: Lt.-Col. J. R. Blundell, RM
Master: D. M. B. Skinner

The Worshipful Company of Cutlers
Warwick Lane, London, EC4M 7BR (Tel: 020-7248 1866; Fax: 020-7248 8426)
Clerk: J. P. Allen
Master: D. Barnes

The Worshipful Company of Distillers
71 Lincoln's Inn Fields, London, WC2A 3JF (Tel: 020-7405 7091; Fax: 020-7405 1453)
Clerk: C. V. Hughes
Master: R. R. Howell

The Worshipful Company of Dyers
10 Dowgate Hill, London, EC4R 2ST (Tel: 020-7236 7197)
Clerk: J. R. Chambers
Prime Warden: E. R. Verney, BA

The Worshipful Company of Farmers
(Correspondence address) Chislehurst Business Centre, 1 Bromley Lane, Chislehurst, Kent, BR7 6LH (Tel: 020-8467 2255; Fax: 020-8467 2666)
Clerk: Miss M. L. Winter
Master: R. A. Brooks

The Worshipful Company of Farmers
3 Cloth Street, London, EC1A 7LD
Clerk: Miss M. L. Winter
Master: R. A. Brooks

The Company of Firefighters
The Insurance Hall, 20 Aldermanbury, London, EC2V 7GF (Tel: 020-7600 1666; Fax: 020-7600 1666)
Clerk: M. Holland Prior
Master: John E. Lawrence, MBE

The Worshipful Company of Fletchers
11 Aldermans Hill, London, N13 4YD (Tel: 020-8882 3055; Fax: 020-8882 5851;
E-mail: john@owen-ward.u-net.com)
Clerk: J. R. Owen-Ward
Master: C. J. Brown

The Worshipful Company of Founders
Number One, Cloth Fair, London, EC1A 7JQ (Tel: 01273-858700; Fax: 01273-858900)
Clerk: A. J. Gillett
Master: A. Newman

The Worshipful Company of Framework Knitters
Whitegarth Chambers, 37 The Uplands, Loughton, Essex, IG10 1NQ (Tel: 020-8502 1964; Fax: 020-8502 5237;
E-mail: clerk@frameworkknitters.co.uk;
Web: www.frameworkknitters.co.uk)
Clerk: H. W. H. Ellis
Master: S. A. F. Smith

London Borough Councils 49

The Worshipful Company of Fuellers
22 Broadfields, Headstone Lane, Hatch End, Middx, HA2 6NH (Tel: 020-8421 6616; Fax: 020-8421 6616; E-mail: fuellers@aol.com; Web: www.fuellers.co.uk)
Clerk: R. A. Riley
Master: R. J. Budge

The Worshipful Company of Furniture Makers
Painters' Hall, 9 Little Trinity Lane, London, EC4V 2AD (Tel: 020-7248 1677; Fax: 020-7248 1688; E-mail: clerk@furnituremkrs.co.uk; Web: www.furnituremkrs.co.uk)
Clerk: Mrs J. A. Wright
Master: S. F. Brown

The Worshipful Company of Gardeners
25 Luke Street, London, EC2A 4AR (Tel: 020-7739 8200; Fax: 020-7613 3412; Web: www.gardenerscompany.org.uk)
Clerk: Col. N. G. S. Gray
Master: A. H. K. Edwards

The Worshipful Company of Girdlers
Girdlers Hall, Basinghall Avenue, London, EC2V 5DD (Tel: 020-7638 0488; Fax: 020-7628 4030; E-mail: girdlers@lineone.net)
Clerk: Lt.-Col. R. Sullivan
Master: F. M. French

The Worshipful Company of Glaziers and Painters of Glass
Glaziers Hall, 9 Montague Close, London, SE1 9DD (Tel: 020-7403 3300; Fax: 020-7407 6036)
Clerk: Col. D. W. Eking
Master: R. A. Stone

The Worshipful Company of Glovers of London
71 Ifield Road, London, SW10 9AU (Tel: 020-7351 4006; Fax: 020-7351 4006; E-mail: gloverslondon@aol.com)
Clerk: Mrs M. Hood
Master: J. D. H. Clarke

The Worshipful Company of Gold and Silver Wyre Drawers
Twizzletwig, The Ballands South, Feltcham, Leatherhead, Surrey, KT22 9EP (Tel: 01372-370104; Fax: 01372-370104; E-mail: liverygswd@ballards.demon.co.uk)
Clerk: T. J. Waller
Master: Peter Yarranton

The Worshipful Company of Gunmakers
The Proof House, 48–50 Commercial Road, London, E1 1LP (Tel: 020-7481 2695; Fax: 020-7481 2040)
Clerk: S. D. O. Duckworth
Master: R. M. Mitchell

The Worshipful Company of Information Technologists
39A Bartholomew Close, London, EC1A 7JN (Tel: 020-7600 1992; Fax: 020-7600 1991; E-mail: assistant@wcit.org.net; Web: www.wcit.org.uk)
Clerk: Mrs G. Davies
Master: John C. Carrington

The Worshipful Company of Innholders
30 College Street, London, EC4R 2RH (Tel: 020-7236 6703; Fax: 020-7236 0059; E-mail: mail@inholders.co.uk; Web: www.innholders.co.uk)
Clerk: D. E. Bulger
Master: A. G. Fisher

The Worshipful Company of Insurers
20 Aldermanbury, London, EC2V 7HY (Tel: 020-7600 4006; Fax: 020-7972 0153)
Clerk: L. J. Walters
Master: D. R. Losse

The Worshipful Company of Launderers
Launderers' Hall, 9 Montague Close, London Bridge, London, SE1 9DD (Tel: 020-7378 1430; Fax: 020-7407 6036)
Clerk: Mrs J. Polek
Master: P. C. Crane

The Worshipful Company of Leathersellers
15 St Helen's Place, London, EC3A 6DQ (Tel: 020-7330 1444; Fax: 020-7330 1445; E-mail: enquiries@leathersellers.co.uk; Web: www.leathersellers.co.uk)
Clerk: J. G. F. Cooke, OBE, RN
Master: T. J. Daniels

The Worshipful Company of Lightmongers
Crown Wharf, 11A Coldharbour, Blackwall Reach, London, E14 9NS (Tel: 020-7515 9055; Fax: 020-7538 5466)
Clerk: D. B. Wheatley
Master: R. Oliver

50 Governed London

The Worshipful Company of Loriners
8 Portland Square, London, E1W 2QR (Tel: 020-7709 0222; Fax: 020-7709 0222)
Clerk: G. B. Forbes
Master: R. H. Walker-Arnott

The Worshipful Company of Masons
22 Cannon Hill, Southgate, London, N14 6LG (Tel: 020-8882 9520; Fax: 020-8882 9520; E-mail: clerk@masonslivery.co.uk; Web: www.masonslivery.co.uk)
Clerk: P. F. Clark
Master: D. Ruffle

Honourable Company of Master Mariners
HQS Wellington, Temple Stairs, Victoria Embankment, London, WC2R 2PN (Tel: 020-7836 8179; Fax: 020-7240 3082; E-mail: info@hcmm.org.uk; Web: www.hcmm.org.uk)
Admiral: HRH The Prince Philip, Duke of Edinburgh, KG, KT, OM, GBE, PC
Clerk: J. A. V. Maddock
Master: Commodore A. D. Barrett, CBE, RD, DL, RNR

The Worshipful Company of Musicians
75 Watling Street, London, EC4M 9BJ
Clerk: Vacant
Master: David Hill

The Worshipful Company of Needlemakers
5 Staple Inn, London, WC1V 7QH
Clerk: M. G. Cook
Master: Brian Hatfield

The Worshipful Company of Painter-Stainers
Painters' Hall, 9 Little Trinity Lane, London, EC4V 2AD (Tel: 020-7236 7070; Fax: 020-7236 7074; E-mail: clerk@painters-hall.co.uk)
Clerk: Col. W. J. Chesshyre
Master: Revd Graham Blacktop

The Company of Parish Clerks
c/o 1 Dean Trench Street, London, SW1P 3HB (Tel: 020-7222 1138; Fax: 020-7222 3468)
Clerk: Lt.-Col. B. J. N. Coombes
Master: S. J. Murphy, MBE

The Worshipful Company of Paviors
3 Ridgemount Gardens, Enfield, Middx, EN2 8QL (Tel: 020-8366 1566; Fax: 020-8366 1566; E-mail: jlwhite@talk21.com)
Clerk: J. L. White
Master: K. C. White

The Worshipful Company of Pewterers
Oat Lane, London, EC2V 7DE (Tel: 020-7606 9363; Fax: 020-7600 3896; E-mail: clerk@pewterers.org.uk; Web: www.pewterers.org.uk)
Clerk: Cdr. A. StJ. Steiner, OBE, RN
Master: M. G. C. Gibbs

The Worshipful Company of Plaisterers
1 London Wall, London, EC2Y 5JU (Tel: 020-7606 1361; Fax: 020-7796 1408; E-mail: clerk@plaistererslivery.co.uk; Web: www.plaistererslivery.co.uk)
Clerk: R. Vickers
Master: A. J. Turner

The Worshipful Company of Plumbers
49 Queen Victoria Street, London, EC4N 4SA (Tel: 020-7236 7816; Fax: 020-7236 7816)
Clerk: Lt.-Col. R. J. A. Paterson-Fox
Master: A. K. Woollanston

The Worshipful Company of Saddlers
40 Gutter Lane, London, EC2V 6BR (Tel: 020-7726 8661; Fax: 020-7600 0386; E-mail: clerk@saddlersco.co.uk; Web: www.saddlersco.co.uk)
Clerk: Gp Capt. W. S. Brereton Martin, CBE
Master: M. A. C. Laurie

The Scientific Instrument Makers
9 Montague Close, London, SE1 9DD (Tel: 020-7407 4832; Fax: 020-7407 1565; E-mail: theclerk@wcsim.co.uk; Web: www.locsim.co.uk)
Clerk: N. J. Watson
Master: J. M. T. Hilton

The Worshipful Company of Scriveners
HQS Wellington, Temple Stairs, Victoria Embankment, London, WC2R 2PN (Tel: 020-7240 0529; Fax: 020-7497 0645; Web: www.scriveners.co.uk)
Clerk: G. A. Hill
Master: P. H. Grove

The Worshipful Company of Shipwrights
Ironmongers Hall, Barbican, London, EC2Y 8AA (Tel: 020-7606 2376; Fax: 020-7600 3515; E-mail: clerk@shipwrights.co.uk)
Permanent Master: HRH The Prince Philip, Duke of Edinburgh, KG, KT, OM, GBE, PC
Clerk: Capt. R. F. Channon, RN
Prime Warden: Vice-Adm. Sir James Wiathnall, KCVO, KBE

London Borough Councils 51

The City of London Solicitors' Company
4 College Hill, London, EC2R 2RB (Tel: 020-7329 2173; Fax: 020-7329 2190; E-mail: mail@citysolicitors.org.uk; Web: www.citysolicitors.org.uk)
Clerk: Miss S. M. Robinson, TD
Master: M. J. Cassidy

The Worshipful Company of Spectacle Makers
Apothecaries' Hall, Black Friars Lane, London, EC4V 6EL (Tel: 020-7236 2932; Fax: 020-7329 3249; E-mail: clerk@spectaclemakers.com; Web: www.spectaclemakers.com)
Clerk: Lt.-Col. J. A. B. Salmon, OBE, LLB
Master: G. W. D. McLaren, FCA, FRSA

The Worshipful Company of Stationers and Newspaper Makers
Ave Maria Lane, London, EC4M 7DD (Tel: 020-7248 2934; Fax: 020-7489 1975; E-mail: admin@stationers.org; Web: www.stationers.org)
Clerk: Brig. D. G. Sharp, AFC
Master: H. F. Chappell

The Worshipful Company of Tallow Chandlers
4 Dowgate Hill, London, EC4R 2SH (Tel: 020-7248 4726; Fax: 020-7236 0844)
Clerk: Brig. W. K. L. Prosser, CBE, MC
Master: C. R. Lambourne, CBE

The Worshipful Company of Turners
182 Temple Chambers, Temple Avenue, London, EC4Y 0HP (Tel: 020-7353 9595; Fax: 020-7353 9933; E-mail: clerk@turnerscompany.demon.co.uk)
Clerk: E. A. Windsor Clive
Master: A. M. Sherred, CB

The Worshipful Company of Upholders
Hall in the Wood, 46 Quail Gardens, Selsdon Vale, Croydon, CR2 8TF (Tel: 020-8656 6811; Fax: 020-8656 6814; E-mail: clerk@codyranch.co.uk; Web: www.codyranch.co.uk)
Clerk: J. P. Cody
Master: R. Colney

The Worshipful Company of Water Conservators
16 St Mary-at-Hill, London, EC2R 8EF (Tel: 020-8421 0305; Fax: 020-8421 0305; E-mail: waterlco@aol.com; Web: www.waterlco.co.uk)
Clerk: R. A. Riley
Master: Vacant

The Worshipful Company of Wax Chandlers
Wax Chandlers Hall, Gresham Street, London, EC2V 7AD (Tel: 020-7606 3591; Fax: 020-7600 5462; E-mail: waxchandlershall@ukonline.co.uk; Web: www.waxchandlershall.co.uk)
Clerk: John R. Williams
Master: The Hon. W. N. Denison

The Worshipful Company of Weavers
Saddlers' House, Gutter Lane, London, EC2V 6BR (Tel: 020-7606 1155; Fax: 020-7606 1119; E-mail: weavers@weaversco.co.uk)
Clerk: Mrs F. Newcombe
Upper Bailiff: P. Littlewood

The Worshipful Company of World Traders
36 Ladbroke Grove, London, W11 2PA (Tel: 020-7792 3410; E-mail: clerk@world-traders.org; Web: www.world-traders.org)
Clerk: N. R. Pullman
Master: B. K. Whalley

The Company of Watermen and Lightermen
Watermen's Hall, 16 St Mary-at-Hill, London, EC3R 8EF (Tel: 020-7283 2373; Fax: 020-7283 0477; E-mail: info@watermenshall.org; Web: www.watermenshall.org)
Clerk: C. Middlemiss
Master: C. G. Newens

The following guilds are located outside the Greater London Area. For their contact details please see Whitaker's Almanack 2002.

The Company of Arbitrators; Chartered Accountants in England and Wales; Chartered Architects; Broderers; Coachmakers and Coach Harness Makers; The Company of Curriers; Engineers; Environmental Cleaners; Fan Makers; Farriers; Feltmakers of London; Fruiterers; Glass Sellers of London; Horners; Joiners and Ceilers; Makers of Playing Cards; Marketors; Pattenmakers; Poulters; Tin Plate Workers (Alias Wire Workers); Tobacco Pipe Makers and Tobacco Blenders; Tax Advisers; The Tylers and Bricklayers Company; Wheelwrights; Woolmen.

52 Governed London

CROYDON

Taberner House, Park Lane, Croydon, CR9 3JS
(Tel: 020-8686 4433; Fax 020-8760 5657;
Web: www.croydon.gov.uk).
Director of Finance: Municipal Offices, Fell Road, Croydon, CR9 1BQ (Tel: 020-8686 4433; Fax 020-8686 7405).
Libraries and Museums: Central Library, Katherine Street, Croydon, CR9 1ET.
Registration of Births, Deaths and Marriages: Register Office, Mint Walk, Croydon CR0 1EA (Tel: 020-8760 5617).

CHIEF OFFICERS

Chief Executive: D. Wechsler
Director of Corporate Services: Miles Smith
Director of Education: Dr. David Sands
Director of Environmental Health and Trading Standards: Don Boon
Director of Finance and IT: Jan Willis
Director of Housing: Mike Davis
Director of Cultural Services: Steve Halsey
Director of Planning and Development: Philip Goodwin
Director of Public Services and Works: K. C. Ollier
Director of Social Services: Hannah Miller
Head of Corporate Construction: K. Herriott
Head of Information Technology: D. Fitze
Head of Policy and Executive Office: Will Tuckley

MEMBERS OF THE COUNCIL

Councillor	Ward
Mayor: P. Hopson, Lab.	Norbury
Deputy Mayor: Rod Matlock, Lab.	Broad Street

Leader of the Council:

Hugh Malyan, Lab.	Beulah
D. Adamson, C.	Selsdon
E. Arram, C.	Ashburton
Ian Atkins, LD	Coulsdon East
Jane Avis, Lab.	South Norwood
Gavin Barwell, C.	Woodcote and Coulsdon West
G. Bass, C.	Purley
Gee Bernard, Lab.	West Thornton
C. Burling, Lab.	Waddon
Alex Burridge, Lab.	Bensham Manor
Jan Buttinger, C.	Kenley
John Calvert, C.	Waddon
Amanda Campbell, Lab.	Addiscombe
P. Cambell, C.	Monks Orchard
R. Chandarana, Lab.	West Thornton
Pat Clouder, Lab.	Thornton Heath
R. Coatman, C.	Fairfield
S. Collins, Lab.	Broad Street
Graham Dare, C.	Waddon
A. Dennis, Lab.	Thornton Heath
B. Finegan, Lab.	Woodside
Mike Fisher, C.	Spring Park
J. Fitzpatrick, Lab.	Addiscombe
S. Fitzsimons, Lab.	Addiscombe
C. Fraser, Lab.	South Norwood
Wally Garratt, Lab.	Thornton Heath
R. Grantham, Lab.	Beulah
Lynne Hale, C.	Sanderstead
Anna Hawkins, C.	Woodcote and Coulsdon West
Steve Hollands, C.	Kenley
Maureen Horden, C.	Heathfield
Karen Jewitt, Lab.	Rylands
M. Jewitt, Lab.	South Norwood
Nick Keable, C.	Croham
Shafi Khan, Lab.	Norbury
Pat Knight, C.	Fairfield
T. Laffin, Lab.	New Addington
Toni Letts, Lab.	Whitehorse Manor
Derek Loughborough, C.	Monks Orchard
H. Maylan, Lab.	Beulah
Maggie Mansell, Lab.	Norbury
Janet Marshall C.	Spring Park
Paul McCombie, C.	Croham
C. McKenzie, Lab.	West Thornton
D. Mead, C.	Selsdon
Margaret Mead, C.	Heathfield
P. Mee, Lab.	Bensham Manor
D. Millard, C.	Purley
T. Newman, Lab.	Woodside
D. Osland, C.	Woodcote and Coulsdon West
Ian Payne, Lab.	Upper Norwood
A. Pelling, C.	Heathfield
J. Perry, C.	Coulsdon East

London Borough Councils 53

Gerry Ryan, Lab.	Whitehorse Manor	
Pat Ryan, Lab.	Upper Norwood	
E. Shaw, C.	Sanderstead	
Paula Shaw, Lab.	Bensham Manor	
A. Slipper, C.	Ashburton	
P. Spalding, Lab.	Broad Street	
Mark Stockwell, C.	Croham	
Phil Thomas, C.	Purley	
Martin Tiedemann, Lab.	Whitehorse Manor	
J. Walker, Lab.	Fieldway	
Mary Walker, Lab.	Fieldway	
Christopher Ward, Lab.	New Addington	
Louisa Woodley, Lab.	Rylands	
C. Wright, C.	Coulsdon East	
M. Wunn, C.	Fairfield	

Political Composition: Lab. 38; C. 31; LD. 1
Parliamentary Constituencies:
Croydon Central; Croydon North; Croydon South.
Population: 337,600
Area: 8,662 hectares.

ABOUT CROYDON

Croydon is the largest of the London boroughs in terms of population. There are approximately 140,000 households in the borough. Outside of central London Croydon is the largest office centre in the south of England and has nearly 3 million square feet of retail space. Many of the borough's residents commute into London with journeys into London's Victoria Station taking less than 15 minutes, but it also remains a major employment centre.

COUNCIL TAX BANDS 2001-2002

Band	Market Value of the Property	Council Tax
A	Up to £40,000	£549.25
B	£40,001 to 52,000	£640.79
C	£52,001 to 68,000	£732.33
D	£68,001 to 88,000	£823.87
E	£88,001 to 120,000	£1006.95
F	£120,001 to 160,000	£1190.04
G	£160,001 to 320,000	£1373.12
H	£320,001 or more	£1647.74

EALING

Town Hall, London W5 2BY (Tel: 020-8579 2424; Fax: 020-8579 5224;
Email: webmaster@ealing.gov.uk;
Web: www.ealing.gov.uk).
Director of Corporate Resources: Town Hall Annex, London, W5 2BY.
Perceval House: 14-16 Uxbridge Road, London, W5 2HL.

CHIEF OFFICERS

Chief Executive: Ms. Gillian Guy
Executive Director of Corporate Resources: Vacant
Executive Director of Education: Alan Parker
Executive Director of Environment Group: John Birch
Executive Director of Regeneration: Chris Dallison
Executive Director of Social Services and Housing: Prof. Norman Tutt

MEMBERS OF THE COUNCIL

Councillor	Ward
Mayor: Ranjit Dheer, Lab.	Mount Pleasant
Deputy Mayor: Kieron Gavan, Lab.	Northfield
Leader of the Council:	
John Cudmore, Lab.	Heathfield
Jasbir Anand, Lab.	Glebe
Joan Ansell, C.	Argyle
Mohammad Aslam, Lab.	Dormers Wells
Tej Ram Bagha, Lab.	Mount Pleasant
Martin Beecroft, Lab.	Walpole
David Bond, Lab.	West End
Elizabeth Brooks, Lab.	Heathfield
Anthony Brown, C.	Ealing Common
Brian Castle C.	Argyle
Umesh Chander, Lab.	Glebe
Julia Clements-Elliott, Lab.	Elthorne

54 Governed London

Edward Coleman, Lab.	Elthorne
Katherine Crawford, Lab.	Vale
John Delaney, Lab.	Springfield
Kamaljit Dhindsa, Lab.	Waxlow
Steven Donnelly, Lab.	Springfield
Peter Downham, C.	Mandeville
Fred Dunckley, Lab.	West End
Laurence Evans, Lab.	Costons
Ian Gibb, C.	Argyle
Richard Gordon, Lab.	Wood End
Tony Gray, Lab.	Victoria
Ian Green, C.	Ealing Common
Phyllis Greenhead, Lab.	Hobbayne
Brenda Hall, C.	Wood End
Eileen Harris, C.	Ealing Common
Joy Hetherington, C.	Costons
Audrey Hider, C.	Pitshanger
Frank Impey, Lab.	West End
Yvonne Johnson, Lab.	Heathfield
Swarn Singh Kang, Lab.	Costons
Manjit Keith, Lab.	Waxlow
Manjit Singh Mahal, Lab.	Northcote
Margaret Majumdar, Lab.	Elthorne
Rajinder Sing Mann, Lab.	Dormers Wells
Shital Manro, Lab.	Horsenden
Andrew Mitchell, LD	Southfield
Glenn Murphy, C.	Mandeville
Diane Murray, Lab.	Ravenor
Inderjeet Singh, Nijhar Lab.	Perivale
Joseph O'Neill, Lab.	Northfield
Diane Pagan, C.	Pitshanger
Rabindara Pathak, Lab.	Glebe
Madhav Patil, Lab.	Mount Pleasant
Christopher Payne, Lab.	Perivale
Margaret Payne, Lab.	Springfield
Ram Perdesi, Lab.	Northcote
Richard Porter, Lab.	Wood End
Philip Portwood, Lab.	Victoria
Ian Potts, C.	Hanger Lane
Royston Price, Lab.	Hobbayne
Rev. N. Richardson, Lab.	Mandeville
Harvey Rose, LD	Southfield
Kieran Ryan, LD	Southfield
Gurdip Singh Sahota, Lab.	Northcote
Stephen Sears, Lab.	Hobbayne
Virendra Sharma, Lab.	Walpole
Gurcharan Singh, Lab.	Waxlow
Jill Stokoe, Lab.	Ravenor
Nigel Sumner C.	Hanger Lane
Leonora Thomson, Lab.	Ravenor
Frederick Varley, Lab.	Hosenden
Surinder Varma, Lab.	Dormers Wells
Peter Wicks, Lab.	Walpole
Paul Woodgate, Lab	Vale
Simon Woodroofe, Lab.	Northfield
Barbara Yerolemou, C.	Hanger Lane
Anthony Young, C.	Pitshanger

Political Composition: Lab. 52; C. 16; LD. 3
Population: 298,000
Area: 5,550.

ABOUT EALING

Ealing encompasses the areas of Ealing, Acton, Hanwell, Southall, Northolt, Perivale and Greenford. Southall is home to one of the major centres in Asian population in the country and there is a substantial African-Caribbean community in Acton. There are nearly 2000 acres of parks and open spaces in Ealing and there is a leisure complex in Park Royal.

COUNCIL TAX BANDS 2001-2002

Band	Market Value of the Property	Council Tax
A	Up to £40,000	£548.57
B	£40,001 to 52,000	£640.46
C	£52,001 to 68,000	£731.96
D	£68,001 to 88,000	£823.45
E	£88,001 to 120,000	£1006.44
F	£120,001 to 160,000	£1189.43
G	£160,001 to 320,000	£1372.42
H	£320,001 or more	£1646.90

ENFIELD

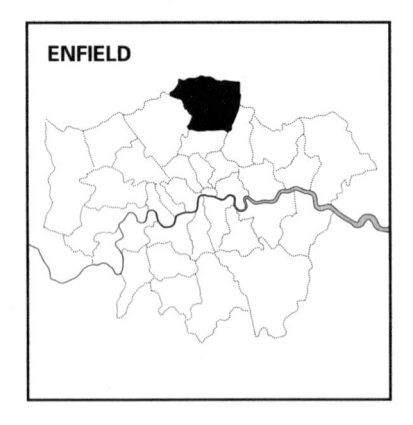

Civic Centre, Silver Street, Enfield, EN1 3XY (Tel: 020-8366 6565; Web: www.enfield.gov.uk).
Occupational Health Service: Kimberley Gardens, Enfield, London EN1 3ST (Tel: 020-8351 8051; Fax 020-8351 8018).
Trading Standards Officer: Gentleman's Row, Enfield, London, EN2 6PS (Tel: 020-8379 8515).
The Register Office: Public Offices, Gentleman's Row, Enfield EN2 6PS (Tel: 020-8367 5757).

London Borough Councils

CHIEF OFFICERS

Chief Executive: David Plank
Acting Director of Corporate Services: David Tullis
Director of Education: Liz Graham
Interim Director of Finance: Peter Leeming
Director of Housing: Donald Graham
Director of Leisure Services: Christine Neyndorff
Director of Environmental Services: John Pryor
Interim Director of Social Services: Stephen Wyld

MEMBERS OF THE COUNCIL

Councillor	Ward
Mayor: Yasemin Brett, Lab.	Arnos
Deputy Mayor: Ivor Wiggett, Lab.	St. Mark's
Leader of the Council: Doug Taylor, Lab.	Green Street
Pamela Adams, C.	Southgate Green
Daniel Anderson, Lab.	Southgate Green
Neil Aves, Lab.	Palmers Green
Brian Barford, Lab.	Huxley
Alan Barker, C.	Highfield
Chris Bond, Lab.	Ponders End
R. Buckley, Lab.	Enfield Wash
David Burrowes, C.	Trent
Stanley Carter, Lab.	Southbury
Bambos Charalambous, Lab.	Palmers Green
Christopher Cole, Lab.	Highfield
J. A. Connew, Lab.	Angel
A. Constantinides, Lab.	Weir Hall
Betty Costello, Lab.	Angel
Wendell Daniel, Ind.	St. Mark's
Don Delman, C.	Merryhills
Tony Dey, C.	Worcester
John Egan, C.	Town
Graham Eustance, C.	Willow
Foston Fairclough, Lab.	Ponders Green
M. Fenton, Lab.	Craig
Jonathan French, C.	Grovelands
Achilleas Georgiou, Lab.	Bowes
Vivien Giladi, Lab.	Arnos
N. Gilmore, C.	Grange
Derek Goddard, Lab.	Jubilee
J. Gorton, Lab.	Bullsmoor
B. Grayston, Lab.	Enfield Wash
Verna Horridge, Lab.	Hoe Lane
J. W. E. Jackson, C.	Village
Dennis Keighley, C.	Winchmore Hill
Bernadette Lappage, Lab.	Enfield Lock
Michael Lavender, C.	Oakwood
Alasdair MacPhail, C.	Town
Alex Mattingly, Lab.	Craig
Joanne McCartney, Lab.	Weir Hall
Clive Morrison, Lab.	St. Alphege
Christopher Murphy, Lab.	St. Alphege
Danny Neary, Lab.	Bullsmoor
Terence Neville, C.	Winchmore Hill
Ayfer Orhan, Lab.	Green Street
Anne Pearce, C.	Trent
Irene Richards, Lab.	Southbury
Colin Robb, Lab.	St. Peter's
J. Rodin, Lab.	Bowes
Lyn Romain, Lab.	Oakwood
Peter Rust, C.	Grovelands
Michael Rye, C.	Willow
George Savva, Lab.	Huxley
Toby Simon, Lab.	Raglan
Edward Smith, C.	Merryhills
Eric Smythe, Lab.	St. Peters
Rita Smythe, Lab.	Jubilee
Geoff Southwell, Lab.	Hoe Lane
Phill Sowter, Lab.	Latymer
Austin Spreadbury, C.	Worcester
Andrew Stafford, Lab.	Latymer
M. Sutters, Lab.	Enfield Lock
Glynis Vince, C.	Grange
Mark Walton, Lab.	Raglan
John Wyatt, C.	Village
J. M. Yates, C.	Chase

Political Composition: Lab. 42; C. 22; Ind. 1; V. 1
Population: 267,000
Area: 8,218.

ABOUT ENFIELD

Enfield is located some 12 miles north of the City on the northern outer edge of the capital. There are numerous parks and open spaces in the borough and there are fourteen conservation areas. Enfield has approximately 113,000 residential dwellings and a substantial number of these are owner-occupied. There are five main shopping centres in the borough along with several out of town superstores and the area is well served by public transport with four overland train services to central London and the Piccadilly underground line.

56 Governed London

COUNCIL TAX BANDS 2001-2002

Band	Market Value of the Property	Council Tax
A	Up to £40,000	£589.82
B	£40,001 to 52,000	£688.12
C	£52,001 to 68,000	£786.43
D	£68,001 to 88,000	£884.73
E	£88,001 to 120,000	£1081.34
F	£120,001 to 160,000	£1277.94
G	£160,001 to 320,000	£1474.55
H	£320,001 or more	£1769.46

GREENWICH

Town Hall, Wellington Street, London, SE18 6PW (Tel: 020-8854 8888; Fax: 020-8921 5074; Web: www.greenwich.gov.uk).
Chief Executive: Town Hall, Wellington Street, London SE18 6PW (Tel: 020-8921 5000).
Head of Legal Services: 29-37 Wellington Street, London SE18 6PW.
Director of Finance: 45-53 Wellington Street, London, SE18 6RA.
Head of Planning and Regeneration: Peggy Middleton House, 50 Woolwich New Road, London, SE18 6HQ.
Director of Strategic Planning, Director of Public Services, Director of Housing: Peggy Middleton House, 50 Woolwich New Road, London SE18 6HQ.
Director of Social Services: Nelson House, 50 Wellington Street, London, SE18 6HQ (Tel: 020-8854 8888).

CHIEF OFFICERS

Chief Executive: Mary Ney
Director of Education Services: George Gyte
Director of Housing Services: Richard Thompson
Director of Social Services: David Behan
Director of Strategic Planning: David McCollum
Director of Public Services: Gurmel Singh-kandola

MEMBERS OF THE COUNCIL

Councillor	Ward
Mayor: T. Malone, Lab.	Tarn
Deputy Mayor: S. Jawaid, Lab.	Charlton
N. R. Adams, Lab.	Kidbrook
D. Austen, Lab.	Glyndon
B. Barwick, Lab.	Lakedale
M. Best, Lab.	Ferrier
C. Boothe, Lab.	Lakedale
G. E. Brighty, C.	Blackheath
P. Brooks, Lab.	Thamesmead Mooring
P. M. Challis, Lab.	Slade
A. Cornforth, Lab.	Rectory Field
J. A. Cove, Lab.	Kidbrook
I. A. Danesi, Lab.	Eynsham
M. Devaux, Lab.	Coldharbour
G. S. Dhillon, Lab.	Woolwich Common
L. L. Duvall, Lab.	Burrage
John Fahy, Lab.	St. Mary's
W. Freeman, Lab.	Well Hall
Janet Gillman, Lab.	New Eltham
Jim Gillman, Lab.	Hornfair
A. H. W. Grant, Lab.	Vanbrugh
D. I. Grant, Lab.	Charlton
B. Groves, Lab.	Eynsham
T. Hales, Lab.	Woolwich Common
H. R. Harris, Lab.	Middle Park
R. C. Harris, C.	Blackheath
M. R. Hayes, Lab.	Sherard
Mick Hayes, Lab.	Shrewsbury
J. Hills, C.	New Eltham
A. C. Hutchinson, Lab.	Slade
B. A. Jones, Lab.	Herbert
J. Kelly, Lab.	Coldharbour
P. J. H. King, C.	Palace
P. Kotz, Lab.	Thamesmead Mooring
R. E. Lewis, Lab.	Hornfair
A. T. Macrae, Lab.	St. Nicholas
C. Mardner, Lab.	Abbey Wood
Q. Marsh, Lab.	Sherard
N. C. McShee, Lab.	St. Mary's
D. O. Mepsted, C.	Trafalgar
A. G. Miles, C.	Deansfield
V. E. Morse, Lab.	Plumstead Common
M. O'Mara, Lab.	West
B. R. O'Sullivan, Lab.	Arsenal
G. Parker, Lab.	Rectory Field
K. M. Patel, Lab.	St. Alfege
M. S. Pattenden, LD	Avery Hill
D. J. Picton, Lab.	Vanbrugh

London Borough Councils   57

D. D. Poston, C.
C. Roberts, Lab.
K. Scott, Lab.
J. Sekhon, Lab.
R. Sidhu, Lab.
J. M. Simpson, C.
C. Slee, Lab.
D. J. Smith, Lab.
D. Steedman, Lab.
B. Taylor, Lab.
J. Wakefield, Lab.
R. Walker, Lab.
B. J. Woodcraft, LD

Eltham Park
St. Alfege
Nightingale
West
Herbert
Eltham Park
St. Nicholas
Ferrier
Abbey Wood
Middle Park
Glyndon
Well Hall
Sutcliffe

Political Composition: Lab. 51; C. 8; LD. 2.
Population: 212,073
Area: 5,043.

ABOUT GREENWICH

Greenwich is the reference point for the World's Time. Set on the banks of the river Thames, Greenwich and is a popular tourist destination outside of central London with attractions such as the Meridian line at the Royal Observatory, The Royal Park, The Royal Naval College and the Cutty Sark Tea Clipper. Greenwich is served by the Docklands Light Railway (DLR) as well as the Jubilee line extension of the London Underground. The Council has introduced a number of projects to regenerate the Borough including a series of developments along the waterfront from Deptford creek to the Greenwich peninsula and Woolwich. These, it is hoped, will bring new employment opportunities, tourism, business as well as housing and leisure facilities.

COUNCIL TAX BANDS 2001-2002

Band	Market Value of the Property	Council Tax
A	Up to £40,000	£607.50 (£644.40)
B	£40,001 to 52,000	£708.75 (£751.80)
C	£52,001 to 68,000	£810.00 (£859.20)
D	£68,001 to 88,000	£911.25 (£966.60)
E	£88,001 to 120,000	£1113.75 (£1181.40)
F	£120,001 to 160,000	£1316.25 (£1396.20)
G	£160,001 to £320,000	£1518.75 (£1611.00)
H	£320,001 or more	£1822.50 (£1933.20)

Figures in brackets represent the amount of Council Tax set for dwellings situated in the area surrounding Gloucester Circus Garden Square.

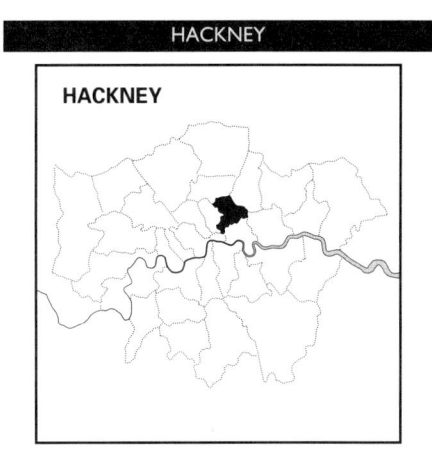

HACKNEY

HACKNEY

Town Hall, Mare Street, London, E8 1EA (Tel: 020-8356 5000; Fax: 020-8356 3202; Web: www.hackney.gov.uk).
Haggerston Park, Queensbridge Road, London E2 8PB (Tel: 020-7739 9725).
Emergency Service (Out of Hours) (Tel: 020-8356 2300/2301/2302/2303).
First Stop Shop: Shoreditch Library, Hoxton Street, London, N1 6LP (Tel: 020-8356 4360).
Revenues and Benefits: Dorothy Hodgkins House, Reading Lane, London, E8 1DS (Tel: 020-8356 5000).
Commercial Standards Unit: 205 Morning Lane, London E9 6LG (Tel: 020-8986 4929).
Core Finance: 298 Mare Street, London, E8 1HE (Tel: 020-8356 2618).
Environmental Health Service Unit: 205 Morning Lane, London E9 6LG (Tel: 020-8356 4771).
Architecture and Planning: 161 City Road, London, EC1V 1NR (Tel: 020-8356 8062).
Leisure and Learning: Edith Cavell Building, Enfield Road, London, N1 5AZ (Tel: 020-8356 5000).
Education: Edith Cavell Building, Enfield Road, London, N1 5AZ (Tel: 020-8356 7341).
Customer and Advice Services: Christopher Addison House, Wilton Way, London, E8 1BJ (Tel: 020-8356 3665).
Estate Management and Development: Christopher Addison House, Wilton Way, London, E8 1BJ (Tel: 020-8356 3671).

58 Governed London

Adult Community Services; Services for Older People; Children and Family Services:
205 Morning Lane, London E9 6LG
(Tel: 020-8356 5000).

CHIEF OFFICERS

Managing Director: Max Caller
Borough Secretary and Solicitor: Christopher Hinde
Borough Treasurer: George Jenkins
Democratic Services Manager: Peter Loveday
Director of Education: Alan Wood
Director of Social Services: Mary Richardson
Head of Communications: Vacant

MEMBERS OF THE COUNCIL

Councillor	Ward
Mayor: S. Siddiqui, Lab.	Kings Park
Deputy Mayor:	
Sharon Patrick, Lab.	Homerton
S. M. Achhala, LD	Northwold
Sylvia Anderson, LD	Clissold
D. Bentley, LD	Dalston
A. Bridgewater, LD	Wick
D. Candlin, C.	Moorfield
J. Carswell, Lab.	North Defoe
Y. C. Chong, Green	North Defoe
R. Cornell, Lab.	Homerton
P. Corrigan, Lab.	Eastdown
Jessica Crowe, Lab.	Rectory
I. Darbyshire, Lab.	Chatham
K. Daws, LD	Wenlock
Meral Ece, LD	Dalston
Lorraine Fahey, C.	Moorfield
A. Gee-Turner, LD	Wick
Julie Grimble, Lab.	Westdown
J. Grosskopf, LD	New River
J. Hudson, Lab.	Clissold
H. Hyman, LD	Victoria
P. Kenyon, Lab.	Brownswood
M. Lewis-Spencer, C.	Northfield
J. Lobenstein, C.	Springfield
Samantha Lloyd, Lab.	Rectory
D. Manion, Lab.	Westdown
Patricia McGuinness, LD	Victoria
Maureen Middleton, C.	New River
Bonnie Miller, Lab.	Leabridge
A. Milton, Lab.	Leabridge
Lindsay Montgomery, C.	Victoria
A. Mulla, Lab.	Leabridge
Sally Mulready, Lab.	Chatham
Vicki Munro, Lab.	Clissold
W. Nicholson, Lab.	Haggerston
C. O'Leary, C.	De Beauvoir
L. Oleforo, Lab.	Rectory
E. Ollerenshaw, C.	Springfield
S. Ogunwobi. Lab.	Kings Park
Bharti Patel, Lab.	Eastdown
I. Peacock, Lab.	South Defoe
F. Pearson, Lab.	De Beauvoir
P. Pearson, LD	Dalston
B. Peretz, C.	Northfield
Hettie Peters, LD	Queensbridge
D. Phillips, Green	New River
Jules Pipe, Lab.	South Defoe
Naomi Russell, Lab.	Chatham
S. Sartain, Lab.	Eastdown
I. Sharer, LD	Northwold
C. Sills. C.	Northfield
Linda Smith, Lab.	Brownswood
Kay Stone, LD	Wenlock
J. Webb, Lab.	Wick
M. Williams, LD	Queensbridge
Andrew Windross, Lab.	De Beauvoir
D. Young, Lab.	Haggerston

Political Composition: Lab. 30, LD. 15, C. 10, Green 2; V. 3
Population: 193,843
Area: 1,950.

ABOUT HACKNEY

Hackney runs north from the City of London to Stamford Hill. It is both an inner city borough and part of the East End. The borough of Hackney was created in 1965 when the metropolitan boroughs of Shoreditch, Stoke Newington and Hackney itself were merged. Hackney is about 30 minutes journey by train from central London with underground stations, Old Street and Manor House and 10 over-ground stations. The borough's first tube line will be the Northern extension of the East London Line, from Whitechapel through Dalston to Highbury and Islington. Four new stations will be at Bishopsgate, Hoxton, Haggerston and Dalston Junction. It is expected that they will be open by 2004.

COUNCIL TAX BANDS 2001-2002

Band	Market Value of the Property	Council Tax
A	Up to £40,000	£615.22
B	£40,001 to 52,000	£717.76
C	£52,001 to 68,000	£820.30
D	£68,001 to 88,000	£922.83
E	£88,001 to 120,000	£1127.90
F	£120,001 to 160,000	£1332.98
G	£160,001 to 320,000	£1538.05
H	£320,001 or more	£1845.66

HAMMERSMITH AND FULHAM

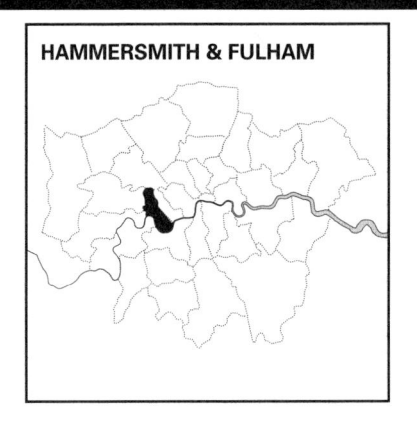

HAMMERSMITH & FULHAM

Town Hall, London, W6 9JU (Tel: 020-8748 3020; Web: www.lbhf.gov.uk).
Advice Centre: 338 Uxbridge Road, London, W12 7LL (Tel: 020-8743 6953).
Director of Housing: Riverview House, Beaver Lane, London, W6 (Tel: 020-8748 3020).
Director of Social Services: 145-155 King Street, London (Tel: 020-8748 3020).
Director of Education: Cambridge House, London (Tel: 020-8748 3020).
Registration of Births, Deaths and Marriages: The Register Office, Nigel Playfair Avenue, London W6 9JY (Tel: 020-8576 5032).

CHIEF OFFICERS

Managing Director: Richard Harbord
Director of Direct Services: Andrew Devenal
Director of Education: Ms. C. Whatford
Director of Environment: Peter Bishop
Director of Finance: Dr. Mark McLarry
Director of Housing Services: E. Elkington
Director of Policy and Administration: Henry Peterson
Director of Social Services: Geoff Alltimes

MEMBERS OF THE COUNCIL

Councillor	Ward
Mayor: A. F. Slaughter, Lab.	Gibbs Green
Deputy Mayor: Christine Graham, Lab.	Coningham
C. Aherne, Lab.	Wormholt
Emile Al-Uzaizi, C.	Palace
A. Alford, C.	Colehill
Chris Allen, Lab.	Grove
B. Bird, Lab.	Sands End
Min Birdsey, Lab.	Magravine
Donal Blaney, C.	Eel Brook
N. Botterill, C.	Sulivan
R. E. Browne MBE, Lab.	White City and Shepherds Bush
S. Burke, Lab.	Wormholt
M. Cartwright, Lab.	Broadway
Joan Caruana, Lab.	Normand
Siobhan Coughlan, Lab.	Addison
S. Cowan, Lab.	Grove
H. Davies, Lab.	Broadway
Fiona Evans, Lab.	Ravenscourt
J. Garrett, Lab.	Sherbrooke
I. Gibbons, Lab.	White City and Shepherds Bush
A. Gray, Lab.	Crabtree
S. Greenhalgh, C.	Town
A. Ground, C.	Palace
Greg Hands, C.	Eel Brook
W. Harcourt, Lab.	College Park and Old Oak
Polly Hicks, Lab.	Brook Green
J. Hillman, Lab.	Starch Green
Sonya Hilton, C.	Avonmore
Lisa Homan, Lab.	Magravine
G. Johnson, Lab.	Brook Green
Ghassan Karian, Lab.	Addison
T. Kennedy Harper, C.	Sherbrooke
Jafar Khaled, Lab.	White City and Shepherds Bush
A. Lillis, C.	Town
Amanda Lloyd Harris, C.	Crabtree
K. Mallinson, Ind.	Avonmore
R. McLaughlin, Lab.	College Park and Old Oak
C. Pavelin, Lab.	Sands End
Dame Sally Powell, Lab.	Wormholt
Hefin Rees, Lab.	Ravenscourt
C. Round, C.	Colehill
Melanie Smallman, Lab.	College Park and Old Oak
Frances Stainton, C.	Walham
T. Stanley, Lab.	Coningham
C. Treloggan, Lab.	Gibbs Green
Dr. Jenny Vaughan, Lab.	Walham
Josie Wicks, Lab.	Coningham
G. Wilkinson, Lab.	Starch Green
D. Williams, Lab.	Normand
G. Wombwell, C.	Sulivan

Political Composition: Lab. 35; C. 14; Ind. Labour 1
Population: 157,000
Area: 1,617.

60 Governed London

ABOUT HAMMERSMITH AND FULHAM

The Borough of Hammersmith and Fulham is located near the heart of London. Until 1965 the boroughs of Hammersmith and Fulham were separate. It is the fourth smallest London Borough and has the fourth highest population density. There are numerous transport links within the borough including the Metropolitan, Piccadilly and District lines of the underground. The A4 also connects Hammersmith to Heathrow airport and the M4. The borough is served by three road bridges-Hammersmith, Putney and Wandsworth. The BBC is the largest employer in the borough with almost 8,000 staff working at Television Centre and the rest of the White City Complex. Hammersmith and Fulham is also home to companies such as Coca Cola, Harper Collins, Haymarket Publications, EMI, and Seagram. House prices in Hammersmith and Fulham are on average the fourth highest in London. The council has therefore made the provision of affordable rented housing one of its key objectives.

COUNCIL TAX BANDS 2001-2002

Band	Market Value of the Property	Council Tax
A	Up to £40,000	£615.53
B	£40,001 to 52,000	£718.11
C	£52,001 to 68,000	£820.70
D	£68,001 to 88,000	£923.29
E	£88,001 to 120,000	£1128.47
F	£120,001 to 160,000	£1333.64
G	£160,001 to 320,000	£1538.82
H	£320,001 or more	£1846.58

HARINGEY

All Departments: Civic Centre, PO Box 264, High Road, London, N22 4LE (Tel: 020 8489 0000; Web: www.haringey.gov.uk).

CHIEF OFFICERS

Chief Executive: David Warwick
Head of Organisational Development and Learning: Gill Davies
Head of Strategy: David Hennings
Director of Finance: Andrew Travers
Director of Education Services: Paul Roberts
Director of Environmental Services: Peter Norton
Director of Housing: Stephen Clarke
Director of Social Services: Anne Burton

MEMBERS OF THE COUNCIL

Councillor	Ward
Mayor: Mary Neuner Lab.	Alexandra
Deputy Mayor: Vivienne Mannheim, Lab.	Bowes Park
Leader of the Council: G. Meehan, Lab.	Woodside
Gina Adamou, Lab.	Harringay
C. Adje, Lab.	White Hart Lane
Lucinda Arnold, Lab.	Bowes Park
Jane Atkinson, Lab.	South Hornsey
D. Basu, Lab.	Seven Sister
Judy Bax, Lab.	Archway
Sally Billot, Lab.	South Hornsey
R. Blanchard, Lab.	Harringay
S. Brasher, Lab.	Bruce Grove
Jean C. Brown, Lab.	Noel Park
Jean E. Brown, Lab.	White Hart Lane
H. Brown, Lab.	Bruce Grove
N. Canver, Lab.	South Tottenham

N. Cleeveley, Lab. — Green Lanes
Lucy Craig, Lab. — Alexandra
T. Davidson, Lab. — Bowes
Maureen Dewar, Lab. — Coleraine
Isidoros Diakides, Lab. — High Cross
D. Dillon, Lab. — Woodside
R. Dodds, Lab. — Park
P. Droussiotis, Lab. — Alexandra
Susan Eedle, Lab. — Fortis Green
Lynne Featherstone, LD — Muswell Hill
P. J. Forrest, C. — Highgate
Nicky Gavron, Lab. — Archway
Julia Glenn, LD — Muswell Hill
B. Haley, Lab. — Green Lanes
B. Harris, Lab. — Tottenham Central
Toby Harris, Lab. — Hornsey Central
S. Horne, Lab. — Hornsey Vale
Josie Irwin, Lab. — Hornsey Vale
H. Jones, Lab. — White Hart Lane
P. Jones, Lab. — West Green
Iris Josiah, Lab. — South Tottenham
A. Knight, Lab. — Seven Sister
Rose Laird, LD — Muswell Hill
W. MacDougall, C. — Highgate
Narendra Makanji, Lab. — Noel Park
R. Muhal, Lab. — West Green
J. Patel, Lab. — Woodside
Sheila Peacock, Lab. — Park
D. Predergast, Lab. — Fortis Green
G. Rahman Khan, Lab. — West Green
S. Reeve, Lab. — Tottenham Central
R. Reynolds, Lab. — Tottenham Central
R. Rice, Lab. — Coleraine
A. Richardson, Lab. — Fortis Green
Irene Robertson, Lab. — Bruce Grove
C. Sandbach, Lab. — Crouch End
C. Sharp, Lab. — Crouch End
Catherine Stafford, Lab. — Hornsey Central
A. Stanton, Lab. — High Cross
Takki Sulaiman, Lab. — Harringay
Bernice Vanier, Lab. — Coleraine
N. Wilmott, Lab. — Crouch End
A. Zaman, Lab. — Noel Park

Political Composition: Lab. 54; LD. 3; C. 2.
Parliamentary Constituencies: Hornsey and Wood Green; Tottenham.
Population: 216,000
Area: 11.5 square miles.

ABOUT HARINGEY

Haringey was formed in 1965 from the boroughs of Hornsey, Tottenham and Wood Green. Bus and rail networks link Haringey to the rest of London as do the Piccadilly and Victoria lines of the Underground. Haringey largely consists of residential areas although hi-tech industry is a rapidly developing trend, notably at the Lee Park Technopark. The Service sector and cultural industries are also flourishing and clothing and textiles are growth sectors.

COUNCIL TAX BANDS 2001-2002

Band	Market Value of the Property	Council Tax
A	Up to £40,000	£640.00
B	£40,001 to 52,000	£746.67
C	£52,001 to 68,000	£853.34
D	£68,001 to 88,000	£960.00
E	£88,001 to 120,000	£1173.33
F	£120,001 to 160,000	£1386.67
G	£160,001 to 320,000	£1600
H	320,001 or more	£1920

HARROW

HARROW

Civic Centre, Station Road, Harrow HA1 2XF
(Tel: 020-8863 5611; Web: www.harrowlb.demon.co.uk).

CHIEF OFFICERS

Chief Executive and Director of Finance: A. G. Redmond
Borough Secretary and Solicitor to the Council: G. Balabanof
Chief Environmental Health Officer: M. Esom
Director of Education: Paul Osburn
Director of Environmental Services: T. Pugh
Director of Social Services: Mrs Ruth Vincent

62 Governed London

Head of Children and Families and Provided Services: Ms. Jo Blake
Head of Contract Services: A. Trehern
Head of Corporate and Information Technology Services: M. Walklate
Head of Environment, Planning and Transportation: B. Hodgson
Head of Financial and Exchequer Services: Ms. C. Cutler
Head of Housing and Environmental Health: M. Wright
Head of Property and Development: G. Easton
Head of School and Community Services: M. Hart
Head of Strategy and Commissioning: D. Burnell
Head of Strategy and Resources (Acting): E. Wingrove

MEMBERS OF THE COUNCIL

Councillor	Ward
Mayor: Bob Currie, Lab.	Roxbourne
Deputy Mayor:	
M. Dharmarajah, Lab.	Roxbourne
A. Alexander, LD	Rayners Lane
D. J. Ashton, C.	Wemborough
Marilyn Ashton, C.	Stanmore Park
Anastasia Attaki, Lab.	Greenhill
Camilla Bath, C.	Stanmore Park
Christine Bednell, C.	Stanmore Park
H. S. Bluston, Lab.	Greenhill
S. Brown, Lab.	Stanmore South
K. Burchell, Lab.	Stanmore South
Lurline Champagnie, C.	Pinner
A. Cocksedge, C.	Pinner
Janet Cowan, C.	Canons
John Cowan, C.	Canons
C. Cox, RA	Wemborough
L. Cox, LD	Roxeth
J. Cripps, RA	Roxeth
C. Davies, Lab.	Kenton West
H. Davies, Lab.	Harrow on the Hill
Margaret Davine, Lab.	Stanmore South
Anne Diamond, LD	Wemborough
Sanjay Dighe, Lab.	Kenton West
A. T. Foulds, Lab.	Kenton East
P. Fox, Lab.	Ridgeway
R. Frogley, Lab.	Kenton West
B. E. Gate, Lab.	Ridgeway
Mary Graham, LD	Harrow Weald
Mitzi Green, Lab.	Centenary
Ann Groves, Lab.	Marlborough
C. Harrison, Lab.	Wealdstone
G. M. Howard, C.	Pinner West
M. Ingram, Lab.	Roxbourne
Mary John, C.	Hatch End
D. M. Kerr, Lab.	Greenhill
Eileen Kinnear, C.	Harrow on the Hill
A. C. Knowles, C.	Hatch End
J. Lammiman, C.	Hatch End
Nicola Lane, LD	Headstone North
P. Lyne, LD	Harrow Weald
Ahmed Marikar, LD	Harrow Weald
Jerry J. Miles, Lab.	Roxeth
Chris Mote, C.	Pinner West
P. Nandhra, LD	Rayners Lane
J. W. Nickolay, C.	Pinner West
C. D. Noyce, LD	Rayners Lane
P. O'Dell, Lab.	Marlborough
A. R. Olins, C.	Pinner
D. Redford, Lab.	Centenary
R. D. Romain, C.	Canons
C. Scowen, C.	Harrow on the Hill
A. Seymour, C.	Headstone North
N. Shah, Lab.	Kenton East
Bob Shannon, Lab.	Wealdstone
E. Silver, C.	Headstone North
Margaret Sims, Lab.	Marlborough
B. Stephenson, Lab.	Headstone South
N. Stillerman, Lab	Ridgeway
Ann Swain, Lab.	Wealdstone
K. Thammaiah, Lab.	Centenary
K. Toms, Lab.	Kenton East
Gillian Travers, Lab.	Headstone South
Anne Whitehead, Lab.	Headstone South

Political Composition: Lab. 32; C. 20; LD. 9; RA. 2.
Population: 210,000
Area: 5,036.

ABOUT HARROW

Harrow is situated in the North west of London and is surrounded by green belt land. Harrow Borough Council has been awarded Beacon Status, given in recognition of the achievements of the Council in 'modern service delivery', particularly its system for handling Council Tax and Housing Benefit. The borough is primarily residential with numerous transport links with the rest of London. It contains more that 50 parks and open spaces. Sights of architectural and historical interest include the Harrow Museum and Heritage Centre. This site is a registered ancient monument and contains a 16th Century Tithe barn and a 14th Century moated manor house.

London Borough Councils 63

COUNCIL TAX BANDS 2001-2002

Band	Market Value of the Property	Council Tax
A	Up to £40,000	£625.97
B	£40,001 to 52,000	£730.29
C	£52,001 to 68,000	£834.62
D	£68,001 to 88,000	£938.95
E	£88,001 to 120,000	£1147.61
F	£120,001 to 160,000	£1356.26
G	£160,001 to 320,000	£1564.92
H	£320,001 or more	£1877.90

HAVERING

Havering Town Hall, Romford, RM1 3BD (Tel: 01708 434343; Fax: 01708 432068; Email: info@havering.gov.uk; Web: www.havering.gov.uk).
Environment and Planning, Development Control, Transportation and Engineering: Mercury House, Mercury Gardens, Romford, RM1 3DS.
Children and Lifelong Learning: Broxhill Centre, Broxhill Road, Harold Hill, Romford, RM4 1XN.
Social Services: Whitworth Centre, Noak Hill Road, Harold Hill, Romford, RM3 7YA (Tel: 01708 434343; Fax: 01708 433010).
Housing: 71-73 Gooshays Gardens, Harold Hill, Romford, RM3 8AF (Tel: 01708 349200; Fax: 01708 349156).
Architectural and Engineering Services: Whitworth Centre, Noak Hill Road, Harold Hill, Romford, RM3 7YA (Tel: 01708 434343; Fax: 01708 433010).
Enterprise Services and Direct Service Organisation: Whitworth Centre, Noak Hill Road, Harold Hill, Romford, RM3 7Y (Tel: 01708 434343; Fax: 01708 433010).
Central Library: Main Road, Romford, RM1 3AR (Tel: 01708 434343; Fax: 01708 432391).

Resources: Havering Town Hall, Romford, RM1 3BD (Tel: 01708 434343).
Legal Services: Ballard Chambers, 26 High Street, Romford, RM1 1HR (Tel: 01708 434343; Fax: 01708 432482).
Registration of Births, Deaths and Marriages: Langtons, Billet Lane, Hornchurch, Essex RM11 1XL (Tel: 01708 434343; Fax: 01708 432391).

CHIEF OFFICERS

Chief Executive: Harold W. Tinworth
Executive Director (Children and Lifelong Learning): Stephen Evans
Executive Director (Community Services): Anthony Douglas
Executive Director (Customer Access and Services): Vacant
Executive Director (Environment and Enterprise Services): Jim Heather Bonfield
Executive Director (Resources): Barry Arden

MEMBERS OF THE COUNCIL

Councillor	Ward
Mayor: Denis O'Flynn, Lab.	Heaton
Deputy Mayor: Maisie Whitelock, Lab.	Hylands
Leader of the Council: Ray Harris, Lab.	Elm Park
Tom Binding, Lab.	South Hornchurch
Edward Cahill, C.	Ardleigh
Eileen Cameron, RA	Hacton
Ivor Cameron, RA	Hacton
Ken Clark, Lab.	Heaton
Jonathan Coles, LD	Harold Wood
Raymond Connelly, Lab.	St. Edward's
Yve Cornell, Lab.	Gooshays
Pam Craig, Lab.	Mawney
Andrew Curtin, C.	Collier Row
Janet Davis, Lab.	Elm Park
Brian E. Eagling, Lab.	Harold Wood
Tony Ellis, Lab.	Rainham
Ray Emmett, Lab.	Airfield
Valerie Evans, RA	Gidea Park
Mark Gadd, C.	Ardleigh Green
P. C. Gardner, C.	Emerson Park
Bill Harrison, Lab.	Gooshays
Linda Hawthorn, RA	Upminster
David Hill, Lab.	Hilldene
Jack Hoepelman, Lab.	Elm Park
Brian F. Kent, Lab.	Rainham
Bob Kilbey, Lab.	Mawney
Geoff Lewis, RA	Cranham East
Joan Lewis, RA	Cranham West
Len Long, RA	South Hornchurch
Eamonn Mahon, Lab.	Brooklands

64 Governed London

Shiela McCole, Lab.
Nigel Meyer, LD
Wilfrid Mills, Lab.
Jean Mitchell, Lab.
E. A. Munday, C.
John Mylod, RA
Patricia Mylod, RA
Barry Norwin, Lab.
Denis O'Flynn, Lab.
Chris Oliver, RA
Chris Purnell, Lab.
Barbara Reith, RA
Ann Roberts, Lab.
Kevin Robinson, Lab.
Paul Rochford, C.
Andrew Rosindell, C.
Gordon Scott-Morris, Con.
Ray Shaw, Lab.
Louise Sinclair, RA
Jeff Stafford, Lab.
Geoffrey Starns, C.
Alby Tebbutt, C.
Wendy Thompson, C.
Owen Ware, RA
Harry Webb, Lab.
Joseph Webster, C.
Michael White, C.
Maisie Whitelock, Lab.
Reg Whitney, RA
Ian Wilkes, RA
Sean Willis, Lab.
Mike Winter, RA
Caroline Wood, Lab.
Mike Wood, Lab.
Malcolm Zetter, LD

Mawney
Oldchurch
Hilldene
Cranham East
Heath Park
St. Andrew's
Upminster
Airfield
Heaton
St. Andrew's
Airfield
Hacton
Hilldene
Gooshays
Emerson Park
Chase Cross
Rise Park
Hylands
Cranham West
Brooklands
Collier Row
Chase Cross
St. Edward's
Upminster
Rainham
Rise Park
Heath Park
Hylands
South Hornchurch
Gidea Park
Heaton
St. Andrew's
Harold Wood
Hylands
Oldchurch

Political Composition: Lab. 31; RA. 16; C. 13; LD. 3
Population: 230,000
Area: 40 square miles.

ABOUT HAVERING

Havering is the second largest borough in Greater London with an area of 40 square miles, 24 of which are green belt. The Borough was created in 1965 in merger of the former Borough of Romford and the Urban District Council of Hornchurch. The name Havering originates from the village of Havering-atte-Bower, where at one time there was a royal palace. Havering is a successful business and commercial Centre with access to the M25 and River Thames frontage of three miles in the south.

COUNCIL TAX BANDS 2001-2002

Band	Market Value of the Property	Council Tax
A	Up to £40,000	£639.33
B	£40,001 to 52,000	£745.89
C	£52,001 to 68,000	£852.44
D	£68,001 to 88,000	£959.00
E	£88,001 to 120,000	£1172.11
F	£120,001 to 160,000	£1385.22
G	£160,001 to 320,000	£1598.33
H	£320,001 or more	£1918.00

HILLINGDON

Civic Centre, Uxbridge, UB8 1UW
(Tel: 01895 250111; Fax 01895 273636;
Web: www.hillingdon.gov.uk).
Borough Information Centre: 14-15 High Street, Uxbridge, UB8 1HD (Tel: 01895 250600).

CHIEF OFFICERS

Chief Executive: Dorian Leatham
Corporate Director of Education, Youth and Leisure Services: Phillip O'Hear
Corporate Director of Environmental Services: Ruth Willis
Corporate Director of Housing Services: Pam Lockley
Corporate Director of Social Services: Graeme Betts

MEMBERS OF THE COUNCIL

Councillor	Ward
Mayor: Catherine Dann, C.	Eastcote
Deputy Mayor: Josephine Barrett, C.	Hillingdon West
Leader of the Council:	
R. Puddifoot, C.	Ickenham
D. Allam, Lab.	Yeading

London Borough Councils

Lynne Allen, Lab.	Botwell	Catherine Stocker, Lab.	Heathrow
Ann Banks, C.	West Drayton	Solveig Stone, C.	Deansfield
D. Banks, C.	Yiewsley	G. R. Tomlin, Lab.	Harlington
R. Barnes, C.	Ickenham	M. Usher, Lab.	Heathrow
R. Benson, C.	Northwood	A. Vernazza, LD	Hillingdon North
J. Bianco, C.	Northwood Hills	A. Way, Lab.	Barnhill
D. Bishop, C.	Northwood Hills	Marion Way, Lab.	Harlington
Lindsay Bliss, Lab.	Barnhill	D. A. Yarrow, C.	Manor
Janet Campbell, LD	Cavendish		
S. Carey, LD	Cavendish		
D. Chand, Lab.	Townfield		
G. Cooper, C.	Uxbridge North		
P. Corthorne, C.	St. Martin's		
G. Courtenay, C.	Cowley		
M. C. Craxton, Lab.	Charville		
Parmjit Dhanda, Lab.	Yeading		
Mahan Dhillon, Lab.	Yeading		
Janet Gardner, Lab.	Wood End		
Jacqueline Griffith, C.	Ickenham		
P. K. Harmsworth, Lab.	Yiewsley		
Shirley Harper-O'Neill, C.	Bourne		
E. Harris, Lab.	Charville		
M. Heywood, C.	Uxbridge North		
R. Hill, Lab.	Townfield		
G. Horn, C.	Eastcote		
D. Horne, Lab.	Hillingdon East		
Sandra Jenkins, C.	Harefield		
J. Jonas, Lab.	Uxbridge South		
A. Kanjee, C.	Northwood		
Mohammed Khursheed, Lab.	Colham		
M. Kilbey, C.	Ruislip		
Maurice Lancaster, C.	Ruislip		
A. G. Langley, C.	Hillingdon West		
J. Major, Lab.	Barnhill		
R. Marshall, Lab.	Cowley		
I. McIntosh, Lab.	Hillingdon East		
D. S. Mills, C.	St. Martin's		
M. Miraj, C.	Manor		
A. Morrison, Lab.	Colham		
J. Morse, Lab.	Bourne		
Caroline Mutton, C.	Harefield		
B. T. Neighbour, Lab.	Harlington		
N. Nunn-Price, Lab.	Botwell		
J. O'Neill, C.	Deansfield		
A. O'Shea, Lab.	Uxbridge South		
J. Oswell, Lab.	Crane		
S. Ouseley, Lab.	Charville		
D. Patel, C.	West Drayton		
C. Pattenden, Lab.	Crane		
D. Payne, C.	Eastcote		
A. Retter, C.	Northwood Hills		
Jill Rhodes, LD	Hillingdon North		
Valerie Robins, C.	Hillingdon West		
P. M. Ryerson, Lab.	Wood End		
S. Seaman-Digby, C.	Northwood		
D. Simmonds, C.	Cowley		
Jeanne Smith, Lab.	Townfield		

Political Composition: C. 33; Lab. 32; LD. 4.
Population: 231,602
Area: 11,240 hectares.

ABOUT HILLINGDON

The London Borough of Hillingdon covers the North west corner of the former County of Middlesex. In 1965 the Borough of Uxbridge and the Urban Districts of Hayes and Harlington, Yiewsley and West Drayton and Ruislip-Northwood were amalgamated to form the London Borough of Hillingdon.

COUNCIL TAX BANDS 2001-2002

Band	Market Value of the Property	Council Tax
A	Up to £40,000	£607.81
B	£40,001 to 52,000	£709.11
C	£52,001 to 68,000	£810.41
D	£68,001 to 88,000	£911.71
E	£88,001 to 120,000	£1114.32
F	£120,001 to 160,000	£1316.92
G	£160,001 to 320,000	£1519.52
H	£320,001 or more	£1823.42

HOUNSLOW

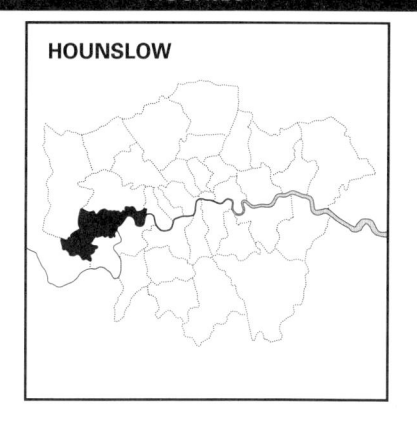

Civic Centre, Lampton Road, Hounslow, TW3 4DN (Tel: 020-8583 2000; Fax: 020-8583 2130; Web: www.hounslow.gov.uk).

66 Governed London

Registration of Births, Deaths and Marriages: The Register Office, 88 Lampton Road, Hounslow TW3 4DW (Tel: 020-8862 5112).

CHIEF OFFICERS

Chief Executive: Mark Gilks
Director of Social Services: Susanna White
Borough Solicitor: Mike Smith
Borough Treasurer: Alan Steele
Director of Cultural and Community Investment: Howard Simmons
Director of Education: Doug Trickett
Director of Environmental Services: John Evans
Director of Housing: Chris Langstaff
Head of Economic Development: Abdul Rashid Craig
Head of Information and Communication: David Hicks
Head of Members Services: Robert Wearing
Head of Public Services: Sandra Harniman
Head of Strategic Personnel: Willie Griffin
Head of Strategic Property: Graham Smith

MEMBERS OF THE COUNCIL

Councillor	Ward
Mayor: Mohinder Gill, Lab.	Heston Central
Deputy Mayor: Melvin Collins, Lab.	Gunnersbury
Govind Agarwal, Lab.	Hounslow South
Philip Andrews, O.	Isleworth South
Norah Atkins, C.	Chiswick Homefields
Ronald Bartholomew, Lab.	Isleworth North
Felicity Barwood, C.	Chiswick Riverside
Rajinder Bath, Lab.	Heston West
L. Bawn, Lab.	Feltham South
Premila Bhanderi, C.	Spring Grove
Kamikar Brar, Lab.	Feltham Central
Tristan Bunnell, Lab.	Gunnersbury
Ruth Cadbury, Lab.	Brentford Clifden
Peter Carey, C.	Spring Grove
Michael Carman, Lab.	Brentford Clifden
John Chatt, Lab.	Feltham North
Mohammed Chaudhary, Lab.	Heston West
Dalbir Cheema, Lab.	Hounslow West
Krishan Chopra, Lab.	Hounslow Heath
Roger Clarke, Lab.	Heston West
John Connelly, Lab.	Hounslow West
Samantha Davies, C.	Turnham Green
Sukhbir Dhaliwal, Lab.	Cranford
Ajmer Dhillon, Lab.	Hounslow Heath
Gopal Dhillon, Lab.	Heston Central
Jagir Dhillon, Lab.	Cranford
Colin Driscoll, Lab.	Feltham Central
Colin Ellar, Lab.	Feltham Central
Raymond Fincher, LD	Hanworth
Darshan Grewal, Lab.	Hounslow West
Herbert Ham, Lab.	Feltham South
Christine Hay, Lab.	Hounslow South
Walter Hill, C.	Hounslow South
Peter Hills, LD	Hanworth
David Hopkins, Lab.	Gunnersbury
John Howliston, Lab.	East Bedfont
David Hughes, Lab.	East Bedfont
Michael Hunt, Lab.	Feltham North
Sahm Jassar, Lab.	Hounslow Central
Harbans Kanwal, Lab.	Cranford
James Kenna, Lab.	Heston West
Ilyas Khwaja, Lab.	Hounslow Central
Robert Kinghorn, C.	Chiswick Riverside
Valerie Lamey, Lab.	Brentford Clifden
Adrian Lee C.	Turnham Green
Paul Lynch, C.	Chiswick Riverside
Amritpal Mann, Lab.	Heston East
Andrew Morgan-Watts, LD	Hanworth
John Murphy, LD	Feltham South
Patricia Nicholas, Lab.	Isleworth South
Barbara Reid, C.	Spring Grove
Devinder Sandhu, Lab.	East Bedfont
Jagdish Rai Sharma, Lab.	Hounslow Heath
Corinna Smart, Lab.	Isleworth North
Vanessa Smith, Lab.	Isleworth South
Patricia Sterne, Lab.	Chiswick Homefields
Peter Thompson, C.	Turnham Green
Janet Tindall, Lab.	Isleworth North
Stuart Walmsley, Lab.	Feltham North
Robert Whatley, Lab.	Hounslow Central

Political Compostiton: Lab. 44; C.11; LD. 4; O. 1.
Population: 213,675
Area: 5,852.

ABOUT HOUNSLOW

The borough stretches from Chiswick in the east to Heathrow Airport in the west. The borough has a lot to offer in terms of culture and history and boasts a variety of historic homes and gardens including Osterley Park, Syon House, Chiswick House, Hogarth's House, Boston Manor House and Gunnersbury Park. Other attractions include Waterman's Arts Centre, The Paul Robeson Theatre and the Kew Bridge Steam Museum. The borough benefits from a variety of cultures and communities with over a quarter of residents from ethnic minorities.

London Borough Councils

COUNCIL TAX BANDS 2001-2002

Band	Market Value of the Property	Council Tax
A	Up to £40,000	£636.58
B	£40,001 to 52,000	£742.68
C	£52,001 to 68,000	£848.77
D	£68,001 to 88,000	£954.87
E	£88,001 to 120,000	£1167.06
F	£120,001 to 160,000	£1379.26
G	£160,001 to 320,000	£1591.45
H	£320,001 or more	£1909.74

ISLINGTON

Town Hall, Upper Street, London N1 2UD (Tel: 020-7226 1234; Web: www.islington.gov.uk).
Education Department: Laycock Street, London N1 1TH (Tel: 020-7457 5753; Fax: 020-7457 5903).
Environment, Leisure, IT, Human Resources, Planning, Finance and Property: Municipal Offices, 222 Upper Street, London, N1 1YR (Tel: 020-7477 4525; Fax: 020-7447 4642).
Housing and Social Services: Highbury House, 5 Highbury Crescent, London N5 1RN (Tel: 020-7477 4293/4294; Fax: 020-7477 4118).
Islington Building Services: Ashburton House, Ashburton Grove, London N7 7DN (Tel: 020-7457 4648; Fax: 020-7457 4948).
Central Library: 2 Fieldway Crescent, London, N5 1PF (Tel: 020-7226 1234).
Play and Youth: Block B Barnsbury Complex, Offord Road, London N1 1TH (Tel: 020-7457 5822; Fax: 020-7457 5547).

CHIEF OFFICERS

Chief Executive: Leisha Fullick
Deputy Chief Execuitve: Nick Sharman
Director of Housing: Andy Jennings
Director of Social Services: Paul Curran
Director of Environment and Conservation: Kevin O'Leary
Director of Finance and Property Services: Mary Hawkins
Director of Law and Public Services: Louise Round
Director of Human Resources Development: Claudette Francis

MEMBERS OF THE COUNCIL

Councillor	Ward
Mayor: J. Trotter, LD	Bunhill
Deputy Mayor: Margot Dunn, LD	Holloway
Leader of the Council: S. Hitchens, LD	St. Peter
G. Allan, LD	Clerkenwell
Jennette Arnold, Lab.	Mildmay
D. Barnes, LD	Quadrant
Rosey Blackmore, Lab.	St. George's
D. Bonner, Lab.	Sussex
M. Boye-Annwomah, Lab.	Mildmay
Janet Burgess, Lab.	Junction
Wally Burgess, Lab.	St. George's
Sheila Camp, Lab.	Hillrise
A. Clinton, Lab.	Hillrise
Joan Coupland, LD	St. Mary
Isobel Cox, LD	St. Mary
Mary Creagh, Lab.	Highbury
Jonathan Dearth, LD	Canonbury East
E. Featherstone, LD	Hillmarton
Bridget Fox, LD	Barnsbury
Paul Fox, LD	Hillrise
R. Greening, Lab.	Gillespie
Edna Griffiths, Lab.	Thornhill
Pat Haynes, Lab.	Mildmay
R. Heseltine, LD	St. Mary
Meg Hillier, Lab.	Sussex
Isabelle Humphreys, LD	Clerkenwell
Talal Karim, Lab.	Junction
J. Kempton, LD	Holloway
Maureen Leigh, Lab.	Highbury
A. Loraine, LD	Barnsbury
Sandy Marks, Lab.	Junction
N. Mason, Lab.	Gillespie
Ruari McCourt, Lab.	Highview
R. McKenzie, Lab.	Tollington
Shonagh Methven, Lab.	St. George's
B. Neave, LD	Clerkenwell
R. Perry, Lab.	Thornhill
Carol Powell, LD	Barnsbury
Mary Powell, LD	St. Peter
Chris Pryce, LD	St. Peter
Jenny Rathbone, Lab.	Highbury
Angela Ribezzo, LD	Canonbury West
Jenny Sands, Lab.	Highview

68 Governed London

D. Sawyer, Lab.
Doreen Scott, LD
Barbara Sidnell, Lab.
Barbara Smith, LD
D. Taylor, LD
Jyoti Vaja, LD
R. Washington, LD
Laura Willoughby, LD
Rose Wooding, LD.

Tollington
Hillmarton
Tollington
Canonbury West
Holloway
Bunhill
Canonbury East
Quadrant
Bunhill

Political Composition: LD. 27, Lab. 25.
Population: 176,393
Area: 1,487 hectares.

ABOUT ISLINGTON

Situated just north of the City, the borough of Islington has strong historical connections with entertainment and craftsmanship. Sadlers Wells is situated in the borough and the area of Clerkenwell is renowned for crafts such as jewellery and clock-making. There are a number of educational institutions in the borough including the City University and the University of North London and the borough is rich in cultural and leisure facilities. Islington is home to Arsenal Football Club and St John's Gate at Clerkenwell is one of the oldest surviving buildings in the borough which houses a collection of paintings, silverware and furniture highlighting periods in the history of St John of Jerusalem.

COUNCIL TAX BANDS 2001-2002

Band	Market Value of the Property	Council Tax
A	Up to £40,000	£584.67
B	£40,001 to 52,000	£682.11
C	£52,001 to 68,000	£779.56
D	£68,001 to 88,000	£877
E	£88,001 to 120,000	£1071.89
F	£120,001 to 160,000	£1266.78
G	£160,001 to 320,000	£1461.67
H	£320,001 or more	£1754

ROYAL BOROUGH OF KENSINGTON AND CHELSEA

KENSINGTON & CHELSEA

Town Hall, Hornton Street, London W8 7NX (Tel: 020-7937 5464; Fax: 020-7938 1445; Web: www.rbkc.gov.uk).

Central Library: Hornton Street, London, W8 5HX (Tel: 020-7937 2542; Fax: 020-7361 2976). Environmental Services, Council Offices, 37 Pembroke Road, London, W8 6PW.
Registration of Births, Deaths and Marriages: The Register Office, Chelsea Old Town Hall, Kings Road, London SW3 5EE (Tel: 020-7361 4100).

CHIEF OFFICERS

Chief Executive and Town Clerk: D. Myers
Executive Director of Education and Libraries: Roger Wood
Executive Director of Environmental Services: M. Stroud
Executive Director of Housing and Social Services: M. Gibb
Executive Director of Planning and Conservation: M. J. French

MEMBERS OF THE COUNCIL

Councillor	Ward
Mayor: L. A. Holt, C.	Courtfield
Deputy Mayor: The Hon. Joanna Gardner, C.	Church
Leader of the Council: M. Cockell, C.	North Stanley
T. Ahern, C.	Campden
J. Atkinson, Lab.	St. Charles
J. Blakeman, Lab.	Colville
S. Blanchflower, Lab.	Avondale
T. Boulton, Lab.	South Stanley
C. Buckmaster, C.	Campden

T. Buxton, C.
Barbara Campbell, C.
D. Campion, C.
Elizabeth Christmas, MBE C.
Prof. Sir Anthony Coates, C.
T. Coleridge, C.
J. Corbet-Singleton, C.
J. Cox, C.
K. Cunningham, Lab.
A. Dalton, C.
I. Donaldson, C.
J. Edge, C.
T. Fairhead, C.
M. Field, C.
A. Fitsgerald, C.
Mrs. Ian Frazer, C.
R. Freeman, C.
The Lady Harsham, CBE, C.
Pat Healy, Lab.
Bridget Hoier, Lab.
S. Hoier, Lab.
Rima Horton, Lab.
D. Hudson C.
M. Lasharie, Lab.
B. Levitt, C.
W. Lightfoot, C.
P. Mason, Lab.
G. Mond, C.
D. Moylan, C.
Dr. J. Munday, C.
N. Paget-Brown, C.
B. Phelps, C.
B. Pope, Lab.
Shireen Ritchie, C.
J. Seidler, C.
S. Shapro, Lab.
S. Stanley, Lab.
Frances Taylor, C.
E. P. Tomlin, C.
R. Walker-Arnott, C.
P. Warrick, C.
Mary Weale, C.
Doreen M. Weatherhead, C.
A. Whitfield, C.
A. Wood, Lab.

Earl's Court
Pembridge
Pembridge
Abingdon
Courtfield
Hans Town
Cheyne
Courtfield
Kelfield
Queen's Gate
Royal Hospital
Royal Hospital
Earl's Court
Abingdon
Church
North Stanley
Campden
Holland
Colville
Golborne
Kelfield
St. Charles
Brompton
Avondale
Holland
Holland
Golborne
Queen's Gate
Queen's Gate
Abingdon
Hans Town
Earl's Court
Colville
Brompton
Redcliffe
Golborne
Avondale
Redcliffe
Norland
Norland
Cheyne
Hans Town
Pembridge
Redcliffe
South Stanley

Political Composition: C. 39; Lab. 15
Population: 179,200
Area: 1,238 hectares.

ABOUT KENSINGTON AND CHELSEA

In 1965 the boroughs of Kensington and Chelsea were united to form the single London Borough of Kensington and Chelsea. It covers five square miles, 70 percent of which is located in conservation areas. It is home to 34 embassies and numerous London Landmarks. The title 'Royal Borough' was granted in 1901 by King Edward VII, in recognition of his mother's (Queen Victoria) wish to recognise her birthplace.

COUNCIL TAX BANDS 2001-2002

Band	Market Value of the Property	Council Tax
A	Up to £40,000	£459.24
B	£40,001 to 52,000	£535.78
C	£52,001 to 68,000	£612.32
D	£68,001 to 88,000	£688.86
E	£88,001 to 120,000	£841.94
F	£120,001 to 160,000	£995.02
G	£160,001 to 320,000	£1148.10
H	£320,001 or more	£1377.72

ROYAL BOROUGH OF KINGSTON UPON THAMES

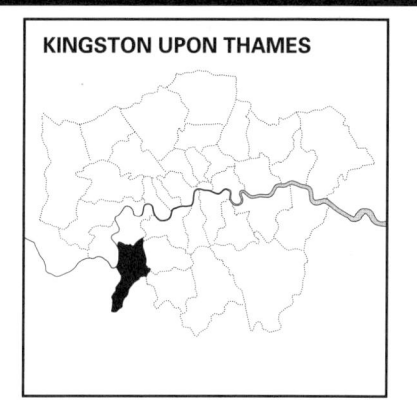

KINGSTON UPON THAMES

Guildhall, Kingston upon Thames, KT1 1EU (Tel:020-8546 2121; Fax: 020-8547 5012; Web: www.kingston.gov.uk).
Tourist Information Centre: The Market House, Market Place, Kingston upon Thames, KT1 1JS (Tel: 020-8547 5592; Fax: 020-8547 5594).
Registration of Births, Deaths and Marriages: 35 Coombe Road, Kingston upon Thames KT2 7BA (Tel: 020-8546 0920).

CHIEF OFFICERS

Chief Executive: Bruce McDonald
Assistant Director (Leisure and Lifelong Learning): Scott Herbertson
Borough Environmental Health Officer: Bob Smart
Chief Trading Standards Officer: Ted Forsyth
Director of Community Services: Roy Taylor, CBE

70 Governed London

Director of Education and Leisure:
John Braithwaite
Director of Environmental Services:
Alan McMillen
Director of Finance: Tony Knights
Head of Democratic Services and Partnerships:
Andrew Bessant
Head of Environmental Care: Tim Darwen
Head of Children and Family Services:
Margie Rooke
Head of Corporate Planning: Chris Field
Head of Housing: Michael England
Head of Legal Services: Sue Jackson
Head of Personnel: Sheila West
Head of Planning and Development: John Allen

MEMBERS OF THE COUNCIL

Councillor	Ward
Mayor: J. Thorn, Lab.	Tolworth West
Deputy Mayor: S. Mama, Lab.	Norbiton
Leader of the Council: K. Davis, C.	Berrylands
M. Amson, C.	St. James's
Patricia Bamford, LD	Chessington South
B. Bennett, LD	Chessington North
D. Booth, C.	Tolworth East
Janet Bowen-Hitchings, C.	Surbiton Hill
P. Brill, LD	Cambridge
T. Brown, Ind.C.	Berrylands
D. Chester, LD	Grove
P. Codd, C.	Coombe
P. Crerar, C.	Coombe
D. Cunningham, C.	Tudor
Leslie Dale, C.	Berrylands
Marian Darke, Lab.	Tolworth West
Rolson Davies, LD	Malden Manor
D. De Lord, C.	St. Mark's
D. Doe, C.	Tudor
D. Edwards, C.	Hill
J. Ellin, Lab.	Canbury
W. Evans, LD	Norbiton Park
R. Faulkner, Lab.	Tolworth South
D. Fraser, C.	St. James's
Julie Haines, LD	Cambridge
A. Hall, Lab.	Tolworth South
Vicki Harris, LD	Chessington North
R. Hayes, LD	Grove
J. Heamon, LD	Cambridge
Chrissie Hitchcock, LD	Grove
E. Humphrey, C.	Hill
Jan Jenner, C.	St. Mark's
P. Johnston, C.	Surbiton Hill
D. Jordan, LD	Norbiton Park
Wendy Malseed, Lab.	Canbury
R. Matthews, C.	St. Mark's

Ian McDonald, LD	Malden Manor
A. McLeay, LD	Burlington
Shiraz Mirza, LD	Chessington South
E. Naylor, Lab.	Norbiton
D. Osbourbe, LD	Burlington
R. Pandya, C.	St. James's
C. Priest, Lab.	Canbury
J. Reay, Lab.	Norbiton
I. Reid, LD	Hook
Mary Reid, LD	Hook
Sally Scrivens, LD	Chessington South
Jane Smith, C.	Surbiton Hill
Gwen Symonds, C.	Tudor
K. Witham, C.	Tolworth East

Political Composition: C. 20; LD. 19; Lab. 10; Ind.C. 1
Population: 144,313
Area: 3,756

ABOUT KINGSTON UPON THAMES

The Royal Borough of Kingston upon Thames is located in South west London on the banks of the river Thames. It is approximately thirty minutes by train to central London and is situated between the two major London airports of Heathrow and Gatwick. The borough consists of the town centre of Kingston and the district centres of New Malden, Surbiton, Tolworth, Chessington and Hook.

COUNCIL TAX BANDS 2001-2002

Band	Market Value of the Property	Council Tax
A	Up to £40,000	£631.07
B	£40,001 to 52,000	£736.24
C	£52,001 to 68,000	£841.43
D	£68,001 to 88,000	£946.60
E	£88,001 to 120,000	£1156.96
F	£120,001 to 160,000	£1367.31
G	£160,001 to 320,000	£1577.67
H	£320,001 or more	£1893.20

London Borough Councils

LAMBETH

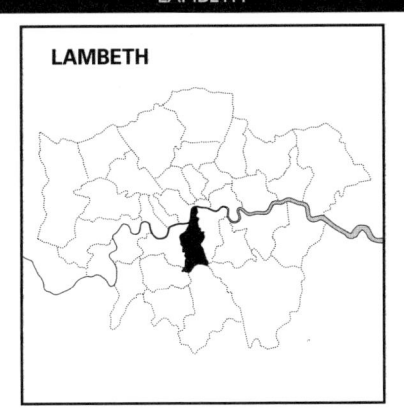

Lambeth Town Hall, Brixton Hill, London SW2 1RW (Tel: 020-7926 1000; Fax: 020-7926 2255; Web: www.lambeth.gov.uk).
Executive Director of Education Services: International House, Canterbury Crescent, Brixton, London SW9 7QE (Tel: 020-7926 1000).
Executive Director of Environmental Services: Blue Star House, London SW2 5SD (Tel: 020-7926 1000).
Executive Director of Finance and Corporate Services: International House, Canterbury Crescent, Brixton, London, SW9 7QE (Tel: 020-7926 1000).
Executive Director of Housing: Hambrook House, Porden Road, London SW2 1RP (Tel: 020-7926 1000).
Executive Director of Social Services and Health Improvement: Mary Seacole House, 91 Clapham High Street, London SW4 7TF (Tel: 020-7926 1000).
Registration of Births, Deaths and Marriages: The Register Office, 361 Brixton Road, London SW9 7DA (Tel: 020-7926 9240).

CHIEF OFFICERS

Chief Executive: Faith Boardman
Acting Executive Director of Education: Michael Peters
Borough Solicitor: Gerard Curran
Executive Director of Housing Services: John Broomfield
Executive Director of Social Services: Lisa Christensen

MEMBERS OF THE COUNCIL

Councillor	Ward
Mayor: Claudette Hewitt, Lab.	Clapham Town
Deputy Mayor: June Fewtrell, LD	Streatham Hill
R. A'Court, C.	Gipsy Hill
M. Abu-Bakr, Lab.	Ferndale
D. Anyanwu, Lab.	Angell
R. Bawden, Lab.	Larkhall
C. Bennet, LD	St. Leonard's
L. Boodram, Lab.	Bishop's Ward
S. Bourne, Lab.	Bishop's Ward
A. Bottrall, LD	Stockwell
Judith Brodie, Lab.	St. Martin's
C. Cattermole, Lab.	Town Hall
Sheila Clarke, LD	Streatham Wells
G. Compton, C.	Gipsy Hill
P. Connolly, Lab.	Knights Hill
K. Craig, Lab.	Larkhall
M. Crichton-Stuart, LD	Oval
C. Crooks, Lab.	Knights Hill
Geraldine Curtis, Lab.	Town Hall
H. David, Lab.	Stockwell
J. Dickson, Lab.	Herne Hill
R. Doven, Lab.	Clapham Park
M. English, Lab.	Clapham Town
J. Feenan, LD	Oval
K. Fitchett, LD	Princes
T. Franklin, Lab.	St. Martin's
R. Giess, LD	St. Leonard's
T. Goddard, Lab.	Tulse Hill
Esther Green, Lab.	Larkhall
Janet Grigg, C.	Gipsy Hill
Daphne Hayes-Moyon, LD	Streatham Wells
J. Heather, LD	Streatham Wells
C. Henley, Lab.	Clapham Town
A. Hogan, Lab.	Angell
R. Jarman, Lab.	Ferndale
J. Kazantis, Lab.	Streatham South
S. Lawman, LD	Princes
Ruth Ling, Lab.	Clapham Park
A. Lumsden, LD	Streatham Hill
D. Malley, Lab.	Streatham South
R. McConnell, LD	Knights Hill
M. McEwan, Lab.	Clapham Park
P. McGlone, Lab.	Ferndale
Kirsty McHugh, Lab.	Herne Hill
A. McKenna, Lab.	Vassall
Jackie Meldrum, Lab.	Tulse Hill
Abigale Melville, Lab.	Stockwell
Julie Minns, Lab.	Thornton
R. O'Brien, LD	Streatham Hill
P. O'Connell, Lab.	Herne Hill
B. Palmer, LD	St. Leonard's
S. Reed, Lab.	Town Hall
D. Sabbagh, Lab.	Vassall

72 Governed London

T. Sargeant, Lab. — Streatham South
A. Sawdon, LD — Oval
Johanna Sherrington, Lab. — Tulse Hill
T. Smith, Lab. — St. Martin's
S. Stevens, Lab. — Angell
P. Truesdale, LD — Bishops Ward
M. Tuffrey, LD — Princes
Kitty Ussher, Lab. — Vassall
Clare Whelan, C. — Thurlow Park
J. Whelan, C. — Thurlow Park

Political Composition: Lab. 40; LD. 18; C. 5; V. 1
Population: 272,500
Area: 2,727 hectares.

ABOUT LAMBETH

Lambeth measures some seven miles north to south and about two and a half miles east to west. There are many important sites and cultural attractions within the borough's boundaries. Lambeth includes the South Bank complex as the most visible element of an expanding arts and leisure industry within the borough. Examples include the Old Vic, the Young Vic, the National Theatre, the Royal Festival Hall and the National Film Theatre. The borough is also home to the London Eye, the Oval Cricket Ground and the Florence Nightingale Museum. Waterloo, Westminster, Lambeth and Wandsworth bridges are all partly located within Lambeth's boundaries, as is Lambeth Palace, the official London residence of the Archbishop of Canterbury. Socially and culturally Lambeth is one of the most diverse communities in Great Britain. 34 per cent of Lambeth's population are from ethnic minorities – the seventh highest figure for a London borough.

COUNCIL TAX BANDS 2001-2002

Band	Market Value of the Property	Council Tax
A	Up to £40,000	£494.00
B	£40,001 to 52,000	£576.33
C	£52,001 to 68,000	£658.67
D	£68,001 to 88,000	£741.00
E	£88,001 to 120,000	£905.67
F	£120,001 to 160,000	£1070.33
G	£160,001 to 320,000	£1238.00
H	£320,001 or more	£1482.00

LEWISHAM

Lewisham Town Hall, London SE6 4RU (Tel: 020-8314 6000; Web: www.lewisham.gov.uk).
Borough Information Centre: 199-201 Lewisham High Street, London SE13.
Education and Culture: 3rd Floor, Lawrence House, 1 Catford Road, London SE6 4RU.
Regeneration: 5th Floor, Lawrence House, 1 Catford Road, London SE6 4RU.
Registration of Births, Deaths and Marriages: 368 Lewisham High Street, London SE13 6LQ (Tel: 020-8690 2128).
Resources: 3rd Floor, Town Hall, London SE6 4RU.
Social Care and Health: 1st Floor, Lawrence House, 1 Catford Road, London SE6 4RU.

CHIEF OFFICERS

Chief Executive: B. Quirk
Director for Regeneration: Patrick Hayes
Director of Education and Culture: Frankie Sulke
Director of Resources: R. Whiteman
Director of Social Care and Health: Zena Peatfield

MEMBERS OF THE COUNCIL

Councillor	Ward
Mayor: Dave Sullivan, Lab.	Horniman
Deputy Mayor: Gavin Moore, Lab.	Blackheath
Jackie Addison, Lab.	Forest Hill
Obajimi Adefiranye, Lab.	Drake
Abdeslam Amrani, Lab.	St. Andrew
Barrie Anderson, C.	St. Mildred
Chris Best, Lab.	Sydenham East
Dave Bodimeade, Lab.	Churchdown
David Britton, C.	St. Mildred

# London Borough Councils 73

Andrew Brown, Lab.	Blackheath	
Joseph Burns, Lab.	Catford	
Liam Carlisle, Lab.	St. Mildred	
Alicia Chater, Lab.	Churchdown	
Fiona Crichlow, Lab.	Crofton Park	
Liam Curran, Lab.	Sydenham East	
Andrew Davies, Lab.	Hither Green	
Sam Dias, Soc.	Pepys	
Kate Donnelly, Lab.	St. Margaret	
Les Eytle, Lab.	Blythe Hill	
Paul Fallon, Lab.	Hither Green	
Peggy Fitzsimmons, Lab.	Rushey Green	
Gurbakhsh Garcha, Lab.	Crofton Park	
Donovan Green, Ind.	Grove Park	
Carl Handley, Lab.	St. Andrew	
Roger Harris, Lab.	Sydenham West	
Colin Hastie, Lab.	Perry Hill	
Jane Hastie, Lab.	St. Margaret	
Mike Holder, Lab.	Perry Hill	
Matthew Huntbach, LD	Downham	
Miriam Iloghalu, Lab.	Ladywell	
Carl Kisicki, LD	Whitefoot	
Helen Klier, Lab.	Rushey Green	
Vanessa Large, Lab.	Grinling Gibbons	
Mee Ling, Lab.	Evelyn	
Madeliene Long, Lab.	Manor Lee	
Jim Mallory, Lab.	Grinling Gibbons	
Paul Maslin, Lab.	Marlowe	
Alyson McGarrigle, Lab.	Churchdown	
Phil Mills, Lab.	Sydenham West	
Man Mohan, Lab.	Grinling Gibbons	
Paul Morris, Lab.	Grove Park	
Pauline Morrison, Lab.	Ladywell	
Paul Newing, Lab.	Ladywell	
Mark Nottingham, Lab.	Evelyn	
Crada Onuegbu, Lab.	Evelyn	
John O'Shea, Lab.	Bellingham	
Stephen Padmore, Lab.	Marlowe	
Ian Page, Soc.	Pepys	
Jarman Parmar, Lab.	Drake	
John Paschoud, Lab.	Forest Hill	
Alan Pegg, Lab.	Sydenham East	
Catherine Priddey, LD	Downham	
Sylvia Scott, Lab.	Blythe Hill	
Terry Scott, Lab.	Drake	
Alan Smith, Lab.	Whitefoot	
Eva Stamirowski, Lab.	Sydenham West	
Ron Stockbridge, Lab.	Bellingham	
Martin Taylor, Lab.	Catford	
Nicholas Taylor, Lab.	Pepys	
Kristine Taylor-Carroll, Lab.	Horniman	
Alan Till, Lab.	Perry Hill	
Ian Walton, LD	Downham	
Ruth Watt, Lab.	Crofton Park	
David Whiting, Lab.	Horniman	
David Wilson, Lab.	Hither Green	
Susan Wise, Lab.	Horniman	

Political Composition: Lab. 58; LD. 4; C. 2; Soc. 2; Ind. 1
Parliamentary Constituencies: Lewisham-Deptford, Lewisham East, Lewisham West.
Population: 241,500
Area: 3,473 hectares.

ABOUT LEWISHAM

Lewisham is situated in the south east of London and enjoys influences from the inner city and the borders of Kent. The area is culturally diverse and a considerable percentage of the population are from ethnic minorities. This is demonstrated by festivals such as People's Day, Black History Month and the Irish Festival which are held annually. Lewisham also hosts the South East London Beer Festival. The area is well served by public transport with numerous rail and bus links and a recently opened Docklands Light Railway line.

COUNCIL TAX BANDS 2001-2002

Band	Market Value of the Property	Council Tax
A	Up to £40,000	£584.51
B	£40,001 to 52,000	£681.93
C	£52,001 to 68,000	£779.35
D	£68,001 to 88,000	£876.77
E	£88,001 to 120,000	£1071.61
F	£120,001 to 160,000	£1266.45
G	£160,001 to 320,000	£1461.28
H	£320,001 or more	£1753.54

74 Governed London

MERTON

Merton Civic Centre, London Road, Morden SM4 5DX (Tel: 020-8543 2222).
Registration of Births, Deaths and Marriages: Morden Cottage, Morden Hall Road, Morden, Surrey SM4 5JA (Tel: 020-8540 5011).

CHIEF OFFICERS

Chief Executive: Roger Paine
Acting Head of Human Resources: Paul Holmes
Head of Legal Services: Julie Belvir
Head of Strategic Policy and Quality: Diane Bailey
Assistant Director (Child Policy and School Effectiveness): Ms. Lorriane O'Reilly
Assistant Director (Community services): Robert Hobbs
Assistant Director (Planning and Resources): Vacant
Director of Education, Leisure and Libraries: Vacant
Director of Environmental Services: Richard Rawes
Director of Financial Services: Mike Parsons
Director of Housing and Social Services: Rea Mattocks
Head of Audit: Chris Johnson
Head of Communications and Member Services: Gene Saunders
Head of Information Technology: Gurnel Bansal
Head of Revenue and Benefits: Mike Teesdale

MEMBERS OF THE COUNCIL

Councillor	Ward
Mayor: S. Pickover, Lab.	Dundonald
Deputy Mayor: Vivien Guy, Lab.	Trinity

Leader of the Council:

A. Judge, Lab	Figges Marsh
J. B. Abrams, Lab.	Graveney
K. Abrams, Lab.	Trinity
S. Assinen, Lab.	Abbey
Barbara Bampton, Lab.	Dundonald
P. Barasi, Lab.	Trinity
N. Beddoe, C.	Raynes Park
R. Bell, C.	Raynes Park
M. Breirly, C.	Raynes Park
D. Cairns, Lab.	Longthornton
K. Carter, Lab.	Abbey
A. Samad Chaudray, Lab.	Longthornton
D. Child, Ind.	Merton Park
J. H. Cole, Lab.	Pollards Hill
D. Connellan, Lab.	Figges Marsh
I. Dysart, LD	West Barnes
Samantha George, C.	Village
Chris Grayling, C.	Hillside
Maurice Groves, C.	Lower Morden
P. Harper, Lab.	Phipps Bridge
N. Harris, LD	West Barnes
R. Harwood, C.	Hillside
P. Holt, Lab.	Colliers Wood
C. Housden, C.	Village
A. Jones, C.	Village
J. Jones, C.	Lower Morden
P. M. Jones, Lab.	Ravensbury
M. Karim Lab.	Abbey
Linda Kirby Lab.	Graveney
S. Knight, Lab.	Colliers Wood
Gillian Lewis-Lavendar, C.	West Barnes
Karen Livingstone, Lab.	Longthornton
C. Lucas, Lab.	Connon Hill
Edith Macauley, Lab.	Lavender
R. Makin, Lab.	Pollards Hill
M. Mannion, Lab.	Connon Hill
Maxi Martin, Lab.	St. Helier
P. McCabe, Lab.	Ravensbury
P. Mors, C.	Lower Morden
I. Munn, Lab.	Phipps Bridge
J. Nelson-Jones, Ind.	Merton Park
Joyce Paton, Lab.	Durnsford
D. Pearce, Lab.	St. Helier
G. Reynolds, Lab.	Colliers Wood
Judy Saunders, Lab.	Phipps Bridge
M. Searle, Lab.	Lavender
Bridget Smith, Ind.	Merton Park
P. Smith, Other	Ravensbury
M. Spacey, Lab.	St. Helier
Geraldine Stanford, Lab.	Figges Marsh
M. Syed, Lab.	Pollards Hill
M. Thompson, Lab.	Durnsford
B. White, Lab.	Cannon Hill
D. T. Williams, C.	Hillside

Political Composition: Lab. 38; C. 13; LD. 2; Ind. 3; Other 1.
Population: 184,315
Area: 3,796.

ABOUT MERTON

The Borough of Merton is located in the South West of London and comprises of the five main towns of Wimbledon, Morden, Mitcham, Raynes Park and Colliers Wood. Merton has a number of large open spaces including Mitcham and Wimbledon Commons with the river Wandle flowing through the Borough. Merton is approximately 13 minutes form Central London and has numerous rail, tube and bus facilities.

COUNCIL TAX BANDS 2001-2002

Band	Market Value of the Property	Council Tax
A	Up to £40,000	£634.66 (647.16)
B	£40,001 to 52,000	£740.44 (755.01)
C	£52,001 to 68,000	£846.22 (862.88)
D	£68,001 to 88,000	£951.99 (970.73)
E	£88,001 to 120,000	£1163.54 (1186.45)
F	£120,001 to 160,000	£1375.10 (1402.17)
G	£160,001 to 320,000	£1586.65 (1617.89)
H	£320,001 or more	£1903.98 (1941.46)

Figures in brackets are for properties within ¾ of a mile of Wimbledon Common. This payment is passed on to the Wimbledon and Putney Common Conservators (WPCC) for the upkeep of the common.

London Borough Councils 75

NEWHAM

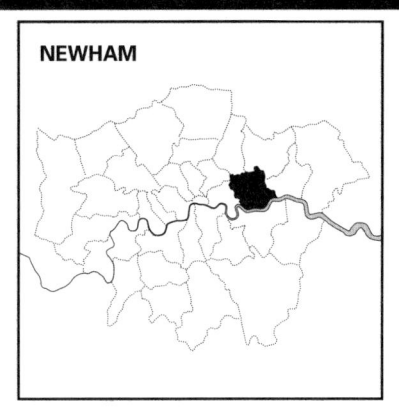

Town Hall, East Ham, London E6 2RP (Tel: 020-8430 2000; Fax: 020-8557 8662 Web: www.newham.gov.uk).
Environment Department: 25 Nelson Street, East Ham, London E6 4EH (Tel: 020-8430 2000; Fax: 020-8472 2284).
Education/Social Services: Broadway House, 322 High Street, London E15 1AJ (Tel: 020-8430 2000).
Housing Department: Bridge House, 320 High Street, London E15 1EW (Tel: 020-8430 2000; Fax: 020-8519 2826).
Environmental Health: Alice Billings House, 2-12 West Ham Lane, London, E15 4SF (Tel: 020-8430 2000; Fax: 020-8557 8869).
Consumer Services: 465 High Street North, Manor Park, London, E12 6TH (Tel: 020-8430 2000; Fax 020-8557 8969).
Leisure Services: 292 Barking Road, East Ham, London, E6 3BA (Tel: 020-8430 2000).
Registration of Births, Deaths and Marriages: Newham Register Office, Passmore Edwards Building, 207 Plashet Grove, East Ham E6 1BT (Tel: 020-8430 2000).

CHIEF OFFICERS

Chief Executive: Dave Burbage
Deputy Chief Executive and Director of Education: Ian Harrison
Director of Environment: Malcolm Smith
Director of Social Services: Ms. Deborah Cameron
Director of Housing: Chris Wood

76 Governed London

MEMBERS OF THE COUNCIL

Councillor	Ward
Mayor: Sukhdev Singh Marway, Lab.	Kensington
Deputy Mayor: J. Riley, Lab.	Stratford
Leader of the Council: Sir R. Wales, Lab.	Canning Town and Grange
M. Ahmad, Lab.	Castle
S. Ahmad, Lab.	Forest Gate
Riaz Ahmed-Mirza, Lab.	Plaistow
N. Ali, Lab.	Upton
S. Ali, Lab.	Kensington
A. Baikie, Lab.	Little Ilford
P. Brickell, Lab.	Forest Gate
L. Brown, Lab.	Custom House and Silver Town
W. Brown, Lab.	Monega
G. Cambage, Lab.	West Ham
A. Chaudhary, Lab.	Park
B. Collier, Lab.	Hudsons
Marie Sylvia Collier, Lab.	Ordnance
I. Corbett, Lab.	Greatfield
R. Crawford, Lab.	Little Ilford
Unmesh Desai, Lab.	St. Stephen's
J. Ejiofor, Lab.	Little Ilford
V. Fone, Lab.	Greatfield
C. Furness, Lab.	Canning Town and Grange
Judith Garfield, Lab	Stratford
D. Gilles, Lab.	Manor Park
A. Griffiths, Lab.	Park
Megan Harris, Lab.	Ordnance
Patricia Holland, Lab.	Custom House and Silver Town
L. Hudson, Lab.	Monega
K. Jenkins, Lab.	Greatfield
A. Kellaway, Lab.	South
Q. Khan, Lab.	Manor Park
Joy Laguda, Lab.	Plaistow
G. Lane, Lab.	Hudsons
June Leitch, Lab.	Central
K. Mangat, Lab.	Wall End
R. Manley, Lab.	West Ham
A. McAlmont, Lab.	New Town
C. McAuley, Lab.	Forest Gate
D. McGladdery, Lab.	Castle
Rupindra Nandra, Lab.	Plashet
D. Pinder, Lab	Custom House and Silver Town
Q. Peppiatt, Lab.	South
S. Ruiz, Lab.	Beckton
Paul Sathianesan, Lab.	Wall End
J. Saunders, Lab.	Park
C. Seddon, Lab.	South
A. Shakoor, Lab.	St. Stephen's
A. Sheikh, Lab.	Upton
A. Singh, Lab.	Manor Park
Mary Skyers, Lab.	Central
E. Sparrowhawk, Lab.	Wall End
A. Taylor, Lab.	Beckton
J. Thorne, Lab.	Plashet
V. Turner, Lab.	Bemersyde
W. Vaughan, Lab.	New Town
G. Vincent, Lab.	Bemersyde
Harvinder Singh Virdee, Lab.	Upton
F. Warwick, Ind.	Plaistow
R. Williams, Lab.	Plashet
N. Wilson, Lab.	Hudsons

Political Composition: Lab. 59; Ind. 1.
Population: 226,000
Area: 3,875.

ABOUT NEWHAM

Newham is part of the East End of London, sitting just north of the river Thames. It has a growing population of over 226,000, over half of which comes from more than 30 ethnic minority groups. Transport links in Newham include road links to the city airport and the Jubilee line extension has stations in Canning Town, West Ham and Stratford. An International Channel Tunnel Rail link is scheduled to open in Stratford in 2003.

Newham borough was formed in 1965 from the old county boroughs of East and West Ham. It experienced a serious economic decline with the closure of the Royal Docks. Considerable Public and Private investment has taken place with the council placing a firm focus on its urban regeneration strategy to encourage business growth, new investment, higher employment levels and a general increase in the standard of living for residents of Newham.

COUNCIL TAX BANDS 2001-2002

Band	Market Value of the Property	Council Tax
A	Up to £40,000	£551.77
B	£40,001 to 52,000	£643.74
C	£52,001 to 68,000	£735.70
D	£68,001 to 88,000	£827.66
E	£88,001 to 120,000	£1011.58
F	£120,001 to 160,000	£1195.51
G	£160,001 to 320,000	£1379.43
H	£320,001 or more	£1655.32

London Borough Councils

REDBRIDGE

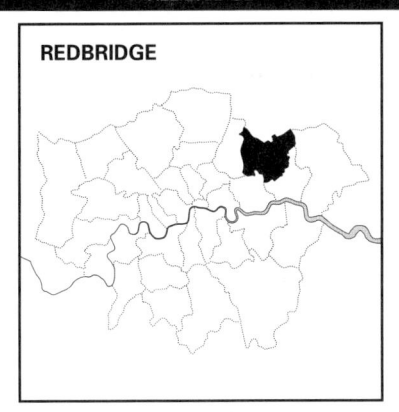

Town Hall, High Road, Ilford IG1 1DD (Tel: 020-8478 3020; Fax: 020-8478 9525).
First Stop Shop: Lynton House, 255-259 High Road, Ilford IG1 1NN (Tel: 020-8708 3440).
Social Services: Ley Street House, 497/499 Ley Street, Ilford IG2 7QX (Tel: 020-8503 8198).
Housing Advice Centre: 17/23 Clements Road, Ilford, IG1 1AG (Tel: 020-8708 4002).
Community Care Advice Centre: Aldborough Road North, Newbury Park, Ilford IG2 7SR (Tel: 020-8503 8833).
Public Protection: 8 Perth Terrace, Perth Road, Ilford IG2 6AT.
Payments and Benefits: Olympic House, 28-42 Clements Road, Ilford, IG1 1BD.
Registration of Births, Deaths and Marriages: Queen Victoria House, 794 Cranbrook Road, Barkingside, Ilford IG1 1JS (Tel: 020-8708 7171).

CHIEF OFFICERS

Chief Executive: Roger Hampson
Chief Leisure Officer: Anita Cacchioli
Chief Administration Officer: Steve Wastell
Chief Children and Families Officer: Patrick Power
Chief Communications Officer: Ms. Maxine Bradley
Chief Community Care Officer: John Powell
Chief Customer Services Officer: David Muggleton
Chief Finance Officer: Geoff Pearce
Chief Legal Officer: Heidi Chottin
Chief Planning Officer: Paul Clark
Corporate Director: Daniel Zammit
Corporate Director: Ms. Lesley Seary
Director of Education: Edwina Grant
Director of Social Services: John Drew

MEMBERS OF THE COUNCIL

Councillor	Ward
Mayor: A. Weinberg, C.	Clayhall
Deputy Mayor: S. Nolan, C.	Snaresbrook
Leader of the Council:	
M. Javed, Lab.	Loxford
K. Axon, C.	Barkingside
F. Banks, LD	Roding
R. I. Barden, C.	Clayhall
I. G. Bond, LD	Roding
G. F. Borrott, C.	Barkingside
A. Boyland, LD	Roding
J. Brindley, Lab.	Valentines
R. Brunnen, C.	Barkingside
A. Burgess, C.	Wanstead
H. Cleaver, LD	Church End
Vanessa Cole, C.	Aldborough
J. Coombes, Lab.	Aldborough
Claire Cooper, C.	Bridge
G. Corfield, C.	Cranbrook
L. Davies, C.	Fullwell
J. Edelman, Lab.	Wanstead
G. Elgin, Lab.	Snaresbrook
C. Elliman, C.	Cranbrook
R. Emmett, C.	Fairlop
J. Fairley-Churchill, Lab.	Hainault
G. George, Lab.	Wanstead
R. Golding, Lab.	Mayfield
P. Goody, C.	Snaresbrook
S. Green, Lab.	Clementswood
M. Hickey, C.	Bridge
L. Hilton, Lab.	Mayfield
M. Hoskins, LD	Church End
R. Hoskins, LD	Church End
L. Huggett, C.	Monkhams
A. Hughes, C.	Fullwell
P. Laugharne, Lab.	Clementswood
P. Lawrence, C.	Bridge
R. Littlewood, Lab.	Seven Kings
J. R. Lovell, C.	Clayhall
F. K. Maravala, Lab.	Loxford
S. Middleburgh, Lab.	Goodmayes
S. Mirza, C.	Cranbrook
A. Moth, C.	Fullwell
R. Newcombe, Lab.	Hainault
G. Nicholson, Lab.	Newbury
F. A. Noor, Lab.	Clementswood
E. Norman, Lab.	Valentines
J. O'Shea, C.	Monkhams
A. Parkash, Lab.	Mayfield
M. Patel, Lab.	Seven Kings
E. Peake, Lab.	Hainault
E. Pearce, Lab.	Seven Kings
D. Radford, Lab.	Goodmayes
J. Ryan, C.	Fairlop
G. Sansun, Lab.	Newbury

78 Governed London

L. Scott, C.
R. Scott, LD
D. Sharma, Lab.
S. Speller, Lab.
G. Staight, LD
M. Stark, C.
V. Tewari, Lab.
K. Turner, Lab.
J. Tyne, LD

Fairlop
Chadwell
Newbury
Loxford
Chadwell
Monkhams
Valentines
Aldborough
Chadwell

Political Composition: Lab. 28; C. 25; LD. 9.
Population: 231,000
Area: 5,652 hectares.

ABOUT REDBRIDGE

Redbridge was formed in 1964 with the joining of Ilford and Wanstead and Woodford, together with parts of Dagenham and Chigwell. Situated in the North East of London, Redbridge boasts 1,200 acres of forest and 600 acres of green parkland.

COUNCIL TAX BANDS 2001-2002

Band	Market Value of the Property	Council Tax
A	Up to £40,000	£580.00
B	£40,001 to 52,000	£676.67
C	£52,001 to 68,000	£773.34
D	£68,001 to 88,000	£870.00
E	£88,001 to 120,000	£1063.33
F	£120,001 to 160,000	£1256.67
G	£160,001 to 320,000	£1450.00
H	£320,001 or more	£1740.00

RICHMOND UPON THAMES

RICHMOND UPON THAMES

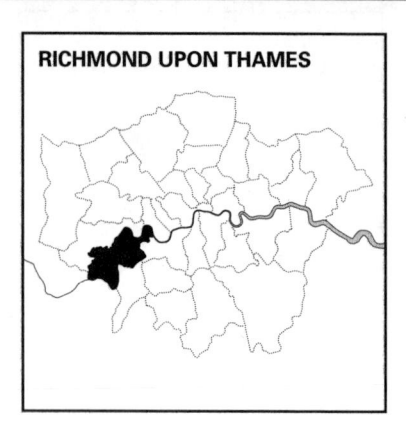

Civic Centre, 44 York Street, Twickenham TW1 3BZ (Tel: 020-8891 1411; Web: www.richmond.gov.uk).
Information Service: Old Town Hall, Whittaker Avenue, Richmond TW9 1TP (Tel: 020-8940 9125; Fax: 020-8940 6899).
Education, Leisure and Arts Department: Regal House, London Road, Twickenham TW1 3QB (020-8891 7500; Fax 020-8891 7714; Email: education@richmond.gov.uk).
Consumer Advice: (020-8891 7770; Fax 020-8891 7726; Email: tradingstds@richmond.gov.uk).
Environmental Health: (020-8891 7726; Email: commercialeh@richmond.gov.uk).
Housing: 44 York Street, Twickenham, TW1 3BZ (020-8891 7400; 020-8891 7717).
Registration of Births, Deaths and Marriages: 1 Spring Terrace, Richmond, Surrey TW9 1LW (Tel: 020-8940 2651).

CHIEF OFFICERS

Chief Executive: Mrs Gillian Norton
Director, Caring for People: Peter Wilson
Director, Environment and Sustainability: Alison Quant
Director of Finance: Mark Maidment
Director, Opportunities for All: Robert Hancock
Corporate Personnel Head of Service: Ross Wood
Chief Education Officer: Anji Phillips
Information Technology, Head of Service: Pat Keane
E-Government/Special Projects, Head of Service: Mike Gravatt

London Borough Councils 79

Housing, Acting Heads: Brian Castle, Rod Birtles
Services for Adults and Older People, Head of Service: Geoff Elford
Services for People with Learning Difficulties, Head of Service: Steve Drew
Services for Children and Families, Head of Service: Terry Earland
Legal Services, Head of Service: Richard Mellor
Environmental and Operational Services, Head of Service: David Streeter
Environment, Planning and Review, Head of Service: John East
Environmental Protection, Head of Service: Martin Esom
Customer Support Services, Head of Service: Tom Fisher
Financial Services, Head of Service: Graham Russell
Revenues, Benefits, Head of Service: Mike Gravatt
Audit Manager: Moyra Molloy
Corporate Policy: Tracy Luck
Democratic Service: Mary Collins
Best Value and Business Planning: Wyn Williams
Communications Manager: Rowena Davison

MEMBERS OF THE COUNCIL

Councillor	Ward
Mayor: Eleanor Stanier, LD	Mortlake
Deputy Mayor: J. Whittall, LD	East Twickenham
Leader of the Council: S. Lourie, LD	Kew
Barbara Alexander, LD	Hampton Hill
T. Arbour, C.	Hampton Wick
A. Barnett, LD	Kew
A. Butler, C.	South Twickenham
J. Cardy, LD	Hampton Nursery
N. Carthew, LD	Richmond Town
Alison Cornish, LD	Richmond Town
D. Cornwell, LD	East Twickenham
M. Daglish, LD	Palewell
M. Elengorn, LD	Teddington
Maria Flemington, C.	East Sheen
Katie Gent, LD	Barnes
M. Gold, Lab.	West Twickenham
Michael Jones, LD	Heathfield
Sue Jones, LD	Ham and Pertersham
B. King, LD	Heathfield
S. Knight, LD	Teddington
M. Kreling, C.	Hampton Hill
N. Lait, C.	South Twickenham
Simon Lamb, C.	Central Twickenham
B. Langford, Lab.	Mortlake
Penelope Lee, LD	Richmond Hill
Liz Mackenzie, Lab.	West Twickenham
Gina MacKinney, LD	Whitton
K. MacKinney, LD	Whitton
L. Mann, LD	East Twickenham
B. Matthews, Lab.	Mortlake
Jean Matthews, C.	Hampton
B. Miller, LD	Ham and Petersham
Jill Miller, LD	Kew
A. Mollett, LD	Richmond Hill
J. Mumford, LD	Teddington
D. Orchard, C.	South Twickenham
Pat Parsons, C.	Hampton Wick
D. Porter, C.	Central Twickenham
G. M. Rae, LD	Hampton Wick
G. Samuel, C.	Hampton Hill
Angela Style, LD	Barnes
Anne Summers, LD	Palewell
W. Treble, LD	Heathfield
N. True, C.	East Sheen
N. Urquhart, C.	Palewell
K. Warren, LD	Whitton
Mary Weber, LD	Richmond Hill
Barbara Westmorland, LD	Barnes
Sir David Williams, LD	Ham and Petersham
B. Woodriff, LD	Hampton
Maureen Woodriff, LD	Hampton Nursery
Anne Woodward, C.	Hampton

Political Composition: LD. 34; C. 14; Lab. 4
Population: 182,766
Area: 5,905 hectares.

ABOUT RICHMOND UPON THAMES

The London Borough of Richmond stretches from Hampton Court Palace to Twickenham Rugby Football Ground to Kew Gardens. It contains numerous parks, historic houses, museums and galleries.

COUNCIL TAX BANDS 2001-2002

Band	Market Value of the Property	Council Tax
A	Up to £40,000	£665.76
B	£40,001 to 52,000	£776.72
C	£52,001 to 68,000	£887.68
D	£68,001 to 88,000	£998.64
E	£88,001 to 120,000	£1220.56
F	£120,001 to 160,000	£1442.48
G	£160,001 to 320,000	£1664.40
H	£320,001 or more	£1997.28

80 Governed London

SOUTHWARK

SOUTHWARK

Town Hall, Peckham Road, London SE5 8UB
(Tel: 020-7525 5000;
Web: www.southwark.gov.uk).
Director of Education and Leisure Services:
Bradenham Close, London (Tel: 020-7525 5007).
Director of Social Services: Mabel Goldwin House, 49 Grange Walk, London
(Tel: 020-7525 3796).
Director of Housing: 9 Larcom Street, London
(Tel: 020-7525 7845).
Registration of Births, Deaths and Marriages:
34 Peckham Road, London SE5 8QA
(Tel: 020-7525 7669).

CHIEF OFFICERS

Chief Executive and Director of Finance:
R. Coomber
Director of Housing: Michael Irvine
Director of Regeneration and Environment:
F. Manson
Director of Social Services: C. Bull
Strategic Director of Education and Lifelong Learning: Dr. Roger Smith

MEMBERS OF THE COUNCIL

Councillor	Ward
Mayor: Hilary Wines, LD	Cathedral
Deputy Mayor: Dora Dixon-Fyle, Lab.	St Giles
Leader of the Council:	
Stephanie Elson, Lab.	St Giles
N. Baar, LD	Rotherhithe
M. Barnard, Lab.	Waverley
Beverley Bassom, LD	Rotherhithe
C. Blango, LD	Dockyard
S. Bosch, LD	Cathedral
Catherine Bowman, LD	Browning
D. Bradbury, C.	Ruskin
R. Bright, LD	Faraday
H. Canagasbey, Ind.	Chaucer
Denise Capstick, LD	Bricklayers
C. Cherrill, Lab.	Barset
C. Claridge, Ind.	Barset
G. Cope, Lab.	Lyndhurst
R. Cornall, Lab.	Lane
N. Dolezal, Lab.	Lyndhurst
N. Duffy, Lab.	Rye
T. Eckersley, C.	Ruskin
Mary Ellery, Lab.	Liddle
J. Friary, Lab.	Brunswick
Norma Gibbes, Lab.	Alleyn
A. Graham, Lab.	Lane
J. Gurling, LD	Newington
J. Halley, LD	Burgess
B. Hargrove, Lab.	Friary
Janet Heatley, Lab.	Bellenden
Jeffrey Hook, LD	Rotherhithe
Kim Humphreys, C.	College
W. Kayada, Lab.	Liddle
P. Kelly, Lab.	Bellenden
Joan Khachik, Lab.	Friary
A. L'Estrange, LD	Riverside
Jelli Ladipo, LD	Newington
S. Lanchashire, Lab.	Chaucer
A. Langely, LD	Faraday
H. Latham, Lab.	Alleyn
Linda Manchester, LD	Abbey
D. McInerny, Lab.	Lyndhurst
K. Mizzi, LD	Burgess
Vicki Naish, Lab.	Brunswick
G. Nash, LD	Bricklayers
D. Noakes, LD	Faraday
B. Olliffe, LD	Riverside
D. Partridge, LD	Dockyard
Michelle Pearce, Lab.	Ruskin
F. Pemberton, Lab.	Friary
Caroline Pidgeon, LD	Newington
A. Ritchie, Lab.	St Giles
W. Rowe, C.	College
A. Shaha, LD	Chaucer
R. Shannon, LD	Browning
A. Simmons, Lab.	Bellenden
B. Skelly, Lab.	Liddle
H. Stanton, LD	Riverside
R. Thomas, LD	Abbey
D. Thorncroft, Lab.	Rye
Viv Todd, Lab.	Waverley
H. Vahib, Lab.	Consort
N. Watson, LD	Browning
I. Wingfield, Lab.	Brunswick
A. Worsley, Lab.	Consort
Anne Yates, LD	Dockyard

Political Composition: Lab. 31; LD. 27; C. 4; Ind. 2
Population: 230,500
Area: 2,888 hectares.

ABOUT SOUTHWARK

The second oldest London borough after the City of London, Southwark is a borough steeped in history. Southwark's Thames-side location brought commercial wealth to the area in its early days, a location which nowadays forms a number of residential developments. Culturally, the borough is rich and is home to the Globe and Rose Theatres and the Bankside Gallery of Modern Art. Leisure and shopping facilities are good and the borough boasts numerous parks and gardens, East Street and Borough markets and Surrey Quays and Elephant and Castle shopping centres. Transport links are excellent and Southwark is home to London Bridge and Waterloo mainline railway stations as well as four stations on the recent Jubilee line extension and bus routes serving the West End, the City and beyond.

COUNCIL TAX BANDS 2001-2002

Band	Market Value of the Property	Council Tax
A	Up to £40,000	£559.67
B	£40,001 to 52,000	£699.61
C	£52,001 to 68,000	£799.56
D	£68,001 to 88,000	£899.50
E	£88,001 to 120,000	£1099.39
F	£120,001 to 160,000	£1299.28
G	£160,001 to 320,000	£1499.17
H	£320,001 or more	£1799.00

London Borough Councils 81

SUTTON

Civic Offices, St. Nicholas Way, Sutton, SM1 1EA (Tel: 020-8770 5000; Fax: 020-8770 5404; Web: www.sutton.gov.uk).
Environment and Leisure: 24 Denmark Road, Carshalton, SM5 2JG.
Learning for Life: The Grove, Carshalton, Surrey SM5 3AL.
Registration of Births, Deaths and Marriages: The Register Office, Russettings, 25 Worcester Road, Sutton, Surrey SM2 6PR (Tel: 020-8770 6790).

CHIEF OFFICERS

Chief Executive: Joanna Simons
Strategic Director, Community Services Group: Eleanor Brazil
Strategic Director, Environment and Leisure Group: Brian Madge
Strategic Director, Finance and Information Group: Vacant
Strategic Director, Learning for Life Group: Dr. Ian Birnbaum

MEMBERS OF THE COUNCIL

Councillor	Ward
Mayor: J. Leach, LD	Beddington North
Deputy Mayor: John Dodwell, LD	Wallington North
R. Aitken, LD.	Beddington South
Sheila Andrews, LD	Wandle Valley
R. Bailey, LD	Wallington South
Angela Baughan, LD	Carshalton Central
R. Bentley, LD	Carshalton Beeches
D. Biss, LD	Belmont
S. Brennan, LD	Sutton Central
D. Brims, LD	Sutton East
Anne Brown, C.	Sutton South

82 Governed London

P. Burstow, LD
Leslie Coman, LD
M. Cooper, LD
Pamela Cooper, LD
Margaret Court, LD
Joan Crowhurst, LD
N. Cull, LD
N. Dologhan, LD
J. Freeman, LD
Anne Gallop, LD
P. Geiringer, C.
Lyn Gleeson, LD
R. Gleeson, LD
C. Hall, LD
P. Hewitt, LD
Lal Hussain, LD
J. Keys, LD
J. Leach, LD
S. Lloyd, Lab.
Janet Lowne, LD
C. Mansell, Lab.
R. Marvelly, LD
G. Miles, LD
J. Morgan, Lab.
Lesley O'Connell, LD
P. Overy, LD
Penny Overy, LD
D. Park, C.
R. Roberts, LD
I. Ruxton, LD
Coleen Saunders, LD
Ruth Shaw, LD
Sheila Siggins, LD
Joyce Smith, Lab.
Sue Stears, LD
S. Theed, LD
A. Theobald, Lab.
R. Thistle: LD
G. Tope, LD
E. Trevor, C.
Myfanwy Wallace, LD
T. Wallace, LD
G. Whitham, C.
J. Woodley, LD
M. Woodley, LD

Rosehill
Worcester Park
Carshalton North
Beddington North
Wandle Valley
Sutton West
Sutton South
Beddington South
North Cheam
Sutton Common
Sutton South
Cheam West
Cheam West
Wallington South
Carshalton North
Sutton East
Wallington North
Beddington North
St. Helier South
Sutton East
St. Helier South
Wallington North
Carshalton Beeches
St. Helier North
Sutton Common
Worcester Park
Rosehill
Cheam South
Worcester Park South
Worcester Park North
Beddington South
North Cheam
Wrythe Green
St. Helier North
Wrythe Green
Wallington South
St. Helier North
Clockhouse
Sutton Central
Cheam South
Sutton West
Belmont
Woodcote
Carshalton Central
Carlshalton Beeches

Political Composition: LD. 45; Lab. 5; C. 5.
Population: 178,189
Area: 4,343 hectares.

ABOUT SUTTON

On the edge of south London with the North Downs to the south and with more trees than any other London borough, Sutton combines the best of city and country. It boasts more than 1,000 acres of open space, yet lies within a few miles of the heart of London. The quality of life has attracted major employers such as Reed Business Publishing, the Crown Agents, Canon, Sainsbury's Homebase and Securicor. Sutton's green image rests on more than the abundance of trees in the borough. Caring for the local environment has become a major priority and Sutton regularly tops the national statistics for recycling.

COUNCIL TAX BANDS 2001-2002

Band	Market Value of the Property	Council Tax
A	Up to £40,000	£581.76
B	£40,001 to 52,000	£678.72
C	£52,001 to 68,000	£775.68
D	£68,001 to 88,000	£872.64
E	£88,001 to 120,000	£1066.56
F	£120,001 to 160,000	£1260.48
G	£160,001 to 320,000	£1454.40
H	£320,001 or more	£1745.28

TOWER HAMLETS

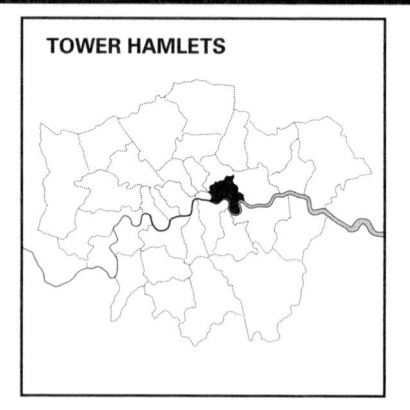

Town Hall, Mulbery Place, 5 Clove Crescent, London E14 2BG (Tel: 020-7364 5000); Fax: 020-7364 4296; Web: www.towerhamlets.gov.uk).
Social Services: 62 Roman Road, London E2 0QJ (Tel: 020-7364 5000).
Planning and Environmental Services: 41-47 Bow Road, London E3 2BS (Tel: 020-7364 5000).

Tower Hamlets Information Service:
18 Lamb Street, London E1 2EA
(Tel: 020-7364 4970).
Registration of Births, Deaths and Marriages:
The Register Office, Bromley Public Hall, Bow Road, London E3 3AA (Tel: 020-8980 8025).

CHIEF OFFICERS

Chief Executive: Eleanor Kelly
Corporate Director of Housing: Sue Benjamis
Corporate Director (Customer Services): Eric Bohl
Corporate Director (Education and Community Services): Ms. Christine Gilbert
Corporate Director (Social Services): Ian Wilson
Solicitor to the Council (Acting): Helen Sidwell

MEMBERS OF THE COUNCIL

Councillors	Ward
Mayor: S. Alom, Lab.	
Deputy Mayor: A. Sardar, Lab.	Bromley
Leader of the Council:	
M. Keith, Lab.	Shadwell
H. Abbas, Lab.	Limehouse
B. Ahmed, Lab.	St. Dunstan's
R. Ahmed, Lab.	East India
M. Ali, Lab.	Weavers
S. Alom, Lab.	Limehouse
A. Asad, Lab.	St. Katherine's
Elizabeth Baunton, LD	Park
D. Bayat, Lab.	Redcoat
Jusna Begum, Lab.	St. Peter's
J. Biggs, Lab.	St. Dunstan's
D. Charles, LD	Park
Betheline Chattopadhyay, Lab.	Bromley
C. Creegan, Lab.	Weavers
Barrie Duffey, LD	Holy Trinity
D. Edgar, Lab.	Limehouse
Ray Gipson, LD	Bow
A. Heslop, Lab.	St. Mary's
Catherine Hinvest, Lab.	Bromley
A. Hoque, Lab.	St. Katherine's
Richard Hunn, Ind.	Grove
Denise Joans, Lab.	St. Katherine's
Diana Johnson, Lab.	Lansbury
M. Keating, Lab.	Lansbury
Janet Ludlow, LD	Grove
J. Mainwaring, Lab.	Millwall
R. Marney, Lab.	St. Peter's
R. Miah, Lab.	St. Peter's
S. Mizan, Lab.	Spitalfields
S. Molyneaux, Lab.	Millwall
K. Morton, Lab.	Lansbury
G. Mortuza, Lab.	Spitalfields
K. Murshid, Lab.	Blackwall
A. Rahman, Lab.	Redcoat
A. Sarder, Lab.	Bromley
A. Shukur, Lab.	Shadwell
J. Snooks, LD	Holy Trinity
B. Son, Lab.	East India
Terry Stacy, LD	Bow
M. Taylor, Lab.	St. James'
Catherine Tuitt, Lab.	Weavers
A. Uddin, Lab.	Spitalfields
M. Uddin, Lab.	St. Dunstan's
S. Ullah, Lab.	Holy Trinity
M. Uz-Zuman, Lab.	St. Mary's
Marian Williams, LD	Bow
S. Wright, Lab.	Blackwall
M. Young, Lab.	Millwall

Political Composition: Lab. 41; LD. 8; Ind. 1
Parliamentary Constituencies: Bethnal Green and Bow, Poplar and Canning Town
Population: 179,834
Area: 1980 hectares.

ABOUT TOWER HAMLETS

Tower Hamlets is located in the East End of London with the Docklands river bend of the Thames at its southern boundary. It is served by the Central, District and new Jubilee Line of the London Underground. The economy of the borough was severely disrupted by the declining prosperity of the Docklands areas. The area has received over £1 billion in UK government assistance and £5 billion in private investment. This has culminated in the rapid re-growth of the local economy with intensive industrial and commercial development of the 530 acres of previously derelict land. The Docklands area is now home to many companies representing the banking, finance and communication sectors.

COUNCIL TAX BANDS 2001-2002

Band	Market Value of the Property	Council Tax
A	Up to £40,000	£520.38
B	£40,001 to 52,000	£607.10
C	£52,001 to 68,000	£693.84
D	£68,001 to 88,000	£780.56
E	£88,001 to 120,000	£954.02
F	£120,001 to 160,000	£1127.48
G	£160,001 to 320,000	£1300.94
H	£320,001 or more	£1561.13

84 Governed London

WALTHAM FOREST

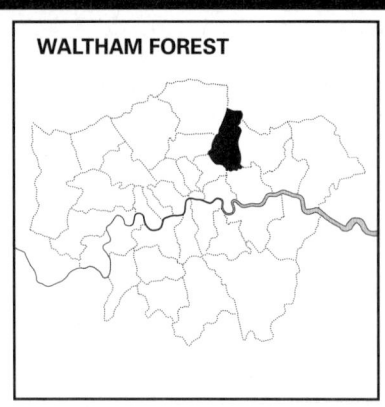

Town Hall, Forest Road, London E17 4JF (Tel : 020-8527 5544;
E-mail: chief.executive@ce.lbwf.gov.uk
Web: www.lbwf.gov.uk).
Planning and Development: Municipal Offices, 16 The Ridge, London E4 6PS (Tel: 020-8527 5544).
Environmental Health Service: 154 Blackhorse Road, Walthamstow, London E17 6NW (Tel: 020-8520 0221;
E-mail: environmentalhealth@lbwf.gov.uk).
Education and Social Services: Municipal Offices, High Road, London, E10 5QJ.
Housing: Willow House, 869 Forest Road, London E17 4UH (Tel: 020- 8527 5544).
Leisure and Regeneration; Legal Services: Sycamore House, PO Box 416, Forest Road, London E17 4SY (Tel: 020-8527 5544).
Community Protection; Trading Standards: 154 Blackhorse Road, London E17 6NW (Tel: 020-8496 2222).
Registration of Births, Deaths and Marriages: 106 Grove Road, Walthamstow, London E17 9BY (Tel: 020-8520 8617).

CHIEF OFFICERS

Chief Executive: S. White
Head of Financial Services: R. Cooke
Head of Planning and Economic Development: A. Bennett
Executive Director of Community Services: R. Wallace
Executive Director of Environmental Services: L. Norton
Executive Director of Corporate Services: C. Badvinatti
Executive Director of Lifelong Learning: S. Hay

MEMBERS OF THE COUNCIL

Councillor	Ward
Mayor: M. Broadley, Lab.	Valley
Deputy Mayor: M. Martin, Lab.	Cathall
L. Ali, Lab.	High Street
D. Arnold, C.	Chingford
P. Atherton, LD	Chapel End
A. Bean, Lab.	Wood Street
R. Belam, LD	Chapel End
T. Bhogal, Lab.	Grove Green
D. Blunt, Lab.	High Street
L. Braham, C.	Hatch End
R. Bruni, Lab.	Lea Bridge
A. Buckley, Lab.	Lea Bridge
S. Buckley, Lab.	Lea Bridge
R. Carey, LD	Higham Hill
P. Dawe, Lab.	Wood Street
K. Dhillon, Lab.	Forest
C. Dunn, Lab.	Wood Street
J. Duran, Lab.	Grove Green
R. Evan, C.	Valley
L. Finlayson, C.	Hale End
M. Fish, C.	Chingford
M. Fitzgerald, C.	Hatch End
J. Gover, C.	Valley
J. Gray, Lab.	Leytonstone
P. Herrington, C.	Endlebury
S. Highfield, Lab.	Cathall
L. Hodges, LD	Leyton
Mladen Jovcic, C.	Endlebury
E. Jones, Lab.	Lloyd
T. Kamal, Lab.	St. James Street
C. Kitson, LD	Cann Hall
I. Leslie, Lab.	Leytonstone
M. Lewis, C.	Chingford
C. Loakes, Lab.	Leytonstone
A. Lock, Lab.	Grove Green
N. Matharoo, Lab.	Lloyd
D. Murray, Lab.	St. James Street
M. Nasim, Lab.	Hoe Street
D. Norman, C.	Hale End
M. O'Connor, Lab.	Lloyd
E. Phillips, LD	Cann Hall
S. Poulson, Lab.	Hoe Street
M. Fazlur Rahman, Lab.	Forest
K. Rayner, LD	Cann Hall
E. Sizer, Lab.	Hoe Street
G. Smith, Lab.	St. James Street
R. Sullivan, LD	Leyton
M. Thompson, Ind.	Larkswood
S. Tucker, Lab.	Forest
C. Tuckley, LD	Leyton
G. Walker, C.	Hatch End
J. Walter, C.	Larkswood
R. Wheatley, LD	High Street

London Borough Councils 85

T. Wheeler, Lab.
E. Williams, C.
P. Woollcott, LD
G. Woolnough, LD

Cathall
Larkswood
Higham Hill
Chapel End

Political Composition: Lab. 30; C. 14; LD. 12; Ind. 1.
Population: 219,417
Area: 15 square miles.

ABOUT WALTHAM FOREST

Waltham Forest is situated in the North East of London. It is mainly a residential borough but contains significant amounts of forest, reservoirs and open spaces. Epping Forest flanks the eastern side of the borough and to the west lies the river Lea and the Lea Valley. The southern areas of Walthamstow, Leyton and Leytonstone contain two thirds of the boroughs total population. The remaining third reside in the northern area of Chingford.

The area is famous for its William Morris Gallery, the only museum dedicated to the Victorian artist and designer and Walthamstow market, the longest daily street market in Europe.

COUNCIL TAX BANDS 2001-2002

Band	Market Value of the Property	Council Tax
A	Up to £40,000	£618.73
B	£40,001 to 52,000	£721.86
C	£52,001 to 68,000	£824.98
D	£68,001 to 88,000	£928.10
E	£88,001 to 120,000	£1134.34
F	£120,001 to 160,000	£1340.59
G	£160,001 to 320,000	£1546.83
H	£320,001 or more	£1856.20

WANDSWORTH

WANDSWORTH

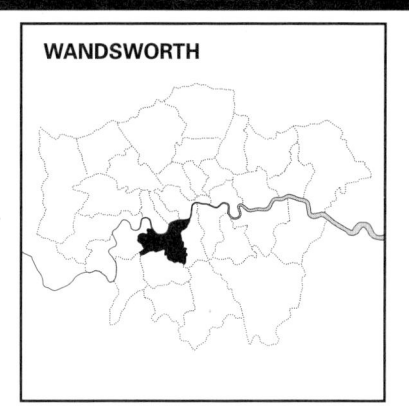

The Town Hall, Wandsworth High Street, London SW18 2PU (Tel: 020-8871 6000).

CHIEF OFFICERS

Borough Planner: I. Thompson
Borough Solicitor: M. Walker
Chief Executive and Director of Administration: G. Jones
Director of Education: P. Robinson
Director of Finance and Deputy Chief Executive: H. Heywood
Director of Housing: R. Sheppard
Director of Leisure and Amenity Services: L. Garrett
Director of Social Services: M. Rundle
Director of Technical Services: W. Myers
Head of Environmental Services: A. R. Waren

MEMBERS OF THE COUNCIL

Councillor	Ward
Mayor: R. Smith, C.	St. John
C. McNaught-Davis, C.	Earlsfield
Leader of the Council:	
E. Lister, C.	Thamesfield
L. Ayonrinde, C.	Balham
P. Beddows, C.	Shaftesbury
A. Belton, Lab.	Latchmere
T. Beresford, C.	St. John
R. Bird, C.	Thamesfield
Jane Briginshaw, Lab.	Furzedown
B. Burn, C.	West Putney
M. Calderbank, C.	West Putney
J. Cousins, C.	Shaftesbury
C. Dawe, C.	Bedford
C. Dixon, C.	Northcote
J. Farebrother, Lab.	Furzedown
S. Finn, C.	Bedford
A. Flook, C.	St. Mary's Park

86 Governed London

J. Garrett, C. — Springfield
A. Gibbons, Lab. — Graveney
R. Govindia, C. — Nightingale
A. Graham, C. — Earlsfield
V. Graham, C. — Fairfield
M. Grimston, C. — West Hill
J. Hallmark, C. — St. Mary's Park
T. Harris, C. — Roehampton
I. Hart, C. — Furzedown
M. Heaster, C. — Nightingale
S. Heath, Lab. — Latchmere
D. Hosain, Lab. — Graveney
E. Howlett, C. — Parkside
C. Humphries, C. — Queenstown
G. Hurley, C. — Balham
B. Jeffrey, C. — West Hill
M. Johnson, Lab. — Latchmere
Martin Johnson, C. — Northcote
S. Khan, Lab. — Tooting
S. King, Lab. — Tooting
L. Lees, C. — Thamesfield
Jan Leigh, C. — Southfield
R. Longmore, C. — Balham
N. Longworth, C. — Southfield
S. Lorch, C. — Southfield
H. Lumby, C. — Roehampton
P. McCausland, C. — St. John
E. McDermott, C. — Nightingale
Leslie McDonnell, C. — East Putney
M. Mervis, C. — Springfield
G. Passmore, C. — Northcote
B. Prichard, C. — East Putney
G. Senior, C. — Shaftesbury
M. Simpson, C. — Roehampton
T. Strickland, C. — Fairfield
Jeremy Swan, C. — Parkside
Pam Tatlow, Lab. — Graveney
K. Tracey, C. — Springfield
R. Vivian, C. — Queenstown
Jane White, Lab. — Tooting
D. Whittingham, C. — East Putney
S. Wilkie, C. — Bedford
S. Williams, C. — St. Mary's Park
N. Zahawi, C. — West Putney

Political Composition: C. 50; Lab. 11
Population: 266,300
Area: 3,432.

ABOUT WANDSWORTH

Wandsworth is in the south west of London and houses a number of areas including Battersea, Earlsfield, Putney and Southfields. Much of the borough lies along the Thames and the Oxford and Cambridge boat race starts in the borough at Putney.

COUNCIL TAX BANDS 2001-2002

Band	Market Value of the Property	Council Tax	
A	Up to £40,000	£301.14	313.63
B	£40,001 to 52,000	£351.33	365.90
C	£52,001 to 68,000	£401.53	418.18
D	£68,001 to 88,000	£451.71	470.45
E	£88,001 to 120,000	£552.09	574.99
F	£120,001 to 160,000	£652.47	679.54
G	£160,001 to 320,000	£752.85	784.08
H	£320,001 or more	£903.42	940.89

(There are two columns as the borough has two council tax groupings, one for the borough generally and one for areas of the borough which are subject to a Conservative levy (right-hand column)).

WESTMINSTER CITY

WESTMINSTER

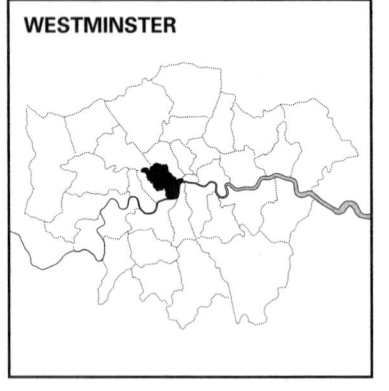

Westminster City Hall, Victoria Street, London SW1E 6QP (Tel: 020-7641 6000; Web: www.westminster.gov.uk).
Registration of Births, Deaths and Marriages: Westminster Council House, Marylebone Road, London NW1 5PT (Tel: 020-7641 1161).

CHIEF OFFICERS

Chief Executive and Director of Finance: Peter Rogers
Director of Education: John Harris
Director of Environment and Leisure: Joe Duckworth
Director of Housing: Vic Baylis
Director of Legal Services: Colin Wilson
Director of Planning and Transportation: Carl Powell
Director of Policy and Communications: Graham Ellis
Director of Social and Community Services: Mrs. Julie Jones

London Borough Councils 87

MEMBERS OF THE COUNCIL

Councillor	Ward
Lord Mayor: H. Marshall, C.	Cavendish
Deputy Lord Mayor:	
M. Page, C.	Cavendish
Leader of the Council:	
S. Milton, C.	Lancaster Gate
A. Allum, C.	Cavendish
A. Barns, C.	Bayswater
Pamela Batty, C.	Hyde Park
Carol Ann Bailey, C.	Churchill
Jenny Bianco, C.	Bryanston
F. Blois, C.	Belgrave
N. Boles, C.	West End
A. Bradley, C.	St. George's
M. Brahams, C.	Bayswater
J. Bull, C.	Bryanston
Susie Burbridge, C.	Maida Vale
M. Caplan, C.	Little Venice
J. Cox, C.	Knightsbridge
C. Cronin, C.	Churchill
R. Davis, C.	Lancaster Gate
P. Dimoldenberg, Lab.	Queen's Park
D. Astaire, C.	Regent's Park
K. Gardner, C.	Lords
Barbara Grahame, Lab.	Church Street
R. Harley, Lab.	Church Street
D. Harvey, C.	Victoria
A. Hooper, C.	Baker Street
L. Hyams, C.	St. James's
T. Joiner, C.	Regent's Park
A. Lazarus, Lab.	Harrow Road
E. Lazarus, C.	Hyde Park
C. Longworth, C	Belgrave
J. Lord, C.	Little Venice
A. Mallinson, C.	Hyde Park
K. Malthouse, C.	St. George's
G. Martin, Lab.	Harrow Road
T. Mitchell, C.	Victoria
C. Nemeth, C.	Lords
A. Nicholl, C.	St. James's
R. Nye, C.	Hamilton Terrace
J. Powell-Tuck, C.	Millbank
J. Predergast, C.	Maida Vale
Murad Qureshi, Lab.	Church Street
Mushtaq Qureshi, Lab.	Queen's Park
R. Raymond-Cox, C.	Maida Vale
G. Rees-Mogg. C.	Knightsbridge
Glenys Roberts, C.	West End
D. Sandys, C.	Millbank
B. Schmeling, C.	Little Venice
A. Segal, C.	St. George's
Jill Selbourne, Lab.	Harrow Road
L. St. John-Howe, C.	Regent's Park
Simon Stockhill, Lab.	Westbourne
R. Tallboys, C.	Lancaster Gate
B. Taylor, Lab.	Queen's Park
Katy Thorne, Lab.	Westbourne
F. Tombolis, C.	Bayswater
G. Walsh, C.	Churchill
J. Warner, C.	Hamilton Terrace
A. Whitley, Lab.	Westbourne
I. Wilder, C.	Baker Street
P. Wright, Lab.	Millbank

Political Composition: C. 47; Lab. 13
Population: 230,000
Area: 2,204 hectares.

ABOUT WESTMINSTER CITY

The City of Westminster occupies an important part of both London and Great Britain as a whole. Buckingham Palace, Downing Street, the Houses of Parliament and most Government departments are within its boundaries. The City is also home to Westminster Abbey, the Roman Catholic Westminster Cathedral and the London Central Mosque. There is culture in the form of the Royal Albert Hall, Royal Opera House and English National Opera and many major theatres and cinemas. There are also countless restaurants, notably in Soho, numerous hotels and many of London's most famous shops. Five major parks and many smaller areas provide light, colour and fresh air.

Over 200,000 people live in Westminster a figure boosted each day to one million by tourists and workers. Half a million people travel into Westminster to their work helped by the fact that four main railway lines terminate here. All Underground lines pass beneath Westminster's streets and coaches go to and from destinations across the United Kingdom from Victoria Coach Station.

The City of Westminster is administered by a directly elected City Council providing social services, housing (22,000 dwellings), libraries, refuse collection and street cleansing. It is also the main highway and planning authority. Sixty percent of Westminster has been designated conservation areas and overall the city contains 9,000 buildings of architectural and historical significance.

As well as being an important place for residents, tourist, government and culture, the City of Westminster is also a key commercial centre with over 30,000 businesses within its boundaries.

COUNCIL TAX BANDS 2001-2002

Band	Market Value of the Property	Council Tax
A	Up to £40,000	£273.00
B	£40,001 to 52,000	£319.00
C	£52,001 to 68,000	£364.00
D	£68,001 to 88,000	£410.00
E	£88,001 to 120,000	£501.00
F	£120,001 to 160,000	£592.00
G	£160,001 to 320,000	£683.00
H	£320,001 or more	£820.00

ORGANISATIONS CONNECTED WITH LOCAL GOVERNMENT IN LONDON

ASSOCIATION OF LONDON GOVERNMENT

59½ Southwark Street, London SE1 0AL (Tel: 020-7934 9999; Fax 020-7934 9991).

The new Association of London Government was created in April 2000. It combines the old Association of London Government, London Borough Grants, Greater London Employers Association, the London Housing Unit and the Transport Committee for London. The new body represents and speaks on behalf of London's 33 councils. Its main committee comprises the elected leaders if all London councils. The objectives of the ALG are to promote economic partnership between the public and private sectors; to develop schemes to improve the environment and quality of life of Londoners; to support local government and to contact Central Government and Europe. Its other functions include the distribution of grants to voluntary organisations in the capital on behalf of the boroughs, and running the London-wide concessionary fares scheme which provides free transport to more than one million elderly and disabled Londoners.

Chief Executive: Martin Pilgrim

AUDIT COMMISSION FOR LOCAL AUTHORITIES AND THE NATIONAL HEALTH SERVICE IN ENGLAND AND WALES

1 Vincent Square, London SW1P 2PN (Tel: 020-7828 1212; Fax: 020-7976 6187); **Press Office:** 26 Grosvenor Gardens, London SW1W 0GT (Tel: 020-7838 4848; Fax: 020-7838 4871)

The Audit Commission for England and Wales is an independent watchdog, promoting proper stewardship of public finance amongst local authorities and local health service bodies. It also has a responsibility to reassure the public and help those responsible for the management and delivery of public services to achieve economy, efficiency and effectiveness through focusing on probity, regularity and value for money.

The Commission carries out work in five principal ways:

- by appointing external auditors to all local authorities including the GLA, health authorities and hospital trusts in England and Wales;
- by undertaking studies which make recommendations for improving economy, efficiency and effectiveness of service;
- by identifying examples of best practice and encouraging their wider adoption;
- by investigating the impact on local authorities of legislation or central government action or advice;
- by inspecting local authority services in line with Best Value legislation

The Commission has a Chair, Deputy Chair and 18 members drawn from a wide range of backgrounds which include local government, the health service, the civil service, the voluntary sector, academia and the private sector. Members are appointed by the Secretary of State for the Environment, Transport and the Regions. The Commission's income derives almost entirely from fees charged for audit work and it is required, taking one year with another, to be self-financing. The Commission has about 200 headquarters staff and employs around 1,200 staff in its auditing agency, District Audit. Audit appointments are made either from District Audit or from one of a number of private firms. Additional responsibilities for the Commission include assisting Ofsted with the inspection of Local Education Authorities and joint reviews with the Social Services Inspectorate.

General Election Results   89

Chair: Dame Helena Shovelton, DBE
Deputy Chairman: Adrienne Fresko
Members: Cllr Richard Arthur, Julie Baddeley, Dr. Judy Curson, Elizabeth Firkin, J. R. Foster, Sir Graham Hart, Dr. Pauline Lane, Gerard Lernos, Rosalynde Lowe, David Moss, Prof. Sue Richards, Nick Skellett, Chris Swinson, Sir Ronald Watson, CBE, Cllr David Williams, Brian Wolfe.

THE LONDON MAYORS' ASSOCIATION

8 Bentinck Street, London W1U 2BJ
(Tel: 020-7486 9041).

The Metropolitan Mayors' and Ex-Mayors' Association was formed in 1901 with the purpose of promoting and discussing general matters affecting the Metropolis and to enable Mayors and former Mayors to meet on a social basis.

In 1950 all the Mayors and former Mayors of the other Boroughs of Greater London were invited to become members and the association changed its name to the London Mayors' Association.

Mayors and former Mayors from all the London Boroughs were entitled to join but the Chairman is always the Lord Mayor of Westminster. Another Mayor is also elected to Chair the Executive Committee which runs the Association on a day to day basis.

President: Honorary Alderman Mrs Calcott-James (Mayor of Wandsworth 1982—1983)

Chairman: The Lord Mayor of Westminster

GENERAL ELECTION RESULTS 2001

The results of voting in each london parliamentary division at the general election of 7 June 2001 are given below. The majority in the 1997 general election, and any by-election between 1997 and 2001, is given below the 2001 result.

Symbols
Sitting MP*
Previously MP in another seat +

Barking
Electorate 55,229
Turnout 25,126 (45.49%) **Lab hold**
Mrs Margaret Hodge (Lab.) 15,302
Mike Weatherley (C.) 5,768
Anura Keppetipola (LD) 2,450
Mark Toleman (BNP) 1,606
Lab. maj 9,534 (37.94%)
5.14% swing Lab. to C.
(1997: Lab. maj 15,896 (48.22%))

Battersea
Electorate 67,495
Turnout 36,804 (54.53%) **Lab hold**
Martin Linton (Lab.) 18,498
Mrs Lucy Shersby (C.) 13,445
Ms Siobhan Vitelli (LD) 4,450
Thomas Barber (Ind.) 411
Lab. maj 5,053 (13.73%)
1.21% swing C. to Lab.
(1997: Lab. maj 5,360 (11.31%))

Beckenham
Electorate 72,241
Turnout 45,562 (63.07%) **C. hold**
Mrs Jacqui Lait (C.) 20,618
Richard Watts (Lab.) 15,659
Alex Feakes (LD) 7,308
Ms Karen Moran (Green) 961
Christopher Pratt (UK Ind.) 782
Rif Winfield (Lib.) 234
C. maj 4,959 (10.88%)
0.89% swing Lab. to C.
(1997 Nov by-election: C. maj 1,227 (3.85%));
(1997: C. maj 4,953 (9.11%))

90 Governed London

Bethnal Green & Bow
Electorate 79,192
Turnout 38,470 (48.58%) **Lab hold**
Ms Oona King (Lab.) 19,380
Shahagir Faruk (C.) 9,323
Ms Janet Ludlow (LD) 5,946
Ms Anna Bragga (Green) 1,666
Michael Davidson (BNP) 1,267
Dennis Delderfield (NBP) 888
Lab. maj 10,057 (26.14%)
0.44% swing C. to Lab.
(1997: Lab. maj 11,285 (25.26%))

Bexleyheath & Crayford
Electorate 63,580
Turnout 40,378 (63.51%) **Lab hold**
Nigel Beard (Lab.) 17,593
David Evennett (C.) 16,121
Nickolas O'Hare (LD) 4,476
Colin Smith (BNP) 1,408
John Dunford (UK Ind.) 780
Lab. maj 1,472 (3.65%)
1.72% swing Lab. to C.
(1997: Lab. maj 3,415 (7.08%))

Brent East
Electorate 58,095
Turnout 28,992 (49.90%) **Lab gain**
Paul Daisley (Lab.) 18,325
David Gauke (C.) 5,278
Ms Nowsheen Bhatti (LD) 3,065
Ms Simone Aspis (Green) 1,361
Ms Sarah Macken (ProLife) 392
Ms Iris Cremer (Soc. Lab.) 383
Ashwin Tanna (UK Ind.) 188
Lab. maj 13,047 (45.00%)
0.01% swing Lab. to C.
(1997: Lab. maj 15,882 (45.03%))

Brent North
Electorate 58,789
Turnout 33,939 (57.73%) **Lab hold**
Barry Gardiner (Lab.) 20,149
Philip Allott (C.) 9,944
Paul Lorber (LD) 3,846
Lab. maj 10,205 (30.07%)
9.77% swing C. to Lab.
(1997: Lab. maj 4,019 (10.53%))

Brent South
Electorate 55,891
Turnout 28,637 (51.24%) **Lab hold**
Paul Boateng (Lab.) 20,984
Carupiah Selvarajah (C.) 3,604
Havard Hughes (LD) 3,098
Mick McDonnell (Soc. All.) 491
Thomas Mac Stiofain (Res. Motor) 460
Lab. maj 17,380 (60.69%)
1.81% swing C. to Lab.
(1997: Lab. maj 19,691 (57.08%))

Brentford & Isleworth
Electorate 84,049
Turnout 44,514 (52.96%) **Lab hold**
Ms Ann Keen (Lab.) 23,275
Tim Mack (C.) 12,957
Gareth Hartwell (LD) 5,994
Nic Ferriday (Green) 1,324
Gerald Ingram (UK Ind.) 412
Danny Faith (Soc. All.) 408
Asa Khaira (Ind.) 144
Lab. maj 10,318 (23.18%)
1.26% swing Lab. to C.
(1997: Lab. maj 14,424 (25.70%))

Bromley & Chislehurst
Electorate 68,763
Turnout 43,231 (62.87%) **C. hold**
Eric Forth (C.) 21,412
Ms Sue Polydorou (Lab.) 12,375
Geoff Payne (LD) 8,180
Rob Bryant (UK Ind.) 1,264
C. maj 9,037 (20.90%)
0.09% swing C. to Lab.
(1997: C. maj 11,118 (21.08%))

Camberwell & Peckham
Electorate 53,694
Turnout 25,104 (46.75%) **Lab hold**
Ms Harriet Harman (Lab.) 17,473
Donnachadh McCarthy (LD) 3,350
Jonathan Morgan (C.) 2,740
Storm Poorun (Green) 805
John Mulrenan (Soc. All.) 478
Robert Adams (Soc. Lab.) 188
Frank Sweeney (WRP) 70
Lab. maj 14,123 (56.26%)
0.91% swing Lab. to LD
(1997: Lab. maj 16,351 (57.43%))

General Election Results 91

Carshalton & Wallington
Electorate 67,337
Turnout 40,612 (60.31%) **LD hold**
Tom Brake (LD) 18,289
Ken Andrew (C.) 13,742
Ms Margaret Cooper (Lab.) 7,466
Simon Dixon (Green) 614
Martin Haley (UK Ind.) 501
LD maj 4,547 (11.20%)
3.26% swing C. to LD
(1997: LD maj 2,267 (4.68%))

Chingford & Woodford Green
Electorate 63,252
Turnout 36,982 (58.47%) **C. hold**
Iain Duncan Smith (C.) 17,834
Ms Jessica Webb (Lab.) 12,347
John Beanse (LD) 5,739
Ms Jean Griffin (BNP) 1,062
C. maj 5,487 (14.84%)
0.99% swing Lab. to C.
(1997: C. maj 5,714 (12.85%))

Chipping Barnet
Electorate 70,217
Turnout 42,456 (60.46%) **C. hold**
***Sydney Chapman (C.) 19,702**
Damien Welfare (Lab.) 17,001
Sean Hooker (LD) 5,753
C. maj 2,701 (6.36%)
2.14% swing Lab. to C.
(1997: C. maj 1,035 (2.09%))

Cities of London & Westminster
Electorate 71,935
Turnout 33,975 (47.23%) **C. hold**
Mark Field (C.) 15,737
Michael Katz (Lab.) 11,238
Martin Horwood (LD) 5,218
Hugo Charlton (Green) 1,318
Colin Merton (UK Ind.) 464
C. maj 4,499 (13.24%)
0.54% swing Lab. to C.
(1997: C. maj 4,881 (12.16%))

Croydon Central
Electorate 77,567
Turnout 45,860 (59.12%) **Lab hold**
Geraint Davies (Lab.) 21,643
David Congdon (C.) 17,659
Paul Booth (LD) 5,156
James Feisenberger (UK Ind.) 545
Ms Lynda Miller (BNP) 449
John Cartwright (Loony) 408
Lab. maj 3,984 (8.69%)
0.85% swing C. to Lab.
(1997: Lab. maj 3,897 (6.99%))

Croydon North
Electorate 76,600
Turnout 41,882 (54.68%) **Lab hold**
Malcolm Wicks (Lab.) 26,610
Simon Allison (C.) 9,752
Ms Sandra Lawman (LD) 4,375
Alan Smith (UK Ind.) 606
Don Madgwick (Soc. All.) 539
Lab. maj 16,858 (40.25%)
2.63% swing C. to Lab.
(1997: Lab. maj 18,398 (35.00%))

Croydon South
Electorate 73,402
Turnout 45,060 (61.39%) **C. hold**
Richard Ottaway (C.) 22,169
Gerry Ryan (Lab.) 13,472
Ms Anne Gallop (LD) 8,226
Mrs Kathleen Garner (UK Ind.) 998
Mark Samuel (Choice) 195
C. maj 8,697 (19.30%)
1.35% swing C. to Lab.
(1997: C. maj 11,930 (22.01%))

Dagenham
Electorate 59,340
Turnout 27,580 (46.48%) **Lab hold**
Jon Cruddas (Lab.) 15,784
Michael White (C.) 7,091
Adrian Gee-Turner (LD) 2,820
David Hill (BNP) 1,378
Berlyne Hamilton (Soc. All.) 262
Robert Siggins (Soc. Lab.) 245
Lab. maj 8,693 (31.52%)
7.82% swing Lab. to C.
(1997: Lab. maj 17,054 (47.16%))

Dulwich & West Norwood
Electorate 70,497
Turnout 38,247 (54.25%) **Lab hold**
Ms Tessa Jowell (Lab.) 20,999
Nick Vineall (C.) 8,689
Ms Caroline Pidgeon (LD) 5,806
Ms Jenny Jones (Green) 1,914
Brian Kelly (Soc. All.) 839
Lab. maj 12,310 (32.19%)
2.29% swing Lab. to C.
(1997: Lab. maj 16,769 (36.76%))

Ealing Acton & Shepherd's Bush
Electorate 70,697
Turnout 37,201 (52.62%) **Lab hold**

92 Governed London

Clive Soley (Lab.) 20,144
Miss Justine Greening (C.) 9,355
Martin Tod (LD) 6,171
Nick Grant (Soc. All.) 529
Andrew Lawrie (UK Ind.) 476
Carlos Rule (Soc. Lab.) 301
Ms Rebecca Ng (ProLife) 225
Lab. maj 10,789 (29.00%)
1.77% swing Lab. to C.
(1997: Lab. maj 15,647 (32.55%))

Ealing North
Electorate 77,524
Turnout 44,957 (57.99%) **Lab hold**
Stephen Pound (Lab.) 25,022
Charles Walker (C.) 13,185
Francesco Fruzza (LD) 5,043
Ms Astra Seibe (Green) 1,039
Daniel Moss (UK Ind.) 668
Lab. maj 11,837 (26.33%)
4.94% swing C. to Lab.
(1997: Lab. maj 9,160 (16.44%))

Ealing Southall
Electorate 82,373
Turnout 46,828 (56.85%) **Lab hold**
Piara Khabra (Lab.) 22,239
Daniel Kawczynski (C.) 8,556
Avtar Lit (Sunrise) 5,764
Baldev Sharma (LD) 4,680
Ms Jane Cook (Green) 2,119
Salvinder Dhillon (Community) 1,214
Mushtaq Choudhry (Ind.) 1,166
Harpal Brar (Soc. Lab.) 921
Mohammed Bhutta (Qari) 169
Lab. maj 13,683 (29.22%)
5.00% swing Lab. to C.
(1997: Lab. maj 21,423 (39.21%))

East Ham
Electorate 71,255
Turnout 37,277 (52.31%) **Lab hold**
*****Stephen Timms (Lab.) 27,241**
Peter Campbell (C.) 6,209
Ms Bridget Fox (LD) 2,600
Rod Finlayson (Soc. Lab.) 783
Ms Johinda Pandhal (UK Ind.) 444
Lab. maj 21,032 (56.42%)
3.95% swing C. to Lab.
(1997: Lab. maj 19,358 (48.53%))

Edmonton
Electorate 62,294
Turnout 34,774 (55.82%) **Lab Co-op hold**
Andy Love (Lab. Co-op.) 20,481

David Burrowes (C.) 10,709
Douglas Taylor (LD) 2,438
Miss Gwyneth Rolph (UK Ind.) 406
Erol Basarik (Reform) 344
Howard Medwell (Soc. All.) 296
Dr Ram Saxena (Ind.) 100
Lab Co-op maj 9,772 (28.10%)
0.97% swing Lab Co-op to C.
(1997: Lab. maj 13,472 (30.04%))

Eltham
Electorate 57,519
Turnout 33,792 (58.75%) **Lab hold**
Clive Efford (Lab.) 17,855
Mrs Sharon Massey (C.) 10,859
Martin Morris (LD) 4,121
Terry Jones (UK Ind.) 706
Andrew Graham (Ind.) 251
Lab. maj 6,996 (20.70%)
1.37% swing Lab. to C.
(1997: Lab. maj 10,182 (23.45%))

Enfield North
Electorate 67,756
Turnout 38,143 (56.29%) **Lab hold**
Ms Joan Ryan (Lab.) 17,888
Nick De Bois (C.) 15,597
Ms Hilary Leighter (LD) 3,355
Ramon Johns (BNP) 605
Brian Hall (UK Ind.) 247
Michael Akerman (ProLife) 241
Richard Course (Ind.) 210
Lab. maj 2,291 (6.01%)
4.15% swing Lab. to C.
(1997: Lab. maj 6,822 (14.31%))

Enfield Southgate
Electorate 66,418
Turnout 41,908 (63.10%) **Lab hold**
Stephen Twigg (Lab.) 21,727
John Flack (C.) 16,181
Wayne Hoban (LD) 2,935
Ms Elaine Graham-Leigh (Green) 662
Roy Freshwater (UK Ind.) 298
Andrew Malakouna (Ind.) 105
Lab. maj 5,546 (13.23%)
5.08% swing C. to Lab.
(1997: Lab. maj 1,433 (3.08%))

Erith & Thamesmead
Electorate 66,371
Turnout 33,351 (50.25%) **Lab hold**
John Austin (Lab.) 19,769
Mark Brooks (C.) 8,602
James Kempton (LD) 3,800

Hardev Dhillon (Soc. Lab.) 1,180
Lab. maj 11,167 (33.48%)
4.21% swing Lab. to C.
(1997: Lab. maj 17,424 (41.90%))

Feltham & Heston
Electorate 73,229
Turnout 36,177 (49.40%) **Lab Co-op hold**
Alan Keen (Lab. Co-op.) 21,406
Mrs Liz Mammatt (C.)8,749
Andy Darley (LD) 4,998
Surinder Cheema (Soc. Lab.) 651
Warwick Prachar (Ind.) 204
Asa Khaira (Ind.) 169
Lab Co-op maj 12,657 (34.99%)
1.11% swing C. to Lab. Co-op
(1997: Lab. maj 15,273 (32.76%))

Finchley & Golders Green
Electorate 76,175
Turnout 43,675 (57.34%) **Lab hold**
Rudi Vis (Lab.) 20,205
John Marshall (C.) 16,489
Ms Sarah Teather (LD) 5,266
Ms Miranda Dunn (Green) 1,385
John de Roeck (UK Ind.) 330
Lab. maj 3,716 (8.51%)
1.08% swing C. to Lab.
(1997: Lab. maj 3,189 (6.34%))

Greenwich & Woolwich
Electorate 62,530
Turnout 32,536 (52.03%) **Lab hold**
*Nick Raynsford (Lab.) 19,691
Richard Forsdyke (C.) 6,258
Russell Pyne (LD) 5,082
Stan Gain (UK Ind.) 672
Miss Kirstie Paton (Soc. All.) 481
Ms Margaret Sharkey (Soc. Lab.) 352
Lab. maj 13,433 (41.29%)
1.79% swing Lab. to C.
(1997: Lab. maj 18,128 (44.87%))

Hackney North & Stoke Newington
Electorate 60,444
Turnout 29,621 (49.01%) **Lab hold**
*Ms Diane Abbott (Lab.) 18,081
Mrs Pauline Dye (C.) 4,430
Ms Meral Ece (LD) 4,170
Chit Yen Chong (Green) 2,184
Sukant Chandan (Soc. Lab.) 756
Lab. maj 13,651 (46.09%)
0.74% swing Lab. to C.
(1997: Lab. maj 15,627 (47.57%))

General Election Results 93

Hackney South & Shoreditch
Electorate 63,990
Turnout 30,347 (47.42%) **Lab hold**
Brian Sedgemore (Lab.) 19,471
Tony Vickers (LD) 4,422
Paul White (C.) 4,180
Ms Cecilia Prosper (Soc. All.) 1,401
Saim Kokshal (Reform) 471
Ivan Beavis (Comm.) 259
William Rogers (WRP) 143
Lab. maj 15,049 (49.59%)
2.60% swing LD to Lab.
(1997: Lab. maj 14,980 (44.39%))

Hammersmith & Fulham
Electorate 79,302
Turnout 44,700 (56.37%) **Lab hold**
Iain Coleman (Lab.) 19,801
Matthew Carrington (C.) 17,786
Jon Burden (LD) 5,294
Daniel Lopez Dias (Green) 1,444
Gerald Roberts (UK Ind.) 375
Lab. maj 2,015 (4.51%)
1.30% swing Lab. to C.
(1997: Lab. maj 3,842 (7.11%))

Hampstead & Highgate
Electorate 65,309
Turnout 35,407 (54.21%) **Lab hold**
Ms Glenda Jackson (Lab.) 16,601
Andrew Mennear (C.) 8,725
Jonathan Simpson (LD) 7,273
Andrew Cornwell (Green) 1,654
Ms Helen Cooper (Soc. All.) 559
Thomas McDermott (UK Ind.) 316
Ms Sister XNunoftheabove (Ind.)144
Ms Mary Teale (ProLife) 92
Amos Klein (Ind.) 43
Lab. maj 7,876 (22.24%)
3.96% swing Lab. to C.
(1997: Lab. maj 13,284 (30.17%))

Harrow East
Electorate 81,575
Turnout 48,077 (58.94%) **Lab hold**
Tony McNulty (Lab.) 26,590
Peter Wilding (C.) 15,466
George Kershaw (LD) 6,021
Lab. maj 11,124 (23.14%)
3.02% swing C. to Lab.
(1997: Lab. maj 9,738 (17.09%))

Harrow West
Electorate 73,505
Turnout 46,648 (63.46%) **Lab hold**

94 Governed London

Gareth Thomas (Lab.) 23,142
Danny Finkelstein (C.) 16,986
Christopher Noyce (LD) 5,995
Peter Kefford (UK Ind.)525
Lab. maj 6,156 (13.20%)
5.42% swing C. to Lab.
(1997: Lab. maj 1,240 (2.36%))

Hayes & Harlington
Electorate 57,561
Turnout 32,403 (56.29%) **Lab hold**
John McDonnell (Lab.) 21,279
Robert McLean (C.) 7,813
Ms Nahid Boethe (LD) 1,958
Gary Burch (BNP) 705
Wally Kennedy (Soc. Alt.) 648
Lab. maj 13,466 (41.56%)
3.39% swing C. to Lab.
(1997: Lab. maj 14,291 (34.78%))

Hendon
Electorate 78,212
Turnout 40,851 (52.23%) **Lab hold**
Andrew Dismore (Lab.) 21,432
Richard Evans (C.) 14,015
Wayne Casey (LD) 4,724
Craig Crosbie (UK Ind.) 409
Ms Stella Taylor (WRP) 164
Michael Stewart (Prog Dem) 107
Lab. maj 7,417 (18.16%)
2.93% swing C. to Lab.
(1997: Lab. maj 6,155 (12.30%))

Holborn & St Pancras
Electorate 62,813
Turnout 31,129 (49.56%) **Lab hold**
Frank Dobson (Lab.) 16,770
Nathaniel Green (LD) 5,595
Mrs Roseanne Serelli (C.) 5,258
Rob Whitley (Green) 1,875
Ms Candy Udwin (Soc. All.) 971
Joti Brar (Soc. Lab.) 359
Magnus Nielsen (UK Ind.) 301
Lab. maj 11,175 (35.90%)
8.31% swing Lab. to LD
(1997: Lab. maj 17,903 (47.11%))

Hornchurch
Electorate 61,008
Turnout 35,557 (58.28%) **Lab hold**
*****John Cryer (Lab.) 16,514**
Robin Squire (C.) 15,032
Ms Sarah Lea (LD) 2,928
Lawrence Webb (UK Ind.) 893
Mr David Durant (Third) 190

Lab. maj 1,482 (4.17%)
4.38% swing Lab. to C.
(1997: Lab. maj 5,680 (12.93%))

Hornsey & Wood Green
Electorate 75,967
Turnout 44,063 (58.00%) **Lab hold**
Ms Barbara Roche (Lab.) 21,967
Ms Lynne Featherstone (LD) 11,353
Jason Hollands (C.) 6,921
Ms Jayne Forbes (Green) 2,228
Ms Louise Christian (Soc. All.) 1,106
Ms Ella Rule (Soc. Lab.) 294
Erdil Ataman (Reform) 194
Lab. maj 10,614 (24.09%)
13.21% swing Lab. to LD
(1997: Lab. maj 20,499 (39.82%))

Ilford North
Electorate 68,893
Turnout 40,234 (58.40%) **Lab hold**
Ms Linda Perham (Lab.) 18,428
Vivian Bendall (C.) 16,313
Gavin Stollar (LD) 4,717
Martin Levin (UK Ind.) 776
Lab. maj 2,115 (5.26%)
0.67% swing Lab. to C.
(1997: Lab. maj 3,224 (6.60%))

Ilford South
Electorate 76,025
Turnout 41,295 (54.32%) **Lab Co-op hold**
Mike Gapes (Lab. Co-op.) 24,619
Suresh Kuma (C.) 10,622
Ralph Scott (LD) 4,647
Harun Khan (UK Ind.) 1,407
Lab Co-op maj 13,997 (33.90%)
2.75% swing C. to Lab. Co-op
(1997: Lab. maj 14,200 (28.39%))

Islington North
Electorate 61,970
Turnout 30,216 (48.76%) **Lab hold**
Jeremy Corbyn (Lab.) 18,699
Ms Laura Willoughby (LD) 5,741
Neil Rands (C.) 3,249
Chris Ashby (Green) 1,876
Steve Cook (Soc. Lab.) 512
Emine Hassan (Reform) 139
Lab. maj 12,958 (42.88%)
6.38% swing Lab. to LD
(1997: Lab. maj 19,955 (55.64%))

General Election Results 95

Islington South & Finsbury
Electorate 59,515
Turnout 28,206 (47.39%) **Lab hold**
*****Chris Smith (Lab.) 15,217**
Keith Sharp (LD) 7,937
Mrs Nicky Morgan (C.) 3,860
Ms Janine Booth (Soc. All.) 817
Thomas McCarthy (Ind.) 267
Charles Thomson (Stuck) 108
Lab. maj 7,280 (25.81%)
7.71% swing Lab. to LD
(1997: Lab. maj 14,563 (41.24%))

Kensington & Chelsea
Electorate 62,007
Turnout 28,038 (45.22%) **C. hold**
Michael Portillo (C.) 15,270
Simon Stanley (Lab.) 6,499
Ms Kishwer Falkner (LD) 4,416
Ms Julia Stephenson (Green) 1,158
Nicholas Hockney (UK Ind.) 416
Ms Josephine Quintavalle (ProLife) 179
Ginger Crab (Wrestling) 100
C. maj 8,771 (31.28%)
2.81% swing Lab. to C.
(1999 Nov by-election: C. maj 6,706 (34.37%);
1997: C. maj 9,519 (25.66%))

Kingston & Surbiton
Electorate 72,687
Turnout 49,093 (67.54%) **LD hold**
Edward Davey (LD) 29,542
David Shaw (C.) 13,866
Phil Woodford (Lab.) 4,302
Chris Spruce (Green) 572
Miss Amy Burns (UK Ind.) 438
John Hayball (Soc. Lab.) 319
Jeremy Middleton (Unrep.)54
LD maj 15,676 (31.93%)
15.92% swing C. to LD
(1997: LD maj 56 (0.10%))

Lewisham Deptford
Electorate 62,869
Turnout 29,107 (46.30%) **Lab hold**
Joan Ruddock (Lab.) 18,915
Ms Cordelia McCartney (C.) 3,622
Andrew Wiseman (LD) 3,409
Darren Johnson (Green) 1,901
Ian Page (Soc. All.) 1,260
Lab. maj 15,293 (52.54%)
1.78% swing Lab. to C.
(1997: Lab. maj 18,878 (56.11%))

Lewisham East
Electorate 58,302
Turnout 30,040 (51.52%) **Lab hold**
Ms Bridget Prentice (Lab.) 16,116
David McInnes (C.) 7,157
David Buxton (LD) 4,937
Barry Roberts (BNP) 1,005
Ms Jean Kysow (Soc. All.) 464
Maurice Link (UK Ind.) 361
Lab. maj 8,959 (29.82%)
1.30% swing Lab. to C.
(1997: Lab. maj 12,127 (32.42%))

Lewisham West
Electorate 60,947
Turnout 30,815 (50.56%) **Lab hold**
Jim Dowd (Lab.) 18,816
Gary Johnson (C.) 6,896
Richard Thomas (LD) 4,146
Frederick Pearson (UK Ind.) 485
Nick Long (Ind.) 472
Lab. maj 11,920 (38.68%)
0.25% swing C. to Lab.
(1997: Lab. maj 14,337 (38.19%))

Leyton & Wanstead
Electorate 61,549
Turnout 33,718 (54.78%) **Lab hold**
Harry Cohen (Lab.) 19,558
Edward Heckels (C.) 6,654
Alex Wilcock (LD) 5,389
Ashley Gunstock (Green) 1,030
Ms Sally Labern (Soc. All.) 709
Michael Skaife D'Ingerthorp (UK Ind.) 378
Lab. maj 12,904 (38.27%)
0.17% swing Lab. to C.
(1997: Lab. maj 15,186 (38.62%))

Mitcham & Morden
Electorate 65,671
Turnout 37,961 (57.80%) **Lab hold**
*****Ms Siobhain McDonagh (Lab.) 22,936**
Harry Stokes (C.) 9,151
Nicholas Harris (LD) 3,820
Tom Walsh (Green) 926
John Tyndall (BNP) 642
Adrian Roberts (UK Ind.) 486
Lab. maj 13,785 (36.31%)
3.83% swing C. to Lab.
(1997: Lab. maj 13,741 (28.66%))

Old Bexley & Sidcup
Electorate 67,841
Turnout 42,133 (62.11%) **C. hold**
Derek Conway (C.) 19,130

96 Governed London

Jim Dickson (Lab.) 15,785
Ms Belinda Ford (LD) 5,792
Mrs Janice Cronin (UK Ind.) 1,426
C. maj 3,345 (7.94%)
0.49% swing Lab. to C.
(1997: C. maj 3,569 (6.95%))

Orpington
Electorate 74,423
Turnout 50,912 (68.4%) **Con hold**
***John Horam (C.) 22,334**
Chris Maines (LD) 22,065
Chris Purnell (Lab.) 5,517
John Youles (UK Ind.) 996
C. maj 269 (0.53%)
2.19% swing C. to LD
(1997: c. maj 2,952 (4.91%)

Poplar & Canning Town
Electorate 75,173
Turnout 34,108 (45.37%) **Lab hold**
Jim Fitzpatrick (Lab.) 20,862
Robert Marr (C.) 6,758
Ms Alexi Sugden (LD) 3,795
Paul Borg (BNP) 1,743
Dr Kambiz Boomla (Soc. All.) 950
Lab. maj 14,104 (41.35%)
3.41% swing Lab. to C.
(1997: Lab. maj 18,915 (48.17%))

Putney
Electorate 60,643
Turnout 34,254 (56.48%) **Lab hold**
***Tony Colman (Lab.) 15,911**
Michael Simpson (C.) 13,140
Tony Burrett (LD) 4,671
Ms Pat Wild (UK Ind.) 347
Ms Yvonne Windsor (ProLife) 185
Lab. maj 2,771 (8.09%)
0.66% swing C. to Lab.
(1997: Lab. maj 2,976 (6.76%))

Regent's Park & Kensington North
Electorate 75,886
Turnout 37,052 (48.83%) **Lab hold**
Ms Karen Buck (Lab.) 20,247
Peter Wilson (C.) 9,981
David Boyle (LD) 4,669
Dr Paul Miller (Green) 1,268
China Mieville (Soc. All.) 459
Alan Crisp (UK Ind.) 354
Ms Charlotte Regan (Ind.) 74
Lab. maj 10,266 (27.71%)
1.63% swing Lab. to C.
(1997: Lab. maj 14,657 (30.96%))

Richmond Park
Electorate 72,663
Turnout 49,151 (67.64%) **LD hold**
Dr Jenny Tonge (LD) 23,444
Tom Harris (C.) 18,480
Barry Langford (Lab.) 5,541
James Page (Green) 1,223
Peter St John Howe (UK Ind.) 348
Raymond Perrin (Ind.) 115
LD maj 4,964 (10.10%)
2.45% swing C. to LD
(1997: LD maj 2,951 (5.19%))

Romford
Electorate 59,893
Turnout 35,701 (59.61%) **Con gain**
Andrew Rosindell (C.) 18,931
*Ms Eileen Gordon (Lab.) 12,954
Nigel Meyer (LD) 2,869
Stephen Ward (UK Ind.) 533
Frank McAllister (BNP) 414
C. maj 5,977 (16.74%)
9.14% swing Lab. to C.
(1997: Lab. maj 649 (1.54%))

Ruislip-Northwood
Electorate 60,788
Turnout 37,141 (61.10%) **C. hold**
John Wilkinson (C.) 18,115
Ms Gillian Travis (Lab.) 10,578
Mike Cox (LD) 7,177
Graham Lee (Green) 724
Ian Edward (BNP) 547
C. maj 7,537 (20.29%)
1.46% swing Lab. to C.
(1997: C. maj 7,794 (17.38%))

Southwark North & Bermondsey
Electorate 73,527
Turnout 36,862 (50.13%) **LD hold**
Simon Hughes (LD) 20,991
Kingsley Abrams (Lab.) 11,359
Ewan Wallace (C.) 2,800
Ms Ruth Jenkins (Green) 752
Ms Lianne Shore (NF) 612
Rob McWhirter (UK Ind.) 271
John Davies (Ind.) 77
LD maj 9,632 (26.13%)
8.91% swing Lab. to LD
(1997: LD maj 3,387 (8.30%))

Streatham
Electorate 76,021
Turnout 36,998 (48.67%) **Lab hold**
Keith Hill (Lab.) 21,041
Roger O'Brien (LD) 6,771

General Election Results 97

Stephen Hocking (C.) 6,639
Mohammed Sajid (Green) 1,641
Greg Tucker (Soc. All.) 906
Lab. maj 14,270 (38.57%)
5.33% swing Lab. to LD
(1997: Lab. maj 18,423 (41.04%))

Sutton & Cheam
Electorate 63,648
Turnout 39,723 (62.41%) **LD hold**
Paul Burstow (LD) 19,382
Lady Olga Maitland (C.) 15,078
Ms Lisa Homan (Lab.) 5,263
LD maj 4,304 (10.84%)
3.19% swing C. to LD
(1997: LD maj 2,097 (4.45%))

Tooting
Electorate 68,447
Turnout 37,591 (54.92%) **Lab hold**
Tom Cox (Lab.) 20,332
Alexander Nicoll (C.) 9,932
Simon James (LD) 5,583
Matthew Ledbury (Green) 1,744
Lab. maj 10,400 (27.67%)
2.45% swing Lab. to C.
(1997: Lab. maj 15,011 (32.56%))

Tottenham
Electorate 65,567
Turnout 31,601 (48.20%) **Lab hold**
David Lammy (Lab.) 21,317
Ms Uma Fernandes (C.) 4,401
Ms Meher Khan (LD) 3,008
Peter Budge (Green) 1,443
Weyman Bennett (Soc. All.) 1,162
Unver Shefki (Reform) 270
Lab. maj 16,916 (53.53%)
0.03% swing Lab. to C.
(2000 Jun by-election: Lab. maj 5,646 (34.39%);
1997: Lab. maj 20,200 (53.58%))

Twickenham
Electorate 74,135
Turnout 49,938 (67.36%) **LD hold**
Dr Vincent Cable (LD) 24,344
Nick Longworth (C.) 16,689
Dean Rogers (Lab.) 6,903
Ms Judy Maciejowska (Green) 1,423
Ray Hollebone (UK Ind.) 579
LD maj 7,655 (15.33%)
3.98% swing C. to LD
(1997: LD maj 4,281 (7.36%))

Upminster
Electorate 56,829
Turnout 33,851 (59.57%) **Con gain**
Mrs Angela Watkinson (C.) 15,410
Keith Darvill (Lab.) 14,169
Peter Truesdale (LD) 3,183
Terry Murray (UK Ind.) 1,089
C. maj 1,241 (3.67%)
5.18% swing Lab. to C.
(1997: Lab. maj 2,770 (6.70%))

Uxbridge
Electorate 58,066
Turnout 33,418 (57.55%) **C. hold**
John Randall (C.) 15,751
David Salisbury-Jones (Lab.) 13,653
Ms Catherine Royce (LD) 3,426
Paul Cannons (UK Ind.) 588
C. maj 2,098 (6.28%)
2.26% swing Lab. to C.
(1997 Jul by-election: C. maj 3,766 (11.82%);
1997: C. maj 724 (1.75%))

Vauxhall
Electorate 74,474
Turnout 33,392 (44.84%) **Lab hold**
Ms Kate Hoey (Lab.) 19,738
Anthony Bottrall (LD) 6,720
Gareth Compton (C.) 4,489
Shane Collins (Green) 1,485
Ms Theresa Bennett (Soc. All.) 853
Martin Boyd (Ind.) 107
Lab. maj 13,018 (38.99%)
4.39% swing Lab. to LD
(1997: Lab. maj 18,660 (47.77%))

Walthamstow
Electorate 64,403
Turnout 34,429 (53.46%) **Lab hold**
Neil Gerrard (Lab.) 21,402
Nick Boys Smith (C.) 6,221
Peter Dunphy (LD) 5,024
Simon Donovan (Soc. Alt.) 806
William Phillips (BNP) 389
Ms Gerda Mayer (UK Ind.) 298
Ms Barbara Duffy (ProLife) 289
Lab. maj 15,181 (44.09%)
0.64% swing C. to Lab.
(1997: Lab. maj 17,149 (42.81%))

98 Governed London

West Ham
Electorate 59,828
Turnout 29,273 (48.93%) **Lab hold**
Tony Banks (Lab.) 20,449
Syed Kamall (C.) 4,804
Paul Fox (LD) 2,166
Ms Jackie Chandler Oatts (Green) 1,197
Gerard Batten (UK Ind.) 657
Lab. maj 15,645 (53.45%)
2.24% swing Lab. to C.
(1997: Lab. maj 19,494 (57.92%))

Wimbledon
Electorate 63,930
Turnout 41,109 (64.30%) **Lab hold**
Roger Casale (Lab.) 18,806
Stephen Hammond (C.) 15,062
Martin Pierce (LD) 5,341
Rajeev Thacker (Green) 1,007
Roger Glencross (CPA) 479
Ms Mariana Bell (UK Ind.) 414
Lab. maj 3,744 (9.11%)
1.47% swing C. to Lab.
(1997: Lab. maj 2,980 (6.17%))

ABBREVIATIONS

C.—Conservative
Lab.—Labour
Lab. Co-op.—Labour and Co-operative
LD—Liberal Democrat
PC—Plaid Cymru
SNP—Scottish National Party
Green—Green Party
UUP—Ulster Unionist Party
DUP—Democratic Unionist Party
SDLP—Social Democratic and Labour Party
SF—Sinn Fein
Alliance—Alliance
WP—Workers' Party
AL—Asian League
Anti-Corrupt—Anti-Corruption Forum
BNP—British National Party
Bean—New Millennium Bean
CPA—Christian Peoples Alliance
Ch. D.—Christian Democrat
Choice—People's Choice
Comm.—Communist Party
Community Independent—Community Candidate Empowering Change
Country—Countryside Party
Customer Direct—Customer Service Party
DefWelfare—Defend The Welfare State Against Blairism
Elvis—Church of the Militant Elvis Party

Ext. Club—Club Extinction Club
FDP—Fancy Dress Party
FP—Freedom Party
Grey—Grey Party
IOW—Isle of Wight Party
Ind.—Independent
Ind. UU—Independent United Unionist
Ind. Vote—Independent—Vote for Yourself Party
JLDP—John Lillburne Democratic Party
JP—Justice Party
KHHC—Kidderminster Hospital and Health Concern
LCA—Legalise Cannabis Alliance
LP—Liberated Party
Left All—Left Alliance
Lib.—Liberal
Loony—Monster Raving Loony Party
Low Excise—Lower Excise Duty Party
Marxist—Marxist Party
Meb. Ker.—Mebyon Kernow
Muslim—Muslim Party
NBP—New Britain Party
NF—National Front
NI Unionist—Northern Ireland Unionist
PF—Pathfinders
PJP—People's Justice Party
PUP—Progressive Unionist Party
Pacifist—Pacifist for Peace, Justice, Cooperation, Environment
Pensioner—Pensioner Coalition
Pro Euro C—Pro Euro Conservative Party
ProLife—ProLife Alliance
Prog Dem—Progress Democratic Party Members Decide Policy
Qari—Qari
R & R Loony—Rock & Roll Loony Party
RP—Rate Payer
Ref. UK—Reform UK
Reform—Reform 2000
Res. Motor—Residents and Motorists of Great Britain
SSP—Scottish Socialist Party
Scot. Ref.—Scottish Freedom Referendum Party
Scot. U.—Scottish Unionist
Soc.—Socialist Party
Soc. Alt.—Socialist Alternative Party
Soc. Lab.—Socialist Labour Party
Socialist—Socialist
Speaker—The Speaker
Stuck—Stuckist

Sunrise—Chairman of Sunrise Radio
Tatton—Tatton Group Independent
Third—Third Way
Truth—Truth Party
UK Ind.—UK Independence Party
UKU—United Kingdom Unionist
Unrep.—Unrepresented People's Party
WFLOE—Women for Life on Earth
WRP—Workers' Revolutionary Party
Wessex Reg.—Wessex Regionalist
Women's Co.—Women's Coalition
Wrestling—Jam Wrestling Party

EUROPEAN PARLIAMENT

European Parliament elections take place at five-yearly intervals; the first direct elections to the Parliament were held in 1979. In mainland Britain MEPs were elected in all constituencies on a first-past-the-post basis until the elections of June 1999; in Northern Ireland three MEPs have been elected by the single transferable vote system of proportional representation since 1979. From 1979 to 1994 the number of seats held by the UK in the European Parliament was 81. At the June 1994 election the number of seats increased to 87 (England 71, Wales 5, Scotland, 8, Northern Ireland 3). At the European Parliament elections held on 10 June 1999, all British MEPs were elected under a 'closed-list' regional system of proportional representation, with England being divided into nine regions (London being one region) and Scotland and Wales each constituting a region. Parties submitted a list of candidates for each region in their own order of preference. Voters voted for a party or an independent candidate, and the first seat in each region was allocated to the party or candidate with the highest number of votes. The rest of the seats in each region were then allocated broadly in proportion to each party's share of the vote. Each region returned the following number of members: East Midlands, 6; Eastern, 8; London, 10; North East, 4; North West, 10; South East, 11; South West, 7; West Midlands, 8; Yorkshire and the Humber, 7; Wales, 5; Scotland, 8.

If a vacancy occurs due to the resignation or death of and MEP, the vacancy is filled by the next available person on that party's list. If an independent MEP resigns or dies, a by-election is held. Where an MEP leaves the party on whose list he/she was elected, there is no requirement to resign and he/she can remain in office until the next general election.

British subjects and citizens of the Irish Republic are eligible for election to the European Parliament provided they are 21 or over and not subject to disqualification. Since 1994, nationals of member states of the European Union have had the right to vote in elections to the European Parliament in the UK as long as they are entered on the electoral register.

MEPs currently receive a salary from the parliaments or governments of their respective member states, set at the level of the national parliamentary salary and subject to national taxation rules. A proposal that all MEPs should be paid the same rate of salary out of the EU budget, and subject to the EC tax rate, was under

100 Governed London

negotiation between the European Parliament and the Council of Ministers at the time of going to press.

Press Office: 2 Queen Anne's Gate, London SW1H 9AA (Tel: 020-7227 4300; Fax: 020-7227 4302; Email: eplondon@europarl.eu.int; Web: www.europarl.org.uk).

LONDON REGION
E.4,940,493 T.23.10%
Lab.	399,466 (35.00%)
C.	372,989 (32.68%)
LD	133,058 (11.66%)
Green	87,545 (7.67%)
UK Ind.	61,741 (5.41%)
Soc. Lab.	19,632 (1.72%)
BNP	17,960 (1.57%)
Lib.	16,951 (1.49%)
Pro Euro C.	16,383 (1.44%)
AHRPE	4,851 (0.43%)
Anti VAT	2,596 (0.23%)
Hum.	2,586 (0.23%)
Hemp	2,358 (0.21%)
NLP	2,263 (0.20%)
WW	846 (0.07%)

Lab. majority: 26,477
(June 1994, Lab. maj. 346,850)

LONDON MEMBERS
Balfe, Richard A. (b. 1944), Lab., London
Bethell, The Lord (b. 1938), C., London
Bowis, John C., obe (b. 1945), C., London
Evans, Robert J. E. (b. 1956), Lab., London
Honeyball, Mrs Mary (b. 1952) Lab., London
Lambert, Ms Jean D. (b. 1950), Green, London
Ludford, The Baroness (b. 1951), LD, London
Moraes, Claude (b. 1965), Lab., London
Tannock, Dr Charles (b. 1957), C., London
Villiers, Ms Theresa (b. 1968), C., London

GOVERNMENT DEPARTMENTS AND PUBLIC OFFICES

In this section you will find information on the Cabinet, Central Government departments and their Executive Agencies. Although these departments and agencies have remits extending further than London we feel that they merit inclusion in order to comprehensively convey the structure of governance in London on a local and national level.

The Civil Service
Under the Next Steps programme, launched in 1988, many semi-autonomous executive agencies have been established to carry out much of the work of the Civil Service. Executive agencies operate within a framework set by the responsible minister which specifies policies, objectives and available resources. All executive agencies are set annual performance targets by their minister. Each agency has a chief executive, who is responsible for the day-to-day operations of the agency and who is accountable to the minister for the use of resources and for meeting the agency's targets. The minister accounts to Parliament for the work of the agency. Nearly 60 per cent of civil servants now work in executive agencies. Customs and Excise, the Inland Revenue, the Crown Prosecution Service and the Serious Fraud Office, which employ a further 17 per cent of civil servants, also operate on 'Next Steps' lines. In January 1999 there were about 463,700 permanent civil servants.

The Senior Civil Service was created in 1996 and comprises about 3,000 staff from Permanent Secretary to the former Grade 5 level, including all agency chief executives. All government departments and executive agencies are now responsible for their own pay and grading systems for civil servants outside the Senior Civil Service.

THE CABINET as at 8 June 2001
Prime Minister, First Lord of the Treasury and Minister for the Civil Service: The Rt. Hon. Anthony (Tony) Blair, MP, since May 1997
Deputy Prime Minister and First Secretary of State: The Rt. Hon. John Prescott, MP, since May 1997
Chancellor of the Exchequer: The Rt. Hon. Gordon Brown, MP, since May 1997
Secretary of State for Foreign and Commonwealth Affairs: The Rt. Hon Jack Straw, MP, since June 2001

Cabinet, Ministers of State   101

Lord Chancellor: The Lord Irvine of Lairg, PC, QC, since May 1997

Secretary of State for the Home Department: The Rt. Hon. David Blunkett, MP, since June 2001

Secretary of State for Education and Skills: The Rt. Hon. Estelle Morris, MP, since June 2001

President of the Council and Leader of the House of Commons: The Rt. Hon. Robin Cook, MP, since June 2001

Minister for the Cabinet Office and Chancellor of the Duchy of Lancaster: The Rt. Hon. Lord MacDonald of Tradeston, CBE

Secretary of State for Scotland: The Rt. Hon. Helen Liddell, MP, since June 2001

Secretary of State for Defence: The Rt. Hon. Geoff Hoon, MP, since October 1999

Secretary of State for Health: The Rt. Hon. Alan Milburn, MP, since October 1999

Parliamentary Secretary to the Treasury (Chief Whip): The Rt. Hon. Hilary Armstrong, MP, since June 2001

Secretary of State for Culture, Media and Sport: The Rt. Hon. Tessa Jowell, MP, since June 2001

Secretary of State for Northern Ireland: The Rt. Hon. Dr John Reid, MP, since June 2001

Secretary of State for Wales: The Rt. Hon. Paul Murphy, MP, since July 1999

Secretary of State for International Development: The Rt. Hon. Clare Short, MP, since May 1997

Secretary of State for Work and Pensions: The Rt. Hon. Alistair Darling, MP, since July 1998

Secretary of State for Environment, Food and Rural Affairs: The Rt. Hon. Margaret Beckett, MP, since June 2001

Leader of the House of Lords: The Rt. Hon. The Lord Williams of Mostyn QC, since June 2001

Secretary of State for Trade and Industry and Women: The Rt. Hon. Patricia Hewitt, MP, since June 2001

Chief Secretary to the Treasury: The Rt. Hon. Andrew Smith, MP, since October 1999

The Minister of State at the Department of Transport, Local Government and the Regions with responsibility for Transport, and the Government Chief Whip in the House of Lords will attend Cabinet meetings although they are not members of the Cabinet.

* Appointed as Lord Privy Seal

MINISTERS OF STATE

Environment, Food and Rural Affairs
The Rt. Hon. Michael Meacher, MP (Environment)
The Rt. Hon. Alun Michael, MP (Rural Affairs)

Cabinet Office
Ms Barbara Roche, MP
Ms Sally Morgan, MP

Culture and Media
The Rt. Hon. Richard Caborn, MP (Sport)
The Rt. Hon. Baroness Blackstone (Arts)

Defence
The Rt. Hon. Adam Ingram, MP (Armed Forces)
Lord Bach (Defence Procurement)

Education and Skills
Stephen Timms, MP, (Schools)
Mrs Margaret Hodge, MP, MBE (Universities)

Transport, Local Government and the Regions
The Rt. Hon. John Spellar, MP (Transport)
The Rt. Hon. Nick Raynsford, MP (Local Government)
Lord Falconer of Thornton, QC (Housing and Planning)

Foreign and Commonwealth Office
Peter Hain, MP (Minister for Europe)
The Rt. Hon. Baroness Symons of Vernham Dean (Trade and FCO)

Health
John Hutton, MP (NHS and Delivery)
Ms Jacqui Smith, MP (Social Care and Mental Health)

Home Office
The Rt. Hon. John Denham, MP, (Police, Courts and Drugs)
The Rt. Hon. Keith Bradley, MP (Prisons)
The Rt. Hon. Jeff Rocker (Asylum and Immigration)

Northern Ireland Office
Ms Jane Kennedy, MP

Scotland Office
George Foulkes, MP

Trade and Industry
Douglas Alexander, MP (E-Commerce and Competitiveness)
The Rt. Hon. Baroness Symons of Vernham Dean (Trade and FCO)
Brian Wilson, MP (Industry and Energy)
Alan Johnson, MP (Employment and Regions)

Treasury
Dawn Primarolo, MP (Paymaster-General)
The Rt. Hon. Paul Boateng, MP (Financial Secretary)
Ms Ruth Kelly, MP (Economic Secretary)

Works and Pensions
The Rt. Hon. Nick Brown, MP (Work)
The Rt. Hon. Ian McCartney, MP (Pensions)

UNDER-SECRETARIES OF STATE
Cabinet: Christopher Leslie, MP

Culture, Media and Sport: Dr Kim Howells, MP

Defence: Dr Lewis Moonie, MP (Veterans)

Education and Skills: Baroness Ashton of Upholland (Early Years and Skill Standards); Ivan Lewis, MP, (Young People and Learning); John Healey, (Adult Skills) MP

Environment, Food and Rural Affairs: Elliot Morley MP (Animal Health and Welfare and Fisheries; The Lord Whitty (Food and Farming)

Foreign and Commonwealth Office: Ben Bradshaw, MP; Baroness Amos; Dr Denis Macshane, MP

Health: Ms Hazel Blears, MP; The Lord Hunt of King's Heath, OBE; Yvette Cooper, MP

Home Office: Ms Bev Hughes, MP (Community and Custodial Sentences); Robert Ainsworth, MP (Anti-Drugs Co-ordination and Organised Crime); Ms Angela Eagle, MP (Europe, Community and Race)

International Development: Hilary Benn, MP

Lord Chancellor's Department: Baroness Scotland of Asthal, QC; Michael Wills, MP; Ms Rosie Winterton, MP

Northern Ireland Office: Des Browne, MP

Works and Pensions: The Baroness Hollis of Heigham, (Child and the Family); Marie Eagle, MP (Disabled People); Malcolm Wicks, MP (Work)

Trade and Industry: Lord Sainsbury of Turville' (Science and Innovation); Ms Melanie Johnson' (Competition, Consumers and Markets), MP; Nigel Griffiths§ (Small Business), MP

Transport, Local Government and the Regions: David Jamieson, MP (Transport); Ms Sally Keeble, MP (Housing, Planning and Regeneration); Dr Alan Whitehead, MP (Local Government and the Regions)

Welsh Office: Don Touhig, MP

§Unpaid

Government Whips – House of Lords
Captain of the Honourable Corps of Gentlemen-at-Arms (Chief Whip): The Rt. Hon. The Lord Carter
Captain of The Queen's Bodyguard of the Yeoman of the Guard (Deputy Chief Whip): The Lord McIntosh of Haringey
Lords-in-Waiting: Lord Davies of Oldham; Bruce Grocott; Lord Filkin, CBE; The Lord Bassam of Brighton
Baronesses-in-Waiting: The Baroness Farrington of Ribbleton;

Government Whips – House of Commons
Parliamentary Secretary to the Treasury (Chief Whip): The Rt. Hon. Hilary Armstrong, MP
Treasurer of HM Household (Deputy Chief Whip): Keith Hill, MP
Comptroller of HM Household: Thomas McAvoy, MP
Vice-Chamberlain of HM Household: Graham Sutcliffe, MP
Lords Commissioners: Mrs Anne McGuire, MP; John Heppell, MP; Tony McNulty, MP; Nick Ainger, MP; Graham Stringer, MP
Assistant Whips: Ian Pearson, MP; Ms Angela Smith, MP; Ivor Caplin, MP; Ms Karen Buck, MP; Fraser Kemp, MP; Philip Woolas, MP; Dan Norris; MP

Law Officers
Attorney-General: Lord Goldsmith, QC, since June 2001
Lord Advocate: Colin Boyd, QC, since February 2000
Solicitor-General: The Rt. Hon. Harriet Harman, MP, since June 2001
Solicitor-General for Scotland: Neil Davidson, QC, February 2000
Advocate-General for Scotland: Dr Lynda Clark, QC, MP, since May 1999

*MINISTRY OF AGRICULTURE, FISHERIES AND FOOD

Nobel House, 17 Smith Square, London SW1P 3JR (Tel: 020-7238 3000; Fax: 020-7238 6591; Email: helpline@inf.maff.gov.uk; Web: www.maff.gov.uk/maffhome.htm).

The Ministry of Agriculture, Fisheries and Food is responsible for government policies on agriculture, horticulture and fisheries in England. The Ministry is responsible for negotiations in the EU on the common agricultural and fisheries policies, and for single European market questions relating to its responsibilities. Its remit also includes international agricultural and food trade policy.

The Ministry exercises responsibilities for the protection and enhancement of the countryside and the marine environment, for flood defence and for other rural issues. It is the licensing authority for veterinary medicines and the registration authority for pesticides. It administers policies relating to the control of animal, plant and fish diseases. It provides scientific, technical and professional services and advice to farmers, growers and ancillary industries, and it commissions research to assist in the formulation and assessment of policy and to underpin applied research and development work done by industry. Responsibility for food safety and standards was transferred to the new Food Standards Agency in April 2000. From April 2001, following a regional service reorganisation, the Farming and Rural Conservation Agency ceased to be an executive agency and reverted to MAFF as part of the Rural Development Service in MAFF's Environment and Rural Development Group. Staff in Wales joined the National Assembly for Wales Agriculture Department.

*Following the General Election, the name of this department became: The Department of Environment, Food and Rural Affairs.

GROUPS/UNITS/DIRECTORATES/DIVISIONS

Establishments Group; Establishments and Office Services Division; Information Technology Directorate; Communications Directorate; Agency Ownership Unit; Finance Department; Financial Policy Division; Procurement and Contracts Division; Audit, Consultancy and Management Services; Resource Management Division; Resource Management Strategy Unit; Business Planning Unit; Legal Department; Investigation Unit; Economics and Statistics; Statistics Division; Chief Scientist's Group; Fisheries Department; Agricultural Crops and Commodities Directorate; European Union and International Policy; Agriculture Group; Food Industry, Competitiveness and Consumers; Plant Variety Rights Office and Seeds Division; Food Safety and Environment Group; Environment and Rural Development Group; Animal Health Group; Chief Veterinary Officer's Group; Veterinary Field Service.

EXECUTIVE AGENCIES

Central Science Laboratory
Sand Hutton, York YO41 1LZ
(Tel: 01904-462000; Fax: 01904-462111;
Email: science@csl.gov.uk;
Web: www.csl.gov.uk).

The Agency provides MAFF with technical support and policy advice on the protection and quality of the food supply and on related environmental issues.

Centre for Environment, Fisheries and Aquaculture Science
Pakefield Road, Lowestoft, Suffolk NR33 0HT
(Tel: 01502-562244; Fax: 01502-513865;
Web: www.cefas.co.uk).

The Agency, established in April 1997, provides research and consultancy services in fisheries science and management, aquaculture, fish health and hygiene, environmental impact assessment, and environmental quality assessment.

Meat Hygiene Service
Foss House, Kings Pool, 1—2 Peasholme Green, York YO1 7PX (Tel: 01904-455501; Fax: 01904-455502; Web: www.foodstandards.gov.uk).

The Agency was launched in April 1995. It protects public health and promotes animal welfare through veterinary supervision and meat inspection in licensed fresh meat establishments.

Pesticides Safety Directorate
Mallard House, Kings Pool, 3 Peasholme Green, York YO1 7PX (Tel: 01904-640500; Fax: 01904-455733;
Email: p.s.d.information@psd.maff.gsi.gov.uk;
Web: www.pesticides.gov.uk).

The Pesticides Safety Directorate is responsible for the evaluation and approval of pesticides and the development of policies relating to them, in order to protect consumers, users and the environment.

Veterinary Laboratories Agency
Woodham Lane, New Haw, Addlestone, Surrey KT15 3NB (Tel: 01932-341111; Fax: 01932-347046; enquiries@vla.maff.gov.uk;
Web: www.maff.gov.uk/vla)

104 Governed London

The Veterinary Laboratories Agency provides scientific and technical expertise in animal health.

Veterinary Medicines Directorate
Woodham Lane, New Haw, Addlestone, Surrey KT15 3LS (Tel: 01932-336911; Fax: 01932-336618).

The Veterinary Medicines Directorate is responsible for all aspects of the authorisation and control of veterinary medicines, including post-authorisation surveillance of residues in meat and animal products, and the provision of policy advice to ministers.

THE CABINET OFFICE

70 Whitehall, London SW1A 2AS (Tel: 020-7270 3000; Web: www.cabinet-office.gov.uk).

The Cabinet Office comprises the Secretariat, which supports Ministers collectively in the conduct of Cabinet business; and units responsible for modernising government and helping to improve the quality, coherence and responsiveness of public services. It is also responsible for Senior Civil Service and public appointments. The Cabinet Office supports the Prime Minister in his capacity as Minister for the Civil Service, with responsibility for day-to-day supervision delegated to the Minister for the Cabinet Office.

PRIME MINISTER'S OFFICE

10 Downing Street, London SW1A 2AA (Tel: 020-7270 3000; Fax: 020-7925 0918; Web: www.number-10.gov.uk).

Secretariat: Economic and Domestic Secretariat; Defence and Overseas Affairs Secretariat; Intelligence Co-ordination Group; European Secretariat; Constitution Secretariat; Central Secretariat; Ceremonial Branch; Public Service Delivery; Central IT Unit; Regulatory Impact Unit; Modernising Government

EXECUTIVE AGENCIES

Civil Service College
11 Belgrave Road, London SW1V 1RB (Tel: 020-7834 6644; Fax: 01344-634451).

The College provides training in management and professional skills for the public and private sectors.

Government Car and Despatch Agency
46 Ponton Road, London SW8 5AX (Tel: 020-7217 3839; Fax: 020-7217 3840; Email: info@gcda.gov.uk; Web: www.gcda.gov.uk).

The Agency provides secure transport and document transfers between government departments.

COI COMMUNICATIONS

Hercules Road, London SE1 7DU (Tel: 020-7928 2345; Fax: 020-7928 5037; Email: enquiries@coi.gov.uk; Web: www.coi.gov.uk).

COI Communications (COI) is a government department which offers consultancy, procurement and project management services to central government for publicity. Administrative responsibility for the COI rests with the Minister for the Cabinet Office.

DEPARTMENT FOR CULTURE, MEDIA AND SPORT

2-4 Cockspur Street, London SW1Y 5DH (Tel: 020-7211 6200; Fax: 020-7211 6032; Email: enquiries@culture.gov.uk; Web: www.culture.gov.uk).

The Department for Culture, Media and Sport was established in April 1992 as the Department of National Heritage and is responsible for government policy relating to the arts, broadcasting, the media, museums and galleries, libraries, sport and recreation, historic buildings and ancient monuments, tourism, and the creative industries. It is also responsible for policy on the National Lottery and the Millennium.

GROUPS/UNITS/DIRECTORATES/ DIVISIONS

Museums, Galleries, Libraries and Heritage Group; Strategy and Communication Group; Corporate Services Group; Creative Industries, Media and Broadcasting Group; Regions, Tourism, Millennium and International Group; Education, Training, Arts and Sport

EXECUTIVE AGENCY

Royal Parks Agency
The Old Police House, Hyde Park, London W2 2UH (Tel: 020-7298 2000; Fax: 020-7298 2005).

Government Departments 105

The Royal Parks Agency is responsible for maintaining and developing the Royal Parks.

MINISTRY OF DEFENCE

Main Building, Whitehall, London SW1A 2HB (Tel 020-7218 9000; Public Enquiry Office: Tel 0870 607 4455; Email: public@ministers.mod.uk; Web www.mod.uk).

*DEPARTMENT FOR EDUCATION AND EMPLOYMENT

Sanctuary Buildings, Great Smith Street, London SW1P 3BT (Tel: 0870-001 2345; Fax: 020-7925 6000; Email: info@dfee.gov.uk; Web: www.dfee.gov.uk).

Caxton House, Tothill Street, London SW1H 9NF (Tel: 020-7273 3000; Fax: 020-7273 5124)

The Department for Education and Employment was formed in July 1995, bringing together the functions of the former Department for Education with the training and labour market functions of the former Employment Department Group. It includes an executive agency, the Employment Service. The Department aims to support economic growth and improve the nation's competitiveness and quality of life by raising standards of educational achievement and skill and by promoting an efficient and flexible labour market.

*Following the General Election, the name of this department became the Department for Education and Skills.

GROUPS/UNITS/DIRECTORATES/DIVISIONS

Employment, Lifelong Learning and International Directorate; Further and Higher Education and Youth Training Directorate; Legal Adviser's Office; Operations Directorate; Personnel and Support Services Directorate; Schools Directorate; Strategy and Communications Directorate

EXECUTIVE AGENCY

The Employment Service
Caxton House, Tothill Street, London SW1H 9NA (Tel: 020-7273 6060; Fax: 020-7273 6099)

The aim of the Employment Service is to help people without jobs to find work and employers to fill their vacancies.

*DEPARTMENT OF THE ENVIRONMENT, TRANSPORT AND THE REGIONS

Eland House, Bressenden Place, London SW1E 5DU.

Great Minster House, 76 Marsham Street, London SW1P 4DR.

Ashdown House, 123 Victoria Street, London SW1E 6DE (Tel: 020-7944 3000; Web: www.detr.gov.uk).

The Department of the Environment, Transport and the Regions (DETR) was formed in June 1997 by the merger of the Department of the Environment and the Department of Transport. It is responsible for policies relating to the environment, housing, transport services, rural affairs, planning, local government, regional development, regeneration, the construction industry and health and safety.

The Department's ministers are based at Eland House.

*Following the General Election, the name of this department became the Department of Transport, Local Government and Regions.

EXECUTIVE AGENCIES

Driver and Vehicle Licensing Agency
Longview Road, Morriston, Swansea SA6 7JL (Drivers Tel: 0870 240 0009; Fax: 01792 783071; Email: drivers.dvla.gtnet.gov.uk; Vehicles Tel: 0870 240 0010; Fax: 01792 782793; Email: vehicles.dvla@gtnet.gov.uk).

The Agency's responsibilities are the issuing of driving licences, the registration and licensing of vehicles in Great Britain, and the collection and enforcement of vehicle excise duty in the UK. The Agency also offers for sale attractive registration marks through the Sale of Marks scheme.

Driving Standards Agency
Stanley House, Talbot Street, Nottingham NG1 5GU (Tel: 0115-901 2500; Web: www.driving-tests.co.uk)

106 Governed London

The Agency is responsible for carrying out theory and practical driving tests for car drivers, motorcyclists, bus and lorry drivers and for maintaining the registers of Approved Driving Instructors and Large Goods Vehicle Instructors, as well as supervising Compulsory Basic Training (CBT) for learner motorcyclists. There are five area offices, which manage over 430 practical test centres across Britain.

Highways Agency
St. Christopher House, Southwark Street, London SE1 0TE (Tel: 0645-556575; Fax: 020-7921 4899; Email: ha-info@highways.gov.uk; Web: www.highways.gov.uk).

The Agency is responsible for the operation, management and maintenance of the motorway and trunk road network and for road construction and improvement.

Maritime and Coastguard Agency
Spring Place, 105 Commercial Road, Southampton SO15 1EG (Tel: 023-8032 9100; Fax: 023-8032 9105; Email: mcamic@mcga.gov.uk; Web: www.mcagency.gov.uk).

The Agency was formed in April 1998 by the merger of the Coastguard Agency and the Marine Safety Agency. Its role is to develop, promote and enforce high standards of marine safety; to minimise loss of life amongst seafarers and coastal users; and to minimise pollution from ships of the sea and coastline.

Planning Inspectorate
Temple Quay House, 2 The Square, Temple Quay, Bristol BS1 6PN (Tel: 0117 327 8000; Email: enquiries@planning-inspectorate.gsi.gov.uk; Web: www.planning-inspectorate.gov.uk).

The Inspectorate is responsible for casework involving planning, housing, roads, environmental and related legislation. It is a joint executive agency of the Department of the Environment, Transport and the Regions and the National Assembly for Wales.

Queen Elizabeth II Conference Centre
Broad Sanctuary, London SW1P 3EE (Tel: 020-7222 5000; Fax: 020-7798 4200; Email: info@qeiicc.co.uk; Web: www.qeiicc.co.uk).

The Centre provides conference and banqueting facilities for both private sector and government use.

Vehicle Certification Agency
1 Eastgate Office Centre, Eastgate Road, Bristol BS5 6XX (Tel: 0117-951 5151; Fax: 0117-952 4103; Email enquiries@vca.gov.uk; Web: www.vca.gov.uk).

The Agency tests and certificates vehicles to UK and international standards.

Vehicle Inspectorate
Berkeley House, Croydon Street, Bristol BS5 0DA (Tel: 0117-954 3200; Fax: 0117-954 3212; Email: enquiries@via.gov.uk; Web: www.via.gov.uk).

The Agency carries out annual testing and inspection of heavy goods and other vehicles and administers the MOT testing scheme.

GOVERNMENT OFFICES FOR THE REGIONS

Regional Co-ordination Unit, 2nd Riverwalk House, 157-161 Millbank, London SW1P 4RR (Tel: 020-7217 3595; Fax: 020-7217 3590; Email: rcusecretariatenquiries@go-regions.gsi.gov.uk; Web: www.rcu.gov.uk).

The Government Offices for the Regions (GOs) were established in 1994 to bring together the English regional services for four departments – Environment, Transport, Education and Employment and Trade and Industry. The merger between Environment and Transport in 1997 reduced this to three parent departments. The role of the GOs is to work with regional partners and local people to maximise competitiveness and prosperity in the regions, and to support integrated policies for an inclusive society. The Regional Co-ordination Unit oversees the Government Offices for the Regions and provides a Whitehall centre of operations for the GO network. There are nine GOs: North East; North West; Yorkshire and Humber; West Midlands; East Midlands' East of England; South West; South East; and London.

Government Departments 107

London
Riverwalk House, 157—161 Millbank, London SW1P 4RR (Tel: 020-7217 3456; Fax: 020-7217 3450).

FOREIGN AND COMMONWEALTH OFFICE

Downing Street West, London SW1A 2AL (Tel: 020-7270 3000; Web: www.fco.gov.uk). King Charles Street, London SW1A 2AH (Tel: 020 7270 1500)

The Foreign and Commonwealth Office provides, mainly through diplomatic missions, the means of communication between the British Government and other governments and international governmental organisations for the discussion and negotiation of all matters falling within the field of international relations. It is responsible for alerting the Government to the implications of developments overseas; for protecting British interests overseas; for protecting British citizens abroad; for explaining British policies to, and cultivating friendly relations with, governments overseas; and for the discharge of British responsibilities to the UK overseas territories.

EXECUTIVE AGENCY
Wilton Park Conference Centre
Wiston House, Steyning, W. Sussex BN44 3DZ (Tel: 01903-815020; Fax: 01903-816373; Email: reception@wiltonpark.org.uk; Web: www.wiltonpark.org.uk).

The Centre organises international affairs conferences and is hired out to government departments and commercial users.

DEPARTMENT OF HEALTH

Richmond House, 79 Whitehall, London SW1A 2NL (Tel: 020-7210 3000; Web: www.open.gov.uk/doh/dhhome.htm).

The Department of Health is responsible for the provision of the National Health Service in England and for social care, including oversight of personal social services run by local authorities in England for children (except day care, which is now the responsibility of the DfEE), the elderly, the infirm, the handicapped and other persons in need. It is responsible for health promotion and has functions relating to public and environmental health, food safety and nutrition. The Department is also responsible for the ambulance and emergency first aid services, under the Civil Defence Act 1948. The Department represents the UK at the European Union and other international organisations including the World Health Organisation. It also supports UK-based healthcare and pharmaceutical industries.

Responsibility for food safety was transferred to the new Food Standards Agency in April 2000.

EXECUTIVE AGENCIES

Medicines Control Agency
Market Towers, 1 Nine Elms Lane, London SW8 5NQ (Tel: 020-7273 0000; Fax: 020-7273 0353; Email: info@mca.gov.uk; Web: www.open.gov.uk/mca/)

The MCA safeguards public health by ensuring that all medicines on the UK market meet appropriate standards of safety, quality and efficiency. This is achieved by a system of licensing, inspection, enforcement and monitoring of medicines after they have been licensed.

Medical Devices Agency
Hannibal House, London SE1 6TQ (Tel: 020-7972 8000; Fax: 020-7972 8108).

The Agency safeguards the performance, quality and safety of medical devices and ensures that they comply with relevant EU directives.

NHS Estates
1 Trevelyan Square, Boar Lane, Leeds LS1 6AE (Tel: 0113-254 7000; Fax: 0113-254 7299; Email: nhs.estates@doh.gov.uk; Web: www.nhsestates.gov.uk).

NHS Estates provides advice and support in the area of healthcare estate and facilities management to the NHS and the healthcare industry.

NHS Pensions
Hesketh House, 200-220 Broadway, Fleetwood, Lancs FY7 8LG (Tel: 01253 774774; Fax: 01253 774860; Web: www.nhspa.gov.uk).

NHS Pensions administers the NHS occupational pension scheme.

HOME OFFICE

50 Queen Anne's Gate, London SW1H 9AT
(Tel: 020-7273 4000; Fax: 020-7273 2190;
Email: gen.ho@gtnet.gov.uk;
Web: www.homeoffice.gov.uk).

The Home Office deals with those internal affairs in England and Wales which have not been assigned to other government departments. The Home Secretary is particularly concerned with the administration of justice; criminal law; the treatment of offenders, including probation and the prison service; the police; immigration and nationality; passport policy matters; community relations; certain public safety matters; and fire and civil emergencies services. The Home Secretary personally is the link between The Queen and the public, and exercises certain powers on her behalf, including that of the royal pardon.

Other subjects dealt with include electoral arrangements; ceremonial and formal business connected with honours; scrutiny of local authority by-laws; granting of licences for scientific procedures involving animals; cremations, burials and exhumations; firearms; dangerous drugs and poisons; general policy on laws relating to shops, liquor licensing, gaming and marriage; theatre and cinema licensing; and race relations policy.

The Home Secretary is also the link between the UK government and the governments of the Channel Islands and the Isle of Man.

EXECUTIVE AGENCIES

Fire Service College
Moreton-in-Marsh, Glos GL56 0RH
(Tel: 01608-650831).

UK Passport Agency
Clive House, Petty France, London SW1H 9HD
(National Enquiry Line: 0870 521 0410;
Web: www.ukpa.gov.uk).

Application forms for British passports are available from main Post Offices, large travel agents and Passport Offices. There are seven regional passport offices based in London, Durham, Liverpool, Newport, Peterborough, Glasgow and Belfast. The Passport Agency is only able to issue and service passports to British nationals who are resident in the UK at the time of application. If a new passport is needed whilst outside the UK, the nearest British Consulate of Embassy should be contacted.

DEPARTMENT FOR INTERNATIONAL DEVELOPMENT

94 Victoria Street, London SW1E 5JL
(Tel: 020-7917 7000; Fax: 020-7917 0019;
Email: enquiry@dfid.gov.uk;
Web: www.dfid.gov.uk).
(From January 2002 this department will be based at: 1 Palace Street, London, SW1E 5HE)

The Department for International Development (DFID) was established in May 1997 from the former Overseas Development Administration of the Foreign and Commonwealth Office. It takes the lead on British policy towards developing countries. It also manages the development assistance budget, including financial aid and technical assistance (specialist staff abroad and training facilities in the UK), whether provided directly to developing countries or through the various multilateral aid organisations, including the EU, the World Bank and the UN agencies.

LAW OFFICERS' DEPARTMENTS

Legal Secretariat to the Law Officers, Attorney-General's Chambers, 9 Buckingham Gate, London SW1E 6JP (Tel: 020-7271 2400; Fax: 020-7271 2430; Email: lslo@gtnet.gov.uk; Web: www. lslo.gov.uk).

The Law Officers of the Crown for England and Wales are the Attorney-General and the Solicitor-General. The Attorney-General, assisted by the Solicitor-General, is the chief legal adviser to the Government and is also ultimately responsible for all Crown litigation. He has overall responsibility for the work of the Law Officers' Departments (the Treasury Solicitor's Department, the Crown Prosecution Service, the Serious Fraud Office and the Legal Secretariat to the Law Officers). He has a specific statutory duty to superintend the discharge of their duties by the Director of Public Prosecutions (who heads the Crown Prosecution Service) and the Director of the Serious Fraud Office. The Director of Public Prosecutions for Northern Ireland is also responsible to the Attorney-General for the performance of his functions. The Attorney-General has additional responsibilities in relation to aspects of the civil and criminal law.

LORD CHANCELLOR'S DEPARTMENT

Selborne House, 54-60 Victoria Street, London SW1E 6QW (Tel: 020-7210 8500; Email: general.queries.lcdhq@gtnet.gov.uk; Web: www.open.gov.uk/lcd).

The Lord Chancellor appoints Justices of the Peace (except in the Duchy of Lancaster) and advises the Crown on the appointment of most members of the higher judiciary. He is responsible for promoting general reforms in the civil law, for the procedure of the civil courts and for legal aid. Since April 2000, civil legal aid is the Community Legal Service. The Lord Chancellor is a member of the Cabinet. He also has ministerial responsibility for magistrates' courts, which are administered locally. Administration of the Supreme Court and county courts in England and Wales was taken over by the Court Service, an executive agency of the department, in 1995.

The Lord Chancellor is also responsible for ensuring that letters patent and other formal documents are passed in the proper form under the Great Seal of the Realm, of which he is the custodian. The work in connection with this is carried out under his direction in the Office of the Clerk of the Crown in Chancery.

The Lord Chancellor is also head of the Judiciary and speaker of the House of Lords.

EXECUTIVE AGENCIES

The Court Service

Southside, 105 Victoria Street, London SW1E 6QT (Tel: 020-7210 2266; Fax: 020-7210 1797; Email: cust.ser.cs@gtnet.gov.uk; Web: www.courtservice.gov.uk).

The Court Service provides administrative support to the Supreme Court, the Crown Court, County Courts and a number of tribunals in England and Wales.

HM Land Registry

Lincoln's Inn Fields, London WC2A 3PH (Tel: 020-7917 8888; Fax: 020-7955 0110).

The registration of title to land was first introduced in England and Wales by the Land Registry Act 1862; HM Land Registry operates today under the Land Registration Acts 1925 to 1986. The object of registering title to land is to create and maintain a register of landowners whose title is guaranteed by the state and so to simplify the transfer, mortgage and other dealings with real property. Registration on sale and certain other transactions is now compulsory throughout England and Wales. The register has been open to inspection by the public since 1990.

Public Trust Office

Stewart House, 24 Kingsway, London WC2B 6JX (Tel: 020-7664 7000; Fax: 020-7664 7702).

Court Funds Office, 22 Kingsway, London WC2B 6LE (Tel: 020-7936 6000; Fax: 020-7936 6882).

The Public Trust Office became an executive agency of the Lord Chancellor's Department in 1994.

The Chief Executive holds the statutory title of Accountant General of the Supreme Court. The Public Trustee, through the Public Trust Office, is a trust corporation created to undertake the business of executorships and trusteeship, acting as executor or administrator of the estate of a deceased person, or as trustee of a will or settlement.

The Public Trustee is also responsible for the performance of all the administrative, but not the judicial, tasks required of the Court of Protection under Part VII of the Mental Health Act 1983, relating to the management and administration of the property and affairs of persons suffering from mental disorder. The Public Trustee also acts as receiver when so directed by the Court, usually where there is no other person willing or able so to act. The Office also deals with the registration of Enduring Powers of Attorney. The Accountant General of the Supreme Court, through the Court Funds Office, is responsible for the investment and accounting of funds in court for persons under a disability, monies in court subject to litigation and statutory deposits. The Office is currently undergoing a process of restructuring and it is possible that the functions described above will be re-allocated to other organisations during 2000/1.

SCOTLAND OFFICE

Dover House, Whitehall, London SW1A 2AU (Tel: 020-7270 6754; Fax: 020-7270 6815; Web: www.scottishsecretary.gov.uk).

The Scotland Office is the Office of the Secretary of State for Scotland, who represents Scottish interests in the Cabinet on matters reserved to the

110 Governed London

UK Parliament, i.e. national financial and economic matters, social security, defence and international relations, and employment.

*DEPARTMENT OF SOCIAL SECURITY

Richmond House, 79 Whitehall, London SW1A 2NS (Tel: 020-7238 0800).

The Department of Social Security (DSS) is responsible for the payment of benefits including child benefit, one-parent benefit, income support and family credit. It administers the Social Fund, and is responsible for assessing the means of applicants for legal aid. It is also responsible for the payment of war pensions and the operation of the child maintenance system. Responsibility for the operation of the national insurance contributions scheme was transferred from the DSS to the Inland Revenue in April 1999.

*Following the General Election the name of this department became the Department for Work and Pensions.

EXECUTIVE AGENCIES

Benefits Agency
Quarry House, Quarry Hill, Leeds LS2 7UA (Tel: 0113-232 4000; Fax: 0113-232 4085; Email: baadmin@baadmin.demon.co.uk; Web: www.dss.gov.uk/ba).

The Agency administers claims for and payments of social security benefits.

Child Support Agency (CSA)
Newcastle Benefits Directory, Benton Park Road, Newcastle upon Tyne NE98 1YX (Helpline: 0845 713 3133; Web: www.dss.gov.uk/csa).

The Agency was set up in April 1993. It is responsible for the administration of the Child Support Act and for the assessment, collection and enforcement of maintenance payments for all new cases.

Information Technology Services Agency
Control Centre, Peel Park, Brunel Way, Blackpool, Lancashire FY4 5ES (Tel: 01253 714114)

The Agency maintains and oversees policies on information technology strategy, procurement, technical standards and security.

War Pensions Agency
Tomlinson House, Norcross, Blackpool, Lancs FY5 3WP (Tel: 01253-851 788; Email: warpensions@gtnet.gov.uk; Web: dss.gov.uk/wpa/index.htm).

The Agency administers the payment of war disablement and war widows' pensions and provides welfare services and support to war disablement pensioners, war widows and their dependants and carers.

DEPARTMENT OF TRADE AND INDUSTRY

1 Victoria Street, London SW1H 0ET (Tel: 020-7215 5000; Fax: 020-7222 0162; Web: www.dti.gov.uk).

The Department is responsible for international trade policy, including the development of UK trade interests in the European Union, GATT, OECD, UNCTAD and other international organisations; the policy in relation to industry and commerce, including industrial relations policy; policy towards small firms; regional industrial assistance; legislation and policy in relation to the Post Office (Consignia is the new name for The Post Office Group); competition policy and consumer protection; the development of national policies in relation to all forms of energy and the development of new sources of energy, including international aspects of energy policy; policy on science and technology research and development; space policy; standards, quality and design; and company legislation.

EXECUTIVE AGENCIES

Companies House
Crown Way, Cardiff CF4 3UZ (Tel: 029-2038 0801).

London Information Centre, 21 Bloomsbury Street, London WC1B 3XD.

37 Castle Terrace, Edinburgh EH1 2EB (Tel: 0131-535 5800; Fax: 0131-535 5820).

Companies House incorporates companies, registers company documents and provides company information.

Employment Tribunals Service
19—29 Woburn Place, London WC1H 0LU (Tel: 020-7273 8666).

Government Departments 111

The Service became an executive agency in 1997 and brought together the administrative support for the employment tribunals and the Employment Appeal Tribunal.

The Insolvency Service
PO Box 203, 21 Bloomsbury Street, London WC1B 3QW (Tel: 020-7637 6731).

The Service administers and investigates the affairs of bankrupts and companies in compulsory liquidation; deals with the disqualification of directors in all corporate failures; regulates insolvency practitioners and their professional bodies; provides banking and investment services for bankruptcy and liquidation estates; and advises Ministers on insolvency policy issues.

National Weights and Measures Laboratory (NWML)
Stanton Avenue, Teddington, Middx TW11 0JZ (Tel: 020-8977 3222; Web www.nwml.gov.uk).

The Laboratory administers weights and measures legislation, carries out type examination, calibration and testing, and runs courses on meteorological topics. The status of the NWML is currently under review.

The Patent Office
Harmsworth House, 13-15 Bouvarie Street, London EC4Y 8DP/Concept House, Cardiff Road, Newport NP10 8QQ (Tel: 08459-500505; Fax: 01633-814444;
Email: enquiries@patent.gov.uk;
Web: www.patent.gov.uk).

The duties of the Patent Office are to administer the Patent Acts, the Registered Designs Act and the Trade Marks Act, and to deal with questions relating to the Copyright, Designs and Patents Act 1988. The Search and Advisory Service carries out commercial searches through patent information. In 1999 the Office granted 2,883 patents and registered 9,655 designs and 33,309 trade marks.

Radiocommunications Agency
Wyndham House, 189 Marsh Wall, London E14 9SX (Tel: 020-7211 0211; Fax: 020-7211 0507;
Email: library.ra@gtnet.gov.uk;
Web: www.radio.gov.uk).

The Agency is responsible for the management of the radio spectrum used for civilian purposes within the UK. It also represents UK radio interests internationally.

HM TREASURY
Parliament Street, London SW1P 3AG
(Tel: 020-7270 5000;
Email: public.enquiries@hm-treasury.gov.uk;
Web: www.hm-treasury.gov.uk).

The Office of the Lord High Treasurer has been continuously in commission for well over 200 years. The Lord High Commissioners of HM Treasury are the First Lord of the Treasury (who is also the Prime Minister), the Chancellor of the Exchequer and five junior Lords (who are government whips in the House of Commons). This Board of Commissioners is assisted at present by the Chief Secretary, the Parliamentary Secretary who is also the government Chief Whip, the Paymaster-General, the Financial Secretary, the Economic Secretary, the Minister of State and the Permanent Secretary.

The Prime Minister is not primarily concerned in the day-to-day aspects of Treasury business; the management of the Treasury devolves upon the Chancellor of the Exchequer and the other Treasury ministers.

The Chief Secretary is responsible for public expenditure planning and control; public sector pay; value for money in the public services; public/private partnerships and procurement policy; strategic oversight of banking, financial services and insurance; departmental investment strategies; welfare reform; devolution; and resource accounting and budgeting. From April 2000 the Chief Secretary also took responsibility for the new Office of Government Commerce which centralises government procurement activities.

The Paymaster-General is responsible for the Inland Revenue, Customs and Excise and the Treasury, with overall responsibility for the Finance Bill. She leads on personal and business taxation, VAT and European/international tax issues. The Paymaster-General's Office is part of the National Investment and Loans Office

The Financial Secretary is responsible for growth and productivity; small firms and venture capital; science, research and development; competition and deregulation policy;

112 Governed London

environmental issues; export credit; most Customs and Excise taxes; vehicle excise duty; and parliamentary financial business.

The Economic Secretary is responsible for National Savings, the Debt Management Office, the National Investment and Loans Office, the Office for National Statistics, the Royal Mint, and the Government Actuary's Department; banking, financial services and insurance; foreign exchange reserves; debt management policy; women's issues; and charity taxation.

EXECUTIVE AGENCIES

National Savings
Charles House, 375 Kensington High Street, London W14 8SD (Tel: 020-7605 9300; Web: www.nationalsavings.co.uk).

National Savings was established as a government department in 1969. It became an executive agency of the Treasury in 1996 and is responsible for the design, marketing and administration of savings and investment products for personal savers and investors. In April 1999 Siemens Business Services took over all the back office functions at National Savings.

Office for National Statistics
1 Drummond Gate, London SW1V 2QQ (Tel: 020-7533 6363; Fax: 020-7533 5719; Email info@statistics.gov.uk; Web: www.statistics.gov.uk).

The Office for National Statistics was created in 1996 by the merger of the Central Statistical Office and the Office of Population, Censuses and Surveys. It is responsible for preparing and interpreting key economic statistics for government policy; collecting and publishing business statistics; publishing annual and monthly statistical digests; providing researchers, analysts and other customers with a statistical service; administration of the marriage laws and local registration of births, marriages and deaths in England and Wales; provision of population estimates and projections and statistics on health and other demographic matters in England and Wales; population censuses in England and Wales; surveys for government departments and public bodies; and promoting these functions within the UK, the European Union and internationally to provide a statistical service to meet European Union and international requirements.

The Office for National Statistics is also responsible for establishing and maintaining a central database of key economic and social statistics produced to common classifications, definitions and standards.

Family Records Centre
1 Myddelton Street, London EC1R 1UW (Tel: 020-8392 5300).

Office of Government Commerce (OGC)
Fleetbank House, 2-6 Salisbury Square, London EC4Y 8JX (Tel 020-7211 1300; Web www.ogc.gov.uk).

The Office of Government Commerce was launched on the 1st April 2000, bringing together the Central Computer and Telecommunications Agency (CCTA), Property Advisers to the Civil Estate (PACE) and The Buying Agency (TBA). It is an office of HM Treasury with a Supervisory Board chaired by the Chief Secretary to the Treasury and made up of Permanent Secretaries, the Head of the National Audit Office and senior external representatives. OGC incorporates six directorates plus an executive agency, which is a trading fund OGC buying.solutions.

OGC works with civil government to achieve best value for money in commercial activities, providing a cross-government approach in procurement for up to 200 government departments, agencies and NDPBs. It aims to deliver value for money gains through dissemination of best practice and the development of Government's collective purchasing power. It introduced the Gateway Process Review, designed to improve the management of construction, IT and property management projects in central and local government.

OGCbuying.solutions
Head Office, Fifth Floor, Royal Liver Building, Pier Head, Liverpool L3 1PE (Tel: 0151-227 4262; Fax: 0151-227 3315; Email: marketing@ogcbs.gsi.gov.uk; Web: www.OGCbuyingsolutions.gov.uk).

Government Departments

OGCbuying.solutions provides a purchasing service to government departments and other public bodies. It is a trading arm of the Office of Government Commerce reporting to the Chief Secretary of the Treasury.

Royal Mint

Llantrisant, Pontyclun CF72 8YT (Tel: 01443-623060; Fax: 01443-623185; Web: www.royalmint.com).

The prime responsibility of the Royal Mint is the provision of United Kingdom coinage, but it actively competes in world markets for a share of the available circulating coin business and about two-thirds of the 20,000 tonnes of coins it produces annually are exported. The Mint also manufactures special proof and uncirculated quality coins in gold, silver and other metals; military and civil decorations and medals; commemorative and prize medals; and royal and official seals.

The Royal Mint became an executive agency of the Treasury in 1990. The Government announced in July 1999 that the Royal Mint would be given greater commercial freedom to expand its business into new areas and develop partnerships with the private sector.

United Kingdom Debt Management Office

Cheapside House, 138 Cheapside, London EC2V 6BB (Tel: 020-7862 6500; Fax: 020-7862 6509).

The UK Debt Management Office was established as an executive agency of the Treasury in April 1998. Its main aim is "to carry out the Government's debt management policy of minimising financing costs over the longer term, taking account of risk, and to manage the aggregate cash needs of the Exchequer in the most cost effective way". The DMO initially took over debt management responsibilities from the Bank of England. Since April 2000 it has also taken responsibility for managing the Exchequer's daily cash needs.

Chief Executive: M. L. Williams

TREASURY SOLICITOR

Queen Anne's Chambers, 28 Broadway, London SW1H 9JS (Tel: 020-7210 3000; Fax: 020-7210 3004).

The Treasury Solicitor's Department provides legal services for many government departments. Those without their own lawyers are provided with legal advice, and both they and other departments are provided with litigation services. The Treasury Solicitor is also the Queen's Proctor, and is responsible for collecting Bona Vacantia on behalf of the Crown. The Department became an executive agency in 1996.

WALES OFFICE

Gwydyr House, Whitehall, London SW1A 2ER (Tel: 020-7270 3000; Fax: 020-7270 0577; Web: www.ossw.wales.gov.uk).

The Welsh Office is the Office of the Secretary of State for Wales, who represents Welsh interests in the Cabinet.

PUBLIC SERVICES
LONDON

EDUCATION
EMERGENCY SERVICES
AMBULANCES
FIRE
POLICE
HEALTH
HOUSING
LIBRARIES
TRANSPORT
UTILITIES

PUBLIC SERVICES LONDON

EDUCATION

BASIC STRUCTURE

As Labour reaches the end of its first four years in power, and begins another term in office, educational provision in London continues in its extended period of far-reaching, turbulent change. The directly elected Greater London Assembly has similarly reached its anniversary, but the first twelve months have not brought the authority closer to acquiring responsibilities for education. The Mayor will, however, be a powerful commentator on the success or failure of London schools and as such is likely to have a considerable impact upon policy.

For the moment however, the basic structure of the educational system remains unchanged. Children begin formal education in nursery schools from the age of three and the primary sector is responsible for education between five and eleven years old, covering Key Stages 1 and 2 of the prescribed National Curriculum, now in its fourteenth year. The secondary sector covers Key Stages 3 and 4 and takes students up to the age of sixteen, the last year of compulsory education for children in the UK. These same schools may accommodate a student's choice of courses post-16. In some London boroughs the small number of post-16 students in individual schools make courses not viable, so provision is concentrated in specialist "Sixth Form Colleges." Further Education Colleges provide a range of academic, vocational and recreational courses for those beyond the compulsory age of schooling. Universities (including the "new" sector that transferred from "polytechnic" status in the past decade) allow the student to proceed along the "higher education" route towards the award of academic degrees and post-graduate research.

LEA RESPONSIBILITIES

Education continues to be administered by LEAs (Local Education Authorities) which coincide with the 33 London boroughs. In fact, education accounts for the highest proportion of local government spending. However, the future for LEAs is far from certain. Government policy speaks of "modernising local education authorities—accelerating the inspection of inner city LEAs and intervening where authorities are seen to be failing—by using contractors if necessary." This has already happened in Hackney, where contractors Nord-Anglia were brought in to replace the east London borough's failing school improvement service.

For the moment however, the main responsibilities of LEAs include:

* Determining their education budget within the constraints imposed by central government.
* Deciding the structure of education in its area—whether to have infant and junior schools; first and middle schools; comprehensives or grammar schools; single sex or coeducational schools.
* Supervising the education service, focusing more on monitoring and evaluating the curriculum and general management of schools.
* Overseeing admissions policies and providing appeals procedures.
* Providing educational psychology and welfare services; free school transport, free school meals, board and lodgings, clothing to pupils who qualify. The Department lays down complex regulations for Education and Employment for many of these services.
* Providing a wide range of central support services from in-service training for teachers and governors, to personnel and financial services.
* Adult Education, Youth Service and the provision of education of the under fives.

EDUCATION AND GOVERNMENT POLICY

The Labour government of recent years has placed much of its effort behind getting the basics right in primary schools. They can claim some success in improving standards of literacy and numeracy through the introduction of dedicated programmes that are, on the whole, welcomed by the teaching profession. By the end of 2001 Labour seem set to meet their 1997 election pledge to cut infant class sizes to below the level of 30. Their manifesto for the next five-year term talks about bringing a "similar transformation in secondary schools."

The following initiatives form the foundation of an ambitious programme that at present has yet to convince a significant proportion of the teaching profession:

- Increasing autonomy for successful schools: further increasing the delegation of budgets; restricting bureaucratic burdens; allowing greater freedoms over the curriculum and teachers' pay and conditions.
- Extending diversity by significantly expanding the specialist schools programme; establishing more faith-based schools and changing the law to allow external sponsors to take responsibility for under-performing schools.
- Setting ambitious targets for performance in tests for 14-year olds in English, Maths, Science and ICT (with the promise of appropriate support and training for teachers and schools).
- Promoting new pathways for pupils beyond 14, particularly those of high ability and those wishing to proceed along more vocational and work-based routes.

Few of these initiatives in themselves provoke complaint from teachers. Instead, it is the pace and style of change that draws the most criticism. The first charge is that the Labour government is becoming increasingly prescriptive in its "guidance" for teachers. The recent decision to specify 300 "problem" spellings for the use of Key Stage Three English teachers is one example. Another is the immensely detailed "advice" given to 11-14 Maths teachers for the implementation of the Key Stage Three Numeracy Policy. The pace of change in the secondary curriculum is a second cause for concern. The Key Stage Three reforms are scheduled with the introduction of new GCSE and "A2" courses—the second year of the replacement for traditional "A" levels. Experience is showing that success in the multiple implementation of such programmes relies heavily upon the quality of change management exhibited by senior managers.

PRIORITIES FOR URBAN EDUCATION

Whereas the above policies relate to all UK schools, cities have particular characteristics that require a specific response from policy-makers. As the largest city in the UK, London has a particular need to address issues that include the cosmopolitan nature of its population; pockets of urban deprivation, poverty and the transient nature of some of its communities. In a major policy initiative that recognised the phenomenon of social exclusion, the Labour government identified early on in its first term an underclass with multiple (and interconnected) difficulties in the areas of health, education and employment. Two particular programmes, "Education Action Zones" and "Excellence In Cities", target social exclusion from the education perspective and seem set to be influential upon London education in this first decade of the new millennium. A new initiative for 2001/2002—*The City Academy*—makes its debut in the borough of Haringey and its progress is sure to be carefully monitored in the months and years to come.

1) EDUCATION ACTION ZONES

Education Action Zones (EAZs) are based on a cluster of about 20 primary, secondary and special schools in a local area. Their task is to stimulate innovation and new approaches and so further lever up standards in schools in deprived areas. The zone is run by a forum of businesses, parents, schools, the local authority and community organisations.

In July 1998, 25 EAZs were created with Newham, Lambeth and Croydon the successful London bids in the first round.

Zones have shown they can deliver improvement, as demonstrated by the summer 1999 exam results. At Key Stage 2, there was a 6 percent average improvement in English and 12 percent improvement in maths in EAZ schools compared to national increases of 5 percent and 10 percent. There was a 2 percent average improvement in the numbers of pupils gaining 1 GCSE A*-G grade in EAZ schools compared to a national increase of 1 percent.

When the Office for Standards in Education inspected the zone in Southwark Central London, they found that Key Stage Two English results had improved at double the national average. The proportion of pupils hitting expected levels climbed by 20 percentage points in 1998-2000.

There is, however, a concession from government that these improvements are largely to be found in the primary rather than the secondary sector. In addition, the zones have yet to produce the hoped-for innovations in practice that can be spread to other schools.

3) EXCELLENCE IN CITIES

The Prime Minister and David Blunkett launched "Excellence in Cities" (EiC) in March 1999. It aimed to concentrate efforts to raise standards in six of the largest city areas around the country, which obviously includes inner London. The EiC LEAs included in the London scheme are: Camden, City of London, Greenwich, Hackney, Hammersmith and Fulham, Haringey, Islington, Kensington and Chelsea, Lambeth, Lewisham, Newham, Southwark, Tower Hamlets, Wandsworth, Waltham Forest and Westminster.

The project bundles up a number of smaller policy initiatives which neatly demonstrates the current administration's philosophy of providing both "pressure and support" in equal measure.

Support largely comes in the form of a radical expansion of the **specialist** and **beacon** schools programmes, giving them a particular focus on inner cities. Specialist schools are existing secondary schools which are designed to provide enrichment programmes in either languages, sports, arts or technology in addition to the National Curriculum. Beacon schools are schools which have been identified as amongst the best performing in the country and represent examples of successful practice which are to be brought to the attention of the rest of the education service, with a view to sharing that practice with others. They work in partnership with other schools to pass on their particular areas of expertise. By 2002/3 it is expected that there will be at least 800 specialist schools and over 1000 beacon schools.

EiC has been running more than a full year in the first 25 areas and early indications of success are encouraging.
- Standards are rising in the first EiC areas faster than in schools nationally.
- The increase in those getting five good GSCEs or their equivalent last year was 2.3 percent compared with 1.3 percent for other areas.
- The biggest increases have been made in the most deprived schools, ie. those with over half their pupils entitled to free school meals.

4) CITY ACADEMIES

City Academies are publicly funded independent secondary schools with sponsors from the private or voluntary sectors or from churches or other faith groups. The first ever City Academy is a good example. Under the control of the Church of England, the former School of St David and St Katherine in Hornsey, Haringey is due for re-opening in its new guise towards the end of 2001.

Each City Academy will have a special focus on a particular area of the curriculum like schools in the **specialist schools programme**. They will be all-ability schools for 11 to 16 or 11 to 18 year olds according to the pattern of local provision, being required to comply with admissions law and the Admissions Code of Practice, which apply to maintained schools. They may select up to 10 percent of pupils on the basis of an aptitude for the specialism.

It is aimed that City Academies will:
- be central to their communities, sharing their facilities with other schools and the wider community.
- have greater freedom to tackle the local problems associated with poor or low pupil performance.
- have a broad, balanced and innovative curriculum, with a special emphasis in one area of the curriculum.
- have curriculum enrichment and study support as an integral part of school life.

STATISTICAL TRENDS—TEACHER RECRUITMENT AND RETENTION

Whereas specific government programmes are making inroads into social exclusion, one fact threatens to make a significantly negative impact on progress. London boasts some of the best and worst class sizes in England. Its growing, and increasingly multi-ethnic, student population is often short of teachers. The statistics tell their own story :
- More than one in eight of England's teachers work in a London school. However, almost half the supply teachers and 16 per cent of all occasional teachers can be found in the capital's schools.
- London also accounted for almost one in three of the unqualified teachers to be found in England's schools in 1999.
- Teachers who train in London have in recent years been less likely than other new teachers to start work in the classroom. According to the latest DfEE figures available, only 70 per cent of those who trained in London in 1997 had started teaching by March 1998. This compared to nearly 75 per cent of those who trained in the North East.

CONCLUSION

The Labour Government has gained its second successive term in office. Education again appears to be a priority in policy terms and the country could well be facing a more radical programme of legislation than in the previous parliament. London will be a prime recipient of measures to reduce still further the level of social exclusion but much rests on schools' ability to recruit and retain qualified class teachers and senior staff. Having found its feet, the Greater London Authority seems set to play an increasing role in passing comment on the capital's educational provision.

120 Public Services London

LOCAL EDUCATION AUTHORITIES

Barking and Dagenham
Town Hall, Barking, Essex, IG11 7LU
(Tel: 020-8227 3181/2; Fax: 020-8227 3471;
Web: www.bardaglea.org.uk)
**Director of Education, Arts and Libraries
Department:** A. Larbalestier

Barnet
The Old Town Hall, Friern Barnet Lane,
London, N11 3DL (Tel: 020-8359 3048;
Fax: 020-8359 3013;
E-mail: lyndsey.stone@barnet.gov.uk;
Web: www.barnet.gov.uk)
**Head of Education Raising Standards and
Chief Education Officer:** Ms Lindsey Stone

Bexley
Hill View, Hill View Drive, Welling, Kent, DA16
3RY (Tel: 020-8303 7777; Fax: 020-8319 4302;
E-mail: committee.els@bexley.gov.uk;
Web: www.bexley.gov.uk)
Director: P. McGee

Brent
Chesterfield House, 9 Park Lane, Wembley,
Middx, HA9 7RW (Tel: 020-8937 3190;
Fax: 020-8937 3023; Web: www.brent.gov.uk)
Director of Education, Arts and Libraries:
Jacky Griffin

Bromley
Civic Centre, Stockwell Close, Bromley, Kent,
BR1 3UH (Tel: 020-8464 3333; Fax: 020-8313
4049; Web: www.bromley.gov.uk)
Director: K. Davis

Camden
Crowndale Centre, 218–220 Eversholt Street,
London, NW1 1BD (Tel: 020-7974 1505;
Fax: 020-7974 1536;
E-mail: r.litchfield@camden.gov.uk)
Director: R. Litchfield

Corporation of London
Education Department, Corporation of London,
PO Box 270, Guildhall, London, EC2P 2EJ
(Tel: 020-7332 1750; Fax: 020-7331 1621;
E-mail: dep.education@corpoflondon.gov.uk)
City Education Officer: D. Smith

City of Westminster
City Hall, 64 Victoria Street, London, SW1E
6QP (Tel: 020-7641 1947; Fax: 020-7641 3406)
Director: J. Harris

Croydon
Taberner House, Park Lane, Croydon, CR9 1TP
(Tel: 020-8760 5452; Fax: 020-8760 5603;
E-mail: education-information@croydon.gov.uk;
Web: www.croydon.gov.uk)
Director: D. Sands

Ealing
Perceval House, 14–16 Uxbridge Road, London,
W5 2HL (Tel: 020-8579 2424; Fax: 020-8280
1291; E-mail: education@ealing.gov.uk)
Director of Education: A. Parker

Enfield
PO Box 56, Civic Centre, Silver Street, Enfield,
Middx, EN1 3XQ (Tel: 020-8379 3201;
Fax: 020-8379 3243)
Director: Ms E. Graham

Greenwich
Riverside House, Woolwich High Street,
London, SE18 6DF (Tel: 020-8921 8038; Fax:
020-8921 8228; Web: www.greenwich.gov.uk)
Director: G. Gyte

Hackney
Edith Cavell Building, Enfield Road, London,
N1 5BA (Tel: 020-8356 8436; Fax: 020-8356
7235; E-mail: tmahoney@hackney.gov.uk;
Web: www.learninglive.co.uk)
Director: A. Ward

Hammersmith and Fulham
Town Hall, King Street, London, W6 9JU
(Tel: 020-8753 3601; Fax: 020-8753 3705;
E-mail: publicity@hafed.org.uk;
Web: www.lbhf.gov.uk)
Director: Ms C. Whatford

Haringey
48 Station Road, Wood Green, London, N22
7TY (Tel: 020-8489 0000; Fax: 020-8489 3864;
E-mail: deborah.bolt@haringey.gov.uk)
Interim Director: S. Jenkin

Local Education Authorities 121

Harrow
PO Box 22, Civic Centre, Station Road, Harrow, Middx, HA1 2UW (Tel: 020-8863 5611; Fax: 020-8427 0870; Web: www.harrow.gov.uk)
Director: P. Osburn

Havering
The Broxhill Centre, Broxhill Road, Harold Hill, Romford, Essex, RM14 1XN
(Tel: 01708-432488; Fax: 01708-432496; E-mail: sevans.ciii@havering.gov.uk)
Executive Director Children and Lifelong Learning: S. Evans

Hillingdon
Civic Centre, High Street, Uxbridge, Middx, UB8 1UW (Tel: 01895-250528; Fax: 01895-250831; E-mail: po'hear@hillingdon.gov.uk)
Corporate Director: P. O'Hear

Hounslow
Civic Centre, Lampton Road, Hounslow, Middx, TW3 4DN (Tel: 020-8583 2901; Fax: 020-8583 2907; E-mail: lesley.crossley@education.hounslow.gov.uk)
Director: D. Trickett

Islington
Laycock Street, Islington, London, N1 1TH (Tel: 020-7527 5666; Fax: 020-7527 5668; E-mail: education@islington.gov.uk)
Director: Jonathon Slater

Kensington and Chelsea
Town Hall, Hornton Street, London, W8 7NX (Tel: 020-7361 3303; Fax: 020-7361 3481; E-mail: edurw@rbkc.gov.uk)
Executive Director Education and Libraries: R. Wood

Kingston upon Thames
Guildhall 2, Kingston upon Thames, KT1 1EU (Tel: 020-8547 5220; Fax: 020-8547 5296; E-mail: john.braithwaite@rbk.kingston.gov.uk)
Director of Education and Leisure:
John Braithwaite

Lambeth
International House, Canterbury Crescent, London, SW9 7QE (Tel: 020-7926 9768; Fax: 020-7926 9778; E-mail: jbringons@lambeth.gov.uk)
Acting Executive Director of Education:
A. Wood

Lewisham
3rd Floor, Laurence House, 1 Catford Road, London, SE6 4RU (Tel: 020-8314 6200; Fax: 020-8314 3039; Web: www.lewisham.gov.uk)
Executive Director for Education and Culture: Vacant

Merton
Civic Centre, London, Morden, Surrey, SM4 5DX (Tel: 020-8545 3251; Fax: 020-8545 3443; E-mail: tony.lenney@merton.gov.uk)
Acting Director of Education, Leisure and Libraries: Tony Lenney

Newham
Broadway House, 322 High Street, Stratford, London, E15 1AJ (Tel: 020-8430 2000; Fax: 020-8430 5043)
Director: Pauline Maddison

Redbridge
Lynton House, 255–259 High Road, Ilford, Essex, IG1 1NN (Tel: 020-8478 3020; Fax: 020-8553 0895; Web: www.redbridge.gov.uk)
Director of Education and Lifelong Learning: E. Grant

Richmond upon Thames
1st Floor, Regal House, London Road, Twickenham, Middx, TW1 3SB
(Tel: 020-8891 7500; Fax: 020-8891 7714; E-mail: education@richmond.gov.uk; Web: www.richmond.gov.uk/education)
Chief Education Officer: Anji Phillips

Southwark
1 Bradenham Close, London, SE17 2QA
(Tel: 020-7525 5050)

Sutton
The Grove, Carshalton, Surrey, SM5 3AL (Tel: 020-8770 6568; Fax: 020-8770 6545; Web: www.sutton.gov.uk)
Strategic Director: Dr I. Birnbaum

122 Public Services London

Tower Hamlets
Town Hall, Mulberry Place, 5 Clove Crescent, London, E14 2BG (Tel: 020-7364 5000; Fax: 020-7364 4976;
E-mail: paul.burgessp@towerhamlets.gov.uk;
Web: www.towerhamlets.gov.uk)
Corporate Director – Education: Ms C. Gilbert

Waltham Forest
Leyton Municipal Offices, High Road, Leyton, London, E10 5QJ (Tel: 020-8527 5544 ext. 5001)
Chief Education Officer: K. J. Evans

Wandsworth
Town Hall, Wandsworth High Street, London, SW18 2PU (Tel: 020-8871 8013;
Fax: 020-8871 8011;
E-mail: eduadminservices@wandsworth.gov.uk)
Director: P. Robinson

UNIVERSITIES

The list below includes contact information for universities in London and their attached colleges.

BRUNEL UNIVERSITY
Uxbridge, Middx UB8 3PH (Tel: 01895-274000; Fax: 01895-232806;
Web: www.brunel.ac.uk/information/html)

300 St Margarets Road, Twickenham, TW1 1PT;
(Web: www.brunel.ac.uk/campus/twickenham)

Borough Road, Isleworth, TW7 5DU;
(Web: www.brunel.ac.uk/campus/asterley)

Englefield Green, Egham, Surrey, TW20 0JZ;
(Web: www.brunel.ac.uk/campus/runnymede)

CITY UNIVERSITY
Northampton Square, London EC1V 0HB
(Tel: 020-70404 5060;
E-mail: registry@city.ac.uk;
Web: www.city.ac.uk)

KINGSTON UNIVERSITY
Kingston upon Thames, Surrey KT1 1LQ
(Tel: 020-8547 2000; Fax: 020-8547 7080;
E-mail: admissions-info@kingston.ac.uk;
Web: www.kingston.ac.uk)

LONDON GUILDHALL UNIVERSITY
31 Jewry Street, London EC3N 2EY
(Tel: 020-7320 1000; Web: www.lgu.ac.uk)

MIDDLESEX UNIVERSITY
White Hart Lane, London N17 8HR
(Tel: 020-8411 5000; Fax: 020-8411 6878;
E-mail: admissions@mdx.ac.uk;
Web: www.mdx.ac.uk)

SOUTH BANK UNIVERSITY
103 Borough Road, London SE1 0AA
(Tel: 020-7928 8989; Fax: 020-7815 8273;
E-mail: registry@sbu.ac.uk;
Web: www.sbu.ac.uk)

THAMES VALLEY UNIVERSITY
St Mary's Road, Ealing, London W5 5RF
(Tel: 020-8579 5000; Fax: 020-8566 1353;
E-mail: learning.advice@tvu.ac.uk;
Web: www.tvu.ac.uk)

UNIVERSITY OF EAST LONDON
Longbridge Road, Dagenham, Essex RM8 2AS
(Tel: 020-8223 3000; Fax: 020-8223 2978;
E-mail: admiss@uel.ac.uk;
Web: www.uel.ac.uk)

UNIVERSITY OF GREENWICH
Bexley Road, Eltham, London SE9 2PQ
(Tel: 020-8331 8000;
E-mail: courseinfo@gre.ac.uk;
Web: www.gre.ac.uk)

Avery Hill
Avery Hill Road, Eltham, London, SE9 2PQ

Dartford
Oakfield Lane, Dartford, Kent, DA1 2SZ

Maritime
30 Park Row, Greenwich, London, SE10 9LS

Medway
Central Avenue, Chatham Maritime, Kent, ME4 4TB

Woolwich
Island Site, Beresford Street, London, SE18 6BU

UNIVERSITY OF LONDON
Senate House, Malet Street, London WC1E 7HU (Tel: 020-7862 8000; Fax: 020-7862 8358;
E-mail: webmaster@admin.lon.ac.uk;
Web: www.lon.ac.uk)

Universities 123

Birkbeck College
Malet Street, London, WC1E 7HX
(E-mail: admissions@bbk.ac.uk;
Web: www.bbk.ac.uk)

British Institute in Paris
9–11 rue de Constantine, 75340 Paris, Cedex 07, France, (E-mail: c.buchanan@admin.lon.ac.uk;
Web: www.bip.lon.ac.uk)

Centre for Defence Studies
King's College London, Strand, London, WC2R 2LS (E-mail: cds@ckl.ac.uk;
Web: www.kcl.ac.uk/kis/schools/hums/war/index)

Courtauld Institute of Art
North Block, Somerset House, Strand, London, WC2R 0RN (E-mail: website@courtauld.ac.uk;
Web: www.courtauld.ac.uk)

Goldsmiths College
Lewisham Way, New Cross, London, SE14 6NW (E-mail: ext-comm@gold.ac.uk;
Web: www.gold.ac.uk)

Heythrop College
Kensington Square, London, W8 5HQ
(E-mail: a.clarkson@heythrop.ac.uk;
Web: www.heythrop.ac.uk)

Imperial College of Science, Technology and Medicine
South Kensington, London, SW7 2AZ
(E-mail: info@ic.ac.uk;
Web: www.ic.ac.uk)

Institute of Advanced Legal Studies
Charles Clore House, 17 Russell Square, London, WC1B 5DR (E-mail: ials@sas.ac.uk;
Web: www.sas.ac.uk)

Institute of Cancer Research
Royal Cancer Hospital, Chester Beatty Laboratories, 17A Onslow Gardens, London, SW7 3AL (E-mail: j.kipling@icr.ac.uk;
Web: www.icr.ac.uk)

Institute of Classical Studies
Senate House, Malet Street, London, WC1E 7HU (E-mail: mpacker@sas.ac.uk;
Web: www.sas.ac.uk)

Institute of Commonwealth Studies
27–28 Russell Square, London, WC1B 5DS
(E-mail: ics@sas.ac.uk;
Web: www.ihr.sas.ac.uk/ics)

Institute of Education
20 Bedford Way, London, WC1H 0AL
(E-mail: l.loughran@ioe.ac.uk;
Web: www.ioe.ac.uk)

Institute of English Studies
Senate House, Malet Street, London, WC1E 7HU (E-mail: ies@sas.ac.uk;
Web: www.sas.ac.uk)

Institute of Germanic Studies
29 Russell Square, London, WC1B 5DP
(E-mail: igs@sas.ac.uk;
Web: www.sas.ac.uk)

Institute of Historical Research
Senate House, Malet Street, London, WC1E 7HU (E-mail: ihr@sas.ac.uk;
Web: www.ihr.info.ac.uk)

Institute of Latin American Studies
31 Tavistock Square, London, WC1H 9HA
(E-mail: ilas@sas.ac.uk;
Web: www.sas.ac.uk/ilas)

Institute of Psychiatry
De Crespigny Park, Denmark Hill, London, SE5 8AF (E-mail: d.heavey@iop.kcl.ac.uk;
Web: www.iop.kcl.ac.uk/main)

Institute of Romance Studies
Senate House, Malet Street, London, WC1E 7HU (E-mail: irs@sas.ac.uk;
Web: www.sas.ac.uk)

Institute of United States Studies
Senate House, Malet Street, London, WC1E 7HU (E-mail: iuss@sas.ac.uk;
Web: www.sas.ac.uk)

King's College London
Strand, London, WC2R 2LS
(E-mail: enquiries@kcl.ac.uk;
Web: www.kcl.ac.uk)

London Business School
Sussex Place, Regent's Park, London, NW1 4SA
(E-mail: jdefries@lbs.ac.uk;
Web: www.lbs.ac.uk)

124 Public Services London

London School of Economics and Political Science
Houghton Street, London, WC2A 2AE
(E-mail: general-course@lse.ac.uk;
Web: www.lse.ac.uk)

London School of Hygiene and Tropical Medicine
Keppel Street, London, WC1E 7HT
(E-mail: registry@lshtm.ac.uk;
Web: www.lshtm.ac.uk)

London School of Jewish Studies
44A Albert Road, London, NW4 2SJ
Web: www.brijnet.org/isjs)

Queen Mary and Westfield College
Mile End Road, London, E1 4NS
(E-mail: admissions@qmn.ac.uk;
Web: www.qmn.ac.uk)

Royal Academy of Music
Marylebone Road, London, NW1 2BS
(E-mail: registry@ram.ac.uk;
Web: www.ram.ac.uk)

Royal Holloway
Egham Hill, Egham, Surrey, TW20 0EX
(E-mail: a.price@rhbnc.ac.uk;
Web: www.rhbnc.ac.uk)

Royal Veterinary College
Royal College Street, London, NW1 0TU
(E-mail: registry@rvc.ac.uk;
Web: www.rvc.ac.uk)

School of Advanced Study
Senate House, Malet Street, London, WC1E 7HU (E-mail: school@sas.ac.uk;
Web: www.sas.ac.uk)

School of Oriental and African Studies
Thornhaugh Street, Russell Square, London, WC1H 0XG (E-mail: study@soas.ac.uk;
Web: www.soas.ac.uk)

School of Pharmacy
29–39 Brunswick Square, London, WC1N 1AX
(E-mail: mistone@ulsop.ac.uk;
Web: www.ulsop.ac.uk)

St George's Hospital Medical School
Cranmer Terrace, London, SW17 0RE
(E-mail: g.jones@sghms.ac.uk;
Web: www.sghms.ac.uk)

University College London
Gower Street, London, WC1E 6BT
(E-mail: degree-info@ucl.ac.uk;
Web: www.ucl.ac.uk)

University Marine Biological Station Millport
Isle of Cumbrae, Scotland, KA28 0EG
(E-mail: milport@gla.ac.uk;
Web: www.gla.ac.uk/acad/marine)

Warburg Institute
Woburn Square, London, WC1H 0AB
(E-mail: apollard@sas.ac.uk;
Web: www.sas.ac.uk)

Wye College
Wye, near Ashford, Kent, TN25 5AH
(E-mail: webmaster@wye.ac.uk;
Web: www.wye.ac.uk)

UNIVERSITY OF NORTH LONDON
166–220 Holloway Road, London N7 8DB
(Tel: 020-7607 2789; Fax: 020-7753 3272;
E-mail: admissions@unl.ac.uk;
Web: www.unl.ac.uk)

UNIVERSITY OF SURREY
Guildford, Surrey GU2 5XH
(Tel: 01483-300800; Fax: 01483-300803;
E-mail: information@surrey.ac.uk;
Web: www.surrey.ac.uk)

UNIVERSITY OF SURREY ROEHAMPTON
Roehampton Lane, London SW15 5PH
(Tel: 020-8392 3000; Fax: 020-8392 3029;
Web: www.roehampton.ac.uk)

Royal College of Art
Kensington Gore, London SW7 2EU
(Tel: 020-7590 4444; Fax: 020-7590 4500;
E-mail: info@rca.ac.uk;
Web: www.rca.ac.uk)

Royal College of Music
London SW7 2BS (Tel: 020-7589 3643;
Fax: 020-7589 7740; E-mail: info@rcm.ac.uk;
Web: www.rcm.ac.uk)

Colleges

Southlands College
80 Roehampton Lane, London, SW15 5SL
(Tel: 020-8392 3401; Fax: 020-8392 3431;
E-mail: southlands@roehampton.ac.uk;
Web: www.roehampton.ac.uk)
Principal: M. Leigh

UNIVERSITY OF WESTMINSTER
309 Regent Street, London W1R 8AL
(Tel: 020-7911 5000;
E-mail: admissions@wmin.ac.uk;
Web: www.wmin.ac.uk)

COLLEGES

The list below includes a selection of colleges in London. Where possible we have included information on what type of college they are, e.g. Further or Higher Education

Babel Technical College
David Game House, 69 Notting Hill Gate, London, W11 3JS (Tel: 020-7221 1483;
Fax: 020-7243 1730;
E-mail: babel@babeltech.ac.uk;
Web: www.babeltech.ac.uk)
Principal: Zed Abaderash
Type of college: Computer and information technology

Barnet College
Wood Street, Barnet, Herts, EN5 4AZ
(Tel: 020-8440 6321; Fax: 020-8441 5236;
E-mail: info@barnet.ac.uk;
Web: www.barnet.ac.uk)
Principal: J. Skitt
Type of college: Further education

Borough College London
210 Borough High Street, London, SE1 1JX
(Tel: 020-7407 2863; Fax: 020-7407 2869;
E-mail: jmc@ukinc.com;
Web: www.ukinc.com/jmc)
Principal: J. Ogunleye

Bromley College
Rookery Lane, Bromley, Kent, BR2 8HE
(Tel: 020-8295 7000; Fax: 020-8295 7099;
E-mail: info@bromley.ac.uk;
Web: www.bromley.ac.uk)
Principal and Chief Executive: R. Pritchard

Building Crafts College
153 Great Titchfield Street, London, W1P 7FR
(Tel: 020-7636 0480; Fax: 020-7323 4532;
Web: www.thecarpenterscompany.co.uk)
Director: J. C. M. Taylor
Type of college: Traditional building crafts, conservation and restoration, fine woodwork, stone masonry

Carshalton College
Nightingale Road, Carshalton, Surrey, SM5 2EJ
(Tel: 020-8770 6800; Fax: 020-8770 6899;
Web: www.carshalton.ac.uk)
Principal: Dr D. Watkins
Type of college: Further and higher education

City and Islington College
Marlborough Building, 383 Holloway Road, London, N7 0RN (Tel: 020-7700 9333; Fax: 020-7700 9222; E-mail: tjupp@candi.ac.uk;
Web: www.candi.ac.uk)
Principal: T. Jupp
Type of college: Further education

Willen House, 8–26 Bath Street, London, EC1V 9PL (Tel: 020-7700 9333; Fax: 020-7250 4026)

Finsbury Park Centre, Prah Road, London, N4 2RA (Tel: 020-7226 9190; Fax: 020-7359 8769)

Sixth Form Centre, Benwell Road, London, N7 7BW (Tel: 020-7609 8401; Fax: 020-7700 7585)

Sixth Form Centre, Annette Road, London, N7 6EX (Tel: 020-7609 8401; Fax: 020-7700 4416)

Bunhill Row, London, EC1Y 8LQ
(Tel: 020-7700 9333; Fax: 020-7588 9024)

Shepperton Arts Centre, Shepperton Road, London, N1 3DH (Tel: 020-7226 6001; Fax: 020-7354 1477)

444 Camden Road, London, N7 0SP

Montem 3D Arts Centre, 179 Hornsey Road, London, N7 6RA (Tel: 020-7263 8309; Fax: 020-7272 8446)

City of London College
71 Whitechapel High Street, London, E1 7PL
(Tel: 020-7247 2166; Fax: 020-7247 1226;
E-mail: registry@clc-london.ac.uk;
Web: www.clc-london.ac.uk)
Principal: R. A. Wright

126 Public Services London

College of Central London
60 Great Ormond Street, London, WC1N 3HR
(Tel: 020-7833 0987; Fax: 020-7837 2959;
E-mail: ccl@btinternet.com;
Web: www.central-college.com)
Principal: N. Kailides
Type of college: Private

Croydon College
Fairfield Campus, College Road, Croydon, Surrey, CR9 1DX (Tel: 020-8686 5700; Fax: 020-8760 5880; E-mail: info@croydon.ac.uk; Web: www.croydon.ac.uk)
Principal and Chief Executive: V. Seddon
Type of college: Further and higher education

Ealing Tertiary College
Southall Centre, Beaconsfield Road, Southall, Middx, UB1 1DP (Tel: 020-8231 6000; Fax: 020-8574 5354; Web: www.etc.ac.uk)
Chief Executive: M. Griffin
Type of college: Further Education

Enfield College
73 Hertford Road, Enfield, Middx, EN3 5HA
(Tel: 020-8443 3434; Fax: 020-8804 7028;
Web: www.enfield.ac.uk)
Principal and Chief Executive: J. Carter

European College
Neil House, 7 Whitechapel Road, London, E1 1DU (Tel: 020-7247 2316/7377 8962; Fax: 020-7247 5907;
E-mail: registrar@europeancollege2000.com;
Web: www.europeancollege2000.com)
Principal: S. Ahmad
Type of college: English and European languages, computer training

Greenwich Community College
95 Plumstead Road, London, SE18 7DQ
(Tel: 020-8488 4800; Fax: 020-8488 4899;
E-mail: info@gcc.ac.uk;
Web: www.gcc.ac.uk)
Principal: G. Pine
Type of college: Further education

Greenwich School of Management
Meridian House, Royal Hill, London, SE10 8RD
(Tel: 020-8516 7800; Fax: 020-8516 7801;
E-mail: enquiries@greenwich-college.ac.uk;
Web: www.greenwich-college.ac.uk)
Principal: W. Hunt
Type of college: Business education

Hammersmith and West London College
Barons Court, Gliddon Road, London, W14 9BL
(Tel: 020-8741 1688; Fax: 020-8741 2491;
E-mail: cic@hwlc.ac.uk;
Web: www.hwlc.ac.uk)
Principal: J. Stone
Type of college: Further education

Hendon College
Grahame Park Way, London, NW9 5RA
(Tel: 020-8200 8300; Fax: 020-8205 7177;
E-mail: info@hendon.ac.uk;
Web: www.hendon.ac.uk)
Principal: J. Skit
Type of college: Further education

Imperial College of Science, Technology and Medicine
Exhibition Road, London, SW7 2AZ
(Tel: 020-7589 5111; Web: www.ic.ac.uk)
Rector: Sir Richard Sykes
Type of college: Science, technology and medicine

Lewisham College
Lewisham Way, London, SE4 1UT
(Tel: 020-8692 0353; Fax: 020-8691 1842;
E-mail: rsi@statt.lewisham.ac.uk;
Web: www.lewisham.ac.uk)
Principal: Ms R. Silver
Type of college: Further education

London College of Business and Computer Studies
159–163 Clapham High Street, London, SW4 7SS (Tel: 020-7720 4414; Fax: 020-7720 2010;
E-mail: lcbcs@telinco.co.uk;
Web: www.lcbcs.ndo.co.uk)
Principal: Mr Tayo Olarewaju
Type of college: Higher and further education

London College of Traditional Acupuncture and Oriental Medicines
HR House, 447 High Road, London, N12 0AZ
(Tel: 020-8371 0820; Fax: 020-8371 0830;
E-mail: enquiries@lcta.com;
Web: www.lcta.com)
Principal: Ms S. Dowie
Type of college: Acupuncture and Oriental herbal medicine

London Tower College
151 Rye Lane, London, SE15 4TL
(Tel: 020-7690 7324; Fax: 020-7503 5361)
Proprietor and Registrar: L. Adeoye
Type of college: Computing, business and law

Colleges 127

Marymount College
22 Brownlow Mews, London, WC1N 2LA
(Tel: 020-7242 7004; Fax: 020-7831 7185;
E-mail: marymount.london@mailbox.ulcc.ac.uk)
Director: P. M. Pelan
Principal: Prof. A. Smith
Type of college: Higher education college of London University

Redbridge College
Little Heath, Romford, Essex, RM6 4XT
(Tel: 020-8548 7400; Fax: 020-8599 8224;
E-mail: info@redbridge.essex.sch.uk)
Principal: Dr J. A. McGrath
Type of college: Further education; special needs

Sir George Monoux College
Chingford Road, Walthamstow, London, E17 5AA (Tel: 020-8523 3544; Fax: 020-8498 2443;
E-mail: info@george-monoux.ac.uk;
Web: www.george-monoux.ac.uk)
Principal: R. Chambers
Type of college: Sixth form

South Thames College
Wandsworth High Street, London, SW18 2PP
(Tel: 020-8918 7000)
Roehampton Centre, 166 Roehampton Lane, London, SW15 4HR (Tel: 020-8918 7676;
Fax: 020-8918 7618)
(E-mail: student-services@south-thames.ac.uk;
Web: www.south-thames.ac.uk)
Principal: Ms J. Scribbins
Type of college: Further education and adult community

Southgate College
High Street, London, N14 6BS
(Tel: 020-8886 6521; Fax: 020-8982 5053;
E-mail: admiss@southgate.ac.uk;
Web: www.southgate.ac.uk)
Principal and Chief Executive: M. Blagden
Type of college: Further education

Southwark College
Surrey Docks Centre, Drummond Road, London, SE16 4EE (Tel: 020-7815 1500;
Fax: 020-7261 1301;
Web: www.southwark.ac.uk)
Principal and Chief Executive: Ms D. Jones
Type of college: Further education

Tower Hamlets College
Poplar Centre, Poplar High Street, London, E14 0AF (Tel: 020-7510 7510; Fax: 020-7538 9153;
E-mail: thc@tower.ac.uk;
Web: www.tower.ac.uk)
Principal: Ms A. Zera
Type of college: Further education

Transatlantic College
138 Kingsland Road, London, E2 8DY
(Tel: 020-8980 2299; Fax: 020-7729 1010)
Principal: Dr P. Efere
Type of college: Housing, welfare, law, social care

West Thames College
London Road, Isleworth, Middx, TW7 4HS
(Tel: 020-8326 2000; Fax: 020-8569 7787;
Web: www.west-thames.ac.uk)
Principal: T. Marriott
Type of college: Further education

Westminster College
Castle Lane, London, SW1E 6DR
(Tel: 020-7828 3771; Fax: 020-7233 8509;
E-mail: admissions@westking.ac.uk;
Web: www.westking.ac.uk)
Head: Ms L. Roberts
Type of college: Languages

Woodhouse College
Woodhouse Road, London, N12 9EY
(Tel: 020-8445 1210; Fax: 020-8445 5210;
E-mail: ggeorge@woodhouse.ndirect.co.uk;
Web: www.woodhouse.org.uk)
Principal: Ms A. Robinson
Type of college: Sixth form

EDUCATIONAL BODIES

The Assessment and Qualifications Alliance
Stag Hill House, Guildford, Surrey, GU2 5XJ
(Tel: 01483-506506; Fax: 01483-300152;
Web: www.aqa.org.uk)
Director-General: Ms K. Tattersall

City and Guilds of London Institute
1 Giltspur Street, London, EC1A 9DD
(Tel: 020-7294 2468; Fax: 020-7294 2400;
E-mail: enquiry@city-and-guilds.co.uk;
Web: www.city-and-guilds.co.uk)
Director-General: N. Carey, PhD.

128 Public Services London

Learning and Skills Development Agency
Citadel Place, Tinworth Street, London, SE11 5EH (Tel: 020-7840 5400; Fax: 020-7840 5401; Web: www.lsagency.org.uk)
Chief Executive: C. Hughes
Chair: Dr T. Melia, CBE

Qualifications and Curriculum Authority
83 Piccadilly, London, W1J 8QA (Tel: 020-7509 5555; Fax: 020-7509 6975;
E-mail: stubbsw@qca.org.uk;
Web: www.open.gov.uk/qca/)
Chairman: Sir William Stubbs

HIGHER EDUCATION
Association of Commonwealth Universities
John Foster House, 36 Gordon Square, London, WC1H 0PF (Tel: 020-7380 6700; Fax: 020-7387 2655; E-mail: info@acu.ac.uk;
Web: www.acu.ac.uk)
Secretary-General: Prof. M. G. Gibbons

Teacher Training Agency
Portland House, Stag Place, London, SW1E 5TT (Tel: 020-7925 3700; Fax: 020-7925 3792;
E-mail: boothc@teach-tta.gov.uk;
Web: www.teach-tta.gov.uk)
Chief Executive: R. Tabberer
Chairman: Prof. C. Booth

Universities UK
Woburn House, 20 Tavistock Square, London, WC1H 9HQ (Tel: 020-7419 4111; Fax: 020-7388 8649; E-mail: info@universitiesuk.ac.uk; Web: www.universities.ac.uk)
President: H. Newby
Chief Executive: Baroness Warwick

INDEPENDENT SCHOOLS
Independent Schools Council
Grosvenor Gardens House, 35–37 Grosvenor Gardens, London, SW1W 0BS (Tel: 020-7798 1500; Fax: 020-7798 1501;
E-mail: national@isis.org.uk;
Web: www.isis.org.uk)
General Secretary: Dr. A. B. Cooke
National Director: D. J. Woodhead

Independent Schools Information Service/ISC
Grosvenor Gardens House, 35–37 Grosvenor Gardens, London, SW1W 0BS (Tel: 020-7798 1500; Fax: 020-7798 1501;
E-mail: national@isis.org.uk;
Web: www.isis.org.uk)
National Director: D. J. Woodhead

SCHOOLS
Education Otherwise
PO Box 7420, London, N9 9SG
(Tel: Helpline: 0870-730 0074;
E-mail: webmaster@education-otherwise.org;
Web: www.education-otherwise.org)
General Secretary: Ms J. Wilkinson

Special Education Needs Tribunal
7th Floor, Windsor House, 50 Victoria Street, London, SW1H 0NW (Tel: 020-7925 6925;
Fax: 020-7925 6926;
E-mail: sen.tribunal@gtnet.gov)
President: T. Aldridge
Secretary: Kevin Mullany

UNITARY AWARDING BODIES
Edexcel Foundation
Stewart House, 32 Russell Square, London, WC1B 5DN (Tel: 0870 2409 800;
Fax: 020-7758 6960;
E-mail: enquiries@edexcel.org.uk;
Web: www.edexcel.org.uk)
Chief Executive: Dr C. Townsend, PhD.

PROFESSIONAL EDUCATION

There are a number of professional bodies in the London area offering courses in and information and advice on professional and vocational qualifications. The list below provides, by subject area in alphabetical order, a list of those bodies which, by providing specialist training or conducting examinations, control entry into a profession, or are responsible for maintaining a register of those with professional qualifications in their sector.

ACCOUNTANCY
Association of Chartered Certified Accountants (ACCA)
29 Lincoln's Inn Fields, London, WC2A 3EE (Tel: 020-7242 6855; Fax: 020-7861 8054;
Web: www.sccaglobal.com)

Chartered Institute of Management Accountants
63 Portland Place, London, W1B 1AB
(Tel: 020-7637 2311;
Web: ww.cimaglobal.com)

Professional Education   129

Chartered Institute of Public Finance and Accountancy (CIPFA)
3 Robert Street, London, WC2N 6BH
(Tel: 020-7543 5600; Fax: 020-7543 5700;
E-mail: webco-ordinator@cipfa.org)

Institute of Chartered Accountants in England and Wales
Chartered Accountants' Hall, PO Box 433, Moorgate Place, London, EC2P 2BJ
(Tel: 020-7920 8100; Fax: 020-7920 0547;
Web: www.icaew.co.uk)

ACTUARIAL SCIENCE
Institute of Actuaries
Staple Inn Hall, High Holborn, London, WC1V 7QJ (Tel: 020-7632 2100; Fax: 020-7632 2111;
E-mail: institute@actuaries.org.uk;
Web: www.actuaries.org.uk)

ARCHITECTURE
The Architectural Association and School of Architecture
34–36 Bedford Square, London, WC1B 3ES
(Tel: 020-7887 4000; Fax: 020-7414 0782)

Architects Registration Board
8 Weymouth Street, London, W1W 5BU
(Tel: 020-7580 5861; Fax: 020-7436 5269;
E-mail: info@arb.org.uk;
Web: www.arb.org.uk)

The Royal Institute of British Architects
66 Portland Place, London, W1B 1AD
(Tel: 020-7580 5533; Fax: 020-7255 1541;
E-mail: admin@inst.riba.org;
Web: www.architecture.com)

The School of Architecture and the Building Arts
19–22 Charlotte Road, London, EC2A 3SG
(Tel: 020-7613 8500; Fax: 020-7613 8599;
E-mail: enquiry@princes-foundation.org;
Web: www.princes-foundation.org)

BANKING
Chartered Institute of Bankers
90 Bishopsgate, London, EC2N 4AS
(Tel: 020-7444 7111)

BUILDING
Institute of Clerks of Works of Great Britain
41 The Mall, London, W5 3TJ (Tel: 020-8579 2917/8; Fax: 020-8579 0554;

E-mail: gensec@icwgb.sagehost.co.uk;
Web: www.icwgb.com)

BUSINESS, MANAGEMENT AND ADMINISTRATION
The Association of MBAs
15 Duncan Terrace, London, N1 8BZ
(Tel: 020-7837 3375)

Institute of Logistic and Transport
11/12 Buckingham Gate, London, SW1E 6LB
(Tel: 020-7592 3110; Fax: 020-7592 3111;
E-mail: enquiry@iolt.org.uk;
Web: www.iolt.org.uk)

Institute of Chartered Secretaries and Administrators
16 Park Crescent, London, W1B 1AH
(Tel: 020-7580 4741; Fax: 020-7323 1132;
E-mail: icsa@dial.pipex.com;
Web: www.icsa.org.uk)

Institute of Chartered Shipbrokers
3 St Helen's Place, London, EC3A 6EJ
(Tel: 020-7628 5559; Fax: 020-7628 5445;
E-mail: info@ics.org.uk;
Web: www.ics.org.uk)

Institute of Healthcare Management
PO Box 33239, London, SW1W 0WN
(Tel: 020-7881 9235; Fax: 020-7881 9236;
E-mail: enquiries@ihm.org.uk;
Web: www.ihm.org.uk)

Institute of Practitioners in Advertising
44 Belgrave Square, London, SW1X 8QS
(Tel: 020-7235 7020; Fax: 020-7245 9904)

Institute of Quality Assurance
12 Grosvenor Crescent, London, SW1X 7EE
(Tel: 020-7245 6722; Fax: 020-7245 6788;
E-mail: iqa@iqa.org; Web: www.iqa.org)

Chartered Institute of Personnel and Development
CIPD House, Camp Road, London, SW19 4UX
(Tel: 020-8971 9000; Fax: 020-8263 3333;
E-mail: cipd@cipd.co.uk;
Web: www.cipd.co.uk)

CHIROPRACTIC
General Chiropractic Council
344–354 Gray's Inn Road, London, WC1X 8BP
(Tel: 020-7713 5155; Fax: 020-7713 5844;

130 Public Services London

E-mail: enquiries@gcc-uk.org;
Web: www.gcc-uk.org)

COMPLEMENTARY MEDICINE
Institute for Complementary Medicine
PO Box 194, London, SE16 7QZ (Tel: 020-7237 5165; Fax: 020-7237 5175;
E-mail: info@icmedicine.co.uk;
Web: www.icmedicine.co.uk)

DANCE
Council for Dance Education and Training (UK)
Tonybee Hall, 28 Commercial Street, London, E1 6LS; E-mail: cdet@btconnect.com;
Web: www.cdet.org.uk)

Imperial Society of Teachers of Dancing
Imperial House, 22–26 Paul Street, London, EC2A 4QE (Tel: 020-7377 1577; Fax: 020-7247 8979; E-mail: admin@istd.org;
Web: www.istd.org)

Royal Academy of Dance
36 Battersea Square, London, SW11 3RA
(Tel: 020-7326 8000; Fax: 020-7924 3129;
Web: www.rad.org.uk)

The Royal Ballet School
155 Talgarth Road, London, W14 9DE
(Tel: 020-8748 6335; Fax: 020-8563 0649;
E-mail: info@royalballetschool.co.uk;
Web: www.royalballetschool.co.uk)

DEFENCE
Royal College of Defence Studies
Seaford House, 37 Belgrave Square, London, SW1X 8NS (Tel: 020-7915 4800; Fax: 020-7915 4999; E-mail: rcdsone@demon.co.uk;
Web: www.mod.uk/rcds)

DENTISTRY
The General Dental Council
37 Wimpole Street, London, W1M 8DQ
(Tel: 020-7887 3800; Fax: 020-7224 3294;
E-mail: information@gdc-uk.org;
Web: www.gdc-uk.org)

DRAMA
The National Council for Drama Training
5 Tavistock Place, London, WC1H 9SS
(Tel: 020-7387 3650; Fax: 020-7383 3060;
E-mail: ncdt@lineone.net;
Web: www.ncdt.co.uk)

ENGINEERING
Chartered Institution of Building Services Engineers
222 Balham High Road, London, SW12 9BS
(Tel: 020-8675 5211; Fax: 020-8675 5449;
E-mail: enquiries@cibse.org;
Web: www.cibse.org)

Institute of Energy
18 Devonshire Street, London, W1G 7AU
(Tel: 020-7580 7124; Fax: 020-7580 4420;
E-mail: info@instenergy.org.uk;
Web: www.instenergy.org.uk)

Institute of Marine Engineers
80 Coleman Street, London, EC2R 5BJ
(Tel: 020-7382 2600; Fax: 020-7382 2670;
E-mail: imare@imare.org.uk;
Web: www.imare.org.uk)

Institute of Materials
1 Carlton House Terrace, London, SW1Y 5DB
(Tel: 020-7451 7300; Fax: 020-7839 1702;
E-mail: admin@materials.org.uk;
Web: www.materials.org.uk)

Institute of Measurement and Control
87 Gower Street, London, WC1E 6AF
(Tel: 020-7387 4949; Fax: 020-7388 8431;
E-mail: education@instmc.org.uk;
Web: www.instmc.org.uk)

Institute of Physics
76 Portland Place, London, W1B 1NT
(Tel: 020-7470 4800; Fax: 020-7470 4848;
E-mail: physics@iop.org; Web: www.iop.org)

Institute of Quality Assurance
12 Grosvenor Crescent, London, SW1X 7EE
(Tel: 020-7245 6722; Fax: 020-7245 6788;
E-mail: iqa@iqa.org; Web: www.iqa.org)

Institution of Civil Engineers
One Great George Street, London, SW1P 3AA
(Tel: 020-7222 7722; Fax: 020-7722 7500;
Web: www.ice.org.uk)

Institution of Electrical Engineers
Savoy Place, London, WC2R 0BL
(Tel: 020-7240 1871; Fax: 020-7240 7735;
E-mail: postmaster@iee.org.uk;
Web: www.iee.org.uk)

Professional Education 131

Institution of Gas Engineers
21 Portland Place, London, W1B 1PY
(Tel: 020-7636 6603; Fax: 020-7636 6602;
E-mail: general@igaseng.demon.co.uk;
Web: www.igaseng.com)

Institution of Incorporated Engineers
Savoy Hill House, Savoy Hill, London, WC2R 0BS (Tel: 020-7836 3357; Fax: 020-7497 9006; E-mail: info@iie.org.uk; Web: www.iie.org.uk)

Institution of Mechanical Engineers
1 Birdcage Walk, London, SW1H 9JJ
(Tel: 020-7222 7899; Fax: 020-7222 4557;
E-mail: enquiries@imeche.org.uk;
Web: www.imeche.org.uk)

Institution of Nuclear Engineers
1 Penerley Road, London, SE6 2LQ
(Tel: 020-8698 1500; Fax: 020-8695 6409;
E-mail: inuce@lineone.net;
Web: www.inuce.co.uk)

Institution of Structural Engineers
11 Upper Belgrave Street, London, SW1X 8BH
(Tel: 020-7235 4535; Fax: 020-7235 4294;
E-mail: mail@istructe.org.uk;
Web: www.istructe.org.uk)

Royal Aeronautical Society
4 Hamilton Place, London, W1V 0BQ
(Tel: 020-7670 4300; Fax: 020-7499 6230;
E-mail: keith.mans@raes.org.uk)

Royal Institution of Naval Architects
10 Upper Belgrave Street, London, SW1X 8BQ
(Tel: 020-7235 4622; Fax: 020-7259 5912;

FOOD AND NUTRITION SCIENCE
Institute of Food Science and Technology
5 Cambridge Court, 210 Shepherd's Bush Road, London, W6 7NJ (Tel: 020-7603 6316;
E-mail: info@ifst.org; Web: www.ifst.org)

FUEL AND ENERGY SCIENCE
Institute of Energy
18 Devonshire Street, London, W1N 2AU
(Tel: 020-7580 7124; Fax: 020-7580 4420;
E-mail: info@instenergy.org.uk;
Web: www.instenergy.org.uk)

Institute of Petroleum
61 New Cavendish Street, London, W1G 7AR
(Tel: 020-7467 7100; Fax: 020-7255 1472;
E-mail: ip@petroleum.co.uk;
Web: www.petroleum.co.uk)

Institution of Gas Engineers
21 Portland Place, London, W1N 3AF
(Tel: 020-7636 6603; Fax: 020-7636 6602;
E-mail: general@igaseng.demon.co.uk;
Web: www.igaseng.com)

HOTELKEEPING, CATERING AND INSTITUTIONAL MANAGEMENT
Hotel and Catering International Management Association
191 Trinity Road, London, SW17 7HN
(Tel: 020-8772 8400; Fax: 020-8772 8500;
E-mail: general@hcima.co.uk;
Web: www.hcima.org.uk)

INSURANCE
Association of Average Adjusters
The Baltic Exchange, St Mary Axe, London, EC3A 8BH (Tel: 020-7623 5501; Fax: 020-7369 1623; E-mail: aaa@be.bex.org;
Web: www.average-adjusters.com)

The Chartered Institute of Loss Adjusters
Peninsular House, 36 Monument Street, London, EC2R 8LJ (Tel: 020-7337 9960;
Fax: 020-7929 3082; E-mail: info@cila.co.uk;
Web: www.cila.co.uk)

Chartered Insurance Institute
20 Aldermanbury, London, EC2V 7HY
(Tel: 020-7417 4425;
E-mail: customer.serv@cii.co.uk;
Web: www.cii.co.uk)

JOURNALISM
The Periodicals Training Council
Queen's House, 55–56 Lincoln's Inn Fields, London, WC2A 3LJ (Tel: 020-7404 4168; Fax: 020-7404 4167; E-mail: training@ppa.co.uk;
Web: www.ppa.co.uk/ptc)

LAW
The General Council of the Bar
3 Bedford Row, London, WC1R 4DB
(Tel: 020-7242 0082; Fax: 020-7831 4778;
E-mail: chairman@barcouncil.org.uk;
Web: www.barcouncil.org.uk)

132 Public Services London

General Council of the Bar, Education and Training Department
2–3 Cursitor Street, London, EC4A 1NE
(Tel: 020-7440 4000; Fax: 020-7440 4002;
E-mail: cach@barcouncil.org.uk;
Web: www.lawzone.co.uk/barcouncil)

Gray's Inn
8 South Square, London, WC1R 5ET
(Tel: 020-7458 7800; Fax: 020-7458 7801;
Web: www.graysinn.org.uk)

The Honourable Society of the Inner Temple
Treasury Office, Inner Temple, London, EC4Y 7HL (Tel: 020-7797 8250; Fax: 020-7797 8178;
E-mail: enquiries@innertemple.org.uk)

Inns of Court School of Law
4 Gray's Inn Place, Gray's Inn, London, WC1R 5DX (Tel: 020-7404 5787; Fax: 020-7831 4188;
E-mail: bvc@icsl.ac.uk; Web: www.icsl.ac.uk)

Law Society of England and Wales
113 Chancery Lane, London, WC2A 1PL
(Tel: 020-7242 1222; Fax: 020-7831 0344;
Web: www.lawsociety.org.uk)

Lincoln's Inn
London, WC2A 3TL
(Tel: 020-7405 1393; Fax: 020-7831 1839;
E-mail: mail@lincolnsinn.org.uk;
Web: www.lincolnsinn.org.uk)

The Middle Temple
London, EC4Y 9AT
(Tel: 020-7427 4800; Fax: 020-7427 4801)

LIBRARIANSHIP AND INFORMATION SCIENCE/MANAGEMENT
The Library Association
7 Ridgmount Street, London, WC1E 7AE
(Tel: 020-7255 0500; Fax: 020-7255 0501;
E-mail: info@la-hq.org.uk;
Web: www.la-hq.org.uk)

MATERIALS STUDIES
Institute of Materials
1 Carlton House Terrace, London, SW1Y 5DB
(Tel: 020-7451 7300)

MEDICINE
Faculty of Accident and Emergency Medicine
Royal College of Surgeons of England, 35–43 Lincoln's Inn Fields, London, WC2A 3PE
(Tel: 020-7405 7071; Fax: 020-7405 0318;
E-mail: faem@compuserve.com;
Web: www.faem.org.uk)

Faculty of Occupational Medicine
6 St Andrew's Place, London, NW1 4LB
(Tel: 020-7317 5890; Fax: 020-7317 5899;
E-mail: fom@facoccmed.ac.uk;
Web: www.facoccmed.ac.uk)

Faculty of Pharmaceutical Medicine
1 St Andrew's Place, London, NW1 4LB
(Tel: 020-7224 0343; Fax: 020-7224 5381;
E-mail: fpm@f-pharm-med.org.uk;
Web: www.fpm.org.uk)

Faculty of Public Health Medicine
4 St Andrew's Place, London, NW1 4LB
(Tel: 020-7935 0243; Fax: 020-7224 6973;
E-mail: enquiries@fphm.org.uk;
Web: www.fphm.org.uk)

General Medical Council
178 Great Portland Street, London, W1W 5JE
(Tel: 020-7580 7642; Fax: 020-7915 3641;
E-mail: gmc@gmc-uk.org;
Web: www.gmc-uk.org)

Royal College of Anaesthetists
48–49 Russell Square, London, WC1B 4JY
(Tel: 020-7813 1900; Fax: 020-7813 1876;
E-mail: info@rcoa.ac.uk;
Web: www.rcoa.ac.uk)

Royal College of General Practitioners
14 Princes Gate, London, SW7 1PU
(Tel: 020-7581 3232; Fax: 020-7225 3047;
E-mail: info@rcgp.org.uk;
Web: www.rcgp.org.uk)

Royal College of Obstetricians and Gynaecologists
27 Sussex Place, London, NW1 4RG
(Tel: 020-7772 6200; Fax: 020-7723 0575;
E-mail: coll.sec@rcog.org.uk;
Web: www.rcog.org.uk)

Royal College of Paediatrics and Child Health
50 Hallam Street, London, W1W 6DE
(Tel: 020-7307 5600; Fax: 020-7307 5601;

Professional Education

E-mail: enquiries@rcpch.ac.uk;
Web: www.rcpch.ac.uk)

Royal College of Pathologists
2 Carlton House Terrace, London, SW1Y 5AF
(Tel: 020-7451 6700; Fax: 020-7451 6701;
E-mail: info@rcpath.org;
Web: www.rcpath.org)

Royal College of Physicians
11 St Andrew's Place, Regent's Park, London, NW1 4LE (Tel: 020-7935 1174; Fax: 020-7487 5218; Web: www.rcplondon.ac.uk)

Royal College of Psychiatrists
17 Belgrave Square, London, SW1X 8PG
(Tel: 020-7235 2351; Fax: 020-7245 2351;
E-mail: rcpsych@rcpsych.ac.uk;
Web: www.rcpsych.ac.uk)

Royal College of Radiologists
38 Portland Place, London, W1N 4QJ
(Tel: 020-7636 4432; Fax: 020-7323 3100;
E-mail: enquiries@rcr.ac.uk;
Web: www.rcr.ac.uk)

Royal College of Surgeons of England
35–43 Lincoln's Inn Fields, London, WC2A 3PN
(Tel: 020-7405 3474; Web: www.rcseng.ac.uk)

Society of Apothecaries of London
14 Blackfriars Lane, London, EC4V 6EJ
(Tel: 020-7236 1189; Fax: 020-7329 3177;
E-mail: clerk@apothecaries.org;
Web: www.apothecaries.org)

United Examining Board
Apothecaries Hall, Blackfriars Lane, London, EC4V 6EJ (Tel: 020-7236 1180; Fax: 020-7329 3177; E-mail: examoffice@apothecaries.org)

MUSIC
Associated Board of the Royal Schools of Music
24 Portland Place, London, W1B 1LU
(Tel: 020-7636 5400; Fax: 020-7367 0234;
E-mail: abrsm@abrsm.ac.uk;
Web: www.abrsm.ac.uk)

Guildhall School of Music & Drama
Silk Street, London, EC2Y 8DT
(Tel: 020-7628 2571; Fax: 020-7256 9438;
Web: www.gsmd.ac.uk)

London College of Music and Media
Thames Valley Univesity, St Mary's Road, London, W5 5RF (Tel: 020-8231 2304; Fax: 020-8231 2546; E-mail: enquiries.lcm2@tvu.ac.uk; Web: www.elgar.tvu.ac.uk)

Royal Academy of Music
Marylebone Road, London, NW1 5HT
(Tel: 020-7873 7373; Fax: 020-7873 7374;
Web: www.ram.ac.uk)

Royal College of Organists
7 St Andrew Street, London, EC4A 3LQ
(Tel: 020-7936 3606; Fax: 020-7353 8244;
E-mail: alandear@rco.org.uk;
Web: www.rco.org,.uk)

Trinity College of Music
King Charles Court, Old Royal Naval College, King Wiliam Walk, Greenwich, London, SE10 9JF (Tel: 020-7935 5773; Fax: 020-7224 6278; E-mail: info@tcm.ac.uk; Web: www.tcm.ac.uk)

NURSING
English National Board for Nursing, Midwifery and Health Visiting
Victory House, 170 Tottenham Court Road, London, W1P 0HA (Tel: 020-7391 6229; Fax: 020-7383 3525; Web: www.enb.org.uk)

The Royal College of Nursing of the United Kingdom
20 Cavendish Square, London, W1G 0RN
(Tel: 020-7409 3333; Fax: 020-7647 3434;
Web: www.rcn.org.uk)

UK Central Council for Nursing, Midwifery and Health Visiting
23 Portland Place, London, W1N 4JT
(Tel: 020-7637 7181; Fax: 020-7436 2924;
E-mail: communications@ukcc.org.uk;
Web: www.ukcc.org.uk)

OPHTHALMIC AND DISPENSING OPTICS
The Association of British Dispensing Opticians
6 Hurlingham Business Park, Sulivan Road, London, SW6 3DU (Tel: 020-7736 0088; Fax: 020-7731 5531; E-mail: general@abdo.org.uk; Web: www.abdo.org.uk)

134 Public Services London

The College of Optometrists
42 Craven Street, London, WC2N 5NG
(Tel: 020-7839 6000; Fax: 020-7839 6800;
E-mail: optometry@college-optometrists.org;
Web: www.college-optometrists.org)

OSTEOPATHY
General Osteopathic Council
Osteopathy House, 176 Tower Bridge Road, London, SE1 3LU (Tel: 020-7357 6655; Fax: 020-7357 0011;
E-mail: info@osteopathy.org.uk;
Web: www.osteopathy.org.uk)

PHARMACY
Royal Pharmaceutical Society of Great Britain
1 Lambeth High Street, London, SE1 7JN
(Tel: 020-7735 9141;
E-mail: careers@rpsgb.org.uk;
Web: www.rpsgb.org.uk)

PRINTING
British Printing Industries Federation
Farringdon Point, 29–35 Farringdon Road, London, EC1M 3JF (Tel: 020-7915 8300; Fax: 020-7405 7784; E-mail: info@bpif.org.uk; Web: www.bpif.org.uk)

PROFESSIONS SUPPLEMENTARY TO MEDICINE
British Association of Art Therapists
Mary Ward House, 5 Tavistock Place, London, WC1H 9SN (Tel: 020-7383 3774; Fax: 020-7387 5513; E-mail: baat@ukgateway.net;
Web: www.baat.co.uk)

British Association of Dramatherapists
41 Broomhouse Lane, London, SW6 3DP
(Tel: 020-7731 0160; Fax: 020-7731 0160;
E-mail: gillian@badth.demon.co.uk)

The British Orthoptic Society
Tavistock House North, Tavistock Square, London, WC1H 9HX (Tel: 020-7387 7992; Fax: 020-7383 2584; E-mail: bos@orthoptics.org.uk; Web: www.orthoptics.org.uk)

The Chartered Society of Physiotherapy
14 Bedford Row, London, WC1R 4ED
(Tel: 020-7306 6666)

College of Occupational Therapists
106–114 Borough High Street, London, SE1 1LB (Tel: 020-7357 6480; Fax: 020-7450 2299; Web: www.cot.co.uk)

The College of Radiographers
207 Providence Square, London, SE1 2EW
(Tel: 020-7740 7200; Fax: 020-7740 7204;
E-mail: info@sor.org; Web: www.sor.org)

The Council for Professions Supplementary to Medicine
Park House, 184 Kennington Park Road, London, SE11 4BU (Tel: 020-7582 0866; Fax: 020-7820 9684)

Institute of Biomedical Science
12 Coldbath Square, London, EC1R 5HL
(Tel: 020-7713 0214; Fax: 020-7436 4946;
E-mail: mail@ibms.org; Web: www.ibms.org)

The Society of Chiropodists and Podiatrists
53 Welbeck Street, London, W1M 7HE
(Tel: 020-7486 3381; Fax: 020-7935 6359;
E-mail: eng@scpod.org;
Web: www.feetforlife.org)

SCIENCE
The Geological Society of London
Burlington House, Piccadilly, London, W1J 0BG
(Tel: 020-7434 9944; Fax: 020-7439 8975;
E-mail: enquiries@geolsoc.org.uk;
Web: www.geolsoc.org.uk)

Institute of Biology
20–22 Queensberry Place, London, SW7 2DZ
(Tel: 020-7581 8333; Fax: 020-7823 9409;
E-mail: info@iob.org; Web: www.iob.org)

Institute of Physics
76 Portland Place, London, W1N 3DH
(Tel: 020-7470 4800)

Royal Society of Chemistry
Burlington House, Piccadilly, London, W1V 0BN (Tel: 020-7437 8656; Fax: 020-7437 8883; E-mail: rsc1@rsc.org; Web: www.rsc.org)

SPEECH AND LANGUAGE THERAPY
The Royal College of Speech and Language Therapists
2 White Hart Yard, London, SE1 1NX
(Tel: 020-7378 1200; Fax: 020-7403 7254;
E-mail: postmaster@rcslt.org)

Professional Education

SURVEYING
Incorporated Society of Valuers and Auctioneers (1968)
3 Cadogan Gate, London, SW1X 0AS
(Tel: 020-7235 2282; Fax: 020-7831 2048)

Institute of Revenues, Rating and Valuation
41 Doughty Street, London, WC1N 2LF
(Tel: 020-7831 3505; Fax: 020-7831 2048;
E-mail: enquiries@irrv.org.uk;
Web: www.irrv.org.uk)

Royal Institution of Chartered Surveyors
12 Great George Street, London, SW1P 3AD
(Tel: 020-7222 7000; Fax: 020-7222 9430;
E-mail: info@rics.org.uk; Web: www.rics.org)

THEOLOGICAL COLLEGES
Allen Hall
28 Beaufort Street, London, SW3 5AA
(Tel: 020-7351 1296; Fax: 020-7349 5601;
E-mail: secretary@allenhall.co.uk)

Campion House College
112 Thornbury Road, Isleworth, Middx, TW7 4NN (Tel: 020-8560 1924; Fax: 020-8569 9645;
E-mail: campionhouse.asterley@compuserve.com;
Web: www.campionhouse.org.uk)

Leo Baeck College
Sternberg Centre for Judaism, 80 East End Road, London, N3 2SY (Tel: 020-8349 5600;
Fax: 020-8343 2558; E-mail: info@lbc.ac.uk;
Web: www.lbc.ac.uk)

London Theological Seminary
104 Hendon Lane, London, N3 3SQ
(Tel: 020-8346 7587;
E-mail: principal@lts.u-net.com;
Web: www.lts.u-net.com)

New London School of Jewish Studies (Jews' College)
Schaller House, Albert Road, London, NW4 2SJ
(Tel: 020-8203 6427; Fax: 020-8203 6420;
E-mail: principal@lsjs.ac.uk;
Web: www.lsjs.ac.uk)

Oak Hill College
Chase Side, London, N14 4PS (Tel: 020-8449 0467; Fax: 020-8441 5996;
E-mail: mailbox@oakhill.ac.uk;
Web: www.oakhill.ac.uk)

Spurgeon's College
South Norwood Hill, London, SE25 6DJ
(Tel: 020-8653 0850;
E-mail: enquiries@spurgeons.ac.uk;
Web: www.spurgeons.ac.uk)

St Edwards College
46 Totteridge Common, London, N20 8ND
(Tel: 020-8959 2553; Fax: 020-8201 1850;
E-mail: recstedwards@aol.com)

TOWN AND COUNTRY PLANNING
The Royal Town Planning Institute
26 Portland Place, London, W1N 4BE
(Tel: 020-7636 9107; Fax: 020-7323 1582;
E-mail: online@rtpi.org.uk;
Web: www.rtpi.org.uk)

TRANSPORT
The Institute of Logistics and Transport
11–12 Buckingham Gate, London, SW1E 6LB
(Tel: 020-7592 3120; Fax: 020-7592 3111;
E-mail: enquiries@iolt.org.uk)

VETERINARY MEDICINE
British Veterinary Association
7 Mansfield Street, London, W1G 9NQ
(Tel: 020-7636 6541; Fax: 020-7436 2970;
E-mail: bvahq@bva.co.uk;
Web: www.bva.co.uk)

Royal College of Veterinary Surgeons
Belgravia House, 62–64 Horseferry Road, London, SW1P 2AF (Tel: 020-7222 2001; Fax: 020-7222 2004; E-mail: admin@rcvs.org.uk;
Web: www.rcvs.org.uk)

EMERGENCY SERVICES

AMBULANCE SERVICE

LONDON AMBULANCE SERVICE (LAS) NHS TRUST

220 Waterloo Road, London SE1 8SD
(Tel: 020 7921 5100).

The London Ambulance Service in one of the largest Ambulance Services in the World. On average, London Ambulance Service Crews take 1.6 million patients to hospital each year. There are seventy ambulance stations spanning the 620 square miles of Greater London. They are divided into 7 sectors. A Chief Executive and a board of directors manage the LAS as a whole. They report to the LAS Trust board.

LAS TRUST BOARD

Trust Board Executive Directors: Mr. Peter Bradley (*Chief Executive*); Mr. Owen Disley (*Assistant Chief Ambulance Officer - Operational Standards*); Mr. Mark Jones (*Director of Finance and Business Planning*); Mrs Wendy Foers (*Director of Human Resources*); Mr. Ian Tighe (*Director of Technology and Trust Secretary*)

Trust Board Non-Executive Directors: Mr. Sigurd Reinton (*Chairman*); Mr. Colin Douglas (*Vice-Chairman*); Lord Toby Harris; Mr. Barry MacDonald; Sarah Waller; Mrs Suzanne Burn

FIRE SERVICE

LONDON FIRE AND EMERGENCY PLANNING AUTHORITY

The London Fire and Civil Defence Authority was responsible for the Capital's fire service and Emergency planning provision. The LFCDA ceased to exist when the Greater London Authority came to power in July 2000. The new body, the London Fire and Emergency Planning Authority comprises of three command areas as did the LFCDA, with an Assistant Chief Fire officer in charge of each one. There will be 17 members of the LFEPA, 9 will be drawn from the London Assembly and 8 will be nominated by the London boroughs. For further information of the LFEPA as part of the Greater London Authority please see the Governed London section.

The London Fire Brigades cover the 620 square miles of Greater London. There are 113 fire stations and one river station divided amongst the three command areas, Eastern, Western and Southern Commands. London's one River Station is at Lambeth. It was built in 1900 with a pontoon on two floors, opposite the Brigade Headquarters at 8 Albert Embankment. It covers the River Thames from Dartford to East Molesey with two fireboats called Fireflash and Firedart.

LONDON FIRE BRIGADE EASTERN COMMAND

Headquarters, 2 Ferns Road, Stratford, London E15 4LX (Tel: 020-7587 2411; Fax: 020-7587 2437; Web: www.london-fire.gov.uk)

Assistant Chief Fire Officer: Malcolm Kelly

Fire Stations: Barking, Bethnal Green, Bow, Chingford, Clerkenwell, Dagenham, Dowgate, East Ham, Edmonton, Enfiled, Hainault, Holloway, Homerton, Hornchurch, Hornsey, Ilford, Islington, Kingsland, Leyton, Leytonstone, Millwall, Plaistow, Poplar, Romford, Shadwell, Shoreditch, Silvertown, Southgate, Stoke Newington, Stratford, Tottenham, Walthamstow, Wennington, Whitechapel, Woodford.

Boroughs served: Barking and Dagenham, City of London, Enfield, Hackney, Haringey, Havering, Islington, Newham, Redbridge, Tower Hamlets, Waltham Forest.

LONDON FIRE BRIGADE SOUTHERN COMMAND

Headquarters, 249/259 Lewisham High Street, London SE13 6NH (Tel: 020-7587 2561; Web: www.london-fire.gov.uk).

Assistant Chief Fire Officer: Mr. L. Gill

Fire Stations: Addington, Battersea, Beckenham, Bexley, Biggin Hill, Brixton, Bromley, Clapham, Croydon, Deptford, Dockhead, Downham, East Greenwich, Eltham, Erith, Forest Hill, Greenwich, Kingston, Lambeth, Lambeth (*River*), Lee Green, Lewisham, Mitcham, New Cross, New Malden, Norbury, Old Kent Road, Orpington, Peckham, Plumstead, Purley, Sidcup, Southwark, Surbiton, Sutton, Tooting, Wallington, Wandsworth, West Norwood, Wimbledon, Woodside, Woolwich.

Boroughs served: Bexley, Bromley, Croydon, Greenwich, Kingston-upon-Thames, Lambeth, Lewisham, Merton, Southwark, Sutton, Wandsworth.

LONDON FIRE BRIGADE WESTERN COMMAND
Headquarters, 591A, Harrow Road, Wembley, Middlesex HA0 2EG (Tel: 020-7587 2700; Web: www.london-fire.gov.uk).

Assistant Chief Fire Officer: Mr M. Overall

Fire Stations: Acton, Barnet, Belsize, Chelsea, Chiswick, Ealing, Euston, Feltham, Finchley, Fulham, Hammersmith, Harrow, Hayes, Heathrow, Hendon, Heston, Hillingdon, Kensington, Kentish Town, Knightsbridge, Manchester Square, Mill Hill, North Kensington, Northolt, Paddington, Park Royal, Richmond, Ruislip, Soho, Southall, Stanmore, Twickenham, Wembley, West Hampstead, Westminster, Willesden.

Boroughs served: Barnet, Brent, Camden, Ealing, Harrow, Hillingdon, Hammersmith and Fulham, Hounslow, Kensington and Chelsea, Richmond upon Thames, Westminster City.

POLICE SERVICE

The Greater London Authority Act 1999 established a new independent Metropolitan Police Authority (MPA) to oversee policing in London. The boundaries of the Metropolitan Police District have been changed to bring them in line with the 32 London boroughs, with areas beyond this becoming part of Surrey, Hertfordshire and Essex police areas. The Home Secretary retains responsibility alongside the MPA for the national and international functions provided by the Metropolitan Police Service (MPS).

The core role of the MPS is to:
- Build communities resistant to crime and disorder
- Divert young people from crime
- Reduce illegal drug dealing
- Police our diverse communities

The MPS also has units involved in providing a number of national and international services. These are:
- The Diplomatic Protection Group
- Royal Protection
- Palace of Westminster
- Anti-terrorist Branch
- Special Branch
- National Identification Service

For further information please see the entry for the MPA in the Governed London section. The MPS set up 41 Police Community Consultative Groups (PCCGs) which operate at borough level aiming to have as diverse a membership as possible. The MPS has also set up 38 Community Safety Units (CSUs) aimed to deal with racist, anti-Semitic and homophobic crime as well as domestic violence.

The City of London Police continues to have a separate police force, the authority for which is a committee of the Corporation of London and includes councillors and magistrates. Police authorities are financed by central and local government grants and a precept on the council tax.

Complaints
The investigation and resolution of a serious complaint against a police officer is subject to the scrutiny of the Police Complaints Authority. An officer who is dismissed, required to resign or reduced in rank, whether as a result of a complaint or not, may appeal to a police appeals tribunal established by the relevant police authority.

METROPOLITAN POLICE SERVICE

New Scotland Yard, Broadway, London SW1H 0BG (Tel: 020-7230 1212; Web: www.met.police.uk).

The Metropolitan Police Force came into existence on 30 September 1829 following Sir Robert Peel's committee recommending the setting up of an organised police force. The Metropolitan Police is one of the largest services in the United Kingdom, serving an area of 620 square miles within a radius of approximately 15 miles of Trafalgar Square. The Metropolitan Police serves a population of over seven million and is divided into 32 Operational Command Units, one for each London Borough. It employs 26,300 officers, 11,100 civil staff and 890 traffic wardens.

Commissioner: J. Stevens, QPM

METROPOLITAN POLICE, SPECIAL CONSTABULARY

The Special Constabulary was originally formed in 1831 to cope with times of emergency. At this time people did not volunteer – they were called up and fines were imposed on people who did not respond. The modern idea of special constables was used extensively during the world wars on a volunteer basis and over 11,000 special constables served during WW2. The Metropolitan Special Constabulary currently employs approximately 1,400 officers.

METROPOLITAN POLICE, RIVER DIVISION
Waterloo: Tel: 020-7321 7278
Wapping: Tel: 020-7275 4425

CITY OF LONDON POLICE

26 Old Jewry, London EC2R 8DJ
(Tel: 020-7601 2222;
Email: postmaster@city-of-london.police.uk;
Web: www.cityoflondon.police.co.uk).
Community Safety (Crime Prevention)
(Tel: 020-7601 2323).

Force Recruitment Tel: 020-7601 2251
Special Constabulary Tel: 020-7601 2713
Fraud Department Tel: 020-7601 2999
Crimestoppers Tel: 0800 555111

The City of London Police Force was formally established by the City of London Police Act 1839. The first commissioner, Daniel Whittle-Harvey, was responsible for about 500 men. In 1842 the Force moved its headquarters from the Corporation's Guildhall to 26 Old Jewry, where it has since remained.

The City of London Police Force is responsible for the safety of everyone who lives and works in or visits London's square mile. There are approximately 6,000 residents in the City of London although this number is swelled daily by an influx of some 350,000 commuters and tourists. The only significant difference between the City of London Police Force and other police forces in the UK is that the Force has retained the link with the local authority for the area – the Corporation of London. Around 1,200 people work for the City of London Police, with approximately one third of these undertaking civilian support duties.

The Operational Support Department co-ordinates the Force's activities to prevent terrorist crime, as well as providing a range of support and specialist uniformed services including the Communications Centre, planning for major operations, traffic patrol, horse and dog sections and firearms experts. The Specialist Crime Department is responsible for co-ordinating crime prevention strategies, providing scientific supports and for investigating major crimes including fraud and money laundering. The City of London Police serves a unique community. Today, the City is host to 565 foreign banks, branches and subsidiaries and contains more corporate headquarters than any other city in Europe.

In January 1999 the Force established a new branch called the Community Safety Branch whose aim is to protect City communities through partnership, support and prevention. The Scientific Support Unit has the remit of examining crime scenes for forensic and fingerprint evidence and to undertake all aspects of photography for the force. Blood, shoeprints, toolmarks, fibres, tyremarks and other trace material may yield valuable intelligence or evidence for investigating officers.

Commissioner: P. Nove

POLICE COMPLAINTS AUTHORITY

10 Great George Street, London SW1P 3AE
(Tel: 020-7273 6450; Fax: 020-7273 6401;
Email: info@pca.gov.uk; Web: www.pca.gov.uk).

The Police Complaints Authority was established under the Police and Criminal Evidence Act 1984 to provide an independent system for dealing with complaints by members of the public against police officers in England and Wales. It is funded by the Home Office. The authority has powers to supervise the investigation of certain categories of serious complaints. It does not deal with police operational matters; these are usually dealt with by the Chief Constable of the relevant force.

NATIONAL POLICE FUNCTIONS

BRITISH TRANSPORT POLICE

15 Tavistock Place, London WC1H 9SJ
(Tel: 020-7388 7541; Web: www.btp.police.uk)

British Transport Police is the national police force for the railways in England, Wales and Scotland, including the London Underground system, Docklands Light Railway, the Midland Metrotram and Croydon Tramlink systems. The Chief Constable reports to the British Transport

Police Committee. The members of the Committee are appointed by the British Railways Board and include representatives of Railtrack and London Underground Ltd as well as independent members. Officers are paid the same as other police forces. There are approximately 2,100 officers.

Chief Constable: I. Johnson
Deputy Chief Constable: J. A. Lake

FORENSIC SCIENCE SERVICE

Headquarters: Priory House, Gooch Street North, Birmingham B5 6QQ (Tel: 0121-607 6800; Fax: 0121-643 3181; Web: www.forensic.gov.uk).

The Forensic Science Service (FSS) provides forensic science support to the police forces in England and Wales for the investigation of scenes of crime, scientific analysis of material, and interpretation of scientific results. The FSS is organised into serious crime, volume crime, drugs and specialist services, supported by intelligence and consultancy services. Laboratories are located at London, Birmingham, Chepstow, Chorley, Huntingdon, and Wetherby.

Chief Executive: Dr J. Thompson

MINISTRY OF DEFENCE POLICE

Wethersfield, Braintree, Essex CM7 4AZ (Tel: 01371-854000; Fax: 01371 854060).

The primary role of the Ministry of Defence Police is the prevention, detection and investigation of crime within the Ministry of Defence and Crown Estate and other locations policed under repayment arrangements. In addition to its policing role, the Ministry of Defence Police also provides a security and guarding service, armed when required, at a number of key defence and other installations. The Chief Constable is also responsible for the professional management and training of the Ministry of Defence Guard Service.

Chief Constable/Chief Executive: Lloyd Clarke
Deputy Chief Constable: Anthony Comben
Head of Secretariat: P. A. Crowther

NCS SERVICE AUTHORITY

Headquarters: PO Box 2600, London SW1V 2WG (Tel: 020-7238 2600; Fax: 020-7328 2602).

The Service Authority is responsible for ensuring the effective operation of the National Crime Squad. It fulfils a similar role to a police authority. It works alongside the National Criminal Intelligence Service Authority. There are 25 members, of whom the chairman and ten others serve as 'core members' on both authorities.

Chairman: Rt. Hon. Sir John Wheeler, JP, DL
Clerk: T. Simmons
Treasurer: P. Derrick

NATIONAL CRIME SQUAD

PO Box 2500, London, SW1V 2WF (Tel: 020-7238 2500; Fax: 020-7238 2520).

The National Crime Squad (NCS) was established on 1 April 1998, replacing the six regional crime squads in England and Wales. It investigates national and international organised and serious crime. It also supports police forces investigating serious crime. The squad is accountable to the National Crime Squad Service Authority.

Director General: William Hughes

POLICE INFORMATION TECHNOLOGY ORGANISATION

New Kings Beam House, 22 Upper Ground, London SE1 9QY (Tel: 020-8358 5678; Fax: 020-8358 5534; Email: information.desk@pito.pnn.police.uk; Web: www.pito.org.uk).

The Police Information Technology Organization (PITO) became a non-departmental public body on 1 April 1998. It develops and manages the delivery of national police information technology services, such as the Police National Computer, co-ordinates the development of local information technology systems where common standards and systems are needed, and provides a procurement service.

Chairman: Sir Edmund Burton
Chief Executive: Vivienne Dews

140 Public Services London

POLICE NATIONAL MISSING PERSONS BUREAU

Headquarters: New Scotland Yard, Broadway, London, SW1H 0BG (Tel: 020-7230 1212)

The Police National Missing Persons Bureau (PNMPB) acts as a central clearing house of information, receiving reports about vulnerable missing persons that are still outstanding after 14 days and details of unidentified persons or remains within 48 hours of being found from all forces in England and Wales. Reports are also received from Scottish police forces, the RUC, and foreign police forces via Interpol.

ROYAL PARKS CONSTABULARY

The Old Police House, Hyde Park, London W2 2UH (Tel: 020-7298 2000; Fax: 020-7298 2059)

The Royal Parks Constabulary is maintained by the Royal Parks Agency, an executive agency of the Department for Culture, Media and Sport, and is responsible for the policing of eight royal parks in and around London. These comprise an area in excess of 5,000 acres. There are approximately 150 officers who are appointed under the Parks Regulations Act 1872 as amended and are paid around 85 per cent of the Metropolitan Police rate.

Chief Officer: vacant
Acting Chief Officer: D. Pollock

POLICE STATIONS

Acton
250 High Street, London, W3 9BH

Addington
Addington Village Road, Croydon, Surrey, CR0 5AO

Albany Street
60 Albany Street, London, NW1 4EE

Arbour Square
East Arbour Street, London, E1 0PU

Barking
6 Ripple Road, Barking, Essex, IG11 7NF

Barkingside
1 High Street, Ilford, Essex, IG6 1QB

Barnet
26 High Street, Barnet, Hertfordshire, EN5 5RU

Battersea
112–118 Battersea Bridge Road, London, SW11 3AP

Beckenham
45 High Street, Beckenham, Kent, BR3 1AW

Belgravia
202–206 Buckingham Palace Road, London, SW1V 6SX

Belvedere
2 Nuxley Road, Belvedere, Kent, DA17 5JF

Bethnal Green
12 Victoria Park Square, London, E2 9NZ

Bexleyheath
2 Arnsberg Way, Bexleyheath, Kent, DA7 4QS

Biggin Hill
195 Main Road, Biggin Hill, TN16 3JU

Bow
111 Bow Road, London, E3 2AN

Brentford
The Half Acre, Brentford, Middx, TW3 8BH

Brick Lane
23–25 Brick Lane, London, E1 6PU

Brixton
367 Brixton Road, London, SW9 7DD

Brockley
4 Howson Road, London, SE4 2AS

Bromley
48 Widmore Road, Bromley, Kent, BR1 3BG

Brompton - Chelsea
2 Lucan Place, London, SW3 3PB

Brompton - Kensington
72 & 74 Earls Court Road, London, W8 6EQ

Camberwell
22a Camberwell Church Street, London, SE5 8QU

Canning Town
23 Tarling Road, London, E16 1HN

Carey Way
Unit 5–7, Towers Business Park, Carey Way, Wembley, Middx, HA9 0LQ

Catford
333 Bromley Road, Southend Village, London, SE6 2RJ

Police Stations

Charing Cross
Agar Street, London, WC2N 4JP

Chelsea
2 Lucan Place, London, SW3

Cheshunt
101 Turner's Hill, Cheshunt, Herts, EN8 9BD

Chingford
King's Head Hill, London, E4 7EA

Chislehurst
47 High Street, Chislehurst, Kent, BR7 5AF

Chiswick
205–211 Chiswick High Road, London, W4 2DR

Clapham
51 Union Grove, London, SW8 2QU

Colindale
Grahame Park Way, London, NW9 5TW

Cray
43–45 High Street, St Mary Cray, Kent, BR5 3NH

Croydon
71 Park Lane, Croydon, Surrey, CR9 1BP

Deptford
116 Amersham Vale, London, SE14 6LG

Ealing
67–69 Uxbridge Road, London, W5 5SJ

Earlsfield
522 Garratt Lane, London, SW17 0NZ

East Dulwich
173–183 Lordship Lane, London, SE22 8HA

East Ham
4 High Street South, London, E6 4ES

Edgware
Whitchurch Lane, Edgware, Middx, HA8 6LA

Edmonton
462 Fore Street, London, N9 0PW

Eltham
20 Well Hall Road, London, SE9 6SF

Enfield
41 Baker Street, Enfield, Middx, EN1 3EU

Erith
22 High Street, Erith, Kent, DA8 1QY

Feltham
34 Hanworth Road, Feltham, Middx, TW13 5BD

Finchley
193 Ballards Lane, London, N3 1LZ

Forest Gate
370 Romford Road, London, E7 8BS

Fulham
Heckfield Place, London, SW6 5NL

Gipsy Hill
66 Central Hill, London, SE19 1DT

Golders Green
1069 Finchley Road, London, NW11 0QE

Greenford
21 Oldfield Lane, Greenford, Middx, UB6 9LQ

Greenwich
31 Royal Hill, London, SE10 8RR

Hackney
4–6 Shepherdess Walk, London, N1 7LF

Ham
18 Ashburnham Road, Ham, Richmond, Surrey, TW10 7NF

Hammersmith
226 Shepherds Bush Road, London, W6 7NX

Hampstead
26 Rosslyn Hill, London, NW3 1PD

Harefield
24 Rickmansworth Road, Harefield, Middx, UB9 6JX

Harlesden
76 Craven Park, London, NW10 8RJ

Harold Hill
Gooshays Drive, Romford, Essex, RM3 8AE

Harrow
74 Northolt Road, South Harrow, Middx, HA2 0DN

Harrow Road
325 Harrow Road, London, W9

Havering
19 Main Road, Romford, Essex, RM1 3BJ

Hayes
755 Uxbridge Road, Hayes, Middx, UB4 8HU

Heathrow Airport
Heathrow Airport, Bath Road, Hounslow, Middx, TW6 2DJ

142 Public Services London

Highgate
407–409 Archway Road, London, N6 4NW

Hillingdon
1 Warwick Place, Uxbridge, Middx, UB8 1PG

Holborn
70 Theobalds Road, London, WC1X 8SD

Holloway
284 Hornsey Road, London, N7 7QY

Hornchurch
74 Station Lane, Hornchurch, Essex, RM12 6NA

Hornsey
98 Tottenham Lane, London, N8 7EJ

Hounslow
5 Montague Road, Hounslow, Middx, TW3 1LB

Ilford
270–294 High Road, Ilford, Essex, IG1 1GT

Isle of Dogs
160–174 Manchester Road, London, E14 9HW

Islington
2 Tolpuddle Street, London, N1 0YY

Kenley
94–96 Godstone Road, Kenley, Surrey, CR8 5AB

Kennington
49 Kennington Road, London, SE1

Kentish Town
60 Albany Road, London, NW1 4EE

Kilburn
38 Salusbury Road, London, NW6 6NN

Kingsbury
5 The Mall, Harrow, Middx, HA3 9TF

King's Cross Road
76 King's Cross Road, London, WC1X 8QH

Kingston
5–7 High Street, Kingston-upon-Thames, Surrey, KT1 1LB

Lavender Hill
176 Lavender Hill, London, SW11 1JX

Lee Road
418 Lee High Road, London, SE12 8RW

Leman Street
74 Leman Street, London, E1

Lewisham
2 Ladywell Road, London, SE13 7UR

Leyton
215 Francis Road, London, E10 6NJ

Leytonstone
470 High Road, London, E11 3HN

Limehouse
29 West India Dock Road, London, E14 8EZ

Marks Gate
78 Rose Lane, Romford, Essex, RM6 5JU

Marylebone
1–9 Seymour Street, London, W1H 7BA

Mitcham
58 Cricket Green, Mitcham, Surrey, CR4 4LA

Morden
4 Crown Parade, Crown Lane, Morden, Surrey, SM4 5DA

Muswell Hill
115 Fortis Green, London, N2 9HW

New Addington
Addington Village Road, Croydon, Surrey, CR0 5AQ

Norbury
1516 London Road, London, SW16 4ES

Northwood
2 Murray Road, Northwood, Middx, HA6 2YW

North Woolwich
Albert Road, London, E16 2JJ

Norwood Green
190 Norwood Road, Southall, Middx, UB2 4JT

Notting Hill
101 Ladbroke Road, London, W11 3PL

Orpington
The Walnuts, Orpington, Kent, BR6 0TW

Paddington
4 Harrow Road, London, W2 1XJ

Paddington Green
2–4 Harrow Road, London, W2 1XJ

Peckham
177 Peckham High Street, London, SE15 5SL

Penge
175 High Street, London, SE20 7DS

Plaistow
444 Barking Road, London, E13 8HJ

Plumstead
200 Plumstead High Street, London, SE18 1JY

Ponders End
204–214 High Street, Ponders End, Middx, EN3 4EZ

Poplar
2 Market Way, London, E14 8ET

Putney
215 Upper Richmond Road, London, SW15 6SH

Rainham
3 New Road, Rainham, Essex, RM13 9PW

Police Stations   143

Richmond
8 Red Lion Street, Richmond, Surrey, TW9 1RW

Roehampton
117 Danebury Avenue, London, SW15 4DH

Rotherhithe
99 Lower Road, London, SE16 2XQ

Ruislip
The Oaks, Manor Road, Ruislip, Middx, HA4 7LE

St Ann's Road
289 St Ann's Road, London, N15 5RD

St John's Wood
20 Newcourt Street, London, NW8 7AA

Shepherds Bush
252–258 Uxbridge Road, London, W12 7JB

Shooters Hill
Shooters Hill, London, SE18 4RF

Shoreditch
4–6 Shepherdess Walk, London, N1 7LF

Sidcup
87 Main Road, Sidcup, Kent, DA14 6ND

Southall
67 High Street, Southall, Middx, UB1 3HG

Southgate
25 Chase Side, London, N14 5BW

South Norwood
11 Oliver Grove, London, SE25 6ED

Southwark
323 Borough High Street, London, SE1 1JL

Stoke Newington
4–6 Sherherdess Walk, London, N1 7LF

Stratford
18 West Ham Lane, London, E15 4SG

Streatham
101 Streatham High Road, London, SW16 1HT

Surbiton
299 Ewell Road, Surbiton, Surrey, KT6 6RD

Sutton
6 Carshalton Road West, Sutton, Surrey, SM1 4RF

Sydenham
179 Dartmouth Road, London, SE26 4RN

Teddington
18 Park Road, Teddington, Middx, TW11 0AQ

Thamesmead
Titmuss Avenue, London, SE28 8BJ

Tooting
251 Mitcham Road, London, SW17 9JQ

Tottenham
398 High Road, London, N17 9JA

Tower Bridge
209 Tooley Street, London, SE1 2JX

Trinity Road
76 Trinity Road, London, SW17 7RJ

Twickenham
41 London Road, Twickenham, Middx, TW1 3SY

Upminster
223 St Mary's Lane, Upminster, Essex, RM14 3BX

Uxbridge
1 Warwick Place, Uxbridge, Middx, UB8 1PG

Vauxhall
49–51 Kennington Road, London, SE1 7QA

Vauxhall – Cavenish Road
47 Cavendish Road, London, SW12 0BL

Wallington
84 Stafford Road, Wallington, Surrey, SM6 9AY

Walthamstow
360 Forest Road, London, E17 5JQ

Walworth
12–18 Manor Place, London, SE17 3RL

Wandsworth
146 High Street, London, SW18 4JJ

Wanstead
Spratt Hall Road, London, E11 2RQ

Wapping
98 Wapping High Street, London, E1 9NE

Wealdstone
78 High Street, Wealdstone, Middx, HA3 7AG

Wembley
603 Harrow Road, Wembley, Middx, HA0 2HH

Westcombe Park
11–13 Combedale Road, London, SE10 0LQ

West Drayton
Station Road, West Drayton, Middx, UB7 7JQ

West End Central
27 Savile Row, London, W1S 2EX

West Hampstead
21 Fortune Green Road, London, NW6 1DX

West Wickham
9 High Street, West Wickham, Kent, BR4 0LP

Whetstone
1170 High Road, London, N20 0LW

Willesden Green
96 High Road, London, NW10 2PP

144 Public Services London

Wimbledon
15 Queen's Road, London, SW19 8NN
Winchmore Hill
687 Green Lanes, London, N21 3RT
Woodford
509 High Road, Woodford Green, Essex, IG8 0SR

Wood Green
347 High Road, London, N22 4HZ
Woolwich
29 Market Street, London, SE18 6QS
Worcester Park
154 Central Road, Worcester Park, Surrey, KT4 8HH

CRIME STATISTICS
Notifiable Offences[1,2] in London recorded by the Police and percentage cleared up
(Rates and percentages)

	Offences Recorded by 100,000 population						Percentage Cleared up					
	London[3]			England and Wales			London[3]			England and Wales		
	1992	1997	1998-99	1992	1997	1998-99	1992	1997	1998-99	1992	1997	1998-99
Violence against the person	514	695	1,733	395	482	963	61	70	44	76	79	71
Sexual offences	80	100	107	58	64	69	58	61	42	75	77	68
Burglary	2,614	1,869	1,632	2,652	1,952	1,826	11	23	13	20	23	19
Robbery	320	362	346	104	121	128	13	24	16	22	27	23
Theft & handling stolen goods	6,377	4,903	5,091	5,581	4,163	4,197	13	19	14	24	24	22
Fraud & Forgery	545	571	1,068	330	258	535	44	41	15	53	48	36
Criminal damage[2]	1,632	1,737	1,800	1,339	1,423	1,685	8	18	13	17	19	17
Drug Offences[4]	29	63	429	27	45	260	98	91	97	98	98	97
Other	92	104	148	50	70	122	88	86	58	94	94	78
All notifiable offences[2]	12,174	10,404	12,354	10,535	8,576	9,785	16	26	22	26	28	29

1 Revised counting rules and expanded coverage of offences from 1 April 1998 have impacted on the offence groups of violence against the person, fraud and forgery, criminal damage and "other" offences
2 Excluding offences of criminal damage valued at £20 or less before 1998-99
3 Metropolitan Police and City of London Police areas
4 Pre-1998-99 figures are drug trafficking only. 1998-99 also includes possession of drugs and other drug offences
Source: Focus on London 2000, National Statistics' Crown Copyright 2001

HEALTH CARE

NATIONAL HEALTH SERVICE

The National Health Service (NHS) came into being on 5 July 1948 under the National Health Service Act 1946, covering England and Wales, and under separate legislation for Scotland and Northern Ireland. The NHS is now administered by the Secretary of State for Health (in England), the National Assembly for Wales, the Scottish Executive and the Secretary of State for Northern Ireland.

The function of the NHS is to provide a comprehensive health service designed to secure improvement in the physical and mental health of the people, and to prevent, diagnose and treat illness. It was founded on the principle that treatment should be provided according to clinical need rather than ability to pay, and should be free at the point of delivery. However prescription charges were provided for by legislation in 1949 and implemented in 1953, followed by some charges for some dental and ophthalmic treatment.

The NHS covers a comprehensive range of hospital, specialist, family practitioner (medical, dental, ophthalmic and pharmaceutical), artificial limb and appliance, ambulance and community health services. Everyone normally resident in the UK is entitled to use any of these services.

The National Health Service and Community Care Act 1990 provided for more streamlined Regional Health Authorities and District Health Authorities, and for the establishment of Family Health Services Authorities (FHSAs) and NHS Trusts). The concept of the "internal market" was introduced into health care whereby care was provided through NHS contracts where health authorities and GP fundholders (collectively known as purchasers) were responsible for purchasing health care from hospitals, non-fundholding GPs, community services and ambulance services (collectively known as providers).

The eight Regional Health Authorities in England were abolished in April 1996 and replaced by 8 Regional Offices of the NHS Executive whose headquarters are based in Leeds. The NHS Executive is part of the Department of Health. The functions of the Regional Offices include financial and performance monitoring of health services purchasers and providers within their region, public health, research and development and workforce development. In 1999, the North Thames, South Thames and Anglia & Oxford regions were reconfigured to form Eastern, London and South East Regions. The London Regional Office covers the same geographical boundaries as the 32 London Boroughs and the City of London.

In 1996, District Health Authorities and Family Health Services Authorities were merged to form Health Authorities which have responsibility for health and health services in their area. They assess the health care needs of their local population and develop integrated strategies for meeting these needs in partnership with GPs and in consultation with NHS Trusts, the public, the Regional Office and others. Health Authority resources are allocated by the NHS Executive to whom they are accountable for their performance. Mergers of Health Authorities in April 2001 will result in 14 Health Authorities in London.

Health Action Zones have been set up in four of the most deprived areas of London covering nearly 2 million Londoners, where extra resources and new ways of working will improve the health of those with the greatest need. HAZs are at: East London and the City, Camden & Islington, Brent, and Lambeth, Southwark and Lewisham.

Under the Health Act of 1999, the NHS internal market in England was replace by teams of GPs and community nurses working together in Primary Care Groups. They operate as a committee of the health authority and are responsible for health improvement, primary and community care development and commissioning secondary care as necessary. From 1 April 2000, Primary Care Groups were able to evolve into Primary Care Trusts if approved by the Secretary of State. These are free standing statutory bodies undertaking many of the functions of Health Authorities. Their main roles are in developing integrated primary and community health services and leading new partnerships between the NHS, local councils, employers and community groups. Two Primary Care Trusts (Hillingdon and Nelson & West Merton) went live on 1 April 2000, followed by Bexley in October 2000 with a further 15 scheduled to launch in April 2001.

The Department of Health and the NHS Executive London Regional Office are dedicated to modernising and improving the quality of health services in London. The NHS Plan (July 2000) has provided both finances and a strategic framework for the modernisation agenda. Innovative ways of improving services are being shared across London's health and care community. These include the 37 organisations

146 Public Services London

providing the Booked Admissions Scheme and a £3.5 billion investment on new and improved hospital buildings. Londoners are able to benefit from national initiatives such as the formation of the National Institute for Clinical Excellence and the publication of National Service Frameworks (NSF) to set national standards and define service models for a defined service or care group. Mental Health and Coronary Heart Disease NSFs have been accompanied by the first National Cancer Plan. The NHS Plan also calls for greater patient and public involvement in the delivery and design of health services.

Local initiatives have included the formation of a London Health Strategy which was launched on 20 May 1999, followed up by the creation of the London Health Commission (for further information see the Governed London section). Dr Sue Atkinson, Regional Director of Public Health, works closely with the Mayor of London as health adviser. All areas of London are now covered by NHS Direct (0845 46 47) which offers medical advice via the telephone.

NHS EXECUTIVE LONDON REGIONAL OFFICE

40 Eastbourne Terrace, London, W2 3QR (Tel 020-7725 5300 Fax 020-7258 0530; Web: www.doh.gov.uk/london).

Regional Chairman: Ian Mills
Regional Director: John Bacon
Communications: Virginia Beardshaw, Mr Jonathan Street

HEALTH AUTHORITIES

Barking & Havering Health Authority
The Clock House, East Street, Barking, Essex IG11 8EY (Tel: 020-8591 9595; Fax: 020-8532 6201)

Barnet Health Authority
Hyde House, The Hyde, Edgware Road, London NW9 6QQ (Tel: 020-8201 4700; Fax: 020-8201 4701)

Bexley and Greenwich Health Authority
221 Erith Road, Bexleyheath, Kent DA7 6HZ (Tel: 020-8298 6000; Fax: 020-8298 6001)

Brent & Harrow Health Authority
Grace House, Harrovian Business Village, Bessborough Road, Harrow, Middlesex HA1 3EX (Tel: 020-8422 6644; Fax: 020-8426 8646)

Bromley Health Authority
Global House, 10 Station Approach, Bromley, Kent BR2 7EH (Tel: 020-8315 8315; Fax: 020-8462 6767)

Camden & Islington Health Authority
Insull Wing, 110 Hampstead Road, London NW1 2LJ (Tel: 020-7853 5353; Fax: 020-7853 5355)

Croydon Health Authority
Knollys House, 17 Addiscombe Road, Croydon, Surrey CR0 6SR (Tel: 020-8401 3900: Fax: 020-8680 2418)

Ealing, Hammersmith & Hounslow Health Authority
1 Armstrong Way, Southall, Middlesex UB2 4SA (Tel: 020-8893 0303; Fax: 020-8893 0398)

East London & The City Health Authority
81-91 Commercial Road, London E1 1RD (Tel: 020-7655 6600; Fax: 020-7655 6666)

Enfield & Haringey Health Authority
Hollbrook House, Cockfosters Road, Barnet, Hertfordshire, EN4 0DR (Tel: 020-8272 5500; Fax: 020-8272 5700)

Hillingdon Health Authority
Kirk House, 97-109 High Street, Yiewsley, West Drayton, Middlesex UB7 7HJ (Tel: 01895 452000; Fax: 01895 452108)

Kensington & Chelsea and Westminster Health Authority
50 Eastbourne Terrace, London W2 6LX (Tel: 020-7725 3333; Fax: 020-7725 3398)

Kingston and Richmond Health Authority
22 Hollyfield Road, Surbiton, Surrey KT5 9AL (Tel: 020-8339 8000; Fax: 020-8339 8100)

Lambeth, Southwark and Lewisham Health Authority
1 Lower Marsh, London SE1 7NT (Tel: 020-7716 7000; Fax 020-7716 7039)

Merton, Sutton and Wandsworth Health Authority
The Wilson, Cranmer Road, Mitcham, Surrey CR4 7TP (Tel: 020-8648 3021; Fax: 020-8646 6240)

NHS Trusts

Redbridge & Waltham Forest Health Authority
Becketts House, 2-14 Ilford Hill, Ilford, Essex IG1 2QX (Tel: 020-8478 5151; Fax: 020-8926 5001)

NHS TRUSTS

Barnet and Chase Farm Hospitals NHS Trust
Chase Farm Hospital, The Ridgeway, Enfield, Middlesex EN2 8JL (Tel: 020-8366 6600; Fax: 020-8366 1361)

Barnet Healthcare NHS Trust
52 Moxon Street, Barnet, Herts EN5 5TS (Tel: 020-8952 2381; Fax: 020-8370 6501)

Barts and The London NHS Trust
The Royal London Hospital, Whitechapel, London E1 1BB (Tel: 020-7377 7000; Fax: 020-7377 7666)

BHB Community Health Care NHS Trust
Trust Headquarters, St George's Hospital, 117 Suttons Lane, Hornchurch, Essex RM12 6RS (Tel: 01708 465000; Fax: 01708 465300)

Brent, Kensington & Chelsea and Westminster Mental Health NHS Trust
30 Eastbourne Terrace, London W2 6LA (Tel: 020-8237 2000; Fax: 020-8746 8978)

Bromley Hospitals NHS Trust
Farnborough Hospital, Farnborough Common, Orpington, Kent BR6 8ND (Tel: 01689 814100; Fax: 01689 862423)

Camden & Islington Community Health Services NHS Trust
St Pancras Hospital, 4 St Pancras Way, London NW1 0PE (Tel: 020-7530 3000; Fax: 020-7530 3104)

Chelsea & Westminster Healthcare NHS Trust
Chelsea & Westminster Hospital, 369 Fulham Road, London SW10 9NH (Tel: 020-8746 8000; Fax: 020-8846 6539)

City & Hackney Community Services NHS Trust
St Leonard's Primary Care Centre, Nuttall Street, London (Tel: 020-7301 3000; Fax: 020-7739 8455)

Community Health South London NHS Trust
Elizabeth Blackwell House, Wardalls Grove, Avonley Road, London SE14 5ER (Tel: 020-7635 5555; Fax: 020-7771 5115)

Croydon and Surrey Downs Community Health NHS Trust
12-18 Lennard Road, Croydon, Surrey CR9 2RS (Tel: 020-8680 2008; Fax: 020-8666 0495)

Ealing Hospital NHS Trust
Uxbridge Road, Southall, Middlesex UB1 3HW (Tel: 020-8574 2444; Fax: 020-8967 5630)

Ealing, Hammersmith and Fulham Mental Health NHS Trust
Ealing Hospital, Uxbridge Road, Southall, Middlesex UB1 3HW (Tel: 020-8354 8354; Fax: 020-8967 5002)

East London and The City Mental Health NHS Trust
St Clements Hospital, 2A Bow Road, London E3 4LL (Tel: 020-7377 7000; Fax: 020-7377 7990)

Enfield Community Care NHS Trust
Avon Villa, Chase Farm Hospital Site, The Ridgeway, Enfield EN2 8JL (Tel: 020-8366 6600; Fax: 020-8366 9166)

Epsom and St Helier NHS Trust
Wrythe Lane, Surrey, Carshalton SM5 1AA (Tel: 020-8296 2000; Fax: 020-8641 9391)

Forest Healthcare NHS Trust
Thorpe Coombe House, 712 Forest Road, Walthamstow, London E17 3HF (Tel: 020-8520 8885; Fax: 020-8535 6787)

Forest Healthcare NHS Trust—Whipps Cross
Management Block, Whipps Cross Hospital, Leytonstone, London E11 1NR (Tel: 020-8539 5522; Fax: 020-8558 8115)

Great Ormond Street Hospital for Children NHS Trust
Great Ormond Street, London WC1N 3JH (Tel: 020-7405 9200; Fax: 0200-7829 8643)

Greenwich Healthcare NHS Trust
Vanbrugh Hill, Greenwich, London, SE10 9HE (Tel: 020-8858 8141; Fax: 020-8312 6159)

148 Public Services London

Guy's & St Thomas' Hospital NHS Trust
Lambeth Palace Road, London SE1 7EH (Tel: 020-7928 9292; Fax: 020-7633 0347)

Hammersmith Hospitals NHS Trust
Hammersmith Hospital, 150 Du Cane Road, London W12 0HS (Tel: 020-8383 3000; Fax: 020-8383 4343)

Haringey Healthcare NHS Trust
St Ann's Hospital, St Ann's Road, London N15 3TH (Tel: 020-8442 6189; Fax: 020-8442 6567)

Harrow and Hillingdon Healthcare NHS Trust
Malt House, 285 Field End Road, Eastcote, Ruislip, Middlesex HA4 9NJ (Tel: 020-8956 3200; Fax: 020-8426 1191)

Havering Hospitals NHS Trust
Harold Wood Hospital, Gubbins Lane, Romford RM3 0BE (Tel: 01708 345533; Fax: 01708 708099)

Hillingdon Hospital NHS Trust
The Hillingdon Hospital, Pield Heath Road, Hillingdon, Middlesex UB8 3NN (Tel: 01895 238282; Fax: 01895 811687)

Homerton Hospital NHS Trust
Homerton Row, London E9 6SR (Tel: 020-8510 5555; Fax: 020-8510 7608)

Hounslow & Spelthorne Community & Mental Health NHS Trust
Phoenix Court, 531 Staines Road, Hounslow TW4 5DP (Tel: 020-8321 2211; Fax: 020-8321 2249)

King's College Hospital NHS Trust
King's College Hospital, Denmark Hill, London SE5 9RS (Tel: 020-7737 4000; Fax: 020-7346 3445)

Kingston & District Community NHS Trust
Woodroffe House, Tolworth Hospital, Red Lion Road, Tolworth, Surrey KT6 7QU (Tel: 020-8390 0102; Fax: 020-8390 1236)

Kingston Hospital NHS Trust
Galsworthy Road, Kingston upon Thames, Surrey KT2 7QB (Tel: 020-8546 7711; Fax: 020-8547 2182)

Lewisham Hospital NHS Trust
1st Floor, Waterloo Block, University Hospital Lewisham, Lewisham High Street, London SE13 6LH (Tel: 020-8333 3000; Fax: 020-8333 3333)

London Ambulance Service NHS Trust
Ambulance Service Headquarters; 220 Waterloo Road, London SE1 8SD (Tel: 020-7921 5100; Fax: 020-7921 5127)

Mayday Healthcare NHS Trust
Mayday University Hospital, London Road, Croydon, Surrey CR7 7YE (Tel: 020-8401 3000; Fax: 020-8665 1974)

Moorfields Eye Hospital NHS Trust
City Road, London EC1V 2PD (Tel: 020-7253 3411 Fax: 020-7253 4696)

Newham Community Services NHS Trust
Sydenham Building, Plaistow Hospital, Samson Street, London E13 9EH (Tel: 020-8586 6200; Fax: 020-8586 6382)

Newham Healthcare NHS Trust
Newham General Hospital, London E13 8SL (Tel: 020-7476 4000; Fax: 020-7363 8181)

North Middlesex Hospital NHS Trust
Sterling Way, Edmonton, London N18 1QX (Tel: 020-8887 2000; Fax: 020-8887 4219)

North West London Hospitals NHS Trust
Watford Road, Harrow, Middlesex HA1 3UJ (Tel: 020-8864 3232; Fax: 020-8869 2009)

Oxleas NHS Trust
Pinewood House, Old Bexley Lane, Bexley, Kent DA5 2BF (Tel: 01322 625700; Fax: 01322 555491)

Parkside Health NHS Trust
Courtfield House, St Charles Hospital, Exmoor Street, London W10 6DZ (Tel: 020-8962 4557; Fax: 020-8962 4545)

Queen Mary's Sidcup NHS Trust
Frognal Avenue, Sidcup, Kent DA14 6LT (Tel: 020-8302 2678; Fax: 020-8308 3052)

NHS Trusts 149

Ravensbourne NHS Trust
Bassetts House, Broadwater Gardens, Farnborough, Orpington, Kent BR6 7UA (Tel: 01689 853339; Fax: 01689 855662)

Redbridge Health Care NHS Trust
King George Hospital, Barley Lane, Goodmayes, Essex IG3 8YB (Tel: 020-8970 8423; Fax: 020-8970 8424)

Riverside Community Health Care NHS Trust
Parsons Green Centre, 5-7 Parsons Green, London SW6 4UL (Tel: 020-8846 6767; Fax: 020-8846 7654)

Royal Brompton and Harefield Hospital NHS Trust
Sydney Street, Chelsea, London SW3 6NP (Tel: 020-7352 8121; Fax: 020-7351 8473)

Royal Free Hampstead NHS Trust
The Royal Free Hospital, Pond Street, Hampstead, London NW3 2QG (Tel: 020-7794 0500; Fax: 020-7830 2468)

Royal Marsden NHS Trust
Fulham Road, Chelsea, London SW3 6JJ (Tel: 020-7352 8171; Fax: 020-7351 3785)

Royal National Orthopaedic Hospital NHS Trust
Brockley Hill, Stanmore, Middlesex HA7 4LP (Tel: 020-8954 2300; Fax: 020-8954 7249)

South London and Maudsley Mental Health NHS Trust
9th Floor, The Tower Building, 11 York Road, London SE1 7NX (Tel: 020-7703 6333)

South London and Maudsley Mental Health NHS Trust (Bethlem Site)
Bethlem Royal Hospital, Monks Orchard Road, Beckenham, Kent BR3 3BX (Tel: 020-8297 0707; Fax: 020-8297 0377)

South West London & St Georges Mental Health NHS Trust
Springfield University Hospital, 61 Glenburnie Road, London SW17 7DJ (Tel: 020-8672 9911; Fax: 020-8767 7608)

South West London Community NHS Trust
Roehampton House, Queen Mary's Hospital, Roehampton Lane, London SW15 5PN (Tel: 020-8789 6611; Fax: 020-8780 1089)

St George's Healthcare NHS Trust
St George's Hospital, Blackshaw Road, London SW17 0QT (Tel: 020-8672 1255; Fax: 020-8672 5304)

St Mary's NHS Trust
St Mary's Hospital, Praed Street, London W2 1NY (Tel: 020-7886 6666; Fax: 020-7886 6200)

Tavistock & Portman NHS Trust
Tavistock Centre, 120 Belsize Lane, London NW3 5BA (Tel: 020-7435 7111; Fax: 020-7431 3709)

Teddington Memorial Hospital NHS Trust
Hampton Road, Teddington, Middlesex TW11 0JL (Tel: 020-8408 8210; Fax: 020-8408 8213)

Tower Hamlets Healthcare NHS Trust
Elizabeth Fry House, Mile End Hospital, Bancroft Road, London E1 4DG (Tel: 020-7377 7920/21; Fax: 020-7377 7931)

University College London Hospitals NHS Trust
Vezey Strong Wing, 112 Hampstead Road, London NW1 2LT (Tel: 020-7387 9300; Fax: 020-7380 9963)

West Middlesex University Hospital NHS Trust
Twickenham Road, Isleworth, Middlesex TW7 6AF (Tel: 020-8560 2121; Fax: 020-8560 2395)

Whittington Hospital NHS Trust
The Whittington Hospital, Highgate Hill, London N19

OTHER ORGANISATIONS CONNECTED WITH HEALTH AND SOCIAL SERVICES IN LONDON

COMMUNITY HEALTH COUNCILS (CHC)

Community Health Councils are statutory bodies, which are independent. They represent the interests of local people to the NHS. They aim to perform the following tasks:
- to provide information about the services available from local health care providers and to review plans for new services
- to make recommendations to healthcare providers about improvements which are in the local community's interest
- to help patients where necessary make official complaints
- to forge links with the local community

ASSOCIATION OF COMMUNITY HEALTH COUNCILS FOR ENGLAND AND WALES

30 Drayton Park, London N5 1PB (Tel: 020-7609 8405; Fax: 020-7700 1152).

The Association was established in 1977. The objectives of the Association are to provide a forum for the exchange of views and for the discussion of matters of common concern to member Community Health Councils. Where appropriate the Association will express views on national health matters to ministers, government departments and other relevant bodies and the Association provides advice and support to CHCs to assist them in the performance of their functions and the meeting of their objectives.

NATIONAL BLOOD SERVICE

North London Centre, Colindale Avenue, Colindale, London NW9 9YR (Tel: 08457 711711).
South Thames Centre, 75 Cranmer Terrace, London SW17 0RB (Tel: 020-8258 8300).

NATIONAL MISSING PERSONS HELPLINE

Roebuck House, 284-286 Upper Richmond Road West, London SW14 7JE (Helpline: 0500 700700; Tel: 020-8392 4590; Fax: 020-8878 7752).

This is the national helpline for people who are trying to trace missing friends and relatives. The National Missing Persons Helpline also run another helpline, Message Home, which is a helpline for people who have runaway or left home to send messages to their families or carers, or to seek confidential help and advice. Message Home: Tel: 020-8392 4550; Helpline: 0800 700740; Fax: 020-8878 7752)

HEALTH AND SAFETY COMMISSION

Rose Court, 2 Southwark Bridge, London SE1 9HS (Tel 020-7717 6000; Fax 020-7717 6644)

The Health and Safety Commission was created under the Health and Safety at Work etc. Act 1974, with duties to reform health and safety law, to propose new regulations, and generally to promote the protection of people at work and of the public from hazards arising from industrial and commercial activity, including major industrial accidents and the transportation of hazardous materials. The members of the Commission are appointed by the Secretary of State for the Environment, Transport and the Regions. The Commission is made up of representatives of employers, trades unions and local authorities, and has a full-time chairman.

Chairman: W. Callaghan

HEALTH AND SAFETY EXECUTIVE

Rose Court, 2 Southwark Bridge, London SE1 9HS (Tel: 020-7717 6000; Fax 020-7717 6717)

The Health and Safety Executive is the Health and Safety Commission's major instrument. Through its inspectorates it enforces health and safety law in the majority of industrial premises. The Executive advises the Commission in its major task of laying down safety standards through regulations and practical guidance for many industrial processes. The Executive is also the licensing authority for nuclear installations and the reporting officer on the severity of nuclear incidents in Britain, and it is responsible for the Channel Tunnel Safety Authority.

Director-General: Mr Timothy Walker

COMMUNITY HEALTH COUNCILS

Barking, Dagenham and Havering,
The Victoria Centre, Pettits Lane, Romford Essex RM1 4HP (Tel: 01708 766412; Fax: 01708 738010)

Community Health Councils 151

Barnet
159 Ballards Lane, London N3 1LJ
(Tel: 020-8349 4364; Fax: 020-8343 3502)

Bexley
11a Upton Road, Bexleyheath, Kent DA6 8LQ
(Tel 020-8301 0920; Fax: 020-8303 1102)

Brent
22-24 Willesden High Road, London NW10 2QD (Tel: 020-8451 4697; Fax: 020-8451 4533)

Bromley
Babbacombe House, 2 Babbacombe Road, Bromley BR1 3LW (Tel: 020-8464 0249; Fax: 020-8313 9899)

Camden
197 Kentish Town Road, London NW5 2JU
(Tel: 020-7530 5266/5255; Fax: 020-7530 5252)

City and Hackney
210 Kingsland Road, London E2 8EB
(Tel: 020-7739 6308; Fax: 020-7729 5943)

Croydon
90 London Road, Croydon, Surrey CR0 2TB
(Tel: 020-8680 1503; Fax: 020-8401 3919)

Ealing
119 Uxbridge Road, London W7 3ST
(Tel: 020-8579 2211; Fax: 020-8579 4257)

Enfield
51-53 Lancaster Road, Enfield Middlesex EN2 0BU (Tel: 020-8366 6665; Fax 020-8366 6650)

Greenwich
23 Anglesea Road, London SE18 6EG
(Tel: 020-8317 9994; Fax: 020-8317 3444)

Hammersmith and Fulham
42 Fulham Palace Road, London W6 9PH
(Tel: 020-8748 0639; Fax: 020-8741 1865)

Haringey
332 High Road, London N15 4BN (Tel: 020-8808 1694; Fax 020-8801 9590)

Harrow
2 Junction Road, Harrow Middlesex HA1 1NL
(Tel: 020-8863 6432; Fax: 020-8424 9780)

Hillingdon
65 Belmont Road, Uxbridge Middlesex UB8 1QT
(Tel: 01895 257858; Fax: 01895 813300)

Hounslow
7-9 Spur Road, Isleworth Middlesex TW7 5BD
(Tel: 020-8568 8558; Fax 020-8568 8418)

Islington
164 Holloway Road, London N7 8DD
(Tel: 020-7609 6096; Fax 020-7609 4015)

Kensington & Chelsea and Westminster
45-47 Praed Street, London W2 1NR
(Tel: 020-7706 7100; Fax: 020-7402 1271)

Kingston
9-13 St James Road, Surbiton Surrey KT6 4QH
(Tel: 020-8399 8467; Fax: 020-8399 8415)

Lambeth
2 Cleaver Street, Kennington, London SE11 4DP
(Tel: 020-7582 3288; Fax: 020-7735 9071)

Lewisham
246 Lewisham High Street, London SE13 6JU
(Tel: 020-8318 3435; Fax: 020-8318 3655)

Merton and Sutton
29 West Street, Sutton Surrey SM1 1SJ
(Tel: 020-8642 6405; Fax: 020-8770 9618)

Newham
128 The Grove, Stratford E15 1NS (Tel: 020-8534 4217/8; Fax 020-8536 0091)

Redbridge
201 Cranbrook Road, Iford Essex IGL 4TD
(Tel: 020-8518 5736; Fax: 020-8518 5738)

Richmond and Twickenham
55 Heath Road, Twickenham TW1 4AW
(Tel: 020-8744 1144; Fax: 020-8744 0682)

Southwark
75 Denmark Hill, London SE5 8RS
(Tel: 020-7703 9498; Fax: 020-7277 1805)

Tower Hamlets
Unit 1 and 2 Albion Yard, Whitechapel Road, London E1 1BW (Tel: 020-7375 1555; Fax 020-7375 0700)

Waltham Forest
772 High Road, Leytonstone, London E11 3AJ
(Tel: 020-8539 7180; Fax 020-8539 0949)

Wandsworth
1 Balham Station Road, London SW12 9SG
(Tel: 020-8673 8820/29; 020-8675 8863)

HOUSING

HOUSING STOCK BY TENURE* 1981-1998 (PERCENTAGES AND 000s)

	1981	1991	1995	1996	1997	1998
LONDON						
Owner-occupied	50	57	57	57	56	56
Rented from local authority	32	24	22	22	20	20
Rented from private owners or with job/business	13	13	15	15	17	17
Rented from registered social landlord	5	5	7	7	7	7
Total dwellings (000s)	2,682	2,928	2,996	3,011	3,025	3,040
GREAT BRITAIN						
Owner-occupied	57	66	67	67	67	—
Rented from local authority or New Town**	30	22	19	19	17	—
Rented from private owners or with job/business	11	9	10	10	11	—
Rented from registered social landlord	11	9	10	10	11	—
Total dwellings (=100%) (000s)	21,085	23,141	23,860	24,037	24,216	—

*At December each year
** Including Scottish Homes, formerly the Scottish Special Housing Association
Source: Focus on London 2000, National Statistics' Crown Copyright 2001

GREATER LONDON—ALL LENDERS SIMPLE AVERAGE HOUSE PRICE SERIES

Annual	New Dwellings Price (£)	1yr % Change	2nd Hand Dwellings Price (£)	1yr % Change	All Dwellings Price (£)	1yr % Change	1st Time Purchasers Price (£)	1yr % Change	Former Owner Occupier Price (£)	1yr % Change
1993	78,084		80,707		81,332		65.554		110,293	
1994	75,200	−3.7	87,563	8.5	87,631	7.7	62,214	−5.1	119,944	8.8
1995	83.933	11.6	88,277	0.8	89,528	2.2	65,912	5.9	122,169	1.9
1996	99,292	18.3	93,321	5.7	94,065	5.1	67,153	1.9	123,043	0.7
1997	116,242	17.1	104,827	12.3	105,819	12.5	73,962	10.1	137,371	11.6
1998	125,079	7.6	114,116	8.9	114,783	8.5	90,160	21.9	145,974	6.3
1999	178,274	42.5	140,347	22.9	142,321	24.0	115,002	27.6	174,899	19.8

Source: DETR 5% Survey of Mortgage lenders, All Lenders, first mortgages. Average of all property prices.
©Crown Copyright

Housing

There are many organisations in London offering advice and information on a wide range of housing and homelessness issues, including:

BRITISH PROPERTY FEDERATION

1 Warwick Row, London SW1E 5ER
(Tel: 020-7828 0111; Fax: 020-7834 3442;
Email: info@bpf.org.uk).

EMPTY HOMES AGENCY

195-197 Victoria Street, London, SW1E 5NE
(Tel: 020-7828 6288; Fax: 020-7828 7006;
E-mail: info@emptyhomes.com;
Web: www.emptyhomes.com).

The Empty Homes Agency is an independent housing charity established in 1992. Its objective is to devise solutions and disseminate good practice on how to tackle the problem of empty homes.

There is a London Empty Homes Hotline which aims to bring London's 100,000 empty homes back into use, the number for which is 0870 901 6303. The Empty Homes Agency estimates that there are in fact 114,000 vacant dwellings in London and 26,729 homeless households. The agency is funded by The Housing Corporation and other bodies and has the backing of the government and local authorities.

HOUSING CORPORATION

149 Tottenham Court Road, London W1P 0BN
(Tel: 020-7393 2000; Fax: 020-7393 2111).

Established by Parliament in 1964, the Housing Corporation regulates, funds and promotes the proper performance of registered social landlords, which are non-profit making bodies run by voluntary committees. There are over 2,200 registered social landlords, most of which are housing associations, and they now provide homes for more than 1.5 million people. Under the Housing Act 1996, the Corporation's regulatory role was widened to embrace new types of landlords, in particular local housing companies. The Corporation is funded by the Department of the Environment, Transport and the Regions.

Chairman: The Rt. Hon Baroness Dean of Thornton-le-Fylde, PC
Deputy Chairman: E. Armitage, OBE

London Regional Office
Waverley House, 7-12 Noel Street, London W1V 4BA (Tel: 020-7292 4400; Fax 020-7292 4401).

Registered Social Landlords (Housing Associations)
Registered Social Landlords or Housing Associations are non-profit making organisations which form the voluntary housing movement. The common aim of housing associations is to provide housing and related services for people on low incomes and in housing need. The term voluntary derives from the nature of housing association provision which is not undertaken through statutory duty but by virtue of the work of people who combine to form an association to meet particular housing needs.

HOUSING MOBILITY AND EXCHANGE SERVICES (HOMES)

242 Vauxhall Bridge Road, London SW1V 1AU (Tel: 020-7963 0210; Fax: 020-7963 0249; Web: www.availablehomes.org).

HOMES works with local authorities and housing associations to help thousands of people move home each year.

Director: Sheila Button

INDEPENDENT HOUSING OMBUDSMAN

Norman House, 105-109 Strand, London WC2R 0AA (Tel: 020-7836 3630; 08457-125973; Fax: 020-7836 3900;
Email: ombudsman@ihos.org.uk;
Web: www.ihos.org.uk).

The Independent Housing Ombudsman was established in 1997 under the Housing Act 1996. The Ombudsman deals with complaints against registered social landlords (not including local authorities) and some private landlords.

Ombudsman: Dr M. Biles
Chair of Board: K. Lampard
General Manager: L. Greenberg

LEASEHOLD ADVISORY SERVICE

8 Maddox Street, London, W1R 9PN
(Tel: 020-7493 3116 Fax: 020-7493 4318;
E-mail info@lease-advice.org;
Web: www.lease-advice.org).

154 Public Services London

The Leasehold Advisory Service is an independent body giving legal advice about residential leaseholding. The service is free of charge and is used by landlords, leaseholders and anyone else concerned with leaseholding.

LONDON HOUSING UNIT

59 ½ Southwark Street, London, SE1 0AL (Tel: 020-7934 9994; Fax: 020-7934 9991; Email: info@alf.gov.uk).

The London Housing Unit provides policy, research and information services on social housing within London Borough Councils. The work of the London Housing Unit includes monitoring the delivery of housing services, assessing the future of housing provision and related issues and encompasses the wider aspects of regeneration, welfare and social policy. The London Housing Unit is part of the Association of London Government.

LONDON RENT ASSESSMENT PANEL/ LEASEHOLD VALUATION TRIBUNAL

Whittington House, 19-30 Alfred Place, London WC1E 7LR (Tel: 020-7446 7700; Fax: 020-7637 1250).

RENT SERVICE

London Region: Chesham House, 4th Floor, 150 Regent Street, London W1R 5FA (Tel: 020-7728 3403; Fax: 020-7728 2949).

The Rent Service is a Next Steps Executive Agency of the Department for the Environment, Transport and the Regions. It is a specialist valuation agency, assessing rents charged to private tenants and has taken over responsibility for the former rent officer service. Its operations cover two areas: establishing 'fair rents' for regulated tenancies, and assessing rents for private sector tenancies where Housing Benefit is to be paid. In London, the Service is divided into six administrative regions as shown below:

Central: 6th Floor, 17 Old Court Place, London W8 4PL (Tel: 020-7361 1850; Fax: 020-7937 0182)

North: 2nd Floor, Nicholas House, River Front, Enfield, Middx., EN1 3TN (Tel: 020-8367 1521; Fax: 020-8366 7564)

North East: 103 Cranbrook Road, Ilford, Essex IG1 4PU (Tel: 020-8478 1693; Fax: 020-8478 9779)

South East: 2nd Floor, Northside House, 69 Tweedy Road, Bromley, Kent BR1 1WA (Tel: 020-8464 2474; Fax: 020-8461 6110)

South West: 1st Floor, Suffolk House, George Street, Croydon, CR0 0YN (Tel: 020-8686 2201/2; Fax: 020-8408 5712/3)

West: 4th Floor, Dawley House, 91-5 Uxbridge Road, London, W5 5TH (Tel: 020-8579 6881; Fax: 020-8840 8170)

SHELTER

88 Old Street, London EC1V 9HU (Tel: 020-7505 2000; Fax: 020-7505 2167; Email: info@shelter.org.uk; Web: www.shelter.org.uk) Freephone 24 hour helpline: 0808 800 4444.

VALUATION OFFICE

New Court, Carey Street, London WC2A 2JE (Tel: 020-7234 1156; Fax: 020-7324 1073).

There are also Valuation Offices in Barking, Bromley, Camden, City, Enfield, Harrow, Lambeth, Tower Hamlets, Westminster, Wimbledon

VALUATION TRIBUNALS

The Valuation Tribunals hear appeals concerning the council tax, non-domestic rating and land drainage rates in England and Wales, and have the residual jurisdiction to hear appeals concerning the community charge, the pre-1900 rating list, disabled rating and mixed hereditaments.

Central London Valuation Tribunal

Floor 2, Black Lion House, 45 Whitechapel Road, London E1 (020-7497 1757; Fax 020-7497 0752).

London North East Valuation Tribunal

Floor 2 Black Lion House, 45 Whitechapel Road, London E1 (020-8554 4004; Fax 020-8518 3342).

London North West Valuation Tribunal

34 Greenhill Way, Harrow HA1 1LE (Tel: 020-8863 6382; Fax 020-8427 9436).

London South East Valuation Tribunal

4th Floor, AMP House, Dingwall Road, Croydon CR0 9XA (020-8681 8843; Fax 020-8681 3892).

London South West Valuation Tribunal

4th Floor, AMP House, Dingwall Road, Croydon CR0 9XA (020-8680 2445; Fax 020-8686 7444).

COUNCIL FOR MUSEUMS, ARCHIVES AND LIBRARIES

16 Queen Anne's Gate, London SW1H 9AA (Tel: 020-7273 1444; Fax: 020-7273 1404).

The Council for Museums, Archives and Libraries is a new strategic agency which will work with museums, archives and libraries throughout the UK.

Chairman: Matthew Evans
Chief Executive: Nevill Mackay

LIBRARIES

Local Authorities are responsible for maintaining and funding libraries within their area. Many libraries now offer not just the traditional services of booklending but also audio-visual and multimedia services. The list below provides contact details of libraries within each London Borough.

BARKING AND DAGENHAM

Head of Library Services: T. Brown
(E-mail: libraries@barking-dagenham.gov.uk)

Central Library
Barking, Essex, IG11 7NB (Tel: 020-8517 8666; Fax: 020-8594 1156)

Fanshawe Library
Barnmead Road, Dagenham, Essex, RM9 5DX (Tel: 020-8270 4244; Fax: 020-8270 4244; E-mail: fanshawlibrary@barking-dagenham.gov.uk)

Marks Gate Library
Rose Lane, Chadwell Heath, Romford, Essex, RM6 5NJ (Tel: 020-8270 4165; Fax: 020-8270 4165; E-mail: mgate@barking-dagenham.gov.uk)

Markyate Library
Markyate Road, Dagenham, Essex, RM8 3HT (Tel: 020-8270 4137; Fax: 020-8270 4137; E-mail: mlibrary@barking-dagenham.org.uk)

Rectory Library
Rectory Road, Dagenham, Essex, RM10 9SA (Tel: 020-8270 6233; Fax: 020-8270 6233; E-mail: rectorylibrary@barking-dagenham.org.uk)

Rush Green Library
Dagenham Road, Rush Green, Romford, Essex, RM7 0TL (Tel: 020-8270 4304; Fax: 020-8270 4304; E-mail: rushgreenlibrary@barking-dagenham.gov.uk)

Thames View Library
2A Farr Avenue, Barking, Essex, IG11 0NZ (Tel: 020-8270 4146; Fax: 020-8270 4146; E-mail: tview@barking-dagenham.gov.uk)

Valence Library
Becontree Avenue, Dagenham, Essex, RM8 3HT (Tel: 020-8227 5292; Fax: 020-8227 5292; E-mail: valencelibrary@barking-dagenham.gov.uk)

156 Public Services London

Wantz Library
Rainham Road North, Dagenham, Essex, RM10 7DX (Tel: 020-8270 4169; Fax: 020-8270 4169; E-mail: wantzlibrary@barking-dagenham.gov.uk)

Whalebone Library
High Road, Chadwell Heath, Romford, Essex, RM6 6AS (Tel: 020-8590 4305; Fax: 020-8270 4305; E-mail: wlibrary@barking-dagenham.gov.uk)

Woodward Library
Woodward Road, Dagenham, Essex, RM9 4SP (Tel: 020-8270 4166; Fax: 020-8270 4166 E-mail: woodwardlibrary@barking-dagenham.gov.uk)

BARNET
Head of Cultural Services: Mrs P. Usher; (Web: www.barnet.gov.uk/profile/librarires/)

Burnt Oak Library
Watling Avenue, Edgware, Middx, HA8 0UB (Tel: 020-8959 3112; E-mail: burnt.oak.library@barnet.gov.uk)

Childs Hill Library
320 Cricklewood Lane, London, NW2 2QE (Tel: 020-8455 5390; E-mail: childshill.library@barnet.gov.uk)

Chipping Barnet Library
3 Stapylton Road, Barnet, Herts, EN5 4QT (Tel: 020-8359 4040; E-mail: chipping.barnet.library@barnet.gov.uk)

Church End Library
24 Hendon Lane, Finchley, London, N3 1TR (Tel: 020-8346 5711; E-mail: church.end.library@barnet.gov.uk)

East Barnet Library
85 Brookhill Road, East Barnet, Herts, EN4 8SG (Tel: 020-8440 4376; E-mail: east.barnet.library@barnet.gov.uk)

East Finchley Library
226 High Road, London, N2 9BB (Tel: 020-8883 2664; E-mail: east.finchley.library@barnet.gov.uk)

Edgware Library
Hale Lane, Edgware, Middx, HA8 8NN (Tel: 020-8359 2626; E-mail: edware.libray@barnet.gov.uk)

Friern Barnet Library
Friern Barnet Road, London, N11 3DS (Tel: 020-8368 2680; E-mail: friern.barnetlibrary@barnet.gov.uk)

General Enquiries
Cultural Services, The Old Town Hall, Friern Barnet Lane, London, N11 3DL (Tel: 020-8359 3164; Fax: 020-8359 3171)

Golders Green Library
156 Golders Green Road, London, NW11 8HE (Tel: 020-8359 2060; E-mail: golders.green.library@banet.gov.uk)

Grahame Park Library
The Concourse, London, NW9 5XL (Tel: 020-8200 0470; E-mail: grahame.park.library@barnet.gov.uk)

Hampstead Garden Suburb Library
15 Market Place, London, NW11 6LB (Tel: 020-8455 1235; E-mail: hampstead.garden.library@barnet.gov.uk)

Hendon Library
The Burroughs, London, NW4 4BQ (Tel: 020-8359 2628)

Local Studies and Archives
Chapel Walk, Egerton Gardens, London, NW4 (Tel: 020-8359 2876; E-mail: hendon.library@barnet.gov.uk)

Mill Hill Library
Hartley Avenue, London, NW7 2HX (Tel: 020-8959 5066; E-mail: mill.hill.library@barnet.gov.uk)

North Finchley Library
Ravensdale Avenue, London, N12 9HP (Tel: 020-8445 4081; E-mail: north.finchley.library@barnet.gov.uk)

Osidge Library
Brunswick Park Road, London, N11 1EY (Tel: 020-8368 0532; E-mail: osidge.library@barnet.gov.uk)

South Friern Library
Colney Hatch Lane, London, N10 1HD (Tel: 020-8883 6513; E-mail: south.friern.library@barnet.gov.uk)

Totteridge Library
109 Totteridge Lane, London, N20 8DZ
(Tel: 020-8445 5288;
E-mail: totteridge.library@barnet.gov.uk)

BEXLEY
Head of Libraries and Cultural Services:
F. V. Johnson
(E-mail: libraries.els@bexley.gov.uk;
Web: www.bexley.gov.uk/service/library)

Barnehurst Library
168 Mayplace Road East, Barnehurst, Kent, DA7 6EJ (Tel: 01322-521663)

Bexley Council Libraries and Cultural Services
Hill View, Hill View Drive, Welling, Kent, DA16 3RY (Tel: 020-8303 7777 ext. 4268; Fax: 020-8308 4926)

Bexley Village Library
Bourne Road, Bexley, Kent, DA1 1LU
(Tel: 01322-522168)

Blackfen Library
Cedar Avenue, Sidcup, Kent, DA15 8NJ
(Tel: 020-8300 3010)

Bostall Library
King Harold's Way, Bexleyheath, Kent, DA7 5RE (Tel: 020-8310 1779)

Central Library
Townley Road, Bexleyheath, Kent, DA6 7HJ
(Tel: 020-8301 5151; Fax: 020-8303 7872)
Head Librarian: G. H. Boulton

Crayford Library
Crayford Road, Crayford, Kent, DA1 4ER
(Tel: 01322-526050)

Erith Library
Walnut Tree Road, Erith, Kent, DA8 1RS
(Tel: 01322-336582)

Local Studies Centre
Hall Place, Bourne Road, Bexley, Kent, DA5 1PQ (Tel: 01322-526574)

North Heath Library
200 Bexley Road, Erith, Kent, DA8 3HF
(Tel: 01322-333663)

Sidcup Library
Hadlow Road, Sidcup, Kent, DA14 4AQ
(Tel: 020-8300 2958)

Slade Green Library
Bridge Road, Slade Green, Erith, Kent, DA8 2HS (Tel: 01322-335027)

Thamesmead Library
Binsey Walk, Thamesmead, London, SE2 9TS
(Tel: 020-8310 9944)

Upper Belvedere Library
Woolwich Road, Upper Belvedere, Kent, DA17 5EQ (Tel: 01322-439760)

Welling Library
Bellegrove Road, Welling, Kent, DA16 3PA
(Tel: 020-8303 2788)

BRENT
Head of Library Service: John Readman
(E-mail: john.readman@brent.gov.uk;
Web: www.brent.gov.uk/services/lib/indxlibs.htm)

Cricklewood Library and Archive
152 Olive Road, London, NW2 6UY
(Tel: 020-8937 3540; Fax: 020-8450 5211)

Grange Road Mobile Library
2–12 Grange Road, London, NW10 2QY
(Tel: 020-8937 3460)
4th Floor, Chesterfield House, 9 Park Lane, Wembley, Middx, HA9 7RJ
(Tel: 020-8937 3149; Fax: 020-8937 3008)

Harlesden Library
Craven Park Road, London, NW10 8SE
(Tel: 020-8965 7132/8937 3570;
Fax: 020-8838 2199)

Neasden Library
277 Neasden Lane, London, NW10 1QJ
(Tel: 020-8937 3580; Fax: 020-8208 3909)

Town Hall Library
Brent Town Hall, Forty Lane, Wembley, Middx, HA9 9HU (Tel: 020-8937 3500;
Fax: 020-8937 3504)

158 Public Services London

Willesden Green Library
95 High Road, London, NW10 2SF
(Tel: 020-8937 3400; Fax: 020-8937 3401)
E-mail: john.readman@brent.gov.uk)

BROMLEY
Chief Librarian: Barry Walkinshaw
(E-mail: reference.library@bromley.gov.uk;
Web: www.bromley.gov.uk)

Anerley Library
Anerley Town Hall, Anerley Road, London,
SE20 8BD (Tel: 020-8778 7457)
Area Manager (West): Tina Alabaster

Beckenham Library
Beckenham Road, Beckenham, BR3 4PE
(Tel: 020-8650 7292)
Area Manager (West): Tina Alabaster

Biggin Hill Library
Church Road, Biggin Hill, TN16 3LB
(Tel: 01959-574468)

Bromley Central Library
High Street, Bromley, Kent, BR1 1EX
(Tel: 020-8460 9955; Fax: 020-8313 9975)
Central Manager: John Wilkins
E-mail: reference.library@bromley.gov.uk)

Burnt Ash Library
Burnt Ash Lane, Bromley, BR1 5AF
(Tel: 020-8460 3405)
Area Manager (West): Tina Alabaster

Chislehurst Library
Red Hill, Chislehurst, BR7 6DA
(Tel: 020-8467 1318)
Area Manager (East): Tim Woolagar

Hayes Library
Hayes Street, Hayes, Middx, BR2 7LH
(Tel: 020-8462 2245)
Area Manager (West): Tina Alabaster

Mottingham Library
31 Mottingham Road, London, SE9 4QZ
(Tel: 020-8857 5406)
Area Manager (East); Tim Woolagar

Orpington Library
The Priory, Church Hill, Orpington, Kent, BR6
0HH (Tel: 01689-831551)
Area Manager (East): Tim Woolagar

Penge Library
186 Maple Road, London, SE20 8HT
(Tel: 020-8778 8772)
Area Manager (West): Tina Alabaster

Petts Wood Library
Frankswood Avenue, Petts Wood, BR5 1BP
(Tel: 01689-821607)
Area Manager (East): Tim Woolagar

Shortlands Library
110 Shortlands Road, Bromley, BR2 0JP
(Tel: 020-8460 9692)
Area Manager (West): Tina Alabaster

Southborough Library
Southborough Lane, Bromley, BR2 8HP
(Tel: 020-8467 0355)
Area Manager (East): Tim Woolagar

St Paul's Cray Library
Mickleham Road, St Paul's Cray, BR5 2RW
(Tel: 020-8800 5454)
Area Manager (East): Tim Woolagar

West Wickham Library
Glebe Way, West Wickham, BR4 0SH
(Tel: 020-8777 4139)
Area Manager (West): Tina Alabaster

CAMDEN
Belsize Library
Antrim Road, London, NW3 4XN
(Tel: 020-7974 6518)

Camden Libraries and Information Services
Crowndale Centre, 218 Eversholt Street,
London, NW1 1BD (Tel: 020-7974 1656;
Fax: 010-7974 1566)

Libraries 159

Chalk Farm Library
Sharpleshall Street, London, NW1 8YN
(Tel: 020-7974 6526)

Heath Library
Keats Grove, London, NW3 2RR
(Tel: 020-7974 6520)

Highgate Library
Chester Road, London, N19 5DH
(Tel: 020-7974 5752)

Holborn Library
32–38 Theobald's Road, London, WC1X 8PA
(Tel: 020-7974 6345/6)

Kentish Town Library
Kentish Town Road, London, NW5 2AA
(Tel: 020-7974 6253)

Kilburn Library
Cotleigh Road, London, NW6 2NP
(Tel: 020-7974 1965)

Local Studies and Archives Centre
32–38 Theobald's Road, London, WC1X 8PA
(Tel: 020-7974 6342)

Queens Crescent Library
165 Queens Crescent, London, NW5 4HH
(Tel: 020-7974 6243)

Regent's Park Library
Compton Close, Robert Street, London, NW1 3QT (Tel: 020-7974 1530)

St Pancras Library
Camden Town Hall, Argyle Street, London, WC1H 8NL (Tel: 020-7974 5833)

Swiss Cottage Central Library
88 Avenue Road, London, NW3 3HA
(Tel: 020-7974 6522)

West Hampstead Library
Dennington Park Road, London, NW6 1AU
(Tel: 020-7974 6610)

CITY OF LONDON
Director of Libraries and Guildhall Art Gallery:
Melvyn Barnes, OBE;
(Web: www.cityoflondon.gov.uk)

Barbican Library
Barbican Centre, London, EC2Y 8DS
(Tel: 020-7638 0569; Fax: 020-7638 2249
E-mail: barbicanliub@corpoflondon.gov.uk)

Camomile Street Library
12–20 Camomile Street, London, EC3A 7EX
(Tel: 020-7247 8895; Fax: 020-7377 2972
E-mail: camomile@corpoflondon.gov.uk)

City Business Library
Brewers Hall Garden, (Off Alderman Square), London, EC2V 5BX (Tel: 020-7332 1812;
Fax: 020-7332 1847)

Guildhall Library
Aldermanbury Lane, London, EC2P 2EG
(Tel: 020-7332 1868)

St Bride Printing Library
Bride Lane, London, EC4Y 8EE
(Tel: 020-7353 4660; Fax: 020-7353 4660
E-mail: stbride@corpoflondon.gov.uk)

Shoe Lane Library
Hill House, Little New Street, London, EC4A 3GR (Tel: 020-7583 7178; Fax: 020-7353 0884
E-mail: shoelane@corpoflondon.gov.uk)

CROYDON
Assistant Director of Libraries: Ms A. Scott
(E-mail: ascott@croydononline.org;
Web: www.croydon.gov.uk/ledept/libraries/cr-libs.htm)

Ashburton Library
Lower Addiscombe Road, Croydon, CR0 6RX
(Tel: 020-8656 4148
E-mail: ashburton@croydononline.org)

Bradmore Green Library
Bradmore Way, Coulsdon, CR5 1PE
(Tel: 01737-553267;
E-mail: bradmoregreen@croydononline.org)

… **160 Public Services London**

Broad Green Library
89 Canterbury Road, Croydon, CR0 3HH
(Tel: 020-8684 4829;
E-mail: broadgreen@croydononline.org)

Coulsdon Library
Brighton Road, Coulsdon, CR5 2NH
(Tel: 020-8660 1548;
E-mail: coulsdon@croydononline.org)

Croydon Central Library
Katharine Street, Croydon, CR9 1ET
(Tel: 020-8760 5400; Fax: 020-8253 1004;
E-mail: www.croydononline.org)

Mobile Library
c/o Selsdon Library
Addington Road, Selsdon, CR2 8LA
(Tel: 020-8657 7210;
E-mail: selsdon@croydononline.org)

New Addington Library
Central Parade, New Addington, CR0 0JB
(Tel: 01689-841248;
E-mail: newaddington@croydononline.org)

Norbury Library
London Road/Beatrice Avenue, Norbury, London, SW16 4UW (Tel: 020-8679 1597;
E-mail: norbury@croydononline.org)

Purley Library
Banstead Road, Purley, CR8 3YH
(Tel: 020-8660 1171;
E-mail: purley@croydononline.org)

Sanderstead Library
Farm Fields, South Croydon, CR2 0HL
(Tel: 020-8657 2882;
E-mail: Sanderstead@croydononline.org)

Selsdon Library
Addington Road, Selsdon, CR2 8LA
(Tel: 020-8657 7210;
E-mail: selsdon@croydononline.org)

Shirley Library
Wickham Road/Hartland Way, Shirley, CR0 8BH (Tel: 020-8777 7650;
E-mail: shirley@croydononline.org)

South Norwood Library
Lawrence Road, South Norwood, London, SE25 5AA (Tel: 020-8653 4545;
E-mail: southnorwood@croydononline.org)

Thornton Heath Library
Brigstock Road, Thornton Heath, CR7 7JB
(Tel: 020-8684 4432;
E-mail: thorntonheath@croydononline.org)

EALING
Library Manager: Mr L. Bowen
(Web: www.ealing.gov.uk)

Acton Library
High Street, London, W3 6NA
(Tel: 020-8752 0999; Fax: 020-8992 6086)
Library Manager: M. Lambert

Central Library
103 Ealing Broadway Centre, London, W5 5JY
(Tel: *Lending:* 020-8567 3670; *Reference:* 020-8567 3656; Fax: 020-8840 2351)
Library Manager: L. Bowen

Greenford Library
Oldfield Lane South, Greenford, Middx, UB6 9LG (Tel: 020-8578 1466; Fax: 020-8575 7800)
Library Manager: F. Hounsell

Hanwell Library
Cherington Road, London, W7 3HL
(Tel: 020-8567 5041)

Jubilee Gardens library
Jubilee Gardens, Southall, Middx, UB1 2TJ
(Tel: 020-8578 1067)

Northfields Library
Northfield Avenue, London, W5 4UA
(Tel: 020-8567 5700; Fax: 020-8567 5572)

Northolt Library
Church Road, Northolt, Middx, UB5 5AS
(Tel: 020-8845 3380)

Perivale Library
Horsenden Lane South, Perivale, Middx, UB6 7NT (Tel: 020-8997 2830)

Pitshanger Library
143–145 Pitshanger Lane, London, W5 1RH
(Tel: 020-8997 0230)

Libraries

Southall Library
Osterley Park Road, Southall, Middx, UB2 4BL
(Tel: 020-8574 3412; Fax: 020-8571 7629)
Library Manager: E. Steverson

West Ealing Library
Melbourne Avenue, Ealing, London, W13 9BT
(Tel: 020-8567 2812; Fax: 020-8567 1736)
Library Manager: H. Farrar

Wood End Library
Whitton Avenue West, Greenford, Middx, UB6 0EE (Tel: 020-8422 3965)

ENFIELD
Assistant Director - Libraries and Culture:
Ms C. Lewis
(Web: www.enfield.gov.uk/libs.htm)

Bowes Road Library
Bowes Road, London, N11 1BD
(Tel: 020-8379 1707; Fax: 020-8368 6025)

Bullsmoor Library
Kempe Road, Enfield, Middx, EN1 1QS
(Tel: 020-8379 1723)

Bush Hill Park Library
Agricola Place, Enfield, Middx, EN1 1DW
(Tel: 020-8379 1709; Fax: 020-8367 2213)

Edmonton Green Library
36–44 South Mall, Edmonton, London, N9 0TN
(Tel: 020-8379 2600; Fax: 020-8379 3753
E-mail: edmonton.library@dial.pipex.com)

Enfield Business Library
Enfield Business Centre, 201 Hertford Road, Enfield, Middx, EN3 5JH (Tel: 020-8443 1701; Fax: 020-8443 2193 E-mail: ebl@dial.pipex.com)

Enfield Central Library
Cecil Road, Enfield, Middx, EN2 6TW
(Tel: 020-8379 8366; Fax: 020-8379 8401;
E-mail: enfield.library@dial.pipex.com)
Area Library Manager: Sheila Barford

Enfield Highway Library
258 Hertford Road, Enfield, Middx, EN3 5BN
(Tel: 020-8379 1710; Fax: 020-8443 5034)

Enfield Libraries
PO Box 58, Civic Centre, Silver Street, Enfield, EN1 3XJ (Tel: 020-8379 3710; Fax: 020-8379 3753)

Library Resources Unit, Bibliographical Services
Town Hall, Green Lane, London, N13 4XD
(Tel: 020-8379 2760; Fax: 020-8379 2761)
Library Resources Unit Manager: Ruth Hellen

Merryhills Library
Enfield Road, Enfield, Middx, EN2 7HL
(Tel: 020-8379 1711; Fax: 020-8367 4715)

Ordnance Road Library
645 Hertford Road, Enfield, Middx, EN3 6ND
(Tel: 020-8379 1725; Fax: 01992-788763;
E-mail: ordnance@enfieldlibrary.demon.co.uk)
Senior Branch Librarian: Alan Lewis

Palmers Green Library
Broomfield Lane, Palmers Green, London, N13 4EY (Tel: 020-8379 2711; Fax: 020-8379 2712;
E-mail: palme@dial.pipex.com)
Area Library Manager: Pam Tuttiet

Ponders End Library
College Court, High Street, Ponders End, Middx, EN3 4EY (Tel: 020-8379 1712;
Fax: 020-8443 5035)

Ridge Avenue Library
Ridge Avenue, Winchmore Hill, London, N21 2RH (Tel: 020-8379 1714; Fax: 020-8364 1352)

Southgate Circus Library
High Street, Southgate, London, N14 6BP
(Tel: 020-8350 1124)

Weir Hall Library
Millfield Arts Complex, Silver Street, Edmonton, London, N18 1PJ (Tel: 020-8379 1717;
Fax: 020-8807 3193)

Winchmore Hill Library
Green Lanes, Winchmore Hill, London, N21 3AP (Tel: 020-8379 1718; Fax: 020-8364 1060)

162 Public Services London

GREENWICH
(E-mail: libraries@greenwich.gov.uk;
Web: www.greenwich.gov.uk)

Abbey Wood Library
Eynsham Drive, London, SE2 9PT
(Tel: 020-8310 4185;
E-mail: libraries@greenwich.gov.uk)

Blackheath Library
Old Dover Road, London, SE3 7BT
(Tel: 020-8858 1131;
E-mail: libraries@greenwich.gov.uk)

Charlton Library, Charlton House
Charlton Road, London, SE7 8RE
(Tel: 020-8317 4466;
E-mail: libraries@greenwich.gov.uk)

Claude Ramsey Library
Thamesmere Leisure Centre, London, SE28 8DT (Tel: 020-8310 4246;
E-mail: libraries@greenwich.gov.uk)

Coldharbour Library
William Barefoot Drive, London, SE9 3AY
(Tel: 020-8857 7346;
E-mail: libraries@greenwich.gov.uk)

East Greenwich Library
Woolwich Road, London, SE10 0RL
(Tel: 020-8858 6656;
E-mail: libraries@greenwich.gov.uk)

Eltham Library
Eltham High Street, London, SE9 1TS
(Tel: 020-8850 2268;
E-mail: libraries@greenwich.gov.uk)

Ferrier Library
Telemann Square, London, SE3 9YR
(Tel: 020-8856 5149;
E-mail: libraries@greenwich.gov.uk)

Greenwich Ethnic Library Service
c/o Plumstead Library, Plumstead High Street, London, SE18 1JL (Tel: 020-8317 1544;
E-mail: libraries@greenwich.gov.uk)

Local History Library
Woodlands, Mycenae Road, London, SE3 7SE
(Tel: 020-8858 4631;
E-mail: local.history@greenwich.gov.uk)

Mobile and Home Service
(Mobile Libraries/Hospitals/Housebound/Homes)
c/o Plumstead Library, Plumstead High Street, London, SE18 1JL (Tel: 020-8317 4466;
E-mail: libraries@greenwich.gov.uk)

New Eltham Library
Southwood Road, London, SE9 3QT
(Tel: 020-8850 2322;
E-mail: libraries@greenwich.gov.uk)

Plumstead Library
Plumstead High Street, London, SE18 1JL
(Tel: 020-8854 1728;
E-mail: libraries@greenwich.gov.uk)

Project Loans (School Library Service)
c/o West Greenwich Library, Greenwich High Road, London, SE10 8NN (Tel: 020-8853 1691;
E-mail: libraries@greenwich.gov.uk)

Slade Library
Erindale, London, SE18 2QQ
(Tel: 020-8854 7900;
E-mail: libraries@greenwich.gov.uk)

West Greenwich Library
Greenwich High Road, London, SE10 8NN
(Tel: 020-8858 4289;
E-mail: libraries@greenwich.gov.uk)

Woolwich Library and Reference Library
Calderwood Street, London, SE18 6QZ
(Tel: 020-8921 5750; *Reference:* 020-8316 6663;
E-mail: libraries@greenwich.gov.uk)

HACKNEY
Head of Library Services: Adrian Whittle
(Web: www.hackney.gov.uk/library/library1.html)

Clapton Library
Northwold Road, London, E5 8RA
(Tel: 020-8356 2570)

Libraries 163

CLR James Library
24–30 Dalston Lane, London, E8 3AZ
(Tel: 020-8356 2571)

Collection enquiries
Hackney Central Library, Mare Street, London, E8 1HG (Tel: 020-8525 2542)

Hackney Central Library
Mare Street, London, E8 1HG
(Tel: 020-8525 2560; Fax: 020-8533 3712)

Homerton Library
Homerton High Street, London, E9 6AS
(Tel: 020-8356 2572)
Library Manager: Anita Kane

Mare Street Library
223 Mare Street, London, E8 3QE
(Tel: 020-8356 2542)
Library Manager: Elizabeth Williams

Principal Library
Hackney Central Library, Mare Street, London, E8 1HG (Tel: 020-8525 2542)

Shoreditch Library
80 Hoxton Street, London, N1 6LP
(Tel: 020-8356 4350)
Library Manager: Stephanie Collins

Stamford Hill Library
Portland Avenue, London, N16 6SB
(Tel: 020-8356 2573)
Library Manager: Sue Comitti

Stoke Newington Library
Stoke Newington Church Street, London, N16 0JS (Tel: 020-8356 5230)
Library Manager: Jackie Obeney

HAMMERSMITH AND FULHAM
Head of Libraries and Archives: N. Bouttell;
(Web: www.lbhf.gov.uk)

Fulham Library
598 Fulham Road, London, SW6 5NX
(Tel: 020-8576 5252; Reference library: 020-7736 3741)
Senior Librarian: N. Boutell

Hammersmith Library
Shepherds Bush Road, London, W6 7AT
(Tel: 020-8753 3823; Fax: 020-8753 3815)
Senior Librarian: Ms J. Samuels

Libraries Administration
Hammersmith Library, Shepherds Bush Road, London, W6 7AT (Tel: 020-8753 3813; Fax: 020-8753 3815)

HARINGEY
Alexandra Park Library
Alexandra Park Road, London, N22 4LU
(Tel: 020-8883 8553)

Coombes Croft Library
Tottenham High Road, London, N17 8AG
(Tel: 020-8808 0022)

Highgate Library
Shepherd's Hill, London, N6 5QT
(Tel: 020-8348 3443)

Hornsey Library
Haringey Park, London, N8 9JA
(Tel: 020-8489 1427)

Marcus Garvey Library
Tottenham Green Centre
1 Philip Lane, London, N15 (Tel: 020-8489 5332)

Muswell Hill Library
Queens Avenue, London, N10 3PE
(Tel: 020-8883 6734)

St Ann's Library
Cissbury Road, London, N15 5PU
(Tel: 020-8800 4390)

Stroud Green Library
Quernmore Road, London, N4 4QR
(Tel: 020-8348 4363)

Wood Green Central Library
High Road, London, N22 6XD
(Tel: 020-8489 2782)

HARROW
Library Service Manager: Bob Mills
(E-mail: library@harrow.gov.uk;
Web: www.harrow.gov.uk)

Bob Lawrence Library
6–8 North Parade, Mollison Way, Edgware, HA8 5QH (Tel: 020-8952 4140;
E-mail: boblawrence.library@harrow.gov.uk)
Library Manager: John Clifford

Central Reference Library
Civic Centre, Station Road, Harrow, Middx, HA1 2UU (Tel: 020-8424 1059; Fax: 020-8424 1971; E-mail: library@harrow.gov.uk)

Civic Centre Library
Station Road, Harrow, Middlesex, HA1 2UU (Tel: 020-8424 1055/6; Fax: 020-8424 1971; E-mail: civiccentre.library@harrow.gov.uk)
Library Manager: Sarah Edis

Gayton Central Lending Library
Gayton Road, Harrow, Middx, HA1 2HL
(Tel: 020-8427 6012/8986;
E-mail: gayton.library@harrow.gov.uk)

Hatch End Library
Uxbridge Road, Hatch End, Middx, HA5 4EA
(Tel: 020-8428 2636;
E-mail: gayton.library@harrow.gov.uk)
Library Manager: John Pennells

Kenton Library
Kenton Lane, Kenton, Middx, HA3 8UJ
(Tel: 020-8907 2463;
E-mail: kenton.library@harrow.gov.uk)

North Harrow Library
429–433 Pinner Road, North Harrow, Middlesex, HA1 4HN (Tel: 020-8427 0611;
E-mail: northharrow.library@harrow.gov.uk)
Library Manager: Stella Davies

Pinner Library
Marsh Road, Pinner, Middx, HA5 5NQ
(Tel: 020-866 7827;
E-mail: pinner.library@harrow.gov.uk)
Library Manager: Pat Watts

Rayners Lane Library
226 Imperial Drive, Rayners Lane, Middx, HA2 7HJ (Tel: 020-8866 9185;
E-mail: Raynerslane.library@harrow.gov.uk)
Library Manager: Carol Manson

Roxeth Library
Northolt Road, South Harrow, Middx, HA2 8EQ (Tel: 020-8422 0809;
E-mail: Roxeth.library@harrow.gov.uk)
Library Manager: Carol Manson

Stanmore Library
8 Stanmore Hill, Stanmore, Middx, HA7 3BQ
(Tel: 020-8954 9955;
E-mail: stanmore.library@harrow.gov.uk)
Library Manager: Richard Young

Wealdstone Library
Grant Road, Wealdstone, Middx, HA3 7SD
(Tel: 020-8427 8670;
E-mail: wealdstone.library@harrow.gov.uk)
Library Manager: Stella Davies

HAVERING
Central Library
St Edward's Way, Romford, Essex, RM1 3AR
(Tel Lending: 01708-432389;
Reference: 01708-432394; Fax: 01708-432391)

Collier Row Library
45 Collier Row Road, Collier Row, Romford, Essex, RM5 3NR (Tel: 01708-760063)

Elm Park Library
St. Nicholas Avenue, Elm Park, Hornchurch, Essex, RM12 4PT (Tel: 01708-451270)

Harold Hill Library
Hilldene Avenue, Harold Hill, Romford, Essex, RM3 8DJ (Tel: 01708-432389; Fax: 01708-432391)

Harold Wood Library
Arundel Road, Harold Wood, Romford, Essex, RM3 0RX (Tel: 01708-342071)

Libraries 165

Hornchurch Library
44 North Street, Hornchurch, Essex, RM11 1LW
(Tel: 01708-452248)

Rainham Library
7–11 The Broadway, Rainham, Essex, RM13 9YW (Tel: 01708-551905)

South Hornchurch Library
Rainham Road, Rainham, Essex, RM13 7RD
(Tel: 01708-554126)

Upminster Library
26 Corbets Tey Road, Upminster, Essex, RM14 2BB (Tel: 01708-222864/221578)

HILLINGDON
Service Manager: Mrs T. Grimshaw;
(Web: www.hillingdon.gov.uk)

Central Library
14–15 High Street, Uxbridge, Middx, UB8 1HD
(Tel: 01895-250714; Reference: 01895-250600;
Fax: 01895-239794;
E-mail: clibrary@hillingdon.gov.uk)
Central Library Manager: Ms S. Lake

Eastcote Library
Field End Road, Eastcote, Middx, HA5 1RL
(Tel: 020-8866 3688)

Harefield Library
Park Lane, Harefield, UB9 6BJ
(Tel: 01895-822171;
E-mail: harefield@library.hillingdon.gov.uk)

Harlington Library
Pinkwell Lane, Hayes, Middx, UB3 1PD
(Tel: 020-8569 1612; Fax: 020-8569 1625)

Hayes End Library
Uxbridge Road, Hayes, Middx, UB4 8JQ
(Tel: 020-8573 4209;
E-mail: hayes.end@library.hillingdon.gov.uk)

Hayes Library
Golden Crescent, Hayes, Middx, UB3 1AQ
(Tel: 020-8573 2855; Fax: 020-8848 0269
E-mail: hayes@library.hillingdon.gov.uk)

Hillingdon Libraries Art and Information
Central Library, 14–15 High Street, Uxbridge,
Middx, UB8 1HD (Tel: 01895-250700;
Fax: 01895-811164)

Ickenham Library
Long Lane, Ickenham, Middx, UB10 8RE
(Tel: 01895-635945;
E-mail: ickenham@library.hillingdon.gov.uk)

Kingshill Library
Bury Avenue, Hayes, Middx, UB4 8LF
(Tel: 020-8845 3773;
E-mail: kingshill@library.hillingdon.gov.uk)

Northwood Hills Library
Potter Street, Northwood, Middx, HA6 1QQ
(Tel: 01923-826690;
E-mail: northwood.hills@library.hillingdon.gov.uk)

Oak Farm Library
Sutton Court Road, Hillingdon, Middx, UB10 9PB (Tel: 01895-234690;
E-mail: oak.farm@library.hillingdon.gov.uk)

Oaklands Gate Library
Green Lane, Northwood, Middx, HA6 3AB
(Tel: 01923-826690;
E-mail: oaklands.gate@library.hillingdon.gov.uk)

Ruislip (Manor Farm) Library
Bury Street, Ruislip, Middx, HA4 7SU
(Tel: 01895-633651; Fax: 01895-677555;
E-mail: manor.farm@library.hillingdon.gov.uk)

Ruislip Manor Library
Victoria Road, Ruislip Manor, Middx, HA4 9BW (Tel: 01895-633668;
E-mail: ruislip.manor@library.hillingdon.gov.uk)

South Ruislip Library
Victoria Road, South Ruislip, Middx, HA4 0JE
(Tel: 020-8845 0188;
E-mail: south.ruislip@library.hillingdon.gov.uk)

West Drayton Library
Station Road, West Drayton, Middx, UB7 7JS
(Tel: 01895-443238;
E-mail: west.drayton@library.hillingdon.gov.uk)

Yeading Library
Yeading Lane, Hayes, Middx, UB4 4EW
(Tel: 020-8573 0261;
E-mail: yeading@library.hillingdon.gov.uk)

Yiewsley Library
High Street, Yiewsley, Middx, UB7 0BE
(Tel: 01895-442539;
E-mail: yiewsley@library.hillingdon.gov.uk)

HOUNSLOW
Borough Librarian: Ms L. Simpson;
(Web: www.cip.org.uk)

Chiswick Library
Dukes Avenue, London, W4 2AB
(Tel: 020-8994 1008)

Hounslow Library
24 Treaty Centre, High Street, Hounslow, TW3 1ES (Tel: 020-8583 4545; Fax: 020-8583 4595)

Hounslow Library, Bibliographical Services
24 Treaty Centre, High Street, Hounslow, TW3 1ES (Tel: 020-8583 4716)

ISLINGTON
Head of Library and Information Service:
Liz Roberts
(E-mail: library.informationunit@islington.gov.uk;
Web: www.islington.gov.uk/libraries)

Archway Library
Hamlyn House, Highgate Hill, London, N19 5PH (Tel: 020-7527 7820; Fax: 020-7527 7833)
Library Managers: Kate Tribe and Nicky Mullen

Arthur Simpson Library
Hanley Road, London, N4 3DL
(Tel: 020-7527 7800; Fax: 020-7527 7806)
Library Manager: Bradley Millington

Central Library
2 Fieldway Crescent, London, N5 1PF
(Tel: 020-7527 6955; Fax: 020-7527 6902;
E-mail: central.library@islington.gov.uk)
Library Manager: Teresa Gibson

Finsbury Library
245 St John Street, London, EC1V 4NB
(Tel: 020-7527 7960; Fax: 020-7527 7988)
Library Manager: Pamela Quantrill

John Barnes Library
275 Camden Road, London, N7 0JN
(Tel: 020-7527 7900; Fax: 020-7527 7907)
Library Manager: Yasmin Webb

Lewis Carroll Children's Library
180 Copenhagen Street, London, N1 0ST
(Tel: 020-7527 7936; Fax: 020-7527 7935)
Library Manager: Sharon Goldstone

Mildmay Library
21–23 Mildmay Park, London, N1 4NA
(Tel: 020-7527 7880; Fax: 020-7527 7892)
Library Manager: Carol Roberts

North Library
Manor Gardens, London (Tel: 020-7527 7840;
Fax: 020-7527 7854)
Library Manager: Carol Levy

South Library
115–117 Essex Road, London, N1 2SL
(Tel: 020-7527 7860; Fax: 020-7527 7869)
Library Manager: Chris Millinston

West Library
Bridgeman Road, London, N1 1BD
(Tel: 020-7527 7920; Fax: 020-7527 7928)

KENSINGTON AND CHELSEA
Head of Libraries and Arts: J. McEachen
(E-mail: information.services@rbkc.gov.uk;
Web: www.rbkc.gov.uk)

Central Library
Phillimore Walk, London, W8 7RX
(Tel: 020-7937 2542; Fax: 020-7361 2976)

Libraries 167

KINGSTON-UPON-THAMES
Head of Library Services: Ms B. Lee;
(Web: www.kingston.gov.uk/libs)

Home and Mobile Library Service
Surbiton Library, Ewell Road, Surbiton, KT6 6AG (Tel: 020-8399 7900)
Library Manager: Ms I. Abrahams

Kingston Library
Bibliographical Services, Fairfield Road, Kingston, Surrey, KT1 2PS (Tel: 020-8547 6420)
ICT Development Manager: S. Cooper

Kingston Library
Fairfield Road, Kingston, Surrey, KT1 2PS (Tel: 020-8547 6413; Fax: 020-8547 6426)
Library Manager: Ms S. Hurlock

New Malden Library
Glaster Road, New Malden, Surrey
(Tel: 020-8547 6540; Fax: 020-8547 6545)
Library Manager: Ms C. Roberts

Old Malden Library
Church Road, Worcester Park, KT4 7RD
(Tel: 020-8337 6344; Fax: 020-8330 3118)
Library Manager: Ms M. Vine

Schools Library Service
The Fairfield Centre, Fairfield East, Kingston upon Thames, KT1 2PT (Tel: 020-8408 9100)
Senior Team Librarian: M. Treacy

Surbiton Library
Ewell Road, Surbiton, Surrey, KT6 6AG
(Tel: 020-8399 2331; Fax: 020-8339 9805)
Senior Library Manager: C. Dale

Tolworth Community Library and IT Learning Centre
37–39 The Broadway, Tolworth, Surbiton, Surrey, KT6 7DJ (Tel: 020-8339 6950; Fax: 020-8339 6955;
E-mail: tolworth.library@rbk.kingston.gov.uk)
Library Manager: Ms V. Gower

Tudor Drive Library
Tudor Drive, Kingston upon Thames, KT2 5QH
(Tel: 020-8546 1198; Fax: 020-8547 2295)
Library Manager Ms S. Montague

LAMBETH
Head of Library Services: David Jones
(Web: www.lambeth.gov.uk)

Central Reference Library
Tate Library, Brixton Oval, Brixton, London, SW2 1JQ (Tel: 020-7926 1067; Fax: 020-7926 1070; E-mail: Ramis@lambeth.gov.uk)
Library Manager: Rodney Amis

Collection enquiries
Bibliographic Services, Herne Hill Library, 188 Herne Hill Road, London, SE24 0AG (Tel: 020-7926 6068)

Lambeth Libraries and Archives
Blue Star House, 234–244 Stockwell Road, Brixton, London, SW9 9SP
(Tel: 020-7926 0750; Fax: 020-7926 0751)

LEWISHAM
Head of Libraries and Information Service:
Ms J. Newton
(Web: www.lewisham.gov.uk)

Blackheath Village Library
3–4 Blackheath Grove, London, SE3 0DD
(Tel: 020-8852 5309)

Catford Library
Laurence House, Catford, London, SE6 4RU
(Tel: 020-8314 6399; Fax: 020-8314 1110)

Central Library
199–201 Lewisham High Street, London, SE13 6LG (Tel: 020-8297 9677; Fax: 020-8297 1169)
Operations Manager: J. Simmons

Crofton Park Library
Brockley Road, London, SE4 2AF
(Tel: 020-8692 1683)

Downham Library
Moorside Road, Downham, BR1 5EP
(Tel: 020-8698 1475)

Forest Hill Library
Dartmouth Road, London, SE23 3HZ
(Tel: 020-8699 2065; Fax: 020-8699 8296)

168 Public Services London

Grove Park Library
Somertrees Avenue, London, SE12 0BX
(Tel: 020-8857 5794)

Lewisham Libraries, Management Services Group
1st Floor, Town Hall Chambers, Rushey Green, Catford, London, SE6 4RU (Tel: 020-8314 8024; Fax: 020-8314 3229)

Lewisham Reference Library
199–201 Lewisham High Street, London, SE13 6LG (Tel: 020-8297 9430; Fax: 020-8297 1169)

Local Studies Centre
199–201 Lewisham High Street, London, SE13 6LG (Tel: 020-8297 0682; Fax: 020-8297 1169)

Manor House Library
Old Road, Lee, London, SE13 5SY
(Tel: 020-8852 0357)

New Cross Library
283–285 New Cross Road, London, SE14 6AS
(Tel: 020-8694 2534)

Sydenham Library
Sydenham Road, London, SE26 5SE
(Tel: 020-8778 7563)

Torridon Road Library
Torridon Road, Catford, London, SE6 1RQ
(Tel: 020-8698 1590)

Wavelengths Library
Giffin Street, Deptford, London, SE8 4RJ
(Tel: 020-8694 2535; Fax: 020-8694 9652)

MERTON

Head of Library and Heritage Services:
J. Pateman
(E-mail: john.pateman@merton.gov.uk;
Web: www.merton.gov.uk)

Donald Hope Library
Cavendish House, High Street, London, SW19 2HR (Tel: 020-8542 1975; Fax: 020-8543 9767)

Merton Heritage Centre
The Canons, Madeira Road, Mitcham, CR4 4HD (Tel: 020-8640 9387; Fax: 020-8640 7266)
Library and Service Manager: Sarah Gould

Merton Library and Heritage Services
Civic Centre, London Road, Morden, SM4 5DX
(Tel: 020-8545 3783; Fax: 020-8545 3629)

Mitcham Library
London Road, Mitcham, CR4 2YR
(Tel: 020-8648 4070; Fax: 020-8646 6360;
E-mail: mitcham.library@merton.uk)
Library and Service Manager:
Dabinder Chaudri

Morden Library
Merton Civic Centre, London Road, Morden, SM4 5DX (Tel: 020-8545 4040;
Fax: 020-8545 4037;
E-mail: morden.library@merton.gov.uk)
Library and Service Manager: Vacant

Pollards Hill Library
South Lodge Avenue, Mitcham, CR4 1LT
(Tel: 020-8764 5877; Fax: 020-8765 0925;
E-mail: pollandshill.library@merton.gov.uk)
Library and Service Manager: Vacant

Raynes Park Library
Approach Road, London, SW20 8BA
(Tel: 020-8542 1893; Fax: 020-8543 6132;
E-mail: raynespark.library@merton.gov.uk)
Library and Service Manager: Patricia Roberts

West Barnes Library
Station Road, New Malden, KT3 6JF
(Tel: 020-8942 2635; Fax: 020-8336 0554;
Library and Service Manager: Alison Williams

Wimbledon Library
35 Wimbledon Hill Road, London, SW19 7NB
(Tel: 020-8946 7432; Fax: 020-8944 6804;
E-mail: wimbledon.library@merton.gov.uk)
Library and Service Manager: Pamela Rew

NEWHAM

Head Librarian: R. McMaster
(Web: www.newham.gov.uk)

Beckton Library
1 Kingsford Way, London, E6 4JQ
(Tel: 020-8430 4063)
Site Manager: A. de Heer

Libraries

Canning Town Library
Barking Road, Canning Town, London, E16 4HQ (Tel: 020-7476 2696; Fax: 020-7511 8693)
Site Manager: Ms J. Udell

Collection enquiries
Technical Services Department, Canning Town Library, Barking Road, London, E16 4HQ (Tel: 020-7511 1332; Fax: 020-7511 8693)
Bibliographical and Financial Services Librarian: Ms N. Parker

Custom House Library
Prince Regent Lane, Custom House, London, E16 3JJ (Tel: 020-7476 1565)
Site Manager: Ms C. Garvey

East Ham Library
High Street South, London, E6 4EL
(Tel: 020-8430 3647)
Site Manager: D. Hemmings

Forest Gate Library
38 Woodgrange Road, Forest Gate, London, E7 0QH (Tel: 020-8534 6952)
Site Manager: Ms M. Newman

Green Street Library
337–341 Green Street, Upton Park, London, E13 9AR (Tel: 020-8472 4101; Fax: 020-8472 0927)
Site Manager: G. Ahadi

Local Studies Library
3 The Grove, Stratford, London, E15 1EL
Archivist: R. Durack

Manor Park Library
Romford Road, Manor Park, London, E12 5JY (Tel: 020-8478 1177; Fax: 020-8514 8221)
Site Manager: M. Blair

Newham Libraries
292 Barking Road, East Ham, London, E6 3BA (Tel: 020-8472 1430; Fax: 020-8557 8845)

North Woolwich Library
St Johns Centre, Albert Road, London, E16 2JD (Tel: 020-7511 2387)
Site Manager: L. Pickard

Plaistow Library
North Street, Plaistow, London, E13 9HL
(Tel: 020-8472 0420; Fax: 020-8471 3148)
Site Manager: Ms E. Norris

Schools Library Service
c/o Canning Town Library
Barking Road, London, E16 4HQ
(Tel: 020-7476 2696; Fax: 020-7511 8693)
Schools Library Manager: Ms J. Stannard

Stratford Library
3 The Grove, Stratford, London, E15 1EL
(Tel: 020-8430 6890; Fax: 020-8430 6886)
Site Manager: Ms H. Allsop

REDBRIDGE
Head Librarian: M. Timms
(E-mail: Martin.Timms@redbridge.gov.uk;
Web: www.redbridge.gov.uk)

Aldersbrook Library
2A Park Road, London, E12 5HQ
(Tel: 020-8989 9319;
E-mail: bob.luxmore@redbridge.gov.uk)
Library Manager: Bob Luxmore

Central Library
Clements Road, Ilford, Essex, IG1 1EA
(Tel: 020-8478 7145; Fax: 020-8553 3299;
E-mail: martin.timms@redbridge.gov.uk)
Library Manager: Martin Timms

Fullwell Cross Library
140 High Street, Barkingside, Ilford, Essex, IG6 2EA (Tel: 020-8550 4457;
E-mail: madeline.barrat@redbridge.gov.uk)
Library Manager: Madeline Barratt and Carol Clarke

Gants Hill Library
490 Cranbrook Road, Gants Hill, Ilford, IG2 6LA (Tel: 020-8554 5211;
E-mail: john.hayward@redbridge.gov.uk)
Library Manager: John Hayward

Goodmayes Library
76 Goodmayes Lane, Goodmayes, Ilford, Essex, IG3 9QB (Tel: 020-8590 8362;
E-mail: anne.brolly@redbridge.gov.uk)
Library Manager: Anne Brolly

Hainault Library
100 Manford Way, Chigwell, Essex, IG7 4DD
(Tel: 020-8500 1204;
E-mail: evelyn.reid@redbridge.gov.uk)
Library Manager: Evelyn Reid

170 Public Services London

Mobile Libraries
Central Library, Clements Road, Ilford, Essex,
IG1 1EA (Tel: 020-8478 7145;
E-mail: Bob.terry@redbridge.gov.uk)
Library Manager: Bob Terry

South Woodford Library
116 High Road, London, E18 2QS
(Tel: 020-8504 1407;
E-mail: geraldine.pote@redbridge.gov.uk)
Library Manager: Geraldine Pote

Wanstead Library
Spratt Hall Road, London, E11 2RQ
(Tel: 020-8989 9462;
E-mail: bob.luxmore@redbridge.gov.uk)
Library Manager: Bob Luxmore

Woodford Green Library
Snakes Lane, Woodford Green, Essex, IG8 0DX
(Tel: 020-8504 4642;
E-mail: jill.fellerman@redbridge.gov.uk)
Library Manager: Jill Fellerman

RICHMOND-UPON-THAMES

Chief Librarian: Jane Battye
(Web: www.richmond.gov.uk/libraries/
library.html)

Castelnau Library
75 Castelnau, London, SW13 9RT
(Tel: 020-8748 3837;
E-mail: castelnau.library@richmond.gov.uk)
Library Administrator: B.Lawrence

East Sheen Library
Sheen Lane, London, SW14 8LP
(Tel: 020-8831 6118;
E-mail: eastsheen.library@richmond.gov.uk)
Library Administrator: J.Preston

Ham Library
Ham Street, Richmond, TW10 7HR
(Tel: 020-8940 8703;
E-mail: ham.library@richmond.gov.uk)
Library Administrator: G.Sharif

Hampton Library
Rosehill, Richmond, TW12 2AB
(Tel: 020-8979 5110;
E-mail: hampton.library@richmond.gov.uk)
Library Administrator: A.Turner

Hampton Hill Library
Windmill Road, Richmond, TW12 1RF
(Tel: 020-8979 3705;
E-mail: hamptonhill.library@richmond.gov.uk)
Library Administrator: L.Brignall

Hampton Wick Library
Bennet Close, Kingston, KT1 4AT
(Tel: 020-8977 1559;
Library Administrator: B.Lawrence

Heathfield Library
Percy Road, Richmond, TW2 6JL
(Tel: 020-8894 1017;
E-mail: heathfield.library@richmond.gov.uk)
Library Administrator: C.Thompson

Kew Library
106 North Road, Richmond, TW9 4HJ
(Tel: 020-8876 8654;
E-mail: kew.library@richmond.gov.uk)
Library Administrator: K.Hacker

Reference Library
Old Town Hall, Whittaker Avenue, Richmond,
TW9 1TP (Tel: 020-8940 5529;
Fax: 020-8940 6899;
E-mail: reference.services@richmond.gov.uk)
Central Reference Librarian: J.Hall

Richmond Lending Library
Little Green, Richmond, TW9 1QL (Tel: 020-
8940 0981; Fax: 020-8940 6857;
E-mail: richmond.library@richmond.gov.uk)
Library Administrator: S.Alderson

**Richmond-upon-Thames Library
and Information Services**
Langholm Lodge, 146 Petersham Road,
Richmond, TW10 6UX (Tel: 020-8831 6118;
Fax: 020-8940 7568)
Library Administrator: Jane Battye

Teddington Library
Waldegrave Road, Teddington, TW11 8LG
(Tel: 020-8977 1284; Fax: 020-8977 8264;
E-mail: teddington.library@richmond.gov.uk)
Library Administrator: A. Painter

Libraries 171

Twickenham Library
Garfield Road, Twickenham, TW1 3JT
(Tel: 020-8892 8091;
E-mail: twickenham.library@richmond.gov.uk)

Whitton Library
141 Nelson Road, Richmond, TW2 7BB
(Tel: 020-8894 9828;
E-mail: whitton.library@richmond.gov.uk)
Library Administrator: D.McCullagh

SOUTHWARK
Arts, Libraries and Museums Service Manager:
A. Olsen
(E-mail: adrian.olsen@southwark.gov.uk;
Web: www.southwark.gov.uk)

Arts, Libraries and Museums Services
15 Spa Road, Bermondsey, London, SE16 3QW
(Tel: 020-7525 1993; Fax: 020-7525 1505)

Blue Anchor Library
Market Place, Southwark Park Road, London, SE16 3UQ (Tel: 020-7231 0475; Fax: 020-7232 1842)

Brandon Library
Maddock Way, Cooks Road, London, SE17 3NH (Tel: 020-7735 3430; Fax: 020-7735 1664)

Camberwell Library
17–21 Camberwell Church Street, London, SE5 8TR (Tel: 020-7703 3763; Fax: 020-7708 4597)

Collection enquiries
Bibliographical Services, 15 Spa Road, London, SE16 3QW (Tel: 020-7525 1571;
Fax: 020-7525 1536)

Dulwich Library
368 Lordship Lane, London, SE22 8NB
(Tel: 020-8693 5171; Fax: 020-8693 5135)

Dulwich Reference Library
368 Lordship Lane, London, SE22 8NB
(Tel: 020-8693 8312; Fax: 020-8693 5153)

East Street Library
168–170 Old Kent Road, London, SE1 5TY
(Tel: 020-7703 0395; Fax: 020-7703 2224)

Education Library Service
Southwark Education Resource Centre, Cator Street, London, SE15 6AA (Tel: 020-7525 2830; Fax: 020-7525 2837)

Grove Vale Library
25–27 Grove Vale, London, BE22 8EQ
(Tel: 020-8693 5734; Fax: 020-8693 0755)

John Harvard Library
211 Borough High Street, London, SE1 1JA
(Tel: 020-7407 0807; Fax: 020-7378 9917)

Kingswood Library
Seeley Drive, London, SE21 8QR
(Tel: 020-8670 4803; Fax: 020-8761 5125)

Local Studies Library
211 Borough High Street, London, SE1 1JA
(Tel: 020-7403 3507; Fax: 020-7403 8633)

Newington Reference Library
155–157 Walworth Road, London, SE17 1RS
(Tel: 020-7708 0516; Fax: 020-7252 6115)

Nunhead Library
Gordon Road, London, SE15 3RW
(Tel: 020-7639 0264; Fax: 020-7277 5721)

Peckham Library
122 Peckham Hill Street, London, SE15 5JR
(Tel: 020-7525 0200; Fax: 020-7525 0202)

Rotherhithe Library
Albion Street, London, SE16 7HY
(Tel: 020-7237 2010; Fax: 020-7394 0672)

Special Library Services
Rotherhithe Library, Albion Street, London, SE16 1JA (Tel: 020-7237 1487; Fax: 020-7237 8417)

SUTTON
Library Manager: Ms J. Selby
(E-mail: sutton.information@sutton.gov.uk;
Web: www.sutton.gov.uk/lfl/library/index.htm)

172 Public Services London

Beddington Library
18 The Broadway, Plough Lane, Beddington, Croydon, CR0 4QR (Tel: 020-8688 5093
E-mail: beddington.library@sutton.gov.uk)

Carshalton Library
The Square, Carshalton, Surrey, SM5 3BN
(Tel: 020-8647 1151;
E-mail: Carshalton.library@sutton.gov.uk)
Library Manager: H. Viola

Cheam Library
Church Road, Cheam, Sutton, Surrey, SM3 8QH
(Tel: 020-8644 9377;
E-mail: Cheam.library@sutton.gov.uk)
Library Manager: C. McCarthy

Middleton Circle Library
Green Wrythe Lane, Carshalton, Surrey, SM5 1JJ
(Tel: 020-8648 6608;
E-mail: middleton.library@sutton.gov.uk)

Ridge Road Library
Ridge Road, Sutton, Surrey, SM3 9LY
(Tel: 020-8644 9696;
E-mail: ridge.library@sutton.gov.uk)
Library Manager: D. Carter

Roundshaw Library
Mollison Drive, Roundshaw, Wallington, Surrey, SM6 9HG (Tel: 020-8770 4901;
E-mail: roundshaw.library@sutton.gov.uk)
Library Manager: T. Ashplant

Sutton Central Library
St Nicholas Way, Sutton, Surrey, SM1 1EA
(Tel: 020-8770 4700; Fax: 020-8770 4777)

Wallington Library
Shotfield, Wallington, Surrey, SM6 0HY
(Tel: 020-8770 4900;
E-mail: wallington.library@sutton.gov.uk)
Library Manager: S. Winser

Worcester Park Library
Stone Place, Windsor Road, Worcester Park, Surrey, KT4 8ES (Tel: 020-8337 1609;
E-mail: worcester.library@sutton.gov.uk)
Library Manager: D. O'nions

TOWER HAMLETS
Head of Libraries: Anne Cunningham
(Web: www.earl.org.uk/partners/tower-hamlets/)

Bethnal Green Reference Library
Cambridge Heath Road, London, E2 0HL
(Tel: 020-8980 6274; Fax: 020-8980 2080;
E-mail: 100633.624@compuserve.com)
Principal Information Librarian: John Jasinski

Bow Library
William Place, London, E3 5ET
(Tel: 020-8980 2282; Fax: 020-8980 2080)
Community Librarians: Lesley Harris/ Sarah Paxton

Cubitt Town Library
Strattondale Street, London, E14 3HG
(Tel: 020-7987 3152; Fax: 020-7538 2795)
Community Librarian: Sandra Murray

Dorset Library
Ravenscroft Street, London, E2 7QX
(Tel: 020-7739 9489; Fax: 020-7729 2548)
Community Librarian: Sheila Brown

Fairfoot Library
102 Campbell Road, London, E3 4EA
(Tel: 020-7987 3338; Fax: 020-7515 7601)
Community Librarians: Lesley Harris/ Sarah Paxton

Lansbury Library
23-27 Market Way, London, E14 6AH
(Tel: 020-7987 3573)
Community Librarian: Barbara Stretch

Stepney Library
Lindly Street, London, E1 3AX
(Tel: 020-7790 5616; Fax: 020-7265 9873)
Community Librarian: Bob Stuart

Limehouse Library
638 Commercial Road, London, E14 7HS
(Tel: 020-7364 2527/2552; Fax: 020-7364 2502)
Community Librarian: Sandra Murray

Tower Hamlets Library
277 Bancroft Road, London, E1 4DQ
(Tel: 020-8980 4366; Fax: 020-8981 9965)
Community Librarian: Anne Cunningham

Libraries 173

Wapping Library
St Peter's Centre, Reardon Street, London, E1
9QN (Tel: 020-7488 3535)
Community Librarian: Steve Avery

Watney Market Library
30–32 Watney Market, London, E1 2PR
(Tel: 020-7790 4039; Fax: 020-7065 9401)
Community Librarian: Steve Avery

Whitechapel and Arts Library
77 Whitechapel High Street, London, E1 7QX
(Tel: 020-7247 5272; Fax: 020-7247 5731)
Community Librarian: Caroline Algar

UPPER NORWOOD JOINT
Upper Norwood Joint Library
Westow Hill, London, SE19 1TJ
(Tel: 020-8670 2551; Fax: 020-8670 5468;
E-mail: unjl@unisonfree.net)

WALTHAM FOREST
Head of Libraries and Cultural Services:
Colin Richardson
(Web: www.lbwf.gov.uk)

Central Library
Information Services, High Street, Walthamstow,
London, E17 7JN (Tel: 020-8520 3031;
Fax: 020-8509 9539)

Hale End Library
Castle Avenue, London, E4 9QD
(Tel: 020-8531 6423; Fax: 020-8527 6995;
E-mail: lib.higham@al.lbwf.gov.uk)

Harrow Green Library
Cathall Road, London, E11 4LF
(Tel: 020-8539 5997;
E-mail: lib.harrow@al.lbwf.gov.uk)

Higham Hill Library
North Countess Road, London, E17 5HF
(Tel: 020-8531 6424;
E-mail: lib.higham@al.lbwf.gov.uk)

Lea Bridge Library
Lea Bridge Road, London, E10 7HU
(Tel: 020-8539 5652;
E-mail: lib.leabridge@al.lbwf.gov.uk)

Leyton Library
High Road, London, E10 5QH
(Tel: 020-8539 1223; Fax: 020-8539 4700;
E-mail: lib.leyton@al.lbwf.gov.uk)

Leytonstone Library
Church Lane, London, E11 1HG
(Tel: 020-8539 2730; Fax: 020-8556 1026;
E-mail: lib.leytonstone@al.lbwf.gov.uk)

North Chingford Library
The Green, London, E4 7EN
(Tel: 020-8529 2993;
E-mail: lib.nching@al.lbwf.gov.uk)

South Chingford Library
Hall Lane, London, E4 8EU (Tel: 020-8529
2332; E-mail: lib.sching@al.lbwf.gov.uk)

St James Street Library
Coppermill Lane, London, E17 7HA
(Tel: 020-8520 1292;
E-mail: lib.stjames@al.lbwf.gov.uk)

Wood Street Library
Forest Road, London, E17 4AA
(Tel: 020-8521 1070;
E-mail: lib.wood@al.lbwf.gov.uk)

WANDSWORTH
Head of Libraries, Museums and Arts:
Ms J. Allen
(E-mail: libraries@wandsworth.gov.uk;
Web: www.wandsworth.gov.uk)

Balham Library
Ramsden Road, London, SW12 8QY
(Tel: 020-8871 7195; Fax: 020-8675 4015)

Battersea Library
265 Lavender Hill, London, SW11 1JB
(Tel: 020-8871 7466; Fax: 020-7978 4376)

Libraries, Museums and Arts
Room 223, Wandsworth Town Hall
High Street, London, SW18 2PU
(Tel: 020-8871 6364; Fax: 020-8871 7630)

Putney Library
Disraeli Road, London, SW15 2DR
(Tel: 020-8871 7090; Fax: 020-8789 6175)

174 Public Services London

WESTMINSTER
Libraries Manager: D. Ruse
(Web: www.westminster.gov.uk/el/libarch/index.html)

Charing Cross Library
4 Charing Cross Road, London, WC2H 0HG
(Tel: 020-7641 4628; Fax: 020-7641 4629)
Site Manager: M. Knowles

Church Street Library
Church Street, London, NW8 8EU
(Tel: 020-7641 5479; Fax: 020-7641 5482)
Site Manager: Ms M. Finn

City of Westminster Archives Centre
10 St Ann's Street, London, SW1P 2DE
(Tel: 020-7641 5180; Fax: 020-7641 5179)
City Archivist: S. Rayner

Home Library Service
Moberly Centre, Kilburn Lane, London, W10 4AH (Tel: 020-7641 4806; Fax: 020-7641 4854)
Library Service Manager: M. Parmiter

Maida Vale Library
Sutherland Avenue, London, W9 2QT
(Tel: 020-7641 3659; Fax: 020-7641 3660)
Site Manager: D. Waller

Marylebone Library
109–117 Marylebone Road, London, NW1 5PS
(Tel: 020-7641 1037; Fax: 020-7641 1044)
Site Manager: Ms L. Tobey

Mayfair Library
25 South Audley Street, London, W1Y 5DJ
(Tel: 020-7641 4903; Fax: 020-7641 4901)
Site Manager: M. Stewart

Paddington Library
Porchester Road, London, W2 5DU
(Tel: 020-7641 4475; Fax: 020-7641 4471)
Site Manager: Ms S. Barnes

Pimlico Library
Rampayne Street, London, SW1V 2PU
(Tel: 020-7641 2983; Fax: 020-7641 2980)
Site Manager: Ms M. Houlihan

Queen's Park Library
666 Harrow Road, London, W10 4NE
(Tel: 020-7641 4575; Fax: 020-7641 4576)
Site Manager: Ms S. Moran

Schools Library Service
62 Shirland Road, London, W9 2EH
(Tel: 020-7641 4321; Fax: 020-7641 4322)
Library Service Manager: N. Fuller

St James's Library
62 Victoria Street, London, SW1E 6QP
(Tel: 020-7641 2989; Fax: 020-7641 2986)
Site Manager: Ms A. Farrell

St John's Wood Library
20 Circus Road, London, NW8 6PD
(Tel: 020-7641 5087; Fax: 020-7641 5089)
Site Managers: Ms A. Lopez

Victoria Library
160 Buckingham Palace Road, London, SW1W 9UD (Tel: 020-7641 4287; Fax: 020-7641 4281)
Site Manager: C. Jones

Westminster Reference Library
35 St Martin's Street, London, WC2H 7HP
(Tel: 020-7641 4636; Fax: 020-7641 4606)
Library Manager: Ms T. Arathoon

TRANSPORT

Ways to get about in London and beyond are many and varied. Within this section you will find statistical data, contact details on the major transport service providers and useful information about how to get in, out and around the capital.

Transport for London (TfL) is the new body responsible for most transport in London. It is an executive arm of the Greater London Authority (GLA). The London boroughs remain the highways and traffic authorities for 95% of roads in London. They are required to develop and put into practice transport strategies in the form of Local Implementation Plans.

The management of the London Underground system remains a controversial issue. The Government at present favours the option of a Public Private Partnership arrangement whereas the Mayor of London's view is that the responsibility for the Underground should remain with the public sector. For further information on the Underground, the Commissioner of Transport for London has outlined in a paper 'Proposed Plan for the London Underground', extended plans on the management of the London Underground system.

TRANSPORT FOR LONDON (TfL)

Windsor House, 42-50 Victoria Street, London SW1H 0TL (Tel: 020-7941 4500).

Transport for London (TfL) is London's integrated transport body. Its role is to implement the Mayor's transport strategy for London and manage the transport services for which the Mayor is responsible. TfL has responsibility for both planning and delivering the provision of transport facilities for all modes of transport throughout Greater London.

* For further information on the role and structure of TfL, see the Governed London Section.

Travel Information Advisor Line (Tel: 020-7222 1234; Email: enquire@TfL.gov.uk; Web: www.transportforlondon.gov.uk).

London Buses: Customer Services Centre, 4th Floor, 172 Buckingham Palace Road, London SW1W 9TN (Tel: 020-7918 4300; 020-7918 3999; E-mail customerservices@tfl-buses.co.uk). London Underground (Tel: 020-7918 4040).

London River Services: Tower Pier, Lower Thames Street, London EC3N 4DT (Tel: 020-7222 1234; Email: enquiries@tfl-river.co.uk).

Docklands Light Railway: (Tel: 020-7918 4000).

Croydon Tramlink: (020-8662 9800).

Public Carriage Office: (Tel: 020-7230 1653).

Travel information and advice for disabled passengers: (Tel: 020-7688 4601).

Lost Property Manager – office open 09.30 and 14.00, Monday to Friday: (Tel: 020-7486 2496; Fax: 020-7918 1028; Email: cservice@dir.co.uk).

People who live, work or visit London on a regular basis will be all too familiar with the concept of 'rush hour'. The table below indicates the numbers of people travelling in London and the modes of transport that they use.

For ease of use, this section has been split up into the following transport modes: Rail, Underground, Road (including Bus, Coach, Taxi, Car), River and Air.

PEOPLE ENTERING LONDON* DURING MORNING PEAK 7-10am, 1981-1997 (000s)

	Surface Rail Total	Of which transfers to LUL and DLR†	LUL and DLR only	LT bus†	Coach/ Minibus	Private Car	Motor/ Pedal cycle	All modes
1981	394	127	336	105	16	173	26	1,050
1986	421	166	381	91	25	166	21	1,105
1988	468	188	411	80	21	160	17	1,157
1991	426	169	347	74	20	155	21	1,042
1997	435	195	373	68	20	142	22	1,059
1998	448	196	394	68	17	140	23	1,088

* Excludes passengers in taxis
† LUL = London Underground Ltd; DLR = Docklands Light Railway; LT = London Transport
Source: Focus on London 2000, National Statistics, © Crown Copyright 2001

COMMISSION FOR INTEGRATED TRANSPORT

5th Floor, Romney House, Tufton Street, London SW1P 3RA (Tel: 020-7944 4101/4813; Fax: 020-7944 2919).

The Commission for Integrated Transport was proposed in the 1998 Transport White Paper and was set up in June 1999. Its role is to provide independent expert advice to the Government in order to achieve a transport system that supports sustainable development. Members of the Commission are appointed by the Secretary of State for the Environment, Transport and the Regions.

RAIL

Greater London is served by an extensive network of rail services which connect London to the rest of the UK, and with the advent of Eurostar services, to Europe. Since 1 April 1994, ownership of operational track and land has been vested in Railtrack, which was floated on the Stock Exchange in 1996. Railtrack is responsible for management of the track and charging train operating companies for access to it. It is also responsible for signalling and timetabling and manages 15 major stations around the network. It does not operate train services.

The independent Rail Regulator is responsible for the licensing of new railway operators, approving access agreements, promoting the use and development of the network, preventing anti-competitive practices and protecting the interests of rail users.

Following privatisation of the rail system, domestic passenger services were divided into 25 train-operating units throughout the UK, which (with the exception of Eurostar) have been franchised to private sector companies via compulsory competitive tendering.

Rail Users' Consultative Committees monitor the policies and performance of train and station operators in their area. They are statutory bodies and have a legal right to make recommendations for changes. The London Transport Users' Committee has a similar role representing users of buses, the Underground, Docklands Light Railway and rail services in the London area.

London Transport Users' Committee, Clements House, 14-18 Gresham Street, London, EC2V 7PR (Tel: 020-7505 9000; Fax: 020-7505 9003);
Director: Rufus Barnes

TRAIN OPERATING COMPANIES SERVING LONDON

The list below provides a general contact point for the head offices of train operating companies serving London. If you have an enquiry relating to train services and timetabling contact National Rail Enquiries on 08457 484950.

Anglia Railways
Press Office, Anglia Railways Train Services Limited, 15-25 Artillery Lane, London E1 7HA (Tel: 020-7465 9009; Fax: 020-7465 9053). Operates services between London and Colchester, Ipswich, Norwich and Harwich and a variety of local services.

c2c
c2c Rail Limited, Central House, Clifftown Road, Southend-on-Sea, Essex SS1 1AB (Tel: 01702-357810; Fax: 01702-357819; Email: custrel@c2crail.co.uk; Web: www.c2c-online.co.uk). Operates services between a variety of busy Essex suburban locations, including Barking, Basildon, Benfleet, Grays, Southend and Upminster.

Chiltern Railways
The Chiltern Railway Company Limited, 2nd Floor, Western House, 14 Rickfords Hill, Aylesbury HP20 2RX (Tel: 01296 332113; Fax: 01296 332100; Web: www.chilternrailways.co.uk). Operates rail passenger services from London Marylebone through High Wycombe and Banbury to Birmingham Snow Hill, and via the London Underground Metropolitan line to Aylesbury.

Connex Rail (South Central)
Connex Communications, Connex Rail, Friars Bridge Court, 41-45 Blackfriars Road, London SE1 8PG (Tel: 020-7620 5505; Fax: 020-7620 5522; Web: www.connex.co.uk). Customer Services, 3 Priory Road, Tonbridge TN9 2AF (Tel: 0870 603 0405; Fax: 0870 603 0405). Operates services from London through West Sussex and along the South Coast to Brighton, Ashford and Bournemouth. Services through West London to Guildford. Through services from Rugby to Gatwick Airport.

Connex Rail (South Eastern)
Connex Communications, Connex Rail, Friars Bridge Court, 41-45 Blackfriars Road, London SE1 8PG (Tel: 020-7620 5505; Fax: 020-7620 5522; Web: www.connex.co.uk). Customer Services, 3 Priory Road, Tunbridge TN9 2AF (Tel: 0870 603 0405; Fax 0870 603 0505). Operates services between South East London, Kent and parts of East Sussex and Surrey.

Eurostar
Eurostar Group, Eurostar House, Waterloo Station, London SE1 8SE (Tel: 020-7922 4486; Fax: 020-7922 4499). Operates high speed services between London, Kent and mainland Europe.

First Great Eastern
First Great Eastern, 35 Artillery Lane, London E1 7LP (Tel: 08459 505000; Email: customer.services@ger.firstgroup.com; Web: www.yourtrain.co.uk). Operates services in East London, Essex and parts of Suffolk. First Great Eastern's three main service groups, Metro, Southend and Mainline, all operate into London Liverpool Street.

First Great Western Trains
Corporate Affairs Manager, First Great Western Trains, Milford House, Milford Street, Swindon SN1 1HL (Tel: 01793-499499/499406; Fax: 01793-499453; Email: customer.relations@gwt.firstgroup.com; Web: www.firstgreatwestern.co.uk). Operates services between London, South Wales, the Cotswolds and the South West.

First North Western
Corporate Affairs, First Floor, Bridgewater House, 58 Whitworth Street, Manchester M1 6LT (0161-228 2141; Fax: 0161-228 5909; Email: customer-relations.nwt@ems.rail.co.uk; Web: www.nwt.rail.co.uk). Operates services between London Euston and the North West of England and North Wales, serving the major centres of Manchester and Liverpool.

Gatwick Express
Marketing and Media Relations, Gatwick Express Limited, 52 Grosvenor Gardens, London SW1W 0AU (Tel: 020-7973 5000; Fax: 020-7973 5048; Web: www.gatwickexpress.co.uk). Operates a dedicated rail/air link between London Victoria Station and London Gatwick Airport.

Great North Eastern Railway
Press Office, Great North Eastern Railway Limited, Headquarters, Station Road, York YO1 6HT (Tel: 01904 653022; Fax: 01904 523022; Customer Enquiry Line: 08457 225225; Email: customer.care@gner.co.uk; Web: www.gner.co.uk). Operates inter-city services on the East Coast mainline between London King's Cross and Scotland.

Midland Mainline
Midland Mainline Limited, Midland House, Nelson Street, Derby DE1 2SA (Tel: 01332-262010; Email: feedback.mml@ems.rail.co.uk; Web: www.mml.rail.co.uk). Operates services between London St. Pancras through Nottingham and Derby to Sheffield and Leeds.

Silverlink
Communications Department, Silverlink Train Services Limited, Melton House, 65-67 Clarendon Road, Watford WD1 1DP (Tel: 01923-207777; Press Office: 01923-246480; Fax: 01923-246480; Web: www.silverlink-trains.com). Silverlink County Services operates services between London Euston, Milton Keynes and Birmingham New Street via Northampton. Silverlink Metro services operate between North Woolwich and Richmond, Willesden Junction and Clapham Junction, Barking and Gospel Oak, with a branch to St. Albans Abbey and a link between Watford and Croxley Green.

South West Trains
South West Trains Limited, Friars Bridge Court, 41-45 Blackfriars Road, London SE1 8NZ (Tel: 020-7928 5151 (Switchboard); 020-7620 5229 (Press Office)). Operates services between London Waterloo and 217 stations throughout south London, Berkshire, Cornwall, Devon, Dorset, East and West Sussex, Hampshire, Somerset, Surrey and Wiltshire.

Thames Trains
Public Affairs, Thames Trains Limited, Venture House, 37 Blagrave Street, Reading RG1 1PZ (Tel: 0118-908 3637; Fax: 0118-957 9648; Email: tatelthames@ems.rail.co.uk; Web: www.thamestrains.co.uk).

178 Public Services London

Operates services between London Paddington and Oxford via Maidenhead and Reading, with certain services extending to Stratford-upon-Avon and via Worcester to Hereford. There is also a service operating between London Paddington and Bedwyn via Reading and Newbury. Thames Trains also run between Reading and London Gatwick Airport via Guildford and Reading and Basingstoke.

Thameslink
Marketing and Communications Manager, Thameslink Rail Limited, Friars Bridge Court, 41-45 Blackfriars Road, London SE1 8NZ (Tel: 020-7620 5002; Fax: 020-7620 5099). Operates services between Bedford, through 5 London stations, to Brighton. London stops include King's Cross Thameslink, Farringdon, City Thameslink, Blackfriars and London Bridge.

Virgin Trains
Corporate Affairs, West Wing Offices, Euston Stations, London NW1 2HS (Tel: 0870 789 1111; Web: www.virgintrains.co.uk). Operates more than 1,600 services a week calling at over 130 stations throughout Great Britain, including London Euston and London Paddington.

WAGN Railway
External Relations Manager, West Anglia Great Northern Railway, Hertford House, 1 Cranwood Street, London EC1V 9QS (Tel: 020-7713 2121; Fax: 020-7713 2116).
Operates services between London King's Cross, Moorgate and Liverpool Street and North East London, Cambridgeshire, Hertfordshire and West Norfolk.

Wales and West
Wales and West Passenger Trains Limited, Brunel House, 2 Fitzalan Road, Cardiff CF4 0SU (Tel: 029-2043 0400; Fax: 029-2043 0214). Operates services between London Paddington and Waterloo and many parts of Great Britain including Manchester, Birmingham, Cardiff, Swansea, Brighton, Exeter, Bath, Liverpool and Penzance.

OTHER TRANSPORT ORGANISATIONS

Association of Train Operating Companies (ATOC)
40 Bernard Street, London WC1N 1BY (Tel: 020-7904 3010; Fax 020-7904 3081).

British Railways Board and Shadow Strategic Rail Authority
55 Victoria Street, London SW1H 0EU (Tel: 020-7960 1500; Fax: 020-7654 6010).
National Rail Enquiries (Tel: 08457 484950).

Office of the Rail Regulator
1 Waterhouse Square, 138-142 Holborn, London EC1N 2TQ (Tel: 020-7282 2000; Fax: 020-7282 2040; Email: orr@dial.pipex.com; Web: www.rail-reg.gov.uk).
Rail Regulator: Tom Winsor

Railtrack plc
Railtrack House, Euston Square, London NW1 2EE (Tel: 020-7557 8000; Fax 020-7557 9000; Web: www.railtrack.co.uk).

Strategic Rail Authority (SRA)
55 Victoria Street, London SW1H 0EU (020-7654 6000; Fax 020-7654 6010; Web: www.sra.gov.uk).

DOCKLANDS LIGHT RAILWAY

Docklands Railway Management, Castor Lane, London, E14 0DS (Tel: 020-7363 9500).

The Docklands Light Railway opened in 1987. It is owned by DLR Ltd, a public body. Following the completion of new lines in 2000, the DLR covers 27 kilometres and 33 stations in and around the Docklands area of east London. Operation of the system was privatised in 1997, when it was franchised to Docklands Railway Management Ltd for seven years. With the establishment of the GLA, DLR Ltd has become part of Transport for London.

UNDERGROUND

There are approximately 2.5 million passenger journeys on the London Underground each day, with over 500 trains serving over 260 stations. The majority of people probably use the underground without giving it a second thought – below are some facts and figures for you to contemplate on your next journey.
- The average speed of an underground train is 33kph
- The maximum tunnel depth below ground level is 221ft
- During the second world war, tube platforms were used as air raid shelters
- Penalty fairs were introduced in 1994
- The opening of the "Twopenny Tube" from Shepherd's Bush to Bank took place in 1900 and now forms part of the Central Line
- The first escalators in service were at Earl's Court in 1911
- Work started on the Jubilee Line extension in 1993. The Jubilee line originally opened in 1979.
- In 1987 a fire at king's Cross station resulted in 31 deaths
- 41 fatalities occurred in a accident at Moorgate station in 1975
- the Circle line was completed in 1884
- the first underground railway took passengers between Paddington and Farringdon in 1863

UNDERGROUND RAIL TRAFFIC IN LONDON 1981-1999

	London Underground passenger journeys (millions)	London Underground passenger kilometres (millions)	Average passenger journey length (km)	Train kilometres (millions)	Occupancy-passengers per train
1981	541	4,088	7.6	50	81.8
1988-89	815	6,292	7.7	51	125.0
1991-92	751	5,895	7.8	53	112.0
1997-98	832	6,479	7.8	62	104.3
1998-99	866	6,716	7.8	61	109.7
% change 1988-89 to 1998-99	4.3	6.7	0.4	20.0	-12.2

Source: Focus on London 2000, National Statistics © Crown Copyright 2001

ROAD

ROAD DISTANCES FROM LONDON

Town/City	Distance from London (miles)
Aberdeen	547
Aberystwyth	238
Birmingham	120
Bristol	120
Cardiff	155
Colchester	61
Dover	79
Edinburgh	413
Exeter	200
Glasgow	412
Inverness	573
Leeds	198
Liverpool	216
Manchester	204
Newcastle	286
Norwich	115
Nottingham	131
Oxford	57
Plymouth	241
Sheffield	169
Southampton	80
York	212

There are many bus routes operating within the London area. London Transport Buses was established in April 1994 and its responsibilities include management of the tendering of bus routes, management of bus stops, stations and shelters and planning the entire bus route network for London.

In London there are 5,400 buses running on 700 routes, with 10,000 bus shelters and 140 bus stations and stands. On a typical weekday there are 4 million bus journeys in the capital, compared with 2.5 million on the London Underground. Flat bus fares are making bus travel simpler and

180 Public Services London

potentially cheaper. The new fares comprise of £1 per single journey in central London and 70p in outer zones.

For bus services linking the main London railway stations, Stationlink provides a daily service to all travellers needing to make cross-London connections. Stationlink currently links Paddington, Marylebone, Euston, King's Cross St. Pancras, Liverpool Street, Fenchurch Street,

London Bridge, Waterloo, Victoria and Victoria Coach stations and routes operate clockwise and anticlockwise, starting and finishing at Paddington. Fares are £1 for adults and 50p for children aged 5-15 years. The service is free to people with elderly or disabled travel permits, holders of British Rail Disabled Persons and Senior Railcards Travelcards, LT cards and Bus Passes which include Zone 1 are also valid.

BUS TRAFFIC IN LONDON, 1981-1999

	Bus passenger journeys (millions)	Bus passenger kilometres (millions)	Average passenger journey length (km)	Bus kilometres (millions)	Occupancy – passengers per bus
1981	1,079	4,023	3.7	280	14.4
1987-88	1,211	4,258	3.5	249	17.1
1988-89	1,206	4,231	3.5	261	16.2
1991-92	1,149	3,996	3.5	301	13.3
1997-98	1,277	4,350	3.4	342	12.7
1998-99	1,267	4,315	3.4	344	12.5
% change 1988-89 to 1998-99	5.1	2.0	-2.9	31.8	-22.6

Source: Focus on London 2000, National Statistics © Crown Copyright 2001

LONDON BUS COMPANIES

First Capital
Chequers Lane, Dagenham, Essex RM9 6QD (Tel: 020-8517 9924; Fax: 020-8595 3369).

London Central
London General House, 25 Raleigh Gardens, Mitcham, Surrey CR4 3NS (Tel: 020-8646 1747; Fax: 020-8640 2317).

Metrobus
Farnborough Hill, Orpington, Kent BR6 6DA (Tel: 01689 861432; Fax: 01689 857324; Email: info@metrobus.co.uk; Web: www.metrobus.co.uk).
Managing Director: Peter Larking

Metroline
118-122 College Road, Harrow, Middx HA1 1DB (Tel: 020-8218 8888; Fax: 020-8218 8899; Email: dofarrell@metroline.co.uk; Web: www.metroline.co.uk).
Chief Executive: Declan O'Farrell

Stagecoach London
2-4 Clements Road, Ilford, Essex IG1 1BA (Tel: 020-8553 3420; Fax: 020-8477 7200; Email: pro-el@stagecoach-london.co.uk; Web: www.stagecoach-london.co.uk).

Stagecoach Selkent
180 Bromley Road, Catford, London SE6 2XA (Tel: 020-8695 0707; Fax: 020-8695 9232).

COACH

Many coaches providing travel from London depart from Victoria Coach station and in addition, there are a number of commuter routes providing frequent services between London and the surrounding counties. The list below gives details of a selection of companies providing leisure and/or commuter coach travel to and from London.

Airlinks
Heathrow Coach Centre, Sipson Road, West Drayton, Middlesex UB 7 0HN (Tel: 0990 747777; Email: info@airlinks.co.uk; Web: www.airlinks.co.uk).
Operates services to and from London airports and other other major UK airports.

Transport

Berry's Coaches (Taunton) Ltd
Wellington New Road, Taunton, Somerset TA1 5NA (Tel: 01823-331356; Fax: 01823-322347; Email: info@berryscoaches.co.uk; Web: www.berryscoaches.co.uk).
Operates an express coach service between London and the West country.

Buzzlines
Unit G1. Lympne Industrial Park, Nr Hythe, Kent CT21 4LR (Tel: 01303-261870; Email: kathryn@buzzlines.co.uk; Web: www.buzzlines.co.uk).
Operates a commuter service between London and Kent.

Chenery Travel
20a Castle Meadow, Norwich (Tel: 01603-630676; Fax: 01603-76523; Web: www.chenerytravel.com/london.html).
Operates services between East Anglia and London Liverpool Street, Temple, Whitehall and Victoria.

Greenline
Greenline Travel Limited, 23-27 Endsleigh Road, Merstham, Redhill Surrey RH1 3LX (Tel: 0870 608 7261; Fax: 01737-643135; Email: enquire@greenline.co.uk; Web: www.greenline.co.uk).
Operates a variety of scheduled services between London and the home counties.

London Coaches Kent
Lower Road, Northfleet, Kent DA11 9BB (Tel: 01474-330300; Fax: 01474-335176; Email: grahamwykes@londoncoaches.demon.co.uk; Web: www.londoncoaches.com).
Operates a number of services between London and Kent.

London United Busways
Busways House, Wellington Road, Twickenham TW2 5NX (Tel: 020-8400 6665; Fax: 020-8943 2688).
Local bus routes in Central and Greater London.

Marshall's Coaches
Firbank Way, Leighton Buzzard, Bedfordshire LU7 4YP (Tel: 020-7837 6663 or 01525 376077; Fax: 01525 850967; Email: bookings@marshalls-coaches.co.uk; Web: www.marshalls-coaches.co.uk)
For all types of private hire UK and Continental.

National Express
(Tel: 08705 808080; Web: www.nationalexpress.co.uk).
Operates a wide range of national services.

Oxford Express
395 Cowley Road, Oxford OX4 2DJ (Tel: 01865 785410; Fax: 01865 711745; Email: info@oxfordbus.co.uk; Web: www.oxfordbus.co.uk).
Operates express services 24 hours every day between London and Oxford and Gatwick and Heathrow airports.

TAXI

Licensed black taxis are found all over London but operate mostly within the central London area. They are strictly regulated by Public Carriage Office, now the responsibility of Transport for London (TfL). A white numbered license plate is displayed inside and on the rear of every licensed Taxi. Every Taxi driver has to pass a series of examinations which tests their knowledge of the streets of central and suburban London. They are also required to pass a medical and driving test.

Drivers are under no duty to accept a hiring of six miles or more, or over 20 miles for a journey from London Heathrow Airport, however, if they do accept such a hiring and the journey is wholly within the London area, the fare indicated by the meter is payable. Alternatively, if the driver accepts a hiring to a destination outside of Greater London, the fare is negotiable. Taxis are most commonly hailed in the street, however, they can be booked in advance: Computer Cab: 020-7286 0286; Dial-a Cab: 020-7253 5000; Radio Taxis: 020-7272 0272.

Public Carriage Office
15 Penton Street, London N1 9PU (Email: pco.tfl@gtnet.gov.uk; Web: www.transportforlondon.gov.uk)
There are also many unregulated mini cab services operating within the London area, some offering specialist services such as women only drivers and services to and from airports. The process of

182 Public Services London

licensing private hire operations, drivers and vehicles by the Public Carriage Office is in the process of implementation.

PARKING

Transport Committee for London (TCfL)
New Zealand House, 80 Haymarket, London SW1Y 4TE (Tel: 020-7747 4700; Fax: 020-7747 4848)

The Transport Committee for London is a part of the Association of London Government. The road Traffic Act 1991 established a new system for parking enforcement in London, giving London boroughs responsibility for all aspects of parking control and enforcement, and to keep the income from tickets in order to pay for the enforcement. TCfL incorporates the Parking Appeals Service, which exists to provide adjudication for disputed parking penalties. Last year it dealt with almost 40,000 appeals making one of the busiest tribunals in Britain.

RIVER

The Port of London Authority has statutory responsibility for the conservancy and safe navigation of 95 miles (150km) of the River Thames from Teddington, Middlesex, to the sea.

PORT OF LONDON AUTHORITY

Baker's Hall, 7 Harp Lane, London EC34 6LB (Tel: 020-7743 7900
Web: www.portoflondon.co.uk).
Chief Executive: S. Cuthbert
The Secretary: G. E. Ennals
Chief Harbour Master: Tel: 01474 562200

Denton Wharf, Mark Lane, Gravesend, Kent (Tel: 01474 562444; Fax: 01474 562403).
London River House, Royal Pier Head, Gravesend, Kent DA12 2BG (Tel: 01474 562200; Fax: 01474 562281).
Thames Barrier Navigation, Control Centre, Unit 28 Bowater Road, London SE18 5TF (Tel: 020-8855 0315; Fax: 020-8854 7422).

In recent years the River Thames has been more frequently used for leisure and commuter transport. London River Services Limited, a subsidiary of Transport for London, aims to develop long term river passenger transport in London and develop new piers and boat services. London River Services Limited is currently responsible for the management of Westminster, Waterloo Festival, Embankment, Blackfriars Bankside, Tower and Greenwich piers.

LONDON RIVER SERVICES LIMITED

Tower Millennium Pier, Lower Thames Street, London EC3N 4DT (Tel: 020-7941 2400; Fax: 020-7941 2410;
Web: www.transportforlondon.gov.uk).

The major services operating on the River Thames are:
- Westminster Tower and Greenwich
- Westminster – St. Katharine's – Westminster
- Westminster to St. Katharine's, Greenwich and Thames Barrier
- Wesminster to Kew, Richmond and Hampton Court
- Embankment to Tower and Greenwich
- Greenland – Savoy via Canary Wharf
- Greenwich to Thames Barrier
- Gravesend and Tilbury to Greenwich
- Cadogan – Blackfriars via Westminster
- Chelsea Harbour – Embankment via Cadogan
- Circular, Luncheon and Evening Cruises
- Woolwich Free Ferry

For travel information, fares and timetabling, call London Travel Information on 020-7222 1234 or visit www.transportforlondon.gov.uk

AIR

There are five major airports serving London, London Gatwick, London Heathrow and London Stansted (regulated and operated by BAA plc/Civil Aviation Authority) and London Luton and London City Airports.

The London Airports are amongst the busiest in the world and below you will see a range of statistical data on the subject of air travel to and from the capital.

The Editor would like to acknowledge BAA plc for allowing us to reproduce statistics from their website: www.baa.co.uk

MAJOR TRAFFIC FLOWS 1999/2000

UK Airport	Terminal Passengers (000's)
London Heathrow	62,271
London Gatwick	30,415
London Stansted	9,902
*London City	1,360.2

* 1998 figure

TOP 5 BUSIEST ROUTES AT BAA AIRPORTS IN 1999/2000

London Heathrow	Terminal Passengers (000's)
New York (JFK)	2,671
Amsterdam	2,273
Dublin	2,167
Paris (Charles de Gaulle)	1,899
Edinburgh	1,586
TOTAL	62,271

London Gatwick	Terminal Passengers (000's)
Orlando	935
Malaga	842
Palma	742
Tenerife	705
Dublin	650
TOTAL	30,415

London Stansted	Terminal Passengers (000's)
Dublin	1,072
Edinburgh	497
Munich	434
Amsterdam	387
Copenhagen	320
TOTAL	9,902

BAA PLC

130 Wilton Road, London SW1V 1LQ (Tel: 020-7834 9449; Fax: 020-7932 6699; Web: www.baa.co.uk).

TOP 5 LEADING AIRLINES AT BAA AIRPORTS IN 1999/2000

London Heathrow

Airline	Passengers (000's)
British Airways	26,123.1
British Midland	5,910.1
Virgin Atlantic	2,432.0
United Airlines	2,159.7
Air Lingus	2,009.6
TOTAL	62,271.0

London Gatwick

Airline	Passengers (000's)
British Airways*	8,934.1
Air 2000	2,131.6
Monarch Airlines	2,094.2
Cityflyer Express	1,693.1
Britannia Airways	1,606.7
TOTAL	30,415.2

* Including EOAG (European Operation at Gatwick)

London Stansted

Airline	Passengers (000's)
Ryanair	3,165.4
Go Airlines	1,887.3
KLM uk	1,336.9
Lufthansa Airlines	441.5
Britannia Airways	322.1
TOTAL	9,901.6

CIVIL AVIATION AUTHORITY

CAA House, 45-59 Kingsway, London WC2B 6TE (Tel: 020-7379 7311; Web: www.caa.co.uk).

The CAA is responsible for the economic regulation of UK airlines and for the safety regulation of UK civil aviation by the certification of airlines and aircraft and by licensing aerodromes, flight crew and aircraft engineers. It also runs the Air Travel Organisers' Licensing (ATOL) consumer protection scheme.

The CAA advises the Government on aviation issues, represents consumer interests, conducts economic and scientific research, produces statistical data, and provides specialist services and other training and consultancy services to clients world-wide.

LONDON CITY AIRPORT

London City Airport Limited, Royal Docks, London E16 2PX (Tel: 020-7646 0088; Email: info@londoncityairport.com; Web: www.londoncityairport.com).

London City Airport operates services to: Amsterdam, Antwerp, Basel, Belfast, Berlin, Berne, Brussels, Dublin, Dundee, Dusseldorf, Edinburgh, Frankfurt, Geneva, Glasgow, Isle of Man, Jersey, Le Havre, Luxembourg, Munster, Nuremburg, Paris, Rennes, Rotterdam, Sheffield, Zurich.

Airlines serving London City Airport include: Aer Lingus, Air France, Crossair, British European, KLM Alps, KLM UK, Lufthansa, Luxair, Sabena, Scot Airways, VLM.

Getting there...
... by Train
Travellers can take the Jubilee line on the London Underground to Canary Wharf to connect with the Airport Shuttlebus services. The Silverlink Metro operates every 30 minutes from Richmond via Canning Town, and Docklands Light Railway (DLR) links Bank and Tower Gateway stations to Canary Wharf and Canning Town where passengers can again connect with the Airport Shuttlebus.

... by Road
Car parking is available adjacent to the terminal building and is available on a long or short stay basis. There is no need to pre-book.
There are two airport shuttlebuses. One runs between the airport and Canning Town on the Jubilee line every 10 minutes and takes only 5 minutes. The second operates every 10 minutes between Liverpool Street Station and London City Airport with the route going via Canary Wharf. Other bus services include routes 69, 473 and 474.

LONDON GATWICK AIRPORT

Passenger Information: (Tel: 0870 002 468; Web: www.baa.co.uk).

London Gatwick Airport welcomes over 32 million passengers each year and is the world's busiest single runway international. It is the second largest airport in the UK and the sixth busiest international airport in the world. There are over 68 schedules airlines and 49 chartered airlines serving over 300 destinations around the world of which, 168 are scheduled destinations. Passengers at Gatwick can travel to 27 US destinations which is more than any other European airport including Heathrow.

Getting there...
... by Train
Gatwick Express trains depart every 15 minutes leaving Gatwick airport between 0500 and 0050 and London Victoria between 0500 and 0001. There is also an hourly service throughout the night. The journey is non-stop to central London and takes 30 minutes. Further information: 0845 530 1530; Web: www.gatwickexpress.co.u.k

Frequent services are also offered to the City with Thameslink, and Olympia with Connex. Gatwick railway station has more that 900 services daily to all parts of the UK. Further Information: 0845 748 4950.

... by Road
London Gatwick Airport is situated 28 miles south of London, linked to the M23 at junction 9 and to the A23 London to Brighton road. Just a 10 minutes drive away, the M25 further connects with the UK's extensive road and motorway network.

For passengers travelling to London Gatwick by road there are petrol station in both terminals which are open 24 hours a day. Parking is available on a short stay (up to 5 hours) or long stay basis (enabling people to park their cars for the duration of their holidays). Valet parking is also available at Gatwick. Tel: 0500 340 089.

For information and pre-booking (Tel: 0845 7740 5000/0800 844 844; Web: www.baa.co.uk)

There are more than 4000 express coach services a day to and from Gatwick Bus and Coach information: 0870 608 2608.

LONDON HEATHROW AIRPORT

Heathrow Airport Limited, 234 Bath Road, Harlington, Hayes, Middlesex UB3 5AP (Tel: 0870 000 0123; Fax: 020-8745 4290; Web: www.heathrowairport.co.uk).

Getting there...
... by Road
The M4 (junction 4), M25 (junction 15) and A4 motorways serve terminals 1, 2 and 3 while terminal 4 can be accessed by M4 (junction 3), M25 (junction 15) and A30. For people travelling

to London Heathrow by road the Department of Environment, Transport and the Regions has set up a journey-planner information line on 01234 276376. There are two petrol stations at London Heathrow, both open 24 hours a day and car parking is available on a Short Stay (up to 5 hours) or Long Stay/Holiday Parking basis. Short Stay car parking is operated by NCP at terminals 2 and 3 (020 8745 7260 – terminal 2; 020 8745 5394 – terminal 3) and Central Parking System at terminals 1 and 4 (020 8745 6520 – terminal 1; 020 8745 7906 – terminal 4). Long Stay/Holiday car parking is operated by Parking Express (APCOA).

There are many bus and coach services connecting London Heathrow with more than 500 destinations across the UK. Most of the coach services operate from the central bus station which can be accessed by the subways that link terminals 1, 2 and 3. For information on coach services and to book tickets call the Travelline on 0990 747777.

... by Train

The Heathrow Express is a non-stop train service operating every 15 minutes between Paddington and London Heathrow. Trains travel at up to 100 miles per hour and journey times are 15 to and from terminals 1, 2 and 3 and 20 minutes to and from terminal 4. For details of timetabling and ticket prices call 0845 600 1515. Train services to and from London Heathrow are also operated by Railair who provide links from Feltham, Reading and Woking. National Rail Enquiries (08457 484950) provides information on all Railair services.

The London Heathrow terminals can also be accessed by two stations on the Piccadilly line of the London Underground, one serving terminals 1, 2 and 3, the other serving terminal 4. The average tube journey time from central London is approximately 50-60 minutes.

LONDON LUTON AIRPORT

Percival House, Percival Way, Luton, Bedfordshire LU2 9LY (Tel: 01582 405100; Email: info@london-luton.co.uk; Web: www.london-luton.com).

London Luton operates scheduled services to the following destinations: Aberdeen, Alicante, Amsterdam, Athens, Barcelona, Belfast, Dublin, Dusseldorf, Edinburgh, Finland, Geneva, Gibraltar, Glasgow, Inverness, Isle of Man, Jersey, Liverpool, Madrid, Malaga, Mahon, Munich, Nice, Palma, Paris, Tenerife and Zurich.

Airlines serving London Luton Airport include: Britannia Airlines, Easyjet, European Air Express, British European, Manx Airlines, Monarch Airlines, Monarch Crown Service, Ryanair.

Getting there...
... by Road

London Luton Airport is situated 30 minutes from north London, 2 miles from the M1 motorway exit at junction 10. The airport is conveniently situated for access to and from north and north-east London, Essex, Kent, Surrey and Sussex.

Parking at London Luton Airport can be on a long, short or executive stay. Long term car parking may be booked in advance.

... by Rail

There are regular services to central London and south Coast and the midlands and northern England are operated by Thameslink and Midland Mainline. The new station and airport terminal are connected by a continuous, free shuttle bus service. The station is approximately 2km from the airport terminal building and the approximate journey time from London King's Cross is 30 minutes.

Virgin Rail Link connects London Luton airport with Milton Keynes Central. For further information telephone 08457 48 49 50.

... by Coach

There are a number of coach services serving London Luton Airport including:

Greenline 757 which runs an express service between London Luton Airport and central London, calling at Brent Cross, Finchley Road, Baker Street, Marble Arch, Hyde Park Corner and Victoria. For further information telephone 0870 608 7261.

Jetlink which operates frequent services connecting London Luton Airport with Amersham, Baldock, Birmingham, Birmingham Airport, Brighton, Cambridge, Coventry, Gatwick Airport, Heathrow Airport, Hemmel Hempstead, High Wycombe, Hitchin, Letchworth, London Colney, Mildenhall, Milton Keynes, Newmarket, Northampton, Norwich, Oxford, Royston, Stanstead Airport and Thetford. For further Information telephone 0870 575 7747; Web: www.gobycoach.com.

Flightlink which operated frequent services connecting London Luton Airport with Leicester, Mansfield and Nottingham (passengers can connect at Heathrow of Birmingham on to the National Express network). For further information telephone 0870 575 7747.

Local Bus services also operate. For more information contact the Airport Information Desk on Tel: 01582 405100 or contact Traveline on 0870 608 2608.

LONDON STANSTED AIRPORT

Stansted Airport Limited, Enterprise House Stansted Airport CM24 1QW (Tel: 0870 000 0303; Fax: 01279 662066; Web: www.baa.co.uk).

Getting there...
...by Road
London Stansted can be accessed via Junction 8 of the M11 and is 20 minutes from Junction 27 of the M25. London Stansted links to Bedfordshire and Hertfordshire via the A505 and A414; to East Anglia via the A11, A12 and A120 and to the North and Midlands by the A1 and A14. Parking is available on a short or long stay basis and car parks are operated by Meteor Parking. Tel: 01279-681192.

Airbus connects London Stansted with London Victoria Coach Station and various other coach services are available serving Bedfordshire, Cambridgeshire, Essex, Norfolk, Oxford and Suffolk. For further information, call 08705 747 777.

...by Train
The Stansted Express offers frequent services, seven days per week between London Stansted and Liverpool Street Station, the journey taking approximately 40 minutes. The service also serves Tottenham Hale Station where travellers can link to London Underground services. There is also an hourly central train service operating between London Stansted, Cambridge and Birmingham. For details, call 08457 484950.

UTILITIES

In England, the Secretary of State for the Environment, Transport and the Regions has overall responsibility for water policy and set the environmental and health and safety standards for the water industry. The Director-General of Water Services, as the independent economic regulator, is responsible for ensuring that the private water companies are able to fulfil their statutory obligation to provide water supply and sewerage services, and for protecting the interests of consumers.

The Minister of Agriculture, Fisheries and Food is responsible for policy relating to land drainage, flood protection, sea defences and the protection and development of fisheries.

The Environment Agency is responsible for water quality and the control of pollution, the management of water resources and nature conservation. The Drinking Water Inspectorate and local authorities are responsible for the quality of drinking water.

WATER

The Water Act 1989 provided for the creation of a privatised water industry under public regulation, and the functions of the regional water authorities were taken over by ten holding companies and the regulatory bodies.

Most of these have public limited company (plc) status and many are now in foreign ownership or are part of larger multi-utility companies. They are represented by Water UK, which also represents the ten water service companies responsible for sewerage and sewage disposal in England and Wales, and the state-owned water authorities of Scotland and Northern Ireland.

Water UK is the trade association for all the water service companies except Mid Kent Water.

THAMES WATER UTILITIES PLC

14 Cavendish Place, London W1M ONU
Chief Executive: Bill Alexander

For further information contact the 24 hour Customer Centre on: 0845 9200 800 (UK or write to Thames Water Customer Centre, PO Box 436, Swindon SN38 1TU).

WATER UK

1 Queen Anne's Gate, London, SW1H 9BT (Tel: 020-7344 1844).
Chief Executive: Ms P. Taylor

OFFICE OF WATER SERVICE

Centre City Tower, 7 Hill Street, Birmingham B5 4UA (Tel: 0121-625 1300; Fax: 0121-625 1400; Email: enquiries@ofwat.gsi.gov.uk; Web: www.ofwat.gov.uk).

The Office of Water Services (Ofwat) was set up under the Water Act 1989 and is a non-ministerial government department headed by the Director-General of Water Services. It is the independent economic regulator of the water and sewerage companies in England and Wales. Ofwat's main duties are to ensure that the companies can finance and carry out the functions specified in the Water Industry Act 1991 and to protect the interests of water customers. There are ten regional customer service committees which are concerned solely with the interests of water customers. Representation of customer interests at national level is the responsibility of the Ofwat National Customer Council (ONCC).

GAS AND ELECTRICITY

The Office of Gas and Electricity Markets is the regulator for the gas industry. It was formed in 1999 by the merger of the Office of Gas Supply and the Office of Electricity Regulation. Under the Competition Act 1998, from 1 March 2000 the Competition Commission has heard appeals against the regulator's decisions regarding anti-competitive agreements and abuse of a dominant position in the marketplace.

The gas industry in Britain was nationalised in 1949 and operated as the Gas Council. The Gas Council was replaced by the British Gas Corporation in 1972 and the industry became more centralised. The British Gas Corporation was privatised in 1986 as British Gas plc.

In 1993 the Monopolies and Mergers Commission found that British Gas's integrated business in Great Britain as a gas trader and the owner of the gas transportation system could be expected to operate against the public interest. In February 1997 British Gas demerged its trading arm and now operates as two separate companies: BG plc, which runs the Transco pipeline business in Britain and oil and gas exploration and production in the UK and abroad; and Centrica plc, which runs the trading, service and retail operations under the British Gas brand name in Great Britain and abroad.

Supply of gas to the domestic market was opened to companies other than British Gas, starting in April 1996. With the electricity market also open, many suppliers now offer their customers both gas and electricity.

ELECTRICITY

Under the Electricity Act 1989, 12 regional electricity companies (RECs), which are responsible for the distribution of electricity from the national grid to consumers, were formed from the former area electricity boards in England and Wales. Four companies were formed from the Central Electricity Generating Board: three generating companies (National Power plc, Nuclear Electric plc and PowerGen plc) and the National Grid Company plc, which owns and operates the transmission system. National Power and PowerGen were floated on the stock market in 1991. Nuclear Electric was split into two parts in 1995; the part comprising the more modern nuclear stations was incorporated into a new company, British Energy, which was floated on the stock market in 1996. Magnox Electric, which owns the magnox nuclear reactors, remained in the public sector and was integrated into British Nuclear Fuels (BNFL) in 1999. Ownership of the National Grid Company was transferred to the RECs and it was subsequently floated in 1995.

Generators sell the electricity they produce into an open commodity market from which buyers purchase. The introduction of competition into the domestic electricity market was completed in May 1999. With the gas market also open, many suppliers now offer their customers both gas and electricity.

The Office of Gas and Electricity Markets is the regulator for the electricity industry. It was formed in 1999 by the merger of the Office of Electricity Regulation and the Office of Gas Supply. Under the Competition Act 1998, from 1 March 2000 the Competition Commission will hear appeals against the regulator's decisions regarding anti-competitive agreements and abuse of a dominant position in the marketplace.

The Electricity Association is the electricity industry's main trade association, providing representational and professional services for the electricity companies. EA Technology Ltd provides distribution and utilisation research, development and technology transfer.

ELECTRICITY ASSOCIATION

30 Millbank, London, SW1P 4RD (Tel: 020-7963 5700; Fax: 020-7963 5959; Email: enquiries@electricity.org.uk; Web: www.electricity.org.uk).

OFFICE OF GAS AND ELECTRICITY MARKETS

Stockley House, 130 Wilton Road, London SW1V 1LQ (Tel: 020-7828 0898; Fax: 020-7932 1600; Web: www.ofgem.gov.uk).

Ofgem is the Office of the Gas and Electricity Markets, regulating the gas and electricity industries in Great Britain. Ofgem's aim is to bring choice and value to all gas and electricity customers by promoting competition and regulating monopolies. Ofgem is governed by an authority and its powers are provided for under the Gas Act 1986, the Electricity Act 1989 and Utilities Act 2000.

Chairman of the Authority and Chief Executive of Ofgem: Callum McCarthy

Executive: Eileen Marshall (*Managing Director, Competition and Trading Arrangements*); John Neilson (*Managing Director, Customers and Supply*); Richard Ramsay (*Managing Director, Regulation and Financial Affairs*); Gill Whittington (*Chief Operating Officer*).

BUSINESS
LONDON

BANKING
FINANCIAL SERVICES REGULATION
INSURANCE
LONDON STOCK EXCHANGE
OMBUDSMEN
BUSINESS AND THE WORKFORCE
TRADE UNIONS AND EMPLOYERS' ASSOCIATIONS
TRAINING AND ENTERPRISE
CHARITY AND THE VOLUNTARY SECTOR
CONFERENCE AND EXHIBITION VENUES

BUSINESS LONDON

History

London is the world's leading financial centre, building on its historic sea-faring routes, sharing the universal language of business, English, and straddling the time zones between East and West. But for all its dominance, the London of the new millennium is entirely different to that of 30 years ago, with its bowler-hatted City gents and clubbish ways of doing business. Modern London is infinitely more cosmopolitan and indeed fragmented, with the historic centre of finance, the Square Mile, ceding its power to the increasingly dominant Canary Wharf in London's Docklands.

Age-old institutions such as the London Stock Exchange have been marginalised with the advance of screen-based trading and e-commerce. Londoners today are more cosmopolitan, with American, Asian and European nationals working in banking, accountancy and law. Ranked as among the world's most expensive cities, with Paris, Tokyo and Moscow, London nevertheless remains a vibrant and pulsating metropolis, setting the pace with its coffee bars and cybercafes.

It is difficult to picture London as it once was: a tiny Roman settlement, squatting on the north side of the Thames in the area where the City of London lies today. Access to the sea and the rise of Empire gave Britain, through London, the means to consolidate its place as a global seat of power. It was this that gave rise to the merchant banker: literally bankers who would finance trade expeditions. Today's merchant banker is more likely to advise on multi-million pound deals in global telecoms or media, but with London continuing to take the lead.

The Economy and Employment

London has long been the generator driving Britain's economy. London's Gross Domestic Product, the measure of total productive activity in the economy, is larger than that of countries including Ireland, Sweden, Denmark, Greece and Austria. London generates GDP of around £180 billion: about a fifth of that for the UK as a whole. Greater London has a labour pool of more than 3.5 million people, supplemented by a further 4 million in the surrounding region. This is the largest regional pool of labour anywhere in Europe. Londoners earn around a third more than the average UK employee (although the cost of living is proportionately higher, too).

Despite the dominance of the financial services industry, the capital remains an eclectic mix. Manufacturing, traditionally associated with regions such as the West Midlands, speaks for over 275,000 jobs in London and accounts for around 12 percent of London's GDP. London has the largest slice of professionals trained in digital media and related skills: 32 percent of the UK total. Some 11,000 businesses operate in the media industries. Advertising and design agencies employ more than 40,000 people in London, earning the UK more than £1.7 billion annually in overseas revenues. London has the largest concentration of software and services companies in the UK and some 80,000 people are employed in computer and related services. London is the biotechnology capital of Europe and the favoured destination for inward investment by pharmaceutical companies. Multinationals such as GlaxoSmithKline (GSK) spend billions of pounds annually on research and development (R&D).

But it is of course finance that powers London's economy. The finance and business service sector accounts for about 40 percent of London GDP compared with about 26 percent for the UK generally, according to research carried out annually for the Corporation of London by the Centre for Economics and Business Research (CEBR). Over 1 million people, more than the population of Frankfurt, work in London's financial services industry. Some 13 percent of all those who work in financial services in the UK are based in the City, contributing to a sector that generates net overseas earnings for Britain of more than £32 billion a year. By the mid-1990s, the City had overtaken UK manufacturing to become Britain's single biggest wealth creator, contributing about a quarter of Britain's economic wealth and generating overseas earnings of more than £17.5 billion a year. Output of financial services doubled between 1986 and 1992. London has 2,900 accountancy firms, led by Big Five firms like KPMG and Ernst & Young, and dozens of big-league law firms, with over 23,000 practising solicitors. City law firms like Clifford Chance generate overseas earnings for Britain approaching £700 million a year. Demand for professional and support staff is satisfied through over 500 recruitment consultancies, from headhunters to outplacement agencies.

Employment in the City has shifted since the 1970s, when rising staff and property costs forced employers to relocate to regional cities like Bristol,

Swindon and Peterborough. Tens of thousands of jobs in printing, telecommunications and manufacturing went elsewhere. Routine clerical work in banking and insurance has given way to "high margin" jobs in corporate finance and fund management. This change has heralded a striking increase in City incomes. In the 1970s, City incomes were typically 10 – 20 percent higher than the national average. By the late 1990s, they were as much as 80 percent higher.

It is a delicate balance, however, as witnessed with the collapse in stock markets in 2000 and into 2001. CEBR predicted that up to 10,000 financial services jobs were under threat in the capital because of the slump in share prices and knock-on effect on merchant banks and professional advisory firms. With a wider economic knock on, as many as 20,000 jobs could be lost over a two-year period. Static earnings and reduced bonuses would impact on commercial rents and house prices.

Banking and Finance
The City dominates global banking and finance. London has 537 foreign banks, more than any other centre worldwide. London is the world's largest fund management centre, with $2,170 billion of institutional equity holdings in 1998. It is also the world's largest foreign exchange market with a daily turnover of more than $600 billion, more than New York and Tokyo combined. London is the world's largest centre for international bank lending (with a 20 percent global market share), international bonds (with 60 percent of primary markets) and international trade in equities (65 percent).

Even today, the gold mines of South Africa and Australia continue to dance to London's tune. Gold and silver prices are fixed daily in London through the London Bullion Market Association. The London Metal Exchange is the biggest exchange of its kind in the world and handles over 90 percent of trading in non-ferrous base metals. The price of crude oil, too, is influenced from London, where two thirds of worldwide business at the International Petroleum Exchange consists of trading in Brent Crude. This is used as the price marker for internationally traded crude oil. The Bank of England is a bedrock of international banking.

The London Stock Exchange drives one of the world's benchmark indices, the FT-SE 100 index of leading shares, although the LSE itself has seen its position weakened by increased competition from electronic exchanges, and by weak management. It has been speculated that the LSE will give up its headquarters on Old Broad Street after 200 years in favour of a smaller base in Docklands or in Paternoster Square, adjacent to St Paul's Cathedral.

London's historic maritime role lives on through the Baltic Exchange on St Mary Axe, the world's largest shipbroking market. The world's only self-regulated shipping market, the exchange maintains professional standards, resolves disputes and provides market information. Its members handle some 30 percent of all dry cargo fixtures, 50 percent of tanker fixtures and the sale and purchase of much of the world's merchant fleet in a market worth some £5 billion annually. As such, the Baltic Exchange plays a pivotal role in maintaining London's standing as an international financial centre.

Maritime services generate almost £1 billion in overseas earnings for the UK annually and provide employment for 14,000 people. A new organisation, Maritime London, was formed in late 2000 to promote London's standing as a provider of financial and business advice to the international maritime community. Specialist services include shipbroking, legal services, finance, insurance, ship classification, arbitration and publishing.

Lloyd's
Shipbroking is intimately bound up with the Lloyd's insurance market, formerly Lloyd's of London, which is headquartered at One Lime Street. Lloyd's dates to the 1680s, when ships' captains and merchants used to arrange insurance while meeting in coffee houses run by one Edward Lloyd. Wealthy individuals would take a share of the risk, signing their names one beneath the other. These "underwriters" live on in the Lloyd's of today which, despite having changed almost beyond recognition, continues to dominate world insurance, generating valuable earnings for the UK. Lloyd's has 12 percent of the world's marine market and 25 percent of the aviation market.

An unparalleled run of disasters in the late 1980s, among them the *Exxon Valdez* tanker spill off Alaska and the *Piper Alpha* oil rig explosion in the North Sea left Lloyd's facing losses running to £8 billion or more. Health claims from American workers who had inhaled asbestos dust threatened to spiral out of control. The modern-day equivalent of those wealthy coffee house patrons, private investors known as "Names", were swamped by ruinous cash-calls as Lloyd's sought to restore its finances. Faced with collapse, insurance claims for years dating back to 1992 and earlier were ring-fenced into a new reinsurance company, Equitas, leaving a streamlined Lloyd's to carve out a new niche. Names have largely been replaced by corporate investors, making Lloyd's more closely resemble a large insurance company. Lloyd's capacity to accept insurance premiums increased by £1 billion in 2001 to reach £11.06 billion, of which £9.09 billion was supplied by corporate members. Lloyd's faces increasing competition from offshore centres like Bermuda. But it continues to be a major driver of London's economy, both in sustaining an entire sub-industry of brokers and underwriters around One Lime Street and as an earner of overseas revenues.

Infrastructure

While bankers in Tokyo and New York still routinely refer to the "City", they will increasingly be dealing with a concentrated patch of land some miles to the east. A decade ago, Canary Wharf in London's Docklands looked a dead loss. The site, which historically dealt with shipping imports from the Canary Islands, was hopelessly impractical, with no direct rail links and a poor supporting infrastructure. Britain was in recession and the location looked doomed. But slowly, the place came right. Transport links came in, led by the Docklands Light Railway and the Jubilee Line extension, and Canary Wharf began to give the Square Mile a run for its money. Big name institutions to decamp to Docklands include Credit Suisse First Boston, Morgan Stanley and Clifford Chance. The UK's new super-regulator, the Financial Services Authority, made Canary Wharf its home. Companies to base themselves here include McGraw-Hill and Northern Trust. The area has become a modern-day successor to Fleet Street, attracting newspapers including the *Daily Mirror*, the *Independent* and the *Daily Telegraph*.

The flagship Canary Wharf tower has been flanked by two 700ft skyscrapers due to be completed in early 2002. The first was secured by Citigroup, which earlier took occupation of an adjacent 17-storey building. The second is the headquarters of HSBC, housing 8,000 people. Lehman Brothers has committed to a new 30-storey tower at Heron Quays, ready for occupation in late 2003. The number of people working at Canary Wharf was set to triple from 27,000 in 1999 to about 100,000 by 2006.

Alarmed at the loss of high-profile names, the Corporation of London, the local authority for the Square Mile, hit back with plans for its own

Introduction 193

building spree. The new Heron Tower, backed by Gerald Ronson, the property entrepreneur, was set to reshape the City skyline, and there was talk of redeveloping land adjacent to Spitalfields Market.

London's three main airports, Heathrow, Gatwick and Stansted, handle more than 100 million passengers a year, making London the number one city in the world for international air travel. Heathrow is the preferred transit point for air travellers from North America, Africa and the Far East. The connecting passenger market is worth more than £1 billion a year to the UK economy. Visitors from abroad inject more than £50 billion into the UK economy each year, in the absence of exceptional circumstances such as the foot and mouth outbreak, which inevitably took its toll of tourist revenues. In stable conditions, tourism accounts for 4 – 5 percent of UK GDP.

While the world might take its lead from London in banking and finance, the threat of competition is always present. Until the mid-1980s, City workers were used to doing business face to face on the floor of the Stock Exchange. The so-called "Big Bang" reforms of 1986 shifted trading onto computers, erasing forever the gentlemanly, face-to-face way of doing business. A rowdier version endured at the London International Financial Futures and Options Exchange (Liffe) where, in its heyday in the early 1990s, some 4,000 traders clad in striped jackets struck deals in an area half the size of a football pitch using an arcane system of hand signals. Liffe's influence was whittled away in the face of competition from cheaper electronic exchanges, notably in Frankfurt, and in November 2000, Liffe switched to screen-based trading, requiring the few remaining floor traders to hang up their jackets for the last time. Liffe remains an important contributor to London's economy, significantly increasing its reach in 2001 by clinching a joint venture with Nasdaq, the US high-tech stock exchange. Physical "open outcry" trading continues at the London Metal Exchange and the International Petroleum Exchange.

A Cosmopolitan Capital

Just as London's finance is primarily international, so has its workforce become increasingly cosmopolitan. Some 40 percent of people working in the City and Canary Wharf work for foreign employers. Old City names like Barings, Warburgs and Morgan Grenfell are in Dutch, Swiss and German hands. London is home to 47,000 Americans, more than 36,000 Germans, more than 30,000 French nationals, 35,000

Business London

Italians, 25,000 Japanese, 24,000 Spaniards and 12,000 Koreans. Many of them work for banks, stockbrokers, legal firms and insurance companies.

With its strategic position straddling the world's time zones, it is hard to imagine the day when London will find itself on the sidelines. Businessmen around the world find a common language in English; Heathrow is their preferred destination. The London markets, regulated without being stifled by red tape, are respected for their integrity. City gents used to do business on a handshake and the motto: "My word is my bond". Even in the increasingly global electronic world, that remains true of London today.

The "Big Five" accountancy firms	London Employees
PricewaterhouseCoopers	12,000
KPMG	5,500
Ernst & Young	4,100
Andersen	4,100
Deloitte & Touche	3,700

The Top 10 UK law firms	Turnover	Total fee earners
1. Clifford Chance	£585m	2,170
2. Linklaters & Alliance	£395m	1,516
3. Freshfields	£380m	1,395
4. Allen & Overy	£322m	1,448
5. Slaughter & May	£243m	606
6. Lovells	£242m	1,100
7. Eversheds	£212m	1,652
8. Herbert Smith	£167m	803
9. Norton Rose	£140m	636
10. DLA	£139.8m	799

Source: The Lawyer

The Top 10 UK General insurance companies	Net Premium Income
1. CGNU	£5bn
2. Royal & SunAlliance	£3.1bn
3. AXA (inc PPP Healthcare)	£2.1bn
4. ZFS Group (inc Eagle Star and Zurich)	£1.5bn
5. Cornhill	£919m
6. Direct Line	£729m
7. Credit Suisse (inc Winterthur, Churchill and NIG)	£637m
8. BUPA	£560m
9. NFU Group (inc Avon)	£496m
10. GE Insurance	£416m

Source: Association of British Insurers Annual Returns based on 1999 UK Net Premium Income.

The Top 10 financial advisors	Value of deals
1. Goldman Sachs	$1.28bn
2. Morgan Stanley Dean Witter	$1.13bn
3. Credit Suisse First Boston	$945m
4. Merrill Lynch	$780m
5. Salomon Smith Barney	$667m
6. JP Morgan	$630m
7. UBS Warburg	$371m
8. Wasserstein Perella	$282m
9. Lehman Brothers	$257m
10. Lazard	$242m

Source: Thomson Financial. Global Ranking. Firms advising on mergers and acquisitions: calendar year 2000

GROSS DOMESTIC PRODUCT AT CURRENT PRICES, BY LOCAL AREA[1,2]
£ millions and £ per head

	£ m 1993	1994	1995	1996	£ per head 1993	1994	1995	1996	£ per head UK=100 1993	1994	1995	1996
UK	540,139	570,944	597,741	629,839	9,282	9,777	10,199	10,711	100	100	100	100
Inner London	56,759	59,390	61,979	65,255	21,440	22,315	23,152	24,099	231	228	227	225
Inner London – West	37,394	39,380	41,385	43,928	39,595	41,367	43,089	44,811	427	423	423	418
Inner London – East	19,365	20,010	20,594	21,327	11,371	11,706	11,997	12,346	123	120	118	115
Outer London	36,369	37,653	38,783	41,402	8,486	8,744	8,957	9,482	91	89	88	89
Outer London – E & NW	9,787	10,198	10,553	11,241	6,410	6,682	6,910	7,350	69	68	68	69
Outer London – South	8,967	9,414	9,811	10,268	8,140	8,489	8,775	9,095	88	87	86	85
Outer London – W & NW	17,615	18,041	18,419	19,893	10,629	10,796	10,932	11,647	115	110	107	109

[1] Based on European System of Accounts 1979 and Blue Book 1997 national totals.
[2] Excluding Extra-Regio and the statistical discrepancy of the income-based measure.
Source: Focus on London 2000, National Statistics © Crown Copyright 2001

SHARE OF GROSS DOMESTIC PRODUCT*, BY INDUSTRY GROUP**
1996

Industry Group	%
Financial & Business Services	38.6
Education, Social Work, Health & Other services	16.3
Distribution, Hotel and Catering etc.	14.2
Manufacturing	10.4
Transport, Storage & Communication	10.3
Public Administration & Defence	4.8
Other Industries†	5.5

*At factor cost before adjustment for financial services.
** Industry breakdown based on SIC 1992.
† Agriculture, mining, energy, construction etc.
Source: Focus on London 2000, National Statistics © Crown Copyright 2001

BANKING

Deposit-taking institutions may be broadly divided into two sectors: the monetary sector, which is predominantly banks, and those institutions outside the monetary sector, of which the most important are the building societies and National Savings. Both sectors are supervised by the Financial Services Authority. As a result of the conversion of several building societies into banks in recent years, the size of the banking sector, which was already substantially greater than the non-bank deposit-taking sector, has increased further.

The main institutions within the British banking system are the Bank of England (the central bank), the retail banks, the merchant banks and the overseas banks. In its role as the central bank, the Bank of England acts as banker to the Government and as a note-issuing authority; it also oversees the efficient functioning of payment and settlement systems.

Since May 1997, the Bank of England has had operational responsibility for monetary policy. At monthly meetings of its monetary policy committee the Bank sets the interest rate at which it will lend to the money markets.

Official Interest Rates 2000-2001

10 February 2000	6.00%
8 February 2001	5.75%
5 April 2001	5.50%
10 May 2001	5.25%
2 August 2001	5.00%

BANK OF ENGLAND

Threadneedle Street, London EC2R 8AH
(Tel: 020-7601 4444; Fax: 020-7601 4771).

The Bank of England was incorporated in 1694 under royal charter. It is the banker of the Government and manages the note issue. Since May 1997 it has been operationally independent and its Monetary Policy Committee has had responsibility for setting short-term interest rates to meet the Government's inflation target. As the central bank of the country, the Bank keeps the accounts of British banks, who also maintain with it a proportion of their sterling deposits, and of most overseas central banks. The Bank has three main areas of activity: Monetary Stability, Market Operations and Financial Stability. Its responsibility for banking supervision has been transferred to the Financial Services Authority.

Governor: The Rt. Hon. E. A. J. George
Deputy Governors: D. Clementi; M. A. King
Non-Executive Directors: R. Bailie, OBE; B. Blow; A. R. F. Buxton; Sir David Cooksey; H. J. Davies; Sir Ian Gibson; Mrs F. A. Heaton; Sir Chips Keswick; Ms S. McKechnie, OBE; Sir Brian Scott Moffat, OBE; W. Morris; J. Neill, CBE, PhD; The Baroness Noakes, DBE (Chairman); Ms K. A. O'Donovan; N. I. Simms; J. Stretton
Monetary Policy Committee: The Governor; the Deputy Governors; C. Allsopp; I. Plenderleith; Dr D. Julius; Dr S. Wadhwani; Prof. Stephen Nickell; C. Bean
Advisers to the Governor: Sir Peter Petrie; D. Brealey
Chief Cashier and Deputy Director, Banking and Market Services: Ms M. V. Lowther
Chief Registrar: G. P. Sparkes
General Manager, Printing Works: Mike Thompson
Secretary: P. D. Rodgers
The Auditor: K. Butler

Merchant Banks

Broadly, a merchant bank is an institution that is involved in investment banking and the negotiation of mergers and acquisitions.

Retail Banks

Retail banks offer a wide variety of financial services to companies and individuals, including current and deposit accounts, loan and overdraft facilities, cash dispenser machines (ATMs), mortgages, cheque guarantee cards, credit cards and debit cards. Several banks also now offer telephone and Internet banking facilities.

Payment Clearings

The Association for Payment Clearing Services (APACS) is an umbrella organisation for payment clearings in the UK. It operates three clearing companies:
—BACS Ltd is the UK's automated clearing house for bulk clearing of electronic debits and credits (e.g. direct debits and salary credits)
—the Cheque and Credit Clearing Company Ltd operates bulk clearing systems for inter-bank cheques and paper credit items in Great Britain
—CHAPS Clearing Company Ltd provides same-day clearing for electronic fund transfers throughout the UK in sterling and globally in euro.

Membership of APACS and the clearing companies is open to any appropriately regulated financial institution providing payment services and meeting the relevant membership criteria.

ASSOCIATION FOR PAYMENT CLEARING SERVICES (APACS)

Mercury House, Triton Court, 14 Finsbury Square, London EC2A 1LQ (Tel: 020-7711 6200; Fax: 020-7256 5527;
E-mail: publicaffairs@apacs.org.uk;
Web: www.apacs.org.uk).

Head of Public Affairs: R. Tyson-Davies

BACS Ltd

De Havilland Road, Edgware, Middx HA8 5QA (Tel: 0870 1650019; Fax: 020-8951 7489; Web: www.apacs.org.uk/bacs.htm).

Chief Executive: G. Younger

CHAPS CLEARING COMPANY LTD

Mercury House, Triton Court, 14 Finsbury Square, London EC2A 1LQ (Tel: 020-7711 6200; Fax: 020-7256 5527;
E-mail: publicaffairs@apacs.org.uk;
Web: www.apacs.org.uk).

Company Manager: Michael Lewis

Authorised Institutions

Banking in the UK is regulated by the Banking Act 1987 as amended by the European Community's Second Banking Co-ordination Directive, which came into effect on 1 January 1993. The Banking Act 1987 established a single category of banks eligible to carry out banking business; these are known as authorised institutions. Authorisation under the Act is granted by the Bank of England; it is an offence for anyone not on its list of authorised institutions to conduct deposit-taking business, unless they are exempted from the requirements of the Act (e.g. building societies). The Government has announced that it will transfer responsibility for banking supervision to the Financial Services Authority. Once the necessary legislation was passed in 1999-2000 the FSA became responsible for the authorisation and supervision of banks and the supervision of clearing and settlement systems.

The implementation of the Second Banking Co-ordination Directive permits banks incorporated in one EU member state to carry on certain banking activities in another member state without the need for authorisation by that state. Consequently, the Bank of England no longer authorises banks incorporated in other EU states with branches in the UK; the authorisation of their home state supervisor is sufficient provided that certain notification requirements are met.

FINANCIAL SERVICES REGULATION

In May 1997 the Government announced plans to establish a new statutory single financial regulator responsible for the supervision of banks, building societies, insurance companies, investment firms and markets. It will replace the current framework, established under a number of different statutes. The new regulator is the Financial Services Authority (FSA).

The FSA is acquiring its full range of responsibilities in two stages. The first stage was completed on 1 June 1998 when the FSA acquired responsibility, under the Bank of England Act 1998, for supervising banks, listed money market institutions and related clearing houses; the Bank of England had previously exercised this responsibility. The second stage will follow on the implementation of the Financial Services and Markets Act 2000, which is expected by the end of November 2001. At that stage the FSA will acquire its full range of powers and will take on responsibility for the regulation and registration functions of the following regulators and supervisors:

Self-Regulating Organisations
Investment Management Regulatory Organisation (IMRO)
Personal Investment Authority (PIA)
Securities and Futures Authority Ltd (SFA)

Others
Building Societies Commission
Friendly Societies Commission
Registry of Friendly Societies

All the above organisations are based at the FSA's offices in Canary Wharf.

The FSA also supervises the recognised professional bodies and recognised investment exchanges and clearing houses, ensuring that they continue to fulfil their regulatory responsibilities.

The new legislation gives the FSA four statutory objectives: to maintain confidence in the UK financial system; to promote public understanding of the financial system; to secure an appropriate degree of protection for consumers; to contribute to the reduction of financial crime.

The new legislation requires the FSA to pursue its objectives in a way that: is efficient and economic in the use of its resources; takes account of the responsibilities of firms' own management; facilitates innovation in financial services; balances restrictions on firms with the benefits of regulation; takes account of the international nature of financial services business and the value of competition between firms; seeks to minimise any adverse effects on competition.

The FSA is currently finalising the details of the new regulatory regime. To help it consult the regulated industry and consumers it has established a Practitioner Forum and Consumer Panel.

Central Register/Public Enquiries
The FSA maintains the Central Register of all firms which are authorised to carry on investment business and authorised deposit takers. The entry for each firm gives its name, address and telephone number; a reference number; its authorisation status; and states which organisation regulates it; and whether it can handle client money. The FSA has issued a series of booklets aimed at providing generic advice to consumers and providing contact points for help and further information. These are also available on the FSA website. The FSA has also established a Consumer Helpline: 0845 606 1234 and Website: www.fsa.gov.uk.

Authorised Institutions
Banking in the UK is regulated by the Banking Act 1987, as amended by the European Community's Second Banking Co-ordination directive, which came into effect on 1st January 1993, now itself part of the Banking Consolidation Directive 2000. The Banking Act 1987 established a single category of banks eligible to take deposits from the public; these are known as authorised institutions. Authorisations under the Act has, since June 1998, been granted by the Financial Services Authority; it is an offence for anyone not on its list of authorised institutions to conduct deposits-taking business, unless they are exempted from the requirements of the Act (e.g. building societies) and certain international development bodies. The FSA is also responsible for supervision of banks and the supervision of clearing and settlement systems.

The implementation of the Second Banking Co-ordination Directive permits banks incorporated and authorised in one EU member state to carry on certain banking activities in other member state without the need for authorisation by that state. Consequently, the FSA no longer authorises banks incorporated in other EU states with branches in the UK; the authorisation of their home state supervisor is sufficient provided that certain notification requirements are met. UK banks, in turn, benefit from these so-called "passporting" arrangements.

FINANCIAL SERVICES AUTHORITY

25 The North Colonnade, Canary Wharf, London E14 5HS (Tel: 020-7676 1000; E-mail: publicenquiries@fsa.gov.uk; Web: www.fsa.gov.uk).

Chairman: Sir Howard Davies

FINANCIAL SERVICES COMPENSATION SCHEME (FSCS)

Lloyds Chambers, 1 Portsoken Street, London E1

A new single compensation scheme is to be established by FSA, under the Financial Services and Markets act, to replace the six existing compensation schemes. The current schemes are the Deposit Protection Scheme, the Building Societies Investor Protection Scheme, the Policyholders Protections Scheme, the Investors Compensation Scheme, the Friendly Societies Protection Scheme and the Section 43 Scheme. FSCA will apply different provisions for claims in respect of insurance, deposits and investment business. FSCS will be operationally independent from FSA but accountable to it.

RECOGNISED PROFESSIONAL BODIES

The FSA is empowered to recognise professional bodies (RPBs) which, as a result, can authorise their members to conduct investment business. Such business must not form the whole or main part of the total business undertaken by the firm.

ASSOCIATION OF CHARTERED CERTIFIED ACCOUNTANTS

29 Lincoln's Inn Fields, London WC2A 3EE (Tel: 020-7396 7000; Web: www.accaglobal.com).

INSTITUTE OF ACTUARIES

Staple Inn Hall, High Holborn, London WC1V 7QJ (Tel: 020-7632 2100; Fax: 020-7632 2111; E-mail: institute@actuaries.rog.uk; Web: www.actuaries.org.uk).

INSTITUTE OF CHARTERED ACCOUNTANTS IN ENGLAND AND WALES

Chartered Accountants' Hall, PO Box 433, Moorgate Place, London EC2P 2BJ (Tel: 020-7920 8100; Web: www.icaew.co.uk).

RECOGNISED INVESTMENT EXCHANGES

Investment exchanges are exempt from needing authorisation under the Financial Services Act. A recognised investment exchange (RIE) is recognised by legislation as providing facilities for trading investment products (e.g. stocks and shares or futures). To be a recognised investment exchange, it must fulfil the following requirements: adequate financial resources; proper conduct of business rules; a proper market in its products; procedures for recording transactions; effective monitoring and enforcement of rules; proper arrangements for the clearing and performance of contracts.

INTERNATIONAL PETROLEUM EXCHANGE (IPE)

International House, 1 St Katharine's Way, London E1W 1UY (Tel: 020-7481 0643; Fax: 020-7481 8485; E-mail: info@ipe.uk.com; Web: www.ipe.uk.com).

FUTURES AND OPTIONS EXCHANGE (LIFFE)

London International Financial, Futures and Options Exchange, Cannon Bridge, London EC4R 3XX (Tel: 020-7623 0444; Web: www.liffe.com).

LONDON METAL EXCHANGE LTD (LME)

56 Leadenhall Street, London EC3A 2DX (Tel: 020-7264 5555; Web: www.lme.co.uk).

LONDON STOCK EXCHANGE

London Stock Exchange plc, Old Broad Street, London EC2N 1HP (Tel: 020-7797 1000; Web: www.londonstockexchange.com).

Financial Bodies 199

OM LONDON EXCHANGE LTD

131 Finsbury Pavement, London EC2A 1NT
(020-7065 8000; Fax 020-7065 8001)

INVESTOR PROTECTION

Following the implementation of the EC Investment Services Directive, recognition by the UK authorities is no longer required for exchanges within the European Economic Area (with certain exceptions).

RECOGNISED CLEARING HOUSES

A recognised clearing house (RCH) is recognised by legislation as providing a service enabling companies trading financial products on a RIE to settle transactions quickly and efficiently. A RCH must satisfy similar criteria to those which apply to be an RIE. There are two RCHs which act as clearing houses for some of the above RIEs. In addition, Crestco also operates a system for dematerialised settlement of share transactions.

CRESTCO LTD

33 Cannon Street, London EC4M 5SB (Tel: 020-7849 0000; Web: www.crestco.co.uk).

LONDON CLEARING HOUSE LTD (LCH)

Aldgate House, 33 Aldgate High Street, London EC3N 1EA (Tel: 020-7426 7000; Fax: 020-7426 7001; Web: www.lch.com).

OTHER FINANCIAL BODIES

ADJUDICATOR'S OFFICE

Haymarket House, 28 Haymarket, London SW1Y 4SP (Tel: 020-7930 2292; Fax: 020-7930 2298; E-mail: adjudicators@gtnet.gov.uk; Web: www.open.gov.uk/adjoff/aodemo1.htm).

The Adjudicator's Office opened in 1993 and investigates complaints about the way the Inland Revenue (including the Valuation Office Agency) and Customs and Excise have handled an individual's affairs.

The Adjudicator: Dame Barbara Mills, DBE, QC
Head of Office: Charlie Gordon

INLAND REVENUE LONDON

New Court, 48 Carey Street, London WC2A 2JE.
Director: R. Massingale

INSURANCE

In addition to the many insurers who operate from Branch and Head offices in London and the famous Lloyd's market based in Lime Street, there is also a distinct separate part of the UK insurance and reinsurance industry called the London Insurance Market. While there is no strict definition for this market it is widely accepted that it is the world's leading market for internationally traded insurance and reinsurance business. This is mainly international, high exposure, non-life (general) risks.

The market is made up of insurance companies, reinsurance companies, syndicates at Lloyd's and Marine Protection and Indemnity Clubs. The market is mainly centred on a small area in the City of London near to the main Lloyd's building although an increasing number of participants from across Europe do so electronically. Usually, the risks are very large and need to be covered by several insurers who each take a proportion of the total amount at risk. It is quite common for UK insurance companies, underwriters at Lloyd's and overseas insurance companies to all share in covering one large piece of business.

The market has been substantially re-structured over the last few years with the number of participating insurers, reinsurers and brokers falling substantially.

Because a number of insurers and underwriters may be involved in the administration work in collecting premiums and handling claims these are processed electronically through two market bureaux, The Lloyd's Policy Signing Office and The London Processing Centre, which is wholly owned by the International Underwriting Association.

It is estimated that around 40,000 people are employed in the market with up to 10,000 more based outside London or involved in ancillary services like accountancy, law and loss adjustment.

The total written gross premium income of the London Insurance Market in 1998 was £14.2 billion. This represents over one-third of the total non-life insurance and reinsurance business written in Britain by the UK insurance industry. Despite its name, participants in the market do not need to be London or UK owned. In fact, the reverse is true. For example, virtually all of the world's top twenty reinsurers are represented in the London Market, and over three-quarters of the companies are foreign-owned and two-fifths of the corporate underwriting capital at Lloyd's comes from overseas. Almost all the companies operating in the market are members of the International Underwriting Association of London (IUA). The IUA was formed in 1999 from a merger of the London International Insurance and Reinsurance Market Association (LIRMA) with the Institute of London Underwriters (ILU).

The challenges for the London Insurance Market are largely the same as those faced by the UK and international insurance industry as a whole. The Financial Services Authority has now taken over the authorisation and regulation of insurance where this is required by law.

Although the UK has chosen not to join the first wave of countries participating in economic and monetary union, the London Market is fully prepared and has been able to trade in the euro since 1 October 1998. Other challenges facing the market include the problems of climate change and global warming and changing legislation in respect of liability for personal injury and damage to property.

INTERNATIONAL UNDERWRITING ASSOCIATION OF LONDON (IUA)

London Underwriting Centre, 3 Minster Court, Mincing Lane, London EC3R 7DD
(E-mail: info@iua.co.uk; Web: www.iua.co.uk).

ASSOCIATION OF BRITISH INSURERS (ABI)

51 Gresham Street, London EC2V 7HQ
(E-mail: info@abi.org.uk; Web: www.abi.org.uk).

LONDON INSURANCE MARKET GROSS WRITTEN PREMIUMS, 1999

	MAT & MAT Reinsurance £m	Home £m	Foreign £m	Non-MAT Treaty Reinsurance £m	Total Business £m
Insurance Companies	1,227	1,715	3,774		6,716
Marine Protection and Indemnity Clubs	726	7	—		733
Lloyd's	2,100	2,840	1,819		6,759
Total	4,053	4,562	5,593		14,208

Insurance Companies

LONDON INSURANCE MARKET ACTIVE PARTICIPANTS IN 2000	
ILU member companies	96
Lloyd's syndicates	123
Marine Protection and Indemnity Clubs	39
Lloyd's Brokers	127

INSURANCE COMPANIES

The following is a list of Insurance Companies with London offices.

ACE Insurance Company of Europe
Mincing Lane, London, EC3R 7XA

AGF Insurance Limited
41 Botolph Lane, London, EC3R 8DL

Albion Insurnace Company Ltd
5 Greenwich View Place, London, E14 9NN

American Re-Insurance Company
77 Gracechurch Street, London, EC3V 0AS
(Tel: 020-7337 2100; Fax: 020-7337 2119)

American International Group
120 Fenchurch Street, London, EC2M 5BP

AON Group Ltd
10 Devonshire Street, London, EC2M 4LE

Avon Insurance plc
130 Fenchurch Street, London, EC3M 5JB

AXA Insurance plc
Royal Exchange, London, EC3V 3LS

AXA Nordstern Art Insurance Limited
78 Leadenhall Street, London, EC3A 3DH
(Tel: 020-7626 5001; Fax: 020-7626 4606)

Sun Life Assurance Society plc
107 Cheapside, London, EC2V 6DU
(Tel: 020-7645 1600

Baptist Insurance Co plc
19–21 Billiter Street, London, EC3M 2RY

Barclays Life Assurance Co Ltd
25 Farringdon Street, London, EC4A 4JA

Britannia Steam Ship Insurance Assurance Ltd
20 St Thomas Street, London, SE1 9RR
(Tel: 020-7407 3588; Fax: 020-7403 3942)

British Aviation Insurance Group
10 St Mary Axe, London, EC3A 8EQ

BUPA
15-19 Bloomsbury Way, London, WC!A 2BA

CAN Maritime Insurance Company Limited
77 Gracechurch Street, London, EC3V 0DL

CGNU Insurance plc
St Helen's, 1 Undershaft, London, EC3P 3DQ

China Insurance Co (UK) Ltd
The Communications Building
48 Leicester Square, London, WC2H 7LT
(Tel: 020-7839 1888; Fax: 020-7839 1188)

Chubb Insurance Company of Europe
106 Fenchurch Street, London, EC3M 5NB

CIGNA Life Insurance Co of Europe S A - N V
38 Trinity Square, London, EC3N 4DJ

City Fire Insurance Company Limited
24B Lime Street, London, EC3M 7HJ
(Tel: 020-7429 2617; Fax: 020-7623 0144)

Clerical Medical Group
15 St James Square, London, SW1Y 4LQ

Cologne Reinsurance Co Ltd
13 Haydon Street, London, EC3N 1DB
(Tel: 020-7481 1533; Fax: 020-7480 6511)

Colonia-Baltica Insurance Management Ltd
69–70 Mark Lane, London, EC3R 7HJ

Cornhill Insurance Plc
32 Cornhill, London, EC3V 3LJ
(Tel: 020-7626 5410; Fax: 020-7929 3562)

DAS Legal Expenses Insurance Co Limited
16 St Helens Place, London, EC3A 6DF

Direct Line Insurance
3 Edridge Road, Croydon, CR9 1AG

Domestic & General Insurance Plc
Swan Court, 2a Mansel Road, London, SW19 4AA (Tel: 020-8946 7777; Fax: 020-8947 0896)

Dowa Insurance Company (Europe) Ltd
9–13 Fenchurch Buildings, London, EC3M 5HR

Eagle Star Insurance Co Ltd
60 St Mary Axe, London, EC3A 8JQ

Eagle Star Insurance Company (Ireland) Limited
Cornwall House, London, EC3N 2BQ

Ecclesiastical Insurance plc
19–21 Billiter Street, London, EC3M 2RY

Equitable Life Assurance Society
Crown House, London, WC2B 4AX

Fortis Insurance Co Ltd
20 Throgmorton Street, London, EC2N 2AT

Friend's Provident Life Office Ltd
15 Old Bailey, London, EC4M 7AP

General and Cologne Life Reinsurance UK Ltd
55 Mark Lane, London, EC3R 7NE

Gerling Global Life Reinsurance Company Ltd
50 Fenchurch Street, London, EC3M 3LE
(Tel: 020-7696 8102; Fax: 020-7696 8126)

Groupama General Insurance
12 Arthur Street, London, EC4R 9BJ

Hibernian Insurance UK Limited
Portsoken House, London, EC3N 1EE

Hiscox Insurance Company Ltd
1 Great St Helen's, London, EC3A 6HX
(Tel: 020-7448 6000)

Independent Insurance Company Limited
Mincing Lane, London, EC3R 7DD

Insurance Company of North America (UK) Ltd
8 Lime Street, London, EC3M 7NA

International Insurance Company of Hanover
2nd Floor, 69-70 Mark Lane, London, EC3R 7HJ (Tel: 020-7480 7300; Fax: 020-7481 3845)

Iron Trades Insurance Company Ltd
Corn Exchange, Mark Lane, London, EC3R 7NE (Tel: 020-7680 1083; Fax: 020-7680 1084)

St James's Place Capital
Spencer House, 27 St James's Street, London, SW1A 1NR (Tel: 020-7514 1907; Fax: 020-7493 3560)

JP Morgan Life Assurance Limited
Finsbury Dials, 20 Finsbury Street, London, EC2Y 9AQ

J Rothschild
27 James Street, London, EC2A 1PD

Koa Insurance Co (Europe) Ltd
8 Devonshire Square, London, EC2M 4PL

Legal & General Assurance Society Ltd
Temple Court, 11 Victoria Street, London, EC4N 4TP (Tel: 020-7528 6200)

Liberity Mutual Insurance Company (UK) Ltd
1 Minster Court, London, EC3R 7YE

Mitsui Marine and Fire Insurance Co Europe Ltd
6th Floor, New London House, 6 London Street, London, EC3R 7LP (Tel: 020-7816 0321; Fax: 020-7816 0220)

Munich Reinsurance Company Ltd
154 Fenchurch Street, London, EC3M 6JJ
(Tel: 020-7626 2566; Fax: 020-7626 4036)

NCM Credit Insurance
63 Queen Victoria Street, London, EC4N 4UA (Tel: 020-7248 6121; Fax: 020-7489 8031)

New Hampshire Insurance Co
120 Fenchurch Street, London, EC3M 5BP
(Tel: 020-7626 7866; Fax: 020-7280 8978)

New India Insurance Co Ltd
14 Fenchurch Avenue, London, EC3M 5BS
(Tel: 020-7480 6626; Fax: 020-7702 2736)

Insurance Companies 203

NIG Corporation Ltd
145 City Road, London, EC1V 1LP

Nippon Insurance Company of Europe
50 Mark Lane, London, EC3R 7QH

Norwich Union Insurance Group
34–36 Lime Street, London, EC3M 7JE

Omnlife Insurance Co Ltd
14 Austin Friars, London, EC2N 2HE

Phillips & Drew Life
14 Finsbury Square, London, EC2A 1PD

Prudential UK plc
Laurence Pountney Hill, London, EC4R 0HH
(Tel: 020-7220 7588; Fax: 020-7548 3725)

QBE International Insurance Limited
Corn Exchange, Mark Lane, London, EC3R 7NE (Tel: 020-7456 0000; Fax: 020-7680 1962)

Reliance National Insurance Company (Europe) Ltd
80b Leadenhall Street, London, EC3A 3DH
(Tel: 020-7283 7110; Fax: 020-7283 7453)

Royal & SunAlliance Insurance plc
30 Berkeley Square, London, W1X 5HA

St Paul International Insurance Company
27 Camperdown Street, London, E1 8DS

Salvation Army General Insurance Ltd
117-121 Judd Street, London, WC1H 9NN

Save & Prosper Insurance Ltd
20 Finsbury Street, London, EC2Y 9AY

Schroder Pensions Ltd
31 Gresham Street, London, EC2V 7HR

Sirius International Insurance Corporation
Marlon House, 71–74 Mark Lane, London, EC3R 7RH (Tel: 020-7265 1651; Fax: 020-7480 5778)

If P & C Insurance Ltd
2nd Floor, 40 Lime Street, London, EC3M 7AW
(Tel: 020-7984 7600; Fax: 020-7984 7629)

Sun Life Financial of Canada Ltd
75 King William Street, London, EC4N 7HA

Swiss Reinsurance Company UK Ltd
71–77 Leadenhall Street, London, EC3A 3DE
(Tel: 020-7623 3456; Fax: 020-7929 4282)

Terra Nova Insurance Co Ltd
41–43 Mincing Lane, London, EC3R 7SP

TIG Reinsurance Company
Suite 4/12, 3 Minster Court, London, EC3R 7DD

Tobacco Insurance Co Ltd
4 Temple Place, London, WC2R 2PG
(Tel: 020-7845 1384; Fax: 020-7845 2114)

The Tokio Marine & Fire Insurance Co (UK) Ltd
150 Leadenhall Street, London, EC3V 4TE
(Tel: 020-7283 8844; Fax: 020-7283 7354)

Tradex Insurance Company Ltd
Glengall Bridge, 14 Pepper Street, London, E14 9QY (Tel: 020-7579 4900; Fax: 020-7519 4923)

Travel & General Insurance Co plc
86 Jermyn Street, London, SW1Y 6JD
(Tel: 020-7930 7714; Fax: 020-7930 7718)

Westminster Motor Insurance Associates Ltd
21 Buckingham Palace Road, London, SW1W 0PN

Winterthur International Insurance Co Ltd
34 Leadenhall Street, London, EC3A 1AT
(Tel: 020-7929 2181)

Yasuda Kasai Insurance Company Ltd
Moorgate Hall
155 Moorgate, London, EC2M 6UB
(Tel: 020-7628 9599; Fax: 020-7628 9323)

Zurich Insurance Company
90 Fenchurch Street, London, EC3M 4JX

LONDON STOCK EXCHANGE

London Stock Exchange plc, Old Broad Street, London EC2N 1HP (Tel: 020-7797 1000); Web: www.londonstockexchange.com).

The London Stock Exchange (the Exchange) is the UK's leading stock exchange and the largest in Europe in terms of the companies on its markets (2,931), their total market capitalisation (£4,666bn) and the value of trading (£8.4bn per day). The Exchange enables companies in the UK and around the world to raise capital by issuing shares, bonds and other securities, and provides a transparent and regulated marketplace for these securities to be bought and sold.

For a company entering the market for the first time there is a choice of Exchange markets, depending upon the size, history and capital requirements of the company. The first is the main market (2,377 companies), which includes techMARK (248 companies, launched in 1999), for innovative technology companies. The second is the Alternative Investment Market (AIM) (554 companies), the Exchange's market for young and growing companies launched in 1995.

Main Market

Companies on the main market come from all business sectors, including information technology, electronics, financial, retail and industrial. The size of companies varies enormously, from those with a market capitalisation of £1 million to more than £130 billion.

techMARK

techMARK is the Exchange's market for innovative technology companies. Sitting within the main market, it groups together companies from a wide range of industrial sectors into a market with its own identity and its own FTSE indices. techMARK is an attribute led-market comprising companies whose business growth and success are dependent on technological development or innovation.

AIM

AIM, the Exchange's Alternative Investment Market for young and growing companies was set up with the objective of offering easier access to equity finance at an earlier stage in a company's growth, by simplifying and minimising the criteria for entry. To be admitted to AIM, a company must be judged to be appropriate to join the market by a 'nominated adviser'. The nominated adviser must be retained by the company at all times while quoted on the market, and is responsible for guiding and helping the company to comply with the market's rules.

Once admitted to the Exchange, all companies are obliged to keep their shareholders informed of their progress, making announcements of a price-sensitive nature through the Exchange's company announcements department.

Regulation

The Financial Services and Markets Act (2000) provides the new framework for regulation in the UK's securities markets, providing a structure for self-regulation within a statutory framework. This legislation supersedes the Financial Services Act (1986).

Most of the statutory powers are held by the Financial Services Authority (FSA), a designated agency created for this purpose. The FSA is accountable to Parliament via the Treasury.

Answerable to the FSA are Recognised Investment Exchanges (RIEs), of which the Exchange is one. As an RIE, the London Stock Exchange has a responsibility to ensure that the operation of each of its markets is orderly and provides proper protection to investors, and to promote and maintain high standards of integrity and fair dealing.

A two-stage admission process applies to companies who want to have their securities admitted to trading on the Exchange's markets for listed securities. The securities need to be admitted to the Official List by the UK Listing Authority, a division of the FSA, and also admitted to trading by the Exchange. Listed companies have to comply with the Exchange's admission and disclosure standards. A different set of standards apply to securities admitted to AIM.

In addition the Exchange's market regulation department regulates trading on the Exchange by monitoring the order book, market makers' quotations, the prices at which business is done, trade reporting and compliance with the Exchange's dealing rules. It liaises closely with other domestic regulators such as the FSA and the Department of Trade and Industry (DTI), and, increasingly, with overseas regulatory authorities. The Exchange has the power to discipline member firms for rule breaches and can impose unlimited fines.

Business and the Workforce

Corporate Structure

The London Stock Exchange has its headquarters in London, and representative offices around the UK. The Exchange is a public company with transferable shares, having changed from a mutual organisation in March 2000.

The company's board is responsible for overall policy and the strategic direction of the Exchange. The board consists of non-executive directors and the Chairman, the Chief Executive and senior executives of the Stock Exchange.

Chairman: Don Cruickshank
Chief Executive: Clara Furse
Executive Directors: Martin Wheatley (Deputy Chief Executive)
Jonathan Howell (Director of Finance)
Non-Executive Directors: Ian Salter (Deputy Chairman) Gary Allen, Baroness Cohen, Oscar Fanjul, Michael Marks, Peter Meinertzhagen, Nigel Stapleton, Robert Webb

OMBUDSMEN

FINANCIAL OMBUDSMAN SERVICE (FOS)

South Quay Plaza, 183 Marsh Wall, London E14 9SR (Tel: 020-7216 0016; E-mail: enquiries@financial-ombudsman.org.uk; Web: www.financial-ombudsman.org.uk).

A new single ombudsman scheme (the Financial Ombudsman Service (FOS) will take over complaints about financial services when the Financial Services and Markets Act 2000 comes into force in late 2001. The FOS will replace eight existing schemes, namely, the ombudsman scheme set up by the IMRO, the PIA Ombudsman Bureau, the SFA scheme, the FSA Complaints Unit and Independent Investigator, the Building Societies Ombudsman, the Banking Ombudsman, the Insurance Ombudsman Bureau and Personal Insurance Arbitration Service. From 1 April 2000, the FOS assumed day-to-day responsibility, under service level agreements, for running 7 of the 8 schemes which it is due to replace.

PENSIONS OMBUDSMAN

6th Floor, 11 Belgrave Road, London SW1V 1RB (Tel: 020-7834 9144; Fax: 020-7630 2219).

The Pensions Ombudsman is appointed and operates under the Pensions Schemes Act 1993 as amended by the Pensions Act 1995, he is responsible to Parliament. He investigates and decides complaints and disputes concerning occupational pension schemes, primarily alleged maladministration by the persons responsible for managing the occupations pension scheme. Personal pension complaints are normally dealt with only if outside the jurisdiction of the Personal Investment Authority.

Pensions Ombudsman: Dr J. T. Farrand

TAKEOVER PANEL

PO Box 226, The Stock Exchange Building, London, EC2P 2JX (Tel: 020-7382 9026).

The Takeover Panel was set up in 1968 in response to concern about practices unfair to shareholders in take-over bids for public and certain private companies. Its principal objective is to ensure equality of treatment, and fair opportunity for all shareholders to consider on its merits an offer that would result in the change of control of a company. It is a non-statutory body that operates the City code on take-overs and mergers.

The chairman, deputy chairmen and members of The Panel are appointed by the Governor of the Bank of England. The remainder are nominated by the banking, insurance, investment, pension fund and accountancy professional bodies and the CBI.

BUSINESS AND THE WORKFORCE

BRITISH TRADE INTERNATIONAL

Kingsgate House, 66-74 Victoria Street, London SW1E 6SW (Tel: 020-7215 5000; Web: www.brittrade.com).

British Trade International has overall responsibility within government for international trade development and the promotion of inward investment. The Chief Executive reports to the Secretary of State for Trade and Industry and the Foreign and Commonwealth Secretary, and to the

Board of British Trade International, chaired jointly by DTI and FCO Ministers. British Trade International operates through two operating arms, Trade Partners UK and Invest UK.

COMPANIES HOUSE LONDON

PO Box 29019, 21 Bloomsbury Street, London WC1B 3XD (Tel: 029-2038 0801; Fax: 029-2038 0900; E-mail: enquiries@companieshouse.gov.uk; Web: www.companies-house.gov.uk).

The key role of Companies House is to provide company information to the public and to maintain the register of companies in the UK by adding, re-registering and striking off companies. There is an information pack available for those wishing to start up their own business and many further guidance booklets are available. The companies house website offers free access to searchable databases of disqualified directors and a companies name and address index. The head office of Companies House is in Cardiff and there are also regional offices in Birmingham, Edinburgh, Glasgow, Leeds and Manchester.

London Information Centre Manager: Lorraine Connelly

COMPETITION COMMISSION

New Court, 48 Carey Street, London WC2A 2JT (Tel: 020-7271 0100; Fax: 020-7271 0367; E-mail: info@competition-commission.org.uk; Web: www.competition-commission.org.uk).

The Commission was established in 1948 as the Monopolies and Restrictive Practices Commission (later the Monopolies and Mergers Commission); it became the Competition Commission in April 1999 under the Competition Act 1998. Its role is to investigate and report on matters which are referred to it by the Secretary of State for Trade and Industry or the Director-General of Fair Trading or, in the case of regulated utilities, by the appropriate regulator. It has no power to initiate its own investigations.

The Appeal Tribunals of the Competition Commission hears appeals against decisions by the Director-General of Fair Trading and the utility regulators in respect of the prohibitions on anti-competitive agreements and abuse of a dominant position to be introduced in March 2000 under the Competition Act 1998.

The Commission has a full-time chairman, two part-time deputy chairmen and about 50 reporting panel members to carry out investigations. All are appointed by the Secretary of State for Trade and Industry.

Chairman: Dr D. Morris, PhD.
Deputy Chairmen:
Prof. P. Geroski MsD. Kingsmill, CBE
President, Appeal Tribunals:
His Hon. Sir Christopher Bellamy, QC
Secretary: R. Foster
Appeal Panel Registrar: Mr C. Dhanowa

CONFEDERATION OF BRITISH INDUSTRY (CBI)

London Region, Centre Point, 103 New Oxford Street, London WC1A 1DU (Tel: 020-7395 8195; Fax: 020-7379 0945; Web: www.cbi.org.uk).

The Confederation of British Industry is an independent non-party political body financed by industry and commerce. It exists primarily to ensure that the Government understands the intentions needs and problems of British Business. The Governing body of the CBI is the 200-strong Council, which meets four times a year in London under the Chairmanship of the President. There are also 13 regional councils and offices one of which concentrates purely on London. Currently, CBI London is focussing on the following issues: promoting the City of London internationally to enhance its position in the face of mounting competition; promoting the interest of its members in Brussels; helping businesses to attain the highest possible environmental performance without cost rising unduly; encouraging a positive approach to London's manufacturing industries to ensure its continued growth.

President: Sir Iain Vallance
Director-General: Digby Jones
Secretary: Peter Forder
CBI London Staff
Director: Jane Calvet-Lee
Assistant Director: Howard Dolan
Assistant Director: Wendy Simpson
Assistant Director: David Tinkler
Assistant Director: John Walter
Assistant Director: Andrew Foote

INVEST UK

1 Victoria Street, London SW1H 0ET (Tel: 020-7215 25; Web: www.invest.uk.com).

Invest UK is the UK's inward investment agency, covering the English regions, Wales, Scotland and Northern Ireland. It comes under the umbrella of British Trade International, which is also responsible for trade development and outward investment. Working with UK network partners, Invest UK offers a free and confidential service to overseas-owned companies looking to establish a presence in the UK,

Chief Executive: William Pedder

LONDON FIRST/ LONDON FIRST CENTRE

1 Hobhouse Court, Suffolk Street, SW1Y 4HH (Tel: 020-7665 1500; Fax: 020-7665 1501; E-mail: mail@london-first.co.uk; Web: www.london-first.co.uk).

London First was set up on the early 1990s as a vehicle to mobilise business leaders to improve and promote London. Funded entirely by over 300 private sector organisations and most of the capital's higher and further education institutions, London First aims to engage business leaders in decision-making about London's future. Its core activities include campaigning for improved transport and environment, and increasing employability of Londoners. London First works in partnership with business, local government, voluntary organisations and other decision-makers to ensure London's position as the leading world class city. Its sister organisation is London First Centre, the inward investment agency for the capital. In over five years of operation, London First Centre has helped over 350 companies from 28 countries around the world locate or expand in the capital. London First's principal sponsors are Argent Group, BAA, British Airways, BT, Canary Wharf plc, Clifford Chance, Ernst and Young, KPMG, Land Securities, MWB Business Exchange, Nelson Bakewell, Orchestream, Paddington Basin Developments, Quintain Estates and Development, Regalian Properties, Resolution Property, Thames Water and Westminster Healthcare.

Chief Executive: Stephen O'Brien
Membership: Michael Rooney
Director of Communications: Anna Barlow; Clare Convey

TRADE PARTNERS UK

Kingsgate House, 66-74 Victoria Street, London SW1E 9SW (Tel: 020-7215 5000; Web: www. tradepartners.gov.uk).

Trade Partners UK is responsible for co-ordinating all trade support provided nationally in the UK, the commercial work of more than 200 diplomatic posts world-wide and trade development and promotion activity organised by the Small Business Service Business Link network in the English regions. A wide range of information, advice and assistance is available to exporters of goods and services and to British firms investing abroad. Support is provided for firms to take part in small and medium sized businesses that are new to exporting. The website provides detailed information and is linked to the TradeUK export sales leads service and national exporters database.

Chief Executive: Sir David Wright

BUSINESS REGISTRATIONS AND DEREGISTRATIONS* (000s AND RATES)

	London			UK		
	1996	1997	1998	1996	1997	1998
Registrations	34.1	37.2	39.7	168.2	182.6	186.3
Deregistrations	29.3	28.3	28.4	165.1	164.5	155.9
Net change	4.7	8.9	8.9	3.1	18.1	30.3
End-year stock	249.8	258.7	258.7	1,603.2	1,621.3	1651.6
Registration rate **	13.9	14.9	14.9	10.5	11.4	11.5
Deregistration rate**	12.0	11.3	11.3	10.3	10.3	9.6
Registration rate†	61	66	70	36	39	40
Deregistration rate†	52	50	50	35	35	33

Enterprises registered for VAT
** Registrations and deregistrations during the year as a percentage of the stock figure at the start of the year.
† Registrations and deregistrations during the year per 10,000 of the resident adult population.
Source: Focus on London 2000, Office for National Statistics © Crown Copyright 2001

LABOUR FORCE

COMPONENTS OF EMPLOYMENT*

	Employees	Self-employed	Others in Employment**	Total Labour Force (=100%) (000s)
Males				
London				
1989	73.6	18.2	0.9	2,010
1999	74.0	17.1	0.6	1,983
UK				
1989	74.3	16.4	1.9	16,434
1999	77.7	14.6	0.9	16,120
Females				
London				
1989	85.8	7.1	0.8	1,546
1999	85.7	7.1	0.7	1,589
UK				
1989	84.8	6.8	1.5	12,330
1999	87.6	6.4	0.9	12,872

* At Spring each year
** Covers people on government-supported employment and training schemes, unpaid family workers (1999 only) and those who did not state their employment status (1989 only).
Source: Focus on London 2000, Office for National Statistics © Crown Copyright 2001

AGE STRUCTURE OF THE LABOUR FORCE

	London			UK		
	1988†	1998†	2006‡	1988†	1998†	2006‡
% aged						
16-25	22.8	13.9	14.4	22.4	15.4	15.0
25-34	26.5	31.5	23.9	24.1	26.4	21.2
35-44	21.7	25.5	29.2	23.5	24.6	27.3
45-59(females)/64 (males)	26.3	26.4	29.5	27.4	30.9	33.3
60 (females)/65 (males) or over	2.7	2.7	3.0	2.6	2.8	3.1
Total Labour Force (000s)	3,492	3,489	3,707	28,345	28,713	30,235

† Percentages of the household population who are in the labour force at Spring each year
‡ The London projections are based on 1994 estimates of the labour force, but the UK projections use 1997 estimates for Great Britain and 1994 estimates for Northern Ireland
Source: Focus on London 2000, Office for National Statistics © Crown Copyright 2001

EMPLOYEES WORKING PART-TIME†‡° (PERCENTAGES)

	Inner London	Outer London	Total London	UK
Males				
1989	4.6	4.5	4.6	4.5
1999	10.0	9.5	9.7	8.4
Females				
1989	26.6	34.3	31.6	43.2
1999	25.9	36.6	32.8	43.7

† Based on respondents' own definition of part-time
‡ At Spring each year
° Basis for calculation of percentages excludes people who do not state whether they worked full or part-time.
Source: Focus on London 2000, National Statistics © Crown Copyright 2001

OCCUPATIONS OF EMPLOYEES, SPRING 1999 (PERCENTAGES AND 000s)

	Males London†	UK	Females London†	UK
Managers & Administrators	22.0	18.9	14.4	10.4
Professional, Associate Professional & Technical	25.9	20.3	25.3	20.7
Clerical & Secretarial	10.3	8.1	29.0	26.0
Craft & related	11.6	17.1	0.9	2.0
Personal & Protective Services	9.2	7.6	14.2	16.8
Sales	6.5	5.6	9.0	12.1
Plant & other Machine Operatives	7.3	14.5	2.1	3.9
Other	7.3	7.8	5.2	8.1
All Employees (000s)‡	1,466	12,531	1,362	11,280

† Resident in London
‡ Includes those who did not state their occupation, but percentages are based on totals that exclude this group.
Source: Focus on London 2000, National Statistics © Crown Copyright 2001

GROSS WEEKLY EARNINGS*, APRIL 1999

		Average Gross Weekly Earnings	10% earned Less than	More than	% earning Under £200	£250	£350	£460
London								
Males	Manual	376.9	207.3	572.4	8.6	19.2	49.2	76.1
	Non-manual	664.6	269.2	1,166.3	3.2	7.9	21.5	38.6
Females	Manual	261.2	155.0	393.2	34.6	56.3	83.3	94.1
	Non-manual	439.1	230.8	682.5	4.9	13.6	40.2	65.7
Great Britain								
Males	Manual	335.0	194.9	500.6	11.1	26.8	62.2	85.4
	Non-manual	525.5	233.5	862.6	5.4	12.5	30.8	51.9
Females	Manual	221.9	140.4	327.8	48.9	71.4	92.8	98.2
	Non-manual	346.9	184.0	540.9	14.5	32.7	61.5	81.1

* Data relates to earnings of full-time employees on adult rates whose pay for the survey period was not affected by absence
Source: Focus on London 2000, National Statistics © Crown Copyright 2001

AVERAGE WEEKLY HOURS* OF FULL TIME EMPLOYEES†

	Males Total including overtime	Overtime	Females Total including overtime	Overtime		Males Totals including overtime	Overtime	Females Total including overtime	Overtime
London					**Great Britain**				
1979**	42.1	4.1	37.3	0.7	1979**	43.2	4.5	37.5	0.6
1989***	40.7	3.3	37.2	1.0	1989***	42.3	4.0	37.6	1.0
1999***	40.2	2.0	37.2	0.7	1999***	41.4	2.7	37.5	0.8

* Including paid overtime.
† At April each year.
**Data from the 1979 New Earning Survey were compiled on the basis of males aged over 21 and females aged over 18.
***Data from the 1989 and 1999 New Earnings survey were compiled on the basis of employees on adult rates.
Source: Focus on London 2000, National Statistics ©Crown Copyright 2001

EARNINGS OF LONDONERS BY BOROUGH*

London Boroughs	Average gross annual earnings (£)	Average hourly earnings excl. overtime (pence)	Increase in total average weekly pay April 99-April 2000 (%)
London Average	29,203	1360	1.0
City of London	45,419	2067	-1.5
Barking and Dagenham	23,929	1087	6.6
Barnet	24,636	1189	6.8
Bexley	22,417	1036	6.1
Brent	23,185	1115	7.6
Bromley	20,185	955	-5.4
Camden	29,895	1436	0.0
Croydon	22,937	1122	4.0
Ealing	25,818	1242	6.3
Enfield	24,554	1174	15.7
Greenwich	23,577	1095	8.0
Hackney	-	-	-
Hammersmith and Fulham	27,721	1329	-4.5
Haringey	21,293	1034	1.5
Harrow	24,675	1182	1.8
Havering	18,785	873	-0.4
Hillingdon	27,982	1229	0.3
Hounslow	26,831	1297	8.1
Islington	32,171	1498	2.2
Kensington and Chelsea	25,924	1262	-4.5
Kingston upon Thames	23,877	1142	6.0
Lambeth	27,981	1353	0.8
Lewisham	21,680	1104	-3.9
Merton	21,128	1016	1.0
Newham	20,943	1060	7.2
Redbridge	21,988	1082	6.5
Richmond Upon Thames	25,162	1247	-1.6
Southwark	27,337	1323	3.4
Sutton	-	1101	1.2
Tower Hamlets	-	1692	3.3
Waltham Forest	21,897	1047	5.4
Wandsworth	-	1142	0.1
City of Westminster	34,278	1552	-1.5

*Data relates to earnings of full-time employees on adult rates whose pay for the survey period was not affected by absence
Source: New Earning Survey 2000, National Statistics © Crown Copyright 2001

TRADE UNIONS AND EMPLOYER'S ASSOCIATIONS

There are over 20 million people in paid employment in the UK and almost 7 million workers belong to unions affiliated to the Trades Union Congress. Trade Unions fulfil a number of different functions including: giving advice to members with work-related problems, negotiating with employers in regard to pay and conditions, helping members take cases to employment tribunals or courts and fight discrimination and help promote equal opportunities. Unions are funded by the contributions of their members.

The following list comprises trade unions based in London, the majority of which are affiliated to the Trades Union Congress.

Trades Union Congress (TUC)
Congress House, 23–28 Great Russell Street, London, WC1B 3LS (Tel: 020-7636 4030; Fax: 020-7636 0632; E-mail: info@tuc.org.uk; Web: www.tuc.org.uk)

The Central Arbitration Committee
Brandon House, 180 Borough High Street, London, SE1 1LW (Tel: 020-7210 3737/8)

TRADE UNIONS

NON-AFFILIATED TRADE UNIONS

British Dental Association
64 Wimpole Street, London, W1G 8YS
(Tel: 020-7935 0875;
E-mail: enquiries@bda-dentistry.org.uk;
Web: www.bda-dentistry.org.uk)
Chief Executive: I.Wylie

Chartered Institute of Journalists
2 Dock Offices, Surrey Quays Road, London, SE16 2XU (Tel: 020-7252 1187; Fax: 020-7252 2302; E-mail: memberservices@ioj.co.uk; Web: www.ioj.co.uk)
General Secretary: C.J. Underwood

Prison Governors' Association
Room 718, Horseferry House, Dean Ryle Street, London, SW1P 2AW (Tel: 020-7217 8591; Fax: 020-7217 8923)
President: M. Newell

Royal College of Midwives
15 Mansfield Street, London, W1M 0BE (Tel: 020-7312 3535; Fax: 020-7312 3536; E-mail: info@rcm.org; Web: www.rcm.org.uk)
General Secretary: Mrs K. Davis

Society of Authors
84 Drayton Gardens, London, SW10 9SB
(Tel: 020-7373 6642; Fax: 020-7373 5768;
E-mail: authorsoc@writers.org.uk;
Web: www.writers.org.uk/society)
General Secretary: M. Le Fanu, OBE

TUC-AFFILIATED TRADE UNIONS

Amalgamated Engineering and Electrical Union (AEEU)
Hayes Court, West Common Road, Bromley, Kent, BR2 7AU (Tel: 020-8462 7755; Fax: 020-8315 8234; Web: www.aeeu.org.uk)
General Secretary: Sir Ken Jackson

Association of First Division Civil Servants (FDA)
2 Caxton Street, London, SW1H 0QH (Tel: 020-7343 1111; Fax: 020-7343 1105; E-mail: head-office@fda.org.uk; Web: www.fda.org.uk)
General Secretary: J. Baume

Association of Flight Attendants – Council 7
United Airlines Cargo Centre, Shoreham Road East, Heathrow Airport, Hounslow, Middx, TW6 3UA (Tel: 020-8276 6723; Fax: 020-8276 6706; E-mail: afa@afalhr.org.uk; Web: www.afrlhr.org.uk)
President: K. Creighan

Association of Magisterial Officers
1 Fellmongers Path, 176 Tower Bridge Road, London, SE1 3LY (Tel: 020-7403 2244; Fax: 020-7403 2274)
General Secretary: Rosie Eagleson

Association Society of Locomotive Engineers and Firemen (ASLEF)
9 Arkwright Road, London, NW3 6AB (Tel: 020-7317 8600)
General Secretary: M. D. Rix

Association of Teachers and Lecturers
7 Northumberland Street, London, WC2N 5DA (Tel: 020-7930 6441; Fax: 020-7930 1359; E-mail: info@atl.org.uk; Web: www.askate.org.uk)
General Secretary: P. Smith

212 Business London

Association of University Teachers
Egmont House, 25–31 Tavistock Place, London, WC1H 9UT (Tel: 020-7670 9700; Fax: 020-7670 9799; E-mail: hq@aut.org.uk; Web: www.aut.org.uk)
General Secretary: D. Triesman

British Actors' Equity Association
Guild House, Upper St Martin's Lane, London, WC2H 9EG (Tel: 020-7379 6000; Fax: 020-73797001; E-mail: info@equity.org.uk; Web: www.equity.org.uk)
General Secretary: I. McGarry

British Air Line Pilots Association (BALPA)
81 New Road, Harlington, Hayes, Middx, UB3 5BG (Tel: 020-8476 4000; Fax: 020-8476 4077; E-mail: balpa@balpa.org.uk; Web: www.balpa.org.uk)
General Secretary: C. Darke

British Orthoptic Society
Tavistock House North, Tavistock Square, London, WC1H 9HX (Tel: 020-7387 7992; E-mail: bos@orthoptics.org.uk; Web: www.orthoptics.org.uk)
Executive Secretary: Mrs A. Armour

Broadcasting, Entertainment, Cinematography and Theatre Union (BECTU)
111 Wardour Street, London, W1V 4AY (Tel: 020-7437 8506; Fax: 020-7437 8268)
General Secretary: R. Bolton

Chartered Society of Physiotherapy
14 Bedford Row, London, WC1R 4ED (Tel: 020-7306 6666; Fax: 020-7306 6611; E-mail: ceo@csphysio.org.uk; Web: www.csp.org.uk)
Chief Executive: P. Gray

Communication Workers Union
150 The Broadway, Wimbledon, London, SW19 1RX (Tel: 020-8971 7200; Fax: 020-8971 7300; E-mail: cproctor@cwu.org; Web: www.cwu.org)
General Secretary: D. Hodgson

Community and District Nursing Association
Thames Valley University, 32-38 Uxbridge Road, Ealing, W5 2BS (Tel: 020-8280 5342; Fax: 020-8280 5341; E-mail: cdna@tvu.ac.uk; Web: www.cdna.tvu.ac.uk)
Chair: Ms A. Duffy

Connect
30 St George's Road, London, SW19 4BD (Tel: 020-8971 6000; Fax: 020-8971 6002; E-mail: eunion@connectuk.org; Web: www.connectuk.org)
General Secretary: S. Petch

Fire Brigades Union
Bradley House, 68 Coombe Road, Kingston upon Thames, Surrey, KT2 7AE (Tel: 020-8541 1765; Fax: 020-8546 5187; E-mail: office@fbu-ho.org.uk)
General Secretary: A. Gilchrist

GMB
22–24 Worple Road, London, SW19 4DD (Tel: 020-8947 3131; Fax: 020-8944 6552; E-mail: john.edmonds@gmb.org.uk; Web: www.gmb.org.uk)
General Secretary: J. Edmonds

Guinness Staff Association
Sun Works Cottage, Park Royal Brewery, London, NW10 7RR (Tel: 020-8963 5249; Fax: 020-8963 5184)
Acting Chair: W. Wardell

Institution of Professionals, Managers and Specialists
75–79 York Road, London, SE1 7AQ (Tel: 020-7902 6600; Fax: 020-7902 6667; E-mail: ipmshq@ipms.org.uk; Web: www.ipms.org.uk)
General Secretary: P. Noon

Iron and Steel Trades Confederation
Swinton House, 324 Gray's Inn Road, London, WC1X 8DD (Tel: 020-7387 6691; Fax: 020-7278 8378; E-mail: istc@istc-tu.org)
General Secretary: M. J. Leahy

Manufacturing, Science and Finance (MSF)
MSF Centre, 33–37 Moreland Street, London, EC1V 8HA (Tel: 020-7505 3000; Fax: 020-7505 3030; Web: www.msf.org.uk)
General Secretary: R. Lyons

Musicians' Union
60–62 Clapham Road, London, SW9 0JJ (Tel: 020-7582 5566; Fax: 020-7582 9805; E-mail: info@musiciansunion.org.uk; Web: www.musiciansunion.org.uk)
General Secretary: D. Scard

NASUWT (National Association of Schoolmasters/Union of Women Teachers)
5 King Street, London, WC2E 8HN (Tel: 020-7420 9670; E-mail: nigel.degruchy@nasuwt.org.uk;

Trade Unions 213

Web: www.teachersunion.org.uk)
General Secretary: N. de Gruchy

NATFHE (University and College Lecturers Union)
27 Britannia Street, London, WC1X 9JP (Tel: 020-7837 3636; Fax: 020-7837 4403; E-mail: hq@natfhe.org.uk; Web: www.natfhe.org.uk)
General Secretary: P. Mackney

National Association of Probation Officers
4 Chivalry Road, London, SW11 1HT (Tel: 020-7223 4887; Fax: 020-7223 3503; E-mail: napo@ukonline.co.uk)
General Secretary: Ms J. McKnight

National League of the Blind and Disabled
Swinton House, 324 Gray Inn Road, WC1X 8DD (Tel: 020-7239 1262; Fax: 020-7278 0436; E-mail: nlbd@istc-tu.org)
General Secretary: J. Mann

National Union of Insurance Workers
27 Old Gloucester Street, London, WC1N 3AF (Tel: 020-7405 6798)
Secretary General: K. Perry

National Union of Journalists (NUJ)
Acorn House, 314–320 Gray's Inn Road, London, WC1X 8DP (Tel: 020-7278 7916; Fax: 020-7837 8143; E-mail: acorn.house@nuj.org.uk)
General Secretary: J. Foster

National Union of Marine, Aviation and Shipping Transport Officers
Oceanair House, 750–760 High Road, E11 3BB (Tel: 020-8989 6677)
General Secretary: B. D. Orrell

National Union of Rail, Maritime and Transport Workers (RMT)
Unity House, 39 Chalton Street, London, NW1 1JD (Tel: 020-7387 4771; Fax: 020-7387 4123; E-mail: b.brown@rmt.org.uk)
General Secretary: J. Knapp

National Union of Teachers (NUT)
Hamilton House, Mabledon Place, London, WC1H 9BD (Tel: 020-7388 6191; Fax: 020-7387 8458; Web: www.teachers.org.uk)
General Secretary: D. McAvoy

Prison Officers' Association
Cronin House, 245 Church Street, London, N9 9HW (Tel: 020-8803 0255; Fax: 020-8803 1761)
General Secretary: B. Caton

Public and Commercial Services Union (PCS)
160 Falcon Road, London, SW11 2LN, (Tel: 020-7924 2727; Fax: 020-7924 1847; Web: www.pcs.org.uk)
General Secretary: B. Reamsbotton

Society of Chiropodists and Podiatrists
53 Welbeck Street, London, W1M 7HE (Tel: 020-7486 3381)
Chief Executive: Ms H. B. De Lyon

Society of Radiographers
2 Carriage Row, 183 Eversholt Street, London, NW1 1BU (Tel: 020-7391 4533)
Chief Executive: Ann Cattell

Transport and General Workers' Union (T&G)
Transport House, 128 Theobalds Road, London, WC1X 8TN (Tel: 020-7611 2500; Fax: 020-7611 2555; E-mail: tgwu@tgwu.org.uk)
General Secretary: W. Morris

Transport Salaried Staffs' Association
Walkden House, 10 Melton Street, London, NW1 2EJ (Tel: 020-7387 2101; E-mail: enquiries@tssa.org.uk; Web: www.tssa.org.uk)
General Secretary: R. A. Rosser

UNiFI
1B Amity Grove, London, SW20 0LG (Tel: 020-8946 9151)
Joint General Secretaries: E. Sweeney; R. Murphy

Union of Construction, Allied Trades and Technicians (UCATT)
UCATT House, 177 Abbeville Road, London, SW4 9RL (Tel: 020-7622 2442; Fax: 020-7720 4081; E-mail: info@ucatt.org.uk; Web: www.ucatt.org.uk)
General Secretary: G. Brumwell

UNISON
1 Mabledon Place, London, WC1H 9AJ (Tel: 020-7388 2366; Fax: 020-7387 6692; Web: www.unison.org.uk)
General Secretary: D. Prentis

Writers' Guild of Great Britain
430 Edgware Road, London, W2 1EH
(Tel: 020-7723 8074; Fax: 020-7706 2413;
E-mail: admin@writersguild.org.uk;
Web: www.writers.org.uk/guild)
Acting General Secretary: Bernie Corbett

EMPLOYERS' ASSOCIATIONS

The following list comprises employers' and trade associations which are based in London.

Advertising Association
Abford House, 15 Wilton Road, London, SW1V 1NJ (Tel: 020-7828 2771; Fax: 020-7931 0376; E-mail: aa@adassoc.org.uk; Web: www.adassoc.org.uk)
Director-General: A. Brown

Association of British Insurers
51 Gresham Street, London, EC2V 7HQ
(Tel: 020-7600 3333)
Director-General: M. Francis

Brewers and Licensed Retailers Association
42 Portman Square, London, W1H 0BB (Tel: 020-7486 4831; Fax: 020-7935 3991;
E-mail: prmail@blra.co.uk; Web: www.blra.co.uk)
Chief Executive Officer: R. Hayward, OBE

British Apparel and Textile Confederation Ltd
5 Portland Place, London, W1B 1PW (Tel: 020-7636 7788; Fax: 020-7636 7515; E-mail: bate@dial.pipex.com)
Director-General: J. R. Wilson

British Bankers' Association
Pinners Hall, 105–108 Old Broad Street, London, EC2N 1EX (Tel: 020-7216 8800; Fax: 020-7216 8811; Web: www.bba.org.uk)
Director-General: T. P. Sweeney

British Clothing Industry Association Ltd
5 Portland Place, London, W1N 3AA (Tel: 020-7636 7788; Fax: 020-7636 7515; E-mail: bcia@dial.pipex.com)
Director: J. R. Wilson

British Office Systems and Stationery Federation
6 Wimpole Street, London, W1G 9SL
(Tel: 020-7637 7692)
Chief Executive: K. Davies

British Plastics Federation
6 Bath Place, Rivington Street, London, EC2A 3JE (Tel: 020-7457 5000; Fax: 020-7457 5045; E-mail: www.bpf.co.uk)
Director-General: P. Davis, OBE

British Ports Association
Africa House, 64–78 Kingsway, London, WC2B 6AH (Tel: 020-7242 1200; Fax: 020-7405 1069; E-mail: info@britishports.org.uk; Web: www.britishsports.org.uk)
Director: D. Whitehead

British Printing Industries Federation
Farrindon Point, 29–35 Farringdon Road, London, EC1M 3JF (Tel: 020-7915 8300; Fax: 020-7405 7784; E-mail: info@bpif.org.uk; Web: www.bpif.org.uk)
Chief Executive: Roy Hill

British Property Federation
7th Floor, 1 Warwick Row, London, SW1E 5ER (Tel: 020-7828 0111; Fax: 020-7834 3442; E-mail: info@bpf.org.uk; Web: www.bpf.org.uk)
Director-General: W. A. McKee

British Retailers Consortium
5 Grafton Street, London, W1X 3LB
(Tel: 020-7647 1500)
Director-General: Ms A. Robinson

British Rubber Manufacturers' Association Ltd
6 Bath Place, Rivington Street, London, EC2A 3JE (Tel: 020-7457 5040; Fax: 020-7972 9008)
Director: A. J. Dorken

Chamber of Shipping Ltd
Carthusian Court, 12 Carthusian Street, London, EC1M 6EZ (Tel: 020-7417 2800; Fax: 020-7726 2080; E-mail: postmaster@british-shipping.org)
Director-General:
Vice-Adm. Sir Christopher Morgan, KBE

Chemical Industries Association Ltd
Kings Buildings, Smith Square, London, SW1P 3JJ (Tel: 020-7834 3399; Fax: 020-7834 4469)
Director-General: Dr E. G. Finer

Commercial Radio Companies Association
The Radiocentre, 77 Shaftesbury Avenue, London, W1D 5DU (Tel: 020-7306 2603; Fax: 020-7306 2603; E-mail: info@crca.co.uk; Web: www.crca.co.uk)
Chief Executive: P. Brown

Employers' Associations

Confederation of Passenger Transport UK
Imperial House, 15–19 Kingsway, London, WC2B 6UN (Tel: 020-7240 3131; Fax: 020-7240 6565; E-mail: cpt@cpt-uk.org; Web: www.cpt-uk.org/cpt)
Director-General: Mrs V. Palmer, OBE

Construction Confederation
Construction House, 56–64 Leonard Street, London, EC2A 4JX (Tel: 020-7608 5004; Fax: 020-7608 5008)
Chief Executive: S. Ratcliffe

Construction Products Association
26 Store Street, London, WC1E 7BT (Tel: 020-7323 3770; Fax: 020-7323 0307; E-mail: enquiries@constprod.org.uk; Web: www.constprod.org.uk)
Chief Executive Officer: M. G. Ankers, FRSA

Dairy Industry Federation
19 Cornwall Terrace, London, NW1 4QP (Tel: 020-7486 7244; Fax: 020-7487 4734; E-mail: jbegg@dif.org.uk)
Director-General: J. Begg

Engineering Employers' Federation
Broadway House, Tothill Street, London, SW1H 9NQ (Tel: 020-7222 7777; Fax: 020-7222 2782; E-mail: enquiries@eef-fed.org.uk; Web: www.eef.org.uk)
Director-General: M. J. Temple

The Federation of Bakers
6 Catherine Street, London, WC2B 5JW (Tel: 020-7420 7190; Fax: 020-7379 0542; E-mail: info@bakersfederation.org.uk; Web: www.bakersfederation.org.uk)
Director: Mr J. S. White

Federation of British Electrotechnical and Allied Manufacturers' Associations (BEAMA)
Westminster Tower, 3 Albert Embankment, London, SE1 7SL (Tel: 020-7793 3000; Fax: 020-7793 3003; E-mail: info@beama.org.uk; Web: www.beama.org.uk)
Director-General: A. A. Bullen

Finance and Leasing Association
Imperial House, 15–19 Kingsway, London, WC2B 6UN (Tel: 020-7836 6511; Fax: 020-7420 9600; E-mail: info@fla.org.uk; Web: www.fla.org.uk)
Director-General: M. A. Hall, MVO

Food and Drink Federation
6 Catherine Street, London, WC2B 5JJ (Tel: 020-7836 2460; Fax: 020-7836 0580)
Director-General: S. Jay

Management Consultancies Association
11 West Halkin Street, London, SW1X 8JL (Tel: 020-7235 3897; Fax: 020-7255 0825; E-mail: will@mca.org.uk; Web: www.mca.org.uk)
Executive Director: B. Petter

National Farmers' Union (NFU)
164 Shaftesbury Avenue, London, WC2H 8HL (Tel: 020-7331 7200; Fax: 020-7331 2380; Web: www.nfu.org.uk)
Director-General: R. Macdonald

National Federation of Retail Newsagents
Yeoman House, Sekforde Street, London, EC1R 0HD (Tel: 020-7253 4225; Fax: 020-7250 0927; E-mail: info@nfrn.org.uk; Web: www.nfrn.org.uk)
Chief Executive: R. Clarke

Newspaper Publishers Association Ltd
34 Southwark Bridge Road, London, SE1 9EU (Tel: 020-7207 2200)
Director: S. Oram

Newspaper Society
Bloomsbury House, 74–77 Great Russell Street, London, WC1B 3DA (Tel: 020-7636 7014; Fax: 020-7580 1972; E-mail: directorate@newspapersoc.org.uk; Web: www.newspapersoc.org.uk)
Director: D. Newell

The Publishers Association
1 Kingsway, London, WC2B 6XD (Tel: 020-7565 7474; Fax: 020-7836 4543; E-mail: mail@publishers.org.uk; Web: www.publishers.org.uk)
Chief Executive: A. R. Williams, OBE

Society of British Aerospace Companies Ltd
Duxbury House, 60 Petty France, London, SW1H 9EU (Tel: 020-7227 1000; Fax: 020-7227 1067; E-mail: post@sbac.co.uk; Web: www.sbac.co.uk)
Director-General: D. Marshall

Society of Motor Manufacturers and Traders Ltd
Forbes House, Halkin Street, London, SW1X 7DS (Tel: 020-7235 7000)
Chief Executive: C. McGowan

Timber Trade Federation
Clareville House, 26–27 Oxendon Street, London, SW1Y 4EL (Tel: 020-7839 1891; Fax: 020-7930 0094; E-mail: ttf@ttf.co.uk; Web: www.ttf.co.uk)
Director-General: P. C. Martin

UK Offshore Operators Association Ltd
2st Floor, 232–242 Vauxhall Bridge Road, London, SW1V 1AU (Tel: 020-7802 2400)
Director-General: J. May

UK Petroleum Industry Association Ltd
9 Kingsway, London, WC2B 6XF (Tel: 020-7240 0289; Fax: 020-7379 3102; E-mail: ukpia@aol.com; Web: www.ukpia.com)
Director-General: M. Webb

ADVISORY, CONCILIATION AND ARBITRATION SERVICE

Brandon House, 180 Borough High Street, London SE1 1LW (Tel: 020-7210 3613; Fax: 020-7210 3708).

Regional Office—London and the South East, Clifton House, 83-117 Euston Road, London NW1 2RB (Tel: 020-7396 0022).

The Advisory, Conciliation and Arbitration Service (ACAS) was set up under the Employment Protection Act 1975 (the provisions now being found in the Trade Union and Labour Relations (Consolidation) Act 1992). ACAS is directed by a Council consisting of a full-time chairman and part-time employer, trade union and independent members, all appointed by the Secretary of State for Trade and Industry. The functions of the Service are to promote the improvement of industrial relations in general, to provide facilities for conciliation, mediation and arbitration as means of avoiding and resolving industrial disputes, and to provide advisory and information services on industrial relations matters to employers, employees and their representatives.

Chairman: Rita Donaghy
Chief Conciliator: Vacant

TRAINING AND ENTERPRISE

BRITISH CHAMBERS OF COMMERCE

Manning House, 22 Carlisle Place, London SW1P 1JA (Tel: 020-7565 2000; E-mail: administrator@britishchambers.org.uk; Web: www.britishchambers.org.uk)

British Chambers of Commerce (BCC) represents, through a UK network of Accredited Chambers of Commerce, across 100 locations, more than 135,000 businesses in all sectors of the economy, and of all sizes. Accredited Chambers seek to represent the interests and support the competitiveness and growth of all businesses in their communities and regions.

London Chamber of Commerce and Industry
33 Queen Street, London EC4R 1AP (Tel: 020-7248 4444; Fax 020-7489 0391; E-mail: lc@londonchamber.co.uk; Web: www.londonchamber.co.uk)

London Chamber of Commerce and Industry states its mission is 'to help London businesses succeed by promoting their interests and expanding their opportunities as members of a world-wide business network'. It is independent of government and has a wide membership of London businesses.

Barnet Chamber of Commerce
23-35 Hendon Lane, Finchley, London N3 1RT (Tel: 020-8343 3833; Fax: 020-8343 3455; Email: barnet@nlcc.co.uk).

Bexley and Greenwich Chamber of Commerce
1 Morden Wharf Road, Tunnel Avenue, Greenwich, London SE10 0NU (Tel: 020-8293).

Croydon and South London Chamber of Commerce
1 Wandle Road, Croydon CR9 (Tel: 020-8680 2165; Fax: 020-8688 4587; Email: info@croydonchamber.freeserve.co.uk).

Ealing Chamber of Commerce
Rover Mews, 42 The Grove, Ealing, London W5 5LH (Tel: 020-8840 6332).

East London Chamber of Commerce
Boardman house, 64 Broadway, London E15 1NT (Tel: 020-8432 0551).

Training and Enterprise 217

Enfield Chamber of Commerce
201 Hertford Road, Enfield, Middx. EN3 5JH (Tel: 020-8443 4464; Fax: 020-8443 3822; Email: enfield@ncll.co.uk).

Hackney Chamber of Commerce
3rd Floor, Netil House, 10-7 Westgate Street, London E8 3RL (Tel: 020-8356 4092; Fax: 020-8356 4086).

Haringey Chamber of Commerce
Lee Valley Technopark, Ashley Road, Tottenham, London N17 9LN (Tel: 020-880 4235; Email: haringey@nlcc.co.uk).

Islington Chamber of Commerce
64 Essex Road, London N1 8LR (Tel: 020-7226 1593; Fax: 020-7226 8437; Email: admin@islchamber.org.uk).

Kensington and Chelsea Chamber of Commerce
Lodge House, 69 Beaufort Street, London SW3 5AH (Tel: 020-7795 0304; Fax: 020-7795 0306).

Kingston Chamber of Commerce
1st Floor, Cheltenham House, 22 Eden Street, Kingston upon Thames, Surrey KT1 1EP (Tel: 020-8296 9595; Fax: 020-8974 8770).

Merton Chamber of Commerce
5th Floor, Tuition House, 27-37 St. George's Road, Wimbledon, London SW19 4EU (Tel: 020-8944 5501; Fax 020-8286 2552).

Newham Chamber of Commerce
(Tel: 020-8534 0363; Fax: 020-8257 2552).

North London Chamber of Commerce
201 Hertford Road, Enfield, Middx. EN3 5JH (Tel: 020-8443 4464; Fax: 020-8443 3822).

Waltham Forest Chamber of Commerce
113 George Lane, London E18 1 AB (Tel: 020-8989 5164).

Wandsworth Chamber of Commerce
125 Upper Richmond Road, Putney, London SW15 2TL (Tel: 020-7780 6541; Fax 020-7780 6501; Email wcc@bllsw.co.uk).

West London Chamber of Commerce
West London Centre, 15/21 Staines Road, Hounslow, Middx. TW3 3HA (Tel: 020-8607 2500).

Worcester Park and District Chamber of Commerce
105 Central Road, Worcester Park, Surrey KT4 8DY (Tel: 020-8296 0444).

BUSINESS LINK

Business Link offers support services to businesses through a network of local advice centres. They offer information and advice on the following: developing of business; selling and marketing, conducting business abroad, Information Communications Technology and E-commerce; money and financial management, legal issues and regulation; and starting up a business.

Business Link for London
Centrepoint, 3rd Floor, 103 New Oxford Street WC1A 1DP (Tel: 0845 600 0787; Fax: 020-7010 0000; Web: businesslink4london.com).
Chief Executive: Judith Rutherford

GREATER LONDON ENTERPRISE (GLE)

28 Park Street, London SE1 9EQ (Tel: 020-7403 0300; Fax: 020-7403 1742;
E-mail: contact@gle.co.uk).

Founded in 1983, GLE is a profitable, commercially run Company, jointly owned by all 33 London Borough Councils. GLE provides services to aid the economic development and regeneration of industries. Services are provided to public, private and voluntary sector clients in London and internationally. The GLE Group includes a number of subsidiaries. They are: GLE Development Capital; GLE Invoice Finance; GLE Properties; GLE Strategies; GLE International and the Joint Venture Unit; GLE Small Business Services.

LEARNING AND SKILLS COUNCIL

DfEE, Room W3B, Moorfoot, Sheffield S1 4PQ

The Learning and Skills Council was established in April 2001 to replace the Further Education Funding Council and the Training and Enterprise Councils. It is a non-departmental public body that advises the government on future National Learning Targets and is responsible for the allocation of £6 billion of public money. Its objective is to ensure that high quality post-16 provision is available to meet the needs of employers, individuals and communities. The LSC operates through 47 local departments, which work to promote the equality of opportunity in the workplace, aiming to ensure that the needs of the most disadvantaged in the labour market are met.

Chairman: B. Sanderson
Chief Executive: J. Harwood

LONDON DEPARTMENTS

London East: Boardman house, 63 Broadway, Stratford, London E15 1NT (Tel: 0845 019 4151).

London North: Damayne House, 1 Fox Lane, Palmers Green, London N13 4AB (Tel: 0845 019 4158).

London South: Canius House, 1 Scarborough Road, Croydon Surrey CR0 1SQ (Tel: 0845 019 4172).

London west: West London Centre, 15-21 Staines Road, Hounslow, Middx. TW3 3HA (0845 019 4164).

ONE LONDON (LEntA)

28 Park Street, London SE1 4EQ (Tel: 020-7248 5555; Fax: 020-7248 8877; E-mail: info@one-london.com; Web: www.one-london.com).

The key function of One London is to assist large companies to work together on issues of job creation and to anticipate social and economic change. This is achieved by providing a business planning service and by establishing projects that examine and provide strategies to tackle various social and economic issues, such as homelessness, racial equality, and unemployment. One London provides support and guidance to new small businesses and offers many services including training and assistance to secure the support of private investors.

Chair: Amanda Jordan
Vice Chair: Michael Hamilton, John Lane plc; David Shelley, HSBC
Managing Director: Peter Thackwray

CHARITY AND THE VOLUNTARY SECTOR

The importance of charities and voluntary organisations as an integral part of modern society is reflected in the size and diversity of the voluntary sector. The areas in which charities are involved continues to grow. In England and Wales, organisations wishing to acquire legal charitable status must be registered with the Charity Commission.

The Charity Commission for England and Wales is a government department with the stated aim of giving the public confidence in the integrity of charity. It is accountable for its decisions to the courts, and for its efficiency to the Home Secretary. There are five Commissioners, appointed by the Home Office and over 500 staff. The Commission has offices in London, Liverpool and Taunton.

There are over 180,000 charities on the Commission's Public Register of Charities, and information about every registered charity is available via the Register of the Commissions website at www.charity-commission.gov.uk.

Additionally, anyone can make an appointment to look at the annual report and accounts of charities with over £10,000 at the Public Register at each of the Commission's three offices.

The Commission carries out a wide range of functions, including the registration, support, monitoring and supervision of charities. It also investigates allegations of wrong-doing by charities.

The Commission can help charities modernise and update their scope of activities and advises charities on ways in which they can run as efficiently and effectively as possible. It is also conducting an on-going Review of the Register to see if there is scope – within the existing law – for interpretation of what is charitable in law.

Charity and the Voluntary Sector 219

Examples of new charitable purposes recognised by the Review so far, include urban and rural regeneration, community capacity building and the relief of unemployment.

A wide range of publications are available free from the Commission covering all aspects of running a charity, including publication in eight languages other than English and Welsh. The Commission also runs an extensive outreach and education programme for trustees and all involved with running charities.

CHARITY COMMISSION

(London Office) Harmsworth House, 13-15 Bouverie Street, London EC4Y 8DP (Tel: 0870-333 0123; Fax: 020-7674 2300; Web: www.charity-commission.gov.uk).

Chief Commissioner: John Stoker
Legal Commissioner: M. Carpenter
Commissioners (part-time): J. Bonds; Ms J. Warburton; Ms J. Unwin
Heads of Legal Sections: J. A. Dutton; G. S. Goodchild; K. M. Dibble; S. Slack
Director of Operations: S. Gillespie
Director of Policy: R. Carter
Director of Resources: B. Richardson
Information Systems Controller: Ms G. Cruickshank

COMMUNITY FUND

St Vincent House, 16 Suffolk Street, London SW1Y 4NL (Tel: 020-7747 5299; Fax: 020-7747 5214; E-mail: enquiries@community-fund.org; Web: www.community-fund.org).

The Community Fund was set up under the National Lottery Act 1993 to distribute funds from the Lottery to support charitable, benevolent and philanthropic organisations. The Chair and Board members are appointed by the Secretary of State for Culture, Media and Sport. The Community Fund's main aim is to help meet the needs of those at greatest disadvantage in society and to improve the quality of life in the community through grants programmes in the UK and an international grants programme for UK-based agencies working abroad.

Chair: Lady Brittan, CBE
Deputy Chairman: Dame Valerie Strachan, DBE
Members: Mrs T. Baring, CBE; Ms R. Bevan; S. Burkeman; J. Carroll; Mrs A. Clark; Ms K. Hampton; Prof. J. Kearney; Ms M. Lee; Mrs B. Lowndes, MBE; Ms S. J. Malley; R. Martineau; N. Stewart, OBE; Mrs E. Watkins; B. Whitaker CBE
Acting Chief Executive: N. Pittman

LONDON BOROUGHS GRANTS (LBG)

59½ Southwark Street, London SE1 0AA (Tel: 020-7934 9999; E-mail: info@alg.gov.uk).

London Boroughs Grants, which is part of the Association of London Government is run by a committee comprising of a representative from all of the thirty three London Borough Councils. It is governed by four key principles which are: to help voluntary organisations tackle poverty in London; to respond to the changing needs of the people of London; to support the voluntary sector in providing high quality services in tackling equality; to support voluntary services provided in more than one London borough.

LONDON VOLUNTARY SERVICE COUNCIL (LVSC)

356 Holloway Road, London, N7 6PA (Tel: 020-7700 8107; Fax: 020-7700 8108; E-mail lvsc@lvsc.org.uk; Web: www.lvsc.org.uk).

Chief Executive: Christine Holloway

LONDON VOLUNTARY SECTOR TRAINING CONSORTIUM (LVSTC)

The Print House, 18 Ashwin Street, London, E8 3DL (Tel: 020-7249 4441; Fax: 020-7923 4280).

NATIONAL ASSOCIATION FOR COUNCILS FOR VOLUNTARY SERVICE

3rd Floor, Arundel Court, 177 Arundel Street, Sheffield S1 2NU (Tel: 0114-278 6636; Fax: 0114-278 7004; E-mail: nacvs@nacvs.org.uk; Web: www.nacvs.org.uk).

NACVS supports a network of over 300 Councils for Voluntary Service throughout England. A Council for Voluntary Service is formed and run by local voluntary and community groups.

NATIONAL ASSOCIATION OF VOLUNTEER BUREAUX (NAVB)

London Development Project, 356 Holloway Road, London N7 6PA (Tel: 020-7700 8128; E-mail: navb@ukf.net).

NAVB is the membership organisation which supports and represents the network of over 400 local Volunteer Bureaux. The head office of the NAVB can be found at New Oxford House, 16 Waterloo Street, Birmingham B2 5UG (Tel: 0121-633 4555; Fax: 0121-633 4043)

NATIONAL CENTRE FOR VOLUNTEERING

Regent's Wharf, 8 All Saints Street, London N1 9RL Information Line: 020-7520 8900 Mondays to Fridays 2-4pm; E-mail: information@thecentre.org.uk; Web: www.volunteering.org.uk).

The National Centre for Volunteering aims to support the voluntary sector through a number of channels including the promotion of best practice, offering training, information, publications and mounting awareness campaigns.

NATIONAL COUNCIL FOR VOLUNTARY ORGANISATIONS (NCVO)

Regent's Wharf, 8 All Saints Street, London, N1 9RL (Tel: 020-7713 6161; Fax: 020-77136300; E-mail ncvo@ncvo-vol.org.uk; Web: www.ncvo-vol.org.uk).

The National Council for Voluntary Organisations is an umbrella body for the voluntary sector in England. NCVO has a growing membership of over 1,400 voluntary organisations.

Chief Executive: Stuart Etherington
Press Officer: Lindsay Wright

NATIONAL COUNCIL FOR VOLUNTARY YOUTH SERVICES

2 Plough Yard, Shoreditch High Street, London EC2A 3LP (Tel: 020-7422 8630; Fax: 020-7422 8631; E-mail: mail@ncvys.org.uk; Web: www.ncvys.org.uk).

NCVYS represents, supports and informs its members from across the voluntary youth sector. It acts as an umbrella body for over 140 national, regional and county-wide members.

Chief Executive: Susanne Rauprich
Press Officer: Laura Trendall

NEW OPPORTUNITIES FUND

Heron House, 322 High Holborn, London WC1V 7PW (Tel: 020-7211 1800; Fax: 020-7211 1750; E-mail: general.enquiries@nof.org.uk; Web: www.nof.org.uk).

The New Opportunities Fund was established under the National Lottery Act 1998 and is responsible for distributing funds allocated from the proceeds of the National Lottery to health, education and environment projects under initiatives determined by the Government.

Chair of the Board: The Baroness Pitkeathley
Members of the Board: Ms J. Barrow; Prof. E. Bolton; Ms N. Clarke; Prof. A. Patmore; D. Mackie; D. Campbell; Prof. S. Griffiths; Ms R. McDonough
Chief Executive: S. Dunmore

REACH

89 Albert Embankment, London SE1 7TP (Tel: 020-7582 6543; Fax: 020-7582 2423; E-mail: volwork@btinternet.com; Web: www.volwork.org.uk).

REACH aims to recruit managerial or professional people with time available and place them as volunteers with voluntary organisations needing their experience.

Chief Executive: Sue Evans

VOLUNTARY SERVICE OVERSEAS (VSO LONDON)

317 Putney Bridge Road, London SW15 2PN (Tel : 020-8780 7200; Fax: 020 8780 7300 Web: www.vso.org.uk).

Founded in 1950, VSO is an international development charity, which works through skilled and experienced volunteers. VSO is now the largest organisation of its kind worldwide and has 2,000 volunteers tackling poverty in 71 of the World's poorest countries.

Charity and the Voluntary Sector   221

COUNCILS FOR VOLUNTARY SERVICE

London
London Voluntary Sector Resource Centre,
356 Holloway Road, London, N7 6PA
(Tel: 020-7700 8107; Fax: 020-7700 8108;
E-mail: lvsc@lvsc.org.uk;
Web: www.lvsc.org.uk)
Director: Ms C. Holloway

Barking & Dagenham
Faircross Community Complex, Hulse Avenue,
Barking, Essex, IG11 9UP (Tel: 020-8591 5275;
Fax: 020-8591 0363;
E-mail: cvsbd@netscapeonline.co.uk)
Director: Miss S. Scott

Barnet
1st Floor, The Annexe, Hertford Lodge, East End Road, London, N3 3QE (Tel: 020-8346 9723; Fax: 020-8343 3698;
E-mail: ce@barnetvsc.org.uk;
Web: www.barnetvsc.org.uk)
Chief Executive: Ms J. Hawkins

Bexley
8 Brampton Road, Bexleyheath, DA7 4EY (Tel: 020-8304 0911; Fax: 020-8298 9583;
E-mail: information@bvsc.co.uk)
Chief Executive: Ms J. Smith

Brent
c/o, Willesden High Road, London, NW10 2QD
(Tel: 01785 501 8167)
Co-ordinator: Lizzie Saunders

Bromley
Community House, South Street, Bromley, BR1 1RH (Tel: 020-8315 1900; Fax: 020-8315 1924;
E-mail: admin@communitylinksbromley.org.uk)
Director: L. Gillians

Camden
293-299 Kentish Town Road, London, NW5 6TJ (Tel: 020-7284 6550; Fax: 020-7284 6551;
Web: www.vac.org.uk)
Director: Ms S. Hensby

Croydon
97 High Street, Thornton Heath, CR7 8RY (Tel: 020-8684 3862; Fax: 020-8665 1334;
E-mail: francis-cva@library.croydon.gov.uk;
Web: www.cvaline.co.uk)
General Manager: S. Phaure

Ealing
24 Uxbridge Road, London, W5 2BP (Tel: 020-8579 6273; Fax: 020-8567 4683;
E-mail: evsc@evsc.demon.co.uk)
Executive Director: Ms Diana Moore

Enfield
Community House, 311 Fore Street, London, N9 0PZ (Tel: 020-8373 6268; Fax: 020-8373 6267)
Director: Ms P. Jeffery

Greenwich
The Old Town Hall, Polytechnic Street, Woolwich, SE18 6PN (Tel: 020-8316 4774; Fax: 020-8316 4755; E-mail: guac@ndirect.co.uk)
Chairman: William Euinu

Hackney
The Print House, 18 Ashwin Street, London, E8 3DL (Tel: 020-7923 1962; Fax: 020-7275 8577;
E-mail: hcvs@post.com)
Director: A. Antigha

Hammersmith & Fulham
Aspen House, 1 Gayford Road, London, W12 9BY (Tel: 020-8762 0862; Fax: 020-8749 3874;
E-mail: vsral@yahoo.co.uk)
Director: Ms P. Harrison

Haringey
Resource Centre, 2 Factory Lane, London, N17 9FL (Tel: 020-8365 1873; Fax: 020-8801 8957)
Director: T. Modu

Harrow
The Lodge, 64 Pinner Road, Harrow, Middx, HA1 4HZ (Tel: 020-8863 6707; Fax: 020-8863 8401; E-mail: havs1@aol.com)
Organising Secretary: Ms M. Nunn

Hillingdon
1st Floor, Kirk House; 97-109 High Street, Yiewsley, UB7 7HJ (Tel: 01895-442722; Fax: 01895-442754)
Director: Mrs C. Coventry

Hounslow
Unit 9, Hounslow Business Park, Alice Way, Hanworth Road, Hounslow, TW3 3UD (Tel: 020-8572 5929; Fax: 020-8572 9027;
E-mail: hvsf@yahoo.co.uk)
Director: M. Tuohy

222 Business London

Islington
322 Upper Street, London, N1 2XQ (Tel: 020-7226 4862; Fax: 020-7359 7442; E-mail: information@ivac.org.uk; Web: www.ivac.org.uk)
Director: D. Abse

Kensington & Chelsea
St Luke's Crypt, Sydney Street, London, SW3 6NH (Tel: 020-7351 3210; Fax: 020-7352 3405; E-mail: csc@chelseasc.demon.co.uk)
Director: Ms S. Copland

Kensington & Chelsea
7 Thorpe Close, London, W10 5XL (Tel: 020-8969 9897; Fax: 020-8960 6392; E-mail: nhsc@nhsc.demon.co.uk)
Director: P. Mesquita

Kingston
Siddeley House, 50 Canbury Park Road, Kingston, KT2 6LX (Tel: 020-8255 3335; Fax: 020-8255 8804; E-mail: info@kva.org.uk; Web: www.kva.org.uk)
General Secretary: H. Garner

Lambeth
95 Acre Lane, London, SW2 5TU (Tel: 020-7737 1419; Fax: 020-7737 4328; E-mail: lvac@lambethvac.org.uk; Web: www.lambethvac.org.uk)
Director: Ms E. Ladimeji

Lewisham
120 Rushey Green, London, SE6 4HQ (Tel: 020-8314 9411; Fax: 020-8314 1315; E-mail: lewcvs@dircon.co.uk; Web: www.lewcvs.dircon.co.uk)
Director: Ms L. Garner

Merton
The Vestry Hall, London Road, Mitcham, CR4 3UD (Tel: 020-8685 1771; Fax: 020-8685 0249; E-mail: info@mvsc.co.uk)
Director: C. Frost

Newham
53 The Broadway, London, E15 4BQ.

Redbridge
1st Floor, North Broadway Chambers, 1 Cranbrook Road, Ilford, Essex, IG1 4DU (Tel: 020-8554 5049; Fax: 020-8478 9420; E-mail: redbridge-cvs@hotmail.com)
Director: P. Champion

Richmond
The Centre for Voluntary Services, 1 Princes Street, Richmond, TW9 1ED (Tel: 020-8255 8500; Fax: 020-8401 1967;
E-mail: action@richmondcvs.org.uk; Web: www.richmondcvs.org.uk)
Chief Executive: C. Whelan

Southwark
64 Camberwell Road, London, SE5 0EN (Tel: 020-7703 8733; Fax: 020-7703 9393; E-mail: mail@savo.org.uk; Web: www.savo.org.uk)
Director: P. Tulloch

Sutton
Unilink House, 21 Lewis Road, Sutton, Surrey, SM1 4BR (Tel: 020-8643 3277; Fax: 020-8643 4178; E-mail: enquiries@suttoncvs.org)
Director: I. Beever

Tower Hamlets
Davenant Centre, 179–181 Whitechapel Road, London, E1 1DN (Tel: 020-7426 9970; Fax: 020-7377 0956; E-mail: jill@towerhamlets.org.uk)
Director: Ms J. Walsh

Waltham Forest
Unit 37, Alpha Business Centre, South Grove Road, London, E17 7NX (Tel: 020-8521 0377; Fax: 020-8521 1672; E-mail: vawf@dial.pipex.com)
Director: M. Wenham

Westminster
37 Chapel Street, London, NW1 5DP (Tel: 020-7723 1216; Fax: 020-7723 8929; E-mail: general@vawestminster.demon.co.uk; Web: www.vawestminster.demon.co.uk)
Director: M. Loughan

CITIZENS' ADVICE BUREAUX

Anyone can obtain advice from a Citizens' Advice Bureau. The service is free. Bureaux offer advice on many legal and financial matters, for example benefit entitlement and debt.

Addington
1a Overbury Crescent, New Addington, Croydon, Surrey, CR0 0LR
(Tel: 01689-846890; Fax: 01689-845105)
Director: Tony Riddeck

Citizens' Advice Bureaux 223

Barking
55 Ripple Road, Barking, Essex, IG11 7NT (Tel: 020-8594 6715; Fax: 020-8591 0440; E-mail: barking.cab@virgin.net)
Chair Management Committee: Brian Cooper

Battersea
14 York Road, London, SW11 3QA (Tel: 020-7228 9462; Fax: 020-7978 5348; E-mail: battersea.cab@virgin.net)
Administrator: Corina Paes

Beckenham & Penge
20 Snowdown Close, Avenue Road, London, SE20 7RU (Tel: 020-8778 0921; Fax: 020-8776 6065)

Beddington & Wallington
16 Stanley Park Road, Wallington, Surrey, SM6 0EU (Tel: 020-8669 3435; Fax: 020-8770 4928)

Bermondsey
8 Market Place, Southwark Park Road, London, SE16 3UQ (Tel: 020-7231 1118; Fax: 020-7231 4410; E-mail: bedmondseycab@aol.com)

Bethnal Green
Tower Hamlets Office, 62 Roman Road, London, E2 0QJ.

Bexleyheath
8 Brampton Road, Bexleyheath, Kent, DA7 4EY (Tel: 020-8303 5100; Fax: 020-8303 9524; E-mail: bexleyheath.cab@btinternet.com)
Manager: Ms Barindar Minhas

Brentford & Chiswick
Town Hall, Heathfield Terrace, London, W4 4JN (Tel: 020-8994 4846; Fax: 020-8995 4674; E-mail: manager@cab.reserve.co.uk)
Manager: A. Rowntree

Camden
94 Avenue Road, London, NW3 3EX (Tel: 020-7586 2694; Fax: 020-7483 1858; E-mail: admin.camdencab@btinternet.com)
Director: Jonathan Merrison

City of London
32 Ludgate Hill, London, EC4M 7DR (Tel: 020-7236 1156; Fax: 020-7329 4547)

Dagenham
339 Heathway, Dagenham, Essex, RM9 5AF (Tel: 020-8592 1084; Fax: 020-8593 2511; E-mail: bureau@dagenham.cabnet.org.uk; Web: www.nacab.org.uk)
Manager: Christopher Evans

Dalston
491–493 Kingsland Road, London, E8 4AU (Tel: 0870-126 4013; Fax: 020-7249 7699; E-mail: manager@dalston-cab.demon.co.uk)

Edmonton
Edmonton Methodist Church, Lower Fore Street, London, N9 0PN (Tel: 020-8807 4253; Fax: 020-8807 1730; E-mail: edmonton.cab@dial.pipex.com)
Manager: Lauren Bennet-Headley

Enfield
10 Little Park Gardens, Enfield, Middx, EN2 6PQ (Tel: 020-8363 0928; Fax: 020-8364 5644; E-mail: enfield.cab@dial.pipex.com)
Manager: Denyse Nott

Feltham
Peoples Centre, High Street, Feltham, Middx, TW13 4AH (Tel: 020-8707 0078; Fax: 020-8707 0077; E-mail: feltham.cab@iname.com)
Manager: Parveen Sohal

Finchley
Hertford Lodge, Annexe East End Road, London, N3 3QE (Tel: 0870-126 4018; Fax: 020-8349 9840; E-mail: finchleycab@dial.pipex.com)
Manager: Pauline Hunter

Fulham
The Pavilion, 1 Mund Street, London, W14 9LY (Tel: 020-7385 1322; Fax: 020-7385 6750; E-mail: manager@fulhamcab.org.uk)
Manager: Rosemary Vase

Ham
Ham Health Clinic, Ashburnham Road, Ham, Richmond, Surrey, TW10 7NS)
Service Manager: Joe Fleming

Hampton
White House Community Centre, 45 The Avenue, Hampton, Middx, TW12 3RN (Tel: 020-8941 8330; Fax: 020-8979 3827; E-mail: hamptoncab.btinternet.com)
Director: Christopher King

Harrow
Civic Centre, Station Road, Harrow, Middx, HA1 2XH (Tel: 020-8427 9443; Fax: 020-8863 3267)
Manager: Gerry Cooper

Hayes
49–51 Station Road, Hayes, Middx, UB3 4BE (Tel: 0870-126 4021; Fax: 020-8606 2939)

Hendon
40–42 Church End, London, NW4 4JT (Tel: 020-8203 5801; Fax: 020-8203 3202; E-mail: hendon.cab@dial.pipex.com)
Managing Director: John Sclocco

Holborn
3rd Floor, Holborn Library, 32–38 Theobalds Road, London, WC1X 8PA (Tel: 020-7404 1497; Fax: 020-7404 1507)

Holloway
Caxton House, 129 St Johns Way, London, N19 3RQ (Tel: 0870-751 0925)
Manager: V. Jennens

Hornchurch
59A Billet Lane, Hornchurch, Essex, RM11 1AX (Tel: 01708-445983; Fax: 01708-443221; E-mail: hornchurch.cab@bigfoot.com)
Area Manager: Mrs H. Ball

Hornsey
7 Hatherley Gardens, London, N8 9JJ (Tel: 020-8374 3704; Fax: 020-8374 2646; E-mail: Sheilasambax@nescapeonline.co.uk)
Director: Jamil Hadj-Nassar

Hounslow
45 Treaty Centre, High Street, Hounslow, Middx, TW3 1ES (Tel: 020-8570 2983)
Manager: Caroline Barker

Kentish Town
242 Kentish Town Road, London, NW5 2AB (Tel: 0845-050 5152; Fax: 020- 7485 1602)
Manager: Maggie Phelps

Kilburn
200 Kilburn High Road, London, NW6 4JD (Tel: 08450 505152)
Manager: R. West

Kingston & Surbiton
Neville House, 55 Eden Street, Kingston-upon-Thames, Surrey, KT1 1BW (Tel: 0870-126 4019; Fax: 020-8255 6053)
Sevice Director: Mrs. P Hare

Lambeth
Ilex House, 1 Barrhill Road, London, SW2 4RJ (Tel: 020-8674 8993; Fax: 020-8678 6593)

Leytonstone
Greater London House, 547–551 High Road, London, E11 4PB (Tel: 020-8988 9620)

Mitcham
326 London Road, Mitcham, Surrey, CR4 3ND (Tel: 020-8288 0450; Fax: 020-8685 9483; E-mail: mitch.cab@btinternet.com)
Manager: Adam Cain

Morden
7 Crown Parade, Crown Lane, Morden, Surrey, SM4 5DA (Tel: 020-8715 0707; Fax: 020-8715 0550)
Manager: Vicki Waddington

New Barnet
30 Station Road, New Barnet, Herts, EN5 1PL (Tel: 020-8449 0975; Fax: 020-8441 2384; E-mail: newbarnetcab@dial.pipex.com)
Manager: Mrs A.E. Martin

Newham
The Advice Arcade 107–109 The Grove, London, E15 1HP (Tel: 020-8536 1710; Fax: 020-8536 1622)
Manager: Kimberley Bachelot

North Cheam
320 Malden Road, North Cheam, Surrey, SM3 8EP (Tel: 020-8770 4851; Fax: 020-8770 4917)
Manager: David Still

Orpington
309a High Street, Orpington, BR6 0NN (Tel: 01689-827732)
Manager: Fleur Jeremiah

Citizens' Advice Bureaux   225

Paddington
441 Harrow Road, London, W10 4RE
(Tel: 020-8960 4481; Fax: 020-8960 4244;
E-mail: paddington.cab@btinternet)
Manager: Shirley Springer

Palmers Green
Town Hall, Green Lanes, London, N13 4XD
(Tel: 020-8350 2963; Fax: 020-8447 9343;
E-mail: palmersgreencab@dial.pipex.com)
Manager: Sue Wagstaff

Peckham
97 Peckham High Street, London, SE15 5RS
(Tel: 020-7639 4471; Fax: 020-7732 2497;
E-mail: admin@peckhamcab.org.uk)
Borough Director: Chris Green

Pimlico
140 Tachbrook Street, London, SW1V 2NE
(Tel: 0870-126 4040)
Manager: P. Tomlinson

Putney & Roehampton
228 Upper Richmond Road, London, SW15 6TG (Tel: 020-8479 0047; Fax: 020-8479 0049;
E-mail: roehampton.cab@btinternet.com;
Web: www.careline.org.uk/CAB)
Bureau Supervisor: Maureen Hussins

Redbridge
Broadway Chambers, 2nd Floor South
1 Cranbrook Road, Ilford, Essex, IG1 4DU
(Tel: 020-8514 1878; Fax: 020-8514 5700;
E-mail: redbridgCAB@aol.com)
Manager: Ms P. J. Watson

Richmond
Linfield House, 26 Kew Road, Richmond, Surrey, TW9 2NA (Tel: 020-8940 2501; Fax: 020-8332 0708; E-mail: richmond.cab@btinternet.com)
Director: Chris King

Romford
7–9 Victoria Road, Romford, Essex, RM1 2JT
(Tel: 0870-120 4200; Fax: 01708-739319)

Ruislip
9 Eastcote Road, Ruislip, Middx, HA4 8BD
(Tel: 0870-126 4021; Fax: 01895-622818;
E-mail: bureau@ruislipcab.cabnet.org.uk;
Web: www.adviceguide.org.uk)
Manager: Ms Kris Fryer

St Helier
5–6 Rose Hill Court Parade, St Helier Avenue, Morden, Surrey, SM4 6JS (Tel: 020-8640 4170; Fax: 020-8648 9128)
Manager: John Harris

Sutton
Central Library, St Nicholas Way, Sutton, Surrey, SM1 1EA (Tel: 020-8643 5291; Fax: 020-8770 4929)
Deputy Manager: Paul Boddy

Sydenham
299 Kirkdale, London, SE26 4QD (Tel: 0870-126 4037; Fax: 020-8776 7499;
E-mail: sydenham.cab@btinternet.com;
Web: www.adviceguide.org.uk)

Thornton Heath
Strand House, Zion Road, Thornton Heath, Surrey, CR7 8RG (Tel: 020-8684 2236; Fax: 020-8683 4790)

Tooting & Balham
4th Floor, Bedford House, 215 Balham High Road, London, SW17 7BQ (Tel: 020-8333 6960; Fax: 020-8378 5892;
Web: www.careline.org.uk/cab)

Tottenham
Town Hall, Town Hall Approach, London, N15 4RY (Tel: 020-8376 3700; Fax: 020-8376 0909)
Manager: Pauline Walcott

Tower Hamlets East
86 Bow Road, London, E3 4DL (Tel: 0870-126 4014; Fax: 020-8981 8761; E-mail: towerhamcab@dial.pipex.com)
Team Leader: Duran A. Hashi

Twickenham
The Advice Centre, 61 Heath Road, Twickenham, Middx, TW1 4AW (Tel: 020-8892 5917; Fax: 020-8744 1167;
E-mail: twickenham.cab@btinternet.com)

Uxbridge
Link 1A, Civic Centre, High Street, Uxbridge, Middx, UB8 1UX (Tel: 0870-126 4021; Fax: 01895-277318;
E-mail: bureau@uxbridgecab.cabnet.org.uk;
Web: www.adviceguide.org.uk)
Manager: Patricia Lee

Walthamstow
167 Hoe Street, London, E17 3AL

Whitechapel
Unit 32 Greatorex Street, London, E1 5NP (Tel: 020-7247 4172; Fax: 020-7375 2256; E-mail: whitechapel@cabx.demon.co.uk)

Woodford
112 High Road, London, E18 2QS (Tel: 020-8502 9194)

Woolwich
Old Town Hall, Polytechnic Street, London, SE18 6NP (Tel: 020-83174988; Fax: 020-8317 7571; Web: www.nacab.org.uk)
Manager: Sue Wells

Yiewsley
106 High Street, Yiewsley, Middx, UB7 7QJ (Tel: 0870-126 4021; Fax: 01895-430421; E-mail: bureau@yiewsleycab.cabnet.org.uk)

CONFERENCE AND EXHIBITION VENUES

The business community increasingly makes use of the many conference and exhibition venues situated in London. The list below provides contact and facilities information on a range of venues which cater for all manner of conference and exhibition requirements, whether for individuals, small groups or large international organisations. Please use the key below to see which specialised facilities each venue has to offer.

Key:
1 = Auditorium
2 = Sound Equipment
3 = Theatre Lighting
4 = Computer Linkup
5 = Audio/Video Equipment
6 = Disabled Facilities
7 = Catering
8 = Accommodation Discounts
Capacity relates to maximum capacity of the venue

CONFERENCE VENUES

Bateaux London
Embankment Pier, Victoria Embankment, London, WC2N 6NU (Tel: 020-7925 2215; Fax: 020-7839 1034; E-mail: info@bateauxlondon.com; Web: www.bateauxlondon.com)
Corporate Account Manager: Ms C. Scarr
Rooms: 3, **Capacity:** 372 — 1, 2, 5, 7

Battersea Park Events Office
Battersea Park, London, SW11 4NJ (Tel: 020-7223 6241; Fax: 020-7223 7919; E-mail: asmith@wandsworth.gov.uk; Web: www.wandsworth.gov.uk)
Events Manager: J. Adam
Capacity: 4000 —

The Berkeley
Wilton Place, Knightsbridge, London, SW1X 7RL (Tel: 020-7235 6000; Fax: 020-7235 4330; E-mail: info@the-berkeley.co.uk; Web: www.savoy-group.co.uk)
Senior Banqueting Account Manager: Ms K. Garland
Rooms: 6, **Capacity:** 200 — 4, 5, 6, 7, 8

Conference and Exhibition Venues 227

The Berkshire
350 Oxford Street, London, W1N 0BY (Tel: 020-7629 7474; Fax: 020-7629 8156; Web: www.radissonedwardian.com)
Conference and Banqueting Sales Manager: N. Jaffer
Rooms: 2, **Capacity:** 16 — 2, 4, 5, 6, 7, 8

Berners Hotel
10 Berners Street, London, W1A 3BE (Tel: 020-7666 2000; Fax: 020-7666 2001; E-mail: berners@berners.co.uk; Web: www.thebernershotel.co.uk)
Conference Co-ordinators: Sabine Hopf
Rooms: 4, **Capacity:** 160 — 2, 4, 5, 6, 7, 8

Bloomsbury Square Training Centre
2–3 Bloomsbury Square, London, WC1A 2RL (Tel: 020-7212 7510; Fax: 020-7212 7550; E-mail: bloomsbury.square@uk.pwcglobal.com; Web: www.bloomsburysquare.co.uk)
Conference Co-ordinator: Antonia Bellew
Rooms: 28, **Capacity:** 110 — 1, 2, 3, 4, 5, 7

The Bonnington in Bloomsbury
Southampton Row, London, WC1B 4BH (Tel: 020-7242 2828; Fax: 020-7831 9170)
Conference Co-ordinator: Ms J. Proud
Rooms: 7, **Capacity:** 120 — 2, 5, 6, 7, 8

The Brewery
Chiswell Street, London, EC1Y 4SD (Tel: 020-7638 8811; Fax: 020-7638 5713; E-mail: thebrewery@chiswellstreet.com; Web: www.thebrewery.chiswellstreet.com)
Conference and Events Manager: Orla Donlan
Rooms: 9, **Capacity:** 900 — 2, 3, 4, 5, 6, 7

The Millennium Hotel
Grosvenor Square, Mayfair, London, W1K 2HP (Tel: 020-7629 9400; Fax: 020-7408 0699; E-mail: sarah.cox@mill-cop.com; Web: www.millennium-hotels.com)
Meetings and Events Business Development Manager: Ms S. Cox
Rooms: 10, **Capacity:** 460 — 2, 3, 4, 5, 6, 7, 8

Brown's Hotel
Albemarle Street, London, W1X 4BP (Tel: 020-7518 4165; Fax: 020-7518 4063; E-mail: brownshotel@brownshotel.com; Web: www.brownshotel.com)
Assistant Banqueting Manager: Sandrine Gosselin
Rooms: 7, **Capacity:** 70 — 5, 7, 8

Cabinet War Rooms
Clive Steps, King Charles Street, London, SW1A 2AQ (Tel: 020-7930 6961; Fax: 020-7839 5897; E-mail: cwr@iwm.org.uk; Web: www.iwm.org.uk)
Marketing Officer: Ms V. Rayner
Rooms: 1, **Capacity:** 50 — 4, 5, 6

Café Royal
68 Regent Street, London, W1R 6EL (Tel: 020-7437 9090; Fax: 020-7439 7672; E-mail: banqueting@caferoyal.demon.co.uk; Web: www.lemeridien-hotels.com)
Conference and Banqueting Director: G. Bush
Rooms: 21, **Capacity:** 700 — 2, 3, 4, 5, 6, 7, 8

Cannizaro House
West Side, Wimbledon Common, London, SW19 4UE (Tel: 020-8879 1464; Fax: 020-8944 6515; E-mail: cannizaro.house@thistle.co.uk)
Event Sales Manager: Brent Wilkinson
Rooms: 6, **Capacity:** 120 — 5, 6, 7, 8

The De Vere
81 Jermyn Street, London, SW1Y 6JF (Tel: 020-7930 2111; Fax: 020-7839 4551)
Conference and Banqueting Administrations Manager: Ms T. Grehan
Rooms: 4, **Capacity:** 100 — 2, 4, 5, 6, 7, 8

Central Hall Westminster
Storey's Gate, London, SW1H 9NH (Tel: 020-7222 8010; Fax: 020-7222 6883; E-mail: events@wch.co.uk; Web: www.wch.co.uk)
Senior Events Manager: Ms C. Williamson
Rooms: 20, **Capacity:** 2500 — 1, 2, 3, 4, 5, 6, 7, 8

The Chelsea Green Hotel
35 Ixworth Place, Chelsea, London, SW3 3QX (Tel: 020-7225 7500; Fax: 020-7225 7555; E-mail: cghotel@dircon.co.uk; Web: www.welcome2london.com)
Operations, Conference and Banqueting Manager: Serena Kelly
Rooms: 2, **Capacity:** 60 — 2, 3, 4, 5, 7, 8

The Chesterfield, Mayfair Hotel
35 Charles Street, Mayfair, London, W1J 5EB (Tel: 020-7491 2622; Fax: 020-7409 1726; E-mail: meetings@chesterfield.redcarnationhotels.com; Web: www.redcarnationhotels.com)
General Manager: Andrew Colley
Rooms: 5, **Capacity:** 120 — 2, 4, 5, 7, 8

228 Business London

Chiswick House
Burlington Lane, Chiswick, London, W4 2RP (Tel: 020-8742 1978; Fax: 020-8742 3104; E-mail: marion.doherty@english-heritage.org.uk; Web: www.heritagehospitality.org.uk)
Hospitality Manager: Ms M. Doherty
Rooms: 4, **Capacity:** 50 —

Churchill Inter-Continental London
30 Portman Square, London, W1A 4ZX (Tel: 020-7486 5800; Fax: 020-7486 1255; E-mail: churchill@interconti.com; Web: www.interconti.com)
Senior Events Manager: C. Poskitt
Rooms: 11, **Capacity:** 300 — 4, 5, 6, 7, 8

City of London Club
19 Old Broad Street, London, EC2N 1DS (Tel: 020-7588 7991; Fax: 020-7374 2020; E-mail: banq@cityclub.co.uk; Web: www.cityclub.co.uk)
Functions Administrator: Ms L. Hasler
Rooms: 9, **Capacity:** 350 — 2, 3, 4, 5, 6, 7

Commonwealth Conference and Events Centre
Kensington High Street, London, W8 6NQ (Tel: 020-7603 3412; Fax: 020-7603 9634; E-mail: conference@commonwealth.org.uk; Web: www.commonwealth.org.uk)
Conference Centre Managers: C. Fielder; B. Thorp
Rooms: 19, **Capacity:** 460 — 1, 2, 3, 4, 5, 6, 7, 8

Congress Centre
23–28 Great Russell Street, London, WC1B 3LS (Tel: 020-7467 1318; Fax: 020-7467 1313; E-mail: congress.centre@tuc.org.uk; Web: www.congresscentre.co.uk)
Conference and Sales Co-ordinator: Ms R. Lyall
Rooms: 17, **Capacity:** 500 — 2, 3, 4, 5, 6, 7

Copthorne Tara, London
Scarsdale Place, Wrights Lane, Kensington, London, W8 5SR (Tel: 020-7937 7211; Fax: 020-7872 2965; E-mail: cathal.leonard@mill-cop.com)
Meetings and Events Manager: C. Leonard
Rooms: 5, **Capacity:** 250 — 2, 4, 5, 6, 7, 8

Ealing Conference and Banqueting Centre
Halls and Events, Perceval House, 14–16 Uxbridge Road, London, W5 2HL (Tel: 020-8758 8293; Fax: 020-8758 8745; E-mail: seniorj@ealing.gov.uk; Web: www.ealing.gov.uk/events)
Marketing Officer: Julia Senior-Smith
Rooms: 12, **Capacity:** 500 — 1, 2, 3, 5, 6, 7, 8

Eltham Palace
Court Yard, Court Road, Eltham, London, SE9 5QE (Tel: 020-8294 2577; Fax: 020-8294 2621)
Hospitality Manager: Ms A. Dadd
Rooms: 10, **Capacity:** 250 — 6, 7

Euston Plaza Hotel
17–18 Upper Woburn Place, Euston, London, WC2H 0HT (Tel: 020-7943 4555; Fax: 020-7943 4501; E-mail: conference@euston-plaza-hotel.com; Web: www.euston-plaza-hotel.com)
Conference and Banqueting Executive: Caroline Saunders
Rooms: 11, **Capacity:** 150 — 2, 5, 6, 7, 8

ExCeL
London, E16 1XL (Tel: 020-7476 0101; Fax: 020-7476 1818; E-mail: info@excel-london.co.uk; Web: www.excel-london.co.uk)
Head of Sales: Giles Nash
Rooms: 66, **Capacity:** 1064 — 2, 3, 4, 5, 6, 7

Posthouse Premier, Bloomsbury
Coram Street, London, WC1 (Tel: 0870-400 9222; Fax: 020-7278 0989; E-mail: Meetings-bloomsbury@forte-hotels.com; Web: www.meetingsatposthouse.com)
Conference Office Manager: A. Taylor
Rooms: 14, **Capacity:** 300 — 2, 4, 5, 6, 7

The Forum
97–109 Cromwell Road, London, SW7 4DN (Tel: 020-7341 3190; Fax: 020-7244 9909; E-mail: forumlondon@interconti.com; Web: www.interconti.com)
Conference and Events Sales Coordinator: T. Munro
Rooms: 8, **Capacity:** 380 — 2, 4, 5, 6, 7, 8

Glaziers Hall
9 Montague Close, London Bridge, London, SE1 9DD (Tel: 020-7403 3300; Fax: 020-7407 6036; E-mail: sales@glaziershall.co.uk; Web: www.glaziershall.co.uk)
Sales and Marketing Executive: Ms D. Dawson
Rooms: 6, **Capacity:** 500 — 1, 2, 4, 5, 6, 7

Conference and Exhibition Venues   229

The Grafton
Tottenham Court Road, London, W1P 9HP
(Tel: 020-7388 4131; Fax: 020-7753 0334;
E-mail: graftcb@radisson.com)
Conference and Banqueting Manager: D. Lord
Rooms: 324, **Capacity:** 150 — 2, 3, 4, 5, 7, 8

The Hatton
51–53 Hatton Garden, London, EC1N 8HN
(Tel: 020-7242 4123; Fax: 020-7242 1818;
E-mail: hatton@etclimited.co.uk)
Head of Sales and Customer Relations:
Ms L. Henderson
Rooms: 23, **Capacity:** 150 — 2, 4, 5, 6, 7

Hilton Hyde Park
129 Bayswater Road, London, W2 4RJ
(Tel: 020-7221 2217; Fax: 020-7229 0557;
E-mail: cb.office@stakis.co.uk;
Web: www.hilton.com)
Revenue Co-ordinator: Ms T. Brown
Rooms: 3, **Capacity:** 100 — 4, 5, 7, 8

HMS Belfast
Morgan's Lane, Tooley Street, London, SE1 2JH
(Tel: 020-7403 6246; Fax: 020-7407 0708;
E-mail: natasha.malcolm@sodexho.co.uk;
Web: www.iwm.co.uk)
Sales Manager: Ms N. Delahayne
Rooms: 4, **Capacity:** 400 — 1, 2, 5, 6, 7, 8

Hotel Antoinette
26 Beaufort Road, Kingston upon Thames, Surrey, KT1 2TQ (Tel: 020-8546 1044; Fax: 020-8547 2595; E-mail: hotelantoinette@btinternet.com; Web: www.hotelantoinette.co.uk)
Food and Beverages Manager: P. Hartnell
Rooms: 7, **Capacity:** 150 — 1, 2, 4, 5, 6, 7, 8

Hotel Inter-Continental
One Hamilton Place, Hyde Park Corner, London, W1V 0QY (Tel: 020-7409 3131; Fax: 020-7491 0926;
E-mail: anastasia—velissarides@interconfi.com;
Web: www.interconti.com)
Conference and Banqueting Sales Manager:
T. Widdowson
Rooms: 8, **Capacity:** 1000 — 2, 3, 4, 5, 6, 7, 8

Hyde Park Ryan Hotel
66 Lancaster Gate, London, W2 3NZ (Tel: 020-7262 5090; Fax: 020-7723 1244;
E-mail: hotel@hydepark-ryan.com;
Web: www.ryan-hotels.com)

General Manager: Ms A. Frigieri
Rooms: 1, **Capacity:** 25 — 2, 4, 5, 7, 8

Imperial College
Conference Office, Prince's Gardens, London, SW7 1LU (Tel: 020-7594 9494; Fax: 020-7594 9504/5; E-mail: conference@icac.ac.uk;
Web: www.imperialcollege-conferencelink.com)
Conference Sales Manager: Ms S. Brace
Rooms: 200, **Capacity:** 740 — 1, 2, 3, 4, 5, 6, 7

Imperial War Museum
Lambeth Road, London, SE1 6HZ (Tel: 020-7416 5394; Fax: 020-7416 5396;
E-mail: swilliams@iwm.org.uk;
Web: www.iwm.org.uk)
Corporate Hospitality Officer: Ms S. Williams
Rooms: 4, **Capacity:** 1000 — 1, 2, 3, 5, 6, 7, 8

Institute of Contemporary Arts (ICA)
Nash House; The Mall, London, SW1Y 5AH (Tel: 020-7766 1413; Fax: 020-7306 0122;
E-mail: hires@ica.org.uk; Web: www.ica.org.uk)
Hires Manager: Ms D. Hay
Rooms: 6, **Capacity:** 350 — 1, 2, 3, 4, 5, 6, 7

Insurance Hall
20 Aldermanbury, London, EC2V 7HY (Tel: 020-7417 4417; Fax: 020-7600 4838;
E-mail: insurance.hall@cii.co.uk;
Web: www.cii.co.uk)
Hall Manager: Ms M. Backhurst
Rooms: 12, **Capacity:** 300 — 1, 3, 4, 5, 6, 7, 8

International Coffee Organisation
22 Berners Street, London, W1T 3DD (Tel: 020-7580 8591; Fax: 020-7580 6129;
E-mail: info@ico.org;
Web: www.icoffee.com)
Conference Organiser: Ms C. Maqueda
Rooms: 3, **Capacity:** 284 — 1, 2, 4, 5, 7, 8

Jarvis International Hotel
Ealing Common, London, W5 3HN (Tel: 020-8896 8400; Fax: 020-8992 7082;
E-mail: jiealing.cem@jarvis.co.uk;
Web: www.jarvis.co.uk)
Conference and Events Sales Manager:
Rachel Watkins
Rooms: 9, **Capacity:** 210 — 1, 2, 3, 4, 5, 6, 7, 8

K + K Hotel George
1–15 Templeton Place, Earl's Court, London, SW5 9NB (Tel: 020-7598 8700; Fax: 020-7370 2285; E-mail: hotelgeorge@kkhotels.co.uk; Web: www.kkhotels.com)
Reservations Manager: Ms D. Glaser
Rooms: 2, **Capacity:** 30 — 4, 5, 7, 8

Lee Valley Leisure Centre
Picketts Lock Lane, Edmonton, London, N9 0AS (Tel: 020-8884 1197; Fax: 020-8884 4975)
Events Manager: R. Garvey
Rooms: 5, **Capacity:** 2000 — 2, 3, 5, 6, 7

Le Meridien Piccadilly
21 Piccadilly, London, W1J 0BH (Tel: 020-7734 8000; Fax: 020-7851 3333; Web: www.le-meridien-piccadilly.com)
Events Manager: Carolina Magdalena
Rooms: 266, **Capacity:** 250 — 2, 3, 4, 5, 6, 7, 8

Le Meridien Waldorf
Aldwych, London, WC2B 4DD (Tel: 020-7836 2400; Fax: 020-7240 9277)
Senior Conference and Events Accounts Manager: Alix Smethirst
Rooms: 13, **Capacity:** 400 — 4, 5, 7, 8

Limelight
136 Shaftesbury Avenue, London, W1D 5EZ (Tel: 020-7287 1426; Fax: 020-7434 3780; E-mail: info@thelimelightclub.com; Web: www.thelimelightclub.com)
Functions Manager: Ms J. Vernol
Rooms: 5, **Capacity:** 860 — 1, 2, 3, 4, 7

London Bridge Hotel
8–18 London Bridge Street, London, SE1 9SG (Tel: 020-7855 2200; Fax: 020-7855 2232; E-mail: sales@london-bridge-hotel.co.uk; Web: www.london-bridge-hotel.co.uk)
Conference Co-ordinator: Susan Clarke
Rooms: 5, **Capacity:** 100 — 5, 6, 7, 8

London Hilton Islington
53 Upper Street, Islington, London, N1 0UY (Tel: 020-7354 7700; Fax: 020-7354 7711; E-mail: cb.office@islington.stakis.co.uk; Web: www.hilton.com)
Conference Co-ordinator: Ms M. Holgren
Rooms: 5, **Capacity:** 24 — 4, 5, 6, 7, 8

London Hilton on Park Lane
22 Park Lane, London, W1K 4BE (Tel: 020-7493 8000; Fax: 020-7208 4145; Web: www.hilton.com)
Banqueting Sales Manager: Eddie Hobson
Rooms: 14, **Capacity:** 1200 — 2, 4, 5, 6, 7, 8

London Kensington Hilton
179–199 Holland Park Avenue, Holland Park, London, W11 4UL (Tel: 020-7603 3355; Fax: 020-7602 9397; E-mail: cb—kensington@hilton.com; Web: www.kensington-hilton.com)
Events Manager: H. Cakan
Rooms: 11, **Capacity:** 400 — 2, 3, 4, 5, 6, 7, 8

London Marriot Hotel, Maida Vale
Plaza Parade, Maida Vale, London, NW6 5RP (Tel: 020-7543 6000; Fax: 020-7543 2495; E-mail: rconferenceandevents.madavale@marriothotel.co.uk; Web: www.marriott.co.uk)
Executive Meeting Manager: Maria Kellensen
Rooms: 3, **Capacity:** 200 — 4, 5, 6, 7, 8

London Marriott Hotel - Marble Arch
134 George Street, London, W1H 6DN (Tel: 020-7723 1277; Fax: 020-7255 942; Web: www.mariotthotels.com)
Senior Executive Meetings Manager: Ms U. Schmoock
Rooms: 5, **Capacity:** 130 — 2, 4, 6, 7, 8

London Transport Museum
The Piazza, Covent Garden, London, WC2E 7BB (Tel: 020-7565 7292; Fax: 020-7565 7253; E-mail: vivienne@ltmuseum.co.uk; Web: www.ltmuseum.co.uk)
Events Co-ordinator: V. Newlands
Rooms: 1, **Capacity:** 400 — 1, 2, 3, 4, 5, 6, 7

London Zoo
Outer Circle, Regent's Park, London, NW1 4RY (Tel: 020-7449 9235; Fax: 020-7586 6177; E-mail: katherine.duffin@zsl.org; Web: www.londonzoo.co.uk)
Conference Executive: Katherine Duffin
Rooms: 6, **Capacity:** 250 — 1, 2, 4, 5, 6, 7

The Marlborough
9–13 Bloomsbury Street, London, WC1B 3QD (Tel: 020-7636 5601)
Conference and Banqueting Sales Manager: Marianne Riddervik
Rooms: 9, **Capacity:** 270 — 2, 4, 5, 6, 7, 8

Conference and Exhibition Venues   231

Mayfair Inter-Continental
Stratton Street, London, W1A 2AW (Tel: 020-7629 7777; Fax: 020-7409 7016)
Group Sales and Catering Manager:
Ms S. Segoura
Rooms: 289, **Capacity:** 250 — 1, 2, 3, 4, 5, 6, 7, 8

Millennium Hotel Knightsbridge
17 Sloane Street, London, SW1X 9NU (Tel: 020-7235 4377; Fax: 020-7235 3705; E-mail: reservations.knightsbridge@mill-cop.com; Web: www.millennium-hotels.com)
Meetings and Events Co-ordinator:
Sandra Merz
Rooms: 4, **Capacity:** 120 — 2, 4, 5, 7, 8

Motcombs Restaurant and Bar
23 Motcomb Street, Belgravia, London, SW1X 8JT (Tel: 020-7235 3092; Fax: 020-7245 6351; E-mail: motcombs@dial.pipex.com; Web: www.motocombs.co.uk)
Sales and Marketing Executive: Maria Paonessa
Rooms: 2, **Capacity:** 50 — 4, 5, 7

The Mountbatten
20 Monmouth Street, Seven Dials, London, WC2H 9HD (Tel: 020-7836 4300; Fax: 020-7240 3540; E-mail: mountc&b@radisson.com; Web: www.radissonedwardian.com)
Conference and Banqueting Sales Manager:
N. Jaffer
Rooms: 4, **Capacity:** 100 — 2, 4, 5, 6, 7, 8

National Maritime Museum
Royal Observatory and Queen's House, Romney Road, Greenwich, London, SE10 9NF (Tel: 020-8312 6693/6674; Fax: 020-8312 6722; E-mail: jcpres@nmm.ac.uk; Web: www.mnn.ac.uk)
Events Manager: Ms L. Cooke
Rooms: 3, **Capacity:** 500 — 1, 2, 3, 4, 5, 6, 7, 8

New Connaught Rooms
61–65 Great Queen Street, Holborn, London, WC2B 5DA (Tel: 020-7242 5938; Fax: 020-7242 4097; E-mail: sales@connaugh.u-net.com; Web: www.newconnaughtrooms.co.uk)
Events and Conference Co-ordinator:
Georgina Woolff
Rooms: 29, **Capacity:** 1000 — 2, 5, 6, 7, 8

Old Town Hall, Stratford
29 Broadway, Stratford, London, E15 4BQ (Tel: 020-8534 7835; Fax: 020-8534 8411; E-mail: maurice.hill@newham.gov.uk)
Assistant Centre Manager: Ms S. Lowe
Rooms: 8, **Capacity:** 500 — 1, 2, 3, 4, 5, 6, 7

The Park Lane Hotel
Piccadilly, London, W1J 7BX (Tel: 020-7499 6321; Fax: 020-7290 7566; E-mail: brigit.radlinger@sheraton.com; Web: www.sheraton.com)
Events Co-ordinator: A. Valentine
Rooms: 8, **Capacity:** 700 — 2, 3, 4, 5, 6, 7, 8

Planet Hollywood
13 Coventry Street, London, W1V 7FE (Tel: 020-7478 1543; Fax: 020-7478 1501/3)
Corporate Sales and Events Co-ordinator:
Ms E. Richards
Rooms: 2, **Capacity:** 500 — 1, 2, 4, 5, 6, 7

Quality Eccleston Hotel
Eccleston Square, London, SW1V 1PS (Tel: 020-7834 8042; Fax: 020-7630 8942; E-mail: admin@gb614.u-net.com; Web: www.choicehotelseurope.com)
Conference and Banqueting Co-ordinator:
Ms L. Beckett
Rooms: 5, **Capacity:** 150 — 1, 5, 7, 8

The Radisson SAS Portman Hotel
22 Portman Square, London, W1H 7BG (Tel: 020-7208 6000; Fax: 020-7224 4928; E-mail: sales@lonza.rdsas.com; Web: www.radissonsas.com)
Conference and Banqueting Co-ordinator:
Ms F. Nigri; Ms L. Luoma
Rooms: 11, **Capacity:** 550 — 2, 4, 5, 6, 8

Really Useful Theatres
Manor House, 21 Soho Square, London, W1V 5FD (Tel: 020-7494 5200; Fax: 020-7434 1217; E-mail: production@stoll-moss.com; Web: www.stoll-moss.com)
Concerts and Hirings Manager: D. Kinsey
Rooms: 13, **Capacity:** 2200 — 1, 2, 3, 6, 7

Regent's College Conference Centre
Regent's Park, Inner Circle, London, NW1 4NS (Tel: 020-7487 7540/1; Fax: 020-7487 7567; E-mail: conferences@regents.ac.uk; Web: www.regents.ac.uk/conferences)
Conference Manager: Ms C. Arouche
Rooms: 20, **Capacity:** 400 — 1, 2, 4, 5, 6, 7

The Ritz, London
150 Piccadilly, London, W1J 9BR (Tel: 020-7493 8181/7300 2246; Fax: 020-7300 2245; E-mail: enquire@theritzlondon.com; Web: www.theritzlondon.com)
Group Sales Co-ordinator: Thierry Rongmail
Rooms: 2, **Capacity:** 50 — 4, 5, 7, 8

Roof Gardens
99 High Street, Kensington, London, W8 5ED (Tel: 020-7937 7994; Fax: 020-7938 2774)
Events Manager: Lucy Baker
Rooms: 1, **Capacity:** 120 — 2, 4, 5, 7

Royal Aeronautical Society
4 Hamilton Place, London, W1J 7BQ (Tel: 020-7670 4316; Fax: 020-7670 4319;
E-mail: roomhire@raes.org.uk)
Sales and Facilities Manager: J. Morris
Rooms: 8, **Capacity:** 280 — 1, 2, 3, 4, 5, 7, 8

Royal Air Force Museum
Grahame Park Way, London, NW9 5LL (Tel: 020-8200 1763; Fax: 020-8358 4981;
E-mail: specialeventsteam@rafmuseum.com;
Web: www.rafmuseum.com)
Special Events Manager: Anne-Marie Henry
Rooms: 9, **Capacity:** 1000 — 1, 2, 3, 4, 5, 6, 7

Royal College of Physicians
11 St Andrew's Place, Regent's Park, London, NW1 4LE (Tel: 020-7935 1174; Fax: 020-7224 0900; E-mail: events@rcplondon.ac.uk;
Web: www.rcplondon.ac.uk)
Events Co-ordinator: Miss A. Bachtler
Rooms: 8, **Capacity:** 300 — 1, 2, 3, 4, 5, 6, 7, 8

Royal Festival Hall
Commercial Department
SBC Royal Festival Hall, Belvedere Road, London, SE1 8XX (Tel: 020-7921 0680; Fax: 020-7921 0892; E-mail: Plochans@rfh.org.uk;
Web: www.sbc.org.uk)
Conference Manager: Patricia Lochans
Rooms: 4, **Capacity:** 2600 — 1, 2, 3, 4, 5, 6, 7

Royal Horticultural Halls and Conference Centre
80 Vincent Square, London, SW1P 2PE (Tel: 020-7828 4125; Fax: 020-7834 2072;
E-mail: horthalls@rhs.org.uk;
Web: www.horticultural-halls.co.uk)
Sales and Marketing Executive: Ms H. Jones
Rooms: 9, **Capacity:** 1800 — 2, 3, 4, 5, 6, 7, 8

Royal Lancaster
Lancaster Terrace, London, W2 2TY (Tel: 020-7262 6737; Fax: 020-7706 3571;
E-mail: banq@royallancaster.com;
Web: www.royallancaster.com)
Administration Manager: Ms F. Barella
Rooms: 3, **Capacity:** 1000 — 2, 3, 4, 5, 6, 7

Royal National Theatre
South Bank, London, SE1 9PX (Tel: 020-7452 3561; Fax: 020-7452 3565;
E-mail: functions@nationaltheatre.org.uk)
Event Hospitality Manager: Olivia Hudson
Rooms: 8, **Capacity:** 1100 — 1, 2, 3, 5, 6, 7

RSA
8 John Adam Street, London, WC2N 6EZ (Tel: 020-7839 5049; Fax: 020-7321 0271;
E-mail: conference@rsa-uk.demon.co.uk;
Web: www.rsa.org.uk)
Conference Administration Manager: Ms N. Kyle
Rooms: 9, **Capacity:** 200 — 1, 2, 3, 4, 5, 6, 7

Shakespeare's Globe
21 New Globe Walk, Bankside, London, SE1 9DT (Tel: 020-7902 1500; Fax: 020-7902 1515)
Exhibition Sales Manager: Ms C. Abbott
Rooms: 5, **Capacity:** 300 — 2, 3, 5, 6, 7

The Thistle Bloomsbury
Bloomsbury Way, London, WC1A 2SD (Tel: 020-7242 5881; Fax: 020-7831 0225;
E-mail: bloomsbury@thistle.co.uk;
Web: www.thistlehotels.com)
Events Services Co-ordinator: Ms L. Bartlett
Rooms: 11, **Capacity:** 100 — 5, 6, 7, 8

Thistle Euston Hotel
Cardington Street, London, NW1 2LP (Tel: 020-7387 4400; Fax: 020-7387 5413;
E-mail: euston@thistle.co.uk;
Web: www.thistlehotels.com)
Conference Manager: A. McLean
Rooms: 5, **Capacity:** 90 — 5, 6, 7, 8

Thistle Hyde Park
Lancaster Gate, London, W2 3NR (Tel: 020-7262 2711; Fax: 020-7262 2147;
E-mail: hyde.park@thistle.co.uk)
Revenue Manager: Ms T. Spillane
Rooms: 2, **Capacity:** 22 — 5, 7, 8

Thistle Kings Cross
100 King's Cross Road, London, WC1X 9DT (Tel: 020-7278 2434; Fax: 020-7833 0798;
E-mail: kings.cross@thislte.co.uk;
Web: www.thistle.co.uk)
Reservations Manager: Ms K. Gilbert
Rooms: 5, **Capacity:** 160 — 2, 4, 5, 6, 7, 8

Conference and Exhibition Venues 233

Thistle Lancaster Gate
75–89 Lancaster Gate, London, W2 3NN (Tel: 020-7402 4272; Fax: 020-7298 0208; Web: www.thistlehotels.com)
Events Sales Manager: Louise Bennett
Rooms: 6, **Capacity:** 100 — **5, 6, 7, 8**

Thistle Westminster
49 Buckingham Palace Road, London, SW1W 0QT (Tel: 020-7834 1821; Fax: 020-7931 7542; E-mail: meetingplan.westminster@thistle.co.uk; Web: www.thistlehotels.com.uk)
Conference, Banqueting and Sales Co-ordinators: Elaine Cruise
Rooms: 6, **Capacity:** 150 — **3, 4, 5, 7, 8**

Tower Bridge Experience
Tower Bridge, London, SE1 2UP (Tel: 020-7407 9222; Fax: 020-7357 7935; E-mail: enquiries@towerbridge.org.uk; Web: www.towerbridge.org.uk)
Corporate Hospitality Executive: Jane Houlding
Rooms: 3, **Capacity:** 300 — **5, 6, 7**

Tower Thistle Hotel
St Katharine's Way, London, E1 9LD (Tel: 020-7481 2575; Fax: 020-7488 1667; E-mail: Tower@thistle.co.uk; Web: www.thistlehotels.com)
Event Services Manager: Ms G. Belcher
Rooms: 19, **Capacity:** 550 — **2, 4, 5, 6, 7, 8**

Westminster Hotel
16 Leinster Square, Bayswater, London, W2 4PR (Tel: 020-7221 9131; Fax: 020-7221 4073; E-mail: Johno@vienna-group.co.uk; Web: www.westminsterhotel@vienna-group.co.uk)
Food and Beverage Manager: Ms L. Hankins
Rooms: 3, **Capacity:** 120 — **2, 5, 6, 7, 8**

LEGAL LONDON

LEGAL SYSTEM
CIRCUIT JUDGES
CROWN COURTS
COUNTY COURTS
MAGISTRATES' COURTS
CORONERS' COURTS
TRIBUNALS
CROWN PROSECUTION SERVICE
PRISON SERVICE
PROBATION SERVICE
LEGAL BODIES

LEGAL LONDON

Introduction

Throughout its history, London has been the centre and focus of the legal system of the United Kingdom. The reasons are manifold but political and economic centralisation as well as London's position as a centre for trade and finance are among the main historical determinants. As the capital, London lies at the heart of the political system of the UK and despite the separate Scottish legal system and the recent devolution of power to the Scottish Parliament and Welsh Assembly, the highest courts in the UK remain in London. A disproportionate amount of legal activity is still conducted in the capital for this reason. London's pre-eminence as an international financial centre can be added as another factor in this equation. Over the years international trade and finance, concentrated in the square mile of the City of London has led to specialised industry of commercial lawyers unrivalled in size and scope in other parts of the country. The London legal community has always embraced this trend and has actively promoted London as a centre for commercial law and dispute resolution.

There are approximately one hundred and fifty courts in London, ranging from magistrates courts and county courts, to the various divisions of the High Courts, the Court of Appeal (unique outside Scotland which has its own Court of Appeal) and the judicial division of the House of Lords (uniquely based in London and the UK's highest judicial authority). This inevitably means that the highest levels of the judiciary in the United Kingdom remain concentrated in London. In addition to this there are a number of specialist tribunals and courts based in London, for example, the Commercial Court, The Technology and Construction Court, the Employment Appeal Tribunal and the Immigration Appeal Tribunal.

Equally important to the London legal market is the fact that many bodies which control and regulate the legal professions remain based in London, namely the Law Society, the Inns of Court and the General Council of the Bar. Further, many industries which may be of interest to lawyers are controlled and/or regulated by bodies based in London. These include the Financial Services Authority, the Stock Exchange (recently merged with the Exchange in Frankfurt), Lloyd's of London, the Competition Commission and government departments such as the Lord Chancellor's Department and the Department of Trade and Industry.

Solicitors

The number of solicitors holding practising certificates and registered with the Law Society in England and Wales is around 80,000 (2001 Law Society figures). Of this number, over 80 per cent work in private practice and those remaining practice either 'in-house' for a company with its own legal department or for central or local government. Some 1,500 solicitors are employed by the Crown Prosecution Service. In addition there are a number of registered solicitors who perform a number of tasks but are not formally in practice. There are approximately 8,500 solicitors' firms operating from around 14,000 offices throughout England and Wales, a large proportion of these being situated in London.

According to Law Society research, about one-third of all solicitors holding practising certificates are employed by organisations based in London, with almost half of all solicitors' firms being based either in London or the south east of England. As one looks at firms which are larger in size, the concentration increases, with 60 percent of 'large firms' (defined as having 26 partners or more) being based in London. The greater number of these large firms are concentrated in the City of London, specialising in corporate or commercial law, often of an international flavour. Further, the commercial law of England and Wales is often chosen as the governing law in situations where the dispute or transaction has not derived from England or Wales. According to the Law Society, some 80 per cent of litigants of the English Commercial Court come from overseas.

In London the largest firms are concentrated in the City of London, and elite group often organised internationally, with offices abroad specialising in both English and local law. According to some surveys, the bulk of solicitors' overseas earnings is earned by these firms alone. City firms are often in a position to dictate the price to the client as a result of their concentration of expertise and consequent ability to deal with a range of transactions for large clients, for example, corporate transactions, corporate finance and associated litigation. Competition amongst these firms is often intense, the largest of which are known informally as the 'magic circle' of firms. The 'magic circle' includes well-known firms, with considerable presence both in London and internationally, such as Clifford Chance, Freshfields Bruckhaus Deringer, Slaughter and May, Linklaters Alliance and Allen and Overy.

238 Legal London

Barristers

There are approximately 10,000 barristers practising in England and Wales, some 6,000 of whom practice in London. The concentration in London of courts and of legal activity generally goes some way to explain these figures. There are currently around 250 sets of barristers chambers in London handling work of all kinds. Despite the many recent changes in the regulation of the legal professions it is still true to say that barristers specialise as independent advocates in whichever area of law they chose to practice and that barristers continue to dominate as advocates in the higher courts, both criminal and civil. The relatively recent development of rights of audience for solicitors in the higher courts and the reforms both of the legal aid system and the civil litigation procedure by virtue of the Courts and Legal Services Act 1990 have, however, led to widespread changes for the bar in London as they have elsewhere. It is common ground among commentators that the bar as an industry is in the process of restructuring, although only the beginnings of this process are currently being witnessed. It is evident that many barristers in London are changing the way they work, whether this takes the form of joining a chambers which specialises in one area of law, undertaking more advisory, non-litigious work, or trying to develop completely new areas of work in, for example, e-commerce or Alternative Dispute Resolution.

THE LEGAL SYSTEM

The Judicature of England and Wales

The supreme judicial authority for England and Wales is the House of Lords, which is the ultimate Court of Appeal from all courts in Great Britain and Northern Ireland (except criminal courts in Scotland) for all cases except those concerning the interpretation and application of European Community law, including preliminary rulings requested by British courts and tribunals, which are decided by the European Court of Justice. Under the Human Rights Act 1998, which is due to come into force on 2 October 2000, the European Convention on Human Rights will be incorporated into British law; unresolved cases will still be referred to the European Court of Human Rights. As a Court of Appeal the House of Lords consists of the Lord Chancellor and the Lords of Appeal in Ordinary (law lords).

Supreme Court of Judicature

The Supreme Court of Judicature comprises the Court of Appeal, the High Court of Justice and the Crown Court. The High Court of Justice is the superior civil court and is divided into three divisions. The Chancery Division is concerned mainly with equity, bankruptcy and contentious probate business. The Queen's Bench Division deals with commercial and maritime law, serious personal injury and medical negligence cases, cases involving a breach of contract and professional negligence actions. The Family Division deals with matters relating to family law. Sittings are held at the Royal Courts of Justice in London. High Court judges sit alone to hear cases at first instance. Appeals from lower courts are heard by two or three judges, or by single judges of the appropriate division. Appeals from the High Court are heard in the Court of Appeal (Civil Division), presided over by the Master of the Rolls, and may go on to the House of Lords.

Criminal Cases

In criminal matters the decision to prosecute in the majority of cases rests with the Crown Prosecution Service, the independent prosecuting body in England and Wales. The Service is headed by the Director of Public Prosecutions, who works under the superintendence of the Attorney-General. Certain categories of offence continue to require the Attorney-General's consent for prosecution.

The Crown Court sits in about 90 centres, divided into six circuits, and is presided over by High Court judges, full-time circuit judges, and part-time recorders and assistant recorders, sitting with a jury in all trials which are contested. The Crown Court deals with trials of the more serious criminal offences, the sentencing of offenders committed for sentence by magistrates' courts (when the magistrates consider their own power of sentence inadequate), and appeals from magistrates' courts. Magistrates usually sit with a circuit judge or recorder to deal with appeals and committals for sentence. Appeals from the Crown Court, either against sentence or conviction, are made to the Court of Appeal (Criminal Division), presided over by the Lord Chief Justice. A further appeal from the Court of Appeal to the House of Lords can be brought if a point of law of general public importance is considered to be involved.

Minor criminal offences (summary offences) are dealt with in magistrates' courts, which usually consist of three unpaid lay magistrates (justices of the peace) sitting without a jury, who are advised on points of law and procedure by a legally-qualified clerk to the justices. In busier courts a full-time, salaried and legally-qualified stipendiary magistrate presides alone. Cases involving people under 18 are heard in youth courts, specially constituted magistrates' courts which sit apart from other courts. Preliminary proceedings in a serious case to decide whether there is evidence to justify committal for trial in the Crown Court are also dealt with in the magistrates' courts. Appeals from magistrates' courts against sentence or conviction are made to the Crown Court. Appeals upon a point of law are made to the High Court, and may go on to the House of Lords.

Civil Cases

Most minor civil cases are dealt with by the county courts. Cases are heard by circuit judges or district judges. For cases involving small claims there are special simplified procedures. Where there are financial limits on county court jurisdiction, claims which exceed those limits may be tried in the county courts with the consent of the parties, or in certain circumstances on transfer from the High Court. Outside London, bankruptcy proceedings can be heard in designated county courts. Magistrates' courts can deal with certain classes of civil case and committees of magistrates license public houses, clubs and betting shops. For the implementation of the Children Act 1989, a new structure of hearing centres was set up in 1991 for family proceedings cases, involving magistrates' courts (family proceedings courts), divorce county courts, family hearing centres and care centres. Appeals in family matters heard in the family proceedings courts go to the Family Division of the High Court; affiliation appeals and appeals from decisions of the licensing committees of magistrates go to the Crown Court. Appeals from county courts are heard in the Court of Appeal (Civil Division), and may go on to the House of Lords.

Coroners' Courts

Coroners' courts investigate violent and unnatural deaths or sudden deaths where the cause is unknown. Cases may be brought before a local coroner (a senior lawyer or doctor) by doctors, the police, various public authorities or members of the public. Where a death is sudden and the cause is unknown, the coroner may order a post-mortem examination to determine the cause of death rather than hold an inquest in court.

Appointments to the Judiciary

Judicial appointments are made by The Queen; the most senior appointments are made on the advice of the Prime Minister and other appointments on the advice of the Lord Chancellor.

Under the provisions of the Criminal Appeal Act 1995, a Commission was set up to direct and supervise investigations into possible miscarriages of justice and to refer cases to the courts on the grounds of conviction and sentence; these functions were formerly the responsibility of the Home Secretary.

High Court and Crown Court Centres

The London area is served by the south-eastern circuit. First-tier centres deal with both civil and criminal cases and are served by High Court and circuit judges. Second-tier centres deal with criminal cases only and are served by High Court and circuit judges. Third-tier centres deal with criminal cases only and are served only by circuit judges. The High Court in Greater London sits at the Royal Courts of Justice.

SOUTH-EASTERN CIRCUIT

First-tier—Chelmsford, **Croydon**, Lewes, Norwich

Second-tier—Chichester, Ipswich, **London (Central Criminal Court),** Luton, Maidstone, Reading, St Albans

240 Legal London

Third-tier—Aylesbury, Basildon, Bury St Edmunds, Cambridge, Canterbury, Guildford, Hove, King's Lynn, **London (Blackfriars, Harrow, Inner London Sessions House, Isleworth, Kingston, Knightsbridge, Middlesex Guildhall, Snaresbrook, Southend, Southwark, Wood Green, Woolwich)**

South-Eastern Circuit Administrator's Office: Kevin Pogson, New Cavendish House, 18 Maltravers Street, London WC2R 3EU (Tel: 020-7947 6052; Fax: 020-7947 7230).

Provincial Administrator:

1st Floor, Steeple House, Church Lane, Chelmsford CM1 1NH (Tel: 01245-257425).

CIRCUIT JUDGES

South-Eastern Circuit—as at 18 May 2001

Presiding Judges, The Hon. Mr Justice Aikens; The Hon. Mr Justice Moses

J. D. R. Adams; M. F. Addison; P. C. Ader; Mrs S. C. Andrew; A. R. L. Ansell; M. G. Anthony; S. A. Anwyl, QC; E. H. Bailey; M. F. Baker, QC; A. F. Balston; G. S. Barham; B. J. Barker, QC; C. J. A. Barnett, QC; W. E. Barnett, QC; R. A. Barratt, QC; K. Bassingthwaighte; *G. A. Bathurst Norman; P. J. L. Beaumont, QC (*Common Serjeant*); N. E. Beddard; R. V. M. E. Behar; Mrs C. V. Bevington; I. G. Bing; M. G. Binning; J. E. Bishop; B. M. B. Black; H. O. Blacksell, QC; J. G. Boal, QC; A. V. Bradbury; P. N. Brandt; G. B. Breen; R. G. Brown; J. M. Bull, QC; *N. M. Butter, QC; The Hon. C. W. Byers; H. J. Byrt, QC; J. Q. Campbell; M. J. Carroll; B. E. F. Catlin; *B. L. Charles, QC; P. C. L. Clark; P. C. Clegg; Miss S. Coates; N. J. Coleman; S. H. Colgan; P. H. Collins; C. C. Colston, QC; S. S. Coltart; Viscount Colville of Culross, QC; J. S. Colyer, QC; C. D. Compston; T. A. C. Coningsby, QC; J. G. Connor; R. D. Connor; M. J. Cook; R. A. Cooke; M. R. Coombe; P. E. Copley; Dr E. Cotran; P. R. Cowell; R. C. Cox; M. L. S. Cripps; C. A. Critchlow; J. F. Crocker; D. L. Croft, QC; D. M. Cryan; P. Curl; Mrs P. M. T. Dangor; A. M. Darroch; G. L. Davies; W. L. M. Davies, QC; M. Dean, QC; P. G. Dedman; J. E. Devaux; M. N. Devonshire, TD; P. Dodgson; P. H. Downes; W. H. Dunn, QC; C. M. Edwards; D. R. Ellis; R. C. Elly; C. Elwen; F. P. L. Evans; Miss D. Faber; J. D. Farnworth; P. Fingret; P. E. J. Focke, QC; P. Ford; G. C. F. Forrester; Ms D. A. Freedman; R. Gee; L. Gerber; C. A. H. Gibson; Miss A. F. Goddard, QC; S. A. Goldstein; C. G. M. Gordon; J. B. Gosschalk; A. A. Goymer; B. S. Green, QC; A. E. Greenwood; D. J. Griffiths; P. Grobel; R. B. Groves, TD, VRD D. F. Hallett; A. B. R. Hallgarten, QC; Miss G. Hallon; J. Hamilton; Miss S. Hamilton, QC; C. R. H. Hardy; B. Hargrove, OBE, QC; M. F. Harris; A. M. Harvey; W. G. Hawkesworth; R. G. Hawkins, QC; J. M. Haworth; R. J. Haworth; R. M. Hayward; A. N. Hitching; H. E. G. Hodge, OBE; D. Holden; K. M. J. Hollis; J. F. Holt; A. C. W. Hordern, QC; K. A. D. Hornby; M. Hucker; Sir David Hughes-Morgan, Bt., CB, CBE; J. G. Hull, QC; M. J. Hyam (*Recorder of London*); D. A. Inman; A. B. Issard-Davies; D. G. A. Jackson; Dr P. J. E. Jackson; T. J. C. Joseph; I. G. F. Karsten, QC; S. S. Katkhuda; C. J. B. Kemp; M. Kennedy, QC; W. A. Kennedy; A. M. Kenny; T. R. King; B. J. Knight, QC; L. G. Krikler; L. H. C. Lait; P. St J. H. Langan, QC; Capt. J. B. R. Langdon, RN; P. H. Latham; R. Laurie; T. Lawrence; D. M. Levy, QC; C. C. D. Lindsay, QC; S. H. Lloyd; F. R. Lockhart; J. A. M. Lowen; Mrs C. M. Ludlow; Capt. S. Lyons; A. G. McDowell; R. J. McGregor-Johnson; B. M. McIntyre; K. A. Machin, QC; R. G. McKinnon; W. N. McKinnon; N. A. McKittrick; K. C. Macrae; T. Maher; F. J. M. Marr-Johnson; D. N. N. Martineau; D. Matheson, QC; N. A. Medawar, QC; D. B. Meier; D. J. Mellor; G. D. Mercer; D. Q. Miller; Miss A. E. Mitchell; F. I. Mitchell; H. M. Morgan; D. Morton Jack; R. T. Moss; Miss M. J. S. Mowat; T. M. E. Nash; M. H. D. Neligan; Mrs M. F. Norrie; Brig. A. P. Norris, OBE; P. W. O'Brien; M. A. Oppenheimer; D. C. J. Paget, QC; Ms M. J. Parker; D. J. Parry; A. Patience, QC; Mrs N. Pearce; Prof. D. S. Pearl; Miss V. A. Pearlman; B. P. Pearson; N. A. J. Philpot; T. D. Pillay; D. C. Pitman; J. R. Platt; J. R. Playford, QC; P. B. Pollock; T. G. Pontius; W. D. C. Poulton; S. Pratt; R. J. C. V. Prendergast; J. E. Prévité, QC; B. H. Pryor, QC; D. W. Radford; J. W. Rant, CB, QC; E. V. P. Reece; J. R. Reid, QC; M. P. Reynolds; M. S. Rich, QC; D. J. Richardson; N. P. Riddell; G. Rivlin, QC; S. D. Robbins; J. M. Roberts; J. M. G. Roberts, QC; D. A. Rodwell, QC; G. H. Rooke, TD, QC; W. M. Rose; P. C. R. Rountree; J. H. Rucker; T. R. G. Ryland; J. E. A. Samuels, QC; R. B. Sanders; A. R. G. Scott-Gall; J. S. Sennitt; D. Serota, QC; J. L. Sessions; D. R. A. Sich; A. G. Simmons; K. T. Simpson; P. R. Simpson; M. Singh, QC; S. P. Sleeman; C. M. Smith, QC; S. A. R. Smith; Miss Z. P. Smith; E. Southwell; S. B. Spence; S. M. Stephens, QC; N. A. Stewart; D. M. A. Stokes, QC; T. M. F. Stow, QC; W. F. C.

County Courts

Thomas; P. J. Thompson; A. G. Y. Thorpe; C. H. Tilling; C. J. M. Tyrer; Mrs A. P. Uziell-Hamilton; J. E. van der Werff; A. O. R. Vick, QC; T. L. Viljoen; J. P. Wadsworth, QC; Miss A. P. Wakefield; R. Wakefield; R. Walker; S. P. Waller; A. R. Webb; C. S. Welchman; A. F. Wilkie, QC; S. R. Wilkinson; Miss J. A. Williams; R. J. Winstanley; D. Worsley; E. G. Wrintmore; M. P. Yelton; M. K. Zeidman, QC K. H. Zucker, QC

COUNTY COURTS

Barnet County Court
St Mary's Court, Regents Park Road, Finchley Central, London N3 1BQ (Tel: 020-8343 4272; Fax: 020-8343 1324; DX: 122570 FINCHLEY (CHURCH END); Web: www.courtservice.gov.uk)
Court Manager: Mrs S. Mosley
District Judges: M. Trent; S. Gerlis; J. Karet

Bow County Court
96 Romford Road, Stratford E15 4EG (Tel: 020-8536 5200; Fax: 020-8503 1152; DX: 97490 STRATFORD (LONDON) 2;
Web: www.courtservice.gov.uk)
Court Manager: Mr I. Anderson
District Judges: R. W. Mullis; D. L. Millard; F. J. Wilkinson; R. H. Naqui-Gregory

Brentford County Court
Alexandra Road, High Street, Brentford, Middx, TW8 0JJ (Tel: 020-8580 7300; Fax: 020-8568 2401; DX: 97840 BRENTFORD 2;
Web: www.courtservice.gov.uk)
Court Manager: J. Bones
District Judges: S. Plaskow; J. Allen; T. Jenkins

Central London County Court
13–14 Park Crescent, London W1B 1HT (Tel: 020-7917 5000; Fax: 020-7917 5014; DX: 97325 REGENTS PARK 2;
Web: www.courtservice.gov.uk)
Court Manager: Mr M. Burke
District Judges: C. P. Wigfield; Mrs S. Hasan; Mrs M. Langley; M. J. Haselgrove; M. Gilchrist; K. A. Price

Clerkenwell County Court
33 Duncan Terrace, Islington, London N1 8AN (Tel: 020-7359 7347; Fax: 020-7354 1166; DX: 58284 ISLINGTON;
Web: www.courtservice.gov.uk)
Court Manager: Mrs T. Warne
District Judges: A. Armon-Jones; R. Southcombe

Croydon County Court
The Law Courts Altyre Road, Croydon, CR9 5AB; (Fax: 020-8760 0432; DX: 97470 CROYDON 6; Web: www.courtservice.gov.uk)
Court Manager: James Malone

Edmonton County Court
Court House, 59 Fore Street, Upper Edmonton, London, N18 2TN (Tel: 020-8807 1666; Fax: 020-8803 0564; DX: 136686 EDMONTON 3; Web: www.courtservice.gov.uk)
Court Manager: P. Joseph
District Judges: G. Silverman; S. Morley; L. Cohen
Circuit Judge: N. Riddell

Ilford County Court
Buckingham Road, Ilford, Essex IG1 1BR (Tel: 020-8478 1132; Fax: 020-8553 2824; DX: 97510 ILFORD 3;
Web: www.courtservice.gov.uk)
Court Manager: Miss K. Langan
District Judges: I. V. Sheratte; A. Thomas

Lambeth County Court
Court House, Cleaver Street, Kennington Road, London, SE11 4DZ (Tel: 020-7735 4425; Fax: 020-7735 8147; DX: 33254 KENNINGTON; Web: www.courtservice.gov.uk)
Court Manager: N. Crew
District Judges: R. M. Jacey; M. Zimmels; A. Worthington

The Mayor's and City of London County Court
Guildhall Buildings, Basinghall Street, London EC2V 5AR (Tel: 020-7796 5400; Fax: 020-7796 5424; DX: 97520 MOORGATE (EC2);
Web: www.courtservice.gov.uk)
Court Manager: Mrs Collins
District Judges: R. Southcombe; M. Trent

Romford County Court
2A Oaklands Avenue, Romford, Essex RM1 4DP (Tel: 01708-750677; Fax: 01708-756653; DX: 97530 ROMFORD 2;
Web: www.courtservice.gov.uk)
Court Manager: J. Ward
District Judges: N. E. Jackson: J. H. G. Chrispin; A. D. Thomas; R. James

Shoreditch County Court
19 Leonard Street, London, EC2A 4AL (Tel: 020-7253 0956; Fax: 020-7490 5613; DX: 121000 SHOREDITCH 2;

242 Legal London

Web: www.courtservice.gov.uk)
Court Manager: Ms A. Latham
District Judge: J. Wright; J. Beattie

Wandsworth County Court
76-78 Upper Richmond Road, Putney, London, SW15 2SU (Tel: 020-8333 4351; Fax: 020-8877 9854; DX: 97540 PUTNEY 2;
E-mail: wandsworth.cty.cm@courtservice.gsi.gov.uk;
Web: www.courtservice.gov.uk)
Court Manager: Mrs T. Wildash
District Judges: I. G. Tilbury; J. Gittens; M. Walker

West London County Court
43 North End Road, West Kensington, London W14 8SZ (Tel: 020-7602 8444; Fax: 020-7602 1820; DX: 97550 WEST KENSINGTON 2;
Web: www.courtservice.gov.uk)
Court Manager: J.Morris
District Judges: N. Madge; E.Habershou

Willesden County Courts
9 Acton Lane, Harlesden, London NW10 8SB (Tel: 020-8963 8200; Fax: 020-8453 0946; DX: 97560 HARLESDEN 2;
Web: www.courtservice.gov.uk)
Court Manager: P. Downer
District Judges: A. J. Morris; D. V. Steel; E. Cohen; C. Dabezies

Woolwich County Court
The Court House 165-167 Powis Street, London SE18 6JW (Tel: 020-8854 2127; Fax: 020-8316 4842; DX: 123450 WOOLWICH 8;
Web: www.courtservice.gov.uk)
Court Manager: Mrs R. Davies
District Judges: M. Lee

CROWN PROSECUTION SERVICE

Crown Prosecution Service London
50 Ludgate Hill, London EC4M 7EX (Tel: 020-7796 800; DX: 300850 LUDGATE EC4)
Area Business Manager: A. Machray

Barking and Stratford CPS
Solar House 1–9 Romford Road, Stratford, London, E15 4LJ (Tel: 020-8221 3500; Fax: 020-8221 3501; DX: 5449 STRATFORD (LONDON)

Crown Courts: Central Criminal Court – Snaresbrook
Magistrates' Courts: Barking; Stratford (Newham)

Barnet and Haringey CPS
6th and 8th Floors, River Park House, 225 High Road, Wood Green, London, N22 8HQ (Tel: 020-8826 4600; Fax: 020-8826 4601; DX: 35699 WOOD GREEN 1)
Branch Crown Prosecutor: Mr D. Levy
Crown Courts: Central Criminal Court – Harrow; Wood Green
Magistrates' Courts: Enfield (Tottenham); Haringey (Highgate, Tottenham); Hendon; Waltham Forest

Brent, Harrow and Uxbridge CPS
2nd Floor, Kings House Kymberley Road, Harrow, Middx, HA1 1YH (Tel: 020-8901 5700; Fax: 020-8901 5739; DX: 4204 HARROW 1)
Crown Courts: Central Criminal Court – Harrow; Isleworth
Magistrates' Courts: Harrow; Uxbridge

Camberwell CPS
8 Gainsford Street, London SE1 2NE (Tel: 020-7378 4100; Fax: 020-7378 4301; DX: 80712 BERMONDSEY)
Crown Courts: Central Criminal Court– Inner London
Magistrates' Courts: Camberwell Green

Croydon CPS
8th Floor, Prospect West 81 Station Road, Croydon, CR0 2RD (Tel: 020-8662 2800; Fax: 020-8662 2828; DX: 2698 CROYDON)
Branch Crown Prosecutor: P. Ragnauth
Crown Courts: Central Criminal Court – Croydon
Magistrates' Courts: Bromley; Croydon; Bexley

Ealing and Hounslow CPS
2nd Floor, Kings House Kymberley Road, Harrow, Middx HA1 1YH (Tel: 020-8901 5700; Fax: 020-8901 5919; DX: 4204 HARROW 1)
Branch Crown Prosecutor: Nazir Afzal
Crown Courts: Central Criminal Court – Isleworth
Magistrates' Courts: Acton; Brentford; Ealing; Feltham

Crown Prosecution Service 243

Greenwich and Bexley CPS
8 Gainsford Street, London SE1 2NE (Tel: 020-7378 4000; Fax: 020-7378 4248; DX: 80712 BERMONDSEY)
Crown Courts: Central Criminal Court – Woolwich
Magistrates' Courts: Bexley; Greenwich; Woolwich

Havering and Redbridge CPS
Solar House 1–9 Romford Road, Stratford, London, E15 4LJ (Tel: 020-8221 3500; Fax: 020-8221 3504/5; DX: 5449 STRATFORD (LONDON))
Crown Courts: Central Criminal Court – Snaresbrook
Magistrates' Court: Havering (Romford); Redbridge (Ilford)

Highbury CPS
Solar House 1–9 Romford Road, Stratford, London E15 4LJ (Tel: 020-8221 3623; Fax: 020-8221 3506; DX: 5449 STRATFORD (LONDON))
Branch Crown Prosecutor: Claire Ward
Crown Courts: Central Criminal Court – Snaresbrook
Magistrates' Court: Highbury Corner

Kingston CPS
17th Floor, Tolworth Tower, Surbiton, Surrey KT6 7DS (Tel: 020-7335 1500; Fax: 020-7335 1601/2/3; DX: 57549 TOLWORTH)
Branch Crown Prosecutor: M. Haddon
Crown Courts: Central Criminal Court – Kingston
Magistrates' Courts: Kingston-upon-Thames; Richmond-upon-Thames; South Western; Wimbledon; Sutton

Thames CPS
50 Ludgate Hill, London EC4M 7EX (Tel: 020-7796 8000; Fax: 020-7796 8268/9; DX: 300850 LUDGATE EC4)
Branch Crown Prosecutor: D. Atkins
Crown Courts: Central Criminal Court – Southwark; Hackney and Tower Hamlets
Magistrates' Courts: Thames

Tower Bridge and City CPS
8 Gainsford Street, London SE1 2NE (Tel: 020-7378 4100; Fax: 020-7378 4201/2; DX: 80712 BERMONDSEY)
Crown Courts: Central Criminal Court – Inner London

Magistrates' Court: City of London; Tower Bridge

CPS Wood Green Branch
5th Floor, River Park House 225 High Road, Wood Green, London N22 8HQ (Tel: 020-8826 4600; Fax: 020-8826 4700; DX: 35699 WOOD GREEN 1)
Branch Crown Prosecutor: D. Levy
Crown Courts: Central Criminal Court – Snaresbrook; Wood Green
Magistrates' Courts: Enfield (Tottenham); Waltham Forest (Walthamstow); Haringey; Barnet/Hendon

West London CPS
50 Ludgate Hill, London EC4M 7EX (Tel: 020-7796 8000; Fax: 020-7796 8028; DX: 300850 LUDGATAE EC4)
Branch Crown Prosecutor: R. Barclay
Crown Courts: Central Criminal Court – Blackfriars
Magistrates' Courts: West London

London Westminster CPS
50 Ludgate Hill, London EC4M 7EX (Tel: 020-7796 8000; Fax: 020-7796 8560/8580; DX: 300850 LUDGATE EC4)
Branch Crown Prosecutor: B. Butler
Crown Courts: Central Criminal Court – Middlesex; Southwark
Magistrates' Courts: Horseferry Road; Bow Street

Youth and City CPS
1st Floor, 8 Gainsford Street, London SE1 2NE (Tel: 020-7378 4100; Fax: 020-7378 4101; DX: 80712 BERMONDSEY)
Branch Crown Prosecutor: Miss H. Bradfield
Crown Courts: Inner London; Southwark Central Criminal Court
Magistrates' Courts: Youth Courts (Inner London and City of London Magistrates Court)

CROWN COURTS

Blackfriars Crown Court
Pocock Street, London SE1 0BJ (Tel: 020-7922 5800; Fax: 020-7922 5815; DX: 400800 LAMBETH 3)
Court Manager: Karl Liddle

244 Legal London

Central Criminal Court
Old Bailey, London EC4M 7EH (Tel: 020-7248 3277; Fax: 020-7248 5735; DX: 46700 OLD BAILEY)
Court Manager: C. Read

Croydon Crown Court
The Law Courts, Altyre Road, Croydon, CR9 5AB (Tel: 020-8410 4700; Fax: 020-8760 0432; DX: 97470 CROYDON 6)
Court Manager: Anne Johnson

Harrow Crown Court
Hailsham Drive, Harrow, Middx HA1 4TU (Tel: 020-8424 2294; Fax: 020-8424 2209; DX: 97335 HARROW 5)
Court Manager: Stuart Hill

Inner London Crown Court
Sessions House, Newington Causeway, London SE1 6AZ (Tel: 020-7234 3100; Fax: 020-7234 3222; DX: 97345 SOUTHWARK 3; Web: www.courtservice.gov.uk)
Court Manager: Mrs J. P. Coles

Isleworth Crown Court
36 Ridgeway Road, Isleworth, Middx TW7 5LP (Tel: 020-8568 8811; Fax: 020-8568 5368; DX: 97420 ISLEWORTH 1)
Court Manager: Mr P Jabbal

Kingston upon Thames Crown Court
6–8 Penrhyn Road, Kingston-upon-Thames, KT1 2BB (Tel: 020-8240 2500; Fax: 020-8240 2675; DX: 97430 KINGSTON-UPON-THAMES 2)
Court Manager: R. Foster

Middlesex Guildhall Crown Court
Little George Street, London, SW1P 3BB (Tel: 020-7799 2131; Fax: 020-7233 1612; DX: 122920 PARLIAMENT SQUARE)
Court Manager: S. Jones

Snaresbrook Crown Court
75 Hollybush Hill, Snaresbrook, London E11 1QW (Tel: 020-8982 5500; Fax: 020-8989 1371; DX: 98240 WANSTEAD 2)
Court Manager: Donna Bolton

Southwark Crown Court
1 English Grounds, Battlebridge Lane, Southwark, London SE1 2HU (Tel: 020-7522 7200; Fax: 020-7522 7300; DX: 39913

LONDON BRIDGE SOUTH)
Court Manager: C. A. Harper

Wood Green Crown Court
Woodall Lane, Lordship Lane, Wood Green, London N22 5LF (Tel: 020-8881 1400; Fax: 020-8881 4802; DX: 130346 WOOD GREEN 3)
Court Manager: Mr U. Bitten

Woolwich Crown Court
2 Belmarsh Road, London SE28 0EY (Tel: 020-8312 7000; Fax: 020-8312 7078; DX: 117650 WOOLWICH 7)
Court Manager: J. Crampsey

FAMILY COURT

Inner London and City Family Proceedings Court
59–65 Wells Street, London W1A 3AE (Tel: 020-7805 3400; Fax: 020-7805 3490; DX: 89268 SOHO SQUARE;
E-mail: familycourt@ilmcl.freeserve.co.uk)
Justices' Clerk: Miss A. F. Damazer

MAGISTRATES' COURTS

Greater London Magistrates' Courts Authority
185 Marylebone Road, London NW1 5QL

Londoners are set to benefit from a better justice system due to the launch of the Greater London Magistrates' Courts Authority under the Access to Justice Act 1999. As from April 2001 the new authority assumed responsibility for the administration of the magistrates' courts in the capital from the 22 Magistrates' Courts Committees. The new authority is more accountable to the people of London as has two elected members from local authorities and two nominated by the Mayor of London.

The Magistrates' Courts in the Greater London area are:

City of London Magistrates' Court
The Justice Rooms 1 Queen Victoria Street, London EC4N 4XY (Tel: 020-7332 1830; Fax: 020-7332 1493; DX: 98943 CHEAPSIDE 2)
Justices' Chief Executive and Clerk to the Justices: J. D. Wignall

Greater London Magistrates' Courts Authority
185 Marylebone Road, London NW1 5QL (Tel: 020-7506 3045; Fax: 020-7723 9481; DX: 41740 Marylebone 2)
Justices' Chief Executive:
Maj. Gen AEG Truluck, CBE

Magistrates' Courts 245

Acton Magistrates' Court
The Court House Winchester Street, Acton, London W3 8PB (Tel: 020-8992 9014; Fax: 020-8993 9647; DX: 82606 WEST EALING)
Justices' Clerk: H. J. Dingwall

Barking Magistrates' Court
The Court House East Street, Barking, Essex IG11 8EW (Tel: 020-8594 5311; Fax: 020-8594 4297; DX: 8518 BARKING 1)
Justices' Clerk: R. Wright

Barnet Magistrates' Court
Justices' Clerk's Office 7C High Street, Barnet, Herts EN5 5UE (Tel: 020-8441 9042; Fax: 020-8441 6753; DX: 8626 BARNET)
Justices' Clerk: J. Clark

Bexley Magistrates' Court
Norwich Place, Bexleyheath, Kent DA6 7NB (Tel: 020-8304 5211; Fax: 020-8303 6849; DX: 100150 BEXLEYHEATH 3)
Justices' Clerk: Mrs C. A. Pilmore-Bedford

Bow Street Magistrates' Court
28 Bow Street, London WC2E 7AS (Tel: 0845-600 8889; Fax: 020-7379 5634; DX: 40041 COVENT GARDEN 2)
Justices' Clerk: Gaynor Houghton-Jones

Brent Magistrates' Court
448 High Road, London NW10 2DZ (Tel: 020-8955 0555; Fax: 020-8955 0543; DX: 110850 WILLESDEN 2)
Justices' Clerk: P. W. H. Lydiate

Brentford Magistrates' Court
Market Place, Brentford, Middx TW8 8EN (Tel: 020-8917 3400; Fax: 020-8917 3448; DX: 133823 FELTHAM 3;
E-mail: alan.baldwin@feltham.olmcs-law.co.uk)
Justices' Clerk: A. J. M. Baldwin

Bromley Magistrates' Court
The Court House, 1 London Road, Bromley, Kent BR1 1RA (Tel: 020-8325 4000; Fax: 020-8325 4006; DX: 119601 BROMLEY 8;
E-mail: admin@bromley.olmcs-law.co.uk;
Web: www.bromleymagscourt.demon.co.uk)
Justices' Clerk: R. J. Haynes

Camberwell Green Magistrates' Court
15 D'Eynsford Road, Camberwell Green, London SE5 7UP (Tel: 020-7805 9860; Fax: 020-7805 9897; DX: 35305 CAMBERWELL GREEN)
Justices' Clerk: Miss B. A. Morse

Croydon Magistates' Court
Barclay Road, Croydon CR9 3NG (Tel: 020-8603 0476; Fax: 020-8680 9801)
Justices' Clerk: Mrs C. J. Bridges

Ealing Magistrates' Court
The Court House, Green Man Lane, Ealing, London W13 0SD (Tel: 020-8579 9311; Fax: 020-8579 2985; DX: 82606 WEST EALING)
Justices' Clerk: H. J. Dingwall

Enfield Magistrates' Court
The Court House Lordship Lane, Tottenham, London N17 6RT (Tel: 020-8808 5411; Fax: 020-8885 4343; DX: 134490 TOTTENHAM 3;
E-mail: postbox@enfield.olms-law.co.uk)
Justices' Clerk: A. P. G. S. Shepstone

Feltham Magistrates' Court
Hanworth Road, Feltham, Middx TW13 5AF (Tel: 020-8890 4811; Fax: 020-8917 3400; DX: 133821 FELTHAM 3)
Justices' Clerk: A. J. M. Baldwin

Greenwich Magistrates' Court
9 Blackheath Road, Greenwich, London SE10 8PG (Tel: 020-8276 1359; Fax: 020-8276 1399; DX: 35203 GREENWICH WEST;
Web: www.greenwich-magistrates.fsnet.co.uk)
Justices' Clerk: Miss B. L. Barnes

Haringey Magistrates' Court
The Court House, Bishops Road, off Archway Road, Highgate, London N6 4HS (Tel: 020-8340 3472; Fax: 020-7348 3343; DX: 1235501/1/2 HIGHGATE 3)
Justices' Clerk: G. Fillingham

Harrow Magistrates' Court
PO Box 164, Rosslyn Crescent, Wealdstone, Harrow, Middx HA1 2JY (Tel: 020-8427 5146; Fax: 020-8863 9518; DX: 30451 HARROW 3)
Justices' Clerk: G. Cropper

246 Legal London

Havering Magistrates' Court
Main Road, Romford, Essex RM1 3BH (Tel: 01708-771771; Fax: 01708-771777; DX: 131527 ROMFORD 8; E-mail: general.office@havering.olmcs-law.co.uk)
Justices' Clerk: T. J. Ring

Hendon Magistrates' Court
Court House, The Hyde, Hendon, London NW9 7BY (Tel: 020-8441 9042; Fax: 020-8205 4595; DX: 8626 BARNET; E-mail: listing.office@hendon.olmcs-law.co.uk)
Justices' Clerk: J. Clark

Highbury Corner Magistrates' Court
51 Holloway Road, London N7 8JA (Tel: 020-7506 3102/3; Fax: 020-7506 3191; DX: 51855 HIGHBURY)
Justices' Clerk: Mrs J. Woolley

Horseferry Road Magistrates' Court
70 Horseferry Road, London SW1P 2AX (Tel: 0845-600 889; Fax: 020-7805 1193; DX: 120551 VICTORIA 6)
Justices' Clerk: Mrs G. Houghton Jones

Kingston-upon-Thames Magistates' Court
19 High Street, Kingston-upon-Thames, Surrey KT1 1JW (Tel: 020-8546 5603; Fax: 020-8481 4848; DX: 119975 KINGSTON-UPON-THAMES 6; E-mail: general@kingston.olmcs-law.co.uk)
Justices' Clerk: A. R. Vickers

Marylebone Magistrates' Court
181 Marylebone Road, London NW1 5QJ (Tel: 020-7706 1261; Fax: 020-7724 9884; DX: 41740 MARYLEBONE 2)
Justices' Clerk: E. Houghton

Richmond-upon-Thames Magistates' Court
Parkshot, Richmond, Surrey TW9 2RF (Tel: 020-8948 2101; Fax: 020-8332 2628; DX: 100257 RICHMOND 2)
Justices' Clerk: D. K. Lowdell

Stratford Magistates' Court
389–397 High Street, London E15 4SB (Tel: 020-8522 5000; Fax: 020-8519 9214; DX: 5417 STRATFORD)
Justices' Clerk: G. K. Norris

Sutton Magistrates' Court
The Court House, Shotfield, Wallington, Surrey SM6 0JA (Tel: 020-8770 5950; Fax: 020-8770 5977; DX: 59957 WALLINGTON)
Justices' Clerk: J. C. Sunderland

Thames Magistrates' Court
58 Bow Road, London E3 4DJ (Tel: 020-8980 1000; Fax: 020-8980 0670; DX: 55654 BOW)
Justices' Clerk: K. T. Griffiths

Tower Bridge Magistrates' Court
211 Tooley Street, London SE1 2JY (Tel: 020-7407 4232; Fax: 020-7378 0712; DX: 39921 LONDON BRIDGE SOUTH)
Justices' Clerk: B.A. Morse

Uxbridge Magistrates' Court
The Court House, Harefield Road, Uxbridge, Middx UB8 1PQ (Tel: 01895-814646; Fax: 01895-274280; DX: 98053 UXBRIDGE 2; Web: www.olmcs-law.co.uk)
Justices' Clerk: P. J. M. Hamilton

Waltham Forest Magistrates' Court
The Court House, 1 Farnan Avenue, Walthamstow, London E17 4NX (Tel: 020-7527 8000; Fax: 020-7527 9063; DX: 124542; E-mail: admin@wfmc.olmc-law.co.uk)
Justices' Clerk: P. F. Cozens

West London Magistrates' Court
181 Talgarth Road, London W6 8DN (Tel: 020-8741 1234; Fax: 020-8700 9344; DX: 124800 HAMMERSMITH 8)
Justices' Clerk: Miss M. H. Parry

Wimbledon Magistates' Court
The Law Courts, Alexandra Road, Wimbledon, London SW19 7JP (Tel: 020-8946 8622; Fax: 020-8946 7030; DX: 116610 WIMBLEDON 4)
Justices' Clerk: E. Packer

Woolwich Magistrates' Court
Market Street, Woolwich, London SE18 6QY (Tel: 020-8276 1359; Fax: 020-8276 1399; Web: www.greewich-magistrates.fsnet.co.uk)
Justices' Clerk: B. L. Barnes

Coroners' Courts

CORONERS' COURTS

City of London Coroners' Court
Milton Court, Moor Lane, London,EC2Y 9BL
(Tel: 020-7332 1598; Fax: 020-7601 2714)
Coroner: D. R. Chambers

Croydon Coroners' Court
Barclay Road, Croydon CR9 3NE (Tel: 020-8681 5019; Fax: 020-8686 3491)
Coroner: P. B. Rose

Croydon Coroners' Court
Queen Mary's Hospital, Frognal Avenue, Sidcup, Kent (Tel: 020-8300 3700 ext 4004; Fax: 020-8308 9388)
Coroner: P. B. Rose

Croydon Coroners' Court
35 London Road, Bromley, Kent BR1 1DG (Tel: 020-8460 6015; Fax: 020-8460 6015)
Coroner: P. B. Rose

Croydon Coroners' Court
Sutton Public Mortuary, Alcorn Close, Sutton, Surrey SM6 0NB (Tel: 020-8641 3240; Fax: 020-8644 1709)
Coroner: P. B. Rose

East London Coroners' Court
Queens Road, Walthamstow, London E17 8QP (Tel: 020-8520 7245/6/7; Fax: 020-8521 0896)
Coroner: Dr E. J. Stearns

East London Coroners' Court
Oldchurch Hospital, Oldchurch Road, Romford, Essex RM7 0BE (Tel: 01708-746431/ 2; Fax: 01708-757032)
Coroner: Dr E. J. Stearns

Hornsey Coroners' Court
Barnet General Hospital Mortuary, Wellhouse Lane, Barnet, Herts EN5 3DJ (Tel: 020-8732 4939; E-mail: hmcwd@freenet.co.uk)
Coroner: W. F. G. Dolman

Hornsey Coroners' Court
Edgware Police Station, Whitchurch Lane, Edgware, Middx HA8 6LA (Tel: 020-8733 3567; Fax: 020-8733 3514;
E-mail: hmcwd@freenet.co.uk)
Coroner: W. F. G. Dolman

Hornsey Coroners' Court
Myddleton Road, Hornsey, London N8 7PY (Tel: 020-8348 4411; Fax: 020-8347 5229; E-mail: hmcwd@freenet.co.uk)
Coroner: W. F. G. Dolman

St Pancras Coroners' Court
Camley Street, London NW1 0PP (Tel: 020-7387 4882; Fax: 020-7383 2485)
Coroner: Dr S. M. T. Chan

St Pancras Coroners' Court
Poplar Coroner's Court, 127 Poplar High Street, London E14 0AAE (Tel: 020-7987 3614; Fax: 020-7538 0565)
Coroner: Dr S. M. T. Chan

Southwark Coroners' Court
1 Tennis Street, London SE1 1YD (Tel: 020-7407 5611; Fax: 020-7378 8401)
Coroner: Mrs Selena Lynch

Westminster Coroners' Court
Battersea Office, 48 Falcon Road, London SW11 2LR (Tel: 020-7228 6044; Fax: 020-7738 0640)
Coroner: Dr P. Knapman

Westminster Coroners' Court
65 Horseferry Road, London SW1P 2ED (Tel: 020-7834 6515; Fax: 020-7828 2837)
Coroner: Dr P. Knapman

TRIBUNALS

Agricultural Land Tribunals
c/o Land Use, Land Tenure and Planning Branch, Ministry of Agriculture, Fisheries and Food, Room 110, Nobel House, 17 Smith Square, London SW1P 3JR (Tel: 020-7238 6991; Fax: 020-7238 5671;
E-mail: gerald.norris@env.maff.gsi.gov.uk)

The Appeals Service
4th Floor, Whittington House, 19–30 Alfred Place, London WC1E 7LW (Tel: 020-7712 2600; Fax: 020-7712 2650;
Web: www.appeals-service.gov.uk)
Chief Executive: N. Ward

Copyright Tribunal
Harmsworth House, 13–15 Bouverie Street, London EC4Y 8DP (Tel: 020-7596 6510; Fax: 020-7596 6526;

248 Legal London

E-mail: copyright.tribunal@patent.gov.uk;
Web: www.patent.gov.uk/dpolicy/copytrib.html)
Secretary: Ms J. Durdin

Data Protection Tribunal
c/o The Home Office, Queen Anne's Gate, London SW1H 9AT (Tel: 020-7273 3755; Fax: 020-7273 3205)
Chairman: J. A. C. Spokes

Employment Tribunals
Central Office (England and Wales), 19–29 Woburn Place, London WC1H 0LU (Tel: 020-7273 8666)
Chief Executive: Roger Heathcote

Employment Appeal Tribunal
Audit House, 58 Victoria Embankment, London EC4Y 0DS (Tel: 020-7273 1041; Fax: 020-7273 1045; Web: www.employmentappeals.gov.uk)
Registrar: Miss V. J. Selio, OBE

Immigration Appellate Authorities
Taylor House, 88 Rosebery Avenue, London EC1R 4QU (Tel: 020-7862 4200)
Tribunal Manager: S. Hill

Land Tribunal
48–49 Chancery Lane, London WC2A 1JR (Tel: 020-7947 7200; Fax: 020-7947 7215; Web: www.courtservice.gov.uk/tribunals/lands)
Registrar: D Scannell

Mental Health Review Tribunal Secretariat
Health Service Directorate, Room 320, Wellington House, 133-155 Waterloo Road, London SE1 8UG (Tel: 020-7972 4503; Fax: 020-7972 4884;
E-mail: margaret.burn@doh.gsi.gov.uk)
Head of the Mental Health Review Tribunal: Margaret Burn

Office of the Social Security and Child Support Commissioners
5th Floor, Newspaper House, 8–16 Great New Street, London EC4A 3NN (Tel: 020-7353 5145; Fax: 020-7936 2171)
Secretary: L. Sadler

Pensions Appeal Tribunals
Central Office (England and Wales), 48–49 Chancery Lane, London WC2A 1JR (Tel: 020-7947 0323/4)

The Solicitors' Disciplinary Tribunal
3rd Floor, Gate House, 1 Farringdon Street, London EC4M 7NS (Tel: 020-7329 4808; Fax: 020-7329 4833;
E-mail: enquiries@solicitorsdt.com)
Clerk: Ms S. Elson

Special Commissioners of Income Tax
15–19 Bedford Avenue, London WC1B 3AS (Tel: 020-7631 4242; Fax: 020-7436 4150/1; Web: www.courtservice.gov.uk/tribunals/comtax/index.htm)
Clerk to Special Commissioners: R. P. Lester

Special Immigration Appeals Commission
Taylor House, 88 Rosebery Avenue, London EC1R 4QU (Tel: 020-7862 4200)
Tribunal Manager: S. Hill

Transport Tribunal
48–49 Chancery Lane, London WC2A 1JR (Tel: 020-7947 7493; Fax: 020-7947 7215)

VAT and Duties Tribunals
15–19 Bedford Avenue, London, WC1B 3AS (Tel: 020-7631 4242; Fax: 020-7436 4150/1; Web: www.courtservice.gov.uk/tribunals/comtax/index.htm)
Registrar: R. P. Lester

CROWN PROSECUTION SERVICE

50 Ludgate Hill, London EC4M 7EX (Tel: 020-7796 8000; Email: enquiries@cps.gov.uk; Web: www.cps.gov.uk)

The Crown Prosecution Service (CPS) is responsible for the independent review and conduct of criminal proceedings instituted by police forces in England and Wales, with the exception of cases conducted by the Serious Fraud Office and certain minor offences.

The Service is headed by the Director of Public Prosecutions (DPP), who works under the superintendence of the Attorney-General, and a chief executive. The Service comprises headquarters in London and York and 42 Areas, each Area corresponding to a police area in England and Wales. Each Area is headed by a Chief Crown Prosecutor, supported by an Area Business Manager.

Director of Public Prosecutions:
D. Calvert-Smith, QC
Chief Executive: M. E. Addison
Directors: C. Newell (*Casework*); G. Patten (*Policy*); J. Graham (*Finance*); L. Carey (*Business Information Systems*); I. Seehra (*Human Resources*)
Head of Communications: Mrs L. Salisbury
Head of Management Audit Services:
Ms R. Read

CPS London
Area HQ, 50 Ludgate Hill, London, EC4M 7EX (Tel: 020-7796 8000).
Chief Crown Prosecutor: Mr Peter Boeuf
Assistant Chief Crown Prosecutors:
Mr. Howard Cohen; Ms Melanie Werrett
Area Business Manager: Mr Alex Machray

THE PRISON SERVICE

The Prison Service in England and Wales is the responsibility of the Home Secretary. The Director General of the Prison Service is responsible for the day-to-day running of the system.

Convicted prisoners are classified according to their assessed security risk and are housed in establishments appropriate to that level of security. Female prisoners are housed in women's establishments or in separate wings of mixed prisons. Remand prisoners are, where possible, housed separately from convicted prisoners. Offenders under the age of 21 are usually detained in a young offenders' institution, which may be a separate establishment or part of a prison.

Every prison establishment also has an independent board of visitors or visiting committee made up of local volunteers. Any prisoner whose complaint is not satisfied by the internal complaints procedures may complain to the Prisons Ombudsman for England and Wales.

HM PRISON SERVICE

Cleland House, Page Street, London SW1P 4LN (Tel: 020-7217 6000; Fax: 020-7217 6403; E-mail: prisons@homeoffice.gsi.gov.uk; Web: www.hmprisonservice.gov.uk).

Director-General: M. Narey
Staff Officer: Ms C. Stuart
Deputy Director-General: P. Wheatley
Director of High Security Prisons: P. Atherton
Director of Security: B. Clark
Director of Personnel: G. Hadley
Director of Finance and Procurement: J. Le Vay
Director of Corporate Affairs; Ms C. Pelham
Director of Resettlement: K. D. Sutton
Head of Prison Health Policy Unit:
Dr F. Harvey
Head of Prison Health Care Task Force:
J. Boyington

PRISONS OMBUDSMAN FOR ENGLAND AND WALES

Ashley House, 2 Monck Street, London SW1P 2BQ (Tel: 020-7276 2876; Fax: 020-7276 2860; Web: www.homeoffice.gov.uk/prisons/prisomb.htm).

250 Legal London

The post of Prisons Ombudsman was instituted in 1994. The Ombudsman is appointed by the Home Secretary and is an independent point of appeal for prisoners' grievances about their lives in prison, including disciplinary issues.

Ombudsman: Stephen Shaw

PAROLE BOARD FOR ENGLAND AND WALES

Abell House, John Islip Street, London SW1P 4LH (Tel: 020-7217 5314; Fax: 020-7217 5793; E-mail: info@paroleboard.gov.uk; Web: www.paroleboard.gov.uk).

The Board was constituted under the Criminal Justice Act 1967 and continued under the Criminal Justice Act 1991. It is an executive non-departmental public body and its duty is to advise the Home Secretary with respect to matters referred to it by him which are connected with the early release or recall of prisoners. Its functions include giving directions concerning the release on licence of prisoners serving discretionary life sentences and of certain prisoners serving long-term determinate sentences.

PRISONS

Belmarsh
Western Way, Thamesmead, London, SE28 0EB (Tel: 020-8317 2436; Fax: 020-8317 2421).
Governor: R. Chapman

Brixton
PO Box 369, Jebb Avenue, London, SW2 5XF (Tel: 020-8674 9811; Fax: 020-8671 7946).
Governor: R. Chapman

Chelmsford
200 Springfield Road, Chelmsford, Essex, CM2 6LQ).
Governor: Ms A. Gomme

Downview
Sutton Lane, Sutton, Surrey, SM2 5PD (Tel: 020-8770 7500; Fax: 020-8770 7673).
Governor: C. Lambert

Feltham
Bedfont Road, Feltham, Middx, TW13 4ND (Tel: 020-8890 0061; Fax: 020-8893 7496).
Governor: Nick Pascoe

High Down
Sutton Lane, Sutton, Surrey, SM2 5PJ (Tel: 020-8643 0063; Fax: 020-8643 2035).
Governor: E. R. Butt

Holloway
Parkhurst Road, London, N7 0NU (Tel: 020-7607 6747; Fax: 020-7700 0269).
Governor: D. Lancaster

Latchmere House
Church Road, Ham Common, Richmond, Surrey, TW10 5HH (Tel: 020-8948 0215; Fax: 020-8332 1359).
Governor: T. Hinchliffe

Pentonville
Caledonian Road, London, N7 8TT (Tel: 020-7607 5353; Fax: 020-7700 0244).
Governor: Gareth Davies

Wandsworth
PO Box 757, Heathfield Road, London, SW18 3HS (Tel: 020-8874 7292; Fax: 020-8877 0358).
Governor: S. Rimmer

Wormwood Scrubs
PO Box 757, Du Cane Road, London, W12 0AE (Tel: 020-8743 0311; Fax: 020-8749 5655).
Governor: S. Moore

NATIONAL PROBATION SERVICE OF ENGLAND AND WALES

The National Probation Service of England and Wales consists of probation officers and supporting staff who are employed by probation committees. There are composed of magistrates and members co-opted from the local community. It contributes to crime reduction through its work with offenders and liaison with the courts and the community.

The National Probation Service of England and Wales strives to develop strong and effective partnerships with organisations in the statutory and independent sector. The aims of the service are to: protect society from crime; to rehabilitate offenders; to supervise offenders effectively; to safeguard the interests of children.

In London there are five probation service areas covering inner, south east, south west and north east London and Middlesex.

Law Centres 251

Inner London
71/73 Great Peter Street, London SW1P 2BN (Tel: 020-7222 5656; Fax: 020-7222 0473).

London, North East
4th Floor, Olympic House, 28/42 Clements Road, Ilford IG1 1BA (Tel: 020-8514 5353).

London, South East
Crosby House, 9-13 Elmfield Road, Bromley BR1 1LT (Tel: 020-8464 3435).

London, South West
45 High Street, Kingston upon Thames KT1 1LQ (Tel: 020-8546 0018; Fax: 020-8549 8990).

Middlesex
Glen House, 4th Floor, 200 Tottenham Court Road, London W1P 9LA (Tel: 020-7436 7121).

OTHER LEGAL BODIES

GENERAL COUNCIL OF THE BAR

3 Bedford Row, London WC1R 4DB (Tel: 020-7242 0082; Fax: 020-7831 9217; Web: www.barcouncil.org.uk)

The General Council of the Bar is the professional body for barristers.

Chief Executive: Niall Morison

LAW CENTRES FEDERATION

Duchess House, 18-19 Warren Street, London W1T 5LR (Tel: 020-7387 8570; Fax: 020-7387 8368)

LAW CENTRES

Brent Community Law Centre: 389 High Road, Willesden, London NW10 2JR (Tel: 020-8451 1122; Fax: 020-8830 2462)

Camden Community Law Centre: 2a Prince of Wales Road, London NW5 3LG (Tel: 020-7485 6672; Fax: 020-7267 6218)

Central London Law Centre: 19 Whitcomb Street, London WC2H 7HA (Tel: 020-7839 2998; Fax: 020-7839 6158)

Greenwich Law Centre: 187 Trafalgar Road, London SE10 9EQ (Tel: 020-8853 2250; Fax: 020-8858 2018)

Hackney Law Centre: 236/8 Mare Street, London E8 1HE (Tel: 020-8985 8364; Fax: 020-8986 9891)

Hammersmith and Fulham Law Centre: 142/4 King Street, London W6 0QU (Tel: 020-8741 4021; Fax: 020-8741 1450)

Hillingdon Law Centre: 12 Harold Avenue, Hayes UB8 4QW (Tel: 020-8561 9400; Fax: 020-8756 0837)

Hounslow Law Centre: 51 Lampton Road, Hounslow TW3 1JG (Tel: 020-8570 9505; Fax: 020-8572 0730)

Islington Law Centre: 161 Hornsey Road, London N7 6DU (Tel: 020-7607 2461; Fax: 020-7700 0072)

North Kensington Law Centre: 74 Golbourne Road, London W10 5PS (Tel: 020-8969 7473; Fax: 020-8968 0934)

North Lambeth Law Centre: 14 Bowden Street, London SE11 5DS (Tel: 020-7582 4373; Fax: 020-7582 2148)

Lewisham Law Cente: 28 Deptford High Street, London SE8 3NU (Tel: 020-8692 5355; Fax: 020-8694 2516)

Newham Rights Centre: 285 Romford Road, Newham, London E7 9HJ (Tel: 020-8968 0417; Fax: 020-8519 7348)

Paddington Law Centre: 439 Harrow Road, London W10 4RE (Tel: 020-8960 3155; Fax: 020-8968 0417)

Plumstead Law Centre: 105 Plumstead High Street, London SE18 1SB (Tel: 020-8855 9817; Fax: 020-8316 7903)

Southwark Law Centre: Hanover Park House, 14-16 Hanover Park, London SE15 5HS (Tel: 020-7732 2008; Fax: 020-7732 2034)

Springfield Law Centre: Springfield Hospital, Glenburnie Road, London SW17 7DJ (Tel: 020-8767 6884; Fax: 020-8767 6996)

252 Legal London

Tottenham Law Centre: 415 Green Lanes, Haringey, London N4 1EZ (Tel: 020-8347 9710; Fax: 020-8347 9613)

Tower Hamlets Law Centre: 341 Commercial Road, London E1 2PS (Tel: 020-7791 0741; Fax: 020-7702 7302)

Wandsworth and Merton Law Centre: 101a Tooting High Street, London SW17 0SU (Tel: 020-8767 2777; Fax: 020-8767 2711)

ASSOCIATE MEMBERS OF THE LAW CENTRES FEDERATION IN LONDON

AIRE (Advice on Individual Rights in Europe): 74 Euro Link Business Centre, Effra Road, London SW2 1BZ (Tel: 020-7924 0927; Fax: 020-7733 6786).

Cambridge House Legal Centre: 137 Camberwell Road, London SE5 0HF (Tel: 020-7701 9499; Fax: 020-7703 3051).

Disability Law Service: Room 241, 49/51 Bedford Row, London WC1R 4LR (Tel: 020-7831 8031; Fax: 020-7831 5582).

Mary Ward Legal Advice Centre: 26-27 Boswell Street, London WC1N 3JZ (Tel: 020-7831 7079).

LAW COMMISSION

Conquest House, 37-38 John Street, Theobalds Road, London WC1N 2BQ (Tel: 020-7453 1220; Fax: 020-7453 1297; E-mail: secretary.lawcomm@gtnet.gov.uk; Web: www.lawcom.gov.uk).

The Law Commission was set up in 1965, under the Law Commissions Act 1965, to make proposals to the Government for the examination of the law in England and Wales and for its revision where it is unsuited for modern requirements, obscure, or otherwise unsatisfactory. It recommends to the Lord Chancellor programmes for the examination of different branches of the law and suggests whether the examination should be carried out by the Commission itself or by some other body. The Commission is also responsible for the preparation of Consolidation and Statute Law (Repeals) Bills.

Chairman: The Hon. Mr Justice Carnwath, CVO
Commissioners: C. Harpum; Prof. H. Beale; Prof. M.Partington; Judge A. Wilkie, QC
Secretary: M. W. Sayers

LAW SOCIETY

113 Chancery Lane, London WC2A 1PL (Tel: 020-7242 1222; Fax: 020-7831 0344; Web: www.lawsociety.org.uk; www.solicitors-online.com).
Greater London Regional Office: Newspaper House, 8-16 Great New Street, London EC4A 3EU (Tel: 020-7316 5556; Fax: 020-7320 5971).

The Law Society is the professional body for solicitors. Chief Executive: Janet Paraskeva

LAW SOCIETY GOVERNMENT GROUP

113 Chancery Lane, London WC2A 1PL (Tel: 020-7242 1222; Web: www.lawsociety.org.uk).

The Law Society Government Group is a part of the Law Society whose aim is to represent the interests of local authority solicitors and to provide support to local government solicitors. All solicitors working in local government automatically become part of this group.

Chairman 2001-2002: Nigel Roberts, West Oxfordshire District Council, Woodgreen, Witney, Oxon OX8 6NB.

LCIA (LONDON COURT OF INTERNATIONAL ARBITRATION)

The International Dispute Resolution Centre, 8 Breams Buildings, Chancery Lane, London EC4A 1HP (Tel: 020 7405 8008; Fax: 020 7405 8009; E-mail: lcia@lcia-arbitration.com Web: www.lcia-arbitration.com/lcia/)

The LCIA is probably the longest-established of all the major international institutions for dispute resolution, but also one of the most modern and forward looking. Its organisation, operation and outlook and the services which it provides are worldwide. Although based in London it is an international institution, offering efficiency, flexibility and neutrality to all parties involved in dispute resolution under its auspices. The LCIA provides cost-effective administration of arbitration, mediation and other methods of ADR in any venue and under any system of law.

Director-General and Registrar:
Adrian Winstanley

LEGAL SERVICES COMMISSION

85 Gray's Inn Road, London WC1X 8TX (Tel: 020-7759 0000; Web: www.legalservices.gov.uk)

The Access to Justice Act 1999 replaced the legal aid system with two new schemes: the Community Legal Service and the Criminal Defence System. It established a Legal Services Commission to run the two schemes and replace the Legal Aid Board. The Commission assumed this role on 1 April 2000. The Community Legal Service fund replaces the legal aid fund in a way that reflects priorities set by the Lord Chancellor and its duty to secure the best possible value for money, to procure or provide a range of legal services. The Commission plans what can be done towards meeting the need for legal services, and liaise with other funders of legal services to facilitate the development of co-ordinated plans for making the best use of all available resources. The intention is to develop comprehensive referral networks of legal service providers of assured quality, offering the widest possible access to information and advice about the law and help with legal problems. The Criminal Defence Service will replace the legal aid system in criminal cases. The new scheme will ensure that people suspected or accused of crime are properly represented, while securing better value for money than is possible under the legal aid scheme. The Criminal Defence Service was launched in April 2001.

Chairman: Peter G. Birch, CBE
Members: Michael Barnes, CBE; Richard Buxton; Anthony Edwards; Philip Ely; Brian Harvey; Juliet Herzog; Sheila Hewitt; Yvonne Mosquito; Steve Orchard, CBE; Richard Penn; Jim Shearer

VALUATION
Valuation Office Agency
New Court, 48 Carey Street, London WC2A 2JE (Tel: 020-7506 1700; Fax: 020-7506 1998; E-mail: custserv.voa@gtnet.gov.uk; Web: www.voa.gov.uk).

Chief Executive: Michael A. Johns

VALUATION TRIBUNALS
Central London Valuation Tribunal
2nd Floor, Black Lion House, 45 Whitechapel Road, London E1 1DU (Tel: 020-7497 1757; Fax: 020-7497 0752; E-mail: central.london.vt@vto.gsx.gov.uk; Web: www.valuationtribunals.gov.uk).

Clerk of the Tribunal: W. R. Shaw

London North East Valuation Tribunal
2nd Floor, Black Lion House, 45 Whitechapel Road, London E1 1DU (Tel: 020-7247 3898; Fax: 020-7247 6598; E-mail: london.northeast.vt@vto.gsx.gov.uk; Web: www.valuationtribunals.gov.uk).

Clerk of the Tribunal: A. Masella

London South West Valuation Tribunal
4th Floor, AMP House, Dingwall Road, Croydon CR0 9XA (Tel: 020-8681 8843; Fax: 020-8686 7444; E-mail: london.south.vt@vto.gsx.gov.uk; Web: www.valuationtribunals.gov.uk).
Clerk of the Tribunal: Peter L. Kain

PUBLIC RECORDS
Public Records Office: Kew, Richmond, Surrey TW9 4DU (Tel: 020-8876 3444; Web: www.pro.gov.uk).

Births Deaths and Marriage Certificates: Family Record Centre, 1 Myddleton Street, London EC1R 1UW (General enquiries) Tel: 020-8392 5300; Certificate Enquiries tel: 0151-471 4200. For your local Registrar of Births, Deaths and Marriages see the Governed London section and your Local Council's entry.

Divorce and Adoption: Family Proceedings Department, First Avenue House, 42-49 High Holborn, London WC1V 6NP

Wills before 1858, Family Record Centre, 1 Myddleton Street, London EC1R 1UW General enquiries (Tel: 020-8392 5300).

Wills after 1858, The Probate Department of the Principal Registry of the Family Division, First Division, First avenue House, 42-49 High Holborn, London WC1V 6NP (Tel: 020-7947 6000.)

LEGAL NOTES

These notes outline certain aspects of the law as they might affect the average person. They are intended only as a broad guideline and are by no means definitive. The law is constantly changing so expert advice should always be taken. In some cases, sources of further information are given in these notes.

It is always advisable to consult a solicitor without delay; timely advice will set your mind at rest but sitting on your rights can mean that you lose them. Anyone who does not have a solicitor already can contact the Citizens' Advice Bureau or the Law Society of England and Wales.

The legal aid and assistance schemes exist to make the help of a lawyer available to those who would not otherwise be able to afford one. Entitlement depends on an individual's means but a solicitor or Citizens' Advice Bureau will be able to advise about entitlement.

Adoption of Children

In England and Wales the adoption of children is mainly governed by the Adoption Act 1976 and the Children Act 1989.

Anyone over 21, or 18 if the natural birth parent wants to adopt with a partner who is 21 or over, can legally adopt a child. Married couples must adopt 'jointly', unless one partner cannot be found, is incapable of making an application, or if a separation is likely to be permanent. Unmarried couples may not adopt 'jointly' although one partner in that couple may adopt. The only organisations allowed to arrange adoptions are the social services departments of local authorities or voluntary agencies which are registered with the local authorities.

Once an adoption has been arranged, a court order is necessary to make it legal. These are obtained from the High Court (Family Division) or from a county, magistrates or family proceedings court. The child's natural parents (or guardians) must consent to the adoption, unless the court dispenses with the consent, e.g. where the natural parent has neglected the child or is incapable of giving consent. Once adopted, the child has the same status as a child born to the adoptive parents and the natural parents cease to have any rights or responsibilities where the child is concerned. The adopted child will be treated as the natural child of the adoptive parents for the purposes of intestate succession, national insurance, family allowances, etc. The adopted child ceases to have any rights to the estates of his/her natural parents. It is an offence for a person other than an adoption agency to make arrangements for the adoption of a child or place a child for adoption unless the proper adopter is a relative or is acting in accordance with a court order. It is also an offence to receive a child who is placed in breach of this rule and it is an offence to make or receive payments for adoption.

Registration and Certificates

All adoptions in England and Wales are registered in the Adopted Children Register kept by the Office of National Statistics. Certificates from the registers can be obtained in a similar way to birth certificates.

Tracing Natural Parents or Children Who Have Been Adopted

An adult adopted person may apply to the Registrar-General for information to enable him/her to obtain a full birth certificate. For those adopted before 12 November 1975 it is obligatory to receive counselling services before this information is given; for those adopted after that date counselling services are optional. There is also an Adoption Contact Register (created after the 1989 Act) in which details of adult adopted people and of their relatives may be recorded. The BAAF (see below) can provide addresses of organisations which offer advice, information and counselling to adopted people, adoptive parents and people who have had their children adopted.

Further information can be obtained from:

British Agencies for Adoption and Fostering (BAAF)
Skyline House, 200 Union Street, London SE1 0LX. Tel: 020-7593 2000

Births (Registration)

The birth of a child must be registered within 42 days of birth at the register office of the district in which the baby was born. In England and Wales it is possible to give the particulars to be registered at any other register office. Responsibility for registering the birth rests with the parents, except in the case of an illegitimate child, when the mother is responsible for registration. Responsibility rests firstly with the parents but if they fail, particulars may be given to the registrar by:

Legal Notes 255

— the occupier of the house in which the baby was born
— a person present at the birth
— the person who is responsible for the child

Failure to register the birth within 42 days without reasonable cause may leave the parents liable to a penalty in England and Wales.

If the parents were married at the time of the birth, either parent may register the birth and details about both parents will be entered on the register. If the parents were unmarried at the time of the birth, the father's details are entered only if both parents attend or if the parents have made a statutory declaration confirming the identity of the father. Copies of the forms necessary to make such a declaration are available at the register offices. A short birth certificate is issued free when the birth is registered.

Still Births

If a baby is stillborn, i.e. born dead after the 24th week of pregnancy, the birth must be registered. The doctor or midwife who attends the birth or afterwards examines the body of the child will issue a Medical Certificate of Stillbirth and this must be presented at the register office.

Re-registration

In certain circumstances it may be necessary to re-register a birth, e.g. where the birth of an illegitimate child is legitimated by the subsequent marriage of the parents. It is also possible to re-register the birth of an illegitimate child so that the father's name is entered on the register.

Birth Abroad

Births of British subjects occurring abroad are registered with consular officers and certificates of birth are subsequently available from the Registrar-General.

Certificates of Births, Deaths and Marriages

Certificates of births, deaths or marriages that have taken place in England and Wales since 1837 can be obtained from the Office of National Statistics (General Register Office). Applications can be made:
— by a personal visit to the Family Records Centre, London
— by postal application to the General Register Office, Southport

Certificates are also available from the Superintendent Registrar for the district in which the event took place or, in the case of marriage certificates, from the minister of the church in which the marriage took place. Any register office can advise about the best way to obtain certificates.

The fees for certificates (from 1 April 2001) are:
— Obtained from Registrar who registered the birth, death or marriage
— Standard certificate, £3.50
— Short certificate of birth other than the first issued at the time of birth registration, £5.00

Obtained from Superintendent Registrar
— Standard certificate, £6.50
— Short certificate of birth, £5.00

From the Family Records Centre, London/by post from the General Register Office, Southport
— Standard certificate of birth, death or marriage Personal application, £6.50

— Standard certificate of adoption:
Personal application, £5.00

— Short certificate of birth:
Personal application, £6.50

— Short certificate of adoption:
Personal application, £5.00

Indexes prepared from the registers are available for searching by the public at the Family Records Centre in London or at a Superintendent Registrar's Office; indexes at the latter relate only to births, deaths and marriages which occurred in that registration district. There is no charge for searching the indexes in the Public Search Room at the Family Records Centre but a general search fee is charged for searches at a Superintendent Registrar's Office. A fee is charged for verifying index references against the records.

The Society of Genealogists has many records of baptisms, marriages and deaths prior to 1837.

Further information can be obtained from:

The General Register Office

Office for National Statistics, Smedley Hydro, Trafalgar Road, Birkdale, Southport, Merseyside PR82HH (Tel: 01704-569824)

Family Records Centre

1 Myddelton Street, London EC1R 1UW

The Society of Genealogists

14 Charterhouse Buildings, Goswell Road, London EC1M 7BA (Tel: 020-7251 8799)

British Citizenship

The British Nationality Act 1981 which came into force on 1 January 1983 established three types of citizenship to replace the single form of Citizenship of the UK and Colonies created by the British Nationality Act 1948. The three forms of citizenship are: British Citizenship; British Dependent Territories Citizenship; and British Overseas Citizenship. Three residual categories were created: British Subjects; British Protected Persons; and British Nationals (Overseas).

British Citizenship

Almost everyone who was a citizen of the UK and colonies and had a right of abode in the UK prior to the 1981 Act became British citizens when the Act came into force. British citizens have the right to live permanently in the UK and are free to leave and re-enter the UK at any time.

A person born on or after 1 January 1983 in the UK (including, for this purpose, the Channel Islands and the Isle of Man) is entitled to British citizenship if he/she falls into one of the following categories:
— he/she has a parent who is a British citizen
— he/she has a parent who is settled in the UK
— he/she is a newborn infant found abandoned in the UK
— his/her parents subsequently settle in the UK
— he/she lives in the UK for the first ten years of his/her life and is not absent for more than 90 days in each of those years
— he/she is adopted in the UK and one of the adopters is a British Citizen

A person born outside the UK may acquire British citizenship if he/she falls into one of the following categories:
— he/she has a parent who is a British citizen otherwise than by descent, e.g. a parent who was born in the UK

— he/she has a parent who is a British citizen serving the Crown overseas
— the Home Secretary consents to his/her registration while he/she is a minor
— he/she is a British Dependent Territories citizen, a British Overseas citizen, a British subject or a British protected person and has been lawfully resident in the UK for five years
— he/she is a British Dependent Territories citizen who acquired that citizenship from a connection with Gibraltar
— he/she is adopted (see above) or naturalised (see below)

Where parents are married, the status of either may confer citizenship on their child. If a child is illegitimate, the status of the mother determines the child's citizenship.

Under the 1981 Act, Commonwealth citizens and citizens of the Republic of Ireland were entitled to registration as British citizens before 1 January 1988. In 1985 citizens of the Falkland Islands were granted British citizenship.

Renunciation of British citizenship must be registered with the Home Secretary and will be revoked if no new citizenship or nationality is acquired within six months. If the renunciation was required in order to retain or acquire another citizenship or nationality, the citizenship may be reacquired once.

British Dependent Territories Citizenship

Under the 1981 Act, this type of citizenship was conferred on citizens of the UK and colonies by birth, naturalisation or registration in British Dependent Territories. British Dependent Territories citizens may be entitled to registration as British citizens on completion of five years' legal residence in the UK.

On 1 July 1997 citizens of Hong Kong who did not qualify to register as British citizens under the British Nationality (Hong Kong) Act 1990 lost their British Dependent Territories citizenship on the handover of sovereignty to China; they may, however, have applied to register as British Nationals (Overseas).

Eligibility for British Dependent Territories citizenship is determined by similar rules to those for acquiring British citizenship, except that the connection is with the dependent territory rather than with the UK.

Legal Notes

British Overseas Citizenship

Under the 1981 Act, this type of citizenship was conferred on any UK and colonies citizens who did not qualify for British citizenship or citizenship of the British Dependent Territories. British Overseas citizenship may be acquired by the wife and minor children of a British Overseas citizen in certain circumstances. British Overseas citizens may be entitled to registration as British citizens on completion of five years' legal residence in the UK.

Residual Categories

British subjects, British protected persons and British Nationals (Overseas) may be entitled to registration as British citizens on completion of five years' legal residence in the UK.

Citizens of the Republic of Ireland who were also British subjects before 1 January 1949 can retain that status if they fulfil certain conditions.

European Union Citizenship

British citizens (including Gibraltarians who are registered as such) are also EU citizens and are entitled to travel freely to other EU countries to work, study, reside and set up a business. EU citizens have the same rights with respect to the United Kingdom.

Naturalisation

Naturalisation is granted at the discretion of the Home Secretary. The basic requirements are five years' residence (three years if the applicant is married to a British citizen), good character, adequate knowledge of the English, Welsh or Scottish Gaelic language, and an intention to reside permanently in the UK.

Status of Aliens

Aliens may not hold public office or vote in Britain and they may not own a British ship or aircraft. Citizens of the Republic of Ireland are not deemed to be aliens. Certain provisions of the Immigration and Asylum Act 1999 came into force on the 11th November 1999. This act makes provision about immigration and asylum and about procedures in connection with marriage on superintendent registrar's certificate.

CONSUMER LAW

Sale of Goods

A sale of goods contract is the most common type of contract. It is governed by the Sale of Goods Act 1979 (as amended by the Sale and Supply of Goods Act 1994). The Act provides protection for buyers by implying terms into every sale of goods contract. These terms are:

— a condition that the seller will pass good title to the buyer (unless the seller agrees to transfer only such title as he has)
— where the seller sells goods by reference to a description, a condition that the goods will match that description and, where the sale is by sample and description, a condition that the bulk of the goods will correspond with such sample and description
— where goods are sold by a business seller, a condition that the goods will be of satisfactory quality if they meet the standard that a reasonable person would regard as satisfactory taking into account any description of the goods, the price, and all other relevant circumstances. The quality of the goods includes their state and condition, relevant aspects being whether they are suitable for their common purpose, their appearance and finish, freedom from minor defects and their safety and durability. This term will not be implied, however, if a buyer has examined the goods and should have noticed the defect or if the seller specifically drew the buyer's attention to the defect
— where goods are sold by a business seller, a condition that the goods are reasonably fit for any purpose made known to the seller by the buyer, unless the buyer does not rely on the seller's judgement, or it is not reasonable for him/her to do so
— where goods are sold by sample, conditions that the bulk of the sample will correspond with the sample in quality, that the buyer will have a reasonable opportunity of comparing the two and that the goods are free from any defect rendering them unsatisfactory which would not be obvious from the sample

Some of the above terms can be excluded from contracts by the seller. The seller's right to do this is, however, restricted by the Unfair Contract Terms Act 1977. The Act offers more protection to a buyer who 'deals as a consumer', that is where the sale is a business sale, the goods are of a type ordinarily bought for private use and the goods are bought by a buyer who is not a business buyer. In a sale by auction or competitive tender, a buyer never deals as consumer. Also, a seller can never exclude the implied term as to title mentioned above.

Hire-purchase Agreements

Terms similar to those implied in contracts of sales of goods are implied into contracts of hire-purchase, under the Supply of Goods (Implied Terms) Act 1973. The 1977 Act limits the exclusion of these implied terms as before.

Supply of Goods and Services

Under the Supply of Goods and Services Act 1982, similar terms are also implied in other types of contract under which ownership of goods passes, e.g. a contract for 'work and materials' such as supplying new parts while servicing a car, and contracts for the hire of goods. These types of contracts have additional implied terms:
— that the supplier will use reasonable care and skill
— that the supplier will carry out the service in a reasonable time (unless the time has been agreed)
— that the supplier will make a reasonable charge (unless the charge has already been agreed)

The 1977 Act limits the exclusion of these implied terms in a similar manner as before.

Unfair Terms

The Unfair Terms in Consumer Contracts Regulations 1994 apply to contracts between business sellers (or suppliers of goods and services) and consumers, where the terms have not been individually negotiated, i.e where the terms were drafted in advance so that the consumer was unable to influence those terms. An unfair term is one which operates to the detriment of the consumer. An unfair term does not bind the consumer but the contract will continue to bind the parties if it is capable of existing without the unfair term. The regulations contain a non-exhaustive list of terms which are regarded as unfair. Whether a term is regarded as fair or not will depend on many factors, including the nature of the goods or services, the surrounding circumstances (such as the bargaining strength of both parties) and the other terms in the contract.

The 1994 Regulations have been replaced by The Unfair Terms in Consumer Contracts Regulations 1999 from October 1999. These new Regulations give the same protection as the 1994 Regulations and stress the importance of plain English in contractual documents.

Trade Descriptions

It is a criminal offence under the Trade Descriptions Act 1968 for a business seller to apply a false trade description of goods or to supply or offer to supply any goods to which a false description has been applied. A 'trade description' includes descriptions of quality, size, composition, fitness for purpose and method, and place and date of manufacture of the goods. It is also an offence to give a false indication of the price of goods.

Fair Trading

The Fair Trading Act 1973 is designed to protect the consumer. It provides for the appointment of a Director-General of Fair Trading, one of whose duties is to review commercial activities in the UK relating to the supply of goods and services to consumers. An example of a practice which has been prohibited by a reference made under this Act is that of business sellers posing in advertisements as private sellers.

Consumer Protection

Under the Consumer Protection Act 1987, producers of goods are liable for any injury or for damage caused by a defect in their product (subject to certain defences).

The Consumer Protection (Cancellation of Contracts Concluded Away from Business Premises) Regulations 1987 allow consumers a seven-day period in which to cancel contracts for the supply of goods and services, where the contracts were made during an unsolicited visit to the consumer's home or workplace. This only applies to certain contracts.

Consumer Credit

In matters relating to the provision of credit (or the supply of goods on hire or hire-purchase), consumers are also protected by the Consumer Credit Act 1974. Under this Act a licence, issued by the Director-General of Fair Trading, is required to conduct a consumer credit or consumer hire business or to deal in credit brokerage, debt adjusting, counselling or collecting. Any 'fit' person may apply to the Director-General of Fair Trading for a licence, which is normally renewable after ten years. A licence is not necessary if such types of business are only transacted occasionally, or if only exempt agreements are involved. The provisions of the Act only apply to 'regulated' agreements, i.e. those that are with individuals or partnerships, those that are not exempt (such as certain local authority

and building society loans), and those where the total credit does not exceed £25,000. Provisions include:
— the terms of the regulated agreement can be altered by the creditor provided the agreement gives him/her the right to do so; in such cases the debtor must be given proper notice of this
— in order for a creditor to enforce a regulated agreement, the agreement must comply with certain formalities and must be properly executed. The debtor must also be given specified information by the creditor or his/her broker or agent during the negotiations which take place before the signing of the agreement. The agreement must state certain information such as the amount of credit, the annual interest rate, the amount and timing of repayments
— if an agreement is signed other than at the creditor's (or credit broker's or negotiator's) place of business and oral representations were made in the debtor's presence during discussions pre-agreement, the debtor has a right to cancel the agreement. Time for cancellation expires five clear days after the debtor receives a second copy of the agreement. The agreement must inform the debtor of his right to cancel and how to cancel
— if the debtor is in arrears (or otherwise in breach of the agreement), the creditor must serve a default notice before taking any action such as repossessing the goods
— if the agreement is a hire-purchase or conditional sale agreement, the creditor cannot repossess the goods without a court order if the debtor has paid one-third of the total price of the goods
— in agreements where the debtor is required to make grossly exorbitant payments or where the agreement grossly contravenes the ordinary principles of fair trading, the debtor may request that the court alter or set aside some of the terms of the agreement. The agreement can also be reopened during enforcement proceedings by the court itself

Where a credit reference agency has been used to check the debtor's financial standing, the creditor must give the agency's name to the debtor, who is entitled to see the agency's file on him. A fee of £1 is payable to the agency.

Proceedings Against the Crown

Until 1947, proceedings against the Crown were generally possible only by a procedure known as a petition of right, which put the litigant at a considerable disadvantage. The Crown Proceedings Act 1947 placed the Crown (not the Sovereign in his/her private capacity, but as the embodiment of the State) largely in the same position as a private individual. The Act did not, however, extinguish or limit the Crown's prerogative or statutory powers, and it granted immunity to HM ships and aircraft. It also left certain Crown privileges unaffected. The Act largely abolished the special procedures which previously applied to civil proceedings by and against the Crown. Civil proceedings may be instituted against the appropriate government department or against the Attorney-General.

DEATHS

When a Death Occurs

If the death (including stillbirth) was expected, the doctor who attended the deceased during their final illness should be contacted. If the death was sudden or unexpected, the family doctor (if known) and police should be contacted. If the cause of death is quite clear the doctor will provide:
— a medical certificate that shows the cause of death
— a formal notice that states that the doctor has signed the medical certificate and that explains how to get the death registered

If the death was known to be caused by a natural illness but the doctor wishes to know more about the cause of death, he/she may ask the relatives for permission to carry out a post-mortem examination. This should not delay the funeral.

In England and Wales a coroner is responsible for investigating deaths occurring in the following circumstances:
— where there is no doctor who can issue a medical certificate of cause of death; or
— when no doctor has treated the deceased during his or her last illness or when the doctor attending the patient did not see him or her within 14 days before death, or after death; or
— when the death occurred during an operation or before recovery from the effect of an anaesthetic; or
— when the death was sudden and unexplained or attended by suspicious circumstances; or
— when the death might be due to an industrial injury or disease, or to accident, violence, neglect or abortion, or to any kind of poisoning; or
— the death occurred in prison or in police custody

The doctor will write on the formal notice that the death has been referred to the coroner; if the post mortem shows that death was due to natural causes, the coroner may issue a notification which gives the cause of death so that the death can be registered. If the cause of death was violent or unnatural, the coroner is obliged to hold an inquest.

Registering a Death

In England and Wales the death must be registered by the registrar of births and deaths for the district in which it occurred; details can be obtained from the telephone directory (under registration of births and deaths and marriages), from the doctor or local council, or at a post office or police station. From April 1997, information concerning a death can be given before any registrar of births and deaths in England and Wales. The registrar will pass the relevant details to the registrar for the district where the death occurred, who will then register the death or, if different in the registration district in which the death took place. In England and Wales the death must normally be registered within five days. If the death has been referred to the coroner/local procurator fiscal it cannot be registered until the registrar has received authority from the coroner/local procurator fiscal to do so. Failure to register a death involves a penalty in England and Wales.

If the death occurred at a house, the death may be registered by:
— any relative of the deceased
— any person present at the death
— the occupier or any inmate of the house or hospital if he/she knew of the occurrence of the death
— any person making the funeral arrangements

The person registering the death should take the medical certificate of the cause of death with them; it is also useful, though not essential, to take the deceased's birth and marriage certificates, medical card (if possible), pension documents and life assurance details. The registrar will issue a certificate for burial or cremation and a certificate of registration of death; both are free of charge. A death certificate is a certified copy of the entry in the death register; these can be provided on payment of a fee and may be required for the following purposes:
— the will
— bank and building society accounts
— savings bank certificates and premium bonds
— insurance policies
— pension claims

If the death occurred abroad or on a foreign ship or aircraft, the death should be registered according to the local regulations of the relevant country and a death certificate should be obtained. The death can also be registered with the British Consul in that country and a record will be kept at the General Register Office. This avoids the expense of bringing the body back.

After 12 months of death or the finding of a dead body, no death can be registered without the consent of the Registrar-General.

Burial and Cremation

In most circumstances in England and Wales a certificate for burial or cremation must be obtained from the registrar before the burial or cremation can take place. If the death has been referred to the coroner, an order for burial or a certificate for cremation must be obtained.

Funeral costs can normally be repaid out of the deceased's estate and will be given priority over any other claims. If the deceased has left a will it may contain directions concerning the funeral; however, these directions need not be followed by the executor.

The deceased's papers should also indicate whether a grave space had already been arranged. Most town churchyards and many suburban churchyards are no longer open for burial because they are full. Most cemeteries are non-denominational and may be owned by local authorities or private companies; fees vary.

If the body is to be cremated, an application form, two cremation certificates (for which there is a charge) or a certificate for cremation if the death was referred to the coroner, and a certificate signed by the medical referee must be completed in addition to the certificate for burial or cremation (the form is not required if the coroner has issued a certificate for cremation). All the forms are available from the funeral director or crematorium. Most crematoria are run by local authorities; the fees usually include the medical referee's fee and the use of the chapel. Ashes may be scattered, buried in a churchyard or cemetery, or kept.

The registrar must be notified of the date, place and means of disposal of the body within 96 hours. If the death occurred abroad or on a foreign ship or aircraft, a local burial or cremation may be arranged. If the body is to be brought back to England or Wales, a death certificate from the relevant country or an authorisation for the removal of the body from the country of death from the coroner or relevant authority will be required. To arrange a funeral in England or Wales an authenticated translation of a foreign death certificate or a death certificate issued in Scotland or Northern Ireland which must show the cause of death, is needed, together with a certificate of no liability to register from the registrar in England and Wales in whose sub-district it is intended to bury or cremate the body. If it is intended to cremate the body a cremation order will be required from the Home Office or a certificate for cremation.

Further information can be obtained from:

The General Register Office

Office for National Statistics, Smedley Hydro, Trafalgar Road, Birkdale, Southport, Merseyside PR8 2HH (Tel: 01704-569824)

DIVORCE AND RELATED MATTERS

There are two types of matrimonial suit: those seeking the annulment of a marriage, and those seeking a judicial separation or divorce. To obtain an annulment, judicial separation or divorce in England and Wales, one or both of the parties must have their permanent home in England and Wales when the petition is started, or have been living in England and Wales for at least a year on the day the petition is started. All cases are commenced in divorce county courts or in the Divorce Registry in London. If a suit is defended it may be transferred to the High Court.

Nullity of Marriage

Various circumstances will render a marriage invalid from the beginning including if: the marriage has not been consummated; one partner had a venereal disease at the time of the marriage and the other did not know about it; the female partner was pregnant with another person's child at the time of the marriage and the male partner did not know of the pregnancy; the parties were within the prohibited degrees of consanguinity, affinity or adoption; the parties were not male and female; either of the parties was already married; either of the parties was under the age of 16; the formalities of the marriage were defective, e.g. the marriage did not take place in an authorised building, and both parties knew of the defect. Declarations of nullity are sought in very few cases.

Separation

A couple may enter into an agreement to separate by consent but for the agreement to be valid it must be followed by an immediate separation; a solicitor should be contacted.

Judicial separation does not dissolve a marriage and it is not necessary to prove that the marriage has irretrievably broken down. Either party can petition for a judicial separation at any time; the grounds listed below as grounds for divorce are also grounds for judicial separation. To petition for judicial separation the parties do not have to prove that they have been married for 12 months or more.

Divorce

Neither party can petition for divorce until at least one year after the date of the marriage. The sole ground for divorce is the irretrievable breakdown of the marriage; this must be proved on one or more of the following grounds:

— the respondent has committed adultery and the petitioner finds it intolerable to live with him/her; however the petitioner cannot rely on an act of adultery by the other party if they have lived together for more than six months after the discovery that adultery had been committed

— the respondent has behaved in such a way that the petitioner cannot reasonably be expected to continue living with him/her

— the respondent deserted the petitioner for two years immediately before the petition. Desertion may be defined as a voluntary withdrawal from cohabitation by the respondent without just cause and against the wishes of the petitioner; where one party is guilty of serious misconduct which forces the other party to leave, the party at fault is said to be guilty of constructive desertion

— the respondent and the petitioner have lived separately for two years immediately before the petition and the respondent consents to the decree

— the respondent and the petitioner have lived separately for five years immediately before the petition

A total period of less than six months during which the parties have resumed living together is disregarded in determining whether the prescribed period of separation or desertion has been continuous (but cannot be included as part of the period of separation).

The Matrimonial Causes Act 1973 requires the solicitor for the petitioner in certain cases to certify whether the possibility of a reconciliation has been discussed with the petitioner.

(The Family Law Act 1996 provides that irretrievable breakdown would be the sole ground for divorce; the partner initiating the divorce would be required to attend an information session about the nature of divorce and the options available; and divorce would be granted after one year, or 18 months if the couple have children, during which time the couple would have the chance to take part in mediation sessions. These changes may not be implemented at all as the pilot schemes have not been very successful).

The Decree Nisi

A decree nisi does not dissolve or annul the marriage but must be obtained before a divorce or annulment can take place. Where the suit is undefended, the evidence normally takes the form of a sworn written statement made by the petitioner which is considered by a district judge. If the judge is satisfied that the petitioner has proved the contents of the petition, he/she will set a date for the pronouncement of the decree nisi in open court; neither party need attend.

If the judge is not satisfied that the petitioner has proved the contents of the petition, or if the suit is defended, the petition will be heard in open court with the parties giving oral evidence.

The Decree Absolute

The decree nisi is usually made absolute after six weeks and on the application of the petitioner. If the judge thinks it may be necessary to exercise any of his/her powers under the Children Act 1989, he/she can in exceptional circumstances delay the granting of the decree absolute. The decree absolute dissolves or annuls the marriage.

Children

Neither parent is now awarded 'custody' of any children of the marriage in England and Wales. Both parents, if married, have 'parental responsibility'. Either parent can exercise this, independently of the other. Any dispute between the parents can be resolved by the courts. In all court cases concerning children, whether connected to a matrimonial suit or not, the welfare of the child is the paramount consideration.

Maintenance, etc.

Either party may be liable to pay maintenance to their former spouse. If there were any children of the marriage, both parents have a legal responsibility to support them financially if they can afford to do so. These so-called ancillary matters, including any property settlements, may be settled before the divorce goes through but currently can go on long after the marriage is dissolved.

The courts are responsible for assessing maintenance for the former spouse, taking into account each party's income and essential outgoings and other aspects of the case. The court also deals with any maintenance for a child which has been treated by the spouses as a 'child of the family', e.g. a stepchild, and any property settlements.

The Child Support Agency (CSA) was set up under the Child Support Act 1991 and is now responsible for assessing the maintenance that absent parents should pay for their natural or adopted children (whether or not a marriage has taken place). The CSA accepts applications only when all the people involved are habitually resident in the UK; the courts will continue to deal with cases where one of the people involved lives abroad. The CSA deals with all new cases, and is gradually taking on cases where the parent with care (or his/her new partner) was already receiving income support, family credit or disability working allowance before 5 April 1993. People with existing court orders or written maintenance agreements made before 5 April 1993 should continue to use the courts. Where it is already collecting child maintenance, the CSA has the power to offer a collection and enforcement service for certain other payments of maintenance.

A formula is used to work out how much child maintenance is payable. The formula ensures that after the payment of child maintenance the absent parent's income, and that of any second family he/she may now have, remains significantly above basic income support rates. Also, no absent parent will normally be assessed to pay more than 30 per cent of his/her net income in current child maintenance, or more than 33 per cent if he/she is also liable for any arrears. Absent parents are normally expected to pay at least a minimum amount of child maintenance.

A scheme has begun to be introduced since the end of 1996 which allows departures from the formula in certain tightly defined circumstances, e.g. the high costs of travel to maintain contact with a child, or to have a property and capital transfer ('clean break' settlement) entered into before April 1993 taken into account; there will also be some additional grounds which may result in liability being increased.

Some cases involving unusual circumstances are treated as special cases and the assessment is modified. Where there is financial need (e.g. because of disability or continuing education), maintenance may be ordered by the court for children even beyond the age of 18.

The level of maintenance is reviewed automatically every two years. Either parent can report a change of circumstances and request a review at any time. An independent complaints examiner for the CSA was appointed in early 1997.

If the absent parent does not pay the child maintenance, the CSA may make an order for payments to be deducted directly from his/her salary or wages; if all other methods fail, the CSA may take court action to enforce the payment.

Court Orders

Magistrates' courts used for domestic proceedings are now called family proceedings courts. A spouse can apply to the family proceedings court for a court order on the ground that the other spouse:
— has failed to pay reasonable maintenance for the applicant
— has failed to make a proper contribution towards the reasonable maintenance of a 'child of the family'
— has deserted the applicant
— has behaved in such a way that the applicant cannot reasonably be expected to live with the respondent

If the case is proved, the court can order:
— periodical payments for the applicant and/or a 'child of the family'
— a lump sum payment to the applicant and/or a 'child of the family'

In deciding what orders (if any) to make, the court must consider guidelines which are similar to those governing financial orders in divorce cases. There are also special provisions relating to consent orders and separation by agreement. An order may be enforceable even if the parties are living together, but in some cases it will cease to have effect if they continue to do so for six months.

Matrimonial Property

Married couples can own property in two ways. The first is according to the title deeds (joint ownership) and the second relates to contributions to the property (beneficial interest). Just because a couple jointly own a property doesn't mean that in the event of divorce the proceeds of matrimonial property will be distributed evenly. When deciding on what financial orders to make, the court will take into consideration the length of the marriage, the parties' ages, the parties' needs, the parties' earning capacity and the needs of children to the marriage.

Cohabiting Couples

Rights for unmarried couples are not the same as for married couples. By virtue of this it is worth considering entering into a contract which establishes how money and property should be divided in the event that the relationship breaks down. These can be drafted by a solicitor and are commonly known as 'separation deeds' or 'cohabitation contracts'.

Domestic Violence

If one spouse has been subjected to violence at the hands of the other, it is now possible to obtain a court order very quickly to restrain further violence and if necessary to have the other spouse excluded from the home. Such orders may also relate to unmarried couples and to a range of other relationships.

Further information can be obtained from any divorce county court, solicitor or Citizens' Advice Bureau, the Lord Chancellor's Department, or the following:

The Principal Registry

First Avenue House, 42-49 High Holborn, London WC1V 6NP (Tel: 020-7947 6000)

The Child Support Agency

Longbenton, Benton Park Road, Newcastle upon Tyne NE98 1ZZ (Tel: 0191-213 5000)

EMPLOYMENT LAW

Pay and Conditions

The Employment Rights Act 1996 consolidates the statutory provisions relating to employees' rights. Employers must give each employee based in Great Britain and employed for more than one month a written statement containing the following information:
— names of employer and employee
— date when employment began
— remuneration and intervals at which it will be paid
— job title or description of job
— hours and place(s) of work
— holiday entitlement and holiday pay
— entitlement to sick leave and sick pay
— details of pension scheme(s)
— length of notice period that employer and employee need to give to terminate employment, or the end date for a fixed-term contract
— details of any collective agreement which affects the terms of employment

264 Legal London

— details of disciplinary and grievance procedures
— if the employee is to work outside the UK for more than one month, the period of such work and the currency in which payment is made

This must be given to the employee within two months of the start of their employment. The Working Time Regulation 1998 and the National Minimum Wage Act now supplement the 1996 Act.

Sick Pay

Employees absent from work through illness or injury are entitled to receive Statutory Sick Pay (SSP) from the employer for a maximum period of 28 weeks in any three-year period. This applies to all employees, both men and women, up to the age of 65.

Deductions From Pay

Employers may not make deductions from an employee's wages without the employee's prior written consent or unless authorised by statute (e.g. deductions for national insurance or tax).

Sunday Trading

The Sunday Trading Act 1994 gave new rights to shop workers. They have the right not to be dismissed, selected for redundancy or to suffer any detriment (such as the denial of overtime, promotion or training) if they refuse to work on Sundays. This does not apply to those who, under their contracts, are employed to work on Sundays.

Disputes

Where it has not been possible to settle a dispute in the workplace, it may be possible for employees to make a complaint to an industrial tribunal. ACAS (the Advisory, Conciliation and Arbitration Service; for entry, see Index) offers advice and conciliation in employment disputes.

Termination of Employment

An employee may be dismissed without notice if guilty of gross misconduct but in other cases a period of notice must be given by the employer. The minimum periods of notice specified in the Employment Rights Act 1996 are:
— at least one week if the employee has been continuously employed for one month or more but for less than two years
— at least two weeks if the employee has been continuously employed for two years or more. A week is added for every complete year of continuous employment up to 12 years
— at least 12 weeks for those who have been continuously employed for 12 years or more
— longer periods apply if these are specified in the contract of employment

If an employee is dismissed with less notice than he/she is entitled to, the employer is generally liable to pay wages for the period of proper notice (or for the period of the contract for those on fixed-term contracts). Generally, no notice needs to be given of the expiry of a fixed-term contract.

Redundancy

An employee dismissed because of redundancy may be entitled to a lump sum. This applies if:
— the employee has at least two years' continuous service
— the employee is actually dismissed by the employer (even in cases of voluntary redundancy)
— dismissal is due to a reduction in the work force

An employee may not be entitled to a redundancy payment if offered a new job by the same employer. The amount of payment depends on the length of service, the salary and the age of the employee.

Unfair Dismissal

Complaints about unfair dismissal are dealt with by an employment tribunal. Since 1 June 1999 any employee, with one years' continuous service subject to exceptions, regardless of their hours of work, can make a complaint to the tribunal. For dismissals prior to that date, it is necessary for the employee to have two years' continuous service in order to bring a complaint (although this requirement has been referred by the House of Lords to the European Court of Justice). At the tribunal the employer must prove that the dismissal was due to one or more of the following reasons:
— the employee's capability for the job
— the employee's conduct
— redundancy
— a legal restriction preventing the continuation of the employee's contract
— some other substantial reason (including breaking the law)

If so, the tribunal must decide whether the employer acted reasonably in dismissing the employee for that reason. If the employee is found to have been unfairly dismissed, the tribunal can order that he/she be reinstated or compensated.

Discrimination

Discrimination in employment on the grounds of sex, race, colour, nationality, ethnic or national origins, married status or (subject to wide exceptions) disability is unlawful. Discrimination includes sexual harassment and gender reassignment (transexuals). The following legislation applies to those employed in Great Britain but not to employees in Northern Ireland or (subject to EC exceptions) to those who work mainly abroad:
— The Equal Pay Act 1970 (as amended) entitles men and women to equality in matters related to their contracts of employment. Those doing like work for the same employer are entitled to the same pay and conditions regardless of their sex
— The Sex Discrimination Act 1975 (as amended by the Sex Discrimination Act 1986) makes it unlawful to discriminate on grounds of sex or marital status. This covers all aspects of employment, including advertising for recruits, terms offered, opportunities for promotion and training, and dismissal procedures
— The Race Relations Act 1976 gives individuals the right not to be discriminated against in employment matters on the grounds of race, colour, nationality, or ethnic or national origins. It applies to all aspects of employment
— The Disability Discrimination Act 1995 makes discrimination against a disabled person in all aspects of employment unlawful. Unlike sex and race discrimination, an employer may show that the treatment is justified and that the employer acted reasonably. Employers with fewer than 15 employees are exempt

The Equal Opportunities Commission, the Commission for Racial Equality and the Disablilty Rights Commission have the function of eliminating such discriminations in the workplace and can provide further information and assistance.

In Northern Ireland similar provisions exist but are constituted in separate legislation. The Fair Employment (Northern Ireland) Act 1989 adds specific provisions aimed at preventing religious discrimination.

Recent Legislation

The Employment Relations Act 1999 has made a number of important changes to the existing law. The main changes are:
— a right of accompaniment. A worker attending a serious disciplinary or grievance hearing will have a right to be accompanied by a trade union representative or co-worker of their choice
— a new scheme of compulsory trade union recognition following a workplace ballot
— greater protection from dismissal for striking employees
— more 'family friendly' measures, including greater rights to maternity leave and parental leave
— the maximum award for unfair dismissal is £51,700 which relates to dismissals occurring on or after 1 February 2001.

ILLEGITIMACY AND LEGITIMATION

The Children Act 1989 gives the mother parental responsibility for the child when she is not married to the father. The father can acquire parental responsibility either by agreement with her (in prescribed form) or by applying to the court. If an illegitimate child is to be adopted, the father's consent is required only where he has been awarded parental rights by the court.

Every child born to a married woman during marriage is presumed to be legitimate, unless the couple are separated under court order when the child is conceived, in which case the child is presumed not to be the husband's child. It is possible to challenge the presumption of legitimacy or illegitimacy through civil proceedings.

Legitimation

Under the Legitimacy Act 1976, an illegitimate person automatically becomes legitimate when his/her parents marry. This applies even where one of the parents was married to a third person at the time of the birth. In such cases it is necessary to re-register the birth of the child.

JURY SERVICE

In England and Wales a person charged with any but the most minor offences is entitled to be tried by jury. There are 12 members of a jury in a criminal case and eight members in a civil case. Jurors are normally asked to serve for ten working days, although jurors selected for longer cases are expected to sit for the duration of the trial.

Every parliamentary or local government elector between the ages of 18 and 70 who has lived in the UK (including, for this purpose, the Channel Islands and the Isle of Man) for any period of at least five years since reaching the age of 13 is qualified to serve on a jury unless he/she is ineligible or disqualified.

England and Wales

Those ineligible for jury service include:
— those who have at any time been judges, magistrates or senior court officials
— those who have within the previous ten years been concerned with the administration of justice
— priests of any religion and vowed members of religious communities
— certain sufferers from mental illness

Those disqualified from jury service include:
— those who have at any time been sentenced by a court in the UK (including, for this purpose, the Channel Islands and the Isle of Man) to a term of imprisonment or custody of five years or more
— those who have within the previous ten years served any part of a sentence of imprisonment, youth custody or detention, been detained in a young offenders' institution, received a suspended sentence of imprisonment or order for detention, or received a community service order
— those who have within the previous five years been placed on probation
— those who are on bail in criminal proceedings

Those who may be excused as of right from jury service include:
— persons over the age of 65
— members and officers of the Houses of Parliament
— members of the National Assembly for Wales
— representatives to the European Parliament
— full-time serving members of the armed forces
— registered and practising members of the medical, dental, nursing, veterinary and pharmaceutical professions
— those who have served on a jury in the previous two years

The court has the discretion to excuse a juror from service, or defer the date of service, if the service would be a hardship to the juror. If a person serves on a jury knowing himself/herself to be ineligible or disqualified, he/she is liable to be fined up to £5,000 if disqualified and up to £1,000 for all other offences. The defendant can object to any juror if he/she can show cause.

A juror may claim travelling expenses, a subsistence allowance and an allowance for other financial loss (e.g. loss of earnings or benefits, fees paid to carers or child-minders) up to a stated limit.

It is an offence for a juror to disclose what happened in the jury room even after the trial is over. A jury's verdict must normally be unanimous, but if no verdict has been reached after two hours' consideration (or such longer period as the court deems to be reasonable) a majority verdict is acceptable if ten jurors agree to it.

Further information can obtained from:

The Court Service

105 Victoria Street, London SW1E 6QT
(Tel: 020-7210 2266)

LANDLORD AND TENANT

When a property is rented to a tenant, the rights and responsibilities of the landlord and the tenant are determined largely by the tenancy agreement but also by statutory provisions. Some of the main provisions are outlined below but it is advisable to contact the Citizens' Advice Bureau or the local authority housing department for further information.

Residential Lettings

The provisions outlined here apply only where the tenant lives in a separate dwelling from the landlord and where the dwelling is the tenant's only or main home. It does not apply to licensees such as lodgers, guests or service occupiers.

The 1996 Housing Act radically changes certain aspects of the legislation referred to below, in particular the grant of assured and assured shorthold tenancies under the Housing Act 1988. It is advisable to check whether the new legislation has come into force before relying on the provisions set out below.

Assured Shorthold Tenancies

If a tenancy was granted on or after 15 January 1989 and before 28 February 1997, the tenant may have an assured tenancy giving that tenant greater rights. The tenant could, for example, stay in possession of the dwelling for as long as the tenant observed the terms of the tenancy. The landlord cannot obtain possession from such a tenant unless the landlord can establish a specific ground for possession (set out in the Housing Act 1988) and obtains a court order. The rent payable is that agreed with the landlord unless the rent has been fixed by the rent assessment committee of the local authority. The tenant or the landlord may request that the committee set the rent in line with open market rents for that type of property. Any rent increases that are to take place should be written into the agreement but failing that, the landlord must give advance notice of the increase.

Under the Housing Act 1996, most new lettings entered into on or after 28 February 1997 will be assured shorthold tenancies. This means that tenants are given limited rights. The landlord must obtain a court order, however, to obtain possession if the tenant refuses to vacate at the end of the tenancy.

Regulated Tenancies

Before the Housing Act 1988 came into force (15 January 1989) there were regulated tenancies; some are still in existence and are protected by the Rent Act 1977. Under this Act it is possible for the landlord or the tenant to apply to the local rent officer to have a 'fair' rent registered. The fair rent is then the maximum rent payable.

Secure Tenancies

Secure tenancies are generally given to tenants of local authorities, housing associations and certain other bodies. This gives the tenant lifelong tenure unless the terms of the agreement are broken by the tenant. In certain circumstances those with secure tenancies may have the right to buy their property. In practice this right is generally only available to council tenants.

Agricultural Property

Tenancies in agricultural properties are governed by the Agricultural Holdings Act 1986 and the Rent (Agricultural) Act 1976, which give similar protections to those described above, e.g. security of tenure, right to compensation for disturbance, etc.

Eviction

Under the Protection from Eviction Act 1977 (as amended by the Housing Act 1988), a landlord must give reasonable notice that he/she is to evict the tenant, and in most cases a possession order, granted in court, is necessary. Notice is generally to be at least four weeks and in prescribed statutory form (notices are available from law stationers). It is illegal for a landlord to evict a person by putting their belongings onto the street, by changing the locks and so on. It is also illegal for a landlord to harass a tenant in any way in order to persuade him/her to give up the tenancy.

Landlord Responsibilities

Under the Landlord and Tenant Act 1985, where the term of the lease is less than seven years the landlord is responsible for maintaining the structure and exterior of the property and all installations for the supply of water, gas and electricity, for sanitation, and for heating and hot water.

Leaseholders

Legally leaseholders have bought a long lease rather than a property and in certain limited circumstances the landlord can end the tenancy. Under the Leasehold Reform Act 1967 (as amended by the Housing Acts 1969, 1974 and 1980), leaseholders of houses may have the right to buy the freehold or to take an extended lease for a term of 50 years. This applies to leases where the term of the lease is over 21 years and where the leaseholder has occupied the house as his/her main residence for the last three years, or for a total of three years over the last ten.

The Leasehold Reform, Housing and Urban Development Act came into force in 1993 and allows the leaseholders of flats in certain circumstances to buy the freehold of the building in which they live.

Responsibility for maintenance of the structure, exterior and interior of the building should be set out in the lease. Usually the upkeep of the interior of his/her part of the property is the responsibility of the leaseholder, and responsibility for the structure, exterior and common interior areas is shared between the freeholder and the leaseholder(s).

If leaseholders are in anyway dissatisfied with treatment from their landlord or with charges made in respect of lease extensions they are entitled to have their situation evaluated by the Leasehold Valuation Tribunal.

Leasehold Advisory Service

70—74 City Road, London, EC1Y 2BJ,
Tel: 020-7490 9580, Fax: 020-7253 2043,
E-mail: info@lease-advice.org;
Web: www.lease-advice.org

Business Lettings

The Landlord and Tenant Acts 1927 and 1954 (as amended) give security of tenure to the tenants of most business premises. The landlord can only evict the tenant on one of the grounds laid down in the 1954 Act, and in some cases where the landlord repossesses the property the tenant may be entitled to compensation.

LEGAL AID

The Access to Justice Act 1999 has transformed what used to known as the Legal Aid system. The Legal Aid Board has been abolished and replaced from 1 April 2000 with the Legal Services Commission (85 Gray's Inn Road, London, WC1X 8TX. Tel: 020-7759 0000). The changeover from the Legal Aid system is set to continue until 2002 with the latest major change being the introduction of the Criminal Defence Service in April 2001 to replace the old system of criminal legal aid. Up-to-date information and further guidance can be obtained from the Legal Services Commission website http://www.legalservices.gov.uk. The Legal Services Commission administers the Community Legal Service fund under which (like the former legal aid) people on low or moderate incomes may qualify for help with the costs of legal advice or representation. Further advice about entitlement to assistance should be sought from a solicitor or Citizens' Advice Bureau. A key element of the reforms has been the introduction of the Community Legal Service which is designed to increase access to legal information and advice by involving a much wider network of funders and providers in giving publicly funded legal services.

Civil Legal Aid

From 1 January 2000, only organisations (solicitors or Citizens' Advice Bureau) with a contract with the Legal Services Commission have been able to give initial help in any civil matter. Moreover, from that date decisions about funding were devolved from the Legal Services Commission to contracted organisations in relation to any level of publicly funded service in family and immigration cases. For other types of case, applications for public funding are made through a solicitor (or other contracted legal services provider) in much the same way as the former Legal Aid. From 1 April 2001 the so-called civil contracting scheme will be extended to cover all levels of service for all types of cases.

Under the new civil funding scheme there are broadly seven levels of service available:
— legal help
— help at court (the first two types of service are limited to advice and assistance with preparing a case, but do not include representation)
— approved family help — either general family help or help with mediation (special levels of service for family cases)
— legal representation — either investigative help or full representation (this covers assistance with representation in court)
— support funding — either investigative support or litigation support (this is a new type of assistance which allows the costs of a privately funded case to be topped up from public funds. It is only available for personal injury claims)
— family mediation
— such other services as are specifically authorised by the Lord Chancellor
— In general, public funding is not available for the following type of cases:
— personal injury (except for the availability of support funding and clinical negligence claims)
— allegations of negligent damage to property
— conveyancing
— boundary disputes
— the making of wills
— matters of trust law
— defamation proceedings
— partnership disputes and company law
— other matters arising out of the carrying on of a business.

Eligibility

Eligibility for funding from the Community Legal Service depends broadly on 5 factors:
— the level of service sought (see above)
— whether the applicant qualifies financially
— the merits if the applicant's case
— a costs-benefits analysis (if the costs are likely to outweigh any benefit that might be gained from the proceedings, funding may be refused)
— whether there is any public interest in the case being litigated (i.e. whether the case has a wider public interest beyond that of the parties involved — for example, a human rights case)

The limits on capital and income above which a person is not entitled to public funding vary with the type of service sought.

To find out if you are eligible, contact a solicitor, who undertakes public funding work. He or she will be able to provide you with the forms necessary to make a claim for public funding. Once forms are complete, your solicitor will send them to the Legal Service Commission. A decision as to eligibility can take 4 weeks or longer, however, it is possible to get a quicker decision if you require urgent public funding.

Contributions

Some of those who qualify for Community Legal Service funding will have to contribute towards their legal costs. Contributions must be paid by anyone who has a disposable income or disposable capital exceeding a prescribed amount. The rules relating to applicable contributions is complex and detailed information can be obtained from the Legal Services Commission, www.legalservices.gov.uk; Tel: 020-7759 0000.

Statutory Charge

A statutory charge is made if a person receives money or property in a case for which they have received legal aid. This means that the amount paid by the Community Legal Service fund on their behalf is deducted from the amount that the person receives. This does not apply if the court has ordered that the costs be paid by the other party (unless the amount paid by the other party does not cover all of the costs) or if the payments are for maintenance.

Contingency or Conditional Fees

This system was introduced by the Courts and Legal Services Act 1990. It offers legal representation on a "no win, no fee" basis. It provides an alternative form of assistance, especially for those cases which are ineligible for funding by the Community Legal Service. The main area for such work is in the field of personal injuries which claims are now largely exempt from public finding (except for clinical negligence claims).

Not all solicitors offer such a scheme and different solicitors may well have different terms. The effect of the agreement is that solicitors will not make any charges until the case is concluded successfully. The charges are usually linked to a percentage of the amount recovered. The merits of a case are usually assessed before the scheme is offered to potential litigants. Should the case be accepted, then the percentage charges will be linked to the risks involved: the higher the risks, the higher the percentage. Any agreement should be in writing and set out the exact terms of the agreement and the effects of success and failure.

Criminal Legal Aid

Criminal legal aid is now administered by the Legal Services Commission. As part of the changes under the Access to Justice Act 1999, in April 2001 the Criminal Defence Service replaced the old system of criminal legal aid under the Legal Aid Act 1988. Up-to-date information and further guidance can be obtained from the Legal Services Commission website http://www.legalservices.gov.uk or from a solicitor or Citizens' Advice Bureau.

The courts will grant criminal legal aid if it is desirable in the interests of justice (e.g. if there are important questions of law to be argued or the case is so serious that if found guilty the person may go to prison) and the person needs help to pay their legal costs.

Criminal legal aid covers the cost of preparing a case and legal representation (including the cost of a barrister) in criminal proceedings. It is also available for appeals against verdicts or sentences in magistrates' courts, the Crown Court or the Court of Appeal. It is not available for bringing a private prosecution in a criminal court.

If granted criminal legal aid, either the person may choose their own solicitor or the court will assign one. Contributions to the legal costs must be paid by anyone who has a disposable income or disposable capital which exceeds a prescribed amount. The rules relating to applicable contributions in complex and detailed information can be obtained from the Legal Services Commission, www.legalservices.gov.uk; Tel: 020-7759 0000.

Duty Solicitors

The Legal Aid Act 1988 also provides free advice and assistance to anyone questioned by the police (whether under arrest or helping the police with their enquiries). No means test or contributions are required for this. The advice or assistance can be from the duty solicitor at the police station, from a person's own solicitor or from any local solicitor (a list is available at police stations).

Duty solicitors are usually available at the magistrates' court, in criminal cases, for advice and/or representation on first appearances. This assistance is not means-tested.

MARRIAGE

Any two persons may marry provided that:
— they are at least 16 years old on the day of the marriage (in England and Wales persons under the age of 18 must generally obtain the

consent of their parents; if consent is refused an appeal may be made to the High Court, the county court or a court of summary jurisdiction)
— they are not related to one another in a way which would prevent their marrying (see below)
— they are unmarried (a person who has already been married must produce documentary evidence that the previous marriage has been ended by death, divorce or annulment)
— they are not of the same sex
— they are capable of understanding the nature of a marriage ceremony and of consenting to marriage
— the marriage would be regarded as valid in any foreign country of which either party is a citizen

Degrees of Relationship

A marriage between persons within the prohibited degrees of consanguinity, affinity or adoption is void.

A man may not marry his mother, daughter, grandmother, granddaughter, sister, aunt, niece, great-grandmother, great-granddaughter, adoptive mother, former adoptive mother, adopted daughter or former adopted daughter. In some circumstances he may now be allowed to marry his former wife's daughter, former wife's granddaughter, father's former wife or grandfather's former wife. A woman may not marry her father, son, grandfather, grandson, brother, uncle, nephew, great-grandfather, great-grandson, adoptive father, former adoptive father, adopted son or former adopted son. In some circumstances she may now be allowed to marry her former husband's son, former husband's grandson, mother's former husband or grandmother's former husband.

Types of Marriage Ceremony

It is possible to marry by either religious or civil ceremony. A religious ceremony can take place at a church or chapel of the Church of England or the Church in Wales, or at any other place of worship which has been formally registered by the Registrar-General.

A civil ceremony can take place at a register office, a registered building or any other premises approved by the local authority.

An application for an approved premises licence must be made by the owners or trustees of the building concerned; it cannot be made by the prospective marriage couple. Approved premises must be regularly open to the public so that the marriage can be witnessed; the venue must be deemed to be a permanent and immovable structure. Open-air ceremonies are prohibited.

Non-Anglican marriages may also be solemnised following the issue of a Registrar-General's licence in unregistered premises where one of the parties is seriously ill, is not expected to recover, and cannot be moved to registered premises. Detained and housebound persons may be married at their place of residence.

MARRIAGE IN THE CHURCH OF ENGLAND OR THE CHURCH IN WALES

Marriage by banns

The marriage must take place in a parish in which one of the parties lives, or in a church in another parish if it is the usual place of worship of either or both of the parties. The banns must be called in the parish in which the marriage is to take place on three Sundays before the day of the ceremony; if either or both of the parties lives in a different parish the banns must also be called there. After three months the banns are no longer valid.

Marriage by common licence

The vicar who is to conduct the marriage will arrange for a common licence to be issued by the diocesan bishop; this dispenses with the necessity for banns. One of the parties must have lived in the parish for 15 days immediately before the issuing of the licence or must usually worship at the church. Affidavits are prepared from the personal instructions of one of the parties and the licence will be given to the applicant in person.

Marriage by special licence

A special licence is granted by the Archbishop of Canterbury in special circumstances for the marriage to take place at any place, with or without previous residence in the parish, or at any time. Application must be made to the Faculty Office of the Archbishop of Canterbury, 1 The Sanctuary, London SW1P 3JT. Tel: 020-7222 5381.

Marriage by certificate

The marriage can be conducted on the authority of the superintendent registrar's certificate, provided that the vicar's consent is obtained. One of the parties must live in the parish or must usually worship at the church.

Marriage by Other Religious Ceremony

One of the parties must normally live in the registration district where the marriage is to take place. In addition to giving notice to the superintendent registrar (see page 665), it may also be necessary to book a registrar to be present at the ceremony.

Civil Marriage

A marriage may be solemnised at any register office, registered building or approved premises in England and Wales. The superintendent registrar of the district should be contacted, and, if the marriage is to take place at approved premises, the necessary arrangements at the venue must also be made.

Notice of Marriage

Unless it is to take place by banns or under common or special licence in the Church of England or the Church in Wales, a notice of the marriage must be given by both parties in person to the superintendent registrar. Notice of marriage may be given in the following ways:

— by certificate. Both parties must have lived in a registration district in England or Wales for at least seven days immediately before giving notice at the local register office. If they live in different registration districts, notice must be given in both districts. The marriage can take place in any register office in England and Wales 16 days after notice has been given

— by licence (often known as 'special licence'). One of the parties must have lived in a registration district in England or Wales for at least 15 days before giving notice at the register office; the other party need only be a resident of, or be physically in, England and Wales on the day notice is given. The marriage can take place one clear day (other than a Sunday, Christmas Day or Good Friday) after notice has been given

A notice of marriage is valid for 12 months. It is not therefore possible to give formal notice of a marriage more than three months before it is to take place, but it should be possible to make an advance (provisional) booking 12 months before the ceremony. In this case it is still necessary to give formal notice three months before the marriage. When giving notice of the marriage it is necessary to produce official proof, if relevant, that any previous marriage has ended in divorce or death by producing a decree absolute or death certificate; it is also useful, but not necessary, to take birth certificates or passports as proof of age and identity.

Solemnisation of the Marriage

On the day of the wedding there must be at least two other people present who are prepared to act as witnesses and sign the marriage register. A registrar of marriages must be present at a marriage in a register office or at approved premises, but an authorised person may act in the capacity of registrar in a registered building.

If the marriage takes place at approved premises, the room must be separate from any other activity on the premises at the time of the ceremony, and no food or drink can be sold or consumed in the room during the ceremony or for one hour beforehand.

The marriage must be solemnised between 8 a.m. and 6 p.m., with open doors. At some time during the ceremony the parties must make a declaration that they know of no legal impediment to the marriage and they must also say the contracting words; the declaratory and contracting words may vary according to the form of service in use but the most basic forms are:

— (declaratory words) 'I declare that I know of no legal reason why I, A. B., may not be joined in marriage to C. D.' Alternatively, the couple may answer 'I am' to the question 'Are you, A. B., free lawfully to marry C. D.?'

— (contracting words) 'I, A. B., take you, C. D., to be my wedded wife [or husband]'

A civil marriage cannot contain any religious aspects, but it may be possible for non-religious music and/or poetry readings to be included. It may also be possible to embellish the marriage vows taken by the couple.

If both parties are Jewish, they may be married in a synagogue, in a private house or elsewhere. The wedding may take place at any time of day and must be registered by the secretary of the synagogue of which the man is a member. The presence of a registrar of marriages is not necessary.

If both parties are members of the Society of Friends (Quakers), they may be married in a Friends' meeting-house. The marriage must be registered by the registering officer of the Society appointed to act for the district in which the meeting-house is situated. The presence of a registrar of marriages is not necessary.

272 Legal London

CIVIL FEES FROM 1 JULY 2001

Registrar
— Attending a marriage at a register office, £34.00
— Attending a marriage at a registered building/ residence of a housebound person, £40.00
— Attending a marriage by Registrar General's licence, £2.00

Superintendent Registrar
— Entering a notice of marriage in marriage notice book, £30.00, payable by each party.
— Entering notice of marriage by Registrar General's licence in marriage notice book, £3.00
— Attending outside office to be given notice of marriage of housebound/detained person, £40.00
— Attending marriage at residence of housebound/detained person, £40.00
— Attending a marriage by Registrar-General's licence, £2.00
— Attending with a registrar a marriage on approved premises, fee set by local authority

Marriage certificate on day of marriage, £3.50

ECCLESIASTICAL FEES SINCE 1 APRIL 2001
(Church of England and Church in Wales*)

Marriage by banns
— For publication of banns, £15.00
— For certificate of banns issued at time of publication, £9.00
— For marriage service, £142.00

Marriage by common licence
Fee for licence, £55.00

Marriage by special licence
Fee for licence, £125.00

Further fees may be payable for additional facilities at the marriage, e.g. the organist's fee.

*Some of these fees may not apply to the Church in Wales

Further information can be obtained from:

The General Register Office

Office for National Statistics, Smedley Hydro, Trafalgar Road, Birkdale, Southport, Merseyside PR8 2HH (Tel: 01704-569824)

RIGHTS OF WAY

On the 30 January 2001, the Countryside and Rights of Way Act 2000 came into force. The first part of the Act is concerned with the rights of access for the public as well as recognising landowner's rights. The second part of the Act improves on existing rights of way legislation and encompasses local authorities' duties, the creation, diversion or abolition of byways and bridleways and other rights of way and the status of nature conservation, wildlife protection, town and village greens and Areas of Outstanding Natural Beauty (AONB) in relation to right of way legislation.

TOWN AND COUNTRY PLANNING

The planning system is important in helping protect the environment, as well as assisting individuals in asserting their land rights. There area a number of Acts governing the development of land and buildings in the UK and advice should always be sought from a Citizen's Advice Bureaux or local planning authority before undertaking building works to your land or property. If you build something which requires planning permission without seeking permission in advance, you may be forced to rectify the situation.

Planning Permission

Planning permission is needed if the work involves:
— making a material change in use, such as dividing off part of the house so that it can be used as a separate home or dividing off part of the house for commercial use, e.g. for a workshop
— going against the terms of the original planning permission, e.g. there may be a restriction on fences in front gardens on an open-plan estate
— building, engineering for mining, except for the permissions below
— new or wider access to a main road
— additions or extensions to flats or maisonettes

Planning permission is not needed to carry out internal alterations or work which does not affect the external appearance of the building.

There are certain types of development for which the Secretary of State for the Environment has granted general permissions, know as "permitted development rights". These include:
— house extensions and additions (including conservatories, loft conversions, garages and dormer windows). Up to 10 per cent or up to 50 cubic metres (whichever is the greater) can

be added to the original house for terraced houses. Up to 15 per cent or 70 cubic metres (whichever is the greater) to other kinds of houses. The maximum that can be added to any house is 115 cubic metres
— buildings such as garden sheds and greenhouses so long as they are no more than 3 metres high (or 4 metres if the roof is ridged), are no nearer to a highway than the house, and at least half the ground around the house remains uncovered by buildings
— adding a porch with a ground area of less than 3 square metres and that is less than 3 metres in height
— putting up fences, walls and gates of under 1 metre in height if next to a road and under 2 metres elsewhere
— laying patios, paths or driveways for domestic use

Other Restrictions

It may be necessary to obtain other types of permissions before carrying out any development. These permissions are separate from planning permission and apply regardless of whether or not planning permission is needed, e.g.:
— building regulations will probably apply if a new building is to be erected, if an existing one is to be altered or extended, or if the work involves building over a drain or sewer The building control department of the local authority will advise on this
— any alterations to a listed building or the grounds of a listed building must be approved by the local authority
— local authority approval is necessary if a building (or, in some circumstances, gates, walls, fences or railings) in a conservation area is to be demolished; each local authority keeps a register of all local buildings that are in conservation areas
— many trees are protected by tree preservation orders and must not be pruned or taken down without local authority consent
— bats and other species are protected and English Nature or the Countryside Council for Wales must be notified before any work is carried out that will affect the habitat of protected species, e.g. timber treatment, renovation or extensions of lofts
— any development in areas designated as a National Park, an Area of Outstanding National Beauty, a National Scenic Area or in the Norfolk or Suffolk Broads is subject to greater restrictions. The local planning authority will advise or refer enquirers to the relevant authority

— If you think you require planning permission, contact your local planning authority. They will advise you and provide you with the correct form for your application. For further information, contact the Department of the Environment, Transport and the Regions.

Voters' Qualifications

Those entitled to vote at parliamentary, European Union (EU) and local government elections are those who are:
— on the electoral roll. Local authorities administer the roll and non-registration can lead to a fine of up to £1,000
— over 18 years old
— Commonwealth (which includes British) citizens or citizens of the Republic of Ireland

British citizens resident abroad are entitled to vote, for 20 years after leaving Britain, as overseas electors in parliamentary and EU elections in the constituency in which they were last resident. Members of the armed forces, Crown servants and employees of the British Council who are overseas and their spouses are entitled to vote regardless of how long they have been abroad.

European Union citizens resident in the UK may vote in EU and local government elections.

The following people are not entitled to vote:
— peers, and peeresses in their own right, who are members of the House of Lords (except that they may vote in EU and local government elections)
— patients detained under mental health legislation (who have criminal convictions)
— those serving prison sentences
— those convicted within the previous five years of corrupt or illegal election practices

Under the representation of the People Act 2000, several new groups of people are permitted to vote for the first time. These include people who live on barges; unconvicted or remand prisoners; people in mental hospitals (other than those with criminal convictions) and homeless people who have made a "declaration of local connection".

Registering to Vote

Voters must be entered on an electoral register, which runs from 16 February in one year to 15 February in the following year. The registration officer for each constituency is responsible for preparing and publishing the register. A registration form is sent to all households in the autumn of each year and the householder is required to provide details of all occupants who are eligible to vote, including ones who will reach their 18th birthday in the year covered by the register. Those who fail to give the required information or who give false information are liable to be fined. A draft register is usually published at the end of November. Any person whose name has been omitted may ask to be registered and should contact the registration officer. Anyone on the register may object to the inclusion of another person's name, in which case he/she should notify the registration officer, who will investigate that person's eligibility. Supplementary electors lists are published throughout the duration of the register.

Voting

Voting is not compulsory in the UK. Those who wish to vote must generally vote in person at the allotted polling station. Those who will be away at the time of the election, those who will not be able to attend in person due to physical incapacity or the nature of their occupation, and those who have changed address during the period for which the register is valid, may apply for a postal vote or nominate a proxy to vote for them. Overseas electors who wish to vote must do so by proxy.

Further information can be obtained from the local authority's electoral registration officer in England and Wales.

Wills and Intestacy

In a will a person leaves instructions as to the disposal of their property after they die. A will is also used to appoint executors (who will administer the estate), give directions as to the disposal of the body, appoint guardians for children and, for larger estates, can operate to reduce the level of inheritance tax. It is best to have a will drawn up by a solicitor but if a solicitor is not employed, the following points must be taken into account:
— if possible the will must not be prepared on behalf of another person by someone who is to benefit from it or who is a close relative of a major beneficiary
— the language used must be clear and unambiguous and it is better to avoid the use of legal terms where the same thing can be expressed in plain language
— it is better to rewrite the whole document if a mistake is made. If necessary, alterations can be made by striking through the words with a pen, and the signature or initials of the testator and the witnesses must be put in the margin opposite the alteration. No alteration of any kind should be made after the will has been executed
— if the person later wishes to change the will or part of it, it is better to write a new will revoking the old. The use of codicils (documents written as supplements or containing modifications to the will) should be left to a solicitor
— the will should be typed or printed, or if handwritten be legible and preferably in ink. Commercial will forms can be obtained from some stationers

The form of a will varies to suit different cases; the following is an example of how a will might be written. The notes after this example explain the terms used and procedures that need to be followed in drawing up a will.

This is the last will and testament of me [Thomas Smith] of [Heather Cottage, Prospero Road, Manchester M1 4DK] which I make this [seventeenth] day of [May 2000] and I revoke all previous wills and testamentary dispositions.

1. I appoint as my executors and trustees [Ann Green of —and Richard Brown of —]. In my will the expression 'my Trustees' means any executors and trustees for the time being of my will and of any trust arising under it.

2. I give all my property to [such of my children as shall survive me by 28 days and if more than one in equal shares or as the case may be].

3. I give to [Pamela Henderson of —] the sum of [£—] and to [Michael Broadbent of —] the sum of [£—] and to [Ruth Walker of —] all of my [jewellery, books or as the case may be]

and

4. I give everything not otherwise disposed of to [Richard Black of —]

Signed by the testator in our joint presence and then by us in his.

Thomas Smith

[Signature of the person making the will]

Elizabeth Wall

[Signature of witness] of 67 Beatrice Lane, Manchester M1 4DK, journalist

William Jones

[Signature of witness] of 17 Paris Road, Manchester M1 4EN, tailor

Specific Gifts and Legacies

Gifts of specific items usually fail if the property is not owned by the person making the will on their death. This problem can be avoided by making a gift of any property fulfilling a particular description, e.g. a car, which is owned at the date of death. It is better in all cases where such gifts are made, to insert a clause which reads 'I give everything not otherwise disposed of to [Richard Black of —], even if it seems that all property has already been disposed of in the will.

Lapsed Legatees

If a person who has been left property in a will dies before the person who made the will, the gift fails and will pass to the person entitled to everything not otherwise disposed of (the residuary estate).

If the person left the residuary estate dies before the person who made the will, their share will generally pass to the closest relative(s) of the person who made the will (as in intestacy) unless the will names a beneficiary such as a charity who will take as a 'long stop' if this gift is unable to take effect for any reason.

It is always better to draw up a new will if a beneficiary predeceases the person who made the will.

Executors

It is usual to appoint two executors, although one is sufficient. No more than four persons can deal with the estate of the person who has died. The name and address of each executor should be given in full (the addresses are not essential but including them adds clarity to the document).

Executors should be 18 years of age or over. An executor may be a beneficiary of the will.

Witnesses

A person who is a beneficiary of a will, or the spouse of a beneficiary at the time the will is signed, must not act as a witness or else he/she will be unable to take his/her gift. Husband and wife can both act as witnesses provided neither benefits from the will. It is better that a person does not act as an executor and as a witness, as he/she can take no benefit under a will to which he/she is witness. The identity of the witnesses should be made as explicit as possible.

Execution of a Will

The person making the will should sign his/her name at the foot of the document, in the presence of the two witnesses. The witnesses must then sign their names while the person making the will looks on. If this procedure is not adhered to, the will will be considered invalid. There are certain exceptional circumstances where these rules are relaxed, e.g. where the person may be too ill to sign, and in these cases the attestation clause which normally reads 'signed by the testator in our joint presence and then by us in his/hers' should be reworded as follows:

'The will was read over to Thomas Smith in our presence when he stated that he understood it. It was then signed on his behalf by Thomas Brown in the presence of the testator and by his direction in our joint presence and then by us in his'.

Capacity to Make a Will

Anyone aged 18 or over can make a will. However, if there is any suspicion that the person making the will is not, through reasons of infirmity or age, fully in command of his/her faculties, it is advisable to arrange for a medical practitioner to examine the person making the will at the time it is to be executed to verify his/her mental capacity and to record that medical opinion in writing, and to ask the examining practitioner to act as a witness. If a person is not mentally able to make a will, the Court may do this for him/her by virtue of the Mental Health Act 1983.

Revocation

A will may be revoked or cancelled in a number of ways:
— a later will revokes an earlier one if it says so; otherwise the earlier will is impliedly revoked by the later one to the extent that it contradicts or repeats the earlier one
— a will is also revoked if the physical document on which it is written is destroyed by the person whose will it is. There must be an intention to revoke the will. It may not be sufficient to obliterate the will with a pen
— a will is revoked when the person marries, unless it is clear from the will that the person intended the will to stand after the marriage
— where a marriage ends in divorce or is annulled or declared void, gifts to the spouse and the appointment of the spouse as executor fail unless the will says that this is not to happen. A former spouse is treated as having predeceased the testator. A separation does not change the effect of a married person's will.

Probate and Letters of Administration

Probate is granted to the executors named in a will and once granted, the executors are obliged to carry out the instructions of the will. Letters of administration are granted where no executor is named in a will or is willing or able to act or where there is no will or no valid will; this gives a person, often the next of kin, similar powers and duties to those of an executor.

Applications for probate or for letters of administration can be made to the Principal Registry of the Family Division, to a district probate registry or to a probate sub-registry. Applicants will need the following documents: the original will (if any); a certificate of death; oath for executors or administrators; particulars of all property and assets left by the deceased; a list of debts and funeral expenses. Certain property, may be disposed of without a grant of probate or letters of administration.

Where to Find A Proved Will

Since 1858 wills which have been proved, that is wills on which probate or letters of administration have been granted, must have been proved at the Principal Registry of the Family Division or at a district probate registry. The Lord Chancellor has power to direct where the original documents are kept but most are filed where they were proved and may be inspected there and a copy obtained. The Principal Registry also holds copies of all wills proved at district probate registries and these may be inspected at Somerset House. An index of all grants, both of probate and of letters of administration, is compiled by the Principal Registry and may be seen either at the Principal Registry or at a district probate registry.

It is also possible to discover when a grant of probate or letters of administration is issued by requesting a standing search. In response to a request and for a small fee, a district probate registry will supply the names and addresses of executors or administrators and the registry in which the grant was made, of any grant in the estate of a specified person made in the previous 12 months or following six months. This is useful for applicants who may be beneficiaries to a will but who have lost contact with the deceased and for creditors of the deceased.

Principal Registry (Family Division)
First Avenue House, 42-49 High Holborn, London, WC1V 6NP (Tel: 020-7947 6000)

INTESTACY

Intestacy occurs when someone dies without leaving a will or leaves a will which is invalid or which does not take effect for some reason. In such cases the person's estate (property, possessions, other assets following the payment of debts) passes to certain members of the family. The relevant legislation is the Administration of Estates Act 1925, as amended by various legislation including the Intestates Estates Act 1952, the Law Reform (Succession) Act 1995, and the Trusts of Land and Appointment of Trustees Act 1996 and Orders made there under. Some of the provisions of this legislation are described below. If a will has been written that disposes of only part of a person's property, these rules apply to the part which is undisposed of.

If the person (intestate) leaves a spouse who survives for 28 days and children (legitimate, illegitimate and adopted children and other descendants), the estate is divided as follows:
— the spouse takes the 'personal chattels' (household articles, including cars, but nothing used for business purposes), £125,000 free of tax (with interest payable at 6 per cent from the time of the death until payment) and a life interest in half of the rest of the estate (which can be capitalised by the spouse if he/she wishes)
— the rest of the estate goes to the children*

If the person leaves a spouse who survives for 28 days but no children:
— the spouse takes the personal chattels, £200,000 free of tax (interest payable as before) and full ownership of half of the rest of the estate
— the other half of the rest of the estate goes to the parents (equally, if both alive) or, if none, to the brothers and sisters of the whole blood*
— if there are no parents or brothers or sisters of the whole blood or their children, the spouse takes the whole estate

If there is no surviving spouse, the estate is distributed among those who survive the intestate as follows:
— to surviving children*, but if none to
— parents (equally, if both alive), but if none to
— brothers and sisters of the whole blood*, but if none to
— brothers and sisters of the half blood*, but if none to
— grandparents (equally, if more than one), but if none to
— aunts and uncles of the whole blood*, but if none to

— aunts and uncles of the half blood*, but if none to
— the Crown, Duchy of Lancaster or the Duke of Cornwall (bona vacantia)

* To inherit, a member of these groups must survive the intestate and attain 18, or marry under that age. If they die under 18 (unless married under that age), their share goes to others, if any, in the same group. If any member of these groups predeceases the intestate leaving children, their share is divided equally among their children.

In England and Wales the provisions of the Inheritance (Provision for Family and Dependants) Act 1975 may allow other people to claim provision from the deceased's assets. This Act also applies to cases where a will has been made and allows a person to apply to the Court if they feel that the will or rules of intestacy or both do not make adequate provision for them. The Court can order payment from the deceased's assets or the transfer of property from them if the applicant's claim is accepted. The application must be made within six months of the grant of probate or letters of administration and the following people can make an application:
— the spouse
— a former spouse who has not remarried
— a child of the deceased
— someone treated as a child of the deceased's family
— someone maintained by the deceased
— someone who has cohabited for two years before the death in the same household as the deceased and as the husband or wife of the deceased

MEDIA LONDON

TELEVISION
RADIO
PRESS
ADVERTISING
PUBLIC RELATIONS
TELECOMMUNICATIONS
POSTAL SERVICES

MEDIA AND COMMUNICATIONS

London has a very high concentration of media activity and in this section you will find numerous contacts from television, radio, press, advertising and public relations.

CROSS-MEDIA OWNERSHIP

There are rules on cross-media ownership to prevent undue concentration of ownership. These were amended by the Broadcasting Act 1996. Radio companies are now permitted to own one AM, one FM and one other (AM or FM) service; ownership of the third licence is subject to a public interest test. Local newspapers with a circulation under 20 per cent in an area are also allowed to own one AM, one FM and one other service, and may control a regional Channel 3 television service subject to a public interest test. Local newspapers with a circulation between 20 and 50 per cent in an area may own one AM and one FM service, subject to a public interest test, but may not control a regional Channel 3 service. Those with a circulation over 50 per cent may own one radio service in the area (provided that more than one independent local radio service serves the area) subject to a public interest test.

Ownership controls on the number of television or radio licences have been removed; holdings are now restricted to 15 per cent of the total television audience or 15 per cent of the total points available in the radio points scheme. Ownership controls on cable operators have also been removed. National newspapers with less than 20 per cent of national circulation may apply to control any broadcasting licences, subject to a public interest test. National newspapers with more than 20 per cent of national circulation may not have more than a 20 per cent interest in a licence to provide a Channel 3 service, Channel 5 or national and local analogue radio services.

BROADCASTING

The British Broadcasting Corporation is responsible for public service broadcasting in London and throughout the UK. Its constitution and finances are governed by royal charter and agreement. On 1 May 1996 a new royal charter came into force, establishing the framework for the BBC's activities until 2006.

The Independent Television Commission and the Radio Authority were set up under the terms of the Broadcasting Act 1990. The ITC is the regulator and licensing authority for all commercially funded television services, including cable and satellite services. The Radio Authority is the regulator and licensing authority for all independent radio services.

BROADCASTING STANDARDS COMMISSION

7 The Sanctuary, London SW1P 3JS (Tel: 020-7808 1000; Fax: 020-7233 0397; Email: bsc@bsc.org.uk; Web: www.bsc.org.uk).

The Broadcasting Standards Commission was set up in April 1997 under the Broadcasting Act 1996 and was formed from the merger of the Broadcasting Complaints Commission and the Broadcasting Standards Council. The Commission considers and adjudicates upon complaints of unfair treatment or unwarranted infringement of privacy in all broadcast programmes and advertisements on television, radio, cable, satellite, Teletext and digital services. It also monitors the portrayal of violence and sex, and matters of taste and decency. Its new code of practice came into force on 1 January 1998.

Chairman: Lord Dubs of Battersea
Deputy Chairmen: Lady Warner
Director: S. Whittle

TELEVISION

All channels are broadcast in colour on 625 lines UHF from a network of transmitting stations. The BBC's transmission network was sold to the Castle Tower Consortium in February 1997; ITV transmission services are owned and operated by National Transcommunications Ltd. Transmissions are available to more than 99 percent of the population.

DIGITAL TELEVISION

Digital broadcasting will increase the number and quality of television channels. It uses digital modulation to improve reception and digital compression to make more effective use of the frequency channels available than PAL, the analogue system currently used.

The Broadcasting Act 1996 provided for the licensing of 20 or more digital terrestrial television channels (on six frequency channels or'multiplexes'). Analogue broadcasting will eventually be discontinued, with the frequencies being sold to mobile telephone companies.

In June 1997 the licences to run the remaining digital multiplexes were awarded by the ITC to British Digital Broadcasting (now called ONdigital), a consortium led by Carlton Communications and Granada. The first digital services went on air in autumn 1998. A set-top digital decoder or an integrated digital television set is required to convert the digital signals into analogue sound and picture waves in order to watch the digital channels. Digital television services are also offered by cable and satellite companies.

BRITISH BROADCASTING CORPORATION

Broadcasting House, Portland Place, London W1A 1AA (Tel: 020-7580 4468).

Television Centre, Wood Lane, London W12 7RJ (Tel: 020-8743 8000).

BBC Information – (0870 010 0322; Web: www.bbc.co.uk).

The BBC was incorporated under royal charter in 1926 as successor to the British Broadcasting Company Ltd. The BBC's current charter came into force on 1 May 1996 and extends to 31 December 2006. The chairman, vice-chairman and other governors are appointed by The Queen-in-Council. The BBC is financed by revenue from receiving licences for the home services and by grant-in-aid from Parliament for the World Service (radio).

Chairman: Sir Christopher Bland *(In the light of Sir Bland's resignation to take up chairmanship of BT, the new chairman was not known at the time of publication)*
Director-General and Editor-in-Chief: G. Dyke

INDEPENDENT TELEVISION

INDEPENDENT TELEVISION COMMISSION

33 Foley Street, London W1P 7IB (Tel: 020-7255 3000; Fax: 020-7306 7800; Email: publicaffairs@itc.org.uk; Web: www.itc.org.uk).

The Independent Television Commission replaced the Independent Broadcasting Authority in 1991. The Commission is responsible for licensing and regulating all commercially funded television services broadcast from the UK. Members are appointed by the Secretary of State for Culture, Media and Sport.

Chairman: Sir Robin Biggam
Chief Executive: Patricia Hodgson
Secretary and Director of Administration: M. Redley

ITV NETWORK CENTRE/ ITV ASSOCIATION

200 Gray's Inn Road, London WC1X 8HF (Tel: 020-7843 8000).

The ITV Network Centre is wholly owned by the ITV companies and undertakes the commissioning and scheduling of those television programmes which are shown across the ITV network. Through its sister organisation, the ITV Association, it also provides a range of services to the ITV companies where a common approach is required.

Chief Executive: Stuart Prebble

INDEPENDENT TELEVISION NETWORK COMPANIES IN LONDON

Carlton Television Ltd
101 St Martin's Lane, London WC2N 4RF (Tel: 020-7240 4000; Fax: 020-7240 4171; Web: www.carlton.com).

Chief Executive: Clive Jones

GMTV Ltd
The London Television Centre, Upper Ground, London SE1 9TT (Tel: 020-7827 7000).

London Weekend Television Ltd
The London Television Centre, Upper Ground, London SE1 9LT (Tel: 020-7620 1620; Web: www.granadamedia.com).

OTHER INDEPENDENT TELEVISION COMPANIES IN LONDON

Channel 5 Broadcasting Ltd
22 Long Acre, London WC2E 9LY
(Tel: 020-7550 5555).

Channel Four Television Corporation
124 Horseferry Road, London SW1P 2TX
(Tel: 020-7396 4444; Web: www.channel4.co.uk).

ITN (Independent Television News)
200 Gray's Inn Road, London WC1X 8XZ
(Tel: 020-7833 3000; Web: www.itn.co.uk).

Teletext Ltd
Unit 24, 101 Farm Lane, London SW6 1QJ
(Tel: 020-7386 5000).

Provides teletext services for the ITV companies and Channel 4.

DIRECT BROADCASTING BY SATELLITE TELEVISION

BRITISH SKY BROADCASTING LTD

Grant Way, Isleworth, Middx TW7 5QD
(Tel: 020-7705 3000; Web: www.sky.com).
Broadcasts 13 channels which are wholly owned by Sky. In addition, Sky Ventures consists of 9 joint venture partnerships which between them broadcast fourteen television channels and forty four audio channels.

Chief Executive and Managing Director:
Tony Ball

Radio 283

RADIO

UK domestic radio services are broadcast across three wavebands: FM (or VHF), medium wave (also referred to as AM) and long wave. In the UK the FM waveband extends in frequency from 87.5 MHz to 108 MHz and the medium wave band extends from 531 kHz to 1602 kHz.

DIGITAL RADIO

Digital radio allows more services to be broadcast to a higher technical quality and provides the data facility for text or pictures. It improves the robustness of high fidelity radio services, especially compared with current FM and AM radio transmissions.

The Broadcasting Act 1996 provided for the licensing of digital radio services (on seven frequency channels or 'multiplexes'). The BBC has been allocated a multiplex capable of broadcasting six to eight national stereo services; BBC digital broadcasts began in the London area in September 1995.

The Radio Authority is responsible for awarding licences for capacity on the non-BBC multiplexes.

THE RADIO AUTHORITY

Holbrook House, 14 Great Queen Street, London WC2B 5DG (Tel: 020-7430 2724; Fax: 020-7405 7062; Email: info@radioauthority.org.uk; Web: www.radioauthority.org.uk).

The Radio Authority was established in 1991 under the Broadcasting Act 1990. It is the regulator and licensing authority for all independent radio services. Members of the Authority are appointed by the Secretary of State for Culture, Media and Sport.

Chairman: Richard Hooper
Chief Executive: A. Stoller
Secretary to the Authority and Director of Legal Affairs: Ms E. Salomon

BBC NETWORK RADIO SERVICES

Radio 1—Frequencies: 97.6—99.8 FM
Radio 2—Frequencies: 88—90.2 FM
Radio 3—Frequencies: 90.2—92.4 FM
Radio 4—Frequencies: 94.6—96.1 FM and 103.5—105 FM; 1449 AM, plus eight local fillers on AM
Radio 5—Frequencies: 693 AM and 909 AM, plus one local filler

Media London

BBC LONDON LIVE

35c Marylebone High Street, London W1M 4AA. (Tel: 020-7224 2424; Fax: 020-7487 2908; Email: londonlive@bbc.co.uk; Web: www.bbc.co.uk/londonlive). **Frequency:** 94.9 FM.

Managing Editor: David Robey

Editor: Sandy Smith

INDEPENDENT RADIO

The Radio Authority began advertising new licences for the development of commercial radio in January 1991. Since then it has awarded three national licences, 137 new local radio licences (including fourteen regional licences) and one additional service licence (to use the spare capacity in an existing channel which is not used by the programme service). The Authority has also issued over 3,000 restricted service licences (for temporary low-powered radio services).

Commercial Radio Companies Association

77 Shaftesbury Avenue, London W1V 7AD (Tel: 020-7306 2603; Fax: 020-7470 0062; Email: info@crca.co.uk; Web: www.crca.co.uk).

Chief Executive: P. Brown

INDEPENDENT NATIONAL RADIO STATIONS IN LONDON

Classic FM, Academic House, 24—28 Oval Road, London NW1 7DQ (Tel: 020-7343 9000) 24 hours a day.
Frequencies: 99.9—101.9 FM

Talk Radio, 76 Oxford Street, London W1N 0TR (Tel: 020-7636 1089) 24 hours a day. **Frequencies:** 1053/1089 AM

Virgin Radio, 1 Golden Square, London W1R 4DJ. (Tel: 020-7434 1215) 24 hours a day. **Frequencies:** 1215/1197/1233/1242/1260 AM

INDEPENDENT LOCAL RADIO STATIONS

963/972 Liberty Radio, 7th Floor, Trevor House, 100 Brompton Road, London SW3 1ER. (Tel: 020-7893 8966) **Frequency:** 963/972 AM

Asian Sound Radio, Globe House, Southall Street, Manchester M3 1LG. (Tel: 0161-288 1000) **Frequencies:** 1377/963 AM

The Bay, PO Box 969, St George's Quay, Lancaster LA1 3LD. (Tel: 01524-848747) **Frequencies:** 96.9/102.3/103.2 FM

Capital FM and Gold, 30 Leicester Square, London WC2H 7LA. (Tel: 020-7766 6000) **Frequencies:** 1548 AM (Gold), 95.8 FM

Choice FM, 291—299 Borough High Street, London SE1 1JG. (Tel: 020-7378 3969) **Frequency:** 96.9 FM

FLR 107.3, Astra House, Arklow Road, London SE14 6EB. (Tel: 020-8691 9202) **Frequency:** 107.3 FM

Heart 106.2 The Chrysalis Building, Bramley Road, London W10 6SP. (Tel: 020-7468 1062) **Frequency:** 106.2 FM

Jazz FM 102.2, 26—27 Castlereagh Street, London W1H 6DJ. (Tel: 020-7706 4100) **Frequency:** 102.2 FM

Kiss 100 FM, Kiss House, 80 Holloway Road, London N7 8JG. (Tel: 020-7700 6100) **Frequency:** 100.0 FM

LBC 1152 AM, 200 Gray's Inn Road, London WC1X 8XZ. (Tel: 020-7973 1152) **Frequency:** 1152 AM

London Greek Radio, Florentia Village, Vale Road, London N4 1TD. (Tel: 020-8800 8001) **Frequency:** 103.3 FM

London Turkish Radio LTR, 185b High Road, Wood Green, London N22 6BA. (Tel: 020-8881 0606) **Frequency:** 1584 AM

Magic 105.4 FM, The Network Building, 97 Tottenham Court Road, London W1P 9HF. (Tel: 020-7504 6000) **Frequency:** 105.4 FM

Millennium Radio, Harrow Manor Way, Thamesmead, London SE2 9XH. (Tel: 020-8311 3112) **Frequency:** 106.8 FM

News Direct 97.3 FM, 200 Gray's Inn Road, London WC1X 8XZ. (Tel: 020-7973 1152) **Frequency:** 97.3 FM

Premier Christian Radio, Glen House, Stag Place, London SW1E 5AG. (Tel: 020-7316 1300) **Frequencies:** 1305/1332/1413 AM

Ritz 1035 AM, 33—35 Wembley Hill Road, London HA9 8RT. (Tel: 020-8733 1300) **Frequency:** 1035 AM

Sunrise Radio, Sunrise House, Sunrise Road, Southall, Middx UB2 4AU. (Tel: 020-8574 6666) **Frequency:** 1458 AM

Virgin 105.8, 1 Golden Square, London W1R 4DJ. (Tel: 030-7434 1215) **Frequency:** 105.8 FM

XFM, 30 Leicester Square, London WC2H 7LA. (Tel: 020-7766 6600) **Frequency:** 104.9 FM

THE PRESS

The press is subject to laws on publication and the Press Complaints Commission was set up by the industry as a means of self-regulation. It is not state-subsidised and receives few tax concessions. The income of most newspapers and periodicals is derived largely from sales and advertising.

PRESS COMPLAINTS COMMISSION

1 Salisbury Square, London EC4Y 8JB (Tel: 020-7353 1248; Fax: 020-7353 8355; Email: pcc@pcc.org.uk; Web: www.pcc.org.uk).

The Press Complaints Commission was founded by the newspaper and magazine industry in 1991 to replace the Press Council. It is a voluntary, non-statutory body set up to operate the press's self-regulation system following the Calcutt report in 1990 on privacy and related matters when the industry feared that a failure to regulate itself might lead to statutory regulation of the press. The Commission's objects are to consider, adjudicate, conciliate and resolve complaints of unfair treatment by the press and to ensure that the press maintains the highest professional standards with respect for generally recognised freedoms, including freedom of expression, the public's right to know and the right of the press to operate free from improper pressure. The Commission judges newspaper and magazine conduct by a code of practice drafted by editors, agreed by the industry and ratified by the Commission.

Chairman: Lord Wakeham
Director: G. Black

NEWSPAPERS

Newspapers are largely financially independent of any political party, though most adopt a political stance in their editorial comments, usually reflecting proprietorial influence. Ownership of the national and regional daily newspapers is concentrated in the hands of large corporations whose interests cover publishing and communications. The rules on cross-media ownership as amended by the Broadcasting Act 1996, limit the extent to which newspaper organisations may become involved in broadcasting.

London has a number of local daily and weekly newspapers in addition to the daily and weekly national newspapers that are published there.

NATIONAL NEWSPAPERS

The list below details all national newspapers which are published in London.

NATIONAL DAILY NEWSPAPERS

Daily Mail
Northcliffe House 2 Derry Street, London, W8 5TT (Tel: 020-7938 6000)
Editor: P. Dacre

Daily Star
Ludgate House 245 Blackfriars Road, London, SE1 9UX (Tel: 020-7928 8000; Fax: 020-7633 0244; Web: www.megastar.co.uk)
Editor: Peter Hill

Daily Telegraph
1 Canada Square, Canary Wharf, London, E14 5DT (Tel: 020-7538 5000;
E-mail: dtnews@telegraph.co.uk;
Web: www.telegraph.co.uk)
Editor: Charles Moore

The Express
Ludgate House 245 Blackfriars Road, London, SE1 9UX (Tel: 020-7928 8000)
Editor: Chris Williams

Financial Times
1 Southwark Bridge, London, SE1 9HL (Tel: 020-7873 3000; Fax: 020-7873 3072; Web: www.ft.com)
Editor: Richard Lambert

The Guardian
119 Farringdon Road, London, EC1R 3ER (Tel: 020-7278 2332; Fax: 020-7837 2114; Web: www.guardian.co.uk)
Editor: Alan Rusbridger

The Independent
1 Canada Square, Canary Wharf, London, E14 5DL (Tel: 020-7293 2000; Fax: 020-7293 2053; E-mail: letters@independent.co.uk; Web: www.independent.co.uk)
Editor-in-Chief: Simon Kelner

The Mirror
1 Canada Square, Canary Wharf, London, E14 5AP (Tel: 020-7293 3000)
Editor: Piers Morgan

Morning Star
1st Floor, Cape House, 787 Commercial Road, London, E14 7HG (Tel: 020-7538 5181; Fax: 020-7538 5125; E-mail: morsta@geo2.poptel.org.uk; Web: www.poptel.org.uk/morning-star)
Editor: J. Haylett

Racing Post
1 Canada Square, Canary Wharf, London, E14 5AP (Tel: 020-7293 3000; Fax: 020-7293 3758; E-mail: editor@racingpost.co.uk; Web: www.racingpost.co.uk)
Editor: A. Byrne

The Sun
1 Virginia Street, London, E98 1SN (Tel: 020-7782 4000; Fax: 020-7782 5605; E-mail: the-sun.co.uk; Web: www.the-sun.co.uk)
Editor: David Yelland

The Times
Times House, 1 Pennington Street, London, E98 1TT (Tel: 020-7782 5000; Web: www.thetimes.co.uk)
Editor: Peter Stothard

WEEKLY NEWSPAPERS

Sunday Express
Ludgate House 245 Blackfriars Road, London, SE1 9UX (Tel: 020-7928 8000; Fax: 020-7922 7300; E-mail: sundaynews@express.co.uk)
Editor: Michael Pilgrim

Independent on Sunday
Independent House 191 Marsh Wall, London, E14 9RS (Tel: 020-7005 2000; Fax: 020-7005 2628)
Editor: Janet Street-Porter

Mail on Sunday
Northcliffe House 2 Derry Street, London, W8 5TS (Tel: 020-7938 6000)

News of the World
1 Virginia Street, London, E98 1NW (Tel: 020-7782 4000)
Editor: Rebekah Wade

The Observer
119 Farringdon Road, London, EC1R 3ER (Tel: 020-7278 2332; Fax: 020-7713 4250; Web: www.observer.co.uk)
Editor: R. Alton

Sunday Business
3 Waterhouse Square 142 Holborn Bars, London, EC1N 2NP (Tel: 020-7961 0000; Fax: 020-7961 0102)

Sunday Mirror
1 Canada Square, Canary Wharf, London, E14 5AP (Tel: 020-7293 3000)

Sunday People
1 Canada Square, Canary Wharf, London, E14 5AP (Tel: 020-7293 3000; Fax: 020-7293 3405)
Editor: Neil Wallis

Sunday Telegraph
1 Canada Square, Canary Wharf, London, E14 5DT (Tel: 020-7538 5000; Fax: 020-7538 7872; E-mail: stnews@telegraph.co.uk; Web: www.telegraph.co.uk)
Editor: D. Lawson

Sunday Times
1 Pennington Street, London, E1 9XN (Tel: 020-7782 5000)

REGIONAL NEWSPAPERS

The list below details all regional newspapers which are based in London and whose audience is the London community.

Barking & Dagenham Express
Newspaper House, 2 Whalebone Lane South, Dagenham, Essex, RM8 1HB (Tel: 020-8517 5577; Fax: 020-8592 7407)
Editor: Dave Russell

Barking & Dagenham Post
Newspaper House, 2 Whalebone Lane South, Dagenham, Essex, RM8 1HB (Tel: 020-8517 5577; Fax: 020-8592 7407)
Editor: Dave Russell

Barking & Dagenham Recorder
539 High Road, Ilford, Essex, IG1 1UD (Tel: 020-8478 4444; Fax: 020-8478 6606; E-mail: bdrec@ser.co.uk; Web: www.ilfordrecorder.co.uk)
Editor: C. Carter

Barnet and Potters Bar Times
71 Church Road, Hendon, London, NW4 4DN (Tel: 020-8359 5959; Fax: 020-8203 9106; E-mail: times@london.newsquest.co.uk; Web: www.barnettimes.co.uk)
Editor: John Killeen

Bexley Borough Mercury
2–4 Leigham Court Road, Streatham, London, SW16 2PD (Tel: 020-8769 4444; Fax: 020-8664 7247)

Bexley & Eltham Leader
Roxby House, Station Road, Sidcup, Kent, DA15 7EJ (Tel: 020-8269 7000; Fax: 020-8269 7272; E-mail: www.independentregionals.com)
Editor: Pip Clarkson

Bexley Times Group
Roxby House, Station Road, Sidcup, Kent, DA15 7EJ (Tel: 020-8269 7000; Fax: 020-8269 7272)
Editor: Pip Clarkson

Bexleyheath & Welling News Shopper
Mega House, Crest View Drive, Petts Wood, Orpington, Kent, BR5 1BT (Tel: 01689-836211; Fax: 01689-890253;
E-mail: ngs@newsquest.media.co.uk;
Web: www.newsquestmedia.co.uk)
Editor: Ivan MacQuisten

Bexleyheath & Welling Times
Roxby House, Station Road, Sidcup, Kent, DA15 7EJ (Tel: 020-8269 7000; Fax: 020-8269 7272)
Editor: Pip Clarkson

Biggin Hill News
Winterton House High Street, Westerham, Kent, TN16 1AL (Tel: 01959-564766; Fax: 01959-562760; E-mail: kbi55@dial.pipex.com)
Editor: Gillie Bowen

Brent Leader
326 Station Road, Harrow, Middx, HA1 2DR (Tel: 020-8763 6666; Fax: 020-8863 0932)

Brentwood Recorder
3 River Chambers, High Street, Romford, Essex, RM1 1JD (Tel: 01708-766044; Fax: 01708-733423)
Editor: Mark Sweetingham

Bromley & Beckenham Leader
Roxby House, Station Road, Sidcup, Kent, DA15 7EJ (Tel: 020-8269 7000; Fax: 020-8269 7272)
Editor: Pip Clarkson

Bromley & Beckenham Times
Roxby House, Station Road, Sidcup, Kent, DA15 7EJ (Tel: 020-8269 7000; Fax: 020-8269 7272)
Editor: Pip Clarkson

Bromley & Hayes News Shopper
Mega House, Crest View Drive, Petts Wood, Orpington, Kent, BR5 1BT (Tel: 01689-885700; Fax: 01689-875367;
E-mail: ngs@newsquestmedia.co.uk;
Web: www.newsquestmedia.co.uk)
Editor: A. Parkes

Bromley News
Winterton House, High Street, Westerham, Kent, TN16 1AL (Tel: 01959-564766; Fax: 01959-562760; E-mail: kbi55@dial.pipex.com)
Editor: Gillie Bowen

Bromley Times Group
Roxby House, Station Road, Sidcup, Kent, DA15 7EJ (Tel: 020-8269 7000; Fax: 020-8269 7272)
Editor: Pip Clarkson

288 Media London

Camden New Journal
40 Camden Road, London, NW1 9DR
(Tel: 020-7419 9000; Fax: 020-7482 7317;
E-mail: letters.cnj@cablenet.co.uk)
Editor: Eric Gordon

Camden Chronicle
161 Tottenham Lane, Hornsey, London, N8 9BU
(Tel: 020-8340 6868; Fax: 020-8340 2444)
Editor: Tony Allcock

Chelsea News
Newspaper House, Winslow Road, Hammersmith, London, W6 9SF (Tel: 020-8741 1622; Fax: 020-8741 1973)
Editor: Paul Mosley

Chingford Guardian
News Centre, 480-500 Larkshall Road, Highams Park, London, E4 9GD (Tel: 020-8498 3400; Fax: 020-8531 2017)
Editor: Pat Stellard

Circuit Newsletter
2nd Floor, Russell Square House, 10-12 Russell Square, London, WC1B 5EE (Tel: 020-7331 2035; Fax: 020-7331 2040/42;
E-mail: sbroadfoot@pcif.org.uk;
Web: www.pcif.org.uk)
Editor: Sarah Broadfoot

City of London Recorder
182-84 High Street North, London, E6 2JD
(Tel: 020-8472 1421; Fax: 020-8471 7908;
E-mail: admin@newhamrecorder;
Web: www.newhamrecorder.co.uk)
Editor: C. Grainger

City Post
Newspaper House, Winslow Road, Hammersmith, London, W6 9SF (Tel: 020-8741 1622; Fax: 020-8741 1973)
Editor: Paul Mosley

City of Westminster Post
Newspaper House, Winslow Road, Hammersmith, London, W6 9SF (Tel: 020-8741 1622; Fax: 020-8741 1973)
Editor: Paul Mosley

Coulsdon & Purley Advertiser
Advertiser House, 19 Bartlett Street, South Croydon, Surrey, CR2 6TB (Tel: 020-8763 6666;
Fax: 020-8763 6633;
E-mail: edit@croydonadvertiser.co.uk)
Editor: M. Starbrook

Croydon Advertiser
Advertiser House, 19 Bartlett Street, South Croydon, Surrey, CR2 6TB (Tel: 020-8763 6666;
Fax: 020-8763 6633;
E-mail: edit@croydonadvertiser.co.uk)
Editor: M. Starbrook

Croydon Guardian
Newspaper House, 34–44 London Road, Morden, Surrey, SM4 5BR (Tel: 020-8646 6336;
Fax: 020-8687 4403;
E-mail: tgeohegan@london.newsquest.co.uk;
Web: www.croydonguardian.co.uk)
Editor: Jo Gumb

Croydon Post
Advertiser House, 19 Bartlett Street, South Croydon, Surrey, CR2 6TB (Tel: 020-8763 6666;
Fax: 020-8763 6633;
E-mail: edit@croydonadvertiser.co.uk)
Editor: M. Starbrook

Dulwich Guardian
Unecol House, 819 London Road, Sutton, Surrey, SM3 9BN (Tel: 020-8329 9306; Fax: 020-8329 9301; E-mail: tcoates@london.newsquaest.co.uk;
Web: www.thisisstreatham.co.uk)
Editor: Tamasin Coates

Ealing Leader
134-136 Broadway, West Ealing, London, W13 0TL (Tel: 020-8579 3131; Fax: 020-8566 1201)
Editor: John Moore

Ealing & Southall Informer
134-136 Broadway, West Ealing, Surrey, W13 0TL (Tel: 01784-433773; Fax: 01784-472608)
Editor: John Moore

East London Advertiser
138 Cambridge Heath Road, London, E1 5QJ
(Tel: 020-7790 8822; Fax: 020-7791 3061;
E-mail: ela.editorial@inuk.co.uk;
Web: www.independentregionals.com)
Editor: Richard Tidiman

Regional Newspapers

Edgware & Mill Hill Times
71 Church Road, Hendon, London, NW4 4DN (Tel: 020-8359 5959; Fax: 020-8203 9106; E-mail: times@london.newsquest.co.uk; Web: www.edgwaretimes.co.uk)
Editor: John Killeen

Eltham & Greenwich Times
Roxby House, Station Road, Sidcup, Kent, DA15 7EJ (Tel: 020-8269 7000; Fax: 020-8269 7272)
Editor: Pip Clarkson

Eltham News Shopper
Mega House, Crest View Drive, Petts Wood, Orpington, Kent, BR5 1BT (Tel: 01689-836211; Fax: 01689-890253; E-mail: nsg@newsquestmedia.co.uk; Web: www.newsquestmedia.co.uk)
Editor: Ivan MacQuisten

Enfield Advertiser
3rd Floor, Refuge House, 9–10 River Front, Enfield, Middx, EN1 3SZ (Tel: 020-8367 2345; Fax: 020-8366 9376)
Editor: Ms J. Woods

Enfield Gazette
3rd Floor, Refuge House, 9–10 River Front, Enfield, Middx, EN1 3SZ (Tel: 020-8367 2345; Fax: 020-8366 9376; E-mail: news@enfieldgazette.demon.co.uk)
Editor: Ms J. Woods

Enfield/Haringey Independent
Guardian House, 480–500 Larkshall Road, London, E4 GGD (Tel: 020-8498 3400; Fax: 020-8531 2017)
Editor: Kate Russell

Epping Forest & Redbridge Independent
Guardian House, 480–500 Larkshall Road, London, E4 9GD (Tel: 020-8498 3400; Fax: 020-8531 2017; E-mail: djackman@london.newsevent.co.uk; Web: www.thisiseppingforest.co.uk)
Editor: M. Oldaker

Epsom & Banstead Informer
19 Bartlett Street, South Croydon, Surrey, CR2 6TB (Tel: 020-8763 6666; Fax: 020-8763 6600)
Editor: Andy O'Hara

Erith & Crayford Times
Roxby House, Station Road, Sidcup, DA15 7EJ (Tel: 020-8269 7000; Fax: 020-8269 7272)
Editor: Pip Clarkson

Evening Standard
Northcliffe House, 2 Derry Street, London, W8 5TT (Tel: 020-7938 6000; Fax: 020-7937 2648; Web: www.thisislondon.com)
Editor: M. Hastings

Fulham and Hammersmith Chronicle
Newspaper House, Winslow Road, Hammersmith, London, W6 9SF (Tel: 020-8741 1622; Fax: 020-8741 1973)
Editor: Ian Patel

Greenwich Borough Mercury
2–4 Leigham Court Road, Streatham, London, SW16 2PD (Tel: 020-8769 4444; Fax: 020-8664 7247)

Greenwich & Charlton News Shopper
Mega House, Crest View Drive, Petts Wood, Orpington, Kent, BR5 1BT (Tel: 01689-836211; Fax: 01689-890253)
Editor: Ivan MacQuisten

Hackney Gazette and North London Advertiser
138 Cambridge Heath Road, London, E1 5QJ (Tel: 020-7790 8822; Fax: 020-7791 0401; Web: www.independentregionals.com)
Editor: N. O'Flynn

Hammersmith Chronicle
Newspaper House, Winslow Road, Hammersmith, London, W6 9SF (Tel: 020-8741 1622; Fax: 020-8741 1973)
Editor: Paul Mosley

Hammersmith & Fulham Independent
Unit 8, Concord Business Centre, Concord Road, London, W3 0TR (Tel: 020-8752 0052; Fax: 020-8896 3654)
Editor: David Hetherington

Hampstead & Highgate Express
100A Avenue Road, Hampstead, London, NW3 3HF (Tel: 020-7433 0000; Fax: 020-7483 5566; E-mail: editorial@hamhigh.co.uk; Web: hamhigh.co.uk)
Editor: Ross Lydall

Haringey Advertiser
3rd Floor, Refuge House, 9–10 River Front, Enfield, Middx, EN1 3SZ (Tel: 020-8367 2345; Fax: 020-8366 9376)
Editor: Ms Justine Woods

Haringey Independent
480-500 Larkshall Road, Highams Park, London, E4 9GD (Tel: 020-8498 3400; Fax: 020-8531 2017; Web: www.thisisharingeyborough.co.uk)
Editor: Kate Russell

Haringey Weekly Herald
161 Tottenham Lane, Hornsey, London, N8 9BU (Tel: 020-8340 6868; Fax: 020-8340 6577)
Editor: Tony Allcock

Harrow Informer
9–11 High Street, Egham, Surrey, TW20 9EA (Tel: 020-8680 4200; Fax: 020-8681 5049; E-mail: barbara@bmpublications.co.uk; Web: www.hupmag.co.uk)
Editor: Barbara Field

Harrow Leader
326 Station Road, Harrow, Middx, HA1 2DR (Tel: 020-8427 4404; Fax: 020-8863 1727)
Editor: Mrs S. Crawley

Harrow Observer
3rd Floor, Refuge House, 9–10 River Front, Enfield, Middx, EN1 3SZ (Tel: 020-8367 2345; Fax: 020-8366 9376)
Editor: Mrs S. Crawley

Heathrow Villager
260 Kingston Road, Staines, Middx, TW18 1PG (Tel: 01784-453196; Fax: 01784-453196)
Editor: I. West

Hendon & Finchley Times
71 Church Road, Hendon, London, NW4 4DN (Tel: 020-8359 5959; Fax: 020-8203 9106; E-mail: times@london.newsquest.co.uk; Web: www.hendontimes.co.uk)
Editor: John Killeen

Highbury & Islington Express
1 Aztec Row, Berners Road, Islington, London, N1 0PW (Tel: 020-7359 4886; Fax: 020-7288 1065; Web: www.islingtonexpress.co.uk)
Editor: R. Lydall

Hillingdon Informer
Gazette House, 28 Bakers Road, Uxbridge, Middsx, UB8 1RG (Tel: 01784-433773; Fax: 01895-451070)
Editor: Andrew Longden

Hornsey, Wood Green & Tottenham Journal
161 Tottenham Lane, Hornsey, London, N8 9BU (Tel: 020-8340 6868; Fax: 020-8340 6577)
Editor: Tony Allcock

Hounslow & Chiswick Informer
Informer House, 2 High Street, Teddington, Middx, TW11 8EW (Tel: 020-8943 5171; Fax: 020-8943 1555)
Editor: Andy O'Hara

Hounslow Leader
134–136 Broadway, London, W13 0TL (Tel: 020-7381 6262; Fax: 020-8566 1201)
Editor: Anthony Longden

Ilford Recorder
539 High Road, Ilford, Essex, IG1 1UD (Tel: 020-8478 4444; Fax: 020-8478 6606; E-mail: ilfordrec@ser.co.uk; Web: www.ilfordrecorder.co.uk)
Editor: C. Carter

Ilford & Redbridge Post
Newspaper House, 2 Whalebone Lane South, Dagenham, Essex, RM8 1HB (Tel: 020-8517 5577; Fax: 020-8592 7407)
Editor: Dave Russell

India Times
Global House, 90 Ascot Gardens, Southall, Middx, UB1 2SB (Tel: 020-8575 0151; Fax: 020-8575 5661)
Editor: Ram Kumar Virka

Islington Chronicle
161 Tottenham Lane, Hornsey, London, N8 9BU (Tel: 020-8340 6868; Fax: 020-8340 2444; Web: www.islingtongazette.co.uk)
Editor: Tony Allcock

Islington Gazette
161 Tottenham Lane, Hornsey, London, N8 9BU (Tel: 020-8340 6868; Fax: 020-8340 6577)
Editor: J. Isherwood

Jobs & Careers
Mega House, Crest View Drive, Petts Wood, Orpington, Kent, BR5 1BT (Tel: 01689-836211; Fax: 01689-890253; E-mail: slg@newsquestmedia.co.uk)
Editor: Roger Mills

Kensington & Chelsea News
Newspaper House, Winslow Road, Hammersmith, London, W6 9SF (Tel: 020-8741 1622; Fax: 020-8741 1973)
Editor: Ian Patel

Kensington News
Newspaper House, Winslow Road, Hammersmith, London, W6 9SF (Tel: 020-8741 1622; Fax: 020-8741 1973)
Editor: Paul Mosley

Kentish Times Newspapers
38–46 Harmer Street, Gravesend, Kent, DA12 2AY (Tel: 020-8269 7000; Fax: 020-8269 7272; E-mail: ktneditorial@innk.co.uk)
Editor: Pip Clarkson

Kentish Times Series & Leader Series
Roxby House, Station Road, Sidcup, Kent, DA15 7EJ (Tel: 020-8269 7000; Fax: 020-8269 7272)
Editor: Pip Clarkson

Kingston Borough Guardian
Unecol House, 819 Condon Road, North Cheam, Surrey, SM3 9BN (Tel: 020-8646 6336; Fax: 020-8329 9357; E-mail: slg@newsquestmedia.co.uk; Web: www.newsquestmedia.co.uk)
Editor: Sean Duccan

Kingston Informer
Informer House, 2 High Street, Teddington, Middx, TW11 8EW (Tel: 020-8943 5171; Fax: 020-8943 1555)
Editor: Andy O'Hara

Lewisham Borough Mercury
2–4 Leigham Court Road, Streatham, London, SW16 2PD (Tel: 020-8769 4444; Fax: 020-8664 7247

Lewisham & Catford News Shopper
Mega House, Crest View Drive, Petts Wood, Orpington, Kent, BR5 1BT (Tel: 01689-836211; Fax: 01689-875367)
Editor: Andrew Parkes

Leyton, Leytonstone Guardian
News Centre, Guardian House, 480–500 Larkshall Road, London, E4 GGD (Tel: 020-8498 3400; Fax: 020-8531 2017)
Editor: Pat Stannard

London Gazette
The Stationery Office, PO Box 7923, London, SE1 5ZH Tel: 020-7394 4580; Fax: 020-7394 4581; Web: www.london-gazette.co.uk)
Managing Editor: D. Mabbutt

Loot
Loot House, 24–32 Kilburn High Road, London, NW6 5TF (Tel: 020-7625 0266; Fax: 020-7625 7921; E-mail: freeads.london@loot.com; Web: www.loot.com)
Editor: Susannah Hughes

Marylebone and Paddington Mercury
Newspaper House, Winslow Road, Hammersmith, London, W6 9SF (Tel: 020-8741 1622; Fax: 020-8741 1973)
Editor: Paul Mosley

New Addington Advertiser
Advertiser House, 19 Bartlett Street, South Croydon, Surrey, CR2 6TB (Tel: 020-8763 6666; Fax: 020-8763 6633; E-mail: edit@croydonadvertiser.co.uk)
Editor: M. J. Starbrook

Newham and Docklands Recorder
184 High Street North, London, E6 2JD (Tel: 020-8472 1421; Fax: 020-8471 7908; Web: www.newhamrecorder.co.uk)
Editor: Colin Graingon

Orpington & Chislehurst & Beckenham News Shopper, Mega House, Crest View Drive, Petts Wood, Orpington, Kent, BR5 1BT (Tel: 01689-836211; Fax: 01689-890253; E-mail: nsg@newsquestmiedia.co.uk; Web: www.newsquestmedia.co.uk)
Editor: Ivan MacQuisten

Orpington & Chislehurst Leader
38–46 Harmer Street, Gravesend, Kent, DA12 2AY (Tel: 01474-363363; Fax: 01474-320316)
Editor: Pip Clarkson

292 Media London

Paddington Mercury
Newspaper House, Winslow Road, Hammersmith, London, W6 9SF (Tel: 020-8741 1622; Fax: 020-8741 1973)
Editor: Paul Mosley

Penge & Sydenham News Shopper
Mega House, Crest View Drive, Petts Wood, Orpington, Kent, BR5 1BT (Tel: 01689-836211; Fax: 01689-890253;
E-mail: ngs@newsquestmedia.co.uk;
Web: www.newsquestmedia.co.uk)
Editor: Ivan MacQuisten

Putney Chronicle
Newspaper House, Winslow Road, Hammersmith, London, W6 9SF (Tel: 020-8741 1622; Fax: 020-8741 1973)
Editor: Paul Mosley

Putney & Wimbledon Times
14 King Street, Richmond, Surrey, TW9 1NF (Tel: 020-8940 6030; Fax: 020-8332 1899;
E-mail: ed@dimbleby.co.uk;
Web: www.dimbleby.co.uk)
Editor: M. Richards

Richmond & Twickenham Informer
Informer House, 2 High Street, Teddington, Middx, TW11 8EW (Tel: 020-8943 5171; Fax: 020-8943 1555)
Editor: Andy O'Hara

Richmond & Twickenham Times
14 King Street, Richmond, Surrey, TW9 1NF (Tel: 020-8940 6030; Fax: 020-8332 1071;
E-mail: ed@dimbleby.co.uk;
Web: www.dimbleby.co.uk)
Editor: Malcolm Richards

Romford & Havering Post
Newspaper House, 2 Whalebone Lane South, Dagenham, Essex, RM8 1HB (Tel: 020-8517 5577; Fax: 020-8592 7407)
Editor: Dave Russell

Romford & Hornchurch Recorder
3 River Chambers, High Street, Romford, Essex, RM1 1JD (Tel: 01708-771500; Fax: 01708-771520)
Editor: M. Sweetingham

Hillingdon Informer
Gazette House, 28 Bakers Road, Uxbridge, UB8 1RG (Tel: 01895-451000; Fax: 01895-451070)
Editor: Anthony Longden

Sidcup & Blackfen Times
38–46 Harmer Street, Gravesend, Kent, DA12 2AY (Tel: 01474-363363; Fax: 01747-320316)
Editor: Pip Clarkson

South London Press
2–4 Leigham Court Road, Streatham, London, SW16 2PD (Tel: 020-8769 4444; Fax: 020-8664 7247)

Southwark News
Unit J104, Tower Bridge Business Complex, Clement's Road, London, SE16 4DG (Tel: 020-7231 5258)
Editor: David Clark

Stratford Express and Docklands Express
138 Cambridge Heath Road, London, E1 5QJ (Tel: 020-7790 8822; Fax: 020-7791 3061;
E-mail: se.editorial@inuk.co.uk)
Editor: Pat O'Conner

Stratford & Newham Express
138 Cambridge Heath Road, London, E1 5QJ (Tel: 020-7790 8822; Fax: 020-7790 0646)
Editor: Pat O'Conner

Streatham & Clapham Guardian
Newspaper House, 34–44 London Road, Morden, Surrey, SM4 5BR (Tel: 020-8646 6336; Fax: 020-8687 4403)

Streatham, Tooting, Brixton & Clapham Mercury
South London Press and Mercury Group, 2–4 Leigham Court Road, London, SW16 2PD (Tel: 020-8769 4444; Fax: 020-8769 1742)

Surrey Comet
Newspaper House, 34–44 London Road, Morden, Surrey, SM4 5BR (Tel: 020-8646 6336; Fax: 020-8687 4403)
Editor: Margaret Strayton

Regional Newspapers 293

Sutton Borough Guardian
Newspaper House, 34–44 London Road, Morden, Surrey, SM4 5BR (Tel: 020-8646 6336; Fax: 020-8687 4403;
E-mail: slg@newsquestmedia.co.uk;
Web: www.newsquestmedia.co.uk)
Editor: Margaret Strayton

Sutton Herald
Trinity House, 51 London Road, Reigate, Surrey, RH2 9PR (Tel: 01737-732000; Fax: 01737-732001)
Editor: Adrian Seal

Tottenham & Wood Green Journal
161 Tottenham Lane, Hornsey, London, N8 9BU (Tel: 020-8340 6868; Fax: 020-8340 2444)
Editor: Tony Allcock

Uxbridge & Hillingdon Leader
3rd Floor, Refuge House, 9–10 River Front, Enfield, Middx, EN1 3SZ (Tel: 020-8567 2345; Fax: 020-8366 9376)
Editor: Richard Parsons

Waltham Forest Guardian
Guardian House, 480–500 Larkshall Road, London, E4 GGD (Tel: 020-8498 3400; Fax: 020-8531 2017;
Web: www.thisiswalthamforest.co.uk)
Editor: Pat Stannard

Waltham Forest Independent
News Centre, Fulbourne Road, Walthamstow, London, E17 4EW (Tel: 020-8531 4141; Fax: 020-8527 3696)
Editor: Peter Dyke

Walthamstow Guardian
News Centre, Fulbourne Road, Walthamstow, London, E17 4EW (Tel: 020-8531 4141; Fax: 020-8527 3696)
Editor: Peter Dyke

Walton & Weybridge Informer
Informer House, 2 High Street, Teddington, Middx, TW11 8EW (Tel: 020-8943 5171; Fax: 020-8943 1555)
Editor: Andy O'Hara

Wandsworth Borough Guardian
Unecol House, 819 London Road, Cheam, Surrey, SM3 9BN (Tel: 020-8646 6336; Fax: 020-8329 9364)
Editor: Ms G. Gray

Wandsworth Borough News
14 King Street, Richmond, Surrey, TW9 1NF (Tel: 020-8940 6030; Fax: 020-8332 1899;
E-mail: ed@dimbleby.co.uk;
Web: www.dimbleby.co.uk)
Editor: M. Richards

Wanstead & Woodford Guardian
Guardian House, 480–500 Larkshall Road, London, E4 GGD (Tel: 020-8498 3400; Fax: 020-8531 2017)
Editor: Leigh Tarrow

West Essex Gazette
8 Simon Campion Court, High Street, Epping, Essex, CH16 4AU (Tel: 01992-572285; Fax: 01992-574039;
E-mail: djackman@london.newsquest.co.uk;
Web: www.eppingguardian.co.uk)
Editor: David Jackman

Westminster Independent Series
Unit 8, Concord Business Centre, Concord Road, London, W3 0TR (Tel: 020-8752 0052; Fax: 020-8896 3654)
Editor: David Hetherington

Westminster & Pimlico News
Newspaper House, Winslow Road, Hammersmith, London, W6 9SF (Tel: 020-8741 1622; Fax: 020-8741 1973)
Editor: Paul Mosley

Wimbledon - Mitcham - Morden Guardian
Unecol House, 819 London Road, Cheam, Surrey, SM3 9BN (Tel: 020-8646 6336; Fax: 020-8329 9364)
Editor: Ms G. Gray

Woolwich & Plumstead News Shopper
Mega House, Crest View Drive, Petts Wood, Orpington, Kent, BR5 1BT (Tel: 01689-836211; Fax: 01689-890253)
Editor: Ivan MacQuisten

Yellow Advertiser East End Series
137 George Lane, South Woodford, London, E18 1AJ (Tel: 020-8989 6688; Fax: 020-8530 4217)
Editor: Hannah Walker

294 Media London

Yellow Advertiser - Havering Services (Romford & Hornchurch Edition)
137 George Lane, South Woodford, London, E18 1AJ (Tel: 020-8989 6688; Fax: 020-8530 4217)
Editor: Hannah Walker

Yellow Advertiser Redbridge Series (Ilford, Redbridge)
137 George Lane, South Woodford, London, E18 1AJ (Tel: 020-8989 6688; Fax: 020-8530 4217)
Editor: Hannah Walker

Yellow Advertiser Waltham Forest Series (Walthamstow, Epping Forest, Chingford)
137 George Lane, South Woodford, London, E18 1AJ (Tel: 020-8989 6688; Fax: 020-8530 4217)
Editor: Hannah Walker

TRADE, PROFESSIONAL AND ACADEMIC PERIODICALS
The list below details popular trade periodicals which are published in London.

ABG Professional Information
40 Bernard Street, London, WC1N 1LD (Tel: 020-7833 3291; Fax: 020-7833 2085;
E-mail: postmaster@theabg.demon.co.uk;
Web: www.accountancymagazine.com)
Editor: B. Singleton-Green

Accountancy Age
VNU House, 32–34 Broadwick Street, London, W1A 2HG (Tel: 020-7316 9000; Fax: 020-7316 9250; E-mail: accountancy—age@vnc.co.uk; Web: www.accountancyage.com)
Editor: Damian Wild

Antique Dealer and Collectors Guide
PO Box 805, London, SE10 8TD (Tel: 020-8691 4820; Fax: 020-8691 2489;
E-mail: antiquedealercollectorsguide@ukbusiness.com;
Web: www.antiquecollectorsguide.co.uk)
Editor: P. Bartlam

Antiques Trade Gazette
115 Shaftesbury Avenue, London, WC2H 8AD (Tel: 020-7420 6600; Fax: 020-7420 6633;
E-mail: editorial@antiquestradegazette.com;
Web: www.antiquestradegazette.com)
Editor: Ivan Macquisten

The Architects' Journal
151 Rosebery Avenue, London, EC1R 4QW (Tel: 020-7505 6700; Fax: 020-7505 6701;
E-mail: austin.williams@construct.emap.com;
Web: www.ajplus.co.uk)
Editor: Isabel Allen

The Architectural Review
151 Rosebery Avenue, London, EC1R 4GB (Tel: 020-7505 6725; Fax: 020-7505 6701;
E-mail: peter.davey@ebc.emap.co.uk;
Web: www.arplus.com)
Editor: P. Davey

The Author
Society of Authors, 84 Drayton Gardens, London, SW10 9SB (Tel: 020-7373 6642; Fax: 020-7373 5768;
E-mail: dparker@societyofauthors.org;
Web: www.societyofauthors.prg)
Editor: D. Parker

The Biochemist
The Biochemical Society, 59 Portland Place, London, W1M 3AJ (Tel: 020-7580 5530; Fax: 020-7323 1136;
E-mail: editorial@portlandpress.com;
Web: www.biochemistry.org)
Editor: Dr F. Burnet

Biologist
Institute of Biology, 20–22 Queensberry Place, London, SW7 2DZ (Tel: 020-7581 8333; Fax: 020-7823 9409; E-mail: biologist@iob.org;
Web: www.iob.org)
Editor: Mrs A. Bailey

The Bookseller
5th Floor, Endeavour House, 189 Shaftesbury Avenue, London, WC2H 8TJ (Tel: 020-7420 6000; Fax: 020-7420 6177;
Web: www.thebookseller.com)
Editor: N. Clee

Trade Periodicals 295

British Dental Journal
64 Wimpole Street, London, W1G 8YS
(Tel: 020-7535 5830; Fax: 020-7535 5843;
E-mail: bdj@bda-dentistry.co.uk;
Web: www.bdj.co.uk)
Editor: Mike Grace

British Journal of Photography
39 Earlham Street, London, WC2H 9LT
(Tel: 020-7306 7000; Fax: 020-7306 7112;
E-mail: bjp.editor@bjphoto.co.uk;
Web: www.bjphoto.co.uk)
Editor: Jon Tarrant

British Journal of Psychiatry
Royal College of Psychiatrists, 17 Belgrave Square, London, SW1X 8PG (Tel: 020-7235 2351; Fax: 020-7259 6507;
Web: www.rcpsych.ac.uk)
Editor: Prof. G. Wilkinson

British Medical Journal
British Medical Association, BMA House, Tavistock Square, London, WC1H 9JR (Tel: 020-7387 4499; Fax: 020-7383 6418;
E-mail: bmj@bmj.com; Web: www.bmj.com)
Editor: Dr R. Smith

British Tax Review
100 Avenue Road, London, NW3 3PF
(Tel: 020-7393 7000; Fax: 020-7393 7020)

Building
Exchange Tower, 2 Harbour Exchange Square, London, E14 9GE (Tel: 020-7560 4000)

Campaign
174 Hammersmith Road, London, W6 7JP
(Tel: 020-8267 4656; Fax: 020-8267 4915;
E-mail: campaign@haynet.com;
Web: www.campaignlive.com)
Editor: Caroline Marshall

Chemistry and Industry
15 Belgrave Square, London, SW1X 8PS
(Tel: 020-7235 3681; Fax: 020-7235 9410;
E-mail: enquiries@soci.org;
Web: www.chemind.org)
Editor: S. Robinson

Chemistry in Britain
Royal Society of Chemistry, Burlington House, Piccadilly, London, W1J 0BA (Tel: 020-7440 3360; Fax: 020-7494 1134;
E-mail: editorial@chembrit.co.uk;
Web: www.chemsoc.org)
Editor: R. Stevenson

Classical Music
241 Shaftesbury Avenue, London, WC2H 8TF
(Tel: 020-7333 1742; Fax: 020-7333 1769;
E-mail: classical.music@rhinegold.co.uk;
Web: www.rhinegold.co.uk)
Editor: Keith Clarke

Community Care
Quadrant House, The Quadrant, Sutton, Surrey, SM2 5AS (Tel: 020-8625 3500; Fax: 020-8652 4739; E-mail: polly.neate@rbi.co.uk;
Web: www.community-care.co.uk)
Editor: Ms P. Neate

Computer Weekly
Quadrant House, The Quadrant, Sutton, Surrey, SM2 5AS (Tel: 020-8652 8642; Fax: 020-8652 8979; E-mail: computerweekly@rbi.co.uk;
Web: www.computerweekly.com)
Editor: Karl Schneider

Computing
VNU House 32-34 Broadwick Street, London, W1A 2HG (Tel: 020-7316 9000)

Construction News
151 Rosebery Avenue, London, EC1R 4GB
(Tel: 020-7505 6868; Fax: 020-7505 6867;
Web: wwwcnplus.co.uk)
Editor: Aaron Morby

Container Management
4th Floor, Regal House, 70 London Road, Twickenham, Middx, TW1 3QS (Tel: 020-8891 1199; Fax: 020-8892 2292;
E-mail: cm.editor@ukgateway.net)
Editor: Ms J. Nunan

Contract Journal
Quadrant House, The Quadrant, Sutton, Surrey, SM2 5AS (Tel: 020-8652 4642; Fax: 020-8652 8958; Web: www.contractjournal.com)
Editor: Rob Willock

Integrated Manufacturing Solutions
St Giles House, 50 Poland Street, London, W1V 4AY (Tel: 020-7970 4119; Fax: 020-7970 4191; E-mail: pgay@centaur.co.uk; Web: www.e4engineering.com)
Editor: P. Gay

Crafts Magazine
Crafts Council, 44A Pentonville Road, London, N1 9BY (Tel: 020-7806 2538; Fax: 020-7837 0858; E-mail: crafts@craftscouncil.org.uk; Web: www.craftscouncil.org.uk)
Editor: G. Rudge

The Criminologist
Tolley House, 2 Addiscombe Road, Croydon, CR9 5AF

The Dentist
Unit 2, Riverview Business Park, Walnut Tree Close, Guildford, Surrey, GU1 4QT (Tel: 01483-304944; Fax: 01483-303191; E-mail: geowarman@aol.com)
Editor: Ms J. Dyer

Design Week
St Giles House, 49–50 Poland Street, London, W1F 7AX (Tel: 020-7970 6666; Fax: 020-7970 6430; E-mail: design-week@centaur.co.uk; Web: www.design-week.co.uk)
Editor: Lynda Relph-Knight

The Director
(Magazine of the Institute of Directors) 116 Pall Mall, London, SW1Y 5ED (Tel: 020-7766 8950; Fax: 020-7766 8840; E-mail: director-ed@iod.co.uk; Web: www.iod.co.uk)
Editor: Ms J. Higgins

Drapers Record
Angel House, 338–346 Goswell Road, London (Tel: 020-7520 1534; Fax: 020-7837 4699; E-mail: dr@fashion.emap.co.uk; Web: www.drapersrecord.com)
Editor: Eric Musgrave

Electrical Review
Ann Berlin House, 9-13 Ewell Road, Cheam, Surrey, SM3 8JT (Tel: 020-8643 6207)

Electrical Times
Ann Berlin House, 9-13 Ewell Road, Cheam, Surrey, SM3 8JT (Tel: 020-8643 6207)

Electronic Engineering
City Reach, 5 Greenwich View Place, Millharbour, London, E14 9NN (Tel: 020-7861 6140)

The Engineer
St Giles House, 50 Poland Street, London, W1F 7AX (Tel: 020-7970 4100; Fax: 020-7970 4189; Web: www.e4engineering.com)
Editor: P. Carslake

Equity Journal
Guild House, Upper St Martin's Lane, London, WC2H 9EG (Tel: 020-7379 6000; Fax: 020-7379 6074; E-mail: mbrown@equity.org.uk; Web: www.equity.org.uk)
Editor: M. Brown

Estates Gazette
151 Wardour Street, London, W1V 4BN (Tel: 020-7437 0141; Web: www.egi.co.uk)
Editor: Peter Bill

Farmers Weekly
Quadrant House, The Quadrant, Sutton, Surrey, SM2 5AS (Tel: 020-8652 4911; Fax: 020-8652 4005; E-mail: farmers.weekly@rbi.co.uk; Web: www.fwi.co.uk)
Editor: S. D. Howe

Financial Management
Chartered Institute of Management Accountants 63 Portland Place, London, W1N 4AB (Tel: 020-7637 2311)

Fishing New International
Meed House, 21 John Street, London, WC1N 2BP (Tel: 020-7470 6200; Fax: 020-7831 9362; E-mail: ian.strutt@informer.com; Web: www.heighway.co.uk)
Editor: Ian Strutt

Flight International
Quadrant House, The Quadrant, Sutton, Surrey, SM2 5AS (Tel: 020-8652 3842; Fax: 020-8652 3840; E-mail: flight.international@rbi.co.uk; Web: www.flightinternational.com)
Editor: Ms C. Reed

Trade Periodicals

Gas Engineering and Management
Institution of Gas Engineers
21 Portland Place, London, W1B 1PY
(Tel: 020-7636 6603; Fax: 020-7636 6602;
E-mail: julie@igaseng.demon.co.uk;
Web: www.igaseng.com)
Editor: Peter Marsden

Hairdressers' Journal International
Quadrant House, The Quadrant, Sutton, Surrey,
SM2 5AS (Tel: 020-8652 8251; Fax: 020-8652 8937)
Editor: Jane Lewis-Orr

The Health Service Journal
Greater London House, Hampstead Road,
London, NW1 7EJ (Tel: 020-7874 0200; Fax: 020-7874 0201)

Heating, Ventilating and Plumbing
Hereford House, Bridle Path, Croydon, Surrey,
CR9 4NL

Index on Censorship
Writers and Scholars International Ltd, 33 Islington High Street, London, N1 9LH
(Tel: 020-7278 2313; Fax: 020-7278 1878;
E-mail: natasha@indexoncensorship.org;
Web: www.indexoncensorship.org)
Editor: Judith Vidal-Hall

The Journalist
National Union of Journalists, Acorn House,
314–320 Gray's Inn Road, London, WC2X 8DP
(Tel: 020-7278 7916)

Journal of Alternative and Complementary Medicine
The White House, Roxby Place, London, SW6 1RS (Tel: 020-7385 9848)
Editor: G. Millar

Journal of the British Astronomical Association
Burlington House, Piccadilly, London, W1J OBQ (Tel: 020-7734 4145; Fax: 020-7439 4629;
Web: www.star.ucl.ac.uk)
Editor: Mrs H. McGee

Justice of the Peace Reports
Harsbury House, 35 Chancery Lane, London,
WC2A 1EL (Tel: 020-7400 2828; Fax: 020-7400 2805; E-mail: jpn@tolley.co.uk;
Web: www.butterworths.com)
Editor: Dr R. Munday

The Lancet
84 Theobald's Road, London, WC1X 8RR
(Tel: 020-7611 4100; Fax: 020-7611 4101)

Law Quarterly Review
100 Avenue Road, London, NW3 3PF
(Tel: 020-7393 7000; Fax: 020-7393 7020;
Web: www.sweetandmaxwell.co.uk)
Editor: Prof. F. Reynolds

The Law Reports
Megarry House, 119 Chancery Lane, London,
WC2A 1PP (Tel: 020-7242 6741; Fax: 020-7831 5247; E-mail: postmaster@iclr.co.uk;
Web: www.lawreports.co.uk)
Editor: R. Williams

Law Society's Gazette
6th Floor, Newspaper House, 8–16 Great New Street, London, EC4A 3BN (Tel: 020-7320 5820; Fax: 020-7831 0869;
E-mail: gazette-editorial@lawsociety.org.uk;
Web: www.lawgazette.co.uk)
Editor: Jonathon Ames

Leisure and Hospitality Business
St Giles House, 49–50 Poland Street, London,
W1F 7AX (Tel: 020-7970 4588; Fax: 020-7970 4891; E-mail: mels@centaur.co.uk;
Web: www.leisureandhospitalitybusiness.co.uk)
Editor: Ms M. Swift

Library Association Record
7 Ridgmount Street, London, WC1E 7AE
(Tel: 020-7255 0500; Fax: 020-7255 0581;
E-mail: record@la-hq.org.uk;
Web: www.la-hq.org.uk/record)
Editor: Elspeth Hyams

Local Government Chronicle
Greater London House, Hampstead Road,
London, NW1 7EJ (Tel: 020-7347 1837; Fax: 020-7347 1830)
Editor: Richard Vize

Machinery Market
Wadham House, 6 Blyth Road, Bromley, Kent,
BR1 3RX (Tel: 020-8460 4224; Fax: 020-8290 1668; E-mail: editorial@machinery—market.co.uk;
Web: www.machinery—market.co.uk)
Editor: Colin Granger

Management Today
174 Hammersmith Road, London, W6 7JP
(Tel: 020-8267 4956; Fax: 020-8267 4966;
E-mail: management.today@haynet.com;
Web: www.clickmt.com)
Editor: Matthew Gwyther

Managing Information
Aslib-Imi, Staple Hall, Stone House Court, London, EC3A 7PB (Tel: 020-7903 0000; Fax: 020-7903 0011; E-mail: graham.coult@aslib.com; Web: www.managinginformation.com)
Editor: Graham Coult

Manufacturing Chemist
Tubs Hill House, London Road, Sevenoaks, Kent, TN13 1BY (Tel: 01732-470028; Fax: 01732-470047;
E-mail: shennessy@wilmington.co.uk)
Editor: Dr. Sarah Houlton

Marketing
174 Hammersmith Road, London, W6 7JP
(Tel: 020-8267 4150; Fax: 020-8267 4504;
E-mail: marketing@haynet.com;
Web: www.marketing.haynet.com)
Editor: Craig Smith

Marketing Week
St Giles House, 49–50 Poland Street, London, W1F 7AX (Tel: 020-7970 4000; Fax: 020-7970 6721; Web: www.marketing-week.co.uk)
Editor: Stuart Smith

Materials Recycling Week
19th Floor, Leon House, 233 High Street, Croydon, Surrey, CR0 9XT (Tel: 020-8277 5540; Fax: 020-8277 5560;
E-mail: recycling@maclaren.emap.co.uk)
Editor: Jane Rayner

Materials World
Institute of Materials, 1 Carlton House Terrace, London, SW1Y 5DB
(Tel: 020-7451 7300; Fax: 020-7451 7319;
E-mail: materials—world@materials.org.uk;
Web: www.materials.org.uk)
Editor: Dr S. Hill

Meat Trades Journal
Quantum House, 19 Scarbrook Road, Croydon, Surrey, CR9 1QH (Tel: 020-8565 4255; Fax: 020-8565 4250; E-mail: mtj@qpp.co.uk; Web: www.mtj.co.uk)
Editor: F. A'Court

Media Week
Quantum House, 19 Scarbrook Road, Croydon, Surrey, CR9 1LX (Tel: 020-8565 4200; Fax: 020-8565 4394; E-mail: mweeked@qpp.co.uk; Web: www.mediaweek.co.uk)
Editor: P. Barrett

Mining Journal
60 Worship Street, London, EC2A 2HD (Tel: 020-7216 6060; Fax: 020-7216 6050; E-mail: editorial@mining-journal.com; Web: www.mining-journal.com/mj)
Editor: Roger Ellis

Motor Transport
Quadrant House, The Quadrant, Sutton, Surrey, SM2 5AS

Municipal Journal
32 Vauxhall Bridge Road, London, SW1V 2SS
(Tel: 020-7973 6400; Fax: 020-7233 5051;
E-mail: m.murray@hemming-group.co.uk)

Musician
241 Shaftesbury Avenue, London, WC2H 8TF
(Tel: 020-7333 1733; Fax: 020-7333 1736;
Web: www.musiciansunion.org.uk)
Editor: B. Blain

Music Journal
Incorporated Society of Musicians, 10 Stratford Place, London, W1C 1AA
(Tel: 020-7629 4413; Fax: 020-7408 1538;
E-mail: membership@ism.org;
Web: www.ism.org)
Editor: N. Hoyle

Music Week
8 Montague Close, London Bridge, London, SE1 9UR (Tel: 020-7940 8500)

Nursing Times
Greater London House, Hampstead Road, London, NW1 7EJ (Tel: 020-787 0200)

Optician
Quadrant House, The Quadrant, Sutton, Surrey, SM2 5AS (Tel: 020-8652 8243; Fax: 020-8652 8993; Web: www.optometryonline.net)
Editor: Chris Bennett

Trade Periodicals 299

Patent World
Informa Professional Publishing 69–77 Paul Street, London, EC2A 4LQ (Tel: 020-7553 1000; Fax: 020-7553 1107;
E-mail: iquaraishi@informa.com;
Web: www.ipworldonline.com)
Editor: I. Quaraishi

People Management
17 Britton Street, London, EC1M 5TP (Tel: 020-7880 6200; Fax: 020-7336 7635;
E-mail: editorial@peoplemanagement.co.uk;
Web: www.peoplemanagement.co.uk)
Editor: S. Crabb

Personal Computer World
VNU House, 32–34 Broadwick Street, London, W1A 2HG (Tel: 020-7316 9000)

Pharmaceutical Journal
Royal Pharmaceutical Society of Great Britain 1 Lambeth High Street, London, SE1 7JN (Tel: 020-7735 9141; Fax: 020-7582 7327;
E-mail: editor@pharmj.org.uk;
Web: www.pharmj.com)
Editor: Olivia Timms

Police Review
Jane's Information Group, 180 Wardour Street, London, W1F 8FS (Tel: 020-7851 9700)

The Practitioner
City Reach, 5 Greenwich View Place, Millharbour, London, E14 9NN (Tel: 020-7861 6479)

Probation Journal
217A Balham High Road, London, SW17 7BP (Tel: 020-8671 0640; Fax: 020-8671 0640;
E-mail: prbjournal@aol.com)
Editor: H. Singh Bhui

Railway Gazette International
Quadrant House, The Quadrant, Sutton, Surrey, SM2 5AS (Tel: 020-8652 8608; Fax: 020-8652 3738; Web: www.railwaygazette.com)
Editor: M. Hughes

Rating and Valuation Reporter
4 Breams Buildings, London, EC4A 1AQ (Tel: 01483-233571; Fax: 01483-234804)

Retail Newsagent
11 Angel Gate, City Road, London, EC1V 2SD (Tel: 020-7689 0600; Fax: 020-7689 0500;
E-mail: rn@newtrade.co.uk;
Web: www.worldofmagazines.co.uk)
Editor: A. Desforges

Retail Week
Maclaren House, PO Box 109, Croydon, CR9 1QH

RUSI Journal
Royal United Services Institute for Defence Studies, Whitehall, London, SW1A 2ET (Tel: 020-7930 5854; Fax: 020-7321 0943;
Web: www.rusi.org)
Editor: Chad Paterson

Screen International
33–39 Bowling Green Lane, London, EC1R 0DA (Tel: 020-7505 8080)

Solicitors Journal
100 Avenue Road, London, NW3 3PF (Tel: 020-7393 7000; Fax: 020-7393 7880;
E-mail: solicitors.journal@sweetandmaxwell.co.uk;
Web: www.sweetandmaxwell.co.uk)
Editor: Ms S. Hart

The Stage
47 Bermondsey Street, London, SE1 3XT (Tel: 020-7403 1818; Fax: 020-7357 9287;
E-mail: editor@thestage.co.uk;
Web: www.thestage.co.uk)
Editor: B. Attwood

Structural Engineer
(Institution of Structural Engineers), 11 Upper Belgrave Street, London, SW1X 8BH (Tel: 020-7235 4535; E-mail: stansfield@istructe.org.uk;
Web: www.istructe.org.uk)
Editor: Ms K. Stansfield

Surveyor
32 Vauxhall Bridge Road, London, SW1V 2SS (Tel: 020-7973 6402; Fax: 020-7973 6677;
E-mail: editorial.surveyor@hemming-group.co.uk;
Web: www.hemming-group.co.uk)
Editor: P. Hughes

Tax Adviser
The Chartered Institute of Taxation, 12 Upper Belgrave Street, London, SW1X 8BB (Tel: 020-7235 9381; Fax: 020-7235 2562;
Web: www.tax.org.uk)
Editor: Andrew Flint

Taxi
Taxi House, 7–11 Woodfield Road, London, W9 2BA (Tel: 020-7432 1429; Fax: 020-7266 2297; E-mail: spessok@comcab.co.uk)
Editor: S. Pessok

The Teacher
National Union of Teachers, Hamilton House, Mabledon Place, London, WC1H 9BD (Tel: 020-7380 4708; Fax: 020-7387 8458; E-mail: teacher@netcomuk.co.uk;
Web: www.teachers.org.uk)
Editor: M. Howard

Teaching History
The Historical Association, 59A Kennington Park Road, London, SE11 4JH (Tel: 020-7735 3901; Fax: 020-7582 4989;
Web: www.history.org.uk)

Television
Royal Television Society, Holborn Hall, 100 Gray's Inn Road, London, WC1X 8AL (Tel: 020-7691 2465; Fax: 020-7430 0924; E-mail: publications@rts.org.uk;
Web: www.rts.org.uk)
Editor: P. Fiddick

Town and Country Planning
Town and Country Planning Association, 17 Carlton House Terrace, London, SW1Y 5AS (Tel: 020-7930 8903; Fax: 020-7930 3280; E-mail: editor@tcpa.org.uk;
Web: www.tcpa.org.uk)
Editor: Nick Matthews

Travel Trade Gazette (UK and Ireland)
1st Floor, City Reach, 5 Greenwich View Place, Millharbour, London, E14 9NN (Tel: 020-7861 6096; Fax: 020-7861 6227; E-mail: phil.davies@unmf.com)
Editor: P. Davies

Veterinary Record
British Veterinary Association, 7 Mansfield Street, London, W1G 9NQ (Tel: 020 7636 6541)

The Weekly Law Reports
Megarry House, 119 Chancery Lane, London, WC2A 1PP (Tel: 020-7242 6471; Fax: 020-7831 5247; E-mail: postmaster@iclr.co.uk;
Web: www.lawreports.co.uk)
Editor: R. Williams

CONSUMER PERIODICALS

The list below details popular consumer periodicals which are published in London.

19
King's Reach Tower, Stamford Street, London, SE1 9LS (Tel: 020-7261 5000; Fax: 020-7261 7634)
Editor: Samantha Warwick

Al Majalla
Arab Press House, 184 High Holborn, London, WC1V 7AP (Tel: 020-7831 8181; Fax: 020-7831 4051; E-mail: almajalla@hhsaudi.com)
Editor: H. Nakshabandi

Amateur Photographer
King's Reach Tower, Stamford Street, London, SE1 9LS (Tel: 020-7261 5100; Fax: 020-7261 5404; E-mail: amateurphotographer@rpcmedia.com;
Web: www.amateurphotographer.com)
Editor: Garry Coward-Williams

Apollo
1 Castle Lane, London, SW1E 6DR (Tel: 020-7233 6640; Fax: 020-7630 7791; E-mail: editorial@apollomag.com;
Web: www.apollomag.com)
Editor: D. Ekserdjian

Arena
3rd Floor, Block A, Exmouth House, Pine Street, London, EC1R 0JL (Tel: 020-7689 9999; Fax: 020-7689 0902/1; E-mail: editorial@arenamag.co.uk)
Editor: Mark Ellen

Art Monthly
4th Floor, 28 Charing Cross Road, London, WC2H 0Db (Tel: 020-7240 0389; Fax: 020-7497 0726; E-mail: info@artmonthly.co.uk;
Web: www.artmonthly.co.uk)
Editor: Ms P. Bickers

Consumer Periodicals 301

Autocar
60 Waldegrave Road, Teddington, Middx, TW11 8LG (Tel: 020-8267 5630; Fax: 020-8267 5759; E-mail: autocar@haynet.com)
Editor: Roy Aherne

BBC Gardener's World Magazine
Woodlands, 80 Wood Lane, London, W12 0TT (Tel: 020-8433 3959; Fax: 020-8433 3986; E-mail: adam.pascoe@bbc.co.uk; Web: www.gardenersworld.com)
Editor: Adam Pascoe

BBC Good Food Magazine
Woodlands, 80 Wood Lane, London, W12 0TT (Tel: 020-8433 2000; Fax: 020-8433 3931; E-mail: good.food.magazine@bbc.co.uk)
Editor: Orlando Murrin

BBC Homes and Antiques
Woodlands, 80 Wood Lane, London, W12 0TT (Tel: 020-8433 3490; Fax: 020-8433 3867)
Editor: Judith Hall

BBC Top Gear
Woodlands, 80 Wood Lane, London, W12 0TT (Tel: 020-8433 3716; Fax: 020-8433 3754; E-mail: Kevin.Blick@bbc.co.uk; Web: www.topgear.com)
Editor: Kevin Blick

BBC Vegetarian Good Food
Woodlands, 80 Wood Lane, London W12 0TT

Bella
H. Baver Publishing, 24-28 Oval Road, Camden, London, NW1 7D (Tel: 020-7241 8000; Fax: 020-7241 8056)

The Big Issue
236–240 Pentonville Road, London, N1 9JY (Tel: 020-7526 3320; Fax: 020-7526 3301; E-mail: london@bigissue.com; Web: www.bigissue.com)
Editor: M. Collin

Boxing Monthly
40 Morpeth Road, London, E9 7LD (Tel: 020-8986 4141; Fax: 020-8986 4145; E-mail: mail@boxing-monthly.demon.co.uk; Web: www.boxing-monthly.co.uk)
Editor: Glyn Leach

Brides and Setting up Home
Vogue House, Hanover Square, London, W1S 1JU (Tel: 020-7499 9080; Fax: 020-7460 6369; Web: www.bridesuk.net)
Editor: Ms S. Boler

Chat
King's Reach Tower, Stamford Street, London, SE1 9LS (Tel: 020-7261 6565; Fax: 020-7261 6534; Web: www.ipcmedia.co.uk)
Editor: Vacant

Classic & Sports Car
Somerset House, Somerset Road, Teddington, Middx, TW11 8RT (Tel: 020-8267 5399; Fax: 020-8267 5318;
E-mail: letters.classicandsportscar@haynet.co.uk)
Editor: James Elliott

Company
National Magazine House, 72 Broadwick Street, London, W1V 2BP (Tel: 020-7439 5000; Fax: 020-7439 5117;
E-mail: company.mail@natmags.co.uk; Web: www.company.co.uk)
Editor: Sam Baker

Computer and Video Games
Priory Court, 30–32 Farringdon Lane, London, EC1R 3AU

Cosmopolitan
National Magazine House, 72 Broadwick Street, London, W1V 2BP (Tel: 020-7439 5000; Web: www.natmags.co.uk)
Editor: Lorraine Candy

302 Media London

Country Homes and Interiors
King's Reach Tower, Stamford Street, London, SE1 9LS (Tel: 020-7261 6451; Fax: 020-7261 6895)
Editor: Deborah Bancer

Country Life
King's Reach Tower, Stamford Street, London, SE1 9LS (Tel: 020-7261 7058; Fax: 020-7261 5139; Web: www.countrylife.co.uk)
Editor: Clive Aslet

Country Living Magazine
National Magazine House, 72 Broadwick Street, London, W1V 2BP (Tel: 020-7439 5000; Fax: 020-7439 5093; Web: www.natmags.co.uk)
Editor: Ms S. Smith

Cycling Weekly
Focus House, Dingwall Avenue, Croydon, CR0 0PH (Tel: 020-8774 0811; Fax: 020-8686 0952; E-mail: cycling@ipcmedia.com)
Editor: R. Garbutt

Daltons Weekly
Ci Tower, St George's Square, New Malden, Surrey, KT3 4JA (Tel: 020-8949 6199; Fax: 020-8949 2718; E-mail: daltons@daltons.co.uk; Web: www.daltons.co.uk)

Dance Theatre Journal
Laban Centre London, Laurie Grove, London, SE14 6NH (Tel: 020-8692 4070; Fax: 020-8694 8749; E-mail: dtj@laban.co.uk; Web: www.dancetheatrejournal.co.uk)
Editor: I. Bramley

Dancing Times
Clerkenwell House, 45–47 Clerkenwell Green, London, EC1R 0EB (Tel: 020-7250 3006; Fax: 020-7253 6679; E-mail: dt@dancing-times.co.uk; Web: www.dancing-times.co.uk)
Editor: Ms M. Clarke

The Ecologist
Unit 18, Chelsea Wharf, 15 Lots Road, London, SW10 0QJ (Tel: 020-7351 3578; Fax: 020-7351 3617; E-mail: kate@theecologist.org; Web: www.theecologist.org)
Editor: Zac Goldsmith

The Economist
25 St James's Street, London, SW1A 1HG (Tel: 020-7830 7000; Fax: 020-7839 2968; Web: www.economist.com)
Editor: B. Emmott

Edinburgh Gazette (Official)
The Stationery Office, PO Box 276, London, SW8 5DT

Elle
Endeavour House, 189 Shaftesbury Avenue, London, WC2H 8JG (Tel: 020-7437 9011; Fax: 020-7208 3599)
Editor: Ms F. McIntosh

Empire
Endeavour House, 189 Shaftesbury Avenue, London, WC2H 8J9 (Tel: 020-7437 9011; Fax: 020-7859 8613; E-mail: empire@ecm.emap.com; Web: www.empireonline.co.uk)
Editor: Ms E. Cochrane

Esquire
National Magazine House, 72 Broadwick Street, London, W1V 2BP (Tel: 020-7439 5000; Fax: 020-7312 3920; Web: www.esquire.co.uk)
Editor: Peter Howarth

Essentials
King's Reach Tower, Stamford Street, London, SE1 9LS (Tel: 020-7261 6970; Fax: 020-7261 5262)
Editor: Karen Livermore

The Face
2nd Floor, Block A, Exmouth House, Pine Street, London, EC1R 0JL

Family Circle
King's Reach Tower, Stamford Street, London, SE1 9LS (Tel: 020-7261 6195; Fax: 020-7261 5929; E-mail: familycircle@ipc.co.uk; Web: www.ipc.co.uk)
Editor: Gillian Carter

FHM
The Network Building, 97 Tottenham Court Road, London, W1T 4TP (Tel: 020-7312 8707; Fax: 020-7504 6300; Web: www.fhm.com)
Editor: A. Noguera

The Field
King's Reach Tower, Stamford Street, London, SE1 9LS (Tel: 020-7261 5198; Fax: 020-7261 5358; E-mail: marcella—bingley@ipcmedia.com; Web: www.thefield.co.uk)
Editor: J. Young

Film Review
9 Blades Court, Deodar Road, London, SW15 2NU (Tel: 020-8875 1520; Fax: 020-8875 1588; E-mail: filmreview@visimag.com; Web: www.visimag.com/filmreview)
Editor: N. Corry

Gay Times
Ground Floor, Worldwide House, 116–134 Bayham Street, London, NW1 0BA (Tel: 020-7482 2576; Fax: 020-7284 0329; E-mail: edit@gaytimes.co.uk; Web: www.gaytimes.co.uk)
Editor: C. Richardson

Geographical Journal
Royal Geographical Society/IBG, 1 Kensington Gore, London, SW7 2AR (Tel: 020-7591 3026; Fax: 020-7591 3001; E-mail: g.lowman@rgs.org; Web: www.rgs.org)
Editor: Hon. Editor: Prof. A. Millington

Good Holiday Magazine
3A High Street, Esher, Surrey, KT10 9RP (Tel: 01372-468140; Fax: 01372-470765)
Editor: John Hill

Good Housekeeping
National Magazine House, 72 Broadwick Street, London, W1V 2BP (Tel: 020-7439 5000)
Editor: Linday Nicholson

The Good Ski Guide
145–147 Ewell Road, Surbiton, Surrey, KT6 6AW (Tel: 020-8786 2950; Fax: 020-8786 2951; E-mail: info@goodskiguide.com; Web: www.goodskiguide.com)
Managing Director: Mike Welby

GQ
Vogue House, Hanover Square, London, W1R 0AD (Tel: 020-7499 9080; Fax: 020-7495 1679; E-mail: djones@condeanst.co.uk)
Editor: D. Jones

Gramophone
38–42 Hampton Road, Teddington, Middx, TW11 0JE (Web: www.gramaphone.co.uk)
Editor: James Jolly

Granta
2–3 Hanover Yard, Noel Road, London, N1 8BE (Tel: 020-7704 9776; E-mail: editorial@granta.com; Web: www.granta.com)
Editor: Ian Jack

The Guardian Weekly
75 Farringdon Road, London, EC1M 3HQ (Tel: 020-7713 4441; Fax: 020-7242 0985; E-mail: weekly@gaurdian.co.uk; Web: www.guardianweekly.co.uk)
Editor: Patrick Ensor

Guiding Magazine
17–19 Buckingham Palace Road, London, SW1W 0PT (Tel: 020-7592 1821; Fax: 020-7828 5791; E-mail: guiding@guides.org.uk; Web: www.guides.org.uk)
Editor: Ms J. Clampett

Harpers and Queen
National Magazine House, 72 Broadwick Street, London, W1V 2BP (Tel: 020-7439 5000; Fax: 020-7439 5482)
Editor: Lucy Yeomans

Having a Baby
National Magazine House, 72 Broadwick Street, London, W1V 2BP (Tel: 020-7439 5000; Fax: 020-7439 5337; E-mail: hab@natmags.co.uk; Web: www.natmags.co.uk)
Editor: Ms L. Murphy

Hello!
69–71 Upper Ground, London, SE1 9PQ (Tel: 020-7667 8700; Fax: 020-7667 8716)
Editor: Phil Hall

History Today
20 Old Compton Street, London, W1D 4TW (Tel: 020-7534 8000; E-mail: p.furtado@historytoday.com; Web: www.historytoday.com)
Editor: P. Furtado

304 Media London

Homes & Gardens
King's Reach Tower, Stamford Street, London, SE1 9LS (Tel: 020-7261 5678; Fax: 020-7261 6247)
Editor: M. Line

Horse & Hound
Room 2018, King's Reach Tower, Stamford Street, London, SE1 9LS (Tel: 020-7261 5306; Fax: 020-7261 5429;
E-mail: jenny—sims@ipcmedia,com;
Web: www.horseandhound.co.uk)
Editor: A. Garvey

House and Garden
Vogue House, Hanover Square, London, W1R 0AD (Tel: 020-7499 9080; Fax: 020-7629 2907)
Editor: Susan Crewe

House Beautiful
Jubilee House, 197 Marsh Walk, London, E14 9SG (Tel: 020-7519 5500; Fax: 020-7519 5518; Web: www.natmags.co.uk)
Editor: Ms L. Norman

Ideal Home
King's Reach Tower, Stamford Street, London, SE1 9LS

i-D Magazine
124 Tabernacle Street, London, EC2A 4SA (Tel: 020-7490 9710)
Editor: Avril Mair

Illustrated London News
20 Upper Ground, London, SE1 9PF

In Britain
Haymarket House, 1 Oxendon Street, London, SW1Y 4EE

Irish Post
Cambridge House, Cambridge Grove, London, W6 0LE (Tel: 020-8741 0649; Fax: 020-8741 3382; E-mail: irishpost@irishpost.co.uk;
Web: www.irishpost.co.uk)
Editor: Ms N. Casey

J17
Endeavour House, 189 Shaftesbury Avenue, London, WC2H 8JG (Tel: 020-7208 3408; Fax: 020-7208 3590)
Editor: Ms S. Wilson

Jazz Journal International
3 and 3A Forest Road, Loughton, Essex, IG10 1DR (Tel: 020-8532 0456; Fax: 020-8532 0440)
Editor: E. Cook

Labour Research
78 Blackfriars Road, London, SE1 8HF (Tel: 020-7928 3649; Fax: 020-7928 0624; E-mail: info@lrd.org.uk; Web: www.lrd.org.uk)
Editor: Clare Ruhemann

The Lady
39–40 Bedford Street, London, WC2E 9ER (Tel: 020-7379 4717; Fax: 020-7836 4620;
Web: www.lady.co.uk)
Editor: Ms A. Usden

Land and Liberty
Suite 427, London Fruit Exchange, Brushfield Street, London, E1 6EL (Tel: 020-7377 8885; Fax: 020-7377 8686;
E-mail: henrygeorge@charity.vfree.com;
Web: www.henrygeorgeuk.cjb.net)
Editor: F. Harrison

Literary Review
44 Lexington Street, London, W1R 3LH (Tel: 020-7437 9392; Fax: 020-7734 1844; E-mail: litrev@dircon.co.uk)
Editor: Nancy Sladek

Loaded
King's Reach Tower, Stamford Street, London, SE1 9LS; Web: www.loadweb.com)
Editor: Keith Kendrick

London Review of Books
28–30 Little Russell Street, London, WC1A 2HN (Tel: 020-7209 1101; Fax: 020-7209 1102; E-mail: edit@lrb.co.uk; Web: www.lrb.co.uk)
Editor: Mary-Kay Wilmers

Majesty
26–28 Hallam Street, London, W1N 6NP (Tel: 020-7436 4006; Fax: 020-7436 3458;
E-mail: majestymagazine@aol.com)

Marie Claire
2 Hatfields, London, SE1 9PG (Tel: 020-7261 5177; Fax: 020-7261 5277)
Editor: Marie O'Riordan

Meteorological Magazine
The Stationery Office, PO Box 276, London, SW8 5DT

Mizz
King's Reach Tower, Stamford Street, London, SE1 9LS

Model Boats
Nexus House, Azalea Drive, Swanley, Kent, BR8 8HU

Moneywise
11 Westferry Circus, Canary Wharf, London, E14 4HE (Tel: 020-7715 8465; Fax: 020-7715 8725; E-mail: matthew—vincent@readersdigest.co.uk; Web: www.moneywise.co.uk)
Editor: M. Vincent

More!
Endeavour House, 189 Shaftesbury Avenue, London, WC2H 8JG (Tel: 020-7208 3165; Fax: 020-7208 3595; E-mail: more.letters@ecm.emap.com)
Editor: Helen Bazuaye (Acting)

Mother and Baby
Greater London House, Hampstead Road, London, NW1 7EJ (Tel: 020-7347 1869; Fax: 020-7347 1888)
Editor: Dani Zur

Nature
Porters South, Crinan Street, London, N1 9SQ (Tel: 020-7833 4000)

New Musical Express (NME)
King's Reach Tower, Stamford Street, London, SE1 9LS

New Scientist
151 Wardour Street, London, W1F 8WE (Tel: 020-7331 2702; Fax: 020-7331 2777; E-mail: enquiries@newscientist.com; Web: www.newscientist.com)
Editor: Jeremy Webb

New Statesman
7th Floor, Victoria Station House, 191 Victoria Street, London, SW1E 5NE (Tel: 020-7828 1232; Fax: 020-7828 1881;

E-mail: info@newstatesman.co.uk; Web: www.newstatesman.co.uk)
Editor: P. Wilby

Newsweek
18 Park Street, London, W1Y 4HH (Tel: 020-7629 8361; Fax: 020-7408 1403; Web: www.newsweek.msnbc.com)
Editor: Bureau Chief: Stryker McGuire

New Woman
Endeavour House, 189 Shaftesbury Avenue, London, WC2H 8JG (Tel: 020-7208 3456; Fax: 020-7208 3585)
Editor: Sara Cremer

OK! Magazine
Ludgate House, 245 Blackfriars Road, London, SE1 9UX (Tel: 020-7928 8000; Fax: 020-7579 4607)
Editor: Martin Townsend

The Oldie
45–46 Poland Street, London, W1F 7NA (Tel: 020-7734 2225; Fax: 020-7734 2226; E-mail: theoldie@theoldie.co.uk; Web: www.theoldie.co.uk)
Editor: R. Ingrams

Opera
36 Black Lion Lane, London, W6 9BE (Tel: 020-8563 8893; Fax: 020-8563 8635; E-mail: editor@operamag.clara.co.uk; Web: www.opera.co.uk)
Editor: John Allison

Opera Now
241 Shaftesbury Avenue, London, WC2H 8TF (Tel: 020-7333 1740; Fax: 020-7333 1769; E-mail: opera.now@rhinegold.co.uk; Web: www.rhinegold.co.uk)
Editor: Ashutosh Khandekar

Parents
Victory House, 14 Leicester Place, London, WC2H 7BP

Parliamentary Debates (Commons) (Hansard)
The Stationery Office, PO Box 29, Norwich, NR3 1GN

Parliamentary Debates (Lords) (Hansard)
The Stationery Office, PO Box 29, Norwich, NR3 1GN

Poetry Review
22 Betterton Street, London, WC2H 9BX
(Tel: 020-7420 9883; Fax: 020-7240 4818;
E-mail: poertyreview@poertysoc.com;
Web: www.poetrysoc.com)
Editor: Peter Forbes

Practical Caravan
60 Waldegrave Road, Teddington, Middx, TW11 8LG (Tel: 020-8267 5693; Fax: 020-8267 5725; E-mail: practical.caravan@haynet.com; Web: www.practicalcaravan.com)
Editor: Carl Rodgerson

Practical Householder
53-79 Highgate Road, London, NW5 1TW (Tel: 020-7331 1000; Fax: 020-7331 1269)
Editor: John Mc Golian

Practical Parenting
King's Reach Tower, Stamford Street, London, SE1 9LS (Tel: 020-7261 5058; Fax: 020-7261 6542)
Editor: Jayne Marsden

Private Eye
6 Carlisle Street, London, W1D 3BN (Tel: 020-7437 4017; Fax: 020-7437 0705; Web: www.private-eye.co.uk)
Editor: I. Hislop

Prospect
4 Bedford Square, London, WC1B 3RA (Tel: 020-7255 1281; Fax: 020-7255 1279; E-mail: editorial@prospect-magazine.co.uk; Web: www.prospect-magazine.co.uk)
Editor: D. Goodhart

The Puzzler
Glenthorne House, Hammersmith Grove, London, W6 0LG

Q
Mappin House, 4 Winsley Street, London, W1V 8HF (Tel: 020-7436 1515; Fax: 020-7312 8247; E-mail: Q@emap.com; Web: www.Q4music.com

Radio Times
Woodlands, 80 Wood Lane, London, W12 0TT (Tel: 0870-608 4455; Fax: 020-8433 3923; E-mail: radio.timers@bbc.co.uk; Web: www.radiotimes.com

The Railway Magazine
King's Reach Tower, Stamford Street, London, SE1 9LS (Tel: 020-7261 5821; Fax: 020-7261 5269; E-mail: railway@ipcmedia.com)
Editor: N. Pigott

Reader's Digest
11 Westferry Circus, Canary Wharf, London, E14 4HE (Tel: 020-7715 8000; Fax: 020-7715 8716; Web: www.readersdigest.co.uk)
Editor: Russell Twisk

Rugby World
King's Reach Tower, Stamford Street, London, SE1 9LS (Tel: 020-7261 6810; Web: www.rugbyworld.com)
Editor: Paul Morgan

Scouting Magazine
Gilwell Park, Chingford, London, E4 7QW (Tel: 020-8433 7100; Fax: 020-8433 7103; E-mail: scouting.magazine@scout.org.uk)
Editor: Anna Sorensen Thomson

She
National Magazine House, 72 Broadwick Street, London, W1V 2BP (Tel: 020-7439 5000; Fax: 020-7312 3981; Web: www.natmags.co.uk)
Editor: Ms A. Pylkkanen

Shoot
King's Reach Tower, Stamford Street, London, SE1 9LS

Shooting Times and Country Magazine
King's Reach Tower, Stamford Street, London, SE1 9LS (Tel: 020-7261 6180; Fax: 020-7261 7179)
Editor: Julian Murray-Evans

Sky Magazine
Endeavour House, 189 Shaftesbury Avenue, London, WC2H 8JG (Tel: 020-7437 9011; Fax: 020-7859 8637; E-mail: sky@ecm.emap.com; Web: www.skymagazine.co.uk)
Editor: M. Hogan

Slimming Magazine
Greater London House, Hampstead Road, London, NW1 7EJ (Tel: 020-7347 1854; Fax: 020-7347 1863; E-mail: claire.selsby@emap.com)
Editor: Alison Hall

Consumer Periodicals 307

Smash Hits
Mappin House, 4 Winsley Street, London, W1M 7AR (Tel: 020-7436 1515)

The Spectator
56 Doughty Street, London, WC1N 2LL (Tel: 020-7405 1706; Fax: 020-7242 0603; E-mail: editor@spectator.co.uk; Web: www.spectator.co.uk)
Editor: B. Johnson

Tatler
Vogue House, Hanover Square, London, W1R 0AD (Tel: 020-7499 9080; Fax: 020-7495 0451; Web: www.tatler.co.uk)
Editor: G. Greig

Time Magazine
Brettenham House, Lancaster Place, London, WC2E 7TL (Tel: 020-7499 4080; Fax: 020-7322 1230; Web: www.time.com)
Editor: C. Redman

Time Out
Universal House, 251 Tottenham Court Road, London, W1P 0AB (Tel: 020-7813 3000; Fax: 020-7813 6001; Web: www.timeout.com)
Editor: Ms L. Lee Davies

The Times Educational Supplement
Admiral House, 66–68 East Smithfield, London, E1W 1BX (Tel: 020-7782 3000; Fax: 020-7782 3202; E-mail: editor@tes.co.uk; Web: www.tes.co.uk)
Editor: Mr R. Doe

The Times Higher Education Supplement
Admiral House, 66–68 East Smithfield, London, E1W 1BX (Tel: 020-7782 3375; Fax: 020-7782 3300; E-mail: editor@thes.co.uk; Web: www.thes.co.uk)

The Times Literary Supplement
Admiral House, 66–68 East Smithfield, London, E1W 1BX (Tel: 020-7782 3000; Fax: 020-7782 3100; E-mail: letters@the-tls.co.uk; Web: www.the-tls.co.uk)
Editor: F. Mount

Tribune
9 Arkwright Road, London, NW3 6AN (Tel: 020-7433 6410; Web: www.tribuneuk.co.uk)
Editor: M. Seddon

TV Times
King's Reach Tower, Stamford Street, London, SE1 9LS (Tel: 020-7261 7000; Fax: 020-7261 7888; E-mail: tvtimes@ipcmedia.com; Web: www.unmissabletv.com)
Editor: Peter Genower

Vacher's Parliamentary Companion
1 Douglas Street, London, SW1P 4PA (Tel: 020-7828 7256; Fax: 020-7828 7269; E-mail: politics@vacherdod.co.uk; Web: www.politicallinks.co.uk)
Publisher: Andrew Cox

Vanity Fair
Vogue House, Hanover Square, London, W1R 0AD (Tel: 020-7499 9080; Fax: 020-7493 1962)
Editor: Graydon Carter

Viz Magazine
The New Boathouse, 136–142 Bramley Road, London, W10 6SR (Tel: 020-7565 3000; Fax: 020-7565 3055; E-mail: viz.comic@virgin.net; Web: www.viz.co.uk)
Editors: S. Donald; G. Dury; S. Thorp

Vogue
Vogue House, Hanover Square, London, W1S 1JU (Tel: 020-7499 9080; Fax: 020-7408 0559; Web: www.vogue.co.uk)
Editor: Alexandra Shulman

The Voice
Blue Star House, 234–244 Stockwell Road, London, SW9 9SP (Tel: 020-7737 7377; Fax: 020-7274 8994; E-mail: mike.best@the-voice.oc.uk; Web: www.voice-online.co.uk)
Editor: Michael Best

What Car?
60 Waldegrave Road, Teddington, Middx, TW11 8LG (Tel: 020-8267 5688; Fax: 020-8267 5750; E-mail: whatcar@haynet.com; Web: www.whatcar.co.uk)
Editor: S. Fowler

Which?
2 Marylebone Road, London, NW1 4DF (Tel: 020-7830 6000)

308 Media London

Woman
King's Reach Tower, Stamford Street, London, SE1 9LS (Tel: 020-7261 7023; Fax: 020-7261 5997; E-mail: woman@ipc.co.uk; Web: www.ipc.co.uk)
Editor: Ms C. Russell

Woman and Home
King's Reach Tower, Stamford Street, London, SE1 9LS

Woman's Journal
King's Reach Tower, Stamford Street, London, SE1 9LS

Woman's Own
King's Reach Tower, Stamford Street, London, SE1 9LS (Tel: 020-7261 5500; Fax: 020-7261 5346)
Editor: Ms T. Tavner

Woman's Realm
King's Reach Tower, Stamford Street, London, SE1 9LS

Woman's Weekly
King's Reach Tower, Stamford Street, London, SE1 9LS (Tel: 0870-444 5000; Fax: 020-7261 6322)
Editor: Gilly Sinvlair

The World of Interiors
Vogue House, Hanover Square, London, W1S 1JU (Tel: 020-7499 9080; Fax: 020-7493 4013; E-mail: interiors@condenast.co.uk)

Yachting Monthly
King's Reach Tower, Stamford Street, London, SE1 9LS (Tel: 020-7261 6040; Fax: 020-7261 7555; E-mail: yachting-monthly@ipcmedia.com; Web: www.yachtingmonthly.com)
Editor: Ms S. Norbury

Zest
National Magazine House, 72 Broadwick Street, London, W1V 2BP (Tel: 020-7439 5000; Fax: 020-7312 3750; Web: www.zest.co.uk)
Editor: Eve Cameron

ZM
National Magazine House, 72 Broadwick Street, London, W1V 2BP

NEWS AGENCIES IN LONDON

News agencies provide general, business, sport and television news to a variety of subscribers including the press, other media, and industrial, commercial, financial and business users.

Associated Press
12 Norwich Street, London EC4A 4BP (Tel: 020-7353 1515; Fax: 020-7353 8118)

Hayters
146-148 Clerkenwell Road, London EC1R 5DP (Tel: 020-7837 7171; Fax: 020-7837 2420)

Parliamentary Monitoring Services
19 Douglas Street, London SW1P 4PA (Tel: 020-7233 8283)

Press Association Ltd
292 Vauxhall Bridge Road, London SW1V 1AE (Tel: 020-7963 7000; Fax: 020-7963 7192)

Reuters Ltd
85 Fleet Street, London EC4P 4AJ (Tel: 020-7250 1122; Fax: 020-7542 7921)

Two-Ten Communications Ltd
Communications House, 210 Old Street, London EC1V 9UN (Tel: 020-7490 8111; Fax: 020-7490 1255)

PUBLISHERS

Allen & Unwin
Osborne House, PO Box 30474, London, NW6 7FG (Tel: 020-8537 1531; Fax: 020-8621 3701; E-mail: allanunwin@compuserve.com; Web: www.allen-unwin.com)

Apple Press
The Old Brewery, 6 Blundell Street, London, N7 9BH (Tel: 020-7700 2929; Fax: 020-7609 6695; E-mail: apple@quarlo.com)

Arnold
338 Euston Road, London, NW1 3BH (Tel: 020-7873 6000; Fax: 020-7873 6325; E-mail: arnold@hodder.co.uk; Web: www.arnoldpublishers.com)

Arrow Books
Random House, 20 Vauxhall Bridge Road, London, SW1V 2SA (Tel: 020-7840 8400; Fax: 020-7233 6127; Web: www.randomhouse.co.uk)

Publishers

Aurum Press
25 Bedford Avenue, London, WC1B 3AT
(Tel: 020-7637 3225; Fax: 020-7580 2469;
E-mail: editorial@aurumpress.co.uk;
Web: www.aurumpress.co.uk)

Bantam Books
61–63 Uxbridge Road, London, W5 5SA
(Tel: 020-8579 2652; Fax: 020-8231 6612;
E-mail: info@transworld-publishers.co.uk;
Web: www.booksattransworld.co.uk)

Barrie & Jenkins
20 Vauxhall Bridge Road, London, SW1V 2SA
(Tel: 020-7840 8400; Fax: 020-7840 8406;
Web: www.randomhouse.co.uk)

Bartholomew
77 Fulham Palace Road, London, W6 8JB
(Tel: 020-8741 7070)

B. T. Batsford
9 Blenheim Court, Brewery Road, London, N7 9NY (Tel: 020-7700 7611; Fax: 020-7700 4552; E-mail: batsford@chrysalisbooks.co.uk;
Web: www.batsford.com)

Berlitz Publishing Co.
4th Floor, 9 Grosvenor Street, London, W1X 9FB (Tel: 020-7518 8300; Fax: 020-7518 8310; E-mail: publishing@berlitz.co.uk;
Web: www.berlitz.co.uk)

A. & C. Black (Publishers) Ltd
35 Bedford Row, London, WC1R 4JH (Tel: 020-7242 0946; Fax: 020-7831 8478;
E-mail: enquiries@acblack.com)

Bloomsbury Publishing
38 Soho Square, London, W1V 5DF
(Tel: 020-7494 2111; Fax: 020-7434 0151;
Web: www.bloomsbury.com)

Boxtree
25 Eccleston Place, London, SW1W 9NF
(Tel: 020-7881 8000; Fax: 020-7881 8280;
Web: www.macmillan.com)

Marion Boyars
24 Lacy Road, London, SW15 1NL (Tel: 020-8788 9522; Fax: 020-8789 8122;
E-mail: marion.boyars@talk21.com;
Web: www.marionboyars.co.uk)

Brimax Children's Books
2–4 Heron Quays, London, E14 4JP (Tel: 020-7531 8400; Fax: 020-7531 8607;
Web: www.brimax.co.uk)

Butterworths Tolley
Halsbury House, 35 Chancery Lane, London, WC2A 1EL (Tel: 020-7400 2500; Fax: 020-7400 2842; Web: www.butterworths.co.uk)

Cadogan Guides
Morris Publications, Network House, 1 Ariel Way, London, W12 7SL (Tel: 020-8600 3550; Fax: 020-8600 3599;
E-mail: guides@morrispub.co.uk;
Web: www.cadoganguides.com)

Jonathan Cape
20 Vauxhall Bridge Road, London, SW1V 2SA (Tel: 020-7840 8400; Fax: 020-7233 6117;
Web: www.randomhouse.co.uk)

Cassell & Co
125 Strand, London, WC2R 0RB (Tel: 020-7420 5555)

Cavendish Publishing
The Glass House, Wharton Street, London, WC1X 9PX (Tel: 020-7278 8000; Fax: 020-7278 8080; E-mail: info@cavendishpublishing.com;
Web: www.cavendishpublishing.com)

Century Publishing Co.
20 Vauxhall Bridge Road, London, SW1V 2SA (Tel: 020-7840 8400; Fax: 020-7233 6127;
Web: www.randomhouse.co.uk)

Chatto & Windus
Random House, 20 Vauxhall Bridge Road, London, SW1V 2SA (Tel: 020-7840 8400; Fax: 020-7932 0077; Web: www.randomhouse.co.uk)

Church House Publishing
Church House, Great Smith Street, London, SW1P 3NZ (Tel: 020-7898 1451; Fax: 020-7898 1449; E-mail: publishing@c-of-e.org.uk;
Web: www.chpublishing.co.uk)

Harcourt Publishers Ltd
32 Jamestown Road, Camden Town, London, NW1 7BY (Tel: 020-7424 4200;
Web: www.harcourt-international.com)

Constable & Robinson Ltd
3 The Lanchesters, 162 Fulham Palace Road, London, W6 9ER (Tel: 020-8741 3663; Fax: 020-8748 7562; E-mail: enquiries@constablerobinson.com; Web: www.constablerobinson.com)

Corgi Books
61–63 Uxbridge Road, London, W5 5SA (Tel: 020-8579 2652; Fax: 020-8231 6612; E-mail: info@transworld-publishers.co.uk)

Darton, Longman & Todd
1 Spencer Court, 140–142 Wandsworth High Street, London, SW18 4JJ (Tel: 020-8875 0155; Fax: 020-8875 0133; E-mail: mail@darton-longman-todd.co.uk)

J. M. Dent & Sons
5 Upper St Martin's Lane, London, WC2H 9EA (Tel: 020-7240 3444; Fax: 020-7240 4822)

Andre Deutsch
20 Mortimer Street, London, W1T 3JW (Tel: 020-7612 0400; Fax: 020-7612 0401)

Dorling Kindersley
80 Strand, London, WC2R 0RL (Tel: 020-7010 3000; Web: www.dk.com/uk)

Doubleday
61–63 Uxbridge Road, London, W5 5SA (Tel: 020-8579 2652; Fax: 020-8579 5479; E-mail: info@transworld-publishers.co.uk; Web: www.booksattransworld.co.uk)

Duckworth & Co.
61 Frith Street, London, W1D 3JL (Tel: 020-7434 4242; Fax: 020-7434 4420; E-mail: info@duckworth-publishers.co.uk; Web: www.ducknet.co.uk)

Ebury Press
20 Vauxhall Bridge Road, London, SW1V 2SA (Tel: 020-7840 8400; Web: www.randomhouse.co.uk)

Egmont Children's Books United
239 Kensington High Street, London, W8 6SA (Tel: 020-7761 3500; Fax: 020-7761 3510; Web: www.egmont.com)

Encyclopaedia Britannica International
16 Golden Square, London, W1F 9TQ (Tel: 020-7815 1000; Fax: 020-7851 1040; E-mail: eng@brittanica.co.uk; Web: www.britannica.co.uk)

Epworth Press
SCM Press, 9–17 St Albans Place, London, N1 0NX (Tel: 020-7359 8033; Fax: 020-7359 0049; E-mail: scmpress@btinternet.com)

Evans Bros.
2A Portman Mansions, Chiltern Street, London, W1U 6NR (Tel: 020-7487 0920; Fax: 020-7487 0921; E-mail: sales@evansbrothers.co.uk; Web: www.evansbooks.co.uk)

Everyman's Publishers Plc
4th Floor, Gloucester Mansions, 140a Shaftesbury Avenue, London, WC2H 8HD (Tel: 020-7539 7600; Fax: 020-7379 4060; E-mail: books@everyman.uk.com; Web: www.everyman.uk.com)

Faber & Faber
3 Queen Square, London, WC1N 3AU (Tel: 020-7465 0045; Fax: 020-7465 0034)

Fourth Estate
77-85 Fulham Palace Road, London, W6 8JB (Tel: 020-8741 4414; Fax: 020-8307 4466; E-mail: general@4thestate.co.uk; Web: www.4thestate.co.uk)

Floodlight Publishing
242 Vauxhall Bridge Road, London, SW1V 1AU (Tel: 020-7630 6314; Fax: 020-7828 3478; Web: www.floodlight.co.uk)

Samuel French
52 Fitzroy Street, London, W1T 5JR (Tel: 020-7387 9373; Fax: 020-7387 2161; E-mail: theatre@samuelfrench-london.co.uk; Web: www.samuelfrench-london.co.uk)

Granta Books
2–3 Hanover Yard, Noel Road, London, N1 8BE (Tel: 020-7704 9776; Fax: 020-7354 3469; E-mail: info@granta.com; Web: www.granta.com)

Publishers

Guinness World Records Ltd
338 Euston Road, London, NW1 3BD (Tel: 020-7891 4567; Fax: 020-7891 4504; E-mail: info@guinessrecords.com; Web: www.guinessworldrecords.com)

Robert Hale
45 Clerkenwell Green, London, EC1R 0HT (Tel: 020-7251 2661; Fax: 020-7490 4958; E-mail: engine@hallbooks.com; Web: www.hallbooks.com)

Hamish Hamilton
27 Wrights Lane, London, W8 5TZ (Tel: 020-7416 3000; Fax: 020-7416 3099; Web: www.penguin.co.uk)

Hamlyn
2–4 Heron Quays, London, E14 4JP (Tel: 020-7531 8400; Fax: 020-7531 8650; E-mail: info-ho@hamlyn.co.uk; Web: www.hamlyn.co.uk)

Harcourt Brace
24 Oval Road, London, NW1 7DX (Tel: 020-7531 8400)

HarperCollins Publishers
77–85 Fulham Palace Road, London, W6 8JB (Tel: 020-8741 7070; Fax: 020-8307 4440; Web: www.fireandwater.com)

William Heinemann
The Random House Group, 20 Vauxhall Bridge Road, London, SW1V 2SA (Tel: 020-7840 8400; Fax: 020-7233 6127; Web: www.randomhouse.co.uk)

William Heinemann
Childrens' Books, 2–4 Heron Quay, London, E14 4JB (Tel: 020-7531 8400; Web: www.randomhouse.co.uk)

Herbert Press
35 Bedford Row, London, WC1R 4JH (Tel: 020-7242 0946; Fax: 020-7831 7489)

Hodder Headline
338 Euston Road, London, NW1 3BH (Tel: 020-7873 6000; Fax: 020-7873 6024)

Michael Joseph
27 Wrights Lane, London, W8 5TZ (Tel: 020-7416 3000; Fax: 020-7416 3099)

Kegan Paul
PO Box 256, London, WC1B 3SW (Tel: 020-7580 5511; Fax: 020-7436 0899; E-mail: books@keganpaul.com; Web: www.keganpaul.com)

Kingfisher Publications Plc
New Penderel House 283–288 High Holborn, London, WC1V 7HZ (Tel: 020-7903 9999; Fax: 020-7242 5009; Web: www.kingfisherpub.com)

Jessica Kingsley Publishers
116 Pentonville Road, London, N1 9JB (Tel: 020-7833 2307; Fax: 020-7837 2917; E-mail: post@jkp.com)

Kogan Page
120 Pentonville Road, London, N1 9JN (Tel: 020-7278 0433; Fax: 020-7837 6348; E-mail: kpinfo@kogan-page.co.uk; Web: www.kogan-page.co.uk)

Roger Lascelles
47 York Road, Brentford, Middx, TW8 0QP (Tel: 020-8847 0935; Fax: 020-8568 3886)

The Law Society of England and Wales
113 Chancery Lane, London, WC2A 1PL (Tel: 020-7242 1222; Fax: 020-7404 1124; E-mail: publishing@lawsociety.org.uk; Web: www.lawsociety.org.uk)

Letts Educational
Aldine House, 9–15 Aldine Place, London, W12 8AW (Tel: 020-8740 2266; Fax: 020-8743 8451; E-mail: mail@lettsed.co.uk; Web: www.letts-education.com)

Frances Lincoln Limited
4 Torriano Mews, Torriano Avenue, London, NW5 2RZ (Tel: 020-7284 4009; Fax: 020-7485 0490; E-mail: reception@frances-lincoln.com)

Little, Brown & Co.
Brettenham House, Lancaster Place, London, WC2E 7EN (Tel: 020-7911 8000; Fax: 020-7911 8100; E-mail: email.uk@littlebrown.com; Web: www.littlebrown.co.uk)

Macmillan Publishers
25 Eccleston Place, London, SW1W 9NF
(Tel: 020-7881 8000; Fax: 020-7881 8001;
Web: www.macmillan.com)

Methuen Publishing Limited
215 Vauxhall Bridge Road, London, SW1V 1EJ
(Tel: 020-7798 1600; Fax: 020-7828 2098;
Web: www.methuen.co.uk)

Harlequin Mills and Boon Ltd
18–24 Paradise Road, Richmond, Surrey, TW9 1SR (Tel: 020-8288 2800; Fax: 020-8288 2898; Web: www.harlequin.com)

Minerva Press
6th Floor, Canberra House, 315–317 Regent Street, London, W1B 2HS (Tel: 020-7580 4114; Fax: 020-7580 9256;
E-mail: publicity&promotions@minerva-press.co.uk;
Web: www.minerva-press.co.uk)

John Murray
50 Albemarle Street, London, W1S 4BD (Tel: 020-7493 4361; Fax: 020-7499 1792;
E-mail: johnmurray@dial.pipex.com;
Web: www.johnmurray.co.uk)

New Holland Publishers
Garfield House, 86 Edgware Road, London, W2 2EA (Tel: 020-7724 7773; Fax: 020-7724 6184;
E-mail: postmaster@nhpub.co.uk)

W. W. Norton & Company
Castle House, 75-76 Wells Street, London, W1T 3QT (Tel: 020-7323 1579; Fax: 020-7436 4553;
E-mail: office@wwnorton.co.uk;
Web: www.wwnorton.co.uk)

Novello & Co.
8-9 Frith Street, London, W1D 3JB (Tel: 020-7434 0066)

Octopus Publishing Group
2–4 Heron Quays, London, E14 4JP (Tel: 020-7531 8400)

Michael O'Mara Books
9 Lion Yard, Tremadoc Road, London, SW4 7NQ (Tel: 020-7720 8643; Fax: 020-7627 8953;
E-mail: enquiries@michaelomarabooks.com;
Web: www.mombooks.com)

Orion Publishing Group
5 Upper St Martin's Lane, London, WC2H 9EA
(Tel: 020-7240 3444; Fax: 020-7240 4822)

Pan Books
25 Eccleston Place, London, SW1W 9NF
(Tel: 020-7881 8000)

Pavilion Books Limited
London House, Great Eastern Wharf, Parkgate Road, London, SW11 4NQ (Tel: 020-7350 1230; Fax: 020-7350 1261;
E-mail: info@pavilionbooks.co.uk;
Web: www.pavilionbooks.co.uk)

Pearson Education
Edinburgh Gate, Harlow, Essex, CM20 2JE (Tel: 01279 623623; Fax: 01279 451059;
Web: www.pearsoned-ema.com)

Penguin Books
80 Strand, London, WC2R 0RJ (Tel: 020-7416 3000; Fax: 020-7416 3099;
E-mail: penguin@penguin.co.uk)

Phaidon Press Limited
Regent's Wharf, All Saints Street, London, N1 9PA (Tel: 020-7843 1000; Fax: 020-7843 1010)

George Philip
2–4 Heron Quay, London, E14 4JB (Tel: 020-7531 8400; Fax: 020-7531 8464;
E-mail: george.philip@philips-maps.co.uk;
Web: www.philips-maps.co.uk)

Piatkus Books
5 Windmill Street, London, W1P 1HF (Tel: 020-7631 0710; Fax: 020-7436 7137; E-mail: info@piatkus.co.uk; Web: www.piatkus.co.uk)

Quartet Books
27 Goodge Street, London, W1P 2LD
(Tel: 020-7636 3992; Fax: 020-7637 1866;
E-mail: quartetbooks@easynet.co.uk)

Quiller Press
46 Lillie Road, London, SW6 1TN (Tel: 020-7499 6529; Fax: 020-7381 8941;
E-mail: greenwood@quiller.conx.co.uk)

Random House Group Ltd
20 Vauxhall Bridge Road, London, SW1V 2SA
(Tel: 020-840 8400;
Web: www.randomhouse.co.uk)

Publishers

Reader's Digest
11 West Ferry Circus, London, E14 4HE
(Tel: 020-7715 8000)

Rough Guides
62–70 Shorts Gardens, London, WC2H 9AH
(Tel: 020-7556 5000; Fax: 020-7556 5050;
E-mail: mail@roughguides.co.uk;
Web: www.roughguides.com)

Routledge
11 New Fetter Lane, London, EC4P 4EE
(Tel: 020-7583 9855; Fax: 020-7842 2298)

Sage Publications
6 Bonhill Street, London, EC2A 4PU
(Tel: 020-7374 0645; Fax: 020-7374 8741;
E-mail: info@sagepub.co.uk;
Web: www.sagepub.co.uk)

Scholastic Children's Books
Commonwealth House
1–19 New Oxford Street, London, WC1A 1NU
(Tel: 020-7421 9000; Fax: 020-7421 9001;
E-mail: publicity@scholastic.co.uk;
Web: www.scholastic.co.uk)

SCM Press
9–17 St Albans Place, London, N1 0NX
(Tel: 020-7359 8033; Fax: 020-7359 0049;
E-mail: scmpress@btinternet.com;
Web: www.scm-canterburypress.co.uk)

Secker & Warburg
20 Vauxhall Bridge Road, London, SW1V 2SA
(Tel: 020-7840 8400; Fax: 020-7233 6117;
Web: www.randomhouse.co.uk)

Serpent's Tail
4 Blackstock Mews, London, N4 2BT
(Tel: 020-7354 1949; Fax: 020-7704 6467;
E-mail: info@serpentstail.com)

Severn House Publishers Ltd
9–15 Sutton High Street, Sutton, Surrey, SM1 1DF (Tel: 020-8770 3930; Fax: 020-8770 3850;
E-mail: info@severnhouse.com;
Web: www.severnhouse.com)

Sidgwick & Jackson
25 Eccleston Place, London, SW1W 9NF
(Tel: 020-7881 8000; Fax: 020-7881 8001;
Web: www.panmacmillan.com)

Souvenir Press
43 Great Russell Street, London, WC1B 3PD
(Tel: 020-7580 9307; Fax: 020-7580 5064;
E-mail: souvenirpress@ukonline.co.uk)

SPCK - The Society for Promoting Christian Knowledge
Holy Trinity Church, Marylebone Road, London, NW1 4DU (Tel: 020-7643 0382; Fax: 020-7643 0391; E-mail: spck@spck.org.uk;
Web: www.spck.org.uk)

Stationery Office Ltd
51 Nine Elms Lane, London, SW8 5DR
E-mail: customer.services@theso.co.uk;
Web: www.clicktso.com)

Sweet & Maxwell
100 Avenue Road, London, NW3 3PF (Tel: 020-7393 7000; Web: www.sweetandmaxwell.co.uk)

Taylor & Francis Books Ltd
11 New Fetter Lane, London, EC4P 4EE
(Tel: 020-7583 0490; Fax: 020-7842 2307;
E-mail: info@tandf.co.uk; Web: www.tandf.co.uk)

Thames & Hudson Ltd
181A High Holborn, London, WC1V 7QX
(Tel: 020-7845 5000; Fax: 020-7845 5050;
E-mail: mail@thameshudson.co.uk;
Web: www.thameshudson.co.uk)

Thorsons
77-85 Fulham Palace Road, London, W6 8JB
(Tel: 020-8741 7070; Fax: 020-8307 4440;
Web: www.thorsons.com)

Times Books
77 Fulham Palace Road, London, W6 8JB
(Tel: 020-8741 7070)

Transworld Publishers
61–63 Uxbridge Road, London, W5 5SA
(Tel: 020-8579 2652; Fax: 020-8579 5479;
E-mail: info@transworld-publishers.co.uk;
Web: www.booksattransworld.co.uk)

Usborne Publishing
Usborne House, 83–85 Saffron Hill, London, EC1N 8RT (Tel: 020-7430 2800; Fax: 020-7430 1562; E-mail: mail@usborne.co.uk;
Web: www.usborne.com)

Viking
27 Wrights Lane, London, W8 5TZ
(Tel: 020-7416 3000; Fax: 020-7416 3290;
Web: www.penguin.co.uk)

Virago Press
Brettenham House, Lancaster Place, London, WC2E 7EN (Tel: 020-7911 8000; Fax: 020-7911 8100; E-mail: email.uk@littlebrown.com; Web: www.virago.co.uk)

Virgin Publishing
Thames Wharf Studios, Rainville Road, London, W6 9HA (Tel: 020-7386 3300; Fax: 020-7386 3360; E-mail: publicity@virgin-pub.co.uk; Web: www.virgin-books.com)

Walker Books
87 Vauxhall Walk, London, SE11 5HJ (Tel: 020-7793 0909; Fax: 020-7587 1123)

Watts Publishing Group Ltd
96 Leonard Street, London, EC2A 4XD (Tel: 020-7739 2929; Fax: 020-7739 2318; E-mail: gm@wattspub.co.uk; Web: www.wattspub.co.uk)

Weidenfeld & Nicholson
5 Upper St Martin's Lane, London, WC2H 9EA (Tel: 020-7240 3444; Fax: 020-7240 4823)

Which? Books
Consumers Association, 2 Marylebone Road, London, NW1 4DF (Tel: 020-7770 7000; Fax: 020-7770 7660; E-mail: books@which.net; Web: www.which.net)

Yale University Press
23 Pond Street, London, NW3 2PN (Tel: 020-7431 4422; Fax: 020-7431 3755; E-mail: anfrew.tuner@yaleup.co.uk; Web: www.yaleup.co.uk)

ADVERTISING

ADVERTISING STANDARDS AUTHORITY

Brook House, 2 Torrington Place, London WC1E 7HW (Tel: 020-7580 5555; Email: enquiries@asa.org.uk; Web: www.asa.org.uk).

Director-General: Christopher Graham

ADVERTISING AGENCIES

The following list comprises a selection of Advertising Agencies/Media Consultancies based in London. Due to the extremely high number of agencies we have not been able to include all of those located in London. Those listed have not been chosen under any specific criteria but are those that responded to our enquiries.

141 London
1st Floor, 121–141 Westbourne Terrace, London, W2 6JR (Tel: 020-7706 2306; Fax: 020-7262 0756; Web: www.bates-dorland.co.uk).
Chief Executive: J. Lee

Abbott Mead Vickers BBDO Ltd
151 Marylebone Road, London, NW1 5QE (Tel: 020-7616 3500; Fax: 020-7616 3600).
Managing Director: C. Snowball

Acumen Partnership
186 Drury Lane, London, WC2B 5RU (Tel: 020-7440 4301; Fax: 020-7440 4310; E-mail: k.hurdwell@acumenpartners.co.uk; Web: www.acumenpartners.co.uk).
Partners: K. Hurdwell; Ms J. Lunnon; Ms G. Evans; A. King; P. Robinson; P. Stewart; S. Kelleher; J. Rooke; J. Arnold

Banks Hoggins O'Shea. FCB Ltd
54 Baker Street, London, W1M 1DJ (Tel: 020-7314 0000; Fax: 020-7314 0001).
Managing Director: S. Olsen

BBA Active Ltd
1 Hampstead West, 224 Iverson Road, London, NW6 2HU (Tel: 020-7625 7575; Fax: 020-7625 7007).
Managing Director: S. Benjamin

Advertising Agencies 315

BANC
Heddon House, 149 Regent Street, London, W1B 4BA (Tel: 020-7437 5552; Fax: 020-7734 3068; E-mail: mailbox@banc.co.uk; Web: banc.co.uk).
Managing Director: M. Cramphorn

Beecham Peplow Noakes Advertising Ltd
3 Duke Street, London, W1M 6BA (Tel: 020-7935 2500; Fax: 020-7486 4050; E-mail: bpn@easynet.co.uk; Web: bpnlebevl.co.uk).
Managing Director: R. Ingham

BMP Solutions in Media Ltd
12 Bishop's Bridge Road, London, W2 6AA (Tel: 020-7258 4082; Fax: 020-7873 4111).
Manaing Director: P. Taylor

BLM Media
50 Marshall Street, London, W1F 9BQ (Tel: 020-7437 1317; Fax: 020-7437 1287; E-mail: blm@blm.co.uk; Web: blm.co.uk).
Managing Partners: N. Lockett; S. Booth; C. Makin

Bygraves Bushell Valladares & Sheldon Ltd
15 New Burlington Street, London, W1S 3BJ (Tel: 020-7734 4445; Fax: 020-7434 0213).
Managing Director: D. Valladares

Capital City Media Limited
Finsbury Business Centre, 40 Bowling Green Lane, London, EC1R 0NE (Tel: 020-7278 0330; Fax: 020-7410 0193;
E-mail: ccm@capitalcitymedia.co.uk).
Joint Directors: M. Richards; A. Bath

Carat Business Ltd
7th Floor, Parker Tower, 43–49 Parker Street, London, WC2B 5PS (Tel: 020-7430 6399; Fax: 020-7430 6373;
Web: www.carat.com).
Managing Director: P. Clarke

Carlson Marketing Group
Alice Court, 116 Putney Bridge Road, London, SW15 2NQ (Tel: 020-8875 0875; Fax: 020-8875 0777; Web: www.carlson-europe.com).
Chairman: Marcus Evans

Citigate Albert Frank
26 Finsbury Square, London, EC2A 1SH (Tel: 020-7282 8000; Fax: 020-7282 8080; E-mail: philip.grepgory@citigateaf.co.uk; Web: www.citigateaf.co.uk).
Managing Director: Philip Gregory

Clark McKay and Walpole
42-46 Weymouth Street, Marylebone, London, W1G 6NR (Tel: 020-7487 9750; Fax: 020-7224 4604; E-mail: j-clark@cmw-uk.com; Web: www.clarkmckayandwalpole.com).
Chairman: J. Clark

The Coltman Media Company Ltd
Aria House, 23 Craven Street, London, WC2N 2516 (Tel: 020-7930 2516; Fax: 020-7930 2660).
Media Director: S. Coltman

The Communications in Business Group Ltd
1 Battersea Church Road, London, SW11 3LY (Tel: 020-7771 7000; Fax: 020-7771 7181).
Chief Executive: T. M. Church

Copeland & Charrington Ltd
Samian House, 85 Borough High Street, London, SE1 1NH (Tel: 020-7407 0440; Fax: 020-7407 0550;
E-mail: office@copeland-charrington.co.uk).
Managing Director: P. Clover

Datamail Direct Advertising Ltd (DDA Ltd)
St Johns House, 366 North End Road, Fulham, London, SW6 1LY (Tel: 020-7381 0222; Fax: 020-7610 1639; Web: www.dda.uk.com).
Managing Director: P. Jewiss

Delaney Lund Knox Warren and Partners
25 Wellington Street, London, WC2E 7DA (Tel: 020-7836 3474; Fax: 020-7240 8739; Web: www.dlkw.co.uk).
Chief Executive: Mark Lund

Duckworth Finn Grubb Waters
41 Great Pulteney Street, London, W1R 3DE (Tel: 020-7734 5888; Fax: 020-7734 3716; Web: www.dfgw.com).
Managing Director: Tom Vick

316 Media London

epb.communications
10 Berners Mews, London, W1P 3LF (Tel: 020-7462 0400; Fax: 020-7462 0401; E-mail: ken.buckfield@epbuk.com; Web: www.epb.com).
Managing Director: K. Buckfield

First City Advertising Ltd
22 Goodge Place, London, W1T 4SL (Tel: 020-7436 7020; Fax: 020-7637 3277).
Managing Director: T. Unwin

Grey Worldwide, London
215–227 Great Portland Street, London, W1W 5PN (Tel: 020-7636 3399; Fax: 020-7637 7473).
Group Managing Directors: Ms J. Barr; B. Cox; S. Richards; C. King

Haygarth Direct
Haygarth House, 28–31 High Street, Wimbledon Village, London, SW19 5BY (Tel: 020-8944 1011; Fax: 020-8946 7712; E-mail: bernice.l@haygarth.co.uk; Web: www.haygarth.co.uk).
Board Directors: D. Lubbock; R. Goldsmith; B. Lovell; S. Morris

HH & S Ltd
67 Brompton Road, London, SW3 1DB (Tel: 020-7225 3300; Fax: 020-7584 6316; Web: www.hhs.co.uk).
Managing Director: M. Halstead

International Marketing & Promotions Ltd
Warwick Building, Kensington Village, Avonmore Road, London, SW14 8HQ (Tel: 020-7931 8000; Fax: 020-7348 3856; Web: www.implondon.co.uk).
Chief Executive Officer/Managing Director: J. Quarrey

Just Media Ltd
Brighton House, 9 Brighton Terrace, London, SW9 8DJ (Tel: 020-7737 8000; Fax: 020-7737 8080; Web: www.justmedia.co.uk).
Managing Director: D. Gibson

J Walter Thompson Company Limited
40 Berkeley Square, London, W1J 5AL (Tel: 020-7499 4040; Fax: 020-7493 8432).
Chief Executive Officer: S. Bolton

Lion
74 Rivington Street, London, EC2A 3AY (Tel: 020-7415 3333; Fax: 020-7739 0757; Web: lion-agency.com).
Managing Director: M. Nohr

Lowe Broadway Ltd
10–11 Percy Street, London, W1T 1DA (Tel: 020-7344 8888; Fax: 020-7344 8889; E-mail: admin@lowebroadway.com; Web: lowebroadway.com).
President: P. Zatland

M & C Saatchi Ltd
36 Golden Square, London, W1F 9EE (Tel: 020-7543 4500; Fax: 020-7543 4501; Web: www.mcsaatchi.com).
Managing Director: T. Duffy

M For Media Ltd
Old Ryde House, 393 Richmond Road, Twickenham, Middx, TW1 2EF (Tel: 020-8892 5779; Fax: 020-8891 6784; Web: www.matthewpoppy.com).
Managing Director: N. Dickinson

Maher Bird Associates Ltd
Academy House, 36 Poland Street, London, W1F 7XX (Tel: 020-7287 1718; Fax: 020-7287 0917; E-mail: stephen.maher@mba.co.uk).
Chief Executive: S. Maher

MBO Ltd
Jubilee House, 2 Jubilee Place, London, SW3 3TQ (Tel: 020-7352 1900; Fax: 020-7352 4700; E-mail: solutions@mbo.co.uk; Web: www.mbo.co.uk).
Chief Executive: J. Taylor

McCann-Erickson Advertising Ltd
McCann-Erickson House, 7–11 Herbrand Street, London, WC1N 1EX (Tel: 020-7837 3737; Fax: 020-7837 3773).
Chairman and Chief Executive: B. Langdon

Media Connections Ltd
15 The Old Power Station, 121 Mortlake High Street, London, SW14 8SN (Tel: 020-8878 4852; Fax: 020-8878 8960; E-mail: mediaconnections@compuserve.com; Web: www.media-connections.co.uk).
Managing Director: E. Hastings

Advertising Agencies 317

Media Insight Limited
40 The Strand, London, WC2N 5RF (Tel: 020-7969 4141; Fax: 020-7316 0241; Web: www.mediainsight.com).
Managing Director: T. Jenner

Media Junction
8 Apollo House, 18 All Saints Road, Notting Hill, London, W11 1HH (Tel: 020-7460 9206; Fax: 020-7460 9209; E-mail: advertising@mediajunction.co.uk).
Managing Director: G. Cooper

The Media Shop Ltd
Dorland House, 14–16 Regent Street, London, SW1Y 4PH (Tel: 020-7766 5000; Fax: 020-7766 5050; E-mail: tms@the.media.shop.co.uk; Web: www.the.media.shop.co.uk).
Chairman and Managing Director: B. Sims

The Mediawise Partnership Ltd
Fairgate House, 78 New Oxford Street, London, WC1A 1HB (Tel: 020-7419 8800; Fax: 020-7419 8801; E-mail: mail@mediawise.co.uk; Web: www.mediawise.co.uk).
Managing Partners: M. Gill; M. Anderson

Mitchell Patterson Grime Mitchell Ltd
137 Regent Street, London, W1R 8PG (Tel: 020-7734 8087; Fax: 020-7434 3081; Web: www.euro-interpartners.com).
Managing Partner: A. Mitchell

Mortimer Whittaker O'Sullivan Advertising
The Carriage Hall, 29 Floral Street, London, WC2E 9TD (Tel: 020-7379 8844; Fax: 020-7379 3396).
Managing Partner: T. Mortimer

Mustoe Merriman Herring Levy
2-4 Bucknall Street, London, WC2E 9AG (Tel: 020-7379 9999; Fax: 020-7379 8487; Web: www.mmhl.co.uk).
Chief Executive: N. Mustoe

New PHD
The Telephone Exchange, 5 North Crescent, Chenies Street, London, WC1E 7PH (Tel: 020-7446 0555; Fax: 020-7446 7100; Web: www.phd.co.uk).
Chief Executive: David Pattison

Ogilvy & Mather Ltd
10 Cabot Square, Canary Wharf, London, E14 4QB (Tel: 020-7345 3000; Fax: 020-7345 9000; Web: www.ogilvy.co.uk).
Chairman & CEO: P. Simons

OgilvyOne
33 St John Street, London, EC1M 4GB (Tel: 020-7566 7000; Fax: 020-7566 5100; Web: www.ogilvyone.com).
Management Partners: M. Dodds; J. Owrid

Ogilvy Primary Contact Limited
33 St. John Street, London, EC1M 4PJ (Tel: 020-7460 6900; Fax: 020-7468 6950; Web: www.primary.co.uk).
Managing Director: K. Dunnell

Optimedia UK
Nations House, 103 Wigmore Street, London, W1U 1QS (Tel: 020-7935 0040; Fax: 020-7486 1985; E-mail: simon.mathews@optimedia.co.uk).
Managing Director/Partner: S. Mathews

Perspectives Red Cell
Swan Court, Swan Street, Old Isleworth, Middx, TW7 6RJ (Tel: 020-8568 4422; Fax: 020-8847 5482; Web: www.perspectivesredcell.com).
Chairman and Chief Executive: J. Williams

Peter Kane & Company Ltd
12 Burleigh Street, London, WC2E 7PX (Tel: 020-7836 4561; Fax: 020-7836 4073; Web: www.peter-kane.co.uk).
Chief Executive: M. Sowerby

Publicis
82 Baker Street, London, W1M 2AE (Tel: 020-7935 4426; Fax: 020-7487 5351).
Managing Director: G. Duncan

Raiper Ltd
The Network Building, 97 Tottenham Court Road, London, W1P 9HF (Tel: 020-7369 8000; Fax: 020-7369 8013; E-mail: bstephens@rapier.ltd.uk).
Chief Executive: J. Stead

318 Media London

Rathbone Media Ltd
Shenfield House, 182 Hutton Road, Shenfield, Brentwood, Essex (Tel: 01277-261363; Fax: 01277-223414).
Managing Director: G. Cole

Retail Marketing Partnership Ltd
Regal Place, Maxwell Road, Fulham, London, SW6 2HD (Tel: 020-7371 5588; Fax: 020-7371 5151; E-mail: retail@rmp.co.uk; Web: www.rmp.co.uk).
Managing Director: Ms S. Lockhart

Ross Levenson Harris Ltd
60–63 Victoria Road, Surbiton, Surrey, KT6 4NQ (Tel: 020-8390 4611; Fax: 020-8399 6557; E-mail: rlh@rlh.co.uk).
Managing Director: C. Ross

RPM3
William Blake House, 8 Marshall Street, London, W1V 2AJ (Tel: 020-7434 4343; Fax: 020-7439 8884).
Managing Director: Mark Brandis

Senior King Ltd
14–15 Carlisle Street, London, W1V 5RE (Tel: 020-7734 5855; Fax: 020-7437 1908; Web: www.seniorkinggroup.co.uk).
Group Development Director: Jeremy Aspinall

Sherrard Media
New Premier House, 150 Southampton Row, London, WC1B 5AL (Tel: 020-7843 6400; Fax: 020-7843 6420; E-mail: media@sherrardmedia.co.uk; Web: www.sherrardmedia.co.uk).
Managing Director: P. Sherrard

Squires Robertson Gill plc
9 Cavendish Place, London, W1M 0BL (Tel: 020-7323 0343; Fax: 020-7580 0586; E-mail: enquiries@srgplc.co.uk).
Media Director: N. Rive

Tullo Marshall Warren Ltd
81 Kings Road, Chelsea, London, SW3 4NX (Tel: 020-7349 4000; Fax: 020-7349 4001; E-mail: direct@tmw.co.uk; Web: www.tmw.co.uk).
Business Development Manager: Richard Marshall

UK Advertising & Marketing Services plc
UKAMS House, Twistleton Court, Priory Hill, Dartford, Kent, DA1 2EN (Tel: 01332-228899; Fax: 01332-288721).
Managing Director: W. Lewis

Walker Media Ltd
Middlesex House, 34-42 Cleveland Street, London, W1P 5FB (Tel: 020-7447 7500; Fax: 020-7447 7501; Web: www.walkermedia.com).
Partners: Ms C. Walker; P. Georgiadis

Walsh Trott Chick Smith
Holden House, 57 Rathbone Place, London, W1P 1AW (Tel: 020-7734 0050; Fax: 020-7734 1172; E-mail: keirc@wtcs.co.uk).
Managing Director: K. Cooper

Warman and Bannister
40 Marsh Wall, London, E14 9TP (Tel: 020-7512 1000; Fax: 020-7512 1999; E-mail: w&b@warban.com; Web: www.warban.com).
Joint Chief Executives: R. Warman; T. Bannister

WCRS
5 Golden Square, London, W1R 4BS (Tel: 020-7806 5000; Fax: 020-7806 5099; E-mail: newbusiness@wcrs.co.uk).
Managing Director: Jason Coward

Western International Media
84 Ecclestone Square, London, SW1X 1PX (Tel: 020-7663 7000; Fax: 020-7663 7001).
Executive Vice President: M. Tunnicliffe

WWAV Rapp Collins Media Ltd
1 Riverside, Mambre Road, London, W6 9WA (Tel: 020-7727 3481; Fax: 020-7221 0420; Web: www.wavrc.media.co.uk).
Managing Director: Peter Mitchell

Zed Media Ltd
2-3 Scala Street, London, W1T 2HN (Tel: 020-7631 2777; Fax: 020-7323 3026).
Managing Director: J. Hyams

PUBLIC RELATIONS/MEDIA CONSULTANCY

The following list comprises a selection of Public Relations Agencies/Media Consultancies based in London. Due to the extremely high number of agencies we have not been able to include all of those located in London. Those listed have not been chosen under any specific criteria but are those that responded to our enquiries.

33 R P M
Unit 226, 28 Old Brompton Road, London, SW7 3SS (Tel: 01423-797800; Fax: 01423-797170; E-mail: pr33rpm@aol.com; Web: www.33rpmpublicrelations.co.uk).
Director: R. Marshall

A Kevorkian Public Relations
5 Accurist House, 44 Baker Street, London, W1M 1DH (Tel: 020-7935 0309; Fax: 020-7486 1416; E-mail: akprouk@aol.com).
Principal: A. Kevorkian

Abel Hadden & Co Ltd
15 Berkeley Street, London, W1J 8DY (Tel: 020-7629 8771; Fax: 020-7629 8772; E-mail: central@ahadden.com; Web: www.ahadden.com).
Directors: Patrick Roberts; Jane Goddard

Accent Communications
Edwards House, 2 Alric Avenue, New Malden, Surrey, KT3 4JN (Tel: 020-8949 6522; Fax: 020-8942 3944; E-mail: accent@breathmail.net).
Director: C. Deane

ANA Communications Ltd
16 Berkeley Street, London, W1J 8DZ (Tel: 020-7629 8118; Fax: 020-7629 8119; E-mail: anna.maclellan@ana-communications.com).
Managing Director: Ms A. Nicholas

Anderson Associates
33 Gordon Road, Beckenham, Kent, BR3 3QE (Tel: 020-8325 1762; Fax: 020-8249 0823; E-mail: andpub@aol.com).
Proprietor: K. Tearle

Andrea Marks Public Relations
146 Edgwarebury Lane, Edgware, Middx, HA8 8NE (Tel: 020-8958 4398; Fax: 020-8905 3727; E-mail: andrea—marks@compuserve.com).
Managing Director: Ms Andrea Marks

ASAP Communications Ltd
2 Tunstall Road, London, SW9 8DA (Tel: 020-7978 9488; Fax: 020-7940 9490; E-mail: info@asapcomms.co.uk; Web: www.asapcomms.com).
Managing Director: Ms Y. Thompson

Athena Medical PR Ltd
500 Chiswick High Road, London, W4 5RG (Tel: 020-8956 2299; Fax: 020-8956 2295; E-mail: ampr@athenamedicalpr.co.uk; Web: www.athenamedicalpr.co.uk).
Managing Director: Ms C. Slater

Avenue Communications
26 Ives Street, London, SE3 2ND (Tel: 020-7589 7463; Fax: 020-7584 0825; E-mail: enquiries@avenuecommunications.com; Web: www.avenuecommunications.com).
Managing Director: Ms E. Aves

BCPR/Beverley Cable PR
11 St Christopher's Place, London, W1U 1NG (Tel: 020-7935 1314; Fax: 020-7935 8314; E-mail: mail@beverleycablepr.co.uk).
Managing Director: Ms B. Cable

B Jane Dickson
70 Royal Hill, London, SE10 8RF (Tel: 020-8694 9056; Fax: 020-8694 9368; E-mail: bjda@compuserve.com).
Principal: Ms B. J. Dickson

Bloomfield Turner Associates
42–44 Carter Lane, London, EC4V 5EA (Tel: 020-7248 1225; Fax: 020-7248 1228; E-mail: info@bloomfieldturner.com; Web: www.bloomfieldturner.com).
Partner: Ms C. Turner

Braben Company
18B Pindock Mews, London, W9 2PY (Tel: 020-7289 1616; Fax: 020-7289 1166; E-mail: alison@braben.co.uk; Web: www.braben.co.uk).
Managing Director: Ms S. Braben

Brook Wilkinson Ltd
87 Notting Hill Gate, London, W11 3JZ (Tel: 020-7229 9907; Fax: 020-7229 8809; E-mail: rbrook@brook-wilkinson.co.uk).
Chairman: Ms R. Brook

320 Media London

Brown Lloyd James
25 Lower Belgrave Street, London, SW1W 0NR (Tel: 020-7591 9610; Fax: 020-7591 9611; E-mail: pr@blj.co.uk; Web: www.brownlloydjames.com).
Chairman: Sir Nicholas Lloyd

BSMG Worldwide (UK)
110 St Martin's Lane, London, WC2N 4RG (Tel: 020-7841 5555; Fax: 020-7847 5777; E-mail: fburr@bsmg.com; Web: www.bsmg.com).
Chief Executive: David Brian

Cairns & Associates Ltd
28–30 Ives Street, London, SW3 2ND (Tel: 020-7584 2776; Fax: 020-7584 2998; E-mail: inforequest@cairnsassociates.co.uk).
Deputy Managing Director: Ms C. Clarke

Cardew & Co
12 Suffolk Street, London, SW1Y 4HQ (Tel: 020-7930 0777; Fax: 020-7925 0647/8; E-mail: cardew@cardew.co.uk).
Chairman: A. Cardew

Cawdell Douglas
10–11 Lower John Street, London, W1R 3PE (Tel: 020-7439 2822; Fax: 020-7287 5488; E-mail: press@cawdelldouglas.co.uk).
Managing Partner: Ms D. Cawdell

Coalition Group Ltd
Devonshire House, 12 Barley Mow Passage, London, W4 4PH (Tel: 020-8987 0123; Fax: 020-8987 0345; E-mail: pr@coalitiongroup.co.uk; Web: www.coalitiongroup.co.uk).
Joint Managing Directors: Ms R. Fitzgerald; T. Linkin

Command Communications Ltd
2–6 Curtain Road, London, EC2A 3NQ (Tel: 020-7247 4457; Fax: 020-7247 4035; E-mail: info@command-group.ltd.uk; Web: www.command-group.ltd.uk).
Managing Director: J. Nicholson

Cypher Press & Promotions
Queens Studios, 117–121 Salusbury Road, London, NW6 6RG (Tel: 020-7372 4474; Fax: 020-7372 4484; E-mail: cypher@newstate.co.uk; Web: www.newstate.co.uk).
General Manager: S. Ward

Denmead Marketing Europe Ltd
11 Russell Garden Mews, London, W14 8EU (Tel: 020-7371 2040; Fax: 020-7371 2028; E-mail: pr@denmeaduk.com).
Managing Director: Ms C. Stott

The Direct Communications Co
Rosedale House, Rosedale Road, Richmond, Surrey, TW9 2SZ (Tel: 020-8939 9040; Fax: 020-8940 9504; E-mail: dccpr@aol.com).
Managing Director: M. Kamlish

Eligo International Ltd
186–188 Queen's Gate, London, SW7 5HL (Tel: 020-7591 0619; Fax: 020-7225 5279; E-mail: info@eligo.net; Web: www.eligo.net).
Managing Director: A. J. Bailey

Ellis Kopel
11 Britannia Road, London, N12 9RU (Tel: 020-8492 0225; Fax: 020-8492 4308; E-mail: e.kopel@btinternet.com).
Principal: E. Kopel

Emma Chapman Publicity
2nd Floor, 18 Great Portland Street, London, W1N 5AB (Tel: 020-7637 0990; Fax: 020-7637 0660; E-mail: pr@ecpub.com).
Company Director: Ms E. Chapman

Englender Ltd
43 South Parade, Mollison Way, Edgware, Middx, HA8 5QL (Tel: 020-8952 5808; Fax: 020-8951 0190).
PR Director: G. Englender

ESL of Network Ltd
38 Grosvenor Gardens, London, SW1W 0EB (Tel: 020-7823 4199; Fax: 020-7823 4335; E-mail: marie-gabrieller@eslnetwork.com).
Senior Consultant: D. Hughes

Euro Strategies Ltd
120 Wilton Road, London, SW1V 1JZ (Tel: 020-7828 7029; Fax: 020-7630 9198; E-mail: info@eurostrategies.co.uk; Web: www.eurostrategies.co.uk).
Managing Director: G. Kelly

Public Relations   321

Europhase Communications
62 Courtfield Gardens, London, SW5 0NQ
(Tel: 020-7565 2584; Fax: 020-7565 2887).
Director: H. McKenna

Faust Talbot PR Ltd
87 Palewell Park, London, SW14 8JJ
(Tel: 020-8392 1085; Fax: 020-8878 5262;
E-mail: faustpr@aol.com).
Proprietor: Ms J. Faust

Fisher Marketing Limited
Media Point, 54 Banstead Road, Carshalton, Surrey, SM5 3NW (Tel: 020-8643 0240; Fax: 020-8770 9511;
E-mail: fmpr@fishermarketing.co.uk;
Web: www.fishermarketing.co.uk).
Managing Director: J. Fisher

Flagship Group
140 Great Portland Street, London, W1W 6QA
(Tel: 020-7299 1500; Fax: 020-7299 1550;
E-mail: diana.solkmann@flagshipgroup.co.uk;
Web: www.flagshipgroup.co.uk).
Chief Executive: Ms D. Soltmann

Food & Other Matters Ltd
58 Blythe Road, London, W14 0HA
(Tel: 020-7371 6466; Fax: 020-7371 4717;
E-mail: carolyn@foodmatters.co.uk).
Managing Director: Ms C. J. Cavele

Garland International
178 Battersea Park Road, London, SW11 4ND
(Tel: 020-7738 8008; Fax: 020-7498 6153;
E-mail: team@garlandintl.co.uk).
Partner: D. Hewett

Gledhill-Gwyer Enterprises
Nightingale Centre, 8 Balham Hill, London, SW12 9EA (Tel: 020-8675 5343; Fax: 020-8675 8457;
E-mail: barbara—gledhill@gwyer.demon.co.uk).
Chief Executive: Dr B. Gledhill

Grandfield Ltd
69 Wilson Street, London, EC2A 2BB
(Tel: 020-7417 4170; Fax: 020-7417 9180;
E-mail: enquiries@grandfield.com;
Web: www.grandfield.com).
Chief Executive: C. Cook

Hammond & Deacon Ltd
64 Linden Gardens, London, W4 2EW
(Tel: 020-8994 4010; Fax: 020-8994 7808;
E-mail: mail@hammond-pr.co.uk).
Managing Director: J. Hammond

Harcourt Public Affairs Ltd
49 Whitehall, London, SW1A 2BX
(Tel: 020-7839 8422; Fax: 020-7930 0037;
E-mail: harcourt.publicaffairs@virgin.net).
Managing Director: Ms C. Cawston

Hards PR
The Hall, Peyton Place, Greenwich, London, SE10 8RS (Tel: 020-8293 7150; Fax: 020-8293 7050; E-mail: mail@hardspr.co.uk;
Web: www.hardspr.co.uk).
Managing Director: R. Hards

Harvard Centro
100 Dean Street, London, W1D 3TE
(Tel: 020-7494 6100; Fax: 020-7494 6111;
E-mail: claire.spence@harvard.co.uk;
Web: www.harvard.co.uk).
Director: F. Butters

Hayes Anderson Ltd
18 Winton Avenue, London, N11 2AT
(Tel: 020-8245 1010; Fax: 020-8245 2557;
E-mail: jhayes@hayesanderson.com).
Managing Director: J. Hayes

Headley Platcha Rolfe Ltd
22 Mount View Road, London, N4 4HX (Tel: 020-8348 1234; E-mail: whitakers@heritage.co.uk;
Web: www.heritage.co.uk/hpr).
Chief Executive Officer: G. Headley

Heady Public Relations Ltd
4 Melina Road, London, W12 9HZ
(Tel: 020-8743 7797; Fax: 020-8749 2498;
E-mail: headypr@aol.com).
Managing Director: Ms H. Heady

IBIKS Public Relations Ltd
Suite 13, St Lukes Enterprise Centre, 85 Tarling Road, London, E16 1HN (Tel: 020-7366 6302; Fax: 020-7366 6301; E-mail: info@ibikspr.com;
Web: www.ibikspr.com).
Managing Consultant: Kunle Thomas

Jackie Cooper Public Relations
91 New Cavendish Street, London, W1W 6XE
(Tel: 020-7208 7208; Fax: 020-7208 7272;
E-mail: info@jcpr.com; Web: www.jcpr.com).
Founding Partners: Ms J. Cooper; R. Phillips

John D. Wood & Co Marketing Department
48 Elizabeth Street, London, SW1W 9PA (Tel: 020-7824 7909; Fax: 020-7824 7910; E-mail: marketing@johndwood.co.uk; Web: www.johndwood.co.uk).
Marketing Director: Richard Page

Keene Public Affairs Consultants Ltd
Victory House, 99–101 Regent Street, London, W1R 7HB (Tel: 020-7287 0652; Fax: 020-7494 0493; E-mail: tony@keenpa.demon.co.uk).
Managing Director: A. G. Richards

Kelso Consulting
89 Great Eastern Street, London, EC2A 3HY (Tel: 020-7729 7595; Fax: 020-7729 9409; E-mail: jamess@kelsopr.com; Web: www.pressquotes.com).
Director: T. Prizeman

Key Communications Ltd
Kings Court, 2–16 Goodge Street, London, W1T 2QA (Tel: 020-7580 0222; Fax: 020-7580 0333; E-mail: davidw@keycommunications.co.uk; Web: www.keycommunications.co.uk).
Managing Director: D. Watson

Kingfisher Public Relations Consultants Ltd
23 Rectory Grove, Croydon, Surrey, CR0 4JA (Tel: 020-8686 5602; Fax: 020-8680 3861; E-mail: mailus@kingfisherpr.co.uk; Web: www.kingfisherpr.co.uk).
Director: J. Fisher

Landmark PR Ltd
23 Earls Court Square, London, SW5 9BY (Tel: 020-7835 1833; Fax: 020-7835 0192; E-mail: info@lmpr.co.uk).
Managing Director: S. Taylor

Lansons Communications
42 St John Street, London, EC1M 4DL (Tel: 020-7490 8828; Fax: 020-7490 5460; E-mail: pr@lansons.com; Web: www.lansons.com).
Chief Executive: Tony Langham

Link Public Relations Ltd
20 Mortlake High Street, London, SW14 8JN (Tel: 020-8392 6629; Fax: 020-8392 6651; E-mail: mail@linkpr.co.uk; Web: www.linkpr.co.uk).
Executive Director: S. Anson

Live PR Ltd
124 Victoria Street, London, SW1E 5LA E-mail: dwrc@livepr.net; Web: www.livepr.net).
Director: R. Clarke

MacLaurin Ltd
22 Berghem Mews, Blythe Road, London, W14 0HN (Tel: 020-7371 3333; Fax: 020-7471 6898; E-mail: ceo@maclaurin.com; Web: www.maclaurin.com).
Chief Executive: B. MacLaurin

Marketeer PLC
2 Dolphin Square, Edensor Road, London, W4 2ST (Tel: 020-8742 3388; Fax: 020-8995 2374; E-mail: keith@marketeer.co.uk; Web: www.marketeer.co.uk).
Chief Executive Officer: K. Searsby

Mason Williams
7–11 Lexington Street, London, W1F 9AF (Tel: 020-7534 6080; Fax: 020-7534 6081; E-mail: john@mason-williams.com; Web: www.mason-williams.co.uk).
Joint Managing Directors: Ms R. Rowe; J. Williams

McQueen Rose Ltd
2 Fox Hill Gardens, London, SE19 2XB (Tel: 020-8653 0066; Fax: 020-8653 3524; E-mail: enquiries@rowlandservices.co.uk; Web: www.rowlandservices.co.uk).
Managing Director: E. M. Rose

Mega Bullet Promotions
Arch 74, Ranelagh Gardens, London, SW6 3UR (Tel: 020-7384 3222; Fax: 020-7384 3223; E-mail: info@megabullet.com; Web: www.platin-m.com).
Director: Ms M. Resen

Midas Public Relations Ltd
7–8 Kendrick Mews, London, SW7 3HG (Tel: 020-7584 7474; Fax: 020-7584 7123; E-mail: info@midaspr.co.uk; Web: www.midaspr.co.uk).
Joint Managing Directors: S. Williams; T. Mulliken

Millham Communications
4 City Road, London, EC1Y 2AA (Tel: 020-7256 5756; Fax: 020-7638 7370; E-mail: millcoms@dircon.co.uk; Web: www.millham.co.uk).
Chairman: D. Millham

Morgan Allen Moore
104–110 Goswell Road, London, EC1V 7DH
(Tel: 020-7253 0802; Fax: 020-7253 0803;
Web: www.morganallenmoore.com).
Managing Director: S. Morgan

Mulberry Marketing Communications Ltd
1 Waterloo Court, Theed Street, London, SE1
8ST (Tel: 020-7928 7676; Fax: 020-7928 7979;
E-mail: info@mulberrymc.com;
Web: www.mulberrymc.com).
Chief Executive Officer: C. Klopper

Panic (Publicity) Ltd
2 Mortimer House, Furmage Street, London,
SW18 4DF (Tel: 020-8871 9980; Fax: 020-
8871 9949; E-mail: Ghislain@panic-uu.com;
Web: www.panic-uu.com).
Managing Director: Ms Ghislain Pascal

Patcom Media Relations
Flat 101, Globe Wharf, 205 Rotherhithe Street,
London, SE16 1XX (Tel: 020-7231 9300; Fax:
020-7231 2990; E-mail: hughp@patcom-media.com;
Web: www.patcom-media.com).
Chief Executive: H. Paterson

Peter Hope Lumley
32 Cromwell Grove, London, W6 7RG
(Tel: 020-7603 5541; Fax: 020-7603 6669).
PR Consultant: P. Hope Lumley

Peter Thompson
Flat 1, 12 Bourchier Street, London, W1V 5HN
(Tel: 020-7439 1210; Fax: 020-7439 1202).
Director: P. Thompson

Phenomenon Communications Ltd
112A Sevenoaks Road, Orpington, Kent, BR6
9JZ (Tel: 01689-855073; Fax: 01689-607944;
E-mail: info@phenomenon.co.uk;
Web: www.phenomenon.co.uk).
Managing Director: D. Owens

Philippa Perry Associates
91 Brick Lane, London, E1 6QL
(Tel: 020-7247 9695; Fax: 020-7247 6069;
E-mail: pnlp@dircon.co.uk).
Director: Ms P. Perry

Pielle Consulting
Museum House, 25 Museum Street, London,
WC1A 1PL (Tel: 020-7323 1587; Fax: 020-7631
0029; E-mail: teampielle@compuserve.com).
Executive Chairman: P. L. Walker

PoLo Public Relations
30 Shrewsbury Avenue, London, SW14 8JZ
(Tel: 020-8876 4242; Fax: 020-8876 8900;
E-mail: info@polopr.co.uk).
Managing Director: Ms P. Lotery

PR21 UK Ltd
67–69 Whitfield Street, London, W1P 5RL (Tel:
020-7436 4060; Fax: 020-7255 2131; E-mail:
bobby.lane@pr21.com; Web: www.pr21.com).
Chief Executive Officer: Ms B. Kaye

PR Direct Ltd
PO Box 53, Richmond, Surrey, TW10 5EZ (Tel:
020-8878 8550; Fax: 020-8878 8559; E-mail:
info@prdirect.net; Web: www.prdirect.net).
Director: Ms E. Boden-Lee

Presswatch Analysis Ltd
Information House, 138–140 Southwark Street,
London, SE1 0SW (Tel: 020-7261 9964; Fax:
020-7928 7688; E-mail: info@presswatch.com;
Web: www.presswatch.com).
General Manager: R. Saunders

PR Newswire Europe
210 Old Street, London, EC1V 9UN (Tel:
020-7490 8111; Fax: 020-7490 1255; E-mail:
sales@prnewswire.eu.com; Web: www.prnewsie.co.uk)

Republic Communications Ltd
Dudley House, 36–38 Southampton Street,
London, WC2E 7HE (Tel: 020-7379 5000;
Fax: 020-7379 5122;
E-mail: jane/deborah@republicpr.com;
Web: www.republicpr.com).
Marketing Directors: Ms J. Howard;
Ms D. Lewis

Richard Franklin Associates
80B Albert Hall Mansions, Kensington, London,
SW7 2AE (Tel: 020-7584 8150;
E-mail: rfa.pr@virgin.net).
Managing Director: R. Franklin

Richman & Associates (Public Relations) Ltd
2 Bloomsbury Place, London, WC1A 2QE
(Tel: 020-7636 7975; Fax: 020-7436 5169;
E-mail: randapr@itl.net).
Managing Director: J. K. Richman

Roche Communications
Edinburgh House, 40 Great Portland Street, London, W1W 7LZ (Tel: 020-7436 1111; Fax: 020-7436 1122).
Managing Director: R. Cohen

Rough House
51 Sheen Road, Richmond, Surrey, TW9 1YH
(Tel: 020-8948 1455; Fax: 020-8948 1433;
E-mail: inquiries@roughhouse.co.uk;
Web: www.roughhouse.co.uk).
Managing Director: G. Fitzgerald

Ruder Finn UK Ltd
Isis House, 74 New Oxford Street, London, WC1A 1BL (Tel: 020-7462 8900; Fax: 020-7462 8999; E-mail: mail@ruderfinn.co.uk; Web: www.ruderfinn.co.uk).
Managing Director: Ms A. Miles

S W C Media Services Ltd
Seedbed Business Centre, Langston Road, Loughton, Essex, IG10 3TQ (Tel: 020-8504 3389; Fax: 020-8506 1011; E-mail: contact@swcmedia.co.uk; Web: www.swcmedia.co.uk).
Managing Director: S. Webb

Sam Weller Associates
155 Upper Street, London, N1 1RA
(Tel: 020-7288 2522; Fax: 020-7288 2533;
E-mail: samweller@swa-pr.co.uk).
Chief Executive: S. Weller

Shine Communications Ltd
101 Goswell Road, London, EC1V 7ER
(Tel: 020-7553 3333; Fax: 020-7553 3330;
E-mail: brilliance@shinecom.com;
Web: www.shineon-line.com).
Managing Director: Ms R. Bell

Sister Public Relations Ltd
27 Lexington Street, London, W1R 3HQ (Tel: 020-7287 9601; Fax: 020-7287 9602; E-mail: sister.pr@virgin.net; Web: www.sister-pr.com).
Managing Director: Ms S. Millar

Spear Communications
36 Bruton Street, London, W1J 6QZ
(Tel: 020-7409 0494; Fax: 020-7409 1018;
E-mail: pr@spear.uk.com).
Managing Director: Ms S. Glasgow

Starfish Communications
Oxford House, 76 Oxford Street, London, W1D 1BS (Tel: 020-7323 2121; Fax: 020-7323 0234; E-mail: speed@star-fish.net;
Web: www.star-fish.net).
Managing Partner: J. Speed

Stratton & Reekie Public Relations Consultancy
46 Broadwick Street, London, W1F 7AF
(Tel: 020-7287 8456; Fax: 020-7287 8455;
E-mail: streek@dircon.co.uk).
Partner: Ms D. Stratton

Synapse Communication Ltd
101 The Foundry Annexe, 65 Glasshill Street, London, SE1 0QR (Tel: 020-7721 8575; Fax: 020-7721 8574; E-mail: tim@synapseltd.co.uk; Web: www.synapseltd.co.uk).
Director: T. Lewis

Tavistock Communications Ltd
1 Angel Court, London, EC2R 7HX (Tel: 020-7600 2288; Fax: 020-7600 5084; E-mail: jcarey@tavistock.co.uk; Web: www.tavistock.co.uk).
Chairman: J. Carey

Tideway Communications
Tapestry Court, Mortlake High Street, London, SW14 8HJ (Tel: 020-8878 0787; Fax: 020-8876 2145; E-mail: tidewaycom@aol.com).
Managing Director: K. Clark

Vanbrugh Financial Communications Ltd
95 Aldwych, London, WC2B 4JF
(Tel: 020-7569 6720; Fax: 020-7569 6721;
E-mail: sophie@vanbrughfinancial.com).
Managing Director: Ms S. Hull

WAT Public Relations
59 Malvern Road, London, E8 3LJ
(Tel: 07000-723 999; Fax: 07000-782 982;
E-mail: info@watpr.com; Web: www.watpr.com).
Managing Director: Ms J. Weisbasm

The Waterfront Partnership
130–132 Tooley Street, London, SE1 2TD
(Tel: 020-7787 1200; Fax: 020-7787 1201;
E-mail: partnership@thewaterfront.co.uk).
Managing Director: N. Finney

Weber Shandwick Worldwide
Aldermary House, 15 Queen Street, London,
EC4N 1TX (Tel: 020-7905 2400; Fax:
020-7950 2877;
E-mail: ebowen-davies@webershandwick.com;
Web: www.webershandwick.com).
Director: Chris Genasi

The Wriglesworth Consultancy
Friars House, 157–168 Blackfriars Road, London,
SE1 8EZ (Tel: 020-7620 2228; Fax: 020-7620
2229; E-mail: enquiries@wriglesworth.com;
Web: www.wriglesworth.com).
Managing Director: Dr. John Wriglesworth

COMMUNICATIONS

TELECOMMUNICATIONS INDUSTRY

London has historically been an attractive market for many industries due to its strategic location and importance as a global player. The communications industry is no exception and although the industry is by no means London-centric, communications and technological innovation in the area have an increasing effect on Londoners, be they consumer or business users.

The UK's mobile market has historically been among the most mature of the world's mobile markets. Liberalisation was introduced early and competition has been actively encouraged by a progressive regulator. The UK now boasts one of the world's most competitive markets with a range of services offered through a number of forward thinking suppliers.

REGULATION

The Regulator is responsible for setting the controls for the UK mobile market and ensuring that none of the industry players indulge in anti-competitive behaviour.

The two government bodies covering the regulation of the mobile industry in the UK are the Radiocommunications Agency and Oftel. The Radiocommunications Agency is part of the Department of Trade and Industry (DTI) and is responsible for radio frequency allocation. The greater part of regulation falls under the jurisdiction of Oftel. Oftel was created by the 1984 Telecommunications Act and empowered to ensure competition in the UK market. It was therefore given authority over licensing procedures, tariffing, interconnection (where one operator has access to another's infrastructure) as well as acting as an arbitrator between operators in disputes. Oftel has authority over the UK's other communications sectors as well.

The policies adopted and enforced by Oftel are largely driven by the European Commission (with the support of the Parliament and Council of Ministers). This follows the European Court of Justice's ruling allowing the European Commission to apply the competition rules of the Treaty of Rome to telecommunications (in 1985). This ruling also prompted the formation of DGXIII (Telecommunications, Information Industries and Innovation) in 1986.

In general, policy has been aimed at providing access to networks and public services and guarantee to harmonised, objective, transparent and non-discriminatory conditions based on the so called "Open Network Provision" (ONP) principles which aim to ensure fair competition and access for new entrants. Among other things that have impacted on the mobile industry, the Commission has addressed:

• Universal Service
This is the stipulation by which services must be provided to all customers irrespective of their location. New entrants often have to contribute to the cost of universal service provision. In the UK in 1996, the government and the EU agreed to offer grants to Vodafone and BT Cellnet to extend their mobile telephony coverage to sparsely populated areas of Scotland.

• Number Portability
This allows the customer to keep his or her telephone number even if they change service provider so the telephone number is seen to belong to the customer not the service provider. Number portability was introduced to the UK's fixed line communications industry in June 1997 and to the mobile industry in January 1999.

• Licensing
The provision of and requirements of the licensing process.

• Incumbent's Tariffs
This provision is to stop incumbent operators abusing their positions as providers of both local, national and long distance services by cross-subsidising one with another.

In the UK the two major pieces of legislation that have shaped the communications industry are the 1981 and the 1984 Telecommunications Acts. The former divided the General Post Office (which prior to this had provided both telecommunications and postal services) into British Telecommunications and the Post Office and made provision for the introduction of competition. The latter established BT as a public limited company and created Oftel as the industry watchdog.

Since its creation, Oftel has licensed hundreds of companies to compete in the various sectors of the UK communications industry. These licenses are divided into the following four categories
- PTO or Public Telecommunications Operator (a total of 39 licensed to date)
- IFS or International Facilities Based Service Provider (110 licensed to date)
- ISVR or International Simple Voice Reseller (179 licensed to date)
- Satellite Services Provider (36 licensed to date)

It must be noted that not all these licenses are current, some operators may have ceased to exist or may never have begun operations.

PTOs can provide either fixed or mobile services and will own their network (the physical infrastructure over which the call is routed). IFS providers also own infrastructure although this is limited by the nature of the services they offer i.e. international calls only. ISVR providers do not own any infrastructure but buy capacity from other operators. Finally, as the name suggests, Satellite Services Providers offer satellite-based services.

Much of the early regulation of the UK telecommunications industry was concerned with the promotion of competition and since this has by and large been achieved in most of the sectors covered by Oftel, the regulator has announced that it intends to take a much "softer" approach in the future. In light of this Oftel's activities can now broadly be described as
- Continuing to review its current customer protection policies to promote the interests of consumers
- Policing the regulation of licenses
- Conducting separate twice yearly reviews of each sector—fixed, mobile, Internet access and interactive broadcasting – to monitor for anti-competitive behaviour, excessive profits and market share

Oftel's three directorates—Regulatory Policy, Compliance and Business Support, conduct these activities. Regulatory Policy Directorate is responsible for developing telecommunications policies. The Compliance Directorate makes sure phone companies meet the obligations of their licenses and existing telecoms regulations. Finally the Business Support Directorate supports the entire organisation.

One aspect of the mobile sector which is currently not covered by Oftel regulation is mobile Internet access. Oftel is currently allowing operators to develop mobile Internet access services unhindered but may impose regulation if mobile Internet access becomes a vital way of accessing information and services.

INDUSTRY PLAYERS

The provision of mobile services in the UK is offered through Network Operators, Service Providers and MVNOs.

The Network Operator owns the license to provide cellular services as well as the physical network. Network operators are responsible for billing and maintaining the networks, can set tariffs and have a direct billing relationship with the end users. There are currently four Network Operators in the UK (*see* table below).

The Service Providers were introduced into the UK market at the very beginning when their role was to increase competition within the market. They buy airtime wholesale from the network operators and sell it onto the end users. This agreement means that they can set their own tariff structures and they have a billing relationship with the end users.

The incumbent operators (those who have been operating since the start) BT Cellnet and Vodafone have an obligation under the terms of their licenses to offer wholesale minutes of airtime to Service Providers. The next two entrants Orange and One2One were never obliged to offer this and although this came up for review in April 1998, both these operators were considered at this time to have insignificant market share. There are around 50 Service Providers still operating in the market including One.Tel, Sainsbury's, Sony Cellular Services and Martin Dawes. In order to maintain a viable business operation many of these Service Providers have diversified their product offer away from pure mobile service offering to other telecom or Internet based services.

Finally, the newest entrants to the market are MVNOs, Mobile Virtual Network Operators. Unlike the Service Providers there is no obligation for the Network operators to open their networks to MVNOs rather it is an entirely commercial agreement where the Network Operator allows the MVNO access to their network. This differs from the Service Provider in that a true MVNO that has its own mobile network code; issues its own SIM cards (Subscriber Identity Module card – the 'brain' of the handset); operates its own mobile switching centre; and has a pricing structure fully independent from the network operator. As these are commercial agreements there are as yet no regulations covering MVNO, but as with mobile Internet access the Regulator is currently observing development closely and may step in as MVNOs become a more important force. To date the most successful MVNO is Virgin which operates on the One2One network although others are emerging including Energis (operating on the Orange network) and Carphone Warehouse which claims to operate on all four networks.

CURRENT MOBILE MARKET

Operator	Ownership	Technology	Launch Date
BT Cellnet	100% BT	Tacs-900 GSM	January 1985 January 1994
Vodafone	100% Vodafone AirTouch	Tacs-900 GSM	January 1985 July 1992
One2One	100% Deutsche Telekom	GSM 1800	September 1993
Orange	100% France Telecom	GSM 1800	April 1994
Hutchison 3G	65% Hutchison Whampoa, 20% DoCoMo & 15% KPN	UMTS	To begin operations 2002

MARKET SHARE

	BT Cellnet	Vodafone	One2One	Orange
Current Subscriber Base	11,158,000	12,279,000	8,981,000	11,030,000
Total Market Share	25.7%	28.3%	20.7%	25.3%

SUBSCRIBER GROWTH

Date	Jan 1997	Jan 1998	Jan 1999	Jan 2000	Mar 2001
Subscriber Base	6,810,000	8,344,000	13,001,000	23,944,000	43,448,000
Penetration Rate	11.7%	14.3%	22.3%	41%	73.8%

Subscriber growth in the UK has been driven by a number of factors. The most important of these are
- Promotion of prepaid services
- Subsidised handsets
- Number portability

PREPAID SERVICES

There are two methods of paying for mobile services in the UK, monthly contracts or pre paid cards. Monthly contracts means that the end user pays a fixed subscription fee each month which entitles them to a number of basic services (for example voicemail) and gives them a certain amount of 'airtime' each month. Prepaid subscribers have access to the same services but pay in advance. Initially this allowed industry players to target additional consumer groups in particular the youth market and those people would normally not pass the credit checks necessary for a contract. It has proved to be a very popular option as it allows people to control their spend and is a low cost entry method to mobile services.

SUBSIDISED HANDSETS

In the UK and other European markets it has become common practice for the Network Operators to subsidise the cost of mobile phones to encourage subscriber acquisition. This has proved to be good news for the end user but a costly practice to Network Operators.

NUMBER PORTABILITY

All UK operators have been obliged to provide number portability since the beginning of 1999. This means that any end user who wishes to change network Operator (or service provider) must be given the option of retaining their existing number i.e. taking their mobile number with them to the new service provider. This was considered to be a barrier to competition. The regulator is currently looking at how the administrative system for number portability can be improved in order to enforce this obligation.

TECHNOLOGY

Services were introduced to the UK in 1985 using an analogue technology called TACS. In 1992 Vodafone launched a new digital "GSM" network. The introduction of GSM was therefore referred to as 2G or second-generation services. BT Cellnet and two more entrants launched GSM service in the following two years making the UK one of Europe's most competitive markets.

The UK was the third European country to license 3G operators after Finland and Spain but was the first to auction its licenses. Auctions are not new to the European communications industry, many of the second and third entrants had to bid for their license, what is spectacular about the UK's 3G auction is the height of the bids. While industry observers have speculated that the auction might reach £4 billion, in the event a total of £22 billion was raised from the sale of spectrum.

There is continued speculation about the impact of the UK's 3G spectrum auction. Since operators must recoup the investment in the license it is expected that this will result in higher costs for the consumer thus hindering the UK's migration to 3G services.

UK 3G LICENSE WINNERS AND TOTAL COST

Hutchison 3G UK	License A	2x 15MHz paired 5MHz unpaired	€7 billion
Vodafone	License B	2x15MHz paired	€9.6 billion
BT Cellnet	License C	2x10 MHz paired 5MHz unpaired	€6.5 billion
One2One	License D	2x10 MHz paired 5MHz unpaired	€6.4 billion
Orange	License E	2x10 MHz paired 5MHz unpaired	€6.6 billion
TOTAL			€36.1 billion

DATA SERVICES

As in the fixed line communications, mobile operators are no longer content to offer connection, voice telephony and standard applications i.e. voicemail, bundled airtime and so on. Competition has driven down price and therefore revenue from the basic services and operators are now seeking to differentiate themselves by offering innovative value added services. The most important of these to date is the development of SMS and WAP applications.

SMS (Short Messaging Services) or 'text messaging' as it is more commonly referred to allows consumers to send and receive text messages up to 160 characters long on their mobile phones. These messages can be personal messages sent from one user to another or can be information based services specified by the end user and sent by the network operator. Most popular SMS information services are sports results and news headlines. Due to its simplicity and popularity among young users the number of SMS messages being sent each day has increased dramatically (see table below).

TOTAL NUMBER OF SMS SENT IN THE UK

Date	December '98	December '99	December '00	March '01
Number of Messages	170 million	271 million	756 million	864 million

SMS is a relatively simple technology but the more complicated offering is WAP, or Wireless Application Protocol. WAP is a language that allows Internet-style data to be viewed from the mobile phone. To date applications have be uninspiring, news and weather reports, sports information, horoscopes etc and uptake much slower than anticipated. However, it is key to Operators' future business plans that users accept and use more sophisticated services to prepare them for the changes that 3G services are expected to herald.

Consumers access this content from Mobile Portals, which like traditional Internet Portals, aggregate and display mobile Internet content in an accessible manner. As could be expected there are a number of independent mobile Internet portals and content sites springing up for UK consumers – the portals offered by the main operators are detailed in the table below.

Operator	WAP Launch	Mobile Portal Launch	Number of WAP Subscribers (Jan 2001)
BT Cellnet	January 2000	"Vizzavi" May 2000	1 million
Vodafone	January 2000	"Genie" September 1997	70,000
One2One	Summer 2000	"T-Motion" February 2001	135,000
Orange	November 1999	"orange.net"	100,000

3G will offer much faster data transfer rates (up to 2Mbps is commonly quoted) which will expand the facility of the network to include full Internet browsing and streamed video content. The question remains as to whether ordinary consumers will want or use these enhanced services.

PMR

There is a fifth operational national mobile network which must be mentioned in a discussion of the communications industry in the UK. Dolphin Telecom operates a national mobile network based on the TETRA standard. PMR (Public Mobile Radio) or PAMR (Public Access Mobile Radio) as it is also referred to differs from other mobile networks in its ability to allow group communication, a single user has the ability to push a button which allows him to broadcast to members of a pre-selected group. Most often PMR is used by the emergency services but the Dolphin network interconnects with the fixed network and is offered primarily to business users as the UK's fifth mobile network. However the take up of services has been much slower than anticipated.

OFTEL
50 Ludgate Hill, London EC4M 7JJ (Tel: 020-7634 8700; Fax: 020-7634 8943; Web: www.oftel.co.uk).

DEPARTMENT OF TRADE AND INDUSTRY (DTI)
Telecommunications Division, 151 Buckingham Palace Road, London SW1W 9SS (Tel: 020-7215 5000; Fax: 020-7215 2909).

BT CELLNET
260 Bath Road Slough, Berkshire SL1 4DX (Tel: 01753-565 000; Fax: 01753-565 010; Web: www.cellnet.co.uk).

DOLPHIN TELECOM
The Crescent, Jays Close, Viables, Basingstoke, Hampshire RG22 4BS (Tel: 01256-811 822; Fax: 01256-474 537; Web: www.dolphin-telecom.co.uk).

HUTCHISON 3G UK
43 New Bond Street; London W1Y 9HB (Tel: 020-7499 1886; Fax: 020-7491 7266).

ORANGE PLC
The Economist Building, 25 St James Street, London, SW1A 1HA (Tel: 020-7766 1766; Fax: 020-7766 1767; Web: www.orange.co.uk).

One2One
Imperial Place, Maxwell Road, Borehamwood WD6 1EA (Tel: 020-8214 2121; Fax: 020-8214 3601; Web: www.one2one.co.uk).

VODAFONE GROUP

The Courtyard, 2 – 4 London Road, Newbury, Berkshire RG14 1JX (Tel: 01635 33251; Fax: 01635 45713; Web: www.vodafone.co.uk).

TELECOMMUNICATIONS COMPANIES

The list below contains a selection of Public Telecommunications Companies based in London.

ACC TELECOM

626 Chiswick High Road, London W4 5RY (Tel: 0800 980 9800; Fax: 020-8400 4444)

AT&T (UK) LTD

Norfolk House, 31 St. James' Square, London SW1Y 4JR (Tel: 0800 064 0001; Fax: 020-7925 8142)

CABLE AND WIRELESS COMMUNICATIONS

26 Red Lion Square, London WC1R 4HQ (Tel: 0500 500 194; Fax: 020-7528 2377)

COLT TELECOMMUNICATIONS

International Headquarters, 15 Marylebone, London NW1 5JD (Tel: 020-7390 3900; Fax: 020-7390 3901)

FIRST TELECOM PLC

Exchange Tower, 1 Harbour Exchange Square, London E14 9EA (Tel: 020-7572 7700; Fax: 020-7572 7001)

GLOBAL ONE

Orion House, 5 Upper St. Martin's Lane, London WC2H 9EA (Tel: 020-7379 4747; Fax: 020-7379 1404)

MFS COMMUNICATIONS LTD.

10 Fleet Place, London EC4M 7RB (Tel: 020-7570 5700; Fax: 020-7571 5711)

NTT EUROPE LTD.

Level 19, City Tower, 40 Basinghall Street, London EC2V 5DE

PRIMUS TELECOMMUNICATIONS LTD.

NIOC House, 4 Victoria Street, London SW1H 0NE (Tel: 0800 086 6000; Fax: 020-7233 0882)

TELIA INTERNATIONAL UK LTD.

114a Cromwell Road, London SW7 4ES (Tel: 020-7416 0306l Fax: 020-7416 0305)

TELSTRA UK Ltd.

44-48 Paul Street, London EC2A 4LB (Tel: 0800 838 848)

WORLDCOM INTERNATIONAL INC

13 City Forum, 250 City Road, London EC1V 2NA (Tel: 020-7750 0000; Fax: 020-7750 3210)

POSTAL SERVICES

Responsibility for running postal services rests in the UK with the Post Office. The Post Office is comprised of three components – Parcelforce, Post Office Counters Ltd and Royal Mail. For further information on the products and services of the Post Office, contact your nearest post office. Alternatively, the main Post Office website provides information on all products and services, along with links to other useful websites.

ROYAL MAIL

Established over 350 years ago, the Royal Mail is the letters 'arm' of the Post Office and provides a number of products and services for both business and residential customers.

PARCELFORCE

Parcelforce Worldwide is the UK's leading carrier of time critical packages, parcels and freight. Parcelforce Worldwide Enquiry Centre (Tel: 0800 224466 – lines open 08.30 – 17.30 Monday – Friday); Parcelforce Worldwide Collections Centre (Tel: 0800 884422 – lines open 08.30 – 17.30 Monday to Friday). Parcelforce can also be contacted via email at parcelforce@parcelforce.co.uk

CULTURAL LONDON

HISTORY TIMELINE
ENGLISH KINGS AND QUEENS
ORDER OF SUCCESSION
ORDER OF PRECEDENCE
SCENES AND SIGHTS OF LONDON
BLUE PLAQUES
CLUBS
MUSEUMS AND GALLERIES
THEATRES
TOURISM
SPORT
CULTURAL, HISTORICAL AND RECREATIONAL ORGANISATIONS

CULTURAL LONDON

The Cultural London section of Whitaker's London Almanack contains a variety of information ranging from London's history, its historic buildings, monuments, scenes and sights to leisure, sport and tourism. London has a rich and vibrant history and a wealth of places to visit and the information listed in this section is merely intended to provide a snapshot of London's cultural, artistic and recreational assets.

HISTORY AND HERITAGE

HISTORY TIME-LINE

BC 54 – Julius Caesar lands his invasion force of five legions and 2,000 cavalry on the South Eastern Coast of England near Deal. The Celts use the Thames as their main line of defence and it is at this time that it is thought that a small Roman settlement on the Thames may have sprung up.

AD 43 – 97 years after Caesar left, the Romans mount their second invasion. During the reign of Claudius, 40,000 roman troops land in Kent and approach the Thames, which is again utilised as the main line of defence.

50 – A bridge is definitely built across the Thames at this time and this is generally recognised as the founding of London. The first recorded name, Londinium, is Roman but is thought to be based on the earlier Celtic name Londinion. Within ten years of the Roman invasion, Londinium is a flourishing town built on two hills, seperated by the river Walbrook.

60 – Tacticus refers to London as 'filled with traders and a celebrated centre of commerce'.

61 – British tribes in the West and North oppose the roman occupation. In a revenge attack for the death of her husband the King of Iceni (a Norfolk Territory), Queen Boudicca (popularly Boadecia), marches on London. The inhabitants of London are massacred and London itself is sacked and burned before Boudicca is finally defeated and commits suicide. London survives the attack due to its established status as a port and commercial centre. The city is rebuilt in the next half century.

200 – a defensive wall is built around the whole city. It consists of a 'v' shaped ditch with 21 bastions around its perimeter. Six main fortified gateways lead out to the Roman roads. By this time London has taken over from Colchester as the capital of the region. The Basilica is built and serves as the Town Hall, Law Courts and Exchange and is larger than the Basilica in Rome.

286 – The Roman Empire is moving in to its decline. Marcus Carausius, commander of the channel fleet, mutinies and assumes the title of Emperor of Britain. His reign lasts six years when he is deposed by his lieutenant Allectus, who names himself emperor.

290 – The London mint is established

296 – Constantius Chlorus is sent by Rome to restore order and Allectus is killed.

410 – Emperor Honorius sends a warning to the people of Britain that they must make preparations to protect themselves in the future. Soon after, the Romans progressively withdraw from Britain to defend Italy. During the 6th Century the Saxons control most of England and London becomes known as Lundenwic. London continues to expand outside the city walls.

604 – St Paul's Cathedral is founded by King Aethelbert. The Christian church is revived and elements of Roman culture such as literacy and learning become important again.

834 – 1014 – The Danish Vikings are a constant threat to the peace and security of Saxon London and mount numerous attacks during this period which leave London in ruins. By 871 The Danes have established London as their winter settlement. They are ousted by King Alfred the Great in 878 and he re-establishes Lundenberg, within the city walls. In 980 the Vikings invade once again but London is recaptured by King Ethelred in 1014.

336 Cultural London

1016 – Ethelred is succeeded briefly by Edmund II and then by the Danish King Canute (Cnut) who is crowned King of All England. During this reign, London replaces Winchester as the capital of England.

1042 – Edward the Confessor becomes King of England. Royal governance is based at Westminster during his reign and the city of London remains the commercial centre.

1065 – Westminster Abbey, rebuilt by Edward the Confessor, is consecrated.

1066 – Edward the Confessor dies. Harold is crowned his successor but is defeated and killed at the battle of Hastings by Duke William of Normandy. William claims his right to the throne and is crowned at Westminster Abbey on the 25 December 1066 whilst standing on the grave of Edward the Confessor. William grants the city of London a charter guaranteeing to preserve the privileges it enjoyed under Edward the Confessor. Neither the Normans nor their successors the Plantagenets succeed in diluting London's autonomy.

1078 – The Building of the Tower of London is started by Gandulf, Bishop of Rochester, for William the Conqueror. Baynard's Castle is built on the river a mile west of the Tower, as is Montfichet Castle, a moated keep near Ludgate.

1077 – 1136 – London is destroyed by fire and requires rebuilding four times. One great fire in 1087 destroys St. Paul's Cathedral which is later rebuilt. The successor of William the Conqueror, William Rufus is responsible for the building of the great hall at Westminster, the reinforcement of the Tower of London and the rebuilding of the Thames Bridge which was destroyed by flood.

1189 – Henry Fitz Ailwyn becomes the first Mayor of London. His term of office lasts until his death in 1212.

1195 – In the absence of Richard I (popularly 'the Lionheart'), John his brother is recognised as regent and the City of London wins the right to be recognised as an 'independent commune'.

1215 – On the 9 May, King John grants a charter to the City confirming its right to choose a Mayor by annual election. This is the foundation of the City's municipal autonomy. Twenty four aldermen begin to advise the Mayor. In later years they represent specific wards.

1348 – The Black Death, believed to have started in Dorchester takes a heavy toll on the population of London. By the end of 1349 it is thought that half of London's population has died as a result of the plague, totalling around 30,000 people.

1381 – The Peasants Revolt takes place when the city gates of London are opened to Wat Tyler's Kentish rebels. The ensuing riots culminate in the lynching of the Archbishop and numerous merchants and clerics. Tyler was subsequently lured to Smithfield and murdered by Mayor Walworth.

1397 – The first of Richard Whittington's four terms as Mayor begins.

1400 – London has become one of the greatest ports in Western Europe. Trading guilds such as the Merchant adventurers promote trade abroad. In order to improve their industries, traders and craftsmen organise themselves into guilds, the successors of which remain today as the City Livery Companies.

1411 – The first Guildhall is built.

1450 – Jack Cade launches his unsuccessful rebellion against the government of Henry VI.

1515 – Major building of Dockyards and shipbuilding at Deptford and Woolwich begins.

1536 – Tudor London – Henry VIII implements the Dissolution of the Monasteries. Vast numbers of the religious buildings and treasurers of London are destroyed as Londoner's enthusiastically embrace Protestantism. Also during Henry's reign the Palace of Sheen, St. James's Palace and Hampton Court Palace are constructed, creating a suburban dimension to the increasingly cramped confines of the 'Walled City'.

History and Heritage

1558 – The reign of Elizabeth I begins, bringing a new period of growth and prosperity for London. The works of Christopher Marlowe, Ben Johnson and William Shakespeare fuel a literary renaissance.

1561 – The spire of St. Paul's Cathedral is lost when it is struck by lightning.

1574 – James Burbage designs the first purpose built playhouse in London. Eventually built south of the River Thames at Southwark the Globe theatre premieres many of Shakespeare's works.

1603 – King James VI of Scotland becomes James I of England and London experiences an influx of Scots. The New River Scheme introduced at this time brings a more reliable water supply to Londoners.

1605 – Guy Fawkes' plot to blow up Parliament is discovered. It is in fact an attempt to assassinate James I, who has caused discontent due to his anti-Catholic laws.

1605 – The Great Frost Fair is held on the Thames

1664–5 – The Great Plague claims an estimated 100,000 lives at a rate of 12,000 a week. The City's cat and dog population is thought to be the source of the epidemic and is exterminated.

1666 – The Great Fire of London. Almost the entire city of London within the walls is consumed with only the Aldgate and Tower areas escaping destruction. 87 Churches, 44 Livery Company Halls and 13,200 houses are destroyed. Among the losses are St. Paul's Cathedral, the Royal Exchange, the Fleet and Bridewell.

1671 – 9,000 houses are rebuilt using bricks and mortar (timber housing is now banned). The opportunity is taken to improve the building laws and infrastructure of London's streets making it one of the safest cities in the world in structural terms.

1675–1711 – Sir Christopher Wren rebuilds St. Paul's Cathedral.

1694 – The Bank of England is founded to raise funds to conduct the war against France.

1715 – The Riot Act is passed to suppress increasing numbers of disturbances in London and England generally. Its impact is limited and fails to prevent the 1743 Gin riots.

1720–1751 – Gin drinking is rife in the slum areas of London and at its height it is estimated that the amount being drunk is equivalent to 2 pints per week for every man, woman and child. This leads to increases in crime, prostitution, poverty and child mortality amongst the poor. Parliament responds to this crisis by significantly increasing the duties on Gin, successfully reducing its consumption.

1721–42 – Robert Walpole is the first politician to live at 10 Downing Street and is commonly regarded at Britain's first Prime Minister.

1760–66 – The last gates to the city and the remaining portions of the walls are demolished.

1780 – In his opposition to proposals for Catholic Emancipation, Lord George Gordon leads a crowd of 50,000 people to the House of Commons. The 'Gordon Riots' which ensue are reported to have caused the deaths of 285 rioters and the destruction of numerous Catholic chapels and private houses.

1829 – Sir Robert Peel creates the Metropolitan Police Service.

1833 – 10,000 Londoners die in a cholera epidemic that leads to a law banning burials within the city boundaries.

1833 – The Horse Omnibus is sanctioned stimulating the spread of the population of London.

1837 – Queen Victoria ascends the throne.

1839 – Admiral Nelson's triumph at the Battle of Trafalgar is celebrated with the construction of Nelson's Column in Trafalgar Square.

1851 – The Great Exhibition is held in the Crystal Palace erected in Hyde Park.

338 Cultural London

1855 – The Metropolitan Board of Works is established with a remit of duties including slum clearance, building regulations, road improvements and main drainage maintenance.

1863 – The Metropolitan Railway opens the first Underground line. It runs between Paddington and Farringdon Street and consists of carriages pulled by steam engines.

1888 – London County Council (LCC) is established in the place of the Board of Works. This is the first directly elected London-wide Government body. At the turn of the century it concentrates its efforts on re-housing by building the first suburban housing estates complemented by an ever growing network of suburban railway lines.

1894 – Tower Bridge opens.

1899 – London Government Act – London is divided into 28 Boroughs. Under the LCC a two tier system of local government is sustained until 1965.

1915–18 – German Zeppelins bomb London. The first Zeppelin raid on London takes place on 31 May 1915. The raid kills 28 people and injures 60 more.

1940 – Sept 7 witnesses the first bombing campaign on London by the German Airforce (Luftwaffe). The Blitz has devastating effects with an estimated 30,000 civilians losing their lives, a further 50,000 injured and 130,000 houses being destroyed.

1951 – The Festival of Britain takes place on the South Bank of the Thames, a site which will eventually become the South Bank Centre.

1956 – The Clean Air Act makes London's infamous 'pea-soupers' a thing of the past. The burning of any fuel which is not smokeless is banned.

1965 – The LCC is replaced by the Greater London Council (GLC) and larger London Boroughs are created.

1982 – The Thames Barrier is completed. It is the world's largest movable flood barrier, spanning 520 metres across the Thames at Woolwich Reach, South East London.

1986 – The GLC is abolished.

1990 – Poll Tax riots take place on the streets of London.

1994 – The Eurostar terminal is completed at Waterloo Station. It is now possible, via the Channel Tunnel, to travel by train from London to Brussels, Paris and Lille.

1997 – 6 September–Following a procession of her coffin through the streets of London, the Funeral of Diana Princess of Wales is held at Westminster Abbey.

1998 – The Government publishes a White Paper 'A Mayor and Assembly for London' on 25 March setting out the Government's proposals for the future governance of London. In the Referendum on 7 May, 72% of those who voted said 'yes' to the proposals. Every borough and the City of London voted in favour. On 3 December the Greater London Authority Bill is published.

1999 – On 11 November the Bill receives Royal Assent to become the Greater London Authority Act.

1999 – On the night of the 31 December, to celebrate the coming of the year 2000, an elaborate show is held at the newly completed Millennium Dome at Greenwich and the immense 'River of Fire' firework display is held on the Thames.

2000 – The Greater London Authority comes into power. May 4 – Independent candidate Ken Livingstone is elected as its first Mayor.

For London events from June 2000 — May 2001 see the events section p 533.

ENGLISH KINGS AND QUEENS 927 TO 1603

HOUSES OF CERDIC AND DENMARK

Reign	
927—939	**Æthelstan** Son of Edward the Elder, by Ecgwynn, and grandson of Alfred Acceded to Wessex and Mercia c.924, established direct rule over Northumbria 927, effectively creating the Kingdom of England Reigned 15 years
939—946	**Edmund I** Born 921, son of Edward the Elder, by Eadgifu Married (1) Ælfgifu (2) Æthelflæd Killed aged 25, reigned 6 years
946—955	**Eadred** Son of Edward the Elder, by Eadgifu Reigned 9 years
955—959	**Eadwig** Born before 943, son of Edmund and Ælfgifu Married Ælfgifu Reigned 3 years
959—975	**Edgar I** Born 943, son of Edmund and Ælfgifu Married (1) Æthelflæd (2) Wulfthryth (3) Ælfthryth Died aged 32, reigned 15 years
975—978	**Edward I (the Martyr)** Born c.962, son of Edgar and Æthelflæd Assassinated aged c.16, reigned 2 years
978—1016	**Æthelred (the Unready)** Born c.968/969, son of Edgar and Ælfthryth Married (1) Ælfgifu (2) Emma, daughter of Richard I, count of Normandy 1013—14 dispossessed of kingdom by Swegn Forkbeard (king of Denmark 987—1014) Died aged c.47, reigned 38 years
1016	**Edmund II (Ironside)** Born before 993, son of Æthelred and Ælfgifu Married Ealdgyth Died aged over 23, reigned 7 months (April—November)
1016—1035	**Cnut (Canute)** Born c.995, son of Swegn Forkbeard, king of Denmark, and Gunhild Married (1) Ælfgifu (2) Emma, widow of Æthelred the Unready Gained submission of West Saxons 1015, Northumbrians 1016, Mercia 1016, king of all England after Edmund's death King of Denmark 1019—35, king of Norway 1028—35 Died aged c.40, reigned 19 years
1035—1040	**Harold I (Harefoot)** Born c.1016/17, son of Cnut and Ælfgifu Married Ælfgifu 1035 recognised as regent for himself and his brother Harthacnut; 1037 recognised as king Died aged c.23, reigned 4 years
1040—1042	**Harthacnut** Born c.1018, son of Cnut and Emma Titular king of Denmark from 1028 Acknowledged king of England 1035—7 with Harold I as regent; effective king after Harold's death Died aged c.24, reigned 2 years
1042—1066	**Edward II (the Confessor)** Born between 1002 and 1005, son of Æthelred the Unready and Emma Married Eadgyth, daughter of Godwine, earl of Wessex Died aged over 60, reigned 23 years

1066 Harold II (Godwinesson)
Born c.1020, son of Godwine, earl of Wessex, and Gytha
Married (1) Eadgyth (2) Ealdgyth
Killed in battle aged c.46, reigned 10 months (January—October)

THE HOUSE OF NORMANDY

1066—1087 William I (the Conqueror)
Born 1027/8, son of Robert I, duke of Normandy; obtained the Crown by conquest
Married Matilda, daughter of Baldwin, count of Flanders
Died aged c.60, reigned 20 years

1087—1100 William II (Rufus)
Born between 1056 and 1060, third son of William I; succeeded his father in England only
Killed aged c.40, reigned 12 years

1100—1135 Henry I (Beauclerk)
Born 1068, fourth son of William I
Married (1) Edith or Matilda, daughter of Malcolm III of Scotland (2) Adela, daughter of Godfrey, count of Louvain
Died aged 67, reigned 35 years

1135—1154 Stephen
Born not later than 1100, third son of Adela, daughter of William I, and Stephen, count of Blois
Married Matilda, daughter of Eustace, count of Boulogne
1141 (February—November) held captive by adherents of Matilda, daughter of Henry I, who contested the crown until 1153
Died aged over 53, reigned 18 years

THE HOUSE OF ANJOU (PLANTAGENETS)

1154—1189 Henry II (Curtmantle)
Born 1133, son of Matilda, daughter of Henry I, and Geoffrey, count of Anjou
Married Eleanor, daughter of William, duke of Aquitaine, and divorced queen of Louis VII of France
Died aged 56, reigned 34 years

1189—1199 Richard I (Coeur de Lion)
Born 1157, third son of Henry II
Married Berengaria, daughter of Sancho VI, king of Navarre
Died aged 42, reigned 9 years

1199—1216 John (Lackland)
Born 1167, fifth son of Henry II
Married (1) Isabella or Avisa, daughter of William, earl of Gloucester (divorced) (2) Isabella, daughter of Aymer, count of Angoulême
Died aged 48, reigned 17 years

1216—1272 Henry III
Born 1207, son of John and Isabella of Angoulême
Married Eleanor, daughter of Raymond, count of Provence
Died aged 65, reigned 56 years

1272—1307 Edward I (Longshanks)
Born 1239, eldest son of Henry III
Married (1) Eleanor, daughter of Ferdinand III, king of Castile (2) Margaret, daughter of Philip III of France
Died aged 68, reigned 34 years

1307—1327 Edward II
Born 1284, eldest surviving son of Edward I and Eleanor
Married Isabella, daughter of Philip IV of France
Deposed January 1327, killed September 1327 aged 43, reigned 19 years

1327—1377 Edward III
Born 1312, eldest son of Edward II
Married Philippa, daughter of William, count of Hainault
Died aged 64, reigned 50 years

1377—1399 Richard II
Born 1367, son of Edward (the Black Prince), eldest son of Edward III
Married (1) Anne, daughter of Emperor Charles IV (2) Isabelle, daughter of Charles VI of France
Deposed September 1399, killed February 1400 aged 33, reigned 22 years

Kings and Queens

THE HOUSE OF LANCASTER

1399—1413 **Henry IV**
Born 1366, son of John of Gaunt, fourth son of Edward III, and Blanche, daughter of Henry, duke of Lancaster
Married (1) Mary, daughter of Humphrey, earl of Hereford (2) Joan, daughter of Charles, king of Navarre, and widow of John, duke of Brittany
Died aged c. 47, reigned 13 years

1413—1422 **Henry V**
Born 1387, eldest surviving son of Henry IV and Mary
Married Catherine, daughter of Charles VI of France
Died aged 34, reigned 9 years

1422—1471 **Henry VI**
Born 1421, son of Henry V
Married Margaret, daughter of René, duke of Anjou and count of Provence
Deposed March 1461, restored October 1470
Deposed April 1471, killed May 1471 aged 49, reigned 39 years

THE HOUSE OF YORK

1461—1483 **Edward IV**
Born 1442, eldest son of Richard of York (grandson of Edmund, fifth son of Edward III, and son of Anne, great-granddaughter of Lionel, third son of Edward III)
Married Elizabeth Woodville, daughter of Richard, Lord Rivers, and widow of Sir John Grey
Acceded March 1461, deposed October 1470, restored April 1471
Died aged 40, reigned 21 years

1483 **Edward V**
Born 1470, eldest son of Edward IV
Deposed June 1483, died probably July—September 1483, aged 12, reigned 2 months (April—June)

1483—1485 **Richard III**
Born 1452, fourth son of Richard of York
Married Anne Neville, daughter of Richard, earl of Warwick, and widow of Edward, Prince of Wales, son of Henry VI
Killed in battle aged 32, reigned 2 years

THE HOUSE OF TUDOR

1485—1509 **Henry VII**
Born 1457, son of Margaret Beaufort (great-granddaughter of John of Gaunt, fourth son of Edward III) and Edmund Tudor, earl of Richmond
Married Elizabeth, daughter of Edward IV
Died aged 52, reigned 23 years

1509—1547 **Henry VIII**
Born 1491, second son of Henry VII
Married (1) Catherine, daughter of Ferdinand II, king of Aragon, and widow of his elder brother Arthur (divorced) (2) Anne, daughter of Sir Thomas Boleyn (executed) (3) Jane, daughter of Sir John Seymour (died in childbirth) (4) Anne, daughter of John, duke of Cleves (divorced) (5) Catherine Howard, niece of the Duke of Norfolk (executed) (6) Catherine, daughter of Sir Thomas Parr and widow of Lord Latimer
Died aged 55, reigned 37 years

1547—1553 **Edward VI**
Born 1537, son of Henry VIII and Jane Seymour
Died aged 15, reigned 6 years

1553 **Jane**
Born 1537, daughter of Frances (daughter of Mary Tudor, the younger daughter of Henry VII) and Henry Grey, duke of Suffolk
Married Lord Guildford Dudley, son of the Duke of Northumberland
Deposed July 1553, executed February 1554 aged 16, reigned 14 days

1553—1558 **Mary I**
Born 1516, daughter of Henry VIII and Catherine of Aragon

342 Cultural London

1558—1603 **Elizabeth I**
Born 1533, daughter of Henry VIII and Anne Boleyn
Married Philip II of Spain
Died aged 42, reigned 5 years
Born 1533, daughter of Henry VIII and Anne Boleyn
Died aged 69, reigned 44 years

BRITISH KINGS AND QUEENS SINCE 1603

THE HOUSE OF STUART

1603—1625 **James I (VI of Scotland)**
Born 1566, son of Mary, queen of Scots (granddaughter of Margaret Tudor, elder daughter of Henry VII), and Henry Stewart, Lord Darnley
Married Anne, daughter of Frederick II of Denmark
Died aged 58, reigned 22 years (see also page 133)

1625—1649 **Charles I**
Born 1600, second son of James I
Married Henrietta Maria, daughter of Henry IV of France
Executed 1649 aged 48, reigned 23 years
Commonwealth Declared 19 May 1649
1649—53 Government by a council of state
1653—8 Oliver Cromwell, Lord Protector
1658—9 Richard Cromwell, Lord Protector

1660—1685 **Charles II**
Born 1630, eldest son of Charles I
Married Catherine, daughter of John IV of Portugal
Died aged 54, reigned 24 years

1685—1688 **James II (VII of Scotland)**
Born 1633, second son of Charles I
Married (1) Lady Anne Hyde, daughter of Edward, earl of Clarendon (2) Mary, daughter of Alphonso, duke of Modena
Reign ended with flight from kingdom December 1688
Died 1701 aged 67, reigned 3 years
Interregnum 11 December 1688 to 12 February 1689

1689—1702 **William III**
Born 1650, son of William II, prince of Orange, and Mary Stuart, daughter of Charles I
Married Mary, elder daughter of James II
Died aged 51, reigned 13 years

1689—1694 **Mary II**
Born 1662, elder daughter of James II and Anne
Died aged 32, reigned 5 years

1702—1714 **Anne**
Born 1665, younger daughter of James II and Anne
Married Prince George of Denmark, son of Frederick III of Denmark
Died aged 49, reigned 12 years

THE HOUSE OF HANOVER

1714—1727 **George I (Elector of Hanover)**
Born 1660, son of Sophia (daughter of Frederick, elector palatine, and Elizabeth Stuart, daughter of James I) and Ernest Augustus, elector of Hanover
Married Sophia Dorothea, daughter of George William, duke of Lüneburg-Celle
Died aged 67, reigned 12 years

1727—1760 **George II**
Born 1683, son of George I
Married Caroline, daughter of John Frederick, margrave of Brandenburg-Anspach
Died aged 76, reigned 33 years

1760—1820 **George III**
Born 1738, son of Frederick, eldest son of George II
Married Charlotte, daughter of Charles Louis, duke of Mecklenburg-Strelitz
Died aged 81, reigned 59 years
Regency 1811—20
Prince of Wales regent owing to the insanity of George III

1820—1830 **George IV**
Born 1762, eldest son of George III
Married Caroline, daughter of Charles, duke of Brunswick-Wolfenbüttel
Died aged 67, reigned 10 years

1830—1837 **William IV**
Born 1765, third son of George III

Married Adelaide, daughter of
George, duke of
Saxe-Meiningen
Died aged 71, reigned 7 years
1837—1901　**Victoria**
Born 1819, daughter of Edward,
fourth son of George III
Married Prince Albert of
Saxe-Coburg and Gotha
Died aged 81, reigned 63 years

THE HOUSE OF SAXE-COBURG AND GOTHA
1901—1910　**Edward VII**
Born 1841, eldest son of Victoria
and Albert
Married Alexandra, daughter of
Christian IX of Denmark
Died aged 68, reigned 9 years

THE HOUSE OF WINDSOR
1910—1936　**George V**
Born 1865, second son of
Edward VII
Married Victoria Mary, daughter
of Francis, duke of Teck
Died aged 70, reigned 25 years
1936　**Edward VIII**
Born 1894, eldest son of
George V
Married (1937) Mrs Wallis
Simpson
Abdicated 1936, died 1972 aged
77, reigned 10 months (20
January to 11 December)
1936—1952　**George VI**
Born 1895, second son of
George V
Married Lady Elizabeth Bowes-
Lyon, daughter of
14th Earl of Strathmore and
Kinghorne
Died aged 56, reigned 15 years
1952—　**Elizabeth II**
Born 1926, elder daughter of
George VI
Married Philip, son of Prince
Andrew of Greece

ORDER OF SUCCESSION
1　HRH The Prince of Wales
2　HRH Prince William of Wales
3　HRH Prince Henry of Wales
4　HRH The Duke of York
5　HRH Princess Beatrice of York
6　HRH Princess Eugenie of York
7　HRH The Earl of Wessex
8　HRH The Princess Royal
9　Peter Phillips
10　Zara Phillips
11　HRH The Princess Margaret, Countess of Snowdon
12　Viscount Linley
13　Viscount Linley's son
14　Lady Sarah Chatto
15　Samuel Chatto
16　Arthur Chatto
17　HRH The Duke of Gloucester
18　Earl of Ulster
19　Lady Davina Windsor
20　Lady Rose Windsor
21　HRH The Duke of Kent
22　Baron Downpatrick
23　Lady Marina Charlotte Windsor
24　Lady Amelia Windsor
25　Lord Nicholas Windsor
26　Lady Helen Taylor
27　Columbus Taylor
28　Cassius Taylor
29　Lord Frederick Windsor
30　Lady Gabriella Windsor
31　HRH Princess Alexandra, the Hon. Lady Ogilvy
32　James Ogilvy
33　Alexander Ogilvy
34　Flora Ogilvy
35　Marina, Mrs Paul Mowatt
36　Christian Mowatt
37　Zenouska Mowatt
38　The Earl of Harewood

ORDER OF PRECEDENCE IN ENGLAND AND WALES
The Sovereign
The Prince Philip, Duke of Edinburgh
The Prince of Wales
The Sovereign's younger sons
The Sovereign's grandsons
The Sovereign's cousins
Archbishop of Canterbury
Lord High Chancellor
Archbishop of York
The Prime Minister
Lord President of the Council
Speaker of the House of Commons
Lord Privy Seal
Ambassadors and High Commissioners
Lord Great Chamberlain
Earl Marshal
Lord Steward of the Household
Lord Chamberlain of the Household
Master of the Horse

344 Cultural London

Dukes, according to their patent of creation:
  (1) of England
  (2) of Scotland
  (3) of Great Britain
  (4) of Ireland
  (5) those created since the Union
Ministers and Envoys
Eldest sons of Dukes of Blood Royal
Marquesses, according to their patent of creation:
  (1) of England
  (2) of Scotland
  (3) of Great Britain
  (4) of Ireland
  (5) those created since the Union
Dukes' eldest sons
Earls, according to their patent of creation:
  (1) of England
  (2) of Scotland
  (3) of Great Britain
  (4) of Ireland
  (5) those created since the Union
Younger sons of Dukes of Blood Royal
Marquesses' eldest sons
Dukes' younger sons
Viscounts, according to their patent of creation:
  (1) of England
  (2) of Scotland
  (3) of Great Britain
  (4) of Ireland
  (5) those created since the Union
Earls' eldest sons
Marquesses' younger sons
Bishops of London, Durham and Winchester
Other English Diocesan Bishops, according to seniority of consecration
Suffragan Bishops, according to seniority of consecration
Secretaries of State, if of the degree of a Baron
Barons, according to their patent of creation:
  (1) of England
  (2) of Scotland
  (3) of Great Britain
  (4) of Ireland
  (5) those created since the Union
Treasurer of the Household
Comptroller of the Household
Vice-Chamberlain of the Household
Secretaries of State under the degree of Baron
Viscounts' eldest sons
Earls' younger sons
Barons' eldest sons
Knights of the Garter
Privy Counsellors
Chancellor of the Exchequer
Chancellor of the Duchy of Lancaster
Lord Chief Justice of England
Master of the Rolls

President of the Family Division
Vice-Chancellor
Lords Justices of Appeal
Judges of the High Court
Viscounts' younger sons
Barons' younger sons
Sons of Life Peers
Baronets, according to date of patent
Knights of the Thistle
Knights Grand Cross of the Bath
Members of the Order of Merit
Knights Grand Cross of St Michael and St George
Knights Grand Commanders of the Indian Empire
Knights Grand Cross of the Royal Victorian Order
Knights Grand Cross of the British Empire
Companions of Honour
Knights Commanders of the Bath
Knights Commanders of St Michael and St George
Knights Commanders of the Indian Empire
Knights Commanders of the Royal Victorian Order
Knights Commanders of the British Empire
Knights Bachelor
Vice-Chancellor of the County Palatine of Lancaster
Official Referees of the Supreme Court
Circuit judges and judges of the Mayor's and City of London Court
Companions of the Bath
Companions of the Star of India
Companions of St Michael and St George
Companions of the Indian Empire
Commanders of the Royal Victorian Order
Commanders of the British Empire
Companions of the Distinguished Service Order
Lieutenants of the Royal Victorian Order
Officers of the British Empire
Companions of the Imperial Service Order
Eldest sons of younger sons of Peers
Baronets' eldest sons
Eldest sons of Knights, in the same order as their fathers
Members of the Royal Victorian Order
Members of the British Empire
Younger sons of the younger sons of Peers
Baronets' younger sons
Younger sons of Knights, in the same order as their fathers
Naval, Military, Air, and other Esquires by office

Women

Women take the same rank as their husbands or as their brothers; but the daughter of a peer marrying a commoner retains her title as Lady or Honourable. Daughters of peers rank next immediately after the wives of their elder brothers, and before their younger brothers' wives. Daughters of peers marrying peers of lower degree take the same order of precedence as that of their husbands; thus the daughter of a Duke marrying a Baron becomes of the rank of Baroness only, while her sisters married to commoners retain their rank and take precedence of the Baroness. Merely official rank on the husband's part does not give any similar precedence to the wife. Peeresses in their own right take the same precedence as peers of the same rank, i.e. from their date of creation.

SCENES AND SIGHTS OF LONDON

There are quite literally thousands of things to see and do in and around London and listed below is a selection of interesting buildings, monuments and attractions.

ALEXANDRA PALACE

Alexandra Palace Way, Wood Green, London N22 7AY (Tel: 020-8365 2121; Email: alexandrapalace@dial.pipex.com; Web: www.alexandrapalace.com).

The Victorian Palace was severely damaged by fire in 1980 but was restored, and reopened in 1988. Alexandra Palace now provides modern facilities for exhibitions, conferences, banquets and leisure activities. There is an ice rink, open daily, a boating lake, the Phoenix Bar and a conservation area.

BARBICAN CENTRE

Silk Street, London EC2Y 8DS (Tel: 020-7638 4141; Fax: 020-7920 9848; Web: www.barbican.org.uk).

Owned, funded and managed by the Corporation of London, the Barbican Centre opened in 1982 and houses the 1,156-seat Barbican Theatre, a 200-seat studio theatre (The Pit), and the 1,989-seat Barbican Hall. There are also three cinemas, two art galleries, a sculpture court, a lending library, conference, trade and banqueting facilities, conservatory, shops, restaurants, cafés and bars.

BLUE PLAQUES

The Royal Society of Arts was the first organisation to erect commemorative plaques at the homes of famous people who had lived in London. The purpose of the scheme has been to draw attention to buildings of interest because of their associations with notable people. The first plaque was erected in 1867 at the birthplace of the poet Byron and 36 plaques had been erected by 1901. In 1901 the London County Council took over the blue plaques scheme. In 1965, when the scheme was taken over by the Greater London Council, there were 298 plaques in existence. By virtue of the Local Government Act 1985, responsibility for the erection and maintenance fell to English Partnerships.

The earliest still surviving plaques are those to Napoleon III in King Street, St James's and John Dryden in Gerrard Street. These were erected by the Royal Society of Arts in 1875. English Heritage has a number of selection criteria when assessing the erection of a blue plaque. The criteria include that there shall be reasonable grounds for believing that the subjects are regarded as eminent by a majority of members of their profession or calling; they shall have made some important positive contribution to human welfare or happiness; they shall have had such exceptional and outstanding personalities that the well-informed passer-by immediately recognises their names; they deserve recognition. Proposals for the commemoration of famous people shall not been considered until they have been dead for 20 years or until the centenary of their birth, whichever is the earlier.

The list below contains details of blue plaques in London, by Borough.

Key:
B = Born at the address given
L = Lived at the address given
D = Died at the address given
W = Worked at the address given
S = Stayed at the address given

BARNET

Blake, William (1757–1827)
Old Wyldes, North End, NW3
S (Poet and artist)

Donat, Robert (1905–58)
8 Meadway, Hampstead Garden Suburb, NW11
L (Actor)

346 Cultural London

Hess, Dame Myra (1890–1965)
48 Wildwood Road, NW11
L (Pianist)

Johnson, Amy (1903–41)
Vernon Court, Hendon Way, NW2
L (Aviator)

Linnell, John (1792–1882)
Old Wyldes, North End, NW3
L (Painter)

Pick, Frank (1878–1941)
15 Wildwood Road, NW11
L (Pioneer of good design for London Transport)

Relph, Harry (1851–1928)
93 Shirehall Park, NW4
L, D ('Little Tich' music hall comedian)

Waugh, Evelyn (1903–66)
145 North End Road, NW11
L (Writer)

BEXLEY
Viscount Castlereagh (1769–1822)
Loring Hall, Water Lane, North Cray
L, D (Statesman)

Morris, William (1834–96)
Red House Lane, Bexleyheath
L (1860–65) (Poet and artist)

Red House
Red House Lane, Bexleyheath
Built in 1859–60 by Philip Webb, architect for William Morris

BRENT
Lucan, Arthur (Arthur Towle) (1887–1954)
11 Forty Lane, Wembley
L (Entertainer and creater of Old Mother Riley)

BROMLEY
Grace, W. G. (1848–1915)
Fairmount, Mottingham Lane, SE9
L (Cricketer)

Kropotkin, Prince Peter (1842–1921)
6 Crescent Road
L (Theorist of anarchism)

Muirhead, Alexander (1848–1920)
20 Church Road, Shortlands
L (Electrical engineer)

CAMDEN
Baillie, Joanna (1762–1851) Bolton House, Windmill Hill, NW3
L (Poet and dramatist)

Barnett, Dame Henrietta (1851–1936)
Heath End House, Spaniards Road, NW3
L (Founder of Hampstead Garden Suburb)

Barnett, Canon Samuel (1844–1913)
Heath End House, Spaniards Road, NW3
L (Social reformer)

Bello, Andres (1781–1865)
58 Grafton Way, W1
L (1810) (Poet, jurist, philologist and Venezuelan Patriot)

Bergman Österberg, Martina (1849–1915)
1 Broadhurst Gardens, NW6
L, W (Pioneer of physical education for women)

Bernal, John Desmond (1901-1971)
44 Albert Street, NW1
L, D (Crystallographer)

Besant, Sir Walter (1836–1901)
Frognal End, Frognal Gardens, NW3
L, D (Novelist and antiquary)

Bliss, Sir Authur (1891–1975)
East Heath Lodge, 1 East Heath Road, NW3
L (1929–39) (Composer)

Bomberg, David (1890–1957)
10 Fordwych Road, NW2
L, W (1928–34) (Painter)

Boult CH, Sir Adrian (1889–1983)
78 Marlborough Mansions, Cannon Hill, NW6
L (1966–77) (Conductor)

Brailsford, Henry Noel (1873–1958)
37 Belsize Park Gardens, NW3
L (Writer, champion of equality and free humanity)

Brain, Dennis (1921–57)
37 Frognal, NW3
L (Horn player)

Blue Plaques 347

Brittain, Vera (1893–1970)
58 Doughty Street, WC1
L (Writer and reformer)

Burne-Jones, Sir Edward C. (Coley) (1833–98)
17 Red Lion Square, WC1
L (Painter)

Buss, Frances Mary (1827-1894)
Camden School for Girls, Sandall Road, NW5
W (1879-94) (Pioneer of Education for Women)

Butt, Dame Clara (1873–1937)
7 Harley Road, NW3
L (1901–29) (Singer)

Butterfield, William (1814–1900)
42 Bedford Square, WC1
L (Architect)

Caldecott, Randolph (1846–86)
46 Great Russell Street, WC2
L (Artist and book illustrator)

Carlyle, Thomas (1795–1881)
33 Ampton Street, WC1
L (Essayist and historian)

Cavendish, Honble Henry (1731–1810)
11 Bedford Square, WC1
L (Natural philosopher)

Cockerell, C. R. (Charles Robert) (1788–1863)
13 Chester Terrace, NW1
L, D (Architect and antiquary)

Constable, John (1776–1837)
40 Well Walk, NW3
L (Painter)

Cruikshank, George (1792–1878)
263 Hampstead Road, NW1
L (1850–78) (Artist)

Dale, Sir Henry (1875–1968)
Mount Vernon House, Mount Vernon, NW3
L (Physiologist)

Dance, George (the younger) (1741–1825)
91 Gower Street, WC1
L, D (Architect)

Daniell, William (1769–1837)
135 St Pancras Way, NW1
L, D (Artist and engraver of Indian scenes)

Darwin, Charles (1809–82)
Biological Sciences Building, University College, Gower Street, WC1
L (1838–42) (Naturalist)

Delius, Frederick (1862–1934)
44 Belsize Park Gardens, NW3
L (1918–19) (Composer)

De Miranda, Francisco (1750–1816)
58 Grafton Way, W1
L (1802–10) (Precursor of Latin American independence)

Dickens, Charles (1812–70)
48 Doughty Street, WC1
L (Novelist)

Disraeli, Benjamin – Earl of Beaconsfield (1804–81)
22 Theobalds Road, WC1
B (Statesman)

Du Maurier, George Louis Palmella Busson (1834–96)
New Grove House, 28 Hampstead Grove, NW3
L (1874–95) (Artist and writer)

Du Maurier, George Louis Palmella Busson (1834–96)
91 Great Russell Street, WC1
L (1863–68) (Artist and writer)

Du Maurier, Sir Gerald (1873–1934)
Cannon Hall, 14 Cannon Place, NW3
L (Actor manager)

Earnshaw, Thomas (1749–1829)
119 High Holborn, WC1
W (Watch and chronometer maker)

Eastlake, Charles (1793–1865)
7 Fitzroy Square, W1
L (Painter and first Director of the National Gallery)

Edwards, John Passmore (1823–1911)
51 Netherhall Gardens, NW3
L (Journalist, editor and builder of free public libraries)

Lord Eldon, John Scott (1751–1838)
6 Bedford Square, WC1
L (Lord Chancellor)

Engels, Friedrich (1820–95)
121 Regent's Park Road, NW1
L (1870–94) (Political philosopher)

Fabian Society
The White House, Osnaburgh Street, NW1
(Society founded in 1884)

Fawcett, Dame Millicent Garrett (1847–1929)
2 Gower Street, WC1
L, D (Pioneer of women's suffrage)

Fenton, Roger (1819–69)
2 Albert Terrace, NW1
L (Photographer)

Ferrier, Kathleen (1912–53)
97 Frognal, NW3
L (Contralto)

Flinders RN, Captain Matthew (1774–1814)
56 Fitzroy Street, W1
L (Explorer and navigator)

Freud, Sigmund (1856–1939)
20 Maresfield Gardens, NW3
L (1938–39) (Founder of psychoanalysis)

Gaitskell, Hugh (1906–63)
18 Frognal Gardens, NW3
L (Statesman)

Galsworthy, John (1867–1933)
Grove Lodge, Admiral's Walk, NW3
L (1918–33) (Novelist and playwright)

Gillies, Sir Harold (1882–1960)
71 Frognal, NW3
L (Pioneer plastic surgeon)

Greenaway, Kate (1846–1901)
39 Frognal, NW3
L, D (Artist)

Gresley, Sir Nigel (1876–1941)
West Offices, King's Cross Station, Pancras Road/Euston Road, N1
W (1923–41) (Locomotive engineer)

Hammond, J. L. and Barbara
Hollycot, Vale of Health, NW3
L (1906–13) (Social historians)

Harmsworth, Alfred – Viscount Northcliffe (1865–1922) 31 Pandora Road, NW6
L (Journalist and newspaper proprietor)

Harrison, John (1693–1776)
Summit House, Red Lion Square, WC1
L, D (Inventor of the marine chronometer)

Hawkins, Sir Anthony Hope (1863–1933)
41 Bedford Square, WC1
L (1903–17) (Novelist)

Herford, Robert Travers (1860–1950)
Dr Williams's Library, 14 Gordon Square, WC1
L, W (Unitarian minister, scholar and interpreter of Judaism)

Hill KCB, Sir Rowland (1795–1879)
Royal Free Hospital, Pond Street, NW3
L (1849–79) (Originator of the Penny Post)

Hodgkin, Thomas (1798–1866)
35 Bedford Square, WC1
L (Physician, reformer and philanthropist)

Hofmann, A. W. (1818–92)
9 Fitzroy Square, W1
L (Professor of chemistry)

Holtby, Winifred (1898–1935)
58 Doughty Street, WC1
L (Writer and reformer)

Howard, John (1726?–90)
23 Great Ormond Street, WC1
L (Prison reformer)

Hughes, Hugh Price (1847–1902)
8 Taviton Street, WC1
L, D (Methodist preacher)

Huxley, Aldous (1894–1963)
16 Bracknell Gardens, NW3
L (Man of science and letters)

Huxley, Julian (1887–1975)
16 Bracknell Gardens, NW3
L (Man of science and letters)

Huxley, Leonard (1860–1933)
16 Bracknell Gardens, NW3
L (Man of science and letters)

Hyndman, Henry Mayers (1842–1921)
13 Well Walk, NW3
L, D (Socialist leader)

Jacobs, W. W. (1863–1943)
15 Gloucester Gate, NW1
L (Author)

Karsavina, Tamara (1885–1978)
108 Frognal, NW3
L (Ballerina)

Keats, John (1795–1821)
Keats House (Wentworth Place), Keats Grove, NW3
L (Poet)

Keynes, John Maynard (1883–1946)
46 Gordon Square, WC1
L (1916–46) (Economist)

Khan, Sir Syed Ahmed (1817–98)
21 Mecklenburgh Square, WC1
L (1869–70) (Muslim reformer and scholar)

Lambert, Constant (1905–51)
197 Albany Street, NW1
L (1947–51) (Composer)

Laughton, Charles (1899–1962)
15 Percy Street, W1
L (1928–31) (Actor)

Lawrence, David Herbert (1885–1930)
1 Byron Villas, Vale of Heath, NW3
L (1915) (Novelist and poet)

Lethaby, William Richard (1857–1931)
Central School of Arts and Crafts, Southampton Row, WC1
(Architect and first principal of this school 1896–1911)

Lethaby, William Richard (1857–1931)
20 Calthorpe Street, WC1
L (1880–91) (Architect)

Macdonald, Ramsay (1866–1937)
9 Howitt Road, NW3
L (1916–25) (Prime Minister)

Madox Brown, Ford (1821–93)
56 Fortess Road, NW5
L (Painter)

Mansfield, Katherine (1888–1923)
17 East Heath Road, NW3
L (Writer)

Marsden, William (1796–1867)
65 Lincoln's Inn Fields, WC2
L (Surgeon, founder of the Royal Free and Royal Marsden Hospitals)

Matthay, Tobias (1858–1945)
21 Arkwright Road, NW3
L (Teacher and pianist)

Maxim, Sir Hiram (1840–96)
57D Hatton Garden, EC1
W (Inventor and engineer)

Mayhew, Henry (1812–87)
55 Albany Street, NW1
L (Founder of 'Punch' and author)

Mazzini, Giuseppe (1805–72)
183 Gower Street, NW1
L (Italian patriot)

Mondrian, Piet Cornelis (1872–1944)
60 Parkhill Road, NW3
L (Painter)

Morris, William (1834–96)
17 Red Lion Square, WC1
L (1856–59) (Poet and artist)

Murry, John Middleton (1889–1957)
17 East Heath Road, NW3
L (Critic)

Nash, Paul (1889–1946)
Queen Alexandra Mansions, Bidborough Street, WC1
L (1914–36) (Artist)

350 Cultural London

Orwell, George (1903–50)
50 Lawford Road, NW5
L (Novelist and political essayist)

Patmore, Coventry (1823–96)
14 Percy Street, W1
L (1863–64) (Poet and essayist)

Pearson, Karl (1857–1936)
7 Well Road, NW3
L (Pioneer statistician)

Perceval, The Hon. Spencer (1762–1812)
59–60 Lincoln's Inn Fields, WC2
L (Prime Minister)

Petrie, Sir William Matthew Flinders (1853–1942)
5 Cannon Place, NW3
L Egyptologist

Plath, Sylvia (1932-1963)
1 Chalcot Square, Primrose Hill, NW1
L (1960-61) (Poet)

Polhill Bevan, Robert (1865–1925)
14 Adamson Road, NW3
L (1900-25) (Camden Town group painter)

The Pre-Raphaelite Brotherhood (1848)
7 Gower Street, WC1
Founded in 1848

Priestley, J. B. (1894–1984)
3 The Grove, N6
L (Novelist, playwrite and essayist)

Rackham, Arthur (1867–1939)
16 Chalcot Gardens, NW3
L (Illustrator)

Rizal, Dr José (1861–96)
37 Chalcot Crescent, NW1
L (Writer and national hero of the Philippines)

Robinson, James (1813–62)
14 Gower Street, WC1
L, W (Pioneer of aneasthesia and dentistry)

Romilly, Samuel (1757–1818)
21 Russell Square, WC1
L (Law reformer)

Romney, George (1734–1802)
Holly Bush Hill, NW3
L (Painter)

Rosetti, Christina Georgina (1830–94)
30 Torrington Square, WC1
L, D (Poetess)

Rossetti, Dante Gabriel (1828–82)
17 Red Lion Square, WC1
L (1851) (Poet and painter)

Roy, Ram Mohun (1772–1833) 4
9 Bedford Square, WC1
L (Indian scholar and reformer)

Salisbury, Robert Gascoyne Cecil, 3rd Marquess of (1830–1903)
21 Fitzroy Square, W1
L (Prime Minister)

Scott, Sir George Gilbert (1811–78)
Admiral's House, Admiral's Walk, NW3
L (Architect)

Sharp, Cecil (1859–1924)
4 Maresfield Gardens, NW3
L (Collector of English folk songs and dances)

Shaw, George Bernard
29 Fitzroy Square, W1
L (1887–98)

Sickert, Walter (1860–1942)
6 Mornington Crescent, NW1
L, W (Painter and etcher)

Siebe, Augustus (1788-1872)
5 Denmark Street, WC2
L, W (Pioneer of the Diving Helmet)

Sitwell, Dame Edith (1887–1964)
Greenhill, Hampstead High Street, NW3
L (Poet)

Sloane, Sir Hans (1660–1753)
4 Bloomsbury Place, WC1
L (1695–1742) (Physician and benefactor of the British Museum)

Smirke, Sir Robert (1781–1867)
81 Charlotte Street, W1
L (Architect)

Smith, Sydney (1771–1845)
14 Doughty Street, WC1
L (Author and wit)

Stephen, Virginia (Virginia Woolf)
(1882–1941) 29 Fitzroy Square, W1
L (1907–11) (Novelist and critic)

Stevens, Alfred (1817–75)
9 Eton Villas, NW3
L (Artist)

Strachey, Lytton (1880–1932)
51 Gordon Square, WC1
L (Critic and biographer)

Tagore, Rabindranath (1861–1941)
3 Villas on the Heath, Vale of Health, NW3
S (1912) (Indian poet)

Tawney, Richard Henry (1880–1962)
21 Mecklenburgh Square, WC1
L (Historian, teacher and political writer)

Thomas, Dylan (1914–53)
54 Delancey Street, NW1
L (Poet)

Turner, Charles (1774–1857)
56 Warren Street, W1
L (Engraver)

Vane, Sir Harry (the younger) (1612–62)
Vane House, Rosslyn Hill, NW3
L (Statesman)

Ventris, Michael (1922–56)
19 North End, NW3
L (Architect and decipherer of Linear B script)

Von Hugel, Baron Friedrich (1852–1925)
4 Holford Road, NW3
L (1882–1903) (Theologian)

Wakley, Thomas (1795–1862)
35 Bedford Square, WC1
L (Reformer and founder of 'The Lancet')

Webb, Beatrice (1858–1943)
10 Netherall Gardens, NW3
L (Social scientist and political reformer)

Webb, Sidney (1859–1947)
10 Netherall Gardens, NW3
L (Social scientist and political reformer)

Wellcome, Sir Henry (1853–1936)
6 Gloucester Gate, NW1
L (Pharmacist, founder of the Wellcome Trust and Foundation)

Willan, Dr Robert (1757–1812)
10 Bloomsbury Square, WC1
L (Dermatologist)

Willis, 'Father' Henry (1821–1901)
9 Rochester Terrace, NW1
L (Organ builder)

Wood, Sir Henry (1869–1944)
4 Elsworth Road, NW3
L (Musician)

Wyatt, Thomas Henry (1807–80)
77 Great Russell Street, WC1
L, D (Architect)

Yeats, William Butler (1865–1939)
23 Fitzroy Road, NW1
L (Irish poet and dramatist)

CITY
Labour Party
Caroone House, Farringdon Street, EC4
Site of the Congregational Memorial Hall; Labour Party was founded here 27 February 1900

CROYDON
Coleridge-Taylor, Samuel (1875–1912)
30 Dagnall Park, SE25
L (Composer)

Conan Doyle, Sir Arthur (1859–1930)
12 Tennison Road, SE25
L (1891–94) (Creator of Sherlock Holmes)

Creed, Frederick George (1871–1957)
20 Outram Road, Addiscombe
L, D (Electrical engineer, inventor of the teleprinter)

Hay, Will (1888-1949)
45 The Chase, Norbury, SW16
L (1927-1934) (Comic actor)

Horniman, Frederick John (1835–1906)
Coombe Cliff Centre, Coombe Road, Croydon
L (Tea merchant, collector and public benefactor)

Horniman, John (1803–93)
Coombe Cliff Centre, Coombe Road, Croydon
L (Tea merchant, collector and public benefactor)

Stanley, W. F. R. (1829–1909)
Stanley Halls, 12 South Norwood Hill, SE25
(Inventor, manufacturer and philanthropist)

Wallace, Alfred Russel (1823–1913)
44 St Peter's Road
L (Naturalist)

Zola, Emile (1840–1902) Queen's Hotel,
122 Church Road, SE19
L (1898–99) (French novelist)

EALING

Blumlein, Alan Dower (1903–42)
37 The Ridings, W5
L (Electronics engineer and inventor)

ENFIELD

Lamb, Charles (1775–1834)
Lamb's Cottage, Church Street, N9
L (Writer)

Lamb, Mary (1764–1847)
Lamb's Cottage, Church Street, N9
L (Writer)

Whitaker, Joseph (1820–95)
White Lodge, Silver Street, Enfield
L, D (Publisher, founder of Whitaker's Almanack)

GREENWICH

Barlow, William Henry (1812–1902)
Highcombe, 145 Charlton Road, SE7
L, D (Engineer)

Chesterfield, Philip – 4th Earl of (1694–1773)
Rangers House, Chesterfield Walk, SE10
L (Statesman and author)

Day-Lewis, C. (1904–72)
6 Crooms Hill, SE10
L (1957–72) (Poet Laureate)

Dyson, Sir Frank (1868–1939)
6 Vanbrugh Hill, SE3
L (1894–1906) (Astronomer Royal)

Eddington OM, Sir Arthur (1882–1944)
4 Bennett Park, SE3
L (Mathematician and astrophysicist)

Gounod, Charles (1818–93)
15 Morden Road, SE3
S (1870) (Composer)

G.P.O. Film Unit, later Crown Film Unit
47 Bennet Park, Blackheath, SE3
W (1933-1943) (Pioneers of documentary film making)

Hawthorne, Nathaniel (1804–64)
4 Pond Road, SE3
S (1856) (American author)

Jefferies, Richard (1848–87)
59 Footscray Road, SE29
L (Naturalist and writer)

McGill, Donald (1875–1962)
5 Bennett Park, SE3
L (Postcard cartoonist)

The Rachel McMillan College
Creek Road, SE8
L (Margaret McMillan CH (1860–1931), pioneer of nursery education)

Morrison, Herbert – Lord Morrison of Lambeth (1888–1965)
55 Archery Road, SE9
L (1929–60) (Cabinet Minister and leader of the the London County Council)

Svevo, Italo (1861–1928)
67 Charlton Church Lane, SE7
L (1903–13) (Writer)

Waugh, Benejamin (1839–1908)
26 Croom's Hill, SE10
L (Founder of the National Society for the Prevention of Cruelty to Children)

Wolfe, General James (1727–59)
Macartney House, Greenwich Park, SE10
L (Victor of Quebec)

Wolseley, Garnet, 1st Viscount (1833–1913)
Rangers House, Chesterfield Walk, SE10
L (Field-Marshal)

HACKNEY

Defoe, Daniel (1661–1731)
95 Stoke Newington Church Street, N16
L (Novelist)

Gosse, Sir Edmund (1849–1928)
56 Mortimer Road, N1
B (Writer and critic)

Gosse, Philip Henry (1810–88)
56 Mortimer Road, N1
L (Zoologist)

Howard, Ebenezer (1850–1928)
50 Durley Road, N16
L (Pioneer of the Garden City Movement)

Lloyd, Marie (1870–1922)
55 Graham Road, E8
L (Music hall artiste)

Priestley, Joseph (1733–1804)
Ram Place, E9
(Scientist, philosopher and theologian)

Priory of St John the Baptist, Holywell
86–88 Curtain Road, EC2

The Theatre
86–88 Curtain Road, EC2
The first London building specially devoted to the performance of plays 1755–98

HAMMERSMITH & FULHAM

Brangwyn, Sir Frank (1867–1956)
Temple Lodge, 51 Queen Caroline Street, W6
L (Artist)

Cobden-Sanderson, Thomas James (1840–1922)
15 Upper Mall, W6
L, D (Founder of Doves Bindery and Doves Press)

Coleridge, Samuel Taylor (1772–1834)
7 Addison Bridge Place, W14
L (Poet and philosopher)

Devine, George (1910–66)
9 Lower Mall, W6
L (Actor; Artisitc Director of the Royal Court Theatre 1956–65)

Elgar, Sir Edward (1857–1934)
51 Avonmore Road, W14
L (1890–91) (Composer)

Gandhi, Mahatma (1869–1948)
20 Baron's Court Road, W14
L (Philosopher and teacher)

Gaudier-Brzeska, Henri (1891–1915)
454 Fulham Road, SW6
L (Sculptor and artist)

The Goossens Family
70 Edith Road, W14
(Family of musicians)

Haggard, Sir Henry Rider (1856–1925)
69 Gunterstone Road, W14
L (1885–88) (Novelist)

Herbert, Sir Alan (1890–1971)
12 Hammersmith Terrace, W6
L, D (Author, humorist and reformist MP)

Johnston, Edward (1872–1944)
3 Hammersmith Terrace, W6
L (1905–12) (Master calligrapher)

Laski, Harold (1893–1950)
5 Addison Bridge Place, W14
L (1926–50) (Teacher and political philosopher)

Ouida (Maria Louisa de la Ramée) (1839–1908)
11 Ravenscourt Square, W6
L (Novelist)

Pissarro, Lucien (1863–1944)
27 Stamford Brook Road, W6
L (Painter, printer and wood engraver)

Ravilious, Eric (1903–42)
48 Upper Mall, W6
L (1931–35) (Artist)

Short, Sir Frank (1857–1945)
56 Brook Green, W6
L (Engraver and painter)

The Silver Studio
84 Brook Green Road, W6

Silver, Arthur (1853–86)
84 Brook Green Road, W6
L (Designer)

Silver, Harry (1881–1971)
84 Brook Green Road, W6
L (Designer)

Silver, Rex (1879–1965)
84 Brook Green Road, W6
L (Designer)

Walker, Sir Emery (1851–1933)
7 Hammersmith Terrace, W6
L (1903–33) (Typographer and antiquary)

Whall, Christopher Whitworth (1849–1924)
19 Ravenscourt Road, W6
L (Stained glass artist)

HARINGEY

Housman, A. E. (1859–1936)
17 North Road, N6
L (Poet and scholar)

Kingsley, Mary (1862–1900)
22 Southwood Lane, N6
L (Traveller and ethnologist)

Savarkar, Vinayak Damodar (1883–1966)
65 Cromwell Avenue, N6
L (Indian patriot and philosopher)

Television
Alexandra Palace, N22
The world's first regular high definition television service was inaugurated here by the BBC
2 November 1936

Waley, Arthur (1889–1966)
50 Southwood Lane, N6
L, D (Poet, translator and Orientalist)

HARROW

Ballantyne, R. M. (1825–94)
Duneaves, Mount Park Road
L (Author of books for boys)

Heath Robinson, W. (1872–1944)
75 Moss Lane, Pinner
L (Illustrator and comic artist)

Shaw, R. Norman
Grims Dyke, Old Redding, Harrow Weald
(Architect)

HOUNSLOW

Forster, E. M. (1879–1970)
Arlington Park Mansions, Sutton Lane, Turnham Green, W4
L (Novelist)

Pope, Alexander (1688–1744)
Mawson Arms PH, 110 Chiswick Lane South, W4
L (1716–19) (Poet)

Zoffany, Johann (1733–1810)
65 Strand-on-the-Green, W4
L (1790–1810) (Painter)

ISLINGTON

Caslon, William (1692–1766)
21–23 Chiswell Street, EC1
The foundry established by William Caslon, typefounder stood on this site 1737–1909

Chamberlain, Joseph (1836–1914)
25 Highbury Place, N5
L (Statesman)

Chisholm, Caroline (1808–77)
32 Charlton Place, N1
L (Philanthropist)

Collins Music Hall
10–11 Islington Green, N1
Music hall located here 1862–1958

Grimaldi, Joseph (1778–1837)
56 Exmouth Market, EC1
L (1818–28) (Clown)

Groom, John (1845–1919)
8 Sekforde Street, EC1
L (Philanthropist)

Irving, Edward (1792–1834)
4 Claremont Square, N1
L (Founder of the Catholic Apostolic church)

Blue Plaques 355

Lamb, Charles 'Elia' (1775–1834)
64 Duncan Terrace, N1
L (Essayist)

Leybourne, George (1842–1884)
136 Englefield Road, N1
L, D (Music hall comedian)

Macneice, Louis (1907–63)
52 Canonbury Park South, N1
L (1947–52) (Poet)

Phelps, Samuel (1804–78)
8 Canonbury Square, N1
L (Tragedian)

Shepherd, Thomas Hosmer (1793–1864)
26 Batchelor Street, N1
L (Artist who portrayed London)

Wesley, John (1703–91)
47 City Road, EC1
L (Evangelist and founder of Methodism)

KENSINGTON AND CHELSEA

Francesca, Jane (Lady Wilde Speranza) (1821-1896)
87 Oakley Street, SW16
L (1887-1896) (Poet and essayist)

Alexander, Sir George (1858–1918)
57 Pont Street, SW1
L (Actor–manager)

Allenby, Field Marshal Viscount Edmund Henry Hynman (1861–1936)
24 Wetherby Gardens, SW5
L

Arnold, Sir Edwin (1832–1904)
31 Bolton Gardens, SW5
L, D (Poet and journalist)

Astafieva, Princess Seraphine (1876–1934)
152 King's Road, SW3
L, W (Ballet dancer)

Baden-Powell, Robert (1857–1941)
9 Hyde Park Gate, SW7
L (Chief Scout of the World)

Bagnold, Enid (1889–1981)
29 Hyde Park Gate, SW7
L (Novelist and playwright)

Bartók, Béla (1881–1945)
7 Sydney Place, SW7
S (Hungarian composer)

Beerbohm, Sir Max (1872–1956)
57 Palace Gardens Terrace, W8
B (Artist and writer)

Belloc, Hilaire (1870–1953)
104 Cheyne Walk, SW10
L (1900–05) (Poet, essayist and historian)

Bennett, Arnold (1867–1931)
75 Cadogan Square, SW1
L (Novelist)

Benson, E. F. (1867–1940)
25 Brompton Square, SW3
L (Writer)

Bonar Law, Andrew (1858–1923)
24 Onslow Gardens, SW7
L (Prime Minister)

Booth, Charles (1840–1916)
6 Grenville Place, SW7
L (Pioneer in social research)

Borrow, George (1803–81)
22 Hereford Square, SW7
L (Author)

Bridge, Frank (1879–1941)
4 Bedford Gardens, W8
L (Composer and musician)

Brunel, Isambard Kingdom (1806–59)
98 Cheyne Walk, SW10
L (Civil engineer)

Brunel, Sir Marc Isambard (1769–1849)
98 Cheyne Walk, SW10
L (Civil engineer)

Burne-Jones, Sir Edward (1833–98)
41 Kensington Square, W8
L (1865–67) (Artist)

Carlile, Prebendary Wilson (1847–1942)
34 Sheffield Terrace, W8
L (Found of the Church Army)

Carter, Howard (1874–1939)
19 Collingham Gardens, SW5
L (Egyptologist and discoverer of the tomb of Tutankhamun)

Chelsea China (1745–1784)
16 Lawrence Street, SW3
Chelsea China was manufactured in a house at the north end of Lawrence Street

Chesterton, Gilbert Keith (1874–1936)
11 Warwick Gardens, W14
L (Poet, novelist and critic)

Chevalier, Albert (1861–1923)
17 St Ann's Villas, W11
B (Music hall comedian)

Churchill KG, Sir Winston (1874–1965)
28 Hyde Park Gate, Kensington Gore, SW7
L, D (Prime Minister)

Clementi, Muzio (1752–1832)
128 Kensington Church Street, W8
L (Composer)

Cole, Sir Henry (1808–82)
33 Thurloe Square, SW7
L (Campaigner and Educator; First Director of the Victoria and Albert Museum)

Compton-Burnett, Dame Ivy (1884–1969)
5 Braemar Mansions, Cornwall Gardens, SW7
L (1934–69) (Novelist)

Crane, Walter (1845–1915)
13 Holland Street, W8
L (Artist)

Cripps, Sir Stafford (1899–1952)
32 Elm Park Gardens, SW10
B (Statesman)

Crookes, Sir William (1832–1919)
7 Kensington Park Gardens, W11
L (Scientist)

Daniell, Thomas (1749–1840)
14 Earls Terrace, W8
L (Topographical artist)

De Morgan, Evelyn (1855–1919)
127 Old Church Street, SW3
L, D (Artist)

De Morgan, William (1839–1917)
127 Old Church Street, SW3
L, D (Ceramic artist and novelist)

Dickinson, Goldsworth Lowes (1862–1932)
11 Edwardes Square, W8
(Author and humanist)

Dilke, Sir Charles Wentworth (1843–1911)
76 Sloane Street, SW1
L (Statesman and author)

Dobson, Frank (1886–1963)
14 Harley Gardens, SW10
L (Sculptor)

Dobson, Henry Austin (1840–1921)
10 Redcliffe Street, SW10
L (Poet and essayist)

Eliot, George (Mary Ann Cross née Evans) (1819–80)
4 Cheyne Walk, SW3
D (Novelist)

Eliot OM, T. S. (1888–1965)
3 Kensington Court Gardens, W8
L, D (Poet)

Fildes, Sir Samuel Luke (1844–1927)
31 Melbury Road, W14
L (1878–1927) (Artist)

Fitzroy, Admiral Robert (1805–65)
38 Onslow Square, SW7
L (Hydrographer and meteorologist)

Fleming, Sir Alexander (1881–1955)
20A Danvers Street, SW3
L (Discoverer of penicillin)

Forbes, Vivian (1891–1937)
Lansdowne House, 80 Lansdowne Road, W11
L, W (Artist)

Ford, Ford Madox (1873–1939)
80 Campden Hill Road, W8
L (Novelist and critic)

Fortune, Robert (1812–80)
9 Gilston Road, SW10
L (1857–80) (Plant collector)

Blue Plaques

Foscolo, Ugo (1778–1827)
19 Edwardes Square, W8
L (1817–8) (Italian poet and patriot)

Franklin, Rosalind (1920–58)
Donovan Court, Drayton Gardens, SW10
L (1951–58) (Pioneer of the study of molecular structures)

Freake, Sir Charles James (1814–84)
21 Cromwell Road, SW7
L (Builder and patron of the arts)

Froude, James Anthony (1818–94)
5 Onslow Gardens, SW7
L (Historian and man of letters)

Gaskell, Mrs Elizabeth Cleghorn (1810–65)
93 Cheyne Walk, SW10
B (Novelist)

Gilbert, Sir W. S. (William Schwenck) (1836–1911)
39 Harrington Gardens, SW7
L (Dramatist)

Gissing, George (1857–1903)
33 Oakley Gardens, SW3
L (1882–84) (Novelist)

Godwin, George (1813–88)
24 Alexander Square, SW3
L (Architect, journalist and social reformer)

Grahame, Kenneth (1859–1932)
16 Phillimore Place, W8
L (1901–08) (Author)

Grainger, Percy (1882–1961)
31 King's Road, SW3
L (Australian composer, folklorist and pianist)

Greaves, Walter (1846–1930)
104 Cheyne Walk, SW10
L (1855–97) (Artist)

Hall, Radclyffe (1880–1943)
37 Holland Street, W8
L (1924–29) (Novelist and poet)

Hansom, Joseph Aloysius (1803–1882)
27 Sumner Place, SW7
L (Architect, founder editor of 'The Builder' and inventor of the Hansom Cab)

Hitchcock, Sir Alfred (1899–1980)
153 Cromwell Road, SW5
L (1926–39) (Film director)

Holman-Hunt OM, William (1827–1910)
18 Melbury Road, W14
L, D (Painter)

Hudson, W. H. (William Henry) (1841–1922)
40 St Luke's Road, W11
L, D (Writer)

Hunt, James Henry Leigh (1784–1859)
22 Upper Cheyne Row, SW3
L (Essayist and poet)

Ireland, John (1879–1962)
14 Gunter Grove, SW10
L (Composer)

James, Henry (1843–1916)
34 De Vere Gardens, W8
L (1886–1902) (Writer)

Earl Jellicoe OM, Admiral of the Fleet (1859–1935)
25 Draycott Place, SW3
L

Jinnah, Mohammed Ali (Quaid i Azam) (1876–1948)
35 Russell Road, W14
S (1895) (Founder of Pakistan)

John, Augustus (1878–1961)
28 Mallord Street, SW3
(Painter)

Jordan, Mrs Dorothy (née Bland) (1762–1816)
30 Cadogan Place, SW1
L (Actress)

Joyce, James (1882–1941)
28 Campden Grove, W8
L (1931) (Author)

Kingsley, Charles (1819–75)
56 Old Church Street, SW3
L (Writer)

358 Cultural London

Kossuth, Louis (1802–94)
39 Chepstow Villas, W11
S (Hungarian patriot)

Lang, Andrew (1844–1912)
1 Marloes Road, W8
L (1876–1912) (Man of letters)

Langtry, Lillie (1852–1929)
Cadogan Hotel, 21 Pont Street, SW1
L (Actress)

Lavery, Sir John (1856–1941)
5 Cromwell Place, SW7
L (1899–1940) (Painter)

Lecky, W. E. H. (William Edward Hartpole) (1838–1903)
38 Onslow Gardens, SW7
L, D (Historian and essayist)

Lord Leighton, Frederick (1830–96)
Leighton House, 12 Holland Park Road, W14
L, D (Painter)

Lewis, Percy Wyndham (1882–1957)
61 Palace Gardens Terrace, W8
L (Painter)

Lind, Jenny (Madame Goldschmidt) (1820–87)
189 Old Brompton Road, SW7
L (Singer)

Lord Macaulay, Thomas Babington (1800–59)
Holly Lodge (now Atkins Buildings, Queen Elizabeth College), Campden Hill, W8
L (Historian and man of letters)

Mallarme, Stephane (1842–98)
6 Brompton Square, SW3
S (1863) (Poet)

Maxwell, James Clerk (1831–79)
16 Palace Gardens Terrace, W8
L (Physicist)

May, Phil (1864–1903)
20 Holland Park Road, W14
L, W (Artist)

Meredith OM, George (1828–1909)
7 Hobury Street, SW10
L (Poet and novelist)

Mill, John Stuart (1806–73)
18 Kensington Square, W8
L (Philosopher)

Millais Bt., PRA, Sir John Everett (1829–96)
2 Palace Gate, W8
L, D (Painter)

Milne, A. A. (1882–1956)
13 Mallord Street, SW3
L (Author)

Monckton Copeman, Sydney (1862–1947)
57 Redcliffe Gardens, SW10
L (Immunologist and developer of smallpox vaccine)

Morgan, Charles (1894–1958)
16 Campden Hill Square, W8
L, D (Novelist and critic)

Nehru, Jawaharlal (1889–1964)
60 Elgin Crescent, W11
L (1910–12) (First Prime Minister of India)

Newbolt, Sir Henry (1862–1938)
29 Campden Hill Road, W8
L (Poet)

Orpen, Sir William (1878–1931)
8 South Bolton Gardens, SW5
L (Painter)

Palmer, Samuel (1805–81)
6 Douro Place, W8
L (1851–61) (Artist)

Pankhurst, Sylvia (1882–1960)
120 Cheyne Walk, SW10
L (Campaigner for women's rights)

Parry, Sir Charles Hubert (1848–1918)
17 Kensington Square, W8
L (Musician)

Peake, Mervyn (1911–68)
1 Drayton Gardens, SW10
L (1960–68) (Author and artist)

Philpot, Glyn (1863–1937)
Lansdowne House, Lansdowne Road, W11
L, W (Artist)

Blue Plaques 359

Place, Francis (1771–1854)
21 Brompton Square, SW3
L (1833–51) (Political reformer)

Playfair, Sir Nigel (1874–1934)
26 Pelham Crescent, SW7
L (Actor-manager)

Pryde, James (1866–1941)
Lansdowne House, 80 Lansdowne Road, W11
L, W (Artist)

Rambert, Dame Marie (1888–1982)
19 Campden Hill Gardens, W8
L (Founder of Ballet Rambert)

Ricketts, Charles (1866–1931)
Lansdowne House, 80 Lansdowne Road, W11
L, W (Artist)

Marquess of Ripon, George Frederick Samuel Robinson (1827–1909)
9 Chelsea Embankment, SW3
L (Statesman and Viceroy of India)

Robinson, F. Cayley (1862–1927)
Lansdowne House, 80 Lansdowne Road, W11
L, W (Artist)

Rossetti, Dante Gabriel (1828–82)
16 Cheyne Walk, SW3
L (Poet and painter)

Rothenstein, Sir William (1872-1945)
1 Pembroke Cottages, Edwardes Square, W8
L (1899-1902) (Painter and writer)

Sargent, Sir Malcolm (1895–1967)
Albert Hall Mansions, Kensington Gore, SW7
L, D (Conductor)

Sartorius, John F. (c.1775–c.1830)
155 Old Church Street, SW3
L (1807–12) (Sporting painter)

Sassoon, Siegfried (1886–1967)
23 Campden Hill Square, W8
L (1925–32) (Writer)

Scott, Captain Robert Falcon (1868–1912)
56 Oakley Street, SW3
L (Antarctic explorer)

Shannon, Charles (1863–1937)
Lansdowne House, Lansdowne Road, W11
L, W (Artist)

Sibelius, Jean (1865–1957)
15 Gloucester Walk, W8
L (1909) (Composer)

Simon, Sir John (1816–1904)
40 Kensington Square, W8
L (Pioneer of public health)

Sloane, Sir Hans (1660–1753)
Kings Mead, King's Road, SW3
The ground to the West of this building was given to the Parish of Chelsea in 1773 by Sloane

Smollett, Tobias (1721–71)
16 Lawrence Street, SW3
L (1750–62) (Novelist)

Stanford, Sir Charles (1852–1924)
56 Hornton Street, W8
L (1894–1916) (Musician)

Staunton, Howard (1810–74)
117 Lansdowne Road, W11
L (1871–74) (British world chess champion)

Steer, Philip Wilson (1860–1942)
109 Cheyne Walk, SW10
L, D (Painter)

Stephen, Sir Leslie (1832–1904)
22 Hyde Park Gate, SW7
L (Scholar and writer)

Stoker, Bram (1847–1912)
18 St Leonard's Terrace, SW3
L (Author)

Stone, Marcus (1840–1921)
8 Melbury Road, W14
L (1877–1921) (Artist)

Stuart, John McDouall (1815–66)
9 Campden Hill Square, W8
L, D (First explorer to cross Australia)

Swinburne, Algernon Charles (1837–1909)
16 Cheyne Walk, SW3
L (Poet)

360 Cultural London

Terry, Dame Ellen (1847–1928)
22 Barkston Gardens, SW5
L (Actress)

Thackeray, William Makepeace (1811–63)
2 Palace Green, W8
L (Novelist)

Thackeray, William Makepeace (1811–63)
16 Young Street, W8
L (Novelist)

Thackeray, William Makepeace (1811–63)
36 Onslow Square, SW7
L (1854–62) (Novelist)

Thompson, Sir Benjamin – Count Rumford (1753–1814)
168 Brompton Road, SW3
L (Inventor and adventurer)

Thorndike, Dame Sybil (1882–1976)
6 Carlyle Square, SW3
L (1921–32) (Actress)

Thornycroft, Sir Hamo (1850–1925)
2A Melbury Road, W14
L (Sculptor)

Tree, Sir Herbert Beerbohm (1853–1917)
31 Rosary Gardens, SW7
L (Actor-manager)

Twain, Mark (Samuel Langhorne Clemens) (1835–1910)
23 Tedworth Square, SW3
L (1896–97) (American writer)

Tweed, John (1863–1933)
108 Cheyne Walk, SW10
L (Sculptor)

Underhill, Evelyn (1875–1941)
50 Campden Hill Square, W8
L (1907–39) (Christian philosopher and teacher)

Warlock, Peter, Philip Arnold Hesseltine (1894–1930)
30 Tite Street, SW3
L (Composer)

Weizmann, Chaim (1874–1952)
67 Addison Road, W14
L (Scientist and statesman. First President of the state of Israel)

Whistler, James Abbot McNeil (1834–1903)
96 Cheyne Walk, SW10
L (Painter and etcher)

Wilberforce, William (1759–1833)
44 Cadogan Place, SW1
D (Opponent of slavery)

Wilde, Oscar O'Flahertie Wills (1854–1900)
34 Tite Street, SW3
L (Wit and dramatist)

Crompton, Colonel (1845-1940)
48 Kensington Court, Kensington, W8
L, W (1891-1939) (Electrical Engineer)

Guizot, Francois (1787-1874)
21 Pelham Crescent, South Kensington, SW7
L (1848-49) (French politican and historian)

Low, Sir David (1891–1963)
Melbury Court, Kensington High Street, W8
L (Cartoonist)

McIndoe, Sir Archibald (1900-1960)
Avenue Court, Dracott Avenue, SW3
L (Reconstructive surgeon)

KINGSTON UPON THAMES

Blyton, Enid (1897–1968)
207 Hook Road, Chessington
L (1920–24) (Children's writer)

Melba, Dame Nellie (1861-1931)
Coombe House, Devey Close (Off Beverley Lane), Kingston upon Thames
L (1906) (Operatic Soprana)

LAMBETH

Barry, Sir Charles (1795–1860)
The Elms, Clapham Common North Side, SW4
L, D (Architect)

Bax, Sir Arnold (1883–1953)
13 Pendennis Road, SW16
B (Composer)

Blue Plaques 361

Baylis, Lilian (1874–1937)
27 Stockwell Park Road, SW9
L, D (Manager of the Old Vic and Sadlers Wells Theatres)

Bentley, John Francis (1839–1902)
43 Old Town, SW4
L (Architect)

Bligh, William (1754–1817)
100 Lambeth Road, SE1
L (Commander of the 'Bounty')

The County Hall
Main Entrance, County Hall, SE1
The home of London government 1922–86; London Chamber of Commerce 1889–1965; Greater London Council 1965–86

Cox, David (1783–59)
34 Foxley Road, SW9
L (Artist)

Ellis, Henry Havelock (1859–1939)
14 Dover Mansions, Canterbury Crescent, SW9
L (Pioneer in the scientific study of sex)

Greet, Sir Philip Ben (1857–1936)
160 Lambeth Road, SE1
L (1920–36) (Actor-manager)

Henderson, Arthur (1863–1935)
13 Rodenhurst Road, SW4
L (Statesman)

Hobbs, Jack (1882–1963)
17 Englewood Road, SW12
L (Cricketer)

Inner London Education Authority
Main Entrance, County Hall, SE1
Home of the Inner London's Education Service from 1922; ILEA succeeding the London School Board (1870–1904) and the LCC (1904–65)

Leno, Dan (1860–1904)
56 Akerman Road, SW9
L (1898–1901) (Music hall comedian)

Macaulay, Thomas Babington (later Lord Macaulay) (1800–59)
5 The Pavement, SW4
L (Historia and man of letters)

Macaulay, Zachary (1768–1838)
5 The Pavement, SW4
L (Philanthropist)

Mee, Arthur (1875–1943)
27 Lanercost Road, SW2
L (Journalist, author and topographer)

Montgomery, Field Marshal – Vicount of Alamein (1887–1976)
Oval House, 52–54 Kennington Oval, SE11
B

Ruskin, John (1819–1900)
26 Herne Hill, SE24
L (Man of letters)

Szabo GC, Violette (1921–45)
18 Burnley Road, SW9
L (Secret agent)

Van Gogh, Vincent (1853–90)
87 Hackford Road, SW9
L (1873–74) (Painter)

Wilberforce, William
Holy Trinity Church, Clapham Common, SW4
(Campaigner for abolition of slavery in the British Dominions)

LEWISHAM

Baird, John Logie (1888-1946)
3 Crescent Wood Road, SE26
L (Television pioneer)

Flecker, James Elroy (1884–1915)
9 Gilmore Road, SE13
B (Poet and dramatist)

Glaisher, James (1809–1903)
20 Dartmouth Hill, SE10
L (Astronomer, meteorologist and pioneer of weather forecasting)

The Horniman Museum and Gardens
London Road, SE23
Given to the people of London in 1901

Ross, Sir James Clark (1800–62)
2 Eliot Place, SE3
L (Polar explorer)

Shackleton, Sir Ernest Henry (1874–1922)
12 Westwood Hill, SE26
L (Antarctic explorer)

Smiles, Samuel (1812–1904)
11 Granville Park, SE13
L (Author)

Tallis, John (1816–76)
233 New Cross Road, SE14
L (Publisher)

Unwin, Sir Stanley (1884–1968)
13 Handen Road, SE12
B (Publisher)

Wallace, Edgar (1875–1932)
6 Tressillian Crescent, SE4
L (Writer)

MERTON

Dowding, Lord, Air Chief Marshal (1882-1970)
3 St Mary's Road, Wimbledon, SW19
L (1941-1951) (Leader of Fighter Command)

Graves, Robert (1895–1985)
1 Lauriston Road, SW19
B (Writer)

Innes, John (1829–1904)
Manor House, Watery Lane, SW20
L (Founder of the John Innes Horticultural Institute)

NEWHAM

Thorne, Will (1857–1946)
1 Lawrence Road, E13
L (Trade union leader and Labour MP)

REDBRIDGE

Attlee, Richard Clement (1883–1976)
17 Monkhams Avenue, Woodford Green
L (Prime Minister)

Mansbridge, Albert (1876–1952)
198 Windsor Road, Ilford
L (Founder of the Workers' Educational Association)

RICHMOND

Fielding, Henry (1707–54)
Milbourne House, Barnes Green, SW13
L (Novelist)

Newman, John Henry (1801–90)
Grey Court, Ham Street, Ham
Later became Cardinal Newman

Schwitters, Kurt (1887–1948)
39 Westmoreland Road, SW13
L (Artist)

Turner RA, J. M. W. (1775–1851)
40 Sandycombe Road, Twickenham
L (Painter)

Woolf, Leonard and Virginia
Hogarth House, Paradise Road
L (Lived here 1915–24 and founded the Hogarth Press in 1917)

RICHMOND UPON THAMES

Beard, John (c.1717–91)
Hampton Branch Library, Rose Hill, Hampton
L (Singer)

Chadwick, Sir Edwin (1801–90)
5 Montague Road, Richmond
L (Public health reformer)

Coward, Sir Noël (1899–1973)
131 Waldegrave Road, Teddington
B (Actor, playwright and songwriter)

de la Mare, Walter (1873–1956)
South End House, Montpelier Row, Twickenham
L (1940–56) (Poet)

Ewart, William (1798–1869)
Hampton Branch Library, Rose Hill, Hampton
L (Promoter of public libraries)

Garrick, David (1717–79)
Garrick's Villa, Hampton Court Road
L (Actor)

Greathead, James Henry (1844-1896)
3 St Mary's Grove, SW13
L (1885-89) (Railway and Tunnelling Engineer)

Hughes, Arthur (1832–1915)
Eastside House, 22 Kew Green, Richmond
L, D (Pre-Raphaelite painter)

Labouchere, Henry (1831-1912)
St James Independent School for Boys, Pope's Villa, 19 Cross Deep, Twickenham
L **(1881-1903)** (Radical MP and journalist)

O'Higgins, Bernardo (1778–1842)
Clarence House, 2 The Vineyard, Richmond
L (General, statesman and liberator of Chile)

Wren, Sir Christopher (1632–1723)
The Old Court House, Hampton Court Green, East Molesey
L (Architect)

SOUTHWARK

Besant, Annie (1847–1933)
39 Colby Road, SE19
L **(1874)** (Social reformer)

Chamberlain, Joseph (1836–1914)
188 Camberwell Grove, SE5
L (Statesman)

Drysdale, Dr Charles Vickery (1874–1961)
153A East Street, SE17
(A founder of the Family Planning Association)

Forester, C. S. (1899–1966)
50 Underhill Road, SE22
L (Novelist)

Karloff, Boris (1887–1969)
36 Forest Hill Road, SE22
B (Actor)

Shaw, Sir Eyre Massey (1830-1908)
Winchester House, 94 Southwark Bridge Road, SE1
L **(1878-1891)** (First Chief Officer of the Metropolitan Fire Brigade)

Moody, Dr Harold (1882–47)
164 Queen's Road, SE15
L, W (Campaigner for racial equality)

Myers, George (1803–75)
131 St George's Road, SE1
L **(1842–53)** (Master builder)

Oliver, Percy Lane (1878–1944)
5 Colyton Road, SE22
L, W (Founder of the first voluntary blood donor service)

Rohmer, Sax, Arthur Henry Ward (1883–1959)
51 Herne Hill, SE24
L (Creator of Dr Fu Manchu)

SUTTON

White, William Hale (Mark Rutherford) (1831–1913) 19 Park Hill, Carshalton
L (Novelist)

TOWER HAMLETS

Barnardo, Dr Thomas John (1845–1905)
58 Solent House, Ben Jonson Road, E1
Began his work for children in a building on this site in 1866

Borough, Stephen (1525–85)
King Edward Memorial Park, Shadwell, E1
(Navigator)

Borough, William (1536–99)
King Edward Memorial Park, Shadwell, E1
(Navigator)

Bradlaugh, Charles (1833–91)
29 Turner Street, E1
L **(1870–77)** (Advocate of free thought)

Cavell, Edith (1865–1915)
London Hospital, E1
W **(1896–1901)** (Pioneer of modern nursing in Belgium and herione of the Great War)

Clayton, Revd. P. T. B. 'Tubby' (1885–1972)
43 Trinity Square, EC3
L (Founder of Toc H)

Cook, Captain James (1728–79)
88 Mile End Road, E1
L (Circumnavigator and explorer)

Flanagan, Bud (1896–1968)
12 Hanbury Street, E1
B (Comedian and Leader of the 'Crazy Gang')

Flying Bomb
Railway Bridge, Grove Road, E3
The first Flying Bomb on London fell here 13 June 1944

Frobisher, Sir Martin (1535?–94)
King Edward Memorial Park, Shadwell, E1
(Navigator)

364 Cultural London

Gandhi, Mahatma (1869–1948)
Kingsley Hall, Powis Road, E3
S (1931) (Philosopher and teacher)

Garthwaite, Anna Maria (1690–1763)
2 Princelet Street, E1
L, W (Designer of Spitalfields Silks)

Gertler, Mark (1891–1939)
32 Elder Street, E1
L (Painter)

The Great Eastern (Launched 1858)
Burrells Wharf, 262 West Ferry Road, E14
Largest steamship of the century was built here

Green, John Richard (1837–83)
St Philip's Vicarage, Newark Street, E1
L (1866–69) (Historian of the English people)

Groser, Revd St John (1890–1966)
Royal Foundation of St Katharine, 2 Butcher Row, E14
L (Priest and social reformer)

Hughes, Mary (1860–1941)
71 Vallance Road, E2
L, W (1926–41) (Friend of all in need)

Mallon CH, Dr Jimmy (1874–1961)
Toynbee Hall, Commercial Street, E1
L (Warden of Toynbee Hall, champion of social reform)

Rosenberg, Isaac (1890–1918)
Whitechapel Library, 77 High Street, E1
(Poet and painter)

Strype Street
10 Leyden Street, E1
Formerly Strype's Yard. The house of John Strype, silk merchant was situated there. At this house his son John (1643–1737) was born and went on to become a historian and biographer

Wainwright, Lincoln Stanhope (1847–1929)
Clergy House, Wapping Lane, E1
L (1884–1929) (Vicar of St Peter's, London Docks)

Willoughby, Sir Hugh (d.1554)
King Edward Memorial Park, Shadwell, E1
(Navigator)

Zangwill, Israel (1864–1926)
288 Old Ford Road, E2
L (Writer and philanthropist)

WALTHAM FOREST

Hilton, James (1900–54)
42 Oakhill Gardens
L (Novelist and scriptwriter)

Plaatje, Sol (1876–1932)
25 Carnarvon Road, E10
L (Black South African writer)

Roe, Alliott Verdon
Railway arches at Walthamstow Marsh Railway Viaduct, Walthamstow Marshes, E17
In July 1909 Roe made the first all-British powered flight from Walthamstow Marshes

WANDSWORTH

Walter, John (1739–1812)
113 Clapham Common North Side, SW4
L (Founder of 'The Times')

Wilson, Edward Adrian (1872–1912)
Battersea Vicarage, 42 Vicarage Crescent, SW11
L (Antarctic explorer and naturalist)

Bateman, H. M. (1887–1970)
40 Nightingale Lane, SW12
L (1910–14) (Cartoonist)

Benes, Dr Edward (1884–1948)
26 Gwendolen Avenue, SW15
L (President of Czechoslovakia)

Burns, John (1858–1943)
110 North Side, Clapham Common, SW4
L (Statesman)

Douglas, Norman (1868–1952)
63 Albany Mansions, Albert Bridge Road, SW11
L (Writer)

Elen, Gus (1862–1940)
3 Thurleigh Avenue, SW12
L (Music hall comedian)

Eliot, George (Mary Ann Cross) (1819–80)
Holly Lodge, 31 Wimbledon Park Road, SW18
L (Novelist)

Hardy, Thomas (1840–1928)
172 Trinity Road, SW17
L (1878–81) (Poet and novelist)

Henty, G. A. (George Alfred) (1832–1902)
33 Lavender Gardens, SW11
L (Author)

Hopkins, Gerard Manley (1844–89)
Gatepost at Manresa House, Holybourne Avenue, SW15
L (Poet)

Knee, Fred (1868–1914)
24 Sugden Road, SW11
L (London Labour Party pioneer and housing reformer)

Lauder, Sir Harry (1870–1950)
46 Longley Road, SW17
L (1903–11) (Music hall artist)

Lloyd George, David (1865–1945)
3 Routh Road, SW18
L (Prime Minister)

Oates, Captain Lawrence (1880–1912)
309 Upper Richmond Road, SW15
L (Antarctic explorer)

O'Casey, Sean (1880–1964)
49 Overstrand Mansions, Prince of Wales Drive, SW11
L (Playwright)

Sargeant Jagger, Charles (1885–1934)
67 Albert Bridge Road, SW11
L, D (Sculptor)

Saunders, Sir Edwin (1814–1901)
Fairlawns, 89 Wimbledon Parkside, SW19
L, D (Dentist to Queen Victoria)

Spurgeon, Charles Haddon (1834–92)
99 Nightingale Lane, SW12
L (Preacher)

Swinburne, Algernon Charles (1837–1909)
11 Putney Hill, SW15
L, D (Poet)

Tate, Harry (Ronald MacDonald Hutchison) (1872–1940)
72 Longley Road, SW17
L (Music hall comedian)

Thomas, Edward (1878–1917)
61 Shelgate Road, SW11
L (Essayist and poet)

Watts-Dunton, Theodore (1832–1914)
11 Putney Hill, SW15
L, D (Poet, novelist and critic)

Wilberforce, William (1759–1833)
111 Broomwood Road, SW11
L (Campaigner)

WESTMINSTER

Asquith, Herbert Henry – 1st Earl of Oxford and Asquith (1852–1928)
20 Cavendish Square, W1
L (Statesman)

Roberts, Earl Fredrick Sleigh (1832–1914)
47 Portland Place, W1
L (Field-Marshal)

Ada, Countess of Lovelace (1815–52)
12 St James's Square, SW1
L (Pioneer of computing)

Adam, Robert (1728–92)
1–3 Robert Street, WC2
L (Architect)

Adelphi Terrace
The Adelphi, WC2
The Adelphi Terrace was built by the brothers Adam in 1768–74

Alma-Tadema OM, Sir Laurence (1886–1912)
44 Grove End Road, NW8
L (1886–1912) (Painter)

Arkwright, Sir Richard (1732–92)
8 Adam Street, WC2
L (Industrialist and inventor)

Arne, Thomas (1710–78)
31 King street, WC2
L (Composer)

Arnold, Matthew (1822–88)
2 Chester Square, SW1
L (Poet and critic)

**Lord Ashfield, Albert Henry Stanley
(1874–1948)**
43 South Street, W1
L (First chairman of London Transport)

Astor, Nancy (1879–1964)
4 St James's Square, SW1
L (First woman to sit in Parliament)

Baron Avebury, Sir John Lubbock (1834–1913)
29 Eaton Place, SW1
B (Scientist)

Bagehot, Walter (1826–77)
12 Upper Belgrave Street, SW1
L (Writer, banker and economist)

Baird, John Logie (1888-1946)
22 Frith Street, W1
(First demonstrated television in this house in 1926)

Bairnsfather, Bruce (1888–1959)
1 Sterling Street, off Montpelier Square, SW7
L (Cartoonist)

Balfe, Michael William (1808–70)
12 Seymour Street, W1
L (Composer)

Banks, Sir Joseph (1743–1820)
32 Soho Square, W1
L (President of the Royal Society)

**Baring, Evelyn – 1st Earl of Cromer
(1841–1917)**
36 Wimpole Street, W1
L, D (Colonial administrator)

Barrie, Sir James (1860–1937)
1–3 Robert Street, WC2
L (Dramatist)

Barrie, Sir James (1860–1937)
100 Bayswater Road, W2
L (Novelist and dramatist)

Basevi, George (1794–1845)
17 Savile Row, W1
L (Architect)

Bazalgette, Sir Joseph William (1819–91)
17 Hamilton Terrace, NW8
L (Civil engineer)

Beardsley, Aubrey (1872–98)
114 Cambridge Street, SW1
L (Artist)

Beatty OM, Earl David (1871–1936)
Hanover Lodge, Outer Circle, NW1
L (Admiral)

Beaufort, Sir Francis (1774–1857)
51 Manchester Street, W1
L (Admiral and hydrographer)

Beecham CH, Sir Thomas (1879–1961)
31 Grove End Road, NW8
L (Conductor and impresario)

Benedict, Sir Julius (1804–85)
2 Manchester Square, W1
L (Musical composer)

Ben-Gurion, David (1886–1973)
75 Warrington Crescent, W9
L (First Prime Minister of Israel)

Bentham, George (1800–84)
25 Wilton Place, SW1
L (Botanist)

Berlioz, Hector (1803–69)
58 Queen Anne Street, W1
S (1851) (Composer)

Bevin, Ernest (1881-1951)
Stratford Mansions, 34 Molton Street, W1
L (1931-39) (Trade Union leader and statesman)

**Lady Bonham Carter, Violet – Baroness
Asquith of Yarnbury (1887–1969)**
43 Gloucester Square, W2
L (Politician and writer)

Boswell, James (1740–95)
122 Great Portland Street, W1
L, D (Biographer)

Bridgeman, Charles
54 Broadwick Street, W1
L (1723–38) (Landscape gardener)

Bridgeman, Sir Orlando (c.1606–74)
Essex Hall, Essex Street, WC2
L (Lord Keeper)

Bright, Richard (1789–1858)
11 Savile Row, W1
L (Physician)

Brooke, Sir Charles Vyner (1874–1963)
13 Albion Street, W2
L (Last Rajah of Sarawak)

Browning, Elizabeth Barrett (1806–61)
99 Gloucester Place, W1
L (Poet)

Browning, Elizabeth Barrett (1806–61)
50 Wimpole Street, W1
L **(1838–46)** (Poet)

Brown, Robert (1773–1858)
32 Soho Square, W1
L (Botanist)

Brummell, Beau (1778–1840)
4 Chesterfield Street, W1
L (Leader of fashion)

Burgoyne, General John (1722–92)
10 Hertford Street, W1
L, D

Burke, Edmund (1729–97)
37 Gerrard Street, W1
L (Author and stateman)

Burma, Earl and Countess Mountbatten
2 Wilton Crescent, SW1
L, W **(1891-1939)** (Last Viceroy and Vicereine of India)

Burnett, Frances Hodgson (1849–1924)
63 Portland Place, W1
L (Writer)

Burney, Fanny (Madam D'Arblay) (1752–1840)
11 Bolton Street, W1
L (Authoress)

Shelley, Percy Bysshe (1792-1822)
15 Poland Street, W1
L **(1811)** (Poet)

Blue Plaques 367

Campbell, Colen (1676–1729)
76 Brook Street, W1
L, D (Architect and author)

Campbell-Bannerman, Sir Henry (1836–1908)
6 Grosvenor Place, SW1
L (Prime Minister)

Canal, Antonio (Canaletto) (1697–1768)
41 Beak Street, W1
L (Venetian painter)

Canning, George (1770–1827)
50 Berkeley Square, W1
L (Statesman)

Cato Street Conspiracy
1A Cato Street, W1
Discovered here 23 February 1820

Cayley, Sir George (1773–1857)
20 Hertford Street, W1
L (Scientist and pioneer of aviation)

Cecil, Viscount of Chelwood (1864–1958)
16 South Eaton Place, SW1
L (Creator of the League of Nations)

Chamberlain, Neville (1869–1940)
37 Eaton Square, SW1
L **(1923–35)** (Prime Minister)

Charles X (1757-1836)
72 South Audley Street, W1
L **(1805-1814)** (Last Bourbon King of France)

Chippendale, Thomas
61 St Martin's Lane, WC2
W **(1753–1813)** (Cabinet maker)

Chopin, Frederic (1810–49)
4 St James's Place, SW1
(From this house in 1848 Frederic Chopin went to the Guildhall to give his last public performance)

Churchill, Lord Randolph (1849–95)
2 Connaught Place, W2
L **(1883–92)** (Statesman)

Clarkson, Willy (1861–1934)
41–43 Wardour Street, W1
L, D (Theatrical wigmaker)

368 Cultural London

Lord Clive of India (1725–74)
45 Berkeley Square, W1
L (Soldier and administrator)

Cobden, Richard (1804–65)
23 Suffolk Street, SW1
D (Statesman)

Cochrane, Thomas – Earl of Dundonald (1775–1860)
Hanover Lodge, Outer Circle, NW1
L (Admiral)

Coleridge, Samuel Taylor (1772–1834)
71 Berners Street, W1
B (Poet and philosopher)

Collins, William Wilkie (1824–89)
65 Gloucester Place, W1
L (Novelist)

Conrad, Joseph (1857–1924)
17 Gillingham Street, SW1
L (Novelist)

Cons, Emma (1837–1912)
136 Seymour Place, W1
L (Philanthropist and founder of the Old Vic)

Crosby, Brass (1725–93)
Essex Hall, Essex Street, WC2
L (Lord Mayor of London)

Cubitt, Thomas (1788–1855)
3 Lyall Street, SW1
L (Master builder)

Curzon, George Nathaniel – Marquess Curzon of Kedleston (1859–1925)
1 Carlton House Terrace, SW1
L (Statesman, Viceroy of India)

Dadd, Richard (1817–86)
15 Suffolk Street, SW1
L (Painter)

Davies, Emily (1830–1921)
17 Cunningham Place, NW8
L (Founder of Girton College, Cambridge)

De Gaulle, General Charles
4 Carlton Gardens, SW1
(President of the French National Committee)

De Quincey, Thomas (1785–1859)
36 Tavistock Street, WC2
(Writer)

Disraeli, Benjamin – Earl of Beaconsfield (1804–81)
19 Curzon Street, W1
D (Stateman)

Don, David (1800–41)
32 Soho Square, W1
L (Botanist)

Dryden, John (1631–1700)
43 Gerrard Street, W1
L (Poet)

Etty, William (1787–1849)
14 Buckingham Street, WC2
L (Painter)

Evans, Dame Edith (1888–1976)
109 Ebury Street, SW1
L (Actress)

Ewart, William (1798–1869)
16 Eaton Place, SW1
L (Reformer)

Faraday, Michael (1791–1867)
48 Blandford Street, W1
W (Man of science)

Fielding, Henry (1707–54)
Essex Hall, Essex Street, WC2
L (Novelist)

Fielding, Henry (1707–54)
19–20 Bow Street, WC2
L (Novelist)

Fielding, Sir John (d.1780)
19–20 Bow Street, WC2
L (Magistrate)

Lord Fisher OM, Admiral of the Fleet (1841–1920)
16 Queen Anne's Gate, SW1
L (1905–10) (First Sea Lord)

Flaxman, John (1755–1826)
7 Greenwell Street, W1
L, D (Sculptor)

Blue Plaques 369

Fleming, Ian (1908–64)
22 Ebury Street, SW1
L (Creator of James Bond)

Fleming, Sir Ambrose (1849–1945)
9 Clifton Gardens, W9
L (Scientist and electrical engineer)

Fox, Charles James (1749–1806)
46 Clarges Street, W1
L (Statesman)

Frampton, George (1860–1928)
32 Queen's Grove, NW8
L, W (1894–1908) (Sculptor)

Franklin, Benjamin (1706–90)
36 Craven Street, WC2
L (American statesman and scientist)

Friese-Greene, William Edward (1855–1921)
136 Maida Vale, W9
L (Pioneer of cinematography)

Frith, W. P. (1819–1909)
114 Clifton Hill, NW8
L, D (Painter)

Fuseli, Henry (1741–1825)
37 Foley Street, W1
L (1788–1803) (Artist)

Gage, Thomas (1721–87)
41 Portland Place, W1
L (Commander of British Forces in North America)

Gainsborough, Thomas (1727–88)
82 Pall Mall, SW1
L (Artist)

Galsworthy, John (1867–1933)
1–3 Robert Street, WC2
L (Novelist and playwright)

Galton, Sir Francis (1822–1911)
42 Rutland Gate, SW7
L (Explorer, statistician, and founder of eugenics)

Garrett Anderson, Elizabeth (1836–1917)
20 Upper Berkeley Street, W1
L (First woman to qualify as a doctor in Britain)

Handel, George Frideric (1685-1759)
25 Brook Street, Maifair, W1
L, D (Composer)

Gibbon, Edward (1737–92)
7 Bentinck Street, W1
L (1773–83) (Historian)

Gibbons, Grinling (1648–1721)
19–20 Bow Street, WC2
L (Wood carver)

Gladstone, William Ewart (1809–98)
11 Carlton House Terrace, SW1
L (Statesman)

Gladstone, W. E. (William Ewart) (1809–98)
73 Harley Street, W1
L (1876–82) (Statesman)

Gladstone, William Ewart (1809–98)
10 St Jame's Square, SW1
L (Prime Minister)

Godley, John Robert (1814–61)
48 Gloucester Place, W1
L, D (Founder of Canterbury, New Zealand)

Gordon Fenwick, Ethel (1857–1947)
20 Upper Wimpole Street, W1
L (1887–1924) (Nursing reformer)

Gray, Henry (1827–61)
8 Wilton Street, SW1
L (Anatomist)

Green, John Richard (1837–83)
4 Beaumont Street, W1
L (Historian of the English people)

Grey, Sir Edward – Viscount Grey of Falloden (1862–1933)
3 Queen Anne's Gate, SW1
L (Foreign Secretary)

Grossmith Sr, George (1847–1912)
28 Dorset Square, NW1
L (Actor and author)

Grossmith Jr, George (1874–1935)
3 Spanish Place, W1
L (Actor-manager)

Grote, George (1794–1871)
12 Savile Row, W1
D (Historian)

370 Cultural London

Lord Haldane (1856–1928)
28 Queen Anne's Gate, SW1
L (Statesman, lawyer and philospher)

Hallam, Henry (1777–1859)
67 Wimpole Street, W1
L (Historian)

Handel, George Frederick (1685–1759)
25 Brook Street, W1
L, D (Musician)

Handley Page, Sir Frederick (1885–1962)
18 Grosvenor Square, W1
L (Aircraft designer and manufacturer)

Handley, Tommy (1892–1949)
34 Craven Road, Paddington, W2
L (Radio comedian)

Harley, Robert – Earl of Oxford (1661–1724)
14 Buckingham Street, WC2
L (Statesman)

Harte, Francis Bret (1836–1902)
74 Lancaster Gate, W2
L (American writer)

Haydon, Benjamin Robert (1786–1846)
116 Lisson Grove, NW1
L (Painter)

Hazlitt, William (1778–1830)
6 Frith Street, W1
D (Essayist)

Heine, Heinrich (1799–1856)
32 Craven Street, WC2
L (1827) (German poet and essayist)

Hendrix, Jimi (1942–70)
23 Brook Street, W1
L (1968–69) (Guitarist and songwriter)

Herzen, Alexander (1812–70)
1 Orsett Terrace, W2
L (1860–63) (Russian political thinker)

Hill, Sir Rowland (1795–1879)
1 Orme Square, W2
L (Postal reformer)

Hill, Octavia (1838–1912)
2 Garbutt Place, W1
(Housing reformer; co-founder of The National Trust)

Hogg, Quintin (1845–1903)
5 Cavendish Square, W1
L (1885–98) (Founder of the Polytechnic, Regent Street)

Hood, Thomas (1799–1845)
1–3 Robert Street, WC2
L (Poet)

Hood, Thomas (1799–1845)
Devonshire Lodge, 28 Finchley Road, NW8
D (Poet)

Lord Hore-Belisha (1893–1957)
16 Stafford Place, SW1
L (Statesman)

Hughes, David Edward (1831–1900)
94 Great Portland Street, W1
L, W (Scientist and inventor)

Hunter, John (1728–93)
31 Golden Square, W1
L (Surgeon)

Hunter, William (1718–83)
Lyric Theatre (rear portion), Great Windmill Street, W1
(Anatomist)

Huskisson, William (1770–1830)
28 St James's Place, SW1
L (Statesman)

Hutchinson, Sir Jonathan (1828–1913)
15 Cavendish Square, W1
L (Surgeon, scientist and teacher)

Huxley, Thomas (1825–95)
38 Marlborough Place, NW8
L (Biologist)

Irving, Sir Henry (1838–1905)
15A Grafton Street, W1
L (1872–99) (Actor)

Irving, Washington (1783–1859)
8 Argyll Street, W1
L (American writer)

Isaacs, Rufus – 1st Marquess of Reading (1860–1935)
32 Curzon Street, W1
L, D (Lawyer and statesman)

Jackson, John Hughlings (1835–1911)
3 Manchester Square, W1
L (Physician)

Jerome, Jerome K (1859–1927)
91–104 Chelsea Gardens, Chelsea Bridge Road, SW1
L (Author)

Johnson, Dr Samuel
Essex Hall, Essex Street, WC2
L (Established an evening club at the 'Essex Head' in 1783)

Johnson, Samuel (1709–84)
8 Russell Street, WC2

Jones, Dr Ernest (1879–1958)
19 York Terrace East, NW1
L (Pioneer psychoanalyst)

Kalvos, Andreas (1792–1869)
182 Sutherland Avenue, W9
L (Greek poet and patriot)

Kelly, Sir Gerald (1879–1972)
117 Gloucester Place, W1
L (1916–72) (Portrait painter)

Lord Kelvin (1824–1907)
15 Eaton Place, SW1
L (Physicist and inventor)

Kempe, Charles Eamer (1837–1907)
37 Nottingham Place, W1
L, W (Stained glass artist)

Kipling, Rudyard (1865–1936)
43 Villiers Street, WC2
L (1889–91) (Poet and story writer)

Kitchener of Khartoum KG, Field Marshal, Earl (1850–1916)
2 Carlton Gardens, SW1
L (1914–15)

Klein, Melanie (1882–1960)
42 Clifton Hill, NW8
L (Psychoanalyst and pioneer of child analysis)

Knight, Harold (1874–1961)
16 Langford Place, NW8
L (Painter)

Knight, Dame Laura (1877–1970)
16 Langford Place, NW8
L (Painter)

Kokoschka, Oskar (1886–1980)
Eyre Court, Finchley Road, NW8
L (Painter)

Lawrence, Susan (1871–1947)
44 Westbourne Terrace, W2
L (Social reformer)

Lawrence, T. E. (1888–1935)
14 Barton Street, SW1
L ('Lawrence of Arabia')

Lear, Edward (1812–88)
30 Seymour Street, W1
L (Artist and writer)

Leigh, Vivien (1913–67)
54 Eaton Square, SW1
L (Actress)

Lindsey, Revd Theophilus (1723–1808)
Essex Hall, Essex Street, WC2
L (Unitarian minister, founded Essex Street Chapel here in 1774)

Lord Lister, Joseph (1827–1912)
12 Park Crescent, W1
L (Surgeon)

Loudon, Jane (1807–58)
3 Porchester Terrace, W2
L (Horticulturalist)

Loudon, John Claudius (1783–1843)
3 Porchester Terrace, W2
L (Horticulturalist)

Lord Lugard (1858–1945)
51 Rutland Gate, SW7
L (1912–19) (Colonial administrator)

Lutyens, Sir Edwin Landseer (1869–1944)
13 Mansfield Street, W1
L, D (Architect)

Lyell, Sir Charles (1797–1875)
73 Harley Street, W1
L (1854–75) (Geologist)

Macaulay, Rose (1881–1958)
Hinde House, 11–14 Hinde Street, W1
L, D (Writer)

Macklin, Charles (1697?–1797)
19–20 Bow Street, WC2
L (Actor)

Macmillan, Douglas (1884–1969)
15 Ranelagh Road, SW1
L (Founder of Macmillan Cancer Relief)

Malone, Edmond (1741–1812)
40 Langham Street, W1
L (1779–1812) (Shakespearian scholar)

Manby, Charles (1804–84)
60 Westbourne Terrace, W2
L (Civil engineer)

Manning, Cardinal Henry Edward (1808–92)
22 Carlisle Place, SW1
L

Manson, Sir Patrick (1844–1922)
50 Welbeck Street, W1
L (Father of modern tropical medicine)

Marconi, Guglielmo (1874–1937)
71 Hereford Road, W2
L (1896–97) (Pioneer of wireless communications)

Marryat, Captain Frederick (1792–1848)
3 Spanish Place, W1
L (Novelist)

Marx, Karl (1818–83)
28 Dean Street, W1
L (1851–56)

Maugham, William Somerset (1874–1965)
6 Chesterfield Street, W1
L (1911–19) (Novelist and playwright)

Maurice, Frederick Denison (1805–72)
2 Upper Harley Street, NW1
L (1862–66) (Christian philosopher and educationalist)

Mayer, Sir Robert (1879–1985)
2 Mansfield Street, W1
L (Philanthropist and patron of music)

Metternich, Prince (1773–1859)
44 Eaton Square, SW1
L (1848) (Austrian statesman)

Meynell, Alice (1847–1922)
47 Palace Court, W2
L (Poet and essayist)

Millbank Prison
Millbank, SW1
Millbank Prison was opened in 1816 and closed in 1890

Lord Milner, Alfred (1854–1925)
14 Manchester Square, W1
L (Statesman)

Mitford, Nancy (1904–73)
Heywood Hill's Bookshop, 10 Curzon Street, W1
W (1942–45) (Writer)

Montefiore, Sir Moses (1784–1885)
99 Park Lane, W1
L (Philanthropist and Jewish leader)

Moore, George (1852–1933)
121 Ebury Street, SW1
L, D (Author)

Moore, Tom (1779–1852)
85 George Street, W1
L (Irish poet)

Morrell, Lady Ottoline (1873–1938)
10 Gower Street, WC1
L (Literary hostess and patron of the Arts)

Morse, Samuel (1791–1872)
141 Cleveland Street, W1
L (1812–15) (American painter and inventor)

Mozart, Wolfgang Amadeus (1756–91)
180 Ebury Street, W1
(Composer)

Napoleon III (1808–73)
1C King Street, SW1
L (1848) (Emperor of the French)

Lord Nelson, Horatio (1758–1805)
147 New Bond Street, W1
L (1797)

Lord Nelson, Horatio (1758–1805)
103 New Bond Street, W1
L (1798)

Newton, Sir Isaac (1642–1727)
87 Jermyn Street, SW1
L (Natural philosopher)

Nicolson, Harold (1886–1968)
182 Ebury Street, SW1
L (Writer and gardener)

Nightingale, Florence (1820–1910)
10 South Street, W1
L, D

Noel-Baker, Philip (1889–1982)
16 South Eaton Place, SW1
L (Olympic sportsman; campaigner for peace and disarmament)

Nollekens, Joseph (1737–1823)
44 Mortimer Street, W1
L, D (Sculptor)

Novello, Ivor (1893–1951)
11 Aldwych, WC2
L, D (Composer and actor-manager)

Oldfield, Ann (1683–1730)
60 Grosvenor Street, W1
W (1725–30) (Actress)

Onslow, Arthur (1691–1768)
20 Soho Square, W1
L (Speaker of the House of Commons 1728–61)

Palgrave, Francis Turner (1824–97)
5 York Gate, NW1
L (1862–75) (Compiler of 'The Golden Treasury')

Palmerston, Henry John Temple, 3rd Viscount (1784–1865)
4 Carlton Gardens, SW1
L (Statesman)

Blue Plaques 373

Palmerston, Henry John Temple, 3rd Viscount (1784–1856)
20 Queen Anne's Gate, SW1
B (Prime Minister)

Lord Palmerston (1784–1865)
Naval and Military Club, 94 Piccadilly, W1
L (Prime Minister and Foreign Secretary)

Patel, Sardar (1875–1950)
23 Aldridge Road Villas, W11
L (Indian statesman)

Peabody, George (1795–1869)
80 Eaton Square, SW1
D (Philanthropist)

Pearson, John Loughborough (1817–97)
13 Mansfield Street, W1
L, D (Architect)

Peel, Sir Robert (1750–1830)
16 Upper Grosvenor Street, W1
L (Manufacturer and reformer)

Pelham, Henry (c.1695–1754)
22 Arlington Street, SW1
L (Prime Minister)

Pepys, Samuel (1633–1703)
12 Buckingham Street, WC2
L (1679–88) (Diarist and Secretary of the Admiralty)

Pepys, Samuel (1633–1703)
14 Buckingham Street, WC2
L (Diarist and Secretary of the Admiralty)

Pinero, Sir Arthur (1855–1934)
115A Harley Street, W1
L (1909–34) (Playwright)

Pitt, William – Earl of Chatham (1708–78)
10 St James's Square, SW1
L (Prime Minister)

Pitt, William (the younger) (1759–1806)
120 Baker Street, W1
L (1803–04) (Prime Minister)

Pitt-Rivers, Lt. Gen. Augustus Henry Lane Fox (1827–1900)
4 Grosvenor Gardens, SW1
L (Anthropologist and archaeologist)

374 Cultural London

Portuguese Embassy
23–24 Golden Square, W1
These two houses were the Portuguese Embassy (1724–47); the Marquess of Pombal, ambassador 1739–44 lived here

Radcliffe, John (1650–1714)
19–20 Bow Street, WC2
L (Physician)

Raglan, Lord Fitzroy Somerset, 1st Baron (1788–1855)
5 Stanhope Gate, W1
L (Commander during the Crimean War)

Rathbone, Eleanor (1782–1946)
Tufton Court, Tufton Street, SW1
L (Pioneer of family allowances)

Lord Reith (1889–1971)
6 Barton Street, SW1
L (1924–30) (First Director-General of the BBC)

Reschid, Mustapha Pasha (1800–58)
1 Bryanston Square, W1
L (1839) (Turkish statesman and reformer)

Reynolds, Sir Joshua (1723–92)
Fanum House, Leicester Square, WC2
L, D (Portrait painter)

Richmond, George (1809–96)
20 York Street, W1
L (1843–96) (Painter)

Rogers, Dr Joseph (1821–89)
33 Dean Street, W1
L (Health care reformer)

Rosebery, 5th Earl (1847–1929)
20 Charles Street, W1
B (Prime Minister and first Chairman of the London County Council)

Rossetti, Dante Gabriel (1828–82)
110 Hallam Street, W1
B (Poet and painter)

Rossi, John Charles Felix (1762–1839)
116 Lisson Grove, NW1
L (Sculptor)

Ross, Sir Ronald (1857–1932)
18 Cavendish Square, W1
L (Nobel Laureate)

Rowlandson, Thomas (1757–1827)
16 John Adam Street, WC2
L (Artist and caricaturist)

Roy, Major-General William (1726–90)
10 Argyll Street, W1
L (Founder of the Ordnance Survey)

Russell, Lord John, 1st Earl (1792–1878)
37 Chesham Place, SW1
L (Twice Prime Minister)

Sackville, Charles – Earl of Dorset (1638–1706)
19–20 Bow Street, WC2
L (Poet)

Sackville-West, Vita (1892–1962)
182 Ebury Street, SW1
L (Writer and gardener)

Salvin, Anthony (1799–1881)
11 Hanover Terrace, NW1
L (Architect)

San Martin, José de (The Liberator) (1778–1850)
23 Park Road, NW1
S (Argentine soldier and statesman)

Santley, Sir Charles (1834–1922)
13 Blenheim Road, NW8
L, D (Singer)

Savage, James (1779–1852)
Essex Hall, Essex Street, WC2
W (Architect)

Sayers, Dorothy L. (1893-1957)
24 Great James Street, WC1
L (1921–1929) (Writer of detective stories)

Scawen-Blunt, Wilfrid (1840–1922)
15 Buckingham Gate, SW1
L (Diplomat, poet and traveller, founder of Crabbet Park Arabian stud)

Schreiner, Olive (1855–1920)
16 Portsea Place, W2
L (Author)

Blue Plaques 375

Site of Scotland Yard
Ministry of Agriculture Building, Whitehall Place, SW1
First headquarters of the Metropolitan Police 1829–90

Scott, Sir Giles Gilbert (1880–1960)
Chester House, Clarendon Place, W2
L (1926–60) (Architect)

Seacole, Mary (1805–81)
157 George Street, W1
L (Jamaican nurse, heroine of Crimean War)

Seferis, George (1900-1971)
51 Upper Brook Street, W1
L (1957-1962) (Greek Ambassador, poet and Nobel laureate)

Shelley, Percy Bysshe (1792–1822)
15 Poland Street, W1
L (Poet)

Shepard, E. H. (1879–1976)
10 Kent Terrace, NW1
L (Painter and illustrator)

Sheraton, Thomas (1751–1806)
163 Wardour Street, W1
L (Furniture designer)

Sheridan, Richard Brinsley (1751–1816)
14 Savile Row, W1
L (Dramatist and Statesman)

Sheridan, Richard Brinsley (1751–1816)
10 Hertford Street, W1
L (1795–1802) (Dramatist and statesman)

Smith, F. E. – Earl of Birkenhead (1872–1930)
32 Grosvenor Gardens, SW1
L (Lawyer and statesman)

Smith, W. H. (1825–91)
12 Hyde Park Street, W2
L (Bookseller and statesman)

Smith MP, William (1756–1835)
16 Queen Anne's Gate, SW1
L (Pioneer of religious liberty)

Sopwith, Sir Thomas (1888–1989)
46 Green Street, W1
L (1934–40 (Aviator and aircraft manufacturer)

Stanfield, Clarkson (1793–1867)
14 Buckingham Street, WC2
L (Painter)

Stanhope, Charles, 3rd Earl (1753–1816)
20 Mansfield Street, W1
L (Reformer and inventor)

Stanley, Edward Geoffrey – Earl of Derby (1799–1869)
10 St James's Square, SW1
L (Prime Minister)

Stanley, Sir Henry Morton (1841–1904)
2 Richmond Terrace, SW1
L, D (Explorer and writer)

Stephenson, Robert (1803–59)
35 Gloucester Square, W2
D (Engineer)

Sterndale Bennett, Sir William (1816–75)
38 Queensborough Terrace, W2
L (Composer)

Still, Sir George Frederic (1868–1941)
28 Queen Anne Street, W1
L (Paediatrician)

Stothard, Thomas (1755–1834)
28 Newman Street, W1
L (Painter and illustrator)

Strang, William (1859–1921)
20 Hamilton Terrace, NW8
L (1900–21) (Painter and etcher)

Street, George Edmund (1824–81)
14 Cavendish Place, W1
L (Architect)

Stuart, Prince Charles Edward
Essex Hall, Essex Street, WC2
S

Taglioni, Marie (1809–84)
14 Connaught Square, W2
L (1875–76) (Ballet dancer)

Talleyrand, Prince (1754–1838)
21 Hanover Square, W1
L (French statesman and diplomatist)

376 Cultural London

Tauber, Richard (1891–1948)
Park West, Edgware Road, W2
L (1947–8) (Lyric tenor)

Tempest, Dame Marie (1864–1942)
24 Park Crescent, W1
L (1899–1902) (Actress)

Lord Tennyson, Alfred (1809–92)
9 Upper Belgrave Street, SW1
L (1880–81) (Poet)

Hood, Thomas (1799-1845)
28 Finchley Road, NW8
L, D (Poet)

Tilak, Lokamanya (1856–1920)
10 Howley Place, W2
L (1918–19) (Indian patriot and philosopher)

Townley, Charles (1737–1805)
14 Queen Anne's Gate, SW1
L (Antiquary and collector)

Treves, Sir Frederick (1886-1907)
6 Wimpole Street, W1
L (1886-1907) (Surgeon)

Trollope, Anthony (1815–82)
39 Montague Square, W1
L (Novelist)

Turing, Alan (1912–54)
2 Warrington Crescent, W9
B (Code-breaker and pioneer of computer science)

Tyburn Tree
Traffic Island at the juction of Edgware and Bayswater Roads, W2

United States Embassy
98 Portland Place, W1
Henry Brook Adams (1838–1918) US historian lived here

Van Buren, Martin (1782–1862)
7 Stratford Place, W1
L (Eighth US President)

Vaughan Williams, Ralph (1872–1958)
10 Hanover Terrace, NW1
L (1953–58) (Composer)

Voysey, C. F. A. (1857–1941)
6 Carlton Hill, NW8
L (Architect and designer)

Walpole, Horace (1717–97)
5 Arlington Street, SW1
L (Connoisseur and man of letters)

Walpole, Sir Robert (1676–1745)
5 Arlington Street, SW1
L (Prime Minister)

Waterhouse, Alfred (1830–1905)
61 New Cavendish Street, W1
L (Architect)

Weisz, Victor 'Vicky' (1913–66)
Welbeck Mansions, 35 Welbeck Street, W1
L (Cartoonist)

Wells, H. G. (1866–1946)
13 Hanover Terrace, NW1
L, D (Writer)

Wesley, Charles (1707–88)
1 Wheatley Street, W1
L, D (Divine and hymn writer)

Wesley, Charles (1757–1834)
1 Wheatley Street, W1
L (Musician)

Wesley, Samuel (1766–1837)
1 Wheatley Street, W1
L (Musician)

Westmacott, Sir Richard (1775–1856)
14 South Audley Street, W1
L, D (Sculptor)

Wheatstone, Sir Charles (1802–75)
19 Park Crescent, W1
L (Scientist and inventor)

Wheeler, Sir Mortimer (1890–1976)
27 Whitcomb Street, WC2
L (Archaeologist)

Winant, John Gilbert (1889–1947)
7 Aldford Street, W1
L (United States Ambassador 1941–46)

Wingfield, Major Walter Clopton (1833–1912)
33 St George's Square, SW1
L (Father of lawn tennis)

Wodehouse, P. G. (1881–1975)
17 Dunraven Street, W1
L (Writer)

Wood, Edward – 1st Earl of Halifax (1881–1959)
86 Eaton Square, SW1
L (Statesman, Viceroy of India and Foreign Secretary)

Wyatville, Sir Jeffry (1766–1840)
39 Brook Street, W1
L, D (Architect)

Wycherley, William (1640?–1716)
19–20 Bow Street, WC2
L (Dramatist)

Wyndham, Sir Charles (1837–1919)
20 York Terrace East, NW1
L, D (Actor-manager)

Young, Thomas (1773–1829)
48 Welbeck Street, W1
L (Man of science)

BRITISH LIBRARY

96 Euston Road, London NW1 2DB
(Tel: 020-7412 7332; Fax: 020-7412 7340; Web: www.bl.uk).

The British Library was established in 1973. It is the UK's national library and occupies a key position in the library and information network. The Library aims to serve scholarship, research, industry, commerce and all other major users of information. Its services are based on collections which include over 16 million volumes, 1 million discs, and 55,000 hours of tape recordings. The Library is now based at two sites: London (St Pancras and Colindale) and Boston Spa, W. Yorks. The Library's sponsoring department is the Department for Culture, Media and Sport.

Access to the reading rooms at St Pancras is limited to holders of a British Library Reader's Pass; information about eligibility is available from the Reader Admissions Office. The exhibition galleries and public areas are open to all, free of charge except for special, temporary exhibitions for which there may be an admission fee.

Opening hours of services vary. Specific information should be checked by telephone.

Reader Admissions (Tel: 020-7412 7677)
Reader Services (Tel: 020-7412 7676)

West European Collections, Slavonic and East European Collections, English Language Collections (Tel: 020-7412 7676); Newspaper Library, Colindale Avenue, London NW9 5HE. (Tel: 020-7412 7353); National Preservation Office (Tel: 020-7412 7612); Special Collections (Tel: 020-7412 7513); Oriental and India Office Collections (Tel: 020-7412 7873); Western Manuscripts (Tel: 020-7412 7513); Map Library (Tel: 020-7412 7702); Music Collections (Tel: 020-7412 7772); Philatelic Collections (Tel: 020-7412 7635); National Sound Archive (Tel: 020-7412 7440); Science and Technology (Tel: 020-7412/7288/7494/7496); British and EPO Patents (Tel: 020-7412 7919); Foreign Patents (Tel: 020-7412 7902); Business (Tel: 020-7412 7454/7977); Social Policy Information Service (Tel: 020-7412 7536).

CEMETERIES

Abney Park, Stamford Hill, N16 (35 acres), tomb of General Booth, founder of the Salvation Army, and memorials to many Non-conformist divines.

Brompton, Old Brompton Road, SW10 (40 acres), graves of Sir Henry Cole, Emmeline Pankhurst, John Wisden.

City of London Cemetery and Crematorium, Aldersbrook Road, E12 (200 acres). Golders Green Crematorium, Hoop Lane, NW11 (12 acres), with Garden of Rest and memorials to many famous men and women.

Hampstead, Fortune Green Road, NW6 (36 acres), graves of Kate Greenaway, Lord Lister, Marie Lloyd.

Highgate, Swains Lane, N6 (38 acres), tombs of George Eliot, Faraday and Marx; guided tours only, west side, £3.00.

Kensal Green, Harrow Road, W10 (70 acres), tombs of Thackeray, Trollope, Sydney Smith, Wilkie Collins, Tom Hood, George Cruikshank, Leigh Hunt, I. K. Brunel and Charles Kemble.

Churchyard of the former Marylebone Chapel, Marylebone High Street, W1, Charles Wesley and his son Samuel Wesley buried; chapel demolished in 1949, now Garden of Rest.

Nunhead, Linden Grove, SE15 (26 acres), closed in 1969, recently restored and opened for burials.

St Marylebone Cemetery and Crematorium, East End Road, N2 (47 acres).

West Norwood Cemetery and Crematorium, Norwood High Street, SE27 (42 acres), tombs of Sir Henry Bessemer, Mrs Beeton, Sir Henry Tate and Joseph Whitaker (Whitaker's Almanack).

CENOTAPH, WHITEHALL, LONDON SW1.

The word 'cenotaph' means 'empty tomb'. The monument, erected 'To the Glorious Dead', is a memorial to all ranks of the sea, land and air forces who gave their lives in the service of the Empire during the First World War. Designed by Sir Edwin Lutyens and erected as a temporary memorial in 1919, it was replaced by a permanent structure unveiled by George V on Armistice Day 1920. An additional inscription was made after the Second World War to commemorate those who gave their lives in that conflict.

CHARTERHOUSE

Charterhouse Square, London EC1M 6AN (Tel: 020-7253 9503; Fax: 020-7251 3929).

A Carthusian monastery from 1371 to 1537, purchased in 1611 by Thomas Sutton, who endowed it as a residence for aged men 'of gentle birth' and a school for poor scholars (removed to Godalming in 1872).

CHELSEA PHYSIC GARDEN

66 Royal Hospital Road, London SW3 4HS (Tel: 020-7352 5646; Fax: 020-7376 3910; Web: www.cpgarden.demon.co.uk).

A garden of general botanical research and education, maintaining a wide range of rare and unusual plants. The garden was established in 1673 by the Society of Apothecaries.

CINEMA

There is a vast number of cinemas in the capital, both independent and those forming part of a national or international chain. Performance and ticket information can be found in the local press, on Teletext and on the Internet. Constraints of space preclude listings of film-houses in London, however, details on the BFI's recently opened IMAX Cinema have been included as this cinema is of technological significance and boasts a building that has already, in its short life, become a unique London landmark.

BFI LONDON IMAX CINEMA

1 Charlie Chaplin Walk, South Bank, London SE1 8XR (Tel: 020-7902 1234; Web: www.bfi.org.uk/imax/).

The BFI London Imax Cinema was opened on 1 May 1999. It cost approximately £20m to build and received £15m from the Arts Council of England's Lottery Fund. Situated on the roundabout adjacent to Waterloo mainline and tube stations, it is the largest and most significant motion picture cinema in the world. The distinctive building was designed by Bryan Avery and the mural featured on the exterior wall is the work of artist Howard Hodgkin. The cinema houses 477 seats and boasts the largest cinema screen in the UK. The cinema shows a range of large format films of an educational nature and many showings are on natural history topics. For performance, ticket and booking information, call the telephone number above.

CLUBS

Alpine Club
55 Charlotte Road, London, EC2A 3QF
(Tel: 020-7613 0755; Fax: 020-7613 0755;
E-mail: sec@alpine-club.org.uk;
Web: www.alpine-club.org.uk)
Hon. Secretary: G. D. Hughes

Anglo-Belgian Club
60 Knightsbridge, London, SW1X 7LF
(Tel: 020-7235 2121; Fax: 020-7245 9470)
Secretary: Patrick R. Bresnan

Army and Navy Club
36 Pall Mall, London, SW1Y 5JN
(Tel: 020-7930 9721; Fax: 020-7930 9991;
E-mail: secretary@therag.co.uk;
Web: www.armynavyclub.co.uk)
Secretary: Cdr. J. A. Holt, MBE

The Athenum
107 Pall Mall, London, SW1Y 5ER
(Tel: 020-7930 4843; Fax: 020-7839 4114;
E-mail: secreatry@hellenist.org.uk)
Secretary: J. H. Ford

Authors' Club
40 Dover Street, London, W1X 3RB
(Tel: 020-7499 8581; Fax: 020-7409 0913)
Secretary: Mrs A. de la Grange

Boodle's
28 St James's Street, London, SW1A 1HJ
(Tel: 020-7930 7166;
E-mail: secreatry@boodles.org)
Secretary: R. R. T. Smith

Caledonian Club
9 Halkin Street, London, SW1X 7DR
(Tel: 020-7235 5162; Fax: 020-7235 4635;
E-mail: office@caledonian-club.org.uk;
Web: www.caledonian-club.org.uk)
Secretary: P. J. Varney

Canning Club
4 St James's Square, London, SW1Y 4JU
(Tel: 020-7827 5757; Fax: 020-7827 5724;
E-mail: canningclub@compuserve.com)
Secretary: T. M. Harrington

Carlton Club
69 St James's Street, London, SW1A 1PJ
(Tel: 020-7493 1164; Fax: 020-7495 4090;
E-mail: secretary@carltonclub.co.uk;
Web: www.carltonclub.co.uk)
Secretary: A. E. Telfer

The Cavalry and Guards Club
127 Piccadilly, London, W1J 7PX
(Tel: 020-7499 1261; Fax: 020-7495 5956;
E-mail: iwh@cavgds.co.uk)
Secretary: Cdr. I. R. Wellesley-Harding, RN

Chelsea Arts Club
143 Old Church Street, London, SW3 6EB
(Tel: 020-7376 3311;
E-mail: secretary@chelseaartsclub.com;
Web: www.chelseaartsclub.com)
Secretary: D. Winterbottom

City Livery Club
20 Aldermanbury, London, EC2V 7HP
(Tel: 020-7814 0200; Fax: 020-7814 0201)
Hon. Secretary: Sir W. C. Hammond, MBE

City of London Club
19 Old Broad Street, London, EC2N 1DS
(Tel: 020-7588 7991; Fax: 020-7374 2020;
E-mail: mail@cityoflondonclub.com;
Web: www.cityclub.co.uk)
Secretary: G. Jones

City University Club
50 Cornhill, London, EC3V 3PD
(Tel: 020-7626 8571)
Secretary: Miss R. C. Graham

380 Cultural London

East India Club
16 St James's Square, London, SW1Y 4LH
(Tel: 020-7930 1000; Fax: 020-7315 2701;
E-mail: eastindi@globalnet.co.uk)
Secretary: M. Howell

Farmers Club
3 Whitehall Court, London, SW1A 2EL
(Tel: 020-7930 3751; Fax: 020-7839 7864)
Secretary: Gp Capt. G. P. Carson

Flyfishers' Club
69 Brook Street, London, W1K 4ER
(Tel: 020-7629 5958)
Secretary: Cdr. T. H. Boycott, OBE, RN

Garrick Club
15 Garrick Street, London, WC2E 9AY
(Tel: 020-7379 6478; Fax: 020-7379 5966)
Secretary: M. J. Harvey

Green Room Club
9 Adam Street, London, WC2N 6AA
(Tel: 020-8276 1341; Fax: 020-8276 1399)
Secretary: D. Lamden

The Hurlingham Club
Ranelagh Gardens, London, SW6 3PR
(Tel: 020-7736 8411)
Secretary: P. H. Covell

The Kennel Club
1–5 Clarges Street, London, W1J 8AB
(Tel: 0870-606 6750; Fax: 020-7518 1050;
E-mail: e-mail-info@the-kennel-club.org.uk;
Web: www.the-kennel-club.org.uk)
Chief Executive: R. French

The Lansdowne Club
9 Firtzmaurice Place, London, W1J 5JD
(Tel: 020-7629 7200; Fax: 020-7409 7839;
E-mail: info@lansdowne-club.co.uk;
Web: www.lansdowneclub.com)
Secretary: Mark Anderson

London Rowing Club
Embankment, Putney, London, SW15 1LB
(Tel: 020-8788 1400; Fax: 020-8874 9056;
E-mail: metregatta@compuserve.com;
Web: www.londonrc.org.uk)
Hon. Secretary: N. A. Smith

MCC (Marylebone Cricket Club)
Lord's Cricket Ground, London, NW8 8QN
(Tel: 020-7289 1611; Fax: 020-7289 9100;
Web: www.lords.org)
Secretary and Chief Executive: R. D. V. Knight

The National Club
c/o Carlton Club, 69 St James's Street, London,
SW1A 1PJ (Tel: 020-8579 0874; Fax: 020-8363
2269; E-mail: suezdm@aol.com)
Hon. Secretary: I. A. Sowton BA

National Liberal Club
Whitehall Place, London, SW1A 2HE
(Tel: 020-7930 9871; Fax: 020-7839 4768;
Web: www.nlc.org.uk)
Secretary: S. J. Roberts

Naval and Military Club
4 St James's Square, London, SW1Y 4JU
(Tel: 020-7827 5757; Fax: 020-7827 5758;
Web: www.navalandmilitaryclub.co.uk)
Secretary: M. G. G. Ebbitt

Naval Club
38 Hill Street, London, W1J 5NS
(Tel: 020-7493 7672; Fax: 020-7629 7995;
E-mail: membership@navalclub.co.uk;
Web: www.navalclub.co.uk)
Chief Executive: Cdr. J. L. L. Prichard, RN

New Cavendish Club
44 Great Cumberland Place, London, W1H 7BS
(Tel: 020-7723 0391; Fax: 020-7262 8411)
General Manager: J. P. Dauvergne

Oriental Club
Stratford House, Stratford Place, London, W1C
1ES (Tel: 020-7629 5126; Fax: 020-7629 0494;
E-mail: sec@orientalclub.org.uk)
Secretary: S. C. Doble

Portland Club
69 Brook Street, London, W1Y 2ER
(Tel: 020-7499 1523)
Secretary: J. Burns, CBE

Pratt's Club
14 Park Place, London, SW1A 1LP (Tel: 020-
7493 0397; E-mail: secreatry@prattsclub.org)
Secretary: G. Snell

The Queen's Club
Palliser Road, London, W14 9EQ
(Tel: 020-7385 3421; Fax: 020-7386 8295;
E-mail: tessa.blazey@queensclub.co.uk;
Web: www.queensclub.co.uk)
Secretary: J. A. S. Edwardes

Railway Club
Room 208, 25 Marylebone Road, London, NW1 5JS (Tel: 01737-812175)
Hon. Secretary: A. G. Wells

Reform Club
104–105 Pall Mall, London, SW1Y 5EW
(Tel: 020-7930 9374; Fax: 020-7930 1857;
E-mail: reform—club@msn.com)
Secretary: R. A. M. Forrest

Roehampton Club
Roehampton Lane, London, SW15 5LR
(Tel: 020-8480 4205; Fax: 020-8480 4265)
Chief Executive: M. Yates

Royal Air Force Club
128 Piccadilly, London, W1V 0PY
(Tel: 020-7399 1000; Fax: 020-7355 1516;
E-mail: admin@rafclub.org.uk;
Web: www.rafclub.org.uk)
Chairman: Air Vice-Marshal P. W. Roser

Royal Automobile Club
89–91 Pall Mall, London, SW1Y 5HS
(Tel: 020-7930 2345; Fax: 020-7976 1086;
E-mail: members@royalautomobileclub.co.uk;
Web: www.royalautomobileclub.co.uk)
Secretary: A. I. G. Kennedy

Royal Ocean Racing Club
20 St James's Place, London, SW1A 1NN
(Tel: 020-7493 2248; Fax: 020-7493 5252;
E-mail: rorc@saintjames.demon.co.uk;
Web: www.rorc.org)
General Manager: D. J. Minords, OBE

Royal Thames Yacht Club
60 Knightsbridge, London, SW1X 7LF
(Tel: 020-7235 2121; Fax: 020-7245 9470;
E-mail: club@royalthames.com;
Web: www.royalthames.com)
Secretary: Capt. D. Goldson, RN

St Stephen's Constitutional Club
34 Queen Anne's Gate, London, SW1H 9AB
(Tel: 020-7222 1382; Fax: 020-7222 8740)
Secretary: L. D. Mawby

Savage Club
1 Whitehall Place, London, SW1A 2HD
(Tel: 020-7930 8118)
Hon. Secretary: The Ven. B. H. Lucas, CB

Savile Club
69 Brook Street, London, W1K 4ER
(Tel: 020-7629 5462; Fax: 020-7499 7087;
E-mail: adminstration@savileclub.co.uk;
Web: www.savileclub.co.uk)
Secretary: N. Storey

Thames Rowing Club
Embankment, Putney, London, SW15 1LB
(Tel: 020-8788 0798; Fax: 020-8788 0798;
E-mail: contact@thamesrc.co.uk;
Web: www.thamesrc.co.uk)
Hon. Secretary: J. R. Elder

Travellers Club
106 Pall Mall, London, SW1Y 5EP
(Tel: 020-7930 8688; Fax: 020-7930 2019;
E-mail: secretary@thetravellersclub.org.uk;
Web: www.csma.org.uk)
Secretary: M. S. Allcock

Turf Club
5 Carlton House Terrace, London, SW1Y 5AQ
(Tel: 020-7930 8555; Fax: 020-7930 7206;
E-mail: mail@turfclub.co.uk)
Secretary: Lt.-Col. O. R. StJ. Breakwell, MBE

United Oxford and Cambridge University Club
71 Pall Mall, London, SW1Y 5HD
(Tel: 020-7930 5151; Fax: 020-7930 9490;
E-mail: uocuc@uocuc.demon.co.uk;
Web: www.uocuc.co.uk)
Secretary: G. R. Buchanan

The University Women's Club
2 Audley Square, London, W1K 1DB
(Tel: 020-7499 2268; Fax: 020-7499 7046;
E-mail: uwc@uwc-london.com;
Web: www.universitywomensclub.com)
Secretary: Adrienne Winchester

382 Cultural London

Victory Services Club
63–79 Seymour Street, London, W2 2HF
(Tel: 020-7723 4474; Fax: 020-7724 1134;
E-mail: office@vsc.co.uk;
Web: www.vsc.co.uk)
General Manager: G. F. Taylor

Wig and Pen Club
229-230 Strand, London, WC2R 1BA
(Tel: 020-7583 7255; Fax: 020-8293 4321)
Chairman: E. Ertan

DOWNING STREET

10 Downing Street, London SW1A 2AA
(Tel: 020-7270 3000; Fax: 020-7925 0918;
Web: www.number-10.gov.uk).

Number 10 Downing Street is the official town residence of the Prime Minister, No. 11 of the Chancellor of the Exchequer and No. 12 is the office of the Government Whips. The street was named after Sir George Downing, Bt., soldier and diplomatist, who was MP for Morpeth from 1660 to 1684. Chequers, a Tudor mansion in the Chilterns near Princes Risborough, was presented by Lord and Lady Lee of Fareham in 1917 to serve, from 1921, as a country residence for the Prime Minister of the day.

GEORGE INN
Borough High Street, London SE1.

The last galleried inn in London, built in 1677. Now run as an ordinary public house.

GREENWICH
Royal Observatory, Greenwich, London SE10 9NF (Tel: 020-8858 6575; Fax: 020-8312 6734; Web: www.rog.nmm.ac.uk).
National Maritime Museum, same address as above Tel: 020-8858 4422; Fax: 020-8312 6632; Web: www.nmm.ac.uk).

The Royal Naval College was until 1873 the Greenwich Hospital. It was built by Charles II, largely from designs by John Webb, and by Queen Anne and William III, from designs by Wren. It stands on the site of an ancient royal palace and of the more recent Palace of Placentia constructed by Humphrey, Duke of Gloucester (1391-1447), son of Henry IV. Henry VIII, Mary I and Elizabeth I were born in the royal palace (which reverted to the Crown in 1447) and Edward VI died there.

Greenwich Park was enclosed by Humphrey, Duke of Gloucester, and laid out by Charles II from the designs of Le Nôtre. On a hill in Greenwich Park is the former Royal Observatory (founded 1675). Its buildings are now managed by the National Maritime Museum and the earliest observatory is named Flamsteed House, after John Flamsteed (1646-1719), the first Astronomer Royal. The Cutty Sark, the last of the famous tea clippers, has been preserved next to Greenwich Pier as a memorial to ships and men of a past Era. Sir Francis Chichester's round-the-world yacht, Gipsy Moth IV, can also be seen.

HISTORIC BUILDINGS

DR JOHNSON'S HOUSE
17 Gough Square, London EC4A 3DE
(Tel: 020-7353 3745;
Email: curator@drjh.dircon.co.uk;
Web: www.drjh.dircon.co.uk).

Home of Samuel Johnson, Poet, essayist, novelist and compiler of a 'Dictionary of the English Language'. Lived at Gough Square for ten years and is buried in Westminster Abbey.

ELTHAM PALACE
Court Yard, Eltham, London SE9 5QE
(Tel: 020-8294 2548; Fax: 020-8294 2621;
Web: www.english-heritage.org.uk).

Eltham Palace combines a 1930s country house and remains of a medieval palace set in moated gardens. It was used as a royal residence until the 16th century. It was eventually bought and rebuilt by the Courtauld family in 1935.

THE GUILDHALL
PO Box 270, London EC2P 2EJ (Tel: 020-7332 1460; Web: www.cityoflondon.gov.uk).

The Guildhall is the centre of civic government of the City. It was built between 1411-1429 and the facade built 1788-9. It is the only secular stone structure dating from before 1666 still standing in the city. The Great Hall is the third largest civic hall in England and was the site of the trial of Lady Jane Grey in 1553. The Guildhall is still used as a venue for the meetings of the Corporation of London elected assembly, the Court of Common Council and for the Honorary Freedom of the City Ceremony as well as for state banquets in honour of royalty and state visits.

HM TOWER OF LONDON
London EC3N 4AB (Tel: 020-7709 0765; Fax: 020-7680 0687; Web: www.hrp.org.uk).

The construction of what we now call 'the Tower of London' was begun by William the Conqueror around 1080 with the building of the White Tower. Over the next two centuries, this was encircled with two curtain walls containing a further twenty one towers and a moat. During the Middle Ages, the Tower was a royal palace and a place of refuge for the monarch, as well as a mint, armoury, zoo, treasury and prison. Under the Tudors, many religious and political prisoners were held here, including Sir Thomas More, Lady Jane Grey and two of Henry VIII's Queens. This period also saw many executions, both inside the castle or outside on Tower Hill. While the appearance of many parts has changed over the centuries, the survival of so many medieval buildings is exceptional. The Tower of London now houses parts of the Royal Armouries collection of arms and armour, and is world-famous as the home of the Crown Jewels.

HORSE GUARDS
Whitehall, London SW1 (Tel: 020-7414 2353; Fax: 020-7414 2352).

Archway and offices built about 1753. The mounting of the guard takes place at 11 a.m. (10 a.m. on Sundays) and the dismounted inspection at 4 p.m. Only those with the Queen's permission may drive through the archway to Horse Guards' Parade (230,000 sq. ft), where the Colour is 'trooped' on The Queen's official birthday.

HOUSES OF PARLIAMENT
House of Commons Information Office, House of Commons, London SW1A 2TT (Tel: 020-7219 4272; Fax 020-7219 5839
Email: hcinfo@parliament.uk;
Web: www.parliament.uk);
House of Lords Information Office, House of Lords, London SW1A 0PW (Tel: 020-7219 3107; Fax: 020-7219 0620;
E-mail: hlinfo@parliament.uk).

The royal palace of Westminster, originally built by Edward the Confessor, was the normal meeting place of Parliament from about 1340. St Stephen's Chapel was used from about 1550 for the meetings of the House of Commons, which had previously been held in the Chapter House or Refectory of Westminster Abbey. The House of Lords met in an apartment of the royal palace.

The fire of 1834 destroyed much of the palace and the present Houses of Parliament were erected on the site from the designs of Sir Charles Barry and Augustus Welby Pugin between 1840 and 1867. The chamber of the House of Commons was destroyed by bombing in 1941 and a new Chamber designed by Sir Giles Gilbert Scott was used for the first time in 1950. Westminster Hall was the only part of the old palace of Westminster to survive the fire of 1834. It was built by William Rufus (1097-9) and altered by Richard II (1394-9). The hammerbeam roof of carved oak dates from 1396-8. The Hall was the scene of the trial of Charles I.

The Victoria Tower of the House of Lords is about 330 ft high, and when Parliament is sitting the Union flag flies by day from its flagstaff. The Clock Tower of the House of Commons is about 320 ft high and contains 'Big Ben', the hour bell said to be named after Sir Benjamin Hall, First Commissioner of Works when the original bell was cast in 1856. This bell, which weighed 16 tons 11 cwt, was found to be cracked in 1857. The present bell (13.5 tons) is a recasting of the original and was first brought into use in 1859. The dials of the clock are 23 ft in diameter, the hands being 9 ft and 14 ft long (including balance piece). A light is displayed from the Clock Tower at night when Parliament is sitting.

For security reasons tours of the Houses of Parliament are available only to those who have made advance arrangements through an MP or peer.

Admission to the Strangers' Gallery of the House of Lords is arranged by a peer or by queue via St Stephen's Entrance. Admission to the Strangers' Gallery of the House of Commons is by Members' order (Members' orders should be sought several weeks in advance), or by queue via St Stephen's Entrance. Queues are usually shorter after 6 p.m. Monday to Wednesday, on Wednesday mornings and on Thursdays after 2 p.m. The House does not always sit on Fridays. Overseas visitors may write to the Parliamentary Education Unit to obtain a permit to tour the Houses of Parliament, or obtain cards of introduction from their Embassy or High Commission to attend the public gallery.

KENSINGTON PALACE

State Apartments, Kensington, London W8 4PX (Tel: 020-7937 9561; Fax: 020-7376 0198; Web: www.hrp.org.uk).

Kensington Palace was built in 1605 and bought by William and Mary in 1689. It was adapted for royal residents by Chrisopher Wren at this time. Kensington Palace is also the birthplace of Queen Victoria. The Orangery was built for Queen Anne in 1704-5 and the formal 'Sunken Garden' opened in 1909. The Royal Ceremonial Dress Collection is housed here and the state apartments are open to the public.

LAMBETH PALACE

Lambeth Palace Road, London SE1 7JU (Tel: 020-7898 1200; Fax: 020-7261 9836; Web: www.archbishopofcanterbury.org).

Lambeth Palace has been the official residence of the Archbishop of Canterbury since 1200. It consists of a 19th-century house with parts dating from the 12th century a mixture of Tudor, Gothic and Neo-gothic architecture. There is also a library and gardens, which are occasionally open to the public. Visits by written application.

LLOYD'S

1 Lime Street, London EC3M 7HA (Tel: 020-7327 1000; Fax: 020-7626 2389; Email: lloyds-external-enquiries@lloyds.com; Web: www.lloydsoflondon.com).

The International insurance market which evolved during the 17th century from Lloyd's Coffee House. The present building was opened for business in May 1986, and houses the Lutine Bell. Underwriting is on three floors with a total area of 114,000 sq. feet.

LORD CHANCELLOR'S RESIDENCE

Lord Chancellor's Office Tours, House of Lords, London, SW1A 0PW. For enquiries call 020-7219 2184.

MARLBOROUGH HOUSE

Pall Mall, London SW1A 5HX (Tel: 020-7839 3411; Fax: 020-7930 0827; Email: info@commonwealth.int; Web: www.the commonwealth.org).

Built by Wren for the first Duke of Marlborough and completed in 1711, the house reverted to the Crown in 1835. In 1863 it became the London house of the Prince of Wales and was the London home of Queen Mary until her death in 1953. In 1959 Marlborough House was given by The Queen as the headquarters for the Commonwealth Secretariat and it was opened as such in 1965. The Queen's Chapel, Marlborough Gate, begun in 1623 from the designs of Inigo Jones for the Infanta Maria of Spain, and completed for Queen Henrietta Maria.

THE QUEEN'S HOUSE

Park Row, Greenwich SE10 9NF (Tel: 020-8858 4422).

The Queen's House was designed for Queen Anne (the wife of James I) by Inigo Jones as part of the Tudor Royal Palace of Placentia. This is now an exhibition venue run by the National Maritime Museum.

LONDON ATTRACTIONS

LONDON EYE

(Web: www.ba-londoneye.com). For further information and advance bookings, call 0870 5000 600.

The London Eye is a 450 ft high observation wheel situated on the South Bank of the River Thames, along from County Hall. The wheel provides a 30 minute ride offering spectacular panoramic views of the capital.

The wheel is 90 ft taller than the previous tallest wheel in Japan's Yokohama Bay, and has 32 pods attached, each with a 25 person capacity – a maximum of 800 passengers at a time (15,000 passengers per day). The wheel has planning permission in its current situation for five years, however, if the ride proves popular it may be able to have a longer life on the South Bank.

LONDON PLANETARIUM
Marylebone Road, London NW1 5LR
(Tel: 020-7487 0200; Fax: 020-7465 0862;
Web: www.madame-tussauds.com).

Open daily, star show and interactive exhibits.

LONDON ZOO
Regent's Park, London NW1 4RY
(Tel: 020-7722 3333; Fax: 020-7449 6579
Web: www.zsl.org/londonzoo).

London Zoo is one of the world's great zoos, committed to the conservation of wildlife and threatened habitats, and successfully breeding species facing extinction. There are daily events and activities at the zoo for people of all ages. The new web of life (www.weboflife.co.uk) exhibit explains biodiversity and the astonishing variety of life on earth.

MADAME TUSSAUD'S
Marylebone Road, London NW1 5LR (Tel: 0870 400 3000; Web: www.madame-tussauds.com).

Waxwork exhibition open daily.

MARKETS

The London markets are mostly administered by the Corporation of London.

Billingsgate (fish), Thames Street site dating from 1875, a market site for over 1,000 years, moved to the Isle of Dogs in 1982.

Borough, SE1 (vegetables, fruit, flowers), established on present site 1756, privately owned and run.

Covent Garden (vegetables, fruit, flowers), established in 1661 under a charter of Charles II, moved in 1973 to Nine Elms Lane.

Leadenhall, EC3 (meat, poultry, fish), built 1881, part recently demolished. London Fruit Exchange, Brushfield Street, built by Corporation of London 1928-9 as buildings for Spitalfields market; not connected with the market since it moved in 1991.

Petticoat Lane, Middlesex Street, E1, a market has existed on the site for over 500 years, now a Sunday morning market selling almost anything.

Portobello Road, W11, originally for herbs and horse-trading from 1870; became famous for antiques after the closure of the Caledonian Market in 1948; Saturdays.

Smithfield, Central Meat, Fish, Fruit, Vegetable and Poultry Markets, built 1851-66, the site of St Bartholomew's Fair from 12th to 19th century, new hall built 1963, market refurbished 1993-4.

Spitalfields, E1 (vegetables, fruit), established 1682, modernised 1928, moved to Leyton in 1991. A much smaller market is still on the original site on Commercial Street, selling arts, crafts, books, clothes and antiques; Sundays.

MONUMENTS

LONDON MONUMENT
(commonly 'The Monument'), Monument Street, London EC3.

Built from designs of Wren, 1671-7, to commemorate the Great Fire of London, which broke out in Pudding Lane on 2 September 1666. The fluted Doric column is 120 ft high; the moulded cylinder above the balcony supporting a flaming vase of gilt bronze is an additional 42 ft; and the column is based on a square plinth 40 ft high (with fine carvings on the west face) making a total height of 202 ft. Splendid views of London from gallery at top of column (311 steps).

MONUMENTS (Sculptor's name in brackets).

Albert Memorial (Durham); Kensington Gore; Royal Air Force (Blomfield), Victoria Embankment; Viscount Alanbrooke, Whitehall; Beaconsfield, Parliament Square; Beatty (Macmillan), Trafalgar Square; Belgian Gratitude (setting by Blomfield, statue by Rousseau), Victoria Embankment; Boadicea (or Boudicca), Queen of the Iceni (Thornycroft), Westminster Bridge; Brunel (Marochetti), Victoria Embankment; Burghers of Calais (Rodin), Victoria Tower Gardens, Westminster; Burns (Steel), Embankment Gardens; Canada Memorial (Granche), Green Park; Carlyle (Boehm), Chelsea Embankment; Cavalry (Jones), Hyde Park; Edith Cavell (Frampton), St Martin's

Place; Cenotaph (Lutyens), Whitehall; Charles I (Le Sueur), Trafalgar Square; Charles II (Gibbons), South Court, Chelsea Hospital; Churchill (Roberts-Jones), Parliament Square; Cleopatra's Needle (68.5ft high, c.1500 bc, erected on the Thames Embankment in 1877-8; the sphinxes are Victorian); Clive (Tweed), King Charles Street; Captain Cook (Brock), The Mall; Crimean, Broad Sanctuary; Oliver Cromwell (Thornycroft), outside Westminster Hall; Cunningham (Belsky), Trafalgar Square; Gen. Charles de Gaulle, Carlton Gardens; Lord Dowding (Faith Winter), Strand; Duke of Cambridge (Jones), Whitehall; Duke of York (124 ft), Carlton House Terrace; Edward VII (Mackennal), Waterloo Place; Elizabeth I (1586, oldest outdoor statue in London; from Ludgate), Fleet Street; Eros (Shaftesbury Memorial) (Gilbert), Piccadilly Circus; Marechal Foch (Mallisard, copy of one in Cassel, France), Grosvenor Gardens; Charles James Fox (Westmacott), Bloomsbury Square; George III (Cotes Wyatt), Cockspur Street; George IV (Chantrey), riding without stirrups, Trafalgar Square; George V (Reid Dick), Old Palace Yard; George VI (Macmillan), Carlton Gardens; Gladstone (Thornycroft), Strand; Guards' (Crimea) (Bell), Waterloo Place; (Great War) (Ledward, figures, Bradshaw, cenotaph), Horse Guards' Parade; Haig (Hardiman), Whitehall; Sir Arthur (Bomber) Harris (Faith Winter), Strand; Irving (Brock), north side of National Portrait Gallery; James II (Gibbons and/or pupils), Trafalgar Square; Jellicoe (Wheeler), Trafalgar Square; Samuel Johnson (Fitzgerald), opposite St Clement Danes; Kitchener (Tweed), Horse Guards' Parade; Abraham Lincoln (Saint-Gaudens, copy of one in Chicago), Parliament Square; Milton (Montford), St Giles, Cripplegate; The Monument (see above); Mountbatten, Foreign Office Green; Nelson (170 ft 2 in), Trafalgar Square, with Landseer's lions (cast from guns recovered from the wreck of the Royal George); Florence Nightingale (Walker), Waterloo Place; Palmerston (Woolner), Parliament Square; Peel (Noble), Parliament Square; Pitt (Chantrey), Hanover Square; Portal (Nemon), Embankment Gardens; Prince Consort (Bacon), Holborn Circus; Queen Elizabeth Gate, Hyde Park Corner; Raleigh (Macmillan), Whitehall; Richard I (Coeur de Lion) (Marochetti), Old Palace Yard; Roberts (Bates), Horse Guards' Parade; Franklin D. Roosevelt (Reid Dick), Grosvenor Square; Royal Artillery (South Africa) (Colton), The Mall; (Great War), Hyde Park Corner; Captain Scott (Lady Scott), Waterloo Place; Shackleton (Sarjeant Jagger),

Kensington Gore; Shakespeare (Fontana, copy of one by Scheemakers in Westminster Abbey), Leicester Square; Smuts (Epstein), Parliament Square; Sullivan (Goscombe John), Victoria Embankment; Trenchard (Macmillan), Victoria Embankment; Victoria Memorial, in front of Buckingham Palace; Raoul Wallenberg (Phillip Jackson), Great Cumberland Place; George Washington (Houdon copy), Trafalgar Square; Wellington (Boehm), Hyde Park Corner, (Chantrey) riding without stirrups, outside Royal Exchange; John Wesley (Adams Acton), City Road; William III (Bacon), St James's Square; Wolseley (Goscombe John), Horse Guards' Parade.

MUSEUMS AND GALLERIES

BARNET

The Museum of Advertising
45 Lyndale Avenue, London, NW2 2QB
(Tel: 020-7435 6540; Fax: 020-7794 6584;
E-mail: library@advertisingarchives.co.uk;
Web: www.advertisingarchives.co.uk)

Barnet Museum
31 Wood Street, Barnet, Herts, EN5 4BE
(Tel: 020-8440 8066)

The Jewish Museum – Finchley
The Sternberg Centre, 80 East End Road, London, N3 2SY (Tel: 020-8349 1143; Fax: 020-8343 2162; E-mail: jml.finchley@lineone.net; Web: www.jewmuseum.ort.org)

Royal Air Force Museum
Grahame Park Way, London, NW9 5L
(Tel: 020-8205 2266; Fax: 020-8200 1751;
E-mail: info@rafmuseum.com;
Web: www.rafmuseum.com)

Church Farmhouse Museum
Greyhound Hill, London, NW4 4JR
(Tel: 020-8203 0130; Fax: 020-8359 2666;
Web: www.earl.org.uk/partners/barnet/churchf.htm)

BAYSWATER

London Toy & Model Museum
21–23 Craven Hill, London, W2 3EN
(Tel: 020-7706 8000)

Museums and Galleries 387

BECKENHAM
Bethlem Royal Hospital Archives and Museum
Monks Orchard Road, Beckenham, Kent, BR3 3BX (Tel: 020-8776 4307)

BOW
The Nunnery
181 Bow Road, London, E3 (Tel: 020-8980 7770)

Matt's Gallery
42-44 Copperfield Street, London, E3 (Tel: 020-8983 1771)

BRENT
The Grange Museum
Neasden Roundabout Neasden Lane, London, NW10 1QB (Tel: 020-8452 8311; Fax: 020-8208 4233; E-mail: grangemuseum@brent.gov.uk; Web: www.brent.gov.uk)

BRENTFORD
The Musical Museum
368 High Street, Brentford, Middx, TW8 0BD (Tel: 020-8560 8108)

BROMLEY
Bromley Galleries
37 East Street, Bromley, Kent, BR1 1QL (Tel: 020-8466 6682; Fax: 020-8464 1561; E-mail: dennisknight@bromleygalleries.com; Web: www.bromleygalleries.com)

Bromley Museum
The Priory Church Hill, Orpington, BR6 0HH (Tel: 01689-873826; E-mail: bromley.museum@bromley.gov.uk; Web: www.bromley.gov.uk)

Crystal Palace Museum
Anerley Hill, London, SE19 2BA (Tel: 020-8676 0700; Fax: 020-8676 0700)

CAMBERWELL
South London Gallery
65 Peckham Road, London, SE5 (Tel: 020-7703 6120)

CAMDEN
British Museum
Great Russell Street, London, WC1B 3DG (Tel: 020-7323 8000; Fax: 020-7323 8616; E-mail: information@thebritishmuseum.ac.uk; Web: www.thebritishmuseum.ac.uk)

Camden Arts Centre
Arkwright Road, London, NW3

Dickens' House Museum
48 Doughty Street, London, WC1N 2LX (Tel: 020-7405 2127; Fax: 020-7831 5175; E-mail: dhmuseum@rmplc.co.uk; Web: www.dickensmuseum.com)

Freud Museum
20 Maresfield Gardens, London, NW3 5SX (Tel: 020-7435 2002; Fax: 020-7431 5452; E-mail: freud@gn.apc.org; Web: www.freud.org.uk)

Jewish Museum
129–131 Albert Street, London, NW1 7NB (Tel: 020-7284 1997; Fax: 020-7267 9008; E-mail: admin@jmus.org.uk; Web: www.jewmusm.ort.org)

Keats House
Keats Grove, London, NW3 2RR (Tel: 020-7435 2062; Fax: 020-7431 9293; E-mail: keatshouse@corpoflondon.gov.uk; Web: www.cityoflondon.gov.uk)

Percival David Foundation of Chinese Art
53 Gordon Square, London, WC1H 0PD (Tel: 020-7387 3909; Fax: 020-7383 5163)

Petrie Museum of Egyptian Archaeology
UCL Malet Place, London, WC1E 6BT (E-mail: petrie.museum@ucl.ac.uk; Web: www.petrie.ucl.ac.uk)

Pollock's Toy Museum
1 Scala Street, London, W1T 2HL (Tel: 020-7636 3452; E-mail: toymuseum@hotmail.com; Web: www.pollocks.wc.net)

Saatchi Gallery
98a Boundary Road, London, NW8 0RH (Tel: 020-7624 8299; Fax: 020-7624 3798)

388 Cultural London

Sir John Soane's Museum
13 Lincolns Inn Fields, London, WC2A 3BP
(Tel: 020-7405 2107; Fax: 020-7831 3957;
Web: www.soane.org)

CITY OF LONDON

Bank of England Museum
(Entrance in Bartholomew Lane)
Threadneedle Street, London, EC2
(Tel: 020-7601 5545; Fax: 020-77601 5808;
E-mail: museum@bankofengland.co.uk)

Barbican Gallery
Silk Street, Barbican, London, EC2Y 8DS
(Tel: 020-7382 7105; Fax: 020-7628 0364;
Web: www.barbican.org.uk)

HMS Belfast
Morgans Lane, Tooley Street, London, SE1 2JH
(Tel: 020-7940 6300; Fax: 020-7403 0719;
E-mail: hmsbelfast@iwm.org.uk)

Museum of London
150 London Wall, London, EC2Y 5HN
(Tel: 020-7600 3699;
Web: www.museumoflondon.org.uk)

St Brides Church Museum
Fleet Street, London, EC4Y 8AU
(Tel: 020-7427 0133; Fax: 020-7583 4867;
E-mail: info@stbrides.com)

CROYDON

Lifetimes Museum
Croydon Clock Tower, Katharine Street, Croydon, Surrey, CR9 1ET (Tel: 020-8253 1030; E-mail: museum@croydon.gov.uk; Web: www.croydon.gov.uk)

Riesco Gallery
Croydon Clock Tower Katharine Street, Croydon, Surrey, CR9 1ET (Tel: 020-8253 1030; E-mail: museum@croydon.gov.uk; Web: www.croydon.gov.uk)

DEPTFORD

Hales Gallery
70 Deptford High Street, London, SE8
(Tel: 020-8694 1194)

DOCKLANDS

Museum in Docklands Project Library & Archive
Unit C14, Poplar Business Park
Prestons Road, London, E14 9RL
(Tel: 020-7515 1162; Fax: 020-7538 0209)

EALING

Pitshanger Manor & Gallery
Walpole Park, Mattock Lane, London, W5 5EQ
(Tel: 020-8567 1227; Fax: 020-8567 0595;
E-mail: pitshanger@ealing.gov.uk;
Web: www.ealing.gov.uk/pitshanger)

ENFIELD

Forty Hall Museum
Forty Hill, Enfield, Middx, EN2 9HA
(Tel: 020-8363 8196; Fax: 020-8367 9098)

FARRINGDON

Eagle Gallery
159 Farringdon Road, London, EC1R 3AL
(Tel: 020-7833 2674; Fax: 020-7624 6597;
E-mail: emmahilleagle@aol.com)

Andrew Mummery Gallery
61-63 Compton Street, London, EC1
(Tel: 020-7251 6265)

GREENFORD

London Motorcycle Museum
Ravenor Farm 29 Oldfield Lane South, Greenford, Middx, UB6 9LB (Tel: 020-8575 6644; E-mail: thelmm@hotmail.com; Web: www.motorcycle-uk.com/lmm.htm)

GREENWICH

The Fan Museum
12 Crooms Hill, London, SE10 8ER
(Tel: 020-8305 1441; Fax: 020-8293 1889;
E-mail: admin@fan-museum.org;
Web: www.fan-museum.org)

Greenwich Borough Museum
232 Plumstead High Street, London, SE18 1JL
(Tel: 020-8855 3240; Fax: 020-8316 5754;
E-mail: beverley.burford@greenwich.gov.uk)

Museums and Galleries 389

Greenwich Citizens Gallery
151 Powis Street, London, SE18 6JL
(Tel: 020-855 3240; Fax: 020-8316 5954;
E-mail: beverley-burford@greenwich.gov.uk)

The Museum Installation
175 Deptford High Street, London, SE8 3NU
(Tel: 020-8692 8778; Fax: 020-8692 8122;
E-mail: moi@dircon.co.uk;
Web: www.moi.org.uk)

National Maritime Museum
Park Row, Greenwich, London, SE10 9NF
(Tel: 020-8858 4422; Fax: 020-8312 6632;
Web: www.nmm.ac.uk)

HACKNEY

Flowers East Gallery
199-205 & 282 Richmond Road, London, E8
(Tel: 020-8985 3333)

The Geffrye Museum
Kingsland Road, London, E2 8EA
(Tel: 020-7739 9893; Fax: 020-7729 5647;
E-mail: info@geffrye-museum.org.uk;
Web: www.geffrye-museum.org.uk)

HAMMERSMITH & FULHAM

CCA Galleries
517–523 Fulham Road, London, SW6 1HD
(Tel: 020-7386 4900; Fax: 020-7386 4919;
E-mail: gallery@ccagalleries.com;
Web: www.ccagalleries.com)

Museum of Fulham Palace
Bishops Avenue, London, SW6 6EA
(Tel: 020-7736 3233; Fax: 020-7736 3233)

HARINGEY

Haringey Museum and Archives Service
Bruce Castle, Lordship Lane, London, N17 8NU
(Tel: 020-8808 8772; Fax: 020-8808 4118;
E-mail: museum.services@haringey.gov.uk;
Web: www.haringey.gov.uk)

HOUNSLOW

Gunnersbury Park Museum
Gunnersbury Park, London, W3 8LQ
(Tel: 020-8992 1612; Fax: 020-8752 0686;
E-mail: gp-museum@cip.org.uk)

Kew Bridge Steam Museum
Green Dragon Lane, Brentford, Middx, TW8 0EN (Tel: 020-8568 4757; Fax: 020-8569 9978;
E-mail: info@kbsm.org; Web: www.kbsm.org.uk)

ISLINGTON

Five Years Gallery
40 Underwood Street, London, N1
(Tel: 020-7608 0331)

Foundation for Women's Art
3rd Floor, 11 Northburgh Street, London, EC1V 0AN (Tel: 020-7251 4881;
E-mail: www.museum-of-womansart.freeserve.co.uk)

Gallery Westland Place
13 Westland Place, London, N1
(Tel: 020-7251 6456)

Islington Museum
Islington Town Hall, Upper Street, London, N1 2UD (Tel: 020-7354 9442; Fax: 020-7527 3049)

London Canal Museum
12–13 New Wharf Road, London, N1 9RT
(Tel: 020-7713 0836;
E-mail: martins@dircon.co.uk;
Web: www.canalmuseum.org.uk)

The Lux Centre
2-4 Hoxton Square, London, N1
(Tel: 020-7684 2785)

One in the Other
41 Dingley Place, London, EC1
(Tel: 020-7253 7882)

Museum of the Order of St John
St John's Gate, St John's Lane, London, EC1M 4DA (Tel: 020-7253 6644; Fax: 020-7336 0587;
Web: www.sja.org.uk/history)

Victoria Miro Gallery
16 Wharf Road, London, N1
(Tel: 020-73336 8109)

Vilma Gold Gallery
66 Rivington Street, London, EC2
(Tel: 020-7613 1609)

White Cube2
48 Hoxton Square, London, N1
(Tel: 020-7930 5373)

KENNINGTON

Daniel Arnaud
123 Kennington Road, London, SE11
(Tel: 020-7735 8292)

KENSINGTON AND CHELSEA

National Army Museum
Royal Hospital Road, Chelsea, London, SW3 4HT (Tel: 020-7730 0717; Fax: 020-7823 6573; E-mail: info@national-army-museum.ac.uk; Web: www.national-army-museum.ac.uk)

Natural History Museum
Cromwell Road, London, SW7 5BD (Tel: 020-7942 5000; E-mail: direct@nhm.ac.net; Web: www.nhm.ac.uk)

Leighton House Art Gallery & Museum
12 Holland Park Road, London, W14 8LZ
(Tel: 020-7602 3316; Fax: 020-7371 2467;
Web: www.rbkc.gov.uk/leightonhousemuseum)

Science Museum
Exhibition Road, London, SW7 2DD
(Tel: 020-7942 4454)

Serpentine Gallery
Kensington Gardens, London, W2 3XA
(Tel: 020-7402 6075; Fax: 020-7402 4103;
Web: www.serpentinegallery.org.uk)

Victoria and Albert Museum
Cromwell Road, South Kensington, London, SW7 2RL (Tel: 020-7942 2000; Fax: 020-7942 2266; Web: www.vam.ac.uk)

LAMBETH

Florence Nightingale Museum
Gassiot House, 2 Lambeth Palace Road, London, SE1 7EW (Tel: 020-7620 0374; Fax: 020-7928 1760; E-mail: curator@florence-nightingale.co.uk; Web: www.florence-nightingale.co.uk)

Hayward Gallery,
Belvedere Road, London, SE1 8XX
(Tel: 020-7928 3144;
E-mail: visual-arts@hayward.org.uk;
Web: www.haywardgallery.org.uk)

The Museum of Garden History
Lambeth Palace Road, London, SE1 7LB
(Tel: 020-7401 8865; Fax: 020-7401 8869;
E-mail: info@museumgardenhistory.org;
Web: www.museumgardenhistory.org)

LEWISHAM

Horniman Museum and Gardens
100 London Road, London, SE23 3PQ
(Tel: 020-8699 1872; Fax: 020-8291 5506;
E-mail: enquiry@horniman.demon.co.uk;
Web: www.horniman.demon.co.uk)

MARYLEBONE

Lisson Gallery
52-4 Bell Street, London, NW1
(Tel: 020-7724 2739;
Web: www.lissongallery.com)

MAYFAIR

The Animation Art Gallery
13-14 Great Castle Street, London, W1N 7AD
(Tel: 020-7255 1456)

Annely Juda Gallery
23 Dering Street, London, W1
(Tel: 020-7629 7578)

Anthony Reynolds Gallery
5 Dering Street, London, W1
(Tel: 020-7491 0621)

Asprey Jacques Gallery
4 Clifford Street, London, W1
(Tel: 020-7287 7675)

Charlotte Street Gallery
28 Charlotte Street, London, W1
(Tel: 020-7255 2828)

Museums and Galleries

Entwistle Gallery
6 Cork Street, London, W1
(Tel: 020-7734 6440;
E-mail: info@entwistle.net)

Flowers Central Gallery
21 Cork Street, London, W1
(Tel: 020-7439 7766)

Gagosian Gallery
8 Heddon Street, London, W1
(Tel: 020-7292 8222;
E-mail: www.gagosian.com)

Greengrassi Gallery
39C Fitzroy Street, London, W1
(Tel: 020-7387 8747)

Laurent Delaye
11 Saville Row, London, W1
(Tel: 020-7287 1546)

Michael Hue-Williams Gallery
First Floor 21 Cork Street, London, W1
(Tel: 020-7434 1318)

Anthony d'Offay Gallery
9, 23 & 24 Dering Street, London, W1
(Tel: 020-7499 4100; Web: www.doffay.com)

Henry Peacock Gallery
38a Foley Street, London, W1
(Tel: 020-7323 4033)

RIBA
66 Portland Place, London, W1
(Tel: 020-7307 3770)

Robert Sandelson Gallery
5 Cork Street, London, W1
(Tel: 020-7439 1001)

Rocket Gallery
13 Old Burlington Street, London, W1
(Tel: 020-7434 3043)

Sadie Coles
35 Heddon Street, London, W1
(Tel: 020-7434 2227;
Web: www.sadiecoles.com)

Sprovieri Gallery
27 Heddon Street, London, W1
(Tel: 020-7734 2066)

Stephen Friedman
21-28 Old Burlington Street, London, W1
(Tel: 020-7494 1434)

Waddington Galleries
11–12 Cork Street, London, W1
(Tel: 020-2437 8611;
Web: www.waddington-galleries.com)

MERTON

Wimbledon Lawn Tennis Museum
Church Road, London, SW19 5AE
(Tel: 020-8946 6131; Fax: 020-8944 6497;
Web: www.wimbledon.org/museum)

Wimbledon Society Museum of Local History
22 Ridgway, London, SW19 4QN
(Tel: 020-8296 9914;
E-mail: mail@wimbledonmuseum.org.uk;
Web: www.wimbledonmuseum.org.uk)

MITCHAM

Wandle Industrial Museum
The Vestry Hall Annexe, London Road, Mitcham, Surrey, CR4 3UD (Tel: 020-8468 0127; Fax: 020-8685 0249;
E-mail: curator@wandle.org;
Web: www.wandle.org)

NEWHAM

Manor Park Museum
Romford Road, London, E12 5JY
(Tel: 020-8514 0274; Fax: 020-8514 8221;
E-mail: tommcallister@newham.gov.uk;
Web: www.newham.gov.uk/leisure/museums/mmp.htm)

NOTTING HILL

K D K Gallery
324 Portobello Road, London, W10 5RU
(Tel: 020-8960 4355)

RICHMOND UPON THAMES

Museum of Richmond
Old Town Hall, Whittaker Avenue, Richmond, Surrey, TW9 1TP (Tel: 020-8332 1141;
Fax: 020-8948 7570;
E-mail: musrich@globalnet.co.uk)

392 Cultural London

Orleans House Gallery
Riverside, Twickenham, Middx, TW1 3DJ
(Tel: 020-8892 0221; Fax: 020-8744 0501;
Web: www.richmond.gov.uk)

ST JAMES'S

White Cube
44 Duke Street, London, SW1
(Tel: 020-7930 5373; Web: www.whitecube.com)

SOHO

Frith Street Gallery
59-60 Frith Street, London, W1
(Tel: 020-7734 6440;
Web: www.frithstreetgallery.co.uk)

SOUTHWARK

The Argent Gallery
Unit 101, Oxo Tower Wharf Barge House Street,
London, SE1 9PH
(Tel: 020-7401 8454)

Bramah Museum of Tea and Coffee
1 Maguire Street, Butlers Wharf, London, SE1
2NQ (Tel: 020-7378 0222; Fax: 020-7378 0219;
E-mail: e.bramagh@virgin.net;
Web: www.bramaghmuseum.co.uk)

Cuming Museum
155-157 Walworth Road, London, SE17 1RS
(Tel: 020-7701 1342; Fax: 020-7703 7415;
E-mail: cuming.museum@southwark.gov.uk;
Web: www.southwark.gov.uk)

Delfina Project Space
51 Southwark Park Road, Lodnon, SE1
(Tel: 020-7357 6600)

Design Museum
Butlers Wharf, Shad Thames, London, SE1 1YD
(Tel: 020-7403 6933; Fax: 020-7378 6540;
E-mail: director@designmuseum.org.uk;
Web: www.designmuseum.org)

Dulwich Picture Gallery
Gallery Road, London, SE21 7AD
(Tel: 020-8693 5254;
Web: www.dulwichpicturegallery.org.uk)

Imperial War Museum
Lambeth Road, London, SE1 6HZ
(Tel: 020-7416 5000; Fax: 020-7416 5374;
E-mail: mail@iwm.org.uk;
Web: www.iwm.org.uk)

Jerwood Gallery
Jerwood Space, 171 Union Street, London, SE1
0LN (Tel: 020-7654 0173; Fax: 020-7654 0176;
E-mail: gallery@jerwoodspace.co.uk;
Web: www.jerwoodspace.co.uk)

Livesey Museum
682 Old Kent Road, London, SE15 1JF
(Tel: 020-7639 5604; Fax: 020-7277 5384;
E-mail: liveseymuseum@southwark.gov.uk)

London Fire Brigade Museum
Winchester House, Southwark Bridge Road,
London, SE1 0EG (Tel: 020-7587 2894;
Fax: 020-7587 2878;
E-mail: museum@london-fire.gov.uk)

The Old Operating Theatre Museum
9A St Thomas Street, London, SE1 9RY
(Tel: 020-7955 4791; Fax: 020-7378 8383;
E-mail: curator@thegarret.org.uk;
Web: www.thegarret.org.uk)

Percy Miller Gallery
39 Snowsfields, London, SE1 (Tel: 020-7207 4578)

The Pumphouse Educational Museum
Lavender Pond, Nature Park Lavender Road, off
Rotherhithe Street, London, SE16 5DZ
(Tel: 020-7231 2976; Fax: 020-7231 2976;
E-mail: c.marais@btclick.com)

Royal Festival Hall
South Bank, London, SE1 (Tel: 020-7921 0600)

Shakespeare Globe Exhibition
Bankside, London, SE1 9DT (Tel: 020-7902
1500; Fax: 020-7902 1515;
E-mail: exhibit@shakespearesglobe.com;
Web: www.shakespeare-globe.org)

Tate Modern
Bankside, London, SE1 (Tel: 020-7887 8008)

TOWER HAMLETS

Anthony Wilkinson Gallery
242 Cambridge Heath Road, London, E2
(Tel: 020-8980 2662)

The Approach Gallery
First Floor, 47 Approach Road, London, E2
(Tel: 020-8983 3878)

Bethnal Green Museum of Childhood
Cambridge Heath Road, London, E2 9PA
(Tel: 020-8983 5200; Fax: 020-8983 5225;
E-mail: d.lees@vam.ac.uk)

Chisenhale Gallery
64 Chisenhale Road, London, E3 5QZ
(Tel: 020-8981 4518; Fax: 020-8980 7169;
E-mail: mail@chisenhale.org.uk;
Web: www.chisenhale.org.uk)

Fordham Gallery
20 Fordham Street, London, E1
(Tel: 020-7247 0410)

Interim Art Gallery
21 Herald Street, London, E2
(Tel: 020-7729 4112)

Nylon Gallery
10 Vyner Street, London, E2
(Tel: 020-9893 5333)

Ragged School Museum
46–50 Copperfield Road, London, E3 4RR
(Tel: 020-8980 6405; Fax: 020-8983 3481;
E-mail: enquiries@raggedschoolmuseum.org.uk;
Web: www.raggedschoolmuseum.org.uk)

The Rossi Gallery
101 Brick Lane, London, E1 6SE
(Tel: 020-7377 9715)

The Showroom
44 Bonner Street, London, E2
(Tel: 020-8983 4115)

Whitechapel Art Gallery
Whitechapel High Street, London, E1 7QX
(Tel: 020-7522 7878; Fax: 020-7377 1685;
E-mail: director@whitechapel.org;
Web: www.whitechapel.org)

TWICKENHAM

The Museum of Rugby
Rugby Road, Twickenham, Middx, TW1 1DZ
(Tel: 020-8892 8877; Fax: 020-8892 2817;
E-mail: museum@rfu.com;
Web: www.rfu.com)

VAUXHALL

Gasworks Gallery
155 Vauxhall Street, London, SE11
(Tel: 020-7582 6848)

Milch Gallery
2-10 Tinworth Street, London, SE11
(Tel: 020-7735 7334)

WALTHAM FOREST

Vestry House Museum
Vestry Road, London, E17 9NH
(Tel: 020-8509 1917;
E-mail: vestry.house@al.lbwf.gov.uk)

William Morris Gallery
Lloyd Park Forest Road, London, E17 4PP
(Tel: 020-8527 3782; Fax: 020-8527 7070;
Web: www.lbwf.gov.uk/wmg)

WANDSWORTH

Wandsworth Museum
The Court House Garratt Lane, London, SW18
4AQ (Tel: 020-8871 7074; Fax: 020-8871 4602;
E-mail: wandsworthmuseum@wandsworth.gov.uk;
Web: www.wandsworth.gov.uk/museum)

WAPPING

The Wapping Project
Wapping Pumping House, Wapping Wall,
London, E1 (Tel: 020-7680 2080)

WESTMINSTER

Royal Academy of Arts
Burlington House, Piccadilly, London, W1S
0BD (Tel: 020-7300 8000; Fax: 020-7300 8001;
Web: www.royalacademy.org.uk)

Cabinet War Rooms
King Charles Street, London, SW1A 2AQ
(Tel: 020-7930 6961; Fax: 020-7839 5897;
E-mail: cwr@iwm.org.uk;
Web: www.iwm.org.uk)

394 Cultural London

Courtauld Institute Galleries
Courtauld Institute of Art Somerset House, Strand, London, WC2R 0RN (Tel: 020-7848 2526; Fax: 020-7848 2589; Web: www.courtauld.ac.uk)

Institute of Contemporary Arts
Nash House The Mall, London, SW1 (Tel: 020-7930 3647)

MCC Museum
Lord's Cricket Ground, London, NW8 8QN (Tel: 020-7289 1611; Fax: 020-7432 1062)

Royal Mews
Buckingham Palace, London, SW1A 1AA (Tel: 020-7839 1377; Fax: 020-7930 9625; E-mail: information@royalcollection.org.uk; Web: www.royal.gov.uk)

Mobile Home Gallery
42 Theobalds Rd, London, WC1 (Tel: 020-7405 7575)

National Gallery
Trafalgar Square, London, WC2N 5DN (Tel: 020-7747 2885; Fax: 020-7747 2423; E-mail: information@ng-london.org.uk; Web: www.nationalgallery.org.uk)

The Photographers' Gallery
5 & 8 Great Newport Street, London, WC2H 7HY (Tel: 020-7831 1772; Fax: 020-7836 9704; E-mail: info@photonet.org.uk; Web: www.photonet.org.uk)

Photology Photography Gallery
1st Floor 24 Litchfield Street, London, WC2H 9NJ (Tel: 020-7836 8600)

Polish Institute & Sikorski Museum
20 Princes Gate, London, SW7 1PT (Tel: 020-7589 9249)

National Portrait Gallery
2 St Martins Place, London, WC2H 0HE (Tel: 020-7306 0055; Fax: 020-7306 0056; Web: www.npg.org.uk)

The Queen's Gallery
Buckingham Palace, London, SW1A 1AA (Tel: 020-7839 1377; Fax: 020-7930 9625; E-mail: information@royalcollection.org.uk; Web: www.royal.gov.uk)

The Sherlock Holmes Museum
221B Baker Street, London, NW1 6XE (Tel: 020-7935 8866; Fax: 020-7738 1269; E-mail: sherlock@easynet.co.uk; Web: www.sherlock-holmes.co.uk)

Tate Britain
Millbank, London, SW1P 4RG (Tel: 020-7887 8000; Fax: 020-7887 8007; Web: www.tate.org.uk)

London's Transport Museum
The Piazza, Covent Garden, London, WC2E 7BB (Tel: 020-7379 6344; Fax: 020-7565 7254; Web: www.ltmuseum.co.uk)

Theatre Museum
1E Tavistock Street, London, WC2E 7PA (Tel: 020-7943 4700; Fax: 020-7943 4777; Web: www.theatremuseum.org.uk)

The Weiss Gallery
1B Albemarle Street, London, W1X 3HF (Tel: 020-7409 0035; Fax: 020-7491 9604; E-mail: mark@weissgallery.com; Web: www.weissgallery.com)

The Wellington Museum
149 Piccadilly, Hyde Park Corner, London, W1V 9FA (Tel: 020-7499 5676; Fax: 020-7493 6576)

Wallace Collection
Hertford House, Manchester Square, London, W1U 3BW (Tel: 020-7563 9500; Fax: 020-7224 2155; E-mail: information@wallace-collection.org.uk)

Westminster Abbey Museum
20 Deans Yard, London, SW1P 3PA (Tel: 020-7654 4831)

Zwemmer Gallery
First Floor 24 Lichfield Street, London, WC2 (Tel: 020-7240 4158)

WIMBLEDON

Wimbledon Windmill Museum
Windmill Road, Wimbledon Common, London, SW19 5NR (Tel: 020-8947 2825; Web: www.wimbledonwindmillmuseum.org.uk)

WOOLWICH

North Woolwich Old Station Museum
Pier Road, North Woolwich, London, E16 2JJ
(Tel: 020-7474 7244; Fax: 020-7473 6065;
E-mail: kathytaylor@newham.gov.uk;
Web: www.newham.gov.uk)

OPEN AIR THEATRE

Inner Circle, Regent's Park, London NW1 4NP
(Booking Line: 020 7486 2431/1933; Fax: 020-7487 4562; Web: www.open-air-theatre.org.uk).

Situated in Regent's Park, the Open Air Theatre is one of the largest theatres in London with seating for 1,187 people. The Theatre was founded in 1932 by Sydney Carroll and Robert Atkins. The existing auditorium was built in 1975 and is famous for its summer seasons of classical theatre including two plays by William Shakespeare, a Broadway musical and a play for children. Audiences may bring picnics or take advantage of the bar, buffet and barbecue facilities.

PARKS

Ashtead Common (500 acres), Surrey

Burnham Beeches and Fleet Wood (540 acres), Bucks. Purchased by the Corporation for the benefit of the public in 1880, Fleet Wood (65 acres) being presented in 1921

Coulsdon Common (133 acres), Surrey

Epping Forest (6,000 acres), Essex. Purchased by the Corporation and opened to the public in 1882. The present forest is 12 miles long by 1 to 2 miles wide, about one-tenth of its original area

Farthing Downs (121 acres), Surrey

Hampstead Heath (789 acres), London NW3. Including Golders Hill (36 acres) and Parliament Hill (271 acres)

Highgate Wood (70 acres), London N6/N10

Kenley Common (138 acres), Surrey

Queen's Park (30 acres), London NW6

Riddlesdown (90 acres), Surrey

Spring Park (51 acres), Kent

West Ham Park (77 acres), London E15

West Wickham Common (25 acres), Kent

Woodredon and Warlies Park Estate (740 acres), Waltham Abbey

Also smaller open spaces within the City of London, including Finsbury Circus Gardens

Maintained by Historic Royal Palaces

Hampton Court Gardens (54 acres), Surrey

Hampton Court Green (17 acres), Surrey

Hampton Court Park (622 acres), Surrey

See also Royal Parks.

ROMAN REMAINS

The city wall of Roman Londinium was largely rebuilt during the medieval period but sections may be seen near the White Tower in the Tower of London; at Tower Hill; at Coopers' Row; at All Hallows, London Wall, its vestry being built on the remains of a semi-circular Roman bastion; at St Alphage, London Wall, showing a succession of building repairs from the Roman until the late medieval period; and at St Giles, Cripplegate. Sections of the great forum and basilica, more than 165 metres square, have been encountered during excavations in the area of Leadenhall, Gracechurch Street and Lombard Street. Traces of Roman activity along the river include a massive riverside wall built in the late Roman period, and a succession of Roman timber quays along Lower and Upper Thames Street. Finds from these sites can be seen at the Museum of London. Other major buildings are the amphitheatre at Guildhall; remains of bath-buildings in Upper and Lower Thames Street; and the temple of Mithras in Walbrook.

ROYAL ALBERT HALL

Kensington Gore, London SW7 2AP
(Tel: 020-7589 3203; Fax: 020-7823 7725;
Email: sales@royalalberthall.com;
Web: www.royalalberthall.com).

The elliptical hall, one of the largest in the world, was completed in 1871. It was constructed in memory of Prince Albert, Consort of Queen Victoria. Designed by British Army Engineer Major General H. Y. D. Scott, the hall seats around 5,000 people. The brick exterior is decorated with a terracotta relief depicting the development of the arts and sciences through history. Since 1941 it has been the venue each summer for the Promenade Concerts founded in 1895 by Sir Henry Wood. Other events include pop and classical music concerts, dance, opera, sporting events, conferences and banquets.

ROYAL HOSPITAL, CHELSEA

Royal Hospital Road, London SW3 4SR (Tel: 020-7730 0161; Fax: 020-7881 5463; Email: chpen2000@aol.com; Web: www.chelseapensioner.org.uk).

Founded by Charles II in 1682, and built by Wren; opened in 1692 for old and disabled soldiers. The extensive grounds include the former Ranelagh Gardens and are the venue for the Chelsea Flower Show each May.

ROYAL OPERA HOUSE

Covent Garden, London, WC2E 9DD; Box Office, 48 Floral Street, London WC2E 7QA (Tel: 020-7304 4000; Fax: 020-7497 1256; Web: www.royaloperahouse.org.uk).

Home of The Royal Ballet (1931) and The Royal Opera (1946), The Royal Opera House is the third theatre to be built on the Covent Garden site. The first, the Theatre Royal at Covent Garden was opened in 1732 and was primarily a playhouse. This theatre was destroyed by fire in 1808 and replaced by the second Theatre Royal which opened in 1809. This Theatre was also destroyed by fire and replaced by the third and present theatre in 1858. The Theatre became the Royal Opera House in 1892. After extensive redevelopment and restoration the Theatre reopened in December 1999.

ROYAL PARKS

The Royal Parks of London are maintained and managed by The Royal Parks Agency. The Old Police House, Hyde Park, London W2 (Tel: 020-7298 2000; Royal Parks Police Tel: 020-7298 2076).

There are seven Royal Parks in London. They are Hyde Park; Kensington Gardens; St. James's Park and The Green Park; Regent's Park and Primrose Hill; Greenwich Park; Richmond Park;

Bushy Park. The Royal Parks Agency also manages Brompton Cemetery and a number of other public open spaces, including Parliament Square and Victoria Tower Gardens. The aims of the Agency are threefold:
* to offer peaceful enjoyment, recreation, entertainment and delight to those that use them.
* to enhance, protect and preserve the parks for this and future generations.
* to manage the parks with levels of efficiency and effectiveness in accordance with the key principals of public service as dictated by the Citizen's Charter.

Bushy Park

Covering an area of 1,100 acres, Bushy Park comprises of woodland areas and many ponds and streams which are fed by the Longford River. The park was created as three separate parks by Henry VIII and Cardinal Wolsey between 1500 and 1537 and is famous for its tree-lined avenues such as Chestnut Avenue leading to the Diana Fountain. Other facilities offered by the park are horse riding, fishing (by permit only), cycling tracks, cricket, hockey and rugby pitches, and a model boat pool.

Stockyard Education Centre, Bushy Park, Hampton Court Road, Hampton Hill, Middlesex TW12 2EJ (Tel: 020-8979 1586).

Greenwich Park

Greenwich Park was created in 1433 and is around 185 acres in size. As well as the Royal Observatory at its centre, the park also contains a deer enclosure and areas of formal gardens. Other facilities include tennis courts, rugby, cricket and hockey pitches, a children's playground and a children's boating pool.

Park Manager, Blackheath Gate, Greenwich Park, London SE10 8QY (Tel: 020-8858 2608).

Hyde Park

Hyde Park was originally formed in 1536 when the land was acquired for hunting purposes. Its most famous features include the Serpentine, a lake of approximately 11.34 hectares which has been used for swimming, boating and fishing; and

'Rotten Row', a riding track. Other facilities include bowling and putting greens, tennis courts, a playground, band concerts, a restaurant, cycle routes and an outdoor riding arena.

Park Manager, Rangers Lodge, Hyde Park, London W2 2UH (Tel: 020-7298 2100).

Kensington Gardens

The Gardens were originally formed in 1689 from land taken from Hyde Park, when William and Mary moved into Nottingham House, now Kensington Palace. The gardens were redesigned and extended by Charles Bridgeman in the Early 18th Century and have received only minor additions and alterations since. These include the Albert Memorial and the Italian Gardens. Other facilities include the Serpentine Gallery, playgrounds and sailing for model boats on Round Pond.

Park Manager, Magazine Storeyard, Magazine Gate, Kensington Gardens, London W2 2UH (Tel: 020- 7298 2117).

Regent's Park and Primrose Hill

The original planning of Regent's park was the responsibility of John Nash, Crown Architect and friend of the Prince Regent in 1811. The site includes the summit of Primrose Hill and boasts views of Westminster and the City. Originally the park was private, but it is now open to the public and incorporates numerous attractions and facilities. These include London Zoo, an Open Air Theatre, bandstands, tennis and netball courts, tennis and golf schools, an athletics track, cricket, softball pitches, rounders pitches, football, rugby, hockey, playgrounds, boating on the main lake and *The Waterbus* on the Regent's Canal.

Park Manager, The Store Yard, Inner Circle, Regent's Park, London NW1 4NR (Tel: 020-7486 7905).

Richmond Park

Richmond Park was enclosed as a hunting ground by Charles I in 1637 and still contains many of the characteristics of a deer park today. The park comprises of a mixture of Wetland, Woodland and numerous herds of Red and Fallow deer. In 1992 the park was given the status of a Site of Special Scientific Interest by English Nature.

Other facilities offered by the park are two public golf courses, horse riding, fishing on Pen Ponds and cycling tracks.

Superintendent's Office, Holly Lodge, Richmond Park, Surrey TW10 5HS (Tel: 020- 8948 3209).

St James's Park and The Green Park

Lying to the east of Buckingham Palace and The Mall, these parks were acquired by Henry VIII in the early 16th Century. Many minor alternations and improvements have taken place through the years but the park as it is today is markedly loyal to the original designs of Crown Architect John Nash in 1827.

Other facilities that the park has to offer are deck chairs, band concerts and a children's playground.

Park Manager, The Storeyard, St. James's Park, Horse Guards Approach, London SW1A 2BJ (Tel: 020-7930 1793).

ST JAMES'S PALACE

Pall Mall, London SW1 (Tel: 020-7930 4832; Fax: 020-7925 0795; Email: press@stjamespalace.gov.uk; Web: www.royal.gov.uk)

Built by Henry VIII; the Gatehouse and Presence Chamber remain; later alterations were made by Wren and Kent. The Chapel Royal is open for services on Sundays at 8.30 a.m. and 11.15 a.m. between the beginning of October and Good Friday (see Marlborough House for summer services in The Queen's Chapel). Representatives of foreign powers are still accredited 'to the Court of St James's'. Clarence House (1825) in the palace precinct is the home of The Queen Mother.

ST PAUL'S CATHEDRAL

The Chapter House, St Paul's Churchyard, London EC4M 8AD (Tel: 020-7246 8348; Fax: 020-7248 3104; Email: chapterhouse@stpaulscathedral.org.uk; Web: stpauls.co.uk).

St Paul's Cathedral was built during the years 1675-1710 at a cost of £747,660. The cross on the dome is 365ft above the ground level, the inner cupola 218ft above the floor. 'Great Paul' in the south-west tower weighs nearly 17 tons. The organ by Father Smith (enlarged by Willis and rebuilt by Mander) is in a case carved by Grinling Gibbons, who also carved the choir stalls.

SOMERSET HOUSE

Strand and Victoria Embankment, London WC2 (Tel: 020-7845 4600; Fax: 020-7836 7613; Email: info@somerset-house.org.uk Web: www.somerset-house.org.uk).

Somerset House was the property of Lord Protector Somerset, at whose attainder in 1552 the palace passed to the Crown, and it was a royal residence until 1692.

The river facade (600 ft long) was built in 1776-86 from the designs of Sir William Chambers. The eastern extension, which houses part of King's College, was built by Smirke in 1829. Somerset House has had many purposes including housing the Royal Academy (1771-1836), the Society of Antiquities and the Register of Births, Deaths and Marriages. After considerable refurbishment, Somerset House is now open to the public offering access to museums, galleries, cafes, shops and restaurants. The South Building houses the Gilbert Collection of decorative arts and the Courtauld Institute Gallery. Concerts are also held in the famous courtyard of Somerset House, one of London's newest open-air venues.

SOUTH BANK CENTRE

Box Office, Level 1, Royal Festival Hall, Belvedere Road, London SE1 8XX (Tel: 020-7921 0600; Fax: 020-7921 0821/0063; Email: boxoffice@rfh.org.uk; Web: www.rfh.org.uk).

The Royal Festival Hall and Hayward Gallery stand on the south bank of the River Thames on a site covering 27 acres of land dedicated to the arts. The South Bank Board directly manages the Royal Festival Hall (2,931 seats, opened in 1951 as part of the Festival of Britain), the Queen Elizabeth Hall (913 seats), the Purcell Room (367 seats), the Voice Box (77 seats), the Saison Poetry Library (housing the Arts Council Collection) and the Hayward Gallery (opened in 1968).

The Royal Festival Hall and Hayward Gallery host a range of concerts and events from jazz, classical, rock, world and folk music, the visual arts, poetry and literature to outdoor events and contemporary dance.

The National Touring Exhibition programme is also based on the South Bank and administered by the Board on behalf of the Arts Council of England, along with the Arts Council Collection of post-war art. The South Bank Centre shares the site with the independently managed Royal National Theatre and the National Film Theatre.

The National Film Theatre (opened 1952), administered by the British Film Institute, has three Auditoria showing over 2,000 films a year. The London Film Festival is held there every November.

The Royal National Theatre (opened 1976) stages classical, modern, new and neglected plays in its auditoria: the 1,160-seat Olivier theatre, the 890-seat Lyttleton theatre and the Cottesloe theatre which seats up to 400.

SOUTHWARK CATHEDRAL

London SE1 9DA (Tel: 020-7367 6700; Fax: 020-7367 6725; Email: cathedral@dswark.org.uk; Web: www.dswark.org).

Southwark Cathedral is mainly 13th century, but the nave is largely rebuilt. The tomb of John Gower (1330-1408) is between the Bunyan and Chaucer memorial windows in the north aisle; Shakespeare's effigy, backed by a view of Southwark and the Globe Theatre, is in the south aisle; the tomb of Bishop Andrewes (died 1626) is near the screen. The retro choir was the scene of the consistory courts of the reign of Mary (Gardiner and Bonner) and is still used as a consistory court. John Harvard, after whom Harvard University is named, was baptised here in 1607, and the chapel by the north choir aisle is his memorial chapel.

RIVER THAMES

The River Thames stretches from the sea as far inland as Teddington in Middlesex. The Port of London Authority is the governing body for the Thames.

There are numerous companies organising trips on the River Thames from sightseeing tours through to dinner cruises and corporate charters. The list below details a selection of companies offering such services.
Bateau London (Tel: 020-7925 2215)
Campion Launches (Tel: 020-8305 0300)

Catamaran Cruisers Ltd (Tel: 020-7987 1185; Fax: 020-7839 1034)
City Cruises (Tel: 020-7237 5134)
London Launches Ltd (Tel: 020-7930 3373)
Turk Launches Ltd (Tel: 020-8546 2434)
Westminster Passenger Services Association (Tel: 020-7930 4097)
Woods River Cruises. Tel: 020-7481 2711; Fax: 020-7481 8300
River Trip Line 0839 123432
(24 hour information on river trips)

BRIDGES

The bridges over the Thames from east to west. (Architect's name in parenthesis).

The Queen Elizabeth II Bridge—opened 1991, from Dartford to Thurrock
Tower Bridge—opened 1894
London Bridge—opened after rebuilding by Rennie, 1831; the new London Bridge opened 1973
Alexandra Bridge—built 1863-6
Southwark Bridge (Rennie)—built 1814-19; rebuilt 1912-21
Blackfriars Railway Bridge—completed 1864
Blackfriars Bridge—built 1760-9; rebuilt 1860-9; widened 1907-10
Waterloo Bridge (Rennie)—opened 1817; rebuilt 1937-42
Hungerford Railway Bridge (Brunel)—suspension bridge built 1841-5; replaced by present railway and footbridge 1863
Westminster Bridge—opened 1750; rebuilt 1854—62
Lambeth Bridge—built 1862; rebuilt 1929-32
Vauxhall Bridge—built 1811-16; rebuilt 1895-1906
Grosvenor Bridge—built 1859-60; rebuilt 1963-7
Chelsea Bridge—built 1851-8; replaced by suspension bridge 1934; widened 1937
Albert Bridge—opened 1873; restructured (Bazalgette) 1884; strengthened 1971-3
Battersea Bridge (Holland)—opened 1772; rebuilt (Bazalgette) 1890
Battersea Railway Bridge—opened 1863
Wandsworth Bridge—opened 1873; rebuilt 1940
Putney Railway Bridge—opened 1889
Putney Bridge—built 1727-9; rebuilt (Bazalgette) 1882-6; starting point of Oxford and Cambridge Boat Race
Hammersmith Bridge—built 1824-7; rebuilt (Bazalgette) 1883-7
Barnes Railway Bridge—built 1846-9; restructured 1893

Chiswick Bridge—opened 1933
Kew Railway Bridge—opened 1869
Kew Bridge—built 1758-9; rebuilt and renamed King Edward VII Bridge 1903
Richmond Lock—lock, weir and footbridge opened 1894
Twickenham Bridge—opened 1933
Richmond Railway Bridge—opened 1848; restructured 1906—8
Richmond Bridge—built 1774-7; widened 1937
Teddington Lock—footbridge opened 1889; marks the end of the tidal reach of the Thames
Kingston Bridge—built 1825-8; widened 1914
Hampton Court Bridge—built 1753; replaced by iron bridge 1865; present bridge built 1933

Two new footbridges are under construction; the Millennium Bridge will link the City and the new Tate Gallery of Modern Art; and a second bridge is being constructed alongside the railway on Hungerford Bridge

THAMES EMBANKMENTS

The Victoria Embankment, on the north side from Westminster to Blackfriars, was constructed by Sir Joseph Bazalgette (1819-91) for the Metropolitan Board of Works, 1864-70; the seats, of which the supports of some are a kneeling camel, laden with spicery, and of others a winged sphinx, were presented by the Grocers' Company and by W. H. Smith, MP, in 1874; the Albert Embankment, on the south side from Westminster Bridge to Vauxhall, 1866-9; the Chelsea Embankment, 1871-4. The total cost exceeded £2,000,000. Bazalgette also inaugurated the London main drainage system, 1858-65. A medallion (Flumini vincula posuit) has been placed on a pier of the Victoria Embankment to commemorate the engineer.

THAMES FLOOD BARRIER

Officially opened in May 1984, though first used in February 1983, the barrier consists of ten rising sector gates, spanning 570 yards from bank to bank of the Thames at Woolwich Reach. When not in use the gates lie horizontally, allowing shipping to navigate the river normally; when the barrier is closed, the gates turn through 90 degrees to stand vertically more than 50 feet above the river bed. The barrier took eight years to complete and can be raised within about 30 minutes.

400 Cultural London

THAMES TUNNELS

The Rotherhithe Tunnel, opened in 1908, connects Commercial Road, London E14, with Lower Road, Rotherhithe; it is 1 mile 332 yards long, of which 525 yards are under the river. The first Blackwall Tunnel (northbound vehicles only), opened in 1897, connects East India Dock Road, Poplar, with Blackwall Lane, East Greenwich. The height restriction on the northbound tunnel is 13ft 4in. A second tunnel (for southbound vehicles only) opened in 1967. The lengths of the tunnels measured from East India Dock Road to the Gate House on the south side are 6,215 ft (old tunnel) and 6,152 ft. Greenwich Tunnel (pedestrians only), opened in 1902, connects the Isle of Dogs, Poplar, with Greenwich; it is 406 yards long. The Woolwich Tunnel (pedestrians only), opened in 1912, connects North and South Woolwich below the passenger and vehicular ferry from North Woolwich Station, London E16, to High Street, Woolwich, London SE18; it is 552 yards long.

THEATRES

Collyer Hall Theatre
Kings College School, Southside Common, London, SW19 4TT
(Tel: 020-8255 5440; Fax: 020-8255 5445)

The Jack Brockley Theatre
410 Brockley Road, London, SE4 2DH
(Tel: 020-8291 1206;
Web: www.brockleyjacktheatre.co.uk)

Upstairs at the Gatehouse
1 North Road, London, N6 4BD
(Tel: 020-8340 3488; Fax: 020-8340 3466;
Web: www.upstairsatthegatehouse.com)

Watermans Art Centre
40 High Street, Brentford, Middx, TW8 0DS
(Tel: 020-8847 5651; Fax: 020-8569 8592;
Web: www.watermans.org.uk)

ARCHWAY

Jackson Lane Theatre
269 Archway Road, London, N6 5AA
(Tel: 020-8340 5226; Fax: 020-8348 2124
Web: www.jacksonslane.org.uk)

BLACKFRIARS

The Mermaid Theatre
The Mermaid Conference and Events Centre, Puddle Dock, London, EC4V 3DB
(Tel: 020-7236 1919; Fax: 020-7236 1819;
Web: www.the-mermaid.co.uk)

BRENT

Tricycle Theatre
269 Kilburn High Road, London, NW6 7JR
(Tel: 020-7372 6611; Fax: 020-7328 0795)
Hotline Number: 020-7328 1000
Seating Capacity: 225

BROMLEY

Bromley Little Theatre
North Street, Bromley, Kent, BR1 1SD
(Tel: 020-8460 3047)

Churchill Theatre
High Street, Bromley, Kent, BR1 1HA
(Tel: 020-8464 7131; Fax: 020-8290 6968;
Web: www.churchilltheatre.co.uk)

Wickham Theatre Trust
Wickham Theatre Centre
Corkscrew Hill, West Wickham, Kent, BR4 9BA
(Tel: 020-8777 9989).
Hotline Number: 020-8777 3037
Seating Capacity: 80–100

CAMDEN

The New Ambassadors Theatre
West Street, London, WC2H 9ND
(Tel: 020-7369 1761; Fax: 020-7836 8012;
Web: www.newambassadors.com)
Hotline Number: 020-7836 6111
Seating Capacity: 418

Bloomsbury Theatre
15 Gordon Street, London, WC1H 0AH
(Tel: 020-7679 2777; Fax: 020-7383 4080;
Web: www.thebloomsbury.com)
Hotline Number: 020-7388 8822
Seating Capacity: 550

Cockpit Theatre
Gateforth Street, London, NW8 8EH
(Tel: 020-7258 2920; Fax: 020-7258 2921)

Theatres 401

Diorama Theatre
34 Osnaburgh Street, Camden Town, London, NW1 3ND (Tel: 020-7916 5467; Fax: 020-7916 5467; Web: www.diorama-arts.org.uk)

Dominion Theatre
268–269 Tottenham Court Road, London, W1T 7AQ (Tel: 0870-0607 7400; Fax: 020-7580 0246; Web: www.london-dominion.co.uk)
Hotline Number: 020-7656 1888
Seating Capacity: 2182

The Donmar Warehouse Theatre
41 Earlham Street, London, WC2 H9L (Tel: 020-7240 4882; Fax: 020-7240 4878; Web: www.donmar-warehouse.com)
Hotline Number: 020-7369 1732
Seating Capacity: 251

Etcetera Theatre Club
265 Camden High Street, London, NW1 7BU (Tel: 020-7482 4857; Fax: 020-7482 0378)

Hampstead Theatre
98 Avenue Road, London, NW3 3EX (Tel: 020-7722 9224; Fax: 020-7722 3860; Web: www.hampstead-theatre.co.uk)
Seating Capacity: 174

The London Palladium
Argyll Street, London, W1F 7TF (Tel: 020 7734 6846).
Hotline Number: 020 7494 5020

New End Theatre
27 New End, London, NW3 1JD (Tel: 020-7794 9963)

Pentameters Theatre
Three Horseshoes, 28 Heath Street, London, NW3 6TE
(Tel: 020-7435 3648)

The Roundhouse
Chalk Farm Road, London, NW1 8EH (Tel: 020-7424 9991; Fax: 020-7424 9992; Web: www.roundhouse.org.uk)
Hotline Number: 020-7424 9800
Seating Capacity: 1400

CITY OF LONDON
The Bridewell Theatre
14 Bride Lane, London, EC4Y 8EQ (Tel: 020-7353 0259; Fax: 020-7583 5289; Web: www.bridewelltheatre.com)
Hotline Number: 020-7936 3456
Seating Capacity: 120-177

CROYDON
Fairfield Halls
Park Lane
Croydon, Surrey, Surrey, CR9 1DG
(Tel: 020-8681 0821; Fax: 020-8603 3838)

EDMONTON
Millfield Theatre
Silver Street, London, N18 1PJ
(Tel: 020-8807 6680; Fax: 020-8803 2801; Web: www.millfieldtheatre.co.uk)

GREENWICH
Bob Hope Theatre
Wythfield Road, Eltham, London, SE9 5TG (Tel: 020-8850 3702; Fax: 020-8850 8763; Web: www.bobhopetheatre.co.uk)
Seating Capacity: 201

Greenwich Theatre
Crooms Hill, London, SE10 8ES
(Tel: 020-8858 4447; Fax: 020-8858 8042; Web: www.greenwichtheatre.org.uk)
Hotline Number: 020-8858 7755
Seating Capacity: 423

HACKNEY
Hackney Empire
291 Mare Street, London, E8 1EJ
(Tel: 020-8510 4500; Fax: 020-8510 4530; Web: www.hackneyempire.co.uk)
Hotline Number: 020-8985 2424
Seating Capacity: 1200

HAMMERSMITH & FULHAM
Bush Theatre
Shepherd's Bush Green, London, W12 8QD (Tel: 020-7602 3703; Fax: 020-7602 3703; Web: www.bushtheatre.co.uk)
Hotline Number: 020-8743 3388
Seating Capacity: 105

The Lyric Theatre Hammersmith
King Street, London, W6 0QL
(Tel: 020-8741 6822; Fax: 020-8741 5965;
Web: www.lyric.co.uk)
Seating Capacity: 555

London Apollo Hammersmith
Queen Caroline Street, Hammersmith, London, W6 9QH (Tel: 020-8748 8660; Fax: 020-8846 9320; Web: www.london-apollo.co.uk)

Shepherds Bush Theatre
Shepherds Bush Green, London, W12 8TT
(Tel: 020-8354 3300; Fax: 020-8743 3218;
Web: www.shepherds-bush-empire.co.uk)

HOUNSLOW

The Tabard Theatre
2 Bath Road, London, W4 1LW
(Tel: 020-8995 6035; Fax: 020-8994 5985)
Hotline Number: 020-8995 6035
Seating Capacity: 49

ISLINGTON

The Courtyard Theatre
The Courtyard, 10 York Way, Kings Cross, London, N1 9AA
(Tel: 020-7833 0870; Fax: 020-7833 0870;
Web: www.thecourtyard.org.uk)
Hotline Number: 020-7833 0876
Seating Capacity: 70

The Kings Head Theatre
115 Upper Street, London, N1 1QN
(Tel: 020-7226 1916; Fax: 020-7226 8507)
Hotline Number: 020-7226 1916
Seating Capacity: 120

The Little Angel
14 Dagmar Pass, London, N1 2DN
(Tel: 020-7226 1787; Fax: 020-7359 7565;
Web: www.littleangeltheatre.com)
Seating Capacity: 100

Old Red Lion Theatre
418 St John Street, London, EC1V 4NJ
(Tel: 020-7837 7816; Fax: 020-7833 9818)

Pop Up Theatre
20–24 Eden Grove, London, N7 8EA
(Tel: 020-7609 3339; Fax: 020-7609 2284;
Web: www.pop-up.net)

Rosemary Branch Theatre
Shepperton Road, London, N1 3DT
(Tel: 020-7704 6665; Fax: 020-7249 4786;
Web: www.rosemarybranch.co.uk)
Hotline Number: 020-7704 6665
Seating Capacity: 50

Sadler's Wells Theatre
Rosebery Avenue, London, EC1R 4TN
(Tel: 020-7863 8198; Fax: 020-7863 8147;
Web: www.sadlers-wells.com)
Hotline Number: 020-7863 8000
Seating Capacity: 1500

St George's Theatre
Tufnell Park Road, London, N7 0PS
(Tel: 020-7607 7978; Fax: 020-7609 2427)

Theatre Futures
39 North Road, London, N7 9DP
(Tel: 020-7700 6877; Fax: 020-7700 7366)

Tower Theatre
Canonbury Place, London, N1 2NQ
(Tel: 020-7226 5111; Fax: 020-7226 5111;
Web: www.tower-theatre.org.uk)
Seating Capacity: 150

Union Chapel Project
Union Chapel, Compton Avenue, London, N1 2XD (Tel: 020-7226 3750; Fax: 020-7354 8343;
Web: www.unionchapel.org.uk)
Hotline Number: 020-7226 1686
Seating Capacity: 50–1000

Y Touring Theatre Co
10 Lennox Road, London, N4 3NW
(Tel: 020-7272 5755; Fax: 020-7272 8413;
Web: www.ytouring.org.uk)

KENSINGTON & CHELSEA

The Chelsea Theatre
Worlds End Place, Kings Road, London, SW10 0DR (Tel: 020-7352 1967; Fax: 020-7352 2024)
Hotline Number: 020-7351 1967
Seating Capacity: 100

The Finborough Theatre
118 Finborough Road, London, SW10 9ED
(Tel: 020-7244 7439; Fax: 020-7835 1853)
Hotline Number: 020-7373 3842
Seating Capacity: 50

The Gate Theatre
11 Pembridge Road, London, W11 3HQ
(Tel: 020-7299 5387; Fax: 020-7221 6055)
Hotline Number: 020-7229 0706
Seating Capacity: 100

Man in the Moon Theatre
392 Kings Road, London, SW3 5UZ
(Tel: 020-7351 5701; Fax: 020-7351 1873)
Hotline Number: 020-7351 2876
Seating Capacity: 68

The Royal Court Theatre
Sloane Square, London, SW1W 8AB
(Tel: 020-7565 5050; Fax: 020-7565 5001;
Web: www.royalcourttheatre.com)

LAMBETH

The Brix at St Matthews
St Matthews Church, Brixton Hill, London, SW2 1JF
(Tel: 020-7738 6604; Fax: 020-7738 6604)

The Landor Theatre
70 Landor Road, London, SW9 9PH
(Tel: 020-7737 7276; Fax: 020-7737 2728;
Web: www.fringetheatre.org.uk)
Hotline Number: 020-7737 7276
Seating Capacity: 55

The Old Vic
103 The Cut, London, SE1 8BN
(Tel: 020-7928 2651; Fax: 020-7261 9161;
Web: www.oldvictheatre.com)
Seating Capacity: 1077

Oval House
52–54 Kennington Oval, London, SE11 5SW
(Tel: 020-7582 0080; Fax: 020-7820 0990;
Web: www.ovalhouse.com)
Hotline Number: 020-7582 7680
Seating Capacity: 150

Royal National Theatre
Upper Ground, London, SE1 9PX
(Tel: 020-7452 3333; Fax: 020-7452 3344;
Web: www.nationaltheatre.org.uk)
Hotline Number: 020-7452 3000
Seating Capacity: 1160, 890 and 350

Young Vic Theatre
66 The Cut, London, SE1 8LZ
(Tel: 020-7633 0133; Fax: 020-7928 1585;
Web: www.youngvic.org)
Hotline Number: 020-7928 6363
Seating Capacity: 40–450

LEWISHAM

Blackheath Halls
23 Lee Road, London, SE3 9RQ
(Tel: 020-8318 9758; Fax: 020-8852 5154;
Web: www.blackheathhalls.com)
Seating Capacity: 650 and 250

The Deptford Albany
Douglas Way, London, SE8 4AG
(Tel: 020-8692 0231; Fax: 020-8469 2253;
Web: www.deptfordnet.org.uk/albany)
Seating Capacity: 239

Lewisham Theatre
Rushey Green, London, SE6 4RU
(Tel: 020-8690 2317; Fax: 020-8314 3144;
Web: www.lewishamtheatre.co.uk)

LOUGHTON

The Corbett Theatre
Rectory Lane, Loughton, Essex, IG10 3RY
(Tel: 020-8508 5983; Fax: 020-8508 7521;
Web: www.east15@ukonline.co.uk)

MERTON

Wimbledon Theatre
93 The Broadway, London, SW19 1QG
(Tel: 020-8543 4549; Fax: 020-8543 6637)

NEWHAM

Theatre Royal Stratford East
Gerry Raffles Square, London, E15 1BN
(Tel: 020-8534 7374; Fax: 020-8534 8381;
Web: www.stratfordeast.org.uk)
Hotline Number: 020-8534 0310
Seating Capacity: 460

404 Cultural London

PUTNEY

The Putney Arts Theatre
Ravenna Road, London, SW15 6AW
(Tel: 020-8788 6943; Fax: 020-8788 6940;
Web: www.putneyartstheatre.org.uk)

REDBRIDGE

Kenneth More Theatre
Oakfield Road, Ilford, Essex, IG1 1BT
(Tel: 020-8553 4464; Fax: 020-8553 5476;
Web: www.kenneth-more-theatre.co.uk)
Seating Capacity: 365

RICHMOND UPON THAMES

The Landmark Arts Centre
Ferry Road, Teddington, Middx, TW11 9NN
(Tel: 020-8977 7558; Fax: 020-8977 4830)
Hotline Number: 020-8977 7558
Seating Capacity: 342

Richmond Theatre
The Little Green, Richmond, Surrey, TW9 1QJ
(Tel: 020-8940 0220; Fax: 020-8948 3601)
Hotline Number: 020-8940 0088
Seating Capacity: 820

Richmond Shakespeare Society
Mary Wallace Theatre, The Embankment, Twickenham, Middx, TW1 3DU
(Tel: 020-8892 2565;
Web: www.rss-mwt.org.uk)

SOUTHWARK

Southwark Playhouse
62 Southwark Bridge Road, London, SE1 0AS
(Tel: 020-7652 2224; Fax: 020-7261 1271;
Web: www.southwark-playhouse.co.uk)

SUTTON

Charles Cryer Studio Theatre
39 High Street, Carshalton, Surrey, SM5 3BB
(Tel: 020-8770 4960; Fax: 020-8770 4969;
Web: www.charlescryer.org.uk)
Seating Capacity: 180

TOOTING

Nomad Puppets/Nomad Studio
37 Upper Tooting Road, London, SW17 7TR

TOWER HAMLETS

The Broomhill Opera
Wilton's Music Hall, Graces Alley, London, E1 8JB (Tel: 020-7702 9555; Fax: 020-7702 1414;
Web: www.broomhill.co.uk)
Seating Capacity: 300

The Space
269 Westferry Road, London, E14 3RS
(Tel: 020-7515 2453; Fax: 020-7987 0444;
Web: www.space.org.uk)
Hotline Number: 020-7515 7799
Seating Capacity: 100–140

WALTHAM FOREST

Waltham Forest Theatre
Lloyd Park Pavillion, Forest Road, London, E17 5EH (Tel: 020-8496 2640; Fax: 020-8521 3577;
Web: www.lbwf.gov.uk)

WANDSWORTH

Bridge Lane Theatre
Bridge Lane, off Battersea Bridge Road, London, SW11 3AD (Tel: 020-7228 5185; Fax: 020-7228 8828)
Hotline Number: 020-7228 8828
Seating Capacity: 500

The Grace Theatre
Latchmere Pub, 503 Battersea Park Road, London, SW11 3BW
(Tel: 020-7924 1517; Fax: 020-7585 2392;
Web: www.fringetheatre.org.uk)
Hotline Number: 020-7794 0022
Seating Capacity: 80

WESTMINSTER

Adelphi Theatre
Strand, London, WC2N 5HZ
(Tel: 020-7836 1166; Fax: 020-7379 5709)
Hotline Number: 020-7344 0055
Seating Capacity: 1500

Albery Theatre
St Martin's Lane, London, WC2N 4AU
(Tel: 020-7438 9700; Fax: 020-7438 9711)

Aldwych Theatre
Aldwych, London, WC2B 4DF
Hotline Number: 020-7416 6003

Apollo Victoria Theatre
17 Wilton Road, London, SW1V 1LG
(Tel: 0870-4000 800; Fax: 020-7834 6910;
Web: www.victoria-apollo.com)
Hotline Number: 020-7416 6059
Seating Capacity: 1524

The London Apollo
29 Shaftesbury Avenue, London, W1V 7DH
(Tel: 020-7437 3435; Fax: 020-7734 4076)

Arts Theatre
6–7 Great Newport Street, London, WC2H 71B
(Tel: 020-7836 3334; Fax: 020-7240 7018;
Web: www.artstheatre.com)

The Canal Café Theatre
Bridge House, Delamere Terrace, London, W2 6ND
(Tel: 020-7289 6056; Fax: 020-7266 1717;
Web: www.canalcafe.co.uk)
Hotline Number: 020-7289 6054
Seating Capacity: 60

The Cochrane Theatre
Southampton Row, London, WC1B 4AP
(Tel: 020-7430 2500; Fax: 020-7831 5476)

Comedy Theatre
7–10 Panton Street, London, SW1Y 4DN
(Tel: 020-7321 5300; Fax: 020-7321 5311;
Web: www.act-arts.co.uk)
Hotline Number: 020-7369 1731
Seating Capacity: 780

Theatre of Comedy
210 Shaftesbury Avenue, London, WC2H 8DP
(Tel: 020-7379 33345; Fax: 020-7836 8181)

Criterion Theatre
2 Jermyn Street, London, SW1Y 4AX
(Tel: 020-7839 8811; Fax: 020-7925 0596)

Delfont Mackintosh Theatres Ltd
Coventry Street, London, W1D 6AS
(Tel: 020-7930 9901; Fax: 020-7930 8970)

The Drill Hall
16 Chenies Street, London, WC1E 7EX
(Tel: 020-7307 5061; Fax: 020-7307 5062)

Drury Lane Theatre
Catherine Street, London, WC2B 5JF

The Duchess Theatre
Catherine Street, London, WC2 B5LA
(Tel: 020 7379 0495; Web: www.rutheatres.com)
Hotline Number: 020-7494 5075

English National Opera
The London Coliseum, St Martins Lane, London, WC2N 4ES
(Tel: 020-7836 0111; Fax: 020-7836 8379;
Web: www.eno.org)

Fortune Theatre
Russell Street, Covent Garden, London, WC2B 5HH (Tel: 020-7836 2238; Fax: 020-7497 5551)

Garrick Theatre
2 Charing Cross Road, London, WC2H OHH
(Tel: 020 7836 9396)
Hotline Number: 020-7494 5080

Gielgud Theatre
Shaftesbury Avenue, London, W1V 6AR
(Tel: 020-7437 6003; Fax: 020-7437 0784)
Hotline Number: 020-7494 5065
Seating Capacity: 882

Her Majesty's Theatre
Haymarket, London, SW1Y 4QL
(Tel: 020-7930 5343; Fax: 020-7930 8467;
Web: www.rutheatres.com)
Hotline Number: 020-7494 5400
Seating Capacity: 1161

Jermyn Street Theatre
16B Jermyn Street, London, SW1Y 6ST
(Tel: 020-7287 2875; Fax: 020-7287 3232;
Web: www.jermynstreettheatre.co.uk)

The Lyceum Theatre
21 Wellington Street, London, WC2E 7DA
(Tel: 020-7420 8100; Fax: 020-7240 4155)

Lyric Theatre
Shaftesbury Avenue, London, W1V 8ES
(Tel: 020-7437 5443; Fax: 020-7437 0783;
Web: www.rutheatres.com)

Open Air Theatre
Inner Circle, Regent's Park, London, NW1 4NP
(Tel: 020-7486 2431; Fax: 020-7487 4562;
Web: www.open-air-theatre.org.uk)
Hotline Number: 020-7486 2431
Seating Capacity: 1200

Palace Theatre
Shaftesbury Avenue, London, W1D 5AY
(Tel: 020-7434 0909; Fax: 020-7734 6157;
Web: www.rutheatres.com)
Hotline Number: 020-7434 0909
Seating Capacity: 1400

Peacock Theatre
Portugal Street, London, WC2A 2HT
(Tel: 020-7863 8216; Fax: 020-7314 9004;
Web: www.sadlers-wells.com)
Hotline Number: 020-7863 8222/8000
Seating Capacity: 1000

Phoenix Theatre
110 Charing Cross Road, London, WC2H 0JP
(Tel: 020-7369 1733)

The Place Theatre
17 Dukes Road, London, WC1H 9PY
(Tel: 020-7380 1268; Fax: 020-7383 2003;
Web: www.theplace.org.uk)

The Players Theatre
The Arches, Villiers Street, London, WC2N 6NG
(Tel: 020-7976 1307; Fax: 020-7839 8067;
Web: www.playerstheatre.co.uk)
Hotline Number: 020-7839 1134
Seating Capacity: 250

The Playhouse Theatre
Northumberland Avenue, London, WC2N 5DE
(Tel: 020-7839 4292; Fax: 020-7839 1195)
Hotline Number: 020-7839 4401
Seating Capacity: 786

Prince Edward Theatre
Old Compton Street, London, W1D 4HS
(Tel: 020-7437 2024; Fax: 020-7734 1454)
Hotline Number: 020-7447 5400
Seating Capacity: 1600

Prince of Wales Theatre
31 Coventry Street, London, W1D 6AS
(Tel: 020-7839 5972)

Queen's Theatre
Shaftesbury Avenue, London, W1D 6BA
(Tel: 020-7734 0869)

Royal Opera House
Covent Garden, London, WC2E 9DD
Tel: 020-7240 1200; Fax: 020-7240 0141;
Web: www.royaloperahouse.org)
Hotline Number: 020-7304 4000
Seating Capacity: 2000

St John's Smith Square
Smith Square, London, SW1P 3HA
(Tel: 020-7222 2168; Fax: 020-7233 1618;
Web: www.sjss.org.uk)
Hotline Number: 020-7222 1061
Seating Capacity: 780

Savoy Theatre
The Strand, London, WC2R 0ET
(Tel: 020-7836 8117; Fax: 020-7379 7322)

Shaftesbury Theatre
10 Shaftesbury Avenue, London, WC2H 8DP
(Tel: 020-7379 3345; Fax: 020-7497 0208)

Really Useful Theatres Ltd
Manor House, 21 Soho Square, London, W1D 3QP (Tel: 020-7494 5200; Fax: 020-7434 1217;
Web: www.rutheatres.com)

Strand Theatre
5 Aldwych, London, WC2B 4LD
(Tel: 020-7836 4144; Web: www.trh.co.uk)
Hotline Number: 020-7930 8800
Seating Capacity: 1050

Studio Theatre
North Westminster Community School, North Wharf Road, London, W2 1LF
(Tel: 020-7641 8424; Fax: 020-7641 8468)

Sunset Strip Theatre
30A Dean Street, London, W1V 5AN
(Tel: 020-7437 7229; Fax: 020-7434 1801;
Web: www.sunsetstrip.co.uk)
Hotline Number: 020-7437 7229
Seating Capacity: 60

The Talk of London
New London Theatre, Parker Street, off Drury Lane, London, WC2B 5PW
(Tel: 020-7405 1516; Fax: 020-7405 1121)

Theatre Royal Haymarket Ltd
18 Suffolk Street, London, SW1Y 4HT
(Tel: 0870-901 3356; Fax: 020-7389 9698;
Web: www.trh.co.uk)

Theatre Royal
Drury Lane, London, WC2B 5JF
(Tel: 020-7836 3687; Fax: 020-7379 6836;
Web: www.rutheatre.com)

Jerwood Vanburgh Theatre
Malet Street, London, WC1E 7HU
(Tel: 020-7636 7076; Fax: 020-7323 3865;
Web: www.rada.org)

Vaudeville
404 Strand, London, WC2R 0NH
(Tel: 020-7836 1820; Fax: 020-7836 1820)

Victoria Palace Theatre
Victoria Street, London, SW1E 5EA
(Tel: 020-7834 1317; Fax: 020-7828 6882)

Westminster Theatre
12 Palace Street, London, SW1E 5JF

Wigmore Hall
36 Wigmore Street, London, W1U 2BP
(Tel: 020-7486 1907; Fax: 020-7224 3800;
Web: www.wigmore-hall.org.uk)
Hotline Number: 020-7935 2141
Seating Capacity: 539

Wyndham's
Charing Cross Road, London, WC2H 0DA
(Tel: 020-7438 9700; Fax: 020-7438 9761)

The Duke of York's Theatre
St Martin's Lane, London, WC2N 4BG
(Tel: 020 7836 4615; Fax: 020 7565 6465)

WESTMINSTER ABBEY

The Chapter Office, Dean's Yard, Westminster Abbey, London SW1P 3PA (Tel: 020-7222 5152; Fax: 020-7233 2072; E-mail: press@westminster-abbey.org; Web: www.westminster-abbey.org).

The original abbey was a Benedictine monastery begun by Edward the Confessor in 1050, however, the present building was built by Henry III in 1245. The abbey contains the chapel of Henry VII, chapter house and cloisters, Edward the Confessor's shrine, tombs of kings and queens and many other monuments, including the grave of 'The Unknown Warrior' and Poets' Corner. The Chapter House was built by Royal Masons around 1250AD, and contains some of the finest medieval wall paintings and sculptures. The octagonal building still has its original floor of glazed tiles. The 11th Century Pyx Chamber houses abbey treasures and the Abbey Museum contains medieval royal effigies.

The Abbey is also the home of the Coronation Chair and has been the venue for numerous Coronoations since the church was established.

WESTMINSTER CATHEDRAL

Cathedral Clergy House, 42 Francis Street, London SW1P 1QW (Tel: 020-7798 9055/6; for service times: 020-7798 9097; Fax: 020-7798 9090; Web: www.westminstercathedral.org.uk).

Westminster Roman Catholic cathedral was built from 1895-1903 in the early Christian Byzantine style, by the architect J. F. Bentley. The campanile is 283 feet high.

WORLD SQUARES FOR ALL

(Trafalgar Square and Parliament Square)

For further information contact the GLA at Romney House, Marsham Street, London SW1P 3PY (Temporary address).

The World Squares for All initiative aims to improve pedestrian access to the historic area around Parliament Square and Trafalgar Square and to redesign, improve and enhance the setting of the listed buildings. The World Squares for All plan, prepared by a team of multi-disciplinary consultants led by Lord Norman Foster, was presented to the Deputy Prime Minister in August 1998. Key features are: no traffic in front of the National Gallery; to improve access to Trafalgar Square; Parliament Square to be transformed; to establish a new gateway between Trafalgar Square and the West End; Whitehall to be transformed and the purpose of the Cenotaph to be respected; Old Palace Yard to be reinforced as a public space. It is thought that work on this will be completed in 2004 at an estimated cost of £70 million.

TOURISM

London Tourist Information Service
(Tel: 0839-337799 or 020-7244 9999;
Fax: 020-7341 9999).

London Tourist Board and Convention Bureau
Glen House, Stag Place, London SW1E 5LT
(Tourist information: 0839-123456).

British Tourist Authority
Thames Tower, Black's Road, London W6 9EL
(Tel: 020-8846 9000; Fax: 020-8563 0302;
Web: britishtouristauthority.org;
www.visitbritain.com).

Chief Executive: J. Hamblin

English Tourism Council
Thames Tower, Black's Road, London W6 9EL
(Tel: 020-8563 3000; Fax: 020-8563 3254;
Web: www.englishtourism.org.uk).
Chief Executive: Mary Lynch

REASONS FOR VISITING* LONDON (PERCENTAGES AND MILLIONS)

	Overseas visits 1991	Overseas visits 1998	Domestic visits 1991	Domestic visits 1998
Holiday	49	50	41	27
Visiting Friends/Relatives	16	17	31	53
Business/Conference	23	22	21	16
Other	12	11	6	4
Total visits** (=100%) (millions)	9.2	13.5	6.6	11.6

* Staying one night or more
** Total visits includes visits made by residents of the Irish Republic, but percentages are based on figures which exclude them.
Source: Focus on London 2000, National Statistics © Crown Copyright 2001

TOP TOURIST ATTRACTIONS, BY NUMBER OF VISITS, 000s, 1998*

Ranking	Attraction	Total visits	Ranking	Attraction	Total visits
1	British Museum	5,620	11	Victoria and Albert Museum	1,110
2	National Gallery	4,770	12	London Zoo	1,053
3	Westminster Abbey	3,000	13	National Portrait Gallery	1,017
4	Madame Tussaud's	2,773	14	Royal Botanical Gardens	1,000
5	Tower of London	2,551	15	Royal Academy of Arts	913
6	Tate Gallery	2,181	16	Hampton Court Palace	605
7	St. Paul's Cathedral	2,000	17	National Maritime Museum	474
8	Natural History Museum	1,905	18	Imperial War Museum	472
9	World of Adventures	1,650	19	Rock Circus	455
10	Science Museum	1,600	20	Photographer's Gallery	400

* The number of visitors to the London Dungeon in 1998 is not available. In 1995 there were 610,000 admissions
Source: Focus on London 2000, National Statistics © Crown Copyright 2001

SPORT

An abundance of sports have developed in London over the centuries, ranging from some of the barbaric events of yesteryear to the sports that are enjoyed today.

ARCHERY

From its early development in ancient times until the 1500s the bow was a popular accoutrement and history shows it as being the most used of all weapons. The bow first appears in Egyptian artwork and folklore.

In 1252 Henry III (1207-1272) decreed that all men between the ages of 15 and 60 shall keep a bow and arrow. By 1388, Richard II (1367-1399) said that all men must practice the sport on Sundays and holidays. Henry VIII (1491-1547) introduced rules for the regulation of archery, and made such alternative pastimes as football and handball unlawful.

Queen Victoria (1819-1901) participated in archery and Henry VIII was a renowned bowman and patron of the sport, organising competitions during his reign. The first archery club in 1537, The Fraternity of St George was co-founded by Henry VIII. In 1787, as the Prince of Wales (later George IV (1762-1830)) established the 'prince's-length' with target distances of 60, 80 and 100 yards and the 'prince's reckoning' of various target rings of 9, 7, 5, 3 and 1 point. He was also patron of the Royal Toxophilite Society, Kentish Bowmen and the Royal British Bowmen and with royal commendation came an increase in the sport's popularity.

Archery was commonly practised at public schools including Harrow and Eton. A Harrow custom called shooting for the 'Silver Arrow' lasted until 1771, when it was abolished because "undesirable characters" were drawn to the school.

The citizens of London and surrounding areas used the fields around the capital from a very early date to practice the sport. This caused problems with the landowners who had enclosed their properties with hedges. Citizens pulled down these hedges which resulted in laws being passed allowing people direct access to the fields.

In 1661 in Hyde Park 400 archers took part in a grand display under the command of Sir E. Hungerford, Knight of the Bath. The Finsbury Archers marched to Hampton court in 1681 to shoot before the King at 160 yards. The King was so pleased with what he saw, he asked for the marshal to be presented and kissed his hand.

The father of modern archery is Sir Ashton Lever, a Lancashire baronet and antiquary, who also was the instigator of the Royal Toxophilite Society, founded in 1781. The formation of this society, prompted many other associations to form throughout England, Scotland and Wales (thought at first to be chiefly around London), with members stemming mainly from the gentry and aristocracy.

Between 1789 and 1793 a series of Annual General Meetings (AGM) for the archers of Great Britain were held in Blackheath. Later AGMs in 1794-5 took place in Dulwich. The Blackheath meetings were dominated by participants from the capital and surrounding areas. On 29 May 1792, there were a total of 13 societies competing against London, Kent and Surrey's 10 best clubs. The York Round for men consists of six dozen arrows at 100 yards, four dozen at 80 yards and two dozen at 60 yards for a total of 144 arrows. The Double York Round uses 288 arrows and has competitors shooting 144 arrows on each of the two days.

Revd Octavius Luard, writer of the archers' register, was convinced that meetings would not be a total success unless women competed. A few women appeared at the meeting on 25-26 July 1851 at Wisden's Cricket Ground in Leamington, where the Women's National Round was established. It consisted on four dozen arrows at 60 yards and two dozen at 50 yards for a total of 72 arrows, making a two-day competition a total of 144 arrows being shot. In 1947 came the Double Hereford for women, with two rounds of six dozen arrows at 80 yards, four dozen at 60 yards and two dozen at 50 yards for a total of 144, with a two-day competition having 288 arrows shot.

A meeting held at York in April 1845 saw women compete in public for the first time. However, in the following year (1846) they were absent once again. Female presence was established at the Grand National Archery Meeting (GNAM) in 1847 and continued from this date.

In 1864 a meeting was held at Alexandra Park, where construction of the Palace was just beginning. There were special trains from Kings Cross to take both the archers and spectators to Wood Green. The Grand National Archery Society received £400 from the Alexandra Park company directors, who considered the contest as a major public attraction.

The year 1875 saw the meeting return to the south east. This time the venue was the cricket ground at Richmond near Kew Gardens. The following year the chosen site was Sandown racecourse, which had just been completed.

Queen Victoria (1819-1901) was patron of the Royal British Bowmen and each year gave £25 each to the ladies and gentlemen for prizes. In 1834, the Queen and her mother HRH the Duchess of Kent became patrons of the St Leonards Archers at Hastings. By doing so the club was entitled to the Royal prefix. Prince Albert became a patron in 1840 and a series of prizes were give by the royal couple.

Today there are many archery clubs around the country, with meetings being contested annually.

Grand National Archery Society
Lilleshall National Sports Centre, Newport, Shropshire TF10 9AT Tel: 01952 677888; Fax: 01952 606019; E-mail: enquiries@gnas.org; Web: www.gnas.org).

BEAR AND BULL BAITING

A sport which today is rightly viewed as barbaric, bear baiting was introduced into England during the reign of King John (1199-1216) by a group of Italians and was displayed for the monarch in Ashby-de-la-Zouch. It is said that both King John and his court were highly delighted with the spectacle.

Elizabeth I (1558-1603) was such a fan of the sport that orders were issued via the Privy Council forbidding theatrical plays being held on Thursdays – the chosen day for bear baiting contests at Bankside.

Hockley in the Hole existed as a sporting arena from the times of Elizabeth I to those of William III (1650-1702) and events held at this venue saw bear and bull baiting, dog fights and gladiatorial contests. There were other sporting arenas located around the capital at Tothill Fields, Westminster, Saffron Hill, Clerkenwell and Marylebone.

Bears used for sport were the property of great nobles who were paid from taxes levied on the peasantry. The peasants were, in turn, given free admission to watch the baiting contests.

Both bears and bulls were chained to a stake in an arena or pit by a 15-foot chain which allowed movement within a 30-foot circle. The dog chosen to attack the bear would be held by the ears until it was filled with rage and would then be released.

For nearly seven centuries this sport was part of English life.

BILLIARDS/SNOOKER

The game of billiards has been attributed to several different countries including France, Spain, Italy and England. Originally the game was played on a table that did not have any pockets and each player had only two balls to use.

There is evidence that a form of billiards was played on a lawn with a stick called a mace and became a feature of Table Billiards. This version grew in popularity among not only English nobility, but also the French.

In London near the end of the 18th century there were a large number of inns, taverns and coffeehouses. These venues were used by famous men associated with the Arts and Sciences as clubs, to debate matters of interest.

A company called the Mail and Stage Coaches travelled to well-known taverns up and down the country. A man named John Thurston travelled throughout the country on the coaches setting up billiard tables, putting on the cloth and carrying out any necessary repairs.

By 1840, there were hundreds of billiard and bagatelle tables in principal inns, taverns and clubs throughout London and the rest of the country, which had been made by Thurston.

Thurston had his first factory in Newcastle Street in the Strand in 1799 and then moved to Catherine Street in 1814. He was the sole appointment granted the Royal Warrant of HM King William IV (1765-1837) in 1833 and again was the sole appointment granted the Royal Warrant of HM Queen Victoria (1819-1901) in 1837. Once again the Royal Warrant was give to Thurston in 1907, this time for HM King Edward VII (1841-1910) followed by another Royal Warrant in 1911 for HM King George V (1865-1936).

His continued improvements to billiards tables saw him earn the Prize Medal at the Great Exhibition in 1851 and 19 years later he moved his factory to 33 Cheyne Walk at Chelsea. In 1892 he designed and made the original 'standard' billiard table that was officially adopted by the Billiards Association.

J. Thurston's Company, now part of E. A. Clare and Son Ltd based in Liverpool, have the only billiard museum in the world and viewing is by appointment only. (Tel: 0151-207 1336).

The game of snooker apparently began in 1875 on a wet and miserable day in Jubbulpore, India. Days would be spent by British officers of the Devonshire regiment around the billiard tables devising new versions of the game.

An officer by the name of Sir Neville Chamberlain stared adding various coloured balls to the table and from this the basic form of snooker was started. It began with 15 red balls, a yellow, green, pink and black and years later the blue and brown were added. Word of this new game made its way back to England during the 1880s thanks to John Roberts, whom while in India in 1885 was introduced to Sir Neville.

The sport's popularity grew and in 1927 Joe Davis won his first World Championship taking home a mere £6 10s 0d. By the time Stephen Hendry took the Embassy World Championship trophy in 1994 the top prize was £180,000.

World Snooker
Ground Floor, Albert House, 111-117 Victoria Street, Bristol BS1 6AX (Tel: 0117-317 8200; Fax: 0117-317 8300;
E-mail: info@worldsnooker.com;
Web: www.worldsnooker.com).

BOXING

Starting in 1867 amateur boxing championships were held in three weight categories – light, middle and heavy. These contests followed the Marquis of Queensberry rules even though these rules were primitive and vague. Due to the way the championships were held, absurd decisions were often handed down. A group of leading London clubs decided to form an authoritative body and revised the rules.

A meeting was held on 21 January 1880 to revise the rules and to form an association. At a second meeting on 25 February a set of rules were drafted and the Amateur Boxing Association (ABA) was formed.

From the 16 agreed upon rules, the decision to have judges award points was so successful that it was quickly used not only by the professional side of the sport, but also throughout the world.

The first championships were held on 18 April 1881 and there were four weight categories – feather (9 stone), light (ten stone), middle (11 stone 4lbs) and heavy (no limit). All entrants paid five shillings and winners received a silver cup. The venue for the contests was St James's Hall (the present site of the Piccadilly Hotel) at Piccadilly, which could hold 2000 spectators and cost 35 guineas to hire.

Boxing rules were revised in 1898 with points being awarded for each round. There were two rounds of three minutes and one round of four minutes with five points being awarded in the first two rounds and seven points in the final round.

At the 1901 championships there were entrants from Ireland, Scotland and Wales, but English boxers won all titles.

In 1902 a boxing tournament was held at the Royal Albert Hall to commemorate the coronation of King Edward VII (1841-1910).

In 1906 it was decided that boxers would be required to take a medical examination before competing in the championships. This decision was brought about from the death of a boxer (though not affiliated to the ABA) at a Battersea Boxing Club novice competition.

Boxing was first included in the Olympic Games at London in 1908, however the number of entrants was not large.

In 1920 a meeting was held at Paris at which the ABA proposed to form a world federation. A constitution was accepted and the new body was called Fédèration Internationale de Boxe Amateur (FIBA). The headquarters for the FIBA are based in Atlanta, Georgia USA.

After creating a world association, the ABA also brought in three new championship weight categories – fly (8 stone), welter (10 stone 7lbs) and light-heavy (12 stone 7lbs).

The ABA enjoyed royal patronage for many years when the Prince of Wales granted the privilege by attending the championships in 1929 at the Royal Albert Hall and in 1936 King George VI became a patron. Following the death of George VI there was no royal patronage until 1953 when HRH the Duke of Edinburgh consented to become patron of the association.

The ABA prepared to re-create an International Association in 1945 and in London the following year more than 20 nations were present for a meeting. A new constitution was approved and it was agreed the new title would be Association Internationale de Box Amateur (AIBA).

In 1947 rule changes saw officials judging each bout and the referee moved inside the ring. Having a referee in the ring did not come into full effect until five years later.

Two new weights were added for the 1951 championships, these being – light-welter (10 stone) and light-middle (11 stone 2lbs).

The Amateur Boxing Association of England Ltd.
Crystal Palace, National Sports Centre, London SE19 2BB (Tel: 020-8778 0251; Fax: 020-8778 9324; E-mail: hq@abae.org.uk).

LONDON PRIZE-RING

The popular sporting venue of 'Great Booth at Tottenham Court' was the site for many bareknuckle fights along with Barnet and Finchley Common.

The Prince of Wales (later George IV) was the person responsible for a fight at Barnet on 17 April 1787 between Daniel Mendoza and Sam 'Bath Butcher' Martin. These two fighters were originally scheduled to do battle at Shepherd's Bush but on the order of a magistrate it was stopped. The Prince arranged for the fight to take place at a secret venue on the 16th so that it could proceed without interference from the magistrates. The location turned out to be a specially built stage at the Barnet Racecourse with 5000 spectators on hand including the Prince's brother the Duke of York. Following the Prince of Wales enthusiasm, the sport saw an increase in popularity as he frequented several matches between 1786 and 1788. However, after witnessing the death of a fighter at Brighton he said he would never watch another match.

Shortly before his coronation in 1820 the prince hired a man named John Jackson to get together 18 leading prize-fighters who would see that order was kept at Westminster Abbey during the ceremony.

This sport was undoubtedly one of London's most dramatic sporting pastimes, but over time its popularity wained.

COCKFIGHTING

The sport of cockfighting became an annual event for schoolboys on Shrove Tuesday. This event would take place in the school itself with desks being moved to make available the necessary space. The schoolmaster who supervised the fights would receive all cocks that were killed in combat and occasionally be given money from all pupils participating.

Henry VIII (1491-1547) had a cockpit built in the palace at Whitehall called the 'Royal Cockpit' thus popularising the sport. Although there is no evidence that he attended many fights, the fact that he acknowledged it was reason enough for society to follow it. Popularity in the sport quickly grew and when Elizabeth I (1533-1603) took the throne it had been firmly established. James I (1566-1625) recognised cockfighting as a national sport and went as far as appointing a 'cockmaster'. It was the cockmaster's responsibility to supervise the breeding, rearing and training of all birds that would appear in the royal arena. Other members of the monarchy who were patrons of the sport included Charles II (1630-1685), William III (1650-1702) and George IV (1762-183).

The 12th Earl of Derby was perhaps the most noted aristocratic figure who ever owned his own birds. After his death on 21 October 1834 an obituary was printed in The Sporting Magazine (December 1834) stating that he was the most celebrated cocker of either ancient or modern days.

Cockfights and horseracing began to be held simultaneously and its popularity increased. Towards the end of the 18th century and the beginning of the 19th cockfighting was an added attraction of race-weeks. During its heyday it attracted far more attention than horseracing.

From time to time authorities took steps to regulate the sport rather than stop it all together. There was a short-lived prohibitory measure in 1654 followed by a restrictive act in 1835, but the sport continued until the passing of the Cruelty to Animals Act in 1849.

CRICKET—LORD'S

The first reference to the game of cricket dates from Guildford around 1550. In Eltham, south-east London, church-warders and overseers fined seven of their parishioners 2 shillings each for playing cricket on the Lord's Day.

The earliest description of a cricket match was written in 1706 by the old Etonian, William Goldwin, who published a collection of poems in Latin. The poem 'In Certamen Pilae' describes a cricket match.

London society enjoyed cricket, but had yet to form any clubs. In 1719, Kent played London in the first county match. However, there are some that consider the matches in 1728 as the first real county matches.

Cricket first earned the patronage of royalty in 1723. Frederick, Prince of Wales (1707-1751), played his first match at Kensington Gardens in September 1735.

The formation in 1787 and the rise of the Marylebone Cricket Club (MCC) were significant events in the game. Other events of major importance are listed below under the heading 'Milestones'.

Cricket owes a great deal to Thomas Lord, the Yorkshireman, who migrated first to Norfolk with his family and then came to London to seek his fortune. He found employment at the White Conduit Club, which was formed at Islington in 1782, as a bowler and handyman.

Prompted by the Earl of Winchilsea, who could be considered the founder of the MCC and Charles Lennox, later the Duke of Richmond, a guarantee against loss was made to Thomas Lord if he would establish a new private cricket ground.

In May 1787, Lord opened his first ground on what is now Dorset Square. The last match played on these grounds was in 1810. In 1808 he developed two fields on the St John's Wood Estate, and for two years Lord had two grounds. As London was spreading outwards, Parliament forced Lord to move again as a decree was passed for the Regent Canal to be cut through the centre of the grounds. Lord found a new site, which is where Lord's now resides. The ground opened in 1814 and was immediately popular with both players and the public.

Thomas Lord sold his share of the ground for £5000 to William Ward (a director of the Bank of England and later an MP for the City of London). His contract with the famous ground ceased in 1825 and he died in Hampshire in 1832, aged 76.

A wooden pavilion was built in 1814 and later enlarged. In 1825, it was destroyed by fire and all the clubs original possessions: records, scorebooks and trophies were lost. A new pavilion was built in 1826 and enlarged again in 1865.

In 1816, E. H. Budd hit the first century at Lord's. The bat used for this milestone is located in the museum (Tel: 020-7289 1611). Both the Ashes urn (the trophy which England and Australia have competed for since England's 1882-3 tour of Australia) and the Widen trophy (awarded to the winners of the England and West Indies Test Series) are permanently housed at Lord's. During the 1840s and 1850s Lord's was also used for pony races once the cricket season ended.

Lord's was purchased in 1866. In 1868 the famous Tavern was built but in 1967 it was torn down and replaced with a public house and banqueting site.

In 1877 international matches between England and Australia started in Melbourne, with early test matches in England being played at The Oval and Old Trafford.

Milestones
1805 first Eton and Harrow match; 1806 first Gentleman v Players match; 1827 first Oxford v Cambridge match; 1837 jubilee of MCC celebrated with a match between North v South; 1846 first telegraph scoreboard installed; 1848 first printing tent erected on the ground and match cards sold; 1864 first groundsman hired; 1866-7 first Grandstand built; 1877 Middlesex County Cricket Club first played; 1884 first test match; 1898 first Board of Control for Test Matches met; 1906 press box built; 1937 MCC 150th anniversary; 1953 HRH The Duke of Edinburgh opened the Memorial Gallery in memory of all cricketers world-wide who lost their lives in the two World Wars; 1962 last Gentleman v Players match; 1963 first Gillette Cup final; 1972 first Benson & Hedges Cup final; 1975 first Prudential World Cup final; 1980 centenary test match between England and Australia; 1997 cricket's governing bodies form the England and Wales Cricket Board; 1999 the Cricket World Cup.

Lord's Cricket Ground
London NW8 8QN (Tel: 020-7432 1200; Web: www.ecb.co.uk
Ticket information: Tel: 0870-533 8833; E-mail: ticketing@mcc.org.uk;
For information regarding tours and entrance to the museum Tel: 020-7432 1033 or Fax: 020-7266 3825; E-mail: Tours@mcc.org.uk).

THE OVAL

For over 150 years The Oval has been the home of Surrey County Cricket Club and has witnessed some of the most significant moments in English sporting history.

In 1845, at the Horns Tavern in Kennington a meeting was held. A proposal transpired to form a cricket club for the county of Surrey and to find and bring together the playing strength of the county. A resolution was passed and a Surrey Club was born, but the formal inauguration was delayed until later that year.

The Duchy of Cornwall, who owned the property in Kennington Oval, was willing to let it for the purpose of a cricket ground. A lease was granted for 31 years at £120 per annum, with an additional charge of £20 for taxes.

The contract for turfing Kennington Oval was awarded to Mr M. Tuttle of Clapham Road for £300, with 10,000 turfs coming from Tooting Common and the first being laid in March 1845.

414 Cultural London

With lack of spectator seating and no pavilion, changes were necessary. By 1880, a stand, pavilion, tavern and scorebox had been erected.

There is a difference of opinion as to when the first match was played at The Oval. The first match officially connected with the Surrey Club was between the Gentlemen of Surrey and the Players of Surrey on 21-22 August 1845. Surrey's first County Championship match occurred on the 5 June 1873 against Sussex and was lost by 29 runs.

The year 1872 saw the first ever F.A. Cup final between The Wanderers and The Royal Engineers which was played at the Oval. The Cup finals continued until 1892, along with international football matches against Scotland and Wales. Rugby Union's first match in England versus Scotland (1872) and the first match between Oxford and Cambridge was played in 1873.

A remarkable run of County Championships were won by Surrey between 1890 and 1899. For over half a century, Surrey however, were not outright champions. Between 1952 and 1958 under the captaincy of Stuart Surridge, they achieved glory again. After rebuilding the amazing team of the 1950s, Surrey were not champions again until 1971.

Their first one-day championship came in 1974 when they won the Benson & Hedges Cup, followed by winning the NatWest Bank Trophy in 1982. Surrey CCC were Sunday League Champions in 1996, Benson & Hedges Cup winners again in 1997 and County Championship victors in 1999.

In 1988, The Oval was re-named The Foster's Oval, as a result of a sponsorship agreement with the Australian brewery.

Past-Presidents of Surrey CCC
1844 W. Strahan; 1856 H. Marshall; 1867 Col. F. Marshall (later General Sir F. Marshall); 1895 Sir Richard Webster (later Lord Alverstone); 1916 Sir Jeremiah Colman; 1923 The Earl of Midleton; 1926 G. H. Longman; 1929 H. D. G. Leveson-Gower; 1940 B. A. Glanvill; 1947 The Earl of Rosebery; 1950 Sir Walter Monkton; 1953 Lord Tedder; 1959 Viscount Monkton; 1965 Lord Nugent; 1969 C. Thain; 1960 M. J. C. Allom; 1978 W. E. Gerrish; 1979 Sir George Edwards, OM, CBE, FRSDL; 1980 A. R. Gover; 1981 W. S. Surridge; 1982 Brig. G. A. Rimbault, CBE, DSO, MC, DL; 1983 M. R. Barton; 1984 Sir Alexander Durie, CBE; 1985 The Rt. Hon. The Lord Carr of Hadley, PC; 1986 M. F. Turner; 1987 A. V. Bedser, CBE; 1988 Sir Michael Sandberg, CBE; 1989 C. G. Howard; 1990 E. A. Bedser; 1991 B. Coleman, OBE; 1992 W. D. Wickson / D. F. Cox; 1993 Sir John Stocker, MC, TD; 1994 J. M. Poland; 1995 P. B. H. Moy, CBE; 1996 J. Paul Getty, KBE; 1997 Mrs Betty Surridge; 1998-9 M. J. Steward, OBE.

The Foster's Oval
Kennington, London SE11 5SS
(Tel: 020-7582 6660; Fax: 020-7735 7769; E-mail: enquiries@surreyccc.co.uk; Web: www.surreyccc.co.uk;
Ticket information: Tel: 020-7582 7764 (9.30am – 4pm Monday to Friday) Fax: 020-7793 7520).

CRYSTAL PALACE

Crystal Palace was originally built in Hyde Park to host the Great Exhibition of 1851 and a year later moved to its current location in south east London. In 1914 King George V watched Burnley play Liverpool and by doing so became the first reigning monarch to attend a Cup Final. Fire completely destroyed the venue in 1936 and it remained derelict until 1951 when an Act of Parliament was passed to redevelop the site.

The building of a National Sports Centre was proposed by Sir Gerald Barry. Work started in 1960 and was completed in 1964.

Crystal Palace has also played host to many athletic meetings over the years featuring the best athletes from around the world including the world record holders Maurice Greene and Michael Johnson of the United States of America.

There are various outdoor and indoor training facilities including: an athletics stadium (consisting of a 400m – 8 lane track, floodlights, a grassed central area, seating capacity of 16,500) four swimming pools (racing, diving, and two for training), an indoor track, indoor arena, four badminton courts, five squash courts, two training halls, boxing hall, two weight rooms, fitness centre, dance studio and climbing wall.

It also houses one of the leading sports injury clinics in the country with consultants and expert specialists.

Crystal Palace
National Sports Centre, Ledrington Road, London SE19 2BB (Tel: 020-8778 0131; Fax: 020-8676 8754;
E-mail: janinec@crystalpalace.co.uk;
Web: www.crystalpalace.co.uk).

FOOTBALL

Around 200 BC in ancient China, a game called Tsu Chu was played using two 30-foot high bamboo poles as goal posts. This was followed with the Greek game Pheninda around the fourth century BC and involved kicking, running and handling a ball. The Romans called their game Haipastum, which was played on rectangular field between two teams, who defended the ends of the field. The ball was thrown amongst players who moved forward at all times in an effort to throw it over the opponents' goal line. Defenders were allowed to tackle and kick. Japan played a game around the fifth century AD called Kemari. It was played on a ground 14 metres square and involved eight players kicking the ball between themselves.

It was during the 15th and 16th centuries that the Italians started a game called Calcio (meaning to kick) in which two sides played in the town square at Florence, on the feast day of St John the Baptist.

There is written confirmation in the 12th century that a ball game was played on Shrove Tuesday at Ashbourne, Derbyshire. The idea was to gain ball possession and deliver it back to the town or parish.

Edwards II and III, Richard II, Henry V and Elizabeth I through the centuries had tried to ban the game, but were unsuccessful in stopping people's interest in the sport.

Modern football came into its own with the expansion of public schools in the mid-19th century. Schools including Harrow, Eton, Charterhouse and Westminster organised games that were a vital part of the curriculum, with emphasis on order, discipline and team spirit.

Ebenezer Cobb Morley was the first Secretary of The Football Association. The main aims were to draw up a set of rules that would be acceptable to its founding members. Captains and representatives from several London teams met on 26 October 1863 in the Freemason's Tavern at Lincoln's Inn Fields to arrange the rules 'for the regulation of the game of football'. However, the first attempt to draw up a set of rules was by Cambridge University in 1848.

The Secretary of The F.A. between 1870 and 1895 was Charles Alcock and in 1871 he decided to start a knock-out competition, similar to the one being played at Harrow. On 20 July 1871 at the office of The Sportsman, off Ludgate Hill in London a meeting was held. Alcock suggested that a Challenge Cup should be started, in which all the clubs belonging to The Association should be invited to attend. The motion was passed and three months later the F.A. Challenge Cup was born.

The first F.A. Cup final was splayed at Kennington Oval on 16 March 1872, before 2000 spectators. The match was between The Wanderers and The Royal Engineers with the aforementioned team winning by a score of 1-0.

On 30 November 1872 the first international match between England and Scotland was played at Partick near Glasgow.

July 1885 saw professional football legalised by The F.A. The formation of the Football League in 1888 and a second division in 1892 followed this.

Once again it was Charles Alcock who was the driving force behind the induction of an England team. It was 1908 before a full England squad went overseas to Austria, Hungary and Bohemia (now part of the Czech Republic) winning all their games. In 1923, Belgium were the first team from the continent to play an international match in England.

England's crowning glory on the international football stage came in 1966 at Wembley on 30 July, when they beat West Germany 4-2 in extra-time to win the World Cup.

The Football Association
25 Soho Square, London W1D 4FA (Tel: 020-7745 4545; E-mail: info@the-fa.org; Web: www.the-fa.org).

LONDON-BASED PROFESSIONAL FOOTBALL TEAMS

Dates shown in brackets indicate when the club was founded.

Arsenal Football Club (1886), Arsenal Stadium, Highbury, London N5 1BU (Tel: 020-7704 4000; Fax: 020-7704 4001; Ticket Office: 020-7704 4242; Email: info@arsenal.co.uk; Web: www.arsenal.co.uk)
Manager: Arsène Wenger
Shirt sponsor: Sega (Dreamcast)

Barnet Football Club (1888), Underhill Stadium, Barnet Lane, Barnet, Herts EN5 2BE (Tel: 020-8441 6932; Fax: 020-8447 0655; Ticket Office: 020-8449 6325)
Shirt sponsor: Maximuscle

416 Cultural London

Brentford Football Club (1889), Griffin Park, Braemar Road, Brentford, Middx TW8 0NT (Tel: 020-8847 2511; Fax: 020-8568 9940; E-mail: enquiries@brentfordfc.co.uk; Web: www.brentfordfc.co.uk)
Manager: Ray Lewington
Shirt sponsor: Patrick

Charlton Athletic Football Club (1905), The Valley, Floyd Road, London SE7 8BL (Tel: 020-8333 4000; Fax: 020-8333 4001; Ticket Office: 020-8333 4010; Web: www.cafa.co.uk)
Manager: Alan Curbishley
Shirt sponsor: Red Bus

Chelsea Football Club (1905), Stamford Bridge, Fulham Road, London SW6 1HS (Tel: 020-7385 5545; Fax: 020-7381 4831; Ticket Office: 020-7386 7799; Web: www.chelseafc.co.uk)
Manager: Claudio Ranieri
Shirt sponsor: Autoglass

Crystal Palace Football Club (1905), Selhurst Park, London SE25 6PU (Tel: 020-8768 6000; Fax: 020-8771 5311; Ticket Office: 020-8771 8841; Web: www.cpfc.co.uk)
Manager: Steve Bruce
Shirt sponsor: Churchill Insurance

Fulham Football Club (1879), Craven Cottage, Stevenage Road, London SW6 6HH (Tel: 020-7893 8383; Fax: 020-7384 4707; Ticket Office: 020-7384 4710; E-mail: enquiries@fulham-fc.demon.co.uk; Web: www.fulhamfc.co.uk)
Manager: Jean Tigana
Shirt sponsor: Demon Internet

Leyton Orient Football Club (1881), Matchroom Stadium, Brisbane Road, London E10 5NE (Tel: 020-8926 1111; Fax: 020-8926 1110; Ticket Office: 020-8926 1008)
Manager: Tommy Taylor
Shirt sponsor: Matchroom Sport

Queens Park Rangers Football Club (1882), Loftus Road Stadium, South Africa Road, London W12 7PA (Tel: 020-8743 0262; Fax: 020-8749 0994; Ticket Office: 020-8740 2575)
Manager: Ian Holloway
Shirt sponsor: Ericsson

Tottenham Hotspur Football Club (founded 1882), Bill Nicholson Way, 748 High Road, London N17 0AP (Tel: 020-8365 5000; Fax: 020-8365 5005; Ticket Office: 020-8365 5050; E-mail: hotspur@globalnet.co.uk; Web: www.spurs.co.uk)
Manager: Glen Hoddle

Watford Football Club (founded 1881), Vicarage Road Stadium, Watford, Herts WD1 8ER (Tel: 01923-496000; Fax: 01923-496001; Ticket Office: 01923-496010; E-mail: yourvoice@watfordfc.com; Web: www.watfordfc.com)
Manager: Gianluca Vialli
Shirt sponsor: Phones 4u

West Ham United Football Club (1895), Boleyn Ground, Green Street, Upton Park, London E13 9AZ (Tel: 020-8548 2748; Fax: 020-8548 2758; Ticket Office: 020-8548 2700; Web: www.whufc.com)
Manager: Glenn Roeder
Shirt sponsor: Dr Marten's

Wimbledon Football Club (1888), Selhurst Park Stadium, South Norwood, London SE25 6PY (Tel: 020-8771 2233; Fax: 020-8768 0640; Ticket Office: 020-8771 8841; Web: www.wimbledon-fc.co.uk)
Manager: Terry Burton

GREYHOUND RACING

Greyhounds can be traced back over 7000 years, with links to the ancient Egyptians and Mesopotamians and were also popular during the Roman Empire. These dogs can reach speeds of up to 61 km/h.

The first attempt to introduce the sport of greyhound racing occurred in 1876, in a field at Hendon, in north London, over a straight course of 400 yards. Even though an enthusiastic article appeared in The Times on 11 September, the novelty of the sport died out.

Attempts were made to entice the dogs onto an oval circuit, but after constant failure the idea of greyhound racing was abandoned for almost a quarter of a century.

Racing made its formal British debut at Belle Vue stadium at Manchester on 24 July 1926. Spectator turnout was low and organisers were faced with a financial loss. A week later, 16,000 people arrived at the stadium and the sport was established as a success. In 1927, racing moved to

London with an event at White City stadium in west London and attracted a crowd of approximately 100,000. Business increased and 30 dog tracks opened by the end of the year. There are currently four dog tracks located in the capital.

The National Greyhound Racing Club was formed in 1928 and rules governing the sport were introduced. Track-side betting is a distinguished part of racing and each course must possess a betting licence.

There are over 70,000 races run a year throughout Great Britain with 3.8 million spectators, track-side bets are in excess of £320 million and an incredible £1.7 billion being spent at various betting shops.

LONDON RACECOURSES

Catford Stadium, Adenmore Road, London SE6 4RJ (Tel: 020-8690 8000/2240; Fax: 020-8314 0223).

Romford Stadium, London Road, Romford, Essex RM7 9DU (Tel: 01708-762345; Fax: 01708-744899).

Walthamstow Stadium, Chingford Road, London E4 8SJ (Tel: 020-8531 4255; Fax: 020-8523 2747).

Wimbledon Stadium, Plough Lane, London SW17 0BL (Tel: 020-8946 8000; Fax: 020-8947 0821).

HORSERACING

It is suggested that horses have been domesticated since 2000BC and therefore could have possibly been raced as early as the bronze age.

Royalty in Britain has had a long association with the sport. King Richard I (1157-1199) imported breeding stock that he had seen in the East and racing was a natural result of this. Evidence shows regular racehorse sales and races were held at Smithfield in London.

As a result of horse losses during the War of the Roses, Henry VIII (1491-1547) set up royal studs at Hampton Court in Surrey, Eltham in south-east London, Tutbury in Staffordshire and Malmesbury in Wiltshire. There was also a racing stable in Greenwich.

Elizabeth I (1533-1603) raced at Croydon in 1574 and Salisbury in 1585. Charles II (1630-1685) not only participated in races, but set rules and served as a judge in disputes. William III (1650-1702) was also keen on the sport and more racecourses sprang up across the country. He restarted the Royal Stud at Hampton Court and hired William Tregonwell Frampton (1641-1727) as 'Keeper of the Running Horses' – a racing manager. The Royal Stud enjoyed success until it was dissolved in 1894.

While still the Prince of Wales, George IV (1762-1830) was the first royal to own a winning horse. At The Derby in 1788, he won with *Sir Thomas*. He was elected to The Jockey Club in 1921, but until his accession in 1936 took little part in racing.

The Princess Royal has won two races—the Diamond Stakes at Ascot in 1987 on *Ten No Trumps* and the Queen Mother's Cup at York on *Insular* in 1988. Princes Charles has also ridden in races, but without the success of his sister.

Racing at the beginning of the 18th century was in the form of matches. Records were kept in private match books, diaries and local records. Racing was transformed by the end of the century with shorter races and younger horses being utilised.

The number of entrants increased for two reasons. Handicapped races were introduced whereby horses would be assessed as to how much weight they should carry which was determined from past performances. The second was the number of sweepstakes that increased quickly from around 1770, as each owner contributed to the prize money. With more entrants running over shorter distances it was more exciting for the spectators and offered greater betting opportunities.

The Jockey Club that began as a London Gentlemen's Club had significant influence on the transformation of racing. It was over a century before the Club centralised the regulatory and administrative aspects of the sport. Starting in 1879 the Club ensured that jockeys were licensed and they could no longer own or partly own horses. Starting machines were introduced in 1896. In 1966 the Club began licensing women trainers, but women jockeys were not licensed until 1972 (amateur) and 1975 (professional). It was not until 1977 that the Jockey Club had elected its first women members.

The British Horseracing Board was founded in 1993 to take over the leadership and strategy of the racing industry. The day-to-day running of the sport is the responsibility of Weatherby's, a family firm going back to 1770, under contract to the British Horseracing Board.

418 Cultural London

There are five racecourses (Ascot, Epsom, Sandown, Windsor and Kempton) around the London area and the two classics held annually near the capital are both at Epsom Downs, Surrey and run over a distance of 1 mile 4 furlongs. The Derby was first run in 1780 and The Oaks first took place in 1779.

British Horseracing Board
42 Portman Square, London W1H 6EN
(Tel: 020-7396 0011; Fax: 020-7935 3626;
E-mail: info@bhb.co.uk; Web: www.bhb.co.uk).

THE LONDON MARATHON

Early in 1980 Chris Brasher (who ran in the 1979 New York marathon and later wrote a major article in The Observer) and Donald Trelford (then editor of The Observer) met with the Greater London Council, the police and a number of athletics' governing bodies. As a result of these meetings The London Marathon was born.

The budget for the first marathon was prepared by Brasher showing an expected expenditure of £75,000. Gillette became the first sponsors and offered £50,000 towards costs.

Brasher and John Disley established charitable status and devised six aims for the marathon:
- To improve the overall standard and status of British marathon running by providing a fast course and strong international competition.
- To show to mankind that, on occasions, the Family of Man can be united.
- To raise money for the provision of recreational facilities in London.
- To help London tourism.
- To prove that when it comes to organising major events, 'Britain is best'.
- To have fun and provide some happiness and sense of achievement in a troubled world.

On 29 March 1981 the first marathon was run. Around 20,000 people had applied to run, but only 7,747 were accepted. A total of 6,255 runners finished with Dick Beardsley of the United States and Inge Simonsen of Norway becoming the joint men's champions, while Joyce Smith became the women's champion and in the process broke the British marathon record.

After a successful first year the 1982 race had more than 90,000 applicants with 18,059 being accepted.

To date, 445,129 runners have completed the 26.2 mile course. More than £134 million has been raised for charity by entrants and The London Marathon has produced a surplus of £9,207,515 for The London Marathon Charitable Trust, which funds recreational projects throughout the capital.

From 1982–93 the race finished on Westminster Bridge, but repair work the following year forced organisers to move the finish line to The Mall, in front of Buckingham Palace, where it remains today.

The following companies have sponsored the marathon. Gillette 1981–3; Mars 1984–8; ADT 1989–92; NutraSweet 1993–5 and Flora 1996–2002.

Included in the marathon is the Flora/DSE Wheelchair London Marathon covering a 26.2 mile course, the Adidas mini marathon (2.65 miles) for boys and girls aged 11–17 and the Adidas mini wheelchair marathon for under 18's.

The 2001 London Marathon took place on the 22 April. Around 41,500 people were accepted to run with 30,071 actually finishing the race within 10 hours. An estimated £24 million was raised for various charities.

Winners of the 2001 race were in the men's race, Abdelkader El Mouaziz of Morocco winning in his fastest ever time of 2hr 7min 11sec, Paul Tergat of Kenya was second and defending champion Antonio Pinto was third. The Women's race was won by Derartu Tulu of Ethiopia in a time of 2hr 23min 56sec. Svetlana Zakharova of Russia was second and Joyce Chepchumba of Kenya was third. Both the winning runners received $55,000. The men's wheelchair race was won by Frenchman Dennis Lemeunir and the Women's Wheelchair race was won for a fifth time by Tanni Grey-Thompson of Great Britain.

The London Marathon
PO Box 1234, London SE1 8RZ (Tel: 020-7620 4117; Fax: 020-7620 4208;
Web: www.london-marathon.co.uk).

OLYMPICS

The modern Olympic Games were first contested in 1896 in Athens, Greece and Great Britain is one of only five countries to have competed in every version of the Games (Summer and Winter).

London hosted its first Games in 1908 from 27 April to 31 October with 22 countries participating. The site chosen as the main venue was the newly constructed complex that became known as White City in West London. Derived during the Games was what would become the standard marathon distance of 26 miles, 385 yards.

In 1948 the Games made a return to London. They were originally awarded to Rome, Italy, but in 1945 the Italian government informed the International Olympic Committee that they would be unable to host the Games because of financial problems.

The main events took place at Wembley from 29 July to 14 August, with 59 countries taking part. Live television broadcasts of the Games were transmitted to some 80,000 homes within range of the stadium.

RACKETS

The game of rackets originated in the 18th century in the Fleet and King's Bench debtor's prisons, where balls were hit against the high prison walls. Both closed and open courts were built, often in association with taverns and the games' popularity increased rapidly when the services and some leading public schools adopted it.

The first world champion was Robert Mackay in 1820 and the longest reigning champion is Geoffrey Atkins (1954-72).

A standard court has a floor measurement of 60' x 30', a front wall height of 32' and a back wall of 12 ½'. All walls have a surface of very hard black plaster.

Rackets has close links with real tennis and is governed by the Tennis and Rackets Association, which was founded in 1907. It's headquarters are based in West London at the Queen's Club.

REAL TENNIS

Real tennis is the oldest of all racquet games and unlike other racket games, it is a product of evolution rather than pure invention.

The forerunner of this games was first played in the 11th century. It started as hand ball played by monks around the cloister of monasteries in Italy and France. As the monks travelled to other monasteries, new rules were adopted and others abandoned.

The game was originally played with bare hands. Later a glove was used and then someone thought of attaching cord to the fingers to form a net, which could be tightened by stretching the hand. The next evolution was attaching the cord to a frame a adding a handle, hence the racket.

The first formal rules came into force in 1599 and bear a remarkable resemblance to those still used today. The court that Charles I (1625-1649) had built at Hampton Court is still used for championship play.

The golden age of tennis was the 16th and 17th centuries. It was the fashionable game of the court in England and France, but prohibited the ordinary citizens from taking part. Henry VIII (1509-1547) was an accomplished player.

The 18th century saw a decline in the game of tennis. In England there was a revival of sorts in the mid-19th century with the construction of many courts. There has been a resurgence in the game within the UK over the last decade with new courts being built around the country.

London area real tennis courts

The Burroughs Club (Middlesex University), Hendon Campus, 2 Campus Way, Greyhound Hill, London NW4 4JF (Tel: 020-8362 6343; Fax: 020-8411 5811).

The Harbour Club, Watermeadow Lane, London SW6 2RR (Tel: 020-7371 7700; Fax: 020-7371 7100).

MCC, The Tennis Court, Lord's Ground, St John's Wood Road, London NW8 8QN (Tel: 020-7432 1013; Fax: 020-7289 9100).

The Queen's Club, Palliser Road, West Kensington, London W14 9EQ (Tel: 020-7385 3421; Fax: 020-7386 8295).

The Royal Tennis Court, 69 Hampton Court Palace, East Molesey, Surrey KT8 9AU (Tel: 020-8977 3015; Fax: 020-8943 5382; E-mail: rtchcp@aol.com).

Tennis and Rackets Association, c/o The Queen's Club, Palliser Road, London W14 9EQ (Tel: 020-7386 3447/8; Fax: 020-7385 7424).

ROWING

Rowing began on the River Thames centuries ago with the wherry being used as the Londoner's water taxi. The wherry had a sharply-angled prow so it could nudge its way through a cluster of boats to reach the landing steps or take itself up the beach at low tide. The men who operated the boats were called 'wherrymen' and with their combined skills with oars and their knowledge of the river, they knew the best routes to take. These boats were operated by licensed men and ferried passengers from Gravesend to Richmond, between Southwark, London and Westminster. The other types of boats that also worked the Thames were the shallop and the livery company barge. The shallop was rowed by six or eight liveried watermen and were owned by wealthy families, including the monarchy. Today the Queen still has royal watermen and a bargemaster. The livery company barges were large vessels that were owned by city livery companies and used for entertaining and displaying wealth on occasions like the Lord Mayor's River Pageant.

Racing competitions started with professional boatmen (those who earned their living transporting people and goods) in the 1700s, with victors receiving substantial prizes. During the 1800s racing became both a popular gambling and spectator sport on the Thames.

Thomas Doggett, an actor and manager at the Drury Lane Theatre at London, offered a coat and badge to the winning waterman over a five-mile course from London Bridge to Chelsea in 1715. The entrants were those who had one year's experience – after their five years of apprenticeship, with the race being held during an incoming tide on the busy river. This was a test of not only watermanship, but also sculling.

The first year of the Boat Race between Oxford and Cambridge Universities was in 1829 at Henley. The s-bend course from Putney to Mortlake over 4.25 miles (6.48km) took place in 1845 and was a test for both oarsmen and coxes. The dark blue of Oxford and the light blue of Cambridge came into effect the same year (1845) that the 'Blues' trophy was introduced.

The Henley Royal Regatta first took place in 1839 and was organised by the town. It has been repeated every year since, apart from during the two world wars (1914-18 and 1939-45). It is Britain's most prestigious regatta and received royal patronage in 1851.

The development of clubs took place in 1818 with the establishment of the Leander club, whose origins began in Lambeth and are now based in Henley. Leander was a club of old Oxford and Cambridge students. The London Rowing Club established in 1856 saw the most significant development along the Thames, bringing with it the best oarsmen from smaller clubs.

The Amateur Rowing Association (ARA) was formed in 1882 from the Metropolitan Rowing Association established in 1879. Most of the founding members were from the London area and included Oxford, Cambridge and Dublin universities boat clubs. Their goals were to govern the sport and form crews that could beat competitors from other countries at the Henley Royal Regatta.

In 1890, the National Amateur Rowing Association was formed as an alternative to the ARA, who excluded menial and manual workers from amateur clubs and regattas. Its size grew considerably and it organised eight autonomous regions, each with its own regatta.

The two associations disputed who would represent Great Britain at the Olympic Games and in the late 1930s set out to settle their differences. Finally in 1953 they decided to merge, but this did not come into effect until 1 January 1956.

British women's rowing began with the colleges of London, Oxford and Cambridge universities, along with clubs like Furnivall Sculling Club (1896) and Weybridge Ladies Amateur Rowing Club (1926).

Today the ARA's membership has approximately 500 clubs with 15,000 members and holds 300 regattas.

Amateur Rowing Association Ltd
The Priory, 6 Lower Mall, London W6 9DJ
(Tel: 020-8748 3632; Fax: 020-8741 4658;
Web: www.ara-rowing.org).

SWIMMING

It is not clear how or where the activity of swimming originated. It is known, however, that the Romans taught their soldiers to swim in the River Tiber.

By a decree of 1571, the University of Cambridge did not allow its members to swim anywhere in the county. There is no specific explanation for this apart from stating it was because of serious and grave reasons.

Swimming began as a formal type of exercise in England in the 18th century, but took place in baths rather than in the sea, rivers or lakes. The Pearless Pool was located at Finsbury in London and was established by a jeweller named William Kemp in 1743 from a natural pond caused by an overflowing spring. Twice a week boys from the nearby Christs Hospital School would come to swim, but by 1850 the pool had been closed.

In 1836 Mr J. Strachan of Westminster established the National Swimming Society (NSA). Their aim was the promotion of health and cleanliness by encouraging swimming and offering free instruction.

The earliest of public schools to engage in the art of swimming was Eton College. A fatal accident of a boy whilst boating in 1839 led George Selwyn and William Evans (masters at the school) to prevail upon the headmaster to adopt the teaching of swimming. After that all the boys had to pass a 250 yard swim before they were allowed to go on a boat on the River Thames. The Baths and Wash-houses Act of 1846 resulted in many towns building public baths.

The Turnhalle at Kings Cross was originally opened in 1866 as a purpose built gymnasium established by Ernest Ravenstein for Germans living in London. A meeting at this venue on 7 January 1869 between Mr Ravenstein and a group of leaders from London swimming clubs saw what may have been the beginning of the Amateur Swimming Association. Another meeting was held in February and it was decided to take the name of the Associated Metropolitan Swimming Clubs. They had established a group to formulate a constitution and on 24 June it was adopted along with a name change to the London Swimming Association (LSA).

The founding members of the LSA were the following swimming clubs: the Alliance, North London, Serpentine, National, West London and St Pancras. The amateur English Men's Mile Championships became their annual event with the first one taking place on the Thames from Putney Aqueduct to Hammersmith Bridge. The venue changed in 1873 to the Serpentine because of river currents and pollution. The second championship to be instituted was the Long distance in 1877 and was known as the Lords and Commons race as the first cup was presented by Members of Parliament. This event was swum until 1939. Today there is a 5km event with winners receiving the House of Commons trophies.

In 1870 the LSA changed its name again to the Metropolitan Swimming Association (MSA). Their main goal was to promote and encourage the art of swimming with the highest values associated with the 'amateur'.

The MSA comprised only of London clubs, but at a meeting in 1873 it was decided the name should change to the Swimming Association of Great Britain (SAGB) to encourage clubs around the country to join.

On 7 April 1884 the Otter Swimming club of London withdrew their membership from the SAGB and along with some smaller clubs formed the Amateur Swimming Union (ASU). On 3 March the SAGB and the ASU decided to establish the Amateur Swimming Association (ASA). This new association set up 135 laws covering procedures for dealing with suspensions and appeals, the conduct of meeting for both council and races, along with organising championship competitions. The ASA as it is known today came into being on 12 April 1886.

Lord Charles Beresford was elected president of the ASA between 1887 and 1889. He obtained royal patronage for the ASA in 1887.

By 1902 there were 595 clubs around the country. Within two years the numbers of clubs increased to 675. The last full year of peace before the start of World War I, there were an amazing 1,409 clubs based throughout the country.

In 1891 the London School Board accepted an offer by the ASA to make use of the services of members who were competent to teach swimming.

The ASA started in 1899 its Professional Certificate and by the 31 December 1900 it had been awarded to 26 male and female candidates from all over England. Minimum age restrictions for this certificate were imposed in 1909 with men being 21 and women at 18. In 1910 the Professional Certificate was thoroughly revised whereby applicants had to pass both a theoretical (instructing the breast stroke, back stroke and breathing) and a practical exam.

The ASA's first formal recognition to women competitors was established in 1901 when they had a 100 yard national competition. By 1912 there was also a race of 200 yards.

On 19 July 1908 at the Olympic Games held at White City in west London saw the formation of Fédération Internationale de Natation (FINA), who are the world governing body of swimming based in Lausanne, Switzerland.

Over the years the ASA has improved the sport in this country with unprecedented success. So much so that many British swimmers are now among an elite group of athletes from around the world.

Amateur Swimming Association
Harold Fern House, Derby Square, Loughborough, Leics LE11 5AL
(Tel: 01509-618700; Fax: 01509-618701; Web: www.britishswimming.org).

TWICKENHAM

For 40 years (1871-1910) the Rugby Football Union (RFU) used various grounds around the country for international matches. The cost of using these different locations was expensive, so the RFU decided to purchase land and build it's own stadium.

422 Cultural London

William Williams, and RFU committee member was given the task of finding a suitable location. A piece of land (10¼ acres) was found near the small town of Twickenham in 1907 and subsequently purchased for £5,572.12s.6d. Construction began on this site in 1908 and by October 1909 the 30,000 capacity stadium was ready.

The first international match was played between England and Wales in January 1910 with over 20,000 spectators.

After England's Grand Slam successes in 1921, 1923 and 1924, work was started again on the stadium with various sections being enlarged. In 1979 the first major work in almost 50 years began with the replacement of the crumbling south terrace and erection of a new south stand. Following the disaster at Hillsborough in 1989, the RFU decided that the stadium would be all-seating only.

Twickenham Stadium is the largest arena in world rugby (a capacity of 74,000).

The Rugby Football Union
Rugby House, Rugby Road, Twickenham, Middx TW1 1DS (Tel: 020-8892 2000; Fax: 020-8892 9816; Web: www.rfu.com; Museum of Rugby and Twickenham Experience Tour: Tel: 020-8892 8877).

LONDON-BASED RUGBY TEAMS

Esher RFC (1923)
The Rugby Ground, 369 Molesey Road, Hersham, Surrey KT12 3PF (Tel: 01932-220295; Fax: 01932-254627; Ticket Office: 01932-220295; Web: www.esherrfc.org).
Coach: Hugh McHardy

Harlequin FC (1866)
Stoop Memorial Ground, Langhorn Drive, Twickenham TW2 7SX (Tel: 020-8410 6000; Fax: 020-8410 6001; Ticket Office: 0871-871 8877; E-mail: mail@quins.co.uk; Web: www.quins.co.uk).
Coaches: J. Kingston and R. Hill

London Irish RFC (1898)
Madejski Stadium, Reading RG2 0FL (Tel: 01932-783034; Fax: 01932-784462; Ticket Office: 0118-968 1000; E-mail: londonirishrfc@aol.com; Web: www.london-irish.com).
Coach: Brendan Venter

London Wasps
Loftus Road Stadium, South Africa Road, London W12 7PA (Tel: 020-8743 0262; Fax: 020-8740 2525; Ticket Office: 020-8740 2545; E-mail: wasps@loftusroadplc.co.uk; Web: www.waspsrfc.co.uk).
Director of Rugby: Nigel Melville
Coaches: John Lambden; Pat Fox

London Welsh RFC (1885)
Old Deer Park, Kew Road, Richmond, Surrey TW9 2AZ
(Tel: 020-8940 2368; Fax: 020-8940 1106; Ticket Office: 020-8940 2368;
E-mail: ron.holley.london-welsh.co.uk; Web: www.london.welsh.co.uk).
Coach: Adrian Davies
Shirt sponsor: Basildon Chemicals

Metropolitan Police RFC (1924)
Metropolitan Police (Imber Court) Sports Club, Ember Lane, East Molesey, Surrey KT8 0BT (Tel: 020-8398 1267; Fax: 020-8398 9755; Ticket Office: 020-8398 1267).
Coach: David Thrower; Simon Deer

Saracens FC (1876)
Vicarage Road Stadium, Vicarage Road, Watford, Herts WD1 8ER (Tel: 01923-475222; Fax: 01923-475275;
E-mail: general@saracens.net; Web: www.saracens.com).
Chief Executive: Francois Pienaar

OTHER LONDON-BASED RUGBY TEAMS —Alphabetical order

(Note: Space limitations mean that we regret we are unable to print all the London based clubs)

Bank of England RFC (Eastern Counties 1); Barclays Bank RFC (Eastern Counties 1); Barnes RFC (Eastern Counties 1); Chiswick RFC (Herts & Middx 1); Civil Service FC (RU) (Herts & Middx 1); Ealing (Herts & Middx 1); East London RUFC (Herts & Middx 1); Economicals RUFC (Herts & Middx 1); Enfield Ignatians RFC (Herts & Middx 1); Eton Manor RFC (Herts & Middx 1); Feltham RFC (Herts & Middx 1); Finchley RFC (Herts & Middx 1); Footscray RUFC (Herts & Middx 1); London Nigerian RFC (Kent 1); Loughton RFC (Kent 1); May and Baker (Kent 1); Merton RFC (Kent 1); Millwall Albion (London 2 North); Old Abbotstonians RFC (London 2 North); Old

Actonians RFC (London 2 North); Old Alleynian FC (London 2 South); Old Ashmoleans RFC (London 2 South); Old Bevonians RFC (London 2 South); Old Cofeians RFC (Division 1); Old Cooperians RUFC (London 3 North East); Old Edwardians RFC (London 3 North East); Old Elthamians RFC (London 3 North West); Old Emanuel RFC (London 3 North West); Old Gaytonians RFC (London 3 North West); Old Grammarians RFC (London 3 North West); Old Haileyburians (London 3 North West) Old Hamptonians RFC (London 3 North West); Old Isleworthians RFC (London 3 North West); Old Johnian RFC (London 3 North West); Old Millhillians RFC (London 3 North West); Old Pauline FC (London 3 North West); Old Rutlishians RFC (London 3 North West); Old Shootershillians RFC (London 3 South East); Old Suttonians RFC (London 3 South East); Old Tiffinian RFC (London 3 South West); Old Tottonians RFC (London 3 South West); Old Wellingtonian RFC (London 3 South West); Old Whitgiftian RFC (London 3 South West); Old Wimbledonians RFC (Surrey 1); Orleans F. P. RFC (Surrey 1); Osterley RFC (Surrey 1); Park House RFC (Surrey 1); Pinner and Grammarians RFC (Surrey 1); Quintin RFC (Surrey 1); Ravens RFC (Surrey 1); Ruislip RFC (Division 1); Staines RFC (Division 1); Sutton and Epsom RFC (Division 1); Wimbledon (Division 1).

WEMBLEY STADIUM

Wembley Stadium cost £750,000 to build and took only 300 working days to complete. The famous twin towers, now demolished were 38.4m (126ft) high. In 1955 floodlights were used when London played Frankfurt in the Inter-Cities Fairs Cup. In 1963 an electronic scoreboard was first used and it was suspended from the new roof. Computerised display boards were first used in March 1988 for the England v Brazil Schools International Match. They measure 25m (82ft) wide by 4.5m (15ft) high and have adjoining advertising panels that are 6m (20ft).

Behind Wembley's famous twin towers on the 28 April 1923, The Football Association's (F.A.) Challenge Cup was played between Bolton Wanderers and West Ham United. This became the permanent home for future F.A. contests. The F.A. final on 20 May between Chelsea and Aston Villa was the last one to be played before demolition of the stadium. The result of the match was Chelsea 1 – Aston Villa 0.

The architects of the new stadium are Sir Norman Foster of Fosters and Partners and HOK Lobb, who have built 50 stadiums throughout the USA. There will be seating for 90,000 and is scheduled for completion in time for the FA Cup Final in 2003. A further £200—£355 million will be spent turning Wembley into the finest sports arena in the world. The National Lottery has given £120 million towards the cost of the new stadium.

Wembley has been the site of many great sporting and non-sporting events over the years. The Rugby League Cup Final was first played in 1929; the first World Speedway Championships were held there in 1936; the XIV Olympic Games in 1948; the European Cup final between AC Milan and Benfica was held in 1963; the World Cup in 1966, when England defeated West Germany 4-2; the Royal International Horse show 1969; the first pop music event in 1972; an exhibition game of American Football between the Minnesota Vikings and St Louis Rams in 1983; Bob Geldof's Live Aid concert in 1985 raising money for African famine victims; the Freddie Mercury Tribute concert in 1992; WBC Heavyweight Boxing in 1995 saw Frank Bruno defeat the American Oliver McCall and in 1996 it was the venue for football's Euro'96.

Wembley National Stadium
Wembley, Middx HA9 0WS
(Web: www.wembleynationalstadium.co.uk).

WIMBLEDON

The All England Lawn Tennis and Croquet Club is a private club founded in 1868 as The All England Croquet Club, with its first grounds off Worple Road at Wimbledon. In the spring of 1877 the Club was re-named The All England Croquet and Lawn Tennis Club and the first lawn tennis Championships were held.

The word 'croquet' was dropped from the name of the Club, as activity in 1882 was confined mostly to lawn tennis. For sentimental reasons in 1899, the word 'croquet' was reinstated to the title and it has remained 'The All England Lawn Tennis and Croquet Club'.

These Championships started with a garden party atmosphere, evident at the first meeting of the Gentlemen's Singles (won by Spencer Gore) but have grown to a highly professional tournament that now attracts over 450,000 spectators.

Ladies' Singles play started in 1884 with Maud Watson becoming the champion. That year also saw the start of the Gentlemen's Doubles. In 1905 an American, May Sutton became the first overseas champion. The Australian, Norman Brookes was the first overseas Gentlemen's champion in 1907.

In 1922 the Club moved to its present location at Church Road and was opened by King George V. The new stadium held 14,000 people and because of this the popularity of the game grew enormously. A total of 20 courts, including the centre court are now used throughout the championships.

The years of 1934 to 1937 were the golden era for British tennis when 11 titles were won. Fred Perry won three singles Championships and Dorothy Round won two.

During World War II the premises of Wimbledon were used for a variety of civil defence and military functions. In October 1940, a bomb hit the Centre Court, which resulted in the loss of 1200 seats.

With the War over, the championships started again in 1946. The person in charge of making sure the tournament went ahead was the newly appointed Secretary, Lt. Col. Duncan Macaulay.

In 1973, 81 members of the Association of Tennis Professionals (ATP) stayed away from the championships as a result of the Yugoslavian Lawn Tennis Association suspending Nikki Pilic earlier in the year. Despite this over 300,000 spectators (throughout the two-week tournament) watched as Jan Kodes of Czechoslovakia and American's Billie Jean King (for the sixth time) became champions.

The championships celebrated their Centenary in 1977 with 41 of the 52 surviving champions parading on Centre Court and being presented with a commemorative medal by H.R.H. The Duke of Kent (the club's President) to mark this milestone.

Each year the championships are bettered as the world's top players continue to strive for what is undoubtedly one of the top honours in the sport – being Wimbledon Champion.

Wimbledon Lawn Tennis Museum – hours of operation 10.30am to 5.00pm (extended hours during the tournament). Tel: 020-8946 6131.

The All England Lawn Tennis and Croquet Club
Church Road, London SW19 5AE
(Tel: 020-8944 1066; Fax: 020-8947 8752;
E-mail: internet@aeltc.com;
Web: www.wimbledon.org).

SPORTS BODIES

THE AMATEUR BOXING ASSOCIATION OF ENGLAND LTD

Crystal Palace National Sports Centre, London, SE19 2BB (Tel: 020-8778 0251; Fax: 020-8778 9324; E-mail: hq@abae.org.uk;
Web: www.amateurboxing.freeserve.co.uk)
Chairman: J. Smart

AMATEUR ROWING ASSOCIATION LTD

The Priory, 6 Lower Mall, London, W6 9DJ
(Tel: 020-8748 3632; Fax: 020-8741 4658;
Web: www.ara-rowing.org)
National Manager: Mrs R. Napp

BRITISH ARM WRESTLING FEDERATION

Unit 4 Nettlefold Place, London, SE27 0JW
(Tel: 020-8761 0597)

BRITISH AUSTRALIAN RULES FOOTBALL LEAGUE

264 High Street, London, W3 9BH
(Tel: 020-8752 1823)

BRITISH BOXING BOARD OF CONTROL LTD

Jack Petersen House, 52A Borough High Street, London, SE1 1XN (Tel: 020-7403 5879; Fax: 020-7378 6670; Web: www.bbbofc.com)
General Secretary: S. J. Block

BRITISH DARTS ORGANISATION

2 Pages Lane, Muswell Hill, London, N10 1PS
(Tel: 020-8883 5544; Fax: 020-8883 0109;
E-mail: 101776.666@compuserve.com;
Web: www.bdodarts.com)
Director: O. A. Croft

Sports Bodies

BRITISH FENCING ASSOCIATION

1 Baron's Gate, 33–35 Rothschild Road, London, W4 5HT (Tel: 020-8742 3032; Fax: 020-8742 3033; E-mail: britishfencing@compuserve.com; Web: www.britishfencing.com)
General Secretary: Miss G. Kenneally

BRITISH HORSEBALL ASSOCIATION

67 Clifford Road, New Barnet, Barnet, Herts, EN5 5NZ (Tel: 020-8441 1799)

BRITISH HORSERACING BOARD

42 Portman Square, London, W1H 0EN (Tel: 020-7396 0011; Fax: 020-7935 3626; E-mail: info@bhb.co.uk; Web: www.bhb.co.uk)
Managing Director: C. Reynolds

BRITISH OLYMPIC ASSOCIATION

1 Wandsworth Plain, London, SW18 1EH (Tel: 020-8871 2677; Fax: 020-8871 9104; E-mail: boa@boa.org.uk; Web: www.olympics.org.uk)
Chief Executive: S. Clegg

BRITISH TENPIN BOWLING ASSOCIATION

114 Balfour Road, Ilford, Essex, IG1 4JD (Tel: 020-8478 1745; Fax: 020-8514 3665)
Chairman: Mrs P. White

BRITISH UNIVERSITIES SPORTS ASSOCIATION

8 Union Street, London, SE1 1SZ (Tel: 020-7357 8555; Fax: 020-7403 0127 Web: www.busa.org.uk)
Chief Executive: G. Gregory-Jones

CENTRAL COUNCIL OF PHYSICAL RECREATION

Francis House, Francis Street, London, SW1P 1DE (Tel: 020-7828 3163; Fax: 020-7630 7046 E-mail: admin@ccpr.org.uk)
Chief Executive: M. Denton

COMMONWEALTH GAMES COUNCIL FOR ENGLAND

Tavistock House, Tavistock Square, London, WC1H 9JZ (Tel: 020-7388 6643; Fax: 020-7388 6744; E-mail: info@cgce.co.uk; Web: www.cgce.co.uk)
Chief Executive: Miss Ann Hogbin

COMMONWEALTH GAMES FEDERATION

Walkden House, 3–10 Melton Street, London, NW1 2EB (Tel: 020-7383 5596; Fax: 020-7383 5506; E-mail: office@thecgf.com; Web: www.thecgf.com)
Chief Executive Officer: Michael Hooper

COUNTRYSIDE ALLIANCE

The Old Town Hall, 367 Kennington Road, London, SE11 4PT (Tel: 020-7840 9200; Fax: 020-7793 8484; E-mail: info@countryside-alliance.org; Web: www.countryside-alliance.org)
Chief Executive: R. Burge

CROQUET ASSOCIATION

c/o The Hurlingham Club, Ranelagh Gardens, London, SW6 3PR (Tel: 020-7736 3148; Fax: 020-7736 3148; E-mail: caoffice@croquet.org.uk; Web: www.croquet.org.uk)
Secretary: N. R. Graves

ENGLAND AND WALES CRICKET BOARD

Lord's Cricket Ground, London, NW8 8QZ (Tel: 020-7432 1200; Fax: 020-7289 5619; Web: www.ecb.co.uk)
Chief Executive: T. Lamb

THE FOOTBALL ASSOCIATION

16 Lancaster Gate, London, W2 3LW (Tel: 020-7262 4542; Fax: 020-7402 0486)
Executive Director: D. Davies

INTERNATIONAL TENNIS FEDERATION

Bank Lane, Roehampton, London, SW15 5XZ (Tel: 020-8878 6464; Fax: 020-8878 7799)
Chief Executive: J. Garnham

426 Cultural London

THE JOCKEY CLUB

42 Portman Square, London, W1H 0EN
(Tel: 020-7486 4921; Fax: 020-7486 8689;
E-mail: info@thejockeyclub.co.uk;
Web: www.thejockeyclub.co.uk)
Senior Steward: C. Spence

KEEP FIT ASSOCIATION

Suite 105, Astra House, Arklow Road, London,
SE14 6EB (Tel: 020-8692 9566; Fax: 020-8692
8383; E-mail: kfa@keepfit.org.uk;
Web: www.keepfit.org.uk)
Chair: Ms A. Bayley

LAWN TENNIS ASSOCIATION

The Queen's Club, London, W14 9EG
(Tel: 020-7381 7000; Fax: 020-7381 5965;
Web: www.lta.org.uk)
Chief Executive: J. A. Crowther

LONDON AMATEUR BOXING ASSOCIATION

58 Comber Grove, London, SE5 0LD
(Tel: 020-7252 7008; Fax: 020-7708 0904)
Hon. Secretary: K. Walters

THE LONDON MARATHON LTD

PO Box 1234, London, SE1 8RZ
(Tel: 020-7620 4117; Fax: 020-7620 4208;
Web: www.london-marathon.co.uk)
Chief Executive: N. Bitel

MCC

Lord's Cricket Ground, London, NW8 8QN
(Tel: 020-7289 1611; Fax: 020-7289 9700;
Web: www.lords.org/mcc)
Chief Executive: R. D. V. Knight

NATIONAL GREYHOUND RACING CLUB LTD

Twyman House, 16 Bonny Street, London, NW1
9QD (Tel: 020-7267 9256; Fax: 020-7482 1023;
E-mail: ngrc@clara.net)
Chief Executive: F. Melville

NATIONAL ICE SKATING ASSOCIATION OF THE UK LTD

National Ice Centre, Lower Parliament Street,
Nottingham, NG1 1LA
E-mail: nisa@iceskating.org.uk;
Web: www.iceskating.org.uk)
Chairman: Mr Haig Oundjian

N F L EUROPE LEAGUE

97–99 Kings Road, London, SW3 4PA
(Tel: 020-7225 3070; Fax: 020-7376 5070)
Chief Financial Adviser

PROFESSIONAL WINDSURFING ASSOCIATION

The Green Room, 1 Burston Road, London,
SW15 6AR (Tel: 020-8780 4698; Fax: 020-8780
4602; E-mail: pwa@ssm-freesports.com;
Web: www.world-windsurfing.com)
Chairman: P. McGain

RICHMOND GYMNASTICS ASSOCIATION

RGA Centre, Townmead Road, Richmond,
Surrey, TW9 4EL (Tel: 020-8878 8682)
Chairman: Mrs L. Gray

RUGBY FOOTBALL UNION

Rugby House, Rugby Road, Twickenham,
Middx, TW1 1DS (Tel: 020-8892 2000;
Fax: 020-8892 9816)
Chief Executive: F. Baron

SANEX WTA TOUR

Bank Lane, London, SW15 5XZ
(Tel: 020-8392 4760; Fax: 020-8392 4765;
Web: www.sanexwta.com)
Vice-President of European Operations:
Ms G. Clark

SOUTH OF ENGLAND ATHLETICS ASSOCIATION

Suite 106, City of London Fruit Exchange,
Brushfield Street, London, E1 6EX
(Tel: 020-7247 2963; Fax: 020-7247 3439;
E-mail: south@seaa.freeserve.co.uk)
Chief Executive: Ms L. Whitehead

Cultural Organisations 427

SPORT ENGLAND

16 Upper Woburn Place, London, WC1H 0QP
(Tel: 020-7273 1500; Fax: 020-7383 5740
E-mail: info@english.sports.gov.uk)
Chief Executive Officer: D. Casey

TENNIS AND RACKETS ASSOCIATION

c/o The Queen's Club, Palliser Road, London, W14 9EQ (Tel: 020-7386 3447/8; Fax: 020-7385 7424; E-mail: ceo@tennis-rackets.net; Web: www.rackets.co.uk)
Chief Executive: James D. Wyatt

UK SPORTS COUNCIL

40 Bernard Street, London, WC1N 1ST
(Tel: 020-7841 9500; Web: www.uksport.gov.uk)
Chief Executive: R. Callicott

WEMBLEY SPORTS ASSOCIATION)

Vale Farm Sports Ground, Watford Road, Wembley, Middx, HA0 3HG (Tel: 020 8868 8818)

CULTURAL, HERITAGE AND LEISURE ORGANISATIONS

ARTS COUNCIL OF ENGLAND

14 Great Peter Street, London SW1P 3NQ
(Tel: 020-7333 0100; Fax: 020-7973 6590;
Email: enquiries@artscouncil.org.uk;
Web: www.artscouncil.org.uk).

The Arts Council is the national body for the arts in England. It distributes public money from government and the lottery to artists and arts organisations, both directly and through the ten Regional Arts Boards. The Council also commissions new work; conducts research; provides advice and information and develops awareness and support for the arts in England. The Arts Council is an independent, non-political body.
Chief Executive: Peter Hewitt
Head of Press and Public Relations: David McNeil

London Arts

2 Pear Tree Court, London EC1R 0DS
(Tel: 020-7608 6100; Fax: 020-7608 4100;
Email: info@lonab.co.uk;
Web: www.arts.org.uk/londonarts).
Chair: Lady Hollick

BRITISH FILM COMMISSION (BFC)

10 Little Poland Street, London W1W 7GJ
(Tel: 020-7861 7860; Fax: 020-7861 7864;
Email: info@bfc.co.uk; Web: www.bfc.co.uk).

The British Film Commission is a division of the Film Council, the strategic government body responsible for commercial and cultural film activity in the UK. The BFC's remit is to promote the UK as an international production centre, encourage the use of locations, facilities, services and personnel, and provide international filmmakers with comprehensive advice and information relating to the practical aspects of filming in the UK.
Commissioner: S. Norris

BRITISH FILM INSTITUTE

21 Stephen Street, London W1P 2LN
(Tel: 020-7255 1444; Fax: 020-7436 7950;
Email: firstname.lastname@bfi.org.uk;
Web: www.bfi.org.uk).

Founded in 1933 the British Film Institute offers opportunities to experience, enjoy and discover more about the world of film and television. Its three main departments are: bfi Education, comprising the bfi National Library, bfi Publishing and Sight and Sound magazine, as well as bfi Education Projects which encourages life-long learning about the moving image; bfi Exhibition, which runs the National Film Theatre on London's South Bank and the annual London Film Festival and supports local cinemas and film festivals UK-wide; and bfi Collections, which preserves the UK's moving image heritage and promotes access to it through a variety of means including film, video and DVD releases and touring exhibitions. The bfi also runs the bfi Lonfon IMAX Cinema at Waterloo, featuring the UK's largest screen.
Patron: HRH The Prince of Wales, KG, KT, GCB
Chair: Joan Bakewell, CBE
Director: Jon Teckman

COMMISSION FOR ARCHITECTURE AND THE BUILT ENVIRONMENT

16th Floor, The Tower Building, 11 York Road, London SE1 7NX (Tel: 020-7960 2400; Fax: 020-7960 2444; Email: enquiries@cabe.org.uk; Web: www.cabe.org.uk).

The Commission for Architecture and the Built Environment (CABE) replaced the Royal Fine Art Commission (RFAC) in August 1999. It has taken over the RFAC's design review function, and is also responsible for promoting the importance of high quality architecture and urban design and encouraging the understanding of architecture through educational and regional initiatives.

Chairman: Stuart Lipton
Chief Executive: Jon Rouse

CORPORATION OF LONDON RECORDS OFFICE

Guildhall, London EC2P 2EJ (Tel: 020-7332 1251; Fax: 020-7710 8682; Email: clro@corpoflondon.gov.uk; Web: www.cityoflondon.gov.uk/archives/clro/).

The Corporation of London Records Office contains the municipal archives of the City of London which are regarded as the most complete collection of ancient municipal records in existence. The collection includes charters of William the Conqueror, Henry II, and later kings and queens to 1957; ancient custumals: Liber Horn, Dunthorne, Custumarum, Ordinacionum, Memorandorum and Albus, Liber de Antiquis Legibus, and collections of statutes; continuous series of judicial rolls and books from 1252 and Council minutes from 1275; records of the Old Bailey and Guildhall sessions from 1603; financial records from the 16th century; the records of London Bridge from the 12th century; and numerous subsidiary series and miscellanea of historical interest. The Readers' Room is open Monday—Friday, 9.30-4.45.

Keeper of the City Records: The Town Clerk
City Archivist: J. R. Sewell, OBE
Deputy City Archivist: Mrs J. M. Bankes

CROWN ESTATE

16 Carlton House Terrace, London SW1Y 5AH (Tel: 020-7210 4377; Fax: 020-7930 8187; Email: pr@crownestate.co.uk; Web: www.crownestate.co.uk).

The Crown Estate includes substantial blocks of urban property, primarily in London, almost 120,000 hectares of agricultural land and extensive marine holdings throughout the United Kingdom. Its origins go back to the reign of King Edward the Confessor and, until the accession of King George III, the Sovereign received its rents and profits. However, since 1760 the annual surplus, after deducting management expenses, has been surrendered by the Sovereign to Parliament to help meet the cost of civil government. In return, the Sovereign receives the Civil List and the Government meets other official expenditure incurred in support of the Sovereign.

First Commissioner and Chairman (part-time): Sir Denys Henderson
Second Commissioner and Chief Executive: Sir Christopher Howes, KCVO, CB
Commissioners (part-time): Mrs H. M. R. Chapman, CBE, FRICS; The Lord De Ramsey; I. D. Grant, CBE; D. E. G. Griffiths, CBE; J. H. M. Norris, CBE; R. R. Spinney, FRICS
Director of Finance and Administration: R. Bright, MA
Director of Urban Estates: D. A. Bickmore, FRICS

ENGLISH HERITAGE

23 Savile Row, London W1S 2ET (Tel: 020-7973 3000; Fax: 020-7973 3001; Web: www.english-heritage.org.uk).

National Monuments Record Centre, Kemble Drive, Swindon SN2 2GZ (Tel: 01793-414600; Fax: 01793-414606).
London Search Room: 55 Blandford Street, London W1H 3AF (Tel: 020-7208 8200; Fax: 020-7224 5333).

English Heritage is a statutory body which gives grants to thousands of listed buildings, cathedrals, churches, archaeological sites, historic parks and gardens and ancient monuments across the country. By the re-use of the nation's historic buildings and by working closely with local authorities and others, it seeks to spark the regeneration of the centres of cities, towns and villages. It has nine Regional Offices across the country and a Centre of Archaeological Excellence at Fort Cumberland in Portsmouth.

English Heritage had a turnover of around £150 million of which £30 million is generated through admissions, membership, retail and catering, sponsorship and fundraising as well as through publications, survey work and archive services. It manages over 400 of the nation's historic houses and monuments attracting 12 million visitors each year. These include Stonehenge, Dover Castle and Kenwood House. On 1 April 1999 English Heritage merged with the Royal Commission on the Historical Monuments of England (RCHME). It is therefore now responsible for the National Monuments Record, which includes all the material gathered since the formation of the RCHME in 1908 and now contains over 12 million photographs, maps and drawings.
Chairman: Sir Neil Cossons OBE
Commissioners: Miss A. Arrowsmith; Mr M. Cairns; Ms B. Cherry; Cllr P. Davis; A. Fane; The Lord Faringdon; Prof. E. Fernie, CBE; Lady Gass; HRH The Duke of Gloucester, KG, GCVO; Mr P. Gough, CBE; L. Grossman; Mrs C. Lycett-Green; Ms K. McLeod; Prof. R. Morris, FSA; Miss S. Underwood
Chief Executive: Ms P. Alexander

FILM COUNCIL

10 Little Portland Street, London W1W 7JG (Tel: 020-7861 7861; Fax: 020-7861 7862).

The Council was created in April 2000 by the Department for Culture, Media and Sport to develop a coherent strategy for the growth and sustainability of film culture and the film industry in the UK. It has £55 million a year to invest in film production, development, policy, distribution, inward investment, training, education and exhibition. Its funding is comprised of lottery money and grant-in-aid.
Chairman: A. Parker
Deputy Chairman: S. Till

HERITAGE OF LONDON TRUST

55 Blandford Street, London W1U 7HN (Tel: 020-7208 8232; Fax: 020-7208 8246; Email: info@heritageoflondon.com; Web: www.heritageoflondon.com).
Director: J. Spicer

HISTORIC ROYAL PALACES

Hampton Court Palace, East Molesey, Surrey KT8 9AU (Tel: 020-8781 9500; Fax: 020-8781 9754; Web: hrp.org.uk).

Historic Royal Palaces was formerly an executive agency of the Department for Culture, Media and Sport; it is now a non-departmental public body with charitable trust status. The Secretary of State for Culture, Media and Sport is still accountable to Parliament for the care and presentation of the palaces, which are owned by the Sovereign in right of the Crown. The chairman of the trustees is appointed by The Queen on the advice of the Secretary of State.

Historic Royal Palaces is responsible for the Tower of London, Hampton Court Palace, Kensington Palace State Apartments and the Royal Ceremonial Dress Collection, Kew Palace with Queen Charlotte's Cottage, and the Banqueting House, Whitehall.
Chairman: The Earl of Airlie, KT, GCVO
Appointed by The Queen: The Lord Camoys, GCVO, DL; Sir Michael Peat, KCVO; H. Roberts, CVO
Appointed by the Secretary of State:
M. Herbert, CBE; Ms A. Heylin, OBE; S. Jones, LVO; Ms J. Sharman
Ex officio: Field Marshal the Lord Inge, GCB (Constable of the Tower of London)
Chief Executive: A. Coppin
Director of Finance: Ms A. McLeish
Director of Human Resources: G. Josephs
Surveyor of the Fabric: R. Davidson
Curator, Historic Royal Palaces: Dr E. Impey
Director, Palaces Group: H. Player
Resident Governor: HM Tower of London, Maj.-Gen. G. Field, CB, OBE

LORD GREAT CHAMBERLAIN'S OFFICE

House of Lords, London SW1A 0PW (Tel: 020-7219 3100; Fax: 020-7219 2500).

The Lord Great Chamberlain is a Great Officer of State, the office being hereditary since the grant of Henry I to the family of De Vere, Earls of Oxford. It is now a joint hereditary office between the Cholmondeley and Carington families. The Lord Great Chamberlain is responsible for the royal apartments of the Palace of Westminster, i.e. The Queen's Robing Room, the Royal Gallery and, in conjunction with the Lord Chancellor and the Speaker, Westminster Hall. The Lord Great

Chamberlain has particular responsibility for the internal administrative arrangements within the House of Lords for State Openings of Parliament and services held in the Chapel of St. Mary Undercroft.
Lord Great Chamberlain: The Marquess of Cholmondeley
Secretary to the Lord Great Chamberlain: Lt. General Sir Michael Willcocks, KCB
Clerks to the Lord Great Chamberlain: Ms Jakki Perodeau; Ms Amanda Feuz

HISTORICAL MANUSCRIPTS COMMISSION

Quality House, Quality Court, Chancery Lane, London WC2A 1HP (Tel: 020-7242 1198; Fax: 020-7831 3550; Email: nra@hmc.gov.uk; Web: www.hmc.gov.uk).

The Commission was set up by royal warrant in 1869 to enquire and report on collections of papers of value for the study of history which were in private hands. In 1959 a new warrant enlarged these terms of reference to include all historical records, wherever situated, outside the Public Records and gave it added responsibilities as a central co-ordinating body to promote, assist and advise on their proper preservation and storage. The Commission is sponsored by the Department for Culture, Media and Sport.

The Commission also maintains the National Register of Archives (NRA), which contains over 43,000 unpublished lists and catalogues of manuscript collections describing the holdings of local record offices, national and university libraries, specialist repositories and others in the UK and overseas. The NRA can be searched using computerised indices which are available in the Commission's search room and on its website.

The Commission also administers the Manorial and Tithe Documents Rules on behalf of the Master of the Rolls.
Chairman: The Lord Bingham of Cornhill, PC

Commissioners: Sir Patrick Cormack, FSA, MP; The Lord Egremont and Leconfield; Sir Matthew Farrer, GCVO; Sir John Sainty, KCB, FSA; Very Revd H. E. C. Stapleton, FSA; Sir Keith Thomas, FBA; The Earl of Scarbrough; Mrs A. Dundas-Bekker; D.Phil, FBA; Mrs S. J. Davies, PhD.; Mrs A. Prochaska, PhD; Miss R. Dunhill, FSA; Dr Caroline Barron, FSA; Prof. T. C. Smout, CBE, PhD., FBA, FRSE, FSASCOT; Prof. Peter Clarke, Mr Victor Gray; Prof. Lola Young
Secretary, C. J. Kitching, PhD., FSA
Resource: Council for Museums, Archives and Libraries
16 Queen Anne's Gate, London SW1H 9AA (Tel: 020-7273 1444; Fax: 020-7273 1404; Web: resource.gov.uk)
Resource: The Council for Museums, Archives and Libraries is a new strategic agency which will work with museums, archives and libraries throughout the UK.
Chairman: Matthew Evans
Chief Executive: Neville Mackay

ROYAL NATIONAL THEATRE BOARD

South Bank, London, SE1 9PX
(Tel: 020-7452 3333; Fax: 020-7452 3344).

The chairman and members of the Board of the Royal National Theatre are appointed by the Secretary of State for Culture, Media and Sport.
Chairman: Sir Christopher Hogg
Members: Ms J. Bakewell, CBE; The Hon. P. Benson; Sir David Hancock, KCB; G. Hutchings; Ms K. Jones; Ms S. MacGregor, OBE; Ben Okri; Andre Ptaszynski; M. Oliver; Sir Tom Stoppard, CBE; Edward Walker-Arnott; P. Wiegand; Prof. Lola Young
Company Secretary: Mrs M. McGregor
Director: T. Nunn, CBE
Executive Director: The Baroness McIntosh of Hudnall

ENVIRONMENTAL
LONDON

**NATURE RESERVES
SIGHTS OF SPECIFIC SCIENTIFIC INTEREST
RIVER THAMES
ENVIRONMENTAL GROUPS
WASTE MINIMISATION AND RECYCLING**

ENVIRONMENTAL LONDON

Environment in London
The establishment of the Greater London Authority (GLA) has changed the way the environment is managed in London. The authority comprises the Mayor, who is responsible for developing sustainable strategies across all of the GLA's functions, including the environment, and the Assembly, which is there to scrutinise the Mayor's policies and act as a check to his powers. The GLA also has the power to conduct its own investigations into environmental issues.

Mayor's responsibilities
The first of the Mayor's four-yearly reports on the state of London's environment is due in 2003. The reports will include information on air quality, energy use and progress towards climate change targets, groundwater levels, traffic levels and emissions. It will be drawn up in consultation with the Environment Agency, which produces a state of the environment report for England and Wales, and local authorities.

Air
Much of London's air quality problems are the result of traffic emissions. The mayor is tasked with developing an integrated transport strategy that will deliver air quality improvements. A draft transport strategy was published in January 2001.

The Mayor is also responsible for working with the boroughs and developing an air quality strategy for London. A draft document was published in January 2001 with a final version due in November 2001. This strategy ties in with the government's National Air Quality Strategy. The aim of which is to map the future ambient air quality in the UK. The strategy is designed to be evolutionary and is regularly monitored and reviewed. Under the strategy, all district and unitary authorities have a duty to review air quality, including likely future air quality, in their areas. This is accompanied by an assessment of whether air quality objectives (set in the strategy) are being, or are likely to be, achieved. If authorities find that any part of their areas breaches the objectives, an air quality management area must be declared and an action plan drawn up for improvements.

Local councils will continue this process and deal with all local pollution episodes, although the Mayor will have the power to ensure they also comply with the London-wide action plan.

Waste
The Mayor must also publish an integrated municipal waste management strategy for London. It covers recovery, recycling, treatment and disposal. The strategy, drawn up in consultation with waste disposal and collection authorities and the private sector, will be reviewed every four years.

The London plan will be in line with the government's national waste strategy – *A way with waste*. This strategy sets a target to reduce the amount of industrial and commercial waste that is landfilled by 85 per cent by 2005 and raises the target recovery rate of municipal waste to 45 per cent by 2010 and the recycling rate for household waste to 30 per cent by the same date. Looking beyond, the government aims to recover value from two thirds of household waste by 2015, at least half of which should be through recycling or composting.

At a local level, the London strategy will have to assess local and best practical environmental options, facilities, resources and economics. Again, the Mayor will have the power to ensure local waste collection and disposal authorities comply with the strategy.

Noise
The Mayor will assess noise levels and develop and ambient noise strategy, the draft of which is due in November. He also has the power to take action and promote efforts that reduce the impact of noise, such as reducing traffic volumes and encouraging low-noise vehicles. However, local councils will continue to deal with neighbourhood noise issues.

Biodiversity
The Mayor issued the draft biodiversity strategy in January 2001 and the final version is expected in February 2002.

Energy
The government has set a target of reducing greenhouse gas emissions by 23% below 1990 levels by 2010. This is almost double the UK's target agreed in the Kyoto Protocol. The Mayor has the responsibility to report on London's contribution to this target. The UK also has a goal of reducing carbon dioxide emissions by 20% below 1990 levels by 2010.

To enable London to contribute to these reductions, the Mayor has chosen to draw up an energy strategy for London to set clear guidance on the efficient use of energy. The draft strategy will be published in September 2001, and will include energy efficiency, fuel poverty and London's contribution to climate change.

Local councils responsibilities
As explained, local councils continue to manage air quality in their areas and are responsible for waste collection. They also promote activity on a local level to draw up sustainable development strategies under Local Agenda 21. Councils were encouraged to develop local plans to ensure the UK meets its commitments under the Agenda 21 agreement that was signed at the 1992 Conference on Environment and Development in Rio (the Earth Summit). Although not a statutory obligation, the government wanted all local councils to adopt Local Agenda 21 by the end of 2000. Not all did, currently 93% have.

Environment also continues to play an important role in the second year of the government's Beacon Council scheme.

LONDON'S LOCAL NATURE RESERVES
Barnet
Coppetts Wood & Glebelands
Oak Hill Wood
Rowley Green Common
Scratchwood and Moat Mount Open
Totteridge Fields
Big Wood & Little Wood

Brent
Fryent Country Park
Welsh Harp

Bromley
Jubilee Country Park
Scadbury Park

Camden
Camley Street Nature Park

Croydon
Bramley Bank
Selsdon Wood
South Norwood Country Park

Ealing
Fox Wood
Islip Manot
Litten Nature Reserve

Long Wood
Northolt Manor
Perivale Wood

Enfield
Covert Way

Greenwich
Oxleas Wood

Hackney
Abney Park Cemetry
Springfield Park

Haringey
Parkland Walk
Queen's Wood
Railway Fields

Harrow
Bentley Priory
Stanmore Common
Stanmore Country Park

Hillingdon
Denham Country Park
Freezeland Court
Yeading Brook Meadows
Yeading Woods

Hounslow
Chiswick Eyot
Duke's Hollow
Gunnersbury Triangle
Hounslow Heath
Pevensey Road

Islington
Barnsbury Wood
Gillespie Park

Kingston upon Thames
Bonesgate Open Space
Castle Hill
Coombe Wood
Edith Gardens Nature Reserve
Hogsmill River Park
Jubilee Wood
Raeburn Open Space
The Wood and Richard Jeffries Bird Sanctuary

Merton
Bennett's Hole
Cannon Hill Common

Fishpond Wood and Beverley Meads
Myrna Close
Sir Joseph Hood Memorial Wood
Wandle Meadow Nature Park

Redbridge
Hainault Lodge

Richmond upon Thames
Barnes Common
Crane Park Island
Ham Lands
Leg of Mutton Reservoir
Oak Avenue Hampton

Southwark
Sydenham Hill Wood and Fern Bank

Sutton
Roundshaw Downs
Ruffet and Bid Woods
Spencer Road Wetlands
Sutton Ecology Centre
The Spinney, Carshalton
Wilderness Island

Waltham Forest
Ainslie Wood

Wandsworth
Battersea Park Nature Areas

Westminster
St John's Wood Church Grounds Wildlife Garden

SSSI SITES IN GREATER LONDON
Abbey Wood, Bexley
Bentley Priory, Harrow
Brent Reservoir (Welsh Harp), Barnet, Brent
Chingford Reservoir, Enfield, Epping Forest, Waltham Forest
Crofton Woods, Bromley
Croham Hurst, Croydon
Denham Lock Wood, Hillingdon
Downe Bank and High Elms, Bromley
Elmstead Pit, Bromley

Epping Forest, Epping Forest, Waltham Forest
Farthing Downs and Happy Valley, Croydon
Fray's Farm Meadows, Hillingdon
Gilbert's Pit, Greenwich
Hainault Forest, Epping Forest, Redbridge
Hampstead Heath Woods, Barnet, Camden, Haringey
Harefield Pit, Hillingdon
Harrow Weald, Harrow
Hornchurch Cutting, Havering
Ingrebourne Marshes, Havering,
Inner Thames Marshes, Havering, Thurrock
Keston and Hayes Commons, Bromley
Mid Colne Valley, Hillingdon, South Bucks
Old Park Woods, Hillingdon
Oxleas Woodlands, Greenwich
Richmond Park, Richmond
Riddlesdown, Croydon
Ruislip Woods, Hillingdon
Ruxley Gravel Pits, Bromley
Saltbox Hill, Bromley
Syon Park, Hounslow
Wansunt Pit, Bexley, Dartford
Walthamstow Marshes, Waltham Forest
Walthamstow Reservoirs, Hackney, Haringey,
Waltham Forest
Wimbledon Common, Merton, Wandsworth

LONDON LAND COVER*, 1988-1991 (THOUSAND HECTARES AND PERCENTAGES)

	Thousands of hectares'	Percentages
Suburban	66	38
Continuous urban	36	20
Semi-natural grass	29	17
Mown grass	13	8
Tilled land	12	7
Deciduous woodland	8	4
Other vegetation	5	3
Inland water	2	1
Estuary	1	1
Other land	3	2
Total	174	100

* Data taken from the Land Cover Map of Great Britain' The satellite classification may involve a degree of imprecision and misallocation and the results should be used with caution.
Source: Focus on London 2000, National Statistics' Crown Copyright 2001

ENVIRONMENT AGENCY

25th Floor, Millbank Tower, 21-24 Millbank, London SW1P 4XL
(Tel: 020-7863 8600; Fax 020-7863 8650).
Rio House, Waterside Drive, Aztec West, Almondsbury, Bristol BS32 4UD
(Tel: 01454 624400; Fax 01454 624409).

The Environment Agency was established in 1996 under the Environment Act 1995 and is a non-departmental public body sponsored by the Department of the Environment, Transport and the Regions, Ministry of Agriculture Fisheries and Food and the National Assembly for Wales. The Agency is responsible for pollution prevention and control in England and Wales, and for the management and use of water resources, including flood defences, fisheries and navigation. It has head offices in London and Bristol and eight regional offices.

Chairman: Sir John Harman
Director of Finance: N. Reader
Director of Personnel: G. Duncan
Director of Environmental Protection: Dr P. Leinster
Director of Water Management: G. Mance
Director of Operations: A. Robertson
Director of Corporate Affairs: H. McCallum
Director of Legal Services: R. Navarro
Chief Scientist: Dr. John Murlis

THE RIVER THAMES

The River Thames is the basis on which the city of London was built. Its freshwater stretches and tributaries provide water supplies for millions of people and the river serves as the main recipient of London's treated waste water. Substantial investment over the last thirty years has greatly improved water quality in the Thames, creating one of the cleanest metropolitan estuaries in the world. There have been 118 species of fish recorded in the tideway, including salmon which had been absent from the river for 140 years.

Historically, the nerve centre of London was the river – as a port, a market and as a source of fish. The foreshores and drawdocks were a hive of activity, and thus formed an important economic centre. Over the years, this role has changed and much of the riverside industry has disappeared. The river remains an important transport route: over 50 million tonnes of freight were shipped in and out of the Port of London in 1997. The Thames Path and other riverside walks encourage people to visit the Thames, but there are still many opportunities for recreation and economic benefit which are being neglected.

Thames21

Thames21 is a joint initiative between Tidy Britain Group, the Port of London Authority (PLA), the Environment Agency, Thames Water and the Corporation of London, to address poor local environmental quality on the Thames and its tributaries throughout London. It was launched officially by Michael Meacher MP in 1998. It continues the work of ThamesClean (established in 1994) and the PLA's Debris Clearance Operation (collecting up to 1,000 tonnes of litter each year from the Thames). The tidal Thames is the cleanest metropolitan estuary in Europe and supports 118 species of fish.

However, it is blighted by thousands of tonnes of litter which is blown, thrown and washed into it. It also exports litter to the marine environment where it pollutes beaches around the UK and the rest of the world. Thames21 aims to prevent and remedy this problem through a range of programmes, including its pioneering Adopt-a-River scheme, work with offenders on community service and improving the condition of the Thames Path National Trail. Over 3,000 volunteers are involved across London, and over 60 reaches of river have been adopted.

THAMES21

C/o Corporation of London, Walbrook Wharf, Upper Thames Street, London EC4R 3TD
(Tel: 020-7248 2916; Fax: 020-7236 1289;
E-mail: thames21.tbg@virgin.net;
Web: www.thames21.org.uk).

Programme Director: Mark Lloyd
(Tel: 020-7236 1281)
Project Officer (Adopt-a-River): Jen Hurst
(Tel: 020-7248 2916)
Project Officer (River Enhancements):
Alistair Maltby (Tel: 020-7684 2124)
Project Officer (Thames Path National Trail):
Deanne Jones (Tel: 020-7236 5657)

OTHER LONDON ENVIRONMENTAL BODIES

BRITISH TRUST FOR CONSERVATION VOLUNTEERS (BTCV)

London Region: 80 York Way, London N1 9AG (Tel: 020-7278 4294; Fax: 020-7278 5095; E-mail: london@btcv.org..uk; Web: www.btcv.org).

The British Trust for Conservation Volunteers (BTCV) in the London region aims to support and encourage Londoners in taking action to protect and improve their environment through programmes of practical conservation and community environmental improvement.

CHARTERED INSTITUTION OF WATER AND ENVIRONMENTAL MANAGEMENT

15 John Street, London WC1N 2EB (Tel: 020-7831 3110; Fax: 020-7405 4967; E-mail: admin@ciwem.org.uk; Web: www.ciwem.org.uk).

The aims and objectives of the Chartered Institution of Water and Environmental Management are to develop and promote the better and integrated management of the environment, to foster a better understanding of water and environmental issues and to enhance the quality of people's lives.

Policy and Technical Manager: Justin Taberham

FRIENDS OF THE EARTH LONDON

26-28 Underwood Street, London N1 7JQ (Tel: 020-7490 1555; Fax: 020-7490 0881; E-mail: pauldz@foe.co.uk; Web: www.foe.co.uk).

Friends of the Earth works to protect and improve conditions for life on earth, now and in the future. In London, work is on a local and regional level on a diverse range of social, economic and environmental issues, using campaigning, lobbying, public information and collaborative working to ensure that London shows the way as a sustainable city.

London Campaigns Co-ordinator: Paul De Zylva

Environmental Bodies 437

GOING FOR GREEN, LONDON

Premier House, 12-13 Hatton Garden, London EC1N 8HG (Tel: 020-7831 4484; Fax: 020-7430 2859; E-mail: jaquelineh@tidybritain.org.uk; Web: www.tidybritain.org.uk).

Going for Green aims to raise environmental awareness for people in London both in the workplace and at home.

National Director for London: Christopher Harris

LONDON 21 SUSTAINABILITY NETWORK

7 Chamberlain Street, London NW1 8XB (Tel: 020-7722 3710; Fax: 020-7722 3959; E-mail: admin@london21.org; Web: www.london 21.org).

LONDON ENVIRONMENTAL EDUCATION FORUM

Policy and Partnerships, Greater London Authority, 4th Floor, Romney House, 43 Marsham Street, London SW1P 3PY (Tel: 020-7983 4311; Fax: 020-7983 4706; E-mail: graham.myers@londongov.uk).

The London Environmental Education Forum develops, promotes and facilitates the delivery of environmental education throughout London.

Contact: Graham Myers

LONDON RIVERS ASSOCIATION

24-31 Greenwich Market, London SE10 9HZ (Tel: 020-8293 9275; Fax: 020-8293 9277; londonriversassociation@btinternet.com).

The London Rivers Association seeks to influence the strategic policy framework for London's waterways, provide a forum for debate and generate new thinking on the future of urban rivers.

Contact: Rose Jaijee/Ian Munt

LONDON TREE OFFICERS ASSOCIATION

3rd Floor, Crowndale Centre, 218 Eversholt Street, London NW1 1BD (Tel: 020-7272 9890; Fax: 020-7272 9890; E-mail: ltoa@dial.pipex.com).

The London Tree Officers Association is involved in improving the management of London's trees and woodlands.

Contact: Becky Hesch

LONDON WILDLIFE TRUST

Central Office, Harling House, 47-51 Great Suffolk Street, London SE1 0BS (Tel: 020-7261 0447; Fax: 020-7261 0538; E-mail: londonwt@cix.co.uk; Web: www.wildlondon.org.uk).

The principal objective of the London Wildlife Trust is to sustain and enhance London's wildlife habitats in order to create a city richer in wildlife. This is achieved through community initiatives, land management, education, campaigning and influencing decision makers in the capital.

PORT OF LONDON AUTHORITY

Baker's Hall, 7 Harp Lane, London EC34 6LB (Tel: 020-7743 7900)

The Port of London Authority is a public trust constituted under the Port of London Act 1908 and subsequent legislation. It is the governing body for the Port of London, covering the tidal portion of the River Thames from Teddington to the seaward limit. The Board comprises a chairman and up to seven but not less than four non-executive members appointed by the Secretary of State for the Environment, Transport and the Regions, and up to four but not less than one executive members appointed by the Board.

Chief Executive: S. Cuthbert
Secretary: G. E. Ennals

SUSTAINABLE LONDON TRUST

7 Chamberlain Street, London NW1 8XB (Tel: 020-7722 3710; Fax: 020-7722 3959; E-mail: slt@gn.apc.org; Web: www.greenchannel.com/slt/index.htm).

THAMES ESTUARY PARTNERSHIP

Department of Geography, Remax House, UCL, 31-32 Alfred Place, London WC1E 7DP (Tel: 020-7679 5299; Fax: 020-7916 8546; E-mail: tep@thamesweb.com; Web: www.thamesweb.com).

The Thames Estuary Partnership is involved in the sustainable use of the Thames Estuary by seeking to achieve a balance between the competing demands being placed on the Estuary. It seeks to do this via information sharing, action plans and a wide range of projects involving government agencies, local communities, local authorities and the voluntary and commercial sector.

Partnership Co-ordinator: Caroline Davis

URBAN POLLUTION RESEARCH CENTRE

Middlesex University, Bounds Green Road, London N11 2NQ (Tel: 020-8411 5229; Fax: 020-8411 6580; E-mail: n.priest@mdx.ac.uk; Web: www.mdx.ac.uk).

The main activity of the Urban Pollution Research Centre is research into all aspects of air and water pollution with special reference to air quality, urban run-off and environmental radionuclides.

Contact: Prof. Nick Priest

WASTE MINIMISATION AND RECYCLING IN LONDON

As households, businesses and industry create increasingly large amounts of waste, London's local authorities are making greater provision for waste minimisation and recycling. In addition to the bottle and can banks that can be seen on most street corners, the recycling concept has grown to encompass composting, door-to-door collection of bulky household items (such as old fridge-freezers which can be used for CFC recycling) and Christmas tree recycling.

Following the 1992 Rio Earth Summit Conference, where world leaders met to discuss ways to prevent future irreversible harm to the planet, Agenda 21 was conceived, laying down targets for the minimising of waste and environmental damage. At a local level, these targets broadly include: reducing the amount of waste produced and sent for disposal; increasing the use of recycling, composting and recovery of waste materials; encouraging the repair and re-use of goods and materials and encouraging households and businesses to buy products with less packaging.

WASTE MANAGEMENT IN LONDON, 1998-99 (MILLION TONNES)

London	Waste (tonnes)
Municipal waste disposal (excluding sweepings), 1998-99	
—Diverted through Recycling or composting	347,148
—Incinerated	520,980
—Landfilled	2,139,370
Total municipal waste	3,007,498
Commercial and industrial waste 1998-99	
—Commercial**	4,000,000
—Industrial**	3,900,000
—Total Commercial and Industrial Waste	7,900,000
Construction and demolition waste, 1999	
—Recycled	10,400,000
—Disposal	3,900,000
—Total Construction and Demolition Waste	14,200,000
Total Waste	25,100,000

* Provisional figures
** The margin of error on the commercial figure is 0.5 million tonnes and for the industrial figure 0.4 million tonnes
Source: Focus on London 2000, National Statistics' Crown Copyright 2001

The Environmental Protection Act 1990 places a duty on all local authorities to issue a Waste Recycling Plan (WRP) and stipulates that each WRP should include data on the authorities arrangements regarding waste collection and recycling. The Department of the Environment, Transport and the Regions has issued guidance notes to a local authorities preparing WRPs.

The list below provides details of the waste and recycling facilities that are available within London's 33 local authority areas. For further information on local government in London please see the Governed London section.

BARNET LBC

Barnet House, 1255 High Road, Whetstone, London N20 0EJ (Tel: 020-8359 2000; Fax: 020-8359 4154; E-mail: dens.lib@barnet.gov.uk; Web: www.barnet.gov.uk).

Barnet LBC encourages residents and local businesses to consider the amount of waste they produce for disposal with the aim of reducing as much of it as possible. The council offers a range of home composting units to residents and schools at competitive prices to help achieve this aim.

In the borough of Barnet there are over 80 recycling sites where recyclable items include glass bottles and jars, newspapers and magazines, cans and tins, textiles, shoes and soft toys. There is a Civic Amenity Site at Brent Terrace, off Tilling Road, London NW2 where there are facilities for recycling paper, glass, cans, textiles, metal, vehicle oil and vehicle batteries, gas cylinders and refrigeration units. The council collects paper for recycling from households with road frontages on a fortnightly basis. In addition, the council promotes Waste Minimisation for businesses with the support of Waste Alert, nation experts in this field. Details can be acquired from Barnet Local Agenda 21 Team (Tel: 020-8359 4662).

BEXLEY LBC

Works and Contracts Department, Crayford Town Hall, 112 Crayford Road, Crayford DA1 4ER (Tel: 020-8303 7777; Fax: 020-8319 9607; Web www.bexley.gov.uk).

There are 57 mini-recycling facilities in the borough of Bexley where materials such as cans, paper and cardboard, glass, metal, oil, textiles, batteries, hardcore, green waste, timber waste, books and shoes can be recycled. There are two municipal dumps/civic amenity sites:

Foots Cray Civic Amenity Site, Maidstone Road, Sidcup, Kent DA14 5HS

Thames Road Civic Amenity Site, Thames Road, Crayford, Kent DA1 5QJ

For further information about recycling and waste minimisation in the area, call the "Green Line" on 020-8319 9619.

BRENT LBC

Brent has approximately 140 recycling sites throughout the borough where a range of materials can be recycled including newspapers, magazines, textiles, glass bottles and jars, food and drinks cans (steel and aluminium), shoes and books.

Full details of all the recycling sites are available on Brent's web site at www.brent.gov.uk/recycling.

Brent has a Civic Amenity Site which is located at First Way, Wembley, Middx, where the full range of materials listed above can be recycled. In addition engine oil and scrap metal can be accepted. There are also facilities for degassing fridges containing CFCs. It is estimated that during 1999/2000, 6,200 tonnes of household waste was recycled.

There is a "Green Box Service" in operation and by the end of January 2001 there were approximately 73,000 households involved. Each household receives a weekly collection of textiles, newspapers and magazines, shoes, food tins and cans, glass bottles and jars, engine oil (in a sealed can) and aluminium foil.

The Waste Management and Recycling section is part of StreetCare which in turn is part of Environmental Services (Tel: 020-8937 5050; Fax: 020-8937 5090; E-mail: streetcare@brent.gov.uk).

BROMLEY LBC

Environmental Service Department, Civic Centre, Stockwell Close, Bromley BR1 3UH.

There are two Civic Amenity Sites in the borough, Waldo Road in Bromley and Churchfields Road in Beckenham. Household and garden waste can be deposited there free of charge, however, to dispose of soil, brick, rubble and construction waste, charges will be applied. At each Civic Amenity Site there are a number of recycling facilities where paper, card, bottles, cans, books, car batteries, wellington boots, fridge freezers, metals and textiles can be recycled. In addition, there are also 50 mini-recycling sites for the recycling of glass, paper, cans and textiles.

CAMDEN LBC

Regis Road Recycling Centre, Regis Road, Kentish Town, London NW5 3EW (Tel: 020-7974 6914/5; Fax: 020-7267 0763).

The London borough of Camden has almost 100 mini-recycling sites throughout the borough where residents can recycle glass and paper, and in most sites, cans, textiles and books. At the recycling centre in Regis Road, residents can bring cardboard, paper, cans, glass bottles, clear plastic bottles, opaque plastic bottles, textiles, books, green waste, metal, white goods, spectacles, car batteries, engine oil, mobile phones, stamps and foil. There is a fortnightly door-to-door paper and multi-material collection covering 40,000 properties within the borough. On special request we collect garden waste, fridge-freezers and other white goods.

CORPORATION OF LONDON

Walbrook Wharf, Upper Thames Street, London EC4R 3TD (Tel: 020-7236 9541; Fax: 020-7236 6560).

The City's residential population is very small and thus, waste recycling schemes are largely deemed to be non cost-effective. Further, security considerations prevent the siting of bottle banks and similar containers in public spaces. However, the City attracts private sector waste recyclers whenever waste materials can be collected for recycling at a profit. Cleansing Services aim to provide waste recycling services if there is strong local need and the necessary service is not available through private sector service providers.

Environmental Bodies 441

Due to the City being a large commercial centre, glass and good quality waste paper are the two commodities most commonly collected by the private sector for recycling. The financial and business sector of the City has an immense concentration of IT equipment which is continuously updated and the Corporation promotes better policies for the recycling or environmentally responsible disposal of such goods through its active membership of the Industry Council of Electronic Equipment Recycling (ICER) Ltd. Cleansing Services are able to provide trade waste customers with a free waste analysis to determine their waste as an aid to fomulating their recycling policies.

CROYDON LBC

Environmental and Recycling Unit, Public Services and Works, Room 18:08, Taberner House, Park Lane, Croydon CR9 3RN (Tel: 020-8760 5524; Fax: 020-8407 1306).

Croydon has approximately 33 recycling sites where paper, glass, textiles, cans and books can be recycled and there are 3 main recycling centres where additional materials can be recycled such as cardboard, metal, car batteries, engine oil, wood and garden waste:

Factory Lane Amenity and Recycling Centre, Factory Lane, West Croydon (Tel 020-8828 8700); Purley Oaks Civic Amenity and Recycling Centre, Brighton Road, South Croydon (Tel: 020-8668 2086); Fishers Farm Civic Amenity and Recycling Centre, North Downs Crescent, New Addington (Tel: 01689 849312).

EALING LBC

Environmental Services, 22—24 Uxbridge Road, London W5 2BP (Tel: 020-8832 6421; Fax: 020-8840 5575); London Borough of Ealing Recycling Office: (Tel: 020-8832 6424).

The following commodities can be recycled in the borough: glass, cans, paper, clothes and shoes, textiles, scrap metal, CFCs, engine oil, garden waste, paint, car batteries and cardboard. Household refuse which cannot be collected as part of the normal household refuse collection service can be disposed of at the borough recycling centres, free of charge.

Acton Waste and Recycling Centre, Stirling Road, London W3.

Greenford Waste and Recycling Centre, Greenford Depot, Greenford Road.

Southall Waste and Recycling Centre, Gordon Road, Southall.

ENFIELD LBC

Waste Reduction Officer, Montagu Road Depot, Edmonton, London N9 0ET (Tel: 020-8379 1788; Fax: 020-8379 1769).

There are numerous recycling facilities throughout the borough, recycling such materials as glass bottles and jars, drinks cans, newspapers and magazines and clothes.

For information about composting activity in the borough contact the Waste Reduction Officer (Tel: 020-8379 1788).

GREENWICH LBC

Waste Services, Directorate of Public Services, Birchmere Business Site, Eastern Way, London SE28 8BF (Tel: 020-8921 4663).

In the borough of Greenwich there are 82 recycling banks for the recycling of textiles, cans, paper, glass and other materials.

Civic Amenity facilities can be found at: Nathan Way Civic Amenity Site, Nathan Way, Thamesmead, London SE28 0AN (Tel: 020-8311 5229). Papers, glass, textiles, oil, scrap metal, green wastes, domestic appliances, cardboard and car batteries can be recycled here.

HACKNEY LBC

Waste Management and Technical Unit, The Portacabin, c/o Maurice Bishop House, Reading Lane, London E8 1HH (Tel: 020-8356 3617; Fax 020-8356 3507).

The borough of Hackney currently has a pilot kerbside-recycling scheme in operation, providing a service to approximately 13,000 residents, with plans to introduce the service to all residents in the future. There are approximately 52 bring sites/mini-recycling centres located around the borough at which residents can recycle glass, magazines and cans. The borough also provides a bulk waste removal service, which provides collection of up to five items free of charge to all residents.

HAMMERSMITH AND FULHAM LBC

Town Hall, King Street, London W6 9JU (Tel: 020-8748 3020).

The borough of Hammersmith and Fulham runs two types of service; kerbside collections and public recycling banks. There is a free weekend amenity skip service available and there are special recycling services for disabled residents of the borough. Bulky items such as fridge freezers can be collected for recycling.

A Civic Amenity Site is based at: Smugglers Way, Wandsworth, London SW18 (Tel: 020-8871 2788).

HARINGEY LBC

The Civic Amenity Centre, Park View Road, London N17 9AY; Recycling Centre, Western Road, Wood Green, London N22 9JJ (Tel: 020-8489 5678 (Customer Care Team)).

The borough has 2 major recycling centres and 27 recycling banks. All of the banks collect glass, paper and cans.

HARROW LBC

Harrow Council Information Office, Station Road, Harrow HA1 2XF (Tel: 020-8424 1778).

For information on recycling facilities in the borough contact: Forward Drive, Wealdstone HA3 8NT (Tel: 020-8424 1778).

HILLINGDON LBC

Civic Centre, High Street, Uxbridge UB8 1UW (Tel: 01895 250111; Fax: 01895 273636); Recycling Office: Central Depot, 128 Harlington Road, Hillingdon, Middx UB8 3EU (01895-277507).

There are nearly 100 recycling sites in the borough and there is also a kerbside recycling initiative which involves the fortnightly collection of recyclables from 16,000 households. Recyclable materials include glass, cans, paper, textiles and metal.

HOUNSLOW LBC

Environmental Services, Civic Centre, Lampton Road, Hounslow TW3 4DN (Tel: 020-8583 5060).

In the borough of Hounslow there are 50 mini-recycling sites where items such as paper, glass, cans and textiles may be recycled. In addition, approximately 71,450 households are covered by a kerbside recycling service via which the following items can be recycled: glass, newspapers and magazines, foil, engine oil, tins and cans, textiles, shoes, flattened cardboard boxes.

Space Waye Civic Amenity Site is based at: Pier Road, North Feltham Trading Estate, Feltham, Middlesex TW14 0TH (Tel: 020-8890 0917). Glass, shoes, books, scrap metal, cardboard, tins, cans, timber, engine oil, car batteries, paper and clothing can be recycled at this site. Green waste is also collected, removed for composting and resold to the public on site.

ISLINGTON LBC

51 Hanley Road, London N4 3TH (Tel: 020-7527 4744; Fax: 020-7527 4642).

The current operations in recycling for the borough includes Mini Recycling Centres (bottle banks) for glass, paper and textiles. There is also a door-to-door- recycling collection for residential properties. For further information contact the **Waste Minimisation officer:** Caroline Brimblescombe

KENSINGTON AND CHELSEA LBC

Waste and Recycling Unit, Council Offices, 37 Pembroke Road, London W8 6PW (Tel: 020-7341 5148; Fax: 020-7341 5200; E-mail: wastemanagement@rbkc.gov.uk).

There are 25 mini-recycling centres located throughout the borough for residents. There are twice-weekly doorstep recycling collections for cans and tins, newspapers and magazines, cardboard, junk mail and telephone directories, rags, plastic bottles, juice and milk cartons and glass bottles and jars.

There are civic amenity skips for the disposal of bulky household waste and green waste sited at Cremorne Wharf, 27 Lots Road, London SW10; Western Riverside Waste Authority, Smugglers Way, Wandsworth SW18 1JS (Tel: 020-8871 2788); Cringle Dock, Cringle Street, Battersea, London SW8 5BA. A Materials Recycling

Facility is located at the Cremorne Wharf site where the following items can be recycled: green garden waste, scrap metal, furniture, fridge freezers, engine oil and household electricals.

KINGSTON UPON THAMES LBC

Guildhall, High Street, Kingston upon Thames, KT1 1EU.

For any queries on waste and recycling within the borough, contact the Recycling Officer (Tel: 020-8547 5567).

LAMBETH LBC

Sustainable Wastes Unit, 4th Floor, Blue Star House, 234-244 Stockwell Road, London SW9 9SP (Tel: 020-7926 2624; Fax 020-7926 6201).

Recycling services in the borough are offered to all households. On-street properties can register for the Green Box Scheme, whereby residents can recycle paper, glass, cans, foil, textiles and oil. For further information residents should call: (Tel: 020-8761 1144). Estate-based properties have access to near-entry based recycling systems, whereby sites are housed near to the entrances of housing blocks to make is easier for residents to recycle. Residents using this scheme can recycle paper, glass and cans. There are currently 200 sites in the borough. A further 23 large on-street recycling sites are rpovided for the recycling of paper, glass, cans and textiles. The provision of these systems ensiures that all residents are within 1km of a recycling facility; the majority are within 500m. The Sustainable Wastes Unit also supports a number of voluntary groups throughout the borough. Current activities supported include community composting schemes, recycling incentive schemes, community campaigns including clean-ups and junk-swaps and computer recycling programmes.

MERTON LBC

Waste Service Review, 13th Floor, London Road, Morden, Surrey SM4 5DX (Tel: 020-8543 2222; Fax: 020-8545 3942).

There are 36 recycling sites in the borough of Merton where materials such as glass, paper, textiles, cans and oil can be recycled. For general information telephone the Environmental Control Line on 020-8545 4157. There is a civic amenity site at Amenity Way, Garth Road, Lower Morden, Surrey SM4 4NJ which is the main facility for tipping large items of waste and recyclables.

NEWHAM LBC

Public Works, Central Depot, Folkestone Road, London E6 6BX (Tel: 020-8430 2000; Fax: 020-8557 8989).

There are 100 recycling sites where people can take a range of materials to be recycled. Items such as bottles, cans, textiles, paper, batteries, shoes, oils and metals. There is a civic amenity site at Jenkins Lane, E6, where refuse from household and commercial collections is put in containers for transport to landfill or incineration sites.

REDBRIDGE LBC

Town Hall, PO Box 2, Ilford IG1 1DD (Tel: 020-8478 3020).

In Redbridge over 92,000 domestic properties receive a weekly refuse collection and approximately 2000 businesses use the Council's Commercial Waste Service. Bulky household waste collections are made and there is also a skip service. There are over 70 recycling sites in the borough and kerbside collections are available to 50 percent of the borough's residents. Recycling targets include: to reduce the total amount of waste produced; to increase the percentage of residents with access to recycling facilities; to establish home composting in 40 percent of all properties with gardens; to involve 100 percent of schools in recycling and anti-litter activities and to respond to 100 percent of community groups who want to get involved in recycling initiatives.

Ilford Recycling Centre is based at 409 High Road, Ilford (Tel: 020-8478 3020 Extn. 2600); Recycling Team (Tel:020-8708 5517/5518 5007).

SUTTON LBC

Environment and Leisure, 24 Denmark Road, Carshalton SM5 2JG (Tel: 020-8770 6248; Fax: 020-8770 6410).

There are 197 recycling sites within the borough of Sutton where the following materials can be recycled: newspapers and magazines, cardboard, plastic bottles, cans, glass bottles and jars, textiles, shoes, books, wood, rubble, engine oil/cooking oil and green waste.

Recycling Manager: Penny Spirling.

TOWER HAMLETS LBC

Waste Disposal and Recycling, Council Offices, Southern Grove, London E3 4PN (Tel: 020-7364 6699; Fax: 020-7364 6922).

Within Tower Hamlets there is a network of over 50 bring-sites where clear/green/brown glass, newspapers, magazines, junk mail, textiles, cardboard and cans can be recycled. A kerbside recycling service is offered to 11,000 houses collecting glass, cans, textiles, paper and cardboard.

The main Civic Amenity site is located at: Northumberland Wharf, Yabsley Street, London E14 9RG. At this site glass, newspapers, magazines, junk mail, food and drink containers, greenwaste, textiles, cardboard, waste engine oils and car batteries can be recycled.

For information on recycling and waste matters within Tower Hamlets, contact Streetline (Tel: 020-8364 3364).

WALTHAM FOREST LBC

Kings Road Recycling Centre, Kings Road, Chingford, London E4 7LH; South Access Road Household Waste Centre, Walthamstow, London E17.

The borough of Waltham Forest has a variety of recycling schemes including: a large recycling centre in Chingford; a green garden waste composting scheme; a network of mini-recycling centres; support for community based projects such as "Community re-paint Waltham Forest", the "Foiled Again" aluminium foil collection scheme, the "Tools for Self Reliance" scheme and the "Renov8" furniture re-use project and a "Sorted" multi-material recycling collection service involving 66,000 homes in the borough.

Materials at the Kings Road Recycling Centre include: cans, glass, textiles, paper, cardboard, garden waste, scrap metal, paint, wood, tools, aluminium foil, engine oil and car batteries and hardcore. At the South Access Road Household Waste Centre the above materials may be recycled, excluding wood.

WANDSWORTH LBC

Leisure and Amenity Services Department, The Town Hall, Wandsworth High Street, London SW18 2PU (Tel: 020-8871 8558; Fax: 020-8871 6383).

Special collection services are offered and items such as unwanted fridges and freezers are collected free of charge. Other bulky items are collected at a small charge and this can be arranged through the Amenity Services Department. Civic Amenity Sites can be found at:

Smugglers Way, Wandsworth, London SW18 (Tel: 020-8871 2788).

Cringle Street, London SW8 (Tel: 020-7622 6233).

At these sites there are facilities for recycling garden waste, wood, scrap metal, fridges and freezers, car batteries, oil, paper and card, glass, textiles, cans and books. Each week there is also a collection of glass, paper and cans for recycling from properties where ordinary rubbish is collected in sacks or dustbins.

There are 39 recycling sites in the borough where glass, paper, cans, textiles and books can be recycled. There is also a weekly recycling service for paper, glass and cans. Residents can call 020-8871 7497 in to join it.

WESTMINSTER CITY LBC

Environmental Services, Contracts Group, Westminster City Hall, 64 Victoria Street, London SW1E 6QP (Tel: 020-7641 7956; Fax: 020-7641 7964).

In the borough of Westminster there are 65 mini-recycling centres where paper, glass, cans and textiles can be recycled. To increase the convenience of recycling the borough is currently in the process of expanding its door-to-door recycling services which collects paper, glass bottles and drinks cans on a weekly basis. There is also a comprehensive range of waste minimisation and recycling services for schools and businesses in the area.

LONDON AND
THE WORLD

**TOURIST BOARDS
EMBASSIES
INTERNATIONAL ORGANISATIONS
EUROPEAN UNION
TIME ZONES
AIR DISTANCES FROM LONDON
INTERNATIONAL DIRECT DIALLING CODES**

LONDON AND THE WORLD

London is well established as a 'World Class' city. It cannot be summed up in any one context as its diversity is so great. It is a business centre, a tourist centre, a cultural centre, a historical centre, a religious centre, an environmental centre, but is also an international centre. None of these facets takes precedence over the others and it is this which gives London its complexity and quality as a world city.

Many international organisations base themselves in London or choose to locate premises in London. There are also people of many nationalities who live, work or travel in London. This section offers information of the institutions and bodies which have an international focus and are based in the London area. It also provides full listings of International time zones and International dialling codes.

CITIES IN EUROPE [1,2], 1997

	Population (000s)	Land area (sq km)	Population density (persons per sq km)	Births (000s)	Crude birth rate (per 1,000 population)	Deaths (000s)	Crude death rate (per 1,000 population)
London [3,4]	7,187	1,578	4,554	105.3	14.7	62.1	8.6
Inner London [3]	2,761	321	8,613	43.7	15.8	21.8	7.9
Outer London [3]	4,427	1,258	3,519	61.6	13.9	40.3	9.1
Birmingham [3]	1,013	265	3,826	14.8	14.6	10.4	10.2
Glasgow [3]	620	175	3,541	7.4	11.5	8.4	13.5
Manchester [3]	430	116	3,690	5.8	13.6	4.9	11.5
Amsterdam [6]	1,132	897	1,262	14.4	12.7	10.3	9.1
Athens	3,449	3,808	906	36.5	10.6	32.9	9.5
Barcelona	4,609	7,733	598	43.0	9.3	41.6	9.0
Berlin [5]	3,442	891	3,964	30.4	8.8	36.4	10.6
Brussels	952	161	5,898	12.8	13.4	10.5	11.0
Lisbon	1,834	1,055	1,738	20.6	11.3	18.5	10.1
Madrid	5,022	7,995	628	48.1	9.6	37.3	7.4
Milan	3,733	1,983	1,883	33.2	8.9	33.3	8.9
Munich [6]	1,231	311	3,965	12.5	10.2	12.4	10.1
Paris	2,122	105	20,135	29.7	14.0	17.0	8.0
Rome	3,792	5,352	709	34.3	9.0	35.1	9.3
Stockholm	1,754	6,490	270	20.6	11.8	15.7	9.0
Vienna	1,600	415	3,856	15.5	9.7	18.5	11.5

1 NUTS 3 area classification unless otherwise stated.
2 NUTS areas are based on national administrative structures which differ greatly. Comparisons should be treated with caution.
3 Figures relate to 1998
4 NUTS 1 area classification.
5 NUTS 2 area classification
6 Figures relate to 1996
Source: Focus on London 2000. National Statistics' Crown Copyright 2001

TOURIST BOARDS

The list below details the London offices of foreign tourist boards.

Anguilla Tourist Office
3 Epirus Road, London, SW6 (Tel: 020-7937 7725)

Antigua and Barbuda Tourist Office
15 Thayer Street, London, W1M 5LD (Tel: 020-7486 7073; Fax: 020-7486 1466; E-mail: antbar@msn.com; Web: www.antigua-barbuda.com)

Austrian National Tourist Office
PO Box 2363, London, W1A 2QB (Tel: 020-7629 0461; Fax: 020-7499 6038; E-mail: info@anto.co.uk; Web: www.austria-tourism.at/)

Barbados Tourism Authority
263 Tottenham Court Road, London, W1T 7LA (Tel: 020-7636 9448; Fax: 020-7637 1496; E-mail: btauk@barbados.org; Web: www.barbados.org)
Regional Manager: Jennifer Barrow

British Virgin Islands Tourist Board
55 Newman Street, London, W1T 3EB (Tel: 020-7947 8200; Fax: 020-7947 8279; E-mail: bvi@bho.fcb.com; Web: www.bviwelcome.com)
Managing Director: David E. Winter

Caribbean Tourism Organisation
42 Westminster Palace Gardens, Artillery Row, London, SW1P (Tel: 020-7222 4335; Fax: 020-7222 4325; E-mail: cto@carib-tourism.com; Web: www.doitcaribbean.com)
Director of Marketing: Jo Spalburg

Catalonia Tourist Board
17 Fleet Street, London, EC4Y (Tel: 020-7583 8855; Fax: 020-7583 8877; E-mail: catalonia@catalantouristboard.co.uk; Web: www.gencat.es/turisme)
Director: David Miro

Cayman Islands Department of Tourism
6 Arlington Street, London, SW1A (Tel: 020-7491 7771; Fax: 020-7409 7773; E-mail: info-uk@caymanislands.ky; Web: www.caymanislands.ky)
Regional Manager: Don McDougall

Cuba Tourist Board
154 Shaftesbury Avenue, London, WC2H 8JT (Tel: 020-7240 6655; Fax: 020-7836 9265; E-mail: cubatouristboard.london@virgin.net)

Cyprus Government Tourist Office
17 Hanover Street, London, W1R 0AA (Tel: 020-7569 8800; Fax: 020-7499 4935; E-mail: ctolon@ctolon.demon.co.uk)
Director: Orestis Rossides

Danish Tourist Board
55 Sloane Street, London, SW1X 9SY (Tel: 020-7259 5958; Fax: 020-7259 5955; E-mail: dtb.london@dt.dk; Web: www.visitdenmark.com)

Dominica Tourist Office
1 Collingham Gardens, London, SW5 (Tel: 020-8350 1000; Fax: 020-8350 1011; Web: www.dominica.dm)

Dubai Department of Tourism and Commerce Marketing
125 Pall Mall, London, SW1Y (Tel: 020-7839 0580; Fax: 020-7839 0582; E-mail: dtcm-uk@dubaitourism.co.uk; Web: www.dubaitourism.co.uk)
Director UK and Ireland: Patrick Macdonald

Egyptian State Tourism Office
Egyptian House, 170 Piccadilly, London, W1V (Tel: 020-7493 5283; Fax: 020-7408 0295; E-mail: egypt@freenetname.co.uk; Web: www.interoz.com/egypt)

Finnish Tourist Board
PO Box 33213, London, SW1Y 5ZS (Tel: 020-7365 2512; Fax: 020-7321 0696; E-mail: finlandinfo@mek.fi; Web: www.finland-tourism.com)
Director: Matti Linnoila

French Tourist Office
178 Piccadilly, London, W1J 9AL (Tel: 09068 244123; Fax: 020-7493 6594; E-mail: info@mdlf.co.uk; Web: www.franceguide.com)
Mananging Director: C.Lepage

Gambia National Tourist Office
57 Kensington Court, London, W8 5DG (Tel: 020-7376 0093; Fax: 020-7938 3644; E-mail: info@thegambia-touristoff.co.uk; Web: www.itsnet.co.uk)
Tourism Attache: Saye Drameh

Tourist Boards 449

German National Tourist Office
PO Box 2695, London, W1A 3TN
(Tel: 09001-600 100; Fax: 020-7495 6129;
E-mail: gntolon@d-z-t.com;
Web: www.germany-tourism.de)
Director UK and Ireland: Rudelf Richter

Government of Gilbraltar
179 The Strand, London, WC2R (Tel:
020-7836 0777; Fax: 020-7420 6612; E-mail:
giblondon@aol.com; Web: www.gilbraltar.gi)

Greece: Hellenic Tourism Organisation
4 Conduit Street, London, W1S 2DJ
(Tel: 020-7734 5997; Fax: 020-7287 1369;
E-mail: got-greektouristoffice@btinternet.com;
Web: www.antor.com/greece)

Grenada Board of Tourism
1 Battersea Church Road, London, SW11 3LY
(Tel: 020-7771 7016; Fax: 020-7771 7181;
E-mail: grenada@cibgroup.co.uk;
Web: www.grenadagrenadlinks.com)
UK Representative: Sharon Bernstein

Hong Kong Tourist Association
6 Grafton Street, London, W1S 4EQ
(Tel: 020-7533 7100; Fax: 020-7533 7111;
E-mail: hktalon@hkta.org;
Web: www.discoverhongkong.com)
Regional Director: Kevin Welch

Hungarian National Tourist Office
46 Eaton Place, London, SW1X 8AL (Tel:
020-7823 1032; Fax: 020-7823 1459;
Web: www.tourist-offices.org.uk)

Iceland Tourist Information Bureau
172 Tottenham Court Road, London, W1P (Tel:
020-8286 8008; Fax: 020-7387 5711; E-mail:
london@icelandair.is; Web: www.goiceland.org)

India Tourist Office
7 Cork Street, London, W1X 2LN
(Tel: 020-7437 3677; Fax: 020-7494 1048)

Irish Tourist Board
150 New Bond Street, London, W1S 2AQ
(Tel: 0800 0397000; Fax: 020-7493 9065;
E-mail: info@irishtouristboard.co.uk;
Web: www.ireland.travel.uk)

Israel Government Tourist Office
UK House, 180 Oxford Street, London, W1N
9DJ (Tel: 020-7299 1111; Fax: 020-7299 1112;
E-mail: information@igto.co.uk;
Web: www.infotour.co.il)

Italian State Tourist Office
1 Princes Street, London, W1R (Tel:
020-7408 1254; Fax: 020-7493 6695; E-mail:
enitlond@glbalnet.co.uk; Web: www.enit.it)
**General Manager UK, Ireland and
Scandinavia:** Mr Piotrippa

Jamaica Tourist Board
1-2 Prince Consort Road, London, SW7 2BZ
(Tel: 020-7224 0505; Fax: 020-7224 0551)

Japan National Tourist Organisation
Heathcoat House, 20 Savile Row, London, W1X
(Tel: 020-7734 9638; Fax: 020-7734 4290;
E-mail: jntolon@dircon.co.uk)

Jersey Tourism & Information Office
7 Lower Grosvenor Place, London, SW1W 0EN
(Tel: 020-7630 8787; Fax: 020-7630 0747;
E-mail: london@jersey.com; Web: www.jersey.com)
UK Sales Manager: Dawn Pinson

Kenya Tourist Office
25 Brook's Mews, London, W1Y
(Tel: 020-7355 3144; Fax: 020-7495 8656;
Web: www.kenya.tourism.org)

Korea National Tourist Organisation
3rd Floor, New Zealand House, Haymarket,
London, SW1Y 4TE (Tel: 020-7321 2535; Fax:
020-7321 0876; E-mail: koreatb@dircon.co.uk;
Web: www.visitkorea.co.uk)
Direcor: D.Kim

Lebanon Tourist & Information Office
90 Piccadilly, London, W1V
(Tel: 020-7409 2031)

Luxembourg Tourist Office
122 Regent Street, London, W1B 5SA
(Tel: 020-7434 2800; Fax: 020-7734 1205;
E-mail: tourism@luxembourg.co.uk;
Web: www.luxembourg.co.uk)
Director: Serge Moes

450 London and the World

Malaysian Tourism Promotion Board
Malaysian House, 57 Trafalgar Square, London, WC2N 5DU (Tel: 020-7930 7932; Fax: 020-7930 9015; E-mail: mtpb.london@tourism.gov.my; Web: www.tourism.gov.my)

Malta Tourist Office
Malta House, 36–38 Piccadilly, London, W1V 0PP (Tel: 020-7292 4900; Fax: 020-7734 1880; E-mail: office.uk@visitmalta.com; Web: www.visitmalta.com)
Director: John Montague

Mauritius Tourism Promotion Authority
32 Elvaston Place, London, SW7 (Tel: 020-7584 3666; Fax: 020-7275 1135; E-mail: mtpa@btinternet.com; Web: www.mauritius.net)
Manager: Sohun Uhoorah

Mexico Tourism Board
Wakefield House, 41 Trinity Square, London, EC3N 4DJ (Tel: 020-7488 9392; Fax: 020-7265 0704; E-mail: info@mexicotravel.co.uk; Web: www.mexicotravel.co.uk)
Regional Director: Manuel Diaz-Cebrian

Monaco Government Tourist & Convention Office
The Chambers, Chelsea Harbour, London, SW10 0XF (Tel: 020-7352 9962; Fax: 020-7352 2103; E-mail: monaco@monaco.co.uk; Web: www.monaco-congres.com)

Moroccan National Tourist Office
205 Regent Street, London, W1R 7DE (Tel: 020-7437 0073; Fax: 020-7734 8172; E-mail: mnto@btconnect.com; Web: www.tourism-in-morocco.com)
Director: Aliel Kasmi

Namibia Tourism
6 Chandos Street, London, W1M (Tel: 020-7636 2924; E-mail: info@naminiatourism.co.uk; Web: www.namibiatourism.co.uk)
Marketing Manager: S. Ailata

Tourism New Zealand
New Zealand House, Haymarket, London, SW1Y 4TQ (Tel: 020-7930 1662; Fax: 020-7839 8929; Web: www.purenz.com)

North Cyprus Tourism Centre
29 Bedford Square, London, WC1B 8EG (Tel: 020-7631 1930; Fax: 020-7631 1873)

Northern Ireland Tourist Board
24 Haymarket, London, SW1Y (Tel: 08701-555 250; Fax: 020-7766 9929; Web: www.ni-tourism.com)

Norwegian Tourist Board
Charles House, 5–11 Lower Regent Street, London, SW1Y (Tel: 020-7839 6255; Fax: 020-7839 6014; E-mail: infouk@ntr.no; Web: www.visitnorway.com)

The Philippine Cultural and Tourism Office
146 Cromwell Road, London, SW7 4EF (Tel: 020-7835 1100; Fax: 020-7835 1926; E-mail: tourism@pdot.co.uk; Web: www.tourism.gov.ph)

Polish National Tourist Office
310–312 Regent Street, London, W1B 3AX (Tel: 020-7580 8811; Fax: 020-7580 8866; E-mail: info@visitpoland.org; Web: www.visitpoland.org)
Director: Jerzy Szegidewicz

Portuguese National Tourist Office
22–25A Sackville Street, London, W1X 2LY (Tel: 09063 640610; Fax: 020-7494 1868; E-mail: tourisminfo@portugaloffice.org.uk; Web: www.portugalinsite.pt)
Director of Tourism: N.Terreira

Romanian National Tourist Office
22 New Cavendish Street, London, W1M 7LH (Tel: 020-7224 3692; Fax: 020-7935 6435; E-mail: uktouroff@romania.freeserve.co.uk; Web: www.romaniatravel.com)
Director: Maria Iordache

Russian Federation, Sport & Tourism
78 Piccadilly, London, W1J 8HP (Tel: 020-7495 7575; Fax: 020-7495 8555; E-mail: inntelmoscow@intel-moscow.co.uk; Web: www.russia-travel.com)

St Kitts & Nevis Tourism Office
10 Kensington Court, London, W8 (Tel: 020-7376 0881; Fax: 020-7937 6742; E-mail: stkitts.nevis@btinternet.com; Web: www.stkitts-nevis.com)
Director UK/Europe: Esther Smith

Tourist Boards 451

St Vincent & The Grenadines Tourist Office
10 Kensington Court, London, W8 5DL
(Tel: 020-7937 6570; Fax: 020-7937 3611;
E-mail: svgtourismeurope@aol.com;
Web: www.svgtourism.com)
Manager UK/Europe: Jasmine Baksh

Scottish Tourist Board
19 Cockspur Street, London, SW1Y 5BL
(Tel: 0131-332 2433; Fax: 020-7930 1817;
Web: www.visitscotland)
Manager, London: Graeme Clark

Seychelles Tourist Office
2nd Floor, Eros House, 111 Baker Street, London, W1M 1FE (Tel: 020-7224 1670; Fax: 020-7486 1352; E-mail: sto@seychelles.uk.com; Web: www.seychelles.uk.com)

Singapore Tourist Board
Carrington House, 126–130 Regent Street, London, W1R (Tel: 020-7437 0033; Fax: 020-734 2191; E-mail: info@stb.org.uk; Web: www.newasia-singapore.comm.sg)
Regional Director: Nicholas Kao

Slovenia Tourist Board
49 Conduit Street, London, W1R 9FB
(Tel: 020-7287 7133; Fax: 020-7287 5476;
E-mail: info@slovenia-tourism.si;
Web: www.slovenia-tourism.si)

Spanish Tourist Office
22–23 Manchester Square, London, W1M 5AP
(Tel: 020-7486 8077; Fax: 020-7486 8034;
E-mail: info.londres@tourspain.es;
Web: www.tourspain.co.uk)

Sri Lanka Tourist Board
Clareville House, 26-27 Oxendon Street, London, SW1Y 4EL (Tel: 020-7930 2627; Fax: 020-7930 9070; E-mail: srilanka@carbernet.co.uk; Web: www.lanka.net/ctb)

Swedish Travel & Tourism Council
11 Montagu Place, London, W1H 2AL
(Tel: 020-7870 5600; Fax: 020-7724 5872;
E-mail: info@swetourism.org.uk;
Web: www.visit-sweden.com)

Switzerland Travel Centre
10th Floor, Swiss Centre, 10 Wardour Street, London, W10 6QF (Tel: 020-7282 1550; Fax: 020-7282 1599; E-mail: sta@stlondon.com)

Thailand Tourism Authority
49 Albermarle Street, London, W1X
(Tel: 0870-900 2007; Fax: 020-7629 5519;
E-mail: info@tat-uk.demon.co.uk;
Web: www.tourismthailand.org)
Director: Thawatchai Arunyik

Tunisian National Tourist Office
77A Wigmore Street, London, W1H
(Tel: 020-7224 5561; Fax: 020-7224 4053;
E-mail: tntolondon@aol.com;
Web: www.tourismtunisia.com)

Turkish Tourist Office
1st Floor, Egyptian House, 170–173 Piccadilly, London, W1J 9EJ (Tel: 020-7629 7771; Fax: 020-7491 0773;
E-mail: tto@turkish.tourism.demon.co.uk;
Web: www.tourist-offices.org.uk/turkey)

Venezuela Tourist Office
Embassy of the Bolivarian, Republic of Venezuelan, 1 Cromwell Road, London, SW7 2HR (Tel: 020-7584 4206; Fax: 020-7584 8887; E-mail: venezlon@venezlon.demon.co.uk; Web: www.venezlon.demon.co.uk)
Tourist Representative: Zhaybel Cardenas

Zambia National Tourist Board
2 Palace Gate, Kensington, London, W8 (Tel: 020-7589 6655; Fax: 020-7584 6346; E-mail: zntb@aol.com; Web: www.zambiatourism.com)
Tourism Promotion Manager:
Donald Pelekamoyo

Zimbabwe Tourist Information
429 The Strand, London, WC2R
(Tel: 020-7240 6169)

EMBASSIES

The list below details the London-based embassies of foreign countries

Embassy of the Islamic State of Afghanistan
31 Princes Gate, London, SW7 1QQ
(Tel: 020-7589 8991; Fax: 020-7581 3452;
E-mail: embassyofafghanistan@compuserve.com;
Web: www.afghan.gov.af)
Charge d'Affaires: Mr. Ahmad Wali MASUD

Embassy of the Republic of Albania
2nd Floor, 24 Buckingham Gate, London, SW1E 6LB (Tel: 020-7828 8897; Fax: 020-7828 8869)
Ambassador Extraordinary and Plenipotentiary:
His Excellency Mr Agim Besim Fagu

Embassy of Algeria
54 Holland Park, London, W11 3RS
(Tel: 020-7221 7800; Fax: 020-7221 0448)
Ambassador Extraordinary and Plenipotentiary:
His Excellency Mr Ahmed Benyamina

American Embassy
24 Grosvenor Square, London, W1A 1AE
(Tel: 020-7499 9000; Fax: 020-7493 3425)

Embassy of the Republic of Angola
98 Park Lane, London, W1Y 3TA
(Tel: 020-7495 1752; Fax: 020-7495 1635)
Ambassador Extraordinary and Plenipotentiary:
His Excellency Senhor Atonio Da Costa Fernandes

High Commission for Antigua and Barbuda
15 Thayer Street, London, W1U 3JT
(Tel: 020-7486 7073; Fax: 020-7486 9970;
Web: www.antigua-barbuda.com)
High Commissioner:
His Excellency Sir Ronald M. Sanders, CMG

Embassy of the Argentine Republic
65 Brook Street, London, W1Y 1YE
(Tel: 020-7318 1300; Fax: 020-7318 1301)
Ambassador Extraordinary and Plenipotentiary:
His Excellency Señor Vicenete E. Berasategui

Embassy of the Republic of Armenia
25A Cheniston Gardens, London, W8 6TG
(Tel: 020-7938 5435; Fax: 020-7938 2595;
E-mail: armembuk@dircon.co.uk)
Ambassador Extraordinary and Plenipotentiary:
His Excellency Dr Vahram Abadjan

Australian High Commision
Australia House, Strand, London, WC2B 4LA
(Tel: 020-7379 4334; Fax: 020-7240 5333;
Web: www.australia.org.uk)
High Commissioner:
His Excellency Mr Michael L'estrange

Austrian Embassy
18 Belgrave Mews West, London, SW1X 8HU
(Tel: 020-7235 3731; Fax: 020-7344 0292;
E-mail: embassy@austria.org.uk;
Web: www.austria.org.uk)
Ambassador Extraordinary and Plenipotentiary:
Dr. Alexandra Christiani

Embassy of the Azerbaijan Republic
4 Kensington Court, London, W8 5DL
(Tel: 020-7938 5482/3412; Fax: 020-7937 1783;
E-mail: sefir@btinternet.com)
Ambassador Extraordinary and Plenipotentiary:
His Excellency Mr Mahmud Mamed-Kuliyev

High Commission for the Commonwealth of the Bahamas
10 Chesterfield Street, London, W1X 8AH
(Tel: 020-7408 4488; Fax: 020-7499 9937)
High Commissioner:
His Excellency Mr Basil G. O'Brien, CMG

Embassy of the State of Bahrain
98 Gloucester Road, London, SW7 4AU
(Tel: 020-7370 5132/3; Fax: 020-7370 7773)
Ambassador Extraordinary and Plenipotentiary:
His Excellency Shaikh Abdul Aziz Bin Mubarak Al Khalfia

High Commission for the People's Republic of Bangladesh
28 Queen's Gate, London, SW7 5JA
(Tel: 020-7584 0081; Fax: 020-7225 2130;
E-mail: bdesh.lon@dial.pipex.com)
High Commissioner:
His Excellency Mr A. H. Mahmood Ali

Barbados High Commission
1 Great Russell Street, London, WC1B 3ND
(Tel: 020-7631 4975; Fax: 020-7323 6872;
E-mail: london@foreign.gov.bb)
High Commissioner:
His Excellency Mr Peter Patrick Simmons

Embassy of the Republic of Belarus
6 Kensington Court, London, W8 5DL
(Tel: 020-7937/3288; Fax: 020-7361 0005;
E-mail: belarus@belemb.freeserve.co.uk;
Web: www.belemb.freeserve.co.uk)
Ambassador: Dr. Valery Sadokho

Belgian Embassy
103 Eaton Square, London, SW1W 9AB
(Tel: 020-7470 3700; Fax: 020-7259 6213;
E-mail: info@belgium-embassy.co.uk;
Web: www.belgium-embassy.co.uk)
Ambassador Extraordinary and Plenipotentiary:
His Excellency Mr Lode Willems

Belize High Commission
22 Harcourt House, 19 Cavendish Square, London, W1G 0PN (Tel: 020-7499 9728; Fax: 020-7491 4139; E-mail: bzhc-lon@btconnect.com; Web: www.belize.gov.bz)
High Commissioner:
His Excellency Mr Assad Shoman

Embassy of Bolivia
106 Eaton Square, London, SW1W 9AD
(Tel: 020-7235 4248/2257; Fax: 020-7235 1286;
E-mail: embollondres@aol.com)
Ambassador Extraordinary and Plenipotentiary:
His Excellency Señor Jaime Quiroga Matos

Embassy of Bosnia and Herzegovina
4th Floor, Morley House, 320 Regent Street, London, W1B 3BF (Tel: 020-7255 3758; Fax: 020-7255 3760; E-mail: ot@totalise.co.uk)
Ambassador Extraordinary and Plenipotentiary:
His Excellency Mr Osman Topcagic

Botswana High Commission
6 Stratford Place, London, W1C 1AY
(Tel: 020-7499 0031; Fax: 020-7495 8595)
High Commissioner:
His Excellency Mr Roy Blackbeard

Brazilian Embassy
32 Green Street, Mayfair, London, W1K 7AT
(Tel: 020-7499 0877; Fax: 020-7399 9100;
E-mail: infobrazil@brazil.org.uk;
Web: www.brazil.org.uk)
Ambassador Extraordinary and Plenipotentiary:
His Excellency Senhor Sergio Silva Do Amaral, KBE

Brunei Darussalam High Commission
19–20 Belgrave Square, London, SW1X 9PG
(Tel: 020-7581 0521; Fax: 020-7235 9717)
High Commissioner:
His Excellency Dato Haji Yusof Hamid

Embassy of the Republic of Bulgaria
186–188 Queen's Gate, London, SW7 5HL
(Tel: 020-7584 9400/9433; Fax: 020-7584 4948;
E-mail: bgembasy@globalnet.co.uk;
Web: www.bulgarianembassy.org.uk)
Ambassador Extraordinary and Plenipotentiary:
His Excellency Mr Valentin Dobrev

Embassy of the Republic of Burundi
26 Armitage Road, London, NW11 8RD
(Tel: 020-8381 4092; Fax: 020-8458 8596)
Ambassador Extraordinary and Plenipotentiary:
His Excellency Monsieur Jonathas Niyungeko

High Commission for the Republic of Cameroon
84 Holland Park, London, W11 3SB
(Tel: 020-7727 0771; Fax: 020-7792 9353)
High Commissioner:
His Excellency Mr Samuel Libock Mbel

Canadian High Commission
Macdonald House, 1 Grosvenor Square, London, W1X 0AB (Tel: 020-7258 6600; Fax: 020-7258 6333; E-mail: ldn@dfait-maeci.gc.ca; Web: www.dfait-maeci.gc.ca/london)
High Commissioner:
His Excellency Jeremy Kinsman

Embassy of Chile
12 Devonshire Street, London, W1N 2DS
(Tel: 020-7580 6392; Fax: 020-7436 5204;
E-mail: echileuk@echileuk.demon.co.uk;
Web: www.echileuk.demon.co.uk)
Ambassador Extraordinary and Plenipotentiary:
His Excellency Señor Cristian Barros

Embassy of the People's Republic of China
49–51 Portland Place, London, W1B 1JL
(Tel: 020-7299 4049; Fax: 020-7637 0399;
Web: www.chinese-embassy.org.uk)
Ambassador Extraordinary and Plenipotentiary:
His Excellency Mr Ma Zhengang

Colombian Embassy
Flat 3A, 3 Hans Crescent, London, SW1X 0LN
(Tel: 020-7589 9177/5037; Fax: 020-7581 1829;
E-mail: colombia@colombia.demon.co.uk;
Web: www.colombia.demon.co.uk)
Ambassador Extraordinary and Plenipotentiary:
His Excellency Mr Victor G. Ricardo

Embassy of the Democratic Republic of the Congo
26 Chesham Place, London, SW1X 8HG
(Tel: 020-7235 6137; Fax: 020-7235 9048)
Ambassador Extraordinary and Plenipotentiary:
vacant

454 London and the World

Costa Rican Embassy
Flat 1, 14 Lancaster Gate, London, W2 3LH
(Tel: 020-7706 8844; Fax: 020-7706 8655;
E-mail: general@emberlon.demon.co.uk;
Web: www.emberlon.demon.co.uk)
Ambassador Extraordinary and Plenipotentiary:
His Excellency Señor Rodolfo Gutierrez

Embassy of the Republic of Côte d'Ivoire
2 Upper Belgrave Street, London, SW1X 8BJ
(Tel: 020-7235 6991; Fax: 020-7259 5320)
Ambassador Extraordinary and Plenipotentiary:
His Excellency Mr Kouadio Adjoumani

Embassy of the Republic of Croatia
21 Conway Street, London, W1T 6BN
(Tel: 020-7387 2022; Fax: 020-7387 0310)
Ambassador Extraordinary and Plenipotentiary:
His Excellency Mr Andrija Kojakovic

Embassy of the Republic of Cuba
167 High Holborn, London, WC1V 6PA
(Tel: 020-7240 2488; Fax: 020-7836 2602)
Ambassador Extraordinary and Plenipotentiary:
His Excellency Señor Jose Fernandez de Cosslo

Cyprus High Commission
93 Park Street, London, W1K 7ET
(Tel: 020-4799 8272; Fax: 020-4791 0691;
E-mail: cyphclondon@dial.pipex.com)
High Commissioner:
His Excellency Mrs Myrna Y. Kleopas

Embassy of the Czech Republic
26 Kensington Palace Gardens, London, W8 4QY (Tel: 020-7243 1115; Fax: 020-7727 9654)
Ambassador Extraordinary and Plenipotentiary:
His Excellency Mr Pavel Siefter

Royal Danish Embassy
55 Sloane Street, London, SW1X 9SR
(Tel: 020-7333 0200; Fax: 020-7333 0270)
Ambassador Extraordinary and Plenipotentiary:
His Excellency Mr Ole Lønsmann Poulsen

Office of the High Commissioner for the Commonwealth of Dominica
1 Collingham Gardens, South Kensington, London, SW5 0HW (Tel: 020-7370 5194/5;
Fax: 020-7373 8743;
E-mail: highcommission@dominica.co.uk;
Web: www.dominica.com)
High Commissioner:
His Excellency Mr George E. Williams

Embassy of the Dominican Republic
139 Inverness Terrace, Bayswater, London, W2 6JF (Tel: 020-7727 6285; Consular: 020-7727 6214; Fax: 020-7727 3693; E-mail: general@embajadom-london.demon.co.uk)
Ambassador Extraordinary and Plenipotentiary:
His Excellency Dr Pedro L Padilla Tonos

Embassy of Ecuador
Flat 3B, 3 Hans Crescent, Knightsbridge, London, SW1X 0LS (Tel: 020-7584 2648/1367/ 8084; Fax: 020-7823 9701;
E-mail: embajada@ecuador.freeserve.co.uk)
Charge d'Affaires: Ricardo Falconi-Pulg

Embassy of the Arab Republic of Egypt
26 South Street, London, W1Y 6DD
(Tel: 020-7499 3304; Fax: 020-7491 1542;
E-mail: etembuk@hotmail.com)
Ambassador Extraordinary and Plenipotentiary:
His Excellency Mr Adel El-Gazzar

Embassy of El Salvador
Mayfair House, 39 Great Portland Street, London, W1W 7JZ (Tel: 020-7436 8282;
Fax: 020-7436 8181;
E-mail: embasalondres@netscapeonline.co.uk)
Ambassador Extraordinary and Plenipotentiary:
His Excellency Mr Mauricio Castro-Aragon

Embassy of the Republic of Estonia
16 Hyde Park Gate, London, SW7 5DG
(Tel: 020-7589 3428; Fax: 020-7589 3430;
E-mail: embassy.london@estonia.gov.uk;
Web: www.estonia.gov.uk)
Ambassador Extraordinary and Plenipotentiary:
His Excellency Mr Raul Mälk

High Commission of the Republic of Fiji
34 Hyde Park Gate, London, SW7 5DN
(Tel: 020-7584 3661; Fax: 020-7584 2838;
E-mail: fijirepuk@compuserve.com)
High Commissioner:
His Excellency Mr Filimone Jitoko

The Embassy of Finland
38 Chesham Place, London, SW1X 8HW (Tel: 020-7838 6200; Fax: 020-7235 3680; E-mail: sanomat.lon@formin.fi; Web: www.finemb.org.uk)
Ambassador Extraordinary and Plenipotentiary:
His Excellency Mr Pertti Salolainen

Embassies 455

French Embassy
58 Knightsbridge, London, SW1X 7JT
(Tel: 020-7201 1000; Fax: 020-7201 1004;
E-mail: info-london@diplomatic.gouv.fr;
Web: www.embafrance-uk.org)
Ambassador Extraordinary and Plenipotentiary:
His Excellency Monsieur Daniel Bernard, CMG, CBE

Embassy of the Republic of Gabon
27 Elvaston Place, London, SW7 5NL
(Tel: 020-7823 9986; Fax: 020-7584 0047)
Ambassador Extraordinary and Plenipotentiary:
Her Excellency Madame Honorne Dossou-Naki

The Gambia High Commission
57 Kensington Court, Kensington, London, W8 5DG (Tel: 020-7937 6316/7/8; Fax: 020-7937 9095; E-mail: gambia@gamhighcom.fonet.co.uk)
Acting High Commissioner:
His Excellency Mr Gibril S. Joof

Embassy of Georgia
3 Hornton Place, London, W8 4LZ
(Tel: 020-7937 8233; Fax: 020-7938 4108;
E-mail: geoemb@dircon.co.uk;
Web: www.embassyofgeorgia.org.uk)
Ambassador Extraordinary and Plenipotentiary:
His Excellency Mr Teimuraz Mamatsashvili

Embassy of the Federal Republic of Germany
23 Belgrave Square, Chesham Place, London, SW1X 8PZ (Tel: 020-7824 1300; Fax: 020-7824 1435; E-mail: mail@german-embassy.org.uk; Web: www.german-embassy.org.uk)
Ambassador Extraordinary and Plenipotentiary:
His Excellency Dr Hans-Friedrich von Ploetz

High Commission for Ghana
Main Chancery, 13 Belgrave Square, London, SW1X 8PN (Tel: 020-7201 5943; Fax: 020-7245 9552; E-mail: giimfa31@men.com)
High Commissioner:
His Excellency Mr James E. K. Aggrey-Orleans

Embassy of Greece
1A Holland Park, London, W11 3TP
(Tel: 020-7229 3850; Fax: 020-7229 7221;
E-mail: london@greekembassy.org.uk;
Web: www.greekembassy.org.uk)
Ambassador Extraordinary and Plenipotentiary:
Alexandros Sandis

High Commission for Grenada
1 Collingham Gardens, Earl's Court, London, SW5 0HW (Tel: 020-7373 7809; Fax: 020-7370 7040;
E-mail: grenada@high-commission.freeserve.co.uk)
High Commissioner:
Her Excellency Ms Ruth Elizabeth Rouse

Embassy of Guatemala
13 Fawcett Street, London, SW10 9HN
(Tel: 020-7351 3042; Fax: 020-7376 5708;
E-mail: embaguatelondon@btinternet.com;
Web: www.guatemala.travel.com.gt)
Ambassador Extraordinary and Plenipotentiary:
His Excellency Seora Marithza Ruiz de Vielman

High Commission for Guyana
3 Palace Court, Bayswater Road, London, W2 4LP (Tel: 020-7229 7684/8; Fax: 020-7727 9809; E-mail: ghc@ie24.net)
High Commissioner:
His Excellency Mr Laleshwar K. N. Singh, CCH

Apostolic Nunciature
54 Parkside, London, SW19 5NE
(Tel: 020-8946 1410; Fax: 020-8947 2494)
Apostolic Nuncio:
His Excellency Archbishop Pablo Puente

Embassy of Honduras
115 Gloucester Place, London, W1U 6JT
(Tel: 020-7486 4880; Fax: 020-7486 4550;
E-mail: hondurassuk@lineone.net)
Ambassador Extraordinary and Plenipotentiary:
His Excellency Seor Hernan Antonio Bermudez-Aguilar

Embassy of the Republic of Hungary
35 Eaton Place, London, SW1X 8BY
(Tel: 020-7235 5218; Fax: 020-7823 1348;
E-mail: office@huemblon.org.uk;
Web: www.huemblon.org.uk)
Ambassador Extraordinary and Plenipotentiary:
His Excellency Mr Gábor Szentiványi, GCVO

Embassy of Iceland
2A Hans Street, London, SW1X 0JE
(Tel: 020-7259 3999; Fax: 020-7245 9649;
E-mail: icemb.london@utn.stjr.is;
Web: www.iceland.org.uk)
Ambassador Extraordinary and Plenipotentiary:
His Excellency Mr Thorsteinn Pálsson

456 London and the World

High Commission for India
India House, Aldwych, London, WC2B 4NA
(Tel: 020-7836 8484; Fax: 020-7836 4331;
E-mail: pnihci@compuserve.com;
Web: www.hcilondon.org)
High Commissioner: Mr Nareshwar Dayal

Embassy of the Republic of Indonesia
38 Grosvenor Square, London, W1K 2HW
(Tel: 020-7499 7661; Fax: 020-7491 4993;
E-mail: kbri@indolondon.freeserve.co.uk;
Web: www.indonesianembassy.org.uk)
Ambassador Extraordinary and Plenipotentiary:
His Excellency Mr Nana S. Sutresna

Embassy of the Islamic Republic of Iran
16 Prince's Gate, London, SW7 1PT
(Tel: 020-7225 3000; Fax: 020-7589 4440;
E-mail: info@iran-embassy.org.uk;
Web: www.iran-embassy.org.uk)
Ambassador Extraordinary and Plenipotentiary:
His Excellency Mr Morteza Saimadi

Iraqi Interests Section
21 Queen's Gate, London, SW7 5JG
(Tel: 020-7584 7141; Fax: 020-7584 7716;
E-mail: iraqyia.london@talk21.com)
Minister/Head of Interests Section:
Dr Mudhafar Amin

Embassy of Ireland
17 Grosvenor Place, London, SW1X 7HR
(Tel: 020-7235 2171; Fax: 020-7245 6961)
Ambassador Extraordinary and Plenipotentiary:
His Excellency Mr Edward Barrington

Embassy of Israel
2 Palace Green, Kensington, London, W8 4QB
(Tel: 020-7957 9500; Fax: 020-7957 9555)
Ambassador Extraordinary and Plenipotentiary:
His Excellency Dr Zvi Shtaubar

Italian Embassy
14 Three Kings Yard, Davies Street, London, W1K 4EH (Tel: 020-7312 2200; Fax: 020-7312 2230; E-mail: emblondon@embitaly.org.uk;
Web: www.embitaly.org.uk)
Ambassador Extraordinary and Plenipotentiary:
His Excellency Signor Luigi Amaduzzi

Jamaican High Commission
1-2 Prince Consort Road, London, SW7 2BZ
(Tel: 020-7823 9911; Fax: 020-7589 5154;
E-mail: jamhigh@jhcuk.com; Web: www.jhcuk.com)
High Commissioner: His Excellency The Hon.
David Muirhead, QC, OJ

Embassy of Japan
101-104 Piccadilly, London, W1J 7JT
(Tel: 020-7465 6500; Fax: 020-7491 9348)
Ambassador Extraordinary and Plenipotentiary:
His Excellency Mr Sadayuki Hayashi

Embassy of the Hashemite Kingdom of Jordan
6 Upper Phillimore Gardens, Kensington,
London, W8 7HA (Tel: 020-7937 3685;
Fax: 020-7937 8795;
Web: www.jordanembassy.uk.gov.jo)
Ambassador Extraordinary and Plenipotentiary:
His Excellency Mr Timoor Daghistani

Embassy of the Republic of Kazakhstan
33 Thurloe Square, London, SW7 2SD
(Tel: 020-7581 4646; Fax: 020-7584 8481)
Ambassador Extraordinary and Plenipotentiary:
Dr. Adil Akhmetov

Kenya High Commission
45 Portland Place, London, W1N 4AS
(Tel: 020-7636 2371/5; Fax: 020-7323 6717)
Acting High Commissioner:
His Excellency Leonard Ngaithe

Embassy of the Republic of Korea
60 Buckingham Gate, London, SW1E 6AJ
(Tel: 020-7227 5500/2; Fax: 020-7227 5503)
Ambassador Extraordinary and Plenipotentiary:
His Excellency Mr Choi Sung-Hong

Embassy of the State of Kuwait
2 Albert Gate, Knightsbridge, London, SW1X 7JU (Tel: 020-7590 3400; Fax: 020-7823 1712)
Ambassador Extraordinary and Plenipotentiary:
His Excellency Mr Khaled Al-Duwaisan, GCVO

Embassy of the Kyrgyz Republic
Ascot House, 119 Crawford Street, London, W1U 6BJ (Tel: 020-7935 1462; Fax: 020-7935 7449; E-mail: email@kyrgyz-embassy.org.uk;
Web: www.kyrgyz-embassy.org.uk)
Ambassador Extraordinary and Plenipotentiary:
Her Excellency Mrs Roza Otunbayeva

Embassy of the Republic of Latvia
45 Nottingham Place, London, W1U 5LY
(Tel: 020-7312 0040. Visa info: 020-7312 0125;
Fax: 020-7312 0042;
E-mail: embassy@embassyoflatvia.co.uk)
Ambassador Extraordinary and Plenipotentiary:
His Excellency Mr Normans Penke

Embassies 457

Lebanese Embassy
15–21 Palace Gardens Mews, London, W8 4RA
(Tel Consulate: 020-7229 7265; Fax: 020-7243 1699; E-mail: emb.leb@btinternet.com)
Ambassador Extraordinary and Plenipotentiary:
His Excellency Mr Jihad Mortada

High Commission of the Kingdom of Lesotho
7 Chesham Place, Belgravia, London, SW1 8HN
(Tel: 020-7235 5686; Fax: 020-7235 5023;
E-mail: lesotholondonhighcom@compuserve.com)
High Commissioner:
Her Excellency Miss Lebbhang Ramohlanka

Embassy of the Republic of Liberia
2 Pembridge Place, London, W2 4XB
(Tel: 020-7221 1036; Fax: 020-7727 2914)
Ambassador Extraordinary and Plenipotentiary:
vacant

The Libyan People's Bureau
61–62 Ennismore Gardens, London, SW7 1NH
(Tel: 020-7589 6120; Fax: 020-7589 6087)
Charge d'Affaires: Mr Isa Baruni Edaeki

Embassy of the Republic of Lithuania
84 Gloucester Place, London, W1U 6AU
(Tel: 020-7486 6401/2; Fax: 020-7486 6403;
E-mail: lzalon@globalnet.co.uk;
Ambassador Extraordinary and Plenipotentiary:
His Excellency Mr Justas V. Paleckis

Embassy of Luxembourg
27 Wilton Crescent, London, SW1X 8SD
(Tel: 020-7235 6961; Fax: 020-7235 9734)
Ambassador Extraordinary and Plenipotentiary:
His Excellency Monsieur Joseph Weyland

Embassy of the Republic of Macedonia
5th Floor, 25 James Street, London, W1U 1DU
(Tel: 020-7935 2823; Fax: 020-7935 3886)
Ambassador Extraordinary and Plenipotentiary:
His Excellency Mr Stevo Crvenkovski

High Commission for the Republic of Malawi
33 Grosvenor Street, London, W1X 0DE
(Tel: 020-7491 4172/7; Fax: 020-7491 9916;
E-mail: kwacha@malawihighcomm.prestel.co.uk)
High Commissioner:
His Excellency Mr Bright McBin Msaka

Malaysian High Commission
45 Belgrave Square, London, SW1X 8QT
(Tel: 020-7235 8033; Fax: 020-7235 5161;
E-mail: mwlondon@btinteret.com)
High Commissioner:
His Excellency Dato' Salim Hashim

High Commission of the Republic of Maldives
22 Nottingham Place, London, W1U 5NJ
(Tel: 020-7224 2135; Fax: 020-7224 2157;
E-mail: maldives.high.commission@virgin.net;
Web: www.visitmaldives.com)
High Commissioner: vacant

Malta High Commission
Malta House, 36–38 Piccadilly, London, W1J 0LE (Tel: 020-7292 4800; Fax: 020-7734 1831)
High Commissioner:
His Excellency Dr George Bonello Du Puis

Embassy of the Islamic Republic of Mauritania
1 Chessington Avenue, London, N3 3DS
(Tel: 020-8343 2829; Fax: 020-8349 0257)
Ambassador Extraordinary and Plenipotentiary:
vacant

Mauritius High Commission
32/33 Elvaston Place, London, SW7 5NW
(Tel: 020-7581 0294/5; Fax: 020-7823 8437;
E-mail: londonmhc@btinternet.com)
High Commissioner:
His Excellency Mr Mohunlall Godgurdhun, QC

Embassy of Mexico
42 Hertford Street, Mayfair, London, W1J 7JR
(Tel: 020-7499 8586; Fax: 020-7495 4035;
E-mail: mexuk@easynet.co.uk;
Web: www.mexicanembassy.co.uk)
Ambassador Extraordinary and Plenipotentiary:
His Excellency Sra. Alma Rosa Moreno

Embassy of Mongolia
7 Kensington Court, London, W8 5DL
(Tel: 020-7937 0150; Fax: 020-7937 1117;
E-mail: embmong@aol.com)
Ambassador Extraordinary and Plenipotentiary:
His Excellency Mr Tsedenjavyn Suhbaatar

Embassy of the Kingdom of Morocco
49 Queen's Gate Gardens, London, SW7 5NE
(Tel: 020-7581 5001/4; Fax: 020-7225 3862;
E-mail: mail@sifamaldn.org)
Ambassador Extraordinary and Plenipotentiary:
His Excellency Mr Mohammed Belmahi

High Commission of the Republic of Mozambique
21 Fitzroy Square, London, W1T 6EL (Tel: 020-7383 3800; Fax: 020-7383 3801; E-mail: mozalon@compuserve.com)
High Commissioner:
His Excellency Dr Eduardo Jose Bagiao Koloma

Embassy of the Union of Myanmar
19A Charles Street, Berkeley Square, London, W1J 5DX (Tel: 020-7499 8841; Fax: 020-7629 4169; E-mail: london@cs.com; Web: www.myanmar.com)
Ambassador Extraordinary and Plenipotentiary:
His Excellency Dr Kyaw Win

High Commission for the Republic of Namibia
6 Chandos Street, London, W1M 0LQ (Tel: 020-7636 6244; Fax: 020-7637 5694; E-mail: namibia-highcomm@btconnect.com)
High Commissioner:
Her Excellency Ms Monica Ndiliawike Nashandi

Royal Nepalese Embassy
12A Kenginston Palace Gardens, London, W8 4QU (Tel: 020-7229 1594/6231/5352; Fax: 020-7792 9861; E-mail: 101642.43@compuserve.com)
Ambassador Extraordinary and Plenipotentiary:
His Excellency Dr Singha B. Basnyat

Royal Netherlands Embassy
38 Hyde Park Gate, London, SW7 5DP (Tel: 020-7590 3200; Fax: 020-7225 0947; E-mail: london@netherlands-embassy.org.uk; Web: www.netherlands-embassy.org.uk)
Ambassador Extraordinary and Plenipotentiary:
His Excellency Baron Willem Oswald Bentinck Van Schoonheten

New Zealand High Commission
New Zealand House, Haymarket, London, SW1Y 4TQ (Tel: 020-7930 8422; Fax: 020-7839 4580; E-mail: publicaffairs@newzealandhc.org.uk; Web: www.newzealandhc.org.uk)
High Commissioner:
His Excellency Rt. Hon. Paul Clayton East, QC

Embassy of Nicaragua
Suite 31, Vicarage House, 58–60 Kensington Church Street, London, W8 4DP (Tel: 020-7938 2373; Fax: 020-7937 0952; E-mail: emb.ofnicaragua@virgin.net; Web: www.freespace.virgin.net/emb.ofnicaragua)
Ambassador Extraordinary and Plenipotentiary:
His Excellency Señor Juan Sacasa

High Commission for the Federal Republic of Nigeria
Nigeria House, 9 Northumberland Avenue, London, WC2N 5BX (Tel: 020-7839 1244; Fax: 020-7839 8746; Web: www.nigeriahouseuk.com)
High Commissioner:
His Excellency Prince Bola Adesombo Ajibola, KBE

Royal Norwegian Embassy
25 Belgrave Square, London, SW1X 8QD (Tel: 020-7591 5500; Fax: 020-7245 6993; E-mail: emblondon@mfa.no; Web: www.norway.org.uk)
Ambassador Extraordinary and Plenipotentiary:
His Excellency Mr Tarald O. Brautaset

Embassy of the Sultanate of Oman
167 Queen's Gate, London, SW7 5HE (Tel: 020-7225 0001; Fax: 020-7589 2505)
Ambassador Extraordinary and Plenipotentiary:
His Excellency Mr Hussain Ali Abdullatif

High Commission for the Islamic Republic of Pakistan
35–36 Lowndes Square, London, SW1X 9JN (Tel: 020-7664 9200; Fax: 020-7664 9224; E-mail: pareplondon@netlineuk.net; Web: www.pakmission-uk.gov.pk)
High Commissioner:
His Excellency Mr Abdul Kader Jaffer

Embassy of the Republic of Panama
Ground Floor and Basement, 40 Hertford Street, London, W1Y 7TG (Tel: 020-7493 4646; Fax: 020-7493 4333; E-mail: emb.pan@lineone.net)
Ambassador Extraordinary and Plenipotentiary:
Her Excellency Seora Ariadne Singares Robinson

Papua New Guinea High Commission
3rd Floor, 14 Waterloo Place, London, SW1Y 4AR (Tel: 020-7930 0922/7; Fax: 020-7930 0828; E-mail: 106655.1056@compuserve.com)
High Commissioner:
His Excellency Sir Kina Bona, KBE

Embassy of Paraguay
Braemar Lodge, Cornwall Gardens, London, SW7 4AQ (Tel: 020-7937 1253/6629; Fax: 020-7937 5687; E-mail: embapar@londrespy.freeserve.co.uk)
Ambassador Extraordinary and Plenipotentiary:
His Excellency Seor Raul Dos Santos

Embassies

Embassy of Peru
52 Sloane Street, London, SW1X 9SP (Tel: 020-7235 1917/2545/3802; Fax: 020-7235 4463; E-mail: postmaster@peruembassy-uk.com; Web: www.peruembassy-uk.com)
Ambassador Extraordinary and Plenipotentiary:
His Excellency Mr Gilbert Chauny

Embassy of the Republic of the Philippines
9A Palace Green, London, W8 4QE (Tel: 020-7937 1600; Fax: 020-7937 2925; E-mail: embassy@philemb.demon.co.uk; Web: www.philemb.demon.co.uk)
Ambassador Extraordinary and Plenipotentiary:
His Excellency Mr Cesar B. Bautista

Embassy of the Republic of Poland
47 Portland Place, London, W1B 1JH (Tel: 020-7580 4324; Fax: 020-7323 4018; E-mail: pol-emb@dircon.co.uk; Web: www.poland-embassy.org.uk)
Ambassador Extraordinary and Plenipotentiary:
His Excellency Dr Stanislaw Komorowski

Portuguese Embassy
11 Belgrave Square, London, SW1X 8PP (Tel: 020-7235 5331; Fax: 020-7245 1287; E-mail: portembassy-london@dialin.net; Web: www.portembassy.gla.ac.uk)
Ambassador Extraordinary and Plenipotentiary:
His Excellency Senhor José Gregrio Faria

Embassy of the State of Qatar
1 South Audley Street, London, W1Y 5DQ (Tel: 020-7493 2200; Fax: 020-7493 2661)
Ambassador Extraordinary and Plenipotentiary:
His Excellency Mr Dasser Bin Hamad Khlifa

Embassy of Romania
Arundel House, 4 Palace Green, London, W8 4QD (Tel: 020-7937 9666; Fax: 020-7937 8069; E-mail: romania@roemb.demon.co.uk)
Ambassador Extraordinary and Plenipotentiary:
His Excellency Mr Radu Onofrei

Embassy of the Russian Federation
13 Kensington Palace Gardens, London, W8 4QX (Tel: 020-7727 8625; Fax: 020-7229 8027; E-mail: harhouse1@harhouse1.demon.co.uk)
Ambassador Extraordinary and Plenipotentiary:
His Excellency Mr Grigory B. Karasin

Embassy of the Republic of Rwanda
Uganda House, 58–59 Trafalgar Square, London, WC2N 5DX (Tel: 020-7930 2570; Fax: 020-7930 2572; E-mail: ambrwanda@compuserve.com; Web: www.ambrwanda.org.uk)
Ambassador Extraordinary and Plenipotentiary:
Her Excellency Rosemary K. Museminali

High Commission for St Christopher and Nevis
2nd Floor, 10 Kensington Court, London, W8 5DL (Tel: 020-7460 6500; Fax: 020-7460 6505)
High Commissioner:
His Excellency Mr James. E. Williams

High Commission for St Lucia
10 Kensington Court, London, W8 5DL (Tel: 020-7937 9522; Fax: 020-7937 8704; E-mail: hcslu@btconnect.com)
High Commissioner:
His Excellency Mr Emmanuel H. Cotter, MBE

High Commission for St Vincent and the Grenadines
10 Kensington Court, London, W8 5DL (Tel: 020-7565 2874; Fax: 020-7937 6040; E-mail: highcommission.svg.uk@cwcom.net)
High Commissioner:
His Excellency Mr Caryle Dennis Dougan, QC

Royal Embassy of Saudi Arabia
30 Charles Street, Mayfair, London, W1J 5DZ (Tel: 020-7917 3000)
Ambassador Extraordinary and Plenipotentiary:
His Excellency Dr Ghazi A. Algosaibi

Embassy of the Republic of Senegal
39 Marloes Road, London, W8 6LA (Tel: 020-7937 7237/938 4048; Fax: 020-7938 2546)
Ambassador Extraordinary and Plenipotentiary:
His Excellency Mr Gabriel Alexandre Sar

High Commission for Seychelles
2nd Floor, Eros House, 111 Baker Street, London, W1U 6RR (Tel: 020-7224 1660; Fax: 020-7487 5756; E-mail: Seychlon@aol.com)
High Commissioner:
His Excellency Mr Bertrand Rassool

Sierra Leone High Commission
Oxford Circus House, 245 Oxford Street, London, W1R 1LF (Tel: 020-7287 9884; Fax: 020-7734 3822)
High Commissioner:
His Excellency Prof. Cyril Patrick Foray

460 London and the World

High Commission for the Republic of Singapore
9 Wilton Crescent, London, SW1X 8SP
(Tel: 020-7235 8315; Fax: 020-7245 6583;
E-mail: schlondon@singcomm.demon.co.uk;
Web: www.mfa.gov.sg/london)
High Commissioner:
His Excellency Prof. Pang Eng Fong

Embassy of the Slovak Republic
25 Kensington Palace Gardens, London, W8 4QY (Tel: 020-7243 0803; Fax: 020-7313 6481;
E-mail: mail@slovakembassy.co.uk;
Web: www.slovakembassy.co.uk)
Ambassador Extraordinary and Plenipotentiary:
His Excellency Mr Frantisek Dlhopolcek

Embassy of the Republic of Slovenia
Suite 1, Cavendish Court, 11–15 Wigmore Street, London, W1U 1AN (Tel: 020-7495 7775;
Fax: 020-7495 7776;
E-mail: slovene-embassy.london@virgin.net;
Web: www.embassy-slovenia.org.uk)
Ambassador Extraordinary and Plenipotentiary:
His Excellency Mr Marjan Setinc

High Commission for the Republic of South Africa
South Africa House, Trafalgar Square, London, WC2N 5DP (Tel: 020-7451 7299; Fax: 020-7451 7284; Web: www.southafricahouse.com)
High Commissioner:
Her Excellency Ms Cheryl Ann Carolus

Spanish Embassy
39 Chesham Place, London, SW1X 8SB
(Tel: 020-7235 5555; Fax: 020-7235 9905)
Ambassador Extraordinary and Plenipotentiary:
His Excellency The Marqués de Tamarn

High Commission for the Democratic Socialist Republic of Sri Lanka
13 Hyde Park Gardens, London, W2 2LU
(Tel: 020-7262 1841/7; Fax: 020-7262 7970;
E-mail: mail@slhc.globalnet.co.uk;
Web: www.users.globalnet.co.uk)
High Commissioner:
His Excellency Mr Mangala Moonesinghe

The Embassy of the Republic of the Sudan
3 Cleveland Row, St James's, London, SW1A 1DD (Tel: 020-7839 8080; Fax: 020-7839 7560)
Ambassador Extraordinary and Plenipotentiary:
His Excellency Dr Hasan Abdin

Kingdom of Swaziland High Commission
20 Buckingham Gate, London, SW1E 6LB
(Tel: 020-7630 6611; Fax: 020-7630 6564)
High Commissioner:
His Excellency Revd Percy S. Mngomezulu

Embassy of Sweden
11 Montagu Place, London, W1H 2AL
(Tel: 020-7917 6400; Fax: 020-7724 4174;
E-mail: embassy@swedmet.met;
Web: www.swedish-embassy.org.uk)
Ambassador Extraordinary and Plenipotentiary:
His Excellency Mr Mats Bergquist, CMG

Embassy of Switzerland
16–18 Montagu Place, London, W1H 2BQ
(Tel: 020-7616 6000; Fax: 020-7724 7001;
E-mail: vertretung@lon.rep.admin.ch;
Web: www.swissembassy.org.uk)
Ambassador Extraordinary and Plenipotentiary:
His Excellency Mr Bruno Spinner

Embassy of the Syrian Arab Republic
8 Belgrave Square, London, SW1X 8PH
(Tel: 020-7245 9012; Fax: 020-7235 4621)
Ambassador Extraordinary and Plenipotentiary:
His Execellency Dr. Sami Glaiel

High Commission for the United Republic of Tanzania
43 Hertford Street, London, W1Y 8DB (Tel: 020-7499 8951/4; Fax: 020-7491 9321; E-mail: balozi@tanzarep.demon.uk/balozi@tazania-online.gov; Web: www.tanzannia-online.gov.uk)
High Commissioner:
His Excellency Dr Abdul-kader A. Shareef

Royal Thai Embassy
29–30 Queen's Gate, London, SW7 5JB
(Tel: 020-7589 2944; Fax: 020-7823 9695;
E-mail: thaiduto@btinternet.com)
Ambassador Extraordinary and Plenipotentiary:
His Excellency Mr Vidhya Rayananonda, KCVO

Tonga High Commission
36 Molyneux Street, London, W1H 6AB
(Tel: 020-7724 5828; Fax: 020-7723 9074;
E-mail: tongohighcommission@btinternet.com)
High Commissioner:
His Excellency Mr Fetu'utolu Tupou

Office of the High Commissioner for the Republic of Trinidad and Tobago
42 Belgrave Square, London, SW1X 8NT
(Tel: 020-7245 9351; Fax: 020-7823 1065;
E-mail: tthc.info@virgin.net)
Acting High Commissioner:
Mrs Sandra McIntyre Trotman

Tunisian Embassy
29 Prince's Gate, London, SW7 1QG
(Tel: 020-7584 8117; Fax: 020-7225 2884;
E-mail: amilcar@globalnet.co.uk)
Ambassador Extraordinary and Plenipotentiary:
His Excellency Mr Khemaies Jhinaoui

Turkish Embassy
43 Belgrave Square, London, SW1X 8PA
(Tel: 020-7393 0202; Fax: 020-7393 0066;
E-mail: turkish.embassy@virgin.net;
Web: www.turkishembassy/london.com)
Ambassador Extraordinary and Plenipotentiary:
His Excellency Mr Korkmaz Haktanir

Embassy of Turkmenistan
2nd Floor South, St George's House, 14–17 Wells Street, London, W1T 3PD (Tel: 020-7255 1071;
Fax: 020-7323 9184;
E-mail: embassy@ashvadlon.demon.co.uk)
Ambassador Extraordinary and Plenipotentiary:
His Excellency Mr Chary Babaev

Uganda High Commission
Uganda House, 58–59 Trafalgar Square, London, WC2N 5DX (Tel: 020-7839 5783; Fax: 020-7839 8925)
High Commissioner:
His Excellency Prof. George Kirya

Embassy of Ukraine
60 Holland Park, London, W11 3SJ
(Tel: 020-7727 6312; Fax: 020-7792 1708;
E-mail: emb—gb@mfa.gov.ua)
Ambassador Extraordinary and Plenipotentiary:
His Excellency Prof. Volodymyr Vassylenko

Embassy of the United Arab Emirates
30 Prince's Gate, London, SW7 1PT
(Tel: 020-7581 1281; Fax: 020-7581 9616;
E-mail: embinfo@cocoon.co.uk)
Ambassador Extraordinary and Plenipotentiary:
His Excellency Mr Easa Saleh Al-Gurg, CBE

Embassy of the Oriental Republic of Uruguay
2nd Floor, 140 Brompton Road, London, SW3 1HY (Tel: 020-7589 8835; Fax: 020-7581 9585;
E-mail: emb@urubri.demon.co.uk)
Ambassador Extraordinary and Plenipotentiary:
His Excellency Dr Miguel J Berthet

Embassy of the Republic of Uzbekistan
41 Holland Park, London, W11 3RP
(Tel: 020-7229 7679; Fax: 020-7229 7029;
E-mail: info@uzbekistanembassy.uk.net;
Web: www.uzbekinstanembassy.uk.net)
Ambassador Extraordinary and Plenipotentiary:
His Excellency Mr Alisher Faizullaev

Venezuelan Embassy
1 Cromwell Road, London, SW7 2HR
(Tel: 020-7584 4206/7; Fax: 020-7589 8887;
E-mail: venezlon@venezlon.demon.co.uk)
Ambassador Extraordinary and Plenipotentiary:
His Excellency Señor Alfredo Toro Hardy

Embassy of the Socialist Republic of Vietnam
12–14 Victoria Road, London, W8 5RD
(Tel: 020-7937 1912; Fax: 020-7937 6108/7565 3853;
E-mail: vp@dsqvnlondon.demon.co.uk)
Ambassador Extraordinary and Plenipotentiary:
His Excellency Mr Vuong Thua Phong

Embassy of the Republic of Yemen
57 Cromwell Road, London, SW7 2ED
(Tel: 020-7584 6607; Fax: 020-7589 3350)
Ambassador Extraordinary and Plenipotentiary:
His Excellency Dr Hussein Abdullah Al-Amri

High Commission for the Republic of Zambia
2 Palace Gate, London, W8 5NG
(Tel: 020-7589 6655; Fax: 020-7581 1353;
E-mail: hc@zhel.org.uk; Web: www.zhel.org.uk)
High Commissioner:
His Excellency Prof. Moses Musonda

High Commission for the Republic of Zimbabwe
Zimbabwe House, 429 Strand, London, WC2R 0JR (Tel: 020-7836 7755; Fax: 020-7379 1167;
E-mail: zimlondon@callnetuk.com;
Web: www.zimbabwelink.com)
High Commissioner: His Excellency Mr Simbarashe Simbanenduku Mumbengegwi

INTERNATIONAL ORGANISATIONS

The list below details London-based international organisations and the London offices of international organisations.

Association of South East Asian Nations
ASEAN Committee in the UK, Indonesian Embassy, 38 Grosvenor Square, London W1X 9AD

Bank for International Settlements
London Agent, Bank of England, Threadneedle Street, London EC2R 8AH (Tel: 020-7601 4444; Fax: 020-7601 4771)

Commonwealth Secretariat
Marlborough House, Pall Mall, London SW1Y 5HX (Tel: 020-7747 6385/86; Fax: 020-7839 9081; Email: info@commonwealth.int; Web: www.thecommonwealth.org)
Secretary-General: Chief Emeka Anyaoku (Nigeria)
Commonwealth Secretary-General:
The Rt. Hon. Donald McKinnon

Commonwealth Foundation
Marlborough House, Pall Mall, London SW1Y 5HY (Tel: 020-7930 3783; Fax: 020-7839 8157; Web: www.commonwealthfoundation.com)
Director: Mr Colin Ball

Commonwealth Institute
Kensington High Street, London W8 6NQ (Tel: 020-7603 4535; Fax: 020-7603 4525; Email: info@commonwealth.org.uk; Web: www.commonwealth.org.uk)
Director-General: David French

European Bank for Reconstruction and Development
One Exchange Square, London EC2A 2JN (Tel: 020-7338 6000; Fax: 020-7338 6100; Web: www.ebrd.com)
President: Jean Lemierre

European Commission Representative Office
8 Storey's Gate, London SW1P 3AT (Tel: 020-7973 1992; Fax: 020-7973 1900/1910; Web: www.cec.org.uk)
Head of Representation: Geoffrey Marsh

International Criminal Organisation
UK Office, NCIS Interpol, PO Box 8000, London SE11 5EN (Tel: 020-7238 8000)
UK Representative: J. M. Abbott, QPM

International Labour Organisation
UK Office, Millbank Tower, 21-24 Millbank, London SW1P 4QP (Tel: 020-7828 6401; Fax: 020-7233-5925; Email: london@ilo-london.org.uk; Web: www.ilo.org)
Director: Peter Brammen

International Maritime Organisation
4 Albert Embankment, London SE1 7SR (Tel: 020-7735 7611; Fax: 020-7587 3210; Email: info@imo.org; Web: www.imo.org)
Secretary-General: W. A. O'Neil

International Red Cross and Red Crescent Movement
British Red Cross, 9 Grosvenor Crescent, London SW1X 7EJ (Tel: 020-7235 5454; Fax: 020-7245 6315; Email: information@redcross.org.uk; Web: www.redcross.org.uk)
Chief Executive: Sir Nicholas Young

League of Arab States
UK Office, 52 Green Street, London W1Y 3YH (Tel: 020-7629 0044; Fax: 020-7493 7943)

United Nations
The United Nations High Commissioner for Refugees (UNHCR)
UK Office, 76 Westminster Palace Gardens, London SW1P 1RL (Tel: 020-7828 9191)

UN Office and Information Centre
Millbank Tower, 21-24 Millbank, London SW1 4QH (Tel: 020-7630 0981; Fax: 020-7976 6478)

World Bank
UK Office, New Zealand House, Haymarket, London SW1Y 4TE (Tel: 020-7930 8511; Fax: 020-7930 8515; Email: scambridge@worldbank.org; Web: www.worldbank.org)
Councellor for UK and Ireland: Sarah Cambridge

EUROPEAN UNION

European Commission Representative Office
8 Storey's Gate, London SW1P 3AT
(Tel: 020-7973 1992).

UK European Parliament Information Office
2 Queen Anne's Gate, London SW1H 9AA
(Tel: 020-7227 4300; Fax: 020-7227 4302;
Email: europarl@eu.int;
Web: www.europarl.org.uk).
Director (UK Office): Chris Piening

European Agency for the Evaluation of Medicinal Products (EMEA)
7 Westferry Circus, Canary Wharf, London E14 4HB (Tel: 020-7418 8400; Fax: 020-7418 8416; Email: mail@emea.eudra.org; Web: www.emea.eu.int).
Executive Director: Thomas Lonngren

London (City) European Information Centre
London Chamber of Commerce, 33 Queen Street, London EC4R 1AP (Tel: 020-7489 1992; Fax: 020-7489 0391; Email: europe@londonchamber.co.uk; Web: www.londonchamber.co.uk).
Head of Information: Marita Weins

London (Westminster) European Information Centre
London Chamber of Commerce and Industry, 25 Maddox Street, London W1R 3AW (Tel: 020-7629 2151; Fax: 020-7629 2057; Email: tony@naslem.win—uk.net).

TIME ZONES

Standard time differences from the Greenwich meridian

+ hours ahead of GMT

− hours behind GMT

* may vary from standard time at some part of the year (Summer Time or Daylight Saving Time)

' some areas may keep another time zone

h hours

m minutes

	h m
Afghanistan	+4 30
*Albania	+1
Algeria	+1
*Andorra	+1
Angola	+1
Anguilla	−4
Antigua and Barbuda	−4
Argentina	−3
*Armenia	+4
Aruba	−4
Ascension Island	0
*Australia	
ACT, NSW (except Broken Hill area) Qld, Tas., Vic, Whitsunday Islands	+10
*Broken Hill area (NSW)	+9 30
*Lord Howe Island	+10 30
Northern Territory	+9 30
*South Australia	+9 30
Western Australia	+8
*Austria	+1
*Azerbaijan	+4
*Bahamas	−5
Bahrain	+3
Bangladesh	+6
Barbados	−4
*Belarus	+2
*Belgium	+1
Belize	−6
Benin	+1
*Bermuda	−4
Bhutan	+6
Bolivia	−4
*Bosnia-Hercegovina	+1
Botswana	+2
Brazil	
western states	−5
central states	−4
N. and NE coastal states	−3
*S. and E. coastal states, including Brasilia	−3

464 London and the World

	h m		h m
Fernando de Noronha Island	-2	*Greenland	-3
British Antarctic Territory	-3	Danmarkshavn, Mesters Vig	0
British Indian OceanTerritory	+5	*Scoresby Sound	-1
Diego Garcia	+6	*Thule area	-4
British Virgin Islands	-4	Djibouti	+3
Brunei	+8	Dominica	-4
*Bulgaria	+2	Dominican Republic	-5
Burkina Faso	0	East Timor	+9
Burundi	+2	Ecuador	-5
Cambodia	+7	Galápagos Islands	-6
Cameroon	+1	*Egypt	+2
Canada		El Salvador	-6
*Alberta	-7	Equatorial Guinea	+1
*'British Columbia	-8	Eritrea	+3
*'Labrador	-4	Estonia	+2
*Manitoba	-6	Ethiopia	+3
*New Brunswick	-4	*Falkland Islands	-4
*Newfoundland	-3 30	Fiji	+12
*Northwest Territories		*Finland	+2
east of 85° W.	-5	*France	+1
85° W.—102° W.	-6	French Guiana	-3
*Nunavut	-7	French Polynesia	-10
*Nova Scotia	-4	Guadeloupe	-4
Ontario		Martinique	-4
*east of 90° W.	-5	Réunion	+4
west of 90° W.	-5	Marquesas Islands	-9 30
*Prince Edward Island	-4	Gabon	+1
Québec		The Gambia	0
east of 63° W.	-4	*Georgia	+3
*west of 63° W.	-5	*Germany	+1
'Saskatchewan	-6	Ghana	0
*Yukon	-8	*Gibraltar	+1
Cape Verde	-1	*Greece	+2
Cayman Islands	-5	Grenada	-4
Central African Republic	+1	Guam	+10
Chad	+1	Guatemala	-6
*Chatham Islands	+12 45	Guinea	0
*Chile	-4	Guinea-Bissau	0
China (inc. Hong Kong and Macao)	+8	Guyana	-4
		Haiti	-5
Christmas Island (Indian Ocean)	+7	Honduras	-6
Cocos (Keeling) Islands	+6 30	*Hungary	+1
Colombia	-5	Iceland	0
Comoros	+3	India	+5 30
Congo (Dem. Rep.)		Indonesia	
Haut-Zaïre, Kasai, Kivu, Shaba	+2	Java, Kalimantan (west and central), Madura, Sumatra	+7
Kinshasa, Mbandaka	+1		
Congo-Brazzaville	+1	Bali, Flores, Kalimantan (south and east), Lombok, Sulawesi, Sumbawa, West Timor	+8
Costa Rica	-6		
Côte d'Ivoire	0		
*Croatia	+1	Irian Jaya, Maluku,	+9
*Cuba	-5	*Iran	+3 30
*Cyprus	+2	*Iraq	+3
*Czech Republic	+1	*Ireland, Republic of	0
*Denmark	+1	*Israel	+2
*Færøe Islands	0	*Italy	+1

Time Zones

	h m		h m
Jamaica	-5	New Caledonia	+11
Japan	+9	*New Zealand	+12
*Jordan	+2	*Cook Islands	-10
*Kazakhstan		Nicaragua	-6
western	+4	Niger	+1
central	+5	Nigeria	+1
eastern	+6	Niue	-11
Kenya	+3	Norfolk Island	+11 30
Kiribati	+12	Northern Mariana Islands	+10
Line Islands	+14	*Norway	+1
Phoenix Islands	+13	Oman	+4
Korea, North	+9	Pakistan	+5
Korea, South	+9	Palau	+9
Kuwait	+3	Panama	-5
*Kyrgyzstan	+5	Papua New Guinea	+10
Laos	+7	*Paraguay	-4
Latvia	+2	Peru	-5
*Lebanon	+2	Philippines	+8
Lesotho	+2	*Poland	+1
Liberia	0	*Portugal	0
Libya	+2	*Azores	-1
*Liechtenstein	+1	*Madeira	0
Line Islands not part of Kiribati	-10	Puerto Rico	-4
Lithuania	+1	Qatar	+3
*Luxembourg	+1	Réunion	+4
*Macedonia	+1	*Romania	+2
Madagascar	+3	*Russia	
Malawi	+2	Zone 1	+2
Malaysia	+8	Zone 2	+3
Maldives	+5	Zone 3	+4
Mali	0	Zone 4	+5
*Malta	+1	Zone 5	+6
Marshall Islands	+12	Zone 6	+7
Ebon Atoll	-12	Zone 7	+8
Mauritania	0	Zone 8	+9
Mauritius	+4	Zone 9	+10
*Mexico	-6	Zone 10	+11
*Nayarit, Sinaloa, S. Baja California	-7	Zone 11	+12
		Rwanda	+2
Sonora	-7	St Helena	0
N. Baja California	-8	St Christopher and Nevis	-4
Micronesia		St Lucia	-4
Caroline Islands	+10	*St Pierre and Miquelon	-3
Kosrae, Pingelap, Pohnpei	+11	St Vincent and the Grenadines	-4
*Moldova	+2	Samoa	-11
*Monaco	+1	Samoa, American	-11
Mongolia	+8	*San Marino	+1
Montserrat	-4	São Tomé and Princípe	0
Morocco	0	Saudi Arabia	+3
Mozambique	+2	Senegal	0
Myanmar	+6 30	Seychelles	+4
*Namibia	+1	Sierra Leone	0
Nauru	+12	Singapore	+8
Nepal	+5 45	*Slovakia	+1
*Netherlands	+1	*Slovenia	+1
Netherlands Antilles	-4	Solomon Islands	+11

	h m
Somalia	+3
South Africa	+2
South Georgia	-2
*Spain	+1
*Canary Islands	0
Sri Lanka	+6
Sudan	+3
Suriname	-3
Swaziland	+2
*Sweden	+1
*Switzerland	+1
*Syria	+2
Taiwan	+8
Tajikistan	+5
Tanzania	+3
Thailand	+7
Togo	0
*Tonga	+13
Trinidad and Tobago	-4
Tristan da Cunha	0
Tunisia	+1
*Turkey	+2
Turkmenistan	+5
*Turks and Caicos Islands	-5
Tuvalu	+12
Uganda	+3
*Ukraine	+2
United Arab Emirates	+4
*United Kingdom	0
*United States of America	
Alaska	-9
Aleutian Islands, east of 169° 30; W.	-9
Aleutian Islands, west of 169° 30; W.	-10
eastern time	-5
central time	-6
Hawaii	-10
mountain time	-7
Pacific time	-8
Uruguay	-3
Uzbekistan	+5
Vanuatu	+11
*Vatican City State	+1
Venezuela	-4
Vietnam	+7
Virgin Islands (US)	-4
Yemen	+3
*Yugoslavia (Fed. Rep. of)	+1
Zambia	+2
Zimbabwe	+2

Source: reproduced with permission from data produced by HM Nautical Almanac Office

AIR DISTANCES FROM LONDON TO WORLD CAPITAL CITIES (MILES)

Abu Dhabi (United Arab Emirates)	3409
Abuja (Nigeria)	3115
Accra (Ghana)	3177
Addis Ababa (Ethiopia)	3673
Algiers (Algeria)	1035
Amman (Jordan)	2280
Amsterdam (Netherlands)	231
Ankara (Turkey)	1765
Asunción (Paraguay)	7100
Athens (Greece)	1500
Baghdàd (Iraq)	2550
Banjul (The Gambia)	2798
Bangkok (Thailand)	5929
Beijing (China)	5053
Beirut (Lebanon)	2162
Berlin (Germany)	593
Bern (Switzerland)	472
Bogotá (Colombia)	5295
Brasilia (Brazil)	6342
Bratislava (Slovakia)	990
Bridgetown (Barbados)	4192
Brussels (Belgium)	217
Bucharest (Romania)	1298
Budapest (Hungary)	923
Buenos Aires (Argentina)	6926
Cairo (Egypt)	2192
Canberra (Australia)	10700
Caracas (Venezuala)	4657
Copenhagen (Denmark)	608
Dakar (Senegal)	3035
Dhaka (Bangladesh)	4969
Dhoa (Qatar)	3253
Dodoma (Tanzania)	4663
Dublin (Republic of Ireland)	279
Freetown (Sierra Leone)	3147
Gaborone (Botswana)	5592
Georgetown (Guyana)	6003
Guatemala City (Guatemala)	6542
Hanoi (Vietnam)	6345
Harare (Zimbabwe)	5160
Havana (Cuba)	4664
Helsinki (Finland)	1147
Islamabad (Pakistan)	3755
Jakarta (Indonesia)	7287
Jerusalem (Israel)	2242
Kàbol (Afghanistan)	3643
Kampala (Uganda)	4566
Kathmandu (Nepal)	4675
Khartoum (Sudan)	3071
Kingston (Jamaica)	4668
Kinshasa (Zaire)	3983
Kuala Lumpur (Malaysia)	6557

Kuwait City (Kuwait)	2903
La Paz (Bolivia)	2356
Libreville (Gabon)	1953
Lilongwe (Malawi)	5007
Lima (Peru)	6951
Lisbon (Portugal)	971
Lomé (Togo)	3172
Lusaka (Zambia)	4985
Luxembourg Ville (Luxembourg)	310
Madrid (Spain)	774
Managua (Nicaragua)	5453
Manama (Bahrain)	3163
Manila (Philippines)	6681
Maseru (Lesotho)	5864
Mbabane (Swaziland)	5790
Mexico City (Mexico)	5544
Mogadishu (Somalia)	4873
Monrovia (Liberia)	3547
Montevideo (Uruguay)	7030
Moscow (Russia)	1557
Muscat (Oman)	3622
Nairobi (Kenya)	4247
Nassau (Bahamas)	4332
New Delhi (India)	5177
Nicosia (Cyprus)	2008
Nuku'alofa (Tonga)	12912
Oslo (Norway)	723
Ottawa (Canada)	3322
Ouagadougou (Burkina Faso)	3663
Panama City (Panama)	4664
Paris (France)	215
Port Louis (Mauritius)	6075
Port Moresby (Papua New Guinea)	9815
Porto Novo (Benin)	3381
Port of Spain (Trinidad and Tobago)	4405
Prague (Czech Republic)	649
Pretoria (South Africa)	5640
Quito (Ecuador)	8779
Rabat (Morocco)	1258
Reykjavík (Iceland)	1167
Riyadh (Saudi Arabia)	3073
Rome (Italy)	896
San José (Costa Rica)	6078
San Salvador (El Salvador)	5564
Sanáa' (Yemen)	4343
Santiago (Chile)	7509
Santo Domingo (Dominican Republic)	4943
Seoul (Korea, Republic of South)	7247
Singapore City (Singapore)	6754
Sofia (Bulgaria)	1258
Sri Jayawardenapura (Sri Lanka)	5413
St. George's (Grenada)	4355
Stockholm (Sweden)	906
Suva (Fiji)	11246
Tegucigalpa (Honduras)	5291
Tehran (Iran)	2741
Teipei (Taiwan)	9245
Tokyo (Japan)	5955
Tripoli (Libya)	1170
Tunis (Tunisia)	1137
Ulaanbator (Mongolia)	6481
Valetta (Malta)	1305
Victoria (Seychelles)	5547
Vienna (Austria)	790
Warsaw (Poland)	912
Washington DC (United States of America)	3672
Wellington (New Zealand)	11865
Yamoussoukro (Cote d'Ivoire)	3209
Yangon (Myanmar)	5582
Yaoundé (Cameroon)	3475

INTERNATIONAL DIRECT DIALLING

International dialling codes are composed of four elements which are dialled in sequence:
(i) the international code
(ii) the country code (*see* below)
(iii) the area code
(iv) the customer's telephone number

Calls to some countries must be made via the international operator. (*Source:* BT)

† Connection is currently unavailable

‡ Calls must be made via the international operator

p A pause in dialling is necessary whilst waiting for a second tone

* Varies in some areas

** Varies depending on carrier

Country	IDD from UK	IDD to UK
Afghanistan	†	†
Albania	00 355	00 44
Algeria	00 213	00*p*44
Andorra	00 376	00 44
Angola	00 244	00 44
Anguilla	00 1 264	011 44
Antigua and Barbuda	00 1 268	011 44
Argentina	00 54	00 44
Armenia	00 374	810 44
Aruba	00 297	00 44
Ascension Island	00 247	00 44
Australia	00 61	00 11 44
Austria	00 43	00 44
Azerbaijan	00 994	810 44
Azores	00 351	00 44
Bahamas	00 1 242	011 44
Bahrain	00 973	0 44
Bangladesh	00 880	00 44
Barbados	00 1 246	011 44
Belarus	00 375	810 44
Belgium	00 32	00 44
Belize	00 501	00 44
Benin	00 229	00*p*44
Bermuda	00 1 441	011 44
Bhutan	00 975	00 44
Bolivia	00 591	00 44
Bosnia-Hercegovina	00 387	00 44
Botswana	00 267	00 44
Brazil	00 55	00 44
British Virgin Islands	00 1 284	011 44
Brunei	00 673	00 44
Bulgaria	00 359	00 44
Burkina Faso	00 226	00 44
Burundi	00 257	90 44
Cambodia	00 855	00 44
Cameroon	00 237	00 44
Canada	00 1	011 44
Canary Islands	00 34	00 44
Cape Verde	00 238	0 44
Cayman Islands	00 1 345	011 44
Central African Republic	00 236	19 44
Chad	00 235	15 44
Chile	00 56	00 44
China	00 86	00 44
Hong Kong	00 852	001 44
Colombia	00 57	009 44
Comoros	00 269	00 44
Congo, Dem. Rep. of	00 243	00 44
Congo, Republic of	00 242	00 44
Cook Islands	00 682	00 44
Costa Rica	00 506	00 44
Côte d'Ivoire	00 225	00 44
Croatia	00 385	00 44
Cuba	00 53	119 44
Cyprus	00 357	00 44
Czech Republic	00 420	00 44
Denmark	00 45	00 44
Djibouti	00 253	00 44
Dominica	00 1 767	011 44
Dominican Republic	00 1 809	011 44
Ecuador	00 593	00 44
Egypt	00 20	00 44
El Salvador	00 503	0 44
Equatorial Guinea	00 240	00 44
Eritrea	00 291	00 44
Estonia	00 372	800 44
Ethiopia	00 251	00 44
Falkland Islands	00 500	0 44
Færøe Islands	00 298	009 44
Fiji	00 679	05 44
Finland	00 358	00 44**
France	00 33	00 44
French Guiana	00 594	00 44
French Polynesia	00 689	00 44
Gabon	00 241	90 44
The Gambia	00 220	00 44
Georgia	00 995	810 44
Germany	00 49	00 44
Ghana	00 233	00 44
Gibraltar	00 350	00 44
Greece	00 30	00 44
Greenland	00 299	009 44
Grenada	00 1 473	011 44
Guadeloupe	00 590	00 44
Guam	00 1 671	001 44
Guatemala	00 502	00 44
Guinea	00 224	00 44

International Direct Dialling 469

Guinea-Bissau	00 245	099 44		Monaco	00 377	00 44
Guyana	00 592	001 44		Mongolia	00 976	00 44
Haiti	00 509	00 44		Montenegro	00 381	99 44
Honduras	00 504	00 44		Montserrat	00 1 664	011 44
Hungary	00 36	00 44		Morocco	00 212	00p44
Iceland	00 354	00 44		Mozambique	00 258	00 44
India	00 91	00 44		Myanmar	00 95	00 44
Indonesia	00 62	001 44**/		Namibia	00 264	00 44
		00844**		Nauru	00 674	00 44
Iran	00 98	00 44		Nepal	00 977	00 44
Iraq	00 964	00 44		Netherlands	00 31	00 44
Ireland, Republic of	00 353	00 44		Netherlands Antilles	00 599	00 44
Israel	00 972	00 44**		New Caledonia	00 687	00 44
Italy	00 39	00 44		New Zealand	00 64	00 44
Jamaica	00 1 876	011 44		Nicaragua	00 505	00 44
Japan	00 81	001 44**		Niger	00 227	00 44
		004144**		Nigeria	00 234	009 44
		006144**		Niue	00 683	00 44
Jordan	00 962	00 44*		Norfolk Island	00 672	0101 44
Kazakhstan	00 7	810 44		Norway	00 47	00 44
Kenya	00 254	00 44		Oman	00 968	00 44
Kiribati	00 686	00 44		Pakistan	00 92	00 44
Korea, North	00 850	00 44		Palau	00 680	011 44
Korea, South	00 82	001 44**/		Panama	00 507	00 44
		00244**		Papua New Guinea	00 675	05 44
Kuwait	00 965	00 44		Paraguay	00 595	00 44**
Kyrgystan	00 996	00 44				003 44**
Laos	00 856	00 44		Peru	00 51	00 44
Latvia	00 371	00 44		Philippines	00 63	00 44
Lebanon	00 961	00 44		Poland	00 48	00 44
Lesotho	00 266	00 44		Portugal	00 351	00 44
Liberia	00 231	00 44		Puerto Rico	00 1 787	011 44
Libya	00 218	00 44		Qatar	00 974	00 44
Liechtenstein	00 423	00 44		Réunion	00 262	00 44
Lithuania	00 370	810 44		Romania	00 40	00 44
Luxembourg	00 352	00 44		Russia	00 7	810 44
Macao	00 853	00 44		Rwanda	00 250	00 44
Macedonia	00 389	99 44		St Christopher and	00 1 869	011 44
Madagascar	00 261	00 44		Nevis		
Madeira	00 351 91	00 44*		St Helena	00 290	0 44
Malawi	00 265	101 44		St Lucia	00 1 758	011 44
Malaysia	00 60	00 44		St Pierre	00 508	00 44
Maldives	00 960	00 44		and Miquelon		
Mali	00 223	00 44		St Vincent and	00 1 784	001 44
Malta	00 356	00 44		the Grenadines		
Mariana Islands,	00 1 670	011 44		Samoa	00 685	0 44
Northern				Samoa, American	00 684	00 44
Marshall Islands	00 692	011 44		San Marino	00 378	00 44
Martinique	00 596	00 44		São Tomé	00 239	00 44
Mauritania	00 222	00 44		and Princípe		
Mauritius	00 230	00 44		Saudi Arabia	00 966	00 44
Mayotte	00 269	10 44		Senegal	00 221	00p44
Mexico	00 52	98 44		Serbia	00 381	99 44
Micronesia,	00 691	011 44		Seychelles	00 248	00 44
Federated				Sierra Leone	00 232	00 44
States of				Singapore	00 65	001 44
Moldova	00 373	810 44		Slovak Republic	00 421	00 44

470 London and the World

Slovenia	00 386	00 44	Turkey	00 90	00 44
Solomon Islands	00 677	00 44	Turkmenistan	00 993	810 44
Somalia	00 252	16 44	Turks and Caicos	00 1 649	0 44
South Africa	00 27	09 44	Islands		
Spain	00 34	00 44	Tuvalu	00 688	00 44
Sri Lanka	00 94	00 44	Uganda	00 256	00 44
Sudan	00 249	00 44	Ukraine	00 380	810 44
Suriname	00 597	00 44	United Arab	00 971	00 44
Swaziland	00 268	00 44	Emirates		
Sweden	00 46	007 44**	Uruguay	00 598	00 44
		00944**	USA	00 1	011 44
		008744**	Alaska	00 1 907	011 44
Switzerland	00 41	00 44	Hawaii	00 1 808	011 44
Syria	00 963	00 44	Uzbekistan	00 998	810 44
Taiwan	00 886	002 44	Vanuatu	00 678	00 44
Tajikistan	00 7	810 44	Vatican City State	00 390	00 44;
Tanzania	00 255	00 44			66982
Thailand	00 66	001 44	Venezuela	00 58	00 44
Tibet	00 86	00 44	Vietnam	00 84	00 44
Togo	00 228	00 44	Virgin Islands (US)	00 1 340	011 44
Tonga	00 676	00 44	Yemen	00 967	00 44
Trinidad and	00 1 868	011 44	Yugoslav Fed. Rep.	00 381	99 44
Tobago			Zambia	00 260	00 44
Tristan da Cunha	00 2 897	‡	Zimbabwe	00 263	00 44
Tunisia	00 216	00 44			

RELIGIOUS
LONDON

CHRISTIANITY
BAHÁ'Í FAITH
BUDDHISM
HINDUISM
ISLAM
JAINISM
JUDAISM
SIKHISM
ZOROASTRIANISM
CHURCHES

RELIGIOUS LONDON

Religion in London

The national church of England (but not of the rest of the United Kingdom) is the Church of England.

About 64 percent of the population of the UK would call itself broadly Christian (in the Trinitarian sense), with 25.1 million people identifying with Anglican churches, 5.8 million with the Roman Catholic Church, 2.6 million with Presbyterian Churches, 1.3 million with the Methodist Churches and 1.96 million with other Christian churches. About 1.3 million people are affiliated to non-Trinitarian churches, e.g. Jehovah's Witnesses, the Church of Jesus Christ of Latter-Day Saints (Mormons), the Church of Christ, Scientist and the Unitarian churches.

A further 7 percent of the population (4.5 million people) are adherents of other faiths, including Hinduism, Islam, Judaism and Sikhism. About 29 percent of the population is non-religious.

AVERAGE CHURCH ATTENDANCE IN LONDON BY DENOMINATION (000s)

Denomination	
Anglican	101.1
Roman Catholic	237.2
Baptist	45.8
Methodist	23.7
Orthodox	16.4
Pentecostal	93.7
United Reformed	16.6
Independent Churches	19.7
New Churches	39.6
Others	24.1
Total	617.9

Adherents of non-Christian faiths and of non-indigenous forms of Christianity form a higher proportion of the population in London than in the UK as a whole, although separate statistics are not available.
Source: Christian Research/Harper Collins Religious—UK Christian Handbook Religious Trends 2000—1; figures in text are for 1998

Inter-Church and Inter-Faith Co-operation

The main umbrella body for the Christian churches in the UK is the Churches Together in Britain and Ireland (formerly the Council of Churches for Britain and Ireland). There is also an ecumenical body for England, Churches Together in England. The Free Churches' Council comprises most of the Free Churches in England and Wales, and the Evangelical Alliance represents evangelical Christians.

The Inter Faith Network for the United Kingdom promotes co-operation between faiths, and the Council of Christians and Jews works to improve relations between the two religions. Churches Together in Britain and Ireland also has a Commission on Inter Faith Relations.

Churches Together in Britain and Ireland
Inter-Church House, 35—41 Lower Marsh, London SE1 7SA (Tel: 020-7523 2121; Fax: 020-7928 0010; E-mail: gensec@ctbi.org.uk; Web: www.ctbi.org.uk).
General Secretary: Dr D. Goodbourn

Churches Together in England
101 Queen Victoria Street, London EC4V 4EN (Tel: 020-7332 8230; Fax: 020-7332 8234; Web: www.freechurch.cte.org.uk).
Secretary: The Revd Bill Snelson

Council of Christians and Jews
5th Floor, Camelford House, 87-89 Albert Embankment, London SE1 7TP (Tel: 020-7829 0090; Fax: 020-7820 0504; E-mail: jcrelalations@ccj.org.uk; Web: www.ccj.org.uk).
Director: Sr M. Shepherd

Evangelical Alliance
Whitefield House, 186 Kennington Park Road, London SE11 4BT (Tel: 020-7207 2100; Fax: 020-7207 2150; E-mail: london@eauk.org; Web: www.eauk.org).
General Director: Revd J. Edwards

Free Churches' Council
27 Tavistock Square, London WC1H 9HH (Tel: 020-7387 8413).
General Secretary: Revd G. H. Roper

Inter Faith Network for the United Kingdom
5-7 Tavistock Place, London WC1H 9SN (Tel: 020-7388 0008; Fax: 020-7387 7968; E-mail: ifnet@interfaith.org.uk; Web: www.interfaith.org.uk).
Director: B. Pearce, OBE

CHRISTIANITY

Christianity is a monotheistic faith based on the person and teachings of Jesus Christ and all Christian denominations claim his authority. Central to its teaching is the concept of God and his son Jesus Christ, who was crucified and resurrected in order to enable mankind to attain salvation.

Jesus' birth, teachings, crucifixion and subsequent resurrection are recorded in the Gospels, which, together with other scriptures that summarise Christian belief, form the New Testament. This, together with the Hebrew scriptures, entitled the Old Testament by Christians, makes up the Bible, the sacred texts of Christianity.

Christians believe that sin distanced mankind from God, and that Jesus was the Son of God, sent to redeem mankind from that sin by his death. The Gospels assure Christians that those who believe in Jesus and obey his teachings will be forgiven their sins and will be resurrected from the dead.

Christian practices vary widely between different Christian churches, but prayer is universal to all, as is charity, giving for the maintenance of the church buildings, for the work of the church, and to the poor and needy. Baptism and the Eucharist are practised by most Christians. Baptism, symbolising repentance and faith in Jesus is an act marking entry into the Christian community; the Eucharist, the ritual re-enactment of the Last Supper, Jesus' final meal with his disciples, is also practised by most denominations.

Most Christians believe that God actively guides the Church.

Christianity in London

Christianity was introduced to England by the Romans and the first Bishop of London, Restitutus, was installed in AD 314. Following the invasion of the pagan Angles, Saxons and Jutes, Pope Gregory sent Augustine to evangelise the English in AD 596 and in AD 604, the first St. Paul's Cathedral was built in by Bishop Mellitus. Conflicts between Church and State during the Middle Ages culminated in the Act of Supremacy in 1534, which repudiated papal supremacy and declared King Henry VIII to be the supreme head of the Church in England. Since 1559 the English monarch has been termed the Supreme Governor of the Church of England.

NON-CHRISTIAN RELIGIONS

London is a multi-faith society comprised of many non-Christian religions.

BAHÁ'Í FAITH

The Bahá'í faith was founded by Mirza Husayn-'Ali, known as Bahá'u'lláh (Glory of God), who was born in Iran in 1817.

The Bahá'í faith recognises the unity and relativity of religious truth and teaches that there is only one God, whose will has been revealed to mankind by a series of messengers, such as Zoroaster, Abraham, Moses, Buddha, Krishna, Christ, Muhammad, the Báb and Bahá'u'lláh, whose common purpose was to bring God's message to mankind. It teaches that all races and both sexes are equal and deserving of equal opportunities and treatment, that education is a fundamental right and encourages a fair distribution of wealth.

Baha'i Community of the United Kingdom
27 Rutland Gate, London SW7 1PD
(Tel: 020-7584 2566; Fax: 020-7584 9402;
E-mail: nsa.bahai.org.uk; Web: www.bahai.org.uk).
Secretary General: The Hon. Barnabas Leith

BUDDHISM

Buddhism originated in northern India in the teachings of Siddhartha Gautama, known to his followers as the Buddha ('the one who knows'). It is most generally accepted that he lived in the sixth/fifth centuries BC. Although Buddhism died out in its country of origin, it spread widely through Asia developing into a number of forms which are superficially very different. This diversity makes it difficult to summarise Buddhist doctrines in a form which would be accepted by all Buddhists, but the following points would likely be accepted by the majority: Buddhists do not believe in one kind of supreme deity central to religions more familiar in the West. Instead, the course of the universe is determined by the law of karma, a form of moral causation. According to this, the good and bad volitions of beings tend to produce pleasant or painful consequences in present and future lives. Karma generally operates to maintain beings in the familiar cycle of rebirth and death (samsara) which is inevitably a state of suffering (dukkha) in the long run notwithstanding the possibility of interludes of happiness and fulfilment. Buddhism teaches that escape from this cycle requires the threefold development of morality (including the practice of qualities such as generosity and patience), concentration (development of the powers of the mind, including loving-kindness and compassion for all beings) and wisdom (insight into the real nature of things, including out own mind and body). The methods of achieving this development vary from one school of Buddhism to another. The Buddhist Society seeks to raise awareness of Buddhist teachings and practice without favouring one school above another. It runs courses, gives lectures and publishes books about Buddhism.

Britain Burma Buddhist Trust
1 Old Church Lane, London NW9 8TG (Tel: 020-8567 7858).

British Buddhist Association
11 Biddulph Road, London, W9 1JA (Tel: 020-7286 5575; Fax: 020-7289 5545).
Director: A. Haviland-Nye

Buddhapadipa Temple
14 Calonne Road, Wimbledon, London SW19 5HJ (Tel: 020-8879 7542; Fax: 020-8894 5788; E-mail: buddhapadipa@hotmail.com; Web: www.buddhapadipa.org).
Abbot: Phra Bhavanakitkoson

Buddhist Society
58 Eccleston Square, London SW1V 1PH (Tel: 020-7834 5858; Fax: 020-7976 5238; E-mail: info@thebuddhistsociety.org.uk; Web: www.thebuddhistsociety.org.uk).
Librarian: R. B. Parsons
General Secretary: R. C. Maddox

Croydon Buddhist Centre
96-98 High Street, Croydon, Surrey CR0 1ND (Tel: 020-8688 8624; E-mail: croydonbc@lineone.net; Web: www.croydonbuddhistcentre.com).
Chairman: Dharmacarini Vijayasri

London Buddhist Centre
51 Roman Road, Bethnal Green, London E2 0HU (Tel: 0845 458 4716; Fax: 020-8980 1960; E-mail: info@lbc.org.uk; www.lbc.org.uk).
Centre Director: Prasannavira

London Buddhist Vihara
Dharmapala Building, The Avenue, Chiswick, London W4 1UD (Tel: 020-8995 9493; Fax: 020-8994 8130; E-mail: london.vihara@virgin.net; Web:londonbuddhistviharra.co.uk).
Head of Vihara: Most Ven. Dr M. Vajiragnana

London Zendo
10 Belmont Street, Chalk Farm, London NW1 8HH (Tel: 020-7485 9576).

Soka Gakkai UK
1 The Green, Richmond, Surrey TW9 1PL (Tel: 020-8992 1120).

Thames Buddhist Vihara
Dulverton Road, Selsdon, Surrey CR2 8PJ (Tel: 020-8657 7120).
Head of Vihara: Ven. P. Somaratana Thera

Vietnamese Buddhist Society
Linh Son Temple, 89 Bromley Road, Catford, London, SE6 2UF (Tel: 020-8771 5933).

West London Buddhist Centre
7 Coleville House, Talbot Road, London W11 1JB (Tel: 020-7727 9382).

HINDUISM

Hinduism has no historical founder but had become highly developed in India by about 1200 bc. Most Hindus hold that satya (truthfulness), ahimsa (non-violence), honesty, physical labour and tolerance of other faiths are essential for good living. They believe in one supreme spirit (Brahman), and in the transmigration of atman (the soul). Most Hindus accept the doctrine of karma (consequences of actions), the concept of samsara (successive lives) and the possibility of all atmans achieving moksha (liberation from samsara) through jnana (knowledge), yoga (meditation), karma (work or action) and bhakti (devotion).

Most Hindus recognise the authority of the Vedas, the oldest holy books, and accept the philosophical teachings of the Upanishads, the Vedanta Sutras and the Bhagavad-Gita.

Brahman is formless, limitless and all-pervading, and is represented in worship by murtis (images or statues). Brahma, Vishnu and Shiva are the most important gods worshipped by Hindus; their respective consorts are Saraswati; Lakshmi and Durga or Parvati, also known as Shakti. There are believed to have been ten avatars (incarnations) of Vishnu, of whom the most important are Rama and Krishna. Other popular gods are Ganesha, Hanuman and Subrahmanyam. All gods are seen as aspects of the supreme God, not as competing deities.

The commonest form of worship is a puja, in which offerings of red and yellow powders, rice grains, water, flowers, food, fruit, incense and light are made to the murti (image) of a deity.

Arya Pratinidhi Sabha (UK) and Arya Samaj London
69a Argyle Road, London W13 0LY (Tel: 020-8991 1732).
President: Prof. S. N. Bharadwaj

Bharatiya Vidya Bhavan
Institute of Indian Art and Culture, 4a Castletown Road, London W14 9HQ (Tel: 020-7381 4608; Web: www.bhavan.co.uk).
Executive Director: Dr M. N. Nandakumara

International Society for Krishna Consciousness (ISKCon)
Bhaktivedanta Manor, Dharam Marg, Hilfield Lane, Aldenham, Watford, Herts WD25 8EZ (Tel: 01923-859578).
Governing Body Commissioner: P. Latai

Swaminarayan Hindu Mission
105—119 Brentfield Road, Neasden, London NW10 8JP (Tel: 020-8965 2651; Fax: 020-8965 6313; E-mail: shm@swaminarayan-baps.org.uk; Web: www.swaminarayan-baps.org.uk).

Vishwa Hindu Parishad (UK)
48 Wharfedale Gardens, Thornton Heath, Surrey CR7 6LB (Tel: 020-8684 9716; Fax: 020-8684 9716).
General Secretary: K. Ruparelia

Vivekananda Centre London
6 Lea Gardens, Wembley, Middlesex, HA9 7SE (Tel: 020-8902 0840; Fax: 020-8903 0763; E-mail: hindu@btinternet.com; Web: www.vivekananda.co.uk).

ISLAM

Islam (which means 'peace arising from submission to the will of Allah' in Arabic) is a monotheistic religion which was taught by the Prophet Muhammad, who was born in Mecca (Makkah) in AD 570.

For Muslims (adherents of Islam), there is one God (Allah), who holds absolute power. His commands were revealed to mankind through the prophets, who include Abraham, Moses and Jesus, but his message was gradually corrupted until revealed finally and in perfect form to Muhammad through the angel Jibril (Gabriel) over a period of 23 years. This last, incorruptible message has been recorded in the Qur'an (Koran), and is held to be the essence of all previous scriptures. The Ahadith are the records of the Prophet Muhammad's deeds and sayings (the Sunnah) as recounted by his immediate followers. The Shari'ah is the sacred law of Islam based upon prescriptions derived from the Qur'an and the Sunnah of the Prophet. There is no central organisation, but the Islamic Cultural Centre, which is the London Central Mosque, and the Imams and Mosques Council are influential bodies; there are many other Muslim organisations in Britain.

East London Mosque Trust Ltd
82 Whitechapel Road, London E1 1JQ (Tel: 020-7247 1357; Fax: 020-7377 9879; E-mail: admin@eastlondonmosque.org.uk; Web: www.eastlondonmosque.org.uk).
Chairman: Abdul Awwal

Imams and Mosques Council
20—22 Creffield Road, London W5 3RP (Tel: 020-8992 6636).
Director of the Council and Principal of the Muslim College: Dr M. A. Z. Badawi

Islamic Cultural Centre and London Central Mosque
146 Park Road, London NW8 7RG (Tel: 020-7724 3363; Fax: 020-7211 0493).
Director: Dr. Dobyan

Muslim Council of Britain
P.O. Box 52, Wembley, Middx HA9 0XW (Tel: 020-8903 9024; Fax: 020-8903 9026; E-mail: admin@mcb.org.uk; Web: www.mcb.org.uk).
Secretary-General: Yousuf Bhailok

Muslim World League
46 Goodge Street, London W1P 1FJ (Tel: 020-7636 7568; Fax: 020-7637 5034; E-mail: mwl@webstar.co.uk).
Deputy Director: G. Rahman

Union of Muslim Organisations of the UK and Eire
109 Campden Hill Road, London W8 7TL (Tel: 020-7221 6608; Fax: 020-7792 2130).
General Secretary: Dr S. A. Pasha

JAINISM

Jainism was founded in the sixth century BC by Vardhamana Jnatiputra, known as Mahavira (The Great Hero), but it traces its roots to a succession of 24 Jinas (those who overcome), of which Mahavira is considered the last.

Jains believe that the universe is eternal and exists as a series of layers, including heaven, the earth and hell. Karma, the fruit of past actions, determines the place of every person and creature within the universe. Moksha (liberation from an endless succession of reincarnations) is achieved by enlightenment, which can be attained only through asceticism.

Institute of Jainology
Unit 18, Silicon Business Centre, 26—28 Wadsworth Road, Greenford, Middx UB6 7JZ. (Tel: 020-8997 2300; Fax: 020-8997 4964).

JUDAISM

The primary authority of Judaism is the Hebrew Bible or Tanakh. The first section (Torah) records how the descendants of Abraham were led by Moses out of their slavery in Egypt to Mount Sinai where God's law was revealed to them as the chosen people. The often two sections are Nevi'im (Prophets) and Ketuvim (Sacred Writings). The Talmud, which consists of commentaries on the Mishnah (the first text of rabbinical Judaism), is also held to be authoritative. Orthodox Jews regard Jewish law as derived from God and therefore unalterable; Reform and Liberal Jews seek to interpret it in the light of contemporary considerations; and Conservative Jews aim to maintain most of the traditional rituals but to allow changes in accordance with tradition.

The Chief Rabbi of the United Hebrew Congregations of the Commonwealth is the rabbinical authority of the Orthodox sector of the Ashkenazi Jewish community. His authority is not recognised by the Reform Synagogues of Great Britain (the largest progressive group), the Union of Liberal and Progressive Synagogues, the Union of Orthodox Hebrew Congregations, the Federation of Synagogues, the Sephardi Community, or the Assembly of Masorti Synagogues. He is, however, generally recognised outside the Jewish community as the public religious representative of the totality of British Jewry. The Chief Rabbi is President of the Beth Din (Court of Judgment) of the United Synagogue. The Board of Deputies of British Jews is the representative body of British Jewry.

Chief Rabbinate
735 High Road, London N12 0US (Tel: 020-8343 6301).
Chief Rabbi: Prof. Jonathan Sacks;
Executive Director: Mrs S. Weinberg

London Beth Din (Court of the Chief Rabbi)
735 High Road, London N12 0US (Tel: 020-8343 6280; Fax: 020-8343 6257;
E-mail: info@londonbethdin.fsnet.co.uk).
Registrar: David Frei;
Dayanim: Rabbi C. Ehrentreu; Rabbi I. Binstock; Rabbi C. D. Kaplin; Rabbi M. Gelley

Board of Deputies of British Jews
Commonwealth House, 1—19 New Oxford Street, London WC1A 1NU (Tel: 020-7543 5400; E-mail: info@bod.org.uk; Web: www.bod.org.uk).
President: E. Tabachnik, QC;
Director-General: N. A. Nagler

Assembly of Masorti Synagogues
1097 Finchley Road, London NW11 0PU (Tel: 020-8201 8772; Fax: 020-8201 8917; E-mail: office@masorti.org.uk; Web: www.masorti.org).
Director: Dr. H. Freedman

Federation of Synagogues
65 Watford Way, London NW4 3AQ (Tel: 020-8202 2263).
Chief Executive: G. D. Coleman

Beth Din of the Federation of Synagogues
65 Watford Way, London NW4 3AQ (Tel: 020-8202 2263; Fax: 020-8203 0610; E-mail: info@kfrosher.org; Web: www.kfrosher.org).
Registrar: Rabbi Z. Unsdorfer;
Dayanim: Dayan Y. Y. Lichtenstein, Dayan B. Berkovits, Dayan M. D. Elzas

Reform Synagogues of Great Britain
The Sternberg Centre for Judaism, 80 East End Road, London N3 2SY (Tel: 020-8349 5640; Fax: 020-8343 5699;
E-mail: admin@reformjudaism.org.uk; Web: www.reformjudiasmorg.uk).
Chief Executive: Rabbi T. Bayfield

Spanish and Portuguese Jews' Congregation
2 Ashworth Road, London W9 1JY (Tel: 020-7289 2573; Fax: 020-7289 2709).
Chief Administrator: H. Miller

Union of Liberal and Progressive Synagogues
The Montagu Centre, 21 Maple Street, London W1T 4BE (Tel: 020-7580 1663; Fax: 020-7436 4184; E-mail: montagu@ulps.org; Web: www.ulps.org).
Executive Director: Rabbi Dr C. H. Middleburgh

Union of Orthodox Hebrew Congregations
140 Stamford Hill, London N16 6QT (Tel: 020-8802 6226; Fax: 020-8809 7092).
Principal Rabbinical Authority: M. C. E. Padwa

United Synagogue Head Office
Alder House, 735 High Road, London N12 0US (Tel: 020-8343 8989; 020-8343 6262; E-mail: george.willna@unitedsynagogue.org.uk; Web: www.unitedsynagogue.org.uk/new).
Chief Executive: George Willman

SIKHISM

The Sikh religion dates from the birth of Guru Nanak in the Punjab in 1469, who taught that there is one God and that different religions are like different roads leading to the same destination. He condemned religious conflict, ritualism and caste prejudices. 'Guru' means teacher but in Sikh tradition has come to represent the divine presence of God giving inner spiritual guidance. Nanak's role as the human vessel of the divine guru was passed on to nine successors, the last of whom (Guru Gobind Singh) died in 1708. The immortal guru is now held to reside in the sacred scripture, Guru Granth Sahib, and so to be present in all Sikh gatherings.

Every gurdwara (temple) manages its own affairs and there is no central body in the UK. The Sikh Missionary Society provides an information service.

Sikh Divine Fellowship
46 Sudbury Court Drive, Harrow, Middx HA1 3TD (Tel: 020-8904 9244).
Secretary: Prof. H. Singh

Sikh Missionary Society UK
10 Featherstone Road, Southall, Middx UB2 5AA (Tel: 020-8574 1902; Fax: 020-8574 1912).
Hon. General Secretary: K. S. Rai

World Sikh Foundation
33 Wargrave Road, South Harrow, Middx HA2 8LL (Tel: 020-8864 9228; Fax: 020-8864 9228).
Managing Editor: Amar Singh Chhatwal

ZOROASTRIANISM

Zoroastrianism was founded by Zarathushtra in Persia around 1500 BC. Zarathushtra's words are recorded in five poems called the Gathas, which, together with other scriptures, forms the Avesta. Zoroastrianism teaches that there is one God, Ahura Mazda (the Wise Lord), and that all creation stems ultimately from God; the Gathas teach that human beings have free will, are responsible for their own actions and can choose between good and evil. Zoroastrians believe that after death, the immortal soul is judged by God, and is then sent to paradise or hell.

In Zoroastrian places of worship, an urn containing fire is the central feature; the fire symbolises the presence of Ahura Mazda in every human being.

World Zoroastrian Organization
135 Tennison Road, London SE25 (E-mail: chairman@w-z-o.org).
Chairman: S. F. Captain

THE CHURCHES

THE CHURCH OF ENGLAND

The Church of England is the established (i.e. state) church in England and the mother church of the Anglican Communion. The Thirty-Nine Articles, a set of doctrinal statements which, together with the Book of Common Prayer of 1662 and the Ordinal, define the position of the Church of England, were adopted in their final form in 1571 and include the emphasis on personal faith and the authority of the scriptures common to the Protestant Reformation throughout Europe.

Structure

The Church of England is divided into the two provinces of Canterbury and York, each under an archbishop. The two provinces are subdivided into 44 dioceses, of which six, all within the province of Canterbury, include parts of Greater London.

Decisions on matters concerning the Church of England are made by the General Synod, established in 1970. It also discusses and expresses opinion on any other matter of religious or public interest.

The Archbishops' Council was established in January 1999. The Council undertakes strategic planning, co-ordinates the work of all the central institutions and oversees the internal and external affairs of the Church of England. It reports frequently to the General Synod and seeks Synodical approval of its decisions.

General Synod of the Church of England

Church House, Great Smith Street, London SW1P 3NZ (Tel: 020-7898 1000; Fax: 020-7898 1369; E-mail: synod@c-of-e.org.uk).
General Secretary: P. Mawer

Archbishop and Primate of All England

Most Revd and Rt. Hon. George L. Carey, PhD, Lambeth Palace, London SE1 7JU.

Church Commissioners

1 Millbank, London SW1P 3JZ (Tel: 020-7898 1000; Fax: 020-7898 1002).

The Church Commissioners were established in 1948 by the amalgamation of Queen Anne's Bounty (established 1704) and the Ecclesiastical Commissioners (established 1836). They are responsible for the management of most of the Church of England's assets, the income from which is predominantly used to pay, house and pension the clergy. The Commissioners own a number of residential estates in central London.

Dioceses which lie within or partly within Greater London.

Chelmsford

8th Bishop
Rt. Revd John F. Perry, Bishopscourt, Margaretting, Ingatestone CM4 0HD (Tel: 01277-352001; Fax: 01277 355374; E-mail: bishopscourt@chelmsford.anglican.org).

Guildford

8th Bishop
Rt. Revd John W. Gladwin, Willow Grange, Woking Road, Guildford GU4 7QS (Tel: 01483-590500; Fax: 01483-590501).

London

132nd Bishop
Rt. Revd and Rt. Hon Richard J. C. Chartres, The Old Deanery, Dean's Court, London EC4V 5AA.

Rochester

106th Bishop
Rt. Revd Dr Michael Nazir-Ali, Bishopscourt, Rochester ME1 1TS (Tel: 01634-830333; Fax: 01634 831136; E-mail: bchoplain@clara.net; Web: www.rochester.anglcon.org).

St Albans

9th Bishop
Rt. Revd Christopher W. Herbert, Abbey Gate House, St Albans AL3 4HD (Tel: 01727-853305; Fax: 01727 846715).

Southwark

9th Bishop
Rt. Revd Dr. Thomas F. Butler, PhD, LLD, Bishop's House, 38 Tooting Bec Gardens, London SW16 1QZ (Tel: 020-8769 3256; Fax: 020-8769 4126; E-mail: bishop.tom@dswars.org.uk; Web: www.dswark.org).

THE ROMAN CATHOLIC CHURCH

The Roman Catholic Church is one world-wide Christian Church acknowledging as its head the Bishop of Rome, known as the Pope (Father). The Pope is held to be the successor of St Peter and thus invested with the power which was entrusted to St Peter by Jesus Christ. A direct line of succession is therefore claimed from the earliest Christian communities.

The Pope exercises spiritual authority over the Church with the advice and assistance of the Sacred College of Cardinals, the supreme council of the Church. He is also advised about the concerns of the Church locally by his ambassadors, who liaise with the Bishops' Conference in each country.

Sovereign Pontiff
His Holiness Pope John Paul II (Karol Wojty'a), born Wadowice, Poland, 18 May 1920; ordained priest 1946; appointed Archbishop of Kraków 1964; created Cardinal 1967; elected Pope 16 October 1978.

Secretariat of State
Secretary of State, HE Cardinal Angelo Sodano
First Section (General Affairs),
Mgr G. B. Re (Archbishop of Vescovio)
Second Section (Relations with other states),
Mgr J.- L. Tauran (Archbishop of Telepte)

Bishops' Conference
The Roman Catholic Church in England and Wales is governed by the Bishops' Conference, membership of which includes the Diocesan Bishops, the Apostolic Exarch of the Ukrainians, the Bishop of the Forces and the Auxiliary Bishops.

The Bishops' Standing Committee has general responsibility for continuity and policy between the plenary sessions of the Conference.

Catholic Bishops' Conference of England and Wales
39 Eccleston Square, London SW1V 1BX (Tel: 020-7630 8220; Fax: 020 7630 5166;
E-mail: secretariat@cbcew.org.uk;
Web: www.catholic-ew.org.uk).
General Secretary: Manager Arthur Roche

Apostolic Nuncio to Great Britain
H. E. Archbishop Pablo Puente, 54 Parkside, London SW19 5NE (Tel: 020-8946 1410; Fax: 020-8974 2494).

The Most Revd Archbishops and bishops in dioceses which lie within or partly within in Greater London (The dioceses of Westminster and Southwark are led by their respective archbishops; the diocese of Brentwood is led by its bishop).

Westminster
Cardinal Cormac Murphy O'Connor, Archbishop's House, Ambrosden Avenue, London SW1P 1QJ
(Tel: 020-7798 9033; Fax: 020-7798 9077;
Web: www.westminsterdiocese.org.uk).

Southwark
Michael G. Bowen, Archbishop's House, 150 St George's Road, London SE1 6HX (Tel: 020-7928 2495;
Web: www.rcsouthwark.co.uk).

Brentwood
Thomas McMahon, Bishop's Office, Cathedral House, Ingrave Road, Brentwood, Essex CM15 8AT (Tel: 01277-232266).

ROMAN CATHOLIC CHURCHES SERVING OTHER NATIONALITIES IN LONDON

Croatian Roman Catholic Church
17 Boutflower Road, London SW11 1RE
(Tel: 020-7223 3530).
Priest: Revd. Fr. Drago Beri'iæ

German Roman Catholic Church
St. Boniface, 47 Adler Street, London E1 1EE
(Tel: 020-7247 9529; Fax: 020-7247 3879).
Parish Priest: Heinz Medoch

Hungarian Roman Catholic Chaplaincy
Dunstan House, 141 Gunnersbury Avenue, London W3 8LE (Tel: 020-8992 2054; Fax: 020-8992 2054).
Snr. Chaplain: Revd. Mgr. George Tutto

Lithuanian Roman Catholic Church of St. Casimir
21 The Oval, London E2 9DT
(Tel: 020-7739 8735;
E-mail: london@ptverijonas.freeserve.co.uk;
Web: www.londdnas.co.uk).
Rector: Revd Petras Tverijonas

Slovenian Roman Catholic Mission
62 Offley Road, London SW9 0LS (Tel: 020-7735 6655; Fax: 020-7735 6655;
E-mail: cikanek@msn.com).
Chaplain: Revd. Stanislav Cikanek

OTHER CHURCHES WITH HEADQUARTERS OR REGIONAL OFFICES IN LONDON

AFRICAN AND AFRO-CARIBBEAN CHURCHES

There are more than 160 Christian churches or groups of African or Afro-Caribbean origin in the UK. These include the Apostolic Faith Church, the Cherubim and Seraphim Church, the New Testament Assembly, the New Testament Church of God, the Wesleyan Holiness Church and the Aladura Churches.

The Afro-West Indian United Council of Churches and the Council of African and Afro-Caribbean Churches UK (which was initiated as the Council of African and Allied Churches in 1979 to give one voice to the various Christian churches of African origin in the UK) are the media through which the member churches can work jointly to provide services they cannot easily provide individually.

Afro-West Indian United Council of Churches
c/o New Testament Church of God, Arcadian Gardens, High Road, London N22 5AA (Tel: 020-8888 9427).
Secretary: Bishop E. Brown

Council of African and Afro-Caribbean Churches UK
31 Norton House, Sidney Road, London SW9 0UJ (Tel: 020-7274 5589; Fax: 020-7274 4726).
Chairman: His Grace The Most Revd Father Olu A. Abiola

THE BAPTIST CHURCH

Baptists trace their origins to John Smyth, who in 1609 in Amsterdam reinstituted the baptism of conscious believers as the basis of the fellowship of a gathered church. Members of Smyth's church established the first Baptist church in England in 1612. They came to be known as 'General' Baptists and their theology was Arminian, whereas a later group of Calvinists who adopted the baptism of believers came to be known as 'Particular' Baptists. The two sections of the Baptists were united into one body, the Baptist Union of Great Britain and Ireland, in 1891. In 1988 the title was changed to the Baptist Union of Great Britain.

Baptists emphasise the complete autonomy of the local church, although individual churches are linked in various kinds of associations. There are international bodies (such as the Baptist World Alliance) and national bodies, but some Baptist churches belong to neither. However, in Great Britain the majority of churches and associations belong to the Baptist Union of Great Britain.

Baptist Union of Great Britain
Baptist House, PO Box 44, 129 Broadway, Didcot, Oxfordshire OX11 8RT.
The General Secretary: The Revd D. R. Coffey

THE HOLY APOSTOLIC CATHOLIC ASSYRIAN CHURCH OF THE EAST

The Holy Apostolic Catholic Assyrian Church of the East traces its beginnings to the middle of the first century. It spread from Upper Mesopotamia throughout the territories of the Persian Empire. The Church is headed by the Catholicos Patriarch and is episcopal in government. The liturgical language is Syriac (Aramaic).

The Church numbers about 400,000 members in the Middle East, India, Europe, North America and Australasia. There are around 1,000 members in the UK.

The Church in Great Britain forms part of the diocese of Europe under Mar Odisho Oraham. Representative in Great Britain, Very Revd Younan Y. Younan, 66 Montague Road, London W7 3PQ (Tel: 020-8579 7259).

THE LUTHERAN CHURCH

Lutheranism is based on the teachings of Martin Luther, the German leader of the Protestant Reformation. The key doctrine is that of justification by faith alone. Lutheranism is one of the largest Protestant denominations and it is particularly strong in northern Europe and the USA. Many Lutheran churches are episcopal, while others have a different form of organisation; unity is based on doctrine rather than structure. Lutheran services in Britain are held in 17 languages, including English, to serve different nationalities. Most Lutheran churches in Britain are members of the Lutheran Council of Great Britain.

Evangelical Lutheran Church of England
110 Warwick Way, London SW1V 1SD (Tel: 020-7834 3033).
Chairman: Revd Marvin Brammeir

Latvian Lutheran Church
17 Ivanhoe House, Balham, London SW12 8PS (Tel: 020-8673 3537).

Lutheran Council of Great Britain
30 Thanet Street, London WC1H 9QH (Tel: 020-7554 2900; Fax: 020-7383 3081; E-mail: enquiries@lutheran.org.uk Web: www.lutheran.org.uk).
General Secretary: Revd T. Bruch
Spiritual Head and Dean: Ringolds Muziks

Swedish Church (Lutheran)
6 Harcourt Street, London W1H 4AG (Tel: 020-7723 5681; Fax: 020-7727 2178; E-mail: office@swedish-church.org.uk; Web: www.swednet.org/swedish.church).
Chief Officer: The Very Revd Lennart Sjöström

THE METHODIST CHURCH

The Methodist movement started in England in 1729 when the Revd John Wesley, an Anglican priest, and his brother Charles met with others in Oxford and resolved to conduct their lives and study by 'rule and method'. In 1739 the Wesleys began evangelistic preaching and the first Methodist chapel was founded in Bristol in the same year. In 1744 the first annual conference was held, at which the Articles of Religion were drawn up. Doctrinal emphasis included repentance, faith, the assurance of salvation, social concern and the priesthood of all believers. After John Wesley's death in 1791 the Methodists withdrew from the established Church. In 1932 the Wesleyan Methodist Church, the United Methodist Church and the Primitive Methodist Church united to form the Methodist Church in Britain as it now exists.

The governing body and supreme authority of the Methodist Church is the Conference.

President of the Conference in Great Britain (2001–2): The Revd C. Le Moignan
Vice-President of the Conference (2001–2): Mrs. A. Leck
Secretary of the Conference: The Revd Dr N. T. Collinson

Methodist Church, Conference Office
25 Marylebone Road, London NW1 5JR (Tel: 020-7486 5502; Fax: 020-7467 5226; E-mail: conferenceoffice@methodistchurch.org.uk; Web: www.methodist.org.uk).

THE (EASTERN) ORTHODOX CHURCH

The Eastern (or Byzantine) Orthodox Church is a communion of self-governing Christian churches recognizing the honorary primacy of the Oecumenical Patriarch of Constantinople. The position of Orthodox Christians is that the faith was fully defined during the period of the Oecumenical Councils. In doctrine it is strongly trinitarian, and stresses the mystery and importance of the sacraments. It is episcopal in government. The structure of the Orthodox Christian year differs from that of western Churches.

EASTERN ORTHODOX CHURCHES IN LONDON

The Patriarchate of Antioch
There are ten parishes served by 13 clergy. In London the Patriarchate is represented by the Revd Fr Samir Gholam, St George's Cathedral, 1a Redhill Street, London NW1 4BG (Tel: 020-7383 0403).

The Greek Orthodox Church (Patriarchate of Constantinople)
The presence of Greek Orthodox Christians in Britain dates back at least to 1677 when Archbishop Joseph Geogirenes of Samos fled from Turkish persecution and came to London. The present Greek cathedral in Moscow Road, Bayswater, was opened for public worship in 1879 and the Diocese of Thyateira and Great Britain was established in 1922. There are now 113 parishes and other communities (including monasteries) in Great Britain, served by six bishops, 113 clergy and about 100 churches.

In London the Patriarchate of Constantinople is represented by Archbishop Gregorios of Thyateira and Great Britain, 5 Craven Hill, London W2 3EN (Tel: 020-7723 4787; Fax: 020-7224 9301).

The Russian Orthodox Church (Patriarchate of Moscow) and The Russian Orthodox Church Outside Russia.
The records of Russian Orthodox Church activities in Britain date from the visit to England of Tsar Peter I in the early 18th century. Clergy were sent from Russia to serve the chapel established to minister to the staff of the Imperial Russian Embassy in London.

In London the Patriarchate of Moscow is represented by Metropolitan Anthony of Sourozh, 67 Ennismore Gardens, London SW7 1NH (Fax: 020-7584 9864) He is assisted by one archbishop, one vicar bishop and 27 clergy. There are 27 parishes and smaller communities.

The Russian Orthodox Church Outside Russia is represented by Archbishop Mark of Berlin, Germany and Great Britain, c/o 57 Harvard

Road, London W4 4ED (Tel: 020-8742 3493). There are eight communities, including two monasteries, served by nine clergy.

Other Nationalities
Most of the Ukrainian parishes in Britain have joined the Patriarchate of Constantinople, leaving a small number of Ukrainian parishes in Britain under the care of other patriarchates (not all of which are recognised by the other Orthodox churches). The Latvian, Polish and some Belorussian parishes are also under the care of the Patriarchate of Constantinople. The Patriarchate of Serbia has 33 parishes and communities served by 12 priests. The Patriarchate of Romania has one parish served by two clergy. The Patriarchate of Bulgaria has one parish served by one priest. The Belorussian Autocephalous Orthodox Church has five parishes served by two priests.

Latvian Orthodox Church Abroad
53 Shakespeare Road, London NW7 4BA (Tel: 020-8959 1413).
Dean of Latvian Church Abroad:
The Very Rev. Alexander Cherney

Romanian Orthodox Church in London
St. Dunstan's in the West, 184A Fleet Street, London EC4A 2AE (Tel: 020-7242 6027; Fax: 020-7735 9515;
E-mail: ppufulete@compuserve.com).
Priest-in-Charge: Revd. S. P. Pufulete

THE ORIENTAL ORTHODOX CHURCHES
The term 'Oriental Orthodox Churches' is now generally used to describe a group of six ancient eastern churches which reject the Christological definition of the Council of Chalcedon (AD 451) and use Christological terms in different ways from the Eastern Orthodox Church.

ORIENTAL ORTHODOX CHURCHES IN THE UK
The Council of Oriental Orthodox Churches
Armenian Vicarage, Iverna Gardens, London W8 6TP (Tel: 020-7937 0152; Fax: 020-7937 9049).
Secretary: Deacon Aziz M. A. Nour (Tel: 020-8368 8447).

The Armenian Orthodox Church (Patriarchate of Etchmiadzin)
The Armenian Orthodox Church is the longest-established Oriental Orthodox community in Great Britain. It is represented by Bishop Nathan Hauhannisian, Armenian Primate of Great Britain, Armenian Vicarage, Iverna Gardens, London W8 6TP (Tel: 020-7937 0152; Fax: 020-7937 9049).

The Coptic Orthodox Church
The Coptic Orthodox Church is the largest Oriental Orthodox community in Great Britain. It has five dioceses (London, Birmingham; Scotland, Ireland and North-East England; the British Orthodox Church; and churches directly under Pope Shenouda III). The senior bishop in Great Britain is Metropolitan Seraphim, 10 Heathwood Gardens, London SE7 8EP (Tel: 020-8854 3090).

London Coptic Orthodox Church
Allen Street, London W8 6UX (Tel: 020-7937 5782; Fax: 020-7798 8335).
Hon. Sec.: Dr. F. Megally

The Eritrean Orthodox Church
78 Edmund Street, Camberwell London SE5 7NR (Tel: 020-7703 5147; Fax: 020-7703 5147).
Priest in Charge: Father Yohannes Sibhatu

The Ethiopian Orthodox Church
The acting head of the Ethiopian Orthodox Church in Europe is Revd Berhanu Beserat, 33 Jupiter Crescent, London NW1 8HA (Tel: 0956-513700).

London Ethiopian Orthodox Church
253b Ladbroke Grove, London W10 6HF (Tel: 020-8960 3848).
Head Priest: Very Revd. Aragawi Wolde Gabriel

The Malankara Orthodox Syrian (Indian) Church
The Malankara Orthodox Syrian Church is part of the Diocese of Europe under Metropolitan Thomas Mar Makarios. His representative in Great Britain is Fr M. S. Skariah, Paramula House, 44 Newbury Road, Newbury Park, Ilford, Essex IG2 7HD (Tel: 020-8599 3836; Fax: 020-8599 3836; Web: www.indian-orthodox.co.uk).
Place of Worship: St Andrew by the Wardrobe Church, Queen Victoria Street, London EC4.

The Syrian Orthodox Church
St. Jacob Baradaeus Parish in London and Environs, 5 Canning Road, Croydon CR0 6QA (Tel: 020-8654 7531; Fax: 020-8654 7531).
Patriarch of Antioch and all the East: H. H. Mar Ignatius Zakka I. Iwas

The **Indian congregation** under the Syrian Patriarch of Antioch is represented by Fr Eldhose Koungampillil, 1 Roslyn Court, Roslyn Avenue, East Barnet, Herts EN4 8DJ (Tel: 020-8368 2794).

St Matthews Westminster, 20 Great Peter Street, Westminster, London SW1 2BU (Tel: 020-7222 3704; Fax: 020-7233 0255).
Priest: Revd Philip Chester

THE RELIGIOUS SOCIETY OF FRIENDS (QUAKERS)
Quakerism is a movement which was founded in the 17th century by George Fox and others in an attempt to revive what they saw as 'primitive Christianity'. The movement was based originally in the Midlands, Yorkshire and north-west England, but there are now Quakers in over 70 countries around the world. The colony of Pennsylvania, founded by William Penn, was originally Quaker.

Emphasis is placed on the experience of God in daily life rather than on sacraments or religious occasions. There is no church calendar. Worship in the British tradition of Quakerism is largely silent and there are no appointed ministers, however, worshippers may speak if inspired to do so; the responsibility for conducting a meeting is shared equally among those present. Social reform and religious tolerance have always been important to Quakers, together with a commitment to non-violence in resolving disputes.

Central Office: Friends House, 173 Euston Road, London NW1 2BJ (Tel: 020-7663 1000; Fax: 020-7663 1001; E-mail: ql@quaker.org.uk; Web: www.quaker.org.uk).

THE SALVATION ARMY
The Salvation Army was founded by a Methodist minister, William Booth, in the east end of London in 1865, and has since become established in 104 countries world-wide. It was first known as the Christian Mission, and took its present name in 1878 when it adopted a quasi-military command structure intended to inspire and regulate its endeavours and to reflect its view that the Church was engaged in spiritual warfare. Salvationists emphasise evangelism, social work and the relief of poverty.

The world leader, known as the General, is elected by a High Council composed of the Chief of the Staff and senior ranking officers known as commissioners.

There are about 1.5 million members, 17,362 active officers (full-time ordained ministers) and 15,669 worship centres and outposts world-wide.
General: J. Gowans

Territorial HQ
101 Newington Causeway, London SE1 6BN (Tel: 020-7367 4500).
Territorial Commander: Commissioner A. Hughes

London Central Division
First Floor, 25/27 Kings Exchange, Tileyard Road, London N7 9AH (Tel: 020-7619 6100; Fax: 020-7619 6111;
E-mail: john.wainwright@salvationarmy.org.uk).
Divisional Commander: Major John Wainwright

London South-East
1 East Court, Enterprise Road, Maidstone, Kent ME15 6JF (Tel: 01622 775000).
Divisional Commander: Major David Jones

London North East
Maldon Road, Hatfield Peverel, Essex CM3 2HL (Tel: 01245 383000).
Divisional Commander: Lt. Col David Phillips

THE SEVENTH-DAY ADVENTIST CHURCH
The Seventh-day Adventist Church was founded in 1863 in the USA. Its members look forward to the second coming of Christ and observe the Sabbath (the seventh day) as a day of rest, worship and ministry. The Church bases its faith and practice wholly on the Bible and has developed 27 fundamental beliefs.

In the British Isles the administrative organisation of the church is arranged in three tiers: the local churches; the regional conferences for south England, north England, Wales, Scotland and Ireland; and the national 'union' conference.

There are 10,492,456 Adventists and 45,715 churches in 205 countries world-wide. In the UK and Ireland there are 20,637 members, 147 ministers and 243 churches.

President of the British Union Conference: Pastor C. R. Perry

South England Conference Office, 25 St. Johns Road, Watford, Herts WD17 1PZ (Tel: 01923 232728; Fax: 01923 250582; E-mail: 102555.2314@compuserve.com; Web: www.secadventist.org.uk).
President: Pastor D. W. McFarlane

THE (SWEDENBORGIAN) NEW CHURCH

The New Church is based on the teachings of the 18th century Swedish scientist and theologian Emmanuel Swedenborg (1688-1772), who believed that Jesus Christ appeared to him and instructed him to reveal the spiritual meaning of the Bible.

The Second Coming of Jesus Christ is believed to have already taken place and is still taking place, being not an actual physical reappearance of Christ, but rather His return in spirit. It is also believed that concurrent with our life on earth is life in a parallel spiritual world, of which we are usually unconscious until death, when our final judgement is our realisation of our individual essential nature.

There are around 30,000 Swedenborgians world-wide, with about 1,300 members, 32 Churches and 14 ministers in the UK

The Swedenborg Movement
98 Abbotts Drive, Wembley, Middx, HA0 3SQ.

The Swedenborg Society
20-21 Bloomsbury Way, London WC1A 2TH. (Tel: 020-7405 7986; Fax: 020-7831 5848).

THE UNITED REFORMED CHURCH

The United Reformed Church was formed by the union of most of the Congregational churches in England and Wales with the Presbyterian Church of England in 1972.

Congregationalism dates from the mid 16th century. It is Calvinistic in doctrine, and its followers form independent self-governing congregations bound under God by covenant, a principle laid down in the writings of Robert Browne (1550—1633).

The Presbyterian Church in England also dates from the mid 16th century, and was Calvinistic and evangelical in its doctrine. It was governed by a hierarchy of courts.

In 1981 a further unification took place, with the Reformed Association of Churches of Christ becoming part of the URC. In 2000 the United Reformed Church and the Congregational Union of Scotland United under the name of the United Reformed Church.

The General Assembly is the central body, and is made up of equal numbers of ministers and lay members.
General Secretary: Revd D. C. Cornick, 86 Tavistock Place, London WC1H 9RT (Tel: 020-7916 2020; Fax: 020-7916 2021; E-mail: agburnam@urc.org.uk; Web: www.urc.org.uk).

NON-TRINITARIAN CHURCHES

CHRISTADELPHIANISM

Christadelphians believe in the Bible as the literal truth and that the Second Coming of Jesus Christ is imminent. Mankind is mortal by nature and only those who have been baptised and saved by their faith in Jesus will be resurrected to eternal life on earth.

Christadelphianism was founded by Dr John Thomas, an Englishman who emigrated to the USA, where he joined a religious group which he left after disagreements on doctrine, taking many of the group with him, the who were later to be called Christadelphians. He founded several magazines and returned to England several times, where several congregations had formed on the basis of his teachings.

There are around 18,700 Christadelphians in the UK and some 282 ecclesias (churches).

The Christadelphian Magazine and Publishing Association
404 Shaftmoor Lane, Birmingham B28 8SZ. (Tel: 0121-777 6324; Fax: 0121-778 5024).

THE CHURCH OF CHRIST, SCIENTIST

The Church of Christ, Scientist was founded by Mary Baker Eddy in the USA in 1879 to 'reinstate primitive Christianity and its lost element of healing'. Christian Science teaches the need for spiritual regeneration and salvation from sin, but is best known for its reliance on prayer alone in the healing of sickness. Adherents believe that such healing is a law, or Science, and is in direct line with that practised by Jesus Christ (revered, not as God, but as the Son of God) and by the early Christian Church.

The denomination consists of The First Church of Christ, Scientist, in Boston, Massachusetts, USA (the Mother Church) and its branch churches in over 60 countries world-wide. Branch churches are democratically governed by their members, while a five-member Board of Directors, based in Boston, is authorised to transact the business of the Mother Church. The Bible and Mary Baker Eddy's book, Science and Health with Key to the Scriptures, are used at services; there are no clergy. Those engaged in full-time healing are called practitioners.

Christian Science Committee on Publication
9 Elysium Gate, 126 New Kings Road, London SW6 4LZ (Tel: 020-7384 8600; Fax: 020-7371 9204; E-mail: joynesh@compub.org; Web: www.tfccs.com).
District Manager: H. Joynes

THE CHURCH OF JESUS CHRIST OF LATTER-DAY SAINTS

The Church (often referred to as 'the Mormons') was founded in New York State, USA, in 1830, and came to Britain in 1837. Mormons are Christians who claim to belong to the 'Restored Church' of Jesus Christ. They believe that true Christianity died when the last original apostle died, but that it was given back to the world by God and Christ through Joseph Smith, the Church's founder and first president. They accept and use the Bible as scripture, but believe in continuing revelation from God and use additional scriptures, including The Book of Mormon: Another Testament of Jesus Christ.

The importance of the family is central to the Church's beliefs and practices.

The Church has no paid ministry; local congregations are headed by a leader chosen from amongst their number.

President of the England London Mission: Steven C. Wheelwright; Elder R. Kerr
London Mission, 64 Exhibition Road, London SW7 2PA (Tel: 020-7584 7553; Fax: 020-7581 5199; Web: www.lds.org.uk).

JEHOVAH'S WITNESSES

The movement now known as Jehovah's Witnesses grew from a Bible study group formed by Charles Taze Russell in 1872 in Pennsylvania, USA. In 1896 it adopted the name of the Watch Tower Bible and Tract Society, and in 1931 its members became known as Jehovah's Witnesses. Jehovah's (God's) Witnesses believe in the Bible as the word of God, and consider it to be inspired and historically accurate. They take the scriptures literally, except where there are obvious indications that they are figurative or symbolic, and reject the doctrine of the Trinity. Witnesses also believe that the earth will remain for ever and that all those approved of by Jehovah will have eternal life on a cleansed and beautified earth; only 144,000 will go to heaven to rule with Christ.

They believe that the second coming of Christ began in 1914 and his thousand-year reign on earth is imminent, and that Armageddon (a final battle in which evil will be defeated) will precede Christ's rule of peace. They refuse to take part in military service, and do not accept blood transfusions. They publish two magazines, The Watchtower and Awake!

There is no paid ministry, but each congregation has elders assigned to look after various duties and every Witness is assigned homes to visit in their congregation.

Watch Tower House, The Ridgeway, London NW7 1RN (Tel: 020-8906 2211; Fax: 020-8371 0051; E-mail: pr@wtbts.org.uk; Web: www.watchtower.org).

UNITARIAN AND FREE CHRISTIAN CHURCHES

Unitarianism has its historical roots in the Judaeo-Christian tradition but rejects the deity of Christ and the doctrine of the trinity. It allows the individual to embrace insights from all the world's faiths and philosophies, as there is no fixed creed. It is accepted that beliefs may evolve in the light of personal experience.

The first avowedly Unitarian place of worship in the British Isles opened in London in 1774.

General Assembly of Unitarian and Free Christian Churches
Essex Hall, 1-6 Essex Street, London WC2R 3HY (Tel: 020-7240 2384; Fax: 020-7240 3089; E-mail: ga@unitarian.org.uk; Web: www.unitarian.org.uk).
General Secretary: J. J. Teagle

SOCIETIES AND INSTITUTIONS

SOCIETIES AND INSTITUTIONS

The list below contains a selection, in alphabetical order, of societies, institutions, charities and professional associations based in London. Where an organisation is very relevant to a particular section of the book, for example, Environmental London, an entry will appear in that section and not in the list below.

2Care
11 Harwood Road, London, SW6 4QP (Tel: 020-7371 0118; Fax: 020-7371 7519).
Chief Executive: Miss E. C. R. O'Sullivan

Action for Blind People
14–16 Verney Road, London, SE16 3DZ (Tel: 020-7635 4800; Fax: 020-7635 4900; E-mail: central@afbp.org; Web: www.afbp.org).
Chief Executive: S. Remington

Actors' Benevolent Fund
6 Adam Street, London, WC2N 6AD (Tel: 020-7836 6378; Fax: 020-7836 8978; E-mail: office@abf.org.uk).
General Secretary: Mrs J. Skerrett

Actors' Charitable Trust
255–256 Africa House, 67–78 Kingsway, London, WC2B 6BD (Tel: 020-7242 0111; Fax: 020-7242 0234; E-mail: tact.actors@virgin.net).
General Secretary: B. Batchelor

Actors' Church Union
St Paul's Church, Bedford Street, London, WC2E 9ED (Tel: 020-720 0344).
Senior Chaplain: Canon W. Hall

Adam Smith Institute
23 Great Smith Street, London, SW1P 3BL (Tel: 020-7222 4995; Fax: 020-7222 7544; E-mail: info@adamsmith.org; Web: www.adamsmith.org).
Director: Dr. M. Pirie

Advertising Standards Authority
2 Torrington Place, London, WC1E 7HW (Tel: 020-7580 5555; Fax: 020-7631 3051; E-mail: inquries@asa.org.uk; Web: www.asa.org.uk).
Director-General: C. Graham

African Medical and Research Foundation
4 Grosvenor Place, London, SW1X 7HJ (Tel: 020-7201 6070; Fax: 020-7201 6170; E-mail: amref.uk@amref.org; Web: www.amref.org).
Executive Director: A. Héroys

Age Concern England
Astral House, 1268 London Road, London, SW16 4ER (Tel: 020-8765 7200; Fax: 020-8765 7211; E-mail: ace@ace.org.uk; Web: www.ageconcern.org.uk).
Director-General: Gordon Lishman

Age Concern Southwark
224-236 Walworth Road, London, SE17 1JE (Tel: 020-7701 9700).
The Chief Executive

Age Conern Westminster
268-272 Edgware Rd, London, W2 1DS (Tel: 020-72248602; Fax: 020-7723 0405).
The Chief Executive: Ms V. Jensen

Alone in London
188 Kings Cross Road, London, WC1X 9DE (Tel: 020-7278 4486; Fax: 020-7837 8599; E-mail: alone@als.org.uk; Web: www.als.org).
Director: Gaynor Quilter

Alzheimer's Society
Gordon House, 10 Greencoat Place, London, SW1P 1PH (Tel: 020-7306 0606; Fax: 020-7306 0808; E-mail: info@alzheimers.org.uk; Web: www.alzheimers.org.uk).
Chief Executive: H. Cayton

Amnesty International United Kingdom
99–119 Rosebery Avenue, London, EC1R 4RE (Tel: 020-7814 6200; Fax: 020-7833 1510; E-mail: info@amnesty.org.uk; Web: www.amnesty.org.uk/).
Director: Ms K. Allen

Ancient Monuments Society
St Ann's Vestry Hall, 2 Church Entry, London, EC4V 5HB (Tel: 020-7236 3934; Fax: 020-7329 3677; E-mail: ancientmonuments@talk21.com; Web: www.ancientmonumentssociety.org.uk).
Secretary: M. J. Saunders, MBE

490 Societies and Institutions

Anglo-Belgian Society
5 Hartley Close, Bickley, Kent, BR1 2TP
(Tel: 020-8467 8442; Fax: 020-8467 8442).
Hon. Secretary: P. R. Bresnan

Anglo-Brazilian Society
32 Green Street, London, W1K 7AU
(Tel: 020-7493 8493;
E-mail: anglo@braziliansociety.freeserve.co.uk).
Secretary: J. Wright

Anglo-Danish Society
Hillgate House, 26 Old Bailey, London, EC4M 7HW.
Chairman: P. J. Willoughby

Anglo-Norse Society
25 Belgrave Square, London, SW1X 8QD
(Tel: 020-7591 5500; Fax: 020-7245 6993).
Chairman: Sir John Robson, KCMG

Anthroposophical Society in Great Britain
Rudolf Steiner House, 35 Park Road, London, NW1 6XT (Tel: 020-7723 4400; Fax: 020-7724 4364;
E-mail: rsh@cix.compulink.co.uk;
Web: www.anth.org.uk).
General Secretary: N. C. Thomas

Anti-Slavery International
Thomas Clarkson House, The Stableyard, Broomgrove Road, London, SW9 9TL
(Tel: 020-7501 8920; Fax: 020-7738 4110;
E-mail: antislavery@antislavery.org;
Web: www.antislavery.org).
Director: M. Dottridge

Architects Benevolent Society
43 Portland Place, London, W1B 1QH
(Tel: 020-7580 2823; Fax: 020-7580 7075;
E-mail: admin@theabs.org.uk).
Secretary: K.Robinson

Architects Registration Board
8 Weymouth Street, London, W1W 5BU
(Tel: 020-7580 5861; Fax: 020-7436 5269;
E-mail: info@arb.org.uk;
Web: www.arb.orf.uk).
Chief Executive and Registrar: Robin Vaughan

Architectural Association (Inc)
34–36 Bedford Square, London, WC1B 3ES
(Tel: 020-7887 4000; Fax: 020-7414 0782).
Chief Executive: Mohsen Inostafari

Architectural Heritage Fund
Clareville House, 26–27 Oxendon Street, London, SW1Y 4EL (Tel: 020-7925 0199;
Fax: 020-7930 0295;
E-mail: ahf@ahfund.org.uk;
Web: www.ahfund.org.uk).
Director: J. Thompson

Army Benevolent Fund
41 Queen's Gate, London, SW7 5HR
(Tel: 020-7591 2000; Fax: 020-7584 0889).
Controller: Maj.-Gen. M. D. Regan, CB, OBE

Army Cadet Force Association
E Block, Duke of York's HQ, London, SW3 4RR
(Tel: 020-7730 9733; Fax: 020-7730 8264
E-mail: acf@armycadets.com;
Web: www.armycadets.com).
General Secretary: Brig. J. E. Neeve

Arthritis Care
18 Stephenson Way, London, NW1 2HD
(Tel: 020-7380 6500; Fax: 020-7380 6505;
Web: www.arthritiscare.org.uk).
Chief Executive: R. Gutch

Artists' General Benevolent Institution and Artists' Orphan Fund
Burlington House, Piccadilly, London, W1V 0DJ
(Tel: 020-7734 1193).
Secretary: Ms A. Connett-Dance

Asian Family Counselling Service
76 Church Road, Hanwell, London, W7 1LB
(Tel: 020-8567 5616; Fax: 020-8567 5616;
E-mail: afcs99@hotmail.com).
Director: R. Atma

ASLIB (The Association for Information Management)
Staple Hall, Stone House Court, London, EC3A 7PB (Tel: 020-7903 0000; Fax: 020-7903 0011;
E-mail: aslib@aslib.com;
Web: www.aslib.com).
Chief Executive: R. Bowes

Association of Accounting Technicians
154 Clerkenwell Road, London, EC1R 5AD
(Tel: 020-7837 8600; Fax: 020-7837 6970;
E-mail: aatuk@dial.pipex.com;
Web: www.aat.co.uk).
Chief Executive: Ms J. Scott Paul

Societies and Institutions 491

Association of Anaesthetists of Great Britain and Ireland
9 Bedford Square, London, WC1B 3RA
(Tel: 020-7631 1650; Fax: 020-7631 4352;
E-mail: info@aagbi.org;
Web: www.aagbi.org).
Chief Executive: Kevin Horlock

Association of British Correspondence Colleges
PO Box 17926, London, SW19 3WB
(Tel: 020-8544 9559; Fax: 020-8540 7657;
E-mail: abcc@msn.com;
Web: www.homestudy.org.uk).
Secretary: Mrs H. Owen

Association of British Dispensing Opticians
199 Gloucester Terrace, London, W2 6HX
E-mail: general@abdo.org.uk;
Web: www.abdo.org.uk).
Registrar: D. S. Baker

Association of British Insurers
51 Gresham Street, London, EC2V 7HQ
(Tel: 020-7600 3333).
Director-General: Mrs M. Francis

Association of British Travel Agents (ABTA)
68–71 Newman Street, London, W1T 3AH
(Tel: 020-7637 2444; Fax: 020-7637 0713;
E-mail: abta@abta.co.uk;
Web: www.abtanet.com).
Chief Executive: I. Reynolds

Association of Business Recovery Professionals
Halton House, 20–23 Holborn, London, EC1N 2JE (Tel: 020-7831 6563; Fax: 020-7405 7049;
E-mail: thoey@r3.org.uk;
Web: www.r3.org.uk).
General Secretary: R. M. Stancombe

Association of Chartered Certified Accountants
29 Lincoln's Inn Fields, London, WC2A 3EE
(Tel: 020-7242 6855; Fax: 020-7831 8054;
Web: www.accaglobal.com).
Chief Executive: Ms A. L. Rose

Association of Consulting Engineers
Alliance House, 12 Caxton Street, London, SW1H 0QL
(Tel: 020-7222 6557; Fax: 020-7222 0750;
E-mail: consult@acenet.co.uk;
Web: www.acenet.co.uk).
Chief Executive: N. Bennett

Association of Corporate Treasurers
Ocean House, 10–12 Little Trinity Lane, London, EC4V 2DJ
(Tel: 020-7213 9728; Fax: 020-7248 2591;
E-mail: enquiries@treasurers.co.uk;
Web: www.treasurers.org).
Director-General: Dr D. Creed

Association of Friendly Societies
10–13 Lovat Lane, London, EC3R 8DT
(Tel: 020-7397 9550; Fax: 020-7397 9551;
E-mail: info@afs.org.uk;
Web: www.afs.org.uk).
General Secretary: Miss M. Poole

Association of Royal Navy Officers
70 Porchester Terrace, London, W2 3TP
(Tel: 020-7402 5231; Fax: 020-7402 5533;
E-mail: ARNO@eurosurf.com;
Web: www.eurosurf.com/ARNO).
Secretary: Lt.-Cdr. I. M. P. Coombes

Association of Sports Historians
Ground Floor Offices, 13–16 Faro Close, Coates Hill Road, Bromley, Kent, BR1 2RR
(Tel: 020-8467 1951).
Chief Executive: C. Harte

Baltic Air Charter Association
The Baltic Exchange, St Mary Axe, London, EC3A 8BH (Tel: 020-7623 5501; Fax: 020-7639 1623; Web: www.baca.org).
Chairman: Capt. N. J. Harris

Baltic Exchange
The Baltic Exchange, St Mary Axe, London, EC3A 8BH (Tel: 020-7623 5501; Fax: 020-7369 1622;
E-mail: enquiries@balticexchange.co.uk;
Web: www.balticexchange.com).
Chief Executive: J. Buckley

Baltic Exchange Charitable Society
13 Norton Folgate, Bishopgate, London, E1 6DB
(Tel: 020-7247 6863;
E-mail: douglas-painter@talk21.com).
Secretary: D. A. Painter

Barnardo's
Tanners Lane, Barkingside, Ilford, Essex, IG6 1QG (Tel: 020-8550 8822; Fax: 020-8551 6870;
Web: www.barnardos.com).
Chief Executive: R. Singleton

492 Societies and Institutions

Barristers' Benevolent Association
14 Gray's Inn Square, London, WC1R 5JP
(Tel: 020-7242 4761; Fax: 020-7831 5366;
E-mail: linda@thebba.swinternet.co.uk).
Secretary: Mrs L. C. Carlier

Battersea Community Arts Centre Trust
Old Town Hall, Lavender Hill, London, SW11
5TF (Tel: 020-7223 6557; Fax: 020-7978 5207;
E-mail: mailbox@bac.org.uk).
The Chief Executive

Battersea Dogs Home
4 Battersea Park Road, London, SW8 4AA
(Tel: 020-7622 3626; Fax: 020-7622 6451;
E-mail: info@dogshome.org;
Web: www.dogshome.org).
Director General: D. A. H. Green

Bibliographical Society
c/o The Wellcome Library, 183 Euston Road,
London, NW1 2BE (Tel: 020-7611 7244;
Fax: 020-7611 8703;
E-mail: jm93@dial.pipex.com;
Web: www.bibsoc.org.uk).
Hon. Secretary: D. Pearson

Biochemical Society
59 Portland Place, London, W1N 3AJ
(Tel: 020-7580 5530; Fax: 020-7637 3626;
E-mail: genadmin@biochemistry.org;
Web: www.biochemistry.org).
Executive Secretary: G. D. Jones

Blue Cross
The Blue Cross Animals Hospital, 1-5 Hugh
Street, London, SW1V 1QQ
(Tel: 020-7834 1128; Fax: 020-78219038;
E-mail: info@bluecross.org.uk;
Web: www.bluecross.org.uk).
The Chief Executive

Book Aid International
39–41 Coldharbour Lane, London, SE5 9NR
(Tel: 020-7733 3577; Fax: 020-7978 8006;
E-mail: info@bookaid.org;
Web: www.bookaid.org).
Director: Mrs S. Harrity, MBE

Book Trust
Book House, 45 East Hill, London, SW18 2QZ
(Tel: 020-8516 2977; Fax: 020-8516 2978;
Web: www.booktrust.org.uk).
Executive Director: C. Meade

Booksellers Association of the UK & Ireland Ltd
Minster House, 272 Vauxhall Bridge Road,
London, SW1V 1BA
(Tel: 020-7834 5477; Fax: 020-7834 8812;
E-mail: mail@booksellers.org.uk;
Web: www.booksellers.org.uk).
Chief Executive: T. E. Godfray

Botanical Society of the British Isles
c/o Department of Botany, The Natural History
Museum, Cromwell Road, London, SW7 5BD
(Tel: 020-7942 5002; E-mail: bsbihgs@aol.com;
Web: www.members.aol.com/bsbihgs).
Hon. General Secretary: Miss Alisa Burns

Britain-Nepal Society
3C Gunnersbury Avenue, London, W5 3NH
(Tel: 020-8992 0173).
Hon. Secretary: Mrs P. Mellor

British Academy of Composers and Songwriters
British Music House, 26 Berners Street, London,
W1T 3LR (Tel: 020-7636 2729; Fax: 020-7636
2212; E-mail: info@britishacademy.com;
Web: www.britishacademy.com).
Chief Executive: C. Green

British Academy of Forensic Sciences
Anaesthetic Unit, The Royal London Hospital,
Whitechapel, London, E1 1BB
(Tel: 020-7377 9201; Fax: 020 377 7126).
Secretary-General: Dr P. J. Flynn

British Antique Dealers' Association
20 Rutland Gate, London, SW7 1BD
(Tel: 020-7589 4128; Fax: 020-7581 9083;
E-mail: enquiry@bada.demon.co.uk;
Web: www.bada.org).
Secretary-General: Mrs E. J. Dean

British Association for Early Childhood Education
136 Lavell Street, London, E1 2JA
(Tel: 020-7539 5400; Fax: 020-7539 5409;
E-mail: office@early-education.org.uk;
Web: www.early-education.org.uk).
Chief Executive: Ms W. Scott

Societies and Institutions 493

British Association for the Advancement of Science
23 Savile Row, London, W1S 2EZ
(Tel: 020-7973 3500; Fax: 020-7973 3063;
E-mail: info@britassoc.org.uk;
Web: www.britassoc.org.uk).
Chief Executive: Dr P. Briggs

British Association of Communicators in Business
42 Borough High Street, London, SE1 1XW
(Tel: 020-7378 7139; Fax: 020-7378 7140;
E-mail: enquiries@bacb.org;
Web: www.bacb.org).
Secretary-General: Mrs K. Jones

British Astronomical Association
Burlington House, Piccadilly, London, W1J ODU (Web: www.ast.cam.ac.uk/-baa).
Assistant Secretary: Miss P. M. Barber

British Board of Film Classification
3 Soho Square, London, W1D 3HD
(Tel: 020-7440 1570; Fax: 020-7287 0141;
E-mail: webmaster@bbfc.co.uk;
Web: www.bbfc.co.uk).
Director: R. Duval

British Commonwealth Ex-Services League
48 Pall Mall, London, SW1Y 5JG
(Tel: 020-7973 7263; Fax: 020-7973 7308).
Secretary-General: Colonel B. G. G. Nicholson OBE, RM

British Consultants Bureau
One Westminster Palace Gardens, 1–7 Artillery Row, London, SW1P 1RJ (Tel: 020-07222 3651; Fax: 020 7222 3664; E-mail: mail@bcb.co.uk).
Director: C. Adams, CBE

British Copyright Council
29–33 Berners Street, London, W1T 3AB
(Tel: 01986-788122; Fax: 01906-788847;
E-mail: copyright@bcc2.demon.co.uk).
Secretary: Ms J. Ibbotson

British Deaf Association
1 Worship Street, London, EC2A 2AB
(Tel: 020-7588 3520; Fax: 020-7588 3527;
E-mail: info@bda.org.uk;
Web: www.bda.org.uk).
Chief Executive: J. McWhinney

British Dental Association
64 Wimpole Street, London, W1G 8YS
(Tel: 020-7935 0875; Fax: 020-7487 5232;
E-mail: enquiries@bda-dentistry.org.uk;
Web: www.bda-dentistry.org.uk).
Chief Executive: Ian Wylie

British Energy Association
34 St James's Street, London, SW1A 1HD
(Tel: 020-7930 1211).
Director: M. Jefferson

British Executive Service Overseas
164 Vauxhall Bridge Road, London, SW1V 4RB
(Tel: 020-7630 0644; Fax: 020-7630 0624;
E-mail: team@beso.org; Web: www.beso.org).
Chief Executive: G. Ramsey, CBE

British Federation of Women Graduates
4 Mandeville Courtyard, 142 Battersea Park Road, London, SW11 4NB
(Tel: 020-7498 8037; Fax: 020-7498 8037;
E-mail: bfwg@bfwg.demon.co.uk;
Web: www.homepages.wyenet.co.uk/bfwg).
Secretary: Mrs A. B. Stein

British Heart Foundation
14 Fitzhardinge Street, London, W1H 6DH
(Tel: 020-7935 0185; Fax: 020-7486 5820;
Web: www.bhf.org.uk).
Director-General: Maj.-Gen. L. F. H. Busk, CB

British Herpetological Society
c/o Zoological Society of London, Regent's Park, London, NW1 4RY (Tel: 020-8452 9578).
Secretary: Mrs M. Green

British Homoeopathic Association
15 Clerkenwell Close, London, EC1R 0AA
(Tel: 020-7566 7800; Fax: 020-7566 7815;
E-mail: info@trusthomeopathy.org;
Web: www.trusthomeopathy.org).
Chief Executive: Sally Penrose

British Hospitality Association
Queens House, 55–56 Lincoln's Inn Fields, London, WC2A 3BH (Tel: 020-7404 7744; Fax: 020-7404 7799; E-mail: bha@bha.org.uk; Web: www.bha-online.org.uk).
Chief Executive: R. G. Cotton

British Humanist Association
47 Theobald's Road, London, WC1X 8SP
(Tel: 020-7430 0908; Fax: 020-7430 1271;
E-mail: info@humanism.org.uk;
Web: www.humanism.org.uk).
Executive Director: R. Ashby

British Institute in Eastern Africa
10 Carlton House Terrace, London, SW1Y 5AH
(Tel: 020-7969 5201; Fax: 020-7969 5401;
E-mail: biea@britac.ac.uk).
London Secretary: Mrs Jeanie Moyo

British Institute of Archaeology at Ankara
10 Carlton House Terrace, London, SW1Y 5AH
(Tel: 020-7969 5204; Fax: 020-7969 5401;
E-mail: biaa@britac.ac.uk;
Web: www.britac.ac.uk/institutes/ankara).
Director: Dr R. J. Matthews

British Institute of Human Rights
8th Floor, King's College London, 75–79 York Road, London, SE1 7AW (Tel: 020-7401 2712; Fax: 020-7401 2695; E-mail: bihr@kcl.ac.uk; Web: www.bihr.org).
Director: Ms S. Cooke

British Institute of Persian Studies
c/o The British Academy, 10 Carlton House Terrace, London, SW1Y 5AH
(Tel: 020-7969 5203; Fax: 020-7969 5401;
E-mail: bips@britac.ac.uk;
Web: www.britac.ac.uk/institutes/bips).
President: Prof. James Allan

British Insurance Brokers' Association
BIBA House, 14 Bevis Marks, London, EC3A 7NT (Tel: 020-7623 9043; Fax: 020-7626 9676;
E-mail: enquiries@biba.org.uk;
Web: www.biba.org.uk).
Chief Executive: R. M. Williams

British Interplanetary Society
27–29 South Lambeth Road, London, SW8 1SZ
(Tel: 020-7735 3160; Fax: 020-7820 1504;
E-mail: bis.bis@virgin.net;
Web: www.bis-spaceflight.com).
Executive Secretary: Ms S. A. Jones

British Israel World Federation
8 Blades Court, Deodar Road, London, SW15 2NU (Tel: 020-8877 9010; Fax: 020-8871 4770;
E-mail: admin@britishisrael.co.uk;
Web: www.britishisrael.co.uk).
Hon. Secretary: M. A. Clark

British Lung Foundation
78 Hatton Garden, London, EC1N 8LD
(Tel: 020-7831 5831; Fax: 020-7831 5832;
E-mail: blf@britishlungfoundation.com;
Web: www.lunguk.org).
Chief Executive: B. Walden

British Medical Association
BMA House, Tavistock Square, London, WC1H 9JP (Tel: 020-7387 4499; Fax: 020-7383 6400;
Web: www.bma.org.uk).
Secretary: Dr E. M. Armstrong

British Music Hall Society
82 Fernlea Road, London, SW12 9RW
(Tel: 020-8673 2175).
Hon. Secretary: Mrs D. Masterton

British Music Information Centre
10 Stratford Place, London, W1C 1BA
(Tel: 020-7499 8567; Fax: 020-7499 4795;
E-mail: info@bmic.co.uk;
Web: www.bmic.co.uk).
Director: M. Greenall

British Naturalists' Association
1 Bracken Mews, London, E4 7UT;
Web: www.bna-naturalists.org).
Hon. Membership Secretary:
Mrs Y. H. Griffiths

British Nuclear Energy Society
1–7 Great George Street, London, SW1P 3AA
(Tel: 020-7665 2241; Fax: 020-7799 1325;
E-mail: andrew@tillbrook@ice.org.uk;
Web: www.bnes.com).
Secretary: A. Tillbrook

British Nutrition Foundation
High Holborn House, 52–54 High Holborn, London, WC1V 6RQ
(Tel: 020-7404 6504; Fax: 020-7404 6747;
E-mail: postbox@nutrition.org.uk;
Web: www.nutrition.org.uk).
Director-General: Prof. R. S. Pickard, Ph.D, CBiol, FIBiol

British Pharmacological Society
16 Angel Gate, City Road, London, EC1V 2SG;
Fax: 020-7417 0114; E-mail: pjc@bps.ac.uk;
Web: www.bps.ac.uk).
President: Prof. N. G. Bowery

Societies and Institutions   495

British Pig Association
Scotsbridge House, Scots Hill, Rickmansworth, Herts, WD3 3BB (Tel: 01923-695295; Fax: 01923-695347; E-mail: bpa@britishpigs.org; Web: www.britishpigs.org).
General Manager: Marcus Bates

British Polio Fellowship
Ground Floor, Unit A, Eagle Office Centre, The Runway, South Ruislip, Middx, HA4 6SE (Tel: 0800-018 0586; E-mail: info@britishpolio.org; Web: www.britishpolio.ork).
Chief Executive: A. Kemp, GQSW

British Records Association
40 Northampton Road, London, EC1R 0HB (Tel: 020-7833 0428; Fax: 020-7833 0416; E-mail: britishrecordsassn@charity.vfree.com).
Hon. Secretary: Mrs E. Hughes

British Red Cross
9 Grosvenor Crescent, London, SW1X 7EJ (Tel: 020-7235 5454; Fax: 020-7245 6315; E-mail: information@redcross.org.uk; Web: www.redcross.org.uk).
Director-General: S. Younger

British Safety Council
70 Chancellor's Road, London, W6 9RS (Tel: 020-8741 1231; Fax: 020-8741 4555; E-mail: mail@britsafe.org; Web: www.britishsafetycouncil.org).
Director-General: Sir Neville Purvis, KCB

British Standards Institution (BSI)
389 Chiswick High Road, London, W4 4AL (Tel: 020-8996 9001; Fax: 020-8996 7001; E-mail: info@bsi-global.com; Web: www.bsi-global.com).
Chairman: V. E. Thomas, CBE

British Union for the Abolition of Vivisection
16A Crane Grove, London, N7 8NN (Tel: 020-7700 4888; Fax: 020-7700 0252; E-mail: info@buav.org; Web: www.buav.org).
Chief Executive: Ms M. Thew

British Veterinary Association
7 Mansfield Street, London, W1G 9NQ (Tel: 020-7636 6541; Fax: 020-7436 2970; E-mail: bvahq@bva.co.uk; Web: www.bva.co.uk).
Chief Executive: J. H. Baird

British Wood Preserving and Damp-Proofing Association
6 The Office Village, 4 Romford Road, London, E15 4EA (Tel: 020-8519 2588; Fax: 020-8519 3444; E-mail: info@bwpda.co.uk; Web: www.bwpda.co.uk).
Director: Dr C. R. Coggins

Buddhist Society
58 Eccleston Square, London, SW1V 1PH (Tel: 020-7834 5858; Fax: 020-7976 5238; E-mail: buddsoc@buddsoc.org.uk; Web: www.buddsoc.org.uk).
General Secretary: R. C. Maddox

Building Societies Association
3 Savile Row, London, W1S 3BP (Tel: 020-7437 0655; Fax: 020-7734 6416; E-mail: info@bsa.org.uk; Web: www.bsa.org.uk).
Director-General: A. Coles

Business and Professional Women UK Ltd
PO Box 26166, London, SW8 4WG (Tel: 020-7627 5040; Fax: 020-7627 5085; E-mail: HQ@bpwuk.org.uk; Web: www.bpwuk.org.uk).
General Secretary: Ms C. Garnier

Business Archives Council
3rd and 4th Floors, 101 Whitechapel High Street, London, E1 7RE (Tel: 020-7247 0024; Fax: 020-7422 0026).
Chairman: Melanie Aspy

Business in the Community
137 Sheperdess Walk, London, N5 2HG (Tel: 0870 600 2482; Fax: 020-7253 1877; E-mail: info@bitc.org.uk).
Chief Executive: Julia Cleverdon

Business in the Community
137 Shepherdess Walk, London, N1 7RQ (Tel: 0870 600 2482; Fax: 020-7253 1877).
Chief Executive: Ms J. Cleverdon, CBE

Business Software Alliance
79 Knightsbridge, London, SW1X 7RB (Tel: 020-7245 0304; Fax: 020-7245 0310; Web: www.bsa.org).
Director: Beth Scott

496 Societies and Institutions

CAFOD (Catholic Fund for Overseas Development)
Romero Close, Stockwell Road, London, SW9 9TY (Tel: 020-7733 7900; Fax: 020-7274 9630; E-mail: hq@cafod.org.uk; Web: www.cafod.org.uk).
Director: J. Filochowski

Camden Community Transport
Arlington Road Works Depot, 211 Arlington Road, London, NW1 7HD (Tel: 020-7911 0959).

Camden Society for People with Learning Difficulties
245 Royal College Street, London, NW1 9LT (Tel: 020-7485 8177; Fax: 020-7267 9099).

Camden Training
57 Pratt Street, London, NW1 0DP (Tel: 020-7482 2103; Fax: 020-7284 2340; E-mail: camdentraining@ndirect.co.uk; Web: www.ndirect.co.uk/-camdentraining).

Cameron Fund
Tavistock House North, Tavistock Square, London, WC1H 9HR (Tel: 020-7388 0796).
Secretary: Mrs J. Martin

Campaign for an Independent Britain
81 Ashmole Street, London, SW8 1NF (Tel: 020-8340 0314; Fax: 020-7582 7021; E-mail: info@cibhq.co.uk; Web: www.cibhq.co.uk).
Hon. Secretary: Sir Robin Williams, Bt.

Campaign for Nuclear Disarmament (CND)
162 Holloway Road, London, N7 8DQ (Tel: 020-7700 2393; Fax: 020-7700 2357; E-mail: enquiries@cnduk.org; Web: www.cnduk.org).
Chair: D. Knight

Canada-United Kingdom Chamber of Commerce
38 Grosvenor Street, London, W1K 4DP (Tel: 020-7258 6572; Fax: 020-7258 6594; E-mail: info@canada-uk.org; Web: www.canada-uk.org).
Executive Director: P. Newton

Cancer Research Campaign
10 Cambridge Terrace, London, NW1 4JL (Tel: 020-7224 1333; Fax: 020-7487 4310; Web: www.crc.org.uk).
Director-General: Prof. J. G. McVie

Capital Housing
318-320 St Paul's Road, London, N1 2LF (Tel: 020-7354 2909; Fax: 020-7359 9690).
Chief Executive: B. Symons

Carers National Association
Ruth Pitter House, 20-25 Glasshouse Yard, London, EC1A 4JT (Tel: 020-7490 8818; Fax: 020-7490 8824; E-mail: info@ukcarers.org; Web: www.carersuk.demon.co.uk).
Chief Executive: Ms D. Whitworth

Cathedrals Fabric Commission for England
Church House, Great Smith Street, London, SW1P 3NZ (Tel: 020-7898 1863; Fax: 020-7898 1881; E-mail: enquiries@cfce.c-of-e.org.uk).
Secretary: Dr R. Gem

Catholic Enquiry Office
The Chase Centre, 114 West Heath Road, London, NW3 7TX (Tel: 020-8458 3316; Fax: 020-8905 5780; E-mail: cms@cms.org.uk; Web: www.cms.org.uk).
Secretary: Fr P. Billington

Catholic Housing Aid Society
209 Old Marylebone Road, London, NW1 5QT (Tel: 020-7723 7273; Fax: 020-7723 5943; E-mail: info@chasnational.org.co.uk; Web: www.chasnational.org.co.uk).
Director: Ms R. Rafferty

Catholic Truth Society
40-46 Harleyford Road, London, SE11 5AY (Tel: 020-7640 0042; Fax: 020-7640 0046; E-mail: info@cts-online.org.uk; Web: www.cts-online.org.uk).
General Secretary: F. Martin

Catholic Union of Great Britain
St Maximilian Kolbe House, 63 Jeddo Road, London, W12 9EE (Tel: 020-8749 1321; Fax: 020-8735 0816; E-mail: phiggs@cathunion.org.uk).
Secretary: P. H. Higgs

Societies and Institutions   497

Central Bureau for International Education and Training
10 Spring Gardens, London, SW1A 2BN (Tel: 020-7389 4487; Fax: 020-7389 4426; Web: www.centralbureau.org.uk).
Director: P. Upton

Central London Dial-a-Ride
Hathaway House, 7D Woodfield Road, London, W9 2BA (Tel: 020-7266 6100; Fax: 020-7266 5079; E-mail: darcen@aol.com; Web: www.dial-a-ride.org.uk).
Company Manager: Janet Cobill

Centre for Economic Policy Research
90-98 Goswell Road, London, EC1V 7RR (Tel: 020-7878 2900; Fax: 020-7878 2999; E-mail: cepr@cepr.org; Web: www.cepr.org).
The Chief Executive: Stephen Yeo

Centre for Metropolitan History
Institute of Historical Research, Senate House, Malet Street, London, WC1E 7HU (Tel: 020-7862 8790; Fax: 020-7862 8793; E-mail: o-myhill@sas.ac.uk; Web: ihr.sas.ac.uk/ihr/associnstits).
Director: Dr D. J. Keene

Centre for Policy on Ageing
12–23 Ironmonger Row, London, EC1V 3QP (Tel: 020-7253 1787; Fax: 020-7490 4206; E-mail: cpa@cpa.org.uk; Web: www.cpa.org.uk).
Director: Dr G. Dalley

Centrepoint
Neil House, 7 Whitechapel Road, London E1 1DU (Tel: 020-7426 5300; Fax: 020-7426 5301; Web: www.centrepoint.org.uk).
Chief Executive: V. O. Adebowale

Centrepoint Soho
Neil House, 7 Whitechapel Road, London E1 1DU (Tel: 020-7426 5300; Fax: 020-7426 5301; Web: www.centrepoint.org).

Chadwick Trust
Department of Civil and Environmental Engineering, University College London, Gower Street, London, WC1E 6BT (Tel: 020-7679 5774; Fax: 020-7679 5789; E-mail: l.fisher@ucl.ac.uk).
Secretary to the Trustees: Helen Fisher

Chartered Institute of Arbitrators
12 Bloomsbury Square, London, WC1A 2LP (Tel: 020-7421 7444; Fax: 020-7404 4023; E-mail: info@arbitrators.org; Web: www.arbitrators.org).
Secretary-General: D. Farrar-Hockley, MC

Chartered Institute of Environmental Health
Chadwick Court, 15 Hatfields, London, SE1 8DJ (Tel: 020-7928 6006).
Director of Professional Services: G. Jures

Chartered Institute of Journalists
2 Dock Offices, Surrey Quays Road, London, SE16 2XU (Tel: 020-7252 1187; Fax: 020-7232 2302; E-mail: memberservices@ioj.com; Web: www.ioj.co.uk).
General Secretary: C. J. Underwood

Chartered Institute of Patent Agents
Staple Inn Buildings, High Holborn, London, WC1V 7PZ (Tel: 020-7405 9450; Fax: 020-7430 0471; E-mail: mail@cipa.org.uk; Web: www.cipa.org.uk).
Secretary: M. C. Ralph

Chartered Institute of Public Finance and Accountancy
3 Robert Street, London, WC2N 6BH (Tel: 020-7543 5600; Fax: 020-7543 5700; Web: www.cipfa.org.uk).
Chief Executive: S. Freer

Chartered Institution of Building Services Engineers
Delta House, 222 Balham High Road, London, SW12 9BS (Tel: 020-8675 5211).
Chief Executive: R. John

498 Societies and Institutions

Chartered Institution of Water and Environmental Management
15 John Street, London, WC1N 2EB
(Tel: 020-7831 3110; Fax: 020-7405 4967;
E-mail: admin@ciwem.org.uk;
Web: www.ciwem.org.uk).
Executive Director: N. Reeves

China Association
Swire House, 59 Buckingham Gate, London, SW1E 6AJ (Tel: 020-7963 9446; Fax: 020-7630 0353; E-mail: Hjacobs@jsslnd.co.uk).
Executive Director: D. F. L. Turner

Christian Aid
PO Box 100, London, SE1 7RT
(Tel: 020-7620 4444; Fax: 020-7620 0719;
E-mail: info@christian-aid.org;
Web: www.christian-aid.org.uk).
Director: Dr D. Mukarji

Church Army
Independents Road, London, SE3 9LG
(Tel: 020-8318 1226).
Chief Secretary: Capt. P. Johanson

Church Mission Society
Partnership House, 157 Waterloo Road, London, SE1 8UU (Tel: 020-7928 8681; Fax: 020-7401 3215; E-mail: info@cms-uk.org;
Web: www.cms-uk.org).
General Secretary: Revd Canon T. J. Dalkin

Church Monuments Society
c/o Society of Antiquaries, Burlington House, Piccadilly, London, W1V 0HS
(Tel: 020-7734 0193; Fax: 020-7287 6967;
E-mail: john@bromilow.screaming.net).
Hon. Secretary: C. J. Easter

Church of England Pensions Board
29 Great Smith, London, SW1P 3PS
(Tel: 020-7898 1800; Fax: 020-7898 1801;
E-mail: enquiries@cepb.c-of-e.org.uk).
Secretary: R. G. Radford

Church Union
Faith House, 7 Tufton Street, London, SW1P 3QN (Tel: 020-7222 6952; Fax: 020-7976 7180;
E-mail: churchunion@carcefree.net;
Web: www.churchunion.care4free.net).
House Manager: Mrs J. Miller

Churches Main Committee
Elizabeth House, 39 Youth Road, London, SE1 7NQ (Tel: 020-7898 1878; Fax: 020-7898 1798;
E-mail: cmc@c-of-e.org.uk;
Web: www.cmainc.org.uk).
Secretary: D. Taylor Thompson, CB

City Business Library (Corporation of London)
Brewers' Hall Garden, London, EC2V 5BX
(Tel: 020-7332 1812; Fax: 020-7332 1847;
Web: www.cityoflondon.gov.uk).
Business Librarian: Garry P. Humphreys

Civic Trust
17 Carlton House Terrace, London, SW1Y 5AW
(Tel: 020-7930 0914; Fax: 020-7321 0180;
E-mail: pride@civictrust.org.uk;
Web: www.civictrust.org.uk).
Chief Executive: Martin Bacon

Clergy Orphan Corporation
1 Dean Trench Street, London, SW1P 3HB
(Tel: 020-7799 3696; Fax: 020-7222 3468).
Registrar: R. A. M. Welsford

College of Optometrists
42 Craven Street, London, WC2N 5NG
(Tel: 020-7839 6000).
Secretary: P. D. Leigh

Combined Cadet Force Association
E Block, The Duke of York's HQ, London, SW3 4RR (Tel: 020-7730 9733; Fax: 020-7730 8264).
Secretary: Brig. J. E. Neeve

Commonwealth Press Union
17 Fleet Street, London, EC4Y 1AA
(Tel: 020-7583 7733; Fax: 020-7583 6868;
E-mail: mark@cpu.org.uk).
Director: M. Robinson

Societies and Institutions 499

Commonwealth Society for the Deaf (Sound Seekers)
34 Buckingham Palace Road, London, SW1W 0RE (Tel: 020-7233 5700; Fax: 020-7233 5800; E-mail: sound.seekers@btinternet.com; Web: www.sound-seekers.org.uk).
Chief Executive: Brig. J. A. Davis

Consumer Council for Postal Services
28–30 Grosvenor Gardens, London, SW1W 0TT (Tel: 020-7259 1200; Fax: 020-7730 3044; E-mail: enquiry@ccps.org.uk; Web: www.ccps.org.uk).
Chief Executives: James Dodds; Gregor McGregor; Jan Scoones

Consumers' Association
2 Marylebone Road, London, NW1 4DF (Tel: 020-7770 7000; Fax: 020-7770 7600; E-mail: which@which.net; Web: www.which.net/).
Director: Ms S. McKechnie, OBE

Contemporary Applied Arts
2 Percy Street, London, W1T 1DD (Tel: 020-7436 2344; Fax: 020-7436 2446; Web: www.caa.org.uk).
Director: Ms M. La Trobe-Bateman

Co-operative Party
77 Weston Street, London, SE1 3SD (Tel: 020-7357 0230; Fax: 020-7407 4476; E-mail: d.jones@co-op-party.org.uk; Web: www.co-op-party.org.uk).
Secretary: P. Hunt

Coroner's Society of England and Wales
44 Ormond Avenue, Hampton, Middx, TW12 2RX (Tel: 020-8979 6805; Fax: 020-8979 6805; E-mail: housec.corsoc@btinternet.com).
Hon. Secretary: M. J. C. Burgess

Council for the Care of Churches
Church House, Great Smith Sreet, London, SW1P 3NZ
(Tel: 020-7898 1866; Fax: 020-7898 1881; E-mail: enquiries@ccc.c-of-e.org.uk).
Secretary: Dr T. Cocke

Council for World Mission
IPALO House, 32–34 Great Peter Street, London, SW1P 2DB
(Tel: 020-7222 4214; Fax: 020-7233 1747; E-mail: council@cwmission.org.uk; Web: www.cwmission.org.uk).
General Secretary: Dr D. P. Niles

Council of Christians and Jews
5th Floor, Camelford House, 87–89 Albert Embankment, London, SE1 7TP (Tel: 020-7820 0090; Fax: 020-7820 0504; E-mail: cjrelations@ccj.org.uk; Web: www.ccj.org.uk).
Director: Sr M. Shepherd

Counsel and Care
Twyman House, 16 Bonny Street, London, NW1 9PG (Tel: 020-7485 1550; Fax: 020-7267 6877; E-mail: advice@counselandcare.org.uk; Web: www.counselandcare.org.uk).
Chief Executive: M. Green

Country Landowners Association
16 Belgrave Square, London, SW1X 8PQ (Tel: 020-7235 0511; Fax: 020-7235 4696; E-mail: mail@cla.org.uk; Web: www.cla.org.uk).
Chief Executive: Mark Pedlington

Countryside Alliance
The Old Town Hall, 367 Kennington Road, London, SE11 4PT
(Tel: 020-7840 9200; Fax: 020-7793 8484; E-mail: info@countryside-alliance.org; Web: www.countryside-alliance.org).
Chief Executive: R. Burge

CPRE (Council for the Protection of Rural England)
Warwick House, 25 Buckingham Palace Road, London, SW1W 0PP (Tel: 020-7976 6433; E-mail: info@cpre.org.uk; Web: www.cpre.org.uk).
Director: Ms K. Parminter

Crafts Council
44A Pentonville Road, London, N1 9BY (Tel: 020-7278 7700; Fax: 020-7837 6891; E-mail: reference@craftscouncil.org.uk; Web: www.craftscouncil.org.uk).
Director: Ms J. Barnes

Crimestoppers Trust
Apollo House, 66A London Road, Morden, Surrey, SW15 2UT
(Tel: 020-8254 3200; Fax: 020-254 3201; E-mail: cst@cromestoppers.uk.org; Web: www.crimestoppers-uk.org).
Director: Roy Clark

500 Societies and Institutions

Crisis
1st Floor, Challenger House, 42 Adler Street, London, E1 1EE (Tel: 020-7655 8300; E-mail: enquiries@crisis.org.uk; Web: www.crisis.org.uk).
Chief Executive: S. Ghosh

Crosslinks
251 Lewisham Way, London, SE4 1XF (Tel: 020-8691 6111; Fax: 020-8694 8023; E-mail: info@crosslinks.org; Web: www.crosslinks.org).
General Secretary: Revd A. Lines

Croydon Almshouse Charities
c/o Street Marshall, 74 High Street, Croydon, CR9 2UU.

Cruse Bereavement Care
126 Sheen Road, Richmond, Surrey, TW9 1UR (Tel: 020-8940 4818; Helpline: 0845-758 5565; Fax: 020-8940 7638; E-mail: info@crusebereavementcare.org.uk; Web: www.crusebereavementcare.org.uk).
Executive Director: Dr C. Easton

Cystic Fibrosis Trust
11 London Road, Bromley, Kent, BR1 1BY (Tel: 020-8464 7211; Fax: 020-8313 0472; E-mail: info@cftrust.org.uk; Web: www.cftrust.org.uk).
Chief Executive: Ms R. Barnes

Design and Industries Association
2 Lawford Road, Grove Park, Chiswick, London, W4 3HS (Tel: 020-8747 0766; Fax: 020-8747 0766; E-mail: info@dia.org.uk; Web: www.dia.org.uk).
Chairman: Paul Williams

Diabetes UK
10 Queen Anne Street, London, W1G 9LH (Tel: 020-7323 1531; Fax: 020-7637 3644; E-mail: info@diabetes.org.uk; Web: www.diabetes.org.uk).
Chief Executive: P. Streets

Diana, Princess of Wales Memorial Foundation
The County Hall, Westminster Bridge Road, London, SE1 7PB
(Tel: 020-7902 5500; Fax: 020-7902 5511; Web: www.theworkcontinues.org.uk).

Diana, Princess of Wales Memorial Fund
County Hall, Westminster Bridge Road, London, SE1 7PB
(Tel: 020-7902 5500; Fax: 020-7902 5511; E-mail: memfund@memfund.org; Web: www.theworkcontinues.org).
Chief Executive: Dr A. Purkis

Dickens Fellowship
Dickens House, 48 Doughty Street, London, WC1 N2L
(Tel: 020-7405 2127; Fax: 020-7831 5175; E-mail: arwilliams33@compuserve.com; Web: www.dickens.fellowship.btinternet.co.uk).
Joint Hon. General Secretaries: Mrs T. Grove, Dr T. Williams

Directory & Database Publishers Association
PO Box 23034, London, W6 0RJ
(Tel: 020-8846 9707; Fax: 0870-168 0552; E-mail: RosemaryPettit@msn.com; Web: www.directory-publisher.co.uk).
Secretary: Ms R. Pettit

Downs Syndrome Association
155 Mitcham Road, London, SW17 9PG
(Tel: 020-8682 4001; Fax: 020-8682 4012; Web: www.downs-syndrome.org.uk).
Chief Executive: Ms C. Boys

Drugscope
32-36 Loman Street, London, SE1 0EE
(Tel: 020-7928 1211; Fax: 020-7928 1771; E-mail: services@drugscope.org.uk; Web: www.drugscope.org.uk).
Chief Executive: Roger Howard

Dulwich Picture Gallery
Gallery Road, London, SE21 7AD
(Tel: 020-8693 5254; Fax: 020-8299 8700; E-mail: dulwichpicturegallery.org.uk; Web: www.dulwichpicturegallery.org.uk).
Director: Desmond Shawe-Taylor

Dyslexia Institute
133 Gresham Road, Staines, Middx, TW18 2AJ
(Tel: 01784-463851; Fax: 01784-460747; E-mail: info@dyslexia-inst.org.uk; Web: www.dyslexia-inst.org.uk).
Chief Executive: Shirley Cramer

Edexcel Foundation
Stewart House, 32 Russell Square, London, WC1B 5DN
(Tel: 0870 240 9800; Fax: 020-7758 6960;
E-mail: enquiries@edexcel.org.uk;
Web: www.edexcel.org.uk).
The Chief Executive: Dr. Townsend

Egypt Exploration Society
3 Doughty Mews, London, WC1N 2PG
(Tel: 020-7242 1880; Fax: 020-7404 6118;
E-mail: eeslondon@talk21.com;
Web: www.ees.ac.uk).
Secretary: Dr P. A. Spencer

Electoral Reform Society
6 Chancel Street, London, SE1 0UU
(Tel: 020-7928 1622; Fax: 020-7401 7789;
E-mail: ers@reform.demon.co.uk;
Web: www.electoral-reform.org.uk).
Chief Executive: Dr K. Ritchie

Empty Homes Agency
195–197 Victoria Street, London, SW1E 5NE
(Tel: 020-7828 6288; Hotline: 0870-901 6303;
Fax: 020-7828 7006;
E-mail: eha@globalnet.co.uk;
Web: www.emptyhomes.com).
Chief Executive: A. Horsey

Energy Saving Trust
21 Dartmouth Street, London, SW1H 9BP
(Tel: 020-7222 0101; Fax: 020-7654 2444;
Web: www.est.org.uk).
Chief Executive: Dr E. Lees

Engineering Industries Association
Broadway House, Tothill Street, London, SW1H 9NS (Tel: 020-7222 2367; Fax: 020-7799 2206;
E-mail: info@eia.co.uk; Web: www.eia.co.uk).
Director: C. J. Mason

English Folk Dance and Song Society
Cecil Sharp House, 2 Regent's Park Road, London, NW1 7AY (Tel: 020-7485 2206;
Fax: 020-7284 0523; E-mail: info@efdss.org;
Web: www.efdss.org).
Chief Executive: Tim Walker

English National Board for Nursing, Midwifery and Health Visiting
Victory House, 170 Tottenham Court Road, London, W1P 0HA
(Tel: 020-7391 6229; Fax: 020-7383 3525;
E-mail: ceo@enb.org.uk;
Web: www.enb.org.uk).
Chief Executive Officer: A. P. Smith, CBE

English-Speaking Union of the Commonwealth
Dartmouth House, 37 Charles Street, London, W1J 5ED
(Tel: 020-7592 1550; Fax: 020-7495 6108;
E-mail: esu@esu.org; Web: www.esu.org).
Director-General: Mrs V. Mitchell, OBE

Evangelical Library
78A Chiltern Street, London, W1M 2HB
(Tel: 020-7935 6997;
E-mail: stlibrary@aol.com;
Web: www.elib.org.uk).
Librarian: S. J. Taylor

Ex-Services Mental Welfare Society
Tyrwhitt House, Oaklawn Road, Leatherhead, Surrey, KT22 0BX
(Tel: 01372-841600; Fax: 01372-841601;
E-mail: contactus@combatstress.org.uk;
Web: www.combatstress.org.uk).
Chief Executive: Cdre. T. Elliott, OBE

F.A.N.Y. (Princess Royal's Volunteer Corps)
Right Wing, The Duke of York's HQ, Turks Row, London, SW3 4RY
(Tel: 020-7730 2058; Fax: 020-7414 5399;
E-mail: fanyhq@cwcom.net;
Web: www.fany.org.uk).
Corps Commander: Mrs L. Rose

Fabian Society
11 Dartmouth Street, London, SW1H 9BN
(Tel: 020-7227 4900; Fax: 020-7976 7153;
E-mail: info@fabian-society.org.uk;
Web: www.fabian-society.org.uk).
General Secretary: M. Jacobs

Faculty of Royal Designers for Industry
RSA, 8 John Adam Street, London, WC2N 6EZ
(Tel: 020-7451 6801; Fax: 020-7839 5805;
E-mail: rdi@rsa-uk.demon.co.uk;
Web: www.rsa.org.uk).
Administrator: Ms J. Thackray

502 Societies and Institutions

Federation of British Artists
17 Carlton House Terrace, London, SW1Y 5BD
(Tel: 020-7930 6844; Fax: 020-7839 7830;
E-mail: vnewlandsmallgalleries@dial.pipex.com;
Web: www.mallgalleries.org.uk).
Chairman: T. Muir

Fire Protection Association
Bastille Court, 2 Paris Garden, London, SE1 8ND (Tel: 020-7902 5300; Fax: 020-7902 5301;
E-mail: fpa@thefpa.co.uk;
Web: www.thefpa.co.uk).
Managing Director: J. O'Neill

Fleet Air Arm Officers' Association
4 St James's Square, London, SW1Y 4JU
(Tel: 020-7930 7722; Fax: 020-7930 7728;
E-mail: faaoa@fleetairarmoa.org;
Web: www.fleetairarmoa.org).
Administration Director:
Cdr. J. D. O. Macdonald

Folklore Society
Warburg Institute, Woburn Square, London, WC1E 0AB (Tel: 020-7862 8564;
E-mail: folklore.society@talk21.com;
Web: www.folklore-society.com).
Hon. Secretary: Dr J. Simpson

Food from Britain
123 Buckingham Palace Road, London, SW1W 9SA (Tel: 020-7233 5111; Fax: 020-7233 9515;
E-mail: foodfrombritain.co.uk;
Web: www.foodfrombritain.com).
Chief Executive: David McNair

Foreign Press Association in London
11 Carlton House Terrace, London, SW1Y 5AJ
(Tel: 020-7930 0445; Fax: 020-7925 0469;
E-mail: secretariat@foreign-press.org.uk;
Web: www.foreign-press.org.uk).
Secretary: Ms D. Crole

Foundation for the Study of Infant Deaths
Artillery House, 11–19 Artillery Row, London, SW1P 1RT (Tel: 020-7222 8001;
Helpline: 020-7233 2090; Fax: 020-7222 8002;
E-mail: fsid@sids.org.uk;
Web: www.sids.org.uk/fsid/).
Director: Mrs J. Epstein

fpa
2–12 Pentonville Road, London, N1 9FP
(Tel: 020-7837 5432; Fax: 020-7837 3034;
Web: www.fpa.org.uk).
Chief Executive: Ms A. Weyman

Franco-British Society
Room 623, Linen Hall, 162–168 Regent Street, London, W1R 5TB (Tel: 020-7734 0815;
Fax: 020-7734 0815).
Executive Secretary: K. Brayn

Friends of the Earth
26–28 Underwood Street, London, N1 7JQ
(Tel: 020-7490 1555;
Web: www.foe.co.uk).
Director: C. Secrett

Friends of the Elderly
40–42 Ebury Street, London, SW1W 0LZ
(Tel: 020-7730 8263; Fax: 020-7259 0154).
Chief Executive: Geoffrey Dennis

Friends of the National Libraries
c/o Department of Manuscripts, The British Library, 96 Euston Road, London, NW1 2DB
(Tel: 020-7412 7559).
Hon. Secretary: M. Borrie, OBE, FSA

Galton Institute
19 Northfields Prospect, London, SW18 1PE
(Tel: 020-8874 7257).
General Secretary: Mrs B. Nixon

Gamblers Anonymous
PO Box 88, London, SW10 0EU
(Tel: 01709-553089).

Garden History Society
70 Cowcross Street, London, EC1M 6EJ
(Tel: 020-7608 2409; Fax: 020-7490 2974;
E-mail: gardenhistorysociety@compuserve.com;
Web: www.gardenhistorysociety.org).
Director: A. Plumridge

Gemmological Association and Gem Testing Laboratory of Great Britain
27 Greville Street, (Saffron Hill entrance), London, EC1N 8TN
(Tel: 020-7404 3334; Fax: 020-7404 8843;
E-mail: gagtl@btinternet.com;
Web: www.gagtl.com).
Director: Dr R. R. Harding

Societies and Institutions 503

General Dental Council
37 Wimpole Street, London, W1G 8DQ
(Tel: 020-7887 3800; Fax: 020-7224 3294;
E-mail: information@gdc-uk.org;
Web: www.gdc-uk.org).
Chief Executive and Registrar:
Anthony Townsend

General Osteopathic Council
Osteopathy House, 176 Tower Bridge Road, London, SE1 3LU
(Tel: 020-7357 6655; Fax: 020-7357 0011;
E-mail: info@osteopathy.org.uk;
Web: www.osteopathy.org.uk).
Registrar: Miss M. J. Craggs

Geological Society of London
Burlington House, Piccadilly, London, W1J 0BG
(Tel: 020-7434 9944; Fax: 020-7439 8975;
E-mail: enquiries@geolsoc.org.uk;
Web: www.geolsoc.org.uk).
Executive Secretary: Edmund Nickless

Geologicals' Association
Burlington House, Piccadilly, London, W1V 9AG (Tel: 020-7434 9298).
Chief Executive Officer: S. Strafford

Grand Lodge of Mark Master Masons
Mark Masons' Hall, 86 St James's Street, London, SW1A 1PL (Tel: 020-7839 5274;
Fax: 020-7930 9750;
E-mail: grandsecretary@markmasonshall.org.uk).
Grand Secretary: T. J. Lewis

Greater London Fund for the Blind
12 Whitehorse Mews, 37 Westminster Bridge Road, London, SE1 7QD (Tel: 020-7620 2066; Fax: 020-7260 2016).

Greek Institute
34 Bush Hill Road, London, N21 2DS
(Tel: 020-8360 7968; Fax: 020-8360 7968).
Director: Dr K. Tofallis

Greenpeace UK
Canonbury Villas, London, N1 2PN
(Tel: 020-7865 8100; Fax: 020-7865 8200;
E-mail: info@greenpeace.org;
Web: www.greenpeace.org.uk).
Executive Director: Stepehn Tindale

Guide Association
17–19 Buckingham Palace Road, London, SW1W 0PT
(Tel: 020-7834 6242; Fax: 020-7828 8317;
E-mail: chq@guides.org.uk;
Web: www.guides.org.uk).
Chief Executive: Mrs T. Ryall

Guild of Aid for Gentlepeople
10 St Christopher's Place, London, W1U 1HZ
(Tel: 020-7935 0641).
Secretary: Miss N. E. Inkson

Guild of Freemen of the City of London
PO Box 153, 40A Ludgate Hill, London, EC4M 7DE (Tel: 020-7223 7638).
Clerk: Col. D. Ivy

Guild of Glass Engravers
35 Ossulton Way, London, N2 0JY
(Tel: 020-8731 9352; Fax: 020-8731 9352;
E-mail: admin.gge@talk21.com).
Secretary: Mrs C. Weatherhead

Guild of Health
PO Box 227, Epsom, KT19 9WQ
(Tel: 020-8786 0517; Fax: 020-8786 0517;
E-mail: gohealth@freeuk.com;
Web: www.gohealth.org.uk).
General Secretary and Chaplain: Revd A. Lynn

Guild of Pastoral Psychology
PO Box 1107, London, W3 6ZP
(Tel: 020-8993 8366; Fax: 020-8993 3148;
E-mail: nvs@gpp.ndo.co.uk;
Web: www.guildofpastoralpsychology.org.uk).
Chairman: Rev. Lyn Phillips

Gurkha Welfare Trust
PO Box 18215, 2nd Floor, 1 Old Street, London, EC1V 9XB
(Tel: 020-7251 5234; Fax: 020-7251 5248;
E-mail: secretary@gwt.org.uk;
Web: www.gwt.org.uk).
Director: E. D. Powell-Jones

Haig Homes
Alban Dobson House, Green Lane, Morden, Surrey, SM4 5NS
(Tel: 020-8685 5777; Fax: 020-8685 5778;
E-mail: haig@haighomes.org.uk;
Web: www.haighomes.org.uk).
Director: A. N. Carlier

504 Societies and Institutions

Hampstead Garden Suburb Institute
Central Square, London, NW11 7BN
(Tel: 020-8455 9951; Fax: 020-8201 8063;
E-mail: office@hgsi.ac.uk;
Web: www.hgsi.ac.uk).
Principal and Chief Executive: Fay Naylor

Hansard Society for Parliamentary Government
St Philips Building North, Sheffield Street, London, WC2A 2EX
(Tel: 020-7955 7459; Fax: 020-7955 7492;
E-mail: hansard@hansard.lse.ac.uk;
Web: www.hansardsociety.org.uk).
Director: Mrs S. Diplock

Harveian Society of London
Lettsom House, 11 Chandos Street, London, W1M 0EB
(Tel: 020-7580 1043; Fax: 020-7580 5793).
Executive Secretary: Col. R. Kinsella-Bevan

Help the Aged
207–221 Pentonville Road, London, N1 9UZ
(Tel: 020-7278 1114; Fax: 020-7278 1116;
E-mail: info@helptheaged.org.uk;
Web: www.helptheaged.org.uk).
Director-General: C. M. Lake, CBE

Hispanic and Luso Brazilian Council
Canning House, 2 Belgrave Square, London, SW1X 8PJ
(Tel: 020-7235 2303; Fax: 020-7235 3587;
E-mail: enquiries@canninghouse.com;
Web: www.canninghouse.com).
Director-General: Philip A. MacLean, CMG

Historic Houses Association
2 Chester Street, London, SW1X 7BB
(Tel: 020-7259 5688; Fax: 020-7259 5590;
E-mail: hha@compuserve.com;
Web: www.hha.org.uk).
Director-General: R. Wilkin

Historical Association
59A Kennington Park Road, London, SE11 4JH
(Tel: 020-7735 3901; Fax: 020-7582 4989;
E-mail: enquiry@history.org.uk;
Web: www.history.org.uk).
Chief Executive: Mrs M. Stiles

Hong Kong Association
Swire House, 59 Buckingham Gate, London, SW1E 6AJ
(Tel: 020-7963 9445; Fax: 020-7630 0353;
E-mail: Dhamer@jsslnd.co.uk).
Executive Director: D. F. L. Turner

Hospital Saturday Fund
24 Upper Ground, London, SE1 9PD
(Tel: 020-7928 6662; Fax: 020-7928 0446;
E-mail: sales@hsf.co.uk;
Web: www.hsf.co.uk).
Chief Executive: K. R. Bradley

Hotel and Catering International Management Association
191 Trinity Road, London, SW17 7HN
(Tel: 020-8772 7400; Fax: 020-8772 7500;
E-mail: library@hcima.co.uk;
Web: www.hcima.org.uk).
Chief Executive: D. Wood

Hounslow Arts Trust
Watermans Arts Centre, 40 High Street, Brentford, TW8 0DS
(Tel: 020-8847 5651; Fax: 020-8569 8592;
E-mail: enquiries@watermans.org.uk;
Web: www.watermans.org.uk).
Director: Jan Lennoy

House of St Barnabas-in-Soho
1 Greek Street, London, W1V 6NQ
(Tel: 020-7434 1846).
Director: Ms W. Taylor

Howard League for Penal Reform
1 Ardleigh Road, London, N1 4HS
(Tel: 020-7249 7373; Fax: 020-7249 7788;
E-mail: howardleague@ukonline.co.uk;
Web: www.howardleague.org).
Director: Ms F. Crook

Huguenot Society of Great Britain and Ireland
The Huguenot Library, University College London, Gower Street, London, WC1E 6BT
(Tel: 020-7697 7094; E-mail: s.massil@ucl.ac.uk;
Web: www.ucl.ac.uk/ucl-info/divisions/library/huguenot.htm).
Hon. Secretary: Mrs M. A. Bayliss

Societies and Institutions 505

Hydrographic Society
c/o University of East London, Longbridge Road, Dagenham, Essex, RM8 2AS
(Tel: 020-8597 1946; Fax: 020-8590 9730; E-mail: hydrosoc@compuserve.com; Web: www.hydrographicsociety.org).
Hon. Secretary: P. J. H. Warden

ICAN (National Educational Charity for Children with Speech and Language Difficulties)
4 Dyers Buildings, Holborn, London, EC1N 2QP (Tel: 0870-010 4066; Fax: 0870-010 4067; E-mail: info@ican,org.uk; Web: www.ican.org.uk).
Chief Executive: Ms G. Edelman

Immigration Advisory Service
County House, 190 Great Dover Street, London, SE1 4YB (Tel: 020-7357 6917; Fax: 020-7403 5875; E-mail: advice@iasuk.org; Web: www.iasuk.org).
Chief Executive: K. Best

Imperial Cancer Research Fund
PO Box 123, Lincoln's Inn Fields, London, WC2A 3PX (Tel: 020-7242 0200; Fax: 020-7269 3610; Web: www.icnet.uk).
Director-General: Sir Paul Nurse, FRS

Incorporated Church Building Society
Fulham Palace, London, SW6 6EA
(Tel: 020-7736 3054; Fax: 020-7736 3880).
Secretary: M. W. Tippen

Incorporated Council of Law Reporting for England and Wales
Megarry House, 119 Chancery Lane, London, WC2A 1PP (Tel: 020-7242 6471;
Fax: 020-7831 5247; E-mail: postmaster@iclr.co.uk; Web: www.lawreports.co.uk).
Secretary: J. Cobbett

Incorporated Society of Musicians
10 Stratford Place, London, W1N 9AE
(Tel: 020-7629 4413; Fax: 020-7408 1538; E-mail: membership@ism.org; Web: www.ism.org).
Chief Executive: N. Hoyle

Independent Schools Council
Grosvenor Gardens House, 35–37 Grosvenor Gardens, London, SW1W 0BS
(Tel: 020-7798 1590; Fax: 020-7798 1591; E-mail: abc@isis.org.uk; Web: www.isis.org.uk).
General Secretary: Dr A. B. Cooke, OBE

Independent Schools Information Service
35–37 Grosvenor Gardens, London, SW1W 0BS
(Tel: 020-7798 1500; Fax: 020-7798 1501; E-mail: national@isis.org.uk; Web: www.isis.org.uk).
Director: D. J. Woodhead

Industrial Christian Fellowship
c/o St Matthews House, 100 George Street, Croydon, CR0 1PE
(Tel: 020-8656 1644; Fax: 020-8656 1644; E-mail: yrq86@dial.pipex.com).
Chairman: Michael Fass

Industrial Society
Robert Hyde House, 48 Bryanston Square, London, W1H 7LN (Tel: 020-7479 2000; Fax: 020-7497 2222; Web: www.indsoc.co.uk).
Chief Executive: W. Hutton

Industry and Parliament Trust
1 Buckingham Place, London, SW1E 6HR
(Tel: 020-7976 5311).
Director: F. R. Hyde-Chambers

Institute for Complementary Medicine
PO Box 194, London, SE16 7QZ
(Tel: 020-7237 5165; Fax: 020-7237 5175; E-mail: icm@icmedicine.co.uk; Web: www.icmedicine.co.uk).
Director: A. Baird

Institute of Actuaries
Staple Inn Hall, High Holborn, London, WC1V 7QJ (Tel: 020-7632 2100; Fax: 020-7632 2111; E-mail: institutes@actuaries.org.uk; Web: www.actuaries.org.uk).
Secretary-General: G. B. L. Campbell

Institute of Administrative Management
40 Chatsworth Parade, Petts Wood, Orpington, Kent, BR5 1RW
(Tel: 01689-875555; Fax: 01689-870891; E-mail: enquiries@instam.org; Web: www.instam.org).
Chief Executive: Alan King

506 Societies and Institutions

Institute of Cancer Research:
Royal Cancer Hospital
123 Old Brompton Road, London, SW7 3RP
(Tel: 020-7352 8133; Fax: 020-7370 5261;
Web: www.icr.ac.uk).
Chief Executive: Dr P. W. J. Rigby

Institute of Chartered Accountants in England and Wales
Chartered Accountants' Hall, PO Box 433, Moorgate Place, London, EC2P 2BJ
(Tel: 020-7920 8100; Fax: 020-7920 0547;
Web: www.icaew.co.uk).
Secretary-General: J. Collier

Institute of Chartered Secretaries and Administrators
16 Park Crescent, London, W1N 4AH
(Tel: 020-7580 4741; Fax: 020-7323 1132;
E-mail: isca@dial.www.ics@org.ukpipex.com).
Chief Executive: M. J. Ainsworth

Institute of Chartered Shipbrokers
3 St Helen's Place, London, EC3A 6EJ
(Tel: 020-7628 5559; Fax: 020-7628 5445;
E-mail: info@ics.org.uk; Web: www.ics.org.uk).
Director: Ms B. Fletcher

Institute of Clerks of Works of Great Britain
41 The Mall, London, W5 3TJ
(Tel: 020-8579 2917; Fax: 020-8579 0554;
E-mail: gensee@icwgb.sagehost.co.uk;
Web: www.lcwgb.com).
General Secretary: Don McGeorge

Institute of Directors
116 Pall Mall, London, SW1Y 5ED
(Tel: 020-7839 1233; Fax: 020-7930 1949;
E-mail: join-iod@iod.co.uk;
Web: www.iod.co.uk).
Chief Executive: A. Wilson

Institute of Economic Affairs
2 Lord North Street, London, SW1P 3LB
(Tel: 020-7799 8900; Fax: 020-7799 2137;
E-mail: iea@iea.org.uk; Web: www.iea.org.uk).
General Director: J. Blundell

Institute of Energy
18 Devonshire Street, London, W1G 7AU
(Tel: 020-7580 7124; Fax: 020-7580 4420;
E-mail: info@instenergy.org.uk;
Web: www.instenergy.org.uk).
Secretary: Miss L. Kingham

Institute of Export
Minerva Business Park, Lynchwood, Peterborough, PE2 6FT (Tel: 020-7247 9812;
E-mail: instutute@export.org.uk;
Web: www.export.org.uk).
Director-General: I. J. Campbell

Institute of Food Science and Technology
5 Cambridge Court, 210 Shepherd's Bush Road, London, W6 7NJ
(Tel: 020-7603 6316; Fax: 020-7602 9936;
E-mail: info@ifst.org;
Web: www.ifst.org).
Chief Executive: Ms H. G. Wild

Institute of Health Services Management
46–48 Grosenor Gardens, London, SW1W 0EB
(Tel: 020-7881 9235; Fax: 020-7881 9236;
E-mail: enquiries@ihm.org.uk;
Web: www.ihm.org.uk).
Director: Ms K. Caines

Institute of Information Scientists
39–41 North Road, London, N7 9DP
(Tel: 020-7619 0624/5; Fax: 020-7619 0627;
E-mail: iis@dial.pipex.com;
Web: www.iis.org.uk).
Director: M F Shearer

Institute of Linguists
Saxon House, 48 Southwark Street, London, SE1 1UN (Tel: 020-7940 3100; Fax: 020-7940 3101;
E-mail: info@iol.org.uk;
Web: www.iol.org.uk).
Director: H. Pavlovich

Institute of Marine Engineers
80 Coleman Street, London, EC2R 5BJ
(Tel: 020-7382 2600; Fax: 020-7382 2670;
E-mail: imare@imare.org.uk;
Web: www.imare.org.uk).
Director-General: K. F. Read

Institute of Masters of Wine
Five Kings House, 1 Queen Street Place, London, EC4R 1QS (Tel: 020-7236 4427; Fax: 020-7213 0499; Web: www.masters-of-wine.org).
Executive Director: L. Jane Caw

Institute of Materials
1 Carlton House Terrace, London, SW1Y 5DB
(Tel: 020-7451 7300).
Chief Executive: Dr B. A. Rickinson

Societies and Institutions 507

Institute of Measurement and Control
87 Gower Street, London, WC1E 6AF
(Tel: 020-7387 4949; Fax: 020-7388 8431;
E-mail: m.yates@instmc.org.uk;
Web: www.instmc.org.uk).
Secretary: M. J. Yates

Institute of Patentees and Inventors
Suite 505A, Triumph House, 189 Regent Street, London, W1B 4JY (Tel: 020-7434 1818;
Fax: 020-7434 1727; E-mail: ipi@invent.org.uk;
Web: www.invent.org.uk/).
Secretary: R. Magnus

Institute of Petroleum
61 New Cavendish Street, London, W1G 7AR
(Tel: 020-7467 7100; Fax: 020-7255 1472;
E-mail: ip@petroleum.co.uk;
Web: www.petroleum.co.uk).
Director-General: J. Pym

Institute of Plant Engineers
77 Great Peter Street, London, SW1P 2EZ
(Tel: 020-7233 2855).
Secretary: P. F. Tye

Institute of Practitioners in Advertising
44 Belgrave Square, London, SW1X 8QS
(Tel: 020-7235 7020; Fax: 020-7245 9904;
E-mail: mark@ipa.org.uk;
Web: www.ipa.org.uk).
Director-General: Nick Phillips

Institute of Sports Medicine
Department of Surgery, Royal Free and University College Medical School, 67–73 Riding House Street, London, W1W 7EJ
(Tel: 020-7813 2832; Fax: 020-7813 2832;
E-mail: m.hobsley@ucl.ac.uk).
Hon. Secretary: Dr W. T. Orton

Institute of Trade Mark Attorneys
Canterbury House, 2–6 Sydenham Road, Croydon, CR0 9XE (Tel: 020-8686 2052;
Fax: 020-8680 5723; E-mail: tm@itma.uk;
Web: www.itma.org.uk).
Secretary: Mrs M. J. Tyler

Institute of Translation and Interpreting
377 City Road, London, EC1V 1ND
(Tel: 020-7713 7600; Fax: 020-7713 7650;
E-mail: info@iti.org.uk;
Web: www.iti.org.uk).
Chairman: Dr. Catherine Greensmith

Institution of Civil Engineers
One Great George Street, London, SW1P 3AA
(Tel: 020-7222 7722; Fax: 020-7222 7500;
E-mail: mike.casebourne@ice.org.uk;
Web: www.ice.org.uk).
Chief Executive: M. Casebourne

Institution of Electrical Engineers
Savoy Place, London, WC2R 0BL
(Tel: 020-7240 1871; Fax: 020-7240 7735;
E-mail: postmaster@iee.org.uk;
Web: www.iee.org.uk).
Chief Executive: Dr A. Roberts

Institution of Gas Engineers
21 Portland Place, London, W1B 1PY
(Tel: 020-7636 6603; Fax: 020-7636 6602;
E-mail: general@igaseng.demon.co.uk;
Web: www.igaseng.com).
Chief Executive: C. Bleach

Institution of Mechanical Engineers
1 Birdcage Walk, London, SW1H 9JJ
(Tel: 020-7222 7899; Fax: 020-7222 4557).
Director-General: Sir Michael Moore, KBE, LVO

Institution of Structural Engineers
11 Upper Belgrave Street, London, SW1X 8BH
(Tel: 020-7235 4535; Fax: 020-7235 4294;
E-mail: mail@istructe.org.uk;
Web: www.istructe.org.uk).
Chief Executive: Dr K. J. Eaton

International African Institute
SOAS, Thornhaugh Street, Russell Square, London, WC1H 0XG (Tel: 020-7898 4420;
Fax: 020-7898 4419; E-mail: iai@soas.ac.uk;
Web: www.oneworld.org/iai/).
Hon. Director: Prof. P. Spencer

International Financial Services
Windsor House, 39 King Street, London, EC2V 8DQ (Tel: 020-7600 1198; Fax: 020-7309 0931;
E-mail: enquiries@ifsl.org.uk;
Web: www.ifsl.org.uk).
Acting Chief Executive: J. R. Nichols

International Friendship League
3 Creswick Road, London, W3 9HE
(Tel: 020-8752 0055; Fax: 020-8752 0066;
E-mail: bookings@ifl—peacelaven.co.uk;
Web: www.ifl-world.org).
Chairman: M. J. A. Prowse

International Hospital Federation
46 Grosvenor Gardens, London, SW1W 0EP
(Tel: 020-7881 9222; Fax: 020-7881 9223;
E-mail: 101662.1262@compuserve.com;
Web: www.ihf.co.uk).
Director-General: Prof. P. G. Svensson

International Institute for Conservation of Historic and Artistic Works
6 Buckingham Street, London, WC2N 6BA
(Tel: 020-7839 5975; Fax: 020-7976 1564;
E-mail: iicon@compuserve.com;
Web: www.iiconservation.org).
Secretary-General: D. Bomford

International Institute for Strategic Studies
Arundel House, 13–15 Arundel Street, Temple Place, London, WC2R 5DY
(Tel: 020-7395 9120; Fax: 020-7395 9186).
Director: Dr J. Chipman

International PEN
9–10 Charterhouse Buildings, Goswell Road, London, EC1M 7AT (Tel: 020-7253 4308; Fax: 020-7253 5711; E-mail: intpen@dircon.co.uk; Web: www.oneworld.org/internatpen).
International Secretary: T. Carlbom

International Students House
1 Park Cresent, London, W1B 1SH
(Tel: 020-7631 8300; Fax: 020-7631 8315;
E-mail: general@ish.org.uk;
Web: www.ish.org.uk).
Executive Director: P. Anwyl

International Underwriting Association
London Underwriting Centre, 3 Minster Court, Minster Lane, London, EC3R 7DD
(Tel: 020-7617 4444; Fax: 020-7617 4440;
E-mail: info@iua.co.uk;
Web: www.iua.co.uk).
Chief Executive: Ms M. L. Rossi

International Union for Land-Value Taxation and Free Trade
Room 427, London Fruit Exchange, Brushfield Street, London, E1 6EL (Tel: 020-7377 8885; Fax: 020-7377 8686;
E-mail: iu@interunion.org.uk;
Web: www.interunion.org.uk).
Hon. Secretary: Mrs B. P. Sobrielo

INTERSERVE
325 Kennington Road, London, SE11 4QH
(Tel: 020-7735 8227; Fax: 020-7587 5362;
E-mail: enquiries@isewi.org;
Web: www.interserve.org/ew).
National Director: R. Clark

Invalids-at-Home
17 Lapstone Gardens, Kenton, Harrow, Middx, HA3 0EB (Tel: 020-8907 1706).
Executive Officer: Mrs S. Lomas

Involvement and Participation Association
42 Colebrooke Row, London, N1 8AF
(Tel: 020-7354 8040;
E-mail: involve@ipa-involve.com;
Web: www.ipa-involve.com).
Director: W. Coupar

Iran Society
2 Belgrave Square, London, SW1X 8PJ
(Tel: 020-7235 5122; Fax: 020-7259 6771;
E-mail: iransoc@rsaa.org.uk;
Web: www.iransoc.dircon.co.uk).
Chairman: M. Nol-Clarke

Irish Genealogical Research Society
The Irish Club, 82 Eaton Square, London, SW1W 9AJ (Tel: 020-7235 4164).
Hon. Librarian: T. G. Chartres

ITRI Ltd
Kingston Lane, Uxbridge, Middx, UB8 3PJ
(Tel: 01895-272406; Fax: 01895-251841;
E-mail: postmaster@itri.co.uk;
Web: www.itri.co.uk).
Managing Director: D. Bishop

Japan Association
Swire House, 59 Buckingham Gate, London, SW1E 6AJ
(Tel: 020-7963 9446/45; Fax: 020-7630 0353;
E-mail: Hjacobs@jssland.co.uk).
Executive Director: D. F. L. Turner

Jewish Historical Society of England
33 Seymour Place, London, W1H 5AP
(Tel: 020-7723 5852; Fax: 020-7723 5852;
E-mail: jhse@dircon.co.uk;
Web: www.jhse.org).
Hon. Secretary: Dr. Gerry Black

Societies and Institutions

Jewish Museum London
Raymond Burton House, 129-131 Albert Street, London, NW1 7NB
(Tel: 020-7284 1997; Fax: 020-7267 9008;
E-mail: admin@jmus.org.uk;
Web: www.jewmusm.ort.org

Justice (British Section of the International Commission of Jurists)
59 Carter Lane, London, EC4V 5AQ
(Tel: 020-7329 5100; Fax: 020-7329 5055;
E-mail: admin@justice.org.uk;
Web: www.justice.org.uk).
Director: Ms A. Owers

King's Fund
11–13 Cavendish Square, London, W1G 0AN
(Tel: 020-7307 2400; Fax: 020-7307 2801;
Web: www.kingsfund.org.uk).
Chief Executive: Rabbi Julia Neuberger

League Against Cruel Sports
83–87 Union Street, London, SE1 1SG
(Tel: 020-7403 6155; Fax: 020-7403 4532;
E-mail: league@compuserve.com;
Web: www.league.uk.com).
Chief Executive: D. Batchelor

League of the Helping Hand
Petersham Hollow, 226 Petersham Road, Petersham, Richmond, Surrey, TW10 7AL
(Tel: 020-8940 7303; Fax: 020-8940 7303;
E-mail: Inga@lhh.org.uk).
Secretary: Mrs I. Goodlad

Leonard Cheshire
30 Millbank, London, SW1P 4QD
(Tel: 020-7802 8200; Fax: 020-7802 8250;
E-mail: info@london.leonard-cheshire.org.uk;
Web: www.leonard-cheshire.org).
Director-General: B. H. Dutton, CB. CBE

Leukaemia Research Fund
43 Great Ormond Street, London, WC1N 3JJ
(Tel: 020-7405 0101; Fax: 020-7405 3139;
E-mail: info@lrf.org.uk; Web: www.lrf.org.uk).
Chief Executive: D. L. Osborne

Liberty (National Council for Civil Liberties)
21 Tabard Street, London, SE1 4LA
(Tel: 020-7403 3888; Fax: 020-7407 5354;
E-mail: info@liberty-human-rights.org.uk;
Web: www.liberty-human-rights.org.uk).
Director: J. Wadham

Linnean Society of London
Burlington House, Piccadilly, London, W1J 0BF
(Tel: 020-7434 4479; Fax: 020-7287 9364;
E-mail: john@linnean.org;
Web: www.linnean.org).
President: Sir David Smith, FRS, FRSE

Listening Books
12 Lant Street, London, SE1 1QH
(Tel: 020-7407 9417; Fax: 020-7403 1377;
E-mail: info@listening-books.org.uk;
Web: www.listening-books.org.uk).
Director: Douglas Kean

Lloyd's of London
1 Lime Street, London, EC3M 7HA
(Tel: 020-7327 1000; Fax: 020-7327 6512;
E-mail: caroline.d.kranyz@lloyds.com;
Web: www.lloyds.com).
Chief Executive Officer: N. E. Prettejohn

Lloyd's Register of Shipping
71 Fenchurch Street, London, EC3M 4BS
(Tel: 020-7709 9166; Fax: 020-7488 4796;
E-mail: lloydsreg@lr.org;
Web: www.lr.org).
Chairman and Chief Executive Officer: D. G. Moorhouse

Local Government Association
Local Government House, Smith Square, London, SW1P 3HZ
(Tel: 020-7664 3000; Fax: 020-7664 3030;
E-mail: info@lga.gov.uk;
Web: www.lga.gov.uk).
Chief Executive: Brian Briscoe

Local Government International Bureau
Local Government House, Smith Square, London, SW1P 3HZ
(Tel: 020-7664 3100; Fax: 020-7664 3128;
E-mail: webmaster@lgib.gov.uk;
Web: www.lgib.gov.uk).
Director: J. Smith

London Academy of Music and Art
Tower House, 226 Cromwell Road, London, SW5 0SR (Tel: 020-7323 9883; Fax: 020-7320 4739; E-mail: enquirys@lamda.org.uk;
Web: www.lamda.org.uk).

510 Societies and Institutions

London and South East Library Region
4th Floor, Gun Court, 70 Wapping Lane, London, E1 9RL
(Tel: 020-7702 2020; Fax: 020-7702 2019;
E-mail: laser@viscount.org.uk;
Web: www.viscount.org.uk/laser).

London Anglers' Association
Isaak Walton House, 2 Hervey Park Road, London, E17 6LJ (Tel: 020-8520 7477; Fax: 020-8520 7477).
Chairman: Mr A. E. Hodges

London Appreciation Society
45 Friars Avenue, London, N20 0XG.
Chairman: Miss Anthea Gray

London Bullion Market Association
6 Frederick's Place, London, EC2R 8BT
(Tel: 020-7796 3067; Fax: 020-7796 4345;
E-mail: mail@lbma.org.uk;
Web: www.lbma.org.uk).
Chief Executive: S. Murray

London Central Mosque Trust
Islamic Cultural Centre, 146 Park Road, London, NW8 7RG (Tel: 020-7724 3363; Fax: 020-7724 0493; E-mail: islamic200@aol.com;
Web: www.islamicculturalcentre.co.uk).
Head of Finance and Accounts: Feizal Mutter

London Chamber of Commerce and Industry Examinations Board
33 Queen Street, London, EC4R 1AP
(Tel: 020-8309 3000; Fax: 020-8302 4169;
E-mail: costservlccicb.org.uk;
Web: www.lccicb.org).
The Chief Executive: Mr Liam Swords

London Chest Hospital Appeal
London Chest Hosptial, Bonner Road, London, E2 9JX
(Tel: 020-8983 2345; Fax: 020-8983 2307;
E-mail: Pat.Gray@bartsandthelondon.nhs.uk).
Senior Manager, Appeals: Mrs Pat Gray

London City Mission
175 Tower Bridge Road, London, SE1 2AH
(Tel: 020-7407 7585; Fax: 020-7403 6711;
E-mail: lcm.uk@btinternet.com;
Web: www.lcm.org.uk).
General Secretary: Revd J. McAllen

London Connection
12 Adelaide Street, London, WC2N 4HW
(Tel: 020-7321 0633; Fax: 020-7839 6277;
E-mail: info@london-connection.org.uk;
Web: www.london-connection.org.uk).
Director: Colin Glover

London Court of International Arbitration
8 Breams Building, Chancery Lane, London, EC4A 1HP
(Tel: 020-7405 8008; Fax: 020-7405 8009;
E-mail: lcia@lcia-arbitration.com;
Web: www.lcia-arbitration.com).
Director General and Registrar: Adrian Winstanley, CBE

London Fish Merchants Ltd
Office 36, Billingsgate Market, Trafalgar Way, London, E14 5ST
(Tel: 020-7515 2655; Fax: 020-7517 3535;
E-mail: lfma@billingsgate-market.com).
Chairman and Chief Executive: Kevin Everett

London Flotilla and President Retired Officers Association
40 Endlesham Road, London, SW12 8JL
(Tel: 020-8673 1879; Fax: 020-8673 1879;
E-mail: richardupton@freenet.co.uk).
Hon. Membership Secretary:
Lt.-Cdr. H. C. R. Upton, RD, RNR

London Goodenough Trust for Overseas Graduates
London House, Mecklenburgh Square, London, WC1N 2AB
(Tel: 020-7837 8888; Fax: 020-7278 7056;
Web: www.lgt.org.uk).
Director: Major General TP Toyne Sewell

London Hostels Association
54 Eccleston Square, London, SW1V 1PG
(Tel: 020-7834 1545; Fax: 020-7834 7146;
E-mail: rgray@london-hostels.co.uk).
General Manager: R. C. Gray

London Housing Foundation
Bramah House, 65-71 Bermondsey Street, London, SE1 3XF
(Tel: 020-74079559; Fax: 020-74079111;
E-mail: kevin.ireland@hacas.co.uk).
Director: Kevin Ireland

Societies and Institutions 511

London International Film School
24-26 Shelton Street, London, WC2H 9UB
(Tel: 020-7836 9642; Fax: 020-7497 3718;
E-mail: film.school@lifs.org.uk;
Web: www.lifs.org.uk).
Director: Ben Gibson

London Investment Banking Association
6 Frederick's Place, London, EC2R 8BT
(Tel: 020-7796 3606; Fax: 020-7796 4345;
E-mail: liba@liba.org.uk;
Web: www.liba.org.uk).
Director-General: Sir Adam Ridley

London Law Trust
c/o Alexanders, 203 Temple Chambers, Temple Avenue, London, EC4Y 0DB
(Tel: 020-7353 6221; Fax: 020-7583 0662).

London Lighthouse
111-117 Lancaster Road, London, W11 1QT
(Tel: 020-7792 1200; Fax: 020-7229 1258).

London Mathematical Society
De Morgan House, 57–58 Russell Square, London, WC1B 4HS
(Tel: 020-7637 3686; Fax: 020-7323 3655;
E-mail: lms@lms.ac.uk; Web: www.lms.ac.uk).
Admistrator: Miss S. M. Oakes

London Medieval Society
61 Beacon Road, Hither Green, London, SE13 6ED (E-mail: r.lutton@unl.ac.uk).
Secretary: Rob Lutton

London Money Market Association
c/o Investec Bank (UK) Limited, 2 Gresham Street, London, EC2V 7QP
(Tel: 020-7597 4485; Fax: 020-7597 4491).
Chairman: Ian Mair

London Playing Fields Society
Fraser House, 29 Albemarle Street, London, W1S 4JB (Tel: 020-7493 3211; Fax: 020-7409 3405; E-mail: lonplayingfields@aol.com).
Chief Executive: Dr C. Goodson-Wickes

London Private Car Hire Association
213 Kenton Road, Harrow, Middx, HA3 0HD
(Tel: 020-8907 9463; Fax: 020-8927 0044;
E-mail: lphca@btinternet.com;
Web: www.lphca.co.uk).
Chairman: Steve Wright, MBE

London Record Society
c/o Institute for Historical Research, Senate House, Malet Street, London, WC1E 7HU
(Tel: 020-7862 8798; Fax: 020-7862 8793;
E-mail: creaton@sas.ac.uk;
Web: www.ihr.sas.ac.uk/ihr/associnstits/lrsmnu.html).
Chairman: H. S. Cobb

London School of Performing Arts and Technology
60 The Crescent, Croydon, CR0 2HN
(Tel: 020-8665 5242; Fax: 020-8665 8676;
E-mail: brit@croydon.school.uk;
Web: www.brit.croydon.sch.uk).
Principal: Roger Durston

London Society
4th Floor, Senate House, Malet Street, London, WC1E 7HU (Tel: 020-7580 5537;
E-mail: londonsociety@hotmail.com;
Web: www.londsoc.org.uk/lonsoc/).
Hon. Secretary: Mrs B. Jones

London Subterranean Survey Association
98 Cambridge Gardens, London, W10 6HS
(Tel: 020-8968 1360;
E-mail: penrm@rbkc.gov.uk).
Hon. Secretary: R. J. Morgan

London Swing Dance Society
31 Rashleigh House, Thanet Street, London, WC1H 9ER (Tel: 020-7387 1011;
E-mail: swinguk@zetnet.co.uk;
Web: www.swingdanceuk.com).
Director: Simon Selmon

London Symphony Orchestra
Barbican Centre, London, EC2Y 8DS
(Tel: 020-7588 1116; Fax: 020-7374 0127;
E-mail: admin@lso.co.uk;
Web: www.lso.co.uk).
Managing Director: Clive Gillinson

London Topographical Society
36 Old Deer Park Gardens, Richmond, Surrey, TW9 2TL (Tel: 020-8940 5419;
Web: www.topsoc.org).
Hon. Secretary: P. Frazer

London Underground Railway Society
54 Brinkley Road, Worcester Park, KT4 8JF
(Tel: 020-8330 1855;
Web: www.lurs.demon.co.uk).
Secretary: E. Felton

512 Societies and Institutions

Lord's Day Observance Society
3 Epsom Business Park, Kiln Lane, Epsom, Surrey, KT17 1JF (Tel: 01372-728300; Fax: 01372-722400; E-mail: info@ldos.co.uk; Web: www.lordsday.co.uk).
General Secretary: J. G. Roberts

MACA – Partnership in Mental Health
25 Bedford Square, London, WC1B 3HW (Tel: 020-7436 6194; Fax: 020-7637 1980; E-mail: maca-bs@maca.org.uk; Web: www.maca.org.uk).
Chief Executive: G. Hitchon

Macmillan Cancer Relief
89 Albert Embankment, London, SE1 7UQ (Tel: 020-7840 7840; Fax: 020-7840 7840; E-mail: information-line@macmillan.org.uk; Web: www.macmillan.org.uk).
Chief Executive: N. Young

Mailing Preference Service
5th Floor, Haymarket House, 1 Oxendon Street, London, SW1Y 4EE (Tel: 020-7766 4410; Fax: 020-7976 1886; E-mail: mps@dma.org.uk; Web: www.mpsonline.org.uk).
Director of Compliance Operations: Ms T. Kelly

Makor-AJY
Balfour House, 741 High Road, London, N12 0BQ (Tel: 020-8446 8020; Fax: 020-8343 9037; E-mail: info@makor.org).
Deputy Director: E. Finestone

Manic Depression Fellowship
Castle Works, 21 St. George's Road, London, SE1 6ES (Tel: 020-7793 2600; Fax: 020-7793 2639).
Chief Executive: Ms K. Campbell

Manorial Society of Great Britain
104 Kennington Road, London, SE11 6RE (Tel: 020-7735 6633; Fax: 020-7582 7022; E-mail: msyb@manor.net; Web: www.msyb.co.uk).
Hon. Chairman: R. A. Smith

Marie Curie Cancer Care
28 Belgrave Square, London, SW1X 8QG (Tel: 020-7235 3325; Fax: 020-7823 2380; E-mail: info@mariecurie.org.uk; Web: www.mariecurie.org.uk).
Chief Executive: Thomas Hughes-Hallett

Marriage Care
Clitherow House, 1 Blythe Mews, Blythe Road, London, W14 0NW (Tel: 020-7371 1341; Fax: 020-7371 4921; E-mail: info@marraigecare.org.uk; Web: www.marriagecare.org.uk).
Chief Executive: Terry Prendergast

Masonic Trust for Girls and Boys
31 Great Queen Street, London, WC2B 5AG (Tel: 020-7405 2644; Fax: 020-7831 4094; Web: www.mtgb.org).
Secretary: Lt.-Col. J. C. Chambers

MCPSPRS Alliance
29–33 Berners Street, London, W1T 3AB (Tel: 020-7580 5544; Fax: 020-7306 4455; Web: www.prs.co.uk).
Chief Executive: J. Hutchinson

Medical Society for the Study of Venereal Diseases
1 Wimpole Street, London, W1M 8AE (Tel: 020-7290 2968; Fax: 020-7290 2989; Web: www.mssvd.org.uk).
Hon. Secretary: Dr Keith Radcliffe

Medical Society of London
Lettson House, 11 Chandos Street, London, W1M 0EB (Tel: 020-7580 1043; Fax: 020-7580 5793).
Registrar: Col. R. Kinsella-Bevan

Medical Women's Federation
Tavistock House North, Tavistock Square, London, WC1H 9HX (Tel: 020-7387 7765; Fax: 020-7387 7765; E-mail: mwf@m-w-f.demon.co.uk; Web: www.medicalwomensfederation.com).
President: Professor Illora Finlay

Medic-Alert Foundation
1 Bridge Wharf, 156 Caledonian Road, London, N1 9UU (Tel: 020-7833 3034).
Chief Executive: Miss J. Friend

MENCAP (The Royal Society for Mentally Handicapped Children and Adults)
12 Golden Lane, London, EC1Y 0RT (Tel: 020-7454 0454; E-mail: information@mencap.org.uk; Web: www.mencap.org.uk).
Chief Executive: F. Heddell, CBE

Societies and Institutions 513

Mental Health Foundation
20–21 Cornwall Terrace, London, NW1 4QL
(Tel: 020-7535 7400; Fax: 020-7535 7474;
E-mail: mhf@mhf.org.uk;
Web: www.mhf.org.uk).
Chair: Christopher Martin

Merchant Navy Welfare Board
19–21 Lancaster Gate, London, W2 3LN
(Tel: 020-7723 3642; Fax: 020-7723 3643;
E-mail: enquiries@mnwb.org.uk;
Web: www.mnwb.org.uk).
General Secretary: Capt. D. A. Parsons

Metropolitan Hospital-Sunday Fund
45 Westminster Bridge Road, London, SE1 7JB
(Tel: 020-7922 0200; Fax: 020-7401 3641;
E-mail: mhsf@peabody.org.uk;
Web: www.mhsf.org.uk).
Secretary: H. F. Doe

Middle East Association
Bury House, 33 Bury Street, London, SW1Y 6AX
(Tel: 020-7839 2137; Fax: 020-7839 6121;
E-mail: mail@the-mea.co.uk;
Web: www.the-mea.co.uk).
Director-General: B. P. Constant

Migraine Trust
45 Great Ormond Street, London, WC1N 3HZ
(Tel: 020-7831 4818;
E-mail: info@migrainetrust.org;
Web: www.migrainetrust.org).
Director: Ms A. Rush

Military Historical Society
National Army Museum, Royal Hospital Road, London, SW3 4HT
(E-mail: pjjobson@hotmail.com).
Secretary: Mr Philip Jobson

MIND (National Association for Mental Health)
Granta House, 15–19 Broadway, London, E15 4BQ (Tel: 020-8519 2122; Fax: 020-8522 1725;
Web: www.mind.org.uk).
Chief Executive: Ms J. Clements

Mineralogical Society
41 Queen's Gate, London, SW7 5HR
(Tel: 020-7584 7516; Fax: 020-7823 8021;
E-mail: info@minersoc.org;
Web: www.minersoc.org).
President: Dr. D. J. Morgan

Modern Churchpeople's Union
MCU Office, 25 Birch Grove, London, W3 9SP
(Tel: 020-8932 4379; Fax: 020-8993 5812;
E-mail: modchruchunion@btinternet,com;
Web: www.modchurchunion.org).
General Secretary: Revd N. P. Henderson

Monumental Brass Society
Lowe Hill House, Stratford St Mary, Colchester, Essex, CO7 6JX
(Tel: 020-8520 5249; Fax: 020-8521 8387;
E-mail: martin.stuchfield@intercitygroup.co.uk;
Web: www.home.clara.net/williamlack).
Hon. Secretary: H. M. Stuchfield

Mothers' Union
Mary Sumner House, 24 Tufton Street, London, SW1P 3RB (Tel: 020-7222 5533; Fax: 020-7222 1591;
E-mail: mu@themothersunion.org;
Web: www.themothersunion.org).
Chief Executive: R. Bailey

Mountbatten Memorial Trust
Estate Office, Broadlands, Romsey, Hants, SO51 9ZE).
Trust Secrtetary: J. B. Moss

Musicians Benevolent Fund
16 Ogle Street, London, W1W 6JA
(Tel: 020-7636 4481; Fax: 020-7637 4307;
E-mail: info@mbf.org.uk;
Web: www.mbf.org.uk).
Secretary: Ms H. Faulkner

NABS
32 Wigmore Street, London, W1U 2RP
(Tel: 020-7299 2888; Fax: 020-7299 2887;
E-mail: nabs@nabs.org.uk;
Web: www.nabs.org.uk).
Director: Miss K. Harris

NACRO (National Association for the Care and Resettlement of Offenders)
169 Clapham Road, London, SW9 0PU
(Tel: 020-7582 6500; Fax: 020-7735 4666).
Chief Executive: Ms H. Edwards

National Art Collections Fund
Millais House, 7 Cromwell Place, London, SW7 2JN (Tel: 020-7225 4800; Fax: 020-7225 4848; E-mail: info@art-fund.org; Web: www.art-fund.org).
Director: D. Barrie

National Association of Teachers of Home Economics and Technology
Hamilton House, Mabledon Place, London, WC1H 9BJ (Tel: 020-7387 1441).
General Secretary: G. Thompson

National Association for maternal and Child Welfare
1st Floor, 40–42 Osnaburgh Street, London, NW4 3ND (Tel: 020-7383 4117).
Administrator: Mrs V. A. Farebrother

National Association of Citizens Advice Bureaux
Myddelton House, 115–123 Pentonville Road, London, N1 9LZ
(Tel: 020-7833 2181; Fax: 020-7833 4371; Web: www.nacab.org.uk).
Chief Executive: D. Harker

National Association of Clubs for Young People
371 Kennington Lane, London, SE11 5QY
(Tel: 020-7793 0787; Fax: 020-7820 9815; E-mail: office@nacyp.org.uk;
Web: www.nacyp.org.uk).
National Director: C. Groves, FIPD, FIMgt

National Association of Local Councils
109 Great Russell Street, London, WC1B 3LD
(Tel: 020-7637 1865; Fax: 020-7436 7451; E-mail: nalc@nalc.gov.uk;
Web: www.nalc.gov.uk).
Chief Executive: J. Findlay

National Asthma Campaign
Providence House, Providence Place, London, N1 0NT (Tel: 020-7226 2260; Fax: 020-7704 0740; Web: www.asthma.org.uk).
Chief Executive: Anne Smith

National Blood Authority
Oak House, Reeds Crescent, Watford, Herts, WD1 1QH (Tel: 01923-486800; Fax: 01923-486801; Web: www.blood.co.uk).
Chairman: M. Fogden, CB

National Campaign for the Arts
Pegasus House, 37–42 Sackville Street, London, W1S 3EH (Tel: 020-7333 0375; Fax: 020-7333 0660; E-mail: nca@artscampaign.org.uk; Web: www.artscampaign.org.uk).
Director: Ms V. Todd

National Consumer Council
20 Grosvenor Gardens, London, SW1W 0DH
(Tel: 020-7730 3469; Fax: 020-7730 0191; E-mail: info@ncc.org.uk;
Web: www.ncc.org.uk).
Director: Ms A. Bradley

National Council for One Parent Families
255 Kentish Town Road, London, NW5 2LX
(Tel: 020-7428 5400; Fax: 020-7482 4851; E-mail: info@oneparentfamilies.org.uk;
Web: www.oneparentfamilies.org.uk).
Director: K.Green

National Council of Women of Great Britain
36 Danbury Street, London, N1 8JU
(Tel: 020-7354 2395; Fax: 020-7354 2395; E-mail: ncwgb@danburystreet.freeserve.org.uk;
Web: www.ncwgb.org).
President: (until October 2001) Dr D. Glick; (from October) Ms M. Birkenhead

National Family Mediation
9 Tavistock Place, London, WC1H 9SN
(Tel: 020-7383 5993;
E-mail: cspa@nfwi.org.uk;
Web: www.womens-institute.co.uk).
Director: Ms T. Fisher

National Federation of Women's Institutes
104 New Kings Road, London, SW6 4LY
(Tel: 020-7371 9300; Fax: 020-7736 3652;
E-mail: hq@nfwi.org.uk;
Web: www.nfwi.org.uk).
General Secretary: Mrs J. Osborne

National Missing Persons Helpline
Roebuck House, 284–286 Upper Richmond Road West, London, SW14 7JE (Tel: 020-8392 4590; Helpline: 0500-700700; Fax: 020-8878 7752; E-mail: admin@missingpersons.org;
Web: www.missingpersons.org).
Co-Founders: Mrs M. Asprey, OBE;
Mrs J. Newman, OBE

National Operatic and Dramatic Association
NODA House, 1 Crestfield Street, London, WC1H 8AU
(Tel: 020-7837 5655; Fax: 020-7833 0609;
E-mail: everyone@noda.org.uk;
Web: www.noda.org.uk).
Chief Executive: M. Pemberton

National Playing Fields Association
Stanley House, St Chads Place, London, WC1X 9HH (Tel: 020-7833 5360; Fax: 020-7833 5365;
E-mail: npfa@npfa.co.uk;
Web: www.npfa.co.uk).
Director: Mrs E. Davies

National Schizophrenia Fellowship
30 Tabernacle Street, London, EC2A 4DD
(Tel: 020-7330 9100; Fax: 020-7330 9102;
E-mail: info@nsf.org.uk;
Web: www.nfs.org.uk).
Chief Executive: C. Prior

National Secular Society Ltd
25 Red Lion Square, London, WC1R 4RL
(Tel: 020-7404 3126; Fax: 020-7404 3126;
E-mail: kpw@secularism.org.uk;
Web: www.secularism.org.uk).
General Secretary: K. P. Wood

National Union of Students
Nelson Mandela House, 461 Holloway Road, London, N7 6LJ
(Tel: 020-7272 8900; Fax: 020-7263 5713;
E-mail: patricia@nus.org.uk).
National President: O James

Societies and Institutions 515

Naval, Military & Air Force Bible Society
Radstock House, 3 Eccleston Street, London, SW1W 9LZ (Tel: 020-7463 1468; Fax: 020-7730 0240; E-mail: nma@sgm.org).
General Secretary: J. M. Hines

Navy Records Society
c/o Department of War Studies, King's College, The Strand, London, WC2R 2LS
(Web: www.navyrecordsociety.com).
Hon. Secretary: Prof. A. D. Lambert

NCH Action for Children
85 Highbury Park, London, N5 1UD
(Tel: 020-7704 7000; Fax: 020-7226 2537).
Chief Executive: D. Mead

New Politics Network
6 Cynthia Street, London, N1 9JF
(Tel: 020-7278 4443; Fax: 020-7278 4425;
E-mail: info@new-politics.net;
Web: www.new-politics.net).
Director: A. Pakes

NHS Confederation
1 Warwick Road, London, SW1E 5ER
(Tel: 020-7959 7273; Fax: 020-7959 7273;
Web: www.nhsconfed.net).
Chief Executive: S. Thornton

North London Dial-a-Ride
Units C/D, Regents Avenue Industrial Estate, Regents Avenue, London, N13 5UR
(Tel: 020-8829 1200; Fax: 020-8829 1221;
E-mail: admin@nldar.freeserve.co.uk;
Web: www.nldar.freeserve.co.uk).

Norwood Ravenswood
Broadway House, 80–82 The Broadway, Stanmore, Middx, HA7 4HB
(Tel: 020-8954 4555; Fax: 020-8420 6800;
E-mail: norwoodravenswood@nwrw.org;
Web: www.nwrw.org).
Chief Executive: Ms N. Brier

516 Societies and Institutions

Nuffield Foundation
28 Bedford Square, London, WC1B 3JS
(Tel: 020-7631 0566; Fax: 020-7323 4877;
Web: www.nuffieldfoundation.org).
Director: A. Tomei

Nutrition Society
10 Cambridge Court, 210 Shepherds Bush Road,
London, W6 7NJ (Tel: 020-7602 0228; Fax: 020-7602 1756; E-mail: mail@nutsoc.org.uk;
Web: www.nutsoc.org.uk).
Hon. Secretary: Dr J. Buttriss

Officers' Pensions Society
68 South Lambeth Road, London, SW8 1RL
(Tel: 020-7820 9988; Fax: 020-7820 9948;
E-mail: memsec@officerspensionsoc.org.uk).
General Secretary: Maj.-Gen. J. C. M. Gordon

OHSA
46 Wimpole Street, London, W1M 7DG
(Tel: 020-7222 1202).
Managing Director: Ms W. Gill

OPAS (Pensions Advisory Service)
11 Belgrave Road, London, SW1V 1RB
(Tel: 020-7233 8080; Fax: 020-7233 8016;
E-mail: opas@iclwcbkiv.co.uk;
Web: www.opas.org.uk).
Chief Executive: M. McLean, OBE

Open-Air Mission
19 John Street, London, WC1N 2DL
Tel: 020-7405 6135; Fax: 020-7405 6135;
E-mail: oamission@btinternet.com;
Web: www.btinternet.com/~oamission).
Secretary: A. N. Banton

Oriental Ceramic Society
30B Torrington Square, London, WC1E 7LJ
(Tel: 020-7636 7985; Fax: 020-7580 6749;
E-mail: ocs-london@beeb,net;
Web: www.ocs-london.com).
President: Rose Kerr

Osteopathic Association Clinic
8–10 Boston Place, London, NW1 6QH
(Tel: 020-7262 1128; Fax: 020-7723 7492).
Clinic Manager: Mrs A. Dalby

Outward Bound Trust
207 Waterloo Road, London, SE1 8XD
(Tel: 020-7928 1991; Fax: 020-7928 3733;
E-mail: enquiries@outwardbound-uk.org;
Web: www.outwardbound-uk.org).
Director: Sir Michael Hobbs, KCVO, CBE

Overseas Development Institute
11 Westminster Bridge Road, London, SE1 7JD
(Tel: 020-7922 0300; Fax: 020-7922 0399;
E-mail: odi@odi.org.uk;
Web: www.odi.org.uk).
Director: S. Maxwell

Parents at Work
45 Beech Street, Barbican, London, EC2Y 8AD
(Tel: 020-7628 3578; Fax: 020-7628 3591;
E-mail: info@parentsatwork.org.uk;
Web: www.parentsatwork.org.uk).
Joint Chief Executives: Ms S. Jackson; Ms S. Monk

Parkinson's Disease Society of the United Kingdom
215 Vauxhall Bridge Road, London, SW1V 1EJ
(Tel: 020-7931 8080; Helpline: 020-7233 5373;
Fax: 020-7233 9908;
E-mail: enquiries@parkinsons.org.uk;
Web: www.parkinsons.org.uk).
Chief Executive: Ms M. G. Baker, MBE

Parliamentary and Scientific Committee
48 Westminster Palace Gardens, 1–7 Artillery Row, London, SW1P 1RR (Tel: 020-7222 7085;
Fax: 020-7222 5355).
Administrative Secretary: Dr A. Whitehouse

Patients Association
PO Box 935, Harrow, Middx, HA1 3YJ
(Tel: 020-8423 9111. Helpline: 020-8423 8999;
Fax: 020-8423 9119;
E-mail: mailbox@patients-association.com;
Web: www.patients-association.com).
Director: M. Stone

Performing Right Society Ltd
Copyright House, 29–33 Berners Street, London,
W1T 3AB (Tel: 020-7580 5544; Fax: 020-7306 4450; Web: www.prs.oc.uk).
Chief Executive: J. Hutchinson

Societies and Institutions 517

Periodical Publishers Association Ltd
Queens House, 28 Kingsway, London, WC2B 6JR (Tel: 020-7404 4166; Fax: 020-7404 4167; E-mail: info:ppa.co.uk; Web: www.ppa.co.uk).
Chief Executive: I. Locks

Philological Society
School of Oriental and African Studies, University of London, Thornhaugh Street, London, WC1H 0XG;
(Web: www.lings.ln.man.ac.uk/html/philsoc).
Hon. Secretary: Prof. N. Sims-Williams

Poetry Society
22 Betterton Street, London, WC2H 9BX (Tel: 020-7420 9880; Fax: 020-7240 4818; E-mail: info@poetrysoc.com; Web: www.poetrysoc.com).
Director: C. Patterson

Policy Studies Institute
100 Park Village East, London, NW1 3SR (Tel: 020-7468 0468; Fax: 020-7388 0914; Web: www.psi.org.uk).
Director: Prof. J. Skea

Prayer Book Society
St James Garlickhythe, Garlick Hill, London, EC4V 2AF (Tel: 01923-824278; Web: www.prayerbookuk.com).
Chairman: C. A. A. Kilmister

Princess Royal Trust for Carers
142 Minories, London, EC3N 1LB (Tel: 020-7480 7788; Fax: 020-7481 4729; E-mail: info@carers.org; Web: www.carers.org).
Chief Executive: Ms A. Ryan

Printing Historical Society
St Bride Institute, Bride Lane, London, EC4Y 8EE.
Hon. Secretary: P. Wickens

Prisoners Abroad
89–93 Fonthill Road, London, N4 3JH (Tel: 020-7561 6820; Fax: 020-7561 6821; E-mail: info@prisonersabroad.org.uk; Web: www.prisonersabroad.org.uk).
Director: C. Laurenzi

Private Libraries Association
Ravelston, South View Road, Pinner, Middx, HA5 3YD;
(Web: www.the-old-school.demon.co.uk/pla.htm).
Hon. Secretary: F. Broomhead

Professional Classes Aid Council
10 St Christopher's Place, London, W1U 1HZ (Tel: 020-7935 0641).
Secretary: Miss N. E. Inkson

Quaker Peace and Social Witness
Friends House, 173–177 Euston Road, London, NW1 2BJ (Tel: 020-7663 1000; Fax: 020-7663 1001; E-mail: qps@quaker.org.uk; Web: www.quaker.org.uk).
General Secretary: Linda Fielding

Queen Victoria Clergy Fund
Church House, Dean's Yard, London, SW1P 3NZ (Tel: 020-7898 1310; Fax: 020-7898 1321).
Secretary: C. D. L. Menzies

Queen's Nursing Institute
3 Albemarle Way, London, EC1V 4RQ (Tel: 020-7490 4227; E-mail: mail@qni.org.uk; Web: www.qni.org.uk).
Director: Mrs J. Hesketh

QUIT (National Society of Non-Smokers)
Victory House, 170 Tottenham Court Road, London, W1T 7NR (Tel: 020-7388 5775; Fax: 020-7388 5995; E-mail: quit@clara.net; Web: www.quit.org.uk).
Chief Executive: P. McCabe

RADAR (Royal Association for Disability and Rehabilitation)
12 City Forum, 250 City Road, London, EC1V 8AF (Tel: 020-7250 3222; Fax: 020-7250 0212; E-mail: radar@radar.org.uk; Web: www.radar.org.uk).
Chief Executive Officer: P. Mansell

Rail Passenger's Council
Clements House, 14–18 Gresham Street, London, EC2V 7NL (Tel: 020-7505 9090; Fax: 020-7505 9004; E-mail: rpc@gtnet.gov.uk).
National Director: Anthony Smith

518 Societies and Institutions

Ramblers' Association
2nd Floor, Camelford House,
87–90 Embankment, London, SE1 7TW
(Tel: 020-7339 8500; Fax: 020-7339 8501;
E-mail: ramblers@london.ramblers.org.uk;
Web: www.ramblers.org.uk).
Chief Executive: Nick Barrett

Regional Studies Association
PO Box 2058, Seaford, East Sussex, BN25 4QU
(Tel: 01323-899698; Fax: 01328-899798;
E-mail: rsa@mailbox.ulcc.ac.uk;
Web: www.regional-studies-assoc.ac.uk).
Chief Executive: Sally Hardy

Regular Forces Employment Association Ltd
49 Pall Mall, London, SW1Y 5JG
(Tel: 020-7321 2011; Fax: 020-7839 0970;
E-mail: ghall@ctp.org.uk;
Web: www.rfea.org.uk).
Chief Executive: Maj.-Gen. M. F. L. Shellard, CBE

Research Defence Society
58 Great Marlborough Street, London, W1V 1DD (Tel: 020-7287 2818; Fax: 020-7287 2627;
E-mail: admin@rds-online.org.uk;
Web: www.rds-online.org.uk).
Executive Director: Dr M. Matfield

Research into Ageing
PO Box 32833, London, N1 9ZQ
(Tel: 020-7843 1550; Fax: 020-7843 1559;
E-mail: ria@ageing.org;
Web: www.ageing.org).
Chief Executive: Mrs E. Mills

Reserve Forces Association
The Duke of York's HQ, London, SW3 4SG
(Tel: 020-7414 5588; Fax: 020-7414 5589;
E-mail: reserveforces.assoc@btinternet.com).
Secretary-General:
Air Vice Marshal A. J. Stables, CB

Richard III Society
4 Oakley Street, London, SW3 5NN
Fax: 01745-550176;
E-mail: neil—trump@richardiii.net;
Web: www.richardiii.net).
Secretary: Miss E. M. Nokes

ROOM: The National Council for Housing and Planning
14-18 Old Street, London, EC1V 9BH
(Tel: 020-7251 2363; Fax: 020-7680 2830).
Director: K. MacDonald

Royal Aeronautical Society
4 Hamilton Place, London, W1J 7BQ
(Tel: 020-7670 4302; Fax: 020-7499 6230).
Director: K. Mans

Royal Agricultural Society of the Commonwealth
2 Grosvenor Gardens, London, SW1W 0DH
(Tel: 020-7259 9678; Fax: 020-7259 9675;
E-mail: rasc@commagshow.org;
Web: www.commagshow.org).
Hon. Secretary: C. Runge, FRICS

Royal Air Force Benevolent Fund
67 Portland Place, London, W1B 1AR
(Tel: 020-7580 8343; Fax: 020-7307 3374;
E-mail: michael.vearncombe@ratbt.org.uk).
Controller: Air Chief Marshal Sir David Cousins, KCB, AFC

Royal Anthropological Institute
50 Fitzroy Street, London, W1T 5BT
(Tel: 020-7387 0455; Fax: 020-7383 4235;
E-mail: admin@therai.org.uk;
Web: www.therai.org.uk).
Director: Hilary Callan

Royal Archaeological Institute
c/o Society of Antiquaries of London, Burlington House, Piccadilly, London, W1J 0JE
(Tel: 020-7479 7092).
Secretary: J. G. Coad, FSA

Royal Artillery Association
Artillery House, Front Parade, Royal Artillery Barracks, London, SE18 4BH
(Tel: 020-8781 3003; Fax: 020-8854 3617).
General Secretary: Lt.-Col. M. G. Felton

Royal Asiatic Society
60 Queen's Gardens, London, W2 3AF
(Tel: 020-7724 4742; Fax: 020-7706 4008;
E-mail: royalasiaticsociety@btinternet.com;
Web: www.royalasiaticsociety.co.uk).
Publications Officer: A. P. A. Belloli

Societies and Institutions 519

Royal British Legion
48 Pall Mall, London, SW1Y 5JY
(Tel: 08457-725725; Fax: 020-7973 7399;
E-mail: info@britishlegion.org.uk;
Web: www.britishlegion.org.uk).
Secretary-General: Brig. I. G. Townsend

Royal Caledonian Schools Trust
80A High Street, Bushey, Watford, Herts, WD2 3DE (Tel: 020-8421 8845; Fax: 020-8421 8845;
E-mail: rcst@caleybushey.demon.co.uk).
Chief Executive: J. Horsfield

Royal Choral Society
Unit 9, 92 Lots Road, London, SW10 0QD
(Tel: 020-7376 3718; Fax: 020-7376 3719;
E-mail: royalchoralsociety@compuserve.com;
Web: www.go.ourworld/royalchoralsociety).
Administrator: H. Body

Royal College of General Practitioners
14 Princes Gate, London, SW7 1PU
(Tel: 020-7581 3232; Fax: 020-7225 3047;
E-mail: info@rcgp.org.uk;
Web: www.rcgp.org.uk).
Hon. Secretary: Dr M. Baker

Royal College of Midwives
15 Mansfield Street, London, W1M 0BE
(Tel: 020-7312 3535; Fax: 020-7312 3536;
E-mail: info@rcm.org.uk;
Web: www.rcm.org.uk).
General Secretary: Mrs K. Davis

Royal College of Nursing
20 Cavendish Square, London, W1G 0RN
(Tel: 020-7409 3333; Fax: 020-7647 3434;
Web: www.rcn.org.uk).
General Secretary: Beverley Malone

Royal College of Obstetricians and Gynaecologists
27 Sussex Place, Regent's Park, London, NW1 4RG (Tel: 020-7772 6200; Fax: 020-7723 0575;
E-mail: coll.sec@rcog.org.uk;
Web: www.rcog.org.uk).
Secretary: Paul A. Barnett

Royal College of Paediatrics and Child Health
50 Hallam Street, London, W1N 6DE
(Tel: 020-7307 5600; Fax: 020-7307 5601;
E-mail: enquiries@rcpch.ac.uk).
Hon. Secretary: Dr P. Hamilton

Royal College of Pathologists
2 Carlton House Terrace, London, SW1Y 5AF
(Tel: 020-7451 6700; Fax: 020-7451 6701;
E-mail: info@rcpath.org;
Web: www.rcpath.org).
Chief Executive: D. Ross

Royal College of Physicians
11 St Andrews Place, London, NW1 4LE
(Tel: 020-7935 1174; Fax: 020-7487 5218;
E-mail: www.rcplondon.ac.uk).
Chief Executive: P. Masterton-Smith

Royal College of Psychiatrists
17 Belgrave Square, London, SW1X 8PG
(Tel: 020-7235 2351; Fax: 020-7245 1231;
E-mail: rcpsych.ac.uk; Web: www.rcpsyph.ac.uk).
Secretary: Mrs V. Cameron

Royal College of Radiologists
38 Portland Place, London, W1N 4JQ
(Tel: 020-7636 4432; Fax: 020-7323 3100;
E-mail: enquiries@rcr.ac.uk;
Web: www.rcr.ac.uk).
General Secretary: A. J. Cowles

Royal College of Veterinary Surgeons
Belgravia House, 62–64 Horseferry Road, London, SW1P 2AF
(Tel: 020-7222 2001; Fax: 020-7222 2004;
E-mail: admin@rcvs.org.uk;
Web: www.rcvs.org.uk).
Registrar: Miss J. C. Hern

Royal Geographical Society (with The Institute of British Geographers)
1 Kensington Gore, London, SW7 2AR
(Tel: 020-7591 3000; Fax: 020-7591 3001;
E-mail: info@rgs.org; Web: www.rgs.org).
Director: Dr R. Gardner

Royal Historical Society
University College London, Gower Street, London, WC1E 6BT
(Tel: 020-7387 7532; Fax: 020-7387 7532;
E-mail: royalhistsoc@ucl.ac.uk;
Web: www.rhs.ac.uk).
Executive Secretary: Mrs J. N. McCarthy

Royal Horticultural Society
80 Vincent Square, London, SW1P 2PE
(Tel: 020-7834 4333; Fax: 020-7821 6060;
E-mail: webmaster@rhs.org.uk;
Web: www.rhs.org.uk).
Director-General: Dr A. Colquhoun

520 Societies and Institutions

Royal Hospital for Neuro-disability
West Hill, Putney, London, SW15 3SW
(Tel: 020-8780 4500; Fax: 020-8789 3098;
E-mail: info@neuro-disability.org.uk;
Web: www.neuro-disability.org.uk).
Chief Executive: Peter Franklyn

Royal Humane Society
Brettenham House, Lancaster Place, London, WC2E 7EP (Tel: 020-7836 8155; Fax: 020-7836 8155;
E-mail: rhs@supanet.co.uk).
Secretary: Maj.-Gen. C. Tyler, CB

Royal Institute of British Architects
66 Portland Place, London, W1N 4AD
(Tel: 020-7580 5533; Fax: 020-7255 1541;
E-mail: admin@inst.riba.org;
Web: www.riba.net).
Director-General: Dr A. Reid.

Royal Institute of International Affairs
Chatham House, 10 St James's Square, London, SW1Y 4LE (Tel: 020-7957 5700; Fax: 020-7957 5710; E-mail: contact@riia.org;
Web: www.riia.org).
Director: C. Gamble, Ph.D.

Royal Institute of Navigation
1 Kensington Gore, London, SW7 2AT
(Tel: 020-7591 3130; Fax: 020-7591 3131;
E-mail: info@rin.org.uk;
Web: www.rin.org.uk).
Director: Gp Capt. D. W. Broughton, MBE

Royal Institute of Oil Painters
17 Carlton House Terrace, London, SW1Y 5BD
(Tel: 020-7930 6844; Fax: 020-7839 7830;
E-mail: vnewlandsmallgalleries@dial.pipex.com;
Web: www.mallgalleries.org.uk).
Secretary: B. Roxby

Royal Institute of Painters in Water Colours
17 Carlton House Terrace, London, SW1Y 5BD
(Tel: 020-7930 6844; Fax: 020-7839 7830;
E-mail: vnewlandsmallgalleries@dial.pipex.com;
Web: www.mallgalleries.org.uk).
Secretary: T. Hunt

Royal Institute of Philosophy
14 Gordon Square, London, WC1H 0AR
(Tel: 020-7387 4130; Fax: 020-7383-4061;
E-mail: I.Purkiss@mailbox.ulcc.ac.uk).
Director: Prof. A. O'Hear

Royal Institute of Public Health
28 Portland Place, London, W1B 1DE
(Tel: 020-7580 2731; Fax: 020-7580 6157;
E-mail: info@riphh.org.uk;
Web: www.riphh.org.uk).
Chief Executive: Ms N. Wilkins

Royal Institution of Great Britain
21 Albemarle Street, London, W1S 4BS
(Tel: 020-7409 2992; Fax: 020-7629 3569;
E-mail: ri@ri.ac.uk;
Web: www.ri.ac.uk).
Director: Prof. S. Greenfield

Royal Institution of Naval Architects
10 Upper Belgrave Street, London, SW1X 8BQ
(Tel: 020-7235 4622; Fax: 020-7259 5912;
E-mail: hq@rina.org.uk;
Web: www.rina.org.uk).
Chief Executive: T. Blakeley

Royal Literary Fund
3 Johnson's Court, off Fleet Street, London, EC4A 3EA (Tel: 020-7353 7150).
General Secretary: Ms E. M. Gunn

Royal Masonic Benevolent Institution
20 Great Queen Street, London, WC2B 5BG
(Tel: 020-7405 8341; Fax: 020-7404 0724;
E-mail: enquiries@rmbi.org.uk;
Web: www.project28.sand.co.uk).
Chief Executive: Mr Peter J. Gray

Royal Medical Benevolent Fund
24 King's Road, London, SW19 8QN
(Tel: 020-8540 9194; Fax: 020-8542 0494;
E-mail: rm.bf@virgin.net;
Web: www.rmbf.co.uk).
Chief Executive Officer: M. Baber

Royal National Institute for Deaf People
19–23 Featherstone Street, London, EC1Y 8SL
(Tel: 020-7296 8000; Fax: 020-7296 8199;
E-mail: helpline@rnid.org.uk;
Web: www.rnid.org.uk).
Chief Executive: J. Strachan

Royal National Institute of the Blind
224 Great Portland Street, London, W1N 6AA
(Tel: 0845-766 9999; Fax: 020-7388 2034;
E-mail: helpline@rnib.org.uk;
Web: www.rnib.org.uk).
Director-General: I. Bruce

Societies and Institutions   521

Royal Naval Association
82 Chelsea Manor Street, London, SW3 5QJ
(Tel: 020-7352 6764; Fax: 020-7352 7385;
E-mail: rna@netcomuk.co.uk;
Web: www.royal-naval-association.co.uk).
General Secretary: Capt. R. McQueen, CBE, RN

Royal Naval Benevolent Society for Officers
1 Fleet Street, London, EC4Y 1BD
(Tel: 020-7427 7471; Fax: 020-7427 7471).
Secretary: Capt. I. B. Sutherland, RN (retd)

Royal Patriotic Fund Corporation
40 Queen Anne's Gate, London, SW1H 9AP
(Tel: 020-7233 1894; Fax: 020-7233 1799).
Secretary: Brig. T. G. Williams, CBE

Royal Pharmaceutical Society of Great Britain
1 Lambeth High Street, London, SE1 7JN
(Tel: 020-7735 9141; Fax: 020-7735 7629;
E-mail: enquiries@rpsgb.org.uk;
Web: www.rpsgb.org.uk).
Secretary: Ms A. M. Lewis, OBE

Royal Philatelic Society London
41 Devonshire Place, London, W1N 1PE
(Tel: 020-7486 1044; Fax: 020-7486 0803;
Web: www.rpsl.org.uk).
Hon. Secretary: D. Gurney

Royal Pinner School Foundation
110 Old Brompton Road, London, SW7 3RB
(Tel: 020-7373 6168).
Secretary: D. Crawford

Royal School of Needlework
Apartment 12A, Hampton Court Palace, Surrey, KT8 9AU (Tel: 020-8943 1432; Fax: 020-8943 4910; E-mail: rnwork@intonet.co.uk;
Web: www.royal-needlework.co.uk).
Principal: Mrs E. Elvin

Royal Society for the encouragement of Arts, Manufactures and Commerce (RSA)
8 John Adam Street, London, WC2N 6EZ
(Tel: 020-7930 5115;
E-mail: general@rsa-uk.demon.co.uk;
Web: www.rsa.org.uk).
Director: Penny Egan

Royal Society of Chemistry
Burlington House, Piccadilly, London, W1V 0BN (Tel: 020-7437 8656; Fax: 020-7437 8883;
E-mail: rsc1@rsc.org; Web: www.rsc.org).
Secretary-General: Dr T. D. Inch

Royal Society of Literature
Somerset House, Strand, London, WC2R 0RN
(Tel: 020-845 4676; Fax: 020-845 4679;
E-mail: info@rslitorg; Web: www.rslit.org).
Secretary: Mrs M. Fergusson

Royal Society of Marine Artists
17 Carlton House Terrace, London, SW1Y 5BD
(Tel: 020-7930 6844; Fax: 020-7839 7830).
Secretary: D. Howell

Royal Society of Painter-Printmakers
Bankside Gallery, 48 Hopton Street, London, SE1 9JH (Tel: 020-7928 7521; Fax: 020-7928 2820; E-mail: bankside@freeuk.com).
President: Prof. D. Carpanini

Royal Society of Portrait Painters
17 Carlton House Terrace, London, SW1Y 5BD
(Tel: 020-7930 6844; Fax: 020-7839 7830;
E-mail: vnewlandsmallgalleries@dial.pipex.com;
Web: www.mallgalleries.org.uk).
Secretary: David Lobley

Royal Society of Tropical Medicine and Hygiene
Manson House, 26 Portland Place, London, W1B 1EY (Tel: 020-7580 2127;
Fax: 020-7436 1389; E-mail: mail@rstmh.org;
Web: www.rstmh.org).
Hon. Secretaries: Prof. R. D. Ward; Dr S. B. Squire

Royal Star and Garter Home for Disabled Sailors, Soldiers and Airmen
Richmond Hill, Richmond-upon-Thames, Surrey, TW10 6RR (Tel: 020-8940 3314;
Fax: 020-8940 1953).
Chief Executive: I. A. Lashbrooke

Royal Statistical Society
12 Errol Street, London, EC1Y 8LX
(Tel: 020-7638 8998; Fax: 020-7256 7598;
E-mail: rss@rss.org.uk;
Web: www.rss.org.uk).
Executive Secretary: I. J. Goddard

Royal Theatrical Fund
11 Garrick Street, London, WC2E 9AR
(Tel: 020-7836 3322; Fax: 020-7379 8273).
Secretary: Mrs R. M. Foster

Royal United Services Institute for Defence Studies
Whitehall, London, SW1A 2ET
(Tel: 020-7930 5854; Fax: 020-7321 0943;
E-mail: defence@rusi.org; Web: www.rusi.org).
Director: Rear-Adm. R. Cobbold, CB

Royal Watercolour Society
Bankside Gallery, 48 Hopton Street, London, SE1 9JH (Tel: 020-7928 7521; Fax: 020-7928 2820).
Secretary: Ms J. Dixey

Salmon and Trout Association
Fishmongers' Hall, London Bridge, London, EC4R 9EL (Tel: 020-7283 5838; Fax: 020-7626 5137;
E-mail: salmon.trout@virgin.net;
Web: www.salmon-trout.org).
Director: C. W. Poupard

SANE
1st Floor, Cityside House, 40 Alder Street, London, E1 1EE (Tel: 020-7375 1002;
Fax: 020-7375 2162; Web: www.sane.org.uk).
Chief Executive: Ms M. Wallace, MBE

Save Britain's Heritage
Gilwell Park, Chingford, London, E4 7QW
(Tel: 020-8433 7100; Fax: 020-8433 7103;
E-mail: info.centre@scout.org.uk;
Web: www.scouts.org.uk).
Secretary: A. Wilkinson

Save the Children Fund
17 Grove Lane, London, SE5 8RD
(Tel: 020-7703 5400; Fax: 020-7703 2278;
Web: www.savethechildren.org.uk).
Director-General: M. Aaronson

SCOPE
6 Market Road, London, N7 9PW
(Tel: 020-7619 7100; Fax: 020-7619 7399;
Web: www.scope.org.uk).
Chief Executive: R. P. Brewster

Scout Association
Baden-Powell House, Queen's Gate, London, SW7 5JS (Tel: 020-7584 7030; Fax: 020-7590 5103; E-mail: baden.powell.house@scout.org.uk; Web: www.scoutbase.org.uk/).
Chief Executive: D. M. Twine

Scripture Gift Mission Incorporated
Radstock House, 3 Eccleston Street, London, SW1W 9LZ (Tel: 020-7730 2155;
E-mail: int@sgm.org).
International Director: H. Q. Davies

Selden Society
Faculty of Laws, Queen Mary and Westfield College, Mile End Road, London, E1 4NS
(Tel: 020-7882 5136; Fax: 020-8981 8733;
E-mail: selden-society@qmw.ac.uk;
Web: www.selden-society.qmw.ac.uk).
Secretary: V. Tunkel

Sense (National Deafblind and Rubella Association)
11–13 Clifton Terrace, London, N4 3SR
(Tel: 020-7272 7774; Fax: 020-7272 6012;
E-mail: enquiries@sense.org.uk;
Web: www.sense.org.uk).
Chief Executive: R. Clark

Shaftesbury Homes and Arethusa
The Chapel, Royal Victoria Patriotic Building, Trinity Road, London, SW18 3SX
(Tel: 020-8875 1555; Fax: 020-8875 1954;
E-mail: shaftesbury.homes@virgin.net).
Chief Executive: Ms A. Chesney

Shaftesbury Society
16 Kingston Road, London, SW19 1JZ
(Tel: 020-8239 5555;
E-mail: info@shaftesburysoc.org.uk;
Web: www.shaftesburysoc.org.uk).
Chief Executive: Ms F. Beckett

Shakespeare Globe Trust
21 New Globe walk, London, SE1 9DT
(Tel: 020-7902 1400; Fax: 020-7902 1460;
E-mail: john@shakespearesglobe.com;
Web: www.shakespeare-globe.org).
Dorector of Development: John Nicholls

Societies and Institutions 523

Shellfish Association of Great Britain
Fishmongers' Hall, London Bridge, London, EC4R 9EL (Tel: 020-7283 8305; Fax: 020-7929 1389; E-mail: sagb@shellfish.org.uk; Web: www.shellfish.org.uk).
Director: Dr P. Hunt

Shelter (The National Campaign for Homeless People)
88 Old Street, London, EC4R 9EL (Tel: 020-7505 2000. Shelterline: 0808-800 4444).
Director: C. Holmes, CBE

Sir Oswald Stoll Foundation
446 Fulham Road, London, SW6 1DT (Tel: 020-7385 2110; Fax: 020-7381 7485; E-mail: stoll446@aol.com).
Chief Executive: R. C. Brunwin

Society for Nautical Research
c/o National Maritime Museum, Greenwich, London, SE10 9NF (Tel: 020-8312 6712; Fax: 020-8312 6722; E-mail: lxveri@nmm.ac.uk; Web: www.snr.org).
Hon. Secretary: Liza Veriy

Society for Psychical Research
49 Marloes Road, London, W8 6LA (Tel: 020-7937 8984; Fax: 020-7937 8984; Web: www.spr.ac.uk).
Secretary: P. Johnson

Society for the Promotion of Hellenic Studies
Senate House, Malet Street, London, WC1E 7HU (Tel: 020-7862 8730).
Executive Secretary: R. W. Shone

Society for the Promotion of Roman Studies
Senate House, Malet Street, London, WC1E 7HU (Tel: 020-7862 8727; Fax: 020-7862 8728; E-mail: romansoc@sas.ac.uk; Web: www.sas.ac.uk/icls/roman).
Secretary: Dr H. M. Cockle

Society for the Protection of Ancient Buildings
37 Spital Square, London, E1 6DY (Tel: 020-7377 1644; Fax: 020-7247 5296; E-mail: info@spab.org.uk; Web: www.spab.org.uk).
Secretary: P. Venning, FSA

Society for the Protection of Unborn Children
5-6 St Matthew Street, London, SW1P 2JT (Tel: 020-7222 5845; Fax: 020-7222 0630; E-mail: enquiry@spuc.org.uk; Web: www.spuc.org.uk).
National Director: J. Smeaton

Society for Theatre Research
c/o the Theatre Museum, 1E Tavistock Street, London, WC2E 7PA (E-mail: e.cottis@btinternet.com; Web: www.str.org.uk).
Joint Hon. Secretaries: Ms E. Cottis; Ms F. Dann

Society of Antiquaries of London
Burlington House, Piccadilly, London, W1J 0BE (Tel: 020-7734 0193; Fax: 020-7287 6967; E-mail: admin@sal.org.uk; Web: www.sal.org.uk).
General Secretary: D. Morgan Evans, FSA

Society of Apothecaries of London
14 Blackfriars Lane, London, EC4V 6EJ (Tel: 020-7236 1189; Fax: 020-7329 3177; E-mail: clerk@apothacaries.org; Web: www.apothacaries.org).
Clerk: R. J. Stringer

Society of Archivists
40 Northampton Road, London, EC1R 0HB (Tel: 020-7278 8630; Fax: 020-7278 2107; E-mail: societyofarchivists@archives.org.uk; Web: www.archives.org.uk).
Executive Secretary: P. S. Cleary

Society of Authors
84 Drayton Gardens, London, SW10 9SB (Tel: 020-7373 6642; Fax: 020-7373 5768; E-mail: info@societyofauthors.org; Web: www.societyofauthors.org).
General Secretary: M. Le Fanu, OBE

Society of Genealogists
14 Chrterhouse Buildings, Goswell Road, London, EC1M 7BA (Tel: 020-7251 8799; Fax: 020-7250 1800; E-mail: info@sog.org.uk; Web: www.sog.org.uk).
Director: R. I. N. Gordon

524 Societies and Institutions

Society of Public Teachers of Law
School of Law, Kings College, Strand, London, WC2R 2LS
(Tel: 020-7848 2849; Fax: 020-7848 2788;
E-mail: peter.niven@tccl.ac.uk;
Web: www.law.warwick.ac.uk/sptl).
Administration Secretary: Peter Niven

Society of Scribes and Illuminators
6 Queen Square, London, WC1N 3AT
(Tel: 01524-251534; Fax: 01524-251534;
E-mail: scribe@calligraphy.org;
Web: www.calligraphy.org).
Hon. Secretary: Mrs G. Hazeldine

Sons of Temperance Friendly Society
176 Blackfriars Road, London, SE1 8ET
(Tel: 020-7928 7384; Fax: 020-7928 7384;
Web: www.sonsoftemperance.co.uk).
Chief Executive: Mrs M. C. Scroby

South London Dial-a-Ride
45 Weir Road, London, SW19 8UG
(Tel: 020-8879 5023; Fax: 020-8944 8611;
E-mail: admin@soldar.org;
Web: www.soldar.org).

Special Trustees for Great Ormond Street Hospital
Great Ormond Street, London, WC1N 3JH
(Tel: 020-7916 5678; Fax: 020-7831 1938;
Web: www.gt-ormond-sthospital.org.uk).

Special Trustees for Guy's Hospital Endowment Funds
Guy's Hospital, St Thomas Street, London, SE1 9RT (Tel: 020-7378 0030).

Special Trustees for St Bartholomew's Hospital
57B West Smithfield, London, EC1A 9DS
(Tel: 020-7607 6110; Fax: 020-7600 6993;
E-mail: bartstrustees@cableclick.net).
Chairman: Mrs Clare Maurice

SSAFA Forces Help
19 Queen Elizabeth Street, London, SE1 2LP
(Tel: 020-7403 8783; Fax: 020-7403 8815;
E-mail: info@ssafa.org.uk;
Web: www.ssafa.org.uk).
Controller: Maj.-Gen. P. Sheppard, CB, CBE

St Dustan's (For Blind ex-Service Men and Women)
12–14 Harcourt Street, London, W1H 4HD
(Tel: 020-7723 5021; Fax: 020-7262 6199).
Chief Executive: Robert Leader

St John Ambulance
1 Grosvenor Crescent, London, SW1X 7EF
(Tel: 020-7235 5231).
Executive Director: L. Martin

Standing Conference of National and University Libraries (SCONUL)
102 Euston Street, London, NW1 2HA
(Tel: 020-7387 0317; Fax: 020-7383 3197;
E-mail: sconul@sconul.ac.uk;
Web: www.sconul.ac.uk).
Secretary: A. J. C. Bainton

Standing Council of the Baronetage
3 Eastcroft Road, West Ewell, Epsom, Surrey, KT19 9TX (Tel: 020-8393 6620; Fax: 020-8393 6620).
Chairman: Sir Brian Barttelot, Bt., OBE, DL

Stone Federation, Great Britain
Construction House, 56–64 Leonard Street, London, EC2A 4JX
(Tel: 020-7608 5094; Fax: 020-7608 5081;
E-mail: enquiries@stone-federation.org.uk;
Web: www.stone-federationgb.org.uk).
Director: Jane Buxey

Strategic Planning Society
17 Portland Place, London, W1B 1PU
(Tel: 020-7636 7737; Fax: 020-7323 1692;
E-mail: enquiries@sps.org.uk;
Web: www.sps.org.uk).
General Manager: D. Lambert

Surrey Archaeological Society
Castle Arch, Guildford, Surrey, GU1 3SX
(Tel: 01483 532454; Fax: 01483-532454;
E-mail: surreyarch@compuserve.com;
Web: www.ourworld.compuserve.com/homepages/surreyarch).
Hon. Secretary: Miss A. J. Monk

Survival International
11–15 Emerald Street, London, WC1N 3QL
(Tel: 020-7242 1441; Fax: 020-7242 1771;
E-mail: info@survival-international.org;
Web: www.survival-international.org).
Director: S. Corry

Societies and Institutions   525

Suzy Lamplugh Trust
14 East Sheen Avenue, London, SW14 8AS
(Tel: 020-8392 1839; Fax: 020-8392 1830;
E-mail: trust@suzylamplugh.org;
Web: www.suzylamplugh.org).
Executive Secretary: P. Lamplugh

Swedenborg Society
20–21 Bloomsbury Way, London, WC1A 2TH
(Tel: 020-7405 7986; Fax: 020-7831 5848;
E-mail: swed.soc@netmatters.co.uk;
Web: www.swedenborg.org.uk).
Secretary: Ms Sarah Harding

Telecommunication Users' Association
Woodgate Studios, 2–8 Games Road, Cockfosters, Barnet, Herts, EN4 9HN
(Tel: 020-8449 8844; Fax: 020-8447 4901;
E-mail: tua@dial.pipex.com;
Web: www.tua.co.uk).
Chairman: W. E. Mieran

Terrence Higgins Trust
52–54 Gray's Inn Road, London, WC1X 8JU
(Tel: 020-7831 0330).
Chief Executive: N. Partridge, OBE

The Air League
Broadway House, Tothill Street, London, SW1H 9NS (Tel: 020-7222 8463; Fax: 020-7222 8462;
E-mail: exec@airleague.co.uk;
Web: www.airleague.co.uk).
Director: E. Cox

The Corporation of Church House
Church House, Dean's Yard, London, SW1P 3NZ (Tel: 020-7898 1310; Fax: 020-7898 1321).
Secretary: C. D. L. Menzies

The Corps of Commissionaires
Market House, 85 Cowcross Street, London, EC1M 6PF
(Tel: 020-7490 1125; Fax: 020-7251 2398;
E-mail: information@the-corps.co.uk;
Web: www.the-corps.co.uk).
Group Managing Director: F. J. Peck

The Edwina Mountbatten Trust
Estate Office, Broadlands, Romsey, Hants, SO51 9ZE
Secretary: J. B. Moss

The Engineering Council
10 Maltravers Street, London, WC2R 3ER
(Tel: 020-7240 7891; Fax: 020-7240 7517;
E-mail: mcshirley@engc.org.uk;
Web: www.engc.org.uk).
Director-General: Malcolm C. Shirley

The Environment Council
212 High Holborn, London, WC1V 7BF
(Tel: 020-7836 2626; Fax: 020-7242 1180;
E-mail: info@envcouncil.org.uk;
Web: www.the-environment-council.org.uk).
Chief Executive: Steve Robinson

The Garwood Foundation
1A Melville Avenue, South Croydon, Surrey, CR2 7HZ (Tel: 020-8681 0460; Fax: 020-8406 8220).
Director of Services: Lucy Sivoli

The Geologists' Association
Burlington House, Piccadilly, London, W1V 9AG (Tel: 020-7434 9298; Fax: 020-7287 0280;
E-mail: geol.assoc@btinternet.com;
Web: www.geologist.demon.co.uk).
Executive Secretary: Mrs S. Stafford

The Library Association
7 Ridgmount Street, London, WC1E 7AE
(Tel: 020-7255 0500; Fax: 020-7255 0501;
E-mail: info@la-hq.org.uk;
Web: www.la-hq.org.uk).
Chief Executive: Bob McKee, Ph.D., FRSA

The London Library
14 St James's Square, London, SW1Y 4LG
(Tel: 020-7930 7705; Fax: 020-7766 4766;
E-mail: membership@londonlibrary.co.uk;
Web: www.londonlibrary.co.uk).
Librarian: A. S. Bell

The Marine Society
202 Lambeth Road, London, SE1 7JW
(Tel: 020-7261 9535; Fax: 020-7401 2537;
E-mail: enq@marine-society.org;
Web: www.marine-society.org).
Director: Capt. J. J. Howard

526 Societies and Institutions

The Mission to Seafarers
St Michael Paternoster Royal, College Hill, London, EC4R 2RL
(Tel: 020-7248 5202; Fax: 020-7248 4761; E-mail: general@missiontoseafarers.org; Web: www.missiontoseafarers.org).
Secretary-General: Revd Canon G. Jones

The National Society
Church House, Great Smith Street, London, SW1P 3NZ (Tel: 020-7898 1518; Fax: 020-7898 1493; E-mail: info@natsoc.c-of-e.org.uk; Web: www.natsoc.org.uk).
General Secretary: Canon J. Hall

The National Trust for Places of Historic Interest and Natural Beauty
36 Queen Anne's Gate, London, SW1H 9AS (Tel: 020-7222 9251; Fax: 020-7222 5097; Web: www.nationaltrust.org.uk).
Director-General: Fiona Reynolds

The Nuffield Trust
59 New Cavendish Street, London, W1G 7LP (Tel: 020-7631 8450; Fax: 020-7631 8451; E-mail: mail@nuffieldtrust.org.uk; Web: www.nuffieldtrust.org.uk).
Secretary: J. Wyn Owen, CB

The Officers' Association
48 Pall Mall, London, SW1Y 5JY
(Tel: 020-7930 0125; Fax: 020-7930 9053; E-mail: postmaster@oaed.org.uk; Web: www.officersassociation.org.uk).
General Secretary: Brig. J. M. A. Norton, OBE, MC

The Physiological Society
PO Box 11319, London, WC1E 7JF
(Tel: 020-7631 1458; Fax: 020-7631 1462; E-mail: admin@physoc.org.uk; Web: www.physoc.org).
Executive Secretary: Mr M. Lewis

The Pilgrim Trust
Cowley House, 9 Little College Street, London, SW1P 3XS (Tel: 020-7222 4723; Fax: 020-7976 0461).
Director: Miss G. Nayler

The Place (Contemporary Dance Trust)
The Place, 17 Duke's Road, London, WC1H 9PY (Tel: 020-7387 0161; Fax: 020-7383 4852; E-mail: placetheatre@easynet.co.uk; Web: www.theplace.org.uk).
General Manager: Sue Hoyle

The Queen's English Society
20 Jessica Road, London, SW18 2QN
(Tel: 020-8874 2200;
Web: www.queens-english-society.co.uk).
Hon. Secretary: Miss P. Raper

The Royal Society for Asian Affairs
2 Belgrave Square, London, SW1X 8PJ
(Tel: 020-7235 5122; Fax: 020-7259 6771; E-mail: info@rsaa.org.uk; Web: www.rsaa.org.uk).
Secretary: D. J. Easton

The Royal Society for the Promotion of Health
RSH House, 38a St George's Drive, London, SW1V 4BH (Tel: 020-7630 0121; Fax: 020-7976 6847; E-mail: rshealth@rshealth.org.uk; Web: www.rsph.org).
Chief Executive: Hugh A. Lowson

The Royal Society of Medicine
1 Wimpole Street, London, W1G 0AE
(Tel: 020-7290 2900; Fax: 020-7290 2992; E-mail: membership@roysocmed.ac.uk; Web: www.rsm.ac.uk).
Executive Director: Dr A. Grocock

The Royal Society of Musicians of Great Britain
10 Stratford Place, London, W1C 1BA
(Tel: 020-7629 6137; Fax: 020-7629 6137).
Secretary: Mrs M. Gibb

The Sea Cadet Association
202 Lambeth Road, London, SE1 7JF
(Tel: 020-7928 8978; Fax: 020-7928 8914; E-mail: schq@sea-cadets.org; Web: www.sea-cadets.org).
Chief Executive: Cdre R. M. Parker, RN

The Socialist Party
52 Clapham High Street, London, SW4 7UN (Tel: 020-7622 3811; Fax: 020-7720 3665; E-mail: spgb@worldsocialism.org).
General Secretary: B. Johnson

Societies and Institutions 527

The Society of Operations Engineers
22 Greencoat Place, London, SW1P 1PR
(Tel: 020-7630 1111; Fax: 020-7630 6677;
E-mail: soe@soe.org.uk;
Web: www.soe.org.uk).
Chief Executive: P. J. G. Corp, CB

The Stroke Association
Stroke House, Whitecross Street, London, EC1Y 8JJ (Tel: 020-7566 0300; Fax: 020-7490 2686;
E-mail: stroke@stroke.org.uk;
Web: www.stroke.org.uk).
Chief Executive Officer: Miss M. Goose

The Tavistock Institute
30 Tabernacle Street, London, EC2A 4UE
(Tel: 020-7417 0407; Fax: 020-7417 0566;
Web: www.tavistockinstitute.org).
Institute Secretary: Vacant

The Theatres Trust
22 Charing Cross Road, London, WC2H 0QL
(Tel: 020-7836 8591; Fax: 020-7836 3302;
E-mail: info@theatrestrust.org.uk;
Web: www.theatrestrust.org.uk).
Director: P. Longman

The Wellcome Trust
The Wellcome Building, 183 Euston Road, London, NW1 2BE
(Tel: 020-7611 8888; Fax: 020-7611 8545;
E-mail: director@wellcome.ac.uk;
Web: www.wellcome.ac.uk).
Director: Dr T. Michael Dexter, FRS

Theosophical Society in England
50 Gloucester Place, London, W1U 8EA
(Tel: 020-7563 9817; Fax: 020-7935 9543;
E-mail: theosophical@freenetname.co.uk;
Web: www.theosophical-society.org.uk).
National President: C. Price

Tower Hamlets and Canary Wharf Further Education Trust
Mulberry Place, 5 Clove Crescent, London, E14 2BG (Tel: 020-7364 4604; Fax: 0207-7364 4311).
Head Administrator: Pasha Kamal

Tower Hill Improvement Trust
Atlee House, 28 Commercial Street, London, E1 6LR (Tel: 020-7377 6614; Fax: 020-7377 9822).

Town and Country Planning Association
17 Carlton House Terrace, London, SW1Y 5AS
(Tel: 020-7930 8903/4/5; Fax: 020-7930 3280;
E-mail: tcpa@tcpa.org.uk;
Web: www.tcpa.org.uk).
Director: Gideon Amos

Tree Council
51 Catherine Place, London, SW1E 6DY
(Tel: 020-7828 9928; Fax: 020-7828 9060;
Web: www.treecouncil.org.uk).
Director: R. Osborne

Trust for London
6 Middle Street, London, EC1A 7PH
(Tel: 020-7606 6145; Fax: 020-7600 1866;
E-mail: traustforlondon@cityparochial.org.uk;
Web: www.cityparochial.org.uk).
Clerk: Bharat Mehta

Trustees for the Royal Free Hospital NHS Trust
The Trustees for the Royal Free Hospital, Pond Street, London, NW3 2QG
(Tel: 020-7794 0500).
The Chief Executive: Martin Else

Turner Society
BCM Box Turner, London, WC1N 3XX
(Web: www.turnersociety.org.uk).
Chairman: Eric Shanes

UK Independence Party
Triumph House, 189 Regent Street, London, W1B 4JX (Tel: 020-7434 4559; Fax: 020-7439 4659; E-mail: mail@ukip.org;
Web: www.ukip.org).
Secretary: Michael Harvey

UK Youth
2nd Floor, Kirby House, 20–24 Kirby Street, London, EC1N 8TS
(Tel: 020-7242 4045; Fax: 020-7242 4045;
E-mail: info@ukyouth.org.uk;
Web: www.ukyouth.org.uk).
Chief Executive: J. Bateman

United Nations Association of Great Britain and Northern Ireland
3 Whitehall Court, London, SW1A 3EL
(Tel: 020-7930 2931; Fax: 020-7930 5893;
E-mail: info@una-uk.org;
Web: www.oneworld.org/una-uk).
Director: M. C. Harper

528 Societies and Institutions

University College London Hospitals Charity
1st Floor Vezey Strong Wing, 112 Hampstead Road, London, NW1 2LT).

USPG (United Society for the Propagation of the Gospel)
Partnership House, 157 Waterloo Road, London, SE1 8XA (Tel: 020-7928 8681; Fax: 020-8928 2371; E-mail: enquiries@uspg.org.uk; Web: www.uspg.org.uk).
Secretary: Rt. Revd M. Rumalshah

Victim Suppport (National Association of Victims Support Schemes)
National Office, Cranmer House, 39 Brixton Road, London, SW9 6DZ (Tel: 020-7735 9166; Helpline: 0845-303 0900; Fax: 020-7582 5712; E-mail: contact@victimsupport.org.uk).
Chief Executive: Dame Helen Reeves, DBE

Victoria Cross and George Cross Association
Horse Guards, Whitehall, London, SW1A 2AX (Tel: 020-7930 3506).
Secretary: Mrs D. Grahame, MVO

Victorian Society
1 Priory Gardens, Bedford Park, London, W4 1TT (Tel: 020-8994 1019; Fax: 020-8995 4895; E-mail: admin@victorian-society.org.uk; Web: www.victorian-society.org.uk).
Director: Dr Ian Dungavell

Victory (Services) Association Ltd and Club
63–79 Seymour Street, London, W2 2HF (Tel: 020-7723 4474; Fax: 020-7724 1134; E-mail: office@vsc.co.uk; Web: www.vsc.co.uk).
General Manager: G. F. Taylor

Viking Society for Northern Research
Department of Scandinavian Studies, University College London, Gower Street, London, WC1E 6BT (Tel: 020-7679 7176; Fax: 020-7679 7750; E-mail: cnr@ucl.ac.uk; Web: www.nott.ac.uk/vaezjj/homepage.html).
Hon. Secretaries: Prof. M. P. Barnes; Dr J. Jesh

VSO (Voluntary Service Overseas)
317 Putney Bridge Road, London, SW15 2PN (Tel: 020-8780 7200; Fax: 020-8780 7300; Web: www.vso.org.uk).
Chief Executive: M. Goldring

War on Want
Fenner Brockway House, 37–39 Great Guildford Street, London, SE1 0ES (Tel: 020-7620 1111; Fax: 020-7261 9291; E-mail: mailroom@waronwant.org; Web: www.waronwant.org).
Director: Ms C. Matheson

WellBeing (The Health Research Charity for Women and Babies)
27 Sussex Place, Regent's Park, London, NW1 4SP (Tel: 020-7772 6400; Fax: 020-7724 7725; E-mail: wellingbeing@rcog.org.uk; Web: www.wellbeing.org.uk).
Director: Mrs Jane Arnell

WES World-Wide Education Service Ltd
Canada House, 272 Field End Road, Eastcote, Ruislip, Middx, HA4 9NA (Tel: 020-8582 0317; Fax: 020-8429 4838; E-mail: wes@wesworldwide.com; Web: www.wesworldwide.com).
Director: Mrs T. Mulder-Reynolds

West London Mission
19 Thayer Street, London, W1V 2QJ (Tel: 020-7935 6179; Fax: 020-7487 3965; E-mail: office@westlondonmission.freeserve.co.uk; Web: www.methodist.org.uk/west.london.mission).
Superintendent: Revd Geoff Cornell

Westminster Foundation for Democracy
2nd Floor, 125 Pall Mall, London, SW1Y 5EA (Tel: 020-7930 0408; Fax: 020-7930 0449; E-mail: wfd@wfd.org; Web: www.wfd.org).
Chief Executive: Mr Trefor Williams, OBE

William Morris Society and Kelmscott Fellowship
Kelmscott House, 26 Upper Mall, London, W6 9TA (Tel: 020-8741 3735; Fax: 020-8748 5207; E-mail: william.morris@care4free.net; Web: www.morrissociety.org).

Wine and Spirit Association
Five Kings House, 1 Queen Street Place, London, EC4R 1XX (Tel: 020-7248 5377; Fax: 020-7489 0322; E-mail: wsa@wsa.org.uk; Web: www.wsa.org.uk).
Director: Q. Rappoport

Societies and Institutions 529

Women's Engineering Society
2 Queen Anne's Gate Buildings, Dartmouth Street, London, SW1H 9BP (Tel: 020-7233 1974; E-mail: info@wes.org.uk; Web: www.wes.org.uk).
Secretary: Mrs C. MacGillivray

Women's Nationwide Cancer Control Campaign
1st Floor, Charity House, 14–15 Perseverance Works, London, E2 8DD (Tel: 020-7729 4688; Fax: 020-7613 0771; E-mail: admin@wnccc.org.uk; Web: www.wnccc.org.uk).
Chief Executive: Ms J. Cohen

Workers' Educational Association
Temple House, 17 Victoria Park Square, London, E2 9PB (Tel: 020-8983 1515; Fax: 020-8983 4840; E-mail: inationaloffice@wea.org.uk; Web: www.wea.org.uk).
General Secretary: R. Lochrie

World Energy Council
5th Floor, Regency House, 1–4 Warwick Street, London, W1R 6LE (Tel: 020-7734 5996; Fax: 020-7734 5926; E-mail: info@worldenergy.org; Web: www.worldenergy.org).
Secretary-General: G. W. Doucet

Young Men's Christian Association (YMCA)
YMCA England, 640 Forest Road, London, E17 3DZ (Tel: 020-8520 5599; Fax: 020-8509 3190; E-mail: press@england.ymca.org.uk).
National Secretary: E. Thomas

Zoological Society of London
Regent's Park, London, NW1 4RY (Tel: 020-7722 3333; Fax: 020-7586 5743; Web: www.zsl.org).
Director-General: Dr Michael Dixon

LONDON EVENTS
OF THE YEAR

EVENTS OF THE YEAR

1 June 2000 to 31 May 2001

LONDON AFFAIRS

June 2000

2. Managers of the Connex rail networks serving south London released figures estimating ticket fraud costing £30m annually. A £475m plan to build a new Wembley Stadium was approved by Brent Council. **6.** A report by the Strategic Rail Authority revealed that South West Trains were fined a record £4m for poor performance in the preceding year. **7.** Tony Blair, the Prime Minister, was jeered and heckled by 10,000 Women's Institute members during a speech at Wembley Arena. Ian Boon, head of the Immigration Services Enforcement Directorate, revealed targets to increase the annual expulsion of illegal immigrants from 12,000 to 57,000 by 2004. **8.** Ken Livingstone, the newly elected Mayor of London, pledged to bring in congestion charges on London drivers by 2002. **9.** The RSPB offered to buy Rainham Marshes from the Ministry of Defence for £1.1m. A £27m estate was left to charity in the will of Mary Coyle and Florance Reakes, two spinsters who shared a flat in Highgate. **15.** The high street clothes retailer C & A announced it was to close 109 of its British Stores, including all those in the capital. **16.** Two Traffic Wardens were fired by APCA Parking Enforcement (Camden) for aggressively responding to citizens' complaints. **19.** A Royal Parks Police spokesman revealed that officials would not stop women from going topless, although it is officially banned. Westminster Council introduced measures to create "quiet zones" in the West End. New bars, clubs, cafes and restaurants will have to pass strict noise tests before being granted a licence. **20.** Ken Livingstone unveiled plans for an £80 fine for drivers caught using the bus lane. Weight and height restrictions were imposed on the bridge linking Kensington High Street and Hammersmith Road. A power cut blacked-out much of West London from 5.09pm to 9.22pm when a substation in Shepherds Bush failed. **21.** Westminster Council pledged to spend an extra £1m on cleaning the borough's streets. **26.** Tony Blair publicly denounced comments by Mo Mowlam, the Cabinet Office minister, that the Royal Family should leave Buckingham Palace. **27.** The RAC voiced its opposition to a car-free day proposed for 22 September. **28.** The Greater London Authority agreed to allow lobbying groups access to its members and staff, contradicting a pre-election pledge by Ken Livingstone. **29.** Islington Arts and Media School, formerly George Orwell Comprehensive, was returned to Ofsted's list of failing schools despite £3m of investment. London Underground revealed it made £294m profit in the preceding 12 months. **30.** Lewisham Council began removing 126 abandoned cars from its streets after receiving nearly 6,000 complaints from residents. Hammersmith Council abandoned width restrictions on the West Kensington Railtrack Bridge.

July 2000

3. The City Corporation's planning committee approved an application to demolish the Grade II* listed former Baltic Exchange Hall, severely damaged in the IRA City bombing in 1992, and replace it with a "gherkin shaped" tower designed by the architect Lord Foster. **4.** Ken Livingstone was inaugurated as Mayor of London. It was revealed that the Queen was to contribute £35m from her civil list payment towards the running costs of the Royal Palaces. The University of East London's Docklands Campus officially opened. **7.** The Halifax revealed that house prices in London had dropped by 2.4% since April, the first drop in 5 years. **10.** A report by the Kings Fund, the health think-tank, estimated there are 5,000 vacant nurses positions in London. **12.** A report by the Drinking Water Inspectorate found 99.87% of tests met with standards, giving London the cleanest tap water in the country. The Home office announced that from July 24 it would financially support all asylum seekers in London, saving local councils, who were previously responsible, £200m. **13.** Staff at Royal Mail's Almeida Street sorting office went on strike. **17.** A report revealed tube delays had increased by 60% in the last year. **18.** Ken Livingstone threatened to seize day-to-day control of Trafalgar Square from Westminster Council unless it agreed to his plans for pedestrianisation. **19.** A report by the shelter and housing association The Peabody Trust showed that 100,000 Londoners found themselves homeless each year. **20.** The Chancellor John Prescott's announcement of a £3.2 billion spending package for London Transport was dismissed by Ken Livingstone as having "an unpleasant sting in the tail" when it was revealed

534 Events of the Year

that the London Transport authority would have to pay the £104m bill for cost over-runs on the Jubilee line. **21.** It was announced that tube fares would rise in line with inflation over the next 2 years. A report claimed there were more than 50,000 illegal minicab drivers in London. **25.** The Met Office published statistics revealing July 2000 as the coldest summer month in 50 years. **27.** A report revealed that London faced a shortfall of at least £10m in funding for HIV and Aids services.

August 2000

4. Over 40,000 people gathered outside Buckingham Palace to celebrate the Queen Mother's 100th birthday. **10.** The London Eye was granted a wedding licence, valid from January 2001, by Lambeth Council. **30.** Scientists released figures showing that London air is cleaner than at any other time since the Industrial Revolution.

September 2000

7. London Mayor, Ken Livingstone, announced plans to charge £5 for motorists driving into central London. The scheme is to be set up by Transport for London and is planned to start in December 2002. **8.** Ford announced its intentions to build a new factory close to its existing plant at Dagenham, producing engines for export and bringing hundreds of new jobs to the area. The plans meant that many of the workers at Dagenham who had been facing redundancy would be offered new jobs instead. **9.** It was revealed that The Environment Agency was preparing to take either the Millennium Bridge Trust, which owns the Millennium Bridge, or its contractors to court for damaging the Thames environment. The Environment Agency wants the court to force them to remove thousands of boulders along the side of the Thames which they believe are damaging conditions for small wildlife and putting walkers in danger of injury.

October 2000

1. Ken Livingstone, Mayor of London, officially took control of Trafalgar and Parliament Squares from the Department for Culture, Media and Sport. **5.** Survivors and families of victims of the Paddington rail crash gathered at Paddington Station and held a minute's silence at 8.11am. **8.** Regulators warned Railtrack that unless they cut delays in their services by March 2001 they would be fined £70 million. A report by The Greater London Authority suggested that the population of London may reach 8.1 million by 2016, an increase of one million. It was announced

that Anthony Mayer was to be appointed as the chief executive of the GLA. London Mayor, Ken Livingstone launched London's biggest consultation exercise as he began a series of six 'Meet the Mayor' public sessions, whereby Londoner's were able to confront him with their concerns. Organisers of the London Marathon revealed that the 2000 Marathon had raised £24 million for charity, making it the biggest annual fund-raising event in the country. A GMB union report found that pay rises of up to 24% were needed to help bridge the gap between the wages of public and private sector workers in London. Officials at Westminster council revealed plans to test high-tech paving blocks which convert exhaust fumes into harmless substances. **9.** Five Greenpeace activists hijacked Londonwaste Ltd, in Edmonton, and set up a platform on top of one of the incinerator's 100m chimneys and the plant had to close after deliveries of refuse were blocked by protestors. It was announced that the Metropolitan Police are to build a multi-million pound regional police headquarters for East London in Barking. Following an investigation into the incident in August 2000, in which a Northern Line train rolled backwards out of control for more than half a mile, recommendations were put forward that all London Underground's 166 new Northern and Jubilee trains had to go through major safety tests, including possible changes to the 'failsafe' braking system. It was announced that London had been allocated a £164 million share of the Government's £800 million neighbourhood renewal fund to boost inner-city areas. **10.** The finance union Unifi called for a significant increase in London weighting payments for lower level finance staff following estimates that, compared to 1990, the cost of living and working in central London has increased by 41%. Plans to rebuild and revitalise the South Bank complex proceeded with the decision to redevelop the Jubilee Gardens in 2002. The South Bank development will include a concert hall, a new BFI Film Centre and a new income generating building called 'The Gateway'. Rupert Perry, chairman of the North London Waste Authority appealed to the Greenpeace activists protesting at Londonwaste Ltd, to call a halt to their protest as tons of medical waste threatened to cause a health hazard at London hospitals. **11.** Former East End gangster, Reggie Kray, was buried in Chingford Mount Cemetery. **12.** A £1 million programme to boost the number of Londoners from ethnic minorities using the NHS was launched. The money will fund the training of health advocates who will act as links between ethnic minority patients and their

GPs, and help develop culturally sensitive services. A research report for the GLA showed that pollution-related deaths were around a third higher than fatal road collisions. Around 226 people a year die in traffic accidents, while there are approximately 380 deaths from transport emissions. Although many of the deaths associated with traffic pollution are among the elderly and the ill, traffic fumes are also believed to have led to more than 300 hospital admissions in London for respiratory conditions, and around half a million for minor breathing problems. **13.** The Greenpeace activists who had been camped out on top of a waste incinerator chimney in Edmonton for four days came down and surrendered to police. **14.** Health Secretary Alan Milburn ordered an urgent investigation into heart and lung transplants at St George's Hospital, Tooting after the death rate amongst patients rose to more than 80%. **16.** More than 200 protesters gathered outside the Israeli Embassy in London to voice their anger against the continuing killing of Palestinians. **17.** A group of parents in Southwark launched a £250,000 appeal to set up their own school after failing to win places for their children at schools of their choice in the borough. **18.** It was revealed that Hackney Council was effectively bankrupt. The Council's treasurer ruled an end to all expenditure on non-statutory services. **19.** Railtrack board members refused to accept Chief Executive Gerald Corbett's resignation. A full scale hunt, involving the RSPCA and the local council, began in Lewisham following several alleged sightings of a kangaroo near the Beckenham Place Park golf club. **20.** A demonstration involving 200 people took place outside Railtrack's head office near Euston Station. The protesters were calling for the railways to be re-nationalised in an attempt to prevent further rail disasters. Parents and children staged a sit-in in two nurseries in east London, following Hackney Council's decision to shut them due to financial restraints. Ken Livingstone and Transport of London ordered a comprehensive review of all bus contracts in London. **22.** It was announced that Railtrack were to receive a five-year grant of £4.7 billion from the rail industry regulator to 'deliver a modern safe railway with greater public accountability'. **24.** Train company Connex was stripped of its south central franchise after extensive criticism over management and performance. The franchise was won by the Govia group which runs Thames Trains. It was announced that a £60 million prison for 600 young offenders is to be built on reclaimed marshland next to high security Belmarsh Prison in Plumstead, south-east London. **25.** Nineteen London firefighters were given bravery awards for their work at the scene of the Paddington train crash. It was announced that teenage pop star Billie Piper was to switch on the Christmas lights in Regent Street. **26.** It was announced that parking meters for motorcycles and scooters were to be introduced as an experiment in some parts of London from January 2001. The official BSE inquiry found that Ministers and Whitehall were guilty of repeatedly misleading the public about the threat to human health posed by mad cow disease, but that there was no deliberate intention to lie or protect farming interests at the expense of the consumer. **27.** The demolition work on Wembley Stadium was put back a month as bankers Chase Manhattan bid to raise the £410 million required to complete the work. **29.** Hammersmith Bridge reopened following a terrorist bomb on 1 June 2000.

November 2000

1. A sit-in demonstration was held at a Crouch End support centre for people with HIV, protesting against its proposed closure. The Thames was put on flood alert following days of heavy rainfall throughout the country. **5.** Almost 400 car enthusiasts took part in the annual London to Brighton run. **8.** The £1.5 million renovation of Wellington Arch at Hyde Park Corner was celebrated in a spectacular dawn fireworks display. All 150 residents of Trowlock Island, near Teddington, and most of the community on Thames Ditton Island had to be evacuated as the Environment Agency issued a severe flood warning. **9.** Plans were unveiled for a 1,280ft glass skyscraper called the London Bridge Tower to be erected in the centre of London. **10.** Prime Minister, Tony Blair, revealed that London nurses were to be paid a 'cost of living' allowance of £1,000 a year to assist with mounting costs of living in London. Defence Secretary Geoff Hoon announced that a new memorial to honour servicemen and women killed since World War II is to be built in London. **13.** The London Police Authority unveiled plans for an eight-month inquiry into discrimination and bullying towards minority officers in the force. **14.** Culture Secretary Chris Smith announced that the statue of Sir Walter Raleigh was to be moved from Westminster to Greenwich to make way for a memorial entitled Women of World War II. The Juniper trains, which cost more than £3 million each and were only weeks old, were withdrawn from London commuter routes because of problems with the black box data recorders. **15.** The National Audit Office announced that it was

536 Events of the Year

to hold an inquiry into the costs of building Portcullis House, the new office block built for MPs in Westminster. Portcullis House is the most expensive office building in Britain at £250 million. Thousands of students marched through London to demand an end to tuition fees. It was revealed that repairs to the Millennium Bridge would cost at least £5 million. **16.** Southwark Council, which technically owns the Millennium Bridge, revealed that they did not have the £5 million required for its repairs. **18.** Family and friends of the 31 people who died in the King Cross fire gathered to pay their respects at the London station 13 years after the disaster. **19.** John Duthie, an amateur poker player from Wandsworth, south London, won £1 million in the final of the Poker Million tournament that took place on the Isle of Wight. **20.** Ken Livingstone cancelled the New Years Eve firework display planned in the centre of London after weeks of negotiation with Tube bosses who said they would not run a service in and out of London after 4pm. **23.** Thousands of London black cabs were recalled for major safety checks after fears were raised over steering faults which could have caused drivers to lose control. Mohammed Al Fayed bought London's last commercial heliport at Battersea for an undisclosed price. **28.** Minister for London, Keith Hill, announced that all firms operating London minicabs would have to be licensed by autumn 2001. **29.** 200 staff were evacuated from the BBC building in Wood Lane, White City, after fire broke out on a seventh-floor wing.

December 2000

1. It was announced that Lewisham Comprehensive, one of the Government's 'fresh-start' schools was to shut. Ken Livingstone announced a £60 million plan to boost the number of police officers in London by 1,250 in an attempt to fight the knife culture that led to the murder of Damilola Taylor. **5.** It was announced that, following the collapse of the New Year's celebrations in central London, 18 boroughs and other organisations will use the money to erect a 'ring of fun' around London, consisting of separate fireworks displays, light shows and street theatre performances. **6.** David Howard, the Lord Mayor of London, announced that the Corporation of London would not pay for repairs to the Millennium Bridge. British Airways announced that they are to cut approximately 1,000 jobs at Gatwick Airport over the next 3 years in a bid to stem heavy losses. **7.** A young City solicitor was suspended after using his work computer to receive an intimate e-mail from a female friend. The e-mail soon made it round the world and the British media began the hunt for Claire Swire, the author. **11.** It was announced that Vauxhall was to end car production at its flagship Luton plant with the loss of around 2,500 jobs. **20.** Metrocab, the second-biggest builder of London taxis suddenly ceased trading, putting the jobs of 250 workers in jeopardy. **14.** A new outdoor ice rink at Somerset House, which is to become an annual Christmas attraction, was opened by the ballerina Darcey Bussell. **15.** London's train companies were hit with record fines of £7 million by rail authorities for providing an 'unacceptable' service even before the current rail crisis. **18.** Oxford Street's John Lewis, was voted London's top shop in the latest findings by the London Customer Service Monitor's quarterly survey. **20.** Central London was brought to a virtual standstill after approximately 1,500 protesters surrounded Parliament to condemn the Hunting Bill which was being given its second reading. It was announced that fanatical Tottenham Hotspur Fan, Daniel Levy, was to buy the controlling interest in the North London club for £22 million from Sir Alan Sugar. **26.** Figures released by the homelessness charity Shelter showed that the number of rough sleepers in British towns and cities had dropped by approximately a third over the past year. **28.** Australian author, Brett De La Mare, was arrested after he flew his paraglider on to the forecourt of Buckingham Palace as a publicity stunt.

January 2001

3. Rail regulator Tim Winsor announced that he had given Railtrack until 18 January to produce plans which would allow train and freight operators to deliver a reliable service. **4.** Government figures showed that wages in London were rising more slowly than in the rest of Britain. Average weekly pay in the capital rose by just one per cent in the year to April 2000 compared with up to 4.7 per cent in other parts of the country. **15.** The Millennium Wheel closed for almost four weeks for routine maintenance checks. Railtrack issued a profit warning after admitting that the rail chaos aftermath of the Hatfield crash had cost the company almost £600 million. **16.** Barclays announced that they were to cut 750 jobs in London and the South-East. It was revealed that a new £5 million centre, funded by the Wellcome Trust, the Office for Science and Technology and the Higher Education Funding Council, dedicated to researching psychiatric disorders, would be developed at the Institute of

Psychiatry in Denmark Hill. **17.** A team at Hammersmith Hospital and Imperial School of Medicine announced that they had discovered an immune cell that could speed the hunt for a cure for leukaemia. **18.** A survey by the Economist Intelligence Unit (EIU) showed London as the most expensive place in Europe to live. **22.** A 34-year-old man collapsed and died minutes after crossing the finishing line of the London Marathon. **24.** Train operator GNER unveiled details of a £4.5 billion bid for the SWT commuter routes out of Waterloo through south-west London to Surrey and Hampshire. Their plans include the relocation of Clapham Junction Station to a new site a third of a mile east towards Waterloo in a bid to modernise the station and ease congestion. Northern Ireland Secretary, Peter Mandelson, resigned from government following revelations about his intervention in a passport application from a Dome sponsor. Researchers at the University of London announced that they had discovered a gene that may protect against lung cancer, after studying people with Down's syndrome. **25.** Statistics from the Public Health Laboratory Service showed that a record number of new cases of HIV were diagnosed in 2000, with more than three quarters of them in London. **29.** Hackney council staff began a three-day strike in protest at cuts to recoup its £40 million deficit. **30.** It was announced that hundreds of office workers were to lose their jobs at city firm ING Barings following a restructuring of the group by its Dutch parent company ING.

February 2001

1. It was announced that the East London line of the London Underground network would be extended northwards to Dalston and Highbury and linked to the mainline rail network. **5.** The transport network in central London was put under considerable strain during a Tube strike over reduced safety standards. **10.** The London Eye officially reopened after being closed for almost 4 weeks while it underwent its annual safety checks. **19.** A review of more than 100,000 breast scans by the West London Breast Screening Service got underway following a serious misdiagnosis. **21.** The Archbishop of Westminster, The Most Reverend Cormac Murphy-O'Connor, was created a cardinal by the Pope John Paul II in a ceremony outside the Vatican watched by approximately 400,000 people. Six tube drivers were suspended for driving busy commuter trains through red lights and ignoring basic safety procedures. **26.** Richmond Park, Bushy Park and Hampton Court Home Park were shut in an attempt to prevent foot-and-mouth disease spreading to deer herds. **27.** The Queen officially opened Portcullis House, the new office block for MP's. The four-day auction of over 15,000 momentos from the Millennium Dome began. **27.** Fulham Football Club was given approval to replace their Craven Cottage ground with a 30,000-seater stadium, despite objections from over 1,500 residents.

March 2001

1. Weather figures revealed that London had endured its wettest six months since 1697. **9.** A second tube strike was planned for 29 March after negotiations over safety standards on the Underground once again broke down. **12.** The British Olympic Association revealed the details of their bid to host the Olympics in London in 2012. **14.** Workmen unearthed a suspected World War II bomb at Gatwick Airport. **20.** Rail Regulators gave Railtrack a deadline of 21 May to get the national rail network back to normal. Rail regulator Tim Winsor warned that if Railtrack failed he would issue an enforcement notice, a legal procedure which would result in the imposition of heavy and unspecified fines. **21.** Ken Livingstone appointed Lord Rogers as Chief Advisor on Architecture to the Greater London Authority. London Underground's most powerful union Aslef called off the 24 hour strike over safety concerns planned for 29 March but the organisation's second largest union Rail Maritime and Transport Union (RMT) vowed to go ahead with the action. **23.** London's stock market dropped more than 200 points in one of its biggest one-day falls in history, triggered by a host of profit warnings and job cut announcements from corporate America. **24.** Cambridge University won the 2001 Boat Race, bringing the total to 77 to 69 in Cambridge's favour. **28.** The controversial application to build the tallest building in Europe at London Bridge Station was submitted to Southwark council, which will decide if the plans can go ahead. **29.** The London Underground was badly affected by industrial action regarding safety regulations. **31.** Prime Minister, Tony Blair, confirmed that there would be no general election on 3 May due to the foot and mouth crisis and that English council elections were to be delayed until 7 June.

538 Events of the Year

April 2001

2. South West Trains won the contract to continue running services in London for 20 years. **11.** The royal parks were reopened to the public after being closed for six weeks due to the foot-and-mouth outbreak.

May 2001

3. South West Trains began a 24 hour strike which affected thousands of commuters. BT announced that it was to sell its St Paul's headquarters in the city in an attempt to reduce its debt mountain. Reassurances were made however, that the move would not result in any job cuts. **10.** It was confirmed that three children at a nursery in Wandsworth had been diagnosed with tuberculosis. **11.** A second 24 hour strike by South West trains got under way. **13.** Approximately 8,000 women sported their bras for a marathon midnight walk through London to raise money for breast cancer charities. **15.** London Guildhall University and the University of North London announced that they were to merge to create the second largest university in Britain in terms of student numbers.

ACCIDENTS AND DISASTERS

June 2000

1. A bomb exploded under Hammersmith Bridge causing widespread damage. No one was hurt. **6.** A Eurostar train travelling from Paris to London derailed near Arras injuring 14 people, including 4 Britons. **7.** 1000 staff and guests were evacuated from the 5 star Marriot Hotel after an accident involving chlorine gas. 2 people died and 26 were injured when a National Express bus from London to Great Yarmouth hit an oncoming car near Newmarket. **9.** All Saints Church in West Dulwich was destroyed by fire. A man lost both legs and an arm after being hit by a train at Southwick Street in Shoreham, West Sussex. **12.** A car transporter carrying 9 new Mercedes turned over blocking 4 lanes of the M25 at Thurrock Lakeside and causing 6 mile tailbacks. Duncan Reidhill, 12, was killed when a garden wall collapsed on him at his home in Templemere, Weybridge. **16.** A Eurostar train from Waterloo to Brussels struck and killed a child at Calais. The M25 was closed in both directions from Leatherhead, Surrey, when a local man threatened to jump from a motorway bridge. **18.** A man fell to his death under a train in Lodge Lane, Addington. **20.** Lee Farrell, 11, of Bermondsey was killed by a street sweeper while riding his bike. **27.** Thames Trains were reprimanded after one of its trains went through a red light, forcing a motorist to swerve on a level crossing. **29.** A 7 year old girl died after being knocked down by a bus in Bethnal Green.

July 2000

10. A Northern Line train rolled backwards for half a mile through Chalk Farm tube station after the driver fell asleep at the controls. **11.** 2 engine covers came off an Airtours Airbus during takeoff at Gatwick and struck aircraft on the runway below. No one was hurt. **21.** The London Eye was closed after a drive wheel fell from the structure into the Thames. **23.** A gas leak in New Bridge Street near Blackfriars Bridge caused extensive disruption to traffic. **25.** Police closed roads in the Holland Park area following a second major gas leak. 3 year old Saulo Pinto Vallejo fell 50 feet from a block of flats and landed in a hedge suffering only minor cuts and bruises.

September 2000

4. Two passenger jets came within seconds of a mid-air collision above Central London. Disaster was averted through the intervention of an air traffic controller.

October 2000

8. A hit and run driver smashed into a crowded bus shelter near Kings Cross Station, injuring 12 people. **10.** A Boeing 767 plane carrying 146 people slid off a runway at Gatwick Airport. None of the passengers or crew were injured. **13.** A group of 23 schoolgirls were taken to hospital after a two-bus crash on the Victoria Embankment. None of the pupils were seriously injured. **15.** Fourteen-year-old Ahmed Ali-Adetuyi was pulled off a live line at Kington-Upon-Thames by two men who had been drinking in a local pub. He suffered serious burns but recovered. **17.** Four people died and 35 were injured when an express train travelling from Kings Cross to Leeds came off the tracks. The accident happened between Welham Green and Hatfield in Hertfordshire. **21.** The recovery operation to remove wreckage from the Hatfield rail crash site began. **22.** The people of Hatfield held a memorial service for the victims of the rail crash. More than 120 firefighters were called in to tackle an intense fire at a foam factory in Croydon. The fire at Zotefoam's warehouse raged for four and a half hours but nobody was hurt. **23.** Two police officers were injured when their car crashed into a parked vehicle and then careered into the central reservation of the North Circular in Brent Cross. **26.** Three people were injured in a train derailment near Virginia Water railway station in Surrey. **28.** Nineteen patients were evacuated from Cromwell Hospital in Kensington following a spillage of a chlorine-based chemical. **29.** Three men were killed and one seriously injured when a car collided with a mechanical road digger in Harrow. **30.** Three trains were involved in separate crashes as they hit trees blown across the tracks.

November 2000

6. A family of four were forced to leap 50ft to escape after a suspected arson attack at their home in Luton. **16.** Nineteen elderly women tourists fell to the bottom of an escalator after it stopped suddenly on the London Underground. Three were taken to hospital to be treated for their injuries.

December 2000

13. 116 passengers were stranded for two hours on a British Airways jet after it slid off the runway at Heathrow and became stuck in the mud. Nobody was injured. **26.** Edson Mitchell, the London based head of Deutsche Bank's global markets division was killed in a plane crash in Maine in the USA. **28.** Charlotte Wilson, 27, from West London was shot dead in a massacre of 20 civilians by rebel forces in Burundi whilst working for Voluntary Services Overseas in Rwanda.

January 2001

2. Chris Coleman, captain of Fulham Football Team, suffered multiple fractures to his right leg that threatened his future as a professional footballer when he crashed his sports car. **28.** Ten people were killed and 33 seriously injured when a Land Rover careered off the M62 in Yorkshire down a railway embankment and into the path of an approaching express train. The express train was derailed but remained upright and continued to move forward, colliding with an oncoming coal train.

March 2001

12. Eight passengers were injured when two rush-hour trains 'clipped' each other just outside Hither Green, when they both headed for the same track.

15. Eleven people were injured when a coach crashed into a branch of Boots the Chemist in Regent Street, near Oxford Circus.

May 2001

1. A six-car train smashed into the buffers at Charing Cross station, causing extensive damage to both the train and the station.

ARTS, MEDIA AND HERITAGE

June 2000

1. The Prince of Wales unveiled a monument at Victoria Embankment in memory of those who lost their lives in the Royal Navy's Fleet Air arm. **8.** The Millennium Bridge, which spans the Thames between St. Paul's and the Tate Modern and cost £18.2m to construct, was officially opened with a fireworks display. **9.** A bronze bust of the Queen Mother was unveiled in St. Paul's Cathedral. **10.** The Millennium Bridge opened to the public but was closed periodically throughout the weekend because it wobbled when large numbers of people crossed simultaneously. **13.** The Millennium Bridge was closed indefinitely for structural work. 200 travellers camped on Hampton Court seriously disrupting the music festival that was due to reach its peak. **14.** The BBC lost the right to show premiership football highlights after ITV paid £183m for the footage. Pieres Yves Gerbeau, Chief Executive of the Millennium Dome, revealed plans to cut jobs in an effort to save £10m. **21.** Victoria Russell, from Hackney, won the BP Portrait Award for her work 'Two Women in White'. **26.** Managers of the Millennium Dome shared £2.5m as an incentive to stop them leaving the project. **27.** The Tate Modern had its millionth visitor, six weeks after it opened. Gerard Hemsworth won the Royal Academy's £25,000 Charles Wollaston Award for his painting 'Between Heaven and Hell'. **28.** Barry Rutter won the £100,000 Creative Britons Award. **29.** Lords Cricket ground had its first ever musical interlude when Jools Holland and Jamaican superstars 'Third World' played during the lunch break of the 1st day of England's 2nd Test against the West Indies.

July 2000

1. 100,000 people descended on Finsbury Park for the annual Gay Pride celebration. **4.** British tennis player Tim Henman lost to the Australian Mark Philippoussis in the 4th round at Wimbledon. **8.** The fourth Harry Potter book 'Harry Potter and the Goblet of Fire' was released, crowds queued on

540 Events of the Year

Tottenham Court Road all night to secure copies. Venus Williams won the women's final at Wimbledon. **9.** Pete Sampras won the men's final at Wimbledon. **10.** It was revealed that flooding over the Easter period would set back the Tate Britain's £32m Millennium arts project by up to 6 months. BBC Director Greg Dyke revealed plans to cut 1,000 jobs and save £750m. **11.** A service was held at St. Paul's Cathedral to celebrate the life of the Queen Mother. **15.** 10 volunteers were imprisoned in a house in East London as Big Brother, Channel Four's hit reality TV show, was launched. **17.** It was confirmed that a £3m fountain to commemorate Diana Princess of Wales was to be built in one of London's Royal Parks. **19.** A pageant was held in celebration of the Queen Mother's 100th birthday. Richmond Council was forced to pay an £11m debt run up by Richmond Theatre. **20.** The National Gallery announced it was to renovate its entrance at a cost of £15m. **25.** Westminster Council banned a video display by the artist Alison Jackson, featuring a Princess Diana look-alike gesturing obscenely, which was to be displayed on a 40 ft screen in Leicester Square. **27.** The Millennium Dome was sold to the Japanese bank Nomura for £105m, less than one seventh of the cost of the project.

September 2000

6. A fifth emergency payment was authorised by the Millennium Commission to prevent the immediate closure of the Millennium Dome. The payment was granted on the condition that the takeover deal agreed with Nomura, the Japanese bank, went ahead. **10.** The Millennium Dome was threatened with early closure after the withdrawal of the £105 million Japanese bid for the Greenwich site. **12.** The 2,000-year-old charred remains of a female gladiator were unearthed at a burial ground in Southwark. **13.** The Millennium Commission agreed to honour the promise of a £47 million payment to the Dome despite the collapse of the takeover deal with Nomura. **17.** It was revealed that Lord Falconer and directors of the Millennium Dome, could face action under company law after publication of a report by PricewaterhouseCoopers. The report showed that the financial records of the Dome were in disarray and that the Dome was insolvent at the time it was awarded the most recent lottery emergency payment. **27.** Lord Falconer admitted that he has misled Parliament during the summer, over the state of the project's finances.

October 2000

5. It was announced that the £32.3 million redevelopment of Tate Britain would open months later than expected, in October 2001, because of a plumbing accident at Easter. **8.** A public meeting was held in Notting Hill where residents' groups called for an end to the Notting Hill Festival which they insisted increased crime levels in the area. **9.** The Government's financial adviser, Lazard, recommended that the Millennium Dome should be demolished to maximise returns on the sale of the site. **11.** Dulwich Picture Gallery received three valuable miniature 17th and 18th century portraits from an anonymous donor. **16.** The Barbican Centre announced a multi-million pound, four-year plan to redesign its public areas. **23.** Work started on the £15 million Hampstead Theatre, due to be completed in 2002, which is to be the first producing theatre to be built in London since the National in 1976. **24.** Tate Modern, which opened in May 2000 announced that it had attracted over 3 million visitors, meaning it had already surpassed the 2000 total reached by the capital's third most popular attraction Madame Tussaud's. Thousands of people had their trips on the London Eye cancelled following a computer problem that prevented it opening. **25.** The designers of the London Eye, David Marks and Julia Barfield, received a special commendation for 'outstanding achievement' in the Prince Philip designers awards scheme. **30.** The Millennium Wheel was closed after 6 of the 32 capsules suffered glass damage during storms.

November 2000

1. The Millennium Dome announced a record number of visitors totalling 650,000 in October. **2.** Pierre-Yves Gerbeau announced that an ice rink would be installed in the Millennium Dome in December. **5.** Peckham's new £4.5 million public library won the £20,000 Stirling Prize for Architecture. **6.** Hundreds of people protested at £18 million of cuts to services in Hackney by blockading Hackney Town Hall. Transport Minister, Lord Macdonald, agreed to new legislation that would give local authorities the right to charge utilities up-front fees for every day that they dig up a stretch of road. **8.** Culture Secretary Chris Smith announced that the Natural History Museum would be given £6 million of Government funding to modernise its palaeontology building and the British Museum was to get £500,000. **16.** The Legacy consortium bidding for the Millennium Dome threatened to pull out unless the Government made a decision on their offer by noon the following day. **27.** A rare manuscript by the 18th-Century composer Felix Mendelssohn was found in West London after lying untouched in a drawer for 50 years. Deputy Mayor Nicky Gavron became the GLA representative on the London Advisory Committee (LAC) of English Heritage. **28.** It was announced that the London Eye was to be illuminated in a flood of rainbow colours in the run-up to Christmas. Madonna held her first live concert in the UK for seven years at the Brixton Academy. **29.** The Queen opened a new £32 million headquarters for the Royal Academy of Dramatic Art (RADA) in London's Bloomsbury. The final of the Miss World contest, held at the Millennium Dome, was won by Miss India, Priyanka Chopra.

December 2000

1. Kylie Minogue switched on the laser lights which were to light up the London Eye in all the colours of the rainbow throughout the Christmas period. **6.** The Queen opened the new £100 million Great Court Development at the British Museum. **16.** The world's longest running play, The Mousetrap, celebrated its 20,000th performance. **21.** It was announced that Swedish dancer and director Matz Skoog was to succeed Derek Deane as Artistic Director of the English National Ballet. He is due to take up this position in September 2001. **31.** The Millennium Dome closed for the final time with the news that more than 6.5 million people had visited the dome in the past year.

January 2001

11. BBC news chief Tony Hall was appointed executive director of the Royal Opera House in succession to Michael Kaiser. **18.** The Natural History Museum pleaded guilty to breaching safety regulations after displaying radioactive rocks in its mineral display.

February 2001

11. Sir Denys Lasdun, the designer of the National Theatre, died aged 86. **15.** Andrew Lloyd Webber and Ben Elton's The Beautiful Game won Best Musical at the Critics' Choice Theatre Awards 2000. **22.** The public viewing for an auction of the contents of the Millennium Dome officially got underway.

March 2001

2. Journalist and author John Diamond died after a four-year battle with cancer. **6.** It was announced that the Hackney Empire was to be restored following a £1.3 million donation from businessman Sir Alan Sugar. **14.** A photograph of Charles Dickens, dating from the early 1850s was discovered during a routine valuation at a London house. **15.** The £23 million music venue Ocean, which has a capacity of over 2,100 opened in Hackney. It was funded partly by the National Lottery as part of a plan to regenerate the area. **22.** The Royal Shakespeare Company was awarded an increase of over £2.5 million a year to its annual Arts Council grant. The increase, effective in April 2002, will increase its subsidy to £12.7 million. **30.** An unexploded bomb caused the closure of the London Eye after builders dredged up a wartime shell from under Hungerford Bridge. It was announced that a third National Audit inquiry into the Millennium Dome would be launched.

April 2001

1. Jacques Herzog and Pierre de Meuron, the architects who turned Bankside power station into Tate Modern, were awarded the $100,000 Pritzker Prize which is awarded to architects who have made 'significant contributions to humanity'. **29.** A concert was held in Trafalgar Square, attended by Nelson Mandela, to celebrate the freedom of South Africa. **30.** Nelson Mandela reopened Southwark Cathedral after a £10 million redevelopment.

May 2001

1. The Victoria and Albert Museum announced that it would drop its entry charges from December 2001. **2.** The National Gallery acquired its first ever Scottish painting, The Archers, an 18th century portrait of two brothers by the Scottish master Henry Raeburn. The Science Museum announced that it would drop its entry charges from December 2001. **11.** Visitor figures for Tate Modern's first year showed that it was the most popular museum of contemporary art in the world and the third most popular visitor attraction in Britain.

CRIME AND LEGAL AFFAIRS

June 2000

1. Ade Adegunloye, 26, was jailed for 5 years for assaulting a female student at knifepoint while she showered. A 20 year old woman was raped at knifepoint in Haggerston Park before being forced by her attackers to withdraw money from a cash point. **2.** Eden Strang, who attacked a group of churchgoers with a samurai sword in November 1999, was found guilty by reason of insanity of the charges brought against him at the Old Bailey. He was committed to a mental institution for an indefinite period. A new initiative launched by the Metropolitan Police seeks to offer advice and support to Police Officers who use drugs rather than instant dismissal. **4.** Jaap Bornkamp, 52, was stabbed to death in New Cross during what Police believe to be a homophobic attack. **7.** An armed man held his 9 month old daughter hostage for 18 hours at his home in Winchmore Hill. **8.** The Home Secretary, Jack Straw, announced the formation of a central agency to treat drug addiction. Thieves broke into the £2m Kensington home of the pop singer Madonna and stole a bag. **9.** Vice Cards advertising prostitutes in West End phone boxes are to be made illegal under measures revealed by the Home Office. A 21 year old pregnant woman was shot in the stomach on Cranbrook Road, Illford. **14.** Tory MP Julie Kirkbride was disturbed in her home by an armed burglar. Jack Straw unveiled plans to extend the confiscation of property as a penalty for an increased range of crimes. A 13 year old boy from Camberwell pleaded guilty to multiple charges of armed robbery. He was given 2 years probation. **15.** Sergeant Belinda Sinclair, who brought sex discrimination charges against the Met, accepted a £10,000 out of court settlement and retired on health grounds. **16.** The Petrol Retailers Association claimed illegal, low grade petrol was being sold by retailers around London at high street prices. Scotland Yard issued an appeal to catch a serial rapist who attacked a 26 year old woman in Homerton in the latest of a series of attacks stretching back to 1998. **19.** John Pitkin, 35, was jailed for 10 years for manslaughter and aggravated burglary. Albert Aldgun, one of Pitkin's victims, died of a heart attack hours after he confronted the burglar at his home in Finsbury Park. A report by Scotland Yard revealed only 255 out of its 13,929 officers and civil staff were freemasons. Colin Bainbridge was jailed for a minimum period of 22 years for the rape and murder of 9 year old Laura Kane in August 1999. Ricky Rising, 19, of Plaistow was shot dead in a pub at 2.15 in the afternoon. **20.** Football Players Thierry Henry, Emmanuel Petit and Patrick Vieira of Arsenal and Marcel Desailly, Frank Leboeuf and Didier Deschamps of Chelsea were put under armed protection after Dutch Police uncovered a plot to murder them by Islamic terrorists. 18 year old Christopher Peterkin was jailed for life for kicking Zardasht Draey, 19, to death outside his home in Fulham. Paul Fursman, a lawyer, was jailed for 3 months and banned from driving for 5 years after pleading guilty to two charges of drink driving. **23.** Graham Thomas of Muswell Hill died after being beaten by a gang with baseball bats. **26.** Melanic Robinson, 20, of Hackney was shot dead while at the wheel of his BMW by the passenger of a motorbike. Scotland Yard came under the democratic control of the Metropolitan Police Authority. Two British Airways staff were arrested after brawling in front of travellers in Heathrow's terminal 1. **29.** Bod Russell, the Libral Democrat MP for Colchester, was mugged at knifepoint in Southwark. **30.** The trial of James Ponting ended. He was sent to Three Bridges regional secure unit indefinitely after severing his mother's head with a combat knife. Christopher Dubbery was jailed for 7 years after killing Austin French with a stolen car in the City of London. Damir Dokic, father of the Australian tennis player Jelena Dokic, attacked journalists at Wimbledon. No charges were pressed.

July 2000

1. 8 year old Sarah Payne was abducted while walking near her home in Kingston, West Sussex. **3.** 4 schoolboys were arrested after smashing up machinery worth £200,000 in a works yard in Tolworth, Surrey. **5.** 6 men were arrested in connection with the stabbing of 3 asylum seekers. **6.** Euan Blair, son of the Prime Minister, was arrested drunk and incapable in Leicester Square. Ronnie Knight, the former husband of the actress Barbara Windsor, was fined £200 for shoplifting goods from a north London supermarket. **7.** Kevin Cobb, 38, a male nurse, was given 7 life sentences for killing a colleague and drugging and raping 2 patients. **10.** A woman was raped by an armed burglar who broke into her flat in Notting Hill. Scotland Yard unveiled plans for a 24 hour fast response team to secure serious crime sites and improve evidence gathering. **11.** Police figures revealed crime in the capital rose by 12.6% in the preceding year. **12.** Justice Cazalet gave doctors permission to discontinue the artificial support of a brain damaged child's life, contrary to the parents' wishes. **13.** Police evicted hundreds of travellers from illegal camps in Horton Park, near Epsom. **14.** Anthony Burt, 63, was sentenced to a 6 month suspended jail sentence for failing to give his son a Christian burial after he dumped the boy's remains on a local rubbish dump. Dariusz Turek, a solicitor, was given a 6 month suspended sentence for assaulting 2 guests at a law society ball. Police seized £7m worth of heroin hidden in a Vauxhall Cavalier in Greenford. **17.** The body of 8 year old Sarah Payne was discovered concealed in woodland in West Sussex. The life sentences of Raphael Rowe, Michael Davis and Randolph Johnson, the "M25 Three", were overturned when Lord Justice Mantell ruled that their convictions for murder were unsafe. **18.** Police blamed the 40% increase in robberies in the capital on a surge of teenage crime. **19.** A bomb planted beside train tracks in Ealing was destroyed by Police in a controlled explosion. Aiden Morley, 26, was beaten to death by a gang in an Islington street. **20.** A security guard delivering money to a bank in Stoke Newington was shot in the leg by masked robbers. **21.** John Shire was cleared of causing death by dangerous driving over the death of Lee Sheekey who was crushed under the wheels of Mr Shire's bus in July 1999. He was fined £750 and given 8 points on his license. Scotland Yard drafted in 160 extra officers to help with enquiries into 7 murders and 21 attempted murders linked to Yardie gangs in London. Murder Squad detectives began the search for 20 year old Polish student Iwona Kaminska. **22.** A woman was raped in Notting Hill on the Grand Union Canal towpath by at least 3 men while their girlfriends reportedly cheered them on. Monty Jackson of Harrow Road Wembley was shot dead when a gang robbed his jewellery shop. **24.** Stephane Dupuis from Brixton was stabbed through the heart and killed when he tried to pursue robbers who had attacked his friend. **26.** A man was injured when a police car crashed demolishing a 10 ft wall in St. Matthews road, Brixton. **27.** A woman was in critical condition after being repeatedly run over in Woodbury Grove, North London. A gunman fired shots at 2 unarmed policemen in Croydon after they tried to stop his car.

August 2000

1. A number of people were injured, one seriously, when gunmen sprayed eight young people with automatic gunfire outside a club in Peckham. **11.** Claire Marsh, 18, of West London was charged with rape, indecently assaulting a woman and conspiracy to commit a robbery on the banks of the Grand Union Canal in Ladbroke Grove in July. She was later convicted. **22.** Paul Trotman, an auxiliary nurse at St George's Hospital in Tooting was mugged and stabbed with his surgical scissors as he was returning from a break. **28.** Two doormen were injured in a shooting outside a nightclub in Essex after trying to break up a fight. **29.** Greg Watson, 21, was stabbed to death in an unprovoked attack at Notting Hill Carnival. A nineteen-year-old man was later charged with his murder. Josephine Martorana, her 18-year-old son and his girlfriend were seriously injured in a shooting in Hoddesdon, Hertfordshire when two men robbed them of their Rolex watches. Mrs Martorana later died in hospital and three men were arrested in connection with her murder.

September 2000

8. Kellie Lyons, 17, and her sister Jean, 19 of North London, were jailed for eight and ten years after befriending an elderly widow from Finsbury and beating her to death with an iron bar in order to steal her savings. **19.** The body of Tim Cressman, a 39-year-old businessman, was discovered at his flat in Fulham. His girlfriend, Jane Andrews, a former aide to the Duchess of York, was later arrested for his murder. **20.** The headquarters of MI6 was damaged when it came under terrorist attack. Two explosions from a rocket-propelled grenade launcher, hit the eighth floor, causing some structural damage. Nobody was injured. **21.** Jane Andrews was arrested by police on suspicion of murdering her boyfriend, Tim Cressman. **29.** Police Constable Alan Paul from Luton, was jailed for five years for raping a young woman who had passed out during a party. **30.** Northumberland Park School in Tottenham became the first school in Britain to have its own policeman stationed on site in an attempt to cut crime and build links between pupils and police.

October 2000

3. Tangor Gokkusu, 16, was murdered by four youths who slashed him across the throat as he stepped off a bus in the city. **5.** The key witness in the Kenneth Noyle road rage case, Alan DeCabral, was murdered in a hitman-style shooting in a car park in Ashford, Kent. **7.** Suhail Rashid of Harrow, North London, was jailed for three and a half years for posing as a doctor at Cambridge University to persuade vulnerable foreign students to submit to intimate medical examinations. **8.** A female doctor was suspended from Basildon Hospital, pending police investigation into a suspected string of mercy killings at the Essex hospital. The man accused of murdering TV presenter Jill Dando in April 1999, Barry Bulsara, was committed for trial. **12.** Robert Sclare, a taxidermist with a shop in Islington, was prosecuted for illegally selling a host of stuffed endangered species including tigers with their litters and leopards. He was later jailed for six months. **13.** The Metropolitan Police Authority awarded the parents of murdered black teenager Stephen Lawrence £320,000 as compensation. Two more people were arrested in connection with an investigation into alleged corruptly awarded contracts by the Millennium Dome operator, NMEC. **14.** Police seized a total of 800 products made from tigers and other endangered species from a Chinese company in Soho. Mohamed Al Fayed lost his bid to see CIA court documents relating to the crash which killed Diana, Princess of Wales and his son Dodi. **16.** David Myers, a 20-year-old Jewish student, was stabbed more than 20 times in an unprovoked attack whilst travelling on a bus in Stamford Hill. The police, treating the case as racist, later arrested and charged Nabil Ould Eddin, 27. **17.** The High Court ruled that the body of James Hanratty, who was hanged in 1962 for the A6 murder, should be exhumed 'in the interests of justice'. **18.** Three boxes of Semtex explosives and a detonation cord were stolen from an RAF van in a hotel car park in Kent. A psychiatric patient with a range of violent convictions absconded from Cane Hill secure unit in south London. **19.** The Metropolitan Police announced plans to fit more than 2,900 incident data recorders (black boxes) into police cars in the next three years to record accidents involving police cars. Sixty-year-old John Pettit was stabbed to death in Pinner, North London, after disturbing a burglar in his home and chasing him across gardens. A man was later arrested and charged with his murder. **20.** Evans-Appiah, an anaesthetist from Leyton, East London, was found guilty of 17 charges of medical incompetence and neglect. **23.** A man was arrested in connection with the murder of John Pettit in Pinner on October 19. Vincent Eggleston, 58, was jailed for seven years after being found guilty of sexually abusing two 14-year-old boys from Pinehurst Children's Home in Camberley. **24.** The Metropolitan Police revealed that the number of 24-hour stations had dropped from 150 in January to 74 in August. **25.** Figures from Scotland Yard revealed that a quarter of crimes committed in London were committed by black people even though they only make up approximately 10 per cent of the city's population. The majority of the crimes committed by black people were carried out by children and teenagers. **26.** It was announced that the Metropolitan Police are to be issued with Polaroid cameras as a way of instantly recording evidence at a crime scene. Sergeant Peter Solley, a highly praised member of the Stephen Lawrence investigation team, was suspended for the alleged rape of a black community worker. He was later charged. An Albanian man was seriously injured after being beaten with a baseball bat by a gang of men in a row over a parking space in Wood Green. **27.** A 15-year-old girl was abducted at knifepoint from a street in South London by two men and subjected to a four hour sex ordeal. A 47-year-old man was found tortured to death in his home in Westbourne Grove. **28.** A police hunt began for a schoolboy, believed to be only 12, suspected of five sex attacks in South London. **30.** Police shot dead a man armed with two knives following a 10-hour siege in Upper Holloway, North London.

November 2000

1. Robert Stewart was jailed for life for bludgeoning his Asian cellmate to death in a racist attack at the Feltham Young Offenders Institution. **2.** Two dangerous psychiatric patients escaped from a north-west London hospital. Wade Hewitt, 26, was stabbed to death by two youths on a bus in Barking. **3.** Three members of the Wandsworth CID were arrested under suspicion of perverting the course of justice, one of whom also faced charges of indecent assault. Twelve years after he was jailed for life, John Duffy, dubbed the Railway Rapist for a number of rapes and attacks in and around London in the 80s, appeared at the Old Bailey to name his accomplice as David Mulcahy. **4.** One man had his nose cut off and another received a gunshot wound to the head in an attack outside a nightclub in Hounslow. **6.** Michael Ashley from Brockley in South London, a blackmailer who threatened to poison Sainsbury's foodstuffs unless the company paid him £150,000 was jailed for five years. **7.** A six-man gang used a JCB digger to try to smash into the concrete vault in the Millennium Dome which houses the De Beers Millennium Diamond collection. However, Scotland Yard and Flying Squad officers, acting on a tip off, were waiting for the raid and arrested a number of the robbers on the scene. Altaf Gani of Acton and Daniel Francis of Hanwell, members of an armed gang who robbed wealthy victims in the West End of their watches and jewellery were jailed for 10 and 12 years respectively. **8.** Detectives questioned 12 men held in connection with the attempted robbery at the Millennium Dome. **10.** It was revealed that police patrolling the streets of London were to start openly wearing bulletproof vests. Linda Bayfield, a childminder from Addiscombe was charged with the murder of eight-month-old Joshua Osborne. Mohammed Sati of Islington, was jailed for 13 years after trying to smuggle £4.8 million of heroin into Britain in a child's cot. A convoy of lorries and tractors, protesting at rising fuel prices left the North East for London. **11.** Security officers foiled a plot by the Real IRA to drive a horsebox packed with explosives into London. **13.** The Metropolitan Police confirmed that it would consider potential officers with minor convictions for the first time. **15.** Jeffrey Archer appeared at Bow Street magistrates' and was ordered to face trial on 12 December 2000 accused of perverting the course of justice. Detectives investigating the disappearance of one of Princess Diana's most valuable wedding gifts arrested her former butler, Harold Brown. Police voiced their fears that a serial sex killer was preying on London women after the disappearance of a fourth woman in west London. **16.** Three prison officers were suspended and another resigned from Pentonville Prison over allegations involving sex, drugs and violence at the jail. Madhusudan Shivadikar, a doctor at Finchley Alternative Medical Centre, whose negligence caused 60 patients to contract hepatitis B, was struck off the medical register for serious professional misconduct. **22.** Fraud officers announced that they were to widen their investigations into corruption at the Millennium Dome to cover four contracts involving the Dome's construction phase. Gilles Van Colle, who was due to give vital evidence in a fraud trial was found shot in the driving seat of his car in an alley way in Mill Hill. **27.** Ten-year-old Damilola Taylor bled to death on a stairwell on a Peckham estate after being stabbed. A project was launched whereby convicted offenders were offered the opportunity of joining a gang cleaning up rubbish on the River Thames rather than go to prison. **30.** The Daily Mail offered a £50,000 award for information leading to the killer or killers of Nigerian schoolboy Damilola Taylor. Armed robbers escaped with £800,000 worth of Gucci watches after storming a shipping warehouse in West London. Yardie gun gangs left four men seriously wounded after a series of shooting with automatic weapons in three separate incidents around London.

December 2000

1. PC Richard Sams was jailed for three years after spraying a motorist with CS gas for driving in the bus lane. **2.** Police hunting the killers of 10-year-old Damilola Taylor arrested two black youths aged 13 and a black woman aged 39, who were later released. Thousands of campaigners for the cancellation of Third World debt gathered in London. **3.** Police arrested a man in connection with the murder of Suzy Lamplugh, an estate agent from Richmond, in July 1986. He was later released. **5.** Police began an investigation into child abuse allegations at the London Oratory School in Fulham. A number of children had claimed that they had been abused by Father David Martin, a former chaplain at the school, who died of a suspected Aids-related disease in 1998. **8.** Gurpal Virdi, the Sikh officer wrongly accused of sending racist hate mail and dismissed from the Metropolitan Police won £150,000 from an employment tribunal. **11.** Detectives began to search a disused brickworks in Worcestershire for the body of estate agent Suzy Lamplugh who disappeared in 1986 after arranging to meet a client at a house in Fulham. **12.** Jeffrey Archer appeared at the Old Bailey and pleaded not guilty to five charges including perjury and perverting the course of justice. **14.** Eleven youths were arrested in dawn raids in connection to the murder of Damilola Taylor. All were later released on police bail. Athlete Diane Modahl lost her damages action over a ban imposed in the wake of drug-taking allegations. **16.** Details of a joint initiative between the Metropolitan Police and bus operators Stagecoach were released whereby police spy cameras are to be fitted to London buses in an attempt to cut crime on London transport. **17.** The unidentified body of a woman, who had been sawn in half, was pulled from the Thames near Battersea. The woman was later identified as Zoe Parker, 24, from Feltham. **18.** Eight football supporters were arrested after clashes following the London derby between Tottenham and Arsenal. **19.** Four armed robbers escaped with thousands of pounds worth of cash and jewellery after breaking into a jewellers in Hayes. **20.** Forty-five people were arrested after bringing the London Eye to a standstill by entering two pods on the attraction and protesting about political prisoners in Turkey. **21.** Robert Loftus, the former head of security at Harrods, was arrested in connection with the theft of audio tapes used during the Neil Hamilton libel trial. **27.** Police announced that more than 400 people had been arrested in the biggest drugs operation ever mounted in London. **29.** A crazed Kenyan passenger forced his way onto the flight deck of a British Airways jumbo jet carrying 380 passengers, causing it to go out of control and go into a steep dive. Disaster was averted when staff managed to overpower and restrain the man.

546 Events of the Year

January 2001

2. Two gunmen burst into the Trocadero centre in Piccadilly, overpowered two guards and escaped with an undisclosed amount of money from the huge Funland amusement arcade. 8. Judge Ann Goddard was injured at the Old Bailey after being attacked by a man accused of murder. 9. Two teenagers were arrested in connection with the murder of Damilola Taylor. They were later released. Police figures revealed that the number of Londoners caught drink-driving over Christmas and the New Year increased by over 16% in 2000, compared to an 11% rise nationally. Two armed robbers raided the Edgware Road branch of the TSB and escaped with £20,000. 10. Nudist campaigner Vincent Bethell walked away from court (naked) after being cleared of causing a public nuisance at Southwark Crown Court. 11. Barry Michael George, the man accused of killing TV presenter Jill Dando appeared briefly at the Old Bailey to plead not guilty. 18. Three year old Najiyah Hussain died after a mix up at Newham General Hospital when she was given nitrous oxide instead of oxygen after suffering a fit.

February 2001

1. Armed police raided an address in Ealing and arrested five men for the suspected manufacture of pipe bombs and recovered a large amount of bomb-making equipment. 2. Five women from London were arrested for attempting to smuggle drugs out of Jamaica on London-bound flights. 12. Four members of the Independent Advisory Group (IAG), set up to advise the Metropolitan Police on community relations, resigned claiming that it was 'just a talking-shop'. Edward Crowley was jailed for life at the Old Bailey for the murder of twelve-year-old Diego Piniero-Villar in Covent Garden on 7 May 2000. 15. Forty-seven London police officers began legal action against Scotland Yard after being accused in an official report of being racist bullies. 18. Detectives investigating the murder of Stephen Lawrence arrested two women on suspicion of attempting to pervert the course of justice. The pair were later released on bail until a date in March. A serving CID officer in the Met was arrested on suspicion of drug offences, including possession of a Class B drug with intent to supply. Figures published by the Home Secretary Jack Straw showed that black people were five times more likely than whites to be stopped and searched by police and that 60% of people arrested for robbery in London in 1999-2000 were black, who represent 7.5 per cent of the capital's population. Appeal Court judges unanimously overturned the libel jury's verdict in the Bruce Grobbelaar case over allegations in the Sun of match-fixing. The former Liverpool goalkeeper was stripped of his £85,000 libel award and branded corrupt by three judges. 19. Police made two further arrests in the long-running investigations of fraudulent contracts at the Millennium Dome. 20. Seven suspected members of an international drug cartel were arrested during dawn raids around London. 23. Special Branch officers foiled what was thought to be a plot to release the nerve gas Sarin on the London Underground by a Middle East group. 24. Police raided 52 brothels in Soho and arrested 28 people, in the largest crackdown on prostitution in many years. 25. Fourteen-year-old Stephen Menary, a Territorial Army cadet, lost his hand and his sight after disturbing a bomb planted at the Territorial Army barracks in White City by dissident Irish terrorists. 26. The trial of Barry Michael George, the man accused of murdering TV presenter Jill Dando opened at the Old Bailey. Detectives investigating the disappearance of London estate agent Suzy Lamplugh 15 years ago resumed a search of land close to an Army barracks in Worcestershire.

March 2001

1. The trial of Barry George was adjourned until 23 April. A second severed torso of a prostitute was discovered in a London waterway in less than two months. 4. A car bomb exploded outside the BBC Television Centre in West London, injuring a London Underground worker. The bomb was thought to be the work of the dissident Irish terrorist group the Real IRA. 5. The discovery of a third woman's body in London waterways in three months led to fears that a serial killer may be at large in London. 8. Police arrested three people in connection with the body found in the Thames two days earlier. 9. Peter Solley, a police sergeant who played a part in the investigation into the murder of Stephen Lawrence was charged with perjury during the Stephen Lawrence inquiry and nine counts of raping a black community worker. A nurse was arrested in connection with the suspicious deaths of four children at Wrexham Park Hospital in Berkshire. 16. Metropolitan Police Deputy Commissioner Ian Blair announced that 3,000 neighbourhood wardens were to be recruited to help police the streets of London. 17. Seven people suffered acid burns after two men returned to a pub in Twickenham after an argument with another group and sprayed strong sulphuric acid around the bar. 18. Police performed a controlled explosion on a suspicious vehicle outside the headquarters of the BBC that

Crime and Legal Affairs 547

later proved to be a false alarm. **20.** Almost 100 people suspected of carrying out racist and homophobic campaigns were arrested during a series of dawn raids across London. **31.** An immigration officer was arrested at London's Waterloo station after detectives seized seven kilos of cocaine valued at £500,000.

April 2001

2. ITN was forced to cancel its 10.30pm news broadcast after police became suspicious of a van abandoned outside the building. No bomb was found. **7.** A demonstration march was held in Bermondsey, South London, by the National Front. Forty-two year old Elizabeth Sherlock was run over and killed after trying to stop thieves stealing her handbag by jumping onto the bonnet of their car outside Euston station. Two people were later charged with her murder. **14.** A bomb, thought to be the work of the Real IRA, exploded on the doorstep of a Royal Mail sorting office in Hendon, south-west London. Nobody was injured. **19.** Figures released by Scotland Yard showed that street crime in London soared in 2000, with offences reaching the 50,000 mark for the first time. **20.** The body of murdered au pair Dana Prokesova was found after lying undiscovered in a garage for six weeks. **22.** Detectives investigating the murder of estate agent Suzy Lumpagh in 1986 prepared to search a forested hillside near Taunton in the hope of finding her body. **23.** The trial of Barry George, the man accused of murdering TV personality Jill Dando reconvened at the Old Bailey.

May 2001

2. London's May Day anti-capitalist protests saw 6,000 police on the streets of London. In total, more than 50 people were injured and more than 60 arrested. **7.** It was announced that, under a new initiative being set up in Southwark from September 2001, police would set up offices in urban comprehensives and patrol the school entrance and surrounding areas as pupils go home. **5.** A couple and their two children were found dead at their home in Harrow. A shotgun was recovered from the house and a police statement revealed that they were not looking for anyone else in connection with the murders. **7.** Ronnie Biggs returned to Britain from Brazil where he has been living since his escape from prison in 1965. He was immediately arrested and taken to top-security Belmarsh prison in south-east London. **8.** Claire Marsh, the 18 year old girl found guilty in August 2000 of the rape of a 37-year old woman beside the Grand Union canal in Ladbroke Grove, was sentenced to seven years in jail. **16.** Jane Andrews, the Duchess of York's former dresser, was jailed for life for the murder of her lover Tom Cressman, when he refused to marry her.

APPOINTMENTS AND RESIGNATIONS

June 2000

7. Ken Livingstone announced George Barlow as Chairman of the London Development agency and Len Duvall as Vice-Chairman.

23. Jimmy Knapp, general secretary of the Rail, Maritime and Transport Workers Union, was appointed to the Board of Transport for London.

July 2000

10. Yasmin Anwar was announced as the chair of the Cultural Strategy group for London.

14. Labour MP Jim Fitzpatrick stepped down as London Party Chairman.

17. Clive Hodson, director of London Buses, quit.

September 2000

6. David Quarmby was appointed Executive Chairman of the Millennium Dome.

October 2000

8. Anthony Mayer was appointed Chief Executive of the Greater London Authority.

10. Robert Kiley was appointed Commissioner of Transport for London.

12. Peter Hendy was appointed Director of Bus, Taxi and River Services in London.

23. Sara Thornton was appointed Assistant Chief Constable of Thames Valley Police.

November 2000

9. Acting Commissioner of Transport Bob Chilton resigned.

27. Deputy Mayor Nicky Gavron was appointed the Greater London Authority representative on the London Advisory Committee (LAC) of English Heritage.

December 2000

7. London Chambers of Commerce chief executive Simon Sperryn resigned.

FORTHCOMING EVENTS 2001-2002

2001

20 July-15 September BBC Henry Wood Promenade Concerts
1 September London Fashion Weekend (Natural History Museum)
2 September Brick Lane Festival
4-5 September City of London Flower Show (Guildhall)
14 September-11 November Martin Kippenberger (Whitechapel Art Gallery)
14 September-12 December Frank Auerbach (Royal Academy of Arts)
15-16 September River Thames Festival
16 September The Spitalfields Show (Old Spitalfields Market)
17 September-2 March Medieval Sculpture (Tate Britain)
20 September-16 December Surrealism: Desire Unbound (Tate Modern)
22 September Public Record Office Open Day: Victorian Times (Public Record Office)
22 September-16 December Rembrandt's Women (Royal Academy of Arts)
25 September-20 October 7th London Festival of Chamber Music
27-30 September 100% Design (Earls Court 2)
30 September Pearly Kings and Queens Harvest Festival (St Mary Le Bow Church)
1-31 October Black History Month (Public Record Office)
2-7 October Horse of the Year Show (Wembley Arena)
9-10 October RHS London Flower Show (Royal Horticultural Society Halls)
11 October International Ballroom Dancing Championships (Royal Albert Hall)
18 October – 6 January The Americans (Barbican Art Gallery)
18 October – 6 January Radical Fashion (Victoria and Albert Museum)
21 October Trafalgar Day Parade – The Sea Cadet Corps
24 October Quit Ceremony and Presentation of the Sheriffs of London (Royal Courts of Justice)
24 October – 13 January Pisanello: Painter to the Renaissance Court (National Gallery)
6 November – 20 January Turner Prize 2001 (Tate Britain)
10 November Lord Mayor's Firework Display (River Thames)
10 November Lord Mayor's Show (City of London)
11 November Remembrance Day Service and Parade
15 November – 13 January Andres Serrano – Placing Time and Evil (Barbican)
20 November – 18 December BBC Lunchtime Concerts (Temple Church)
29 November Spanish Riding School of Vienna (Wembley Arena)
November London Film Festival
4-6 December Online Information 2001 (Olympia)
11 December Rugby: The Varsity Match
24 December Christmas Eve (Guards Chapel)
25 December Christmas Day Services (St Martin-in-the-Fields Church)

2002

1 January The New Year's Day Parade (Parliament Square)
3-13 January 48th London Boat Show (Earls Court Exhibition Centre)
12-27 January London International Mime Festival
16-20 January Art 2002 (Business Design Centre)
28 January Chinese New Year Celebrations (Gerrard Street and Leicester Square)
17 February International Napoleonic Fair
18 February – 19 May American Sublime (Tate Britain)
2-3 March London International Dive Show
2-3 March Sailboat and Windsurf Show (Alexandra Palace)
March National Science Week (British Museum)
23 March Head of the River Race (River Thames)
7–10 May 2002 16th International Composer Festival (Royal Academy of Music)
May 2002 Covent Garden Festival
3 May – 18 August George Romney (1734-1802) (National Portrait Gallery)
17–19 March London Book Fair
5-16 April World Pianp Competition (South Bank)
14 April London Marathon

Forthcoming Events 2001-2002   549

18–19 May London Tattoo (Wembley Arena)
5-26 June Spitalfields Festival
20 June – 4 September The Dutch Italianates 1600-1700 (Dulwich Picture Gallery)
20 June – 15 September Lucian Freud (Tate Britain)
8 June Trooping the Colour – The Queen's Birthday Parade (Horse Guards Palace)

24 June – 7 July Wimbledon Lawn Tennis Championships
25 June – 11 July City of London Festival
19 July – 14 September BBC Henry Wood Promenade Concerts
6 August – 29 September Houses of Parliament Tour
25-26 August Western Union Notting Hill Carnival

ASTRONOMY
AND TIDES

ASTRONOMY AND TIDES

ASTRONOMICAL DATA

Lighting-up Time

The legal importance of sunrise and sunset is that the Road Vehicles Lighting Regulations 1989 (SI 1989 No. 1796) make use of the front and rear position lamps on vehicles compulsory during the period between sunset and sunrise. Headlamps on vehicles are required to be used during the hours of darkness on unlit roads or whenever visibility is seriously reduced. The hours of darkness are defined in these regulations as those between half an hour after sunset and half an hour before sunrise.

In all laws and regulations, sunset refers to the local sunset, i.e. the time at which the Sun sets at the place in question. This common-sense interpretation has been upheld by legal tribunals. Thus the necessity for providing for different latitudes and longitudes is evident.

Sunrise and Sunset

The times of sunrise and sunset are those when the Sun's upper limb, as affected by refraction, is on the true horizon of an observer at sea-level. Assuming the mean refraction to be 34', and the Sun's semi-diameter to be 16', the time given is that when the true zenith distance of the Sun's centre is 90°+34'+16' or 90° 50', or, in other words, when the depression of the Sun's centre below the true horizon is 50'. The upper limb is then 34' below the true horizon, but is brought there by refraction. An observer on a ship might see the Sun for a minute or so longer, because of the dip of the horizon, while another viewing the sunset over hills or mountains would record an earlier time. Nevertheless, the moment when the true zenith distance of the Sun's centre is 90° 50' is a precise time dependent only on the latitude and longitude of the place, and independent of its altitude above sea-level, the contour of its horizon, the vagaries of refraction or the small seasonal change in the Sun's semi-diameter; this moment is suitable in every way as a definition of sunset or sunrise for all statutory purposes.

Twilight

Light reaches us before sunrise and continues to reach us for some time after sunset. The interval between darkness and sunrise or sunset and darkness is call twilight. Astronomically speaking, twilight is considered to begin or end when the Sun's centre is 18' below the horizon, as no light from the Sun can then reach the observer. As thus defined, twilight may last several hours; in high latitudes at the summer solstice the depression of 18' is not reached, and twilight lasts from sunset to sunrise. The need for some sub-division of twilight is met by dividing the gathering darkness into four stages.

- Sunrise or sunset, as defined above
- Civil twilight, which begins or ends when the Sun's centre is 6' below the horizon. This marks the time when operations requiring daylight may commence or must cease. In England it varies from about 30 to 60 minutes after sunset and the same interval before sunrise
- Nautical twilight, which begins or ends when the Sun's centre is 12' below the horizon. This marks the time when it is, to all intents and purposes, completely dark
- Astronomical twilight, which begins or ends when the Sun's centre is 18' below the horizon. This marks theoretical perfect darkness. It is of little practical importance, especially if nautical twilight is tabulated

To assist observers the durations of civil, nautical and astronomical twilights are given at intervals of ten days. The beginning of a particular twilight is found by subtracting the duration from the time of sunrise, while the end is found by adding the duration to the time of sunset.

554 Astronomical Data

JANUARY 2002
SUNRISE AND SUNSET (GMT)

	0° 05'	51° 30'
	h m	h m
1	8 06	16 02
2	8 06	16 03
3	8 06	16 04
4	8 05	16 05
5	8 05	16 06
6	8 05	16 08
7	8 04	16 09
8	8 04	16 10
9	8 04	16 12
10	8 03	16 13
11	8 02	16 14
12	8 02	16 16
13	8 01	16 17
14	8 00	16 19
15	7 59	16 20
16	7 59	16 22
17	7 58	16 24
18	7 57	16 25
19	7 56	16 27
20	7 55	16 28
21	7 54	16 30
22	7 52	16 32
23	7 51	16 34
24	7 50	16 35
25	7 49	16 37
26	7 48	16 39
27	7 46	16 41
28	7 45	16 42
29	7 43	16 44
30	7 42	16 46
31	7 40	16 48

MOON PHASES

	d	h	m
Last Quarter	6	03	55
New Moon	13	13	29
First Quarter	21	17	46
Full Moon	28	22	50

DURATION OF TWILIGHT AT 51.5°N (MINUTES)

January	1st	11th	21st	31st
Civil	40	39	38	36
Nautical	83	81	79	76
Astronomical	123	121	118	115

FEBRUARY 2002
SUNRISE AND SUNSET (GMT)

	0° 05'	51° 30'
	h m	h m
1	7 39	16 49
2	7 37	16 51
3	7 36	16 53
4	7 34	16 55
5	7 33	16 57
6	7 31	16 59
7	7 29	17 00
8	7 27	17 02
9	7 26	17 04
10	7 24	17 06
11	7 22	17 08
12	7 20	17 10
13	7 18	17 11
14	7 17	17 13
15	7 15	17 15
16	7 13	17 17
17	7 11	17 19
18	7 09	17 21
19	7 07	17 22
20	7 05	17 24
21	7 03	17 26
22	7 01	17 28
23	6 59	17 30
24	6 57	17 31
25	6 55	17 33
26	6 52	17 35
27	6 50	17 37
28	6 48	17 38

MOON PHASES

	d	h	m
Last Quarter	4	13	33
New Moon	12	07	41
First Quarter	20	12	02
Full Moon	27	09	17

DURATION OF TWILIGHT AT 51.5°N (MINUTES)

February	1st	11th	21st	28th
Civil	36	35	34	33
Nautical	76	74	73	72
Astronomical	115	113	111	111

Astronomical Data

MARCH 2002
SUNRISE AND SUNSET (GMT)

	0° 05'	51° 30'
	h m	h m
1	6 46	17 40
2	6 44	17 42
3	6 42	17 44
4	6 40	17 45
5	6 37	17 47
6	6 35	17 49
7	6 33	17 51
8	6 31	17 52
9	6 29	17 54
10	6 26	17 56
11	6 24	17 58
12	6 22	17 59
13	6 20	18 01
14	6 17	18 03
15	6 15	18 05
16	6 13	18 06
17	6 10	18 08
18	6 08	18 10
19	6 06	18 11
20	6 04	18 13
21	6 01	18 15
22	5 59	18 16
23	5 57	18 18
24	5 55	18 20
25	5 52	18 21
26	5 50	18 23
27	5 48	18 25
28	5 45	18 27
29	5 43	18 28
30	5 41	18 30
31	5 39	18 32

MOON PHASES

	d	h	m
Last Quarter	6	01	24
New Moon	14	02	02
First Quarter	22	02	28
Full Moon	28	18	25

DURATION OF TWILIGHT AT 51.5°N (MINUTES)

March	1st	11th	21st	31st
Civil	34	33	33	34
Nautical	72	72	73	75
Astronomical	111	112	114	118

APRIL 2002
SUNRISE AND SUNSET (GMT)

	0° 05'	51° 30'
	h m	h m
1	5 36	18 33
2	5 34	18 35
3	5 32	18 37
4	5 30	18 38
5	5 27	18 40
6	5 25	18 42
7	5 23	18 43
8	5 21	18 45
9	5 18	18 47
10	5 16	18 48
11	5 14	18 50
12	5 12	18 52
13	5 10	18 53
14	5 07	18 55
15	5 05	18 57
16	5 03	18 58
17	5 01	19 00
18	4 59	19 02
19	4 57	19 03
20	4 55	19 05
21	4 53	19 07
22	4 50	19 08
23	4 48	19 10
24	4 46	19 12
25	4 44	19 13
26	4 42	19 15
27	4 40	19 17
28	4 38	19 18
29	4 37	19 20
30	4 35	19 22

MOON PHASES

	d	h	m
Last Quarter	4	15	29
New Moon	12	19	21
First Quarter	20	12	48
Full Moon	27	03	00

DURATION OF TWILIGHT AT 51.5°N (MINUTES)

April	1st	11th	21st	30th
Civil	34	35	36	38
Nautical	75	78	82	88
Astronomical	118	125	135	149

556 Astronomical Data

MAY 2002
SUNRISE AND SUNSET (GMT)

	0° 05'	51° 30'
	h m	h m
1	4 33	19 23
2	4 31	19 25
3	4 29	19 26
4	4 27	19 28
5	4 25	19 30
6	4 24	19 31
7	4 22	19 33
8	4 20	19 34
9	4 18	19 36
10	4 17	19 38
11	4 15	19 39
12	4 14	19 41
13	4 12	19 42
14	4 10	19 44
15	4 09	19 45
16	4 07	19 47
17	4 06	19 48
18	4 05	19 50
19	4 03	19 51
20	4 02	19 53
21	4 01	19 54
22	3 59	19 55
23	3 58	19 57
24	3 57	19 58
25	3 56	19 59
26	3 55	20 01
27	3 54	20 02
28	3 53	20 03
29	3 52	20 04
30	3 51	20 06
31	3 50	20 07

MOON PHASES

	d	h	m
Last Quarter	4	07	16
New Moon	12	10	45
First Quarter	19	19	42
Full Moon	26	11	51

DURATION OF TWILIGHT AT 51.5°N (MINUTES)

May	1st	11th	21st	31st
Civil	38	40	43	45
Nautical	88	95	103	112
Astronomical	149	170	212	TAN

TAN = twilight all night

JUNE 2002
SUNRISE AND SUNSET (GMT)

	0° 05'	51° 30'
	h m	h m
1	3 49	20 08
2	3 48	20 09
3	3 47	20 10
4	3 47	20 11
5	3 46	20 12
6	3 46	20 13
7	3 45	20 14
8	3 45	20 14
9	3 44	20 15
10	3 44	20 16
11	3 43	20 17
12	3 43	20 17
13	3 43	20 18
14	3 43	20 19
15	3 43	20 19
16	3 42	20 20
17	3 42	20 20
18	3 42	20 20
19	3 43	20 21
20	3 43	20 21
21	3 43	20 21
22	3 43	20 21
23	3 43	20 22
24	3 44	20 22
25	3 44	20 22
26	3 44	20 22
27	3 45	20 22
28	3 45	20 21
29	3 46	20 21
30	3 47	20 21

MOON PHASES

	d	h	m
Last Quarter	3	00	05
New Moon	10	23	46
First Quarter	18	00	29
Full Moon	24	21	42

DURATION OF TWILIGHT AT 51.5°N (MINUTES)

June	1st	11th	21st	30th
Civil	45	47	48	47
Nautical	112	119	122	120
Astronomical	TAN	TAN	TAN	TAN

TAN = twilight all night

Astronomical Data

JULY 2002
SUNRISE AND SUNSET (GMT)

	0° 05'		51° 30'	
	h	m	h	m
1	3	47	20	21
2	3	48	20	20
3	3	49	20	20
4	3	49	20	20
5	3	50	20	19
6	3	51	20	18
7	3	52	20	18
8	3	53	20	17
9	3	54	20	17
10	3	55	20	16
11	3	56	20	15
12	3	57	20	14
13	3	58	20	13
14	3	59	20	12
15	4	00	20	11
16	4	02	20	10
17	4	03	20	09
18	4	04	20	08
19	4	05	20	07
20	4	07	20	06
21	4	08	20	05
22	4	09	20	03
23	4	11	20	02
24	4	12	20	01
25	4	13	19	59
26	4	15	19	58
27	4	16	19	56
28	4	18	19	55
29	4	19	19	53
30	4	21	19	52
31	4	22	19	50

MOON PHASES

	d	h	m
Last Quarter	2	17	19
New Moon	10	10	26
First Quarter	17	04	47
Full Moon	24	09	07

DURATION OF TWILIGHT AT 51.5°N (MINUTES)

July	1st	11th	21st	31st
Civil	47	46	43	41
Nautical	120	113	104	96
Astronomical	TAN	TAN	211	175

TAN = twilight all night

AUGUST 2002
SUNRISE AND SUNSET (GMT)

	0° 05'		51° 30'	
	h	m	h	m
1	4	24	19	49
2	4	25	19	47
3	4	27	19	45
4	4	28	19	44
5	4	30	19	42
6	4	31	19	40
7	4	33	19	38
8	4	34	19	37
9	4	36	19	35
10	4	37	19	33
11	4	39	19	31
12	4	41	19	29
13	4	42	19	27
14	4	44	19	25
15	4	45	19	23
16	4	47	19	21
17	4	49	19	19
18	4	50	19	17
19	4	52	19	15
20	4	53	19	13
21	4	55	19	11
22	4	57	19	09
23	4	58	19	07
24	5	00	19	05
25	5	01	19	03
26	5	03	19	00
27	5	04	18	58
28	5	06	18	56
29	5	08	18	54
30	5	09	18	52
31	5	11	18	49

MOON PHASES

	d	h	m
Last Quarter	1	10	22
New Moon	8	19	15
First Quarter	15	10	12
Full Moon	22	22	29
Last Quarter	31	02	31

DURATION OF TWILIGHT AT 51.5°N (MINUTES)

August	1st	11th	21st	31st
Civil	41	38	37	35
Nautical	95	88	82	78
Astronomical	172	150	136	126

558 Astronomical Data

SEPTEMBER 2002
SUNRISE AND SUNSET (GMT)
0° 05' 51° 30'

	h	m	h	m
1	5	12	18	47
2	5	14	18	45
3	5	16	18	43
4	5	17	18	40
5	5	19	18	38
6	5	20	18	36
7	5	22	18	34
8	5	24	18	31
9	5	25	18	29
10	5	27	18	27
11	5	28	18	25
12	5	30	18	22
13	5	32	18	20
14	5	33	18	18
15	5	35	18	15
16	5	36	18	13
17	5	38	18	11
18	5	40	18	08
19	5	41	18	06
20	5	43	18	04
21	5	44	18	02
22	5	46	17	59
23	5	48	17	57
24	5	49	17	55
25	5	51	17	52
26	5	52	17	50
27	5	54	17	48
28	5	56	17	45
29	5	57	17	43
30	5	59	17	41

OCTOBER 2002
SUNRISE AND SUNSET (GMT)
0° 05' 51° 30'

	h	m	h	m
1	6	01	17	39
2	6	02	17	36
3	6	04	17	34
4	6	05	17	32
5	6	07	17	30
6	6	09	17	27
7	6	10	17	25
8	6	12	17	23
9	6	14	17	21
10	6	15	17	18
11	6	17	17	16
12	6	19	17	14
13	6	20	17	12
14	6	22	17	10
15	6	24	17	08
16	6	26	17	05
17	6	27	17	03
18	6	29	17	01
19	6	31	16	59
20	6	32	16	57
21	6	34	16	55
22	6	36	16	53
23	6	38	16	51
24	6	39	16	49
25	6	41	16	47
26	6	43	16	45
27	6	45	16	43
28	6	46	16	41
29	6	48	16	39
30	6	50	16	37
31	6	52	16	36

MOON PHASES

	d	h	m
New Moon	7	03	10
First Quarter	13	18	08
Full Moon	21	13	59
Last Quarter	29	17	03

MOON PHASES

	d	h	m
New Moon	6	11	18
First Quarter	13	05	33
Full Moon	21	07	20
Last Quarter	29	05	28

DURATION OF TWILIGHT AT 51.5°N (MINUTES)

September	1st	11th	21st	31st
Civil	35	34	33	33
Nautical	78	75	73	72
Astronomical	125	119	114	112

DURATION OF TWILIGHT AT 51.5°N (MINUTES)

October	1st	11th	21st	31st
Civil	33	33	34	35
Nautical	72	72	73	74
Astronomical	112	111	111	113

Astronomical Data

NOVEMBER 2002
SUNRISE AND SUNSET (GMT)

	0° 05'		51° 30'	
	h	m	h	m
1	6	53	16	34
2	6	55	16	32
3	6	57	16	30
4	6	59	16	28
5	7	00	16	27
6	7	02	16	25
7	7	04	16	23
8	7	06	16	22
9	7	08	16	20
10	7	09	16	19
11	7	11	16	17
12	7	13	16	16
13	7	14	16	14
14	7	16	16	13
15	7	18	16	11
16	7	20	16	10
17	7	21	16	09
18	7	23	16	07
19	7	25	16	06
20	7	26	16	05
21	7	28	16	04
22	7	30	16	03
23	7	31	16	02
24	7	33	16	01
25	7	34	16	00
26	7	36	15	59
27	7	37	15	58
28	7	39	15	57
29	7	40	15	56
30	7	42	15	56

DECEMBER 2002
SUNRISE AND SUNSET (GMT)

	0° 05'		51° 30'	
	h	m	h	m
1	7	43	15	55
2	7	45	15	54
3	7	46	15	54
4	7	47	15	53
5	7	49	15	53
6	7	50	15	52
7	7	51	15	52
8	7	52	15	52
9	7	53	15	52
10	7	55	15	51
11	7	56	15	51
12	7	57	15	51
13	7	58	15	51
14	7	58	15	51
15	7	59	15	51
16	8	00	15	52
17	8	01	15	52
18	8	02	15	52
19	8	02	15	52
20	8	03	15	53
21	8	03	15	53
22	8	04	15	54
23	8	04	15	54
24	8	05	15	55
25	8	05	15	56
26	8	05	15	56
27	8	06	15	57
28	8	06	15	58
29	8	06	15	59
30	8	06	16	00
31	8	06	16	01

MOON PHASES

	d	h	m
New Moon	4	20	34
First Quarter	11	20	52
Full Moon	20	01	34
Last Quarter	27	15	46

MOON PHASES

	d	h	m
New Moon	4	07	34
First Quarter	11	15	49
Full Moon	19	19	10
Last Quarter	27	00	31

DURATION OF TWILIGHT AT 51.5°N (MINUTES)

November	1st	11th	21st	31st
Civil	35	36	38	39
Nautical	75	77	79	81
Astronomical	113	116	119	121

DURATION OF TWILIGHT AT 51.5°N (MINUTES)

December	1st	11th	21st	31st
Civil	39	40	40	40
Nautical	81	83	84	83
Astronomical	121	123	124	124

TIDAL DATA

CONSTANTS

The constant tidal difference may be used in conjunction with the time of high water at London Bridge to find the time of high water at any of the ports or places listed below. These tidal differences are very approximate and should be used only as a guide to the time of high water at the places below. More precise local data should be obtained for navigational and other nautical purposes.

All data allow high water time to be found in Greenwich Mean Time; this applies also to data for the months when British Summer Time is in operation and the hour's time difference should be allowed for. Parts marked with * are in a different time zone and the standard time zone difference also needs to be added/subtracted to give local time. The columns headed Springs and Neaps show the height, in metres, of the tide datum for mean high water springs and mean high water neaps respectively.

Port	Diff.		Springs	Neaps
	h	m	m	m
*Antwerp	+0	50	5.8	4.8
(Prosperpolder)				
Avonmouth	−6	45	13.2	9.8
Belfast	−2	47	3.5	3.0
*Boulogne	−2	44	8.9	7.2
*Calais	−2	04	7.2	5.9
*Cherbourg	−6	00	6.4	5.0
Cowes	−2	38	4.2	3.5
Dartmouth	+4	25	4.9	3.8
*Dieppe	−3	03	9.3	7.3
Dover	−2	52	6.7	5.3
Dublin	−2	05	4.1	3.4
Dun Laoghaire	−2	10	4.1	3.4
*Dunkirk	−1	54	6.0	4.9
*Flushing	−0	15	4.7	3.9
Folkestone	−3	04	7.1	5.7
Harwich	−2	06	4.0	3.4
*Le Havre	−3	55	7.9	6.6
*Hook of Holland	−0	01	2.1	1.7
Hull (Albert Dock)	−7	40	7.5	5.8
Immingham	−8	00	7.3	5.8
Larne	−2	40	2.8	2.5
Londonderry	−5	37	2.7	2.1
Lowestoft	−4	25	2.4	2.1
Margate	−1	53	4.8	3.9
Newhaven	−2	46	6.7	5.1
*Ostend	−1	32	5.1	4.2
Plymouth	+4	05	5.5	4.4
Portland	+5	09	2.1	1.4
Portsmouth	−2	38	4.7	3.8
Ramsgate	−2	32	5.2	4.1
Richmond Lock	+1	00	4.9	3.7
*Rotterdam	+1	45	2.0	1.7
St Helier	+4	48	11.0	8.1
St Malo	+4	27	12.2	9.2
St Peter Port	+4	54	9.3	7.0
Sheerness	−1	19	5.8	4.7
Shoreham	−2	44	6.3	4.9
Southampton	−2	54	4.5	3.7
(1St high water)				
Spurn Head	−8	25	6.9	5.5
Swansea	−7	35	9.5	7.2
Tilbury	−0	49	6.4	5.4
Tyne River	−10	30	5.0	3.9
(North Shields)				
Walton-on-the-	−2	10	4.2	2.8
Naze				
*Zeebrugge	−0	55	4.8	3.9

TIDAL PREDICTIONS

The data below are daily predictions of the time and height of high water at London Bridge. The time of the data is Greenwich Mean Time; this applies also to data for the months when British Summer Time is in operation and the hour's time difference should be allowed for. The datum of predictions for each port shows the difference of height, in metres from Ordnance data (Newlyn). This tidal information is reproduced with the permission of the UK Hydrographic Office and the Controller of HMSO. Crown copyright reserved.

JANUARY 2002 Highwater GMT

LONDON BRIDGE
Year 2002 Zone Time UT(GMT)

		hr		ht m	hr		ht m
1	Tu	02	48	6.9	15	14	7.1
2	We	03	32	6.9	16	01	7.2
3	Th	04	15	6.8	16	48	7.1
4	Fr	04	59	6.8	17	37	7.0
5	Sa	05	46	6.6	18	28	6.7
6	Su	06	37	6.4	19	25	6.4
7	Mo	07	38	6.2	20	29	6.2
8	Tu	08	49	6.1	21	36	6.1
9	We	09	59	6.1	22	40	6.2
10	Th	11	04	6.3	23	38	6.4
11	Fr	12	02	6.5	–	–	–
12	Sa	00	31	6.6	12	56	6.7
13	Su	01	20	6.7	13	46	6.8
14	Mo	02	04	6.7	14	31	6.8
15	Tu	02	43	6.7	15	12	6.8
16	We	03	17	6.6	15	48	6.6
17	Th	03	48	6.5	16	21	6.5
18	Fr	04	19	6.5	16	54	6.5
19	Sa	04	53	6.4	17	30	6.4
20	Su	05	31	6.3	18	09	6.3
21	Mo	06	14	6.2	18	54	6.1
22	Tu	07	02	6.0	19	44	6.0
23	We	07	59	5.8	20	42	5.9
24	Th	09	03	5.8	21	48	5.8
25	Fr	10	13	5.9	22	58	6.0
26	Sa	11	23	6.1	–	–	–
27	Su	00	01	6.3	12	26	6.5
28	Mo	00	57	6.6	13	22	6.8
29	Tu	01	47	6.8	14	13	7.1
30	We	02	35	7.0	15	02	7.3
31	Th	03	20	7.1	15	49	7.4

FEBRUARY 2002 Highwater GMT

LONDON BRIDGE
Year 2002 Zone Time UT(GMT)

		hr		ht m	hr		ht m
1	Fr	04	03	7.1	16	35	7.4
2	Sa	04	46	7.1	17	20	7.3
3	Su	05	29	7.0	18	06	7.0
4	Mo	06	13	6.7	18	55	6.6
5	Tu	07	03	6.4	19	51	6.1
6	We	08	08	6.1	20	58	5.8
7	Th	09	28	5.9	22	09	5.8
8	Fr	10	43	5.9	23	14	5.9
9	Sa	11	47	6.2	–	–	–
10	Su	00	11	6.2	12	43	6.5
11	Mo	01	03	6.5	13	33	6.7
12	Tu	01	48	6.6	14	17	6.8
13	We	02	28	6.6	14	57	6.8
14	Th	03	02	6.6	15	30	6.6
15	Fr	03	32	6.5	15	59	6.6
16	Sa	04	00	6.5	16	28	6.5
17	Su	04	30	6.5	17	00	6.6
18	Mo	05	04	6.5	17	36	6.5
19	Tu	05	42	6.4	18	17	6.4
20	We	06	26	6.3	19	03	6.1
21	Th	07	18	6.0	19	57	5.9
22	Fr	08	20	5.8	21	01	5.7
23	Sa	09	31	5.8	22	18	5.7
24	Su	10	53	6.0	23	34	6.0
25	Mo	12	06	6.4	–	–	–
26	Tu	00	36	6.4	13	06	6.8
27	We	01	29	6.8	13	58	7.2
28	Th	02	17	7.1	14	46	7.4

MARCH 2002 Highwater GMT

LONDON BRIDGE
Year 2002 Zone Time UT(GMT)

		hr		ht m	hr		ht m
1	Fr	03	02	7.2	15	32	7.6
2	Sa	03	44	7.3	16	15	7.5
3	Su	04	25	7.4	16	58	7.3
4	Mo	05	06	7.2	17	39	7.0
5	Tu	05	47	6.9	18	21	6.6
6	We	06	32	6.5	19	07	6.1
7	Th	07	29	6.0	20	08	5.6
8	Fr	08	58	5.6	21	37	5.4
9	Sa	10	23	5.7	22	49	5.6
10	Su	11	28	6.0	23	48	6.0
11	Mo	12	24	6.4	–	–	–
12	Tu	00	41	6.3	13	13	6.7
13	We	01	27	6.6	13	57	6.8
14	Th	02	07	6.7	14	34	6.8
15	Fr	02	42	6.6	15	05	6.7
16	Sa	03	11	6.5	15	33	6.6
17	Su	03	38	6.5	16	00	6.6
18	Mo	04	06	6.6	16	31	6.6
19	Tu	04	38	6.6	17	05	6.6
20	We	05	15	6.6	17	44	6.5
21	Th	05	59	6.4	18	29	6.2
22	Fr	06	50	6.1	19	22	5.8
23	Sa	07	52	5.8	20	25	5.6
24	Su	09	05	5.7	21	46	5.6
25	Mo	10	32	5.9	23	10	6.0
26	Tu	11	48	6.4	–	–	–
27	We	00	13	6.4	12	47	6.9
28	Th	01	06	6.8	13	38	7.3
29	Fr	01	54	7.2	14	25	7.5
30	Sa	02	38	7.3	15	09	7.6
31	Su	03	21	7.5	15	52	7.5

APRIL 2002 Highwater GMT

LONDON BRIDGE
Year 2002 Zone Time UT(GMT)

		hr		ht m	hr		ht m
1	Mo	04	03	7.4	16	32	7.3
2	Tu	04	43	7.3	17	10	7.0
3	We	05	25	7.0	17	48	6.6
4	Th	06	08	6.5	18	27	6.1
5	Fr	07	02	6.0	19	17	5.6
6	Sa	08	32	5.6	20	59	5.3
7	Su	09	59	5.6	22	19	5.5
8	Mo	11	02	6.0	23	19	5.9
9	Tu	11	57	6.4	–	–	–
10	We	00	11	6.3	12	45	6.7
11	Th	00	58	6.5	13	28	6.8
12	Fr	01	39	6.6	14	04	6.8
13	Sa	02	14	6.6	14	35	6.7
14	Su	02	45	6.5	15	04	6.6
15	Mo	03	13	6.5	15	32	6.6
16	Tu	03	43	6.6	16	04	6.6
17	We	04	17	6.6	16	39	6.6
18	Th	04	56	6.6	17	18	6.4
19	Fr	05	41	6.4	18	03	6.2
20	Sa	06	33	6.1	18	56	5.8
21	Su	07	36	5.9	20	01	5.6
22	Mo	08	51	5.8	21	24	5.7
23	Tu	10	17	6.1	22	44	6.0
24	We	11	27	6.6	23	46	6.5
25	Th	12	23	7.0	–	–	–
26	Fr	00	39	6.9	13	14	7.3
27	Sa	01	28	7.2	14	01	7.5
28	Su	02	14	7.3	14	45	7.4
29	Mo	02	59	7.4	15	27	7.3
30	Tu	03	42	7.4	16	06	7.1

562 Tidal Data

MAY 2002 Highwater GMT

LONDON BRIDGE
Year 2002 Zone Time UT(GMT)

		hr		ht m	hr		ht m
1	We	04	24	7.2	16	44	6.9
2	Th	05	07	6.9	17	20	6.5
3	Fr	05	52	6.5	17	58	6.1
4	Sa	06	44	6.0	18	44	5.7
5	Su	08	02	5.6	20	05	5.4
6	Mo	09	24	5.6	21	38	5.5
7	Tu	10	27	5.9	22	41	5.8
8	We	11	21	6.2	23	34	6.1
9	Th	12	08	6.5	–	–	–
10	Fr	00	21	6.4	12	51	6.7
11	Sa	01	03	6.5	13	28	6.7
12	Su	01	41	6.6	14	03	6.7
13	Mo	02	16	6.6	14	35	6.7
14	Tu	02	50	6.6	15	09	6.7
15	We	03	25	6.6	15	43	6.6
16	Th	04	03	6.7	16	20	6.6
17	Fr	04	44	6.6	17	01	6.4
18	Sa	05	32	6.5	17	47	6.2
19	Su	06	25	6.3	18	40	6.0
20	Mo	07	28	6.1	19	46	5.8
21	Tu	08	42	6.1	21	05	5.9
22	We	09	57	6.3	22	16	6.2
23	Th	11	02	6.6	23	18	6.5
24	Fr	11	58	7.0	–	–	–
25	Sa	00	13	6.9	12	50	7.2
26	Su	01	04	7.1	13	37	7.3
27	Mo	01	53	7.2	14	22	7.2
28	Tu	02	40	7.2	15	05	7.1
29	We	03	25	7.2	15	45	7.0
30	Th	04	09	7.0	16	22	6.7
31	Fr	04	52	6.8	16	58	6.5

JUNE 2002 Highwater GMT

LONDON BRIDGE
Year 2002 Zone Time UT(GMT)

		hr		ht m	hr		ht m
1	Sa	05	36	6.4	17	36	6.2
2	Su	06	24	6.1	18	20	5.9
3	Mo	07	21	5.8	19	18	5.7
4	Tu	08	29	5.7	20	35	5.6
5	We	09	35	5.8	21	46	5.7
6	Th	10	31	6.0	22	44	5.9
7	Fr	11	22	6.2	23	36	6.1
8	Sa	12	08	6.4	–	–	–
9	Su	00	23	6.3	12	51	6.6
10	Mo	01	07	6.5	13	31	6.7
11	Tu	01	49	6.6	14	11	6.7
12	We	02	30	6.7	14	50	6.7
13	Th	03	11	6.8	15	29	6.7
14	Fr	03	54	6.8	16	10	6.6
15	Sa	04	39	6.8	16	52	6.5
16	Su	05	27	6.7	17	38	6.4
17	Mo	06	19	6.5	18	29	6.3
18	Tu	07	18	6.4	19	31	6.1
19	We	08	24	6.3	20	40	6.1
20	Th	09	31	6.3	21	47	6.2
21	Fr	10	35	6.5	22	51	6.4
22	Sa	11	33	6.7	23	50	6.7
23	Su	12	27	6.9	–	–	–
24	Mo	00	45	6.9	13	17	7.0
25	Tu	01	37	7.0	14	04	7.0
26	We	02	26	7.0	14	47	6.9
27	Th	03	13	7.0	15	28	6.8
28	Fr	03	56	6.9	16	04	6.7
29	Sa	04	37	6.7	16	39	6.5
30	Su	05	17	6.5	17	15	6.4

JULY 2002 Highwater GMT

LONDON BRIDGE
Year 2002 Zone Time UT(GMT)

		hr		ht m	hr		ht m
1	Mo	05	56	6.3	17	55	6.2
2	Tu	06	39	6.0	18	41	6.0
3	We	07	28	5.9	19	35	5.8
4	Th	08	23	5.8	20	37	5.7
5	Fr	09	24	5.8	21	41	5.8
6	Sa	10	25	6.0	22	44	5.9
7	Su	11	22	6.2	23	42	6.1
8	Mo	12	15	6.4	–	–	–
9	Tu	00	35	6.4	13	04	6.6
10	We	01	25	6.6	13	50	6.7
11	Th	02	13	6.8	14	35	6.8
12	Fr	02	59	7.0	15	18	6.8
13	Sa	03	45	7.0	16	01	6.8
14	Su	04	31	7.1	16	43	6.8
15	Mo	05	17	7.0	17	27	6.7
16	Tu	06	06	6.8	18	13	6.6
17	We	06	58	6.6	19	06	6.4
18	Th	07	57	6.3	20	08	6.2
19	Fr	09	02	6.2	21	17	6.1
20	Sa	10	08	6.2	22	27	6.2
21	Su	11	10	6.3	23	33	6.4
22	Mo	12	07	6.5	–	–	–
23	Tu	00	32	6.6	13	00	6.7
24	We	01	26	6.8	13	49	6.8
25	Th	02	15	6.9	14	33	6.8
26	Fr	03	01	6.9	15	13	6.8
27	Sa	03	42	6.8	15	47	6.7
28	Su	04	18	6.7	16	19	6.6
29	Mo	04	51	6.5	16	50	6.5
30	Tu	05	24	6.4	17	26	6.4
31	We	06	00	6.3	18	05	6.3

AUGUST 2002 Highwater GMT

LONDON BRIDGE
Year 2002 Zone Time UT(GMT)

		hr		ht m	hr		ht m
1	Th	06	41	6.1	18	50	6.1
2	Fr	07	28	6.0	19	42	5.9
3	Sa	08	23	5.8	20	42	5.7
4	Su	09	28	5.8	21	51	5.7
5	Mo	10	38	5.9	23	03	5.9
6	Tu	11	43	6.2	–	–	–
7	We	00	08	6.3	12	41	6.5
8	Th	01	05	6.6	13	32	6.7
9	Fr	01	56	7.0	14	19	6.9
10	Sa	02	44	7.2	15	03	7.0
11	Su	03	30	7.3	15	45	7.1
12	Mo	04	15	7.3	16	26	7.1
13	Tu	04	59	7.2	17	07	7.1
14	We	05	44	7.0	17	50	6.9
15	Th	06	30	6.6	18	36	6.6
16	Fr	07	22	6.2	19	32	6.2
17	Sa	08	27	5.9	20	47	5.9
18	Su	09	41	5.7	22	10	5.8
19	Mo	10	49	5.9	23	20	6.1
20	Tu	11	50	6.2	–	–	–
21	We	00	20	6.5	12	44	6.5
22	Th	01	14	6.8	13	32	6.7
23	Fr	02	02	7.0	14	16	6.8
24	Sa	02	44	7.0	14	54	6.8
25	Su	03	21	6.8	15	27	6.7
26	Mo	03	52	6.7	15	54	6.6
27	Tu	04	20	6.5	16	23	6.5
28	We	04	48	6.5	16	54	6.5
29	Th	05	21	6.4	17	29	6.4
30	Fr	05	59	6.3	18	10	6.3
31	Sa	06	41	6.1	18	58	6.0

Tidal Data

SEPTEMBER 2002 Highwater GMT

LONDON BRIDGE
Year 2002 Zone Time UT(GMT)

		hr		ht m	hr		ht m
1	Su	07	33	5.8	19	56	5.8
2	Mo	08	35	5.6	21	05	5.7
3	Tu	09	53	5.6	22	27	5.8
4	We	11	14	5.9	23	45	6.2
5	Th	12	17	6.4	–	–	–
6	Fr	00	45	6.7	13	10	6.7
7	Sa	01	37	7.1	13	57	7.0
8	Su	02	24	7.4	14	40	7.2
9	Mo	03	09	7.5	15	22	7.3
10	Tu	03	52	7.5	16	03	7.3
11	We	04	34	7.3	16	43	7.3
12	Th	05	16	7.0	17	24	7.1
13	Fr	05	57	6.6	18	08	6.7
14	Sa	06	42	6.1	19	00	6.2
15	Su	07	42	5.6	20	21	5.7
16	Mo	09	13	5.4	21	55	5.7
17	Tu	10	28	5.6	23	05	6.0
18	We	11	29	6.0	–	–	–
19	Th	00	03	6.5	12	23	6.4
20	Fr	00	55	6.8	13	10	6.7
21	Sa	01	40	7.0	13	53	6.9
22	Su	02	20	7.0	14	30	6.8
23	Mo	02	54	6.8	15	01	6.7
24	Tu	03	21	6.7	15	27	6.6
25	We	03	46	6.6	15	53	6.5
26	Th	04	13	6.6	16	23	6.5
27	Fr	04	44	6.5	16	57	6.5
28	Sa	05	20	6.4	17	38	6.4
29	Su	06	02	6.2	18	26	6.1
30	Mo	06	52	5.8	19	24	5.8

OCTOBER 2002 Highwater GMT

LONDON BRIDGE
Year 2002 Zone Time UT(GMT)

		hr		ht m	hr		ht m
1	Tu	07	54	5.6	20	33	5.7
2	We	09	12	5.5	21	58	5.8
3	Th	10	43	5.8	23	21	6.3
4	Fr	11	49	6.3	–	–	–
5	Sa	00	21	6.8	12	41	6.8
6	Su	01	13	7.2	13	28	7.1
7	Mo	01	59	7.5	14	13	7.3
8	Tu	02	44	7.5	14	56	7.4
9	We	03	26	7.5	15	38	7.5
10	Th	04	07	7.3	16	20	7.4
11	Fr	04	47	7.0	17	02	7.1
12	Sa	05	26	6.6	17	47	6.7
13	Su	06	05	6.1	18	39	6.1
14	Mo	06	54	5.6	20	03	5.6
15	Tu	08	42	5.3	21	34	5.6
16	We	10	00	5.5	22	40	6.0
17	Th	11	00	5.9	23	37	6.4
18	Fr	11	53	6.4	–	–	–
19	Sa	00	26	6.8	12	41	6.7
20	Su	01	11	7.0	13	23	6.8
21	Mo	01	49	6.9	14	00	6.8
22	Tu	02	21	6.8	14	31	6.6
23	We	02	48	6.7	14	59	6.6
24	Th	03	14	6.6	15	27	6.5
25	Fr	03	42	6.6	15	58	6.6
26	Sa	04	14	6.6	16	34	6.6
27	Su	04	50	6.5	17	16	6.4
28	Mo	05	33	6.2	18	05	6.2
29	Tu	06	23	5.9	19	04	5.9
30	We	07	24	5.6	20	13	5.8
31	Th	08	41	5.6	21	36	5.9

NOVEMBER 2002 Highwater GMT

LONDON BRIDGE
Year 2002 Zone Time UT(GMT)

		hr		ht m	hr		ht m
1	Fr	10	08	5.9	22	53	6.4
2	Sa	11	15	6.4	23	53	6.8
3	Su	12	09	6.8	–	–	–
4	Mo	00	45	7.2	12	59	7.1
5	Tu	01	33	7.4	13	46	7.3
6	We	02	18	7.4	14	32	7.4
7	Th	03	01	7.4	15	17	7.4
8	Fr	03	42	7.2	16	01	7.3
9	Sa	04	22	6.9	16	46	7.0
10	Su	05	00	6.6	17	32	6.6
11	Mo	05	38	6.2	18	25	6.1
12	Tu	06	22	5.8	19	37	5.7
13	We	07	51	5.4	21	00	5.7
14	Th	09	21	5.5	22	05	5.9
15	Fr	10	23	5.8	23	00	6.2
16	Sa	11	16	6.1	23	50	6.5
17	Su	12	04	6.4	–	–	–
18	Mo	00	34	6.7	12	47	6.6
19	Tu	01	12	6.7	13	26	6.6
20	We	01	46	6.7	14	00	6.6
21	Th	02	17	6.7	14	33	6.6
22	Fr	02	48	6.6	15	06	6.6
23	Sa	03	19	6.6	15	41	6.6
24	Su	03	53	6.6	16	20	6.6
25	Mo	04	31	6.5	17	04	6.5
26	Tu	05	14	6.3	17	54	6.3
27	We	06	03	6.1	18	51	6.1
28	Th	07	02	5.9	19	57	6.0
29	Fr	08	15	5.8	21	11	6.1
30	Sa	09	34	6.0	22	22	6.4

DECEMBER 2002 Highwater GMT

LONDON BRIDGE
Year 2002 Zone Time UT(GMT)

		hr		ht m	hr		ht m
1	Su	10	41	6.4	23	24	6.7
2	Mo	11	40	6.7	–	–	–
3	Tu	00	18	7.0	12	34	7.0
4	We	01	08	7.2	13	25	7.2
5	Th	01	55	7.2	14	14	7.3
6	Fr	02	40	7.1	15	01	7.3
7	Sa	03	22	7.0	15	48	7.1
8	Su	04	02	6.8	16	33	6.9
9	Mo	04	40	6.6	17	18	6.6
10	Tu	05	18	6.3	18	05	6.3
11	We	05	59	6.0	18	58	5.9
12	Th	06	53	5.7	20	02	5.7
13	Fr	08	11	5.6	21	09	5.7
14	Sa	09	26	5.6	22	08	5.8
15	Su	10	26	5.8	23	01	6.0
16	Mo	11	19	6.0	23	49	6.2
17	Tu	12	07	6.3	–	–	–
18	We	00	32	6.4	12	51	6.4
19	Th	01	12	6.6	13	32	6.5
20	Fr	01	51	6.6	14	11	6.6
21	Sa	02	28	6.7	14	51	6.7
22	Su	03	05	6.6	15	31	6.8
23	Mo	03	42	6.6	16	13	6.8
24	Tu	04	21	6.6	16	58	6.7
25	We	05	03	6.5	17	45	6.6
26	Th	05	50	6.3	18	38	6.4
27	Fr	06	43	6.2	19	36	6.3
28	Sa	07	46	6.1	20	42	6.2
29	Su	08	58	6.1	21	51	6.2
30	Mo	10	09	6.2	22	56	6.4
31	Tu	11	15	6.4	23	54	6.6

564

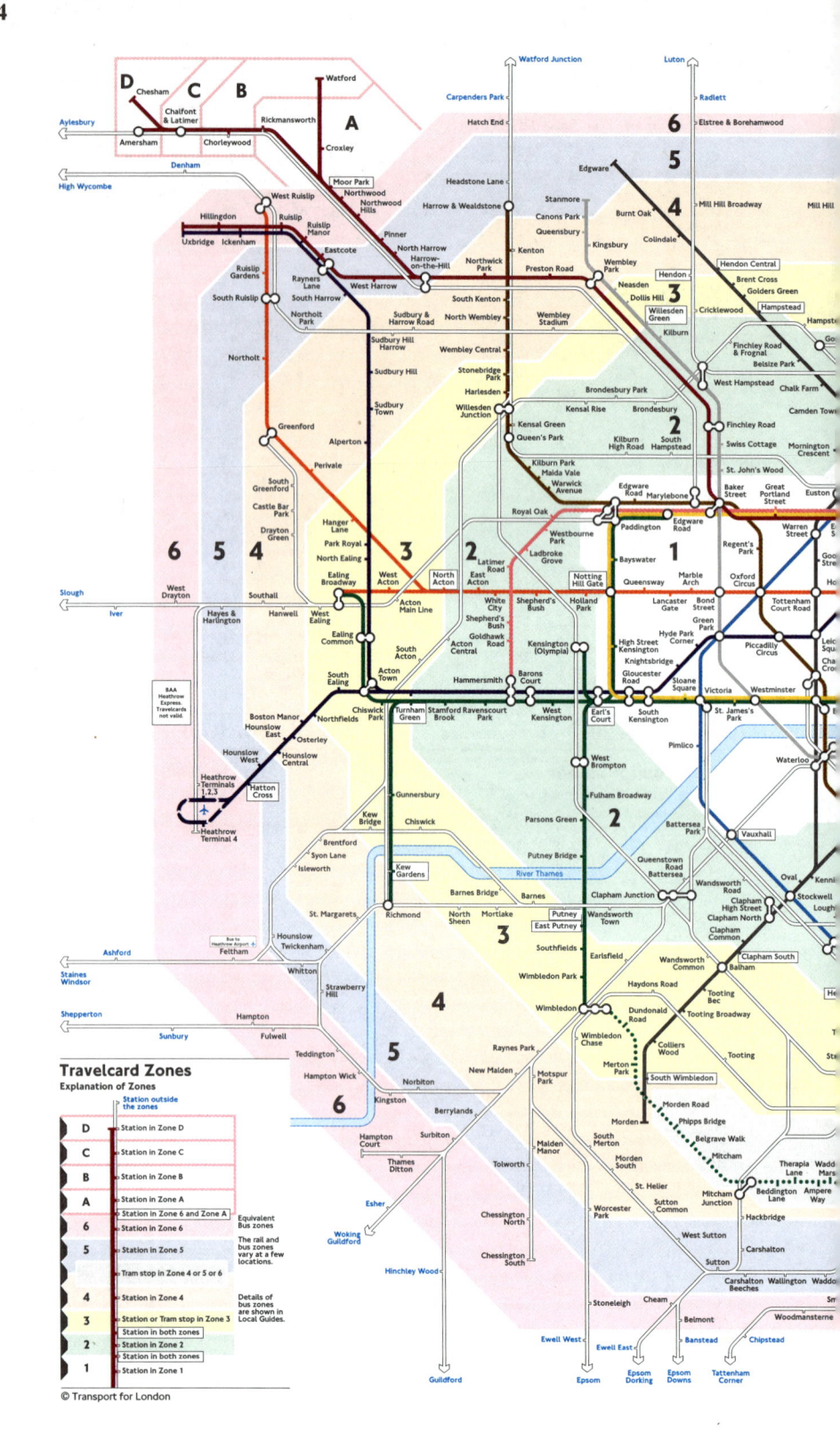

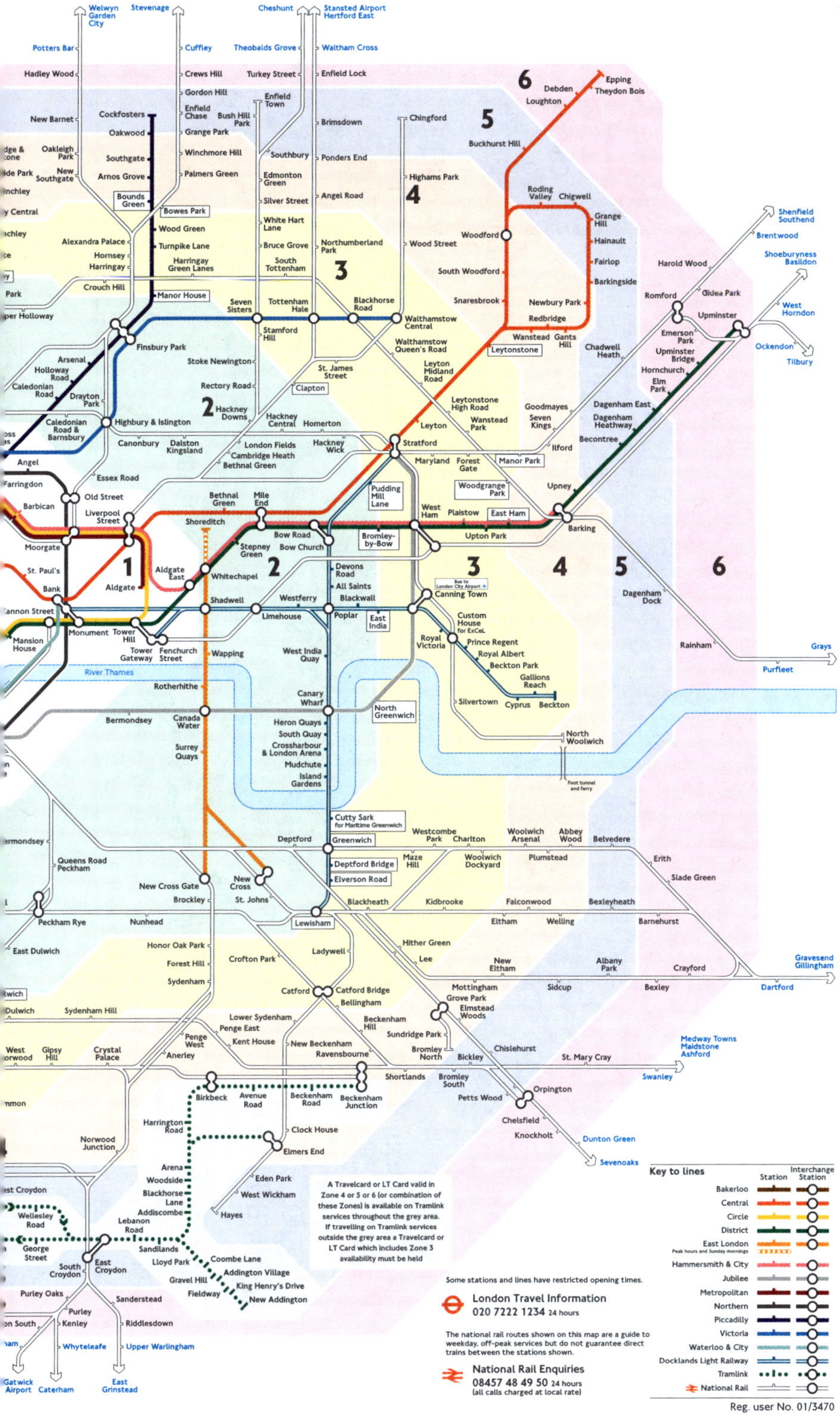

Welwyn Garden City
Stevenage
Cheshunt
Stansted Airport Hertford East
Potters Bar
Cuffley
Theobalds Grove
Waltham Cross
Hadley Wood
Crews Hill
Turkey Street
Enfield Lock
Gordon Hill
Enfield Town
Enfield Chase
Bush Hill Park
New Barnet
Cockfosters
Oakwood
Grange Park
Brimsdown
Chingford
Epping
Debden
Theydon Bois
Loughton
Buckhurst Hill
Oakleigh Park
Southgate
Winchmore Hill
Southbury
Ponders End
New Southgate
Arnos Grove
Palmers Green
Edmonton Green
Angel Road
Highams Park
Roding Valley
Chigwell
Grange Hill
Bounds Green
Silver Street
Bowes Park
Wood Green
White Hart Lane
Alexandra Palace
Turnpike Lane
Bruce Grove
Northumberland Park
Woodford
Hainault
Wood Street
Hornsey
Harringay
Harringay Green Lanes
South Tottenham
Fairlop
Harold Wood
Shenfield Southend
Brentwood
Shoeburyness Basildon
South Woodford
Barkingside
Crouch Hill
Manor House
Seven Sisters
Tottenham Hale
Blackhorse Road
Snaresbrook
Newbury Park
Romford
Gidea Park
Walthamstow Central
Redbridge
Upminster
West Horndon
Finsbury Park
Stamford Hill
Walthamstow Queen's Road
Wanstead
Gants Hill
Leytonstone
Chadwell Heath
Emerson Park
Ockendon
Tilbury
Upminster Bridge
Arsenal
Stoke Newington
St. James Street
Leyton Midland Road
Hornchurch
Holloway Road
Caledonian Road
Rectory Road
Clapton
Elm Park
Drayton Park
Hackney Downs
Leytonstone High Road
Goodmayes
Dagenham East
Wanstead Park
Seven Kings
Dagenham Heathway
Caledonian Road & Barnsbury
Highbury & Islington
Hackney Central
Homerton
Leyton
Canonbury
Dalston Kingsland
London Fields
Hackney Wick
Stratford
Becontree
Ilford
Cambridge Heath
Bethnal Green
Maryland
Forest Gate
Manor Park
Angel
Essex Road
Farringdon
Old Street
Pudding Mill Lane
Woodgrange Park
Upney
Barbican
Bethnal Green
Mile End
West Ham
Plaistow
East Ham
Liverpool Street
Shoreditch
Barking
Moorgate
Bow Road
Bromley-by-Bow
Upton Park
Stepney Green
Bow Church
St. Paul's
Aldgate East
Devons Road
Whitechapel
All Saints
Dagenham Dock
Bank
Aldgate
Bus to London City Airport
Canning Town
Shadwell
Westferry
Blackwall
Cannon Street
Limehouse
Poplar
East India
Custom House for ExCeL
Monument
Tower Hill
Royal Victoria
Prince Regent
Mansion House
Royal Albert
Rainham
Grays
Tower Gateway
Fenchurch Street
Wapping
West India Quay
Beckton Park
Purfleet
River Thames
Gallions Reach
Rotherhithe
Canary Wharf
Silvertown
Cyprus
Beckton
North Greenwich
Bermondsey
Canada Water
Heron Quays
South Quay
North Woolwich
Surrey Quays
Crossharbour & London Arena
Mudchute
Island Gardens
Foot tunnel and ferry
Cutty Sark for Maritime Greenwich
Westcombe Park
Charlton
Woolwich Arsenal
Abbey Wood
Belvedere
Deptford
Greenwich
Queens Road Peckham
Maze Hill
Woolwich Dockyard
Plumstead
Erith
Deptford Bridge
Elverson Road
New Cross
New Cross Gate
Slade Green
Brockley
St. Johns
Blackheath
Kidbrooke
Falconwood
Bexleyheath
Peckham Rye
Nunhead
Lewisham
Eltham
Welling
Barnehurst
Hither Green
East Dulwich
Honor Oak Park
Ladywell
Crofton Park
Lee
Forest Hill
New Eltham
Albany Park
Crayford
Gravesend Gillingham
Sydenham
Catford
Catford Bridge
Mottingham
Sidcup
Bexley
Dartford
Bellingham
Grove Park
Sydenham Hill
Lower Sydenham
Elmstead Woods
Beckenham Hill
Penge East
Sundridge Park
Kent House
Penge West
West Norwood
Gipsy Hill
Crystal Palace
New Beckenham
Chislehurst
Medway Towns Maidstone Ashford
Anerley
Ravensbourne
Bromley North
Bickley
St. Mary Cray
Swanley
Shortlands
Bromley South
Birkbeck
Avenue Road
Beckenham Road
Beckenham Junction
Orpington
Petts Wood
Harrington Road
Chelsfield
Clock House
Norwood Junction
Knockholt
Elmers End
Dunton Green
Sevenoaks
Arena
Woodside
Eden Park
West Wickham
Blackhorse Lane
Addiscombe
Hayes
Wellesley Road
Lebanon Road
George Street
East Croydon
Sandilands
South Croydon
Lloyd Park
Coombe Lane
Addington Village
Gravel Hill
King Henry's Drive
Fieldway
New Addington
Purley Oaks
Sanderstead
Purley
Kenley
Riddlesdown
Whyteleafe
Upper Warlingham
Gatwick Airport
Caterham
East Grinstead
1
2
3
4
5
6
A Travelcard or LT Card valid in Zone 4 or 5 or 6 (or combination of these Zones) is available on Tramlink services throughout the grey area. If travelling on Tramlink services outside the grey area a Travelcard or LT Card which includes Zone 3 availability must be held
Some stations and lines have restricted opening times.
London Travel Information
020 7222 1234 24 hours
The national rail routes shown on this map are a guide to weekday, off-peak services but do not guarantee direct trains between the stations shown.
National Rail Enquiries
08457 48 49 50 24 hours
(all calls charged at local rate)
Key to lines
Station
Interchange Station
Bakerloo
Central
Circle
District
East London
Peak hours and Sunday mornings
Hammersmith & City
Jubilee
Metropolitan
Northern
Piccadilly
Victoria
Waterloo & City
Docklands Light Railway
Tramlink
National Rail
Reg. user No. 01/3470

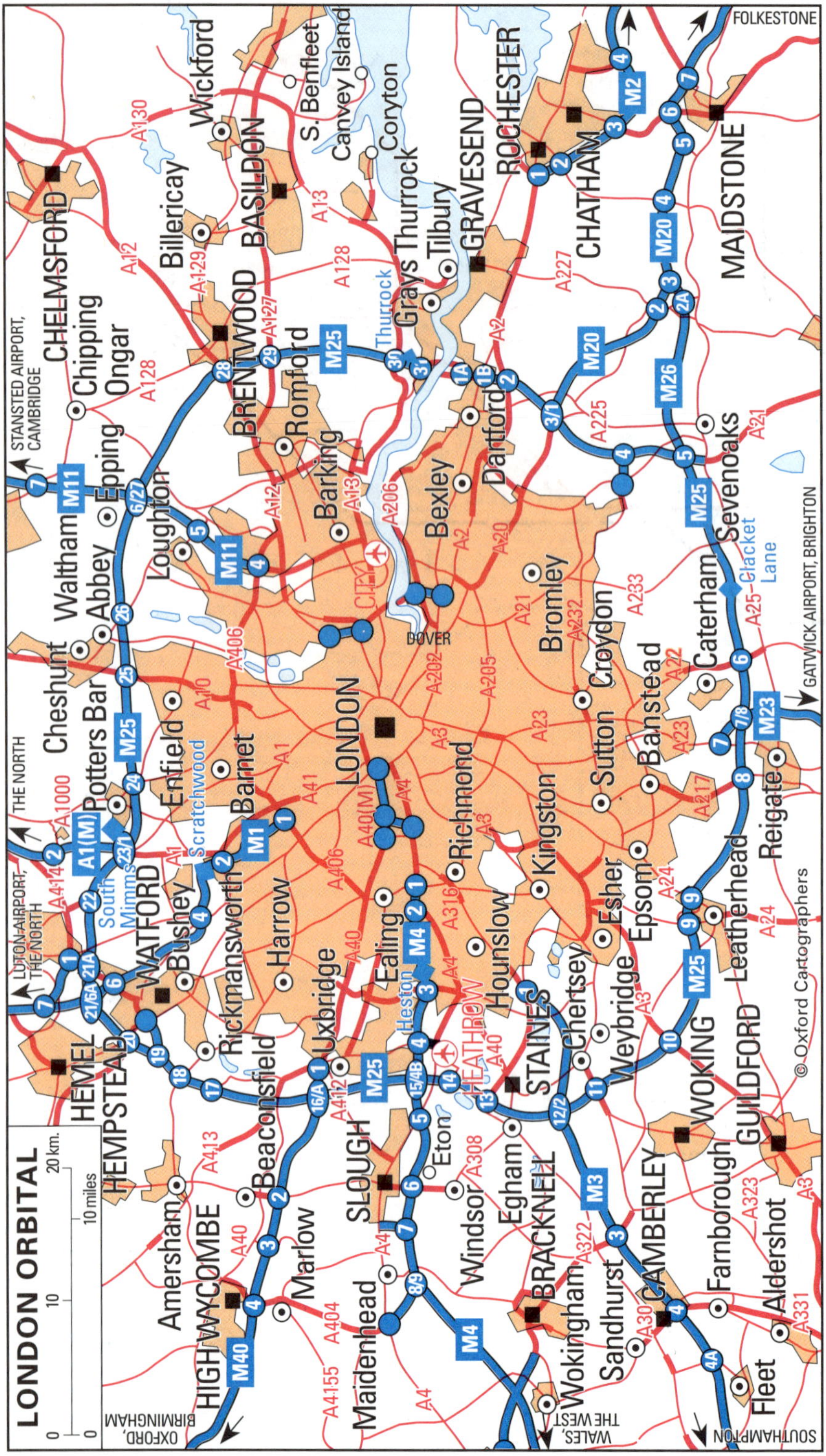
LONDON ORBITAL
0 10 20 km.
0 10 miles
OXFORD, BIRMINGHAM
WALES, THE WEST
SOUTHAMPTON
LUTON AIRPORT, THE NORTH
THE NORTH
STANSTED AIRPORT, CAMBRIDGE
FOLKESTONE
GATWICK AIRPORT, BRIGHTON
DOVER
CHELMSFORD
Chipping Ongar
Epping
Waltham Abbey
Cheshunt
Potters Bar
South Mimms
HEMEL HEMPSTEAD
WATFORD
Bushey
Enfield
Scratchwood
Barnet
Loughton
Billericay
Wickford
BASILDON
BRENTWOOD
Romford
Barking
S. Benfleet
Canvey Island
Coryton
Thurrock
Grays Thurrock
Tilbury
GRAVESEND
ROCHESTER
CHATHAM
MAIDSTONE
Sevenoaks
Dartford
Bexley
Bromley
Croydon
Caterham
Clacket Lane
Banstead
Sutton
Reigate
Leatherhead
Epsom
Esher
Kingston
Richmond
Hounslow
LONDON
CITY
Ealing
Harrow
Rickmansworth
Uxbridge
Heston
HEATHROW
STAINES
Chertsey
Weybridge
WOKING
GUILDFORD
Beaconsfield
Amersham
HIGH WYCOMBE
Marlow
SLOUGH
Eton
Windsor
Egham
Maidenhead
BRACKNELL
Wokingham
Sandhurst
CAMBERLEY
Farnborough
Aldershot
Fleet
M25
M11
M1
A1(M)
M4
M40
M3
M23
M20
M26
M2
A40(M)
© Oxford Cartographers

Index

A
Accountancy
 education and training 128-9
 firms 194
Action zones, education 118
Actuarial Science, education and training 129
Adjudicator's Office 199
Adoption
 Adoption and Fostering, agencies 254
 legal notes 254
Advertising
 agencies 314-18
 Standards Authority 314
Advisory, Conciliation and Arbitration Service 216
Afghanistan Embassy 452
African and Afro-Caribbean Churches 481
Afro-West Indian United Council of Churches 481
Agricultural Land Tribunal 247
Agriculture, Fisheries and Food, Ministry of 102-4
Air travel
 Airlinks 180
 airports 184-6
 Civil Aviation Authority 183
 distances from London 466-7
 statistics 183
Albanian Embassy 452
Albert Bridge 399
Albert Hall 395-6
Aldermen 44
Alexandra, Bridge 399
Alexandra, Palace 345
Algerian Embassy 452
Ambassadors 452-6
Ambulance Service 136
Anglia Railways 176
American Embassy 452
Angolan Embassy 452
Anguillan Tourist Office 448
Antigua and Barbuda
 Embassy 452
 Tourist Office 448
Apostolic Nuncio of Great Britain 455
Appeals Service, Tribunal 247
Aquaculture, Environment, Fisheries and, Centre for 103
Archbishop of Canterbury 479
Archery 409
Architecture and the Built Environment, Commission for 428
Architecture, education and training 129
Archives, Museums, Libraries and, Council for 155
Argentinian, Embassy 452
Armenian Embassy 452
Arsenal Football Club 415
Arts Council of England 427
Arya Pratinidhi Sabha 476
Asian Sound Radio 284
Associations
 Amateur Boxing 411, 424
 Amateur Rowing 424
 for Payment Clearing Services 196
 of Chartered Certified Accountants 198
 of Community Health Councils for England and Wales 150
 of London Government 88
 of South East Asian Nations 462
 of Train Operating Companies 178
Astronomical data 553-9
Athletics Association, South of England 426
ATOC 178
Audit Commission for Local Authorities and the National Health Service in England and Wales 88-9
Australian Embassy 452
Austria
 Embassy 452
 National Tourist Office 448
Azerbaijan, Embassy 452

B
BAA plc 183
BACS ltd 196
Bahá'í Faith 474
Bahamas, Embassy 452
Bahrain, Embassy 452
Bangladesh, Embassy 452
Banking
 Bank for International Settlement 462
 Bank of England 195
 education and training 129
 retail banks 195-6
 UK system 195
Baptist Church 481
 Union of Great Britain 481
Barbados
 High Commission 452
 Tourism Authority 448
Barbican Centre 345
Barbuda, Antigua and
 Embassy 452
 Tourist Office 448
Barking, MP 89

Barking and Dagenham
  Borough Council 34-5
  map 34
Barking and Havering, Health Authority 146
Barnes Bridge 399
Barnet
  Borough Council 35-6
  Football Club 415
  Health Authority 146
  map 35
  waste and recycling facilities 439-40
Bar, The, General Council 251
Battersea
  bridges 399
  MP 89
Bay, The, local radio 284
BBC
  local radio stations 284
  network services 284
  organisation 282
  television 282
Bear Baiting 410
Beckenham, MP 89
Belarus, Embassy 452
Belgian Embassy 453
Belize, Embassy 453
Benefits Agency 110
Bermondsey, Southwark North and, MP 96
Berry's Coaches 181
Beth Din, Federation of Synagogues 477
Bethnal Green and Bow, MP 90
Bexley
  Borough Council 37-8
  map 37
  waste and recycling facilities 440
Bexley and Greenwich, Health Authority 146
Bexleyheath and Crayford, MP 90
BFI London Imax Cinema 378-9
Bharatiya Vidya Bhavan 476
Billiards 410-11
Billingsgate Market 383
Birth statistics 4
Bishops' Conference of England and Wales 480
Blackfriars bridges 399
Blood Service, National 150
Blue plaque sites 345-77
Board of Deputies of British Jews 477
Bolivian Embassy 453
Borough councils
  chief officers 34-87
  council members 34-87
  development of 34
  maps 33-86
  political composition of 34-87
  population 34-87
  tax bands 34-87
Borough Grants, London 219

Borough Market 385
Bosnia and Hercegovina, Embassy 453
Botswana, Embassy 453
Bow, Bethnal Green and, MP 90
Boxing
  Amateur Association 424
  Board of Control 424
  development of 411
Brazilian Embassy 453
Brent
  Borough Council 38-9
  map 38
  MPs 90
  waste and recycling facilities 440
Brent and Harrow Health Authority 146
Brentford and Isleworth, MP 90
Brentford Football Club 415
Bridges 399
Britain Burma Buddhist Trust 475
British
  Agencies for Adoption and Fostering 254
  Boxing Board of Control 424
  Broadcasting Corporation 282
  Buddhist Association 475
  Darts Organisation 424
  Fencing Association 425
  Film Commission 427
  Film Institute 427
  Horseracing Board 425
  Library 377
  Olympic Association 425
  Property Federation 153
  Railways Board 178
  Sky Broadcasting 283
  Telecom 251, 328-9
  Tenpin Bowling Association 425
  Tourist Authority 408
  Trade International 205-6
  Transport Police 138-9
  Trust for Conservation Volunteers 437
  Universities Sports Association 425
British Virgin Islands, Tourist Board 448
Broadcasting 281-5
  Standards Commission 281
Bromley and Chislehurst, MP 90
Bromley
  Borough Council 40-1
  Health Authority 146
  map 40
  waste and recycling facilities 440
Brunei Darussalam, High Commission 453
Brushfield Street Market 385
BT 328-9
  Cellnet 327
Buddhapadipa Temple 475

Buddhism
   Britain Burma Buddhist Trust 475
   British Burma Trust 475
   Buddhist centres 475
   Buddhist Society 475
   Buddhist Vihara, London 475
   origin and development 474-5
   Soka Gakkai 475
   Thames Buddhist Vihara 475
   Vietnam Society 475
   West London Society 476
Building, education and training 129
Building societies, Commission 197
Built Environment, Architecture and, Commission for 428
Bulgarian Embassy 453
Bull Baiting 410
Burroughs Club 419
Burundi, Embassy 453
Buses
   coach travel 180-1
   companies 180-1
   services 180
   traffic statistics 180
Bushy Park 396
Business
   development of 191-3
   education and training 129
   Registration and Deregistration statistics 207
   workforce organisations 205-7
Business Link for London 217
Buzzlines 181

C
C2C (Railway) 176
Cabinet, The 100-1
   Office 104
Cable and Wireless Communications 329
Camberwell and Peckham, MP 90
Camden
   Borough Council 41-2
   map 41
   waste and recycling facilities 440
Camden and Islington Health Authority 146
Cameroon, High Commission, Embassy 453
Canada, Embassy 453
Canning Town, Poplar and, MP 96
Capital FM and Gold 284
Caribbean Tourist organisation 448
Carlton Television Ltd. 282
Carshalton and Wallington, MP 91
Catalonia Tourist Board 448
Catford Stadium 417
Cayman Islands, Department of Tourism 448
CBI 206
Cenotaph, The 378

Central
   Council for Physical Recreation 425
   Mosque 476
   Office of Information 104
   Science Laboratory 103
Chambers of Commerce 216-17
Channel 5 Broadcasting Ltd. 283
Channel Four Television Corporation 283
Chaps Clearing Company Ltd 196
Charity Commission 219
Charity organisations 218-22
Charlton Athletic Football Club 416
Chartered Certified Accountants, Association of 198
Chartered Institution of Water and Environment Management 437
Charterhouse 378
Cheam, Sutton and, MP 97
Chelsea
   Bridge 399
   Football Club 416
   Physic Garden 378
Chelsea, Kensington and
   map 68
   MP 95
   Royal Borough 58-9
   waste and recycling facilities 442-3
Chelsea, Kensington, Westminster and, Health Authority 146
Chenery Travel (coaches) 181
Chief Rabbinate 477
Children, legal notes 262-3
Child Support Agency 262
Chilean Embassy 453
Chiltern Railways 176
China, Peoples' Republic, Embassy 453
Chingford and Woodford Green, MP 91
Chipping Barnet, MP 91
Chiropractic, education and training 129
Chislehurst, Bromley and, MP 90
Chiswick Bridge 399
Choice FM radio 284
Christianity
   Christians and Jews, Council for 473
   in London 475
   origin and beliefs 474
Christian Science Committee on Publication 486
Churches
   African and Afro-Caribbean 481
   attendance 473
   Baptist 481
   Christ, Scientist 486-7
   Church Commissioners 479
   Churches Together in Britain and Ireland 473
   Churches Together in England 473
   Church of Christ, Scientist 486-7

570 Index

Church of England 479
Church of Jesus Christ of Latter-Day Saints 486
  dioceses 479
  Jesus Christ of Latter-Day Saints 486
  Lutheran 481-2
  Methodist 482
  Orthodox 482-4
  Roman Catholic 479-80
  Seventh-Day Adventist 484-5
  United Reform 485
Cinemas 378-9
Circuit, South Eastern 239-40
  judges 240-1
Citizens' Advice Bureaux 222-6
City Airport 184
City, East London and, Health Authority 146
Cities of London
  Aldermen 44
  Common Council 44-5
  Corporation of 42-51
  guilds 45-51
  map 42
  Police 138
Cities of London and Westminster, MP 91
Civil Aviation Authority 183
Civil Service College 104
Classic FM 284
Clearing House, London, Ltd. 199
Clearing Houses, Recognised 199
Clubs 379-82
Coach travel 180-1
Coastguard, Maritime and, Agency 106
Cockfighting 412
Colleges 125-7
Colombian Embassy 453
Commercial Radio Companies Association 284
Commission for Architecture and the Built Environment 428
Commission for Integrated Transport 176
Commonwealth
  Foundation 462
  Games 425
  Institute 462
  Secretariat 462
Community, Fund 219
Community Health Councils 150
Community Health Councils, Association of, for England and Wales 150
Companies House 206
Competition Commission 206
Complementary Medicine, education and training 130
Confederation of British Industry 206
Conference venues 226-33
Congo, Democratic Republic, Embassy 453
Connex Rail 176-7

Conservation, Volunteers, British Trust for 437
Constituencies, parliamentary 89-99
Consumer Law 257-9
Copyright Tribunal 247-8
Coroners' courts 239, 247
Corporation of London 42-5
Corporation of London Records Office 428
Costa Rica, Embassy 454
Côte d'Ivoire, Embassy 454
Council of African and Afro-Caribbean Churches 481
Councils
  for Christians and Jews 473
  for Museums, Archives and Libraries 155
Countryside Alliance 425
Court
  International Arbitration 252
  Service, The 109
Courts
  Coroners' 239, 247
  county 241-2
  crown 243-4
  magistrates' 244-5
  Supreme Court of Judicature 238
Covent Garden, Market 385
Crayford, Bexleyheath and, MP 90
Cresto Ltd 199
Cricket 412-14
Crime Squad, National 139
Criminal Organisation, International 462
Croatia, Embassy 454
Croquet Association 425
Crown
  Court Centres 239
  courts 243-4
  Estate 428
  Prosecution Service 248-9
Croydon
  Borough Council 52-3
  Buddhist Centre 475
  Health Authority 146
  map 52
  MPs 91
  waste and recycling facilities 441
Crystal Palace 414
  Football Club 416
Cuba
  Embassy 454
  Tourist Board 448
Culture, Media and Sport, Department for 104
Cyprus
  Embassy 454
  tourist offices 448, 449
Czech Republic, Embassy 454

D

Dagenham, MP 91

Dagenham, Barking and
  Borough Council 34-5
  map 34
Dance, education and training 130
Darts, British Organisation 424
Data Protection Tribunal 248
Data services 328
Death
  legal notes 259-61
  statistics 4
Debt Management Office, United Kingdom 113
Defence
  Ministry of 103
  Studies, Royal College of 130
Denmark
  Embassy 454
  Tourist Board 448
Dentistry, education and training 130
Deprivation statistics 5
Development Agency 11
Dioceses, Church of England 479
Dispensing Optics, education and training 133
Distances from London
  air 466-7
  road 179
Divorce, legal notes 261-3
Docklands Light Railway 178
Dominican Republic
  Embassy 454
  Tourist Office 448
Downing Street 382
Drama, education and training 130
Driver and Vehicle Licensing Agency 105
Driving Standards Agency 105-6
Dr Johnson's House 382
Dubai, Department of Tourism and Commerce Marketing 448
Dulwich and West Norwood, MP 91

E
Ealing
  Borough Council 53-4
  map 53
  MPs 92
  waste and recycling facilities 441
Ealing Acton and Shepherd's Bush, MP 91-2
Ealing, Hammersmith and Hounslow, Health Authority 146
Earnings, gross weekly 209
East Ham, MP 92
East London and the City, Health Authority 146
East London Mosque Trust 476
Ecuador, Embassy 454
Edmonton, MP 92
Education
  action zones 118
  agencies 127-8

colleges 125-7
'Excellence in Cities' 118-19
government policy 117-19
LEA authorities 120-2
LEA responsibilities 117
professional 128-35
system 117
universities 122-5
urban priorities 118
Education and Employment, Department of 105
Egypt
  Embassy 454
  Tourism Office 448
Election Results, General, 2001 89-99
Electricity
  Association 188
  supply 188
Electricity Markets, Gas and, Office of 188
El Salvador, Embassy 454
Eltham
  MP 92
  Palace 382
Embassies 452-61
Emergency Planning, Fire and, Authority 136
Emergency services 136-44
Emigration 5
Employment
  age structure 208
  Appeal Tribunal 248
  by occupation 209
  employer associations 214-16
  legal notes 263-5
  part-time 208
  Service, The 105
  Tribunal 248
Employment, Education and, Department of 105
Empty Homes Agency 153
Enfield
  Borough Council 54-6
  map 54
  MPs 92
  waste and recycling facilities 441
Enfield and Haringey Health Authority 146
Engineering, education and training 130-1
English
  Heritage 428-9
  Tourism Council 408
Enterprise, Greater London 217
Environment
  Agency 436
  Fisheries and Aquaculture, Centre for 103
  Transport and the Regions,
    Department of 105-6
  Water and, Management, Chartered
    Institution of 437
Environmental Education, London Forum 437
Erith and Thamesmead, MP 92-3

572 Index

Eritrean Orthodox Church 483
Esher RFC 422
Estonia, Embassy 454
Ethiopian Orthodox Church 483
European
   Agency for the Evaluation of Medicinal Products 463
   Bank for Reconstruction and Development 462
   cities 447
   Commission Representative Office 462
   Information Centres 463
   Parliament 99-100
   Union 463
Eurostar 177
Evangelical Alliance 473
Evangelical Lutheran Church of England 481
Environment 11
Exhibition centres 226-33
Expenditure, household 6

F

Family Court 244
Family Records Centre 112, 256
Federation of Synagogues 477
Feltham and Heston, MP 93
Fencing Association, British 425
Fiji, High Commission 454
Film
   Commission, British 427
   Council 429
   Institute, British 427
Financial Service
   advisers 194
   Authority 198
   Compensation Scheme 198
Financial Services Regulation 197-8
Finchley and Golders Green, MP 93
Finland
   Embassy 454
   Tourism Board 448
Fire and Emergency Planning Authority 12
Fire Service
   College 108
   Emergency Planning Authority 136
   Fire Brigade commands 136-7
First Capital (buses) 180
First Great Eastern (Railway) 177
First Great Western Trains 177
First North Western (Railway) 177
Fisheries, Agriculture, Food and, Ministry of 102-4
Fisheries, Environment, Aquaculture and, Centre for 103
FLR (radio) 284
Food, Agriculture, Fisheries and, Ministry of 102-4

Food and Nutrition Science, education and training 131
Football
   Association 425
   development of 415
   teams 416
Foreign and Commonwealth Office 107
Forensic Science Service 139
France
   Embassy 455
   Tourist Office 448
Free Churches' Council 473
Friendly Societies
   Commission 197
   Registry of 197
Friends of the Earth 437
Friends, Religious Society 484
Fuel and Energy Science, education and training 131
Fulham Football Club 416
Fulham, Hammersmith and Borough Council 59-60
   MP 93
   waste and recycling facilities 442
Futures and Options Exchange 198

G

Gabon, Embassy 455
Galleries 386-95
Gambia
   Embassy 455
   National Tourist Office 448
Gas and Electricity Markets, Office of 188
Gas supply 187
Gatwick
   Airport 184
   Express 177
Genealogy, Society of 256
General Council of the Bar 251
General Register Office, The 256
General Synod, Church of England 479
George Inn 382
Georgia, Embassy 455
Germany
   National Tourist Office 449
Germany, Federal Republic of, Embassy 455
Ghana, Embassy 455
Gibraltar, Government of, Tourist Office 449
GMTV 282
Going for Green 437
Golders Green, Finchley and, MP 93
Government
   Car and Despatch Agency 104
   Commerce, Office of 112
   departments 100-13
   ministers 100-2
   Offices for the Regions 106-7

Government of Gibraltar Tourist Office 449
Greater London
    Authority 8-32
    constituencies 30-1
Greater London Authority 8-32
    elections 10
    London List members 31-2
    map 8
    structure 10-11
Greater London Enterprise 217
Greater London Magistrates' Courts
    Authority 244
Great North Eastern Railway 177
Greece
    Embassy 455
    Hellenic Tourism organisation 449
Greek Orthodox Church 482
Greenline (coaches) 181
Green Park 396
Greenwich
    Borough Council 56-7
    map 56
    Observatory 382
    Park 396
    Royal Naval College 382
    waste and recycling facilities 441
Greenwich and Woolwich, MP 93
Greenwich, Bexley and, Health Authority 146
Grenada
    Board of Tourism 449
    High Commission 455
Grenadines, St Vincent and
    High Commission 459
    Tourism Office 451
Greyhound Racing 416-17
    National Club 426
Gross Domestic Product 194
Grosvenor Bridge 399
Guatemala, Embassy 455
Guildhall, The 382-3
Guilds 45-51
Guyana, Embassy 355

H
Hackney
    Borough Council 57-8
    map 57
    MPs 93
    waste and recycling facilities 441-2
Hammersmith and Fulham
    Borough Council 59-60
    map 59
    MP 93
    waste and recycling facilities 442
Hammersmith Bridge 399
Hammersmith, Ealing, Hounslow and, Health
    Authority 146

Hampstead and Highgate, MP 93
Hampton Court Bridge 399
Harbour Club 419
Haringey
    Borough Council 60-1
    map 60
    waste and recycling facilities 442
Haringey, Enfield and, Health Authority 146
Harlequin FC 422
Harlington, Hayes and, MP 94
Harrow
    Borough Council 61-3
    map 61
    MPs 93-4
    waste and recycling facilities 442
Harrow, Brent and, Health Authority 146
Havering
    Borough Council 63-4
    map 63
Havering, Barking and, Health Authority 146
Hayes and Harlington, MP 94
Health
    authorities 146-7
    Department of 107
Heart Radio 284
Hendon, MP 94
Heritage of London Trust 429
Heston, Feltham and, MP 93
High commissioners 452-61
High Court Centres 239
Highgate, Hampstead and, MP 93
Highways Agency 106
Hillingdon
    Borough Council 64-5
    Health Authority 146
    map 64
    waste and recycling facilities 442
Hinduism
    Bharatiya Vidya Bhavan 476
    origin and development 476
    Swaminarayan Hindu Mission 476
    Vishnu Hindu Parishad 476
Historic
    buildings 382-5
    royal palaces 429
Historical Manuscripts, Royal
    Commission on 430
HM Land Registry 109
Holborn and St Pancras, MP 94
Home Office 108
Honduras, Embassy 455
Hong Kong, Tourism Association 449
Hornchurch, MP 94
Hornsey and Wood Green 94
Horse Guards 383
Horseracing 417-18
Horseracing Board, British 425

Hotel-keeping, education and training 131
Hounslow
　Borough Council 65-7
　map 65
　waste and recycling facilities 442
Hounslow, Ealing, Hammersmith and, Health Authority 146
Household statistics 5, 6
Houses of Parliament 383-4
Housing
　average prices 152
　Corporation 153
　Ombudsman 153
　Organisations Mobility and Exchange Service 153
　regulation and provision 153
　Rent Service 154
　stock by tenure 152
　Unit, London 154
Housing Corporation 153
Hungary
　Embassy 455
　National Tourism Office 449
Hungerford Bridge 399
Hyde Park 396

I

Iceland
　Embassy 455
　Tourism Information Bureau 449
Ice Skating, National Association of the UK 426
Ilford, MPs 94
Illegitimacy, legal notes 265
Imams and Mosques Council 476
Immigration 5
Immigration Appellate Authorities 248
IMRO 197
Independent Radio 284
Independent Television
　Commission 282
　companies 282-3
　News 283
India
　High Commission 456
　Tourist Office 449
Indonesia, Embassy 456
Industry, Trade and, Department of 110-11
Information Science, education and training 132
Information Technology Organisation, Police 139
Information Technology Services Group 110
Inland Revenue 199
Institute of Actuaries 198
Institute of Chartered Accountants in England and Wales 198
Institutional Management, education and training 129

Institutions 489-529
Insurance
　companies 194, 200-3
　education and training 131
　London Market 200-1
Integrated Transport, Commission for 176
Inter-Church and Inter-faith Co-operation 473
Interest rates 195
International
　Development, Department for 108
　Direct Dialling 468-70
　Labour Organisation 462
　Maritime Organisation 462
　Petroleum Exchange 198
　Tennis Federation 425
Intestacy, legal notes 276-7
Investment, Management Regulatory Organisation 197
Iran, Embassy 456
Iraqi Interests Section 456
Ireland
　Embassy 456
　Tourist Board 449
Islam
　Central Mosque 476
　East London Mosque Trust 476
　Imams and Mosques Council 476
　Islamic Cultural Centre 476
　Muslim Council of Britain 476
　origin and development 476
Isleworth, Brentford and, MP 90
Islington
　Borough Council 67-8
　map 67
　MPs 94-5
　waste and recycling facilities 443
Islington, Camden and, Health Authority 146
Israel
　Embassy 456
　Government Tourist Office 449
Italy
　Embassy 456
　State Tourist Office 449
　ITV Network Centre 282

J

Jainism 477
Jamaica
　High Commission 456
　Tourist Board 449
Japan
　Embassy 456
　National Tourist organisation 449
Jazz FM 284
Jehovah's Witnesses 486
Jersey, Tourism and Information Office 449
Jews, Christians and, Council for 473

Index 575

Jockey Club, The 426
Jordan, Embassy 456
Journalism, education and training 131
Judaism
    Beth Din Federation of Synagogues 477
    Chief Rabbinate 477
    Christians and Jews Council 473
    Federation of Synagogues 477
    Masorti Synagogues 477
    origin and development 477
    Union of Liberal and Progressive Synagogues 477
    United Synagogue 478
Jury service 265-6

K
Kazakhstan Embassy 456
Keep Fit Association 426
Kensington
    Gardens 397
    Palace 384
Kensington and Chelsea
    MP 95
    Royal Borough Council 68-69
    waste and recycling facilities 442-3
Kensington, Chelsea and Westminster, Health Authority 146
Kenya
    High Commission 456
    Tourist Office 449
Kew Bridges 399
Kings, (since 927 AD) 339-43
Kingston and Richmond Health Authority 146
Kingston and Surbiton, MP 95
Kingston upon Thames
    Bridge 399
    map 69
    Royal Borough Council 69-70
    waste and recycling facilities 443
Kiss 100 FM 284
Korea
    Embassy 456
    National Tourism organisation 449
Krishna Consciousness, International Society for 476
Kuwait, Embassy 456
Kyrgyz Republic, Embassy 456

L
Labour Force, components 208
Labour Organisation, International 462
Lambeth
    Borough Council 71-2
    Bridge 399
    map 71
    Palace 384
    waste and recycling facilities 443

Lambeth, Southwark and Lewisham Health Authority 146
Land
    Registry, HM 109
    Tribunal 248
    utilisation 435
Language Therapy, education and training 134
Latvia
    Embassy 456-7
    Lutheran Church 481
    Orthodox Church Abroad 483
Law
    Centres 251-2
    Centres Federation 251
    Commission 252
    education and training 131-2
    firms 194
    Officers' Departments 108
    Society 252
    Society, Government Group 252
Lawn Tennis
    Association 426
    Museum 424
LBC Radio 284
Leadenhall Market 385
League of Arab States 462
Learning and Skills Council 218
Leasehold
    Advisory Service 153-4
    Valuation Tribunal 154
Lebanon
    Embassy 457
    Tourist and Information Office 449
Legal London
    legal notes
    adoption 254
    births 254
    children 262-3
    citizenship 256-7
    consumer law 257-9
    deaths 259-61
    divorce 261-3
    employment 263-5
    illegitimacy 265
    intestacy 276-7
    jury service 265-6
    landlord and tenant 266-8
    legal aid 268-9
    legitimacy 2265
    marriage 269-72
    rights of way 272
    tenancy 266-8
    voters' qualifications 273
    wills 274-6
Legal Services Commission 253
Legal system
    appointments 239

576 Index

barristers 238
civil cases 239
criminal cases 238-9
outline 237
solicitors 237
Lesotho, High Commission 457
Lewisham
  Borough Council 72-3
  map 72
  MPs 95
Lewisham, Lambeth, Southwark and, Health Authority 146
Leyton and Wanstead, MP 95
Leyton Orient Football Club 416
Liberia, Embassy 457
Liberty Radio 284
Librarianship, education and training 132
Libraries 155-74
Libraries, Archives, Museums and, Council for 155
Libya, People's Bureau 457
Lithuania
  Embassy 457
  Roman Catholic Church 480
Lloyd's of London 384
Local Education Authorities 120-2
London
  21 Sustainability Network 437
  air distances from 466-7
  blue plaque sites 262-85
  Bridge 399
  Central (buses) 180
  Clearing House Ltd. 199
  Coaches Kent 181
  Corporation of, waste and recycling facilities 440-1
  Court of International Arbitration 252
  Enterprise Agency 218
  Eye, The 384
  First Centre 207
  Government, Association of 88
  Greek Radio 284
  history 335-8
  Irish RFC 422
  Marathon, The 418, 426
  Mayors' Association, The 89
  Metal Exchange 198
  Monument 385
  Rivers Association 437
  River Services Ltd. 182
  Transport 175
  Turkish Radio 284
  Wasps 422
  Weekend Television 282
  Welsh RFC 422
  Wildlife Trust 438
  Zendo 475

Lord Chancellor
  Department 109
  Residence 384
Lord Great Chamberlain's Office 429-30
Lord Mayor's Day 43
Lord's Cricket Ground 412-13
Lutheran Church 481-2
  Council of Great Britain 482
Luton Airport 185-6
Luxembourg
  Embassy 457
  Tourist Office 449

M

Macedonia, Embassy 457
Madame Tussaud's 385
Magic Radio 284
Magistrates Courts 244-5
Malankara Orthodox Syrian Church 483
Malawi, High Commission 457
Malaya, Tourism Promotion Board 338
Maldives, High Commission 457
Malta
  High Commission 457
  Tourist Office 450
Management, education and training 129
Maps
  Greater London Authority 8
  London borough councils 33-86
  London orbital 566-7
  public transport 564-5
Marathon, London 418, 426
Maritime and Coastguard Agency 106
Markets 385
Marlborough House 384
Marriage, legal notes 269-72
Marshall's Coaches 181
Masorti Synagogues, Assembly of 477
Material Studies, education and training 132
Mauritania, Embassy 457
Mauritius
  High Commission 457
  Tourism Promotion Authority 450
Mayoral election
  candidates 13-14
  constituency results 15-29
Mayoralty 43
MCC 426
  Tennis Club 419
Meat Hygiene Service 103
Media consultancies 319
Media, Culture, Sport and, Department for 104-5
Medical Devices Agency 107
Medicinal Products, European Agency for Evaluation 463
Medicine
  Complementary, education and training 130

Control Agency 107
  education and training 132-3
  supplementary professions 133
Mental Health Review Tribunal 248
MEPs 100
Merchant banks 195
Merton
  Borough Council 74-5
  map 74
  waste and recycling facilities 443
Merton, Sutton and Wandsworth, Health Authority 146
Metal Exchange, London 198
Methodist Church 482
  Conference Office 482
Metrobus 180
Metroline (buses) 181
Metropolitan Police
  Authority 12
  RFC 422
  River Division 105
  Service 137
  Special Constabulary 137
Mexico
  Board of Tourism 450
  Embassy 457
Midland Mainline 177
Migration 5
Millennium, Radio 284
Ministry of Defence Police 139
Missing Persons Helpline, National 150
Mitcham and Morden, MP 95
Mobile telephones 326-8, 330-1
Monaco, Government Tourist and Convention Office 450
Mongolia, Embassy 457
Monuments 385-6
Moon phases 554-9
Morden, Mitcham and, MP 95
Morocco
  Embassy 457
  National Tourist Office 450
Mortality rates 4
Mozambique, Embassy 458
Museums 386-95
Museums, Archives, Libraries and, Council for 155
Music, education and training 133
Muslim
  Council of Britain 476
  Organisations of the UK and Eire, Union of 476
  World League 476
Myanmar, Embassy 458

N
Namibia
  Embassy 458
  Tourism 450
National
  Association, of Volunteer Bureaux 220
  Association for Councils for Voluntary Service 219
  Blood Service 150
  Centre for Volunteering 220
  Council for Voluntary Organisations 220
  Council for Voluntary Youth Services 220
  Crime Squad 139
  Express 181
  Greyhound Racing Club 426
  Ice Skating Association of the UK 426
  Missing Persons Bureau 139
  Missing Persons Helpline 150
  Savings 113
National Health Service
  Community Health Councils 150-1
  regional offices 146
  structure 146
  trusts 147-9
Nature Reserves 434-5
NCS Service Authority 139
Nepal, Royal, Embassy 458
Netherlands, Embassy 458
Nevis, St Christopher and, High Commission 459
Nevis, St Kitts and, Tourism Office 450
Newham
  Borough Council 75-6
  map 75
  waste and recycling facilities 443
New Opportunities Fund 220
News Agencies 308
News Direct 285
Newspapers
  national 285-6
  regional 221-6
New Zealand
  High Commission 458
  Tourism 450
NFL Europe League 426
NHS Estates 107
NHS Pensions 107
Nicaragua, Embassy 458
Nigeria, Embassy 458
Northern Ireland, Tourist Board 450
Norway
  Embassy 458
  Tourist Board 450
Nursing, education and training 133
Nutrition Science, Food and, education and training 131

O

Office for National Statistics 112
Office of
    Gas and Electricity Markets 188
    Passenger Rail Franchising 177
    Telecommunications 325
    the Rail Regulator 178
    Water Service 188
Oftel 325, 329
OGC buying solutions 112-13
Old Bexley and Sidcup, MP 95-6
Olympics 418-19
Oman, Sultanate of, Embassy 458
Ombudsmen
    Financial Service 205
    Housing 153
    Insurance 159
    Pensions 205
    Prison Service 249-50
OM London Exchange Ltd 199
Open Air Theatre 395
Opthalmics, education and training 133
Order of
    Precedence 343-5
    Succession 343
Orpington, MP 96
Orthodox Churches 482-4
Osteopathy, education and training 134
Oval Cricket Ground 413-14
Oxford Express (coaches) 181

P

Pakistan, High Commission 458
Panama, Embassy 458
Papua New Guinea, High Commission 458
Paraguay, Embassy 458
Parcelforce 331
Parking 182
Parks 395, 396-7
    Royal 396-7
Parliament
    constituencies 88-99
    Houses of 383
Parole Board for England and Wales 250
Passenger Rail Franchising, Office of 177
Patent Office 111
Payment Clearing Services, Association for 196
Peckham, Camberwell and, MP 90
Pensions
    Appeal Tribunal 248
    Ombudsman 205
Periodicals
    consumer 300-8
    trade 294-300
Personal Investment Authority 197
Peru, Embassy 459
Pesticides Safety Directorate 103

Petticoat Lane Market 385
Pharmacy, education and training 134
Philippines
    Cultural and Tourist Office 450
    Embassy 459
Planetarium, The 385
Planning Inspectorate 106
Poland
    Embassy 459
    National Tourist Office 450
Police
    British Transport 138-9
    City of London 138
    Complaints Authority 138
    crime statistics 144
    Forensic Science Service 139
    Information Technology organisation 139
    Metropolitan 12, 137
    Ministry of Defence 139
    National Crime Squad 139
    National Missing Persons Bureau 140
    NCS Service 139
    Police Service, the 137-40
    Royal Parks Constabulary 140
    stations 140-4
Pollution 433
    Urban Research Centre 438
Poplar and Canning Town, MP 96
Population
    by age 3
    by ethnic groups 4
    trends 3
Portobello Road Market 385
Port of London Authority 182, 438
Portugal
    Embassy 459
    National Tourist Office 450
Postal services 331
Precedence, Order of 343-5
Premier Christian Radio 285
Press, The 285-314
Prime Minister's Office 104
Primrose Hill 397
Printing, education and training 134
Prison Service
    Ombudsman 249-50
    prisons 250
Prize Ring, London 412
Probation Service, 251-2
Professional Windsurfing Association 426
Public
    offices 102-13
    relations consultancies 319-25
    Telecommunication Service 329-30
Public Carriage Office 181-2
Public Records Office 2533
Publishers 308-14

Putney
   bridges 399
   MP 96
Q
Qatar, Embassy 459
Quakers, The 484
Queen Elizabeth II
   Bridge 399
   Conference Centre 106
Queen's Club 419
Queen's House 384
Queens Park Rangers Football Club 416
Queens (since 927 AD) 339-43
R
Rackets 419
Radio
   Authority, The 283
   BBC 283-4
   Channel 5 Broadcasting 283
   digital 283-4
   independent stations 284-5
Rail
   companies 176-8
   Railway Board, British 178
   Regulator, Office of 178
   transport 176-8
Railtrack plc 178
Reach 220
Real Tennis 419
Records Office, Corporation of London 428
Recycling, local authority facilities 439-44
Redbridge
   Borough Council 77-8
   map 77
   waste and recycling facilities 443
Redbridge and Waltham Forest, Health Authority 147
Red Crescent 462
Red Cross 462
Reform Synagogues of Great Britain 477
Regent's Park 397
Regent's Park and Kensington North, MP 96
Regional Office, London 153
Regions, the, Environment, Transport and, Department of 105-6
Registry of Friendly Societies 197
Religion 473-86
Religious Society of Friends 484
Rent Association Panel 154
Rent Service 154
Retail banks 195-6
Richmond
   Borough Council 78-79
   bridges 399
   Gymnastic Association 426
   Kingston and, Health Authority 146
   Lock 399
   map 78
   Park 397
Richmond Park, MP 96
Rights of way 272
Ritz Radio 285
Rivers Association, London 437
River Services, London Ltd. 182
Road transport 179-82
Roman Catholic Church 479-80
Romania
   Embassy 459
   National Tourist Office 450
   Orthodox Church in London 483
Roman remains 395
Romford
   MP 96
   Stadium 417
Rowing 419-20
   Association, Amateur, The 424
Royal
   Albert Hall 395-6
   Commission on Historical Manuscripts 430
   Hospital, Chelsea 396
   Mail 331
   Mint 113
   National Theatre Board 430
   Opera House 396
   Parks 396-7
   Parks Agency 104-5
   Parks Constabulary 140
   Tennis Court 419
Rugby Football Union 422, 426
Rugby teams 422-3
Ruislip-Northwood, MP 96
Russian Federation
   Embassy 459
   Sport and Tourism 450
Russian Orthodox Church 482-3
Rwanda, Embassy 459
S
Salvation Army, London divisions 484
Sanex WTA Tour 426
Saracens FC 422
Saudi Arabia, Royal Embassy 459
Science, education and training 134
Scotland, Tourist Board 451
Scotland Office 109-10
Securities, and Futures Authority 197
Senegal, Embassy 459
Seventh Day Adventist Church 484-5
Seychelles
   High Commission 459
   Tourist Office 339
Shelter 154
Shepherd's Bush, Ealing Acton and, MP 91-2

580 Index

Shoreditch, Hackney South and, MP 93
Sidcup, Old Bexley and, MP 95-6
Sierra Leone, High Commission 459-60
Sikhism
    Divine Fellowship 478
    Missionary Society 478
    origin and development 478
    World Fellowship 478
Silverlink 177
Singapore
    High Commission 460
    Tourist Office 451
Slovak Republic, Embassy 460
Slovenia
    Catholic Mission 480
    Embassy 460
    Tourist Board 451
Smithfield Market 385
Snooker 410-11
Social Security, Department of 110
Societies 489-529
Soka Gakkai UK 475
Solicitors' Disciplinary Tribunal 248
Somerset House 398
South Africa, High Commission 460
South Bank Centre 398
South East Nations, Association of 462
Southwark
    Borough Council 80-1
    Bridge 399
    Cathedral 398
    map 80
Southwark, Lambeth, Lewisham and, Health Authority 146
Southwark North and Bermondsey, MP 96
South West Trains 177
Spain
    Embassy 460
    Tourist Office 451
Spanish and Portuguese Jews' Congregation 478
Special
    Commissioners of Income Tax Tribunal 248
    Constabulary 137-8
    Immigration Appeals Tribunal 248
Speech Therapy, education and training 134
Spitalfields Market 385
Sport 409-24
    Bodies 424-7
    Culture, Media and, Department for 105-6
    England 427
Sri Lanka
    High Commission 460
    Tourist Board 451
SSSI sites 435
Stagecoach (buses) 180
Stagecoach Selkent 180
Stansted Airport 186

Statistics
    church attendance 473
    crime 144
    deprivation 5
    employment 208-10
    European cities 447
    finance 194, 200, 201
    household expenditure 6
    housing 152
    land utilisation 435
    migration 5
    mobile phones 327
    mortality rates 4
    population 3
    tourism 408
    transport 175
    travel 179, 180, 183
    waste management 439
St Christopher and Nevis, High Commission 459
St James's Palace 397
St James's Park 397
St Kitts and Nevis, Tourism Office 451
St Lucia, High Commission 459
St Matthews Westminster 484
Stock Exchange, The 204-5
Stoke Newington, Hackney North and, MP 93
St Pancras, Holborn and, MP 94
St Paul's Cathedral 397-8
Strategic Rail Authority 178
Strategic Rail Authority, Shadow 178
Streatham, MP 96-7
St Vincent and the Grenadines
    High Commission 459
    Tourism Office 451
Succession, Order of 343
Sudan, Embassy 460
Sunrise 554-9
Sunrise Radio 285
Sunset 554-9
Supreme Court of Judicature 238
Surbiton, Kingston and, MP 95
Surveying, education and training 135
Sustainable London Trust 438
Sutton
    Borough Council 81-2
    map 81
    waste and recycling facilities 443
Sutton and Cheam, MP 97
Sutton, Merton, Wandsworth and, Health Authority 146
Swaminarayan Hindu Mission 476
Swaziland, High Commission 460
Sweden
    Church 482
    Embassy 460
    Travel and Tourism Council 451
Swimming 420-1

Switzerland
    Embassy 460
    Travel Centre 451
Synagogues, Federation of 477
Syria, Embassy 460
Syrian Orthodox Church 484

T
Takeover Panel 205
Tanzania, High Commission 460
Taxi services 181-2
Teddington Lock 399
Telephones
    companies 330-1
    international dialling codes 468-70
    mobile 330-1
Teletext Ltd. 283
Television
    BBC 282
    digital 281-2
    Independent 282-3
Tenancy, legal notes 266-8
Tennis
    International Federation 425
    Royal 419
    Tennis and Rackets Association 427
Tenpin Bowling Association, British 425
Thailand
    Royal Embassy 460
    Tourism Authority 451
Thames
    Buddhist Vihara 475
    Embankments 399
    Estuary Partnership 438
    Flood Barrier 399
    River 398-400, 436
    Trains 178-9
    Tunnel 400
    Water Utilities plc 187
Thameslink 178
Thamesmead, Erith and, MP 92-3
Theatres 400-7
Theological colleges 135
Tidal
    constants 560
    predictions 560-3
Time zones 463-6
Tobago, Trinidad and, High Commission 461
Tonga, High Commission 461
Tooting, MP 97
Tottenham, MP 97
Tottenham Hotspur Football Club 416
Tourism
    Information Centre 408
    statistics 408
    Tourist Boards 448-51
Tower Bridge 399

Tower Hamlets
    Borough Council 82-3
    map 82
    waste and recycling facilities 444
Tower of London 383
Town and Country Planning, education and training 135
Trade and Industry, Department of 110-11
Trade Unions 211-14
    Trades Union Congress 211
Train Operating Companies, Association of 178
Transport
    air 182-6
    bus 175
    Committee for London 182
    education and training 135
    for London 11
    London 175
    rail 176-8
    taxi 181-2
    Tribunal 248
    underground 179
    Users' Committee 176
Transport, Environment, the Regions and, Department of 105-6
Treasury 111-13
    Solicitor 113
Tree Officers Association, London 438
Tribunals
    Agricultural Land 247
    Appeals Service 247
    Copyright 247-8
    Data Protection 248
    Employment 248
    Employment Appeal 248
    Land 248
    Mental Health Review 248
    Pensions Appeal 248
    Solicitors' Disciplinary 248
    Special Commissioners of Income Tax 248
    Special Immigration Appeals 248
    Transport 248
    Valuation 253
    VAT and Duties 248
Trinidad and Tobago, High Commission 461
Tunisia
    Embassy 461
    National Tourist Office 451
Turkey, National Tourist Office 451
Turkmenistan, Embassy 461
Twickenham
    Bridge 399
    MP 97
    Stadium 421-2
Twilight, duration of 554-9

582 Index

U
Uganda, High Commission 461
UK
   European Parliament Office 463
   Passport Agency 108
   Sports Council 427
Ukraine, Embassy 461
Underground rail traffic, statistics 179
Union of Liberal and Progressive Synagogues 478
Union of Orthodox Hebrew Congregation 478
Unitarian and Free Christian Churches 486
   General Assembly 486
United
   Arab Emirates, Embassy 461
   Busways 181
   Nations 462
   Nations, Office and Information Centre 462
   Reform Church 485
   Synagogue 478
Universities 122-5
Upminster, MP 97
Urban Pollution Research Centre 438
Uruguay, Embassy 461
Uxbridge, MP 97
Uzbekistan, Embassy 461

V
Valuation
   Office 154
   Office Agency 253
   tribunals 154, 253
VAT and Duties Tribunal 248
Vauxhall
   Bridge 399
   MP 97
Vehicle
   Certification Agency 106
   Inspectorate 106
Venezuela
   Embassy 461
   Tourist Office 451
Veterinary
   Laboratory Agency 103
   Medicine Directorate 104
   Medicine, education and training 135
Vietnam
   Buddhist Society 475
   Embassy 461
Virgin Radio 285
Virgin Trains 178
Vishnu Hindu Parishad 476
Vivekananda Centre 476
Voluntary, Organisations 218-22
Voluntary Organisations, National
   Council for 220
Voluntary Sector Training Consortium 219
Voluntary Service
   Council 219
   councils 221-2
   National Association for Councils for, 219
   Voluntary Service Overseas 220
Volunteer Bureaux, National Association of 220
Volunteering, National Centre for 220
Voters' qualifications, legal notes 273
VSO 220

W
WAGN Railway 178
Wales and West (Railway) 178
Wales Office 113
Wallington, Carshalton and, MP 91
Waltham Forest
   Borough Council 84-5
   map 84
   waste and recycling facilities 444
Waltham Forest, Redbridge and, Health Authority 147
Walthamstow
   MP 97
   Stadium 417
Wandsworth
   Borough Council 85-6
   Bridge 399
   map 85
   waste and recycling facilities 444
Wandsworth, Merton, Sutton and, Health Authority 146
Wanstead, Leyton and, MP 95
War Pensions Agency 110
Waste management
   local authority facilities 439-44
   statistics 439
Water and Environment Management, Chartered Institution of 437
Water Services 187
Water UK 187
Waterloo Bridge 399
Watford Football Club 416
Wembley Stadium 423
West Ham
   Football Club 416
   MP 98
West London Buddhist Centre 359
Westminster
   Abbey 407
   Borough Council 86-8
   Bridge 399
   Cathedral 407
   map 86
   waste and recycling facilities 444
Westminster, Cities of London and, MP 91
Westminster, Kensington, Chelsea and, Health Authority 146
West Norwood, Dulwich and, MP 91

Wildlife Trust 438
Wills, legal notes 274-6
Wilton Park Conference Centre 107
Wimbledon
   All England Tennis Club 424
   Football Club 416
   Lawn Tennis Museum 424
   MP 98
   Stadium 417
Windsurfing Association, Professional 426
Woodford Green, Chingford and, MP 91
Wood Green, Hornsey and, MP 94
Woolwich, Greenwich and, MP 93
World Bank 462
World Sikh Fellowship 478
World Squares for All 407

X
XFM Radio 285

Y
Yemen, Embassy 461
Youth Services, Voluntary, National Council for 220

Z
Zambia
   High Commission 461
   National Tourist Board 451
Zendo, London 475
Zimbabwe, High Commission 461
Zimbabwe Tourist Information 451
Zoological Gardens 385
Zoroastrianism 478